FINANCIAL ACCOUNTING

AN INTRODUCTION TO CONCEPTS, METHODS, AND USES

NINTH EDITION

FINANCIAL ACCOUNTING

AN INTRODUCTION TO CONCEPTS, METHODS, AND USES

CLYDE P. STICKNEY | *Dartmouth College*
ROMAN L. WEIL | *University of Chicago*

THE DRYDEN PRESS
A DIVISION OF HARCOURT COLLEGE PUBLISHERS
FORT WORTH   PHILADELPHIA   SAN DIEGO   NEW YORK   AUSTIN   ORLANDO   SAN ANTONIO
TORONTO   MONTREAL   LONDON   SYDNEY   TOKYO

Publisher	Mike Roche
Acquisitions Editor	Bill Schoof
Market Strategist	Charles Watson
Developmental Editor	Jennifer Langer
Project Editor	Clarinda
Art Director	Linda Beaupré
Production Manager	Darryl King
Indexer	Cherie B. Weil

ISBN: 0-03-025962-2
Library of Congress Catalog Card Number: 99-63421

Address for Domestic Orders
The Dryden Press, 6277 Sea Harbor Drive, Orlando, FL 32887-6777
800-782-4479

Address for International Orders
International Customer Service
The Dryden Press, 6277 Sea Harbor Drive, Orlando, FL 32887-6777
407-345-3800
(fax) 407-345-4060
(e-mail) hbintl@harcourtbrace.com

Address for Editorial Correspondence
The Dryden Press, 301 Commerce Street, Suite 3700, Fort Worth, TX 76102

Web Site Address
http://www.harcourtcollege.com

THE DRYDEN PRESS, DRYDEN, and the DP LOGO are registered trademarks of Harcourt, Inc.

Printed in the United States of America

9 0 1 2 3 4 5 6 7 8   048   9 8 7 6 5 4 3 2 1

The Dryden Press
Harcourt College Publishers

Whatever be the detail with which you cram your students, the chance of their meeting in after-life exactly that detail is infinitesimal; and if they do meet it, they will probably have forgotten what you taught them about it. The really useful training yields a comprehension of a few general principles with a thorough grounding in the way they apply to a variety of concrete details. In subsequent practice the students will have forgotten your particular details; but they will remember by an unconscious common sense how to apply principles to immediate circumstances.

Alfred North Whitehead
The Aims of Education and Other Essays

THE DRYDEN PRESS SERIES IN ACCOUNTING

The ninth edition of "FACMU" (as we have come to know it) has the same principal objectives as the previous editions:

- To help students develop a sufficient understanding of the basic concepts underlying financial statements so that they can apply the concepts to new and different situations.
- To train students in accounting terminology and methods so that they can interpret, analyze, and evaluate financial statements currently published in corporate annual reports.

Most introductory financial accounting textbooks share these, or similar, objectives. The critical differences among textbooks are the relative emphases on concepts, methods, and uses.

1. **Concepts** This book emphasizes the rationale for, and implications of, important accounting concepts. To learn accounting, the student must develop the ability to conceptualize the transactions that accounting summarizes and the process of summarization. Without such conceptualization, students will have difficulty focusing on relevant issues in new and different situations.

   Accordingly, each chapter begins by identifying important accounting concepts. Several numerical examples illustrating their application then follow. The end-of-chapter material includes numerous short exercises to check the students' ability to apply the concepts to different problem situations.

2. **Methods** We place sufficient emphasis on accounting procedures so that students can interpret, analyze, and evaluate published financial statements. The text does not emphasize procedures to such an extent that students become bogged down in detail. All writers of accounting textbooks must decide just how much accounting procedure to include. We believe students will learn most effectively through practice and working the problems and exercises. Too much emphasis on accounting procedures, however, lulls students into the security of thinking they understand accounting concepts when they do not. We have for many years used the mixture of concepts and procedures in this book and have found it effective in the classroom.

   Understanding the accounting implications of an event requires that students construct the journal entry for that event. Throughout this book we use journal entries in describing the nature of accounting events. Moreover, most chapters contain exercises and problems that require the analysis of transactions with debits and credits. Do not conclude by a glance at this text, however, that it is primarily procedural. We want students to learn concepts; the procedures enhance the learning of concepts.

3. **Uses** This book attempts to bridge the gap between the preparation of financial statements and their use in various decision situations. The chapters consider the effects of alternative accounting principles on the measurement of earnings and financial position and the appropriate and inappropriate interpretations of them. Numerous user-oriented problems and cases based on financial statement data of actual companies appear at the end of most chapters.

CHANGES IN THIS EDITION

The ninth edition represents the most significant revision yet of this book. Before describing these changes, we emphasize that we have not changed the basic philosophy of the book as described in the preceding section. We use accounting procedures to cement understanding of accounting concepts so that users of financial statements will make more intelligent interpretations and decisions.

1) Reorganization of Chapter Sequence. We have revised the sequence and content of chapters for a more effective conceptual and pedagogical flow. The placement of material in this edition as compared to the eighth edition is as follows:

Current Edition	Previous Edition
Chapter 1: Introduction to Business Activities and Overview of Financial Statements and the Reporting Process	Same
Chapter 2: Balance Sheet: Presenting the Investments and Financing of a Firm	Same
Chapter 3: Income Statement: Reporting the Results of Operating Activities	Chapter 3 plus parts of Chapter 4
Chapter 4: Statement of Cash Flows: Reporting the Effects of Operating, Investing, and Financing Activities on Cash Flows	Chapter 5
Chapter 5: Introduction to Financial Statement Analysis	Chapter 6
Chapter 6: Receivables and Revenue Recognition	Chapters 4 and 7
Chapter 7: Inventories: The Source of Operating Profits	Chapters 4 and 8
Chapter 8: Plant, Equipment, and Intangible Assets: The Source of Operating Capacity	Chapter 9
Chapter 9: Liabilities: Introduction	Chapter 10
Chapter 10: Liabilities: Off-Balance Sheet Financing, Leases, Deferred Income Taxes, Retirement Benefits, and Derivatives	Chapter 11
Chapter 11: Marketable Securities and Investments	Chapters 7 and 13
Chapter 12: Earnings, Comprehensive Income, and Shareholders' Equity	Chapters 4 and 12
Chapter 13: Statement of Cash Flows: Another Look	Chapter 14
Chapter 14: Significance and Implications of Alternative Accounting Principles	Chapter 15

Our rationales for the principal changes to this edition are:

■ Reorganizing Chapter 4

Chapter 4 of the previous edition extended the accrual concept to manufacturers, long-term contractors, and other types of businesses. We found that students had difficulty grasping these extensions of the accrual concept so early in the course. Our new Chapter 6 includes a comprehensive discussion of revenue recognition and related receivables for various types of businesses. The application of accrual concepts to manufacturers now appears with inventories and cost of goods sold in Chapter 7. Chapter 4 of the eighth edition also included the reporting of non-recurring income items, which this edition places in Chapter 12 in an expanded discussion of reporting comprehensive income and other income items.

■ **Moving Marketable Securities**

We have moved coverage of marketable securities from Chapter 7 of the eighth edition to Chapter 11 of this edition. The similar accounting for marketable securities available for sale and investments in securities available for sale suggest their coverage in the same chapter.

■ **Sequence of Investments in Securities and Shareholders' Equity**

We have switched the sequence of Investments in Securities (now in Chapter 11) and Shareholders' Equity (now in Chapter 12). Chapter 12's discussion of comprehensive income uses unrealized gains and losses on marketable equity securities, now discussed in Chapter 11, to illustrate the required disclosures.

2) The concept of the **quality of earnings** now provides a principal means for evaluating alternative accounting principles discussed in Chapters 6 to 12. Chapter 6 describes three avenues firms might use to manage their earnings: selecting their accounting principles, applying their accounting principles, and timing asset acquisitions and dispositions. Subsequent chapters discuss particular accounting principles in light of this quality-of-earnings framework.

3) Each chapter incorporates pronouncements of the Financial Accounting Standards Board for reporting in the United States as well as applicable pronouncements of the International Accounting Standards Committee.

4) **New to This Edition** We have incorporated in the text brief terminology notes, conceptual notes, or practical notes that enhance understanding of the topic being discussed.

5) **New to This Edition** Most chapters now include cases appropriate for MBA and executive programs in addition to many new exercises and problems. Examples of new cases are Computer Needs (case **3.49**), Boston Chicken (case **6.36**), America Online (case **8.50**), Merck (case **12.43**), Wendy's (case **12.44**), Kellogg's (case **12.45**), and Petite-Mart (case **14.19**). In addition, this edition includes a revised version of the W.T. Grant case (case **5.33**).

6) **New to This Edition** Advanced topics now appear on our Web Site for this book located at www.harcourtcollege.com for optional use in your course. Topics on the Web Site include:

   ■ foreign currency translation,

   ■ pension benefits,

   ■ consolidation when a minority interest is present,

   ■ a balance sheet approach to deferred tax accounting, and

   ■ general price-level accounting.

   Each topic contains reading material and exercises or problems. Instructors desiring to include any of these topics in their courses can direct students to the Web Site to obtain reading and assignment material. Solutions to these exercises and problems are included in the Instructor's Manual. To visit the Web Site, (1) go to www.harcourtcollege.com; (2) go to the pull-down menu for disciplines and select "accounting"; (3) select the icon for *Financial Accounting* by Stickney and Weil; (4) select "Student." There you will find a variety of material we have designed to help you and we expect the amount ot material there to grow over time.

7) **New to This Edition** The ninth edition is now in full color, designed to stimulate students and increase user friendliness.

ORGANIZATION

This book comprises four major parts:

- Part One: "Overview of Financial Statements," consisting of Chapter 1.
- Part Two: "Accounting Concepts and Methods," Chapters 2 through 5.
- Part Three: "Measuring and Reporting Assets and Equities," Chapters 6 through 13.
- Part Four: "Synthesis," Chapter 14.

In our view, the four parts are tiers, or steps, in the learning process. Part One presents a general overview of the principal financial statements. Part Two discusses the basic accounting model accountants use to generate the principal financial statements. Part Three considers the specific accounting principles or methods used in preparing the financial statements. Finally, Part Four synthesizes material covered in Chapters 1 to 13. This organization reflects the view that learning takes place most effectively when the student starts with a broad picture, then breaks up that broad picture into smaller pieces until achieving the desired depth, and finally synthesizing so that the relation between the parts and the whole retains its perspective.

Chapter 1 presents a brief description of the principal activities of a business firm (goal setting and strategy formulation, investing, financing, and operating) and shows how the three principal financial statements—the balance sheet, the income statement, and the statement of cash flows—report the results of these activities. Chapter 1 also provides an overview of the financial reporting environment. Many students feel deluged with the multitude of new terms and concepts after reading Chapter 1. However, most of these same students admit later that the broad overview helped piece material together as they later explored individual topics at greater length.

Chapters 2 through 4 present the basic accounting model that generates the three principal financial statements. In each case, the discussion begins with a description of the important concepts underlying each statement. The chapter then describes and illustrates procedures accountants use to generate the financial statements. Each chapter uses the balance sheet equation or changes in the balance sheet equation to motivate understanding of the preparation procedures. Although these chapters emphasize debit/credit procedures, instructors can use the balance sheet equation approach to communicate the basics of statement preparation. Each of these chapters includes one or more simple problems that students can work using the balance sheet approach to prepare the three principal financial statements. Chapter 3, unlike treatments in other texts, integrates the accounting entries for transactions during a period with the related adjusting entries at the end of the period. When textbooks discuss these two types of entries in separate chapters, students often lose sight of the fact that measurement of net income and financial position requires both kinds of entries.

We continue to put coverage of the statement of cash flows early in the text (Chapter 4). This placement serves two purposes. First, it elevates the statement to its rightful place among the three principal financial statements. Students can thereby integrate the concepts of profitability and cash flow more effectively and begin to understand that one does not necessarily accompany the other. Covering this statement at the end of the course (in many cases, when time is running out) can lead students to think the cash flow statement less important. Placing this chapter early in the book forces the student to cement understanding of the basic accounting model from Chapters 2 and 3. Preparing the statement of cash flows requires the student to "work backward" from the balance sheet and income statement to reconstruct the transactions that took place. This edition includes *two new features* to its coverage of the statement of cash flows:

1) emphasis on both the indirect and the direct method of calculating cash flow from operations
2) the use of both the columnar worksheet and the T-account worksheet for preparing the statement.

Chapter 5 describes and illustrates tools for analyzing the financial statements. The discussion structures the various financial statement ratios in a multi-level format that students have found minimizes the need to memorize formulas. Instructors who incorporate annual reports of actual companies throughout their course will find that analysis of the financial statements of such companies at this point in the course serves as an effective synthesis. An appendix to Chapter 5 illustrates procedures for preparing pro forma financial statements. This topic helps cement understanding of the relationship among the three principal financial statements.

Chapters 6 through 12 discuss the various generally accepted accounting principles that accountants use in generating the financial statements. Each chapter not only describes and illustrates the application of the various accounting methods but also considers their effects on the financial statements. This approach reflects the view that students should be able to interpret and analyze published financial statements and to understand the effect of alternative accounting methods on such assessments.

Some of the specific changes to Chapters 6–12 of this edition include:

- an integrated discussion of revenue recognition for various types of businesses along with the related treatment of receivables (Chapter 6),
- asset impairments related to goodwill (Chapter 8),
- constructive liabilities (Chapter 9),
- nature and accounting for derivatives (Chapter 10), and
- comprehensive income (Chapter 12).

Chapter 13 explores the statement of cash flows in greater depth by presenting a comprehensive illustration using transactions discussed in Chapters 6 through 12. Instructors have flexibility in structuring their coverage of the statement of cash flows by covering Chapter 4 early in the course and Chapter 13 at the end of the course or by covering both chapters at the end of the course.

Some students who have used the previous editions of this book report that Chapter 14, which synthesizes much of the material in the first thirteen chapters, is the most useful in the book. This chapter explicitly considers the combined effects of alternative accounting methods on the financial statements. The chapter also summarizes the effect of various accounting principles discussed in earlier chapters on the quality of earnings. The self-study problem and problems 16 and 17 at the end of Chapter 14 provide thorough review for the entire book. Case **14.19** requires students to evaluate the quality of earnings for many of the topics discussed throughout the book.

An appendix to the book describes compound interest and present value computations for students not previously exposed to this topic.

The end of the book includes a comprehensive glossary of accounting terms. It serves as a useful reference tool for accounting and other business terms and provides additional descriptions of a few topics, such as accounting changes and inventory profit, considered only briefly in the text.

RELATED MATERIALS ACCOMPANYING THE TEXTBOOK

The following supplementary materials are available with the textbook:

Instructor's Manual   The instructor's manual presents suggested outlines for courses of varying lengths, a list of chapter objectives, helpful teaching hints, detailed lecture and discussion outlines, including the numbers of particularly germane questions, exercises, problems, and cases.

Solutions Manual   The solutions manual provides full solutions for all end-of-chapter and Web site assignment items, including questions, exercises, problems, and cases. We give computations wherever possible, allowing the instructor to show how to reach a particular answer.

Study Guide   This study guide, by LeBrone C. Harris and James E. Moon, lists highlights from each chapter and provides numerous short true/false, matching, multiple-choice questions, and exercises, with answers.

Test Bank   Prepared by Bobbe Barnes of the University of Colorado, the test bank is thoroughly expanded and revised and now includes multiple-choice items, matching questions, short essay questions, and problems.

Computerized Test Bank   All items in the test bank are available in EXAMaster software format for Windows.

Lecture Presentation Software in PowerPoint   Sample lectures have been created by Gordon Duke of the University of Minnesota to aid in lecture preparations using this text. Software is available on CD-ROM for a Windows format.

Spreadsheet Template Software   At least three problems per chapter have a corresponding template where basic problem data appear on a Microsoft Excel® Spreadsheet to reduce tedium in solving problems and increase student awareness of basic software applications.

Solutions Transparencies   Solutions acetates accompany all numerical end-of-chapter exercises, problems, and cases.

Teaching Transparencies   A selection of 100 textbook illustrations are available in transparency acetate form.

The Dryden Press will provide complimentary supplements or supplement packages to those adopters qualified under our adoption policy. Please contract your sales representative to learn how you may qualify. If as an adopter or potential user you receive supplements you do not need, please return them to your sales representative or send them to:

Attn: Returns Department
Troy Warehouse
465 South Lincoln Drive
Troy, MO 63379

ACKNOWLEDGMENTS

We gratefully acknowledge the helpful criticisms and suggestions of the following people who used the previous edition or reviewed the manuscript for this edition:

Andrew W. Alford University of Pennsylvania
Matthew Anderson Michigan State University
Gary C. Biddle University of Washington
Peggy Bishop University of Pennsylvania
Germain B. Boer Vanderbilt University
Paul R. Brown New York University
Robert Bushman University of North Carolina
Alvin H. Carley University of Pennsylvania
Kevin M. Devine Xavier University
Gordon Duke University of Minnesota
Kirsten M. Ely Emory University
Merle Erikson University of Chicago
Carol Ann Frost Dartmouth College
Bertrand N. Horwitz SUNY Binghamton
Jennifer J. Jones University of Chicago
A. Ronald Kucic University of Denver
James A. Largay III Lehigh University
Laureen A. Maines Duke University
Edward Maydew University of Chicago
Janette Moody The Citadel
Alan Mayer-Sommer Georgetown University
Aritit Mukherji University of Minnesota
Patricia C. O'Brien University of Waterloo
Eugene Orza Major League Baseball Players' Association
Glen E. Owen University of California, Santa Barbara
Glenn Pfeiffer Chapman College
Gordon S. Potter Cornell University
Alan Reinstein Wayne State University
Anne J. Rich Quinnipiac College
Katherine Schipper University of Chicago
Katherine Schrand University of Pennsylvania
Stephen E. Sefcik University of Washington
Thomas I. Selling Thunderbird
Galen Sevcik University of Arizona
Lawrence Singleton George Washington University
Virginia E. Soybel Babson College
Steve Sung Washington University, St. Louis
Brent Trueman University of California, Berkeley
Bob Virgil Edward Jones and Co.
Peter Wilson Duke University
Stephen A. Zeff Rice University

Thomas Horton and Daughters, Inc., permits us to reproduce material from *Accounting: The Language of Business*. Problems **45** to **47** in Chapter 3 derive from ones prepared by George H. Sorter. These problems involve working backward from one financial statement to another, and we have found them useful in cementing understanding. Stan

Baiman provided us with a series of excellent problems on the statement of cash flows for use in Chapters 8 through 12. Katherine Schipper provided us ideas and data for several cases. Steve Zeff provided us with numerous thought-provoking problems, which we have used or adapted for use in many of the chapters in this edition.

We thank J. Scott Whisenant and Alice Cash for their review of the text throughout the production process of the ninth edition. Their observations were invaluable.

We thank Katherine Xenophon-Rybowiak, Tammy Stebbins, and Gloria Langer for helping us to prepare the manuscript for this edition and Cherie Weil for preparing the index.

We thank the following at The Dryden Press who assisted with various aspects of this revision including publisher Mike Roche, developmental editor Jennifer Langer, marketing strategist Charles Watson, senior project editor Jim Patterson, assistant manager art and designer Linda Beaupré, permissions editor Linda Blundell, and manufacturing manager Kim Samuels.

We thank Cindy Miller and Gail Gavin of Clarinda Publication Services for coordinating the production of the book, as well as Kimm Livengood and the compositors at The Clarinda Company for their excellent work on page-makeup.

Finally, Sidney Davidson. What can we say? For over twenty-five years he has taught us and guided us and wrote with us. Thank you.

BRIEF CONTENTS

CONTENTS

CHAPTER 5

Introduction to Financial Statement Analysis   231

PART THREE
MEASURING AND REPORTING ASSETS AND EQUITIES USING GENERALLY ACCEPTED ACCOUNTING PRINCIPLES   301
CHAPTER 6

Receivables and Revenue Recognition   303

CHAPTER 7

Inventories: The Source of Operating Profits   352

CHAPTER 8

Plant, Equipment, and Intangible Assets: The Source of Operating Capacity   410

PART ONE

A C M U F

OVERVIEW OF FINANCIAL STATEMENTS

1

INTRODUCTION TO BUSINESS ACTIVITIES AND OVERVIEW OF FINANCIAL STATEMENTS AND THE REPORTING PROCESS

CHAPTER 1

LEARNING OBJECTIVES

1. Develop a general understanding of four principal activities of business firms: (a) establishing goals and strategies, (b) obtaining financing, (c) making investments, and (d) conducting operations.
2. Develop a general understanding of the purpose and content of the three principal financial statements that business firms prepare to measure and report the results of their business activities: (a) balance sheet, (b) income statement, and (c) statement of cash flows.
3. Develop a sensitivity to financial reporting issues, including the following: (a) the multiple uses of financial accounting reports, (b) the alternative approaches to establishing accounting measurement and reporting standards, (c) the role of the independent audit of a business firm's financial statements, and (d) the role of financial reporting in an efficient capital market.

Let's begin candidly. Do you expect to enjoy this introductory course in financial accounting? Many students come into this course expecting accounting to be dull, to deal with meticulous detail, and to lack opportunities for creative thinking. Film and television characterizations of accountants and the procedural emphasis of some accounting courses foster these images.

We think accounting will surprise you. Accounting is the language of business. Business activity has undergone rapid change and faced exciting challenges during the last decade. Consider, for example, advances in information technologies, global integration of business across national boundaries, economic recessions, frequent bankruptcies, and increased concern for the environment. The pace of change in the future will not likely lessen, and its direction will remain uncertain. Accounting strives to make some sense of this complexity by measuring the results of business activities and aggregating these measurements in the form of financial statements that users can understand and interpret.

You will likely not become an accountant (although some students will). Rather, you will probably use financial accounting as a tool for making production, marketing, investment, financing, or other business decisions. The goal of your study (and of this book) is to help you develop sufficient understanding of financial accounting so that you can use accounting data effectively. Although most professors (and textbook authors) probably agree with the goal just stated for this financial accounting course, we might disagree on the most effective way to accomplish the goal. The usual question raised is, How much accounting do students need to know in order to analyze and interpret financial statements effectively?

Various course offerings in financial accounting place different weights on three key elements of its study: concepts, methods, and uses. We find that students become intelligent users of financial accounting information by mastering the accounting concepts that underlie the financial statements. Understanding accounting concepts not only enhances interpretations of the financial statements as currently prepared but also permits extrapolation to other measurement methods and to reporting formats encountered in other countries. Accounting methods link accounting concepts and the financial statements. The accountant uses these methods to accumulate data about business transactions and to synthesize and summarize these data in the financial statements. Thus, a certain level of exposure to accounting methods enhances an understanding of accounting concepts, which in turn aids users in interpreting financial information. The relative emphasis that we place on concepts, methods, and uses in this book results from our own experience in teaching the introductory financial accounting course. We hope that you will find this mixture effective in both motivating your study of financial accounting and enhancing your understanding of financial statements.

This chapter overviews the whole book. We begin by studying how a typical firm carries out its business activities. We next see how the firm measures the results of these business activities and reports them in the financial statements. We then raise several issues about the financial reporting process. This chapter introduces material that later chapters will cover in greater depth. At this point in your study of financial accounting, you will not fully understand all of the concepts and terms discussed in this chapter. As the chapter title suggests, the objective is to develop the big picture of the concepts, methods, and uses discussed later.

OVERVIEW OF BUSINESS ACTIVITIES

Firms prepare financial statements for various external users: owners, lenders, regulators, and employees. The statements attempt to present meaningful information about a firm's business activities. Understanding these financial statements requires an understanding of the business activities that they attempt to portray.

Example 1   Joe Soft and Jane Ware, while working toward degrees in computer science, develop computer software for monitoring automobile engine performance. They copyright the software and want to set up their own firm to manufacture and sell it. They decide to call the firm SoftWare Corporation.

The following sections describe some of the more important business activities that the management of SoftWare Corporation must understand.

ESTABLISHING CORPORATE GOALS AND STRATEGIES

A firm's **goals** state the targets, or end results, toward which the firm directs its energies. A firm's **strategies** state the means for achieving these goals. The firm sets goals and strategies in light of the economic, institutional, and cultural environment in which it intends to operate. For example, a firm might set goals to

- maximize the return to the owners of the firm;
- provide a stimulating and stable lifetime working environment for employees; and
- contribute to and integrate with national goals and policies.

Management sets strategies for a firm as a whole. For example, a firm might choose to operate in one industry or several industries. It might integrate backward into production of raw materials or forward into distribution of products to customers. It might operate in the United States only or also in other countries.

Management also sets strategies for each business unit or product. For example, a firm might attempt to find a niche for each of its products. Such a strategy might permit the firm to obtain favorable selling prices for its products relative to competitors so that it can pass along cost increases to its customers. (Common business terminology refers to this as a "product differentiation strategy.") Alternatively, the firm might choose primarily to emphasize cost control and might strive to be the low-cost producer in its industry. Such a strategy might permit it to charge aggressively low prices and generate high volumes. (Terminology refers to this as a "low-cost leadership strategy.") Some products lend themselves more naturally to one strategy or the other, whereas the firm might pursue either or both strategies for other products.

When establishing goals and strategies, the firm must consider external factors, such as the following:

1. Who are the firm's competitors, and what goals and strategies do they pursue?
2. What barriers, such as patents or large investments in buildings and equipment, might preclude new firms from entering the industry? Or are entry barriers low?
3. Is the demand for products within the industry increasing rapidly, such as for Internet software, or is the demand relatively stable, such as the demand for groceries?
4. Is the industry subject to government regulation, such as for food and pharmaceutical products, or is it unregulated?

SoftWare Corporation sets a goal to develop a continuing stream of quality software products that it can manufacture and market profitably, thereby increasing the value of the firm and the wealth of its owners. Its strategies to accomplish this goal include the following:

1. SoftWare Corporation will manufacture all software itself so as to ensure product quality.
2. The firm's sales staff will carry out the sale and servicing of the software to provide close working relations with customers.
3. The firm will invest in research and development to promote the ongoing creation of new products.

OBTAINING FINANCING

Before SoftWare Corporation can embark on its business activities, it must obtain the necessary financing. Such **financing activities** involve obtaining funds from two principal sources: owners and creditors.

Owners Owners provide funds to a firm and in return receive some evidence of their ownership. When a firm is a corporation, shares of common stock provide evidence of ownership, and the owners are called *shareholders* or *stockholders*.[1] The firm need not repay the owners at a particular future date. Instead, the owners receive distributions, called **dividends,** from the firm only when the firm decides to pay them. The owners also have a claim on all the firm's increases in value resulting from future profitable operations.

Creditors   Unlike owners, creditors provide funds but require that the firm repay the funds, usually with interest, at a specific date. The length of time that elapses until repayment varies.

Long-term creditors may provide funds and not require repayment for 20 years or more. A bond usually evidences such borrowings. In a bond agreement, the borrowing company promises to pay to the creditors, at specific dates in the future, interest on the amounts borrowed and then to repay the amount borrowed at the end of some stated period of years.

Banks usually lend for periods between several months and several years. A note, in which the borrowing company promises to repay the amount borrowed plus interest at some future date, provides evidence of bank borrowings.

Suppliers of raw materials do not always view themselves as supplying funds to a firm. Yet when they sell raw materials but do not require payment for 30 days, they implicitly provide funds—the firm gets raw materials now but need not pay cash until later. Likewise, employees paid weekly or monthly and governmental units requiring only monthly or quarterly tax payments provide funds by not demanding payment hourly or daily.

All firms must choose the proportion of funds they will obtain from owners, long-term creditors, and short-term creditors. Finance courses cover such financing decisions. Many firms that fail do so because they have not arranged their sources of funds to be sufficiently long term.

MAKING INVESTMENTS

Once a firm has obtained funds, it usually invests them to carry out its business activities. Such **investing activities** involve acquisitions of the following:

1. Land, buildings, and equipment. These investments, which provide a firm with a capacity to manufacture and sell its products, usually take years to provide all of the potential services for which the firm acquired them.
2. Patents, licenses, and other contractual rights. These investments provide a firm with the legal right to use certain property or processes in pursuing its business activities.
3. Common shares or bonds of other firms. A firm might purchase shares or bonds of another firm (thereby becoming one of its owners or creditors). A firm might acquire these holdings for a few months with temporarily excess cash or might invest for longer-term purposes, such as to secure a source for critical raw materials or gain entrance into an emerging technology.
4. Inventories. To satisfy the needs of customers as they arise, firms must maintain an inventory of products to sell. A firm does not usually invest in specific inventory items for long because it will soon sell the items to customers. Because firms must have at least small amounts of inventory on hand, however, they must continually invest some of their funds in inventory items.
5. Accounts receivable from customers. When a firm sells its products but does not require customers to pay immediately, the firm provides financing to its customers. Carrying

---

[1]When a firm operates as a partnership, its owners are partners. When a firm operates as a sole proprietorship, its owner is a sole proprietor. This book focuses on the corporate form of legal entity.

some amount of accounts receivable may be in the best interest of the firm if by doing so, the firm increases its sales and profits. In extending credit to customers, the firm forgoes collecting its cash right away, but if it did not extend the credit, it might not make the sale in the first place. Insofar as the firm delays the collection of needed cash from its customers, it must obtain funds elsewhere. Carrying accounts receivable, therefore, requires an investment of funds.

6. Cash. Most firms will leave a portion of their funds as cash in checking accounts so that they can pay their current bills.

Managerial accounting and corporate finance courses cover the techniques that firms use to make investment decisions.

CARRYING OUT OPERATIONS

A firm obtains financing and invests the funds in various resources to generate profit. The **operating activities** of the firm comprise the following:

1. Purchasing. The purchasing department of a merchandising firm acquires products needed by its retail stores. The purchasing department of a manufacturing firm acquires raw materials needed for production.
2. Production. The production department in a manufacturing firm combines raw materials, labor services, and other manufacturing inputs to produce the products, or outputs, of a firm. A firm that offers services combines various labor services in creating its product.
3. Marketing. The marketing department oversees selling and distributing a firm's products to customers.
4. Administration. The administrative activity of a firm supports purchasing, production, marketing, and other operating departments. Administrative activities include data processing, legal services, research and development, and other support services.

Managerial accounting, marketing, and production courses cover the appropriate bases for making operating decisions.

SUMMARY OF BUSINESS ACTIVITIES

Figure 1.1 summarizes the four principal business activities discussed in this section. Figure 1.1 distinguishes between the short term and the long term. Although the time line dividing short- from long-term activities varies somewhat among firms, most accountants use one year as the dividing line.

PRINCIPAL FINANCIAL STATEMENTS

The financial statements that individuals outside a firm most frequently use appear in a firm's **annual report to shareholders.** The annual report to shareholders typically includes a letter from the firm's management summarizing the activities of the past year and assessing the firm's prospects for the coming year; firms refer to this section as the **MD&A,** the **management discussion and analysis.** The annual report also frequently includes promotional materials, such as pictures of the firm's products and employees. The section of the annual report containing the financial statements includes the following:

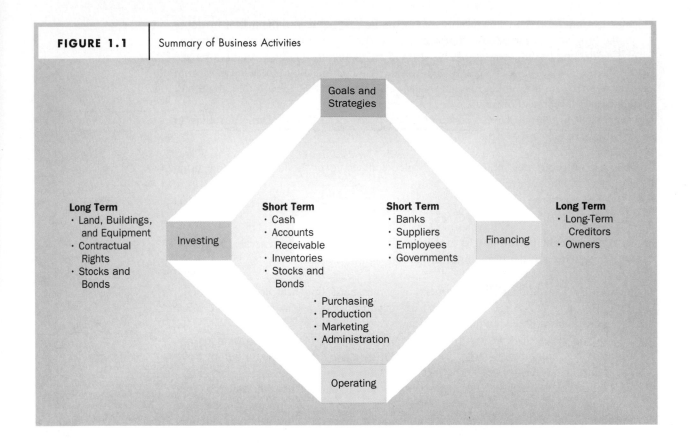

FIGURE 1.1 | Summary of Business Activities

1. Balance sheet
2. Income statement
3. Statement of cash flows
4. Notes to the financial statements, including various supporting schedules
5. Opinion of the independent certified public accountant

The following sections of this chapter briefly discuss each of these five items.

BALANCE SHEET

The **balance sheet** presents a snapshot of the investing and financing activities of a firm at a moment in time. Exhibit 1.1 presents a comparative balance sheet for SoftWare Corporation as of December 31, Year 0, and December 31, Year 1.

The owners formed SoftWare Corporation on December 31, Year 0. The balance sheet on December 31, Year 0, depicts SoftWare Corporation on that day. The owners provided $500,000 in funds, long-term creditors provided $400,000, and suppliers provided $100,000. The firm invested these funds in inventories, land, buildings, equipment, and a patent; it left $70,000 in the firm's checking account.

The balance sheet on December 31, Year 1, presents the financial position of SoftWare Corporation at the end of the first year. The amounts for most items in the balance sheet changed between the beginning and the end of the year. Note several aspects of the balance sheet.

EXHIBIT 1.1	SOFTWARE CORPORATION Comparative Balance Sheet

	December 31	
	Year 0	Year 1
ASSETS		
Current Assets		
Cash	$ 70,000	$ 200,000
Accounts Receivable from Customers	—	180,000
Inventories (at manufacturing cost)	100,000	270,000
Total Current Assets	$ 170,000	$ 650,000
Noncurrent Assets (at acquisition cost)		
Land	$ 30,000	$ 30,000
Buildings (net of accumulated depreciation)	400,000	380,000
Equipment (net of accumulated depreciation)	250,000	230,000
Patent (net of accumulated amortization)	150,000	120,000
Total Noncurrent Assets	$ 830,000	$ 760,000
Total Assets	$1,000,000	$1,410,000
LIABILITIES AND SHAREHOLDERS' EQUITY		
Current Liabilities		
Accounts Payable to Suppliers	$ 100,000	$ 130,000
Salaries Payable to Employees	—	30,000
Income Taxes Payable to Federal Government	—	40,000
Total Current Liabilities	$ 100,000	$ 200,000
Noncurrent Liabilities		
Bonds Payable to Lenders (due Year 20)	400,000	450,000
Total Liabilities	$ 500,000	$ 650,000
Shareholders' Equity		
Common Stock	$ 500,000	$ 600,000
Retained Earnings	—	160,000
Total Shareholders' Equity	$ 500,000	$ 760,000
Total Liabilities and Shareholders' Equity	$1,000,000	$1,410,000

Concepts of Assets, Liabilities, and Shareholders' Equity   The balance sheet presents a listing of a firm's assets, liabilities, and shareholders' equity.

Assets are economic resources with the ability or potential to provide future benefits to a firm. For example, a firm can use cash to purchase inventory or equipment. The firm can sell inventory to customers for an amount it hopes will provide a profit. The firm can use equipment to transport inventory to customers.

Liabilities are creditors' claims on the assets of a firm. SoftWare Corporation has purchased inventories from its suppliers but has not paid for a portion of the purchases. As a result, these creditors have provided funds to the firm and have a claim on its assets. Employees have provided labor services for which the firm has not made payment as of December 31, Year 1. These employees likewise have provided funds to the firm and have a claim on its assets. Creditors' claims, or liabilities, result from a firm's having previously received benefits (cash, inventories, labor services) for which the firm must pay a specified amount on a specified date.

Shareholders' equity is the owners' claim on the assets of a firm. Unlike creditors, the owners have only a residual interest; that is, owners have a claim on all assets in excess of those required to meet creditors' claims. The shareholders' equity generally comprises two parts: contributed capital and retained earnings. **Contributed capital** reflects the funds invested by shareholders for an ownership interest. The owners initially contributed $500,000 for shares of SoftWare Corporation's common stock. They invested an additional $100,000 during Year 1 for more shares of stock. **Retained earnings** represent a firm's earnings that exceed the dividends it has distributed to shareholders since its formation. In other words, retained earnings represent assets reinvested by management for the benefit of shareholders. Management attempts to direct the use of a firm's assets so that over time it receives more assets than it consumes in operations. This increase in assets, after any claims of creditors, belongs to the firm's owners. Most firms use a large percentage of the assets generated by earnings to replace assets and to grow rather than to pay dividends.

Equality of Assets and Liabilities Plus Shareholders' Equity   As the balance sheet for SoftWare Corporation shows, assets equal liabilities plus shareholders' equity.

$$\text{Assets} = \text{Liabilities} + \text{Shareholders' Equity}$$

A firm must invest somewhere every dollar of resources it obtains from financing. The balance sheet therefore views the same resources from two angles: as a listing of the assets the firm holds and as a listing of the parties (creditors and owners) who provided financing and who, therefore, have a claim on those assets. Thus,

$$\text{Assets} = \text{Liabilities} + \text{Shareholders' Equity,}$$

or

$$\text{Investing} = \text{Financing}$$
$$\text{Resources} = \text{Sources of Resources}$$
$$\text{Resources} = \text{Claims on Resources}$$

The asset mix (that is, the proportion of total assets represented by accounts receivable, inventories, equipment, and other assets) reflects a firm's investment decisions, and the mix of liabilities plus shareholders' equity reflects a firm's financing decisions.

Balance Sheet Classification   The balance sheet classifies assets and liabilities as being either current or noncurrent.

Current assets include cash and assets that a firm expects to turn into cash, sell, or consume within approximately one year from the date of the balance sheet. Cash, temporary investments in securities, accounts receivable from customers, and inventories are the most common current assets. *Current liabilities* represent obligations a firm expects to pay within one year. Examples are notes payable to banks, accounts payable to suppliers, salaries payable to employees, and taxes payable to governments.

Noncurrent assets, typically held and used for several years, include land, buildings, equipment, patents, and long-term investments in securities. *Noncurrent liabilities* and *shareholders' equity* are a firm's longer-term sources of funds.

Balance Sheet Valuation Assets, liabilities, and shareholders' equity items appear on the balance sheet at dollar amounts that accountants might measure on one of two bases: (1) a **historical valuation,** which reflects the acquisition cost of assets or the amounts of funds originally obtained from creditors or owners, or (2) a **current valuation,** which reflects the current cost of acquiring assets or the current market value of creditors' and owners' claims on a firm. As Chapter 2 discusses, accountants can more easily verify historical valuations and will disagree less often as to their amounts, whereas financial statement users probably find current valuations more relevant. Making current valuations, however, requires greater subjectivity.

The balance sheet reports cash as the amount of cash on hand or in the bank (a current valuation). Accounts receivable appear at the present value of the amount of cash the firm expects to collect from customers (often, approximating a current valuation). Liabilities generally appear at the present value of the cash required to pay liabilities (a current valuation).

The remaining assets appear either at acquisition cost or at acquisition cost net of accumulated depreciation or amortization (a historical valuation). For example, inventories and land usually appear at the amount of cash or other resources that the firm originally sacrificed to acquire those assets. Buildings, equipment, and patents appear at acquisition cost, adjusted downward to reflect the portion of the assets' services that the firm has used since acquisition.[2]

Common stock appears at the amount invested by owners when the firm first issued common stock (a historical valuation). Retained earnings shows the sum of all prior years' earnings in excess of dividends (a combination of historical and current valuations). Chapters 3 and 12 further discuss the valuation, or measurement, of retained earnings.

INCOME STATEMENT

The second principal financial statement is the **income statement.** Exhibit 1.2 shows the income statement for SoftWare Corporation for Year 1. This statement presents the results of the operating activities of a firm for a specific time period, one year in Exhibit 1.2. The income statement indicates the **net income** or **earnings** for that time period. Net income is the difference between revenues and expenses. Note several aspects of the income statement.

Concepts of Net Income, Revenue, and Expense The terms *net income* and *earnings* are synonyms used interchangeably in corporate annual reports and throughout this text. Generating a profit from operating activities is the primary goal of most business firms. The income statement reports a firm's success in achieving this goal for a given time span. The income statement reports the sources and amounts of a firm's revenues and the nature and amount of a firm's expenses. The excess of revenues over expenses equals the earnings for the period.

Revenues measure the inflows of assets (or reductions in liabilities) from selling goods and providing services to customers. During Year 1, SoftWare Corporation sold software and provided consulting and financing services. From its customers, SoftWare Corporation received either cash or promises that it would receive cash in the future,

---

[2]Sometimes, balance sheet amounts for inventories, buildings, land, equipment, and patents will reflect amounts lower than historical cost when these items decline in value after the firm acquires them. Later chapters discuss these exceptions.

EXHIBIT 1.2	SOFTWARE CORPORATION Income Statement for Year 1

Revenue	
Sale of Software	$2,250,000
Sale of Consulting Services	140,000
Interest on Accounts Receivable from Customers	10,000
Total Revenues	$2,400,000
Expenses	
Cost of Goods Sold	$1,465,000
Selling Expenses	400,000
Administrative Expenses	200,000
Interest Expense	50,000
Income Tax Expense	85,000
Total Expenses	$2,200,000
Net Income	$ 200,000

called Accounts Receivable from Customers. Both are assets. Thus the firm generated revenues and increased assets.

Expenses measure the outflow of assets (or increases in liabilities) used in generating revenues. Cost of Goods Sold (an expense) measures the cost of inventories sold to customers. Selling expenses measure the cash payments made or the liabilities incurred to make future cash payments for marketing services received during the period. For each expense, either an asset decreases or a liability increases (or both).

A firm strives to generate an excess of net asset inflows from revenues over net asset outflows from expenses required to generate the revenues. Net income indicates a firm's accomplishments (revenues) relative to the efforts required (expenses) in pursuing its operating activities. When expenses for a period exceed revenues, a firm incurs a **net loss.**

Classification of Revenues and Expenses

The income statement for SoftWare Corporation classifies revenues by the nature of the good or service sold (software, consulting services, financing services) and classifies expenses by the department that carried out the firm's operating activities (production, marketing, administration). Interest expense on long-term bonds and income tax expense appear separately. Alternatively, the firm might classify expenses by the nature of the expense (for example, salaries, depreciation, utilities). Firms classify revenues and expenses in their income statements in different ways.

Relation to Balance Sheet

The income statement links the balance sheet at the beginning of the period with the balance sheet at the end of the period. Recall that the balance sheet amount for retained earnings represents the sum of prior earnings of a firm in excess of dividends. The amount of net income helps explain the change in retained earnings between the beginning and the end of the period. During Year 1, SoftWare Corporation had net income of $200,000. It declared and paid dividends of $40,000. Retained earnings during Year 1, therefore, changed as follows:

Retained Earnings, December 31, Year 0	$ 0
Add Net Income for Year 1	200,000
Subtract Dividends Declared and Paid during Year 1	(40,000)
Retained Earnings, December 31, Year 1	$160,000

SUMMARY OF BALANCE SHEET AND INCOME STATEMENT

Recall Figure 1.1, which summarizes the principal business activities of a firm: setting goals and strategies, financing, investing, and operating. Figure 1.2 summarizes the relation between these business activities and the balance sheet and income statement.

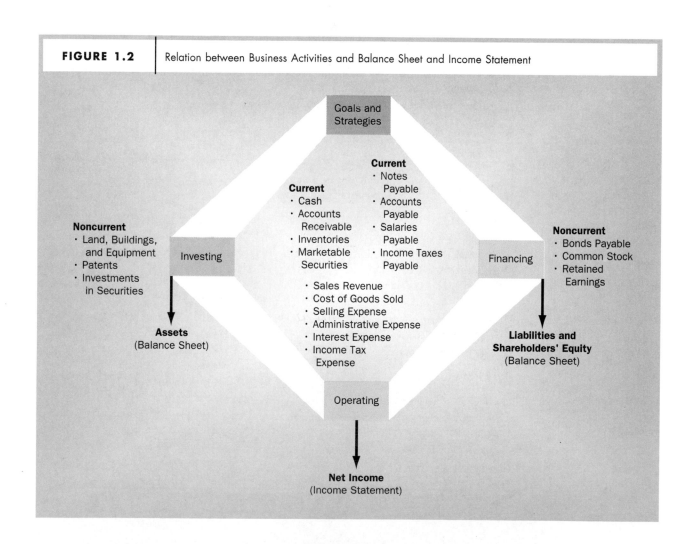

FIGURE 1.2 | Relation between Business Activities and Balance Sheet and Income Statement

STATEMENT OF CASH FLOWS

The third principal financial statement is the **statement of cash flows.** Exhibit 1.3 presents the statement of cash flows for SoftWare Corporation for Year 1. This statement reports the net cash flows relating to operating, investing, and financing activities for a period of time. Operations led to an increase in cash of $50,000. (Recall that not all revenues result in an immediate increase in cash and that not all expenses result in an immediate decrease in cash.) Acquiring noncurrent assets used cash of $30,000. Financing activities led to a $110,000 net increase in cash. Of what significance is a statement explaining or analyzing the change in cash during a period of time? The following example illustrates the usefulness.

Example 2   Diversified Technologies Corporation began business four years ago. In its first four years, it generated net income of $100,000, $300,000, $800,000, and $1,500,000, respectively. The company retained all of its earnings for growth (reflected on the balance sheet as an increase in net assets and an increase in retained earnings). Early in the fifth year, the company learned that despite paying no dividends, it was running out of cash. A careful study of the problem revealed the company was expanding accounts receivable, inventories, buildings, and equipment so fast that operations and external financing were not generating cash quickly enough to keep pace with the growth.

This example illustrates a common phenomenon for business firms. A firm might not generate cash in sufficient amounts or at the proper times to finance all ongoing or growing operations. If a firm is to continue operating successfully, it must generate more cash than it spends. In some cases it can borrow from creditors to replenish its cash, but future operations must generate cash to repay these loans.

EXHIBIT 1.3	SOFTWARE CORPORATION Statement of Cash Flows for Year 1

Operations		
Revenues Providing Cash	$2,220,000[a]	
Expenses Using Cash	(2,170,000)[a]	
Cash Flow from Operations		$ 50,000
Investing		
Sale of Noncurrent Assets	—	
Acquisition of Noncurrent Assets	(30,000)	
Cash Flow from Investing		(30,000)
Financing		
Issue of Bonds	$ 50,000	
Issue of Common Stock	100,000	
Dividends	(40,000)	
Reduction in Debt and Common Stock	—	
Cash Flow from Financing		110,000
Net Change in Cash for Year 1		$130,000

[a]Chapter 4 discusses the computation of cash generated from operations and its relation to net income.

| FIGURE 1.3 | Inflows and Outflows of Cash |

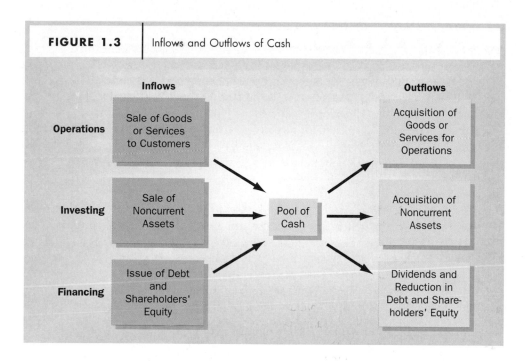

Classification of Items in the Statement of Cash Flows   Exhibit 1.3 classifies the inflows and outflows of cash using three of the principal business activities described earlier in the chapter. Figure 1.3 depicts these various sources and uses of cash.

1. Operations. Most firms expect their primary source of cash to be the excess of cash they receive from customers over the amount of cash they pay to suppliers, employees, and others in carrying out the firms' operating activities.
2. Investing. Firms that expect either to maintain current operating levels or to grow must continually acquire buildings, equipment, and other noncurrent assets. Just to keep productive capacity constant requires cash to replace assets used up. To grow requires even more. A firm can obtain some of the cash needed from selling existing land, buildings, and equipment. The firm's cash needs, however, usually exceed the cash proceeds of such disposals.
3. Financing. Firms obtain additional financing to support operating and investing activities by issuing bonds or common stock. The firm uses cash to pay dividends and to retire old financing, such as long-term debt when it comes due.

Relation to Balance Sheet and Income Statement   The statement of cash flows explains the change in cash between the beginning and the end of the period. The statement also sets forth the major investing and financing activities of the period. Thus, the statement of cash flows helps explain changes in various items on the comparative balance sheet. The statement of cash flows likewise parallels the income statement: the statement of cash flows shows how operations affected cash for the period, and the income statement shows how the same operations affected revenues and expenses.

PROBLEM 1.1 FOR SELF-STUDY

Preparing a balance sheet and an income statement. The accounting records of Gateway 2000, a manufacturer and direct marketer of personal computers, reveal the following (amounts in thousands):

	December 31	
	Year 3	**Year 4**
Balance Sheet Items		
Accounts Payable CL	$411,788	$488,717
Accounts Receivable CA	449,723	510,679
Buildings and Equipment (net of accumulated depreciation) NCA	227,477	315,038
Cash CA	447,718	593,601
Common Stock SE	290,829	295,535
Computer Software Development Cost (net of accumulated amortization) NCA	31,873	39,998
Goodwill from Corporate Acquisitions NCA	35,631	118,121
Inventories CA	278,043	249,224
Land NCA	14,888	21,431
Long-term Debt SE	7,244	7,240
Notes Payable CL	15,041	13,969
Other Current Assets CA	74,216	152,531
Other Current Liabilities CL	207,336	315,292
Other Noncurrent Liabilities NCL	50,857	98,081
Retained Earnings SE	410,870	634,509
Royalties Payable CL	125,270	159,418
Short-term Cash Investments CA	0	38,648
Taxes Payable CL	40,334	26,510
Income Statement Items		**For Year 4**
Cost of Goods Sold Exp (O)		$5,217,239
Income Tax Expense Exp (O)		93,823
Interest Expense Exp F		1,740
Interest Revenue Revenue I		28,929
Sales Revenue (O)		6,293,680
Selling and Administrative Expenses Revenue (O)		786,168

a. Prepare a comparative balance sheet for Gateway 2000 as of December 31, Year 3 and Year 4. Classify the balance sheet items into the following categories: current assets, noncurrent assets, current liabilities, noncurrent liabilities, and shareholders' equity.

b. Prepare an income statement for Gateway 2000 for the year ending December 31, Year 4. Classify income statement items into revenues and expenses.

c. Calculate the amount of dividends declared and paid to common shareholders during the year ending December 31, Year 4.

d. Did the increase in cash between December 31, Year 3, and December 31, Year 4, primarily result from operating activities, investing activities, or financing activities? Explain.

OTHER ITEMS IN ANNUAL REPORTS

SUPPORTING SCHEDULES AND NOTES

The balance sheet, income statement, and statement of cash flows present information condensed to ease comprehension by the typical reader. Some readers desire additional details omitted from these condensed versions. Firms therefore usually include with their financial statements additional schedules that provide more detail for some of the items reported in the three main statements. For example, most firms present separate schedules to explain the change in contributed capital and retained earnings.

Every set of published financial statements also contains explanatory notes as an integral part of the statements. As later chapters make clear, a firm must select the accounting methods followed in preparing its financial statements from a set of generally accepted methods. The notes indicate the actual accounting methods the firm uses and also disclose additional information that elaborates on items presented in the three principal statements. To understand fully a firm's balance sheet, income statement, and statement of cash flows requires understanding the notes. No such notes appear here for the financial statements of SoftWare Corporation because they would not mean much at this stage. Do not let this omission lead you to conclude that the notes are unimportant.

AUDITOR'S OPINION

Regulatory bodies generally require firms whose shares of common stock publicly trade in the capital markets to obtain an audit of their financial statements by an independent auditor. The annual report to the shareholders contains the opinion of the independent auditor, or certified public accountant, on the financial statements, supporting schedules, and notes.

The auditor's opinion generally follows a standard format, with some variations to meet specific circumstances. An auditor's opinion on the financial statements of SoftWare Corporation might be as follows:

> We have audited the accompanying balance sheet of SoftWare Corporation as of December 31, Year 0 and Year 1, and the related statements of net income and cash flows for the year then ended. These financial statements are the responsibility of the Corporation's management. Our responsibility is to express an opinion on these financial statements based on our audits.
>
> We conducted our audit in accordance with generally accepted auditing standards. Those standards require that we plan and perform the audit to obtain reasonable assurance about whether the financial statements are free of material misstatement. An audit includes examining, on a test basis, evidence supporting the amounts and disclosures in the financial statements. An audit also includes assessing the accounting principles used and significant estimates made by management, as well as evaluating the overall financial statement presentation. We believe that our audit provides a reasonable basis for our opinion.
>
> In our opinion, the financial statements referred to above present fairly, in all material respects, the financial position of SoftWare Corporation as of December 31, Year 0 and Year 1, and the results of its operations and its cash flows for the year then ended in conformity with generally accepted accounting principles.

The opinion usually contains three paragraphs. The first paragraph indicates the financial presentations covered by the opinion and indicates that the responsibility for the financial statements rests with management. The second paragraph affirms that the auditor has followed auditing standards and practices generally accepted by the accounting profession unless otherwise noted and described. Exceptions to the statement that the auditor conducted the examination "in accordance with generally accepted auditing standards" are rare. There are occasional references to the auditor's having relied on financial statements examined by other auditors, particularly for subsidiaries or for data from prior periods.

The auditor's opinion expressed in the third paragraph is the heart of the report. It may be an **unqualified** or a **qualified opinion.** Most opinions are unqualified; that is, the auditor describes no exceptions or qualifications to its opinion that the statements "present fairly . . . the financial position . . . and the results of its operations and its cash flows . . . in conformity with generally accepted accounting principles." Qualifications to the opinion result primarily from material uncertainties regarding realization or valuation of assets, outstanding litigation or tax liabilities, or accounting inconsistencies between periods caused by changes in the application of accounting principles.

A qualification so material that the auditor cannot express an opinion as to the fairness of the financial statements as a whole must result in either a **disclaimer of opinion** or an **adverse opinion.** Disclaimers of opinion and adverse opinions rarely appear in published annual reports.

FINANCIAL REPORTING ISSUES

The preceding overview of business activities and the principal financial statements raises financial reporting questions, such as the following:

1. Who is the target audience for a firm's financial accounting reports (for example, owners, creditors, regulators, or competitors)? What level of accounting knowledge should the firm assume about its readers in preparing its financial accounting reports? (For example, what knowledge does the proverbial small investor from Peoria possess? the sophisticated Wall Street analyst?)
2. Who should decide which alternative accounting measurement and reporting standards, or methods, firms can use in preparing financial statements and which they cannot use? For example, should a governmental body, practicing accountants, financial statement users, or the reporting firms make these decisions? Should standard-setters require all firms to use the same accounting methods, or should they permit firms to select their accounting methods from a set of allowable methods? On what basis, or by what approach, should the standard-setting body establish acceptable accounting methods?
3. What role does an audit of a firm's financial statements serve? Who should select the auditor? How often should the firm change auditors?
4. How do capital markets react to information in the financial statements? Do market participants accept information as presented in the financial statements, or do they adjust reported information to eliminate unusual or nonrecurring items and filter out differences in accounting methods between firms?

This section briefly describes several of the more important financial reporting issues raised by these questions. The responses to these questions, which later chapters develop more fully, provide insight into the institutional environment in which financial reporting operates.

USERS AND USES OF FINANCIAL ACCOUNTING REPORTS

Consider the following list of potential **users and uses of financial accounting reports:**

1. An investor in a firm's common stock
2. A bank that lends, either short term or long term, to a firm
3. A customer to whom a firm provides a critical raw material
4. A labor union that represents a firm's employees in compensation negotiations
5. An antitrust regulator interested in the market share and profitability of a firm relative to its competitors
6. A competitor interested in the market share and profitability of a firm's products
7. A court of law attempting to measure profits that one firm lost because another firm wrongfully injured it
8. An income tax agency assessing taxes on the income of a firm

Should firms prepare financial accounting reports that meet the particular needs of each of these user groups, or should they prepare one set of general-purpose financial statements? Targeted reports probably satisfy particular user needs more fully, but perhaps they do so at an unjustifiably high cost to the reporting firms and to those with other needs. Incorporating the information needed by various users into a single set of general-purpose financial statements may increase their length and complexity to the point of inhibiting understandability.

A related question concerns the level of accounting understanding that firms should assume users possess. Detailed financial statements and notes may provide useful information to security analysts but may confuse passive investors who simply cash their dividend checks. Perhaps passive investors ignore details and consider them harmless. Should firms provide condensed and detailed versions of their financial statements and permit users to select the set they find meaningful?

AUTHORITY FOR ESTABLISHING ACCEPTABLE ACCOUNTING STANDARDS

Firms use various accounting methods, or standards, in preparing their financial statements. A governmental body might set such accounting standards and use the legislative power of the government to enforce them. With this approach to standard setting, one would worry that government employees might represent neither preparer nor user perspectives and thereby might specify accounting standards that were either impracticable to apply or irrelevant to user needs. One would also worry that a government body could encounter political pressures in **establishing acceptable accounting standards** that both meet the information needs of financial statement users and permit the government to raise needed tax revenues.

A private-sector body lacks legal enforcement power for its accounting standards but can more likely incorporate viewpoints of various preparer and user groups. Placing the standard-setting process in the private sector does not, however, eliminate political pressures. Firms reporting about themselves sometimes prefer to report less accounting information when it is costly to prepare or when it provides competitors with otherwise-secret information. Users desire more accounting information because they do not bear the cost of preparing the additional information and can ignore information that turns out to be unhelpful. The standard-setting body must deal with these conflicting viewpoints in gaining acceptance for its pronouncements.

A second issue concerns the desired degree of **uniformity in selecting accounting methods** across firms. Should standard-setters require all firms to follow the same accounting method for similar transactions? Such an approach might confuse financial statement users less than if standard-setting bodies permitted firms a choice of several alternative methods. Requiring uniformity also reduces a firm's flexibility to manage reported earnings through its selection of accounting methods. An opposing argument is that because the economic characteristics of firms differ, management should be free, within certain prescribed limits, to select those accounting methods that best capture the firm's particular economics. This view suggests greater **flexibility in selecting accounting methods.**

A third issue concerns the approach that standard-setting bodies should follow in establishing acceptable accounting methods. One approach requires the **conformity of financial reporting to income tax reporting,** so that the government tax authorities would effectively establish acceptable accounting methods. This approach results in firms using one set of accounting methods to measure both net income and taxable income. Financial statements that will help the government raise tax revenues differ, however, from those statements that users want to use to assess the financial position and operating performance of a firm. Financial reports prepared for one purpose need not provide information useful for another. Such an approach also raises concerns about using a governmental body to set accounting standards.

Another approach establishes a broad theoretical structure for financial reporting and then deduces the accounting methods most consistent with this theoretical structure. Such a theoretical structure might start with a set of financial reporting objectives and then specify a set of concepts and general principles that evolve from these objectives. Standard-setting bodies would then determine which of several alternative accounting methods most consistently matches the theoretical structure. The advantage to this **deductive theory-based approach to setting acceptable accounting methods** is that a common core of theory would guide the standard-setting process, presumably resulting in more consistent standards across time and across financial statement items. Standard setting would likely encounter two difficulties with this approach, however. One difficulty relates to obtaining consensus on the theoretical framework to begin with. Unlike the natural sciences, accounting theory does not exist in the physical world and simply await discovery. Rather, the various preparer and user groups must reach a consensus on the accounting measurement and reporting methods that provide the most useful information. Obtaining this consensus results in part from a political process in which each side lobbies for its position. This **political-lobbying approach** to standard setting could lead to a theoretical structure so general, or broad, that it would not guide standard-setters to specific answers for specific questions, leading them to allow several different accounting methods for similar transactions.

A third approach recognizes the political nature of the standard-setting process. The standard-setting body would select those accounting methods most favored by preparers, users, and others involved with financial accounting reports. This approach follows democratic principles, with the standard-setting body serving as a type of "accounting court" to judge between conflicting positions. This approach also has shortcomings. How does the standard-setting body trade off conflicting positions? Should the positions taken by business firms or those taken by financial statement users count more? As various participants in the standard-setting process gain or lose political power over time, the standards might reflect preparers' concerns at some times and users' preferences at other times. How should the process deal with inconsistency in accounting standards over time?

THE ROLE OF AN AUDIT OF A FIRM'S FINANCIAL STATEMENTS

An audit of a firm's financial statements involves (1) an assessment of the capability of a firm's accounting system to accumulate, measure, and synthesize transactional data properly, and (2) an assessment of the operational effectiveness of this accounting system. The auditor obtains evidence for the first assessment by studying the procedures and internal controls built into the accounting system. The auditor obtains evidence for the second assessment by examining a sample of actual transactions.

Employees of a firm might conduct such audits (referred to as **internal audits**). The employees' knowledge and familiarity with the activities of their firm probably enhance the quality of the audit work and increase the likelihood that the audit will generate suggestions for improving operations. Because internal auditors work for the firm, however, their audits do not add to the firm's financial statements the degree of credibility that an external, independent audit provides. The managers of a firm have incentives to report as favorable a picture as possible in the financial statements. An **external audit** by independent auditors somewhat controls management's optimistic inclinations.

Either a firm might select its external auditor or the government could appoint such an auditor. Allowing firms to select their external auditor creates a market for audit services. Competition tends to drive out inefficient audit firms and constrain audit fees. Competition might also lead audit firms to differentiate themselves on the quality of audit work or range of services, thereby increasing the value of the audit product. Granting firms the freedom to select their external auditor may, however, lead them to opinion shopping—that is, searching for an auditor who will agree with a firm's wishes. Government appointment of the auditor eliminates a firm's tendency to shop but results in losing the benefits of a competitive market for auditor services. Some observers suggest that regulators should require firms to change auditors periodically, say every five years.

EFFICIENCY OF CAPITAL MARKETS

Empirical research during the last two decades provides support for the notion that capital markets are efficient. In an **efficient capital market,** prices react quickly and unbiasedly to new information. The research suggests that market prices incorporate new information within a day or two—or even faster—of its release to the market. An efficient capital market implies that users of financial statements cannot analyze those financial statements weeks or months later to find undervalued or overvalued securities. Market prices quickly impound any new financial information. The research also suggests that market participants do not interpret financial statement data naively. Rather, they adjust for nonrecurring items and differences in accounting methods across firms. An efficient capital market suggests that requiring increased disclosure of the accounting methods that a firm uses helps investors more than does requiring uniform methods for all firms.

As evidence that market prices do not necessarily reflect economic values continually, critics of capital market efficiency point to the sharp market-wide increases and decreases in security prices experienced in recent years and to the rapid increases in market prices of securities of certain firms that are takeover targets. Believers in efficient capital markets suggest that such criticism reflects a lack of understanding of the implications of efficiency in capital markets. *Efficient capital markets* means merely that market prices reflect all publicly available information. Such prices can change quickly and by large amounts when information and understandings of markets change dramatically fast.

Even if capital markets are efficient, critics point out that the analysis and interpretation of financial statements still have a role to play. Someone, presumably sophisticated security analysts, must analyze financial statements soon after their release and, through buying and selling recommendations, inject new information into security prices. Critics further point out that financial statements serve information needs outside of a capital market setting, such as credit analyses by lenders, antitrust investigations by regulators, and pricing studies by competitors.

SUMMARY OF FINANCIAL REPORTING ISSUES

The preceding sections raise several financial reporting issues that have no uniquely correct resolutions. We introduced you in a general way to the environment in which financial reporting operates, to begin sensitizing you to the unresolved issues. Later chapters discuss each of these issues. The next two sections describe the financial reporting process in the United States and, to a lesser extent, in other countries.

THE FINANCIAL REPORTING PROCESS IN THE UNITED STATES

The **Securities and Exchange Commission (SEC),** an agency of the federal government, has the legal authority to set acceptable accounting methods, or standards, in the United States. The SEC looks to the **Financial Accounting Standards Board (FASB),** a private-sector body, for leadership in establishing such standards. The seven-member FASB contains financial statement users, practicing accountants, and representatives from business firms, academia, and the government. Board members work full-time for the FASB and sever all relations with their previous employers. Thus, a private-sector body containing representatives from a broad set of constituencies establishes acceptable accounting standards.[3]

Common terminology refers to the pronouncements of the FASB (and its predecessors) as **generally accepted accounting principles (GAAP).** The FASB issues its major pronouncements in the form of *Statements of Financial Accounting Standards.* The FASB has issued more than 135 statements since it began operating in 1973. For some financial reporting topics, the FASB requires the use of a uniform accounting method by all firms. In other cases, firms enjoy some freedom to select from a limited set of alternative methods. Thus, the current standard-setting approach lies somewhere between uniformity and flexibility, with a mild tilt toward uniformity.

With the exception of one method of accounting for inventories and cost of goods sold (discussed in Chapter 7), the accounting methods that firms use for financial reporting can differ from the methods used in calculating taxable income. Permitting different methods recognizes that the goal of providing useful information to financial statement users may differ from the taxation authorities' goals of raising revenues efficiently.

The FASB combines the deductive theory-based approach and the political-lobbying approach in setting accounting standards. As the FASB contemplates a reporting issue, it follows a rigorous due-process procedure to ensure that it receives inputs from various preparer and user groups. Involving these constituencies in the deliberations also identifies concerns and increases the likelihood of acceptance of the final reporting standards.

The FASB recognizes that it needs some theoretical structure to guide its deliberations. The Board has developed a conceptual framework to use, not as a rigorous deductive scheme but as a guiding mechanism for setting accounting standards. The conceptual framework contains guidance about the following:

1. Objectives of financial reporting
2. Qualitative characteristics of accounting information

---

[3]You may want to visit the Web site of the Financial Accounting Standards Board at www.fasb.org to learn more about the purpose, procedures, and pronouncements of the FASB.

3. Elements of financial statements
4. Recognition and measurement principles

The FASB reports the components of its conceptual framework in *Statements of Financial Accounting Concepts.* Figure 1.4 summarizes the **financial reporting objectives** established by the FASB and their relation to the principal financial statements.

1. Financial reporting should provide information useful for making rational investment and credit decisions. This general-purpose objective simply states that financial reporting should aim primarily at investors and creditors and should strive to be useful to these individuals in their decision making.
2. Financial reporting should provide information to help investors and creditors assess the amount, timing, and uncertainty of future cash flows. This objective flows from the first by defining "useful information" more fully. It states that investors and creditors primarily want to know about the cash they will receive from investing in a firm. The ability of the firm to generate cash flows affects the amount of cash that will likely flow to investors and creditors.
3. Financial reporting should provide information about the economic resources of a firm and the claims on those resources. The balance sheet attempts to accomplish this objective.
4. Financial reporting should provide information about a firm's operating performance during a period. The income statement attempts to accomplish this objective.
5. Financial reporting should provide information about how an enterprise obtains and uses cash. The statement of cash flows accomplishes this objective.
6. Financial reporting should provide information about how management has discharged its stewardship responsibility to owners. Stewardship refers to the prudent use of resources entrusted to a firm. No single statement helps in assessing stewardship. Rather, owners assess stewardship using information from all three financial statements and the notes.
7. Financial reporting should include explanations and interpretations to help users understand the financial information provided. Supporting schedules and notes to the financial statements attempt to satisfy this objective.

AN INTERNATIONAL PERSPECTIVE

The processes followed in setting accounting principles in countries other than the United States vary widely. In some countries, the measurement rules followed in preparing the financial statements match those followed in computing taxable income. Thus, the legislative branch of the government sets acceptable accounting principles. In other countries, an agency of the government sets acceptable accounting principles, but the measurement rules differ from those used in computing taxable income. In still other countries, the accounting profession, through its various boards and committees, plays a major role in setting accounting principles. Not surprisingly, the differing objectives of these standard-setting bodies (for example, taxation, accomplishment of government policy objectives, fair reporting to investors) result in diverse sets of accounting principles across countries.

FIGURE 1.4 Summary of Reporting Process and Principal Financial Statements

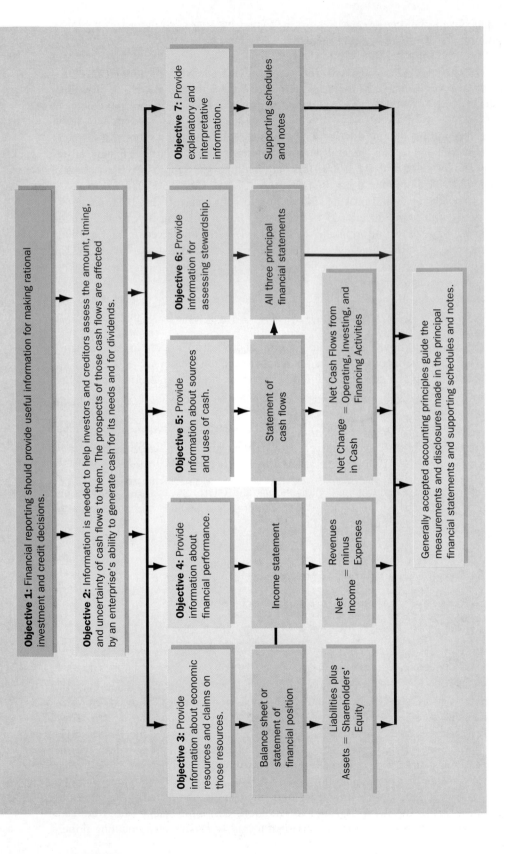

Objective 1: Financial reporting should provide useful information for making rational investment and credit decisions.

Objective 2: Information is needed to help investors and creditors assess the amount, timing, and uncertainty of cash flows to them. The prospects of those cash flows are affected by an enterprise's ability to generate cash for its needs and for dividends.

Objective 3: Provide information about economic resources and claims on those resources.

Balance sheet or statement of financial position

Assets = Liabilities plus Shareholders' Equity

Objective 4: Provide information about financial performance.

Income statement

Net Income = Revenues minus Expenses

Objective 5: Provide information about sources and uses of cash.

Statement of cash flows

Net Change in Cash = Net Cash Flows from Operating, Investing, and Financing Activities

Objective 6: Provide information for assessing stewardship.

All three principal financial statements

Objective 7: Provide explanatory and interpretative information.

Supporting schedules and notes

Generally accepted accounting principles guide the measurements and disclosures made in the principal financial statements and supporting schedules and notes.

The globalization of capital markets in recent years has increased the need for comparable and understandable financial statements across countries. To address this need, the **International Accounting Standards Committee (IASC),** a voluntary association of professional accounting organizations from many countries, has played an important role in developing acceptable accounting principles worldwide. Although the IASC has no legal authority, it encourages its members to exert influence on the standard-setting process within their own countries to reduce diversity. Stock exchanges in several countries now allow firms from other countries to list their securities on the exchanges as long as the financial statements of these firms reflect pronouncements of the IASC. Standard-setting boards in several countries now accept IASC pronouncements as allowable accounting principles within their countries. It is too early to assess the extent to which the responsibility and authority for setting acceptable accounting standards will remain within individual countries or will shift to the IASC.[4]

SUMMARY

This chapter provides an overview of business activities and relates them to the principal financial statements included in annual reports to shareholders. The chapter raises more questions than it answers. It provides you with a broad overview of the various financial statements before you examine the concepts and procedures that underlie each statement.

Chapters 2 through 4 discuss and illustrate the concepts and procedures underlying the balance sheet, income statement, and statement of cash flows. Chapter 5 considers techniques for analyzing and interpreting these financial statements. Chapters 6 through 13 explore more fully the principles of accounting for individual assets, liabilities, and shareholders' equities. Chapter 14 provides a synthesis for the material in Chapters 6 through 13.

Now we turn to the study of financial accounting. To comprehend the concepts and procedures in the book, you should study the numerical examples presented in each chapter and prepare solutions to several problems, including the self-study problems. You may find the glossary of terms at the back of the book useful.

SOLUTION TO SELF-STUDY PROBLEM

SUGGESTED SOLUTION TO PROBLEM 1.1 FOR SELF-STUDY

(Gateway 2000: preparing a balance sheet and an income statement)
a. See Exhibit 1.4.
b. See Exhibit 1.5.
c. Gateway 2000 did not declare or pay a dividend to the common shareholders during Year 4 because the change in retained earnings equals net income, as the following analysis shows (amounts in thousands):

Retained Earnings, May 31, Year 3	$410,870
Plus Net Income for Year 4	223,639
Less Dividend Declared	0
Retained Earnings, May 31, Year 4	$634,509

[4]You may want to visit the Web site of the International Accounting Standards Committee at www.iasc.org.uk to learn more about the purpose, procedures, and pronouncements of the IASC.

EXHIBIT 1.4	GATEWAY 2000 Comparative Balance Sheet December 31, Year 3 and Year 4 (Problem 1.1 for Self-Study)

	December 31	
	Year 3	Year 4
ASSETS		
Current Assets		
Cash	$ 447,718	$ 593,601
Short-term Cash Investments	0	38,648
Accounts Receivable	449,723	510,679
Inventories	278,043	249,224
Other Current Assets	74,216	152,531
Total Current Assets	$1,249,700	$1,544,683
Noncurrent Assets		
Land	$ 14,888	$ 21,431
Buildings and Equipment (net of accumulated depreciation)	227,477	315,038
Computer Software Development Cost (net of accumulated		
amortization)	31,873	39,998
Goodwill from Corporate Acquisitions	35,631	118,121
Total Noncurrent Assets	$ 309,869	$ 494,588
Total Assets	$1,559,569	$2,039,271
LIABILITIES AND SHAREHOLDERS' EQUITY		
Current Liabilities		
Accounts Payable	$ 411,788	$ 488,717
Notes Payable	15,041	13,969
Royalties Payable	125,270	159,418
Taxes Payable	40,334	26,510
Other Current Liabilities	207,336	315,292
Total Current Liabilities	$ 799,769	$1,003,906
Noncurrent Liabilities		
Long-term Debt	$ 7,244	$ 7,240
Other Noncurrent Liabilities	50,857	98,081
Total Noncurrent Liabilities	$ 58,101	$ 105,321
Total Liabilities	$ 857,870	$1,109,227
Shareholders' Equity		
Common Stock	$ 290,829	$ 295,535
Retained Earnings	410,870	634,509
Total Shareholders' Equity	$ 701,699	$ 930,044
Total Liabilities and Shareholders' Equity	$1,559,569	$2,039,271

EXHIBIT 1.5	GATEWAY 2000 Income Statement For the Year Ended December 31, Year 4 (Problem 1.1 for Self-Study)

Revenues	
Sales	$6,293,680
Interest Revenue	28,929
Total Revenues	$6,322,609
Expenses	
Cost of Goods Sold	$5,217,239
Selling and Administrative Expenses	786,168
Interest Expense	1,740
Income Tax Expense	93,823
Total Expenses	$6,098,970
Net Income	$ 223,639

d. Gateway 2000 experienced only minor changes in accounts related to financing activities (notes payable, long-term debt, common stock). The firm experienced increases in accounts related to investing activities (land, buildings and equipment, computer software development costs, goodwill from acquisitions), which would likely have reduced cash. Thus, the increase in cash primarily resulted from profitable operations. Note, though, that the increase in cash and short-term investments of cash of $184,531 [= ($593,601 + $38,648) − $447,718] is less than net income for the year of $223,639.

KEY TERMS AND CONCEPTS

Goals and strategies
Financing activities
Dividends
Investing activities
Operating activities
Annual report to shareholders
Management discussion and analysis (MD&A)
Balance sheet
Assets
Liabilities
Shareholders' equity
Contributed capital
Retained earnings
Historical valuation
Current valuation
Income statement
Net income, earnings
Revenue
Expense

Net loss
Statement of cash flows
Unqualified, qualified opinion
Disclaimer of opinion
Adverse opinion
Users and uses of financial accounting reports
Establishing acceptable accounting standards
Uniformity versus flexibility in selecting accounting methods
Conformity of financial reporting to income tax reporting
Deductive theory–based approach versus political-lobbying approach to setting acceptable accounting methods
Internal audits versus external audits
Efficient capital market
Securities and Exchange Commission (SEC)

Financial Accounting Standards Board
  (FASB)
Generally accepted accounting principles
  (GAAP)
*Statement of Financial Accounting
  Standards*

*Statement of Financial Accounting
  Concepts*
Financial reporting objectives
International Accounting Standards
  Committee (IASC)

QUESTIONS, EXERCISES, PROBLEMS, AND CASES

QUESTIONS

1. Review the meaning of the terms and concepts listed in Key Terms and Concepts.
2. The chapter describes four activities common to all entities: setting goals and strategies, financing activities, investing activities, and operating activities. How would these four activities likely differ for a charitable organization versus a business firm?
3. "The photographic analogy for the balance sheet is a snapshot and for the income statement and statement of cash flows is a motion picture." Explain.
4. "Asset valuation and income measurement are closely related." Explain.
5. A student states, "It is inconceivable to me that a firm could report increasing net income yet run out of cash." Clarify this seeming contradiction.
6. Does an unqualified, or "clean," opinion of an independent auditor indicate that the financial statements are free of errors and misrepresentations? Explain.
7. Suggest reasons why the format and content of financial accounting reports tend to be more standardized than the format and content of accounting reports that firms prepare for their internal decision-making, planning, and control purposes.
8. In France, Germany, and Japan, governmental entities establish acceptable accounting standards and generally require conformity between financial reporting and tax reporting. Describe the advantages and disadvantages of this approach to standard setting.
9. "Prescribing a single method of accounting for a particular financial statement item will result in uniform reporting across firms." Do you agree? Why or why not?
10. "Politics is inherent to the accounting standard-setting process." Explain.
11. "The efficiency of capital markets eliminates the need for financial accounting reports." Do you agree? Why or why not?

EXERCISES

12. **Preparing a personal balance sheet.** Prepare a balance sheet of your personal assets, liabilities, and owner's equity. How does the presentation of owner's equity on your balance sheet differ from that in Exhibit 1.1?
13. **Classifying financial statement accounts.** The balance sheet or income statement classifies various items in one of the following ways:

    CA—Current assets

    NA—Noncurrent assets

    CL—Current liabilities

    NL—Noncurrent liabilities

    CC—Contributed capital

    RE—Retained earnings

    NI—Income statement item (revenue or expense)

    X—Item generally not appearing on a balance sheet or an income statement

Using the letters, indicate the classification of each of the following items:
   a. Factory
   b. Interest revenue
   c. Common stock issued by a corporation
   d. Goodwill developed by a firm (see glossary)
   e. Automobiles used by sales staff
   f. Cash on hand
   g. Unsettled damage suit against a firm
   h. Commissions earned by sales staff
   i. Supplies inventory
   j. Note payable, due in three months
   k. Increase in market value of land held
   l. Dividends
   m. Employee payroll taxes payable
   n. Note payable, due in six years

14. **Balance sheet relations.** Selected balance sheet amounts for Sports Authority, a retailer of sports equipment and apparel at discount prices, for four recent years appear below (amounts in millions):

	Year 8	Year 9	Year 10	Year 11
Noncurrent Assets	$157	$212	$309	?
Shareholders' Equity	?	278	310	$334
Total Assets	?	?	754	?
Current Liabilities	197	228	?a	?b
Current Assets	306	?	?a	?b
Noncurrent Liabilities	14	?	?	188
Total Liabilities and Shareholders' Equity	?	524	?	812

aCurrent Assets − Current Liabilities = $176.
bCurrent Assets − Current Liabilities = $99.

   a. Compute the missing balance sheet amounts for each of the four years.
   b. How did the structure of total assets (that is, the proportion of current versus noncurrent assets) change over the four-year period? What might account for such a change?
   c. How did the structure of total liabilities plus shareholders' equity change over the four-year period? What might account for such a change?

15. **Balance sheet relations.** Selected balance sheet amounts for TJX Cos., Inc., a retailer of name-brand apparel at discount prices, for four recent years appear below (amounts in millions):

	Year 8	Year 9	Year 10	Year 11
Total Assets	$1,600	?	?	$2,610
Noncurrent Liabilities	273	$ 703	?	228
Noncurrent Assets	?	1,059	$ 899	?
Total Liabilities and Shareholders' Equity	?	2,674	?	?
Current Liabilities	720	?	1,182	1,218
Shareholders' Equity	?	$ 765	1,127	?
Current Assets	1,008	?	1,662	1,683

a. Compute the missing balance sheet amounts for each of the four years.
b. How did the structure of total assets (that is, the proportion of current versus non-current assets) change between Year 8 and Year 9? What factors might account for such a change?
c. How did the structure of total liabilities plus shareholders' equity change between Year 8 and Year 9? What factors might account for such a change?
d. How did the structure of total assets change between Year 9 and Year 10? What factors might account for such a change?
e. How did the structure of total liabilities plus shareholders' equity change between Year 9 and Year 10? What factors might account for such a change?

16. **Balance sheet relations.** Selected balance sheet amounts for Procter & Gamble, a consumer products company, for four recent years appear below (amounts in millions):

	Year 6	Year 7	Year 8	Year 9
Current Assets	$ 8,435	?[a]	$ 9,975	$ 9,988
Noncurrent Assets	?	?	14,960	?
Total Assets	?	$24,025	?	?
Current Liabilities	6,733	7,642	8,287	?[c]
Noncurrent Liabilities	5,999	?	9,207	?
Contributed Capital	?	1,149	?	1,399
Retained Earnings	6,719	7,922	?[b]	?[d]
Total Liabilities and Shareholders' Equity	20,468	?	?	25,535

[a]Current Assets − Current Liabilities = $1,724.
[b]Net loss for Year 8 is $656, and dividends are $1,117.
[c]Current Assets − Current Liabilities = $1,948.
[d]Net income for Year 9 is $2,524, and dividends are $1,240.

a. Compute the missing balance sheet amounts for each of the four years.
b. What is the likely explanation for the increase in total assets between Year 6 and Year 7?
c. What transactions might explain the changes in noncurrent liabilities and retained earnings between Year 7 and Year 8?
d. What transactions might explain the changes in the mix of financing between Year 8 and Year 9?

17. **Balance sheet relations.** Selected balance sheet amounts for Anheuser-Busch, a manufacturer of beer and operator of theme parks, for four recent years appear below (amounts in millions):

	Year 6	Year 7	Year 8	Year 9
Current Assets	$ 1,546	?	$1,466	?
Noncurrent Assets	?	$9,080	8,998	$10,143
Total Assets	10,547	?	?	?
Current Liabilities	1,489	?	?	1,501
Noncurrent Liabilities	4,643	4,915	?	?
Shareholders' Equity	?	4,434	4,029	4,042
Total Liabilities and Shareholders' Equity	?	10,591	?	?
Current Assets/Current Liabilities	?	?	1.024	1.055

  a. Compute the missing amounts for each of the four years.

  b. Identify changes in the component structure of total assets and in the component structure of total liabilities plus shareholders' equity over the four-year period. Suggest the events or transactions that might explain these changes.

18. **Balance sheet relations.** Selected balance sheet amounts for Texas Instruments (TI), a computer hardware and software company, for four recent years appear below (amounts in millions):

	Year 5	Year 6	Year 7	Year 8
Current Assets	?	$2,626	$3,314	?
Noncurrent Assets	$2,628	?	2,679	?
Total Assets	?	5,185	?	?
Current Liabilities	1,568	?	2,001	$2,199
Noncurrent Liabilities	1,486	?	1,677	1,751
Contributed Capital	?	1,031	?	1,127
Retained Earnings	766	916	?[a]	?[b]
Total Liabilities and Shareholders' Equity	5,009	?	?	?
Current Assets/Current Liabilities	?	1.58	?	1.83

[a]Net income for Year 7 was $472, and dividends were $81.
[b]Net income for Year 8 was $691, and dividends were $86.

  a. Compute the missing amounts for each of the four years.

  b. Identify changes in the component structure of total assets and in the component structure of total liabilities and shareholders' equity over the four years above. Suggest the events or transactions that might explain these changes.

19. **Retained earnings relations.** Olin Corporation manufactures a diversified line of chemical products. Its sales tend to vary with changes in the business cycle. Selected data from its financial statements for four recent years appear below (amounts in millions):

	Year 6	Year 7	Year 8	Year 9
Retained Earnings, Beginning of Year	$499	?	$388	$238
Net Income	(13)[a]	$ 9	?	91
Dividends Declared and Paid	51	56	58	?
Retained Earnings, End of Year	?	388	238	269

[a]Net loss

  a. Compute the missing amounts for each year.

  b. What is the likely reason for the variations in net income and net loss?

  c. Why might Olin Corporation continue to pay and even increase its dividend, given the variability in earnings?

20. **Retained earnings relations.** Selected data affecting retained earnings for Volvo Group, a Swedish automobile manufacturer, for four recent years appear on the following page (amounts in millions of Swedish kronor):

	Year 3	Year 4	Year 5	Year 6
Retained Earnings, January 1	25,634	?	?	37,922
Net Income	5,665	4,940	?	?
Dividends Declared and Paid	815	?	1,203	1,203
Retained Earnings, December 31	?	34,338	37,922	35,669

a. Compute the missing amounts for each of the four years.

b. Retained earnings increased but at a decreasing rate between Year 3 and Year 5 and declined between Year 5 and Year 6. What is the apparent explanation for these changes?

21. **Relating net income to balance sheet changes.** The comparative balance sheets for Home Depot, a retailer of products for the home, as of December 31, Year 2, December 31, Year 3, and December 31, Year 4, appear below (amounts in millions):

HOME DEPOT
Comparative Balance Sheet
December 31, Year 2, Year 3, and Year 4

	December 31		
	Year 2	**Year 3**	**Year 4**
Total Assets	$7,354	$9,342	$11,229
Liabilities	$2,290	$3,289	$ 4,015
Common Stock	2,485	2,646	2,784
Retained Earnings	2,579	3,407	4,430
Total Liabilities and Shareholders' Equity	$7,354	$9,342	$11,229

Home Depot declared and paid dividends of $110 million during Year 3 and $139 million during Year 4.

a. Compute net income for Year 3 and Year 4 by analyzing the change in retained earnings.

b. Demonstrate that the following relation holds:

Net Income = Increase in Assets − Increase in Liabilities
− Increase in Contributed Capital + Dividends

22. **Relating net income to balance sheet changes.** The comparative balance sheets for Nestlé, a Swiss consumer foods company, for Year 4, Year 5, and Year 6 appear below (amounts in millions of Swiss francs):

NESTLÉ
Comparative Balance Sheets
December 31, Year 4, Year 5, and Year 6

	December 31		
	Year 4	**Year 5**	**Year 6**
Total Assets	SF39,209	SF41,205	SF41,436
Liabilities	21,760	22,395	21,470
Common Stock	353	371	371

(continued)

NESTLÉ
(continued)

	December 31		
	Year 4	Year 5	Year 6
Retained Earnings	17,096	18,439	19,595
Total Liabilities and Shareholders' Equity	SF39,209	SF41,205	SF41,436

Dividends declared and paid were SF617 during Year 5 and SF740 during Year 6.

a. Compute net income for Year 5 and Year 6 by analyzing the change in retained earnings.

b. Demonstrate that the following relation holds:

$$\text{Net Income} = \text{Increase in Assets} - \text{Increase in Liabilities} - \text{Increase in Contributed Capital} + \text{Dividends}$$

23. **Income statement relations.** Selected income statement information for Dell Computer, a manufacturer of personal computers, for three recent years appears below (amounts in millions):

	Year 4	Year 5	Year 6
Sales	$5,296	?	$12,327
Interest Revenue	6	$ 33	52
Cost of Goods Sold	4,229	6,093	?
Marketing and Administrative Expenses	595	826	1,202
Research and Development Expense	95	126	204
Income Tax Expense	111	216	424
Net Income	?	531	944

a. Compute the missing amounts for each of the three years.

b. Prepare a common-size income statement for each year, in which sales is equal to 100 percent and each revenue, expense, and net income are expressed as a percentage of sales. What factors appear to explain the change in the ratio of net income to sales?

24. **Income statement relations.** Selected income statement information for Circuit City Stores, a retailer of electronic products, for three recent years appears below (amounts in millions):

	Year 6	Year 7	Year 8
Sales	$7,029	?	$8,871
Cost of Goods Sold	5,394	$5,903	?
Marketing and Administrative Expenses	1,322	1,511	1,849
Interest Expense	25	30	27
Income Tax Expense	108	84	64
Net Income	?	136	104

a. Compute the missing amounts for each of the three years.

b. Prepare a common-size income statement for each year, in which sales equals 100 percent and each expense and net income are expressed as a percentage of sales. What factors appear to explain the change in the ratio of net income to sales?

25. **Statement of cash flows relations.** Selected data from the statement of cash flows for Delta Airlines for Year 2, Year 3, and Year 4 appear below (amounts in millions):

	Year 2	Year 3	Year 4
Inflows of Cash			
Increase in Short-term Debt	$ 746	0	0
Issue of Long-term Debt	2,313	?	$ 975
Issue of Common Stock	0	$ 1,127	0
Increase in Cash from Operations	10,519	12,196	12,528
Sale of Property and Equipment	43	87	103
Outflows of Cash			
Acquisition of Property and Equipment	3,082	1,414	?
Decrease in Short-term Debt	0	801	0
Decrease in Long-term Debt	794	519	547
Dividends	89	138	120
Decrease in Cash for Operations	?	11,519	11,204
Increase (Decrease) in Cash	(713)	1,130	122

a. Prepare a statement of cash flows for Delta Airlines for the three years using the format in Exhibit 1.3.

b. Comment on the relation among cash flows from operating, investing, and financing activities during the three years.

26. **Statement of cash flows relations.** Selected data from the statement of cash flows for Nike, a manufacturer of athletic footwear and sports apparel, for three recent years appear below (amounts in millions):

	Year 8	Year 9	Year 10
Inflows of Cash			
Proceeds from Bank Borrowings	$ 23	$ 388	$ 26
Revenues from Operations Increasing Cash	6,184	6,087	9,633
Issue of Common Stock	2	69	12
Total Inflows	$6,209	$6,544	$ 9,671
Outflows of Cash			
Acquisition of Property, Plant, and Equipment	$ 240	$ 496	$ 595
Expenses for Operations Decreasing Cash	5,844	5,764	9,115
Dividends	79	101	127
Repurchase of Common Stock	—	—	170
Total Outflows	$6,163	$6,361	$10,007
Increase (Decrease) in Cash	$ 46	$ 183	$ (336)

a. Prepare a statement of cash flows for Nike for each of the three years using the format in Exhibit 1.3.

b. Net income was $553 in Year 8, $796 in Year 9, and $400 in Year 10. Why do the amounts for cash flow from operations computed in part **a** differ from these net income amounts?

27. **Relations between financial statements.** Compute the missing information in each of the four independent cases below. The letters in parentheses refer to the following:

> BS—Balance sheet
>
> IS—Income statement
>
> SCF—Statement of cash flows

a.	Accounts Receivable, Jan. 1, Year 2 (BS)	$ 630
	Sales on Account for Year 2 (IS)	3,290
	Collections from Customers on Account during Year 2 (SCF)	2,780
	Accounts Receivable, Dec. 31, Year 2 (BS)	?
b.	Income Taxes Payable, Jan. 1, Year 2 (BS)	$ 1,240
	Income Tax Expense for Year 2 (IS)	?
	Payments to Governmental Entities during Year 2 (SCF)	8,290
	Income Taxes Payable, Dec. 31, Year 2 (BS)	1,410
c.	Building (net of depreciation), Jan. 1, Year 2 (BS)	$ 89,000
	Depreciation Expense for Year 2 (IS)	?
	Sale of Building during Year 2 (SCF)	17,600
	Building (net of depreciation), Dec. 31, Year 2 (BS)	102,150
d.	Retained Earnings, Jan. 1, Year 2 (BS)	$ 76,200
	Net Income for Year 2 (IS)	14,200
	Dividends Declared and Paid during Year 2 (SCF)	?
	Retained Earnings, Dec. 31, Year 2 (BS)	83,300

PROBLEMS AND CASES

28. **Preparing a balance sheet and income statement.** The accounting records of America Online reveal the following (amounts in thousands):

	June 30	
BALANCE SHEET ITEMS	**Year 7**	**Year 8**
Cash	$124,000	$ 631,000
Accounts Receivable	65,000	104,000
Other Current Assets	134,000	195,000
Property, Plant, and Equipment (net of depreciation)	233,000	363,000
Investment in Securities (noncurrent)	277,000	921,000
Accounts Payable to Suppliers	68,000	87,000
Other Current Liabilities	485,000	807,000
Long-term Debt	140,000	722,000
Common Stock	647,000	1,013,000
Retained Earnings (Deficit)	(507,000)	(415,000)
INCOME STATEMENT ITEMS		**For Year 8**
Sales Revenue		$2,600,000
Interest Revenue		21,000
Cost of Goods Sold		1,678,000
Research and Development Expense		175,000

(continued)

INCOME STATEMENT ITEMS (continued)	For Year 8
Selling and Administrative Expenses	604,000
Depreciation Expense	14,000
Interest Expense	58,000
DIVIDEND INFORMATION	
Dividends Declared and Paid	$ 0

a. Prepare an income statement for America Online for the year ending June 30, Year 8. Refer to Exhibit 1.2 for help in designing the format of the statement.

b. Prepare a comparative balance sheet for America Online on June 30, Year 7, and June 30, Year 8. Refer to Exhibit 1.1 for help in designing the format of the statement.

c. Prepare an analysis of the change in retained earnings during the year ending June 30, Year 8.

29. **Preparing a balance sheet and income statement.** The accounting records of Ben and Jerry's Homemade Ice Cream, Inc. (Ben and Jerry's), reveal the following for a recent year (amounts in thousands):

	December 31	
BALANCE SHEET ITEMS	Year 6	Year 7
Accounts Payable	$ 5,219	$ 7,873
Accounts Receivable	5,044	6,940
Bonds Payable (due Year 20)	10,313	4,602
Cash	796	6,704
Common Stock	6,532	12,959
Inventories	10,083	9,000
Other Current Assets	518	1,091
Other Current Liabilities	2,623	4,249
Other Noncurrent Assets	559	21
Property, Plant, and Equipment	17,299	19,300
Retained Earnings	9,570	13,310
Salaries Payable	42	63
INCOME STATEMENT ITEMS		For Year 7
Administrative Expense		$ 4,798
Cost of Goods Sold		68,500
Income Tax Expense		2,765
Interest Expense		736
Sales Revenue		97,005
Selling Expense		16,466

a. Prepare a comparative balance sheet for Ben and Jerry's as of December 31, Year 6 and Year 7. Classify each balance sheet item into one of the following categories: current assets, noncurrent assets, current liabilities, noncurrent liabilities, and shareholders' equity.

b. Prepare an income statement for Ben and Jerry's for Year 7. Separate income items into revenues and expenses.

c. Prepare a schedule explaining the change in retained earnings between the beginning and the end of Year 7.

d. Compare the amounts on Ben and Jerry's balance sheet on December 31, Year 6, and December 31, Year 7. Identify the major changes and suggest possible explanations for these changes.

30. Preparing a balance sheet and an income statement. The accounting records of Wal-Mart Stores, Inc., reveal the following (amounts in millions):

	December 31	
BALANCE SHEET ITEMS	**Year 1**	**Year 2**
Accounts Payable	$ 4,104	$ 5,907
Accounts Receivable	898	900
Bank Loan Payable (due Year 2 and Year 3)	1,646	1,882
Bonds Payable (due Year 16)	7,960	9,709
Building (net of accumulated depreciation)	6,128	8,163
Cash	20	45
Common Stock	766	769
Equipment (net of accumulated depreciation)	4,307	4,675
Income Taxes Payable	183	365
Land	2,741	3,036
Merchandise Inventory	11,196	14,393
Other Current Liabilities	1,473	1,819
Other Noncurrent Assets	1,151	1,607
Retained Earnings	10,309	12,368
INCOME STATEMENT ITEMS		**For Year 2**
Cost of Merchandise Sold		$65,586
Depreciation Expense		1,070
Income Tax Expense		1,581
Interest Expense		706
Other Operating Expenses		11,788
Sales		83,412
DIVIDEND INFORMATION		
Dividends Declared and Paid during Year 2		$622

a. Prepare a comparative balance sheet for Wal-Mart Stores, Inc., as of December 31, Year 1 and Year 2. Classify each balance sheet item into one of the following categories: current assets, noncurrent assets, current liabilities, noncurrent liabilities, and shareholders' equity.

b. Prepare an income statement for Wal-Mart Stores, Inc., for Year 2. Separate income items into revenues and expenses.

c. Prepare a schedule explaining, or accounting for, the change in retained earnings between the beginning and the end of Year 2.

31. Relations between net income and cash flows. The ABC Company starts the year in fine shape. The firm makes widgets—just what the customer wants. It makes them for $0.75 each and sells them for $1.00. The ABC Company keeps an inventory equal to shipments of the past 30 days, pays its bills promptly, and collects cash from customers within 30 days after the sale. The sales manager predicts a steady increase in sales of 500 widgets each month beginning in February. It looks like a great year, and it begins that way.

January 1	Cash, $875; receivables, $1,000; inventory, $750
January	In January the firm sells, on account for $1,000, 1,000 widgets costing $750. Net income for the month is $250. The firm collects receivables outstanding at the beginning of the month. Production equals 1,000 units at a total cost of $750. The books at the end of January show the following:
February 1	Cash, $1,125; receivables, $1,000; inventory, $750
February	This month's sales jump, as predicted, to 1,500 units. With a corresponding step-up in production to maintain the 30-day inventory, ABC Company makes 2,000 units at a cost of $1,500. All receivables from January sales are collected. Net income so far is $625. Now the books look like this:
March 1	Cash, $625; receivables, $1,500; inventory, $1,125
March	March sales are even better, increasing to 2,000 units. Collections are on time. Production, to adhere to the inventory policy, is 2,500 units. Operating results for the month show net income of $500. Net income to date is $1,125. The books show the following:
April 1	Cash, $250; receivables, $2,000; inventory, $1,500
April	In April, sales jump another 500 units to 2,500, and the manager of ABC Company shakes the sales manager's hand. Customers are paying right on time. Production is pushed to 3,000 units, and the month's business nets $625 for a net income to date of $1,750. The manager of ABC Company takes off for Miami before the accountant's report is issued. Suddenly a phone call comes from the treasurer: "Come home! We need money!"
May 1	Cash, $0; receivables, $2,500; inventory, $1,875

a. Prepare an analysis that explains what happened to ABC Company. (*Hint:* Compute the amount of cash receipts and cash disbursements for each month during the period January 1 to May 1.)
b. How can a firm show increasing net income but a decreasing amount of cash?
c. What insights are provided by the problem about the need for all three financial statements—balance sheet, income statement, and statement of cash flows?
d. What actions would you suggest that ABC Company take to deal with its cash flow problem?

32. **Balance sheet and income statement relations.** (Prepared by Professor Wesley T. Andrews Jr. and reproduced, with adaptation, by permission.)[5]

Once upon a time many, many years ago, a feudal landlord lived in a small province of central Europe. The landlord, called the Red-Bearded Baron, lived in a castle high on a hill. This benevolent fellow took responsibility for the well-being of many peasants who occupied the lands surrounding his castle. Each spring, as the snow began to melt, the Baron would decide how to provide for all his serf dependents during the coming year.

One spring, the Baron was thinking about the wheat crop of the coming growing season. "I believe that 30 acres of my land, being worth five bushels of wheat per

[5]*Accounting Review* (April 1974). Reproduced by permission of the American Accounting Association.

acre, will produce enough wheat for next winter," he mused, "but who should do the farming? I believe I'll give Ivan the Indefatigable and Igor the Immutable the task of growing the wheat." Whereupon he summoned Ivan and Igor, two gentry noted for their hard work and not overly active minds, for an audience.

"Ivan, you will farm on the 20-acre plot of ground, and Igor will farm the 10-acre plot," the Baron began. "I will give Ivan 20 bushels of wheat for seed and 20 pounds of fertilizer. (Twenty pounds of fertilizer are worth two bushels of wheat.) Igor will get 10 bushels of wheat for seed and 10 pounds of fertilizer. I will give each of you an ox to pull a plow, but you will have to make arrangements with Feyador, the Plowmaker, for a plow. The oxen, incidentally, are only three years old and have never been used for farming, so they should have a good 10 years of farming ahead of them. Take good care of them, because an ox is worth 40 bushels of wheat. Come back next fall and return the oxen and the plows along with your harvest." Ivan and Igor bowed and withdrew from the Great Hall, taking with them the things provided by the Baron.

The summer came and went. After the harvest Ivan and Igor returned to the Great Hall to account to their master for the things given them in the spring. Ivan, pouring 223 bushels of wheat onto the floor, said, "My Lord, I present you with a slightly used ox, a plow broken beyond repair, and 223 bushels of wheat. I, unfortunately, owe Feyador, the Plowmaker, three bushels of wheat for the plow I got from him last fall. And, as you might expect, I used all the fertilizer and seed you gave me last spring. You will also remember, my Lord, that you took 20 bushels of my harvest for your own personal use."

Igor, who had been given 10 acres of land, 10 bushels of wheat, and 10 pounds of fertilizer, spoke next. "Here, my Lord, is a partially used-up ox, the plow for which I gave Feyador, the Plowmaker, three bushels of wheat from my harvest, and 105 bushels of wheat. I, too, used all my seed and fertilizer last spring. Also, my Lord, you took 30 bushels of wheat several days ago for your own table. I believe the plow is good for two more seasons."

"Knaves, you did well," said the Red-Bearded Baron. Blessed with this benediction, the two serfs departed. After the servants had taken their leave, the Red-Bearded Baron, watching the two hungry oxen slowly eating the wheat piled on the floor, began to contemplate what had happened. "Yes," he thought, "they did well, but I wonder which one did better?"

a. What measuring unit should the Red-Bearded Baron use to measure financial position and operating performance?
b. Prepare a balance sheet for Ivan and for Igor at both the beginning and the end of the period.
c. Prepare an income statement for Ivan and for Igor for the period.
d. Prepare a schedule reconciling the change in owner's equity between the beginning and the end of the period.
e. Did Ivan or Igor perform better during the period? Explain.

PART TWO

ACCOUNTING CONCEPTS AND METHODS

2

BALANCE SHEET: PRESENTING THE INVESTMENTS AND FINANCING OF A FIRM

CHAPTER 2

LEARNING OBJECTIVES

1. Understand the accounting concepts of assets, liabilities, and shareholders' equity, including the conditions under which firms recognize such items (recognition issues), the amounts at which firms report these items (valuation issues), and the manner in which firms disclose them on the balance sheet (classification issues).
2. Understand the dual-entry recording framework and learn to apply it to a series of transactions, leading to the balance sheet.
3. Develop skills to analyze a balance sheet, focusing on the relations between assets, liabilities, and shareholders' equity that one would expect for financially healthy firms in different industries.

The balance sheets of many savings and loan associations (S&Ls) during the late 1980s included loans receivable with maturities of as long as 20 or 30 years from the date of the balance sheet. Yet these S&Ls obtained a major portion of their financing from balances in saving accounts and certificates of deposit (both S&L liabilities), funds that customers could withdraw either immediately or within a few months of the date of the balance sheet. An imbalance between the maturity structure of assets and the maturity structure of liabilities and shareholders' equity can result in financial difficulty or even bankruptcy, as occurred for many S&Ls. This chapter discusses important concepts underlying the balance sheet, illustrates procedures for preparing the balance sheet, and demonstrates relations the user should look for when analyzing the balance sheets of healthy firms in different industries. This chapter and the book take the perspective of a financial statement user. An understanding of the principal concepts underlying the balance sheet aids the user in analyzing and interpreting published balance sheets. Understanding the accounting methods (or procedures) that accountants follow in preparing the balance sheet helps with the comprehension of the concepts.

UNDERLYING CONCEPTS

Chapter 1 introduced the balance sheet, one of the three principal financial statements. Common terminology in some countries refers to this financial statement as a *statement of financial position*. The balance sheet presents a snapshot of the investments of a firm (assets) and the financing of those investments (liabilities and shareholders' equity) as of a specific time. The balance sheet shows the following balance, or equality:

$$\text{Assets} = \text{Liabilities} + \text{Shareholders' Equity}$$

This equation states that a firm's assets balance with the financing of those assets by creditors and owners. The balance sheet presents resources from two angles: a listing of the specific forms in which a firm holds them (for example, cash, inventory, equipment); and a listing of the people or entities that provided the financing and therefore have a claim on the assets (for example, suppliers, employees, governments, shareholders). Accountants often refer to the sum of liabilities plus shareholders' equity as total equities. The introduction to the balance sheet in Chapter 1 left several questions unanswered:

1. Which resources does a firm recognize as assets?
2. What valuations does it place on these assets?
3. How does it classify, or group, assets within the balance sheet?
4. Which claims against a firm's assets appear on the balance sheet as liabilities?
5. What valuations does a firm place on these liabilities?
6. How does a firm classify liabilities within the balance sheet?
7. What valuation does a firm place on shareholders' equity, and how does it disclose the shareholders' equity within the balance sheet?

To answer these questions, one must consider several accounting concepts underlying the balance sheet. This discussion not only provides a background for understanding the statement as currently prepared but also permits the reader to assess alternative methods of measuring financial position.

ASSET RECOGNITION

An asset is a resource that has the potential for providing a firm with a future economic benefit—the ability to generate future cash inflows or to reduce future cash outflows. A firm will recognize a resource as an asset only if (1) the firm has acquired rights to its use in the future as a result of a past transaction or exchange, and (2) the firm can measure or quantify the future benefits with a reasonable degree of precision.[1] All assets are future benefits; however, not all future benefits are assets.

Example 1   Miller Corporation sold merchandise and received a note from the customer, who agreed to pay $2,000 within four months. This note receivable is an asset of Miller Corporation because Miller has a right to receive a definite amount of cash in the future as a result of the previous sale of merchandise.

Example 2   Miller Corporation acquired manufacturing equipment costing $40,000 and agreed to pay the seller over three years. After the final payment, but not until then,

---

[1]Financial Accounting Standards Board, *Statement of Financial Accounting Concepts No. 6,* "Elements of Financial Statements," 1985, par. 25. See the glossary for the Board's actual definition of an asset.

legal title to the equipment will transfer to Miller Corporation. Even though Miller Corporation will not possess legal title for three years, the equipment is Miller's asset because Miller has the rights and responsibilities of ownership and can maintain those rights as long as it makes payments on schedule.

Example 3   Miller Corporation has developed a good reputation with its employees, customers, and citizens of the community. Management expects this good reputation to provide benefits to the firm in its future business activities. A good reputation, however, is generally not an accounting asset. Although Miller Corporation has made various expenditures in the past to develop the reputation, the future benefits are too difficult to quantify with a sufficient degree of precision to allow Miller to recognize an asset.

Example 4   Miller Corporation plans to acquire a fleet of new trucks next year to replace those that are wearing out. These new trucks are not assets now because Miller Corporation has made no exchange with a supplier and, therefore, has not established a right to the future use of the trucks.

Most of the difficulties that accountants encounter in deciding which items to recognize as assets relate to mutually unexecuted or partially executed contracts. In Example 4, suppose that Miller Corporation entered into a contract with a local truck dealer to acquire the trucks next year at a cash price of $60,000. Miller Corporation has acquired rights to future benefits, but the contract remains unexecuted by both the truck dealer (who must deliver the trucks) and Miller Corporation (who must pay the agreed cash price). Accounting does not generally recognize mutually unexecuted contracts, sometimes called **executory contracts.** Miller Corporation will recognize an asset for the trucks when it receives them next year.

To take the illustration one step further, assume that Miller Corporation advances the truck dealer $15,000 of the purchase price at the time it signs the contract. Miller Corporation has acquired rights to future benefits and has exchanged cash. Current accounting practice treats the $15,000 advance on the purchase of equipment as an asset reported under a title such as Advances to Suppliers. The trucks would not be assets at this time, however, because Miller Corporation has not yet received sufficient future rights to the services of the trucks to justify their inclusion in the balance sheet. Similar asset-recognition questions arise when a firm leases buildings and equipment for its own use under long-term leases or when a firm contracts with a transport company to deliver all of the firm's products to customers for some period of years. Later chapters discuss these issues more fully.

ASSET VALUATION

Accounting must assign a monetary amount to each asset in the balance sheet. The accountant might use several methods of computing this amount.

Acquisition or Historical Cost   The amount of cash paid (or the cash equivalent value of other forms of payment) in acquiring an asset is the **acquisition (historical) cost** of the asset. The accountant can typically ascertain this amount by referring to contracts, invoices, and canceled checks related to the acquisition of the asset. Nothing compels a firm to acquire a given asset, so accountants assume that the firm expects the future benefits from an asset that it does acquire to be at least as large as the acquisition cost. Historical cost, then, sets the lower limit on the value of the asset's future benefits to the firm at the time of acquisition.

Current Replacement Cost   Each asset might appear on the balance sheet at the current cost of replacing it. Because **current replacement cost** represents the amount currently required to acquire, or enter into, the rights to receive future benefits from the asset, accountants refer to it as an **entry value.**

For assets purchased frequently, such as merchandise inventory, the accountant can often calculate current replacement cost by consulting suppliers' catalogs or price lists. But accountants measure the replacement costs of assets purchased less frequently—assets such as land, buildings, and equipment—with difficulty. A major obstacle to using current replacement cost as the valuation basis is the absence of well-organized secondhand markets for many used assets. When a firm cannot easily find similar used assets for sale, ascertaining current replacement cost requires finding the cost of a similar new asset and then adjusting that amount downward for the services of the asset already used. Difficulties can arise, however, in finding a similar asset. With technological improvements and other quality changes, equipment purchased currently will likely differ from equipment that a firm acquired 10 years earlier but still uses. Consider, for example, the difficulties in ascertaining the current replacement cost of a five-year-old computer, computer software package, or cellular phone. Thus there may be no similar equipment on the market to indicate replacement cost. Alternatively, when the replacement cost of the specific asset is not readily available, the accountant might substitute the current replacement cost of an asset capable of rendering equivalent services. This approach, however, requires subjectivity in identifying assets with equivalent service potential.

Current Net Realizable Value   The net amount of cash (selling price less selling costs) that a firm would receive currently if it sold each asset separately is the **current net realizable value.** This amount is an **exit value** because it reflects the amount the firm would receive currently if it sold the asset, or exited ownership. In measuring net realizable value, one generally assumes that the firm sells the asset in an orderly fashion rather than through a forced sale at some distress price.

Measuring net realizable value entails difficulties similar to those encountered in measuring current replacement cost. Without well-organized secondhand markets for used equipment, the accountant cannot readily measure net realizable value, particularly for equipment specially designed for a firm's needs. In this case, the current selling price of the asset (value in exchange) will generally be less than the value of the future benefits to the firm from using the asset (value in use).

Present Value of Future Net Cash Flows   Another possible valuation basis is the **present value** of future net cash flows. An asset is a resource that provides a future benefit. This future benefit is the ability of an asset either to generate future net cash receipts or to reduce future cash expenditures. For example, accounts receivable from customers will lead directly to future cash receipts. The firm can sell merchandise inventory for cash or promises to pay cash. The firm can use equipment to manufacture products that it can sell for cash. A building that the firm owns reduces future cash outflows for rental payments. Because these cash flows represent the future services, or benefits, of assets, the accountant might base asset valuations on them.

Because cash can earn interest over time, today's value of a stream of future cash flows, called the *present value,* is worth less than the sum of the cash amounts that a firm will receive or save over time. The balance sheet shows asset valuations measured as of a current date. If future cash flows are to measure an asset's value as of that date, then the accountant must discount the future net cash flows to find their present value as of the date of the balance sheet. Chapters 9 and 10 and the appendix discuss the discounting methodology. The following example presents the general approach.

Example 5   Miller Corporation sold merchandise to a reliable customer, General Models Company, who promised to pay $10,000 one year after the date of sale. General Models Company signed a promissory note to that effect and gave the note to Miller Corporation. Miller Corporation judges that the current borrowing rate of General Models Company is 10 percent per year; that is, if Miller Corporation made a loan to General Models Company, the loan would carry an interest rate of 10 percent. Miller Corporation is to receive $10,000 one year from today. The $10,000 includes both the amount lent initially plus interest on that amount for one year. Today's value of the $10,000 to be received in one year is not $10,000 but about $9,090; that is, $9,090 plus 10 percent interest on $9,090 equals $10,000 (= 1.10 × $9,090). Hence, the present value of $10,000 to be received one year from today is $9,090. (Miller Corporation is indifferent between receiving approximately $9,090 today and $10,000 one year from today.) The asset represented by General Models Company's promissory note has a present value of $9,090. If the balance sheet states the note at the present value of the future cash flows, it would appear at approximately $9,090 on the date of sale.

Using discounted cash flows in the valuation of individual assets requires solving several problems. One is the difficulty caused by the uncertainty of the amounts of future cash flows. The amounts a firm will receive can depend on whether competitors introduce new products, the rate of inflation, and other factors. A second problem is allocating the cash receipts from the sale of a single item of merchandise inventory to all of the assets involved in its production and distribution (for example, equipment, buildings, sales staff's automobiles). A third problem is selecting the appropriate rate to use in discounting the future cash flows to the present. Is the interest rate at which the firm could borrow the appropriate one? Or should the firm use the rate at which it could invest excess cash? Or is the appropriate rate the firm's cost of capital (a concept introduced in managerial accounting and finance courses)? In the example above, the appropriate rate is General Models' borrowing rate.

SELECTING THE APPROPRIATE VALUATION BASIS

The valuation basis selected depends on the purpose of the financial report.

Example 6   Miller Corporation prepares its income tax return for the current year. The *Internal Revenue Code and Regulations* specify that firms must use acquisition or adjusted acquisition cost valuations in most instances.

Example 7   A fire recently destroyed the manufacturing plant, equipment, and inventory of Miller Corporation. The firm's fire insurance policy provides coverage in an amount equal to the cost of replacing the assets destroyed. Current replacement cost at the time of the fire is appropriate for supporting the insurance claim.

Example 8   Miller Corporation plans to dispose of a manufacturing division that has operated unprofitably. In deciding on the lowest price to accept for the division as a unit, the firm considers the net realizable value of each asset.

Example 9   Brown Corporation is considering the purchase of Miller Corporation. The highest price that Brown Corporation should pay is the present value of the future net cash flows to be realized from owning Miller Corporation.

Example 10   Miller Corporation discovers that the demand for land it owns has declined so much that the original cost of the land exceeds the sum of all expected rental receipts for the indefinite future. Generally accepted accounting principles (GAAP) require Miller Corporation to show the land on the balance sheet at the net present value of the expected cash flows, discounted using a rate adjusted for the risk of the expected cash flows—the more certain the cash flows, the lower the discount rate.[2]

GENERALLY ACCEPTED ACCOUNTING ASSET VALUATION BASES

The asset valuation basis appropriate for financial statements issued to shareholders and other investors is perhaps less obvious. The financial statements currently prepared by publicly held firms use two valuation bases for assets that have not declined substantially in value since the firm acquired them, one basis for monetary assets and a different basis for nonmonetary assets.

Monetary assets, such as cash and accounts receivable, generally appear on the balance sheet at their net present value—their current cash, or cash equivalent, value. Cash appears at the amount of cash on hand or in the bank. Accounts receivable from customers appear at the amount of cash the firm expects to collect in the future. If the time until a firm collects a receivable spans more than one year, the firm discounts the expected future cash inflow to a present value. Most firms collect their accounts receivable, however, within one to three months. The amount of future cash flows (undiscounted) approximately equals the present (discounted) value of these flows; thus accounting ignores the discounting process on the basis of a lack of materiality.

Nonmonetary assets, such as merchandise inventory, land, buildings, and equipment, generally appear at acquisition cost, in some cases adjusted downward to reflect the assets' services that have been consumed and to recognize some declines in market value. Chapters 3, 7, and 8 discuss these adjustments, called *depreciation* when the firm has used some of the services from the asset and called *holding losses* when market value has declined even more than the amount of the depreciation. Some nonmonetary, financial assets, such as holdings of marketable securities, appear on the balance sheet at current market value.

The acquisition cost of an asset includes more than its invoice price. Acquisition cost includes all expenditures made or obligations incurred in order to put the asset into usable condition. Transportation costs, installation costs, handling charges, and any other necessary and reasonable costs incurred until the firm puts the asset into service are part of the total cost assigned to the asset. For example, the accountant might calculate the cost of an item of equipment as follows:

Invoice Price of Equipment	$12,000
Less: 2 Percent Discount for Prompt Cash Payment	(240)
Net Invoice Price	$11,760
Transportation Cost	326
Installation Costs	735
Total Cost of Equipment	$12,821

The accountants records the acquisition cost of this equipment as $12,821.

---

[2]Financial Accounting Standards Board, *Statement of Financial Accounting Standards No. 121,* "Accounting for the Impairment of Long-Lived Assets and for Long-Lived Assets to Be Disposed Of," 1995.

Instead of disbursing cash or incurring a liability, the firm might give (or swap or barter) other forms of consideration (for example, common stock, merchandise inventory, or land) in acquiring an asset. In these cases, the accountant measures acquisition cost by the market value of the consideration given or the market value of the asset received, whichever market value the accountant can more reliably measure.

Example 11 Miller Corporation issued 1,000 shares of its common stock in the acquisition of a used machine. The common stock of Miller Corporation traded on a stock exchange for $15 per share on the day of the exchange. The accountant records the machine on the books of Miller Corporation for $15,000.

Foundations for Acquisition Cost Accounting's use of acquisition cost valuations for nonmonetary assets rests on three important concepts or conventions. First, accounting assumes that a firm is a **going concern.** In other words, accounting assumes a firm will remain in operation long enough to carry out all of its current plans. The firm will realize any increases in the market value of assets held in the normal course of business when the firm receives higher prices for its products. Accounting generally assumes that the current values of the individual assets are largely unimportant. Second, acquisition cost valuations provide more objectivity than do the other valuation methods. **Objectivity** in accounting refers to the ability of several independent measurers to come to the same conclusion about the valuation of an asset. Different accountants will likely agree on the acquisition cost of an asset. Differences among measurers can arise in ascertaining an asset's current replacement cost, current net realizable value, or present value of future cash flows. For independent accountants to reach consensus in auditing the financial statements requires objectivity. Third, acquisition cost generally provides more conservative valuations of assets (and measures of earnings) than do the other valuation methods. Many accountants believe that financial statements will less likely mislead users if balance sheets report assets at lower rather than higher amounts. Thus, **conservatism** has evolved as a convention to justify acquisition cost valuations (and subsequent downward, but not upward, adjustments to acquisition cost valuations).

The general acceptance of these valuation bases does not justify them. Research has not provided guidance as to the valuation basis—acquisition cost, current replacement cost, current net realizable value, or present value of future net cash flows—most relevant to financial statement users.

ASSET CLASSIFICATION

The classification of assets within the balance sheet varies widely in published annual reports. The following discussion gives the principal asset categories.

Current Assets Cash and other assets that a firm expects to realize in cash or to sell or consume during the normal operating cycle of the business are current assets. The operating cycle refers to the period of time during which a given firm converts cash into salable goods and services, sells those goods and services to customers, and receives cash from customers in payment for their purchases. The operating cycle for most manufacturing, retailing, and service firms spans one to three months, whereas for firms in some industries, such as building construction or liquor distilling, the operating cycle may span several years. Except for firms with an operating cycle longer than one year, conventional accounting practice uses one year as the dividing line between current assets and noncurrent assets. Current assets include the following: cash; marketable securities held for the short term; accounts and notes receivable; inventories of merchandise, raw materials, supplies, work in process, and finished goods; and prepaid operating costs, such as prepaid insurance and prepaid rent. Prepaid costs, or prepayments, are current assets because if the firm did not pay for them in advance, it would use current assets within the next operating cycle to acquire those services.

Investments   A second section of the balance sheet, labeled Investments, includes long-term (noncurrent) investments in securities of other firms. For example, a firm might purchase shares of common stock of a supplier to help ensure continued availability of raw materials. Or it might acquire shares of common stock of a firm in another area of business activity to permit the acquiring firm to diversify its operations. When one corporation (the parent) owns more than 50 percent of the voting stock in another corporation (the subsidiary), it usually prepares a single set of consolidated financial statements; that is, the firm merges, or consolidates, its specific assets, liabilities, revenues, and expenses with those of the subsidiary in the financial statements. The securities shown in the Investments section of the balance sheet therefore represent investments in firms whose assets and liabilities the parent or investor firm has not consolidated with its own. Chapter 11 discusses consolidated financial statements.

Property, Plant, and Equipment   The phrase *property, plant, and equipment* (sometimes called **plant, or fixed, assets**) designates the tangible, long-lived assets used in a firm's operations over a period of years and generally not acquired for resale. This category includes land, buildings, machinery, automobiles, furniture, fixtures, computers, and other equipment. The balance sheet shows these items (except land) at acquisition cost reduced by the cumulative (or "accumulated," to use common accounting terminology) depreciation since the firm acquired the assets. (Chapter 8 discusses additional downward adjustments if the assets have declined substantially in value, beyond that indicated by depreciation calculations.) Frequently, only the net balance, or book value, appears on the balance sheet. Land usually appears at acquisition cost.

Intangible Assets   Such items as patents, trademarks, franchises, and goodwill are **intangible assets.** Accountants generally do not recognize as assets those expenditures that a firm makes in *developing* intangibles because of the difficulty of ascertaining the existence and value of future benefits. Consider, for example, the difficulty of identifying whether future benefits exists when a firm expends cash to research new technologies or advertise its products. Accountants do, however, recognize as assets those specifically identifiable intangibles that firms *acquire* in market exchanges from other entities—intangibles such as a patent acquired from its holder. Accounting's recognition of an asset in the latter case presumes that a firm would not purchase a patent, trademark, or other intangible from another entity unless the firm expected future benefits. The exchange between an independent purchaser and seller provides objective evidence of the value of the future benefits. Chapter 8 discusses more fully the accounting used for internally developed intangibles versus that used for externally purchased intangibles, a topic that remains controversial.

P R O B L E M   2 . 1   F O R   S E L F - S T U D Y

Asset recognition and valuation.   The transactions listed below relate to Coca-Cola Company. Indicate whether or not each transaction immediately gives rise to an asset of the company under GAAP. If accounting recognizes an asset, state the account title and amount.

a. The company spends $10 million to develop a new soft drink. No commercially feasible product has yet evolved, but the company hopes that such a product will evolve in the near future.

b. The company signs a contract with United Can Corporation for the purchase of $4 million of soft-drink cans. It makes a deposit of $400,000 on signing the contract.

c. The company spends $2 million for advertisements that appeared during the past month: $500,000 to advertise the Coca-Cola name and $1,500,000 for specific brand advertisements, such as those for Diet Coke.

d. The company issues 50,000 shares of its common stock, valued on the market at $2.5 million, in the acquisition of all the outstanding stock of Coring Glass Company, a supplier of soft-drink bottles.

e. The company spends $800,000 on educational-assistance programs for its middle-level managers to obtain MBAs. Historically, 80 percent of the employees involved in the program receive their MBAs and remain with the company 10 years or more thereafter.

f. The company acquires land and a building by signing a mortgage payable for $150 million. Because the company has not yet paid the mortgage, the title document for the land and building remains in the vault of the holder of the mortgage note.

LIABILITY RECOGNITION

A liability arises when a firm receives benefits or services and in exchange promises to pay the provider of those goods or services a reasonably definite amount at a reasonably definite future time. The firm usually pays cash but may give goods or services.[3] All liabilities are obligations; not all obligations, however, are accounting liabilities.

Example 12 Miller Corporation borrowed $4 million by issuing long-term bonds. On December 31 of each year it must make annual interest payments of 10 percent of the amount borrowed, and it must repay the $4 million principal in 20 years. This obligation is a liability because Miller Corporation received the cash and must repay the debt in a definite amount at a definite future time.

Example 13 Miller Corporation purchased merchandise inventory and agreed to pay the supplier $8,000 within 30 days. This obligation is a liability because Miller Corporation received the goods and must pay a definite amount at a reasonably definite future time.

Example 14 Miller Corporation provides a three-year warranty on its products. The obligation to maintain the products under warranty plans creates a liability. The selling price for its products implicitly includes a charge for future warranty services. As customers pay the selling price, Miller Corporation receives a benefit (that is, the cash collected). Past experience provides a basis for estimating the amount of the liability. Miller Corporation can estimate the proportion of customers who will seek services under

[3]*SFAC No. 6*, par. 35. See the glossary for the Board's actual definition of a liability.

the warranty agreement and the expected cost of providing the warranty services. Thus, Miller Corporation can measure the amount of the obligation with a reasonable degree of accuracy and will show it as a liability.

Example 15   Miller Corporation received an advance of $600 from a customer for products that Miller Corporation will manufacture next year. The cash advance creates a liability of $600. Miller Corporation must manufacture and deliver the products next year or return the cash advance.

Example 16   A customer has sued Miller Corporation, claiming damages of $10 million from faulty products manufactured by Miller Corporation. The case has not yet gone to trial. Accounting typically does not recognize unsettled lawsuits as liabilities because of uncertainty regarding both the need to pay and the amount of any payment. GAAP require the recognition of a liability when the payment is probable. As Chapter 9 discusses, most accountants would interpret "probable" to mean greater than 80 or 85 percent.

Example 17   Miller Corporation signed an agreement with its employees' labor union, promising to increase wages by 6 percent and to provide for medical and life insurance. Although this agreement creates an obligation, it does *not* immediately create an accounting liability. Employees have not yet provided labor services that would require the firm to pay wages and insurance. As employees work, a liability arises.

The most troublesome questions of liability recognition relate to obligations under mutually unexecuted contracts. The labor union agreement in Example 17 is a mutually unexecuted contract. Other examples include some leases, purchase order commitments, and employment contracts. Accounting does not usually recognize as liabilities the obligations created by mutually unexecuted contracts. Chapter 10 discusses the accounting treatment of these off-balance sheet financing arrangements.

LIABILITY VALUATION

Most liabilities are monetary, requiring payments of specific amounts of cash. Those due within one year or less appear at the amount of cash the firm expects to pay to discharge the obligation. If the payment dates extend more than one year into the future (for example, as in the case of the bonds in Example 12), the liability appears at the present value of the future cash outflows.

A liability that requires delivering goods or rendering services, rather than paying cash, is nonmonetary. The warranty liability in Example 14 above is nonmonetary and appears on the balance sheet at the estimated cost of providing the warranty services. The cash advance in Example 15 is also nonmonetary but appears on the balance sheet at the amount of cash received. The seemingly inconsistent valuation of these two nonmonetary liabilities results from accounting's view that the warranty liability relates to products that the firm has already sold, whereas the cash advance relates to products that the firm will manufacture and deliver to customers next year. Other examples of nonmonetary liabilities arising from cash advances include amounts received by magazine publishers for future magazine subscriptions, by theatrical and sports teams for future performances or games, and by landlords for future rental services. The title frequently used for liabilities of this type is Advances from Customers.

LIABILITY CLASSIFICATION

The balance sheet typically classifies liabilities in one of the following categories.

Current Liabilities Obligations that a firm expects to pay or discharge during the normal operating cycle of the firm, usually one year, are current liabilities. In general, the firm uses current assets to pay current liabilities. This category includes liabilities to merchandise suppliers, employees, and governmental units. It also includes notes and bonds payable to the extent that they will require the use of current assets within the next year.

Long-Term Debt Obligations having due dates, or maturities, more than one year after the balance sheet date are long-term debt. Long-term debt includes bonds, mortgages, and similar debts, as well as some obligations under long-term leases.

Other Long-Term Liabilities Obligations not properly considered as current liabilities or long-term debt appear as other long-term liabilities, which include such items as deferred income taxes and some retirement obligations.

PROBLEM 2.2 FOR SELF-STUDY

Liability recognition and valuation. The transactions listed below relate to the New York Times Company. Indicate whether or not each transaction immediately gives rise to a liability of the company under GAAP. If the company recognizes a liability, state the account title and amount.

a. The company receives $10 million for newspaper subscriptions covering the one-year period beginning next month.

b. The company receives an invoice for $4 million from its advertising agency for television advertisements that appeared last month promoting the *New York Times*.

c. The company signs a one-year lease for rental of new delivery vehicles. It pays $50,000 of the annual rental of $80,000 at the signing.

d. Attorneys have notified the company that a New York City resident, seriously injured by one of the company's delivery vehicles, has sued the company for $10 million. Company lawyers have predicted that the court is likely to find the company liable in the lawsuit, but the company carries sufficient insurance to cover any losses.

e. Refer to part **d** above. Assume now that the company carries no insurance against such losses.

f. A two-week strike by employees has closed down newspaper publishing operations. As a result, the company could not deliver subscriptions totaling $2 million.

SHAREHOLDERS' EQUITY VALUATION AND DISCLOSURE

The shareholders' equity in a firm is a residual interest[4]—that is, the owners have a claim on all assets not required to meet the claims of creditors.[5] The valuation of the assets and liabilities included in the balance sheet therefore determines the valuation of total shareholders' equity.

---

[4]Although shareholders' equity is equal to assets minus liabilities, accounting provides an independent method for computing the amount. This and the next chapter present this method.

[5]*SFAC No. 6*, par. 49.

The remaining question concerns the manner of disclosing this total shareholders' equity. Accounting distinguishes between capital contributed by owners and earnings retained by a firm. The balance sheet for a corporation generally separates the amount that shareholders contribute directly for an interest in the firm (that is, common stock) from earnings the firm subsequently realizes in excess of dividends declared (that is, retained earnings).

In addition, the balance sheet usually further disaggregates the amount received from shareholders into the **par or stated value** of the shares and the amounts contributed in excess of par value or stated value. The par or stated value of a share of stock is an amount assigned to comply with the corporation laws of each state and rarely equals the market price of the shares at the time the firm issues them. As a result, the distinction between par or stated value and amounts contributed in excess of par or stated value contains little information, nor does it have economic significance. (Chapter 12 discusses details of accounting for shareholders' equity.)

Example 18 Stephens Corporation legally incorporated on January 1, Year 1. It issued 15,000 shares of $10-par value common stock for $10 cash per share. During Year 1, Stephens Corporation generated net income of $30,000 and paid dividends of $10,000 to shareholders. The shareholders' equity section of the balance sheet of Stephens Corporation on December 31, Year 1, is as follows:

Common Stock (par value of $10 per share, 15,000 shares issued and outstanding)	$150,000
Retained Earnings	20,000
Total Shareholders' Equity	$170,000

Example 19 Instead of issuing $10-par value common stock as in Example 18, Stephens Corporation issued 15,000 shares of $1-par value common stock for $10 cash per share. (The market price of a share of common stock depends on the economic value of the firm, not on the par value of the shares.) The shareholders' equity section of the balance sheet of Stephens Corporation on December 31, Year 1, is as follows:

Common Stock (par value of $1 per share, 15,000 shares issued and outstanding)	$ 15,000
Additional Paid-in Capital (or Capital Contributed in Excess of Par Value)	135,000
Retained Earnings	20,000
Total Shareholders' Equity	$170,000

Firms legally organized as partnerships or sole proprietorships, instead of as corporations, do not make a distinction between contributed capital and retained earnings in their balance sheets. Rather, the owners' equity section of the balance sheet combines each owner's share of capital contributions and each owner's share of earnings in excess of distributions.

Example 20 Refer to Examples 18 and 19. Assume that William Kinsey and Brenda Stephens organized this business firm as a partnership, with Kinsey and Stephens as equal partners. The owners' equity section of the firm's balance sheet on December 31, Year 1, is as follows:

William Kinsey, Capital	$ 85,000
Brenda Stephens, Capital	85,000
Total Owners' Equity	$170,000

A sole proprietorship would, by definition, have only one owner.

ACCOUNTING PROCEDURES FOR PREPARING THE BALANCE SHEET

With the concepts underlying the balance sheet in mind, we can now consider how accounting applies these concepts in preparing this financial statement. We want to help you develop a sufficient understanding of the accounting process involved in generating the balance sheet so that you can interpret and analyze it effectively.

DUAL EFFECTS OF TRANSACTIONS ON THE BALANCE SHEET EQUATION

The balance sheet equation maintains the equality between total assets and total liabilities plus shareholders' equity by reporting the effects of each transaction in a dual manner. Any single transaction will have one of the following four effects or some combination of these effects:

1. It increases both an asset and a liability or shareholders' equity.
2. It decreases both an asset and a liability or shareholders' equity.
3. It increases one asset and decreases another asset.
4. It increases one liability or shareholders' equity and decreases another liability or shareholders' equity.

To understand the dual effects of various transactions on the balance sheet equation, consider the following transactions for Miller Corporation during January:

(1) On January 1, the firm issues 10,000 shares of $10-par value common stock for $100,000 cash.
(2) On January 5, it pays $60,000 cash to purchase equipment.
(3) On January 15, Miller Corporation purchases merchandise inventory costing $15,000 from a supplier on account.
(4) On January 21, it pays the supplier in (3) $8,000 of the amount due.
(5) On January 25, the supplier in (3) accepts 700 shares of common stock at par value in settlement of the $7,000 amount still owed.
(6) On January 31, the firm pays $600 cash for a one-year insurance premium for coverage beginning February 1.
(7) On January 31, Miller Corporation receives $3,000 from a customer for merchandise to be delivered during February.

Exhibit 2.1 illustrates the dual effects of these transactions on the balance sheet equation. Note that after each transaction, assets equal liabilities plus shareholders' equity.

The dual effects reported for each transaction represent an outflow and an inflow. For example, the firm issues common stock to shareholders and receives cash. The firm makes a cash expenditure and receives equipment. The firm promises to make a future

EXHIBIT 2.1	MILLER CORPORATION Illustration of Dual Effects of Transactions on Balance Sheet Equation

Transaction	Assets	=	Liabilities	+	Shareholders' Equity
(1) On January 1, Miller Corporation issues 10,000 shares of $10–par value common stock for $100,000 cash	+$100,000	=	$ 0	+	$100,000
Subtotal	$100,000	=	$ 0	+	$100,000
(2) On January 5, the firm pays $60,000 cash to purchase equipment	− 60,000 + 60,000				
Subtotal	$100,000	=	$ 0	+	$100,000
(3) On January 15, the firm purchases merchandise inventory costing $15,000 from a supplier on account	+ 15,000		+15,000		
Subtotal	$115,000	=	$ 15,000	+	$100,000
(4) On January 21, the firm pays the supplier in **(3)** $8,000 of the amount due.	− 8,000		− 8,000		
Subtotal	$107,000	=	$ 7,000	+	$100,000
(5) On January 25, the supplier in **(3)** accepts 700 shares of common stock in settlement of the $7,000 still owed.			− 7,000	+	7,000
Subtotal	$107,000	=	$ 0		$107,000
(6) On January 31, the firm pays $600 cash for a one-year insurance premium for coverage beginning February 1.	+ 600 − 600				
Subtotal	$107,000	=	$ 0	+	$107,000
(7) On January 31, the firm receives $3,000 from a customer for merchandise to be delivered during February.	+ 3,000		+ 3,000		
Total—January 31	$110,000	=	$ 3,000	+	$107,000

cash payment to a supplier and receives merchandise inventory. Most transactions and events recorded in the accounting system result from exchanges. The accounting records reflect the inflows and outflows arising from these exchanges.

PURPOSE AND USE OF ACCOUNTS

We could prepare a balance sheet for Miller Corporation as of January 31 using the information from the preceding analysis. Total assets are $110,000. To prepare a balance sheet, however, would require tracing each transaction's effects on total assets to ascertain what portion of the $110,000 represents cash, merchandise inventory, and equipment. Likewise, the effects of each transaction on total liabilities and shareholders' equity would require retracing to ascertain which liability and shareholders' equity amounts compose the $110,000 total. Even just a few transactions during the accounting period make this approach to preparing a balance sheet cumbersome. Most firms have thousands of transactions during the accounting period, necessitating a more practical approach to accumulating amounts for the balance sheet. To keep track of the changes that take place in each balance sheet item, the accounting system uses a device called an *account.*

Requirement for an Account   A balance sheet item can only increase, decrease, or remain the same during a period of time. Thus, an account must provide for accumulating the increases and decreases (if any) that occur during the period for a single balance sheet item. The total additions during the period increase the balance carried forward from the previous statement, the total subtractions decrease it, and the result is the new balance for the current balance sheet.

Form of an Account   The account may take many possible forms, and accounting practice commonly uses several. Perhaps the most useful form of the account for textbooks, problems, and examinations is the **T-account.** Actual practice does not use this form of the account, except perhaps for memoranda or preliminary analyses. However, the T-account satisfies the requirement of an account and is easy to use. As the name indicates, the T-account looks like the letter T, with a horizontal line bisected by a vertical line. The name or title of the account appears on the horizontal line. One side of the space formed by the vertical line records increases in the item and the other side records decreases. Dates and other information can appear as well.

T-Account Form

The form that the account takes in actual records depends on the type of accounting system in use. In manual systems, the account may take the form of a single sheet of paper with columns for recording increases and decreases;[6] in computer systems, the account may be a group of similarly coded items in a file. Whatever its form, an account contains the opening balance as well as increases and decreases that result from the transactions of the period.

Placement of Increases and Decreases in the Account   Given the two-sided account, we must choose the side used to record increases and the side for decreases. Long-standing custom follows three rules:

1. Accounting places increases in assets on the left side and decreases in assets on the right side.
2. Accounting places increases in liabilities on the right side and decreases in liabilities on the left side.
3. Accounting places increases in shareholders' equity on the right side and decreases in shareholders' equity on the left side.

This custom reflects the fact that in the balance sheet equation, assets appear to the left of the equal sign and liabilities and shareholders' equity appear to the right. Following this format, asset balances should appear on the left side of accounts; liability and shareholders' equity balances should appear on the right. Asset balances will appear on the left only if the left side of the account records asset increases. Similarly, liability and

---

[6]A collection of such sheets in a book, sometimes loose-leaf, is a *ledger.*

shareholders' equity balances appear on the right only if accounting records liability and shareholders' equity increases on the right side of accounts. When the accountant properly analyzes each transaction into its dual effects on the accounting equation and follows the three rules for recording the transaction, every transaction results in recording equal amounts in entries on the left-hand and the right-hand sides of the various accounts.

Debit and Credit   Accountants use two convenient abbreviations: debit (Dr.) and credit (Cr.). **Debit,** used as a verb, means "record an entry on the left side of an account" and, used as a noun or adjective, means an "entry on the left side of an account." **Credit,** used as a verb, means "record an entry on the right side of an account" and, used as a noun or adjective, means "an entry on the right side of an account."[7] Often, however, accountants use the word **charge** instead of debit, both as a noun and as a verb. In terms of balance sheet categories, a debit or charge indicates (1) an increase in an asset, (2) a decrease in a liability, or (3) a decrease in a shareholders' equity item. A credit indicates (1) a decrease in an asset, (2) an increase in a liability, or (3) an increase in a shareholders' equity item.

To maintain the equality of the balance sheet equation, the accountant must be sure that the amounts debited to various accounts for each transaction equal the amounts credited to various accounts. Likewise, the sum of balances in accounts with debit balances at the end of each period must equal the sum of balances in accounts with credit balances.

Summary of Account Terminology and Procedure   The following T-accounts summarize the conventional use of the account form and the terms *debit* and *credit:*

Any Asset Account

√ Beginning Balance Increases + Dr.	Decreases − Cr.
√ Ending Balance	

Any Liability Account

Decreases − Dr.	Beginning Balance Increases + Cr. √
	Ending Balance √

Any Shareholders' Equity Account

Decreases − Dr.	Beginning Balance Increases + Cr. √
	Ending Balance √

Customarily, a checkmark in an account indicates a balance.

---

[7]The origin of the terms *debit* and *credit* and their abbreviations, Dr. and Cr. (always with initial capital letters), is Great Britain. In early British balance sheets, amounts receivable from customers (then called *debitors*) formed the major assets, whereas amounts payable to suppliers and others (then and now called *creditors*) formed the major liabilities.

EXHIBIT 2.2	MILLER CORPORATION Summary T-Accounts Showing Transactions during January

	Assets		=	Liabilities		+	Shareholders' Equity	
	Increases (Dr.)	Decreases (Cr.)		Decreases (Dr.)	Increases (Cr.)		Decreases (Dr.)	Increases (Cr.)
(1) Issue common stock for cash	100,000							100,000
(2) Purchase equipment with cash	60,000	60,000						
(3) Purchase merchandise on account	15,000				15,000			
(4) Pay cash to supplier in **(3)**		8,000		8,000				
(5) Issue common stock to supplier in **(3)**					7,000			7,000
(6) Pay insurance premium in advance	600	600						
(7) Receive cash from customer in advance	3,000				3,000			
Balance	✓ 110,000				3,000 ✓			107,000 ✓

REFLECTING THE DUAL EFFECTS OF TRANSACTIONS IN THE ACCOUNTS

We can now see how the dual effects of transactions change the accounts. We use three separate T-accounts: one for assets, one for liabilities, and one for shareholders' equity. The dual effects of the transactions of Miller Corporation for January, described earlier in the chapter, appear in the T-accounts shown in Exhibit 2.2.

The amount entered on the left side of (or debited to) the accounts for each transaction equals the amount entered on the right side of (or credited to) the accounts. Recording equal amounts of debits and credits for each transaction ensures that the balance sheet equation will always balance. At the end of January, the assets account has a debit balance of $110,000. The balances in the liabilities and shareholders' equity accounts sum to a credit balance of $110,000.

To provide a direct computation of the amount of each asset, liability, and shareholders' equity item requires a separate account for each balance sheet item, rather than one for each of the three broad categories. The recording procedure is the same, except that it debits and credits specific asset or equity accounts.

Exhibit 2.3 records the transactions of Miller Corporation for January using separate T-accounts for each balance sheet item. The numbers in parentheses refer to the seven transactions during January for Miller Corporation. Most accountants would use the checkmark to indicate a balance, as in Exhibit 2.2, rather than spell out the word *balance,* as we do in Exhibit 2.3.

The total assets of Miller Corporation of $110,000 as of January 31 comprise $34,400 in cash, $15,000 in merchandise inventory, $600 in prepaid insurance, and $60,000 in equipment. Total liabilities plus shareholders' equity of $110,000 comprise $3,000 of advances from customers and $107,000 of common stock.

EXHIBIT 2.3	MILLER CORPORATION Individual T-Accounts Showing Transactions

Cash (Asset)

Increases (Dr.)	Decreases (Cr.)
(1) 100,000	60,000 **(2)**
(7) 3,000	8,000 **(4)**
	600 **(6)**
Balance 34,400	

Merchandise Inventory (Asset)

Increases (Dr.)	Decreases (Cr.)
(3) 15,000	
Balance 15,000	

Prepaid Insurance (Asset)

Increases (Dr.)	Decreases (Cr.)
(6) 600	
Balance 600	

Equipment (Asset)

Increases (Dr.)	Decreases (Cr.)
(2) 60,000	
Balance 60,000	

Accounts Payable (Liability)

Decreases (Dr.)	Increases (Cr.)
(4) 8,000	15,000 **(3)**
(5) 7,000	
	0 Balance

Advance from Customer (Liability)

Decreases (Dr.)	Increases (Cr.)
	3,000 **(7)**
	3,000 Balance

Common Stock (Shareholders' Equity)

Decreases (Dr.)	Increases (Cr.)
	100,000 **(1)**
	7,000 **(5)**
	107,000 Balance

One can prepare the balance sheet using the amounts shown as balances in the T-accounts. The balance sheet of Miller Corporation after the seven transactions of January appears in Exhibit 2.4.

EXHIBIT 2.4	MILLER CORPORATION Balance Sheet, January 31

ASSETS

Current Assets

Cash	$ 34,400
Merchandise Inventory	15,000
Prepaid Insurance	600
Total Current Assets	$ 50,000

Property, Plant, and Equipment

Equipment	60,000
Total Assets	$110,000

LIABILITIES AND SHAREHOLDERS' EQUITY

Current Liabilities

Advance from Customer	$ 3,000

Shareholders' Equity

Common Stock	107,000
Total Liabilities and Shareholders' Equity	$110,000

P R O B L E M   2 . 3   F O R   S E L F - S T U D Y

T-accounts for various transactions. Set up T-accounts for the following accounts:

- Cash
- Merchandise Inventory
- Prepaid Rent
- Equipment
- Accounts Payable

- Bonds Payable
- Land
- Buildings
- Common Stock—Par Value
- Additional Paid-in Capital

Indicate whether each account is an asset, a liability, or a shareholders' equity item, and enter in the T-accounts the transactions described below.

1. The firm issues 20,000 shares of $10-par value common stock for $12 cash per share.
2. The firm issues $100,000 principal amount of bonds for $100,000 cash.
3. The firm acquires, with $220,000 in cash, land costing $40,000 and a building costing $180,000.
4. The firm acquires, on account, equipment costing $25,000 and merchandise inventory costing $12,000.
5. The firm signs an agreement to rent equipment from its owner and pays $1,500 rental in advance.
6. The firm pays $28,000 to the suppliers in (4).

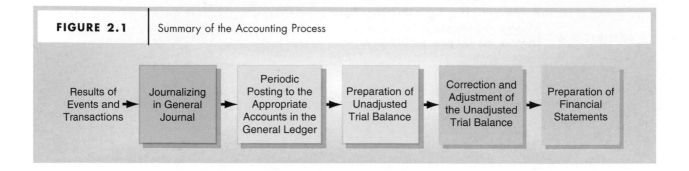

FIGURE 2.1 | Summary of the Accounting Process

Results of Events and Transactions ➤ Journalizing in General Journal ➤ Periodic Posting to the Appropriate Accounts in the General Ledger ➤ Preparation of Unadjusted Trial Balance ➤ Correction and Adjustment of the Unadjusted Trial Balance ➤ Preparation of Financial Statements

AN OVERVIEW OF THE ACCOUNTING PROCESS

The double-entry framework records the results of various transactions and events in the accounts to enable the periodic preparation of financial statements. The accounting system designed around this recording framework generally involves the following operations:

1. Entering the results of each transaction in a book, called the *general journal,* in the form of a journal entry, a process called *journalizing.*
2. Copying the amount from the journal entries in the general journal to the accounts in the general ledger, a process called *posting.*
3. Preparing a trial balance of the accounts in the general ledger.
4. Making adjusting and correcting journal entries to the accounts listed in the trial balance and posting them to the appropriate general ledger accounts.
5. Preparing financial statements from a trial balance after adjusting and correcting entries.

Figure 2.1 shows these operations, which the next sections describe further and illustrate using the transactions of Miller Corporation during January.

JOURNALIZING

Accounting initially records each transaction in the general journal in the form of a **journal entry.** The standard journal entry is as follows:

Date	Account Debited	Amount Debited
	Account Credited	Amount Credited
	Explanation of transaction or event being journalized.	

Sometimes the date appears on a separate line.

The **general journal** is merely a book or other record containing a listing of journal entries in chronological order, like a diary. The general journal, often called the *book of original entry,* contains the first record of each transaction in the accounting system.

The journal entries for the seven transactions of Miller Corporation during January are as follows:

(1) Jan. 1	Cash	100,000	
	Common Stock		100,000
	Issue 10,000 shares of $10-par value common stock for cash.		

(2) Jan. 5	Equipment		60,000	
	Cash			60,000
	Purchase equipment costing $60,000 in cash.			
(3) Jan. 15	Merchandise Inventory		15,000	
	Accounts Payable			15,000
	Purchase merchandise inventory costing $15,000 on account.			
(4) Jan. 21	Accounts Payable		8,000	
	Cash			8,000
	Pay liabilities of $8,000 with cash.			
(5) Jan. 25	Accounts Payable		7,000	
	Common Stock			7,000
	Issue 700 shares of $10-par value common stock in settlement of $7,000 account payable.			
(6) Jan.31	Prepaid Insurance		600	
	Cash			600
	Pay one-year fire insurance premium of $600 in advance.			
(7) Jan. 31	Cash		3,000	
	Advance from Customer			3,000
	Receive $3,000 from customer for merchandise to be delivered in February.			

Journal entries provide the first mechanical step in helping you to understand the effects of various transactions on a firm's financial statements and to prepare solutions to the problems at the end of each chapter of this book. You cannot be sure that you understand a business transaction until you can analyze it into its required debits and credits and prepare the proper journal entry. Later, you will see that after the accountant records the journal entry, all the remaining steps in the record-keeping process are procedural, not requiring intellectual analysis. Once an accountant has recorded a proper journal entry for a transaction, the financial statements resulting after all the mechanical record-keeping steps will properly reflect the effects of that transaction. Throughout, this text uses journal entries as tools of analysis.

POSTING

At periodic intervals (for example, weekly or monthly), the accountant enters, or posts, transactions recorded in the general journal to the individual accounts in the general ledger. In manual systems, the **general ledger** is a book with a separate page for each account. In computerized systems, the general ledger takes the form of access numbers in a computer file. The T-account described earlier serves as a useful surrogate for a general ledger account. Exhibit 2.3 shows the posting of the journal entries from the general journal of Miller Corporation to the general ledger accounts.

Like journal entries, T-accounts help in preparing solutions to accounting problems and appear throughout this text.

TRIAL BALANCE PREPARATION

A **trial balance** lists each of the accounts in the general ledger with its balance as of a particular date. The trial balance of Miller Corporation on January 31 appears in Exhibit 2.5.

An equality between the sum of debit account balances and the sum of credit account balances helps check the accuracy of the arithmetic in the dual-entry recording procedure carried out during the period. If the trial balance fails to balance, one must retrace the steps followed in processing the accounting data to locate the source of the error.

EXHIBIT 2.5	MILLER CORPORATION Unadjusted Trial Balance, January 31	

Account	Amounts in Accounts with Debit Balances	Amounts in Accounts with Credit Balances
Cash	$ 34,400	
Merchandise Inventory	15,000	
Prepaid Insurance	600	
Equipment	60,000	
Advance from Customer		$ 3,000
Common Stock		107,000
Totals	$110,000	$110,000

TRIAL BALANCE AFTER ADJUSTMENT AND CORRECTION

The accountant must correct any errors detected in the processing of accounting data. The most frequent type of adjustment accounts for unrecorded events that help to measure net income for the period and financial position at the end of the period. For example, at the end of February, the accountant will adjust downward the Prepaid Insurance account to reflect the coverage that expired during February. Chapter 3 discusses this type of adjustment more fully. Most corrections and adjustments involve preparing a journal entry, entering it in the general journal, and then posting it to the general ledger accounts.

FINANCIAL STATEMENT PREPARATION

One can prepare the balance sheet and the income statement from the trial balance after adjustments and corrections. Because Miller Corporation does not require correcting or adjusting entries, the balance sheet presented in Exhibit 2.4 is correct as presented. Subsequent chapters will consider the accounting procedures for preparing the income statement and the statement of cash flows.

The results of various transactions and events flow through the accounting system beginning with the journalizing operation and ending with the financial statements. The audit of the financial statements by the independent auditor typically flows in the opposite direction. The auditor begins with the financial statements prepared by management and then traces various items back through the accounts to the corresponding source documents (for example, sales invoices and canceled checks) that support the entries made in the general journal. Thus one can move back and forth among source documents, journal entries, general ledger postings, and the financial statements.

BALANCE SHEET ACCOUNT TITLES

This section describes the balance sheet account titles commonly used. The descriptions should help in understanding the nature of various assets, liabilities, and shareholders' equities as well as in selecting appropriate account names to use when solving problems. One can use alternative account titles. The list does not show all the account titles that are used in this book or that appear in the financial statements of publicly held firms. Many beginning students become overly concerned about precise wording for account titles. We require of our students only that the titles be descriptive and unambiguous and that students use the identical (or similar) account titles for identical (or similar) items. Later chapters discuss more fully the use of some of the account titles described below.

ASSETS

Cash: coins and currency and items such as bank checks and money orders (the latter items are merely claims against individuals or institutions but by custom are called *cash*), bank deposits against which the firm can draw checks, and time deposits, usually savings accounts and certificates of deposit.

Marketable Securities: government bonds or corporate stocks and bonds that the firm plans to hold for a relatively short time. The word *marketable* implies that the firm can buy and sell them readily through a security exchange such as the New York Stock Exchange.

Accounts Receivable: amounts due from customers of a business from the sale of goods or services. The collection of cash occurs sometime after the sale. These accounts are also known as "charge accounts" or "open accounts." The general term Accounts Receivable used in the balance sheet describes the figure representing the total amount receivable from all customers. The firm, of course, keeps a separate record for each customer.

Notes Receivable: amounts due from customers or from others to whom a firm has made loans or extended credit. The customer or other borrower puts the claim into writing in the form of a formal note (which distinguishes the claim from an open account receivable).

Interest Receivable: interest—on assets such as promissory notes or bonds—that has accrued (or come into existence) through the passing of time but that the firm has not yet collected as of the date of the balance sheet.

Merchandise Inventory: goods on hand purchased for resale, such as canned goods on the shelves of a grocery store or suits on the racks of a clothing store.

Raw Materials Inventory: unused materials for manufacturing products.

Supplies Inventory: lubricants, abrasives, and other incidental materials used in manufacturing operations; stationery, computer disks, pens, and other office supplies; bags, twine, boxes, and other packaging supplies; gasoline, oil, spare parts, and other delivery supplies.

Work-in-Process Inventory: partially completed manufactured products.

Finished Goods Inventory: completed, but unsold, manufactured products.

Advances to Suppliers: payments made in advance for goods or services that a firm will receive at a later date. If the firm does not make a cash expenditure when it places an order, it does not recognize an asset.

Prepaid Rent: rent paid in advance for the future use of land, buildings, or equipment. In parallel with the previous account title, one could call this Advances to Landlord.[8]

Prepaid Insurance: insurance premiums paid for future coverage. One could call this Advances to Insurance Company.

Investment in Securities: bonds or shares of common or preferred stock that the firm plans to hold for a relatively long time, typically longer than one year.

Land: land used in operations or occupied by buildings used in operations.

---

[8]Prepaid Rent is an ambiguous account title, even though virtually all firms with such an item use this account title. This account title could just as aptly describe the liability of the landlord who has an obligation to a tenant who paid rent in advance. We urge our students not to use the title Prepaid Rent but instead Advances to Landlord, for the asset of the tenant, and Advances from Tenants, for the liability of the landlord.

Buildings: factory buildings, store buildings, garages, warehouses, and so forth.

Equipment: lathes, ovens, machine tools, boilers, computers, bins, cranes, conveyors, automobiles, and so forth.

Furniture and Fixtures: desks, tables, chairs, counters, showcases, scales, and other selling and office equipment.

Accumulated Depreciation: the cumulative amount of the cost of long-term assets (such as buildings and equipment) allocated to the costs of production or to current and prior periods in measuring net income. The amount in this account reduces the acquisition cost of the long-term asset to which it relates when measuring the net book value of the asset shown in the balance sheet.

Leasehold: the right to use property owned by someone else.

Organization Costs: amounts paid for legal and incorporation fees, for printing the certificates for shares of stock, and for accounting and other costs incurred in organizing a business so that it can function. GAAP requires firms to expense organization costs in the year incurred.[9]

Patents: rights granted for up to 17 years by the federal government to exclude others from manufacturing, using, or selling certain processes or devices. Under current GAAP, the firm must expense research and development costs in the year incurred rather than recognize them as assets with future benefits.[10] As a result, a firm that develops a patent will not normally show it as an asset. On the other hand, a firm that purchases a patent from another firm or from an individual will recognize the patent as an asset. Chapter 8 discusses this inconsistent treatment of internally developed and externally purchased patents.

Goodwill: the amount that is greater than the sum of the current values assignable to individual identifiable assets and liabilities of a business enterprise being acquired by another firm. Accounting generally does not recognize as assets the good reputation and other desirable attributes that a firm creates or develops for itself. However, when one firm acquires another firm, accounting recognizes these desirable attributes as assets insofar as they cause the amount paid for the acquired firm to exceed the sum of the values assigned to all the other assets and liabilities identified in the acquisition.

LIABILITIES

Accounts Payable: amounts owed for goods or services acquired under an informal credit agreement. These accounts are usually payable within one or two months. The same items appear as Accounts Receivable on the creditor's books.

Notes Payable: the face amount of promissory notes given in connection with loans from a bank or with the purchase of goods or services. The same items appear as Notes Receivable on the creditor's (lender's) books.

Interest Payable: interest—on obligations—that has accrued or accumulated with the passage of time but that the firm has not yet paid as of the date of the balance sheet. The liability for interest customarily appears separately from the face amount of the obligation. The same items appear as Interest Receivable on the creditor's books.

Income Taxes Payable: the estimated liability for income taxes, accumulated and unpaid, based on the taxable income of the business from the beginning of the taxable year to the date of the balance sheet.

Advances from Customers: the general name used to indicate payments received in advance for goods or services a firm will furnish to customers in the future; a nonmonetary

---

[9]American Institute of Certified Public Accountants, *Statement of Position 98-5,* "Reporting the Cost of Start-up Activities," 1998.

[10]Financial Accounting Standards Board, *Statement of Financial Accounting Standards No. 2,* "Accounting for Research and Development Costs," 1974.

liability. The firm has an obligation to deliver goods or services, not return the cash. Even so, the firm records this liability at the amount of cash it receives. If the firm does not receive cash when a customer places an order, it does not record a liability; the contract is mutually unexecuted.

Advances from Tenants, or Rent Received in Advance: another example of a nonmonetary liability. For example, a firm owns a building that it rents to a tenant. The tenant prepays the rental charge for several months in advance. The firm cannot include the amount applicable to future months as a component of income until the firm renders a rental service with the passage of time. Meanwhile the advance payment results in a liability payable in services (that is, in the use of the building). On the records of the tenant, the same amount appears as an asset, Prepaid Rent (or Advances to Landlord).

Mortgage Payable: long-term promissory notes that the borrower has protected by pledging specific pieces of property as security for payment. If the borrower does not pay the loan or interest according to the agreement, the lender can require the sale of the property to generate funds to repay the loan.

Bonds Payable: amounts borrowed by a business for a relatively long period of time under a formal written contract or indenture. The borrower usually obtains the loan from a number of lenders, all of whom receive written evidence of their share of the loan.

Convertible Bonds: bonds payable that the holder can convert into, or trade in for, shares of common stock. The bond indenture specifies the number of shares the lenders will receive when they convert their bonds into stock, the dates when conversion can occur, and other details.

Capitalized Lease Obligations: the present value of the commitment to make future cash payments in return for the right to use property owned by someone else. Chapter 10 discusses the conditions under which a firm recognizes lease obligations as liabilities.

Deferred Income Taxes: particular income tax amounts that are delayed beyond the current accounting period. Chapter 10 discusses this item, which appears on the balance sheet of most U.S. corporations.

SHAREHOLDERS' EQUITY

Common Stock: amounts received equal to the par or stated value of a firm's principal class of voting stock.

Preferred Stock: amounts received for the par value of a class of a firm's stock that has some preference relative to the common stock, usually in the area of dividends and assets in the event of corporate liquidation. Sometimes preferred shareholders may convert the stock into common stock.

Additional Paid-in Capital: in the issuance of common or preferred stock, the amounts received in excess of par value or stated value. Some firms use for this account the alternative title "Capital Contributed in Excess of Par (or Stated) Value."

Retained Earnings: since the time a business began operations, the increase in net assets (= all assets − all liabilities) that results from its generating earnings in excess of net assets (usually cash) distributed as dividend declarations. When a firm declares dividends, net assets decrease (liability for dividends payable increases), and retained earnings decrease by an equal amount. As Chapters 4 and 12 discuss, a firm does not generally hold net assets generated from retained earnings as cash.

Treasury Shares: the cost of shares of stock that a firm originally issued but subsequently reacquires. Treasury shares do not receive dividends, and accountants do not identify them as outstanding shares. The cost of treasury shares almost always appears on the balance sheet as a deduction from the total of the other shareholders' equity accounts. Chapter 12 discusses the accounting for treasury shares.

Journal entries, T-accounts, and balance sheet preparation. Electronics Appliance Corporation begins operations on September 1. The firm engages in the following transactions during the month of September:

(1) September 1: Issues 4,000 shares of $10-par value common stock for $12 cash per share.
(2) September 2: Gives 600 shares of $10-par value common stock to acquire a patent from another firm. The two entities agree on a price of $7,200 for the patent.
(3) September 5: Pays $10,000 as two months' rent in advance on a factory building that is leased for the three years beginning October 1. Monthly rental payments are $5,000.
(4) September 12: Purchases raw materials on account for $6,100.
(5) September 15: Receives a check for $900 from a customer as a deposit on a special order for equipment that Electronics plans to manufacture. The contract price is $4,800.
(6) September 20: Acquires office equipment with a list price of $950. After deducting a discount of $25 in return for prompt payment, it issues a check in full payment.
(7) September 28: Issues a cash advance totaling $200 to three new employees who will begin work on October 1.
(8) September 30: Purchases factory equipment costing $27,500. It issues a check for $5,000 and assumes a long-term mortgage liability for the balance.
(9) September 30: Pays $450 for the labor costs of installing the new equipment in **(8)**.

a. Prepare journal entries for each of the nine transactions.
b. Set up T-accounts and enter each of the nine transactions.
c. Prepare a balance sheet for Electronics Appliance Corporation as of September 30.

ANALYSIS OF THE BALANCE SHEET

The balance sheet reflects the effects of a firm's investing and financing decisions. In general, firms attempt to balance the term structure of their financing with the term structure of their investments (that is, use short-term financing for current assets and long-term financing for noncurrent assets). **Term structure** refers to the length of time that must elapse before an asset becomes cash or before a liability or a shareholders' equity item requires cash.[11] One tool for studying the term structure of a firm's assets and the term structure of its financing is a **common-size balance sheet.** In a common-size balance sheet, the analyst expresses each balance sheet item as a percentage of total assets or total liabilities plus shareholders' equity. Exhibit 2.6 presents common-size balance sheets for Wal-Mart Stores (discount stores and warehouse clubs), American Airlines (airline), Merck (pharmaceuticals), and Interpublic Group (advertising services).

Wal-Mart Stores maintains a large percentage of its assets in merchandise inventories, which it expects to sell within a period of one to two months. It therefore uses a high proportion of short-term financing (that is, accounts payable).

---

[11]In financial economics, *term structure* has a different meaning.

EXHIBIT 2.6	Common Size Balance Sheets for Selected Companies

	Wal-Mart Stores	American Airlines	Merck	Interpublic Group
Assets				
Cash	0.2%	7.7%	14.9%	9.9%
Accounts Receivable	2.7	5.0	16.3	61.2
Inventories	47.8	3.8	10.4	—
Prepayments	4.8	0.8	3.8	1.9
Total Current Assets	55.5%	17.3%	45.4%	73.0%
Investments in Securities	—	—	11.0	1.0
Property, Plant, and Equipment	41.6	68.2	36.9	6.8
Intangible Assets	2.9	14.5	6.7	19.2
Total Assets	100.0%	100.0%	100.0%	100.0%
Liabilities and Shareholders' Equity				
Accounts Payable	22.4%	6.2%	14.7%	52.3%
Notes Payable	3.2	6.4	3.6	5.6
Other Current Liabilities	6.8	16.7	11.3	8.7
Total Current Liabilities	32.4%	29.3%	29.6%	66.6%
Long-term Debt	21.2	36.3	5.2	6.1
Other Noncurrent Liabilities	1.1	11.0	13.4	6.2
Total Liabilities	54.7%	76.6%	48.2%	78.9%
Shareholders' Equity	45.3	23.4	51.8	21.1
Total Liabilities and Shareholders' Equity	100.0%	100.0%	100.0%	100.0%

American Airlines, on the other hand, invests a large percentage of its assets in property, plant, and equipment. It finances these assets with long-term sources of financing (long-term debt plus shareholders' equity). Airlines tend to use more long-term debt than shareholders' equity to finance the acquisition of equipment because (1) the equipment serves as collateral for the borrowing (that is, the lender can repossess or confiscate the equipment if the airline fails to make debt payments on time) and (2) long-term debt usually has a lower explicit cost to the firm than do funds provided by shareholders.

Merck also invests a high proportion of its assets in property, plant, and equipment. Pharmaceutical companies tend to maintain capital-intensive, automated manufacturing facilities to ensure quality control of their products. Unlike airlines, however, pharmaceutical companies tend not to carry much long-term debt. One reason for not using debt results from the nature of the resources of a pharmaceutical company. Key resources include its research scientists, who could leave the firm at any time, and its patents on pharmaceutical products, which competitors could render worthless by developing new, superior products. Given the risk inherent in these resources, which do not appear on the balance sheet, pharmaceutical firms tend not to add risk on the financing side of their balance sheets by taking on debt, which requires fixed interest and principal payments. In addition, since pharmaceutical companies have historically generated the highest ratios of profitability and operating cash flow of all industry groups, they do not need to borrow to finance operating and investing activities.

Interpublic Group provides advertising services for clients. It purchases time or space in various media (television, newspapers, magazines), for which it incurs an obligation (accounts payable). It develops advertising copy for clients and sells them media time or space to promote their products, resulting in a receivable from the clients (accounts receivable). Service firms such as Interpublic Group have few assets other than their employees, which accounting does not recognize as assets. Thus, current receivables dominate the asset side of the balance sheet and current payables dominate the financing side of the balance sheet.

Financial analysts may become concerned when a firm's percentage of short-term financing begins to exceed its percentage of current assets. Such firms use short-term financing for noncurrent assets. Like savings and loan associations during the late 1980s, such firms may face difficulties obtaining sufficient cash from these assets to meet short-term commitments to creditors. The only firm in Exhibit 2.6 to have a financing structure unbalanced in this way is American Airlines.

AN INTERNATIONAL PERSPECTIVE

The format of the balance sheet in some countries differs from that discussed in this chapter. In Germany, France, and some other European countries, property, plant, and equipment and other noncurrent assets appear first, followed by current assets. On the equities side, shareholders' equity appears first, followed by noncurrent and current liabilities. Exhibit 2.7 presents the balance sheet of BMW, the German automobile manufacturer, for two recent years. Note that this balance sheet maintains the equality of investments and financing. Note also that some terms differ from those commonly used in the United States.

Term Used in Exhibit 2.7	Common Term Used in the United States
Tangible Fixed Assets	Property, Plant, and Equipment
Financial Assets	Investment in Securities
Trade Receivables	Accounts Receivable
Liquid Funds	Cash
Subscribed Capital	Common Stock
Capital Reserve	Additional Paid-in Capital
Profit Reserves, Net Income Available for Distribution	Retained Earnings
Bonds	Bonds Payable
Due to Banks	Notes Payable to Banks
Trade Payables	Accounts Payable

In the United Kingdom, the following form of the balance sheet equation characterizes the balance sheet.

| EXHIBIT 2.7 | BMW
Balance Sheets (in millions of deutsche marks) | | | |

| | | December 31 | | |
		Year 9		Year 10
Assets				
Intangible Assets	Dm	8	Dm	5
Tangible Fixed Assets		6,163		6,339
Financial Assets		198		363
Total Fixed Assets	Dm	6,369	Dm	6,707
Inventories	Dm	2,390	Dm	2,544
Lease Receivables		5,294		6,306
Trade Receivables		2,006		2,284
Marketable Securities		2,084		2,138
Liquid Funds		2,227		2,205
Total Current Assets	Dm	14,001	Dm	15,477
Prepayment and Other Assets	Dm	319	Dm	317
Total Assets	Dm	20,689	Dm	22,501
Shareholders' Equity And Liabilities				
Subscribed Capital	Dm	835	Dm	849
Capital Reserve		749		775
Profit Reserves		3,593		4,037
Net Income Avalable for Distribution		194		199
Total Shareholders' Equity	Dm	5,371	Dm	5,860
Bonds	Dm	6,158	Dm	7,003
Due to Banks		543		604
Trade Payables		1,335		1,463
Other Liabilities and Provisions		7,282		7,571
Total Liabilities	Dm	15,318	Dm	16,641
Total Shareholders' Equity and Liabilities	Dm	20,689	Dm	22,501

$$\begin{matrix} \text{Noncurrent} \\ \text{Assets} \end{matrix} + \left(\begin{matrix} \text{Current} \\ \text{Assets} \end{matrix} - \begin{matrix} \text{Current} \\ \text{Liabilities} \end{matrix} \right) - \begin{matrix} \text{Noncurrent} \\ \text{Liabilities} \end{matrix} = \begin{matrix} \text{Shareholders'} \\ \text{Equity} \end{matrix}$$

Exhibit 2.8 presents a balance sheet for Ranks Hovis McDougall PLC, a consumer products company, for two recent years. This form of balance sheet does not permit a direct comparison of investments with financing. The analyst must rearrange such balance sheets to obtain the desired information. A balance sheet for Ranks Hovis McDougall PLC in the format discussed in this chapter appears in Exhibit 2.9. Note that the amount for current liabilities roughly equals the amount for current assets and that the total for noncurrent liabilities and shareholders' equity roughly equals the amount for noncurrent assets. Terms used in the balance sheet in Exhibit 2.8 also differ from those discussed in this chapter.

EXHIBIT 2.8	RANKS HOVIS McDOUGALL PLC Comparative Balance Sheet in U.K. Format (in millions of pounds)		

	August 31	
	Year 7	**Year 8**
Fixed Assets		
Brand Names	—	£ 678.0
Tangible Assets	£ 422.3	463.7
Investments	3.4	0.7
Total Fixed Assets	£ 425.7	£1,142.4
Current Assets		
Stocks	£ 168.6	£ 184.6
Debtors	215.6	234.3
Cash	46.2	65.2
Creditors Due within One Year		
Borrowings	(53.0)	(45.1)
Other	(286.7)	(347.3)
Net Current Assets	£ 90.7	£ 91.7
Total Assets Less Current Liabilities	£ 516.4	£1,234.1
Creditors Due after More Than One-Year		
Borrowings	£(133.7)	£ (139.8)
Other	(78.6)	(96.6)
Provisions for Liabilities	(38.9)	(19.0)
Total Assets Less Total Liabilities	£ 265.2	£ 978.7
Capital and Reserves		
Called-up Share Capital	£ 91.4	£ 93.2
Share Premium Account	28.0	27.5
Revaluation Reserve	24.9	622.6
Other Reserves	107.3	184.9
Minority Interests	13.6	50.5
Total Shareholders' Equity	£ 265.2	£ 978.7

Term Used in Exhibit 2.8	Common Term Used in the United States
Tangible Assets	Property, Plant, and Equipment
Stocks	Inventories
Debtors	Accounts Receivable
Borrowings	Notes Payable, Bonds Payable
Called-up Share Capital	Common Stock
Share Premium Account	Additional Paid-in Capital
Other Reserves	Retained Earnings

Two accounts reported in Exhibit 2.8 seldom appear on balance sheets in the United States and most other countries: Brand Names and Revaluation Reserve. Common practice

EXHIBIT 2.9	RANKS HOVIS McDOUGALL PLC Comparative Balance Sheet in U.S. Format (in millions of pounds)

	August 31	
	Year 7	Year 8
Assets		
Cash	£ 46.2	£ 65.2
Debtors	215.6	234.3
Stocks	168.6	184.6
Total Current Assets	£430.4	£ 484.1
Investments	3.4	0.7
Tangible Assets	422.3	463.7
Brand Names	—	678.0
Total Assets	£856.1	£1,626.5
Liabilities And Shareholders' Equity		
Borrowings	£ 53.0	£ 45.1
Other	286.7	347.3
Total Current Liabilities	£339.7	£ 392.4
Borrowings	133.7	139.8
Other	78.6	96.6
Provisions for Liabilities	38.9	19.0
Total Liabilities	£590.9	£ 647.8
Shareholders' Equity		
Called-up Share Capital	£ 91.4	£ 93.2
Share Premium Account	28.0	27.5
Revaluation Reserve	24.9	622.6
Other Reserves	107.3	184.9
Minority Interest	13.6	50.5
Total Shareholders' Equity	£265.2	£ 978.7
Total Liabilities and Shareholders' Equity	£856.1	£1,626.5

in most countries reports nonmonetary assets (for example, inventories and property, plant, and equipment) at acquisition, or historical, cost. Common practice also does not recognize as assets those expenditures that firms make to develop brand names, a good reputation, and other intangibles. Accounting standards in the United Kingdom and in a few other countries permit the periodic revaluation of property, plant, and equipment to current market values. Firms obtain appraisals of the market values of their tangible fixed assets at periodic intervals (every three to five years). They then reflect the revaluation in the accounts with a journal entry such as the following:

Tangible Fixed Assets .... Amount	
Revaluation Reserve	Amount
To revalue tangible assets to current market value.	

At the end of Year 7, Ranks Hovis McDougall PLC reports a balance in the Revaluation Reserve account of £24.9 million, suggesting that the current market values of its property, plant, and equipment exceed acquisition cost by £24.9 million. The journal entry to record a decrease in market values reverses the debit and credit accounts in the entry above.

Accounting standards in the United Kingdom also permit the reporting of the current market value of brand names. Firms must obtain an independent appraisal of such values. Ranks Hovis McDougall PLC recognized brand names as an asset for the first time during Year 8. It made the following journal entry:

Brand Names	678.0	
Revaluation Reserve		678.0
To recognize the current market value of brand names.		

The revaluation reserve changed as follows during Year 8:

Revaluation Reserve, August 31, Year 7	£ 24.9
Plus Recognition of Brand Names	678.0
Less Decrease in Market Value of Tangible Fixed Assets (Plug)[12]	(80.3)
Revaluation Reserve, August 31, Year 8	£622.6

An analyst wanting to convert the balance sheets of Ranks Hovis McDougall PLC to U.S. accounting standards would make the following restatements.

End of Year 7:		
Revaluation Reserve	24.9	
Tangible Fixed Assets		24.9
To convert tangible fixed assets from current market values to historical costs.		
End of Year 8:		
Revaluation Reserve	622.6	
Tangible Fixed Assets (Plug)	55.4	
Brand Names		678.0
To convert tangible fixed assets from current market values to historical costs and eliminate brand names from assets.		

You will likely find the discussion of different balance sheet formats, terminology, and restatement entries discussed in this section somewhat difficult to follow at this early stage in your study of financial accounting. The principal message of this section is that a solid grasp of important balance sheet concepts, as discussed throughout most of this

---

[12]The accountant knows definite amounts for all numbers in this calculation except for the decrease in market value. By taking the known amounts for the beginning balance plus additions (£24.9 + £678.0 = £702.9) and subtracting this from the ending amount (£622.6), we can find the missing amount (£622.6 − £702.9 = −£80.3), the decrease for this year. Accountants generally refer to this process as *plugging* and to the amount so found as a *plug*.

chapter, should permit you to apply those concepts to balance sheets that differ from those commonly found in the United States.

SUMMARY

The balance sheet comprises three major classes of items: assets, liabilities, and shareholders' equity.

Resources become accounting assets when a firm has acquired the rights to their future use as a result of a past transaction or exchange and when it can measure the value of the future benefits with a reasonable degree of precision. Monetary assets appear, in general, at their current cash, or cash equivalent, values. Nonmonetary assets appear at acquisition cost, in some cases adjusted downward for the cost of services that a firm has consumed. Liabilities represent obligations of a firm to make payments of a reasonably definite amount at a reasonably definite future time for benefits already received. Shareholders' equity, the difference between total assets and total liabilities, for corporations typically comprises contributed capital and retained earnings.

Recording the effects of each transaction in a dual manner in the accounts maintains the equality of total assets and total liabilities plus shareholders' equity. The following summarizes the double-entry recording framework:

Asset Accounts		=	Liability Accounts		+	Shareholders' Equity Accounts	
Increases (Debits)	Decreases (Credits)		Decreases (Debits)	Increases (Credits)		Decreases (Debits)	Increases (Credits)

The accountant initially records the dual effects of each transaction in journal entry form in the general journal. The accountant periodically transfers or posts the amounts in these journal entries to the appropriate asset, liability, and shareholders' equity accounts in the general ledger. A trial balance of the ending balances in the general ledger accounts provides a check on the arithmetic accuracy of the double-entry recording procedure. At the end of each accounting period, the accountant adjusts or corrects the account balances in the trial balance as needed by making an entry in the general journal and posting it to the accounts in the general ledger. The adjusted and corrected trial balance then provides the information needed to prepare the financial statements. Chapter 3 discusses the procedures for preparing the income statement. Chapter 4 discusses the statement of cash flows.

When analyzing a balance sheet, one looks for a reasonable match between the term structure of assets and the term structure of liabilities plus shareholders' equity. The proportion of short-term versus long-term financing should bear some relation to the proportion of current assets versus noncurrent assets.

SOLUTIONS TO SELF-STUDY PROBLEMS

SUGGESTED SOLUTION TO PROBLEM 2.1 FOR SELF-STUDY

(Coca-Cola Company; asset recognition and valuation)

a. Accounting does not recognize research and development expenditures as assets under GAAP because of the uncertainty of future benefits that a firm can measure with reasonable precision.

b. Deposit on Containers, $400,000. This is a partially executed contract, which accountants recognize as an asset to the extent of the partial performance.

c. Although GAAP allow firms to capitalize advertising expenditures as assets, common practice immediately expenses all advertising costs because of the uncertainty of future benefits that firms can measure with reasonable precision.

d. Investment in Common Stock, $2.5 million. As Chapter 11 discusses more fully, this corporate acquisition may qualify as a uniting of interests in some countries, in which case the valuation would likely differ from $2.5 million.

e. Accounting does not recognize an asset for the same reasons as in part **a** above.

f. Land and Building, $150 million. The accountant must allocate the aggregate purchase price between the land and the building because the building is depreciable and the land is not. Legal passage of title is not necessary to justify recognition of an asset. Coca-Cola has acquired the rights to use the land and building and can sustain those rights as long as it makes the required payments on the mortgage obligation.

SUGGESTED SOLUTION TO PROBLEM 2.2 FOR SELF-STUDY

(New York Times Company; liability recognition and valuation)

a. Subscription Fees Received in Advance, $10 million.

b. Accounts Payable, $4 million. Other account titles are also acceptable.

c. Accounting does not recognize a liability in this case because the one-year rental period is much shorter than the life of the vehicles. Chapter 10 discusses the criteria for recognition of leases as liabilities.

d. Accounting does not recognize a liability because there is a very low probability, given the insurance coverage, that the firm will make a future cash payment.

e. GAAP require the recognition of a liability when a cash payment is "probable." GAAP provide no specific guidelines as to how high the probability needs to be to recognize a liability. Anecdotal evidence suggests that practicing accountants use 80 to 85 percent.

f. It is likely that the $2 million was previously recorded in the account Subscription Fees Received in Advance. The strike will probably extend the subscription period by two weeks. Thus, the firm has already recognized a liability.

SUGGESTED SOLUTION TO PROBLEM 2.3 FOR SELF-STUDY

(T-accounts for various transactions)

Cash (A)

(1)240,000	220,000 (3)
(2)100,000	1,500 (5)
	28,000 (6)

Merchandise Inventory (A)

(4) 12,000	

Prepaid Rent (A)

(5) 1,500	

Land (A)

(3) 40,000	

Buildings (A)

(3)180,000	

Equipment (A)

(4) 25,000	

Accounts Payable (L)

(6) 28,000	37,000 (4)

Bonds Payable (L)

	100,000 (2)

Common Stock— Par Value (SE)

	200,000 (1)

Additional Paid-in Capital (SE)

	40,000 (1)

SUGGESTED SOLUTION TO PROBLEM 2.4 FOR SELF-STUDY

(Electronics Appliance Corporation; journal entries, T-accounts, and balance sheet preparation)

a. Journal entries for the nine transactions follow:

(1) Sept. 1	Cash	48,000	
	Common Stock		40,000
	Additional Paid-in Capital		8,000
	Issue 4,000 shares of $10-par value common stock for $12 cash per share.		
(2) Sept. 2	Patent	7,200	
	Common Stock		6,000
	Additional Paid-in Capital		1,200
	Issue 600 shares of $10-par value common stock in the acquisition of a patent.		
(3) Sept. 5	Prepaid Rent	10,000	
	Cash		10,000
	Prepay rent for October and November on factory building.		
(4) Sept. 12	Raw Materials Inventory	6,100	
	Accounts Payable		6,100
	Purchase raw materials costing $6,100 on account.		
(5) Sept. 15	Cash	900	
	Advances from Customers		900
	Receive an advance of $900 from a customer as a deposit on equipment to be manufactured in the future.		
(6) Sept. 20	Equipment	925	
	Cash		925
	Acquire equipment with a list price of $950, after a discount, for $925.		
(7) Sept. 28	Advances to Employees	200	
	Cash		200
	Give cash advances of $200 to employees beginning work on Oct. 1.		
(8) Sept. 30	Equipment	27,500	
	Cash		5,000
	Mortgage Payable		22,500
	Acquire equipment for $5,000 cash and assume a $22,500 mortgage for the balance of the purchase price.		
(9) Sept. 30	Equipment	450	
	Cash		450
	Pay installation cost of $450 on equipment acquired in **(8)**.		

b. Exhibit 2.10 presents T-accounts for Electronics Appliance Corporation and shows the recording of the nine entries in the accounts. The letters A, L, and SE after the account titles indicate the balance sheet category of the accounts.

c. Exhibit 2.11 presents a balance sheet as of September 30.

EXHIBIT 2.10	ELECTRONICS APPLIANCE CORPORATION T-Accounts and Transactions during September (Problem 2.4 for Self-Study)

Cash (A)

(1) 48,000	10,000	**(3)**
(5) 900	925	**(6)**
	200	**(7)**
	5,000	**(8)**
	450	**(9)**
√ 32,325		

Advances to Employees (A)

(7) 200	
√ 200	

Raw Materials Inventory (A)

(4) 6,100	
√ 6,100	

Prepaid Rent (A)

(3) 10,000	
√ 10,000	

Equipment (A)

(6) 925	
(8) 27,500	
(9) 450	
√ 28,875	

Patent (A)

(2) 7,200	
√ 7,200	

Accounts Payable (L)

	6,100 **(4)**
	6,100 √

Advances from Customers (L)

	900 **(5)**
	900 √

Mortgage Payable (L)

	22,500 **(8)**
	22,500 √

Common Stock (SE)

	40,000 **(1)**
	6,000 **(2)**
	46,000 √

Additional Paid-in Capital (SE)

	8,000 **(1)**
	1,200 **(2)**
	9,200 √

EXHIBIT 2.11	ELECTRONICS APPLIANCE CORPORATION Balance Sheet, September 30 (Problem 2.4 for Self-Study)

ASSETS

Current Assets

Cash	$32,325	
Advances to Employees	200	
Raw Materials Inventory	6,100	
Prepaid Rent	10,000	
Total Current Assets		$48,625
Property, Plant, and Equipment		
Equipment		28,875
Intangibles		
Patent		7,200
Total Assets		$84,700

LIABILITIES AND SHAREHOLDERS' EQUITY

Current Liabilities

Accounts Payable	$ 6,100	
Advances from Customers	900	
Total Current Liabilities		$ 7,000
Long-Term Debt		
Mortgage Payable		22,500
Total Liabilities		$29,500
Shareholders' Equity		
Common Stock, $10 Par Value . .	$46,000	
Additional Paid-in Capital	9,200	
Total Shareholders' Equity		$55,200
Total Liabilities and		
Shareholders' Equity		$84,700

KEY TERMS AND CONCEPTS

Executory contract	Par or stated value
Acquisition (historical) cost	T-account
Current replacement cost (entry value)	Debit
Current net realizable value (exit value)	Credit
Present value	Charge
Monetary assets	Journal entry
Nonmonetary assets	General journal
Going concern	General ledger
Objectivity	Trial balance
Conservatism	Term structure
Plant, or fixed, assets	Common-size balance sheet
Intangible assets	

QUESTIONS, EXERCISES, PROBLEMS, AND CASES

QUESTIONS

1. Review the meaning of the terms and concepts listed above in Key Terms and Concepts.

2. Conservatism is generally regarded as a convention in accounting. Indicate whom this might hurt.

3. One of the criteria for the recognition of an asset or a liability is that there be an exchange. What justification can you see for this requirement?

4. Accounting typically does not recognize either assets or liabilities for mutually unexecuted contracts. What justification can you see for this treatment?

5. Accounting treats cash discounts taken on the purchase of merchandise or equipment as a reduction in the amount recorded for the assets acquired. What justification can you see for this treatment?

6. A group of investors owns an office building that it rents unfurnished to tenants. It purchased the building five years previously from a construction company. At that time it expected the building to have a useful life of 40 years. Indicate the procedures you might follow to ascertain the valuation amount for this building under each of the following valuation methods:

    a. Acquisition cost
    b. Adjusted acquisition cost
    c. Current replacement cost
    d. Current net realizable value
    e. Present value of future net cash flows

7. Some of the assets of one firm correspond to the liabilities of another firm. For example, an account receivable on the seller's balance sheet is an account payable on the buyer's balance sheet. For each of the following items, indicate whether it is an asset or a liability and give the corresponding account title on the balance sheet of the other party to the transaction:

    a. Advances by Customers
    b. Bonds Payable
    c. Interest Receivable
    d. Prepaid Insurance
    e. Rental Fees Received in Advance

EXERCISES

8. **Asset recognition and valuation.** The following transactions relate to Eli Lilly and Company, a pharmaceutical firm. Indicate whether or not each transaction immediately gives rise to an asset of the company under GAAP. If accounting recognizes an asset, state the account title and amount.
   a. The firm sends a check for $12,000,000 to an insurance company for liability insurance. The period of coverage begins next month.
   b. The firm issues a check for $500,000 as a deposit on specially designed scientific equipment. The equipment will have a total purchase price of $2,000,000 and will be completed and delivered next year.
   c. The firm acquires shares of common stock in Genetic Engineering, Inc., a leading firm in genetics research, for $325,000. Eli Lilly holds these shares with the expectation of developing long-term relations with this genetic engineering firm.
   d. The firm acquires chemicals, used as raw materials in its pharmaceutical products, at a list price of $800,000, with payment made in time to secure a 2 percent discount for prompt payment. Eli Lilly treats cash discounts as a reduction in the acquisition cost of inventory.
   e. The firm hires a well-known scientist to manage its research and development activities. Employment begins next month. One-twelfth of the annual salary of $480,000 is payable at the end of each month worked.
   f. The firm purchases bonds with a face value of $3,000,000 for $3,200,000. The bonds mature in 20 years and require interest payments of 8 percent annually. Eli Lilly made the investment with temporarily excess cash and intends to sell the bonds when it needs cash.
   g. The firm receives an order from Revco Drug Stores for $15,000 of pharmaceutical products.
   h. The firm receives notice that a supplier has shipped by freight raw materials billed at $200,000 with payment due in 30 days. Eli Lilly obtains title to the goods as soon as the supplier ships them to the buyer.

9. **Asset recognition and valuation.** The transactions listed below relate to IBM Corporation, a manufacturer of electronic equipment. Indicate whether or not each transaction immediately gives rise to an asset of IBM Corporation under GAAP. If accounting recognizes an asset, give the account title and amount.
   a. The firm invests $8,000,000 in a government bond. The bond has a maturity value of $10,000,000 in three years, and IBM intends to hold the bond to maturity.
   b. The firm sends a check for $600,000 to a landlord for two months' rent in advance on warehouse facilities.
   c. The firm writes a check for $1,000,000 to obtain an option to purchase a tract of land. The price of the land is $10,000,000.
   d. The firm signs a four-year employment agreement with its president for $2,500,000 per year. The contract period begins next month.
   e. The firm purchases a patent on a laser printer from its creator for $1,200,000.
   f. The firm receives a patent on a new computer processor that it developed. The firm spent $3,200,000 to develop the patented invention.
   g. The firm received notice that a supplier had shipped by freight memory chips billed at $12,000,000, with payment due in 30 days. The seller retains title to the memory chips until received by the buyer.

10. **Asset recognition and valuation.** The transactions listed below relate to General Mills, Inc., a consumer foods company. Indicate whether or not each transaction

immediately gives rise to an asset under GAAP. If accounting recognizes an asset, state the account title and amount.

a. The firm spends $3,400,000 to develop and test-market a new breakfast cereal. It intends to launch the new product nationally next month.

b. The firm spends $2,800,000 to acquire rights to manufacture and sell a new low-cholesterol, salt-free cake mix developed by a local Minneapolis resident.

c. The firm spends $1,800,000 to obtain options to purchase land as future sites for its Red Lobster and Olive Garden restaurant chains.

d. The firm spends $760,000 for television advertisements that appeared last month.

e. The firm issues shares of its common stock currently selling on the market for $3,500,000 for 30 percent of the shares of Pizza-to-Go Restaurants, Inc., a regional, family-owned pizza chain. Recent appraisals suggest that a 30 percent share of Pizza-to-Go is worth between $3,200,000 and $4,000,000. General Mills intends to hold these shares as a long-term investment.

f. The firm acquires land and a building costing $2,000,000 by paying $800,000 in cash and signing a promissory note for the remaining $1,200,000 of the purchase price. General Mills expends $60,000 for a title search and other legal fees, $8,000 in recording fees with the state of Minnesota, and $120,000 to destroy the building. General Mills intends to use the land for a parking lot.

11. **Asset recognition and valuation.** The transactions below relate to Office Depot, an office supply retailer. Indicate whether or not each transaction immediately gives rise to an asset under GAAP. If the accounting recognizes an asset, state the account title and amount.

a. The firm rents retail space in a local shopping center for the five-year period beginning next month. Office Depot pays $250,000, which includes $120,000 as rent for the first year and $130,000 as a security deposit against future damages and unpaid rent.

b. The firm spends $10,000 to install petitions between administrative and retail space, $6,500 to paint the walls colors that are consistent with other Office Depot stores, and $20,000 to install carpeting.

c. The firm purchases display counters with a list price of $30,000. It pays for the display counters in time to take a 2 percent discount for prompt payment. Costs to transport the display counters to the new location total $1,200, and costs to install them total $800.

d. The firm hires a store manager at an annual salary of $60,000.

e. The firm spends $1,500 in newspaper and television advertisements that appeared this month.

f. The firm purchases inventory with an invoice price of $160,000. It pays for merchandise with an original invoice price of $120,000 in time to take a 2 percent discount for prompt payment. It has not yet paid for the remainder of the merchandise purchased. The firm treats cash discounts taken as a reduction in the acquisition cost of merchandise. An inspection of the merchandise reveals that merchandise with an original invoice price of $12,000 is defective. Office Depot returns this merchandise to the supplier, having not yet paid for it.

12. **Asset recognition and valuation.** In each of the following transactions, give the title(s) and amount(s) of the asset(s) that would appear on the balance sheet.

a. A firm purchases an automobile with a list price of $20,000. The dealer allows a discount of $1,600 from the list price for payment in cash. Dealer preparation charges on the automobile amount to an extra $350. The dealer collects a 6 percent sales tax on the price paid for the automobile and preparation charges. In addition, the dealer collects a $125 fee to be remitted to the state for this year's license plates and $500 for a one-year insurance policy provided by the dealer's insurance agency. The firm pays a body shop $190 for painting the firm's name on the automobile.

b. A firm acquires land that a certified real estate appraiser appraised at $5 million. The firm pays for the land by giving up shares in the Microsoft Corporation at a time when equivalent shares traded on the NASDAQ have a market value of $5,200,000.

c. A firm acquires land that a certified real estate appraiser appraised at $5 million. The firm pays for the land by giving up shares in Small Timers, Inc., whose shares are traded only on the Pacific Stock Exchange. The last transaction in shares of Small Timers, Inc., occurred four days before this asset swap. Using the prices of the most recent trades, the shares of stock of Small Timers, Inc., given in exchange for the land have a market value of $5,200,000.

13. **Liability recognition and valuation.** The transactions listed below relate to Travelers Insurance Company. Indicate whether or not each transaction immediately gives rise to a liability of the company under GAAP. If accounting recognizes a liability, state the account title and amount.

a. The firm receives $6,500,000 from customers for insurance coverage beginning next month.

b. The firm hires its president under a three-year contract beginning next month. The contract calls for $750,000 of compensation each year.

c. The firm receives a bill from its attorneys for $1,200,000 to cover services rendered in defending the company in a successful lawsuit.

d. The firm issues additional common stock, with a par value of $3,000,000, for $7,600,000.

e. The firm has not yet paid employees who earned salaries and commissions totaling $950,000 during the most recent pay period. The employer must also pay payroll taxes of 8 percent of the compensation earned.

f. The firm received a legal notice that it is subject to a lawsuit by a group of customers who allege that the company improperly canceled their insurance. The suit claims damages of $6,000,000.

14. **Liability recognition and valuation.** The transactions below relate to Kansas City Royals, Inc., owner of a professional baseball team, and Kauffman Stadium. Indicate whether or not each of the following transactions immediately gives rise to a liability of the firm under GAAP. If accounting recognizes a liability, state the account title and amount.

a. The firm signs a five-year contract with Joe Superstar for $7,400,000 per year. The contract period begins on February 1 of next year.

b. The firm receives $2,700,000 from sales of season tickets for the baseball season starting April 1 of next year.

c. The firm issues bonds in the principal amount of $8,000,000 for $8,400,000. The bonds mature in 20 years and bear interest at 8 percent per year. The firm intends to use the proceeds to expand Kauffman Stadium.

d. The firm receives a bill for utility services received last month totaling $3,400.

e. The firm receives notice that a former player has filed suit against Kansas City Royals, Inc., alleging nonperformance of contractual terms. The player claims $10,000,000 in damages.

f. The firm orders new uniforms for the team for the baseball season beginning next spring. The contract calls for a $10,000 deposit upon signing the contract and a $15,000 payment on delivery of the uniforms in February of next year. The firm signs the contract and sends a check for $10,000.

15. **Liability recognition and valuation.** The transactions below relate to the activities of a local college. Indicate whether or not each of the following transactions immediately gives rise to a liability under GAAP. If accounting recognizes a liability, state the account title and amount.
    a. The college issues bonds with a principal amount and issue price of $10,000,000. The college must pay interest at a rate of 7 percent of the principal amount each year and repay the principal in 15 years. The college intends to use the proceeds to construct a new dormitory.
    b. The college contracts with a construction company to build the dormitory in part **a** for a contract price of $12,000,000. The college pays $2,000,000 on signing the contract and must pay the remainder as construction progresses. Construction begins next month and should take three years to complete.
    c. The college institutes a guaranteed tuition plan for students entering next fall. The tuition for the academic year beginning next fall is $15,000 per year. Although the college expects tuition to increase each year, any entering student who pays $45,000 in advance will receive rights to a four-year undergraduate education without additional tuition payments. The college receives $1,800,000 from students who are entering next fall and who signed up for the guaranteed tuition plan.
    d. The college bookstore receives textbooks, for the coming academic year, with an invoice price of $170,000.
    e. The college owes employees $280,000 in compensation for the last pay period. The college is also responsible for payment of payroll taxes of 6 percent of compensation.
    f. The college receives a grant from the Carnegie Foundation for $1,500,000 to enhance undergraduate teaching. The college intends to disburse the funds to faculty members to develop new teaching materials.
16. **Liability recognition and valuation.** Indicate whether or not each of the following events immediately gives rise to a liability under GAAP. If accounting recognizes a liability, state the account title and amount.
    a. A paving company agrees to pave the parking lot owned by a firm. The agreed price for the work is $12,000. Consider this event from the standpoint of the firm owning the parking lot.
    b. A symphony orchestra receives a check for $400 for a two-year, future season ticket to the orchestra's performances. Consider this event from the standpoint of the symphony orchestra.
    c. A construction company agrees to build a bridge for $4 million. It receives a down payment of $500,000 on signing the contract; it is entitled to the remainder when it completes the bridge.
    d. A firm issues, for $180,000, additional common stock with a par value of $100,000.
    e. A firm receives a 60-day, 10 percent loan of $30,000 from a local bank.
    f. A firm signs a contract to purchase at least $10,000 worth of merchandise during the next year.
    g. Refer to part **f**. The firm places an order for $2,500 of merchandise with the supplier.
    h. Refer to part **g**. The firm receives the merchandise ordered.
17. **Balance sheet classification.** GAAP classify items on the balance sheet in one of the following ways:
    (1) Asset
    (2) Liability
    (3) Shareholders' equity

(4) Item that would not appear on the balance sheet as conventionally prepared under GAAP.

Using these numbers, indicate the appropriate classification of each of the following items:

a. Salaries payable
b. Retained earnings
c. Notes receivable
d. Unfilled customers' orders
e. Land
f. Interest payable
g. Work-in-process inventory
h. Mortgage payable
i. Organization costs
j. Advances by customers
k. Advances to employees
l. Patents
m. Good credit standing
n. Common stock

18. **Balance sheet classification.** GAAP classify items on the balance sheet in one of the following ways:
(1) Asset
(2) Liability
(3) Shareholders' equity
(4) Item that would not appear on the balance sheet as conventionally prepared under GAAP.

Using these numbers, indicate the appropriate classification of each of the following items:

a. Preferred stock
b. Furniture and fixtures
c. Potential liability under lawsuit (case has not yet gone to trial)
d. Prepaid rent
e. Capital contributed in excess of par value
f. Cash on hand
g. Goodwill
h. Estimated liability under warranty contract
i. Raw materials inventory
j. Rental fees received in advance
k. Bonds payable
l. Prepaid insurance
m. Income taxes payable
n. Treasury stock

PROBLEMS AND CASES

19. **Journal entries for various transactions.** Present journal entries for each of the following transactions of Brackin Corporation during October, its first month of operations.
(1) October 2: Issues 600,000 shares of $10-par value common stock for $16 cash per share.
(2) October 3: Acquires a building costing $3,000,000. The firm makes a down payment of $300,000 and signs an 8 percent note maturing in three years for the balance.

(**3**) October 8: Acquires equipment costing $40,000 for cash.

(**4**) October 15: Acquires on account merchandise inventory costing $130,000 from various suppliers.

(**5**) October 18: Issues a check for $800 for insurance coverage for the period beginning November 1.

(**6**) October 20: Receives a check for $2,200 from a customer for merchandise to be delivered on November 5.

(**7**) October 26: Pays invoices totaling $90,000 from the purchases on October 15, after deducting a 2 percent discount for prompt payment. The firm treats cash discounts as a reduction in the acquisition cost of inventory.

(**8**) October 30: Pays the remaining invoices from the purchases on October 15 after the discount period has lapsed.

20. **Journal entries for various transactions.** Present journal entries for each of the following transactions of Schneider Corporation. You may omit dates and explanations for the journal entries.

  (**1**) Issues 50,000 shares of $10-par value common stock at par value for cash.

  (**2**) Acquires land and building costing $225,000 with the payment of $50,000 cash and the assumption of a 20-year, 8 percent mortgage for the balance. The land appears at $40,000 and the building at $185,000 on the balance sheet.

  (**3**) Purchases a used crane for $13,200 cash.

  (**4**) Acquires raw materials costing $8,600 on account.

  (**5**) Returns defective raw materials purchased in (**4**) and costing $900 to the supplier. The account has not yet been paid.

  (**6**) Pays the supplier in (**4**) and (**5**) the amount due, less a 2 percent discount for prompt payment. The firm treats cash discounts as a reduction in the acquisition cost of raw materials.

  (**7**) Obtains a fire insurance policy providing $500,000 coverage beginning next month. It pays the one-year premium of $4,950.

  (**8**) Issues a check for $8,000 to acquire a patent from another firm.

  (**9**) Issues a check for $1,800 for three months' rent in advance for office space.

  (**10**) Purchases a patent on a machine process for $90,000 cash.

  (**11**) Purchases office equipment for $2,700, making a down payment of $250 and agreeing to pay the balance in 30 days.

  (**12**) Pays $825 to Express Trucking Company for delivering the equipment purchased in (**3**).

21. **Journal entries for various transactions.** Express the following transactions of Winkle Grocery Store, Inc., in journal entry form. You may omit explanations for the journal entries.

  (**1**) Receives $30,000 from John Winkle in return for 1,000 shares of the firm's $30-par value common stock.

  (**2**) Gives a 60-day, 8-percent note to a bank and receives $5,000 cash from the bank.

  (**3**) Rents a building and pays the annual rental of $12,000 in advance.

  (**4**) Acquires display equipment costing $8,000 and issues a check in full payment.

  (**5**) Acquires merchandise inventory costing $25,000. The firm issues a check for $12,000, with the remainder payable in 30 days.

  (**6**) Signs a contract with a nearby restaurant under which the restaurant agrees to purchase $2,000 of groceries each week. The firm receives a check for the first two weeks' orders in advance.

(7) Obtains a fire insurance policy providing $50,000 coverage beginning next month. It pays the one-year premium of $1,200.

(8) Pays $600 for advertisements that will appear in newspapers next month.

(9) Places an order with suppliers for $35,000 of merchandise to be delivered next month.

22. Journal entries for various transactions. Express the following independent transactions in journal entry form. If an entry is not required, indicate the reason. You may omit explanations for the journal entries.

(1) A firm purchases, for $103,500, bonds of the Summers Company with a face value of $80,000 and annual interest at the rate of 6 percent.

(2) A fire insurance company receives a check for $6,390 for premiums on policy coverage over the next two years.

(3) A corporation issues 12,000 shares of $12-par value common stock in exchange for land, building, and equipment. The land appears at $15,000, the building at $105,000, and the equipment at $60,000 on the balance sheet.

(4) A manufacturing firm signs a contract agreeing to purchase 200 dozen machine tool parts over the next two years at a price of $60 per dozen.

(5) A firm issues 6,000 shares of $1-par value preferred stock in the acqustion of a patent from another firm. The two entities agree on a price of $7,500 for the patent.

(6) A movie theater issues a coupon book, redeemable in future movie viewings, for $650 cash.

(7) A firm receives notice that a customer is suing it for $250,000 in damages suffered because of defective merchandise.

(8) A firm returns defective merchandise inventory it purchased on account for $4,000 to the supplier for full credit. The firm had not yet paid for these items.

23. Journal entries for various transactions. The transactions below relate to Wendy's International, Inc., a restaurant chain. Express each transaction in journal entry form. If an entry is not required, indicate the reason. You may omit explanations for the journal entries.

(1) The firm places an order for restaurant supplies totaling $1,600,000 to be delivered next month.

(2) The firm receives the supplies ordered in transaction **(1)** on open account.

(3) The firm discovers supplies received in transaction **(2)** costing $40,000 are defective and returns them to the supplier for full credit.

(4) The firm pays for some of the purchases in transactions **(1)** and **(2)** originally invoiced for $1,400,000 in time to take advantage of 2 percent discounts for prompt payment. The firm treats discounts taken as a reduction in the cost of supplies.

(5) The firm pays for the remaining purchases—see transactions **(1)** through **(4)**—after the discount period has lapsed.

(6) The firm places an order, totaling $900,000, for refrigerated salad bars for its restaurants. It pays $200,000 on signing the contract and agrees to pay the remainder at delivery.

(7) The firm receives the salad bars ordered in transaction **(6)** and pays the amount due.

(8) The firm pays $27,000 to install the salad bars in its restaurants.

(9) The firm discovers that salad bars costing $22,000 are defective and returns them to the supplier, expecting a cash refund.

(10) The firm receives a check for $22,000 from the supplier in transaction **(9)**.

24. Effect of transactions on balance sheet equation. Indicate the effects of the following transactions on the balance sheet equation using this format:

Transaction Number	Assets	=	Liabilities	+	Shareholders' Equity
(1)	+ $30,000		$0		$30,000
Subtotal	$30,000	=	$0	+	$30,000

(1) A firm issues 3,000 shares of $10-par value common stock at par for cash.

(2) It purchases merchandise costing $18,900 on account.

(3) The firm acquires store equipment costing $12,700. It issues a check for $2,000, with the balance payable over three years under an installment contract.

(4) The firm issues a check for $1,800 covering two months' rent in advance.

(5) Refer to transaction **(3)**. The firm issues common stock with a market value of $10,700 in full settlement of the installment contract.

(6) The firm pays the merchandise supplier in transaction **(2)** the amount due.

25. Preparation of worksheet for balance sheet transactions. Veronica Regaldo creates a new business firm in Mexico on January 2, Year 8, to operate a retail store. Transactions of Regaldo Department Stores during January in preparation for opening its first retail store in February appear below:

(1) January 2: Receives Ps500,000 from Veronica Regaldo for all of the common stock of Regaldo Department Stores. The stock has no par or stated value.

(2) January 5: Pays another firm Ps20,000 for a patent and pays the Mexican government Ps4,000 to register the patent.

(3) January 10: Orders merchandise from various suppliers at a cost of Ps200,000. See transactions **(5)**, **(6)**, and **(7)** below for later information regarding these merchandise orders.

(4) January 15: Signs a lease to rent land and a building for Ps30,000 a month. The rental period begins February 1. Regaldo pays Ps60,000 for the first two months' rent in advance.

(5) January 20: Receives the merchandise ordered on January 10. Regaldo delays payment for the merchandise until it receives an invoice from the supplier—see transaction **(7)** below.

(6) January 21: Discovers that merchandise costing Ps8,000 is defective and returns the items to the supplier.

(7) January 25: Receives invoices for $160,000 of the merchandise received on January 20. After subtracting an allowed discount of 2 percent of the invoice for paying promptly, Regaldo pays the suppliers the amount due of Ps156,800 (.98 × Ps160,000). The firm treats cash discounts taken as a reduction in the acquisition cost of the merchandise.

(8) January 30: Obtains fire and liability insurance coverage from Windwards Islands Insurance Company for the period beginning February 1, Year 8. It pays the one-year insurance premium of Ps12,000.

a. Create a worksheet with columns labeled Transaction Number, Cash, Inventories, Other Assets, Liabilities, Common Stock, and Retained Earnings. Indicate the effect of each of the eight transactions above on these balance sheet accounts.

b. Prepare a balance sheet for Regaldo Department Stores on January 31, Year 8.

26. T-account entries for various transactions. Set up T-accounts for the following accounts. Indicate whether each account is an asset, a liability, or a shareholders' equity item, and enter the transactions described below.

- Cash

- Merchandise Inventory

- Prepaid Insurance

- Buildings
- Equipment
- Accounts Payable
- Note Payable
- Advances from Customers
- Mortgage Payable
- Common Stock—Par Value
- Additional Paid-in Capital

(1) A firm issues 20,000 shares of $5-par value stock for $12 cash per share.

(2) The firm acquires a building costing $500,000. It makes a cash payment of $80,000 and assumes a long-term mortgage for the balance of the purchase price.

(3) The firm acquires on account equipment costing $20,000 and merchandise inventory costing $35,000.

(4) The firm obtains a three-year fire insurance policy and pays the $3,000 premium in advance.

(5) The firm issues a 90-day, 6 percent note to the bank for a $20,000 loan.

(6) The firm pays $22,000 to the suppliers in (3).

(7) The firm receives an order for $6,000 of merchandise to be shipped next month. The customer pays $600 at the time of placing the order.

27. **T-account entries and balance sheet preparation.** Patterson Manufacturing Corporation begins operations on January 1. See the assumptions given at the end of the list. The firm engages in the following transactions during January:

(1) Issues 15,000 shares of $10-par value common stock for $210,000 in cash.

(2) Issues 28,000 shares of common stock in exchange for land, building, and equipment. The land appears at $80,000, the building at $220,000, and the equipment at $92,000 on the balance sheet.

(3) Issues 2,000 shares of common stock to another firm to acquire a patent.

(4) Acquires raw materials with a list price of $75,000 on account from suppliers.

(5) Acquires manufacturing equipment with a list price of $6,000. It deducts a $600 discount and pays the net amount in cash. The firm treats cash discounts as a reduction in the acquisition cost of equipment.

(6) Pays freight charges of $350 for delivery of the equipment in (5).

(7) Discovers that raw materials with a list price of $800 are defective and returns them to the supplier for full credit. The raw materials had been purchased on account—see (4)—and no payment had been made as of the time that the goods were returned.

(8) Signs a contract for the rental of a fleet of automobiles beginning February 1. Pays the rental for February of $1,400 in advance.

(9) Pays invoices for $60,000 of raw materials purchased in (4) with an original list price of $60,000, after deducting a discount of 3 percent for prompt payment. The firm treats cash discounts as a reduction in the acquisition cost of raw materials.

(10) Obtains fire and liability insurance coverage from Southwest Insurance Company. The two-year policy, beginning February 1, carries a $400 premium that has not yet been paid.

(11) Signs a contract with a customer for $20,000 of merchandise that Patterson plans to manufacture. The customer advances $4,500 toward the contract price.

(12) Acquires a warehouse costing $60,000. The firm makes a down payment of $7,000 and assumes a long-term mortgage for the balance.

(13) Discovers that raw materials with an original list price of $1,500 are defective and returns them to the supplier. This inventory was paid for in **(9).** The returned raw materials are the only items purchased from this particular supplier during January. A cash refund has not yet been received from the supplier.

(14) On January 31, the firm purchases 6,000 shares of $10-par value common stock of the General Cereal Corporation for $95,000. This purchase is a short-term use of excess cash. The shares of General Cereal Corporation trade on the New York Stock Exchange.

The following assumptions will help you resolve certain accounting uncertainties: (i) transactions **(2)** and **(3)** occur on the same day as transaction **(1)**; and (ii) the invoices paid in **(9)** are the only purchases for which suppliers made discounts available to the purchaser.

a. Enter these transactions in T-accounts. Indicate whether each account is an asset, a liability, or a shareholders' equity item. Cross-reference each entry to the appropriate transaction number.

b. Prepare a balance sheet as of January 31.

28. T-Account entries and balance sheet preparation. Idaho Products Corporation begins operations on April 1. The firm engages in the following transactions during April:

(1) Issues 20,000 shares of $5-par value common stock for $12 per share in cash.

(2) Issues 500 shares of $100-par value preferred stock at par value for cash.

(3) Gives $40,000 in cash and 5,000 shares of common stock in exchange for land and a building. The land appears at $25,000 and the building at $75,000 on the balance sheet.

(4) Acquires equipment costing $46,000. It makes a cash payment of $8,000 and gives an 8 percent note, due in one year, for the balance.

(5) Pays transportation costs of $1,200 on the equipment in **(4).**

(6) Pays installation costs of $1,800 on the equipment in **(4).**

(7) Acquires, on account, merchandise inventory costing $60,000.

(8) Pays license fees of $1,300 in advance for the year beginning May 1.

(9) Discovers that merchandise costing $1,900 from the acquisition in **(7)** is defective and returns it to the supplier for full credit. The firm has not yet paid this account.

(10) Purchases a patent from the creator for $30,000.

(11) Signs an agreement to manufacture a specially designed machine for a customer for $60,000, with the machine to be delivered in January of next year. At the time of signing, the customer advances $12,000 of the contract price.

(12) Pays invoices totaling $40,000 from the purchases in **(7),** after deducting a 2 percent discount for prompt payment. The firm treats cash discounts as a reduction in the acquisition cost of inventory.

a. Enter the transactions in T-accounts. Indicate whether each account is an asset, a liability, or a shareholders' equity item. Cross-reference each entry to the appropriate transaction number.

b. Prepare a balance sheet for Idaho Products Corporation as of April 30.

29. T-account entries and balance sheet preparation. Soybel Corporation begins operations on January 1. During January it engages in the following transactions:

(1) Issues 20,000 shares of $5-par value common stock for $150,000.

(2) Issues at face value cash bonds with a face and maturity value of $250,000.

(3) Acquires land and a building costing $300,000. Issues a check for $220,000, with the remainder payable over 20 years. It assigns $60,000 to the land and $240,000 to the building.

(4) Acquires equipment with a gross invoice price of $90,000. After deducting a discount of 2 percent for immediate cash payment, the firm pays the net amount due.

(5) Acquires on account merchandise costing $75,000.

(6) Discovers that merchandise costing $8,000 is defective and returns it to the supplier. The firm has not yet made a payment to this supplier.

(7) Obtains an insurance policy for a one-year period beginning February 1. Pays the premium of $3,200 for the one-year period.

(8) Receives an order from a customer for $2,500 of merchandise to be delivered in February. The customer sends a check for $900 with the order.

(9) Pays merchandise suppliers in (5) $64,000 of the amounts due. The firm will pay the remaining suppliers in February.

   a. Enter these transactions in T-accounts. Indicate whether each account is an asset, a liability, or a shareholders' equity item. Cross-reference each entry to the appropriate transaction number.

   b. Prepare a balance sheet for Soybel Corporation as of January 31.

30. **T-account entries and balance sheet preparation.** The following transactions occur during May for Computer Graphic, Inc., a computer software company, in preparation for its opening on June 1:

   (1) May 1: Issues 10,000 shares of $10-par value common stock for cash to a group of investors for $150,000.

   (2) May 1: Issues 6,000 shares of $10-par value common stock in exchange for graphics software.

   (3) May 1: Issues 100 shares of $10-par value common stock to another firm to acquire a patent.

   (4) May 5: Signs a lease to rent office space for the one year beginning June 1 and pays the first month's rent of $18,000 in advance.

   (5) May 10: Purchases, for cash, office equipment costing $12,000.

   (6) May 15: Orders stationery with the firm's letterhead at a cost of $900.

   (7) May 18: Receives an order from a customer for graphics software with a selling price of $6,000. The customer makes a deposit of $1,500, with the remainder due when Computer Graphic delivers the software in June.

   (8) May 20: Purchases, on account, blank software disks costing $4,900.

   (9) May 30: Receives the stationery ordered on May 15 and pays the $900 invoice.

   (10) May 30: Pays the invoice for the purchases in transaction (8) in time to take advantage of a 2 percent discount for prompt payment. The firm treats cash discounts taken as a reduction in the cost of the items purchased.

   a. Enter these transactions in T-accounts. Indicate whether each account is an asset, a liability, or a shareholders' equity item. Cross-reference each entry to the appropriate transaction number.

   b. Prepare a balance sheet for Computer Graphic, Inc., as of May 30.

31. **T-account entries and balance sheet preparation.** Joshua Blacksmith plans to open a bakery on September 1, specializing in natural-grain breads, pastries, and other baked goods. He will operate the bakery under the name of Blacksmith's Bakery, Inc. The cash account during August showed the following:

Date	Description	Amount
Cash Receipts		
(1) August 10	Investment made by J. Blacksmith for 2,000 shares of $1-par value common stock	$2,000
(2) August 20	Advance from local grocery store for order to be shipped September 1	220
(3) August 25	Grant received from local chamber of commerce to encourage small business	500
Cash Disbursements		
(4) August 12	Expenditure made for a sign that Blacksmith's Bakery, Inc., will place outside its bakery	(450)
(5) August 15	Cost of used baking ovens from a bankrupt restaurant	(580)
(6) August 18	Rent prepaid on banking and retail space for the month beginning September 1	(800)
(7) August 25	Expenditure for baking and packaging supplies	(390)
(8) August 30	Expenditure for advertising to appear in local newspapers in September	(120)
		$ 380

In addition to the cash transactions above, you learn the following from Joshua Blacksmith:

(9) Baking and packaging supplies costing $240 were purchased on August 28 but not paid for by the end of August.

(10) A bill for services rendered in painting the Blacksmith Bakery, Inc., sign in the amount of $750 remains unpaid at the end of August.

(11) The firm has received an insurance premium notice totaling $390 for coverage beginning September 1.

a. Enter these transactions in T-accounts. Indicate whether each account is an asset, a liability, or a shareholders' equity item. Cross-reference each entry to the appropriate transaction number.

b. Prepare a balance sheet for Blacksmith's Bakery, Inc., as of August 31.

32. **Effect of recording errors on the balance sheet equation.** Using the notation O/S (overstated), U/S (understated), or No (no effect), indicate the effects on assets, liabilities, and shareholders' equity of *failing to record* each of the following independent transactions or events. For example, a failure to record the issuance of common stock for $10,000 cash would be shown as follows:

■ Assets—U/S $10,000

■ Liabilities—No

■ Shareholders' equity—U/S $10,000

(1) A firm purchases merchandise costing $8,000 on account.

(2) A firm acquires a machine costing $20,000. It makes a 25 percent down payment, with the remainder payable over four years.

(3) A firm places an order for $5,500 of merchandise with a supplier.

(4) A firm receives a check for $600 from a customer for merchandise to be delivered next month.

(5) A firm issues a check for $1,200 to cover rental of a warehouse for the next two months.

(6) A firm issues common stock with a market value of $2,500 in the acquisition of a patent.

(7) A firm pays a note payable for $4,000. The note had previously been correctly recorded on the books in the amount of $4,000.

(8) A firm pays $5,000 for an option to purchase a tract of land. The price of the land is $40,000. The firm can exercise the option within 90 days.

33. **Effect of recording errors on the balance sheet equation.** Using the notation O/S (overstated), U/S (understated), or No (no effect), indicate the effects on assets, liabilities, and shareholders' equity of *failing to record* each of the following independent transactions or events. For example, a failure to record the issuance of common stock for $10,000 cash would be shown as follows:

- Assets—U/S $10,000

- Liabilities—No

- Shareholders' Equity—U/S $10,000

(1) A firm acquires a building costing $800,000 by paying $40,000 in cash and signing a 20-year mortgage for the balance of the purchase price.

(2) A firm returns defective merchandise to a supplier and receives a cash refund of the $800 purchase price.

(3) A firm places an order for a machine costing $3,500. Payment is due on delivery of the machine next month.

(4) Holders of a firm's bonds originally issued for their principal amount of $10,000 exchange these bonds for common stock of the firm valued at $10,000. Consider this transaction from the viewpoint of the firm exchanging its common stock for the bonds.

(5) A firm issues a check for $900 for insurance coverage on automobiles for the next three months.

(6) A firm receives notice that it is a defendant in a lawsuit by a customer who is suing for damages of $250,000. The lawsuit is scheduled for trial in nine months.

(7) A firm purchases, for $2,000, shares of its outstanding common stock held by a shareholder.

(8) A firm pays accounts payable recorded on the books for $3,000 in time to take advantage of a 2 percent discount for prompt payment.

34. **Effect of recording errors on the balance sheet equation.** A firm recorded various transactions with the journal entries shown below. Using the notation O/S (overstated), U/S (understated), or No (no effect), indicate the effects on assets, liabilities, and shareholders' equity of any errors in recording each of these transactions. For example, if a firm recorded the issue of $10,000 of common stock by debiting Cash and crediting Bonds Payable, the effects of the error are shown as follows:

- Assets—No

- Liabilities—O/S $10,000

- Shareholders' equity—U/S $10,000

(1)	Building	10,000	
	Cash		2,000
	Note Receivable		8,000

To record acquisition of equipment for $2,000 cash and signing of an $8,000 promissory note for the balance.

(2)	Equipment	4,000	
	Cash		1,000
	Note Payable		3,000

To record the placing of an order for equipment to be delivered next month. The firm made a $1,000 deposit with the order.

(3)	Cash	800	
	Accounts Receivable		800

To record an advance from a customer on merchandise to be shipped next month. The customer did not owe the firm any amounts at the time of this transaction.

(4)	Prepaid Rent	1,000	
	Rent Payable		1,000

To record the signing of a rental agreement for warehouse space for a one-year period beginning next month. The monthly rental fee of $1,000 is due on the first day of each month.

(5)	Patent	2,500	
	Cash		2,500

To record the issuance of common stock in the acquisition of a patent.

(6)	Merchandise Inventories	4,900	
	Cash		4,900

To record the acquisition of office equipment for cash.

35. **Balance sheet format, terminology, and accounting methods.** Exhibit 2.12 presents a balance sheet for Marks and Spencer, PLC, a department store chain headquartered in the United Kingdom. This balance sheet appears in the format and uses terminology and accounting methods commonly found in the United Kingdom.
   a. Prepare a balance sheet for Marks and Spencer on March 30, Year 4, and March 30, Year 5, following the format, terminology, and accounting methods commonly found in the United States. Use the category Other Noncurrent Assets for assets that do not fit any typical U.S. grouping.
   b. Comment on the term structure of Marks and Spencer's investments relative to its financing.

36. **Balance sheet format, terminology, and accounting methods.** Exhibit 2.13 presents a balance sheet for United Breweries Group, a Danish brewing company. This balance sheet appears in the format and uses the terminology and accounting methods commonly found in Denmark.
   a. Prepare a balance sheet for United Breweries Group on September 30, Year 8, and September 30, Year 9, following the format, terminology, and accounting methods commonly found in the United States.
   b. Comment on the term structure of United Breweries Group's investments relative to its financing.

EXHIBIT 2.12	MARKS AND SPENCER Balance Sheet (in millions of pounds) (Problem 35)

	March 30	
	Year 4	Year 5
Fixed Assets		
Land and Buildings	£2,094	£2,193
Fixtures, Fittings, and Equipment	375	419
Total Fixed Assets	£2,469	£2,612
Current Assets		
Stocks	£ 374	£ 351
Debtors (Note 1)	538	618
Investments	28	29
Cash at Bank and in Hand	266	293
Total Current Assets	£1,206	£1,291
Current Liabilities		
Creditor Amounts Falling Due within One Year		
(Note 2)	925	897
Net Current Assets	£ 281	£ 394
Total Assets Less Current Liabilities	£2,750	£3,006
Creditor Amounts Falling Due within One Year	565	550
Other Noncurrent Liabilities and Provisions	4	19
Net Assets	£2,181	£2,437
Capital and Reserve		
Called-Up Share Capital	£675	£ 680
Share Premium Account	50	69
Revaluation Reserve (Note 3)	458	460
Profit and Loss Account	998	1,228
Total Capital Employed	£2,181	£2,437

Note 1: Debtors include the following:

Amounts Falling Due within One Year:		
Accounts Receivable	£ 192	£ 212
Prepayments	134	142
Amounts Falling Due after One Year:		
Accounts Receivable	174	217
Prepayments	38	47
	£ 538	£ 618

Note 2: Creditor amounts falling due within one year include the following:

Accounts Payable	£ 187	£ 168
Bank Loans	100	107
Other	638	622
	£ 925	£ 897

Note 3: The revaluation reserve arises from the restatement of land and buildings to current market value. None of the restatement affected net income.

EXHIBIT 2.13	UNITED BREWERIES GROUP Balance Sheet (in millions of kronor) (Problem 36)

	September 30	
	Year 8	Year 9
ASSETS		
Fixed Assets		
Tangible Fixed Assets	Kr 3,934	Kr 4,106
Investments in Securities	422	573
Total Fixed Assets	Kr 4,356	Kr 4,679
Current Assets		
Stocks	Kr 1,290	Kr 1,393
Trade Debtors	1,413	1,444
Prepayments	317	285
Securities	3,018	3,460
Cash at Bank and in Hand	810	1,224
Total Current Assets	Kr 6,848	Kr 7,806
Total Assets	Kr 11,204	Kr 12,485
LIABILITIES		
Capital and Reserves		
Share Capital	Kr 976	Kr 976
Revaluation Reserves (Note 1)	416	561
Other Reserves (Note 2)	3,169	3,672
Total Capital and Reserves	Kr 4,561	Kr 5,209
Provisions (Note 3)	Kr 1,149	Kr 1,425
Long-term Debt	Kr 1,805	Kr 1,723
Short-term Debt		
Bank Debt	Kr 619	Kr 986
Trade Creditors	913	902
Other	2,157	2,240
Total Short-term Debt	Kr 3,689	Kr 4,128
Total Capital and Liabilities	Kr 11,204	Kr 12,485

Note 1: The Revaluation Reserves result from restating tangible fixed assets to current market values.

Note 2: Other Reserves represent cumulative net income in excees of dividends.

Note 3: Provisions represent noncurrent liabilities for income taxes and miscellaneous obligations.

37. **Interpreting balance sheet changes.** Exhibit 2.14 presents a common-size balance sheet for Staples, Inc., an office supply retailer, for two recent years.
   a. Identify the ways in which the structure of Staples' assets and the structure of its financing correspond to what one would expect of a retail store chain.
   b. Identify the major changes in the structure of Staples' assets and its financing over the two-year period and suggest possible reasons for the changes.
   c. "An increase in the common-size balance sheet percentage between two year-ends for a particular balance sheet item (for example, cash) does not necessarily mean that its dollar amount increased." Explain.

EXHIBIT 2.14	STAPLES, INC. Common-Size Balance Sheet (Problem 37)

| | **January 31** | |
	Year 6	**Year 7**
ASSETS		
Cash	5.9%	14.6%
Accounts Receivable	9.3	6.2
Inventories	45.5	44.5
Other Current Assets	3.6	2.6
Total Current Assets	64.3%	67.9%
Property, Plant, and Equipment	24.8	23.4
Other Assets	10.9	8.7
Total Assets	100.0%	100.0%
LIABILITIES AND SHAREHOLDERS' EQUITY		
Current Liabilities		
Accounts Payable	23.6%	26.1%
Notes Payable	.4	1.6
Other Current Liabilities	9.7	10.6
Total Current Liabilities	33.7%	38.3%
Noncurrent Liabilities		
Bonds Payable	21.9%	20.7%
Other Noncurrent Liabilities	1.8	1.6
Total Noncurrent Liabilities	23.7%	22.3%
Total Liabilities	57.4%	60.6%
Shareholders' Equity		
Common Stock	28.4%	24.2%
Retained Earnings	14.2	15.2
Total Shareholders' Equity	42.6%	39.4%
Total Liabilities and Shareholders' Equity	100.0%	100.0%

38. **Interpreting balance sheet changes.** Exhibit 2.15 presents a common-size balance sheet for Kroger Company, a grocery store chain, for two recent years.
    a. In what ways is the common-size balance sheet of Kroger Company on January 31, Year 7, typical of a grocery store chain?
    b. What is the likely reason for the changes in the financing of Kroger Company between January 31, Year 7, and January 31, Year 8?

39. **Market value versus book value of shareholders' equity.** Firms prepare their balance sheets using GAAP for the recognition and valuation of assets and liabilities. Accountants refer to the total common shareholders' equity appearing on the balance sheet as the *book value of shareholders' equity.* The *market value of shareholders' equity* equals the number of shares of common stock outstanding times the market price per share. Financial analysts frequently examine the ratio of the market value of

EXHIBIT 2.15	KROGER COMPANY Common-Size Balance Sheet (Problem 38)		

		January 31	
		Year 7	Year 8
ASSETS			
Cash		2.5%	4.6%
Accounts Receivable		5.7	5.6
Inventories		32.5	32.7
Prepayments		7.6	10.6
Total Current Assets		48.3%	53.5%
Property, Plant, and Equipment		47.9	41.4
Other Assets		3.8	5.1
Total Assets		100.0%	100.0%
LIABILITIES AND SHAREHOLDERS' EQUITY			
Current Liabilities			
Accounts Payable		22.5%	23.7%
Note Payable		7.8	7.6
Other Current Liabilities		13.8	15.7
Total Current Liabilities		44.1%	47.0%
Noncurrent Liabilities			
Bonds Payable		22.1%	102.4%
Other Noncurrent Liabilities		8.4	8.7
Total Noncurrent Liabilities		30.5%	111.1%
Total Current Liabilities		74.6%	158.1%
Shareholders' Equity			
Preferred Stock		2.8%	5.4%
Common Stock		9.5	2.2
Additional Paid-in Capital		24.5	(54.6)
Retained Earnings		(11.4)	(11.1)
Total Shareholders' Equity		25.4%	(58.1)%
Total Liabilities and Shareholders' Equity		100.0%	100.0%

shareholders' equity to the book value of shareholders' equity, referred to as the *market-to-book ratio,* in assessing current market prices. Recent theoretical and empirical research suggests that the size of the market-to-book ratio is related to (1) a firm's ability to generate higher rates of profitability than its competitors, (2) its rate of growth, and (3) its use of GAAP in measuring assets and liabilities, which net to the book value of shareholders' equity.

Exhibit 2.16 presents balance sheet information for five firms at the end of a recent year. It also shows their market-to-book ratios. These ratios differ from 1.0 in part because the rates of profitability and growth of these five firms differ from

EXHIBIT 2.16	Balance Sheets for Selected Companies (amounts in millions) (Problem 39)

	Coca-Cola	Bristol-Myers Squibb	Bankers Trust	International Paper	Walt Disney
ASSETS					
Cash and Marketable Securities	$ 1,531	$ 2,423	$79,048	$ 270	$ 1,510
Accounts and Notes Receivable	1,525	2,043	11,249	2,241	1,671
Inventories	1,047	1,397	—	2,075	2,264
Other Current Assets	1,102	847	—	244	—
Total Current Assets	$ 5,205	$ 6,710	$90,297	$ 4,830	$ 5,445
Investments in Securities	3,928	—	—	1,032	630
Property, Plant, and Equipment	4,080	3,666	915	9,941	5,814
Other Noncurrent Assets	660	2,534	5,804	2,033	937
Total Assets	$13,873	$12,910	$97,016	$17,836	$12,826
LIABILITIES AND SHAREHOLDERS' EQUITY					
Accounts Payable	$ 2,564	$ 693	$24,939	$ 1,204	$ 2,475
Short-term Borrowing	2,083	725	55,166	2,083	—
Other Current Liabilities	1,530	2,856	5,502	747	967
Total Current Liabilities.	$ 6,177	$ 4,274	$85,607	$ 4,034	$ 3,442
Long-term Debt	1,426	644	6,455	4,464	2,937
Other Noncurrent Liabilities	1,035	2,288	—	2,824	939
Total Liabilities	$ 8,638	$ 7,206	$92,062	$11,322	$ 7,318
Preferred Stock	—	—	$ 645	—	—
Common Stock	$ 1,600	$ 451	1,401	$ 1,914	$ 945
Retained Earnings	10,708	7,299	3,324	4,711	5,849
Treasury Stock	(7,073)	(2,046)	(416)	(111)	(1,286)
Total Shareholders' Equity	$ 5,235	$ 5,704	$ 4,954	$ 6,514	$ 5,508
Total Liabilities and Shareholders' Equity	$13,873	$12,910	$97,016	$17,836	$12,826
Market Value/Book Value Ratio	12.6	5.2	1.0	1.3	4.4

those of their competitors. This problem does not provide you with sufficient information to assess the impact of these two factors on the market-to-book ratio. The ratios also differ from 1.0 because of the use of GAAP for assets and liabilities, which this chapter discussed. Identify the GAAP that most likely explain the market-to-book ratios for each of the six firms (that is, identify which accounting principles cause the book values of assets and liabilities to differ from the market value of shareholders' equity).

Additional information regarding the five companies follows:

(1) *Coca-Cola (Coke):* Coke markets soft drinks worldwide. It has grown primarily by internal expansion rather than by acquiring other soft-drink firms. Coke maintains less than 50 percent ownership in a large number of its bottlers.

(2) *Bristol-Myers Squibb (Bristol):* Bristol generates approximately 75 percent of its revenues from prescription drugs and medical devices and 25 percent from nonprescription health products, toiletries, and beauty aids.

(3) *Bankers Trust (Bankers):* Bankers obtains funds primarily from depositors (reported on the Accounts Payable line in Exhibit 2.16) and invests them in short-term liquid assets or lends them to businesses and consumers. It also engages in investment activities on its own account.

(4) *International Paper (IP):* IP has the largest holdings of forest lands of any nongovernmental entity in the United States. It processes timber into wood products for the construction industry and processes pulp from the timber into various types of commodity and specialty papers.

(5) *Walt Disney (Disney):* Disney produces motion picture films and operates theme parks.

40. **Market value versus book value of shareholders' equity.** Firms prepare their balance sheets using GAAP for the recognition and valuation of assets and liabilities. Accountants refer to the total common shareholders' equity appearing on the balance sheet as the *book value of shareholders' equity.* The *market value of shareholders' equity* equals the number of shares of common stock outstanding times the market price per share. Financial analysts frequently examine the ratio of the market value of shareholders' equity to the book value of shareholders' equity, referred to as the *market-to-book ratio,* in assessing current market prices. Recent theoretical and empirical research suggests that the size of the market-to-book ratio is related to (1) a firm's ability to generate higher rates of profitability than its competitors, (2) its rate of growth, and (3) its use of GAAP in measuring assets and liabilities, which net to the book value of shareholders' equity.

Exhibit 2.17 presents balance sheet information for six firms at the end of a recent year. It also shows their market-to-book ratios. These ratios differ from 1.0 in part because the rates of profitability and growth of these six firms differ from those of their competitors. This problem does not provide you with sufficient information to assess the impact of these two factors on the market-to-book ratio. The ratios also differ from 1.0 because of the use of GAAP for assets and liabilities, which this chapter discussed. Identify the GAAP that most likely explain the market-to-book ratios for each of the six firms (that is, identify which accounting principles cause the book values of assets and liabilities to differ from the market value of shareholders' equity).

Additional information regarding the six companies follows:

(1) Merck is a pharmaceutical company headquartered in the United States. Merck recently acquired a large, prescription drug-management firm.

(2) Nestlé is a consumer products company headquartered in Switzerland. In addition to its chocolate products, it manufactures and distributes beverages (Nestea, Poulin Springs mineral water), frozen foods (Stouffers), milk products (infant formulas), and pet foods (Alpo).

(3) Promodes is a French company that operates chains of supermarkets (Champion), hypermarkets (Continent, Continente), convenience stores (Promocash, Punt&Cash), and restaurant supply stores (Prodirest).

(4) Deutsche Bank is a German commercial bank that provides both traditional commercial banking services (deposit taking, loan making) and investment banking services (investment management, financial consulting).

EXHIBIT 2.17	Common-Size Balance Sheets for Selected Companies (Problem 40)

	Merck	Nestlé	Promodes	Deutsche Bank	British Airways	New Oji Paper Co.
ASSETS						
Cash and Marketable Securities	8.9%	11.5%	12.9%	44.2%	6.5%	2.1%
Accounts and Notes Receivable	11.1	18.9	22.6	50.4	13.5	19.8
Inventories	8.3	13.4	18.4	—	.7	8.5
Other Current Assets	3.6	1.4	—	—	—	1.5
Total Current Assets	31.9%	45.2%	53.9%	94.6%	20.7%	31.9%
Investments in Securities	9.8	7.1	8.7	2.7	6.6	24.5
Property, Plant, and Equipment	25.6	43.7	28.3	1.2	72.7	43.6
Other Noncurrent Assets	32.7	4.0	9.1	1.5	—	—
Total Assets	100.0%	100.0%	100.0%	100.0%	100.0%	100.0%
LIABILITIES AND SHAREHOLDERS' EQUITY						
Accounts Payable	12.7%	11.2%	44.3%	66.5%	9.4%	10.2%
Short-term Borrowing	3.5	18.1	3.3	16.0	5.3	16.2
Other Current Liabilities	5.4	9.6	12.6	4.9	15.6	10.7
Total Current Liabilities	21.6%	38.9%	60.2%	87.4%	30.3%	37.1%
Long-term Debt	5.2	6.7	7.7	1.2	36.8	16.9
Other Noncurrent Liabilities	19.8	9.2	4.1	8.0	4.0	4.8
Total Liabilities	46.6%	54.8%	72.0%	96.6%	71.1%	58.8%
Common Stock	24.9%	3.0%	.8%	1.7%	8.1%	17.3%
Retained Earnings	67.1	42.7	27.2	1.7	20.8	23.9
Treasury Stock	(38.6)	(.5)	—	—	—	—
Total Shareholders' Equity	53.4%	45.2%	28.0%	3.4%	28.9%	41.2%
Total Liabilities and Shareholders' Equity	100.0%	100.0%	100.0%	100.0%	100.0%	100.0%
Market Value/Book Value Ratio	9.1	3.3	4.6	1.7	2.4	1.4

(5) British Airways is headquartered in the United Kingdom and provides air transportation services.

(6) New Oji Paper Co. is a Japanese forest-products company. It purchases wood pulp from Canada and the United States and processes it into various papers for sale in Japan.

CHAPTER 3

INCOME STATEMENT: REPORTING THE RESULTS OF OPERATING ACTIVITIES

LEARNING OBJECTIVES

1. Understand the accrual basis of accounting and why accountants believe that the accrual basis usually provides measures of operating performance superior to those provided by the cash basis of accounting.
2. Deepen your understanding of the accrual basis of accounting by examining when firms recognize revenues and expenses and how they measure these two components of net income.
3. Build on your skills in recording transactions in the accounts by extending the recording process studied in Chapter 2 to include income statement items.
4. Understand the need for end-of-the-period adjusting entries under the accrual basis of accounting and extend your skills in the recording process to include adjusting entries.
5. Develop skills to analyze the income statement, focusing on the relations between revenues, expenses, and net income for various types of businesses.

The income statement, the second principal financial statement, provides a measure of the operating performance of a firm for some particular period of time. **Net income,** or earnings, equals revenues minus expenses.

Revenues measure the net assets (assets less liabilities) that flow into a firm when it sells goods or renders services. **Expenses** measure the net assets that a firm consumes in the process of generating revenues. As a measure of operating performance, revenues reflect the services rendered by a firm, and expenses indicate the efforts required.

This chapter considers the measurement principles and accounting procedures that underlie the income statement. We begin by considering the concept of an accounting period, the span of time over which accountants measure operating performance. Next, the chapter describes and illustrates two common approaches to measuring operating performance, the cash basis and the accrual basis. It then illustrates the accounting procedures used in applying the accrual basis of accounting for a merchandising firm. Finally, the chapter discusses relations between revenues, expenses, and net income for different types of businesses.

THE ACCOUNTING PERIOD CONVENTION

The income statement reports operating performance for a specific time period. Years ago, the length of this period varied among firms. Firms prepared income statements at the completion of some activity, such as after the round-trip voyage of a ship between England and the Colonies or after the completion of a construction project.

The operating activities of most modern firms do not divide so easily into distinguishable projects. Instead, the income-generating activity occurs continually. For example, a firm acquires a plant and uses it in manufacturing products for a period of 40 years or more. A firm purchases delivery equipment and uses it in transporting merchandise to customers for four, five, or more years. If preparing the income statement awaited the completion of all operating activities, the firm might prepare the report only when it ceased to exist and the report would be too late to help a reader appraise operating performance. An **accounting period** of uniform length facilitates timely comparisons and analyses among firms. One might think of an accounting period as the time elapsing between balance sheet dates. Balance sheets prepared at the end of the day on December 31 of one year and at the end of the day on December 31 of the next year bound a calendar-year accounting period. Balance sheets prepared at the end of the day on November 30 and at the end of the day on December 31 bound a one-month accounting period for December.

An accounting period of one year underlies the principal financial statements distributed to shareholders and potential investors. Most firms prepare their annual reports using the calendar year as the accounting period. Many firms, however, use a **natural business year or fiscal period** to attempt to measure performance at a time when they have concluded most operating activities for the period. The ending date of a natural business year varies from one firm to another and usually occurs when inventories are at their lowest level during the year. For example, JCPenney, a retailer, uses a natural business year ending near the end of January, which comes after the Christmas shopping season and before the start of the Easter season. Winnebago Industries, a manufacturer of recreational vehicles, uses a year ending August 31, the end of its model year.

Firms frequently prepare reports of performance for periods shorter than a year to indicate progress during the year. These are known as *interim reports* or *reports for interim periods*. Preparing interim reports does not eliminate the need to prepare an annual report.

ACCOUNTING METHODS FOR MEASURING PERFORMANCE

Some operating activities both start and finish within a given accounting period. For example, a firm might purchase merchandise from a supplier, sell it to a customer on account, and collect the cash, all within the same accounting period. These cases present few difficulties in measuring performance. The difference between the cash received from customers and the cash disbursed to acquire, sell, and deliver the merchandise represents earnings from this series of transactions.

Many operating activities, however, start in one accounting period and finish in another. A firm uses, over several years, buildings and equipment acquired in one period. In an extreme example, firms purchase merchandise in one accounting period, pay for it in a second, sell it during a third, and collect cash from customers in a fourth. Moreover, the events need not occur in that order. Cash payments can precede or follow the acquisition of goods; cash collection can precede or follow the sale of goods. To measure performance for a specific accounting period requires measuring the amount of revenues and expenses from operating activities already begun by the beginning of the period and other activities not yet complete at the end of the period. Two approaches to measuring operating performance are (1) the cash basis of accounting and (2) the accrual basis of accounting.

CASH BASIS OF ACCOUNTING

Under the **cash basis of accounting,** a firm recognizes revenues, from selling goods and providing services, in the period when it receives cash from customers. It reports expenses in the period when it makes cash expenditures for merchandise, salaries, insurance, taxes, and similar items. To understand the measurement of performance under the cash basis of accounting, consider the following information.

Donald and Joanne Allens open a hardware store on January 1, Year 1. The firm receives $20,000 in cash from the Allens and borrows $12,000 from a local bank. It must repay the loan on June 30, Year 1, with interest charged at the rate of 8 percent per year. The firm rents a store building on January 1 and pays two months' rent of $4,000 in advance. On January 1, it also pays the premium of $2,400 for property and liability insurance coverage for the year ending December 31, Year 1. During January it acquires merchandise costing $40,000, of which it purchases $26,000 for cash and $14,000 on account. Sales to customers during January total $50,000, of which $34,000 is for cash and $16,000 is on account. The acquisition cost of the merchandise sold during January is $32,000, and various employees receive $5,000 in salaries.

Example 1 Exhibit 3.1 presents an income statement for Allens' Hardware Store for the month of January, Year 1, using the cash basis of accounting. Cash receipts of $34,000 from sales of merchandise represent the portion of the total January sales, $50,000, that the firm collects during January. Whereas the firm acquires merchandise costing $40,000 during January, it disburses only $26,000 cash to suppliers and therefore subtracts only this amount in measuring net income under the cash basis. In measuring performance, the firm also subtracts the amounts of cash expenditures made during January for salaries, rent, and insurance, without regard to whether the firm fully consumes the services by the end of the month. Cash expenditures for merchandise and services exceeded cash receipts from customers during January by $3,400. Note that under the cash basis, the income statement does not include cash received from owners or from borrowing, both of which are financing transactions.

As a basis for measuring performance for a particular accounting period (here, January, Year 1, for Allens' Hardware Store), the cash basis of accounting has three weaknesses.

Inadequately Matches Revenues and Expenses First, the cash basis does not adequately match the cost of the efforts required in generating revenues with those revenues. The performance of one period mingles with the performance of preceding and succeeding periods. The store rental payment of $4,000 provides rental services for both January and February, but the cash basis subtracts the full amount in measuring performance during January. Likewise, the annual insurance premium provides coverage for the full year, whereas the cash basis of accounting subtracts none of this insurance cost in measuring performance during February through December.

The longer the period over which a firm receives future benefits, the more deficient becomes the cash basis for reporting. Consider, for example, a capital-intensive firm's investments in buildings and equipment that it will use for 20 or more years. The length of time between the purchase of these assets and the collection of cash for goods produced and sold can span many years and distort the measurement of performance during both the period of the cash expenditure and subsequent periods.

EXHIBIT 3.1	ALLENS' HARDWARE STORE Income Statement for the Month of January, Year 1 Cash Basis of Accounting

Cash Receipts from Sales of Merchandise		$34,000
Less Cash Expenditures for Merchandise and Services:		
Merchandise	$26,000	
Salaries	5,000	
Rent.	4,000	
Insurance	2,400	
Total Cash Expenditures		37,400
Excess of Cash Expenditures over Cash Receipts		$ (3,400)

Unnecessarily Delays the Recognition of Revenues   Second, the cash basis of accounting unnecessarily postpones the time when the firm recognizes revenue. A firm should recognize revenue when it has finished the difficult parts of the operating process. The operating process involves the following actions by the seller:

- Acquiring goods and labor
- Persuading the customer to buy the goods or services
- Delivering the goods or services to the customer
- Collecting cash from the customer
- Waiting, in the case of sales of goods, until the period of warranty (or right to return) expires

The most difficult parts of the operating process for manufacturing and retailing firms are persuading the customer to buy the goods and delivering the goods. The most difficult parts for service firms are persuading the customer to use the services and then rendering the services. Most firms find that collecting cash and dealing with warranties and returns are relatively routine or, at least, predictable. In these cases, recognizing revenue at the time of cash collection may result in reporting the effects of operating activities one or more periods after the critical revenue-generating activity has occurred. For example, sales to customers during January by Allens' Hardware Store totaled $50,000. Under the cash basis of accounting, the firm will not recognize $16,000 of this amount until it collects the cash, during February or even later. If the firm checks the creditworthiness of customers before making the sales on account, it will probably collect the cash and therefore need not postpone recognition of the revenue until the time it actually collects the cash.

Provides Opportunities to Distort the Measurement of Operating Performance   A third criticism of the cash basis is that it provides an opportunity for firms to distort the measurement of operating performance by timing their cash expenditures. Firms might delay cash expenditures near the end of the accounting period in an effort to increase earnings and appear more profitable. Firms might accelerate cash expenditures to appear less profitable and perhaps discourage competitors from entering the industry or labor unions from negotiating higher wages for employees.

Lawyers, accountants, and other professionals are the principal users of the cash basis of accounting. These professionals have relatively small investments in inventories and multiperiod assets, such as buildings and equipment, and usually collect cash from clients

EXHIBIT 3.2	ALLENS' HARDWARE STORE Income Statement for the Month of January, Year 1 Accrual Basis of Accounting

Sales Revenue		$50,000
Less Expenses:		
Cost of Goods Sold	$32,000	
Salaries Expense	5,000	
Rent Expense	2,000	
Insurance Expense	200	
Interest Expense	80	
Total Expenses		39,280
Net Income		$10,720

soon after they render services. Most of these firms actually use a modified cash basis of accounting, under which they treat the costs of buildings, equipment, and similar items as assets when purchased. They then recognize a portion of the acquisition cost as an expense when they consume services of these assets. Except for the treatment of these long-lived assets, such firms recognize revenues at the time they receive cash and recognize expenses when they disburse cash.

Most individuals use the cash basis of accounting for the purpose of computing personal income and personal income taxes. When a firm, such as one in merchandising or manufacturing, uses inventories as an important factor in generating revenues, the Internal Revenue Code prohibits the firm from using the cash basis of accounting in its income tax returns.

ACCRUAL BASIS OF ACCOUNTING

The **accrual basis of accounting** typically recognizes revenue when a firm sells goods (manufacturing and retailing firms) or renders services (service firms). At these points the firm has usually accomplished the most difficult part of the operating process. The costs of assets used in producing revenues lead to expenses in the period when the firm recognizes the revenues that the costs helped produce. Thus accrual accounting attempts to match expenses with associated revenues. If the costs of assets used do not easily match with particular revenues, these costs appear as expenses of the period when the firm uses the services of the assets.

Example 2 Exhibit 3.2 presents an income statement for Allens' Hardware Store for January of Year 1 using the accrual basis of accounting. The firm recognizes the entire $50,000 of sales during January as revenue, even though it has received only $34,000 in cash by the end of January. The firm will probably collect the remaining accounts receivable of $16,000 in February or later periods. Therefore, the sale of the goods, rather than the collection of cash from customers, triggers the recognition of revenue.[1] The merchandise sold during January cost $32,000. Recognizing this amount as an expense

---

[1]This example assumes that the firm collects all its receivables from sales. Later, we relax this assumption and assume merely that the firm collects a predictable proportion of its sales on account. When the firm collects a predictable proportion of its sales on account, we can still say that the sale triggers revenue recognition, but the amount of the revenue results from calculations about expected cash collections.

(cost of goods sold) matches the cost of the merchandise sold with revenue from sales. Of the advance rental payment of $4,000, only $2,000 applies to the cost of services consumed during January. The remaining rental of $2,000 applies to the month of February and will therefore appear on the balance sheet on January 31 as an asset. Likewise, only $200 of the $2,400 insurance premium represents coverage used up during January. The remaining $2,200 of the insurance premium provides coverage for February through December and will become an expense during those months. In the meantime it appears as an asset on the balance sheet on January 31. The interest expense of $80 represents one month's interest on the $12,000 bank loan at an annual rate of 8 percent (= $12,000 × .08 × 1/12). Although the firm will not pay this interest until the loan comes due on June 30, Year 1, the firm benefited from using the funds during January; it should therefore recognize one month of the total interest cost on the loan as an expense of January. The firm reports its obligation to pay the $80 as a liability on the balance sheet on January 31. The salaries, rent, insurance, and interest expenses, unlike the cost of merchandise sold, do not associate directly with revenues recognized during the period. These costs therefore become expenses of January to the extent that the firm consumed services during the month.

The accrual basis of accounting provides a better measure of operating performance for Allens' Hardware Store for the month of January than does the cash basis for two reasons:

1. Revenues more accurately reflect the results of sales activity during January.
2. Expenses more closely match reported revenues.

Likewise, the accrual basis will provide a superior measure of performance for future periods because activities of those periods will bear their share of the costs of rental, insurance, and other services the firm will consume. Thus the accrual basis focuses on inflows of net assets from operations (revenues) and the use of net assets in operations (expenses), independent of whether those inflows and outflows of net assets are currently in the form of cash.

Many accountants argue that the accrual basis provides fewer opportunities than the cash basis to distort the measurement of earnings. The matching of expenses with associated revenues serves as a guiding principle that constrains a firm's efforts to time the recognition of expenses to suit its particular reporting objectives. As later chapters make clear, however, timing revenue recognition and measuring related expenses under the accrual basis both often involve judgment. Thus opportunities for earnings management are present even under the accrual basis.

Most business firms, particularly those involved in merchandising and manufacturing activities, use the accrual basis of accounting. The next section examines the measurement principles of accrual accounting.

PROBLEM 3.1 FOR SELF-STUDY

Cash versus accrual basis of accounting. Thompson Hardware Store commences operations on January 1, Year 5. J. Thompson invests $10,000, and the firm borrows $8,000 from a local bank. The firm must repay the loan on June 30, Year 5, with interest at the rate of 9 percent per year.

The firm rents a building on January 1 and pays two months' rent in advance in the amount of $2,000. On January 1, it also pays the $1,200 premium for property and liability insurance coverage for the year ending December 31, Year 5.

The firm purchases $28,000 of merchandise inventory on account on January 2 and pays $10,000 of this amount on January 25. A physical inventory indicates that the cost of merchandise on hand on January 31 is $15,000.

During January, the firm makes cash sales to customers totaling $20,000 and sales on account totaling $9,000. The firm collects $2,000 from these credit sales by the end of January.

The firm pays other costs during January as follows: utilities, $400; salaries, $650; and taxes, $350.

a. Prepare an income statement for January, assuming that Thompson uses the accrual basis of accounting and recognizes revenue at the time goods are sold (delivered).

b. Prepare an income statement for January, assuming that Thompson uses the cash basis of accounting.

c. Which basis of accounting do you believe provides a better indication of the operating performance of the firm during January? Why?

MEASUREMENT PRINCIPLES OF ACCRUAL ACCOUNTING

Under the accrual basis of accounting, one must consider when a firm recognizes revenues and expenses (timing questions) and how much it recognizes (measurement questions).

TIMING OF REVENUE RECOGNITION

Figure 3.1 depicts the operating process for the acquisition and sale of merchandise. A firm could recognize revenue, a measure of the increase in net assets from selling goods or providing services, at the time of purchase, sale, or cash collection, at some point(s) between these events, or even continually. Answering the timing question requires a set of criteria for revenue recognition.

Criteria for Revenue Recognition The accrual basis of accounting recognizes revenue when both of the following events have occurred:

1. A firm has performed all, or most of, the services it expects to provide.
2. The firm has received cash or some other asset capable of reasonably precise measurement, such as a receivable.

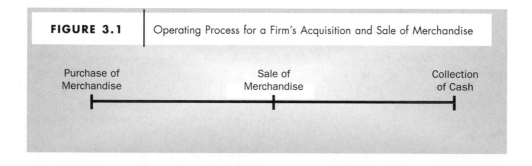

| **FIGURE 3.1** | Operating Process for a Firm's Acquisition and Sale of Merchandise |

Purchase of Merchandise   Sale of Merchandise   Collection of Cash

Most firms involved in selling goods and services recognize revenue at the time of sale (delivery). The firm has transferred the goods to a buyer or has performed the services. The firm estimates that future services, such as for warranties, will not generate significant costs or, if they are significant, the firm can estimate the amounts with reasonable precision. Similarly, the firm estimates that purchasers' returns will not involve significant amounts or, if they are significant, that the firm can estimate the amounts with reasonable precision. An exchange between an independent buyer and seller provides an objective measure of the amount of revenue.

If the firm makes the sale on account, past experience and an assessment of credit standings of customers provide a basis for predicting the amount of cash the firm will collect. Thus the time of sale usually meets the criteria for revenue recognition. In general, the firm will recognize revenue when it has no further significant uncertainty about the amount and timing of cash collection from the sales transaction. An example of a firm that should *not* recognize revenue at the time of sale is a software developer shipping a new product. The developer can estimate neither how many of the customers will return the product nor the cost of debugging the software once customers start to use it. Hence, that developer cannot estimate with reasonable precision the eventual net cash inflows.

MEASUREMENT OF REVENUE

A firm measures the amount of revenue by the cash or cash-equivalent value of other assets it receives from customers. As a starting point, this amount is the agreed-upon price between buyer and seller at the time of sale. If a firm recognizes revenue in a period before it collects the cash, however, it may need to make adjustments to the agreed-upon price in measuring revenue to recognize the effects of the time delay.

Uncollectible Accounts   If a firm expects not to collect some portion of the sales for a period, it must adjust the amount of revenue recognized during that period for estimated uncollectible accounts arising from those sales. This adjustment of revenue occurs in the period when the firm recognizes revenue and not in the later period when it identifies specific customers' accounts as uncollectible. If the firm postpones the adjustment, earlier decisions to extend credit to customers will affect income of subsequent periods. A failure to recognize anticipated uncollectibles at the time of sale incorrectly measures the performance of the firm for both the period of sale and the period when the firm judges the account uncollectible. Chapter 6 considers these problems further.

Sales Discounts and Allowances   Customers may take advantage of discounts for prompt payment, and the seller may grant allowances for unsatisfactory merchandise. In these cases, the firm will eventually receive cash in a smaller amount than the stated selling price. The firm must estimate these amounts and make appropriate reductions, at the time of sale, in measuring the amount of revenue it recognizes.

Sales Returns   Customers may return goods. If so, the firm will eventually receive cash in an amount smaller than the original sales price. The firm must estimate the expected returns and make appropriate reductions in revenue measured at the time of sale.

Delayed Payments   Firms sometimes permit customers to delay payment for purchases of goods or services but make no provision for explicit interest charges. In such cases, the selling price probably includes an implicit interest charge for the right to delay payment. The accrual basis of accounting recognizes this interest element as interest revenue during the periods between sale and collection. Recognizing all revenue entirely in the period of sale results in recognizing too soon the return for services rendered over time in lending cash. When a firm delays cash collection beyond one year, generally accepted accounting principles require it to report revenue for the current period at an amount less than the selling price. The reduction accounts for interest between the sale and the collection of cash. For the period of sale, the firm recognizes as revenue only the present value, at the time of sale, of the amount it expects to receive.

For most accounts receivable, the period between sale and collection spans only two to three months. Such transactions usually imply an insignificant amount of interest. As a result, accounting practice makes no reduction for interest on delayed payments for receivables that a firm expects to collect within one year or less. This procedure provides a practical expedient rather than adherence to the underlying accounting theory.

TIMING OF EXPENSE RECOGNITION

Assets provide future benefits to a firm. Expenses measure the assets consumed in generating revenue. Assets are **unexpired costs,** and expenses are **expired costs** or "gone assets." We focus on when the asset expiration takes place. The critical question is, "When do the benefits of an asset expire, leaving the balance sheet, and become expenses, entering the income statement as reductions in shareholders' equity?"

Balance Sheet	**Income Statement**
Assets or Unexpired Costs ⟶	Expenses or Expired Costs (which reduce shareholders' equity on the balance sheet)

Criteria for Expense Recognition Accountants recognize expenses as follows:

1. If an asset expiration associates directly with a particular revenue, that expiration becomes an expense in the period when the firm recognizes the revenue. This treatment—the **matching principle**—matches cost expirations with revenues.
2. If an asset expiration does not clearly associate with revenues, that expiration becomes an expense of the period when the firm consumes the benefits of that asset in operations.

Product Costs The matching principle most clearly applies to the cost of goods sold because the firm can easily associate the asset expiration with the revenue from selling the goods. At the time of sale, the asset physically changes hands. The firm recognizes sales revenue, and the cost of the goods sold becomes an expense.

A merchandising firm purchases inventory and later sells it without changing its physical form. The inventory appears as an asset stated at acquisition cost on the balance sheet. Later, when the firm sells the inventory, the same amount of acquisition cost appears as an expense (cost of goods sold) on the income statement.

A manufacturing firm, on the other hand, incurs various costs as it changes the physical form of the goods it produces. These costs incurrences are not yet expenses—gone assets—but represent the transformation of one form of asset into another. A firm incurs three types of costs in manufacturing: (1) direct material costs, (2) direct labor costs, and (3) manufacturing overhead costs (sometimes called "indirect manufacturing costs"). A firm incurs direct material and direct labor costs because it manufactures particular products, so the firm can associate those costs with the particular products manufactured. Manufacturing overhead includes a mixture of costs that provide a firm with a capacity to produce. Examples of manufacturing overhead costs are expenditures for supervisors' salaries, utilities, property taxes, and insurance on the factory, as well as depreciation on manufacturing plant and equipment. The firm uses the services of each of these items during a period when it creates new assets—the inventory of goods it works on or holds for sale.

The manufacturing process transfers the benefits from direct material, direct labor, and manufacturing overhead to the asset represented by units of inventory. Because the firm shows the inventory items as assets until it sells them to customers, the various direct material, direct labor, and manufacturing overhead costs incurred in producing the goods remain as assets on the balance sheet in the manufacturing inventory under the titles Work-in-Process Inventory and Finished Goods Inventory. Such costs, called **product costs,** are assets transformed from one form to another. They remain on the balance sheet as assets until the firm sells the goods that they embody; then, they become expenses. Chapter 7 discusses more fully the accounting for manufacturing costs.

Marketing Costs   The costs a firm incurs in marketing or selling its products during a period relate primarily to the units it sells during the period. In generating current revenue, a firm incurs costs for salaries and commissions of the sales staff, for sales literature used, and for advertising. Because these marketing costs associate with the revenues of the period, accounting reports them as expenses in the period when the firm uses their services. One might argue that some marketing costs, such as advertising and other sales promotion, provide future-period benefits for a firm and that therefore the firm should continue to treat them as assets. Accountants find it difficult to distinguish the portion of the cost relating to the current period (an expense) from the portion relating to future periods (an asset). They therefore treat most marketing activity costs as expenses of the period when the firm uses the services. Even when such costs enhance the future marketability of a firm's products, accounting treats these marketing costs as **period expenses** rather than assets—an expedient rather than a strict following of concepts.

Administrative Costs   Since the costs incurred in administering the activities of a firm do not closely associate with units produced or sold, accounting treats them, like marketing costs, as period expenses. Examples include the president's salary, accounting and information systems costs, and the costs of conducting various supportive activities such as legal services, employee training, and corporate planning.

MEASUREMENT OF EXPENSES

Expenses represent assets consumed during the period, so the amount of an expense equals the cost of the asset consumed. The basis for expense measurement is the same as for asset measurement. Because accounting reports assets primarily at acquisition cost on the balance sheet, it measures expenses by the acquisition cost of the assets sold or used during the period.

SUMMARY

Over sufficiently long time periods, the *amount* of net income equals cash inflows minus cash outflows from operating, investing, and debt servicing activities; that is, the amount of net income equals the difference between the cash received from customers and the amount of cash paid to suppliers, employees, and other providers of goods and services. Users of financial statements, however, desire information about a firm's operating performance for short time periods, such as a year or less. Thus accountants must slice up this total amount of net income and allocate a portion to each period. Using the *timing* of cash flows to dictate the allocation of this total income usually provides a poor measure of operating performance. Cash receipts from customers do not always occur in the same accounting period as the related cash expenditures to the providers of goods and services. The accrual basis allocates this total net income so that outflows of net assets more closely match inflows of net assets of the period, independent of whether the net assets are currently in the form of cash.

The accrual basis determines the timing of income recognition. The accrual basis typically recognizes revenue at the time of sale (delivery). Costs that associate directly with particular revenues become expenses in the period when a firm recognizes the revenues. A firm treats the cost of acquiring or manufacturing inventory items in this manner. Costs that do not closely associate with particular revenue streams become expenses of the period when a firm consumes the goods or services in operations. Most marketing and administrative costs receive this treatment.

The next section considers the accounting procedures for preparing the income statement.

PROBLEM 3.2 FOR SELF-STUDY

Revenue and expense recognition. A firm uses the accrual basis of accounting and recognizes revenues at the time it sells goods or renders services. Indicate the amount of revenue or expense that the firm recognizes during April in each of the following transactions:

a. Collects $4,970 cash from customers during April for merchandise sold and delivered in March.

b. Sells merchandise to customers during April for $14,980 cash.

c. Sells to customers during April merchandise totaling $5,820 that the firm expects to collect in cash during May.

d. Pays suppliers $2,610 during April for merchandise received by the firm and sold to customers during March.

e. Pays suppliers $5,440 during April for merchandise received and sold to customers during April.

f. Receives from suppliers and sells to customers during April merchandise that cost $2,010 and that the firm expects to pay for during May.

g. Receives from suppliers during April merchandise that cost $1,570 and that the firm expects to sell to customers and to pay for during May.

OVERVIEW OF ACCOUNTING PROCEDURES

RELATION BETWEEN BALANCE SHEET AND INCOME STATEMENT

Chapter 2 discussed the balance sheet, which reports the assets of a firm and the financing of those assets by creditors and owners at a specific moment in time. This chapter discusses the income statement, which measures for a period of time the excess of revenues (net asset inflows) over expenses (net asset outflows) from selling goods and providing services. Firms may distribute net assets to shareholders each period as a dividend. Accountants view dividends as a distribution of net assets generated by earnings and not as a cost incurred in generating earnings. Thus, dividends are not expenses on the income statement. The Retained Earnings account on the balance sheet measures the cumulative excess of earnings over dividends since the firm began operations. The following disaggregation of the balance sheet equation shows the relation of revenues, expenses, and dividends to the components of the balance sheet.

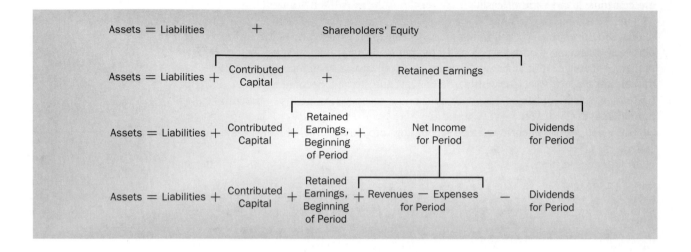

PURPOSE AND USE OF INDIVIDUAL REVENUE AND EXPENSE ACCOUNTS

The accountant could record revenue and expense amounts directly in the Retained Earnings account. For example, the sale of merchandise on account has at least two pairs of effects on the balance sheet:

1. The inflow of assets—accounts receivable, in this example, or cash, in other cases—causes an increase in assets (accounts receivable) and an increase in retained earnings (sales revenue).
2. The transfer of goods to customers causes a decrease in assets (merchandise inventory) and a decrease in retained earnings (cost of goods sold).

Recording revenues and expenses directly in the Retained Earnings account would make measuring the mere amount of net income easy. The following equation would derive net income:

$$\text{Net Income} = \frac{\text{Retained Earnings,}}{\text{End of Period}} - \frac{\text{Retained Earnings,}}{\text{Beginning of Period}} + \text{Dividends}$$

The income statement does not, however, report just the amount of net income. One can derive the amount of net income, as the equation above shows, using balance sheet amounts (and the amount of dividends, if any). The income statement reports the sources and amounts of a firm's revenues and the nature and amounts of a firm's expenses that generate earnings for the period. Knowing the components of a firm's net income helps both in understanding the causes of past performance and in forecasting future performance. Knowing the purpose of the income statement—to help explain why income was what it was—will help you understand the need for some of the procedures for preparing it.

To help prepare the income statement, accountants maintain individual revenue and expense accounts during the accounting period. These accounts begin the accounting period with a zero balance. During the period, the accountant records revenues and expenses in the accounts. At the end of the period, the balances in revenue accounts represent the cumulative revenues for the period. Similarly, at the end of the period, the balances in expense accounts represent the cumulative expenses for the period. The accountant reports these revenues and expenses, which aggregate to the period's net income, in the income statement.

Revenues and expenses are components of retained earnings, temporarily labeled with descriptive account titles so that the accountant can prepare an income statement. After preparing the income statement at the end of the period, the accountant transfers the balance in each revenue and expense account to the Retained Earnings account. Common terminology describes this transfer as *closing the revenue and expense accounts* because after closing (or transfer), each revenue and expense account has a zero balance. Retained earnings will increase by the amount of net income (or decrease by the net loss) for the period.

Maintaining separate revenue and expense accounts during the period and transferring their balances to the Retained Earnings account at the end of the period will have the same end result as initially recording revenues and expenses directly in the Retained Earnings account. Using separate revenue and expense accounts facilitates preparation of the income statement, which shows specific types of revenues and expenses. Once revenue and expense accounts serve their purpose, the need for separate accounts for a given accounting period ends. The accountant closes these accounts, so that they begin the following accounting period with a zero balance, ready for the revenue and expense entries of the new period.

The **closing process** transfers the balances in revenue and expense accounts to retained earnings. The term *closing* describes the process of reducing the balance to zero in each revenue and expense account. Because revenue and expense accounts accumulate amounts for only a single accounting period, accountants often refer to them as **temporary accounts.** In contrast, the accounts on the balance sheet reflect the cumulative changes in each account from the time the firm first began business. The balance sheet accounts remain open each period. Because the balances in these accounts at the end of one period carry over as the beginning balances for the following period, accountants often describe them as **permanent accounts.**

DEBIT AND CREDIT PROCEDURES FOR REVENUES, EXPENSES, AND DIVIDENDS

Because revenues, expenses, and dividends increase or decrease retained earnings, the recording procedures for these items are the same as for any other transaction affecting shareholders' equity accounts.

Shareholders Equity	
Decreases (Debit)	Increases (Credit)
Expenses	Revenues
Dividends	Issues of Capital Stock

A transaction generating revenue increases net assets (increase in assets or decrease in liabilities) and increases shareholders' equity. The usual journal entry to record a revenue transaction is therefore as follows:

Asset (A) Increase or Liability (L) Decrease . . . .   Amount
    Revenue (SE) . . . .   Amount
Typical entry to recognize revenue.

A transaction generating an expense decreases net assets (decrease in assets or increase in liabilities) and decreases shareholders' equity. The usual journal entry to record an expense transaction is therefore as follows:

Expense (SE) . . . .   Amount
    Asset (A) Decrease or Liability (L) Increase . . . .   Amount
Typical entry to record expense.

Dividends result in a decrease in net assets and a decrease in shareholders' equity. As Chapter 12 discusses, a firm may pay dividends either in cash or in other assets. Although the accounting procedures for dividends do not depend on the form of the distribution, we assume that the firm pays dividends in cash unless we have contrary information. The usual entry to record the declaration of a dividend by the board of directors of a corporation is as follows:

Retained Earnings (SE) . . . .   Amount
    Dividends Payable (L) . . . .   Amount
Typical entry to record dividend declaration.

When the firm pays the dividend, the journal entry is as follows:

Dividends Payable (L) . . . .   Amount
    Cash (A) . . . .   Amount
Typical entry to record dividend payment.

Note again that dividends are not expenses, even though the journal entries resemble those for expenses. They are not costs incurred in generating revenues. Rather, they represent distributions of assets, arising from current and previous years' operations, to the owners of the firm. Because dividends are not expenses, they do not affect the measurement of net income for the period.

Before we illustrate the recording procedures for revenues and expenses, we will briefly review the steps in the accounting process.

REVIEW OF THE ACCOUNTING PROCESS

The steps in the accounting process, discussed in Chapter 2, are listed below.

Journalizing   The accountant records each transaction or series of transactions during the period in journal entry form in the general journal (or in a special journal that supplements the general journal).

Posting   Periodically, the accountant posts **general journal entries** to the accounts in the general ledger.

Trial Balance   At the end of the accounting period, the accountant calculates the balance in each general ledger account and prepares a trial balance. A trial balance lists all accounts in the general ledger and their balances. If the firm has carried out the accounting process properly, the total of amounts in accounts having debit balances will equal the total of amounts in accounts having credit balances.

Adjusting Entries   During the period, some accounting events may escape the recording process or enter it partially or incorrectly. The accountant corrects these omissions or errors before preparing financial statements at the end of the period. The usual term for these correcting entries is **adjusting entries.** Adjusting entries result in reporting revenues and expenses in appropriate accounts with correct amounts for the period and reporting assets, liabilities, and shareholders' equities in appropriate accounts with correct amounts at the end of the period. Adjusting entries generally require entries in at least one income statement account and one balance sheet account. The accountant prepares the income statement only after making all adjusting entries to properly measure net income for the period.

Closing Entries   After preparing the income statement, the accounting process closes revenue and expense accounts at the end of the accounting period by transferring the balance in each account to the Retained Earnings account. After closing entries, the revenue and expense accounts have zero balances and the Retained Earnings account increases by the amount that revenues exceed expenses (or decreases if expenses exceed revenues) for the period.

Other Statement Preparation   Finally, the accountant prepares the balance sheet, the statement of cash flows, and any desired supporting schedules (for example, an analysis of changes in the Property, Plant, and Equipment account or the Retained Earnings account).

ILLUSTRATION OF THE ACCOUNTING PROCESS FOR A MERCHANDISING FIRM

Stephen's Shoe Store, Inc., began business in Year 1. A trial balance taken from its general ledger accounts on January 1, Year 4, the first day of the accounting period, appears in Exhibit 3.3. The trial balance designates asset accounts as (A), liability accounts as (L), and shareholders' equity (including revenue and expense) accounts as (SE). Trial balances do not usually contain such designations. Note that the revenue and expense accounts do not appear in this trial balance; they have zero balances at the beginning of an accounting period.

We have not previously considered one of the accounts in the trial balance, Accumulated Depreciation. The amount in this account appears on the balance sheet as a deduction from Building and Equipment. (See Exhibit 3.9 for the balance sheet presentation of this account.) This presentation—showing a subtraction from another account—results in a special term for this account (and others like it): **contra account.** A contra account accumulates amounts subtracted from the amount in another account. The illustration that follows discusses the nature and use of contra accounts. The trial balance designates asset contra accounts as (XA).

EXHIBIT 3.3	STEPHEN'S SHOE STORE, INC. Trial Balance January 1, Year 4

	Accounts with Debit Balances	Accounts with Credit Balances
Cash (A)	$ 30,000	
Accounts Receivable (A)	63,000	
Merchandise Inventory (A)	175,000	
Land (A)	100,000	
Building and Equipment (A)	525,000	
Accumulated Depreciation (XA)		$ 85,000
Accounts Payable (L)		135,000
Bonds Payable (L)		100,000
Common Stock (SE)		250,000
Additional Paid-in Capital (SE)		200,000
Retained Earnings (SE)		123,000
Total	$893,000	$893,000

JOURNALIZING

The transactions of Stephen's Shoe Store during Year 4 and the appropriate journal entries at the time of the transactions follow.

1. The firm purchases merchandise on account costing $355,000.

(**1**) Merchandise Inventory (A)	355,000	
Accounts Payable (L)		355,000

2. The firm sells merchandise during the year at a total selling price of $625,000. It receives $225,000 immediately, with the remainder sold on account.

(**2**) Cash (A)	225,000	
Accounts Receivable (A)	400,000	
Sales Revenue (SE)		625,000

3. The cost of merchandise sold during Year 4 is $390,000.

(**3**) Cost of Goods Sold (SE)	390,000	
Merchandise Inventory (A)		390,000

4. The firm pays salaries in cash of $110,000 for employee services received during the year.

| (**4**) Salaries Expense (SE) . . . . | 110,000 | |
| Cash (A) . . . . | | 110,000 |

5. The firm collects cash of $325,000 from customers who had purchased on account.

| (**5**) Cash (A) . . . . | 325,000 | |
| Accounts Receivable (A) . . . . | | 325,000 |

6. The firm makes payments of $270,000 to merchandise suppliers for purchases on account.

| (**6**) Accounts Payable (L) . . . . | 270,000 | |
| Cash (A) . . . . | | 270,000 |

7. The firm pays a premium of $1,500 on January 1, Year 4, for a three-year property and liability insurance policy.

| (**7**) Prepaid Insurance (A) . . . . | 1,500 | |
| Cash (A) . . . . | | 1,500 |

The account debited in this entry, made on January 1, Year 4, is an asset account because the insurance provides three years of coverage beginning on that date. The entry to reduce the Prepaid Insurance account and to record the insurance expense for Year 4 is one of the adjusting entries made at the end of the accounting period.

8. The company rents out for one year, beginning on December 1, Year 4, warehouse space not needed in its operations. The firm receives the annual rental of $600 at that time.

| (**8**) Cash (A) . . . . | 600 | |
| Advances from Tenants (L) . . . . | | 600 |

9. On December 31, Year 4, the firm pays annual interest at 8 percent on the long-term bonds outstanding: .08 × $100,000 = $8,000.

| (**9**) Interest Expense (SE) . . . . | 8,000 | |
| Cash (A) . . . . | | 8,000 |

10. A customer who had purchased merchandise on account for $10,000 has experienced financial difficulty and has been unable to pay for the goods on time. The customer now promises to pay $10,000 in 90 days with interest at 9 percent per year. As evidence of that promise, the customer gives a promissory note. On November 1, Year 4, Stephen's Shoe Store accepts the 90-day note for $10,000 bearing interest at 9 percent in settlement of the open account receivable.

| (**10**) Notes Receivable (A) . . . . | 10,000 | |
| Accounts Receivable (A) . . . . | | 10,000 |

11. The board of directors declares a cash dividend of $15,000 on December 28, Year 4. The firm will pay the dividend on January 20, Year 5.

(**11**) Retained Earnings (SE) 15,000
        Dividends Payable (L) 15,000

P R O B L E M   3 . 3   F O R   S E L F - S T U D Y

Journalizing transactions during a period. Harris Equipment Corporation began operations on January 2, Year 2, with the issuance of 10,000 shares of $10-par value common stock for $15 cash per share. The firm engages in the following transactions during Year 2:

1. January 2, Year 2: Acquires a building costing $80,000 and equipment costing $40,000. It pays cash in the amount of $60,000 and assumes a 10 percent mortgage for the balance of the purchase price. Interest is payable on January 2 of each year, beginning one year after the purchase.

2. January 2, Year 2: Obtains a two-year fire insurance policy on the building and equipment. It pays the insurance premium of $1,200 for the two-year period in advance (debit an asset account).

3. During Year 2: Acquires merchandise on account totaling $320,000. It makes payments to these suppliers during Year 2 totaling $270,000.

4. During Year 2: Makes sales of merchandise totaling $510,000, of which $80,000 is for cash and $430,000 is on account. Collections from credit customers during Year 2 total $360,000.

5. During Year 2: Pays employees' salaries totaling $80,000.

6. During Year 2: Pays utility bills totaling $1,300.

7. November 1, Year 2: Receives a $600 cash advance from a customer toward the purchase price of merchandise to be delivered during January, Year 3.

8. November 1, Year 2: Receives a $1,000, 9 percent, 90-day note from a customer to settle an open account receivable.

9. December 1, Year 2: Rents out a portion of its building for a three-month period. The firm received the rent for the period, $900, in advance (credit a revenue account for the full amount received).

Give the journal entries to record these nine transactions during Year 2. (The next self-study problem analyzes adjusting entries at the end of Year 2.) Omit explanations for the journal entries.

POSTING

The next step in the accounting process posts the entries in the general journal to the appropriate general ledger accounts. In this illustration, the posting operation takes place on December 31, Year 4. The T-accounts in Exhibit 3.4 show the opening balances from the trial balance in Exhibit 3.3 and the effects of transactions (**1**) through (**11**) of Stephen's Shoe Store.

TRIAL BALANCE PREPARATION

Accountants use the term **unadjusted trial balance** to refer to the trial balance prepared at the end of the accounting period before adjusting and closing entries. Exhibit 3.5 presents the unadjusted trial balance of Stephen's Shoe Store as of December 31, Year 4. The amounts in the unadjusted trial balance come directly from the ending balances in the T-accounts in Exhibit 3.4.

ADJUSTING ENTRIES

The general journal entries made during the year result from transactions between the firm and outsiders (for example, suppliers, employees, customers, and governmental units). Other events continually occur for which no specific transaction signals the requirement for a journal entry but that still affect the net income for the period and the financial position at the end of the period. For example, a firm continually uses buildings and equipment in the process of generating revenue. Because the firm uses the services of these assets during the period, a portion of their acquisition cost becomes an expense. Similarly, insurance coverage expires continually throughout the year. Because the firm gradually uses the services of the asset, it records a portion of the asset, Prepaid Insurance, as an expense.

Other kinds of events affect the revenues and expenses of the period but do not involve a cash transaction with an outsider until a subsequent period:

- Administrative employees earn salaries and wages during the last several days of the current accounting period, but the firm will not pay them until early in the next accounting period. Such salaries and wages, although paid in the next period, are expenses of the current period, when the firm uses the labor services.
- Interest accrues on a firm's notes receivable or notes payable with the passage of time. The firm will collect or pay interest in a subsequent period, but it recognizes a portion of the interest as revenue or expense in the current period.

Adjusting entries prepared at the end of the accounting period change the balances in the general ledger accounts so that revenue and expense accounts reflect correct amounts for measuring net income for the period and assets, liabilities, and shareholders' equity accounts report correct amounts for measuring financial position at the end of the period. The following sections illustrate several examples of adjusting entries for Stephen's Shoe Store.

Recognition of Accrued Revenues and Receivables
A firm earns revenues as it renders services. For example, it earns rent as a tenant uses its rental property. As time passes, a firm earns interest as a borrower uses its funds. Recording these amounts as they accrue day by day is usually not convenient, however.

At the end of the accounting period, the firm may have earned revenue but has made no entry, either because it has not yet received cash or because the time has not yet arrived to send a formal invoice to the customer. A claim has come into existence that, although not due immediately, should appear on the balance sheet as an asset and on the income statement as a revenue of the period. The adjusting entry for interest eventually receivable by the lender recognizes on the balance sheet the right to receive cash in an amount equal to the interest already earned and to recognize the same amount as revenue on the income statement for the period.

EXHIBIT 3.4

Stephen's Shoe Store, Inc
T-Accounts Showing Beginning Balances, Transactions during Year 4, and Ending Balances before Adjusting Entries

Cash (A)

Debit		Credit	
Bal. 1/1	30,000	110,000	(4)
(2)	225,000	270,000	(6)
(5)	325,000	1,500	(7)
(8)	600	8,000	(9)
Bal. 12/31	191,100		

Accounts Receivable (A)

Debit		Credit	
Bal. 1/1	63,000	325,000	(5)
(2)	400,000	10,000	(10)
Bal. 12/31	128,000		

Notes Receivable (A)

Debit		Credit	
Bal. 1/1	0		
(10)	10,000		
Bal. 12/31	10,000		

Merchandise Inventory (A)

Debit		Credit	
Bal. 1/1	175,000	390,000	(3)
(1)	355,000		
Bal. 12/31	140,000		

Prepaid Insurance (A)

Debit		Credit	
Bal. 1/1	0		
(7)	1,500		
Bal. 12/31	1,500		

Land (A)

Debit		Credit	
Bal. 1/1	100,000		
Bal. 12/31	100,000		

Building and Equipment (A)

Debit		Credit	
Bal. 1/1	525,000		
Bal. 12/31	525,000		

Accumulated Depreciation (XA)

Debit		Credit	
		85,000	Bal. 1/1
		85,000	Bal. 12/31

Accounts Payable (L)

Debit		Credit	
(6)	270,000	135,000	Bal. 1/1
		355,000	(1)
		220,000	Bal. 12/31

Dividends Payable (L)

	0 Bal. 1/1
	15,000 (11)
	15,000 Bal. 12/31

Common Stock (SE)

	250,000 Bal. 1/1
	250,000 Bal. 12/31

Sale Revenue (SE)

	0 Bal. 1/1
	625,000 (2)
	625,000 Bal. 12/31

Salaries Expense (SE)

Bal. 1/1 0	
(4) 110,000	
Bal. 12/31 110,000	

Advances from Tenants (L)

	0 Bal. 1/1
	600 (8)
	600 Bal. 12/31

Additional Paid-in Capital (SE)

	200,000 Bal. 1/1
	200,000 Bal. 12/31

Cost of Goods Sold (SE)

Bal. 1/1 0	
(3) 390,000	
Bal. 12/31 390,000	

Interest Expense (SE)

Bal. 1/1 0	
(9) 8,000	
Bal. 12/31 8,000	

Bonds Payable (L)

	100,000 Bal. 1/1
	100,000 Bal. 12/31

Retained Earnings (SE)

(11) 15,000	123,000 Bal. 1/1
	108,000 Bal. 12/31

EXHIBIT 3.5	STEPHEN'S SHOE STORE, INC. Unadjusted Trial Balance December 31, Year 4

	Accounts with Debit Balances	Accounts with Credit Balances
Cash (A)	$ 191,100	
Accounts Receivable (A)	128,000	
Notes Receivable (A)	10,000	
Merchandise Inventory (A)	140,000	
Prepaid Insurance (A)	1,500	
Land (A)	100,000	
Building and Equipment (A)	525,000	
Accumulated Depreciation (XA)		$ 85,000
Accounts Payable (L)		220,000
Dividends Payable (L)		15,000
Advances from Tenants (L)		600
Bonds Payable (L)		100,000
Common Stock (SE)		250,000
Additional Paid-in Capital (SE)		200,000
Retained Earnings (SE)		108,000
Sales Revenue (SE)		625,000
Cost of Goods Sold (SE)	390,000	
Salaries Expense (SE)	110,000	
Interest Expense (SE)	8,000	
Totals	$1,603,600	$1,603,600

Stephen's Shoe Store received a 90-day note from a customer on November 1, Year 4 (see transaction (10) above). At year-end, the note appears on the trial balance. Interest earned during November and December, however, does not appear in the unadjusted trial balance because the customer has not yet paid it, nor does the note require the customer to pay the interest until the maturity date in Year 5. The note earns interest at the rate of 9 percent per year.

General Principle for Interest Calculations By convention in business practice, interest rates on loans almost always refer to annual interest rates. Also, to simplify the calculation of interest, convention assumes a year equal to 12 months of 30 days each, or 360 days. Stephen's Shoe Store earns interest revenue of $150 during November and December. This amount equals the $10,000 principal times the 9 percent annual interest rate times the elapsed 60 days divided by 360 days: $150 = $10,000 × .09 × 60/360. The adjusting entry to recognize the asset, Interest Receivable, and the interest earned follows:

(12) Interest Receivable (A)	150	
Interest Revenue (SE)		150

Recognition of Accrued Expenses and Payables   As a firm receives various services, it reflects their cost in the financial statements, whether it has made payment or received an invoice. Daily recording of these amounts, however, is frequently not convenient. The accountant must therefore adjust expenses and liabilities at the end of the accounting period for the transactions purposefully not recorded until then.

Salaries and wages earned during the last several days of the accounting period but not paid until the following accounting period illustrate this type of adjustment. According to payroll records, salaries that the employees of Stephen's Shoe Store earned during the last several days of Year 4 and that the firm has not yet recorded by year-end total $6,000. The adjusting entry is as follows:

(13) Salaries Expense (SE)	6,000	
Salaries Payable (L)		6,000

Other examples of this type of adjusting entry include costs incurred for utilities, taxes, and interest.

Allocation of Prepaid Operating Costs   Another type of adjustment arises because a firm acquires assets for use in operations but does not completely use them during the accounting period when acquired. For example, Stephen's Shoe Store paid $1,500 on January 1, Year 4, for a three-year insurance policy (see transaction **(7)** above). During Year 4, one-third of the coverage expired, so $500 of the premium should leave the asset account on the balance sheet and become an insurance expense, reducing net income and retained earnings. The balance sheet on December 31, Year 4, should show only $1,000 of prepaid insurance as an asset because this portion of the premium is a future benefit—the asset of insurance coverage the firm will receive over the next two years.

The nature of the adjusting entry to record an asset expiration as an expense depends on the recording of the original payment. If the payment resulted in a debit to an asset account, the adjusting entry must reduce the asset and increase the expense for the services used up during the accounting period. Stephen's Shoe Store recorded in entry **(7)** the payment of the insurance premium on January 1, Year 4, as follows:

(7) Prepaid Insurance (A)	1,500	
Cash (A)		1,500

The adjusting entry is, therefore, as follows:

(14) Insurance Expense (SE)	500	
Prepaid Insurance (A)		500

Insurance expense for Year 4 is $500, and prepaid insurance of $1,000 appears as an asset on the balance sheet on December 31, Year 4.

Instead of debiting an asset account at the time of paying the premium, some firms debit an expense account. For example, Stephen's Shoe Store might have recorded the original premium payment as follows:

(7a) Insurance Expense (SE)	1,500	
Cash (A)		1,500

Because many operating costs become expenses in the period when a firm makes the expenditure (for example, monthly rent), this second procedure for recording expenditures during the year sometimes reduces the number of adjusting entries the firm must make at year-end. In the situation with the insurance policy, however, not all of the $1,500 premium paid is an expense of Year 4. If Stephen's Shoe Store had originally recorded the payment of the insurance premium as in **(7a)**, then the adjusting entry would be as follows:

(14a) Prepaid Insurance (A)	1,000	
Insurance Expense (SE)		1,000

After the original entry in **(7a)** and the adjusting entry in **(14a),** insurance expense for Year 4 appears in the accounts at $500 and prepaid insurance at $1,000. The end result of these two approaches to recording the original payment of the premium is the same. The adjusting entries, however, differ. (See Problem 3.5 for Self-Study at the end of the chapter.)

Recognition of Depreciation   When a firm purchases assets such as buildings, machinery, furniture, and trucks, it debits their acquisition cost to appropriate asset accounts. Although these assets may provide services for a number of years, their future benefits expire as time passes. Accounting spreads an asset's cost over the periods of the asset's estimated useful life. The term *depreciation* refers to the charge made to the current operations for the portion of the cost of such assets consumed during the current period. Depreciation involves nothing new in principle; it is identical to the procedure, presented previously, for prepaid operating costs. For example, the cost of a building is a prepayment for a series of future services, and depreciation allocates the cost of the services to the periods in which the firm receives and uses the services.

Various accounting methods allocate the acquisition cost of long-lived assets to the periods of benefit. The most widely used method, the straight-line method, allocates an equal portion of the acquisition cost, less estimated salvage value, to each period of the asset's estimated useful life. The straight-line depreciation method computes the depreciation charge for each period as follows:

$$\frac{\text{Acquisition Cost} - \text{Estimated Salvage Value}}{\text{Number of Periods in Estimated Useful Life}} = \text{Depreciation Charge for Each Period}$$

Internal records indicate that the Building and Equipment account of Stephen's Shoe Store comprises a store building with an acquisition cost of $400,000 and a group of items of equipment with an acquisition cost of $125,000. At the time the firm acquired the building, it had an estimated 40-year useful life and zero salvage value. Depreciation expense for each year of the building's life is

$$\frac{(\$400,000 - \$0)}{40 \text{ years}} = \$10,000 \text{ per year.}$$

At the time the firm acquired the equipment, it had an estimated useful life of six years and an estimated salvage value of $5,000. Annual depreciation is

$$\frac{(\$125,000 - \$5,000)}{6 \text{ years}} = \$20,000 \text{ per year.}$$

The adjusting entry to record depreciation of $30,000 (= $10,000 + $20,000) for Year 4 is

| **(15)** Depreciation Expense (SE) .... | 30,000 | |
| Accumulated Depreciation (XA) .... | | 30,000 |

Because the credit in the entry above records the portion of the asset's cost that has expired, or become an expense, during Year 4, we could credit the Building and Equipment account in entry **(15)**. Instead, we credit the Accumulated Depreciation account, a contra-asset account, and then deduct the balance in this account from the acquisition cost of the assets in the Building and Equipment account on the balance sheet, achieving the same end result. Using the contra account enables the financial statements to show both the acquisition cost of the assets in use and the portion of that amount that the firm has previously recognized as an expense. Showing both acquisition cost and accumulated depreciation amounts separately provides a rough indication of the relative age of the firm's long-lived assets. (See Exercise **26** at the end of the chapter.)

Note that Depreciation Expense (an income statement account) includes depreciation for the current accounting period only, whereas Accumulated Depreciation (a balance sheet account) includes the cumulative depreciation charges since the firm acquired the assets.

Valuation of Liabilities   When a firm receives cash from customers before it sells merchandise or renders services, it incurs a liability. For example, Stephen's Shoe Store received $600 on December 1, Year 4, as one year's rent on warehouse space. When it received the cash, it credited the liability account Advances from Tenants (see transaction **(8)** above). The firm has earned one month's rent as of December 31, Year 4. The adjusting entry is as follows:

(16) Advances from Tenants (L)	50	
Rent Revenue (SE)		50
Recognizes one month's rent revenue and reduces liability from $600 to $550.		

The firm has not yet earned the remaining $550 of the collections for rent, so the amount must appear on the December 31, Year 4, balance sheet as a liability.

Correction of Errors   The process of checking, reviewing, and auditing at the end of the accounting period may uncover various errors and omissions. For example, the firm may have recorded one month's sales during the year as $38,700 instead of $37,800. Or it may not have recorded the sale to a specific customer. At the end of the accounting period, the accountant makes entries to correct for these errors. There were no such errors in the accounts of Stephen's Shoe Store.

Accrual of Income Taxes   The last adjusting entry typically made is to recognize income tax expense for the period. Governments usually assess income taxes on revenues minus expenses after making all other adjusting entries. The recording of transactions **(1)** to **(11)** and adjusting entries **(12)** to **(16)** results in adjusted revenues and expenses, or income before income taxes, of $80,700. Assume that the income tax rate is

40 percent. Income tax expense for Year 4 is $32,280 (= .40 × $80,700). The adjusting entry is:

(17) Income Tax Expense (SE)	32,280	
Income Tax Payable (L)		32,280

Recognizes income tax expense using an income tax rate of 40 percent on net income before taxes of $80,700.

<hr>

P R O B L E M   3 . 4   F O R   S E L F - S T U D Y

Journalizing adjusting entries at the end of the period.   Refer to the data for Harris Equipment Corporation in Problem 3.3 for Self-Study. Give the adjusting entries on December 31, Year 2, to reflect the following items. You may omit explanations to the journal entries.

10. The building acquired on January 2, Year 2 (see transaction **(1)** in Problem 3.3 for Self-Study), has a 20-year estimated life and zero salvage value. The equipment has a seven-year estimated life and $5,000 salvage value. The firm uses the straight-line depreciation method.

11. The firm recognizes insurance expense on the fire insurance policy obtained on January 2, Year 2 (see transaction **(2)** in Problem 3.3 for Self-Study).

12. After the firm takes a physical inventory at the end of the year, it finds the cost of merchandise sold during Year 2 to be $180,000 (see transaction **(3)** in Problem 3.3 for Self-Study).

13. The firm recognizes interest expense on the mortgage liability for Year 2 (see transaction **(1)** in Problem 3.3 for Self-Study).

14. Salaries earned by employees during the last three days of December total $800. The firm will pay them on January 4, Year 3.

15. The firm recognizes interest revenue on the note receivable (see transaction **(8)** in Problem 3.3 for Self-Study).

16. The firm makes an adjusting entry to record the proper amount of rent revenue for Year 2 (see transaction **(9)** in Problem 3.3 for Self-Study).

17. The firm declares dividends of $25,000. It will pay the dividend on January 15, Year 3.

18. The income tax rate is 40 percent of net income before income taxes.

TRIAL BALANCE AFTER ADJUSTING ENTRIES

The accountant posts the adjusting entries in the general ledger in the same manner as entries made during the period. After making the adjusting entries, the accountant prepares a trial balance of the general ledger accounts. This **adjusted trial balance** helps in preparing the financial statements. Refer to Exhibit 3.6. The first three sets of debit and credit columns in Exhibit 3.6 present the trial balance data before and after adjusting entries for Stephen's Shoe Store. The exhibit indicates the effect of the adjustment process on the various accounts. The parenthetical numbers identify the debit and credit components of each adjusting entry.

PREPARING THE INCOME STATEMENT

The adjusted trial balance shows all revenue and expense accounts with their correct amounts for the period. The accountant can prepare the income statement by listing all the revenue accounts, listing all the expense accounts, and showing the difference between the sum of the revenues and the sum of the expenses as net income. The upper panel of Exhibit 3.7 presents an income statement for Stephen's Shoe Store for Year 4 in a *single-step* format. This format derives net income in a single subtraction of total expenses from total revenues.

Another income statement format frequently used is *a multiple-step* income statement. The multiple-step format presents several subtotals before reporting the amount of net income. The lower panel of Exhibit 3.7 presents an income statement for Stephen's Shoe Store for Year 4 in one common multiple-step format. Revenues and expenses related to the firm's principal business activity, the retailing of shoes, appear in a separate section that results in reporting the amount of *operating income* for the year. Revenues and expenses related only peripherally to operations, usually investing and financing activities, appear in a separate section. Income taxes appear in a third section. Multiple subtractions result in various subtotals before arriving at net income. One often sees other multiple-step formats as well.

CLOSING OF TEMPORARY ACCOUNTS

Revenue and expense accounts are temporary labels for portions of retained earnings. Once the accountant has prepared the adjusted trial balance, the revenue and expense accounts have served their purpose for the current period, and the accounting process closes these accounts. The closing process transfers the balances in the temporary revenue and expense accounts to retained earnings. To close temporary accounts with debit balances (primarily expense accounts), credit each temporary account with an amount equal to its balance at the end of the period and debit retained earnings. The usual closing entry for a temporary account with a debit balance is as follows:

Retained Earnings (SE)	X	
Account with Debit Balance (SE) (use specific account title,		
usually an expense).		X

To close temporary accounts with credit balances (primarily revenue accounts), debit each temporary account and credit retained earnings. The usual closing entry for a temporary account with a credit balance is as follows:

Account with Credit Balance (SE) (use specific account title, usually a revenue)	X	
Retained Earnings (SE)		X

Closing entries reduce the balances in all temporary accounts to zero. The former debit (credit) balances in temporary accounts become debits (credits) in the Retained Earnings account.

A separate entry could close each temporary revenue and expense account. However, closing all revenue and expense accounts in a single entry, as follows, saves recording time.

EXHIBIT 3.6	STEPHEN'S SHOE STORE, INC. Trial Balance before and after Adjusting Entries and after Closing Entries[a] December 31, Year 4

| | Unadjusted Trial Balance | | Adjusting Entries | |
Accounts	Debit	Credit	Debit	Credit
Cash (A)	$ 191,100			
Accounts Receivable (A)	128,000			
Notes Receivable (A)	10,000			
Interest Receivable (A)			$ 150 (12)	
Merchandise Inventory (A)	140,000			
Prepaid Insurance (A)	1,500			$ 500 (14)
Land (A)	100,000			
Building and Equipment (A)	525,000			
Accumulated Depreciation (XA)		$ 85,000		30,000 (15)
Accounts Payable (L)		220,000		
Salaries Payable (L)				6,000 (13)
Income Tax Payable (L)				32,280 (17)
Dividends Payable (L).		15,000		
Advances from Tenants (L)		600	50 (16)	
Bonds Payable (L)		100,000		
Common Stock (SE)		250,000		
Additional Paid-in Capital (SE)		200,000		
Retained Earnings (SE)		108,000		
Sales Revenue (SE).		625,000		
Interest Revenue (SE)				150 (12)
Rent Revenue (SE)				50 (16)
Cost of Goods Sold (SE)	390,000			
Salaries Expense (SE)	110,000		6,000 (13)	
Interest Expense (SE)	8,000			
Insurance Expense (SE)			500 (14)	
Depreciation Expense (SE)			30,000 (15)	
Income Tax Expense (SE)			32,280 (17)	
Totals	$1,603,600	$1,603,600	$68,980	$68,980

[a]This convenient tabular form is often called a *worksheet*.

Adjusted Trial Balance		Closing Entries		Post-Closing Trial Balance	
Debit	Credit	Debit	Credit	Debit	Credit
$ 191,100				$ 191,100	
128,000				128,000	
10,000				10,000	
150				150	
140,000				140,000	
1,000				1,000	
100,000				100,000	
525,000				525,000	
	$ 115,000				$ 115,000
	220,000				220,000
	6,000				6,000
	32,280				32,280
	15,000				15,000
	550				550
	100,000				100,000
	250,000				250,000
	200,000				200,000
	108,000		$ 48,420 (18)		156,420
	625,000	$625,000 (18)			
	150	150 (18)			
	50	50 (18)			
390,000			390,000 (18)		
116,000			116,000 (18)		
8,000			8,000 (18)		
500			500 (18)		
30,000			30,000 (18)		
32,280			32,280 (18)		
$1,672,030	$1,672,030	$625,200	$625,200	$1,095,250	$1,095,250

EXHIBIT 3.7	STEPHEN'S SHOE STORE, INC. Income Statement for the Year Ending December 31, Year 4 Single-Step Format

Revenues

Sales Revenue	$625,000	
Interest Revenue	150	
Rent Revenue	50	
Total Revenues		$625,200

Less Expenses

Cost of Goods Sold	$390,000	
Salaries Expense	116,000	
Interest Expense	8,000	
Insurance Expense	500	
Depreciation Expense	30,000	
Income Tax Expense	32,280	
Total Expenses		576,780
Net Income		$ 48,420

	STEPHEN'S SHOE STORE, INC. Income Statement for the Year Ending December 31, Year 4 Multiple-Step Format

Sales Revenue	$ 625,000
Cost of Goods Sold	(390,000)
Salaries Expense	(116,000)
Insurance Expense	(500)
Depreciation Expense	(30,000)
Operating Income	$ 88,500
Interest Revenue	150
Rent Revenue	50
Interest Expense	(8,000)
Net Income Before Income Taxes	$ 80,700
Income Tax Expense	(32,280)
Net Income	$ 48,420

(18) Sales Revenue (SE)	625,000	
Interest Revenue (SE)	150	
Rent Revenue (SE)	50	
Cost of Goods Sold (SE)		390,000
Salaries Expense (SE)		116,000
Interest Expense (SE)		8,000
Insurance Expense (SE)		500
Depreciation Expense (SE)		30,000
Income Tax Expense (SE)		32,280
Retained Earnings (SE)		48,420

The amount credited to the Retained Earnings account is the difference between the amounts debited to revenue accounts and the amounts credited to expense accounts in the closing process (see the Closing Entries column of Exhibit 3.6). This amount represents the net income for the period (see Exhibit 3.7).

Accounting Terminology The accountant calls the amount credited to retained earnings in the closing entry a *plug*. As we pointed out in the preceding chapter, often when one makes a journal entry, one knows all debits and all but one of the credits (or vice versa). Because the double-entry recording procedure requires equal debits and credits, one can find the unknown quantity by subtracting the sum of the known credits from the sum of all debits (or vice versa). Accounting calls this process *plugging*.

Alternative Closing Procedure An alternative closing procedure uses a temporary Income Summary account. This procedure first closes individual revenue and expense accounts to an Income Summary account. The accountant prepares the income statement using information on the individual revenues and expenses in the Income Summary account. Finally, the procedure closes the balance in the Income Summary account, representing net income for the period, to the Retained Earnings account.

For example, the entry to close the Sales Revenue account under this alternative procedure is as follows:

(18a) Sales Revenue (SE)	625,000	
Income Summary (SE)		625,000

The entry to close the Cost of Goods Sold account is as follows:

(18b) Income Summary (SE)	390,000	
Cost of Goods Sold (SE)		390,000

After the accountant makes similar closing entries for the other revenue and expense accounts, the Income Summary account will have a credit balance of $48,420. The final step is to transfer this balance to the Retained Earnings account.

(18c) Income Summary (SE)	48,420	
Retained Earnings (SE)		48,420

The end result of both closing procedures is the same. Revenue and expense accounts, as well as the Income Summary account (if the accountant uses one), have zero balances after closing entries, and the Retained Earnings account increases by the net income for the period of $48,420. Exhibit 3.8 shows the Income Summary account for Stephen's Shoe Store after closing all revenue and expense accounts at the end of the period.[2]

Trial Balance after Closing Entries The accountant could prepare a trial balance after closing entries. Such a trial balance shows revenue and expense accounts with zero balances and balance sheet accounts at their end-of-period balances. A **post-closing**

---

[2]Students ask, "When should we use an Income Summary account in working problems?" We answer, "Whenever you find doing so convenient." We almost always do so because a neat Income Summary account, with labels added to each of the numbers, serves as a first draft of the income statement itself.

EXHIBIT 3.8	STEPHEN'S SHOE STORE, INC. Illustration of Income Summary Account

Income Summary Account (SE)				Retained Earnings (SE)		
Cost of Goods Sold	390,000	625,000	Sales Revenue		123,000	Beginning
Salaries Expense	116,000	150	Interest Revenue			Balance
Interest Expense	8,000	50	Rent Revenue Dividends 15,000		48,420	Net Income
Insurance Expense	500	625,200			156,420	Ending
Depreciation Expense	30,000					Balance
Income Tax Expense	32,280					
To Close Income						
Summary Account	48,420					
	625,200					

trial balance for Stephen's Shoe Store appears in the last set of debit and credit columns in Exhibit 3.6.

FINANCIAL STATEMENT PREPARATION

The post-closing trial balance provides information for preparing the balance sheet and any desired supporting schedules. Exhibit 3.9 gives the comparative balance sheets for December 31, Year 3 and Year 4, for Stephen's Shoe Store. Exhibit 3.10 presents an analysis of changes in retained earnings.

PROBLEM 3.5 FOR SELF-STUDY

Preparing adjusting entries.   To achieve efficient recording of day-to-day cash receipts and disbursements relating to operations, a firm may credit all cash receipts to revenue accounts and debit all cash disbursements to expense accounts. The efficiency stems from treating all receipts in the same way and all disbursements in the same way. As a result, the firm can employ lower-paid clerks to make the routine and repetitive entries for receipts and disbursements. In the day-to-day recording of transactions, the clerk does not need to be concerned with whether a specific cash transaction reflects settlement of a past accrual, a revenue or expense correctly assigned to the current period, or a prepayment relating to a future period. At the end of the period, higher-paid accountants analyze the existing account balances and construct the adjusting entries required to correct them. This process results in temporarily incorrect balances in some balance sheet and income statement accounts during the accounting period.

Construct the adjusting entry required for each of the following scenarios.

a. On September 1, Year 2, a tenant paid $24,000 rent for the one-year period starting at that time. The tenant debited the entire amount to Rent Expense and credited Cash.

The tenant made no adjusting entries for rent between September 1 and December 31. Construct the adjusting entry to be made on December 31, Year 2, to recognize the proper balances in the Prepaid Rent and Rent Expense accounts. What is the amount of Rent Expense for Year 2?

b. The tenant's books for December 31, Year 2, after adjusting entries, show a balance in the Prepaid Rent account of $16,000. This amount represents rent for the period January 1 through August 31, Year 3. On September 1, Year 3, the tenant paid $30,000 for rent for the one-year period starting September 1, Year 3. The tenant debited this amount to Rent Expense and credited Cash but made no adjusting entries for rent during Year 3. Construct the adjusting entry required on December 31, Year 3. What is Rent Expense for Year 3?

c. The tenant's books for December 31, Year 3, after adjusting entries, show a balance in the Prepaid Rent account of $20,000. This amount represents rent for the period January 1 through August 31, Year 4. On September 1, Year 4, the tenant paid $18,000 for rent for the six-month period starting September 1, Year 4. The tenant debited this amount to Rent Expense and credited Cash but made no adjusting entries during Year 4. Construct the adjusting entry required on December 31, Year 4. What is Rent Expense for Year 4?

d. Whenever the firm makes payments for wages, it debits Wage Expense. At the start of April, the Wages Payable account had a balance of $5,000, representing wages earned but not paid during the last few days of March. During April, the firm paid $30,000 in wages, debiting the entire amount to Wage Expense. At the end of April, analysis of amounts earned since the last payday indicates that employees have earned wages of $4,000 that they have not received. These are the only unpaid wages at the end of April. Construct the required adjusting entry. What is Wage Expense for April?

e. A firm purchased an insurance policy providing one year's coverage from May 1, Year 1, and debited the entire amount to Insurance Expense. After the firm made adjusting entries, the balance sheet for December 31, Year 1, correctly showed Prepaid Insurance of $3,000. Construct the adjusting entry that the firm must make on January 31, Year 2, if the firm closes its books monthly and prepares a balance sheet for January 31, Year 2.

f. The record-keeping system for an apartment building instructs the bookkeeper always to credit rent revenue when the firm collects a payment from tenants. At the beginning of Year 3, the liability account Advances from Tenants had a credit balance of $25,000, representing collections from tenants for rental services to be rendered during Year 3. During Year 3, the firm collected $250,000 from tenants; it debited Cash and credited Rent Revenue. It made no adjusting entries during Year 3. At the end of Year 3, analysis of the individual accounts indicates that of the amounts already collected, $30,000 represents collections for rental services to be provided to tenants during Year 4. Present the required adjusting entry. What is Rent Revenue for Year 3?

g. When the firm acquired new equipment costing $10,000 on January 1, Year 1, the bookkeeper debited Depreciation Expense and credited Cash for $10,000 but made no further entries for this equipment during Year 1. The equipment has an expected service life of five years and an estimated salvage value of zero. Construct the adjusting entry required before the accountant can prepare a balance sheet for December 31, Year 1.

EXHIBIT 3.9	STEPHEN'S SHOE STORE, INC. Comparative Balance Sheet December 31, Year 3 and Year 4

	December 31, Year 3	December 31, Year 4
ASSETS		
Current Assets		
Cash	$ 30,000	$191,100
Accounts Receivable	63,000	128,000
Notes Receivable	—	10,000
Interest Receivable	—	150
Merchandise Inventory	175,000	140,000
Prepaid Insurance	—	1,000
Total Current Assets	$268,000	$470,250
Property, Plant, and Equipment		
Land	$100,000	$100,000
Building and Equipment (at Acquisition cost)	$525,000	$525,000
Less Accumulated Depreciation	(85,000)	(115,000)
Building and Equipment (net)	440,000	410,000
Total Property, Plant, and Equipment	$540,000	$510,000
Total Assets	$808,000	$980,250
LIABILITIES AND SHAREHOLDERS' EQUITY		
Current Liabilities		
Accounts Payable	$135,000	$220,000
Salaries Payable	—	6,000
Income Tax Payable	—	32,280
Dividends Payable	—	15,000
Advances from Tenants	—	550
Total Current Liabilities	$135,000	$273,830
Long-Term Debt		
Bonds Payable	100,000	100,000
Total Liabilities	$235,000	$373,830
Shareholders' Equity		
Common Stock (at par value)	$250,000	$250,000
Additional Paid-in Capital	200,000	200,000
Retained Earnings	123,000	156,420
Total Shareholders' Equity	$573,000	$606,420
Total Liabilities and Shareholders' Equity	$808,000	$980,250

EXHIBIT 3.10	STEPHEN'S SHOE STORE, INC. Analysis of Changes in Retained Earnings for the Year Ending December 31, Year 4

Retained Earnings, December 31, Year 3		$123,000
Net Income	$48,420	
Less Dividends	15,000	
Increase in Retained Earnings		33,420
Retained Earnings, December 31, Year 4		$156,420

INTERPRETING AND ANALYZING THE INCOME STATEMENT

The income statement provides information for assessing the operating profitability of a firm. One tool for analysis, a **common-size income statement,** expresses each expense and net income as a percentage of revenues. A common-size income statement permits an analysis of changes or differences in the relations between revenues, expenses, and net income and identifies relations that the analyst should explore further.

TIME SERIES ANALYSIS

Exhibit 3.11 presents a common-size income statement for Boise Cascade Corporation, a forest products company, for a recent three-year period. The changes in sales from the preceding year were as follows: Year 9, +5.9 percent; Year 10, −3.5 percent; Year 11, −5.6 percent.

Boise Cascade experienced substantially decreased profitability during this three-year period. The most important symptom of the decline appears to be an increase in the cost-of-goods-sold percentage. Forest products companies use capital-intensive manufacturing facilities. As a consequence, depreciation and other costs of maintaining these manufacturing facilities do not change significantly as the level of output changes. Boise Cascade Corporation experienced decreased sales in Year 10 and Year 11 because of a recession in the economy. Its cost-of-goods-sold percentage increased because of decreased use of its plant facilities.

EXHIBIT 3.11	BOISE CASCADE CORPORATION Common-Size Income Statement

	Year 9	Year 10	Year 11
Sales	100.0%	100.0%	100.0%
Cost of Goods Sold	(78.8)	(84.4)	(90.9)
Selling and Administrative Expenses	(9.4)	(10.0)	(10.4)
Interest Expense	(2.2)	(2.8)	(4.4)
Income Tax Expense	(3.8)	(1.0)	1.2
Net Income	5.8%	1.8%	(4.5)%

EXHIBIT 3.12	Common-Size Income Statements for Three Retailers		

| | **May** | | |
	The Limited	**Dept. Stores**	**Wal-Mart**
Sales	100.0%	100.0%	100.0%
Cost of Goods Sold	(70.9)	(69.0)	(79.2)
Selling and Administrative Expenses	(17.4)	(20.4)	(14.3)
Interest Expense	(1.0)	(3.0)	(0.6)
Income Tax Expense	(4.1)	(2.7)	(2.2)
Net Income	6.6%	4.9%	3.7%

The percentage for selling and administrative expenses also increased, probably because of the presence of certain costs that remained fixed despite the decreased level of sales (for example, salaries of selling and administrative staff and depreciation on selling and administrative facilities). The percentage for interest expense increased because the firm did not decrease its level of debt, despite the decrease in sales. The income tax percentage decreased because of a decreased pretax profit margin.

CROSS-SECTION ANALYSIS

A common-size income statement also provides information about differences in company strategies. Exhibit 3.12 presents common-size income statements for The Limited (specialty retailer), May Department Stores (department stores), and Wal-Mart (discount stores and warehouse clubs).

The Limited has the highest net-income-to-sales percentage. The Limited has a lower cost-of-goods-sold percentage than Wal-Mart, reflecting its specialty, fashion-oriented product line and higher markups than Wal-Mart. May Department Stores ranks second on the net-income-to-sales percentage. Its cost-of-goods-sold percentage resembles that of The Limited, reflecting the movement of department stores to a multiple, mini-boutiques merchandising strategy. May Department Stores, however, has a higher selling-and-administrative-expense percentage than The Limited, arising from the overhead cost of maintaining and staffing its comparatively larger retail stores. Wal-Mart's high cost-of-goods-sold percentage results from its low-price strategy—its lower markups on cost. It gains an advantage on the selling-and-administrative-expense percentage, however, from the lower overhead in its stores.

We explore interpretation and analysis of the income statement more fully in Chapters 5 and 6.

SUMMARY

Measurement of net income for a period inevitably affects financial position at the end of a period. Revenues result from selling goods or rendering services to customers and lead to increases in assets or decreases in liabilities. Expenses indicate that the firm has used assets and other services in generating revenue. Expenses decrease assets or increase liabilities. Because revenues represent increases in shareholders' equity, revenue transactions result in credits (increases) to a shareholders' equity account for the specific type of revenue and in debits either to an asset or to a liability account. Expenses represent decreases in shareholders' equity and result in debits (decreases) to a shareholders' equity account for the specific type of expense and credits either to an asset or to a liability account. The revenue and expense accounts accumulate the revenues earned and expenses recognized during the period.

Some events will not enter the regular day-to-day recording process during the period because no explicit transaction between the firm and some external party (such as a customer, creditor, or governmental unit) has taken place to require a journal entry. Such events require adjusting entries at the end of the period so that the firm's periodic income and its financial position properly appear in the financial statements reported on an accrual basis.

After providing the necessary information to prepare an income statement for the period, the accounting process transfers, or closes, the balances in these temporary accounts to the Retained Earnings account. Exhibit 3.13 summarizes the relation between cash inflows/outflows and the recognition of revenues/expenses.

Interpreting the income statement involves studying the relation between revenues, expenses, and net income both over time and across firms. Changes in economic conditions, technologies, government policies, competitive conditions, and similar factors can affect relations between these items over time. The design and successful implementation of a firm's strategy for competing within its markets affect relations between these items across firms.

EXHIBIT 3.13	Relation of Cash Flows (Receipts and Expenditures) to Recognition of Revenues and Expenses

| | Journal Entry Each Year | | |
Transaction	Year 1	Year 2	Year 3

1. Cash received from customer in Year 1 for services to be performed in Year 2	(T)[a] Cash X
	    Liability ... X
		(A)[b] Liability X
		    Revenue X	

2. Cash received from customer in Year 2 for services to be performed in Year 2		(T) Cash ..... X Revenue X	

3. Services performed in Year 2 for which cash will not be received until Year 3		(A) Accounts
		    Receivable .. X
		    Revenue X
			(T) Cash X
			    Accounts
			    Receivable ..X

4. Cash expended in Year 1 for services consumed in Year 2	(T) Asset X
	    Cash X
		(A) Expense ... X
		    Asset X	

5. Cash expended in Year 2 for services consumed in Year 2		(T) Expense ... X Cash X	

6. Services consumed in Year 2 for which cash will not be expended until Year 3		(A) Expense ... X
		    Liability X
			(T) Liability ... X
			    Cash X

[a](T) is a transaction entry made during the period.
[b](A) is an adjusting entry made at the end of a period.

SOLUTIONS TO SELF-STUDY PROBLEMS

SUGGESTED SOLUTION TO PROBLEM 3.1 FOR SELF-STUDY

(J. Thompson; cash versus accrual basis of accounting.)
a. and **b.**

	a. Accrual Basis	b. Cash Basis
Sales Revenue	$29,000	$22,000
Less Expenses:		
Cost of Merchandise Sold	$13,000	—
Payments on Merchandise Purchased	—	$10,000
Rental Expense	1,000	2,000
Insurance Expense	100	1,200
Interest Expense	60	—
Utilities Expense	400	400
Salaries Expense	650	650
Taxes Expense	350	350
Total Expenses	$15,560	$14,600
Net Income	$13,440	$ 7,400

c. The accrual basis gives a better measure of operating performance because it matches revenue generated during January with costs incurred in generating that revenue. The cash basis mixes operating and financing activities together, principally with regard to sales and purchases on account. Note that the capital contributed by Thompson and the bank loan received do not give rise to revenue under either basis of accounting because they are financing, not operating, activities.

SUGGESTED SOLUTION TO PROBLEM 3.2 FOR SELF-STUDY

(Revenue and expense recognition.)
a. None
b. $14,980
c. $5,820
d. None
e. $5,440
f. $2,010
g. None

SUGGESTED SOLUTION TO PROBLEM 3.3 FOR SELF-STUDY

(Harris Equipment Corporation; journalizing transactions during a period.)

(1) Jan. 2, Year 2	Building	80,000	
	Equipment	40,000	
	Cash		60,000
	Mortgage Payable		60,000
(2) Jan. 2, Year 2	Prepaid Insurance	1,200	
	Cash		1,200

(3) During Year 2	Merchandise Inventory	320,000	
	Accounts Payable		320,000
During Year 2	Accounts Payable	270,000	
	Cash		270,000
(4) During Year 2	Cash	80,000	
	Accounts Receivable	430,000	
	Sales Revenue		510,000
During Year 2	Cash	360,000	
	Accounts Receivable		360,000
(5) During Year 2	Salaries Expense	80,000	
	Cash		80,000
(6) During Year 2	Utilities Expense	1,300	
	Cash		1,300
(7) Nov. 1, Year 2	Cash	600	
	Advances from Customers		600
(8) Nov. 1, Year 2	Note Receivable	1,000	
	Accounts Receivable		1,000
(9) Dec. 1, Year 2	Cash	900	
	Rent Revenue		900

SUGGESTED SOLUTION TO PROBLEM 3.4 FOR SELF-STUDY

(Harris Equipment Corporation; journalizing adjusting entries at the end of the period.)

(10)	Depreciation Expense	9,000	
	Accumulated Depreciation		9,000
	($80,000 − $0)/20 = $4,000; ($40,000 − $5,000)/7 = $5,000.		
(11)	Insurance Expense	600	
	Prepaid Insurance		600
(12)	Cost of Goods Sold	180,000	
	Merchandise Inventory		180,000
(13)	Interest Expense	6,000	
	Interest Payable		6,000
	$60,000 × 0.10 = $6,000		
(14)	Salaries Expense	800	
	Salaries Payable		800
(15)	Interest Receivable	15	
	Interest Revenue		15
	$1,000 × 0.09 × 60/360		
(16)	Rent Revenue	600	
	Advances from Tenants		600
(17)	Retained Earnings	25,000	
	Dividends Payable		25,000
(18)	Income Tax Expense	93,046	
	Income Tax Payable		93,046
	.40($510,000 + $900 − $600 + $15 − $80,000 − $1,300 − $9,000 − $600 − $180,000 − $6,000 − $800) = $93,046.		

SUGGESTED SOLUTION TO PROBLEM 3.5 FOR SELF-STUDY

(Preparing adjusting entries.)

a. The Prepaid Rent account on the year-end balance sheet should represent eight months of prepayments. The rent per month is $2,000 (= $24,000/12), so the balance required in the Prepaid Rent account is $16,000 (= 8 × $2,000). Rent Expense for Year 2 is $8,000 (= 4 × $2,000 = $24,000 − $16,000).

Prepaid Rent	16,000	
Rent Expense		16,000
To increase the balance in the Prepaid Rent account, reducing the amount in the Rent Expense account.		

b. The Prepaid Rent account on the balance sheet for the end of Year 3 should represent eight months of prepayments. The rent per month is $2,500 (= $30,000/12), so the required balance in the Prepaid Rent account is $20,000 (= 8 × $2,500). The balance in that account is already $16,000, so the adjusting entry must increase it by $4,000 (= $20,000 − $16,000).

Prepaid Rent	4,000	
Rent Expense		4,000
To increase the balance in the Prepaid Rent account, reducing the amount in the Rent Expense account.		

The Rent Expense account will have a balance at the end of Year 3 before closing entries of $26,000 (= $30,000 − $4,000). This amount comprises $16,000 (= $2,000 × 8) for rent from January through August and $10,000 (= $2,500 × 4) for rent from September through December.

c. The Prepaid Rent account on the balance sheet at the end of Year 4 should represent two months of prepayments. The rent per month is $3,000 (= $18,000/6), so the required balance in the Prepaid Rent account is $6,000 (= 2 × $3,000). The balance in that account is $20,000, so the adjusting entry must reduce it by $14,000 (= $20,000 − $6,000).

Rent Expense	14,000	
Prepaid Rent		14,000
To reduce the balance in the Prepaid Rent account, increasing the amount in the Rent Expense account.		

The Rent Expense account will have a balance at the end of Year 4 before closing entries of $32,000 (= $18,000 + $14,000). This amount comprises $20,000 (= $2,500 × 8) for rent from January through August and $12,000 (= $3,000 × 4) for rent from September through December.

d. The Wages Payable account should have a credit balance of $4,000 at the end of April, but it has a balance of $5,000 carried over from the end of March. The adjusting entry must reduce the balance by $1,000, which requires a debit to the Wages Payable account.

| Wages Payable .... | 1,000 | |
| Wage Expense .... | | 1,000 |

To reduce the balance in the Wages Payable account, reducing the amount
in the Wage Expense account.

Wage Expense is $29,000 (= $30,000 − $1,000).

e. The Prepaid Insurance account balance of $3,000 represents four months of coverage. Thus the cost of insurance is $750 (= $3,000/4) per month. The adjusting entry for a single month is as follows:

| Insurance Expense .... | 750 | |
| Prepaid Insurance .... | | 750 |

To recognize cost of one month's insurance cost as expense of the month.

f. The Advances from Tenants account has a balance of $25,000 carried over from the start of the year. At the end of Year 3, it should have a balance of $30,000. Thus the adjusting entry must increase the balance by $5,000, which requires a credit to the liability account.

| Rent Revenue .... | 5,000 | |
| Advances from Tenants .... | | 5,000 |

To increase the balance in the Advances from Tenants account, reducing
the amount in the Rent Revenue account.

Rent Revenue for Year 3 is $245,000 (= $250,000 − $5,000).

g. The Depreciation Expense for the year should be $2,000 (= $10,000/5). The balance in the Accumulated Depreciation account should also be $2,000; thus, the firm must reduce (credit) the Depreciation Expense account by $8,000 (= $10,000 − $2,000). The adjusting entry not only reduces recorded Depreciation Expense but also sets up the asset account and its accumulated depreciation contra account.

Equipment	10,000	
Accumulated Depreciation		2,000
Depreciation Expense		8,000

To reduce Depreciation Expense, setting up the asset and its contra
account.

KEY TERMS AND CONCEPTS

Net income or net loss
Revenue
Expense
Accounting period
Natural business year or fiscal period
Cash basis of accounting
Accrual basis of accounting
Unexpired costs
Expired costs
Matching principle
Product costs

Period expense
Closing process
Temporary and permanent accounts
Dividends
General journal entries
Adjusting entries
Contra account
Unadjusted trial balance
Adjusted trial balance
Post-closing trial balance
Common-size income statement

QUESTIONS, EXERCISES, PROBLEMS, AND CASES

QUESTIONS

1. Review the meaning of the terms and concepts listed above in Key Terms and Concepts.
2. What factors would a firm likely consider in its decision to use the calendar year versus a fiscal (natural business) year as its accounting period?
3. Which of the following types of businesses are likely to have a natural business year different from the calendar year? Explain.
   a. A ski resort in Vermont
   b. A professional basketball team
   c. A grocery store
4. Distinguish between a revenue and a cash receipt. Under what conditions will they be the same?
5. Distinguish between an expense and a cash expenditure. Under what conditions will they be the same?
6. "Cash flows determine the amount of revenue and expense but not the timing of their recognition." Explain.
7. "Accrual accounting focuses on the use rather than the financing of assets." Explain.
8. "The valuation of assets and liabilities relates closely to the measurement of revenues and expenses." Explain.
9. "Revenue and expense accounts are useful accounting devices, but they could be dispensed with." What is an alternative to using them?
10. Why does the accountant close revenue and expense accounts at the end of each accounting period?
11. Before a firm closes its books for an accounting period, what types of accounts will have nonzero balances? After closing, what types of accounts will have nonzero balances?
12. If a firm has properly recorded each transaction occurring during an accounting period, why is there a need for adjusting entries at the end of the period?
13. What is the purpose of using contra accounts? What is the alternative to using them?

EXERCISES

14. **Revenue recognition.** JCPenney uses the accrual basis of accounting and recognizes revenue at the time it sells goods. Indicate the amount of revenue the firm recognizes during the month of May in each of the following transactions. The firm does the following:
    a. Collects $2,450,000 cash from customers during May for merchandise sold and delivered in April.
    b. Sells merchandise during May for $16,940,000 cash.
    c. Sells merchandise to customers during May on account, for which the firm will collect $2,925,000 cash from customers in June.
    d. Collects $18,000 cash from customers during May as a down payment for merchandise the firm will sell and deliver in June.
    e. Rents a store building to a toy shop for $8,000 a month, effective May 1. JCPenney receives a check for $16,000 for two months' rent on May 1.
    f. Same as part **e,** except that it receives the check from the tenant in June.
15. **Revenue recognition.** Assume that a firm uses the accrual basis of accounting and recognizes revenue at the time it sells goods or renders services. Indicate the amount

of revenue the firm recognizes in each of the months of April, May, and June relating to the following cash receipts during May. The firm does the following:

a. Collects $6,500 from customers for merchandise sold and delivered in April.

b. Collects $28,600 from customers for merchandise sold and delivered in May.

c. Collects $2,200 from customers for merchandise the firm will deliver in June.

d. Collects $1,800 from subscribers for subscription fees to monthly magazines for the one-year period beginning April 1.

e. Same as part **d,** except that the subscription period begins May 1.

f. Same as part **d,** except that the subscription period begins June 1.

16. **Revenue recognition.** Indicate which of the following transactions or events immediately gives rise to the recognition of revenue under the accrual basis of accounting.

a. The receipt of an order by Magnavox from Wal-Mart for televisions

b. The shipment by *Sports Illustrated* of magazines that subscribers paid for in advance

c. The issue of 20-year bonds by Apple Computer

d. The completion of a batch of athletic shoes by Nike

e. The sale of tickets by the Boston Symphony Orchestra for a concert in two weeks

f. Same as part **e,** except the sale is made by Ticketmaster, a ticket agent

g. The earning of interest by Microsoft on a certificate of deposit prior to maturity

h. The collection of cash by The Limited from its customers for sales made on account last month

i. The rendering of audit services by Arthur Andersen to a client on account

17. **Expense recognition.** Indicate the effect on assets and the amount of expense recognized (if any) by Computervision from each of the following related events, assuming that the firm uses the accrual basis of accounting:

a. The purchasing department notifies the stockroom that the supply of Apple Macintosh computers has reached the minimum point and requires reordering.

b. Computervision sends a purchase order to Apple Computer for $400,000 of computers.

c. Computervision receives an acknowledgment of the order. Apple Computer indicates that it will deliver the computers in 15 days but that the price has increased to $406,000.

d. The shipment of computers arrives at the receiving department of Computervision in the correct quantity.

e. The purchase invoice arrives. The amount of $406,000 is subject to a 2 percent discount if paid within 10 days. Computervision treats cash discounts taken as a reduction in the acquisition cost of inventory.

f. On inspection, Computervision discovers defective computers with a gross invoice price of $14,000 and returns them to Apple Computer.

g. Computervision pays the balance of the amount due Apple Computer in time to obtain the discount.

h. Computervision sells the computers to customers for $500,000.

18. **Expense recognition.** Assume that Hewlett-Packard (HP) uses the accrual basis of accounting and recognizes revenue at the time it sells goods or renders services. Indicate the amount of expense recognized during March (if any) from each of the following transactions or events:

a. HP pays an insurance premium of $18,000 on March 1 for one year's coverage beginning on that date.

b. On April 3, HP receives a utilities bill totaling $4,600 for services during March.

c. HP purchases on account supplies costing $7,000 during March. It makes payment for $5,000 of these purchases on account in March and pays the remainder in April. On March 1, supplies were on hand that cost $3,000. On March 31, supplies that cost $3,500 were still on hand.

d. Same as part **c**, except that $2,000 of supplies were on hand March 1.

e. In January, HP paid property taxes of $48,000 on an office building for the year.

f. On March 29, HP paid an advance of $250 on the April salary to an employee.

19. **Expense recognition.** Assume that a firm uses the accrual basis of accounting and recognizes revenue at the time it sells goods or renders services. Indicate the amount of expense the firm recognizes in each of the months of April, May, and June relating to the following cash expenditures during May:

a. $3,300 for advertising that appeared in magazines during April

b. $4,500 for sales commissions on sales made during May

c. $1,600 for rent on office equipment for the month of June

d. $1,200 for an insurance premium for coverage from May 1 until October 30

e. $3,000 as a deposit on a computer to be delivered on June 30

f. $3,600 for property taxes on an office building for the current calendar year

20. **Income recognition.** Demski Company acquired used trucks costing $125,000 from various sources. It incurred $8,000 in costs to prepare the trucks for sale. It then sold these trucks to Gator Corporation. Delivery costs paid by Demski Company totaled $6,000. Gator Corporation had agreed to pay $150,000 cash for these trucks. Finding itself short of cash, however, Gator Corporation offered some of its bonds to Demski Company. The bonds have a face value of $160,000, mature in five years, and promise 8 percent interest per year. At the time Gator Corporation made the offer it could have sold the bonds in public bond markets for $147,000.

Demski Company accepted the offer and held the bonds for three years. During the three years, it received interest payments of $12,800 per year, or $38,400 total. At the end of the third year, Demski Company sold the bonds for $153,000.

a. What profit or loss did Demski Company recognize at the time of the sale of trucks to Gator Corporation?

b. What profit or loss would Demski Company have recognized at the time of the sale of trucks if it had sold the bonds for $147,000 immediately on receiving them?

c. What profit or loss would Demski Company have recognized at the time of the sale of trucks if it had held the bonds to maturity, receiving $12,800 each year for five years and $160,000 at the time the bonds matured?

21. **Identifying missing half of journal entries.** In the business world, many transactions are routine and repetitive. Because accounting records business transactions, many accounting entries are also routine and repetitive. Knowing one-half of an entry in the double-entry recording system often permits a reasoned guess about the other half. The items below give the account name for one-half of an entry. Indicate your best guess as to the nature of the transaction being recorded and the name of the account of the routine other half of the entry. Also indicate whether the transaction increases or decreases the other account.

a. Debit: Cost of Goods Sold

b. Debit: Accounts Receivable

c. Credit: Accounts Receivable

d. Debit: Accounts Payable

e. Credit: Accounts Payable

f. Credit: Accumulated Depreciation

g. Debit: Retained Earnings

h. Credit: Prepaid Insurance

     i. Debit: Property Taxes Payable

     j. Debit: Merchandise Inventory

     k. Debit: Advances from Customers

     l. Credit: Advances to Suppliers

22. **Asset versus expense recognition.** Give the journal entry that Midland Grocery Stores should make on the receipt of each of the following invoices, assuming that it has made no previous entry.

     a. From Eastern Electric Supply Company, $430 for lightbulbs purchased for use in its stores

     b. From Price Waterhouse, certified public accountants, $1,500 for services in filing income tax returns

     c. From General Electric Company, $14,720 for refrigerators Midland purchased for its stores

     d. From White Stationery Company, $450 for office supplies Midland purchased

     e. From Showy Sign Company, $790 for a neon sign acquired

     f. From Sidley & Austin, attorneys, $2,000 for legal services in changing from the corporate to the partnership form of organization

     g. From Bell Telephone Company, $90 for telephone service for next month

     h. From Madison Avenue Garage, $73 for repairs to a forklift truck

     i. From Commonwealth Edison, $190 for electricity used for lighting last month

23. **Journal entries for notes receivable and notes payable.** The Restaurant Supply Company receives a $60,000, three-month, 8 percent promissory note, dated December 1, Year 6, from Wendy's to apply on its open accounts receivable.

     a. Present journal entries for the Restaurant Supply Company from December 1, Year 6, through collection at maturity. The Restaurant Supply Company closes its books quarterly. Include the closing entry.

     b. Present journal entries for Wendy's from December 1, Year 6, through payment at maturity. Wendy's closes its books quarterly. Include the closing entry.

24. **Journal entries for office supply inventories.** On January 1, Year 4, the Office Supplies Inventory account of Kelly Services Company had a balance of $48,700. During the ensuing quarter, Kelly Services Company purchases supplies on account for $137,900. On March 31, Year 4, it finds that inventory still on hand amounts to $37,400. Present journal entries to record these acquisitions and adjustments at the end of March in accordance with each of the following sets of instructions, which might be established in an accounting systems manual.

     a. Debit an asset account at the time Kelly Services acquires supplies.

     b. Debit an expense account at the time Kelly Services acquires supplies.

25. **Journal entries for rental receipts and payments.** Arizona Realty Company rents office space to Hagen Consultants at the rate of $900 per month. Arizona Realty Company has received all rentals due through April 30, Year 3. The following transactions occurred on the dates indicated:

     a. May 1, Year 3: Collection, $900

     b. June 1, Year 3: Collection, $1,800

     c. August 1, Year 3: Collection, $2,700

     Present journal entries for these transactions and for adjusting and closing entries from May 1 to August 31 (inclusive) as they relate to both companies, assuming that each company closes its books monthly.

26. **Using accumulated depreciation to estimate asset age.**

     a. Machine A costs $15,000, has accumulated depreciation of $9,000 as of year-end, and is being depreciated on a straight-line basis over 10 years with an estimated salvage value of zero. How long ago was machine A acquired?

b. Machine B has accumulated depreciation (straight-line basis) of $8,000 at year-end. The depreciation charge for the year is $4,000. The estimated salvage value of the machine at the end of its useful life is $2,000. How long ago was machine B acquired?

27. **Effect of recording errors on financial statements.** Using the notation O/S (overstated), U/S (understated), and NO (no effect), indicate the effects (direction and amount) on assets, liabilities, and shareholders' equity as of December 31, Year 3, of the following independent errors or omissions. Ignore income tax implications.

   a. On December 1, Year 3, a firm debits Prepaid Rent for $1,800 for six months' rent on an automobile. It made no adjusting entry on December 31, Year 3.

   b. A firm debits Administrative Expenses for $9,000 for a computer acquired on July 1, Year 3. The computer has an expected useful life of three years and zero estimated salvage value.

   c. A company rents out excess office space for the six-month period beginning January 1, Year 3. It receives a rental check for this period of $1,500 on December 26, Year 2, and correctly credits Rental Fees Received in Advance. It makes no further journal entries relating to this rental during Year 3.

   d. A firm earns interest on Notes Receivable of $300 as of December 31, Year 3, but makes no entry to recognize this interest.

   e. A firm receives a check for $250 from a customer on December 31, Year 3, in settlement of an account receivable. It makes no journal entries to record this check.

   f. A firm records as $740 an expenditure of $470 for travel during December, Year 3.

28. **Effect of recording errors on financial statements.** Forgetful Corporation neglected to make various adjusting entries on December 31, Year 8. Indicate the effects on assets, liabilities, and shareholders' equity on December 31, Year 8, of failing to adjust for the following independent items as appropriate, using the notation O/S (overstated), U/S (understated), and NO (no effect). Also, give the amount of the effect. Ignore income tax implications.

   a. On December 15, Year 8, Forgetful Corporation received a $1,400 advance from a customer for products to be manufactured and delivered in January, Year 9. The firm recorded the advance by debiting Cash and crediting Sales Revenue and has made no adjusting entry as of December 31, Year 8.

   b. On July 1, Year 8, Forgetful Corporation acquired a machine for $5,000 and recorded the acquisition by debiting Cost of Goods Sold and crediting Cash. The machine has a five-year useful life and zero estimated salvage value.

   c. On November 1, Year 8, Forgetful Corporation received a $2,000 note receivable from a customer in settlement of an accounts receivable. It debited Notes Receivable and credited Accounts Receivable on receipt of the note. The note is a six-month note due April 30, Year 9, and bears interest at an annual rate of 12 percent. Forgetful Corporation made no other entries related to this note during Year 8.

   d. Forgetful Corporation paid its annual insurance premium of $1,200 on October 1, Year 8, the first day of the year of coverage. It debited Prepaid Insurance $900, debited Insurance Expense $300, and credited Cash for $1,200. It made no other entries related to this insurance during Year 8.

   e. The Board of Directors of Forgetful Corporation declared a dividend of $1,500 on December 31, Year 8. The dividend will be paid on January 15, Year 9. Forgetful Corporation neglected to record the dividend declaration.

   f. On December 1, Year 8, Forgetful Corporation purchased a machine on account for $50,000, debiting Machinery and crediting Accounts Payable for $50,000. Ten days later, the account was paid, and the company took the allowed 2 percent discount. Cash was credited $49,000, Miscellaneous Revenue was credited $1,000, and Accounts Payable was debited $50,000. It is the policy of Forgetful Corporation to record cash discounts taken as a reduction in the cost of assets. On December 28, Year 8, the machine was installed for $4,000 in cash; Maintenance Expense was debited and Cash was credited for $4,000. The machine started operation on January 1, Year 9. Since the machine was not placed into operation until January 1, Year 9, as appropriate, no depreciation expense was recorded for Year 8.

29. **Reconstructing accounting records.** An employee of K9 Supplies Company removes most of the financial records of the company on October 31, as well as all of the cash on hand. The company had correctly recorded all transactions through October 31. From supplementary records, the company obtains the following information:
    (1) According to the bank, cash in the bank was $3,290.
    (2) Amounts payable to creditors totaled $3,620.
    (3) K9's initial contribution to the business was $12,000, and the total shareholders' equity at the time of the theft was $14,500.
    (4) Cost of merchandise on hand was $9,740.
    (5) A one-year fire insurance policy was purchased on October 1 for $1,200.
    (6) Furniture and fixtures are rented from the Anderson Office Supply Company for $300 per month. The rental for October has not been paid.
    (7) A note for $1,500 was given to K9 Supplies Company by a customer. Interest due at October 31 was $75.
    (8) Payments due from other customers amounted to $1,510.
    (9) K9 purchased a license from the city for $600 on September 1. The license allows retail operations for one year.
    a. Prepare a well-organized balance sheet presenting the financial position immediately preceding the theft.
    b. What is the probable cash shortage?

PROBLEMS AND CASES

30. **Cash versus accrual basis of accounting.** Argenti Corporation began operations on January 1, Year 6. The firm's cash account revealed the following transactions for the month of January.

Date	Transaction	Amount
Cash Receipts		
Jan. 1	Investment by Mary Argenti for 100 percent of Argenti Corporation's Common Stock	$50,000
Jan. 1	Loan from Upper Valley Bank, due June 30, Year 6, with interest at 6 percent per year	20,000
Jan. 15	Advance from a customer for merchandise scheduled for delivery in February, Year 6	800
Jan. 1–31	Sales to customers	40,000
Cash Disbursements		
Jan. 1	Rental of retail space at a monthly rental of $2,500	(5,000)
Jan. 1	Purchase of display equipment (five-year life, zero salvage value)	(30,000)
Jan. 1	Premium on property and liability insurance for coverage from January 1 to December 31, Year 6	(2,400)
Jan. 15	Payment of utility bills	(850)
Jan. 16	Payment of salaries	(2,250)
Jan. 1–31	Purchase of merchandise	(34,900)
	Balance, January 31, Year 6	$35,400

The following information relates to Argenti Corporation as of January 31, Year 6:

(1) Customers owe the firm $7,500 from sales made during January.

(2) The firm owes suppliers $4,400 for merchandise purchased during January.

(3) Unpaid utility bills total $760, and unpaid salaries total $2,590.

(4) Merchandise inventory on hand totals $7,200.

a. Prepare an income statement for January, assuming that Argenti Corporation uses the accrual basis of accounting and recognizes revenue at the time it sells goods to customers.

b. Prepare an income statement for January, assuming that Argenti Corporation uses a cash basis of accounting.

c. Which basis of accounting do you believe provides a better indication of the operating performance of the firm during January? Why?

31. **Cash versus accrual basis of accounting.** Management Consultants, Inc., opens a consulting business on July 1, Year 2. Roy Bean and Sarah Bower each contribute $5,000 cash for shares of the firm's common stock. The corporation borrows $6,000 from a local bank on August 1, Year 2. The loan is repayable on July 31, Year 3, with interest at the rate of 9 percent per year.

The firm rents office space on August 1, paying two months' rent in advance. It pays the remaining monthly rental fees of $1,600 per month on the first of each month, beginning October 1. The firm purchases office equipment with a four-year life for cash on August 1 for $12,000.

The firm renders consulting services for clients between August 1 and December 31, Year 2, totaling $45,000. It collects $39,000 of this amount by year-end.

It incurs and pays other costs by the end of the year as follows: utilities, $350; salaries, $28,200; supplies, $650. It has unpaid bills at year-end as follows: utilities, $50; salaries, $1,800; supplies, $40. The firm used all the supplies it had acquired.

a. Prepare an income statement for the five months ended December 31, Year 2, assuming that the corporation uses the accrual basis of accounting and recognizes revenue at the time services are rendered.

b. Prepare an income statement for the five months ended December 31, Year 2, assuming that the corporation uses the cash basis of accounting.

c. Which basis of accounting do you believe provides a better indication of the operating performance of the consulting firm for the period? Why?

32. **Cash versus accrual basis of accounting.** J. Hennessey opens a retail store on January 1, Year 8. Hennessey invests $20,000 for all of the common stock of Hennessey Retail Store, Inc. The store borrows $10,000 from a local bank. The loan is repayable on December 31, Year 9, with interest at the rate of 12 percent per year.

The store purchases $84,000 of merchandise on account during Year 8 and pays $76,000 of the amount by the end of Year 8. A physical inventory taken on December 31, Year 8, indicates $12,000 of merchandise on hand.

During Year 8, the store makes cash sales to customers totaling $30,000 and sales on account totaling $70,000. Of the sales on account, the store collects $56,000 by December 31, Year 8.

The store incurs and pays other costs as follows: salaries, $20,000; utilities, $1,500. It has unpaid bills at year-end as follows: salaries, $1,400; utilities, $120.

a. Prepare an income statement for Year 8 assuming that the company uses the accrual basis of accounting and recognizes revenue at the time of sale.

b. Prepare an income statement for Year 8 assuming that the company uses the cash basis of accounting.

c. Which basis of accounting do you believe provides a better indication of operating performance for the retail store during Year 8? Why?

d. Prepare a balance sheet on December 31, Year 8.

33. **Worksheet preparation of income statement and balance sheet.** Refer to the information for Regaldo Department Stores as of January 31, Year 8 in problem **25** of Chapter 2. Regaldo Department Stores opened for business during February, Year 8. It uses the accrual basis of accounting. Transactions and events during February were as follows.

  (1) February 1: Purchased display counters and computer equipment for Ps90,000. The firm borrowed Ps90,000 from a local bank to finance the purchases. The bank loan bears interest at a rate of 12 percent each year and is repayable with interest on February 1, Year 9.

  (2) During February: Purchased merchandise on account totaling Ps217,900.

  (3) During February: Sold merchandise costing Ps162,400 to various customers for Ps62,900 cash and Ps194,600 on account.

  (4) During February: Paid to employees compensation totaling Ps32,400 for services rendered during the month.

  (5) During February: Paid utility (electric, water, gas) bills totaling Ps2,700 for services received during February.

  (6) During February: Collected Ps84,600 from customers from sales on account (see transaction **(3)** above).

  (7) During February: Paid invoices from suppliers of merchandise (see transaction **(2)** above) with an original purchase price of Ps210,000 in time to receive a 2 percent discount for prompt payment and Ps29,000 to other suppliers after the discount period had elapsed. The firm treats discounts taken as a reduction in the acquisition cost of merchandise.

  (8) February 28: Compensation that employees earned during the last several days in February and that the firm will pay early in March totaled Ps6,700.

  (9) February 28: Utility services that the firm used during February and that the firm will not pay until March totaled Ps800.

  (10) February 28: The display counters and computer equipment purchased in transaction **(1)** have an expected useful life of five years and zero salvage value at the end of the five years. The firm depreciates such equipment on a straight-line basis over the expected life.

  (11) February 28: The firm recognizes an appropriate portion of the prepaid rent as of January 31 (see problem **25** in Chapter 2).

  (12) February 28: The firm recognizes an appropriate portion of the prepaid insurance as of January 31 (see problem **25** in Chapter 2).

  (13) February 28: The firm amortizes (that is, recognizes as an expense) the patent over 60 months (see problem **25** in Chapter 2).

  (14) February 28: The firm recognizes an appropriate amount of interest expense on the loan in transaction **(1)** above.

  (15) February 28: The firm is subject to an income tax rate of 30 percent of net income before income taxes. The income tax law requires firms to pay income taxes on the fifteenth day of the month after the end of each quarter (that is, April 15, July 15, October 15, and January 15).

  a. Create a worksheet with a column for each of the balance sheet accounts on January 31, Year 8 (see problem **25** in Chapter 2). Leave space to add asset, liability, and shareholders' equity accounts as needed. Enter the amounts from the balance sheet on January 31, Year 8.

  b. Enter each of the 15 transactions or events listed above in the various accounts, creating additional accounts as needed. Use a single revenue account and a single expense account, but label each entry affecting a revenue account (for example, sales revenue) and an expense account (for example, salary expense). Be sure to indicate whether the transaction increases (+) or decreases

($-$) each account. Use the numbers of the 15 transactions to cross-reference your entries on the worksheet. Be sure that you enter the dual effects of each transaction so that you maintain the balance sheet equality of assets with liabilities and shareholders' equity.

   c. Prepare an income statement for the month of February, Year 8.

   d. Prepare a balance sheet as of February 28, Year 8.

34. **Miscellaneous transactions and adjusting entries.** Present journal entries for each of the following independent sets of data.

   a. On January 15, Year 2, a company receives an $18,000, two-month, 6 percent note. Present adjusting entries at the end of each month and the entry for collection at maturity.

   b. A company uses one Merchandise Inventory account to record the beginning inventory and purchases during the period. The balance in this account on December 31, Year 2, is $620,000. The inventory of merchandise on hand at that time is $50,000. Present the adjusting entry.

   c. A company rents out part of its building for office space at the rate of $1,200 a month, payable in advance for each calendar quarter of the year. It receives the quarterly rental for the first quarter one month late, on February 1, Year 2. Present collection and adjusting entries for the quarter. Assume that the company closes its books monthly.

   d. A company leases branch office space at $2,000 a month beginning July 1, Year 2. It makes payments on the first day of each six-month period. The company made a payment of $12,000 on July 1, Year 2. Present payment and adjusting entries through August 31, Year 2. Assume that the company closes its books monthly.

   e. The balance of the Prepaid Insurance account on October 1, Year 2, was $600. On December 1, Year 2, the company renews its only insurance policy for another three years, beginning on that date, by paying $11,700. Present journal entries for renewal and adjusting entries through December 31, Year 2. Assume that the company closes its books quarterly.

   f. The Office Supplies on Hand account had a balance of $400 on December 31, Year 2. The firm records purchases of supplies in the amount of $1,420 in the Office Supplies Expense account during the month. The physical inventory of office supplies on December 31, Year 2, totals $420. Present any necessary adjusting entry at December 31, Year 2.

   g. A firm constructs an office building at a cost of $820,000. It estimates that the building will have a useful life of 40 years from the date of occupancy, October 31, Year 2, and a residual value of $100,000. Present the adjusting entry for the depreciation of the building for Year 2. Assume that the company closes its books annually on December 31.

35. **Miscellaneous transactions and adjusting entries.** Give the journal entry to record (1) each of the following transactions as well as (2) any necessary adjusting entries on December 31, Year 6, assuming that the firm uses a calendar-year accounting period and closes its books on December 31. You may omit explanations for the journal entries.

   a. Sung Corporation gives a 60-day note to a supplier on December 2, Year 6. The note in the face amount of $6,000 replaces an open account receivable of the same amount. The note is due on January 30, Year 7, with interest at 10 percent per year.

   b. Allstate Insurance Company sells a two-year insurance policy on September 1, Year 6, receiving the two-year premium of $18,000 in advance.

   c. Blaydon Company acquires a machine on October 1, Year 6, for $40,000 cash. It expects the machine to have a $4,000 salvage value and a four-year life.

d. Pyke Electronics Company acquires an automobile on July 1, Year 6, for $24,000 cash. It expects the automobile to have a $3,000 salvage value and a three-year life.

e. Devine Company rents needed office space for the three-month period beginning December 1, Year 6. It pays the three months' total rent of $12,000 on this date.

f. Hall Corporation begins business on November 1, Year 6. It acquires office supplies costing $7,000 on account. Of this amount, it pays $5,000 by year-end. A physical inventory indicates that office supplies costing $1,500 are on hand on December 31, Year 6.

36. **Miscellaneous transactions and adjusting entries.** Give the journal entry to record (1) each of the following transactions as well as (2) any necessary adjusting entries on December 31, Year 3, assuming that the firm uses a calendar-year accounting period and closes its books on December 31. You may omit explanations for the journal entries.

a. Gale Company rents out excess office space on October 1, Year 3. It receives on that date the annual rental of $48,000 for the period from October 1, Year 3, to September 30, Year 4, and credits a liability account.

b. Whitley Company receives a $10,000, two-month, 6 percent note on December 1, Year 3, in full payment of an open account receivable.

c. The balance in the Prepaid Insurance account of Pierce Company on January 1, Year 3, was $500. On March 1, Year 4, the company renews its only insurance policy for another two years, beginning on that date, by paying the $6,600 two-year premium. It debits an asset account for the payment.

d. The Repair Parts Inventory account of Kelly Company showed a balance of $4,000 on January 1, Year 3. During Year 3, the firm purchases parts costing $14,900 and charges them to Repair Expense. An inventory of repair parts at the end of December reveals parts costing $3,800 on hand.

e. Roberts Company acquires an office machine on July 1, Year 3, at a cost of $200,000. It estimates that the machine will have a 10-year life and a $20,000 residual value. It uses the straight-line depreciation method.

f. Lovejoy Company pays its property taxes for the year ending December 31, Year 3, of $12,000 on September 1, Year 3. It debits an expense account at the time of the payment.

37. **Preparation of T-account entries and adjusted trial balance.** Jennifer Langer and Gloria Langer organize a corporation known as the Sisters' Collection Agency on January 1, Year 3. The firm collects overdue accounts receivable of various clients on a commission basis. The following transactions occur during January:

(1) Jennifer Langer contributes office supplies of $2,000 and cash of $8,000. She receives stock certificates for 500 shares with a par value of $20 a share.

(2) Gloria Langer contributes cash of $4,000 and office equipment valued at $6,000. She receives stock certificates for 500 shares.

(3) The Langer agency collects $1,200 on an account turned over to it by Z-Mart Stores. It earns a commission of 50 percent of the amount collected.

(4) The firm pays salaries of $1,500 during January.

(5) The firm receives a bill from Lyband and Linn, certified public accountants, for $800 to cover the cost of installing a computer system.

(6) The firm pays the amount due Z-Mart Stores (see transaction **(3)** above).

(7) The firm leases an office for the year, beginning February 1, Year 3, and pays the rent for two months in advance. It writes a check for $1,000.

(8) The firm purchases an automobile on January 31 for $15,000; it pays $2,500 by check and signs an installment contract, payable to the Scotch Automobile Sales Company, for the balance.

   a. Open T-accounts and record the transactions during January.

   b. Prepare an adjusted, preclosing trial balance as of January 31, Year 3. Indicate, by the letters **R** or **E,** which accounts are revenue and which are expense accounts.

38. **Preparation of T-account entries, adjusted trial balance, income statement, and balance sheet.** The unadjusted, preclosing trial balance of Kleen Cleaners, Inc., at February 28, Year 6, appears in Exhibit 3.14. The firm has not made adjusting entries or closed its books since December 31, Year 5. A summary of the transactions for the month of March, Year 6, follows.

   (1) Sales: for cash, $15,000; on account, $4,900

   (2) Collections on account, $11,200

   (3) Purchases of outside work (cleaning done by wholesale cleaners) on account, $700

   (4) Purchases of supplies on account, $3,100

   (5) Payments on account, $4,600

   (6) March rent paid, $800

   (7) March salaries and wages paid, $10,930

   Adjusting entries required at the end of March relate to the following:

   (8) Supplies used (for the quarter), $5,610

EXHIBIT 3.14	KLEEN CLEANERS, INC. Unadjusted, Preclosing Trial Balance February 28, Year 6 (Problem 38)

Cash	$ 3,400	
Accounts Receivable	15,200	
Supplies on Hand	4,800	
Prepaid Insurance	1,200	
Equipment	65,000	
Accumulated Depreciation		$ 9,680
Accounts Payable		7,900
Common Stock		20,000
Retained Earnings		40,000
Sales Revenue		46,060
Salaries and Wages Expense	26,600	
Cost of Outside Work	2,040	
Advertising Expense	400	
Repairs Expense	500	
Rent Expense	1,200	
Power, Gas, and Water Expense	880	
Supplies Expense	—	
Depreciation Expense	—	
Miscellaneous Expense	2,420	
	$123,640	$123,640

(9) Depreciation (for the quarter), $2,560

(10) Bills received but not recorded or paid by the end of the month: advertising, $300; maintenance on equipment, $80; power, gas, and water, $420

(11) Insurance expired (for the quarter), $300

   a. Open T-accounts and enter the trial balance amounts.

   b. Record the transactions for the month of March and adjusting entries at the end of March in the T-accounts, opening additional T-accounts as needed. Cross-reference the entries using the numbers of the transactions above.

   c. Prepare an adjusted, preclosing trial balance at March 31, Year 6, and an income statement for the three months ending March 31, Year 6.

   d. Enter closing entries in the T-accounts using an Income Summary account.

   e. Prepare a balance sheet as of March 31, Year 6.

39. Preparation of T-account entries, adjusted trial balance, income statement, and balance sheet. The adjusted, post-closing trial balance of Bosworth Computer Repair Services at June 30, Year 8, appears in Exhibit 3.15. A summary of the transactions during July follows.

(1) Performed repair services, for which it received $2,250 cash immediately.

(2) Performed additional repair work, $500, and sent bills to customers for this amount.

(3) Paid creditors $1,000.

(4) Took out insurance on equipment on July 1 and issued a check to cover one year's premium of $240.

(5) Paid $150 for a series of advertisements that appeared in the local newspaper during July.

(6) Issued a check for $325 for rent of shop space for July.

(7) Paid telephone bill of $90 for the month.

(8) Collected $250 of the amount charged to customers in item **(2)**.

(9) Paid salaries to employees of $1,100 for the month.

Adjusting entries required at the end of July relate to the following:

(10) The cost of insurance expired during July is $20.

(11) The cost of repair parts used during the month is $450.

(12) The cost of office supplies used during July is $100.

EXHIBIT 3.15	BOSWORTH COMPUTER REPAIR SERVICES Adjusted, Post-Closing Trial Balance June 30, Year 8 (Problem 39)	
Cash	$ 4,800	
Repair Parts Inventory	1,500	
Office Supplies Inventory	200	
Equipment	5,500	
Accumulated Depreciation		$ 750
Accounts Payable		6,250
Common Stock		1,250
Retained Earnings		3,750
	$12,000	$12,000

(13) Depreciation of equipment for the month is $75.

    a. Open T-accounts and insert the July 1 balances.

    b. Record the transactions for the month of July and adjusting entries at the end of July in the T-accounts, opening additional T-accounts for individual revenue and expense accounts as needed. Cross-reference the entries using the numbers of the transactions above.

    c. Prepare an adjusted, preclosing trial balance at July 31, Year 8, and an income statement for the month of July.

    d. Enter closing entries in the T-accounts using an Income Summary account.

    e. Prepare a balance sheet as of July 31, Year 8.

40. Preparation of T-account entries, adjusted trial balance, income statement, and balance sheet. The unadjusted, preclosing trial balance of Jones Shoe Repair Shop, Inc., at February 28, Year 2, appears in Exhibit 3.16. The firm has not made adjusting entries or closed its books since December 31, Year 1. A summary of the transactions during the month of March, Year 2, follows.

(1) Sales for cash total $22,000; sales on account total $14,900.

(2) Collections on account total $18,200.

(3) Purchases of outside work (repair work done by another shoe repair shop for Jones) total $1,200, on account.

(4) Purchases of supplies, on account, total $3,700.

(5) Payments on account total $5,800.

(6) Payments for March rent total $1,000.

(7) Payments for March salaries and wages total $11,900.

Adjusting entries required at the end of March relate to the following:

(8) Supplies used for the quarter total $6,820.

EXHIBIT 3.16	JONES SHOE REPAIR SHOP, INC. Unadjusted, Preclosing Trial Balance February 28, Year 2 (Problem 40)	

Cash	$ 6,060	
Accounts Receivable	15,200	
Supplies Inventory	4,800	
Prepaid Insurance	900	
Equipment	65,000	
Accumulated Depreciation		$ 11,460
Accounts Payable		6,120
Common Stock		15,000
Retained Earnings		47,360
Sales Revenue		46,060
Salaries and Wages Expense	26,600	
Cost of Outside Work	2,040	
Advertising Expense	900	
Rent Expense	1,200	
Power, Gas, and Water Expense	880	
Supplies Expense	—	
Depreciation Expense	—	
Miscellaneous Expense	2,420	
	$126,000	$126,000

(9) Depreciation for the quarter totals $2,820.

(10) Bills received but not yet recorded or paid by the end of the month total as follows: advertising, $400; power, gas, and water, $520.

(11) Insurance expired for the quarter totals $400.

  a. Open T-accounts and enter the trial balance amounts.

  b. Record the transactions for the month of March and adjusting entries at the end of March in the T-accounts, opening additional T-accounts as needed. Cross-reference the entries using the numbers of the transactions above.

  c. Prepare an adjusted, preclosing trial balance at March 31, Year 2, and an income statement for the three months ending March 31, Year 2.

  d. Enter closing entries in the T-accounts using an Income Summary account.

  e. Prepare a balance sheet as of March 31, Year 2.

41. Preparation of journal entries, T-accounts, adjusted trial balance, income statement, and balance sheet. The adjusted, post-closing trial balance of Rybowiak's Building Supplies on June 30, Year 9, appears in Exhibit 3.17. The firm made the following transactions during July:

(1) Sold merchandise on account for a total selling price of $85,000.

(2) Purchased merchandise inventory on account from various suppliers for $46,300.

(3) Paid rent for the month of July of $11,750.

(4) Paid salaries to employees during July of $20,600.

(5) Collected accounts receivable of $34,150.

(6) Paid accounts payable of $38,950.

(7) Paid miscellaneous expenses of $3,200.

Adjusting entries required at the end of July relate to the following:

(8) The firm paid the premium on a one-year insurance policy on March 1, Year 9, with coverage beginning on that date. This is the only insurance policy in force on June 30, Year 9.

(9) The firm depreciates its equipment over a 10-year life. Estimated salvage value of the equipment is negligible.

EXHIBIT 3.17	RYBOWIAK'S BUILDING SUPPLIES Adjusted, Post-Closing Trial Balance June 30, Year 9 (Problem 41)

Cash	$ 44,200	
Accounts Receivable	27,250	
Merchandise Inventory	68,150	
Prepaid Insurance	400	
Equipment	210,000	
Accumulated Depreciation		$ 84,000
Accounts Payable		33,100
Note Payable		5,000
Salaries Payable		1,250
Common Stock		150,000
Retained Earnings		76,650
	$350,000	$350,000

(10) Employees earned salaries of $1,600 during the last two days of July but were not paid. These are the only unpaid salaries at the end of July.

(11) The note payable is a 90-day, 12-percent note issued on June 30, Year 9.

(12) Merchandise inventory on hand on July 31, Year 9, totals $77,950.

    a. Prepare general journal entries to reflect the transactions and other events during July. Indicate whether each entry records a transaction (T) during the month or is an adjusting entry (A) at the end of the month.

    b. Set up T-accounts and enter the opening balances in the accounts on June 30, Year 9. Record the entries from part **a** in the T-accounts, creating additional accounts as required. Cross-reference the entries using the numbers of the transactions above.

    c. Prepare an adjusted, preclosing trial balance at July 31, Year 9.

    d. Prepare an income statement for the month of July.

    e. Enter the appropriate closing entries at the end of July in the T-accounts, assuming that the firm closes its books each month. Use an Income Summary account.

    f. Prepare a balance sheet as of July 31, Year 9.

42. Preparation of adjusting entries. Exhibit 3.18 presents an unadjusted, preclosing trial balance for Reliable Appliance Company on July 31, Year 3. The company closes its books monthly. Additional data include the following:

EXHIBIT 3.18	RELIABLE APPLIANCE COMPANY Unadjusted, Preclosing Trial Balance July 31, Year 3 (Problem 42)	
Accounts Payable		$ 25,904
Accounts Receivable	$ 36,514	
Accumulated Depreciation		16,428
Advances by Customers		1,080
Cash	18,000	
Common Stock		80,000
Equipment	5,280	
Depreciation Expense	—	—
Dividends Payable	—	—
Furniture and Fixtures	24,000	
Income Tax Expense	—	—
Income Tax Payable		7,000
Insurance Expense	—	—
Leasehold	21,600	
Merchandise Cost of Goods Sold	—	—
Merchandise Inventory	99,000	
Miscellaneous Expense	376	
Prepaid Insurance	900	
Rent Expense	—	—
Retained Earnings		28,588
Salaries and Commissions Expense	4,040	
Salaries and Commissions Payable		1,000
Sales		50,000
Supplies Inventory	290	
	$210,000	$210,000

(1) The company calculates depreciation on equipment at 20 percent of cost per year (assume zero salvage value).

(2) The company calculates depreciation on furniture and fixtures at 25 percent of cost per year (assume zero salvage value).

(3) The leasehold represents long-term rent paid in advance by Reliable Appliance Company. The monthly rental charge is $1,800.

(4) During the month, the company mistakenly recorded one invoice of $260 for the purchase of merchandise on account from the Hinsdale Company as $620. The firm has not yet paid the account.

(5) Commissions unpaid at July 31, Year 3, are $1,210. The firm has paid all salaries. The balance in the Salaries and Commissions Payable account represents the amount of commissions unpaid at July 1.

(6) The company recently delivered merchandise with a sales price of $490 to a customer and charged Accounts Receivable, although the customer had previously paid $490 in advance.

(7) The balance in the Prepaid Insurance account relates to a two-year policy that went into effect on January 1, Year 3.

(8) The company declared a dividend of $2,500 on July 31, Year 3.

(9) The inventory of merchandise on July 31, Year 3, was $61,200.

Present adjusting entries at July 31, Year 3. Use only the accounts listed in the trial balance.

43. **Preparation of adjusting entries.** Exhibit 3.19 presents an unadjusted, preclosing trial balance for Williamson Corporation on December 31, Year 9. The firm closes its books annually. Additional data include the following:

(1) The firm calculates depreciation on equipment using an eight-year life and zero estimated salvage value.

EXHIBIT 3.19	WILLIAMSON CORPORATION Unadjusted, Preclosing Trial Balance December 31, Year 9 (Problem 43)

Accounts Payable		$ 8,900
Accounts Receivable	$ 14,700	
Accumulated Depreciation		14,950
Advances by Customers		290
Cash	6,920	
Common Stock		10,000
Depreciation Expense	—	—
Equipment	50,000	
Income Tax Expense	—	—
Income Tax Payable	—	—
Marketing and Administrative Expenses	45,600	
Merchandise Cost of Goods Sold	—	—
Merchandise Inventory	110,000	
Prepaid Rent	1,200	
Retained Earnings		42,480
Salaries Payable		1,800
Sales Revenue		150,000
	$228,420	$228,420

(2) The amount shown for Advances by Customers represents the amount received from a customer during December, Year 8, for goods shipped to that customer during February, Year 9.

(3) The firm received from a customer a cash payment of $860 relating to a previous sale on account. The firm incorrectly credited Accounts Payable when it received the cash.

(4) The amount appearing in the Prepaid Rent account relates to prepayments as of January 1, Year 9. The firm charged rental payments during Year 9 totaling $15,000 to Marketing and Administrative Expenses. Prepaid rent on December 31, Year 9, totals $1,400.

(5) Unpaid salaries as of December 31, Year 9, total $2,250.

(6) The inventory of merchandise on December 1, Year 9, totals $15,200.

(7) The income tax rate is 30 percent.

Present adjusting entries on December 31, Year 9. Use only the accounts listed in the trial balance.

44. **Preparation of closing entries.** Exhibit 3.20 presents the adjusted, preclosing trial balance of Creative Photographers, Inc., at June 30, Year 2.

  a. Present the journal entries to close the revenue and expense accounts directly to Retained Earnings as of June 30, Year 2.

EXHIBIT 3.20	CREATIVE PHOTOGRAPHERS, INC. Adjusted, Preclosing Trial Balance June 30, Year 2 (Problem 44)	
Accounts Payable		$ 10,923
Accounts Receivable	$ 11,700	
Accumulated Depreciation		5,985
Advertising Expense	4,500	
Cameras and Equipment	46,500	
Cash	8,982	
Common Stock		30,000
Depreciation Expense—Cameras and Equipment	540	
Depreciation Expense—Furniture and Fixtures	315	
Electricity Expense	900	
Equipment Repairs Expense	540	
Furniture and Fixtures	28,800	
Insurance Expense	990	
Photographic Supplies Expense	5,850	
Photographic Supplies on Hand	10,170	
Prepaid Insurance	810	
Rent Expense	4,275	
Retained Expense		42,414
Revenue—Commercial Photography		54,270
Revenue—Printing Service		14,040
Salaries Expense	32,400	
Telephone Expense	360	
	$157,632	$157,632

b. Set up in T-account form the revenue, expense, and retained earnings accounts. Insert the trial balance amounts, and record the closing entries from part **a.**

45. Working backward to the balance sheet at the beginning of the period. (Problems **45** through **47** derive from problems by George H. Sorter.) The following data relate to the Prima Company.

(1) Post-closing trial balance at December 31, Year 2:

Debits	
Cash	$ 10,000
Marketable Securities	20,000
Accounts Receivable	25,000
Merchandise Inventory	30,000
Prepayments for Miscellaneous Services	3,000
Land, Buildings, and Equipment	40,000
Total Debits	$128,000
Credits	
Accounts Payable (for merchandise)	$ 25,000
Interest Payable	300
Taxes Payable	4,000
Note Payable (6 percent, long-term)	20,000
Accumulated Depreciation	16,000
Capital Stock	50,000
Retained Earnings	12,700
Total Credits	$128,000

(2) Income and retained earnings data for Year 2:

Sales		$200,000
Less Expenses:		
Cost of Goods Sold	$ 130,000	
Depreciation Expense	4,000	
Taxes Expense	8,000	
Other Operating Expense	47,700	
Interest Expense	1,200	
Total Expenses		190,900
Net Income		$ 9,100
Less Dividends		5,000
Increase in Retained Earnings		$ 4,100

(3) Summary of cash receipts and disbursements in Year 2:

Cash Receipts		
Cash Sales	$ 47,000	
Collection from Credit Customers	150,000	
Total Receipts		$197,000

Cash Disbursements

Payment to Suppliers of Merchandise	$128,000
Payment to Suppliers of Miscellaneous Services	49,000
Payment of Taxes	7,500
Payment of Interest	1,200
Payment of Dividends	5,000
Purchase of Marketable Securities	8,000
Total Disbursements	$198,700
Excess of Disbursements over Receipts	$ 1,700

(4) Purchases of merchandise during the period, all on account, were $127,000. All "Other Operating Expenses" were credited to Prepayments.

Prepare a balance sheet for January 1, Year 2. (*Hint:* Set up T-accounts for each of the accounts in the trial balance, and enter the ending balances in the T-accounts. Starting with information from the income statement and statement of cash receipts and disbursements, reconstruct the transactions that took place during the year and enter the amounts in the appropriate T-accounts.)

46. **Working backward to cash receipts and disbursements.** The Secunda Company's trial balance at the beginning of Year 2 and the adjusted, preclosing trial balance at the end of Year 2 appear in Exhibit 3.21. The company purchases all goods and services acquired during the year on account. The Other Operating Expenses account

EXHIBIT 3.21 THE SECUNDA COMPANY
Trial Balance
January 1 and December 31, Year 2   (Problem 46)

	1/1/Year 2	12/31/Year 2
Debits		
Cash	$ 20,000	$ 9,000
Accounts Receivable	36,000	51,000
Merchandise Inventory	45,000	60,000
Prepayments	2,000	1,000
Land, Buildings, and Equipment	40,000	40,000
Cost of Goods Sold	—	50,000
Interest Expense	—	3,000
Other Operating Expenses	—	29,000
Total Debits	$143,000	$243,000
Credits		
Accumulated Depreciation	$ 16,000	$ 18,000
Interest Payable	1,000	2,000
Accounts Payable	30,000	40,000
Mortgage Payable	20,000	17,000
Capital Stock	50,000	50,000
Retained Earnings	26,000	16,000
Sales	—	100,000
Total Credits	$143,000	$243,000

includes depreciation charges and expirations of prepayments. The company debits dividends declared during the year to Retained Earnings.

Prepare a schedule showing all cash transactions for Year 2. (*Hint:* Set up T-accounts for each of the accounts listed in the trial balance, and enter the amounts shown as of January 1, Year 2, and December 31, Year 2. Starting with the entries in revenue and expense accounts, reconstruct the transactions that took place during the year, and enter the amounts in the appropriate T-accounts. The Retained Earnings account in the trial balance does not yet reflect the effects of earnings activities because the firm has not yet made closing entries.)

47. **Working backward to the income statement.** Tertia Company presents incomplete post-closing trial balances (Exhibit 3.22), as well as a statement of cash receipts and disbursements (Exhibit 3.23). Prepare a combined statement of income and retained earnings for Year 2. (*Hint:* Set up T-accounts for each of the balance sheet accounts listed in the trial balance, and enter the amounts shown as of January 1, Year 2, and December 31, Year 2. Starting with the cash receipts and disbursements for the year, reconstruct the transactions that took place during the year, and enter them in the appropriate T-accounts. The Retained Earnings account reflects the effect of earnings activities for the year because the firm has made closing entries.)

48. **Reconstructing the income statement and balance sheet.** (Adapted from a problem by Stephen A. Zeff.) Portobello Co., a firm that sells merchandise to retail customers, is in its tenth year of operation. On December 28, Year 10, three days before the close of its fiscal year, a flash flood devastated the company's administrative office and destroyed almost all of its accounting records. The company was able to save the balance sheet on December 31, Year 9 (see Exhibit 3.24), the checkbook, the bank

EXHIBIT 3.22	TERTIA COMPANY Trial Balance January 1 and December 31, Year 2 (Problem 47)

	1/1/Year 2	12/31/Year 2
Debits		
Cash	$?	$?
Accounts and Notes Receivable	36,000	41,000
Merchandise Inventory	55,000	49,500
Interest Receivable	1,000	700
Prepaid Miscellaneous Services	4,000	5,200
Building, Machinery, and Equipment	47,000	47,000
Total Debits	$?	$?
Credits		
Accounts Payable (miscellaneous services)	$ 2,000	$ 2,500
Accounts Payable	34,000	41,000
Property Taxes Payable	1,000	1,500
Accumulated Depreciation	10,000	12,000
Mortgage Payable	35,000	30,000
Capital Stock	25,000	25,000
Retained Earnings	76,000	?
Total Credits	$183,000	$211,200

EXHIBIT 3.23	TERTIA COMPANY Statement of Cash Receipts and Disbursements For Year 2 (Problem 47)

	Year 2
Cash Receipts	
1. Collection from Credit Customers	$144,000
2. Cash Sales	63,000
3. Collection of Interest	1,000
	$208,000
Less Cash Disbursements	
4. Payment to Suppliers of Merchandise	$114,000
5. Repayment on Mortgage	5,000
6. Payment of Interest	500
7. Prepayment to Suppliers of Miscellaneous Services	57,500
8. Payment of Property Taxes	1,200
9. Payment of Dividends	2,000
	$180,200
Increase in Cash Balance for Year	$ 27,800

statements, and some soggy remains of the specific accounts receivable and accounts payable balances. Based on a review of the surviving documents and a series of interviews with company employees, you obtain the following information.

(1) The company's insurance agency advises that a four-year insurance policy has six months to run as of December 31, Year 10. The policy cost $12,000 when the company paid the four-year premium during Year 7.

(2) During Year 10, the company's board of directors declared $6,000 of dividends, of which the firm paid $3,000 in cash to shareholders during Year 10 and will pay the remainder during Year 11. Early in Year 10 the company also paid dividends of $1,800 cash that the board of directors had declared during Year 9.

(3) On April 1, Year 10, the company received from Appleton Co. $10,900 cash, which included principal of $10,000 and interest, in full settlement of Appleton's nine-month note dated July 1, Year 9. According to the terms of the note, Appleton paid all interest at maturity on April 1, Year 10.

(4) The amount owed by the company to merchandise suppliers on December 31, Year 10, was $20,000 less than the amount owed on December 31, Year 9. During Year 10, the company paid $115,000 to merchandise suppliers. The cost of merchandise inventory on December 31, Year 10, based on a physical count, was $18,000 larger than the balance in the Merchandise Inventory account on the December 31, Year 9, balance sheet. On December 8, Year 10, the company exchanged shares of its common stock for merchandise inventory costing $11,000. The company's policy is to purchase all merchandise on account.

(5) The company purchased delivery trucks on March 1, Year 10, for $60,000. To finance the acquisition, it gave the seller a $60,000 four-year note that bears interest at 10 percent per year. The company must pay interest on the note each six months, beginning September 1, Year 10. The company made the required payment on this date. The delivery trucks have an expected useful life of 10

EXHIBIT 3.24	PORTOBELLO CO. Balance Sheet December 31, Year 9 (Problem 48)	

Assets

Cash		$ 18,600
Accounts Receivable		33,000
Notes Receivable		10,000
Interest Receivable		600
Merchandise Inventories		22,000
Prepaid Insurance		4,500
Total Current Assets		$ 88,700
Computer System:		
At Cost		$ 78,000
Less Accumulated Depreciation		(26,000)
Net		$ 52,000
Total Assets		$140,700

Liabilities and Shareholders' Equity

Accounts Payable		$ 36,000
Dividend Payable		1,800
Salaries Payable		6,500
Taxes Payable		10,000
Advances from Customers		600
Total Liabilities		$ 54,900
Common Stock		$ 40,000
Retained Earnings		45,800
Total Shareholders' Equity		$ 85,800
Total Liabilities and Shareholders' Equity		$140,700

years and an estimated salvage value of $6,000. The company uses the straight-line depreciation method.

(6) The company's computer system has a six-year total expected life and zero expected salvage value.

(7) The company makes all sales on account and recognizes revenue at the time of shipment to customers. During Year 10, the company received $210,000 cash from its customers. The company's accountant reconstructed the Accounts Receivable subsidiary ledger, the detailed record of the amount owed to the company by each customer. It showed that customers owed the company $51,000 on December 31, Year 10. A close examination revealed that $1,400 of the cash received from customers during Year 10 applies to merchandise that the company will not ship until Year 11. Also, $600 of the cash received from customers during Year 9 applies to merchandise not shipped to customers until Year 10.

(8) The company paid $85,000 in cash to employees during Year 10. Of this amount, $6,500 relates to services that employees performed during Year 9, and $4,000 relates to services that employees will perform during Year 11. Employees performed the remainder of the services during Year 10. On December 31,

Year 10, the company owes employees $1,300 for services performed during the last several days of Year 10.

(9) The company paid $27,000 in cash for property and income taxes during Year 10. Of this amount, $10,000 relates to income taxes applicable to Year 9, and $3,000 relates to property taxes applicable to Year 11. The company owes $4,000 in income taxes on December 31, Year 10.

(10) The company entered into a contract with a management consulting firm for consulting services. The total contract price is $48,000. The contract requires the company to pay the first installment of $12,000 cash on January 1, Year 11, and the company intends to do so. The consulting firm had performed 10 percent of the estimated total consulting services under the contract by December 31, Year 10.

Prepare an income statement for Year 10 and a balance sheet on December 31, Year 10. (*Hint:* Set up T-accounts for each of the accounts on the December 31, Year 9, balance sheet, and enter the appropriate amounts at that time. Next, enter the information for each of the 10 items, listed above, in the T-accounts, adding income statement and additional balance sheet accounts as needed.)

49. **Reconstructing the income statement and balance sheet.** Computer Needs, Inc., operates a retail store that sells computer hardware and software. It began operations on January 2, Year 8, and operated successfully during its first year, generating net income of $8,710 and ending the year with $15,600 in its bank account. Exhibit 3.25 presents an income statement for Year 8, and Exhibit 3.26 presents a balance sheet as of the end of Year 8.

As Year 9 progressed, the owners and managers of Computer Needs, Inc., felt that they were doing even better. Sales seemed to be running ahead of Year 8, and customers were always in the store. Unfortunately, a freak lightning storm hit the store on December 31, Year 9, and completely destroyed the computer on which Computer Needs, Inc., kept its records. It now faces the dilemma of figuring how much income it generated during Year 9 in order to assess its operating performance and figure out how much income taxes it owes for the year.

You are asked to prepare an income statement for Year 9 and a balance sheet at the end of Year 9. To assist in this effort, you obtain the following information.

(1) The bank at which Computer Needs, Inc., maintains its account provided a summary of the transactions during Year 9, as shown in Exhibit 3.27.

EXHIBIT 3.25	COMPUTER NEEDS, INC. Income Statement For the Year Ended December 31, Year 8 (Problem 49)

Sales	$152,700
Cost of Goods Sold	(116,400)
Selling and Administrative Expenses	(17,400)
Depreciation	(2,800)
Interest	(4,000)
Income Taxes	(3,390)
Net Income	$ 8,710

EXHIBIT 3.26	COMPUTER NEEDS, INC. Balance Sheet December 31, Year 8 (Problem 49)

Assets

Cash	$ 15,600
Accounts Receivable	32,100
Inventories	46,700
Prepayments	1,500
Total Current Assets	$ 95,900
Property, Plant and Equipment:	
At Cost	$ 59,700
Less Accumulated Depreciation	(2,800)
Net	$ 56,900
Total Assets	$152,800

Liabilities and Shareholders' Equity

Accounts Payable—Merchandise Suppliers	$ 37,800
Income Tax Payable	3,390
Other Current Liabilities	2,900
Total Current Liabilities	$ 44,090
Mortgage Payable	50,000
Total Liabilities	$ 94,090
Common Stock	$ 50,000
Retained Earnings	8,710
Total Shareholders' Equity	$ 58,710
Total Liabilities and Shareholders' Equity	$152,800

EXHIBIT 3.27	COMPUTER NEEDS, INC. Analysis of Changes in Bank Accounts For the Year Ended December 31, Year 9 (Problem 49)

Balance, January 1, Year 9	$ 15,600
Receipts:	
Cash from Cash Sales	37,500
Checks Received from Third-Party Credit Cards and Customers	151,500
Disbursements:	
To Merchandise Suppliers	(164,600)
To Employees and Other Providers of Selling and Administrative Activities	(21,000)
To U.S. Government for Income Taxes for Year 8	(3,390)
To Bank for Interest ($4,000) and Principal on Mortgage ($800)	(4,800)
To Supplier of Equipment	(6,000)
Balance, December 31, Year 9	$ 4,810

(2) Collections received during January, Year 10, from third-party credit card companies and from customers for sales made during Year 9 totaled $40,300. This is your best estimate of accounts receivable outstanding on December 31, Year 9.

(3) A physical inventory of merchandise was taken on January 1, Year 10. Using current catalogs from suppliers, you estimate that the merchandise has an approximate cost of $60,700.

(4) Computer Needs, Inc., had paid its annual insurance premium on October 1, Year 9 (included in the amounts in Exhibit 3.27). You learn that $1,800 of the insurance premium applies to coverage during Year 10.

(5) Based on depreciation claimed during Year 8 and new equipment purchased during Year 9, you approximate that depreciation expense for Year 9 was $3,300.

(6) Bills received from merchandise suppliers during January, Year 10, totaled $45,300. This is your best estimate of accounts payable outstanding to these suppliers on December 31, Year 9.

(7) Other Current Liabilities represent amounts payable to employees and other providers of selling and administrative services. Other Current Liabilities as of December 31, Year 9, total $1,200.

   a. Prepare an income statement for Computer Needs, Inc., for Year 9 and a balance sheet on December 31, Year 9. The income tax rate is 28 percent. (*Hint:* Set up T-accounts, enter the balance sheet amounts on December 31, Year 8, and then enter the information in items (1) to (7) above.)

   b. How well did Computer Needs, Inc., perform during Year 9?

50. **Interpreting common-size income statements.** Exhibit 3.28 presents common-size income statements for the three leading firms in the office supplies industry: Office Depot, Office Max, and Staples. Exhibit 3.28 also indicates the growth rate in combined sales for the three firms for each year and the share of combined sales realized by each of the three firms.

   a. Staples has the highest net-income-to-sales percentage of the three firms. Identify the expense-to-sales percentages that give Staples this advantage, and suggest reasons for them.

   b. Office Depot and Office Max have similar net-income-to-sales percentages, but the individual expense-to-sales percentages differ. Identify the expense-to-sales percentages that differ, and suggest reasons for the differences.

EXHIBIT 3.28	Income Statement Data for Office Products Retailers (Problem 50)

Common-Size Income Statements

	Office Depot		Office Max		Staples	
	Year 7	Year 8	Year 7	Year 8	Year 7	Year 8
Sales	100.0%	100.0%	100.0%	100.0%	100.0%	100.0%
Cost of Goods Sold	(77.5)	(76.6)	(78.3)	(76.9)	(76.2)	(75.9)
Gross Profit	22.5%	23.4%	21.7%	23.1%	23.8%	24.1%
Selling and Administrative						
Expense	(18.5)	(18.9)	(18.1)	(19.0)	(18.6)	(18.8)
Interest Expense	(.5)	(.6)	—	(.2)	(.8)	(1.2)
Net Income before Taxes	3.5%	3.9%	3.6%	3.9%	4.4%	4.1%
Income Tax Expense	(1.4)	(1.5)	(1.4)	(1.5)	(1.7)	(1.6)
Net Income	2.1%	2.4%	2.2%	2.4%	2.7%	2.5%

	Year 6	Year 7	Year 8
Percentage of Combined Sales for the Three Firms			
Office Depot	48.6%	45.9%	42.9%
Office Max	23.2	24.1	24.0
Staples	28.1	30.0	33.1
	100.0%	100.0%	100.0%
Growth Rate In Combined Sales of Three Firms	34.7%	21.0%	18.5%
Combined Sales (in millions)	$10,945	$13,243	$15,692

STATEMENT OF CASH FLOWS: REPORTING THE EFFECTS OF OPERATING, INVESTING, AND FINANCING ACTIVITIES ON CASH FLOWS

1. Understand why using the accrual basis of accounting to prepare the balance sheet and income statement creates the need for a statement of cash flows.
2. Understand the types of transactions that result in cash flows from operating, investing, and financing activities.
3. Develop an ability to prepare a statement of cash flows from a comparative balance sheet and income statement.
4. Develop an ability to analyze the statement of cash flows, including the relation among cash flows from operating, investing, and financing activities for various businesses.

What do Boston Market, Montgomery Ward, and United Press International have in common? Each of these firms filed for bankruptcy during the early to mid-1990s. Yet each of these firms operated profitably for most of the years preceding its bankruptcy filing. The bankruptcies occurred because these firms were unable to generate sufficient cash to cover operating costs, debt service costs, and capital expenditures. This chapter discusses the statement of cash flows, which reports the impact of a firm's operating, investing, and financing activities on cash flows during an accounting period. The FASB requires that the statement of cash flows explain changes in cash and cash equivalents. Cash equivalents represent short-term, highly liquid investments in which a firm has temporarily placed excess cash. Throughout this text, we use the term *cash flows* to refer to cash and cash equivalents.[1]

OVERVIEW OF THE STATEMENT OF CASH FLOWS

Exhibit 4.1 presents a statement of cash flows for Wal-Mart Stores for three recent years. Note the following aspects of this statement.

---

[1]See Financial Accounting Standards Board (FASB), *Statement of Financial Accounting Standards No. 95,* "Statement of Cash Flows," 1987.

EXHIBIT 4.1	WAL-MART STORES Statement of Cash Flows (amounts in millions)		

	Year 7	Year 8	Year 9
Operations			
Net Income	$ 2,681	$ 2,740	$ 3,056
Depreciation	1,070	1,304	1,463
(Increase) Decrease in Receivables	(84)	(61)	(58)
(Increase) Decrease in Inventories	(3,171)	(2,077)	99
(Increase) Decrease in Other Current Assets	(147)	(77)	38
Increase (Decrease) in Accounts Payable	1,914	448	1,208
Increase (Decrease) in Other Current Liabilities	643	106	124
Cash Flow from Operations	$ 2,906	$ 2,383	$ 5,930
Investing			
Fixed Assets Acquired	$ (3,734)	$ (3,566)	$ (2,643)
Other Investing Transactions	(58)	234	575
Cash Flow from Investing	$ (3,792)	$ (3,332)	$ (2,068)
Financing			
Increase in Short-term Borrowing	$ 220	$ 660	0
Increase in Long-term Borrowing	1,250	1,004	$ 632
Issue of Capital Stock	0	0	0
Decrease in Short-term Borrowing	0	0	(2,458)
Decrease in Long-term Borrowing	(107)	(207)	(615)
Acquisition of Capital Stock	0	0	0
Dividends	(391)	(458)	(481)
Other Financing Transactions	(61)	(12)	(140)
Cash Flow from Financing	$ 911	$ 987	$ (3,062)
Change in Cash	$ 25	$ 38	$ 800
Cash—Beginning of Year	20	45	83
Cash—End of Year	$ 45	$ 83	$ 883

THE STATEMENT EXPLAINS THE REASONS FOR THE CHANGE IN CASH BETWEEN BALANCE SHEET DATES

The last two lines of the statement of cash flows report the amount of cash on Wal-Mart's balance sheet at the beginning and the end of each year. The remaining lines show the inflows and outflows of cash during the year, which explain the net change between the two balance sheet dates. Thus, the statements of cash flows reports flows, or changes over time, whereas the balance sheet reports amounts at a moment in time.

THE STATEMENT CLASSIFIES THE REASONS FOR THE CHANGE IN CASH AS AN OPERATING, INVESTING, OR FINANCING ACTIVITY

Various inflows and outflows of cash during the year appear in the statement of cash flows in one of three categories: operating, investing, or financing. Figure 4.1 presents the major types of cash flows, which the following sections describe.

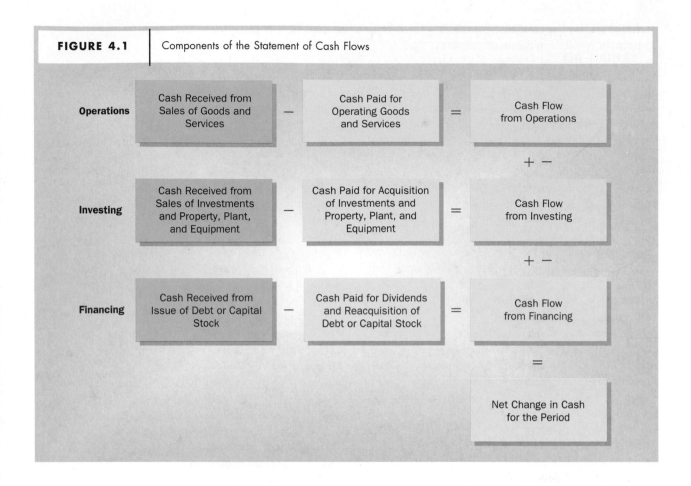

FIGURE 4.1 | Components of the Statement of Cash Flows

Operations Selling goods and providing services are the most important ways for a financially healthy company to generate cash. Assessed over several years, the cash flow from operations indicates the extent to which operating activities have generated more cash than they have used. A firm can use the excess **cash flow from operations** to acquire buildings and equipment, pay dividends, retire long-term debt, and conduct other investing and financing activities.

Investing The second section of the statement of cash flows shows the amount of **cash flows from investing activities.** The acquisition of noncurrent assets, particularly property, plant, and equipment, usually represents a major ongoing use of cash. A firm must replace such assets as they wear out, and it must acquire additional noncurrent assets if it is to grow. A firm obtains part of the cash needed to acquire noncurrent assets from sales of existing noncurrent assets. Such cash inflows seldom, however, cover the entire cost of new acquisitions. Firms not experiencing rapid growth can usually finance capital expenditures with cash flow from operations. Firms growing rapidly must often borrow funds or issue common stock to finance their acquisitions of noncurrent assets.

Financing A firm obtains cash from short- and long-term borrowing and from issues of common or preferred stock. It uses cash to pay dividends to shareholders, to repay short- or long-term borrowing, and to reacquire shares of outstanding common or preferred stock. The amount of **cash flow from financing activities** is the third major component reported in the statement of cash flows.

Refer to Exhibit 4.1. Wal-Mart reported positive cash flow from operations in each of the three years. In Year 7 and Year 8, however, cash flow from operations was less than the cash outflows needed to acquire additional property, plant, and equipment. Although Wal-Mart is profitable and generating positive cash flows from operations, its rapid expansion of new stores required still more cash. The financing section of the statement of cash flows shows that Wal-Mart engaged in short- and long-term borrowing to make up the difference. During Year 9, cash flow from operations increased significantly, whereas cash expenditures on new stores declined. This pattern is typical of a firm experiencing a slowdown or decline in its rate of growth. Wal-Mart used the excess cash primarily to repay short-term debt.

Cash flows do not always fit unambiguously into only one of these three categories of cash flows. For example, the accountant might conceivably classify cash received from interest and dividend revenues generated by investments in securities as an operating activity. The logic for this treatment is that interest and dividends appear as revenues in the income statement, the financial statement that reports the results of a firm's operations. Alternatively, cash received from interest and dividends might appear as an investing activity. The logic for this treatment is that cash flows related to the purchase and sale of investments in securities appear as investing activities. The Financial Accounting Standards Board's *Statement of Financial Accounting Standards No. 95* requires firms to classify the receipt of cash from interest and dividend revenues as an operating activity but the cash related to the purchase and sale of investments in securities as an investing activity.[2]

Similar ambiguities arise with interest expense on debt. Should the cash outflow for interest expense appear as an operating activity (to achieve consistency with its inclusion in the income statement as an expense) or as a financing activity (to achieve consistency with the classification of debt issues and retirements as a financing activity)? FASB *SFAS No. 95* requires that firms classify interest expense as an operating activity but the issue or redemption of debt as a financing activity.[3] Dividends that a firm pays to its shareholders appear, however, as a financing activity.[4] The classification of interest expense on debt as an operating activity and dividends paid on common or preferred stock as a financing activity appears inconsistent. The FASB's likely rationale is that accountants treat interest as an expense in computing net income, whereas dividends represent a distribution of assets generated by net income, not an expense reducing net income.

Similar ambiguities arise in classifying purchases and sales of marketable securities (treated as investing, not operating, activities) and increases and decreases in short-term bank borrowings (treated as financing, not operating, activities). Later chapters discuss these items more fully.

Firms sometimes engage in investing and financing transactions that do not directly involve cash. For example, a firm may acquire a building by assuming a mortgage obligation or might exchange a tract of land for equipment. Holders of a firm's debt might convert the debt into common stock. These transactions do not appear in the statement of cash flows as an investing or a financing transaction because they are not factors in explaining the change in cash. Firms must disclose noncash investing and financing activities in a separate schedule or note.[5]

---

[2]Ibid., para. 16, 17, 22.

[3]Ibid., para. 19, 20, 23.

[4]Ibid., para. 20.

[5]Ibid., para. 32.

THE STATEMENT RECONCILES NET INCOME WITH CASH FLOW FROM OPERATIONS

The first line in the operating section of the statement of cash flows shows the amount of net income for each year from the income statement. Accountants use the accrual basis of accounting to compute net income, as discussed in Chapter 3. Firms typically recognize revenues at the time of sale, or delivery, of products and then attempt to match expenses with revenues in measuring net income. The receipt of cash from customers may precede, coincide with, or occur after the time of sale. Thus, cash receipts from customers during any particular accounting period will likely differ from the amount of sales revenue. Likewise, firms might disburse cash to suppliers, employees, and other providers of goods and services prior to, concurrent with, or subsequent to the recognition of expenses. Cash outflows for operating costs during any particular accounting period will likely differ from the amount of expenses appearing in the income statement. The operating section of the statement of cash flows shows the adjustments required to convert net income, measured on an accrual basis, to the amount of net cash flow generated from operations during the period.

Refer to Exhibit 4.1. Wal-Mart shows an addition to net income each year for depreciation. Depreciation appears as an expense on the income statement because using a portion of the service potential of buildings and equipment is a necessary cost of operating retail stores. The events causing the firm to recognize depreciation expense, however, consume not cash but other assets (buildings, equipment). The firm used cash sometime previously in acquiring the fixed assets. Wal-Mart debits Depreciation Expense and credits Accumulated Depreciation each year. Subtracting depreciation expense in arriving at the amount of net income on the first line and then adding the same amount on the second line of the statement of cash flows results in a zero net effect on cash flow from operations. Thus, the adjustment for depreciation removes a noncash expense.

Another large adjustment for Wal-Mart is for the change in inventories. Net income on the first line includes a subtraction for the cost of goods sold. As Wal-Mart increases the number of its stores, purchases of inventories likely exceed the cost of goods sold. Thus, the cash outflow for inventories each year likely exceeds the cost of goods sold. Wal-Mart shows the additional cash outflow to build inventories as a subtraction from net income when computing cash flow from operations. Later sections of this chapter discuss these and other adjustments to net income to compute cash flow from operations.

Wal-Mart's presentation of cash flow from operations follows the **indirect method,** meaning that cash flow from operations is the net result of adjusting net income for noncash items. Most firms report cash flow from operations using the indirect method. An acceptable alternative presentation, called the **direct method,** lists the cash received from customers and the cash expenditures to various providers of goods and services. Cash flow from operations is identical under the two methods. Students sometimes experience difficulty understanding the logic of the adjustments under the indirect method on their first exposure to the statement of cash flows, whereas the direct method is more understandable. We include discussion of both the indirect and the direct methods in this chapter.

PROBLEM 4.1 FOR SELF-STUDY

Classifying cash flows by type of activity.   Indicate whether each of the following transactions of the current period would appear as an operating, investing, or financing activity in the statement of cash flows. If any transaction would not appear in the statement of cash flows, suggest the reason.

a. Disbursement of $96,900 to merchandise suppliers.

b. Receipt of $200,000 from issuing common stock.

c. Receipt of $49,200 from customers for sales made this period.

d. Receipt of $22,700 from customers this period for sales made last period.

e. Receipt of $1,800 from a customer for goods the firm will deliver next period.

f. Disbursement of $16,000 for interest expense on debt.

g. Disbursement of $40,000 to acquire land.

h. Issue of common stock with market value of $60,000 to acquire land.

i. Disbursement of $25,300 as compensation to employees for services rendered this period.

j. Disbursement of $7,900 to employees for services rendered last period but not yet paid for.

k. Disbursement of $53,800 for a patent purchased from its inventor.

l. Acquisition of a building by issuing a note payable to a bank.

m. Disbursement of $19,300 as a dividend to shareholders.

n. Receipt of $12,000 from the sale of equipment that originally cost $20,000 and had $8,000 of accumulated depreciation at the time of sale.

o. Disbursement of $100,000 to redeem bonds at maturity.

p. Disbursement of $40,000 to acquire shares of IBM common stock.

q. Receipt of $200 in dividends from IBM relating to the shares of common stock acquired in transaction **p.** above.

PREPARING THE STATEMENT OF CASH FLOWS

Firms could prepare their statement of cash flows directly from entries in their cash account. To do so would require them to classify each transaction affecting cash as an operating, investing, or financing activity. As the number of transactions affecting cash increases, however, this approach become cumbersome. Most firms design their accounting systems to accumulate the information needed to prepare income statements and balance sheets. They then use a work sheet at the end of the period to transform information from the income statement and balance sheet into a statement of cash flows.

We illustrate two approaches for preparing the statement of cash flows in this chapter. One uses a columnar work sheet and serves well for relatively simple situations involving few transactions. The columnar work sheet approach also enhances an understanding of this financial statement as you encounter it for the first time. The other approach, illustrated later in the chapter, uses a T-account work sheet. This approach builds on the use of T-accounts from Chapters 2 and 3. It works well as the number and the complexity of transactions affecting a particular account increase. The benefits of using the T-account work sheet will become clearer as we explore more-complicated accounting topics in later chapters.

ALGEBRAIC FORMULATION

Fundamental to the preparation of a statement of cash flows is an understanding of how changes in cash relate to changes in noncash accounts. Reexamine the accounting equation, using the following notation:

C—cash

N$A—noncash assets

L—liabilities

SE—shareholders' equity

Δ—the change in an item; it may be positive (an increase) or negative (a decrease) from the beginning of a period to the end of the period.

The accounting equation states:

$$\text{Assets} = \text{Liabilities} + \text{Shareholders' Equity}$$

$$C + N\$A = \quad L \quad + \quad SE \qquad \text{Equation (1), Balance Sheet Equation}$$

Furthermore, this equation must be true for balance sheets constructed at both the start of the period and the end of the period. If the start-of-the-period and end-of-the-period balance sheets maintain the accounting equation, then the following equation must also be valid:

$$\Delta C + \Delta N\$A = \Delta L + \Delta SE \qquad \text{Equation (2), Balance Sheet Change Equation}$$

Rearranging terms in this equation, we obtain the equation for changes in cash:

$$\Delta C = \Delta L + \Delta SE - \Delta N\$A \qquad \text{Equation (3), Cash Change Equation}$$

The left-hand side of the **Cash Change Equation** (3) represents the change in cash. The right-hand side of the equation, reflecting changes in all noncash accounts, must also net to the change in cash. The equation states that the increases in cash (left-hand side) equal the increases in liabilities plus the increases in shareholders' equity less the increases in noncash assets (right-hand side). For example, a loan from a bank or other lender increases cash and increases a liability. The issue of common stock increases cash and increases shareholders' equity. The purchase of equipment decreases cash and increases noncash assets. Increases in noncash assets carry a negative sign on the right-hand side of the equation. *Thus, we can identify the causes of the change in cash by studying the changes in noncash accounts and classifying those changes as operating, investing, and financial transactions.* These activities underlie both the columnar work sheet and the T-account work sheet discussed in subsequent sections.

DATA FOR ILLUSTRATIONS

To illustrate the preparation of the statement of cash flows in this chapter, we use information for Solinger Electric Corporation for Year 4. Exhibit 4.2 presents the balance sheet at the beginning and end of Year 4. Exhibit 4.3 presents the income statement for Year 4. Solinger Electric Corporation declared and paid $7,000 in dividends during Year 4.

ILLUSTRATION OF COLUMNAR WORKSHEET

The upper panel of Exhibit 4.4 presents a **columnar work sheet** for the preparation of the statement of cash flows for Solinger Electric Company. This work sheet involves the following steps.

Step 1   Compute the change in each balance sheet account between the beginning and the end of the year. Enter the changes in the noncash balance sheet accounts in the first column of the work sheet using the following rules regarding signs:

- Increases in noncash assets reduce cash and therefore appear with negative signs.
- Decreases in noncash assets increase cash and therefore appear with positive signs.

Repeated for convenience:

$$\Delta C = \Delta L + \Delta SE - \Delta N\$A \qquad \text{Equation (3), Cash Change Equation}$$

EXHIBIT 4.2	SOLINGER ELECTRIC CORPORATION Comparative Balance Sheets for December 31, Year 3 and 4

	December 31	
	Year 3	Year 4
ASSETS		
Current Assets		
Cash	$ 30,000	$ 6,000
Accounts Receivable	20,000	55,000
Merchandise Inventory	40,000	50,000
Total Current Assets	$ 90,000	$111,000
Noncurrent Assets		
Buildings and Equipment (Cost)	$100,000	$225,000
Accumulated Depreciation	(30,000)	(40,000)
Total Noncurrent Assets	$ 70,000	$185,000
Total Assets	$160,000	$296,000
EQUITIES		
Current Liabilities		
Accounts Payable—Merchandise Suppliers	$ 30,000	$ 50,000
Accounts Payable—Other Suppliers	10,000	12,000
Salaries Payable	5,000	6,000
Total Current Liabilities	$ 45,000	$ 68,000
Noncurrent Liabilities		
Bonds Payable	$ 0	$100,000
Shareholders' Equity		
Common Stock	$100,000	$100,000
Retained Earnings	15,000	28,000
Total Shareholders' Equity	$115,000	$128,000
Total Equities	$160,000	$296,000

- Increases in liability and shareholders' equity accounts increase cash and appear with positive signs.
- Decreases in liability and shareholders' equity accounts decrease cash and appear with negative signs.

Enter the net change in cash on the last line of the columnar work sheet. As the equation for changes in balance sheet accounts above shows, the net change in noncash accounts (right-hand side of the equation) should equal the change in cash. The net

EXHIBIT 4.3

SOLINGER ELECTRIC CORPORATION
Income Statement
For Year 4

Sales Revenue	$125,000
Cost of Goods Sold	(60,000)
Depreciation Expense	(10,000)
Salary Expense	(20,000)
Interest Expense	(4,000)
Other Expenses	(11,000)
Net Income	$ 20,000

EXHIBIT 4.4

SOLINGER ELECTRIC CORPORATION
Columnar Work Sheet for Preparation of the Statement of Cash Flows
For Year 4

	Balance Sheet Changes	Operations	Investing	Financing
(Increase) Decrease in Assets				
(1) Accounts Receivable	$ (35,000)	$(35,000)		
(2) Merchandise Inventories	(10,000)	(10,000)		
(3) Buildings and Equipment	(125,000)		$(125,000)	
(4) Accumulated Depreciation	10,000	10,000		
Increase (Decrease) in Liabilities And Shareholders' Equity				
(5) Accounts Payable—Merchandise Suppliers	$ 20,000	$ 20,000		
(6) Accounts Payable—Other Suppliers	2,000	2,000		
(7) Salaries Payable	1,000	1,000		
(8) Bonds Payable	100,000			$100,000
(9) Common Stock	—			—
(10) Retained Earnings	13,000	20,000		(7,000)
(11) Increase (Decrease) in Cash	$ (24,000)	$ 8,000	$(125,000)	$ 93,000

	Income Statement +	Operating Balance Sheet Changes =	Cash Receipts −	Cash Disbursements =	Cash Flow from Operations
Revenues	$125,000	$(35,000)	$90,000		
Cost of Goods Sold	(60,000)	(10,000)			
		20,000		$(50,000)	
Depreciation Expense	(10,000)	10,000		—	
Salary Expense	(20,000)	1,000		(19,000)	
Other Expenses	(11,000)	2,000		(9,000)	
Interest Expense	(4,000)			(4,000)	
Net Income	$ 20,000 +	$(12,000) =	$90,000 −	$ 82,000 =	$8,000

Repeated for convenience:

$$\Delta C = \Delta L + \Delta SE - \Delta N\$A \qquad \text{Equation (3), Cash Change Equation}$$

---

change in noncash balance sheet accounts of a negative $24,000 equals the decrease in cash of $24,000 for the year.

Step 2 Classify the change in each balance sheet account as an operating, investing, or financing activity and enter it in the appropriate column of the work sheet using the same sign as in the first column. Most of the changes in noncash accounts studied to this point in the book affect only one of these three categories of activities. Retained earnings, however, increases for net income (an operating activity) and decreases for dividends (a financing activity) and appears in two columns. We discuss below the adjustment appearing on each line of the columnar work sheet. Because the operating section of the statement of cash flows under the indirect method begins with net income (see Exhibit 4.1 for Wal-Mart), we begin our discussion with the change in retained earnings on line **(10)**.

Line (10) Retained earnings increased by $13,000 during Year 4. Exhibit 4.3 indicates that Solinger Electric Corporation generated net income of $20,000. It declared and paid dividends of $7,000. We enter the increase in retained earnings from net income in the Operations column as a positive amount and the dividend in the Financing column as a negative amount. The presumption at this point is that Solinger Electric Corporation generated cash flow from operations equal to net income. As we discussed above, however, we must adjust net income measured on an accrual basis for the noncash effects of revenues and expenses. We discuss these adjustments next.

Line (1) Accounts receivable increase each year for sales made on account and decrease for collections from customers. By entering net income on line **(10)** in the Operations column, we presume that Solinger Electric Corporation received cash from customers equal to sales revenue. If accounts receivable increased during the year, the firm collected less cash than sales made on account. We must therefore enter the increase in accounts receivable as a negative amount in the Operations column.

Line (2) Merchandise inventories increase each year for purchases of inventories and decrease for the cost of goods sold. When we enter net income on line **(10),** we presume that Solinger Electric Corporation used cash to purchase inventory in an amount equal to the cost of goods sold. Because the firm purchased more inventory than it sold, we must subtract the increase in inventories to show the additional cash outflow required. We cannot conclude, however, that Solinger Electric Corporation actually paid for the additional inventory in cash during Year 4. We must first consider the change in accounts payable to merchandise suppliers, which we consider when discussing line **(5).**

Line (3) The building and equipment account (at cost) increased $125,000 during the year. This account increases for new buildings and equipment acquired and decreases for old buildings and equipment sold. The accounting records of Solinger Electric Corporation will provide detailed information about the increases and decreases during the year. We have no indication that the firm sold buildings and equipment during Year 4.

One such indication would be the disclosure of a gain or loss on sale of buildings and equipment in the income statement. We therefore assume that the firm must have purchased new buildings and equipment costing $125,000. We enter this amount as a cash outflow in the Investing column.

Line (4)   The accumulated depreciation account increased $10,000 during the year. Recall that this account normally has a credit balance and shows the depreciation recognized to date on buildings and equipment still in use. This account increases for depreciation recognized during the current period on buildings and equipment in service. It decreases for the accumulated depreciation on any buildings and equipment sold during the year and therefore removed from the accounting records. The discussion for line **(3)** suggests that Solinger Electric Corporation did not sell buildings and equipment during Year 4. The increase in the accumulated depreciation account must therefore represent depreciation expense for the year. We enter this amount as an addition in the Operations column. As an earlier section discusses, depreciation is an expense that did not use cash *during the current period*. The firm used cash when it acquired the buildings and equipment. When it did so, it entered the cash outflow in the Investing column (as we did on line **(3)** above for acquisition during Year 4). Because depreciation expense reduces net income on line **(10)** but does not use cash, we add back the depreciation to net income when computing cash flow from operations. The addback offsets the subtraction and shows that depreciation has a zero net effect on cash flow from operations.

Line (5)   Accounts payable to merchandise suppliers increases each period for new purchases on account and decreases for cash payments made to merchandise suppliers. On line **(2)** we converted the cost of goods sold subtracted in computing net income to the amount of purchases of merchandise during the year. We presumed above that Solinger Electric Corporation paid for all of these purchases during the year. The increase in accounts payable indicates that the firm did not pay for the full amount of purchases. We thus enter the increase in accounts payable as a positive amount in the Operations column. The following summarizes the adjustments made for merchandise:

Cost of Goods Sold (from the Income Statement)	$(60,000)
Less Increase in Merchandise Inventories	(10,000)
= Purchases of Merchandise Inventories	$(70,000)
Plus Increase in Accounts Payable for Merchandise	20,000
= Cash Payments Made for Purchases of Merchandise Inventories	$ 50,000

Line (6)   Accounts payable to other suppliers increases for goods (other than merchandise) and services received on account and decreases for cash payment made. The income statement in Exhibit 4.3 indicates that other expenses totaled $11,000 during Year 4. The increase in accounts payable to other suppliers means that Solinger Electric Corporation received $2,000 more in goods and services than payments made to these suppliers. Thus, we enter the $2,000 increase in accounts payable to other suppliers in the Operations column. Cash payments to these suppliers therefore total $9,000 (= −$11,000 + $2,000).

> *Repeated for convenience:*
>
> $$\Delta C = \Delta L + \Delta SE - \Delta N\$A \qquad \text{Equation (3), Cash Change Equation}$$

Line (7) Salaries payable increased by $1,000, indicating that Solinger Electric Corporation paid $1,000 less in salaries than the amount of salary expense. The $1,000 addition in the Operations column converts the salary expense of $20,000 subtracted in computing net income—line **(10)**—to cash payments made to employees of $19,000 (= −$20,000 + $1,000).

Line (8) The Bonds Payable account increases for new bonds issued and decreases for outstanding bonds redeemed. We have no evidence that Solinger Electric Corporation redeemed bonds during Year 4. Thus, we assume that it issued new bonds for $100,000. We enter the $100,000 in the Financing column.

Line (9) The Common Stock account did not change during the year. It is possible that transactions occurred affecting this account but that their net effect was zero. Lacking information regarding any such transactions, we assume that Solinger Electric Corporation made no entries in this account during the year.

Step 3 The final step in the preparation of the columnar work sheet is to sum the entries in the Operations, Investing, and Financing columns and net the three sums to ensure that they equal the net change in cash. The reconciliation is as follows:

Cash Flow from Operations	$ 8,000
Cash Flow from Investing	(125,000)
Cash Flow from Financing	93,000
Net Change in Cash	$ (24,000)

The columnar work sheet provides the information needed to prepare the statement of cash flows. Exhibit 4.5 presents the statement of cash flows for Solinger Electric Corporation for Year 4. The presentation of cash flow from operations follows the indirect method, starting with net income and then converting it to cash flow from operations. Cash flow from operations of $8,000 was less than net income of $20,000 primarily because cash collections from customers were less than sales revenue during the year. Cash flow from operations was not sufficient to finance the acquisition of buildings and equipment. The firm incurred long-term debt to finance these capital expenditures. As the discussion in Chapter 2 makes clear, firms tend to use long-term financing when acquiring long-term assets.

EXHIBIT 4.5	SOLINGER ELECTRIC CORPORATION Statement of Cash Flows for Year 4 Indirect Method

Operations

Net Income	$ 20,000	
Additions:		
Depreciation Expense Not Using Cash	10,000	
Increased Accounts Payable:		
To Suppliers of Merchandise	20,000	
To Other Suppliers	2,000	
Increased Salaries Payable	1,000	
Subtractions:		
Increased Accounts Receivable	(35,000)	
Increased Merchandise Inventory	(10,000)	
Cash Flow from Operations		$ 8,000
Investing		
Acquisition of Buildings and Equipment		(125,000)
Financing		
Dividends Paid	$ (7,000)	
Proceeds from Long-term Bonds Issued	100,000	
Cash Flow from Financing		93,000
Net Change in Cash for Year		$ (24,000)
Cash, January 1, Year 4		30,000
Cash, December 31, Year 4		$ 6,000

PROBLEM   4 . 2   FOR   SELF - STUDY

Preparing a columnar work sheet for a statement of cash flows. Exhibit 4.6 presents a comparative balance sheet for Robbie Corporation as of December 31, Year 1 and Year 2. During Year 2 the firm sold no plant and equipment. It declared and paid dividends of $2,000. Prepare a columnar work sheet for the preparation of a statement of cash flows. Use the format shown in the upper panel of Exhibit 4.4.

EXTENSION OF THE COLUMNAR WORK SHEET

Although most firms present the operating section of their statements of cash flows using the indirect method, students often find the presentation confusing on initial exposure. The lower panel of Exhibit 4.4 shows the computation of cash flow from operations using the direct method. This analysis involves the following steps.

Step 1   List the revenue and expense accounts from the income statement and enter their amounts for the year in the first column.

Repeated for convenience:

$$\Delta C = \Delta L + \Delta SE - \Delta N\$A \qquad \text{Equation (3), Cash Change Equation}$$

EXHIBIT 4.6	ROBBIE CORPORATION Comparative Balance Sheet December 31, Year 1 and Year 2 (all dollar amounts in thousands) (Problem 4.2 for Self-Study)

	December 31			December 31	
	Year 1	**Year 2**		**Year 1**	**Year 2**
ASSETS			**LIABILITIES AND SHAREHOLDERS' EQUITY**		
Current Assets			**Current Liabilities**		
Cash	$10	$ 25	Accounts Payable	$30	$ 37
Accounts Receivable	15	22	Total Current Liabilities	$30	$ 37
Merchandise Inventories	20	18	**Long-Term Debt**		
Total Current Assets	$45	$ 65	Bonds Payable	10	18
Noncurrent Assets			Total Liabilities	$40	$ 55
Property, Plant, and Equipment	$50	$ 66	**Shareholders' Equity**		
Less Accumulated Depreciation	(25)	(31)	Common Stock	$10	$ 20
Total Property, Plant, and			Retained Earnings	20	25
Equipment	$25	$ 35	Total Shareholders' Equity	$30	$ 45
Total Assets	$70	$100	Total Liabilities and Shareholder's Equity	$70	$100

Step 2   For each of the work sheet entries in the Operations column in the upper panel of Exhibit 4.4, identify the revenue or expense account to which it most closely relates. Enter the amount, using the same sign as above, in the second column in the lower panel, labeled Operating Balance Sheet Changes. We discuss each adjustment next.

Change in Accounts Receivable   Accounts receivable on the balance sheet relate to sales revenue on the income statement. The increase in accounts receivable means that Solinger Electric Corporation collected $35,000 less cash than sales on account. Thus, cash receipts from customers during Year 4 totaled $90,000 (= $125,000 − $35,000).

Change in Merchandise Inventories and Accounts Payable— Merchandise Suppliers   Merchandise inventory on the balance sheet relates to cost of goods sold on the income statement. The increase in inventories indicates, as we discussed above, that Solinger Electric Corporation purchased more merchandise inventories than it sold. Accounts payable to merchandise suppliers also relates to cost of goods sold. The increase in accounts payable to merchandise suppliers means that cash disbursements for purchases were $20,000 less than merchandise purchased during the year. The lower panel of Exhibit 4.4 shows that the firm disbursed $50,000 for merchandise during the year.

Change in Accumulated Depreciation   The change in accumulated depreciation results from the recognition of depreciation expense. This expense does not use cash. Entering depreciation as a positive amount in the second column of Exhibit 4.4 offsets its subtraction as an expense in the first column and shows that depreciation does not affect cash.

Change in Salaries Payable   The change in salaries payable ties to salary expense on the income statement. The increase in salaries payable during the year indicates that Solinger Electric Corporation paid only $19,000 in cash for employee compensation.

Change in Accounts Payable—Other Suppliers   Without more specific information, we must assume that accounts payable to other suppliers links with other expenses on the income statement. Entering the $2,000 increase in accounts payable to other suppliers converts other expenses of $11,000 on the income statement to the $9,000 of cash disbursed during the year.

The third and fourth columns in the lower panel of Exhibit 4.4 provide the information for preparing the operating section of the statement of cash flows following the direct method. Exhibit 4.7 presents the statement of cash flows using the direct method.

EXHIBIT 4.7	SOLINGER ELECTRIC CORPORATION Statement of Cash Flows for Year 4 Direct Method	

Operations		
Cash Receipts from Customers	$ 90,000	
Cash Disbursed to:		
Suppliers of Merchandise	(50,000)	
Employees for Salaries	(19,000)	
Lenders for Interest	(4,000)	
Other Suppliers of Goods and Services	(9,000)	
Cash Flow from Operations		$ 8,000
Investing		
Acquisition of Buildings and Equipment		(125,000)
Financing		
Dividends Paid	$ (7,000)	
Long-term Bonds Issued	100,000	
Cash Flow from Financing		93,000
Net Change in Cash		$(24,000)
Cash, January 1, Year 4		30,000
Cash, December 31, Year 4		$ 6,000

> *Repeated for convenience:*
>
> $$\Delta C = \Delta L + \Delta SE - \Delta N\$A \qquad \text{Equation (3), Cash Change Equation}$$

P R O B L E M   4 . 3   F O R   S E L F - S T U D Y

Computing cash flow from operations using the direct method. Refer to Problem 4.2 for Self-Study. Exhibit 4.6 presents a comparative balance sheet for Robbie Corporation as of December 31, Year 1 and Year 2. Exhibit 4.8 presents an income statement for Robbie Corporation for Year 2. Compute the amount of cash flow from operations using the format shown in the lower panel of Exhibit 4.4.

ILLUSTRATION OF T-ACCOUNT WORK SHEET

The columnar work sheet works well when the change in each balance sheet account affects only one of the three types of activities in the statement of cash flows: operations, investing, or financing. When the change in any particular account affects more than one of these activities, we must study each of the entries in the account during the period and classify it in the appropriate category. The columnar work sheet approach becomes cumbersome for these more-realistic situations. Using the columnar work sheet can also lead to errors and omissions as a consequence of overlooking some portion of the entry for more complex transactions. The T-account work sheet approach for preparing the statement of cash flows, discussed next, provides built-in checks to ensure the full recognition of the effects of each transaction on various accounts. The T-account work sheet is also a direct extension of the T-accounts used in Chapters 2 and 3. The accountant prepares a T-account work sheet, like the columnar work sheet discussed earlier, at the end of the period after preparing the balance sheet and income statement. The work sheet provides the information for preparing the statement of cash flows.

We begin by illustrating the preparation of a T-account work sheet using the same data used thus far in the chapter for Solinger Electric Corporation. We then add some complexities to illustrate the use of the T-account work sheet in a more realistic situation.

EXHIBIT 4.8	ROBBIE CORPORATION Income Statement For Year 2 (all dollar amounts in thousands) (Problem 4.3 for Self-Study)

Sales Revenue	$180
Cost of Goods Sold	(140)
Selling and Administrative Expenses	(25)
Depreciation Expense	(6)
Interest Expense	(2)
Net Income	$ 7

Step 1   Obtain balance sheets for the beginning and end of the period covered by the statement of cash flows. Exhibit 4.2 presents the comparative balance sheets of Solinger Electric Corporation for December 31, Year 3 and Year 4, discussed earlier in the chapter.

Step 2   Prepare a **T-account work sheet.** An example of such a T-account work sheet appears in Exhibit 4.9. The top of the work sheet shows a master T-account titled Cash. Note that this T-account has sections labeled Operations, Investing, and Financing, which we use to classify transactions that affect cash. Enter the beginning and ending amounts of cash in the master T-account. (The beginning and ending amounts of cash for Solinger Electric Corporation are $30,000 and $6,000, respectively.) The number at the top of the T-account is the opening balance; the one at the bottom is the closing balance. The check

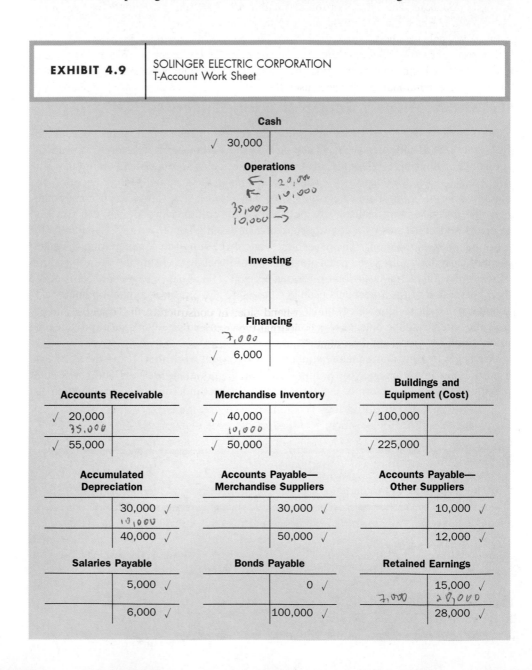

EXHIBIT 4.9	SOLINGER ELECTRIC CORPORATION T-Account Work Sheet

Cash

√ 30,000

Operations

20,000
10,000
35,000
10,000

Investing

Financing

7,000

√ 6,000

Accounts Receivable		**Merchandise Inventory**		**Buildings and Equipment (Cost)**	
√ 20,000		√ 40,000		√ 100,000	
35,000		10,000			
√ 55,000		√ 50,000		√ 225,000	

Accumulated Depreciation		**Accounts Payable— Merchandise Suppliers**		**Accounts Payable— Other Suppliers**	
	30,000 √		30,000 √		10,000 √
	10,000				
	40,000 √		50,000 √		12,000 √

Salaries Payable		**Bonds Payable**		**Retained Earnings**	
	5,000 √		0 √		15,000 √
				7,000	20,000
	6,000 √		100,000 √		28,000 √

Repeated for convenience:

$$\Delta C = \Delta L + \Delta SE - \Delta N\$A \qquad \text{Equation (3), Cash Change Equation}$$

---

marks indicate that the figures are balances. The master T-account, Cash, represents the left-hand side of Equation (3) for changes in cash.

After preparing the master T-account for Cash (as at the top of Exhibit 4.9), complete the work sheet by preparing T-accounts for each noncash asset, liability, and shareholders' equity account. The lower portion of Exhibit 4.9 shows the T-accounts for each noncash account. Enter the beginning and ending balances in each account for the period given in the balance sheet (see Exhibit 4.2). The sum of the changes in these individual T-accounts expresses the right-hand side of Equation (3) for changes in cash. To see the parallel between the columnar work sheet and the T-account work sheet, observe the following: the columnar work sheet uses the net change in each account, whereas the T-account work sheet uses the beginning and ending balances, which net to the change for the period.

Step 3 Explain the change in the master cash account between the beginning and the end of the period by accounting for the change in each noncash account during the period. Accomplish this step by reconstructing the entries originally recorded in the accounts during the period and entering them into the same accounts on the T-account work sheet as the accounts originally used during the period. The only extension is that entries in the master account for cash require classification as an operating, investing, or financing activity. Once this procedure has accounted for the net change in each of the noncash accounts, it will have generated sufficient information to account for the net change in cash. In other words, if the reconstructed transactions explain the changes in the right-hand side of the Cash Change Equation (3), they will have explained the causes of the changes in cash itself on the left-hand side. In constructing the T-account work sheet, we make analytic entries, that is, journal-type entries that we do not actually enter into a firm's record-keeping system. These analytic entries appear on the work sheet; once we have completed the T-account work sheet and the statement of cash flows, the analytic entries have served their purpose, and we discard them or, perhaps, save them in a file for later reference.

The amounts debited to various accounts on the T-account work sheet must equal amounts credited to various accounts. A common source of error when preparing the T-account work sheet results from the partial recording of a transaction in which debits do not equal credits. The error becomes evident only on completion of the work sheet when the preparer discovers that the entries in one or more accounts on the T-account work sheet do not explain the change in the account during the period. The preparer must then retrace each of the entries to discover the source of the error. A careful initial recording of analytic entries in the T-account work sheet can save considerable time afterward.

Reconstructing the transactions during the year usually proceeds more easily by accounting first for supplementary information. Our earlier illustration for Solinger Electric Corporation used the following information for Year 4:

1. Net income is $20,000.
2. Depreciation expense is $10,000.
3. Dividends declared and paid total $7,000.

The analytic entry to record the information concerning net income is as follows:

---

(1) Cash (Operations: Net Income)   20,000
        Retained Earnings   20,000
Analytic entry recorded in T-account work sheet.

To understand this analytic entry, review the process of recording revenues and expenses and the closing entries for those temporary accounts from Chapter 3. All of the journal entries that together record the process of earning $20,000 in net income are equivalent to the following single journal entry:

Net Assets (= All Assets Minus All Liabilities)   20,000
        Retained Earnings   20,000
Summary entry equivalent to recording earnings of $20,000.

The summary journal entry debits Net Assets. We assume at this stage of preparing the statement of cash flows that all of the net assets generated by the earnings process were cash. Thus, in analytic entry **(1)**, the debit shows a provisional increase in cash from operations in an amount equal to net income for the period. This is an analytic entry; we make entry **(1)** on a separate work sheet to help reconstruct the transactions affecting cash.

Recall from our earlier discussion that not all of the items recognized as expenses and deducted in calculating net income decrease cash. To calculate the net amount of cash from operations, we must add back to the provisional increase in cash any amounts of the expenses that do not use cash (but instead use other noncash net assets in this period). For example, one expense that does not require an operating cash outflow this period is depreciation, illustrated in entry **(2)**:

---

(2) Cash (Operations: Depreciation Expense Addback)   10,000
        Accumulated Depreciation   10,000
Analytic entry recorded in T-account work sheet.

Depreciation expense, deducted in calculating net income, did not reduce cash this period. Some time ago, the firm used cash to acquire the fixed assets now being depreciated. The use of cash appeared on the statement for the earlier period in the Investing section. This analytic entry adds back depreciation expense to net income in calculating the amount of cash flow from operations.

Next, record the supplementary information concerning dividends of $7,000 declared and paid:

---

(3) Retained Earnings   7,000
        Cash (Financing: Dividends)   7,000
Analytic entry recorded in T-account work sheet.

Dividends reduce retained earnings and cash. As an earlier section discussed, paying dividends appears on the statement of cash flows as a financing activity.

> *Repeated for convenience:*
>
> $$\Delta C = \Delta L + \Delta SE - \Delta N\$A \qquad \text{Equation (3), Cash Change Equation}$$

Once the T-account work sheet reflects the supplementary information, one must make inferences about the reasons for the remaining changes in the noncash accounts on the balance sheet. (The preparer of a statement of cash flows for an actual firm will likely not need to make such inferences because sufficient information regarding the change in each account will probably appear in the firm's accounting records.) Explanations for the changes in noncash accounts appear below, in balance sheet order.

The Accounts Receivable account shows an increase of $35,000. The analytic entry to record this information in the work sheet is as follows:

(4) Accounts Receivable	35,000	
Cash (Operations: Subtractions)		35,000
Analytic entry recorded in T-account work sheet.		

The operations of the period generated sales, but not all of these sales resulted in an increase in cash. Some of the sales increased accounts receivable. Because we start the statement of cash flows with net income, provisionally assuming that all sales generated cash, we must subtract that portion of revenues that did not produce cash (that is, the excess of sales on account over cash collections from customers) in deriving the amount of actual cash from operations.

The next noncash account showing a change, Merchandise Inventory, shows an increase during the year of $10,000. As the operations of the firm have expanded, so has the amount carried in inventory. The analytic entry in the work sheet to explain the change in Merchandise Inventory is as follows:

(5) Merchandise Inventory	10,000	
Cash (Operations: Subtractions)		10,000
Analytic entry recorded in T-account work sheet.		

Solinger Electric Corporation found it necessary to increase the amount of inventory carried to make possible increased future sales. An increase in inventory is ordinarily an operating use of cash, and the preparation process provisionally assumes that the firm used cash to acquire all inventory. Later, the process will adjust for the amounts that were acquired on account (and will use cash later) or that were paid for in advance (and used cash already, in a prior period). Because we start the statement of cash flows with net income, in deriving the amount of cash from operations we must subtract from net income the increase in inventories during the year (that is, the excess of purchases over the cost of goods sold).

The next noncash account, Buildings and Equipment (Cost), shows a net increase of $125,000 (= $225,000 − $100,000). Because we have no other information, we must assume that the firm acquired buildings and equipment costing $125,000 during the year. The analytic entry is as follows:

---

(6) Buildings and Equipment (Cost) 125,000
  Cash (Investing: Acquisitions of Buildings and Equipment) 125,000
Analytic entry recorded in T-account work sheet.

The next noncash account showing a change is Accounts Payable—Merchandise Suppliers. As the amounts carried in inventory increase, so do amounts owed to suppliers of inventory. The analytic entry to explain the increase in the amount of Accounts Payable—Merchandise Suppliers is as follows:

---

(7) Cash (Operations: Additions) 20,000
  Accounts Payable—Merchandise Suppliers 20,000
Analytic entry recorded in T-account work sheet.

Ordinarily, acquiring inventory requires cash, and earlier we assumed that the firm paid cash in the period of acquisition for all inventory it acquired. Suppliers who allow a firm to pay later for goods and services received now in effect supply the firm with cash. Thus, an increase in the amount of accounts payable for inventory results from a transaction in which inventory increases but cash does not decrease. This is equivalent to saying that an increase in payables provides cash, even if it is only temporary. Accounting classifies the increase in cash resulting from increased payables for inventory as an operating source of cash.

The next noncash account showing a change is Accounts Payable—Other Suppliers. As the scope of operations has increased, so has the amount owed to others. The analytic entry to explain the increase in the amount of Accounts Payable—Other Suppliers is as follows:

---

(8) Cash (Operations: Additions) 2,000
  Accounts Payable—Other Suppliers 2,000
Analytic entry recorded in T-account work sheet.

The reasoning behind this analytic entry is the same as for analytic entry **(7)**. Creditors who permit a firm to increase amounts owed temporarily provide cash.

The same reasoning applies to an increased amount of Salaries Payable, the next noncash account showing a change. The analytic entry to record the increase in Salaries Payable is as follows:

---

(9) Cash (Operations: Additions) 1,000
  Salaries Payable 1,000
Analytic entry recorded in T-account work sheet.

Employees who do not demand immediate payment for earned salaries temporarily provide their employer with cash.

Repeated for convenience:

$$\Delta C = \Delta L + \Delta SE - \Delta N\$A \qquad \text{Equation (3), Cash Change Equation}$$

Bonds Payable, the final noncash account with a change not yet explained, shows a net increase of $100,000 for the year. In the absence of explicit information, one can deduce that the firm issued long-term bonds during the year. The analytic entry is as follows:

---

(10) Cash (Financing: Long-Term Bond Issue) 100,000

        Bonds Payable 100,000

Analytic entry recorded in T-account work sheet.

Exhibit 4.10 presents the completed T-account work sheet for Solinger Electric Corporation for Year 4. The ten analytic entries explain all changes in the noncash T-accounts. If the work is correct, the causes of the change in the Cash account will appear in the entries in the master Cash account.

Step 4 The final step is to use the information provided in the master T-account for Cash in the completed work sheet to prepare a formal statement of cash flows. Exhibit 4.5 presents the Solinger Electric Corporation statement, which we prepared earlier using the columnar work sheet approach.

DEPRECIATION DOES NOT PROVIDE CASH

Because the indirect method adds depreciation expense to net income to calculate cash provided by operations, readers of financial statements might incorrectly conclude that depreciation expense provides cash. However, as Exhibit 4.4 illustrates, the recording of depreciation expense does not affect cash. A noncash asset decreases, and a shareholders' equity account decreases. Cash from operations results from selling goods and services to customers. If a firm makes no sales, there will be no cash provided by operations regardless of how large the depreciation charge may be.

To understand that **depreciation does not provide cash,** refer to the income statement of Solinger Electric Corporation (Exhibit 4.3) and the operations section of the statement of cash flows (Exhibit 4.5). Exhibit 4.11 reproduces them in condensed form. Ignore income taxes for a moment. Suppose that depreciation for Year 4 had been $25,000 rather than $10,000. The condensed income statement and cash flow from operations would then appear as in Exhibit 4.12. Note that the total cash flow provided by operations, which is receipts from customers minus all expenses that used cash, remains $8,000. Transactions involving long-term assets affect cash only when (1) a firm acquires a long-term asset for cash or (2) it sells the asset for cash.

At a more sophisticated level, when the firm considers income taxes, depreciation does affect cash flow. Depreciation affects the calculation of net income reported in the financial statements, and as a deduction, it also reduces taxable income on tax returns. The larger the amount of depreciation on tax returns, the smaller is the taxable income and the smaller the current payment for income taxes. Chapters 8 and 10 discuss the effect of depreciation on income taxes.

EXHIBIT 4.10	SOLINGER ELECTRIC CORPORATION T-Account Work Sheet

Cash

✓	30,000				

Operations

Net Income	**(1)**	20,000	35,000	**(4)**	Increased Accounts Receivable
Depreciation Expense Addback	**(2)**	10,000	10,000	**(5)**	Increased Merchandise Inventory
Increased Accounts Payable to Merchandise Suppliers	**(7)**	20,000			
Increased Accounts Payable to Other Suppliers	**(8)**	2,000			
Increased Salaries Payable	**(9)**	1,000			

Investing

		125,000	**(6)**	Acquistion of Buildings and Equipment

Financing

Long-Term Bond Issue	**(10)**	100,000	7,000	**(3)**	Dividends
✓	6,000			

Accounts Receivable			Merchandise Inventory			Buildings and Equipment (Cost)		
✓	20,000		✓	40,000		✓	100,000	
(4)	35,000		**(5)**	10,000		**(6)**	125,000	
	55,000		✓	50,000		✓	225,000	

Accumulated Depreciation			Accounts Payable— Merchandise Suppliers			Accounts Payable— Other Suppliers		
	30,000	✓		30,000	✓		10,000	✓
	10,000	**(2)**		20,000	**(7)**		2,000	**(8)**
	40,000	✓		50,000	✓		12,000	✓

Salaries Payable			Bonds Payable			Retained Earnings		
	5,000	✓		0	✓			15,000	✓
	1,000	**(9)**		100,000	**(10)**	**(3)**	7,000	20,000	**(1)**
	6,000	✓		100,000	✓			28,000	✓

Repeated for convenience:

$$\Delta C = \Delta L + \Delta SE - \Delta N\$A \qquad \text{Equation (3), Cash Change Equation}$$

EXHIBIT 4.11

SOLINGER ELECTRIC CORPORATION
Year 4
Depreciation, $10,000

Income Statement

Revenues	$125,000
Expenses Except Depreciation	(95,000)
	$30,000
Depreciation Expense	(10,000)
Net Income	$ 20,000

Cash Flow from Operations

Net Income	$20,000
Additions:	
Depreciation	10,000
Other	23,000
Subtractions	(45,000)
Cash Flow Provided by Operations	$ 8,000

EXHIBIT 4.12

SOLINGER ELECTRIC CORPORATION
Year 4
Depreciation, $25,000

Income Statement

Revenues	$125,000
Expenses Except Depreciation	(95,000)
	$ 30,000
Depreciation Expense	(25,000)
Net Income	$ 5,000

Cash Flow from Operations

Net Income	$ 5,000
Additions:	
Depreciation	25,000
Other	23,000
Subtractions	(45,000)
Cash Flow Provided by Operations	$ 8,000

To overcome some of these interpretative problems of the indirect method, the FASB permits firms to use the direct method in reporting cash flow from operations in the statement of cash flows. A note to the financial statements, however, must reconcile net income with cash flow from operations (that is, the indirect method).

As we discussed earlier, most firms prepare the operating section of the statement of cash flows using the indirect method, perhaps because it reconciles net income with cash flow from operations. To simplify the illustrations in this book, we use the indirect method in preparing the statement of cash flows. The lower portion of Exhibit 4.4 shows the calculation of cash flow from operations using the direct method.

Preparing a T-account work sheet for a statement of cash flows. Refer to Problem 4.2 for Self-Study. Prepare a T-account work sheet for the preparation of a statement of cash flows.

EXTENSION OF THE ILLUSTRATION

The illustration for Solinger Electric Corporation considered so far in this chapter is simpler than the typical published statement of cash flows in at least four respects:

1. There are only a few balance sheet accounts requiring explanation.
2. Several types of more complex transactions that affect cash flow from operations do not arise.
3. Each transaction recorded in Step **3** involves only one debit and one credit.
4. Except for the Retained Earnings account, each explanation of a noncash account change involves only one analytic entry on the work sheet.

Most of the complications that arise in interpreting published statements of cash flows relate to accounting events that are discussed in later chapters. These chapters will illustrate the corresponding effects on the statement of cash flows. We can, however, explain here one complication, caused by supplementary disclosure.

Suppose that the firm sold some of its buildings and equipment during the year at their book value. That is, when the firm disposed of existing buildings and equipment, the cash proceeds from disposition equaled acquisition cost less the accumulated depreciation of the assets. With this assumption, no gain or loss on the disposition arises.

Reconsider the Solinger Electric Corporation example with the following new information. Solinger Electric Corporation sold some equipment during Year 4. The firm originally paid $10,000 for this equipment and then sold it for $3,000 at a time when accumulated depreciation on the equipment was $7,000. The actual entry made during the year to record the sale of the equipment was as follows:

Cash	3,000	
Accumulated Depreciation	7,000	
Buildings and Equipment (Cost)		10,000
Journal entry for sale of equipment.		

Assume that the comparative balance sheets as shown in Exhibit 4.2 are correct and thus the net decrease in cash for Year 4 is still $24,000. The entries in the T-accounts must differ to reflect this new information. The following analytic entry in the T-account work sheet recognizes the effect of the sale of equipment:

(1a) Cash (Investing: Sale of Equipment)	3,000	
Accumulated Depreciation	7,000	
Buildings and Equipment (Cost)		10,000
Analytic entry recorded in T-account work sheet.		

Repeated for convenience:

$$\Delta C = \Delta L + \Delta SE - \Delta N\$A \qquad \text{Equation (3), Cash Change Equation}$$

The debit to Cash (Investing: Sale of Equipment) shows the proceeds of the sale. As a result of analytic entry **(1a)**, the T-accounts for Buildings and Equipment (Cost) and Accumulated Depreciation appear as follows:

Buildings and Equipment (Cost)				Accumulated Depreciation			
✓	100,000					30,000	✓
		10,000	**(1a)**	**(1a)**	7,000		
✓	225,000					40,000	✓

When the time comes to explain the change in Buildings and Equipment (Cost) account, the T-account indicates both a total increase of $125,000 and a credit (decrease) entry **(1a)** of $10,000 to recognize the sale of equipment. To explain the net increase in the Buildings and Equipment (Cost) account, given the decrease already entered, one must assume that the firm acquired new buildings and equipment for $135,000 during the period.

The reconstructed analytic entry to complete the explanation of the change in this account is as follows:

(6a) Buildings and Equipment (Cost)   135,000

      Cash (Investing: Acquisition of Buildings and
          Equipment)   135,000

Analytic entry recorded in T-account work sheet.

Likewise, when the time comes to explain the change in the T-account for Accumulated Depreciation, there is a net credit change of $10,000 and a debit entry **(1a)** of $7,000 to recognize the sale. Thus the depreciation charge for Year 4 must have been $17,000. The reconstructed analytic entry to complete the explanation of the change in the Accumulated Depreciation account is as follows:

(2a) Cash (Operations: Depreciation Expense Addback)   17,000

      Accumulated Depreciation   17,000

Analytic entry recorded in T-account work sheet.

Exhibit 4.13 presents a revised T-account work sheet for Solinger Electric Corporation incorporating the new information on the sale of equipment.

EXHIBIT 4.13	SOLINGER ELECTRIC CORPORATION Revised T-Account Work Sheet

Cash

✓	30,000		

Operations

Net Income	**(1)**	20,000	35,000	**(4)**	Increased Accounts Receivable
Depreciation Expense Addback	**(2a)**	17,000	10,000	**(5)**	Increased Merchandise Inventory
Increased Accounts Payable to Merchandise Suppliers	**(7)**	20,000			
Increased Accounts Payable to Other Suppliers	**(8)**	2,000			
Increased Salaries Payable	**(9)**	1,000			

Investing

Sale of Equipment	**(1a)**	3,000	135,000	**(6a)**	Acquistion of Buildings and Equipment

Financing

Long-Term Bond Issue	**(10)**	100,000	7,000	**(3)**	Dividends
	✓	6,000			

Accounts Receivable			**Merchandise Inventory**			**Buildings and Equipment (Cost)**			
✓	20,000		✓	40,000		✓	100,000		
(4)	35,000		**(5)**	10,000		**(6a)**	135,000	10,000	**(1a)**
✓	55,000		✓	50,000		✓	225,000		

Accumulated Depreciation				**Accounts Payable— Merchandise Suppliers**				**Accounts Payable— Other Suppliers**			
		30,000	✓			30,000	✓			10,000	✓
(1a)	7,000	17,000	**(2a)**			20,000	**(7)**			2,000	**(8)**
		40,000	✓			50,000	✓			12,000	✓

Salaries Payable				**Bonds Payable**				**Retained Earnings**			
		5,000	✓			0	✓			15,000	✓
		1,000	**(9)**			100,000	**(10)**	**(3)**	7,000	20,000	**(1)**
		6,000	✓			100,000	✓			28,000	✓

Another complication arises when firms sell buildings and equipment for an amount different from their book values. Assume, for example, that Solinger Electric Corporation sold the equipment discussed above for $2,000 instead of $3,000. The entry made during the year to record the sale of the equipment is as follows:

Repeated for convenience:

$$\Delta C = \Delta L + \Delta SE - \Delta N\$A \qquad \text{Equation (3), Cash Change Equation}$$

Cash	2,000	
Loss on Sale of Equipment	1,000	
Accumulated Depreciation	7,000	
Buildings and Equipment (Cost)		10,000
Journal entry to record sale of equipment.		

This entry removes from the accounting records all amounts related to the equipment sold, which includes its acquisition cost of $10,000 and the $7,000 of depreciation recognized while Solinger Electric Corporation used the equipment. Accountants refer to the net amount appearing on the books for such equipment as its *book value.* The entry also records the cash received from the sale of the equipment. The difference between the cash proceeds and the book value of the equipment is a loss of $1,000 [= $2,000 − ($10,000 − $7,000)].

The following analytic entry on the T-account work sheet would recognize the effect of the sale of equipment for $2,000:

(1a) Cash (Investing: Sale of Equipment)	2,000	
Cash (Operations: Loss on Sale of Equipment Addback)	1,000	
Accumulated Depreciation	7,000	
Buildings and Equipment (Cost)		10,000
Entry recorded in T-account work sheet.		

The debit to Cash (Investing: Sale of Equipment) shows the $2,000 proceeds of sale. The debit to Cash (Operations: Loss on Sale of Equipment Addback) for $1,000 adds back to net income the loss on sale of equipment that did not use cash. Like the depreciation expense addback, the debit to Cash (Operations: Loss on Sale of Equipment Addback) does not represent a source of cash (ignoring income taxes). The addback merely offsets the subtraction for the loss in computing net income. One might view the recognition of a loss on the sale of equipment as indicating that the firm took insufficient depreciation during the accounting periods before the sale. If the firm had known for certain that it would sell the equipment for $2,000, it would have recognized another $1,000 of depreciation during the periods while it used the equipment. The sale of the equipment would then have resulted in no gain or loss. The firm would have shown the $1,000 additional depreciation as an addback to net income in computing cash flow from operations during the periods while it used the equipment.

Extending this illustration still further, assume that Solinger Electric Corporation sold the equipment for $4,500. The entry made to record the sale of equipment is as follows:

Cash	4,500	
Accumulated Depreciation	7,000	
Buildings and Equipment (Cost)		10,000
Gain on Sale of Equipment		1,500
Journal entry to record sale of equipment.		

This entry, like that above for sale at a loss, removes the amounts on the books for the equipment and records the cash proceeds. In this case the cash proceeds exceed the book value of the equipment, resulting in a gain on the sale.

The following analytic entry in the T-account work sheet would recognize the effect of the sale of equipment for $4,500:

(1a) Cash (Investing: Sale of Equipment)	4,500	
Accumulated Depreciation	7,000	
Buildings and Equipment (Cost)		10,000
Cash (Operations: Gain on Sale of Equipment Subtraction)		1,500
Analytic entry recorded in T-account work sheet.		

The debit to Cash (Investing: Sale of Equipment) shows the $4,500 proceeds of sale. The credit to Cash (Operations: Gain on Sale of Equipment Subtraction) reduces net income for the gain on sale of equipment that did not provide an operating cash inflow. Unless we subtract the $1,500 gain in the operations section of the work sheet, we overstate the amount of cash inflow from this transaction, as the following analysis summarizes:

Operations

Net Income (Gain on Sale of Equipment)	$ 1,500
Subtraction for Gain on Sale of Equipment Not Providing an Operating Cash Inflow	(1,500)
Cash Flow from Operations	$ 0

Investing

Sale of Equipment	$ 4,500
Net Change in Cash from Transaction	$ 4,500

One might interpret the recognition of a gain on the sale of equipment as indicating that the firm took too much depreciation during the accounting periods before the sale. If the firm had known for certain that it would sell the equipment for $4,500, it would have recognized $1,500 less depreciation during the periods while it used the equipment. The sale of the equipment would then have resulted in no gain or loss. The firm would have shown $1,500 less depreciation as an addback to net income in computing cash flow from operations. The $1,500 credit in the operating section of the T-account work sheet in effect adjusts for the excess depreciation.

PROBLEM 4.5 FOR SELF-STUDY

Preparing a statement of cash flows.   Exhibit 4.14 presents a comparative balance sheet for Gordon Corporation as of December 31, Year 1 and Year 2. The following information pertains to Gordon Corporation for Year 2:

1. Net income was $200,000.
2. Dividends declared and paid were $120,000.
3. Depreciation expense totaled $80,000.
4. The firm sold buildings and equipment, which originally cost $55,000 and had accumulated depreciation of $40,000, for $10,000.

a. Prepare a T-account work sheet for the preparation of a statement of cash flows.
b. Prepare a formal statement of cash flows.

Repeated for convenience:

$$\Delta C = \Delta L + \Delta SE - \Delta N\$A \qquad \text{Equation (3), Cash Change Equation}$$

EXHIBIT 4.14	GORDON CORPORATION Comparative Balance Sheet December 31, Year 1 and Year 2 (all dollar amounts in thousands) (Problem 4.5 for Self-Study)

	December 31	
	Year 1	**Year 2**
ASSETS		
Current Assets		
Cash	$ 70	$ 40
Accounts Receivable	320	420
Merchandise Inventories	360	470
Prepayments	50	70
Total Current Assets	$ 800	$1,000
Property, Plant, and Equipment		
Land	$ 200	$ 250
Buildings and Equipment (net of accumulated depreciation of $800 and $840)	1,000	1,150
Total Property, Plant, and Equipment	$1,200	$1,400
Total Assets	$2,000	$2,400
LIABILITIES AND SHAREHOLDERS' EQUITY		
Current Liabilities		
Accounts Payable	$ 320	$ 440
Income Taxes Payable	60	80
Other Current Liabilities	170	360
Total Current Liabilities	$ 550	$ 880
Noncurrent Liabilities		
Bonds Payable	$ 250	$ 200
Total Liabilities	$ 800	$1,080
Shareholders' Equity		
Common Stock	$ 500	$ 540
Retained Earnings	700	780
Total Shareholders' Equity	$1,200	$1,320
Total Liabilities and Shareholders' Equity	$2,000	$2,400

Standard No. 7 of the International Accounting Standards Committee recommends the preparation of a statement of cash flows that reports cash flows from operating, investing, and financing activities.[6] Standard-setting bodies in most countries have adopted this standard, so that firms in these countries prepare a statement of cash flows following the format illustrated in this chapter.

USING INFORMATION IN THE STATEMENT OF CASH FLOWS

The statement of cash flows provides information that helps the reader in (1) assessing the impact of operations on liquidity and (2) assessing the relations among cash flows from operating, investing, and financing activities.

IMPACT OF OPERATIONS ON LIQUIDITY

Perhaps the most important factor not reported on either the balance sheet or the income statement is how the operations of a period affected cash flows. Increased earnings do not always generate increased cash flow. When increased earnings result from expanding operations (in contrast to merely increases in selling price or reductions in cost), they usually lead to decreased cash flow from operations. A growing, successful firm—such as Wal-Mart, discussed in connection with Exhibit 4.1—may have increasing amounts for accounts receivable and inventories, resulting in a lag between earnings and cash flows. If a firm's payments for wages and inventories do not lag earnings as much as do its collections of receivables, and they usually do not lag earnings by as much, the firm will find itself perpetually short of cash for wages and accounts payable. Successful, growing businesses will need permanent financing from long-term debt issues or common stock issues to cover short-term cash needs. Some successful firms find themselves constantly short of cash because they have not adequately obtained long-term financing to cover perpetual short-term needs.

On the other hand, increased cash flow can accompany reduced earnings. Consider, for example, a firm that is experiencing operating problems and reduces the scope of its activities. Such a firm likely will report reduced net income or even losses. However, it might experience positive cash flow from operations because it collects accounts receivable from prior periods but does not replace inventories, thus saving cash.

RELATIONS AMONG CASH FLOWS FROM OPERATIONS, INVESTING, AND FINANCING ACTIVITIES

The relations among the cash flows from each of the three principal business activities likely differ depending on the characteristics of the firm's products and the maturity of its industry. Consider each of the four following patterns of cash flows.

---

[6]International Accounting Standards Committee, *International Accounting Standard No. 7,* "Cash Flow Statements," 1994.

Repeated for convenience:

$$\Delta C = \Delta L + \Delta SE - \Delta N\$A \qquad \text{Equation (3), Cash Change Equation}$$

Cash Flows from:	A	B	C	D
Operations	$ (3)	$ 7	$15	$ 8
Investing	(15)	(12)	(8)	(2)
Financing	18	5	(7)	(6)
Net Cash Flow	$ 0	$ 0	$ 0	$ 0

Case A illustrates a typical new, rapidly growing firm. It does not yet operate profitably, and it experiences buildups of its accounts receivable and inventories. Thus it has negative cash flow from operations. To sustain its rapid growth, the firm must invest heavily in plant and equipment. During this stage, the firm must rely on external sources of cash to finance both its operating and its investing activities. See, for example, the statement of cash flows for Sun Microsystems for Year 5 and Year 6 in Exhibit 4.15 (discussed more fully below) and for Amazon.com in Exercise 14 and Yahoo, Inc., in Exercise 15 at the end of the chapter.

Case B illustrates a firm that is somewhat more seasoned than the one in Case A but that is still growing. It operates profitably, but because its rapid growth has begun to slow, it generates positive cash flow from operations. However, this cash flow from operations falls short of the amount the firm needs to finance acquisitions of plant and equipment. The firm therefore requires external financing. See, for example, the statement of cash flows for Wal-Mart Stores for Year 7 and Year 8 in Exhibit 4.1 and for Sun Microsystems for Year 7 in Exhibit 4.15.

Case C illustrates the cash flow pattern of a mature, stable firm. It generates a healthy cash flow from operations—more than enough to acquire new plant and equipment. It uses the excess cash flow to repay financing from earlier periods and, perhaps, to pay dividends. See, for example, the statement of cash flows for Wal-Mart Stores for Year 9 in Exhibit 4.1. Firms such as Coca-Cola, Procter and Gamble, and Ford show a similar pattern.

Case D illustrates a firm in the early stages of decline. Its cash from operations has begun to decrease but remains positive because of decreases in accounts receivable and inventories. It cuts back significantly on capital expenditures because it is in a declining industry. It uses some of its excess cash flow to repay outstanding financing, and the remainder is available for investment in new products or other industries. Steel companies typically show this pattern of cash flows.

These four cases do not, of course, cover all of the patterns of cash flows found in corporate annual reports. They illustrate, however, how the characteristics of a firm's products and industry can affect the interpretation of information in the statement of cash flows.

Exhibit 4.15 presents a statement of cash flows for Sun Microsystems for four recent years. The rapid increase in net income and fixed assets acquired suggests that the firm operates in high-growth markets. The fact that depreciation expense makes up such a high proportion of net income suggests that the firm is relatively capital-intensive. During Year 5 and Year 6 the firm had negative cash flow from operations. Even though Sun earned positive net income in these years, increases in accounts receivable and inventories caused

EXHIBIT 4.15	SUN MICROSYSTEMS Statement of Cash Flows (in millions)			
	Year 5	**Year 6**	**Year 7**	**Year 8**
Operations				
Net Income	$ 6	$ 12	$ 36	$ 66
Depreciation	4	6	25	51
Working Capital Provided by Operations	$ 10	$ 18	$ 61	$ 117
(Increase) Decrease in Receivables	(18)	(24)	(58)	(117)
(Increase) Decrease in Inventories	(16)	(21)	(32)	(77)
(Increase) Decrease in Other Current Assets	(1)	(18)	(31)	(30)
Increase (Decrease) in Accounts Payable—Trade	4	21	33	58
Increase (Decrease) in Other Current Liabilities	9	6	35	52
Cash Flow from Operations	$(12)	$(18)	$ 8	$ 3
Investing				
Fixed Assets Acquired	$(15)	$(36)	$ (76)	$(117)
Other Investing Transactions	(2)	(2)	(23)	(32)
Cash Flow from Investing	$(17)	$(38)	$ (99)	$(149)
Financing				
Increase in Short-term Borrowing	$ 3	$ 11	$ 21	$ 0
Increase in Long-term Borrowing	5	1	121	—
Issue of Capital Stock	45	47	96	63
Decrease in Short-term Borrowing	0	0	0	(6)
Decrease in Long-term Borrowing	(1)	(2)	0	0
Other Financing Transactions	3	3	0	0
Cash Flow from Financing	$ 55	$ 60	$238	$ 57
Change in Cash	$ 26	$ 4	$147	$ (89)
Cash, January 1	4	30	34	181
Cash, December 31	$ 30	$ 34	$181	$ 92

a negative cash flow from operations. Cash flow from operations was positive in Year 7 and Year 8. In each of the four years, however, cash flow from operations fell short of the amounts Sun needed to finance acquisitions of fixed assets. Sun Microsystems relied on additional common stock and long-term debt to finance those investing activities.

Interpreting the statement of cash flows requires an understanding of the economic characteristics of the industries in which a firm conducts its operations. Examining the statement of cash flows over several years is usually more informative than analyzing the amounts for any single year.

SUMMARY

The statement of cash flows reports the effects of a firm's operating, investing, and financing activities on cash flows. Information in the statement helps in understanding

1. how operations affect the liquidity of a firm,
2. the level of capital expenditures needed to support ongoing and growing levels of activity, and
3. the major changes in the financing of a firm.

To prepare the statement of cash flows requires analyzing changes in balance sheet accounts during the accounting period, as represented by the Cash Change Equation (3). As a by-product of correct double-entry recording of all transactions, the net change in cash will equal the net change in all noncash accounts. The columnar work sheet to prepare the statement of cash flows works well when the entire change in a particular balance sheet account affects only one of the three cash flow categories: operating, investing, or financing. The T-account work sheet works well in more complicated situations, when changes in balance sheet accounts affect more than one of the cash flow categories. The T-account work sheet requires the preparer to reconstruct the entries made in the noncash accounts during the period. Explaining the net change in the noncash accounts will also explain the net change in cash.

The statement of cash flows usually presents cash flow from operations in the indirect format, beginning with net income for the period. The statement then adjusts for revenues not providing cash, for expenses not using cash, and for changes in operating working capital accounts. The result is cash flow from operations. Some firms follow a more direct approach to calculating cash flow from operations by listing all revenues that provide cash and subtracting all expenses that use cash. The cash flows from investing activities and financing activities appear after cash flow from operations.

Interpreting a statement of cash flows requires an understanding of the economic characteristics of the industries in which a firm conducts its activities, including capital intensity, growth characteristics, and similar factors.

PROBLEM 4.6 FOR SELF-STUDY

Effect of transactions on the statement of cash flows. Exhibit 4.16 shows a simplified statement of cash flows for a period. Numbers appear on nine of the lines in the statement. Other lines are various subtotals and grand totals; ignore these in the remainder of the problem. Assume that the accounting cycle is complete for the period and that the firm has prepared all of the financial statements. It then discovers that it has overlooked a transaction. It records that transaction in the accounts and corrects all of the financial statements. For each of the following transactions, indicate which of the numbered lines of the statement of cash flows change, and state the amount and direction of the change. If net income, line (1), changes, be sure to indicate whether it decreases or increases. Ignore income tax effects. (*Hint:* First, construct the entry the firm would enter in the general journal to record the transaction in the accounts. Then, for each line of the journal entry, identify the line of Exhibit 4.16 affected.)

a. Depreciation expense of $2,000 on an office computer
b. Purchase of machinery for $10,000 cash
c. Declaration of a cash dividend of $6,500 on common stock; the firm paid the dividend by the end of the fiscal year
d. Issue of common stock for $12,000 cash
e. Proceeds of the sale of a common stock investment, a noncurrent asset, for $15,000 cash; the firm sold the investment for its book value of $15,000

EXHIBIT 4.16	Simplified Statement of Cash Flows (Problem 4.6 for Self-Study)

Operations

Net Income	(1)
Additions to Net Income to Compute Cash	
Flow from Operations	+(2)
Subtractions from Net Income to Compute Cash	
Flow from Operations	−(3)
Cash Flow from Operations [= (1) + (2) − (3)]	S1

Investing

Proceeds from Dispositions of "Investing" Assets	+(4)
Cash Used to Acquire "Investing" Assets	−(5)
Cash Flow from Investing [= (4) − (5)]	S2

Financing

Cash Provided by Increases in Debt or Capital Stock	+(6)
Cash Used to Reduce Debt or Capital Stock	−(7)
Cash Used for Dividends	−(8)
Cash Flow from Financing [= (6) − (7) − (8)]	S3
Net Change in Cash [= S1 + S2 + S3]	(9)
Cash, Beginning of the Period	S4
Cash, End of the Period [= (9) + S4]	S5

SOLUTIONS TO SELF-STUDY PROBLEMS

SUGGESTED SOLUTION TO PROBLEM 4.1 FOR SELF STUDY

(Classifying cash flows by type of activity.)

- **a.** Operating
- **b.** Financing
- **c.** Operating
- **d.** Operating
- **e.** Operating
- **f.** Operating
- **g.** Investing
- **h.** Item does not affect cash flows during the current period and would therefore not appear in the statement of cash flows. The firm must disclose this transaction in a separate schedule or a note to the financial statements.
- **i.** Operating
- **j.** Operating
- **k.** Investing
- **l.** Item does not affect cash flows during the current period and would therefore not appear in the statement of cash flows. The firm must disclose this transaction in a separate schedule or note to the financial statements.
- **m.** Financing
- **n.** Investing

	ROBBIE CORPORATION
EXHIBIT 4.17	Columnar Work Sheet for Preparation of the Statement of Cash Flows For Year 2 (all dollar amounts in thousands) Problem 4.2 for Self-Study

(INCREASE) DECREASE IN ASSETS	Balance Sheet Changes	Operations	Investing	Financing
Accounts Receivable	$ (7)	$ (7)		
Merchandise Inventories	2	2		
Buildings and Equipment	(16)		$(16)	
Accumulated Depreciation	6	6		
INCREASE (DECREASE) IN LIABILITIES AND SHAREHOLDERS' EQUITY				
Accounts Payable—Merchandise Suppliers	7	7		
Bonds Payable	8			$ 8
Common Stock	10			10
Retained Earnings	5	7		(2)
Increase (Decrease) in Cash	$15	$15	$(16)	$16

   o. Financing
   p. Investing
   q. Operating

SUGGESTED SOLUTION TO PROBLEM 4.2 FOR SELF-STUDY

(Robbie Corporation; preparing a columnar work sheet for a statement of cash flows.) Exhibit 4.17 presents a completed columnar work sheet for Robbie Corporation.

SUGGESTED SOLUTION TO PROBLEM 4.3 FOR SELF-STUDY

(Robbie Corporation; computing cash flow from operations using the direct method.) Exhibit 4.18 presents the calculation of cash flow from operations using the direct method.

	ROBBIE CORPORATION
EXHIBIT 4.18	Computing Cash Flow from Operations Using the Direct Method For Year 2 (all dollar amounts in thousands) Problem 4.3 for Self-Study

	Income Statement +	Operating Balance Sheet Changes	Cash = Receipts −	Cash Disbursements =	Cash Flow from Operations
Sales	$180	$(7)	$173		
Cost of Goods Sold	(140)	2			
		7		$(131)	
Depreciation Expense	(6)	6			
Selling and Administrative Expenses	(25)			(25)	
Interest Expense	(2)			(2)	
Net Income	$ 7 +	$ 8	= $173 −	$(158) =	$15

EXHIBIT 4.19	ROBBIE CORPORATION T-Account Work Sheet (all dollar amounts in thousands) (Problem 4.4 for Self-Study)

Cash

✓	10	

Operations

(2)	2	7	(1)
(4)	6		
(5)	7		
(8)	7		

Investing

		16	(3)

Financing

(6)	8	2	(9)
(7)	10		
✓	25		

Accounts Receivable		**Merchandise Inventories**		**Property, Plant and Equipment**	
✓	15	✓	20	✓	50
(1)	7		2 (2)	(3)	16
✓	22	✓	18	✓	66

Accumulated Depreciation		**Accounts Payable**		**Bonds Payable**	
	25 ✓		30 ✓		10 ✓
	6 (4)		7 (5)		8 (6)
	31 ✓		37 ✓		18 ✓

Common Stock		**Retained Earnings**	
	10 ✓		20 ✓
	10 (7)	(9) 2	7 (8)
	20 ✓		25 ✓

SUGGESTED SOLUTION TO PROBLEM 4.4 FOR SELF-STUDY

(Robbie Corporation; preparing a T-account work sheet for a statement of cash flows.)
Exhibit 4.19 presents a completed T-account work sheet for Robbie Corporation.

SUGGESTED SOLUTION TO PROBLEM 4.5 FOR SELF-STUDY

(Gordon Corporation; preparing a statement of cash flows.)
Exhibit 4.20 presents a completed T-account work sheet for Gordon Corporation. Exhibit 4.21 presents a formal statement of cash flows.

EXHIBIT 4.20	GORDON CORPORATION T-Account Work Sheet (all dollar amounts in thousands) (Problem 4.5 for Self-Study)

Cash

√ 70	

Operations

(1) 200	100 ✓ (5)
(3) 80 ✓	110 ✓ (6)
(4) 5	20 ✓ (7)
(10) 120 ✓	
(11) 20 ✓	
(12) 190 ✓	

Investing

(4) 10	50 (8)
	245 (9)

Financing

(14) 40	120 (2)
	50 (13)
√ 40	

Accounts Receivable		**Merchandise Inventory**		**Prepayments**	
√ 320		√ 360		√ 50	
(5) 100		(6) 110		(7) 20	
√ 420		√ 470		√ 70	

Land		**Buildings and Equipment**		**Accumulated Depreciation**	
√ 200		√ 1,800			800 √
(8) 50		(9) 245	55 (4)	(4) 40	80 (3)
√ 250		√ 1,990			840 √

Accounts Payable		**Income Taxes Payable**		**Other Current Liabilities**	
	320 √		60 √		170 √
	120 (10)		20 (11)		190 (12)
	440 √		80 √		360 √

Bonds Payable		**Common Stock**		**Retained Earnings**	
	250 √		500 √		700 √
(13) 50			40 (14)	(2) 120	200 (1)
	200 √		540 √		780 √

EXHIBIT 4.21	GORDON CORPORATION Statement of Cash Flows for Year 2 (all dollar amounts in thousands) (Problem 4.5 for Self-Study)

Operations

Net Income	$200	
Additions:		
Depreciation Expense	80	
Loss on Sale of Equipment	5	
Increase in Accounts Payable	120	
Increase in Income Taxes Payable	20	
Increase in Other Current Liabilities	190	
Subtractions:		
Increase in Accounts Receivable	(100)	
Increase in Merchandise Inventories	(110)	
Increase in Prepayments	(20)	
Cash Provided by Operations		$385
Investing		
Buildings and Equipment Sold	$ 10	
Acquisition of Land	(50)	
Acquisition of Buildings and Equipment	(245)	
Cash Used for Investing		(285)
Financing		
Common Stock Issued	$ 40	
Dividends Paid	(120)	
Repayment of Bonds	(50)	
Cash Used for Financing		(130)
Net Decrease in Cash		$ (30)
Cash, Beginning of Year 2		70
Cash, End of Year 2		$ 40

SUGGESTED SOLUTION TO PROBLEM 4.6 FOR SELF-STUDY

(Effect of transactions on the statement of cash flows.)

Preparing the journal entry for each transaction aids in understanding the effect on the nine lines in Exhibit 4.16.

a. Depreciation Expense	2,000	
Accumulated Depreciation		2,000

This entry involves a debit to an income statement account, so line (1) declines by $2,000. Depreciation expense reduces net income but does not affect cash line (9). Thus, line (2) must increase by $2,000 for the addback of depreciation expense to net income. This addback eliminates the effect of depreciation on both cash flow from operations and cash.

b. Machinery	10,000	
Cash		10,000

This entry involves a credit to Cash, so line (9) decreases by $10,000. Because line (9) is the net change in cash for the period, some other line must change as well. Acquisitions of equipment represent Investing activities, so line (5) increases by $10,000. Note that line (5) has a negative sign, so increasing this line reduces cash.

c. Retained Earnings	6,500	
Cash		6,500

This entry involves a credit to Cash, so line (9) decreases by $6,500. Dividends are a financing activity, so line (8) increases by $6,500.

d. Cash	12,000	
Common Stock		12,000

The debit to Cash means that line (9) increases by $12,000. Issuing stock is a financing transaction, so line (6) increases by $12,000.

e. Cash	15,000	
Investment in Securities		15,000

The debit to Cash means that line (9) increases by $15,000. Selling investments in securities is an investing activity, so line (4) increases by $15,000.

KEY TERMS AND CONCEPTS

Cash flow from operations
Cash flow from investing activities
Cash flow from financing activities
Indirect method
Direct method

Cash Change Equation
Columnar work sheet
T-account work sheet
Depreciation does not provide cash

QUESTIONS, EXERCISES, PROBLEMS, AND CASES

QUESTIONS

1. Review the meaning of the terms and concepts listed above in Key Terms and Concepts.
2. "One can most easily accomplish the reporting objective of the income statement under the accrual basis of accounting and the reporting objective of the statement of cash flows by issuing a single income statement using the cash basis of accounting." Evaluate this proposal.
3. "The accrual basis of accounting creates the need for a statement of cash flows." Explain.
4. "The statement of cash flows provides information about changes in the structure of a firm's assets and equities." Explain.

5. A student remarked: "The direct method of computing cash flow from operations is easier to understand than the indirect method. Why do the vast majority of firms follow the indirect method in preparing their statements of cash flows?" Respond to this student.

6. The statement of cash flows classifies cash expenditures for interest expense as an operating activity but classifies cash expenditures to redeem debt as a financing activity. Explain this apparent paradox.

7. The statement of cash flows classifies cash expenditures for interest on debt as an operating activity but classifies cash expenditures for dividends to shareholders as a financing activity. Explain this apparent paradox.

8. The statement of cash flows classifies changes in accounts payable as an operating activity but classifies changes in short-term bank borrowing as a financing activity. Explain this apparent paradox.

9. The acquisition of equipment by assuming a mortgage is a transaction that firms cannot report in their statement of cash flows but must report in a supplemental schedule or note. Of what value is information about this type of transaction? What is the reason for its exclusion from the statement of cash flows?

10. One writer stated, "Depreciation expense is a firm's chief source of cash for growth." A reader criticized this statement by replying: "The fact remains that if companies had elected, in any year, to charge off $10 million more depreciation than they did charge off, they would not thereby have added one dime to the total of their cash available for expanding plants or for increasing inventories or receivables. Therefore, to speak of depreciation expense as a source of cash is incorrect and misleading." Comment on these statements, taking into account income tax effects.

11. A firm generated net income for the current year, but cash flow from operations was negative. How can this happen?

12. A firm operated at a net loss for the current year, but cash flow from operations was positive. How can this happen?

13. The sale of equipment for an amount of cash greater than the book value of the equipment results in a cash receipt equal to the book value of the equipment plus the gain on the sale. Why does the accountant subtract the gain on sale of equipment from net income when computing cash flow from operations?

EXERCISES

14. **Calculating and interpreting cash flows.** Amazon.com sells books over the Internet. The changes in its balance sheet accounts for two recent years appear below (amounts in thousands):

	Year 4	Year 5
Cash	$5,252 Increase	$103,561 Increase
Marketable Securities	—	15,256 Increase
Inventories	554 Increase	8,400 Increase
Prepayments	307 Increase	2,977 Increase
Property, Plant, and Equipment (at cost)	1,360 Increase	15,283 Increase
Accumulated Depreciation	286 Increase	4,742 Increase
Accounts Payable—Merchandise Suppliers	2,753 Increase	29,845 Increase
Other Current Liabilities	2,010 Increase	7,603 Increase
Long-term Debt	—	78,202 Increase
Common Stock	8,201 Increase	52,675 Increase
Retained Earnings	5,777 Decrease	27,590 Decrease

a. Prepare columnar work sheets for the statement of cash flows for Year 4 and Year 5. Amazon.com did not declare or pay dividends during either year.

b. Prepare a statement of cash flows for Year 4 and Year 5. The balance in cash was $6,248 at the end of Year 4 and $109,809 at the end of Year 5.

c. Discuss the relation between net income and cash flow from operations and the relation between cash flow from operating, investing, and financing activities during the two years.

15. **Calculating and interpreting cash flows.** Yahoo, Inc., is an Internet service provider. The changes in its balance sheet accounts for two recent years appear below (amounts in thousands):

	Year 8	Year 9
Cash	$ 28,250 Increase	$28,991 Increase
Marketable Securities (current asset)	60,689 Increase	32,917 Decrease
Accounts Receivable	4,267 Increase	5,904 Increase
Prepayments	384 Increase	5,509 Increase
Property, Plant, and Equipment (at cost)	3,155 Increase	14,930 Increase
Accumulated Depreciation	552 Increase	2,554 Increase
Investments in Securities (noncurrent asset)	10,477 Increase	9,053 Increase
Accounts Payable	1,086 Increase	3,605 Increase
Other Current Liabilities	6,447 Increase	11,598 Increase
Common Stock	103,796 Increase	36,980 Increase
Retained Earnings	4,659 Decrease	23,267 Decrease

a. Prepare columnar work sheets for the statement of cash flows for Year 8 and Year 9. Yahoo, Inc., did not declare or pay dividends during either year. It sold marketable securities during Year 9 at no gain or loss.

b. Prepare a statement of cash flows for Year 8 and Year 9. The balance in cash was $33,547 at the end of Year 8 and $62,538 at the end of Year 9.

c. Discuss the relation between net income and cash flow from operations and the relation between cash flow from operating, investing, and financing activities during the two years.

16. **Preparing a columnar work sheet for a statement of cash flows from changes in balance sheet accounts.** The comparative balance sheets of The Coca-Cola Company show the following information for the current year (amounts in millions):

Change	Amount	Direction
Cash	$ 453[a]	Increase
Accounts Receivable	282	Increase
Inventories	2	Decrease
Prepayments	38	Increase
Property, Plant, and Equipment (at cost)	1,291[b]	Increase
Accumulated Depreciation	210[b]	Increase
Accounts Payable	347	Increase
Short-term Borrowing	411	Increase
Other Current Liabilities	248	Increase
Bonds Payable	195[c]	Increase
Common Stock	1,104	Decrease
Retained Earnings	1,755[d]	Increase

[a]Cash was $1,078 million at the beginning of the year and $1,531 million at the end of the year.
[b]The firm sold for $70 million during the year equipment costing $150 million and with accumulated depreciation of $80 million.
[c]The firm retired during the year bonds with a face value and book value of $150 million, at no gain or loss.
[d]The firm declared and paid dividends totaling $1,006 million during the year.

a. Prepare a columnar work sheet for the statement of cash flows for the current year.
b. Comment on the most important reasons for the change in cash during the year.

17. **Preparing a statement of cash flows from changes in balance sheet accounts.** The comparative balance sheets of Delta Airlines show the following information for a recent year (amounts in millions):

Change	Amount	Direction
Cash	$ 462[a]	Decrease
Accounts Receivable	26	Decrease
Inventories	11	Increase
Prepayments	19	Increase
Investments in Securities	345	Increase
Property, Plant, and Equipment (at cost)	1,219[b]	Increase
Accumulated Depreciation	363[b]	Increase
Accounts Payable	14	Increase
Notes Payable	88	Increase
Other Current Liabilities	32	Decrease
Long-term Debt	674	Increase
Common Stock	187	Decrease
Retained Earnings	186[c]	Increase

[a]Cash was $530 million at the beginning of the year and $68 million at the end of the year.
[b]Delta Airlines sold for $30 million equipment originally costing $151 million on which the firm had previously recognized $96 million of depreciation.
[c]Net income was $303 million.

a. Prepare a statement of cash flows for Delta Airlines for the year.

b. Discuss briefly the pattern of cash flows from operating, investing, and financing activities for Delta Airlines for the year.

18. **Calculating and interpreting cash flow from operations.** The following items appear in the financial statements of Upjohn, a pharmaceutical company, for Year 2 (amounts in millions):

Sales	$3,275
Depreciation Expense	163
Income Taxes	154
Other Expenses	2,469

The changes in the current asset and current liability accounts were as follows:

Accounts Receivable	$ 3	Decrease
Merchandise Inventories	46	Increase
Prepayments	195	Increase
Accounts Payable	58	Increase
Other Current Liabilities	62	Increase

a. Compute the amount of cash flow from operations.

b. Comment on the major reasons why cash flow from operations exceeds net income.

19. **Calculating and interpreting cash flow from operations.** Selected data for L.A. Gear, an athletic shoe company, appear below (amounts in millions):

	Year 8	Year 9	Year 10	Year 11
Net Income (Loss)	$22	$55	$31	$(68)
Depreciation Expense	1	1	3	7
Increase (Decrease) in:				
Accounts Receivable	35	51	56	(48)
Inventories	51	73	21	(20)
Prepayments	2	13	1	25
Accounts Payable	7	18	(4)	(15)
Other Current Liabilities	12	13	7	7

a. Compute the amount of cash flow from operations for each of the four years.

b. Discuss briefly the most important reasons why cash flow from operations differs from net income or net loss for each year.

20. **Calculating and interpreting cash flows.** Kelly Services is the largest temporary-help firm in the United States. Selected data for Kelly Services for three recent years appear below (amounts in thousands):

	Year 3	Year 4	Year 5
Net Income	$39,225	$44,559	$61,057
Depreciation Expense	13,977	16,614	17,309
Inc. (Dec.) in Marketable Securities	(31,571)	(9,614)	(2,265)
Inc. (Dec.) in Accounts Receivable	32,273	39,116	59,317
Inc. (Dec.) in Prepayments	2,340	2,656	9,137
Inc. (Dec.) in Salaries Payable	14,793	14,465	34,460
Inc. (Dec.) in Other Current Liabilities	(21,203)	12,600	20,241
Acquisition of Property, Plant, and Equipment	32,449	16,056	18,433
Dividends Paid	21,999	23,846	26,570
Common Stock Issued	1,617	1,031	373

   a. Prepare a comparative statement of cash flows for Kelly Services for the three years.

   b. Discuss the relation between net income and cash flow from operations and the pattern of cash flow from operating, investing, and financing activities during the three years.

21. **Working backward from changes in the Buildings and Equipment account.** The comparative balance sheets of American Airlines show a balance in the Buildings and Equipment account at cost on December 31, Year 4, of $17,369 million; at December 31, Year 3, the balance was $16,825 million. The Accumulated Depreciation account shows a balance of $5,465 million at December 31, Year 4, and of $4,914 million at December 31, Year 3. The statement of cash flows reports that expenditures for buildings and equipment for the year totaled $1,314 million. The income statement indicates a depreciation charge of $1,253 million for the year. The firm sold buildings and equipment during the year at their book value.

   Calculate the acquisition cost and accumulated depreciation of the buildings and equipment that were retired during the year and the proceeds from the disposition.

22. **Effects of gains and losses from sales of equipment on cash flows.** Exhibit 4.22 presents an abbreviated statement of cash flows for Largay Corporation for the current year (amounts in thousands). After preparing this statement of cash flows for the current year, you discover that the firm sold an item of equipment on the last day of the year but failed to record it in the accounts or to deposit the check received from the purchaser. The equipment originally cost $50,000 and had accumulated depreciation of $40,000 at the time of sale. Recast the statement of cash flows above assuming that Largay Corporation sold the equipment for cash in the following amounts (ignore income taxes):

   a. $10,000

   b. $12,000

   c. $8,000

23. **Effect of various transactions on the statement of cash flows.** Exhibit 4.16 shows a simplified statement of cash flows for a period. Numbers appear on nine of the lines in the statement. Other lines are various subtotals and grand totals; ignore these in the rest of the problem. Assume that the accounting cycle is complete for the period and that the firm has prepared all of the financial statements. It then discovers that it has overlooked a transaction. It records that transaction in the accounts and corrects all of the financial statements. For each of the following transactions, indicate which of the numbered lines of the statement of cash flows change and the

EXHIBIT 4.22	LARGAY CORPORATION Statement of Cash Flows for the Current Year (Exercise 22)

OPERATIONS

Net Income	$100
Depreciation Expense	15
Changes in Working Capital Accounts	(40)
Cash Flow from Operations	$ 75

INVESTING

Acquisition of Buildings and Equipment	(30)

FINANCING

Repayment of Long-term Debt	(40)
Change in Cash	$ 5
Cash, Beginning of Year	27
Cash, End of Year	$ 32

amount and direction of the change. If net income—line (1)—changes, be sure to indicate whether it decreases or increases. Ignore income tax effects.

a. Amortization of a patent, treated as an expense, $600

b. Acquisition of a factory site financed by issuing capital stock with a market value of $50,000 in exchange

c. Purchase of inventory on account for $7,500

d. Uninsured fire loss of merchandise inventory totaling $1,500

e. Collection of an account receivable totaling $1,450

f. Issue of bonds for $10,000 cash

g. Sale of equipment for its book value of $4,500

PROBLEMS AND CASES

24. **Preparing and interpreting the statement of cash flows using a columnar work sheet.** The accounting records of The GAP, a clothing retailer, for Year 6 and Year 7 indicate the following changes in its balance sheet accounts (amounts in millions):

	Year 6	Year 7
Cash	$ 94 Decrease	$428 Increase
Marketable Securities (current asset)	46 Increase	46 Decrease
Merchandise Inventories	96 Increase	154 Increase
Prepayments	1 Increase	56 Increase
Property, Plant, and Equipment (at cost)	372 Increase	466 Increase
Accumulated Depreciation	215 Increase	270 Increase
Other Noncurrent Assets	51 Increase	15 Increase
Accounts Payable—Merchandise Suppliers	114 Increase	134 Increase
Notes Payable to Banks (current liability)	18 Increase	45 Increase
Income Taxes Payable	26 Increase	7 Decrease
Other Current Liabilities	90 Increase	123 Increase
Bonds Payable	—	577 Increase
Common Stock	360 Decrease	524 Decrease
Retained Earnings	369 Increase	455 Increase

Income statement data for The GAP appear below:

	Year 6	Year 7
Sales	$5,284	$6,508
Cost of Goods Sold	(3,285)	(4,022)
Selling and Administrative Expenses	(1,250)	(1,632)
Income Tax Expense	(296)	(320)
Net Income	$ 453	$ 534

a. Prepare a columnar work sheet for the statement of cash flows for Year 6 and Year 7 (see the upper panel of Exhibit 4.4 for the desired format). The GAP sold marketable securities during Year 7 at their book value (that is, at no gain or loss). The firm did not sell property, plant, and equipment during either year. Treat changes in other noncurrent assets as an investing activity.

b. Prepare a statement of cash flows for Year 6 and Year 7 using the indirect method for computing cash flow from operations. The balance in cash was $486 at the end of Year 6 and $914 at the end of Year 7.

c. Compute cash flow from operations for Year 6 and Year 7 using the direct method (see the lower panel of Exhibit 4.4 for the desired format). The GAP includes depreciation in selling and administrative expenses. Your analysis should show how much cash The GAP collected from customers and how much cash The GAP paid to merchandise suppliers, to governments for income taxes, and to other providers of goods and services.

d. Comment on the pattern of cash flows from operating, investing, and financing activities.

25. **Preparing and interpreting the statement of cash flows using a columnar work sheet.** The accounting records of Circuit City for Year 7 and Year 8 indicate the following changes in balance sheet accounts (amounts in millions):

	Year 7	Year 8
Cash	$159 Increase	$ 86 Decrease
Accounts Receivable	208 Increase	66 Increase
Merchandise Inventories	69 Increase	19 Increase
Prepayments	8 Decrease	15 Decrease
Property, Plant, and Equipment (at cost)	209 Increase	291 Increase
Accumulated Depreciation	99 Increase	116 Increase
Accounts Payable—Merchandise Suppliers	117 Increase	44 Increase
Notes Payable to Banks (current asset)	92 Decrease	27 Increase
Other Current Liabilities	71 Decrease	9 Decrease
Bonds Payable	31 Increase	19 Decrease
Common Stock	428 Increase	25 Increase
Retained Earnings	125 Increase	91 Increase

Income statement data appear below:

	Year 7	Year 8
Sales	$7,664	$8,871
Cost of Goods Sold	(5,903)	(6,827)
Selling and Administrative Expenses	(1,511)	(1,849)
Interest Expense	(30)	(27)
Income Tax Expense	(84)	(64)
Net Income	$ 136	$ 104

a. Prepare a columnar work sheet for the statement of cash flows for Circuit City for Year 7 and Year 8 (see the upper panel of Exhibit 4.4 for the desired format). The firm did not sell property, plant, and equipment during either year. It includes depreciation in selling and administrative expenses. It retired bonds during the year at their book value.

b. Prepare a statement of cash flows for Circuit City for Year 7 and Year 8 using the indirect method of computing cash flow from operations. The balance in cash was $203 at the end of Year 7 and $117 at the end of Year 8.

c. Calculate the amount of cash collected from customers each year.

d. Calculate the amount of cash paid to suppliers of merchandise each year.

e. Calculate the amount of cash paid to suppliers of selling and administrative services during each year.

f. Comment on the pattern of cash flows from operating, investing, and financing activities cach year.

26. **Preparing and interpreting a statement of cash flows using a columnar work sheet.** Exhibit 4.23 presents a comparative balance sheet for Swan Corporation as of the beginning and the end of the current year. The firm made no dispositions of property, plant, and equipment during the year, nor did it declare or pay dividends.

EXHIBIT 4.23	SWAN CORPORATION Comparative Balance Sheet (Problem 26)

	January 1	December 31
ASSETS		
Current Assets		
Cash	$ 12,000	$ 15,000
Accounts Receivable	144,000	156,000
Merchandise Inventories	190,000	210,000
Total Current Assets	$346,000	$381,000
Property, Plant, and Equipment	$700,000	$775,000
Less Accumulated Depreciation	(246,000)	(325,000)
Total Property, Plant, and Equipment	$454,000	$450,000
Total Assets	$800,000	$831,000

(continued)

EXHIBIT 4.23 *(continued)*	SWAN CORPORATION Comparative Balance Sheet (Problem 26)

	January 1	December 31
LIABILITIES AND SHAREHOLDERS' EQUITY		
Current Liabilities		
Accounts Payable	$190,000	$165,000
Income Taxes Payable	20,000	25,000
Total Current Liabilities	$210,000	$190,000
Long-Term Debt		
Bonds Payable	100,000	96,000
Total Liabilities	$310,000	$286,000
Shareholders' Equity		
Common Stock	$210,000	$215,000
Retained Earnings	280,000	330,000
Total Shareholders' Equity	$490,000	$545,000
Total Liabilities and Shareholders' Equity	$800,000	$831,000

a. Prepare a columnar work sheet for the statement of cash flows for Swan Corporation for the current year (see the upper panel of Exhibit 4.4 for the desired format).
b. Prepare a statement of cash flows for the current year using the indirect method of computing cash flow from operations.
c. Comment on the pattern of cash flows from operating, investing, and financing activities.

EXHIBIT 4.24	HALE COMPANY Comparative Balance Sheet (Problem 27)

	January 1	December 31
ASSETS		
Cash	$ 52,000	$ 58,000
Accounts Receivable	93,000	106,000
Inventory	151,000	162,000
Land	30,000	30,000
Buildings and Equipment (cost)	790,000	830,000
Less Accumulated Depreciation	(460,000)	(504,000)
Total Assets	$656,000	$682,000
LIABILITIES AND SHAREHOLDERS' EQUITY		
Accounts Payable for Inventory	$136,000	$141,000
Interest Payable	10,000	8,000
Mortgage Payable	120,000	109,000
Common Stock	250,000	250,000
Retained Earnings	140,000	174,000
Total Liabilities and Shareholders' Equity	$656,000	$682,000

EXHIBIT 4.25	HALE COMPANY Statement of Income and Retained Earnings for the Current Year (Problem 27)

Sales Revenues		$1,200,000
Expenses		
Cost of Goods Sold	$788,000	
Wages and Salaries	280,000	
Depreciation	54,000	
Interest	12,000	
Income Taxes	22,000	
Total		$1,156,000
Net Income		$ 44,000
Dividends on Common Stock		(10,000)
Addition to Retained Earnings for Year		$ 34,000
Retained Earnings, January 1		140,000
Retained Earnings, December 31		$ 174,000

27. **Preparing and interpreting a statement of cash flows using a T-account work sheet.** Condensed financial statement data for Hale Company for the current year appear in Exhibits 4.24 and 4.25. During the current year, the firm sold for $5,000 equipment costing $15,000 with $10,000 of accumulated depreciation.
   a. Prepare a statement of cash flows for Hale Company for the year using the indirect method of computing cash flow from operations. Support the statement with a T-account work sheet.
   b. Calculate the amount of cash received from customers during the year.
   c. Calculate the amount of cash paid to suppliers of inventory during the year.
   d. Calculate the amount of cash paid to lenders for interest during the year.
   e. Comment on the pattern of cash flows from operations, investing, and financing activities.
28. **Preparing and interpreting a statement of cash flows using a T-account work sheet.** Financial statement data for Dickerson Manufacturing Company for the current year appear in Exhibit 4.26.
   Additional information includes the following:

   (1) Net income for the year was $568,000; dividends declared and paid were $60,000.
   (2) Depreciation expense for the year was $510,000 on buildings and machinery.
   (3) The firm sold for $25,000 machinery originally costing $150,000 with accumulated depreciation of $120,000.
   a. Prepare a statement of cash flows for Dickerson Manufacturing Company for the year using the indirect method to compute cash flow from operations. Support the statement with a T-account work sheet.
   b. Comment on the pattern of cash flows from operating, investing, and financing activities.

	EXHIBIT 4.26	DICKERSON MANUFACTURING COMPANY Comparative Balance Sheet (Problem 28)

	January 1	December 31
ASSETS		
Current Assets		
Cash	$ 358,000	$ 324,000
Accounts Receivable	946,000	1,052,000
Inventory	1,004,000	1,208,000
Total Current Assets	$2,308,000	$2,584,000
Noncurrent Assets		
Land	$ 594,000	$ 630,000
Buildings and Machinery	8,678,000	9,546,000
Less Accumulated Depreciation	(3,974,000)	(4,364,000)
Total Noncurrent Assets	$5,298,000	$5,812,000
Total Assets	$7,606,000	$8,396,000
LIABILITIES AND SHAREHOLDERS' EQUITY		
Current Liabilities		
Accounts Payable	$ 412,000	$ 558,000
Taxes Payable	274,000	290,000
Other Short-term Payables	588,000	726,000
Total Current Liabilities	$1,274,000	$1,574,000
Noncurrent Liabilities		
Bonds Payable	1,984,000	1,934,000
Total Liabilities	$3,258,000	$3,508,000
Shareholders' Equity		
Common Stock	$1,672,000	$1,704,000
Retained Earnings	2,676,000	3,184,000
Total Shareholders' Equity	$4,348,000	$4,888,000
Total Liabilities and Shareholders' Equity	$7,606,000	$8,396,000

29. **Preparing an income statement and a statement of cash flows.** The year's condensed financial statement data for Vincent Company appear in Exhibit 4.27. Expenditures on new plant and equipment for the year amounted to $60,000.
    a. Prepare an income statement (including a reconciliation of retained earnings) for the year.
    b. Prepare a statement of cash flows for Vincent Company using the indirect method of computing cash flow from operations. Support the statement of cash flows with a T-account work sheet.
    c. Comment on the pattern of cash flows from operating, investing, and financing activities.
30. **Preparing and interpreting a statement of cash flows using a T-account work sheet.** Exhibit 4.28 presents a comparative balance sheet for Clark Corporation as of the beginning and the end of the current year. Additional information related to the year appears below Exhibit 4.28.

EXHIBIT 4.27	VINCENT COMPANY Post-Closing Trial Balance Comparative Data (Problem 29)		
		January 1	**December 31**
Debits			
Cash		$ 42,000	$ 38,000
Accounts Receivable		130,000	113,000
Merchandise Inventory		216,000	202,000
Plant and Equipment (cost)		872,000	850,000
Total Debits		$ 1,260,000	$ 1,203,000
Credits			
Accounts Payable		$ 61,000	$ 53,000
Accumulated Depreciation		473,000	540,000
Long-term Debt		250,000	275,000
Capital Stock		300,000	300,000
Retained Earnings		176,000	35,000
Total Credits		$ 1,260,000	$ 1,203,000
Income Statement Data			
Sales			$ 1,300,000
Gain on Sale of Equipment			6,000
Cost of Goods Sold (excluding depreciation)			910,000
Selling and Administrative Expenses			428,000
Depreciation Expense			85,000
Interest Expense			24,000

EXHIBIT 4.28	CLARK CORPORATION Comparative Balance Sheet (Problem 30)		
		January 1	**December 31**
ASSETS			
Current Assets			
Cash		$ 42,000	$ 38,000
Accounts Receivable		146,000	166,000
Merchandise Inventories		162,000	178,000
Total Current Assets		$350,000	$ 382,000
Property, Plant, and Equipment		$180,000	$ 266,000
Less Accumulated Depreciation		(62,000)	(78,000)
Total Property, Plant, and Equipment		$118,000	$ 188,000
Total Assets		$468,000	$ 570,000

(continued)

EXHIBIT 4.28 (continued)	CLARK CORPORATION Comparative Balance Sheet (Problem 30)

LIABILITIES AND SHAREHOLDERS' EQUITY

Current Liabilities

Accounts Payable	$182,000	$ 199,000
Income Taxes Payable	20,000	25,000
Total Current Liabilities	$202,000	$ 224,000
Long-Term Debt		
Bonds Payable	20,000	50,000
Total Liabilities	$222,000	$ 274,000
Shareholders' Equity		
Common Stock	$ 50,000	$ 50,000
Retained Earnings	196,000	246,000
Total Shareholders' Equity	$246,000	$ 296,000
Total Liabilities and Shareholders' Equity	$468,000	$ 570,000

Net Income	$60,000
Dividends Declared and Paid	10,000
Property, Plant, and Equipment Acquired:	
For Cash	80,000
By Exchanging for Long-Term Debt	20,000
Proceeds from Sales of Property, Plant, and Equipment at Book Value	8,000

    a. Prepare a statement of cash flows for Clark Corporation for the current year, supporting the statement with a T-account work sheet.

    b. Comment on the pattern of cash flows from operating, investing, and financing activities.

31. **Preparing a statement of cash flows over a two-year period using a T-account work sheet.** Condensed financial statement data of Quebec Company for December 31, Year 1, Year 2, and Year 3, appear in Exhibits 4.29 and 4.30.

    a. Prepare a statement of cash flows for Quebec Company for Year 2 using the indirect method of computing cash flow from operations. Support the statement with a T-account work sheet. The original cost of the property, plant, and equipment sold during Year 2 was $216,000. The firm sold these assets for cash at their net book value.

    b. Prepare a statement of cash flows for Year 3 using the indirect method of computing cash flow from operations. Support the statement with a T-account work sheet. The firm sold equipment during the year at a loss of $4,000. Expenditures on new property, plant, and equipment amounted to $636,000 during Year 3.

    c. Comment on the pattern of cash flows from operating, investing, and financing activities for each year.

EXHIBIT 4.29	QUEBEC COMPANY Post-Closing Trial Balance Comparative Data (Problem 31)		

	12/31/Year 1	12/31/Year 2	12/31/Year 3
Debits			
Cash	$ 110,000	$ 174,000	$ 194,000
Accounts Receivable	220,000	240,000	210,000
Merchandise Inventories	250,000	230,000	280,000
Total Current Assets	$ 580,000	$ 644,000	$ 684,000
Property, Plant, and Equipment	3,232,000	3,358,000	3,750,000
Total Debits	$3,812,000	$4,002,000	$4,434,000
Credits			
Accounts Payable	$ 162,000	$ 160,000	$ 166,000
Accumulated Depreciation	1,394,000	1,440,000	1,490,000
Bonds Payable	212,000	180,000	270,000
Common Stock	754,000	846,000	1,028,000
Retained Earnings	1,290,000	1,376,000	1,480,000
Total Credits	$3,812,000	$4,002,000	$4,434,000

EXHIBIT 4.30	QUEBEC COMPANY Income and Retained Earnings Statement Data (Problem 31)	

Sales	$1,820,000	$1,940,000
Interest and Other Revenue	10,000	14,000
Cost of Goods Sold (excluding depreciation)	740,000	826,000
Selling and Administrative Expenses	640,000	602,000
Depreciation	174,000	192,000
Loss on Sale of Equipment	—	4,000
Federal Income Taxes	110,000	132,000
Dividends Declared	80,000	94,000

32. **Working backward through the statement of cash flows.** Quinta Company presents the post-closing trial balance shown in Exhibit 4.31 and the statement of cash flows shown in Exhibit 4.32 for Year 5. The firm sold investments, equipment, and land for cash at their net book value. The accumulated depreciation of the equipment sold was $20,000.

Prepare a balance sheet for the beginning of the year, January 1, Year 5.

EXHIBIT 4.31	QUINTA COMPANY Post-Closing Trial Balance December 31, Year 5 (Problem 32)

Debit Balances

Cash	$ 25,000
Accounts Receivable	220,000
Merchandise Inventories	320,000
Land	40,000
Buildings and Equipment	500,000
Investments (noncurrent)	100,000
Total Debits	$1,205,000

Credit Balances

Accumulated Depreciation	$ 200,000
Accounts Payable	280,000
Other Current Liabilities	85,000
Bonds Payable	100,000
Common Stock	200,000
Retained Earnings	340,000
Total Credits	$1,205,000

EXHIBIT 4.32	QUINTA COMPANY Statement of Cash Flows for Year 5 (Problem 32)

Operations

Net Income		$ 200,000
Additions:		
Depreciation Expense	60,000	
Increase in Accounts Payable	25,000	
Subtractions:		
Increase in Accounts Receivable	(30,000)	
Increase in Merchandise Inventories	(40,000)	
Decrease in Other Current Liabilities	(45,000)	
Cash Flow from Operations		$ 170,000
Investing		
Sale of Investments	$ 40,000	
Sale of Buildings and Equipment	15,000	
Sale of Land	10,000	
Acquisition of Buildings and Equipment	(130,000)	
Cash Flow from Investing		(65,000)
Financing		
Common Stock Issued	$ 60,000	
Bonds Issued	40,000	
Dividends Paid	(200,000)	
Cash Flow from Financing		(100,000)
Net Change in Cash		$ 5,000

33. **Preparing and interpreting the statement of cash flows using the indirect method. (Adapted from a problem by L. Morrissey.)** RV Suppliers, Inc., founded in January, Year 1, manufactures "Kaps." A "Kap" is a relatively low-cost camping unit attached to a pickup truck. Most units consist of an extruded aluminum frame and a fiberglass skin.

After a loss in its initial year, the company was barely profitable in Year 2 and Year 3. It realized more substantial earnings in Years 4 and 5, as the financial statements in Exhibits 4.33 and 4.34 show. However, in Year 6, ended just last month, the company suffered a loss of $13,400. Sales dropped from $424,000 in Year 5 to $247,400 in Year 6. The outlook for Year 7 is not encouraging. Potential buyers continue to shun pickup trucks in preference for more energy-efficient, small foreign and domestic automobiles.

EXHIBIT 4.33	RV SUPPLIERS, INC. Balance Sheet (all dollar amounts in thousands) (Problem 33)

	Dec 31 Year 4	Dec 31 Year 5	Dec 31 Year 6
ASSETS			
Cash	$ 14.0	$ 12.0	$ 5.2
Accounts Receivable	28.8	55.6	24.2
Inventories	54.0	85.6	81.0
Tax Refund Receivable	0	0	5.0
Prepayments	4.8	7.4	5.6
Total Current Assets	$101.6	$160.6	$121.0
Property, Plant, and Equipment—Net (Note 1)	30.2	73.4	72.2
Total Assets	$131.8	$234.0	$193.2
LIABILITIES AND SHAREHOLDER'S EQUITY			
Current Liabilities			
Bank Notes Payable	$ 10.0	$ 52.0	$ 70.0
Accounts Payable	31.6	53.4	17.4
Income Taxes Payable	5.8	7.0	0
Other Current Liabilities	4.2	6.8	4.4
Total Current Liabilities	$ 51.6	$119.2	$ 91.8
Shareholders' Equity			
Capital Stock	$ 44.6	$ 44.6	$ 44.6
Retained Earnings	35.6	70.2	56.8
Total Shareholders' Equity	$ 80.2	$114.8	$101.4
Total Liabilities and Shareholders' Equity	$131.8	$234.0	$193.2
Note 1: Analysis of Changes in Property, Plant, and Equipment	Year 4	Year 5	Year 6
Balance in Property, Plant, and Equipment (net) at Beginning of Year	$ 18.9	$ 30.2	$ 73.4
Acquisitions	13.4	48.4	12.2
Depreciation Expense	(1.7)	(4.8)	(8.0)
Book Value of Property, Plant, and Equipment Sold	(.4)	(.4)	(5.4)
Balance in Property, Plant and Equipment (net) at End of Year	$ 30.2	$ 73.4	$ 72.2

EXHIBIT 4.34	RV SUPPLIERS, INC. Income Statement (all dollar amounts in thousands) (Problem 33)			

	Year 4	Year 5	Year 6
Net Sales	$266.4	$424.0	$ 247.4
Cost of Goods Sold	(191.4)	(314.6)	(210.6)
Gross Margin	$ 75.0	$109.4	$ 36.8
Operating Expenses[a]	(35.5)	(58.4)	(55.2)
Income (Loss) before Income Taxes	$ 39.5	$ 51.0	$ (18.4)
Income Taxes	(12.3)	(16.4)	5.0
Net Income (Loss)	$ 27.2	$ 34.6	$ (13.4)

[a]Includes depreciation expense of $1.7 in Year 4, $4.8 in Year 5, and $8.0 in Year 6.

How did the company finance its rapid growth during the year ended December 31, Year 5? What were the sources and uses of cash during the year? Similarly, how did the company manage its financial affairs during the abrupt contraction in business during the year just ended last month? Property, plant, and equipment were sold during the year at their book value. (*Hint:* Prepare a statement of cash flows for Year 5 and Year 6 to assist in responding to these questions.)

34. **Inferring cash flows from trial balance data.** Exhibit 4.35 presents trail balance excerpts for Heidi's Hide-Out, a bar and video-game club, with private rooms for rent for parties. The trial balance at the beginning of the year is post-closing, meaning that the firm closed its income statement accounts at the end of the previous year and has not yet entered income transactions for the current year. The trial balance at the end of the year is adjusted preclosing, meaning that the firm has made all adjusting entries for the year to properly measure net income but has not yet closed its income statement accounts to retained earnings. Heidi's deals with

- many employees, to some of whom it has made advances on wages and to some of whom it owes wages for past work;

- many landlords, to some of whom it has made advance payments and to some of whom it owes rent for past months;

- many customers, some of whom have paid for special parties not yet held and some of whom have not yet paid for parties they have held; and

- many suppliers of goods, including food and beverages, some of whom Heidi's has paid for orders not yet received and some of whom have delivered goods for which Heidi's has not yet paid.

Heidi's and its customers, suppliers, and employees settle all transactions with cash, never with noncash assets.

a. Calculate the amount of cash received from retail customers during the current year.

b. Calculate the amount of cash Heidi's paid landlords during the current year for the rental of space.

c. Calculate the amount of cash Heidi's paid employees during the current year.

EXHIBIT 4.35	HEIDI'S HIDE-OUT Selected Detail from Trial Balances For the Current Year (Problem 34)				

	Post-Closing Trial Balance Beginning of Year		Adjusted Preclosing Trial Balance End of Year	
	Debits	**Credits**	**Debits**	**Credits**
Accounts Payable to Suppliers of Retail Merchandise		$ 8,000		$ 7,700
Accounts Receivable from Retail Customers	$ 8,000		$ 8,900	
Advances from Retail Customers		9,000		10,000
Advances to Employees	1,000		1,500	
Advances to Landlords	5,000		5,600	
Advances to Suppliers of Retail Merchandise	10,000		10,500	
Cost of Retail Merchandise Sold			90,000	
Inventory of Retail Merchandise	11,000		10,000	
Rent Expense			33,000	
Rent Payable to Landlords		6,000		5,300
Sales Revenue from Retail Customers				120,000
Wage Expense			20,000	
Wages Payable to Employees		2,000		1,800
All Other Accounts (Net)		10,000		34,700
Totals	$35,000	$35,000	$179,500	$179,500

    d. Calculate the amount of cash Heidi's paid suppliers of retail merchandise, which includes food and beverages it sells to retail customers, during the current year.

35. Inferring cash flows from balance sheet and income statement data. (Based on a problem prepared by Stephen A. Zeff.) You work for the Plains State Bank in Miles City, Montana, as an analyst specializing in the financial statements of small businesses seeking loans from the bank. Digit Retail Enterprises, Inc., provides you with its balance sheet on December 31, Year 4 and Year 5 (Exhibit 4.36), and its income statement for Year 5 (Exhibit 4.37). The firm's independent accountant has audited these financial statements and found them to be in conformity with generally accepted accounting principles. Digit Retail Enterprises acquired no new property, plant, and equipment during the year.

    a. Calculate the amount of cash received from customers during the year.

    b. Calculate the acquisition cost of merchandise purchased during the year.

    c. Calculate the amount of cash paid to suppliers of merchandise during the year.

    d. Calculate the amount of cash paid to salaried employees during the year.

    e. Calculate the amount of cash paid to insurance companies during the year.

    f. Calculate the amount of cash paid to landlords for rental of space during the year.

    g. Calculate the amount of dividends paid during the year.

    h. Calculate the amount of cash received when property, plant, and equipment were sold during the year.

EXHIBIT 4.36	DIGIT RETAIL ENTERPRISES, INC. Balance Sheet (Problem 35)

	December 31, Year 4	December 31, Year 5
ASSETS		
Current Assets		
Cash	$ 36,000	$ 50,000
Accounts Receivable	23,000	38,000
Notes Receivable	7,500	—
Interest Receivable	100	—
Merchandise Inventory	48,000	65,000
Prepaid Insurance	9,000	12,000
Prepaid Rent	2,000	—
Total Current Assets	$125,600	$165,000
Property, Plant, and Equipment		
At Cost	$100,000	$ 90,000
Less Accumulated Depreciation	(20,000)	(35,000)
Net	$ 80,000	$ 55,000
Total Assets	$205,600	$220,000
LIABILITIES AND SHAREHOLDERS' EQUITY		
Current Liabilities		
Accounts Payable—Merchandise Suppliers	$ 18,000	$ 20,000
Salaries Payable	2,100	2,800
Rent Payable	—	3,000
Advances from Customers	8,500	6,100
Note Payable	—	5,500
Dividends Payable	4,200	2,600
Other Current Liabilities	1,300	3,700
Total Current Liabilities	$ 34,100	$ 43,700
Shareholders' Equity		
Common Stock	$160,000	$164,500
Retained Earnings	11,500	11,800
Total Shareholders' Equity	$171,500	$176,300
Total Liabilities and Shareholders' Equity	$205,600	$220,000

36. **Interpreting the statement of cash flows.** Exhibit 4.38 presents a statement of cash flows for Nike, Inc., maker of athletic shoes, for three recent years.

   a. Why did Nike experience increasing net income but decreasing cash flow from operations during this three-year period?

   b. What is the likely explanation for the changes in Nike's cash flow from investing during the three-year period?

   c. How did Nike finance its investing activities during the three-year period?

   d. Evaluate the appropriateness of Nike's use of short-term borrowing during Year 9.

EXHIBIT 4.37	DIGIT RETAIL ENTERPRISES, INC. Income Statement For Year 5 (Problem 35)

Sales Revenue	$270,000
Gain on Sale of Property, Plant, and Equipment	3,200
Interest Revenue	200
Total Revenues	$273,400
Less Expenses:	
Cost of Goods Sold	$145,000
Salaries Expense	68,000
Rent Expense	12,000
Insurance Expense	5,000
Depreciation Expense	20,000
Other Expenses	13,800
Total Expenses	$263,800
Net Income	$ 9,600

EXHIBIT 4.38	NIKE, INC. Statement of Cash Flows (amounts in millions) (Problem 36)

	Year 7	Year 8	Year 9
Operations			
Net Income	$ 167	$ 243	$ 287
Depreciation and Amortization	15	17	34
Other Addbacks and Subtractions	(5)	5	3
Working Capital Provided by Operations	$ 177	$ 265	$ 324
(Increase) Decrease in Accounts Receivable	(38)	(105)	(120)
(Increase) Decrease in Inventories	(25)	(86)	(275)
(Increase) Decrease in Other Operating Current Assets	(2)	(5)	(6)
Increase (Decrease) in Accounts Payable	21	36	59
Increase (Decrease) in Other Current Operating Liabilities	36	22	32
Cash Flow from Operations	$ 169	$ 127	$ 14
Investing			
Sale of Property, Plant, and Equipment	$ 3	$ 1	$ 2
Acquisition of Property, Plant, and Equipment	(42)	(87)	(165)
Acquisition of Investment	(1)	(3)	(48)
Cash Flow from Investing	$ (40)	$ (89)	$(211)
Financing			
Increase in Short-term Debt	—	—	$ 269
Increase in Long-term Debt	—	$ 1	5
Issue of Common Stock	$ 3	2	3
Decrease in Short-term Debt	(96)	(8)	—
Decrease in Long-term Debt	(4)	(2)	(10)
Dividends	(22)	(26)	(41)
Cash Flow from Financing	$(119)	$ (33)	$ 226
Change in Cash	$ 10	$ 5	$ 29
Cash, Beginning of Year	74	84	89
Cash, End of Year	$ 84	$ 89	$ 118

	EXHIBIT 4.39	BOISE CASCADE CORPORATION Statement of Cash Flows (amounts in millions) (Problem 37)

	Year 5	Year 6	Year 7
Operations			
Net Income (Loss)	$(154)	$ (77)	$ (63)
Depreciation	266	268	236
Other Addbacks (Subtractions)	(56)	(43)	41
(Inc.) Dec. in Accounts Receivable	(46)	—	(68)
(Inc.) Dec. in Inventories	(3)	(31)	6
Inc. (Dec.) in Accounts Payable	9	15	55
Inc. (Dec.) in Other Current Liabilities	50	(1)	9
Cash Flow from Operations	$ 66	$ 131	$ 216
Investing			
Sale of Property, Plant, and Equipment	$ 202	$ 24	$ 171
Acquisition of Property, Plant, and Equipment	(283)	(222)	(271)
Other Investing Transactions	(31)	9	(75)
Cash Flow from Investing	$(112)	$(189)	$(175)
Financing			
Inc. (Dec.) in Short-term Borrowing	$ (54)	$ 27	$ 25
Inc. in Long-term Debt	131	84	139
Inc. In Preferred Stock	191	287	—
Dec. in Long-term Debt	(164)	(269)	(116)
Dividends	(55)	(67)	(84)
Other Financing Transactions	(5)	(2)	2
Cash Flow from Financing	$ 44	$ 60	$ (34)
Change in Cash	$ (2)	$ 2	$ 7
Cash—Beginning of Year	22	20	22
Cash—End of Year	$ 20	$ 22	$ 29

37. **Interpreting the statement of cash flows.** Exhibit 4.39 presents a statement of cash flows for Boise Cascade Corporation, a forest products company, for three recent years.
   a. Boise Cascade operated at a net loss each year but generated positive cash flow from operations. Explain.
   b. What is the likely explanation for the changes in Boise Cascade's cash flow from investing activities during the three-year period?
   c. What is the likely explanation for the changes in long-term financing during Year 5 and Year 6?

38. **Interpreting the statement of cash flow relations.** Exhibit 4.40 presents statements of cash flow for eight companies for a recent year:
   a. American Airlines (airline transportation)
   b. American Home Products (pharmaceuticals)
   c. Interpublic Group (advertising and other marketing services)
   d. Procter & Gamble (consumer products)

   e. Reebok (athletic shoes)
   f. Texas Instruments (electronics)
   g. The Limited (specialty retailing)
   h. Upjohn (pharmaceuticals)

   Discuss the relation between net income and cash flow from operations and the pattern of cash flows from operating, investing, and financing activities for each firm.

EXHIBIT 4.40

Statements of Cash Flows for Selected Companies
(amounts in millions)
(Problem 38)

	American Airlines	American Home Products	Interpublic Group	Procter & Gamble	Reebok	Texas Instruments	The Limited	Upjohn
OPERATIONS								
Net Income (Loss)	$ (110)	$ 1,528	$ 125	$2,211	$ 254	$ 691	$ 455	$ 491
Depreciation	1,223	306	61	1,134	37	665	247	175
Other Addbacks (Subtractions)	166	71	23	196	(4)	(9)	—	7
(Inc.) Dec. in Receivables	37	14	(66)	40	(65)	(197)	(102)	6
(Inc.) Dec. in Inventories	(27)	(157)	16	25	(82)	(60)	(74)	(21)
Inc. (Dec.) in Payables	34	325	59	98	35	330	118	63
Inc. (Dec.) in Other Current Liabilities	54	(185)	(15)	(55)	(2)	112	110	(11)
Cash Flow from Operations	$ 1,377	$ 1,902	$ 203	$3,649	$ 173	$ 1,532	$ 754	$ 710
INVESTING								
Capital Expenditures (net)	$(2,080)	$ (473)	$ (79)	$(1,841)	$ (62)	$(1,076)	$ (430)	$ (224)
Sale (Acq.) of Marketable Securities	290	24	3	23	—	(47)	—	(287)
Sale (Acq.) of Other Businesses	—	(9,161)	—	(295)	—	—	(60)	308
Other Investing	36	(5)	(85)	105	(4)	—	—	(1)
Cash Flow from Investing	$(1,754)	$(9,615)	$(161)	$(2,008)	$ (66)	$(1,123)	$ (490)	$ (204)
FINANCING								
Inc. (Dec.) in Short-term Borrowing	$ (380)	$ 8,640	$ 35	$ (281)	$ 37	$ (1)	$ (322)	$ 5
Inc. in Long-term Debt	730	—	42	414	—	1	150	15
Inc. in Capital Stock	1,081	38	19	36	13	110	17	—
Dec. in Long-term Debt	(1,069)	—	(15)	(797)	(3)	(88)	—	(46)
Acq. of Treasury Stock	—	(314)	(37)	(14)	(112)	—	—	(32)
Dividends	(49)	(903)	(36)	(949)	(25)	(79)	(102)	(264)
Other Financing	82	11	(14)	1	(12)	4	—	37
Cash Flow from Financing	$ 395	$ 7,472	$ (6)	$(1,590)	$(102)	$ (53)	$ (257)	$ (285)
Change in Cash	$ 18	$ (241)	$ 36	$ 51	$ 5	$ 356	$ 7	$ 221
Cash—Beginning of Year	45	1,937	256	2,322	79	404	34	281
Cash—End of Year	$ 63	$ 1,696	$ 292	$ 2,373	$ 84	$ 760	$ 41	$ 502

INTRODUCTION
TO FINANCIAL
STATEMENT ANALYSIS

1. Understand the relation between the expected return and risk of investment alternatives and the role financial statement analysis can play in providing information about returns and risk.
2. Understand the usefulness of the rate of return on assets (ROA) as a measure of a firm's operating profitability independent of financing and the insights gained by disaggregating ROA into profit-margin and assets-turnover components.
3. Understand the usefulness of the rate of return on common shareholders' equity (ROCE) as a measure of profitability that incorporates a firm's particular mix of financing and the insights gained by disaggregating ROCE into profit-margin, assets-turnover, and leverage-ratio components.
4. Understand the strengths and weaknesses of earnings per common share as a measure of profitability.
5. Understand the distinction between short-term liquidity risk and long-term liquidity (solvency) risk and the financial statement ratios used to assess these two dimensions of risk.
6. Develop skills to interpret effectively the results of an analysis of profitability and risk.
7. (Appendix) Develop skills to prepare pro forma financial statements.
8. (Appendix) Understand the usefulness of pro forma financial statements in the valuation of a firm.

Chapters 1 through 4 discussed the purpose, underlying concepts, preparation, and uses of the three principal financial statements: the balance sheet, the income statement, and the statement of cash flows. Chapters 6 through 12 explore the generally accepted accounting principles that accountants use in preparing these statements.

Before embarking on our study of accounting principles, we introduce, in this chapter, tools and techniques for analyzing financial statements. Most financial statement analysis attempts to assess the profitability and risk of a firm. The analyst examines relations between various financial statement items, expressed in the form of financial statement ratios. This chapter describes several commonly used financial statement ratios and illustrates their usefulness in assessing a firm's profitability and risk.

Such analyses permit the analyst (1) to evaluate the past performance and current financial position of a firm (primarily a backward-looking exercise) and (2) to project its likely future performance and condition (primarily a forward-looking exercise).

Assessments by management of the performance of competitors, assessments by shareholders of the performance of management, and assessments by government antitrust regulators of the performance of a firm use *historical* data. This chapter emphasizes such analyses. An examination of the financial statement effects of changes in strategies or policies, such as adding new products or substituting debt financing for equity financing, emphasizes the analysis of *projected* data. Management prepares a set of pro forma financial statements based on these new strategies or policies to study their impact. Analysts also use pro forma financial statements in valuing a firm, such as in evaluating an acquisition candidate. The appendix to this chapter discusses the preparation and use of pro forma financial statements.

OBJECTIVES OF FINANCIAL STATEMENT ANALYSIS

The first question the analyst asks in analyzing a set of financial statements is, "What do I look for?" The response to this question requires an understanding of investment decisions.

To illustrate, assume that you recently inherited $25,000 and must decide what to do with the bequest. You narrow the investment decision to purchasing either a certificate of deposit at a local bank or shares of common stock of Horrigan Corporation, currently selling for $70 per share. You will base your decision on the **return** you anticipate from each investment and the **risk** associated with that return.

The bank currently pays interest at the rate of 5 percent annually on certificates of deposit. Because the bank is unlikely to go out of business, you are virtually certain of earning 5 percent each year. The return from investing in the shares of Horrigan Corporation's common stock has two components. First, the firm paid a cash dividend in its most recent year of $.625 per share, and you anticipate that it will continue to pay this dividend in the future. Also, the market price of the stock will likely change between the date you purchase the shares and the date in the future when you sell them. The difference between the eventual selling price and the purchase price, often called a capital gain (or loss, if negative), is a second component of the return from buying the stock.

The common stock investment involves more risk than does the certificate of deposit investment. The future profitability of the firm will likely affect future dividends and market price changes. If competitors introduce new products that erode Horrigan Corporation's share of its sales market, future income might be less than you currently anticipate. If Horrigan Corporation makes important discoveries or introduces successful new products, future income might be greater than you currently anticipate.

Economy-wide factors such as inflation and changes in international tensions will also affect the market price of Horrigan Corporation's shares. Also, specific industry factors, such as raw materials shortages or government regulatory actions, may influence the market price of the shares. Because most individuals prefer less risk to more risk, you will probably expect a higher return if you purchase Horrigan Corporation's shares than if you invest in a certificate of deposit.

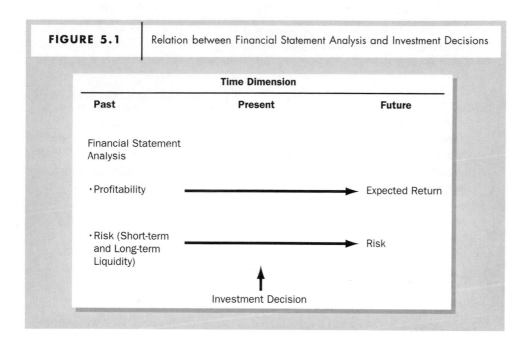

Theoretical and empirical research has shown that the expected return from investing in a firm relates, in part, to the expected profitability of the firm.[1] The analyst studies a firm's past earnings to understand its operating performance and to help forecast its future profitability.

Investment decisions also require that the analyst assess the risk associated with the expected return.[2] A firm may find itself short of cash and unable to repay a short-term loan coming due. Or the amount of long-term debt in the capital structure may be so large that the firm has difficulty meeting the required interest and principal payments. The financial statements provide information for assessing how these and other elements of risk affect expected return.

Most financial statement analysis, therefore, explores some aspect of a firm's profitability or its risk or both. Figure 5.1 summarizes the relation between financial statement analysis and investment decisions.

USEFULNESS OF RATIOS

Readers may have difficulty answering questions about a firm's profitability and risk from the raw information in financial statements. For example, one cannot assess the profitability of a firm by noting the amount of net income. Comparing earnings with the assets or capital required to generate those earnings can help. The analyst expresses these (and other useful) relations between items in the financial statements in the form of ratios. Some ratios compare items within the income statement; some use only balance sheet data; others relate items from more than one of the three principal financial statements.

---

[1]Ray Ball and Phillip Brown, "An Empirical Evaluation of Accounting Income Numbers," *Journal of Accounting Research* (Autumn 1968), 159–78; Jane A. Ou and Stephen H. Penman, "Financial Statement Analysis and the Prediction of Stock Returns," *Journal of Accounting and Economics* (November 1989), 295–329.

[2]Modern finance distinguishes between systematic (market) risk and nonsystematic (firm-specific) risk. The discussion in this chapter does not distinguish between these two dimensions of risk.

EXHIBIT 5.1	HORRIGAN CORPORATION Comparative Income Statements (all dollar amounts in millions)		

| | For the Year Ended December 31 | | |
	Year 2	**Year 3**	**Year 4**
Sales Revenue	$210	$310	$475
Less Expenses:			
Cost of Goods Sold	$119	$179	$280
Selling	36	42	53
Administrative	15	17	22
Depreciation	12	14	18
Interest	5	10	16
Total	$187	$262	$389
Net Income before Taxes	$ 23	$ 48	$ 86
Income Tax Expense	7	14	26
Net Income	$ 16	$ 34	$ 60

Ratios aid financial statement analysis because they conveniently summarize data in a form easy to understand, interpret, and compare.

Ratios, by themselves out of context, provide little information. For example, does a rate of return on common shareholders' equity of 8.6 percent indicate satisfactory performance? After calculating the ratios, the analyst must compare them with some standard. The following list provides several possible standards:

1. The planned ratio for the period
2. The corresponding ratio during the preceding period for the same firm
3. The corresponding ratio for a similar firm in the same industry
4. The average ratio for other firms in the same industry

Later sections of this chapter discuss difficulties encountered in using each of these bases for comparison.

The following sections describe several ratios useful for assessing profitability and various dimensions of risk. To demonstrate the calculation of various ratios, we use data for Horrigan Corporation for Years 2 through 4 appearing in Exhibit 5.1 (comparative income statements), Exhibit 5.2 (comparative balance sheets), and Exhibit 5.3 (comparative statements of cash flows). Our analysis for Horrigan Corporation examines changes in its various ratios over the three-year period. We call such an analysis a **time-series analysis,** in contrast with a **cross-section analysis,** which involves comparing a given firm's ratios with those of other firms for a specific period. Several problems at the end of the chapter involve cross-section analysis (see Exercises 11, 12, 13, 17, and 18 and Problem 28).

ANALYSIS OF PROFITABILITY

A firm engages in operations to generate net income. This section discusses three measures of **profitability:**

EXHIBIT 5.2	HORRIGAN CORPORATION Comparative Balance Sheets (all dollar amounts in millions)

	December 31			
	Year 1	Year 2	Year 3	Year 4
ASSETS				
Cash	$ 10	$ 14	$ 8	$ 12
Accounts Receivable (net)	26	36	46	76
Inventories	14	30	46	83
Total Current Assets	$ 50	$ 80	$100	$171
Land	$ 20	$ 30	$ 60	$ 60
Building	150	150	150	190
Equipment	70	192	276	313
Less Accumulated Depreciation	(40)	(52)	(66)	(84)
Total Noncurrent Assets	$200	$320	$420	$479
Total Assets	$250	$400	$520	$650
LIABILITIES AND SHAREHOLDERS' EQUITY				
Accounts Payable	$ 25	$ 30	$ 35	$ 50
Salaries Payable	10	13	15	20
Income Taxes Payable	5	7	10	20
Total Current Liabilities	$ 40	$ 50	$ 60	$ 90
Bonds Payable	50	50	100	150
Total Liabilities	$ 90	$100	$160	$240
Common Stock ($10 par value)	$100	$150	$160	$160
Additional Paid-in Capital	20	100	120	120
Retained Earnings	40	50	80	130
Total Shareholders' Equity	$160	$300	$360	$410
Total Liabilities and Shareholders' Equity	$250	$400	$520	$650

1. Rate of return on assets
2. Rate of return on common shareholders' equity
3. Earnings per share of common stock

RATE OF RETURN ON ASSETS

The **rate of return on assets (ROA)** measures a firm's performance in using assets to generate earnings independent of the financing of those assets. Previous chapters described three principal business activities: investing, financing, and operating. The rate of return on assets relates the results of operating performance to the investments of a firm without regard to how the firm financed the acquisition of those investments.

The calculation of ROA is as follows:

$$\text{ROA} = \frac{\text{Net Income} + \text{Interest Expense Net of Income Tax Savings}}{\text{Average Total Assets}}$$

EXHIBIT 5.3	HORRIGAN CORPORATION Comparative Statements of Cash Flows (all dollar amounts in millions)

| | **For the Year Ended December 31** | | |
	Year 2	**Year 3**	**Year 4**
OPERATIONS			
Net Income	$ 16	$ 34	$ 60
Additions:			
Depreciation Expense	12	14	18
Increase in Accounts Payable	5	5	15
Increase in Salaries Payable	3	2	5
Increase in Income Taxes Payable	2	3	10
Subtractions:			
Increase in Accounts Receivable	(10)	(10)	(30)
Increase in Inventories	(16)	(16)	(37)
Cash Flow from Operations	$ 12	$ 32	$ 41
INVESTING			
Purchase of Land	$ (10)	$ (30)	—
Purchase of Building	—	—	$(40)
Purchase of Equipment	(122)	(84)	(37)
Cash Flow from Investing	$(132)	$(114)	$(77)
FINANCING			
Issuance of Bonds	—	$ 50	$ 50
Issuance of Common Stock	$ 130	30	—
Dividends	(6)	(4)	(10)
Cash Flow from Financing	$ 124	$ 76	$ 40
Net Change in Cash	$ 4	$ (6)	$ 4
Cash, Beginning of Year	10	14	8
Cash, End of Year	$ 14	$ 8	$ 12

In the numerator, ROA uses an earnings figure that recognizes income before any payments or distributions to the suppliers of capital. Because firms compute net income after subtracting interest expense on debt, the analyst must add back the interest expense to net income if the numerator is to exclude the costs of financing. Because firms can deduct interest expense in calculating taxable income, interest expense does not reduce *aftertax* net income by the full amount of interest expense. Thus, to calculate the numerator of ROA, the analyst adds back interest expense reduced by the income taxes that interest deductions save.

For example, Horrigan Corporation reported interest expense for Year 4 (see Exhibit 5.1) of $16 million. The income tax rate is 30 percent of pretax income. Because Horrigan can deduct interest in computing taxable income, it saved income taxes of $4.8 million (= .30 × $16 million). The net after-tax cost of interest expense was $11.2 million (= $16.0 million − $4.8 million). To compute income before payments of interest to lenders, the analyst adds back to net income $11.2 million. The analyst need not add back dividends paid to shareholders because the firm does not deduct them as an expense in calculating net income; net income already represents an amount before payments to suppliers of shareholders' equity capital.

Because we are computing the earnings rate for a year, the measure of investment for the denominator should reflect the average amount of assets in use during the year. A crude but usually satisfactory figure for average total assets is one-half the sum of total assets at the beginning and at the end of the year.

CONCEPTUAL NOTE

Most financial economists would subtract average noninterest-bearing liabilities (for example, accounts payable, salaries payable) from average total assets in the denominator of ROA. Economists realize that when liabilities do not provide for explicit interest charges, the creditor adjusts the terms of the contract, such as setting a higher selling price or lower discount, for those who do not pay cash immediately. This ratio requires in the numerator the income amount before a firm accrues any charges to suppliers of funds. We cannot measure the interest charges implicit in the noninterest-bearing liabilities; items such as cost of goods sold and salary expense are somewhat larger because of these charges. Thus, implicit charges reduce the measure of operating income in the numerator. Subtracting average noninterest-bearing liabilities from average total assets likewise reduces the denominator for assets financed with such liabilities. The examples and problems in this book use average total assets in the denominator of the rate of return on assets, making no adjustment for noninterest-bearing liabilities.

The calculation of rate of return on assets for Horrigan Corporation for Year 4 is as follows:[3]

$$\frac{\text{Net Income} + \text{Interest Expense Net of Income Tax Savings}}{\text{Average Total Assets}} = \frac{\$60 + (\$16 - \$4.8)}{.5(\$520 + \$650)} = 12.2 \text{ percent}$$

Thus, for each dollar of assets used, the management of Horrigan Corporation earned $.122 during Year 4 before payments to the suppliers of capital. The rate of return on assets was 8.9 percent in Year 3 and 6.0 percent in Year 2. Thus the rate of return increased steadily during this three-year period.

One might question the rationale for a measure of return that excludes the costs of financing. After all, the firm must finance the assets and must cover the cost of the financing if it is to be profitable.

The rate of return on assets has particular relevance to lenders, or creditors, of a firm. These creditors have a senior claim on earnings and assets relative to common shareholders. Creditors receive their return via contractual interest payments. The firm typically pays these amounts before it makes payments, often as dividends, to any other suppliers of capital. When extending credit or providing debt capital to a firm, creditors want to be sure that the firm can generate a rate of return on that capital (assets) exceeding its cost.

Common shareholders find the rate of return on assets useful in assessing financial leverage, which a later section of this chapter discusses.

---

[3]Throughout the remainder of this chapter, we omit reference to the fact that the amounts for Horrigan Corporation are in millions; for example, "$60" means "$60 million," and "16 shares" means "16 million shares."

DISAGGREGATING THE RATE OF RETURN ON ASSETS

To study changes in the rate of return on assets, the analyst can disaggregate ROA into the product of two other ratios. Improving either of these ratios will improve the overall rate of return. The disaggregation follows:

$$
\begin{array}{c}
\text{Rate of} \\
\text{Return} \\
\text{on Assets}
\end{array}
=
\begin{array}{c}
\text{Profit Margin Ratio} \\
\text{(before interest expense} \\
\text{and related} \\
\text{income tax effects)}
\end{array}
\times
\begin{array}{c}
\text{Total Assets} \\
\text{Turnover} \\
\text{Ratio}
\end{array}
$$

Or:

$$
\frac{\begin{array}{c}\text{Net Income} + \\ \text{Interest Expense} \\ \text{Net of Income} \\ \text{Tax Savings}\end{array}}{\begin{array}{c}\text{Average Total} \\ \text{Assets}\end{array}}
=
\frac{\begin{array}{c}\text{Net Income} + \\ \text{Interest Expense} \\ \text{Net of Income} \\ \text{Tax Savings}\end{array}}{\text{Sales}}
\times
\frac{\text{Sales}}{\begin{array}{c}\text{Average Total} \\ \text{Assets}\end{array}}
$$

The **profit margin ratio** measures a firm's ability to control the level of expenses relative to sales. By holding down costs, a firm can increase the profits from a given amount of sales and thereby improve its profit margin ratio. The **total assets turnover ratio** measures a firm's ability to generate sales from a particular level of investment in assets. The smaller the amount of assets the firm needs to generate a given level of sales, the better (larger) will be the assets turnover. The total assets turnover measures a firm's ability to control the level of investment in assets for a particular level of sales.

Exhibit 5.4 disaggregates the rate of return on assets for Horrigan Corporation into profit margin and total assets turnover ratios for Year 2, Year 3, and Year 4. Much of the improvement in the rate of return on assets between Year 2 and Year 3 results from an increase in the profit margin ratio from 9.3 percent to 13.2 percent. The total assets turnover ratio remained relatively stable between these two years. On the other hand, one can attribute most of the improvement in the rate of return on assets between Year 3 and Year 4

EXHIBIT 5.4	HORRIGAN CORPORATION Disaggregation of Rate of Return on Assets for Year 2, Year 3, and Year 4

	$\dfrac{\begin{array}{c}\textbf{Net Income plus}\\\textbf{Interest Expense}\\\textbf{Net of Income}\\\textbf{Tax Savings}\end{array}}{\textbf{Average Total Assets}}$	=	$\dfrac{\begin{array}{c}\textbf{Net Income plus}\\\textbf{Interest Expense}\\\textbf{Net of Income}\\\textbf{Tax Savings}\end{array}}{\textbf{Sales}}$	×	$\dfrac{\textbf{Sales}}{\textbf{Average Total Assets}}$
Year 2:	$\dfrac{\$16 + (\$5 - \$1.5)}{.5(\$250 + \$400)}$	=	$\dfrac{\$16 + (\$5 - \$1.5)}{\$210}$	×	$\dfrac{\$210}{.5(\$250 + \$400)}$
	6.0%	=	9.3%	×	0.65
Year 3:	$\dfrac{\$34 + (\$10 - \$3)}{.5(\$400 + \$520)}$	=	$\dfrac{\$34 + (\$10 - \$3)}{\$310}$	×	$\dfrac{\$310}{.5(\$400 + \$520)}$
	8.9%	=	13.2%	×	0.67
Year 4:	$\dfrac{\$60 + (\$16 - \$4.8)}{.5(\$520 + \$650)}$	=	$\dfrac{\$60 + (\$16 - \$4.8)}{\$475}$	×	$\dfrac{\$475}{.5(\$520 + \$650)}$
	12.2%	=	15.0%	×	0.81

to the increased total assets turnover. The firm increased sales from each dollar invested in assets from \$.67 of sales per dollar in Year 3 to \$.81 of sales from each dollar invested in assets during Year 4. The increased total assets turnover, coupled with an improvement in the profit margin ratio, permitted Horrigan Corporation to increase its rate of return on assets during Year 4. To pinpoint the causes of the changes in Horrigan Corporation's profitability over this three-year period, we must analyze the changes in the profit margin ratio and total assets turnover ratio further. We will examine this analysis shortly.

Firms improve their rate of return on assets by increasing the profit margin ratio, the rate of assets turnover, or both. Some firms, however, have limited flexibility to alter one or the other of these components. For example, a firm selling commodity products in a highly competitive market may have little opportunity to increase its profit margin. Such a firm would likely take actions to improve its assets turnover (for example, tightening inventory controls to shorten the holding period for inventories) when attempting to increase its rate of return on assets. The activities of other firms might require substantial investments in property, plant, and equipment. The need for such investment might constrain the firm's ability to increase its rate of return on assets by increasing its assets turnover. Such a firm might have more flexibility to take actions that increase the profit margin (for example, creating brand loyalty for its products).

ANALYZING CHANGES IN THE PROFIT MARGIN RATIO

Changes in a firm's expenses relative to sales cause the profit margin ratio to change. To see the relation, one can express individual expenses and net income as a percentage of sales. Exhibit 5.5 presents such an analysis, which Chapter 3 described as a common-size income statement, for Horrigan Corporation. This analysis alters the conventional income statement format by subtracting interest expense (net of its related income tax effects) as the last expense item. The percentages on the line Income before Interest and Related

EXHIBIT 5.5	HORRIGAN CORPORATION Common-Size Income Statement for Year 2, Year 3, and Year 4		
	Year Ended December 31		
	Year 2	**Year 3**	**Year 4**
Sales Revenue	100.0%	100.0%	100.0%
Less Operating Expenses:			
Cost of Goods Sold	56.7%	57.7%	58.9%
Selling	17.1	13.6	11.2
Administrative	7.1	5.5	4.6
Depreciation	5.7	4.5	3.8
Total	86.6%	81.3%	78.5%
Income before Income Taxes and Interest	13.4%	18.7%	21.5%
Income Taxes at 30 Percent	4.1	5.5	6.5
Income before Interest and Related Income Tax Effect	9.3%	13.2%	15.0%
Interest Expense Net of Income Tax Effect	1.7	2.2	2.4
Net Income	7.6%	11.0%	12.6%

Income Tax Effect correspond to the profit margin ratios (before interest and related tax effects) in Exhibit 5.4.

The analysis in Exhibit 5.5 indicates that the improvement in Horrigan Corporation's profit margin ratio over the three years resulted primarily from decreased selling, administrative, and depreciation expenses as a percentage of sales. The analyst should explore further with management the reasons for these decreasing percentages.

- Does the decrease in selling expenses as a percentage of sales reflect an advertising expenditure reduction that could hurt future sales?
- Does the decrease in depreciation expense as a percentage of sales reflect a failure to expand plant and equipment as sales increased?
- On the other hand, do these decreasing percentages result from economies of scale as the firm spreads fixed marketing, administrative, and depreciation expenses over a larger number of units?[4]

Neither the amount nor the trend in a particular ratio should, by itself, cause the analyst to invest in a firm. Ratios indicate areas requiring additional analysis. For example, the analyst should further explore the increasing percentage of cost of goods sold to sales. The increase may reflect a pricing policy of reducing gross margin (selling price less cost of goods sold) to increase the volume of sales, a policy successfully designed to generate increased profits even though the gross margin percentage declines. On the other hand, the replacement cost of inventory items may have increased without accompanying increases in selling prices. Or, the firm may have accumulated excess inventories that are physically deteriorating or are becoming obsolete.

ANALYZING CHANGES IN THE TOTAL ASSETS TURNOVER RATIO

The total assets turnover ratio aggregates the effects of the turnover ratios for the individual asset components. The analyst generally calculates three separate assets turnover ratios: accounts receivable turnover, inventory turnover, and fixed asset turnover.

Accounts Receivable Turnover   The rate at which accounts receivable turn over indicates how quickly a firm collects cash. The **accounts receivable turnover ratio** equals sales revenue divided by average accounts receivable during the period. In theory the numerator should include only sales made on account. Most firms, except some retailers (such as fast-food outlets) that deal directly with final consumers, sell their goods and services on account. Other firms sell both for cash and on account. Such firms seldom disclose the proportions of cash and credit sales in their financial statements or notes. Thus, the analyst uses sales revenue in the numerator of the accounts receivable turnover ratio, recognizing that the inclusion of sales made for cash will increase the numerator and thereby overstate the turnover ratio. For Horrigan Corporation, the accounts receivable turnover ratio for Year 4 is as follows:

$$\frac{\text{Sales}}{\text{Average Accounts Receivable}} = \frac{\$475}{.5(\$46 + \$76)} = 7.8 \text{ times per year}$$

The analyst often expresses the accounts receivable turnover in terms of the average number of days that elapse between the time that the firm makes the sale and the time that it

---

[4]*Operating leverage* is the term used to describe this phenomenon, which managerial accounting and managerial economics textbooks discuss more fully.

later collects the cash, sometimes called "days accounts receivable are outstanding" or "days outstanding for receivables." To calculate this ratio, divide 365 days by the accounts receivable turnover ratio. The days outstanding for accounts receivable for Horrigan Corporation during Year 4 average 46.8 days (= 365 days/7.8 times per year). Thus, on average, it takes slightly more than 1.5 months after the date of sale to collect receivables. Whether this represents good performance or bad depends on the terms of sale. If the terms of sale are "net 30 days," the accounts receivable turnover indicates that collections do not accord with the stated terms. Such a result warrants a review of the credit and collection activity to ascertain the cause and to guide corrective action. If the firm offers terms of "net 60 days," the ratio indicates that the firm handles accounts receivable well.

Inventory Turnover   The **inventory turnover ratio** indicates how fast firms sell their inventory items, measured in terms of rate of movement of goods into and out of the firm. Inventory turnover equals cost of goods sold divided by the average inventory during the period. The inventory turnover for Horrigan Corporation for Year 4 is as follows:

$$\frac{\text{Cost of Goods Sold}}{\text{Average Inventory}} = \frac{\$280}{.5(\$46 + \$83)} = 4.3 \text{ times per year}$$

Items remain in inventory about 85 days (= 365 days/4.3 times per year) before sale.

Managing inventory turnover involves two opposing considerations. Firms prefer to sell as many goods as possible with a minimum of capital tied up in inventories. An increase in the rate of inventory turnover between periods indicates reduced costs of financing the investment in inventory. On the other hand, management does not want to have so little inventory on hand that shortages result in lost sales. Increases in the rate of inventory turnover caused by inventory shortages could signal a loss of customers, thereby offsetting any advantage gained by decreased investment in inventory. Firms must balance these opposing considerations in setting the optimum level of inventory and, thus, the accompanying rate of inventory turnover.

Some analysts calculate the inventory turnover ratio by dividing sales, rather than cost of goods sold, by the average inventory. As long as the ratio of selling price to cost of goods sold remains relatively constant, either measure will identify changes in the trend of the inventory holding period. Using sales in the numerator will lead, however, to incorrect measures of the inventory turnover ratio for calculating the average number of days that inventory is on hand until sale.

Fixed Asset Turnover   The **fixed asset turnover ratio** measures the relation between the investment in fixed assets—property, plant, equipment—and sales. The fixed asset turnover ratio for Horrigan Corporation for Year 4 is as follows:

$$\frac{\text{Sales}}{\text{Average Fixed Assets}} = \frac{\$475}{.5(\$420 + \$479)} = 1.1 \text{ times per year}$$

Thus $1.00 invested in fixed assets during Year 4 generated $1.10 in sales.

Some analysts find the reciprocal of this ratio helpful in comparing the operating characteristics of different firms. The reciprocal ratio measures dollars of fixed assets required to generate one dollar of sales. For Horrigan Corporation, this reciprocal is $.95. Horrigan requires $.95 of fixed assets to generate $1.00 of sales. Compare fixed assets per dollar of sales of AT&T, for example, with that of Safeway Stores in a recent year. AT&T has $2.70 of fixed assets per dollar of sales while Safeway Stores, a retailer with relatively modest fixed assets, requires only $.16 (i.e., only 16¢) of fixed assets per dollar of sales. AT&T has large asset requirements to generate sales; Safeway does not.

Interpret changes in the fixed asset turnover ratio cautiously. Firms often invest in fixed assets (for example, new production facilities) several periods before these assets

	Year 2	Year 3	Year 4

EXHIBIT 5.6 — HORRIGAN CORPORATION
Asset Turnover Ratios for Year 2, Year 3, and Year 4

	Year 2	Year 3	Year 4
Total Assets Turnover	0.65	0.67	0.81
Accounts Receivable Turnover	6.80	7.60	7.80
Inventory Turnover	5.40	4.70	4.30
Fixed Asset Turnover	0.80	0.80	1.10

generate sales from products manufactured in their plants. Thus, a low or decreasing rate of fixed asset turnover may indicate an expanding firm preparing for future growth. On the other hand, a firm anticipating a decline in product sales could cut back its capital expenditures. Such an action could increase the fixed asset turnover ratio.

Summary of Asset Turnovers We noted earlier that the total assets turnover ratio for Horrigan Corporation remained stable between Year 2 and Year 3 but increased in Year 4. Exhibit 5.6 presents the four turnover ratios discussed for Horrigan Corporation over this three-year period. The accounts receivable turnover ratio increased steadily over the three years, indicating either more careful screening of credit applications or more effective collection efforts. The inventory turnover ratio decreased during the three years. Coupling this result with the increasing percentage of cost of goods sold to sales shown in Exhibit 5.5 indicates possibly excessive investments in deteriorating and obsolete inventories.

Most of the increase in the total assets turnover between Year 3 and Year 4 results from an increase in the fixed asset turnover ratio. We note in the statement of cash flows for Horrigan Corporation in Exhibit 5.3 that total capital expenditures on land, buildings, and equipment decreased over the three-year period, possibly accounting for the increase in the fixed asset turnover ratio. The analyst should ask, "What caused this decrease?"

SUMMARY OF THE ANALYSIS OF THE RATE OF RETURN ON ASSETS

The rate of return on assets helps one assess a firm's performance in using assets to generate earnings, independent of the financing of those assets. The rate of return on assets results from the interaction of its separate components: profit margin and total assets turnover.

- The profit margin ratio results from the relation of the various expenses to sales.
- Total assets turnover reflects the effects of turnover ratios for accounts receivable, inventory, and fixed assets.

The analysis for Horrigan Corporation revealed the following:

1. The rate of return on assets increased over the three-year period from Year 2 to Year 4.
2. An increasing profit margin over all three years and an improved total assets turnover during Year 4 help to explain the improved rate of return on assets.
3. Decreases in the percentages of selling, administrative, and depreciation expenses to sales largely explain the improved profit margin. The analyst should question whether

these decreases resulted from the firm's curtailing selling and administrative efforts, a cutback that might adversely affect future sales and operations.

4. The changes in the total assets turnover reflect the effects of increasing accounts receivable and fixed asset turnover ratios and a decreasing inventory turnover ratio. The increasing fixed asset turnover, coupled with the decreased depreciation expense percentage, might relate to a reduced level of investment in new property, plant, and equipment, a reduction that could hurt future productive capacity. The analyst should question whether the decreasing rate of inventory turnover, coupled with the increasing percentage of cost of goods sold to sales, indicates the buildup of obsolete inventory or some other inventory-control problem.

PROBLEM 5.1 FOR SELF-STUDY

Analyzing the rate of return on assets. Exhibit 5.7 presents profitability ratios for Abbott Corporation for three recent years.

a. Identify the likely reason for the decreasing rate of return on assets. Use common-size income statement percentages and individual asset turnover ratios in your interpretations.

b. What is the likely explanation for the decreasing cost of goods sold to sales percentage coupled with the increasing inventory turnover ratio?

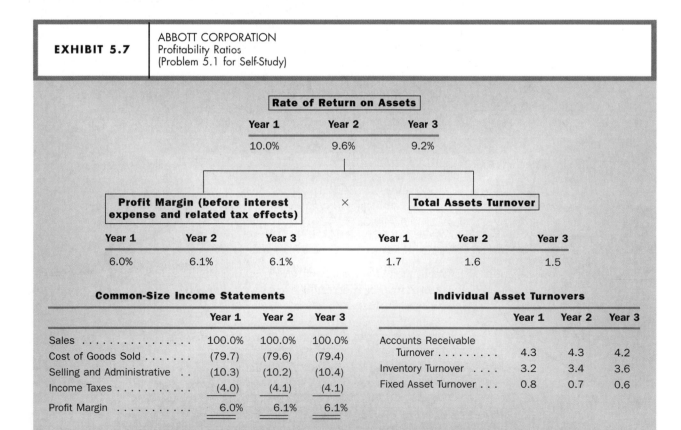

EXHIBIT 5.7 — ABBOTT CORPORATION Profitability Ratios (Problem 5.1 for Self-Study)

Rate of Return on Assets

Year 1	Year 2	Year 3
10.0%	9.6%	9.2%

Profit Margin (before interest expense and related tax effects) × **Total Assets Turnover**

Year 1	Year 2	Year 3		Year 1	Year 2	Year 3
6.0%	6.1%	6.1%		1.7	1.6	1.5

Common-Size Income Statements

	Year 1	Year 2	Year 3
Sales	100.0%	100.0%	100.0%
Cost of Goods Sold	(79.7)	(79.6)	(79.4)
Selling and Administrative	(10.3)	(10.2)	(10.4)
Income Taxes	(4.0)	(4.1)	(4.1)
Profit Margin	6.0%	6.1%	6.1%

Individual Asset Turnovers

	Year 1	Year 2	Year 3
Accounts Receivable Turnover	4.3	4.3	4.2
Inventory Turnover	3.2	3.4	3.6
Fixed Asset Turnover	0.8	0.7	0.6

RATE OF RETURN ON COMMON SHAREHOLDERS' EQUITY

The **rate of return on common shareholders' equity (ROCE)** measures a firm's performance in using and financing assets to generate earnings and is of primary interest to common shareholders. Unlike the rate of return on assets, the rate of return on shareholders' equity explicitly considers financing costs. Thus this measure of profitability incorporates the results of operating, investing, and financing decisions. The calculation of the rate of return on common shareholders' equity is as follows:

$$\text{ROCE} = \frac{\text{Net Income} - \text{Dividends on Preferred Stock}}{\text{Average Common Shareholders' Equity}}$$

The Numerator   To calculate the amount of earnings assignable to common shareholders' equity, the analyst subtracts all amounts required to compensate other providers of capital for the use of their funds. Expenses subtracted in computing net income already include amounts for interest expense, so the analysis requires no further adjustment for interest. Because expenses exclude all dividends, the analyst must subtract from net income any earnings allocable to preferred stock equity, usually the dividends on preferred stock declared during the period, to measure the returns solely to the common shareholders. Note that the analyst should not subtract dividends on common stock, because such dividends represent distributions to common shareholders of a portion of the returns generated for them during the period.

The Denominator   The capital provided by common shareholders during the period equals the average par value of common stock, capital contributed in excess of par value on common stock, and retained earnings for the period. (Alternatively, subtract average preferred shareholders' equity from average total shareholders' equity.)

The rate of return on common shareholders' equity of Horrigan Corporation for Year 4 is as follows:

$$\frac{\text{Net Income} - \text{Dividends on Preferred Stock}}{\text{Average Common Shareholders' Equity}} = \frac{\$60 - \$0}{.5(\$360 + \$410)} = 15.6 \text{ percent}$$

The rate of return on common shareholders' equity was 7.0 percent in Year 2 and 10.3 percent in Year 3. The rate of return on common shareholders' equity increased over the three years.

RELATION BETWEEN RETURN ON ASSETS AND RETURN ON COMMON SHAREHOLDERS' EQUITY

Figure 5.2 graphs the two measures of rate of return discussed thus far for Horrigan Corporation for Year 2, Year 3, and Year 4. In each year, the rate of return on common shareholders' equity exceeds the rate of return on assets. What accounts for this relation, a normal one for profitable firms?

The rate of return on assets measures the profitability of a firm before any payments to the suppliers of capital. Each of the various providers of capital have a claim on some portion of this return on assets. The share allocated to creditors equals any contractual interest to which they have a claim (net of tax savings the firm realizes from deducting interest for tax purposes). The share allocated to preferred shareholders, if any, equals the stated dividend amounts on the preferred stock. Any remaining earnings belong to the common shareholders; that is, common shareholders have a residual claim on all

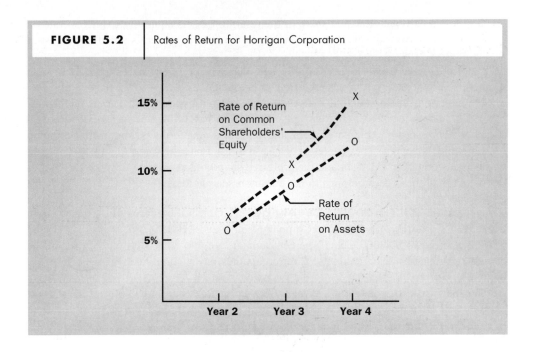

FIGURE 5.2 | Rates of Return for Horrigan Corporation

earnings after creditors and preferred shareholders receive amounts contractually owed them. Thus,

$$
\text{Rate of Return on Assets} \rightarrow \begin{bmatrix} \text{Return to} & \text{Return to} & \text{Return to} \\ \text{Creditors} & , & \text{Preferred} & , & \text{Common} \\ \text{(interest)} & \text{Shareholders} & \text{Shareholders} \\ & \text{(dividends)} & \text{(residual)} \end{bmatrix}
$$

We can now see that the rate of return on common shareholders' equity will exceed the rate of return on assets whenever the rate of return on assets exceeds the aftertax cost of debt (assuming, as here, that the firm has no preferred stock outstanding). For Year 4, the rate of return on assets was 12.2 percent and the aftertax cost of liabilities was 5.6 percent [= (1.0 − 0.3)($16)/.5($160 + $240); see Exhibits 5.1 and 5.2]. This return to assets exceeding the cost of aftertax debt belongs to the common shareholders.

The common shareholders earned a higher return, but they undertook more risk in their investment. The risk results from the firm's incurring debt obligations with fixed payment amounts and dates. The next section discusses this phenomenon, called *financial leverage.*

FINANCIAL LEVERAGE

The term **financial leverage** describes financing with debt and preferred stock to increase the potential return to the residual common shareholders' equity. Financial leverage works as follows:

1. A firm obtains funds from creditors, preferred shareholders, and common shareholders.
2. The firm invests the funds in various assets. Each period the firm generates a return on the assets. The rate of return on assets measures this return before allocating any amounts to the suppliers of capital.

3. Creditors receive an allocated share of the return on assets equal to the interest rate on the amount borrowed. The cost of this debt to the firm, however, is the aftertax cost of the interest expense.
4. Preferred shareholders receive an allocated share of the return on assets equal to the preferred dividend rate on the preferred stock outstanding.
5. The common shareholders have a residual claim on all earnings in excess of the cost of debt and preferred shareholder financing. As long as a firm earns a rate of return on assets that exceeds the cost of debt and preferred shareholder capital, the common shareholders benefit. They benefit because the difference between the amount earned on assets financed with debt and the preferred shareholders' capital exceeds the cost of that capital; the excess belongs to the common shareholders.

Illustration of Financial Leverage   Exhibit 5.8 explores this phenomenon. Leveraged Company and No-Debt Company both have $100,000 in assets. Leveraged Company borrows $40,000 at a 10 percent annual rate. No-Debt Company raises all its capital from common shareholders. Both companies pay income taxes at the rate of 30 percent.

Consider, first, a good earnings year. Both companies earn $10,000 before interest charges (but after taxes, except for tax effects of interest charges).[5] This represents a rate of return on assets for both companies of 10 percent (= $10,000/$100,000). Leveraged Company's net income is $7,200 [= $10,000 − ((1.0 − 0.3 tax rate) × (.10 interest rate × $40,000 borrowed))], representing a rate of return on common shareholders' equity of 12.0 percent (= $7,200/$60,000). Net income of No-Debt Company is $10,000, representing a rate of return on shareholders' equity of 10 percent. Leverage increased the rate of return to shareholders of Leveraged Company because the capital contributed by the long-term debtors earned 10 percent but required an aftertax interest payment of only 7 percent [= (1.0 − 0.3 tax rate) × (.10 interest rate)]. This additional 3 percent return on each dollar of assets financed by creditors increased the return to the common shareholders, as the following analysis shows.

RATE OF RETURN TO COMMON SHAREHOLDERS

Excess Return on Assets Financed with Debt:	
(.10 − .07) × ($40,000)	$ 1,200
Return on Assets Financed by Common Shareholders:	
(.10) × ($60,000).	6,000
Total Return to Common Shareholders	$ 7,200
Common Shareholders' Equity	$60,000
Rate of Return on Common Shareholders' Equity:	
$7,200/$60,000	12%

Although leverage increased the return to common stock equity during the good earnings year, a larger increase would occur if the firm financed a greater proportion of its assets with long-term borrowing, simultaneously increasing the firm's risk level. For example, assume that the firm financed its assets of $100,000 with $50,000 of long-term borrowing and $50,000 of shareholders' equity. Net income of Leveraged Company in this case would be $6,500 [= $10,000 − ((1.0 − 0.3 tax rate) × (.10 × $50,000 borrowed))]. The rate of return on common stock equity would be 13 percent (= $6,500/$50,000). This compares with a rate of return on common stock equity of 12 percent when long-term debt was only 40 percent of the total capital provided. Increasing

---

[5]Income before taxes and before interest charges is $14,286; $10,000 = (1.0 − .3) × $14,286.

leverage from 40 percent to 50 percent, assuming the interest rate on the borrowings stayed constant, increased the rate of return from 12 percent to 13 percent.

This 13 percent rate of return on common stock equity has the following components:

RATE OF RETURN TO COMMON SHAREHOLDERS

Excess Return on Assets Financed with Debt:	
$(.10 - .07) \times (\$50,000)$	$ 1,500
Return on Assets Financed by Common Shareholders:	
$(.10) \times (\$50,000)$	5,000
Total Return to Common Shareholders	$ 6,500
Common Shareholders' Equity	$50,000
Rate of Return on Common Shareholders' Equity:	
$\$6,500/\$50,000$	13%

Financial leverage increases the rate of return on common stock equity when the rate of return on assets exceeds the aftertax cost of debt. The greater the proportion of debt in the capital structure, however, the greater is the risk the common shareholders bear. In addition, a firm cannot increase debt without increasing the cost of debt. As it adds more debt to the capital structure, the risk of insolvency or bankruptcy becomes greater. *Insolvency* refers to a condition in which the firm has insufficient cash to pay its current debts, whereas *bankruptcy* refers to a legal condition in which liabilities usually exceed assets. Lenders, including investors in a firm's bonds, require a higher and higher return (interest rate) to compensate for this additional risk. At some point, the aftertax cost of debt will exceed the rate of return earned on assets. At this point, leverage no longer increases the potential rate of return to common stock equity. For most large manufacturing firms, liabilities represent between 30 percent and 60 percent of total capital.

Exhibit 5.8 also demonstrates the effect of leverage in a neutral earnings year and in a bad earnings year. In the neutral earnings year, leverage neither increases nor decreases the rate of return to common shareholders because the return on assets is 7 percent and the aftertax cost of long-term debt is also 7 percent. In the bad earnings year, the return on assets of 4 percent falls below the 7 percent aftertax cost of debt. The difference between the cost of debt and the return generated on assets financed with that debt reduces the return to the common shareholders. The return on common shareholders' equity then drops below the rate of return on assets, to only 2 percent. Clearly, financial leverage—borrowing—can work in two ways. It can enhance owners' rate of return in good years, but owners run the risk that bad earnings years will be even worse than these years would have been without the borrowing.

DISAGGREGATING THE RATE OF RETURN ON COMMON SHAREHOLDERS' EQUITY

The rate of return on common shareholders' equity disaggregates into several components (in a manner similar to that of the disaggregation of the rate of return on assets):

Rate of Return on Common Shareholders' Equity	=	Profit Margin Ratio (after interest expense and preferred dividends)	×	Total Assets Turnover Ratio	×	Leverage Ratio

The profit margin percentage indicates the portion of the sales dollar left over for the common shareholders after covering all operating costs and subtracting all claims of creditors and preferred shareholders. The total assets turnover indicates the sales generated from each dollar of assets. The **leverage ratio** indicates the relative proportion of capital provided by

EXHIBIT 5.8 Effects of Financial Leverage on Rate of Return on Common Shareholders' Equity (income tax rate is 30 percent of pretax income)

	Long-Term Financing Equals $100,000		Income after Taxes but before Interest Charges[a]	Aftertax Interest Charges[b]	Net Income	Rate of Return on Total Assets[c] (percent)	Rate of Return on Common Shareholders' Equity (percent)
	Borrowing at 10 Percent Per Year	Shareholders' Equity					
Good Earnings Year							
Leveraged Company	$40,000	$ 60,000	$10,000	$2,800	$ 7,200	10.0%	12.0%
No-Debt Company	—	100,000	10,000	—	10,000	10.0%	10.0%
Neutral Earnings Year							
Leveraged Company	40,000	60,000	7,000	2,800	4,200	7.0%	7.0%
No-Debt Company	—	100,000	7,000	—	7,000	7.0%	7.0%
Bad Earnings Year							
Leveraged Company	40,000	60,000	4,000	2,800	1,200	4.0%	2.0%
No-Debt Company	—	100,000	4,000	—	4,000	4.0%	4.0%

[a]Not including any income tax savings caused by interest charges. Income before taxes and interest for *good* year is $14,286, for *neutral* year is $10,000, for *bad* year is $5,714.

[b]$40,000 (borrowed) × .10 (interest rate) × [1 − .30 (income tax rate)]. The numbers shown in the preceding column for aftertax income do not include the effects of interest charges on taxes.

[c]In each year, the rate of return on total assets is the same, for both companies, as the rate of return on common shareholders' equity for No-Debt Company: 10 percent, 7 percent, and 4 percent, respectively.

EXHIBIT 5.9	HORRIGAN CORPORATION Disaggregation of Rate of Return on Common Shareholders' Equity

	Rate of Return on Common Shareholders' Equity	=	Profit Margin	×	Total Assets Turnover	×	Leverage Ratio
Year 2	7.0%	=	7.6%	×	0.65	×	1.4
Year 3	10.3%	=	11.0%	×	0.67	×	1.4
Year 4	15.6%	=	12.6%	×	0.81	×	1.5

common shareholders contrasted with the capital provided by creditors and preferred shareholders. The larger the leverage ratio, the smaller is the proportion of capital that common shareholders provide and the larger is the proportion that creditors and preferred shareholders provide. Thus, the larger the leverage ratio, the greater is the extent of financial leverage.

The disaggregation of the rate of return on common shareholders' equity ratio for Horrigan Corporation for Year 4 is as follows:

$$\frac{\$60}{.5(\$360 + 410)} = \frac{\$60}{\$475} \times \frac{\$475}{.5(\$520 + 650)} \times \frac{.5(\$520 + 650)}{.5(\$360 + 410)}$$

$$15.6\% \quad = 12.6\% \times \quad 0.81 \quad \times \quad 1.5$$

Exhibit 5.9 disaggregates the rate of return on common shareholders' equity for Horrigan Corporation for Year 2, Year 3, and Year 4. Most of the increase in the rate of return on common shareholders' equity results from an increasing profit margin over the three-year period and an increase in total assets turnover in Year 4. The leverage ratio remained reasonably stable over this period.

PROBLEM 5.2 FOR SELF-STUDY

Analyzing the rate of return on common shareholders' equity. Refer to the profitability analysis for Abbott Corporation in Problem 5.1 for Self-Study. Consider the following additional data.

	Year 1	Year 2	Year 3
Profit Margin (after subtracting financing costs)	5.1%	4.9%	4.6%
Total Assets Turnover	1.7	1.6	1.5
Leverage Ratio	1.6	1.8	2.1
Rate of Return on Common Shareholders' Equity[a]	14.0%	14.2%	14.2%

[a]Amounts do not exactly equal the product of the three preceding ratios due to rounding.

a. What is the likely explanation for the increasing rate of return on common shareholders' equity?

b. Is financial leverage working to the advantage of the common shareholders in each year?

EARNINGS PER SHARE OF COMMON STOCK

Earnings per share of common stock provides a third measure of profitability. Earnings per share equals net income attributable to common stock divided by the average number of common shares outstanding during the period. Earnings per share for Horrigan Corporation for Year 4, based on 16 million weighted-average shares outstanding,[6] follows:

$$\frac{\text{Net Income} - \text{Preferred Stock Dividends Declared}}{\text{Weighted Average Number of Common Shares Outstanding during the Period}} = \frac{\$60 - \$0}{16 \text{ shares}} = \$3.75 \text{ per share}$$

Earnings per share were \$1.28 (= \$16/12.5) for Year 2 and \$2.19 (= \$34/15.5) for Year 3.

A firm with securities outstanding that holders can convert into or exchange for shares of common stock may report two earnings-per-share amounts: **basic earnings per share** (the amount that results from the calculations above) and **fully diluted earnings per share.** Convertible bonds and convertible preferred stock permit their holders to exchange these securities directly for shares of common stock. Many firms have employee stock-option plans, which allow employees to acquire shares of the company's common stock. When holders convert their securities or when employees exercise their options, the firm will issue additional shares of common stock. Then, the amount shown as basic earnings per share will probably decrease. Accountants refer to such decreases as *dilution.* When a firm has securities outstanding that, if exchanged for shares of common stock, would decrease basic earnings per share by 3 percent or more, generally accepted accounting principles require a dual presentation: basic earnings per share and fully diluted earnings per share.[7]

Firms that do not have convertible or other potentially dilutive securities outstanding compute earnings per share in the conventional manner. Firms with outstanding securities that have the potential for materially diluting earnings per share as conventionally computed must present dual earnings-per-share amounts.

Interpreting Earnings per Share

Accountants and financial analysts criticize earnings per share as a measure of profitability because it does not consider the amount of assets or capital required to generate that level of earnings. Two firms with the same earnings and earnings per share will not be equally profitable if one of the firms requires twice the amount of assets or capital to generate those earnings as does the other firm.

In comparing firms, earnings-per-share amounts have limited use. For example, assume that two firms have identical earnings, common shareholders' equity, and rates of return on common shareholders' equity. One firm may have a lower earnings per share simply because it has a larger number of shares outstanding (perhaps due to the use of a lower par value for its shares or to different earnings retention policies; see Exercise **20** at the end of this chapter).

Price-Earnings Ratio

Financial analysts often compare earnings-per-share amounts with the market price of the stock. They usually express this comparison as a price-earnings ratio (= market price per share/earnings per share). For example, the common stock of Horrigan Corporation sells for \$70 per share at the end of Year 4. The price-earnings

---

[6]Exhibit 5.2 indicates that the par value of a common share is \$10 and that the common stock account has a balance of \$160 million throughout Year 4. The shares outstanding were therefore 16 million.

[7]Financial Accounting Standards Board, *Statement of Financial Accounting Standards No. 128,* "Earnings per Share," 1997.

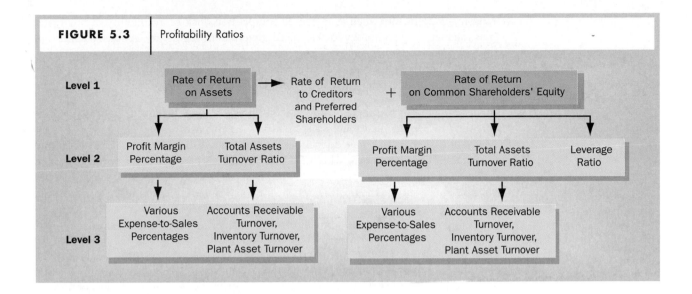

FIGURE 5.3 | Profitability Ratios

ratio, often called the P/E ratio, is 18.7 to 1 (= $70/$3.75). The analyst often expresses the relation by saying, "The stock sells at 18.7 times earnings."

Tables of stock prices and financial periodicals often present price-earnings ratios. The analyst must interpret these published P/E ratios cautiously, however. In cases in which a firm's earnings include unusual, nonrecurring gains and losses, the reader must ascertain whether the published ratio uses only income from recurring operations or final net income that includes the unusual items in the denominator. To serve their intended purpose, P/E ratios should use normal, ongoing earnings data in the denominator. The appendix to this chapter discusses more fully the use of earnings per share in the valuation of firms.

SUMMARY OF PROFITABILITY ANALYSIS

This chapter has introduced three broad measures for assessing a firm's profitability. Because the rate of return on assets and the rate of return on common shareholders' equity relate earnings to some measure of the capital required to generate those earnings, we have focused most of our attention on these two profitability measures.

Figure 5.3 summarizes the analysis discussed. Most generally (Level 1), the analysis concerns overall measures of profitability and the effectiveness of financial leverage. On the next level (Level 2), we disaggregate the overall measures of profitability into profit margin, asset turnover, and leverage components. On the third level, we further disaggregate the profit margin and asset turnover ratios to gain additional insights into reasons for changes in profitability. The depth of analysis required for an analyst to understand a particular case depends on the relative size of the observed differences or changes in profitability.

ANALYSIS OF RISK

Analysts deciding between investments must consider the comparative risks. Various factors affect the risk of business firms:

1. Economy-wide factors, such as increased inflation or interest rates, unemployment, or recessions

2. Industry-wide factors, such as increased competition, lack of availability of raw materials, changes in technology, or increased government regulatory actions, such as antitrust or clean environment policies
3. Firm-specific factors, such as labor strikes, loss of facilities due to fire or other casualty, or poor health of key managerial personnel

Ultimately, analysts assess whether a firm will likely become bankrupt; creditors and investors may lose the capital they provided to a bankrupt firm.

Analysts assessing risk generally focus on the relative liquidity of a firm. Cash and near-cash assets provide a firm with the resources needed to adapt to the various types of risk; that is, liquid resources provide a firm with financial flexibility. Cash is also the connecting link that permits the operating, investing, and financing activities of a firm to run smoothly and effectively.

Assessing liquidity requires a time horizon. Consider the three questions that follow:

1. Does a firm have sufficient cash to repay a loan if it is due tomorrow?
2. Will the firm have sufficient cash to repay the same loan if it is due in six months?
3. Will the firm have sufficient cash to repay the same loan if it is due in five years?

In answering the first question, the analyst probably focuses on the amount of cash on hand and in the bank relative to the obligation coming due tomorrow. In answering the second question, the analyst compares the amount of cash expected from operations during the next six months, as well as from any new borrowings, with the obligations maturing during that period. In answering the third question, the analyst shifts the focus to the longer-run cash-generating ability of a firm relative to the amount of long-term debt that is maturing.

MEASURES OF SHORT-TERM LIQUIDITY RISK

This section discusses four measures for assessing **short-term liquidity risk:** (1) the current ratio, (2) the quick ratio, (3) the cash flow from operations to current liabilities ratio, and (4) working capital turnover ratios.

Current Ratio The **current ratio** equals current assets divided by current liabilities. Recall that current assets comprise cash and assets that a firm expects to turn into cash, sell, or consume within approximately one year of the balance sheet date. Current liabilities include obligations that will require cash (or the rendering of services) within approximately one year. Thus, the current ratio indicates a firm's ability to meet its short-term obligations. The current ratios of Horrigan Corporation on December 31, Year 1, Year 2, Year 3, and Year 4, appear below:

	Current Ratio	=	Current Assets / Current Liabilities
December 31, Year 1	$50 / $40	=	1.25 to 1.0
December 31, Year 2	$80 / $50	=	1.60 to 1.0
December 31, Year 3	$100 / $60	=	1.67 to 1.0
December 31, Year 4	$171 / $90	=	1.90 to 1.0

Although the analyst generally prefers an excess of current assets over current liabilities, changes in the trend of the ratio can mislead. For example, when the current ratio exceeds 1 to 1, an increase of equal amount in both current assets and current liabilities (by acquiring inventory on account) results in a decline in the ratio, whereas equal decreases (by paying an accounts payable) result in an increased current ratio.[8]

In a recessionary period, a business may contract and use cash, a current asset, to pay its current liabilities. When the current ratio exceeds one, such action will increase it. In a boom period, firms sometimes conserve cash by delaying payment of current liabilities, causing the reverse effect. Thus, a high current ratio may accompany deteriorating business conditions, whereas a falling ratio may accompany profitable operations.

Furthermore, management can manipulate the current ratio. It can take deliberate steps to produce a financial statement that presents a better current ratio at the balance sheet date than the average, or normal, current ratio. For example, near the end of its fiscal year a firm might delay normal purchases on account. Or, it might collect receivables for loans to officers, classified as noncurrent assets, and use the proceeds to reduce current liabilities. When the current ratio exceeds one, the usual situation, such actions will increase the current ratio. Analysts refer to these manipulations as *window dressing.*

 Although analysts commonly use the current ratio in statement analysis, its trends do not necessarily indicate substantial changes, and management can easily manipulate it.

Quick Ratio   A variation of the current ratio is the **quick ratio** (sometimes called the **acid test ratio**). The quick ratio includes in the numerator of the fraction only those current assets that a firm could convert quickly into cash. The numerator customarily includes cash, marketable securities, and receivables. Some businesses can convert their inventory of merchandise into cash more quickly than other businesses can convert their receivables. The facts in each case will indicate whether the analyst should include receivables or exclude inventories. The denominator includes all current liabilities.

Assuming that the quick ratios of Horrigan Corporation include accounts receivable but exclude inventory, the quick ratios on December 31, Year 1, Year 2, Year 3, and Year 4, are as follows:

	Quick Ratio	=	Cash, Marketable Securities, and Accounts Receivable / Current Liabilities
December 31, Year 1	$36/$40	=	.90 to 1.0
December 31, Year 2	$50/$50	=	1.00 to 1.0
December 31, Year 3	$54/$60	=	.90 to 1.0
December 31, Year 4	$88/$90	=	.98 to 1.0

---

[8]The general rule is that adding equal amounts to both the numerator and the denominator of a fraction moves that fraction closer to the number 1, whereas subtracting equal amounts from both the numerator and the denominator of a fraction makes that fraction diverge from the number 1. To be even more general, adding *a* to (subtracting *a* from) the numerator while adding *b* to (subtracting *b* from) the denominator of the fraction makes the fraction converge to (diverge from) the fraction *a/b*.

Whereas the current ratio increased steadily over the period, the quick ratio remained relatively constant. The increase in the current ratio resulted primarily from a buildup of inventories.

Cash Flow from Operations to Current Liabilities Ratio   Some analysts criticize the current ratio and the quick ratio because they use amounts at a specific time. If financial statement amounts at that time are unusually large or small, the resulting ratios will not reflect normal conditions.

The **cash flow from operations to current liabilities ratio** overcomes these deficiencies. The numerator of this ratio is cash flow from operations for the year. The denominator is average current liabilities for the year. The cash flow from operations to current liabilities ratios for Horrigan Corporation for Year 2, Year 3, and Year 4 are as follows:

	Cash Flow from Operations to Current Liabilities Ratio $=$	Cash Flow from Operations / Average Current Liabilities
Year 2	$\dfrac{\$12}{.5(\$40 + \$50)}$ $=$	26.7%
Year 3	$\dfrac{\$32}{.5(\$50 + \$60)}$ $=$	58.2%
Year 4	$\dfrac{\$41}{.5(\$60 + \$90)}$ $=$	54.7%

A healthy firm commonly has a ratio of 40 percent or more.[9] Thus the liquidity of Horrigan Corporation improved dramatically between Year 2 and Year 3.

Working Capital Turnover Ratios   During the operating cycle, a firm

1. purchases inventory on account from suppliers,
2. sells inventory on account to customers,
3. collects amounts due from customers, and
4. pays amounts due to suppliers.

This cycle occurs continually for most businesses. The number of days that a firm holds inventories (that is, 365 days/inventory turnover ratio) indicates the length of the period between the purchase and the sale of inventory during each operating cycle. The number of days that a firm's receivables remain outstanding (that is, 365 days/accounts receivable turnover ratio) indicates the length of the period between the sale of inventory and the collection of cash from customers during each operating cycle.

Firms must finance their investments in inventories and accounts receivable. Suppliers typically provide a portion of the needed financing. The number of days that a firm's accounts payable remain outstanding (that is, 365 days/accounts payable turnover ratio) indicates the length of the period between the purchase of inventory on account and the payment of cash to suppliers during each operating cycle. The **accounts payable**

---

[9]Cornelius Casey and Norman Bartczak, "Using Operating Cash Flow Data to Predict Financial Distress: Some Extensions," *Journal of Accounting Research* (Spring 1985), 384–401.

turnover ratio equals purchases on account divided by average accounts payable. Although firms do not disclose their purchases, the analyst can approximate the amount as follows:

Beginning Inventory + Purchases = Cost of Goods Sold + Ending Inventory

Rearranging terms yields the following:

Purchases = Cost of Goods Sold + Ending Inventory − Beginning Inventory

The purchases of Horrigan Corporation appear below:

	Purchases	=	Cost of Goods Sold	+	Ending Inventory	−	Beginning Inventory
Year 2	$135	=	$119	+	$30	−	$14
Year 3	$195	=	$179	+	$46	−	$30
Year 4	$317	=	$280	+	$83	−	$46

The accounts payable turnover ratio for Year 4 is as follows:

$$\frac{\text{Purchases}}{\text{Average Accounts Payable}} = \frac{\$317}{.5(\$35 + \$50)} = 7.5$$

The accounts payable turnover was 4.3 for Year 2 and 5.5 for Year 3. The average number of days that payables were outstanding was 84.9 days for Year 2, 66.4 days for Year 3, and 48.7 days for Year 4. Thus, the days payable declined during the three years.

Interpreting the accounts payable turnover ratio involves opposing considerations. An increase in the accounts payable turnover ratio indicates that a firm pays its obligations to suppliers more quickly, requiring cash and even wasting cash if the firm makes payments earlier than it needs to. On the other hand, a faster accounts payable turnover means a smaller relative amount of accounts payable that the firm must pay in the near future. Most firms want to extend their payables as long as they can, but they also want to maintain their reputations for honorable dealings. Ethical businesses, then, delay paying and negotiate hard for favorable payment terms.

A comparison of the days outstanding for inventories, accounts receivable, and accounts payable reveals the following:

Year	Days Inventory Held	Days Accounts Receivable Outstanding	Days Accounts Payable Outstanding
Year 2	67.6	53.7	84.9
Year 3	77.7	48.0	66.4
Year 4	84.9	46.8	48.7

The increased number of days that the firm held inventories suggests increased short-term liquidity risk, but the reduction in the number of days that accounts receivable remain outstanding reduced short-term liquidity risk. Interpreting the decreased number of days that accounts payable remain outstanding involves the opposing considerations discussed above. Clearly, however, in Year 4 Horrigan Corporation must obtain more short-term financing for its investments in inventories than in Year 2. The cash flow from operations to current liabilities ratio, discussed in the preceding section, suggests that operations have provided more than sufficient cash flow to finance this increased financing need.

Summary of Short-Term Liquidity Analysis   The current and quick ratios measure liquidity at a particular date. These ratios for Horrigan Corporation indicate satisfactory conditions at the end of each year, although they indicate a buildup of inventories.

The cash flow from operations to current liabilities and the working capital turnover ratios measure short-term liquidity for a period of time. The increase in the number of days the firm held inventory, coupled with a decrease in the number of days it delayed paying its accounts payable, suggests an increased need for short-term financing. However, Horrigan Corporation's increased profitability and accounts receivable turnover ratio resulted in an increasing cash flow from operations to current liabilities ratio, well above the 40 percent typically found for a financially healthy firm.

P R O B L E M   5 . 3   F O R   S E L F - S T U D Y

Analyzing short-term liquidity risk.   Refer to the profitability ratios for Abbott Corporation in Problems 5.1 and 5.2 for Self-Study. Consider the following additional data:

	Year 1	Year 2	Year 3
Current Ratio	1.4	1.3	1.2
Quick Ratio	1.0	0.9	1.0
Cash Flow from Operations to Current Liabilities Ratio	38.2%	37.3%	36.4%
Days Accounts Receivable Outstanding	84.9	84.9	86.9
Days Inventories Held	114.1	107.4	101.4
Days Accounts Payable Outstanding	58.6	59.1	58.8

a. What is the likely explanation for the decreasing current ratio coupled with the stable quick ratio?
b. What is the likely explanation for the decline in the cash flow from operations to current liabilities ratio?
c. What is your assessment of the short-term liquidity risk of Abbott Corporation at the end of Year 3?

MEASURES OF LONG-TERM LIQUIDITY RISK

Analysts use measures of **long-term liquidity risk** to evaluate a firm's ability to meet interest and principal payments on long-term debt and similar obligations as they come due. If a firm cannot make the payments on time, it becomes insolvent and may have to reorganize or liquidate.

A firm's ability to generate profits over several years provides the best protection against long-term liquidity risk. If a firm is profitable, it will either generate sufficient cash from operations or obtain needed capital from creditors and owners. The measures of profitability discussed previously therefore apply for this purpose as well. Analysts measure long-term liquidity risk with debt ratios, the cash flow from operations to total liabilities ratio, and the interest coverage ratio.

Debt Ratios The debt ratio has several variations, but the **long-term debt ratio** commonly appears in financial analysis. It reports the portion of the firm's long-term capital that debt-holders furnish. To calculate this ratio, divide total long-term debt by the sum of total long-term debt and total shareholders' equity.

Another form of the debt ratio is the **debt-equity ratio.** To calculate the debt-equity ratio, divide total liabilities (current and noncurrent) by total equities (= liabilities plus shareholders' equity = total assets). Some analysts compute the long-term debt ratio, as defined above, but call it the debt-equity ratio. Be sure you know the definition that the writer (or speaker) has in mind when you read (or hear) this term. No other financial statement ratio has so many variations in practice.

Exhibit 5.10 shows the two forms of the debt ratio for Horrigan Corporation on December 31, Year 1, Year 2, Year 3, and Year 4. In general, the higher these ratios, the higher is the likelihood that the firm will be unable to meet fixed interest and principal payments in the future. Most firms must decide how much financial leverage, with its attendant risk, they can afford to take on. Funds obtained from issuing bonds or borrowing from a bank have a relatively low interest cost but require fixed, periodic payments that increase the likelihood of insolvency or even bankruptcy.

In assessing the debt ratios, analysts customarily vary the standard in relation to the stability of the firm's earnings and cash flows from operations. The more stable the earnings and cash flows, the higher is the debt ratio they deem acceptable or safe. Public utilities have high debt-equity ratios, frequently on the order of 60 to 70 percent. Banks have even higher debt ratios. The stability of earnings and cash flows of firms in these industries makes these ratios acceptable to many investors. These investors might find such high leverage unacceptable for firms with less stable earnings and cash flows, such as a computer software developer or a biotechnology firm. Horrigan Corporation has debt ratios about average for an industrial firm.

Because several variations of the debt ratio appear in corporate annual reports, the analyst should take care when comparing debt ratios among firms.

EXHIBIT 5.10	HORRIGAN CORPORATION Debt Ratios

$\dfrac{\text{Long-term}}{\text{Debt Ratio}} = \dfrac{\text{Total Long-term Debt}}{\text{Total Long-term Debt} + \text{Shareholders' Equity}}$		$\text{Debt-Equity Ratio} = \dfrac{\text{Total Liabilities}}{\text{Total Liabilities} + \text{Shareholders' Equity}}$	
Dec. 31, Year 1	$\dfrac{\$\ 50}{\$210} = 24\%$	Dec. 31, Year 1	$\dfrac{\$\ 90}{\$250} = 36\%$
Dec. 31, Year 2	$\dfrac{\$\ 50}{\$350} = 14\%$	Dec. 31, Year 2	$\dfrac{\$100}{\$400} = 25\%$
Dec. 31, Year 3	$\dfrac{\$100}{\$460} = 22\%$	Dec. 31, Year 3	$\dfrac{\$160}{\$520} = 31\%$
Dec. 31, Year 4	$\dfrac{\$150}{\$560} = 27\%$	Dec. 31, Year 4	$\dfrac{\$240}{\$650} = 37\%$

Cash Flow from Operations to Total Liabilities Ratio

Cash Flow from Operations to Total Liabilities Ratio The debt ratios do not consider the availability of liquid assets to cover various levels of debt. The **cash flow from operations to total liabilities ratio** overcomes this deficiency. This cash flow ratio resembles the one for assessing short-term liquidity risk, but here the denominator includes all liabilities (both current and noncurrent). The cash flow from operations to total liabilities ratios for Horrigan Corporation are as follows:

	Cash Flow from Operations to Total Liabilities Ratio	=	Cash Flow from Operations / Average Total Liabilities
Year 2	$\dfrac{\$12}{.5(\$90 + \$100)}$	=	12.6%
Year 3	$\dfrac{\$32}{.5(\$100 + \$160)}$	=	24.6%
Year 4	$\dfrac{\$41}{.5(\$160 + \$240)}$	=	20.5%

A financially healthy company normally has a cash flow from operations to total liabilities ratio of 20 percent or more. Thus the long-term liquidity risk decreased significantly between Year 2 and Year 3 but increased again in Year 4.

Interest Coverage Ratio The number of times that earnings cover interest charges also measures long-term liquidity risk. The **interest coverage ratio** equals income before interest and income tax expenses divided by interest expense. For Horrigan Corporation, the interest coverage ratios for Year 2, Year 3, and Year 4 are as follows:

	Interest Coverage Ratio	=	Income before Interest and Income Taxes / Interest Expense
Year 2	$\dfrac{\$16 + \$5 + \$7}{\$5}$	=	5.6 times
Year 3	$\dfrac{\$34 + \$10 + \$14}{\$10}$	=	5.8 times
Year 4	$\dfrac{\$60 + \$16 + \$26}{\$16}$	=	6.4 times

Thus, whereas the bonded indebtedness increased sharply during the three-year period, the growth in income before interest and income taxes provided increasing coverage of the fixed interest charges.

This ratio attempts to indicate the relative protection that operating profitability provides bondholders, permitting them to assess the probability that a firm will fail to meet required interest payments. If bond indentures require periodic repayments of principal on long-term liabilities, the denominator of the ratio might include such repayments. The ratio would then be called the *fixed charges coverage ratio*.

One can criticize the interest or fixed charges coverage ratios as measures for assessing long-term liquidity risk because they use earnings rather than cash flows in the numerator. Firms pay interest and other fixed payment obligations with cash, not with earnings. When the value of the ratio is relatively low (for example, two to three times), the analyst should use some measure of cash flows, such as cash flow from operations, in the numerator.

Summary of Long-Term Liquidity Analysis Long-term liquidity analysis focuses on the amount of debt (particularly long-term debt) in the capital structure of a firm and the adequacy of earnings and cash flows to service this debt (that is, to provide interest and principal payments as they mature). Although both short- and long-term debt of Horrigan Corporation increased over the three-year period, increases in sales, earnings, and cash flows from operations all appear to be increasing sufficiently to cover the current levels of debt.

PROBLEM 5.4 FOR SELF-STUDY

Analyzing long-term liquidity risk. Refer to the profitability and short-term liquidity risk ratios for Abbott Corporation in Problems 5.1, 5.2, and 5.3 for Self-Study. Consider the following additional data:

	Year 1	Year 2	Year 3
Long-term Debt Ratio	27.2%	33.8%	43.3%
Debt-Equity Ratio	37.5%	44.4%	52.4%
Cash Flow from Operations to Total Liabilities Ratio	16.3%	13.4%	11.1%
Interest Coverage Ratio	6.7	5.1	4.1

a. What is the likely explanation for the decrease in the cash flow from operations to total liabilities ratio?
b. What is the likely explanation for the decrease in the interest coverage ratio?
c. What is your assessment of the long-term liquidity risk of Abbott Corporation at the end of Year 3?

LIMITATIONS OF RATIO ANALYSIS

The analyst should be aware of limitations in the computations discussed in this chapter, such as the following:

1. Because ratios use financial statement data as inputs, the same factors that cause financial statements themselves to have shortcomings will affect the ratios computed from them. Such shortcomings, at least for some purposes, include the use of acquisition cost for assets rather than current replacement cost or net realizable value and the latitude permitted firms in selecting from among various generally accepted accounting principles.
2. Changes in many ratios correlate with each other. For example, the current ratio and the quick ratio often change in the same direction and proportionally. The analyst need not compute all the ratios to assess a particular dimension of profitability or risk.

3. When comparing the size of a ratio between periods for the same firm, one must recognize conditions that have changed between the periods being compared (for example, different product lines or geographic markets served, changes in economic conditions, changes in prices, changes in accounting principles, and corporate acquisitions).

4. When comparing ratios of a particular firm with those of similar firms, one must recognize differences between the firms (for example, use of different methods of accounting, differences in the methods of operations and types of financing).

Financial statement ratios alone cannot provide direct indicators of good or poor management. Such ratios indicate areas that the analyst should investigate further. For example, a decrease in the turnover of merchandise inventory, ordinarily considered an undesirable trend, may reflect the accumulation of merchandise to keep retail stores open during anticipated shortages. Such shortages may force competitors to restrict operations or to close down. The analyst must combine ratios derived from financial statements with an investigation of other facts before drawing conclusions.

AN INTERNATIONAL PERSPECTIVE

Analyzing the financial statements of a non-U.S. firm requires consideration of the following:

1. The format and terminology of financial statements in other countries often differs from that used in statements in the United States.

2. Economic, political, and cultural factors in other countries can differ from those in the United States in ways that affect the interpretation of financial statement ratios.

3. Firms in other countries may use accounting principles different from those that U.S. firms use.

SUMMARY

For convenient reference, Exhibit 5.11 summarizes the calculation of the financial statement ratios discussed in this chapter.

This chapter began with the question of whether you should invest your inheritance in a certificate of deposit or in the shares of common stock of Horrigan Corporation. Analysis of Horrigan Corporation's financial statements indicates that it has been a growing, profitable company with few indications of either short-term or long-term liquidity problems. You need at least three additional inputs before making the investment decision. First, you should consult sources of information other than the financial statements (for example, articles in the financial press, capital spending plans, and new product introduction plans by competitors) to understand a firm's future profitability and risk. Second, you must decide your attitude toward, or willingness to assume, risk.

EXHIBIT 5.11	Summary of Financial Statement Ratios	

Ratio	Numerator	Denominator
Profitability Ratios		
Rate of Return on Assets	Net Income + Interest Expense (net of tax effects)[a]	Average Total Assets during the Period
Profit Margin Ratio (before interest effects)	Net Income + Interest Expense (net of tax effects)[a]	Sales
Various Expense Ratios	Various Expenses	Sales
Total Assets Turnover Ratio	Sales	Average Total Assets during the Period
Accounts Receivable Turnover Ratio	Sales	Average Accounts Receivable during the Period
Inventory Turnover Ratio	Cost of Goods Sold	Average Inventory during the Period
Fixed Asset Turnover Ratio	Sales	Average Fixed Assets during the Period
Rate of Return on Common Shareholders' Equity	Net Income − Preferred Stock Dividends	Average Common Shareholders' Equity during the Period
Profit Margin Ratio (after interest expense and preferred dividends)	Net Income − Preferred Stock Dividends	Sales
Leverage Ratio	Average Total Assets during the Period	Average Common Shareholders' Equity during the Period
Earnings per Share of Common Stock[b]	Net Income − Preferred Stock Dividends	Weighted-Average Number of Common Shares Outstanding
Short-term Liquidity Ratios		
Current Ratio	Current Assets	Current Liabilities
Quick or Acid Test Ratio	Highly Liquid Assets (cash, marketable securities, and receivables)[c]	Current Liabilities
Cash Flow from Operations to Current Liabilities Ratio	Cash Flow from Operations	Average Current Liabilities during the Period
Accounts Payable Turnover Ratio	Purchases[d]	Average Accounts Payable during the Period
Days Accounts Receivable Outstanding	365 days	Accounts Receivable Turnover Ratio
Days Inventories Held	365 days	Inventory Turnover Ratio
Days Accounts Payable Outstanding	365 days	Accounts Payable Turnover Ratio
Long-term Liquidity Ratios		
Long-term Debt Ratio	Total Long-term Debt	Total Long-term Debt Plus Shareholders' Equity
Debt-Equity Ratio	Total Liabilities	Total Equities (total liabilities plus shareholders' equity)
Cash Flow from Operations to Total Liabilities Ratio	Cash Flow from Operations	Average Total Liabilities during the Period
Interest Coverage Ratio	Income before Interest and Income Taxes	Interest Expense

[a]If the parent company does not own all of a consolidated subsidiary, the calculation also adds back to net income the minority interest share of earnings. See Chapter 11 for discussion of minority interest.

[b]This calculation is more complicated when there are convertible securities, options, or warrants outstanding.

[c]The calculation could conceivably exclude receivables for some firms and include inventories for others.

[d]Purchases = Cost of Goods Sold + Ending Inventories − Beginning Inventories.

EXHIBIT 5.12	COX CORPORATION Income and Retained Earnings Statement for Year 2 (Problem 5.5 for Self-Study)

Sales Revenue		$30,000
Less Expenses:		
Cost of Goods Sold	$18,000	
Selling	4,500	
Administrative	2,500	
Interest	700	
Income Taxes	1,300	
Total Expenses		27,000
Net Income		$ 3,000
Less Dividends:		
Preferred	$ 100	
Common	700	800
Increase in Retained Earnings for Year 2		$ 2,200
Retained Earnings, December 31, Year 1		4,500
Retained Earnings, December 31, Year 2		$ 6,700

Third, you must decide if you think the stock market price of the shares makes them an attractive current purchase.[10] Before making buy/sell recommendations to investors, analysts compare their assessments of the firm's profitability and risk to the firm's share price. Analysts might recommend the purchase of shares of a poorly run company whose shares they judge underpriced rather than recommend shares of a well-run company whose shares they judge overpriced in the market. At this stage in the investment decision, the analysis requires intuition, judgment, and experience.

PROBLEM 5.5 FOR SELF-STUDY

Computing profitability and risk ratios. Exhibit 5.12 presents an income statement for Cox Corporation for Year 2, and Exhibit 5.13 presents comparative balance sheets as of December 31, Year 1 and Year 2. Using information from these financial statements, compute the following ratios. The income tax rate is 30 percent. Cash flow from operations totals $3,300.

a. Rate of return on assets
b. Profit margin ratio (before interest and related tax effects)
c. Cost of goods sold to sales percentage
d. Selling expense to sales percentage
e. Total assets turnover

---

[10]Finance texts discuss other important factors in the investment decision. Perhaps the most important question is how a particular investment fits in with the investor's entire portfolio. Modern research suggests that the suitability of a potential investment depends more on the attributes of the other components of an investment portfolio and the risk attitude of the investor than it does on the attributes of the potential investment itself.

EXHIBIT 5.13	COX CORPORATION Comparative Balance Sheets December 31, Year 1 and Year 2 (Problem 5.5 for Self-Study)

	December 31	
	Year 1	Year 2
ASSETS		
Current Assets		
Cash	$ 600	$ 750
Accounts Receivable	3,600	4,300
Merchandise Inventories	5,600	7,900
Prepayments	300	380
Total Current Assets	$10,100	$13,330
Property, Plant, and Equipment		
Land	$ 500	$ 600
Buildings and Equipment (net)	9,400	10,070
Total Property, Plant, and Equipment	$ 9,900	$10,670
Total Assets	$20,000	$24,000
LIABILITIES AND SHAREHOLDERS' EQUITY		
Current Liabilities		
Notes Payable	$ 2,000	$ 4,000
Accounts Payable	3,500	3,300
Other Current Liabilities	1,500	1,900
Total Current Liabilities	$ 7,000	$ 9,200
Noncurrent Liabilities		
Bonds Payable	4,000	2,800
Total Liabilities	$11,000	$12,000
Shareholders' Equity		
Preferred Stock	$ 1,000	$ 1,000
Common Stock	2,000	2,500
Additional Paid-in Capital	1,500	1,800
Retained Earnings	4,500	6,700
Total Shareholders' Equity	$ 9,000	$12,000
Total Liabilities and Shareholders' Equity	$20,000	$24,000

f. Accounts receivable turnover
g. Inventory turnover
h. Fixed asset turnover
i. Rate of return on common shareholders' equity
j. Profit margin ratio (after interest and preferred dividends)
k. Leverage ratio
l. Current ratio (both dates)
m. Quick ratio (both dates)
n. Cash flow from operations to current liabilities ratio

o. Accounts payable turnover
p. Long-term debt ratio (both dates)
q. Debt-equity ratio (both dates)
r. Cash flow from operations to total liabilities ratio
s. Interest coverage ratio

APPENDIX 5.1: PRO FORMA FINANCIAL STATEMENTS AND VALUATION

Firms often project financial statement amounts for a year or more into the future. For example, a firm might project future sales, net income, assets, and cash flows to ascertain whether operations will generate sufficient cash flows to finance capital expenditures or whether the firm will need to borrow more. A firm might change its product lines or pricing policies and might want to estimate the impact on rates of return. A firm might project future financial statement amounts for an acquisition target to ascertain the price it should pay.

Accountants use the term **pro forma financial statements** to refer to financial statements prepared under a particular set of assumptions. One set of assumptions might be that historical patterns (for example, growth rates or rates of return) will continue. Alternatively, the pro forma financial statements might reflect new assumptions about growth rates, debt levels, profitability, and so on. This appendix describes and illustrates procedures for preparing pro forma financial statements, then shows you how to use them to value firms.

PREPARATION OF PRO FORMA FINANCIAL STATEMENTS

The preparation of pro forma financial statements requires the analyst to make assumptions about the future. The usefulness of the pro forma financial statements depends on the reasonableness of those assumptions. Various computer spreadsheet programs ease the calculations required in preparing these statements, but the warning "garbage-in, garbage-out" certainly applies—the results will have quality and validity no better than the input assumptions. Careful analysts bring together, preferably in a single section of their spreadsheet, a list of all assumptions made and assumed values for parameters. Well-prepared pro forma statements allow the analyst to vary critical assumptions to see how the results vary.

The preparation of pro forma financial statements typically begins with the income statement, followed by the balance sheet and then the statement of cash flows. The level of operating activity usually dictates the required amount of assets, which in turn affects the required level of financing. Amounts for the statement of cash flows come directly from the income statement and comparative balance sheets.

We follow the steps below in preparing pro forma financial statements:

1. Project operating revenues.
2. Project operating expenses (excluding the cost of financing and income taxes).
3. Project the assets required to support the level of projected operating activity.
4. Project the financing (liabilities and shareholders' equity) required to fund the level of assets in step **3.**
5. Project the cost of financing the debt projected in step **4,** income tax expense, net income, dividends, and the change in retained earnings.

6. Project the statement of cash flows from amounts on the projected balance sheet and income statement.

Exhibit 5.14 summarizes these six steps. To illustrate the preparation of pro forma financial statements, we use the data for Horrigan Corporation discussed previously in this chapter. We project amounts for Year 5.

Step 1: Project Operating Revenues

The projections begin with sales. The analyst studies the historical pattern of changes in sales and assesses whether this pattern will continue in the future. Among the questions raised are the following:

1. Does the firm plan to change product lines or pricing policies, make acquisitions of other companies, or take other actions that would alter the historical sales pattern?
2. Does the firm expect competitors to alter their strategies or new competitors to enter the market and thereby change the market shares?
3. Will conditions in the economy affect the firm's sales? For example, do the firm's sales fluctuate with economic cycles, do they remain steady, or do they fluctuate with other variables, such as local population growth?

The assumption about sales drives most other items in the pro forma financial statements, which makes this assumption perhaps the most important.

Exhibit 5.1 indicates that sales revenues for Horrigan Corporation increased from $210 million to $475 million between Year 2 and Year 4, a compound annual growth rate of 50.4 percent. This growth rate suggests a temporary high-growth phase, which will not continue indefinitely. Won't new competitors enter the market? Do any signs indicate that the firm's products have reached market saturation, which will slow future growth? We assume here that this growth rate will continue for at least one more year. Thus, projected sales for Year 5 are $714 million (= $475 million $\times$ 1.504).

Step 2: Project Operating Expenses

Projecting operating expenses requires understanding the behavior of various operating costs. Does the expense item tend to vary with the level of sales, a behavior pattern characterized as a *variable cost?* Alternatively, does the expense item tend to remain relatively constant for a particular time period regardless of the level of sales, a behavior pattern characterized as a *fixed cost?* Does the expense item have both variable- and fixed-cost characteristics, a pattern described as a *mixed cost* or a *step cost?* Does the firm have some discretion to change the amount of a fixed cost item in the short term in response to current conditions (for example, maintenance or advertising expenditures), or is there little discretion to change the level of fixed costs (for example, depreciation on equipment)? Understanding the behavior of each expense item aids in projecting its amount.

Exhibit 5.5 presents a common-size income statement for Horrigan Corporation for Year 2, Year 3, and Year 4. We use these common-size percentages in projecting operating expenses.

Cost of Goods Sold

The cost of goods sold percentage has increased slightly during the last three years. We learn from management that the increase was a result of a pricing policy to keep prices low to maintain the high growth rate in sales. For sales revenue, we assume that the historical growth rate will continue. Thus, we project the cost of goods sold percentage to increase to 60 percent of sales. Projected cost of goods sold is $428 million (= .60 $\times$ $714 million).

EXHIBIT 5.14 | Preparing Pro Forma Financial Statements

Statement of Income and Retained Earnings

STEP 1: Project Operating Revenues

Sales Revenue
Other Revenues

STEP 2: Project Operating Expenses

Cost of Goods Sold
Selling and Administrative Expenses
Net Income before Interest Expense
and Income Taxes

STEP 5: Project Cost of Financing, Income
Tax Expense, and the Change in
Retained Earnings

Interest Expense
Income Tax Expense
Net Income
Dividends
Change in Retained Earnings

Operations

Net Income
Depreciation
Other Adjustments
Change in Receivables
Change in Inventories
Change in Other Current Assets
Change in Accounts Payable
Change in Other Current Liabilities
CASH FLOW FROM OPERATIONS

Balance Sheet

STEP 3: Project Assets

Cash
Accounts Receivable
Inventories
Other Current Assets
Investments
Fixed Assets
Other Assets

STEP 4: Project Liabilities and
Contributed Capital

Accounts Payable
Notes Payable
Other Current Liabilities
Long-Term Debt
Other Liabilities
Contributed Capital

STEP 5: Project Retained Earnings

Retained Earnings

Statement of Cash Flows

STEP 6: Project the Statement of Cash Flows

Investing

Acquisition of Fixed Assets
Sale of Investments
Acquisition of Investments
Other Investing Transactions
CASH FLOW FROM INVESTING

Financing

Change in Notes Payable
Change in Long-term Debt
Change in Common Stock
Dividends
Other Financing Transactions
CASH FLOW FROM FINANCING

Selling Expense

The ratio of selling expense to sales decreased during the last three years. The decrease occurred because the firm compensated its sales staff based on a fixed salary each year but added few new salespeople. Thus, an increased sales level coupled with a relatively fixed compensation level caused the selling expense percentage to decrease. Horrigan Corporation indicates that it began switching to a commission-based compensation scheme in Year 4 and expects to fully implement this new system in Year 5. The firm expects selling expenses to average approximately 10 percent of sales in the future. Thus, projected selling expenses for Year 5 are $71 million (= .10 × $714 million).

Administrative Expense

The ratio of administrative expense to sales similarly decreased during the last three years. Discussions with management suggest that the decrease resulted from spreading the relatively fixed salaries of administrative personnel over a larger sales level. Management indicates that the administrative personnel are not yet working at capacity, so that additional increases in sales do not require additional administrative personnel. We assume that the administrative expense percentage for Year 5 will decrease slightly, to 4.5 percent of sales. Thus, projected administrative expenses for Year 5 are $32 million (= .045 × $714 million).

Depreciation Expense

The decrease in the ratio of depreciation expense to sales resulted from spreading the relatively fixed cost of operating capacity over ever-larger sales. Expenditures on depreciable assets have increased each year but at a decreasing rate (see the expenditures on buildings and equipment in Exhibit 5.3) and at a rate smaller than the increase in sales. The analyst must assess whether the firm has sufficient operating capacity to sustain a 50.4 percent growth rate in sales or whether it must acquire additional buildings and equipment. We note from the income statement in Exhibit 5.1 that depreciation expense increased approximately 22 percent annually during the last three years. Depreciable assets on the balance sheet increased at a similar rate during the last three years. Thus, we assume a growth rate in depreciation expense (and depreciable assets on the balance sheet) of 22 percent. Projected depreciation expense for Year 5 is $22 million (= $18 million × 1.22).

Step 3: Project Assets

The projection of total assets on the balance sheet requires the analyst to make assumptions consistent with those underlying the pro forma income statement. One approach assumes a total assets turnover (that is, sales/average total assets) similar to that of previous years. For example, the total assets turnover of Horrigan Corporation was .81 during Year 4. If the firm maintains this assets turnover during Year 5, then the calculation of its total assets at the end of Year 5 results from solving the following equation:

$$\frac{\text{Total Assets}}{\text{Turnover}} = \frac{\text{Sales}}{\text{Average Total Assets}} = \frac{\$714}{.5(\$650 + x)} = .81$$

Solving for the unknown in the equation yields projected total assets at the end of Year 5 of $1,113. The analyst can then use common-size balance sheet percentages to allocate this total to individual balance sheet accounts.

The above approach yields an unreasonable amount for total assets in this case relative to the historical growth rate in total assets. An alternative approach uses the historical annual growth rate in total assets of 37.5 percent during the last three years. This approach yields total assets of $894 million (= $650 million × 1.375). The analyst can then apply common-size balance sheet amounts to allocate this $894 million to individual balance sheet items.

A third approach combines both assets turnovers and growth rates in separately analyzing each asset rather than applying an overall estimate to total assets. We illustrate this
approach next. We will compute last the amount of cash at the end of Year 5 as the residual (or plug) necessary to equate total assets and total liabilities plus shareholders' equity.

Accounts Receivable

The accounts receivable turnover has trended upward during the last three years, from 6.8
to 7.8. Most of the increase occurred between Year 2 and Year 3. We assume an accounts
receivable turnover of 8.0 for Year 5. We solve the following equation to project accounts
receivable at the end of Year 5.

$$\text{Accounts Receivable Turnover Ratio} = \frac{\text{Sales}}{\text{Average Accounts Receivable}} = \frac{\$714}{.5(\$76 + x)} = 8.0$$

Projected accounts receivable at the end of Year 5 are $103 million.

Inventory

We use the inventory turnover to project the ending inventory for Year 5. The inventory
turnover ratio declined from 5.4 to 4.3 between Year 2 and Year 4. We assume an
inventory turnover of 4.1 for Year 5.

$$\text{Inventory Turnover Ratio} = \frac{\text{Cost of Goods Sold}}{\text{Average Inventories}} = \frac{\$428}{.5(\$83 + x)} = 4.1$$

Projected inventories at the end of Year 5 are $126 million.

Property, Plant, and Equipment

We could use the fixed asset turnover to project property, plant, and equipment in a
manner similar to that used for accounts receivable and inventories above. Yet the fixed
asset turnover, like the total assets turnover, changed dramatically during the last three
years and provides unreasonable projections for property, plant, and equipment relative to
the historical growth rate. We instead use the historical growth rates for depreciation
expense and depreciable assets of 22 percent. Projected property, plant, and equipment at
the end of Year 5 is $584 million (= $479 million × 1.22).

Step 4: Project Liabilities and Shareholders' Equity

We project next the financing side of the balance sheet. The projection of liabilities and
shareholders' equity flows directly from the projection of the level of operating activity
estimated in the first two steps and the projection of total assets estimated in the preceding step.

Accounts Payable

The accounts payable turnover increased from 4.3 to 7.5 during the last three years. The
analyst should attempt to learn whether the increase resulted from the firm's attempts to
pay its suppliers more quickly, from pressure by suppliers to pay more quickly, or for
some other reason. Such a clarification helps the analyst in projecting the likely accounts payable turnover during Year 5. Assume that the increase results from the firm's
efforts to take advantage of cash discounts for prompt payment within 45 days of purchase. Paying within 45 days of purchase suggests an accounts payable turnover of 8.1
(that is, 365/45 = 8.1). We solve the following equation to project accounts payable at
the end of Year 5.

$$\begin{array}{l}\text{Accounts}\\\text{Payable}\\\text{Turnover}\end{array} = \frac{\text{Purchases}}{\text{Average Accounts Payable}} = \frac{\$428 + \$126 - \$83}{.5(\$50 + x)} = 8.1$$

Projected accounts payable at the end of Year 5 is $66 million.

Salaries Payable

The projected amount for salaries payable should consider both salary levels and the number of days since the last pay period as of the end of Year 5. Obtaining information on these items from published sources may sometimes be difficult. We project that salaries payable will grow at its historical annual growth rate: 26 percent during the last three years. Thus, projected salaries payable are $25 (= $20 × 1.26) million.

Income Taxes Payable

Income taxes payable at the end of each year have averaged 75 percent of income tax expense for each of the last two years. We assume a continuation of this pattern. We cannot project income taxes payable at this stage because we do not yet know income tax expense for Year 5. We must delay this projection until the next step.

Bonds Payable

Horrigan Corporation issued $50 million of bonds during each of the last two years. We assume that the firm will again issue $50 million of bonds in Year 5. We can alter this assumption at a later stage if the firm does not need to borrow.

Contributed Capital

We assume no change in common stock or additional paid-in capital during Year 5.

Step 5: Project Interest Expense, Income Tax Expense, Net Income, Dividends, and the Change in Retained Earnings

Interest Expense

Interest expense usually bears a relatively fixed relation to the level of borrowing. Interest expense for Horrigan Corporation averages approximately 10 percent of bonds payable. We assumed above that Horrigan Corporation will continue its historical pattern of adding $50 million to long-term debt early in Year 5. Thus, projected interest expense for Year 5 is $20 million (=.10 × $200 million).

Income Tax Expense

The projections of sales, operating expenses, and interest expense yields income before income taxes of $141 (= $714 − $428 − $71 − $32 − $22 − $20). Income tax expense remained a steady 30 percent of income before income taxes during the last three years. We maintain this income tax rate in projecting income tax expense for Year 5. Projected income tax expense is $42 (= .30 × $141). We can now project income tax payable on the balance sheet as $32 (= .75 × $42).

Retained Earnings

Retained earnings increase by the $99 million of net income and decrease by dividends declared and paid. Horrigan Corporation paid dividends totaling 17 percent of net income during Year 4. We assume a continuation of this dividend policy during Year 5, resulting in a dividend of $17 (= .17 × $99) million. (Corporate finance texts discuss the interaction of dividend and borrowing policies, including the wisdom of declaring cash dividends during periods when a firm engages in net, new long-term borrowing.) Thus, retained earnings at the end of Year 5 are $212 (= $130 + $99 − $17) million.

EXHIBIT 5.15	HORRIGAN CORPORATION Pro Forma Income Statement for Year 5 (amounts in millions)

	Year 4 Actual	Assumption	Year 5 Pro Forma
Sales	$475	Growth Rate = 50.4%	$714
Less Expenses:			
Cost of Goods Sold	$280	60.0% of Sales	$428
Selling	53	10.0% of Sales	71
Administrative	22	4.5% of Sales	32
Depreciation	18	Growth Rate = 22.0%	22
Interest	16	10.0% of Bonds Payable[a]	20
Total Expenses	$389		$573
Net Income before Taxes	$ 86		$141
Income Tax Expense	26	30.0% of Net Income before Taxes	42
Net Income	$ 60		$ 99

[a]Including new bonds issued at the beginning of Year 5; see text.

The preparation of pro forma financial statements through the first five steps results in a projected income statement (see Exhibit 5.15) and a projected balance sheet (see Exhibit 5.16). The only item on the balance sheet not yet projected is cash. We set cash as the plug that equates projected total assets with projected liabilities and shareholders' equity. Projected liabilities and shareholders' equity total $815 million. Projected assets other than cash equal $813 million (= $103 + $126 + $584). Projected cash is $2 (= $815 − $813). The balance in Horrigan Corporation's cash account at the end of the last four years has averaged approximately $11 million. The analyst may view a projected balance in cash at the end of Year 5 of $2 million as insufficient to operate the firm effectively. If so, then the analyst might change the financing assumptions made earlier. Perhaps the firm should increase long-term borrowing by $60 million instead of $50, borrow $10 million on a short-term loan, or issue additional common stock.

The preparation of pro forma financial statements usually requires the analyst to plug some account to equate assets with liabilities plus shareholders' equity and have income statement amounts articulate with projected balance sheet amounts. Cash is often the plug, but not necessarily. The analyst might assume that a firm needs a certain minimum amount of cash. The analyst might assume that the firm will invest cash in excess of this balance in marketable securities or borrow if projected cash flows suggest a balance in cash less than the minimum.

Step 6: Project the Statement of Cash Flows

The analyst can prepare a pro forma statement of cash flows directly from the pro forma income statement and pro forma balance sheet. Exhibit 5.17 presents the pro forma statement of cash flows for Horrigan Corporation for Year 5. Note that the decrease in cash during Year 5 of $10 reconciles to the change in cash on the pro forma balance sheet. The only item not explicitly discussed previously is the cash outflow for acquisitions of property, plant, and equipment. The calculation of this amount is as follows:

EXHIBIT 5.16	HORRIGAN CORPORATION Pro Forma Balance Sheet December 31, Year 5 (amounts in millions)

	December 31, Year 4 Actual	Assumption	December 31, Year 5 Pro Forma
ASSETS			
Cash	$ 12	Residual	$ 2
Accounts Receivable	76	Turnover = 8.0	103
Inventories	83	Turnover = 4.1	126
Total Current Assets	$171		$231
Property, Plant, and Equipment (net)	479	Growth Rate = 22%	584
Total Assets	$650		$815
LIABILITIES AND SHAREHOLDERS' EQUITY			
Accounts Payable	$ 50	Turnover = 8.1	$ 66
Salaries Payable	20	Growth Rate = 26%	25
Income Taxes Payable	20	75% of Income Tax Expense	32
Total Current Liabilities	$ 90		$123
Bonds Payable	150	Increase = $50	200
Total Liabilities	$240		$323
Common Stock	$160	No Change	$160
Additional Paid-in Capital	120	No Change	120
Retained Earnings	130	17% Dividend Payout Ratio	212
Total Shareholders' Equity	$410		$492
Total Liabilities and Shareholders' Equity	$650		$815

Property, Plant, and Equipment (net) December 31, Year 4 (Exhibit 5.16)	$479
Plus Acquisition during Year 5 (plug)	127
Less Depreciation Expense for Year 5 (Exhibit 5.15)	(22)
Property, Plant, and Equipment (net) December 31, Year 5 (Exhibit 5.16)	$584

A common source or error in preparing pro forma financial statements is to fail to reconcile the change in property, plant, and equipment (net) on the balance sheet with the amount for depreciation expense on the income statement and the statement of cash flows and the amount for acquisitions on the statement of cash flows.

Analysis of Pro Forma Financial Statements

The analyst can calculate various financial statement ratios from the pro forma financial statements. Exhibit 5.18 presents financial statement ratios for Horrigan Corporation based on its actual amounts for Year 2, Year 3, and Year 4 and on its pro forma amounts for Year 5. The pro forma amounts indicate a continuing increase in profitability. The rate of return on assets increases because of both an increasing profit margin and an increasing total assets turnover. The rate of return on common shareholders' equity increases because of improved operating profitability and increased financial leverage. The increased debt, however, does not appear to increase the short- or long-term liquidity risk

	HORRIGAN CORPORATION
EXHIBIT 5.17	Pro Forma Statement of Cash Flows for Year 5 (amounts in millions)

OPERATIONS

Net Income	$ 99
Depreciation	22
(Increase) Decrease in Accounts Receivable	(27)
(Increase) Decrease in Inventories	(43)
Increase (Decrease) in Accounts Payable	16
Increase (Decrease) in Salaries Payable	5
Increase (Decrease) in Income Taxes Payable	12
Cash Flow from Operations	$ 84

INVESTING

Acquisition of Property, Plant, and Equipment	$(127)
Cash Flow from Investing	$(127)

FINANCING

Issue of Long-term Debt	$ 50
Dividends	(17)
Cash Flow from Financing	$ 33
Change in Cash	$ (10)
Cash, December 31, Year 4	12
Cash, December 31, Year 5	$ 2

of Horrigan Corporation. The projected increases in the cash flow and interest coverage ratios offset the slight increases in debt levels.

VALUATION

Managers, security analysts, and others analyze financial statements (both historical and pro forma) to form judgments about the market value of a firm. This section briefly describes the relation between financial statement items and market values. The analyst typically values a firm by several approaches to ascertain if a small range of values emerges. Entire textbooks and courses consider the valuation approaches introduced below.

Present Value of Future Cash Flows

Chapter 2 defined an *asset* as a resource with the potential to generate future cash inflows (or to reduce future cash outflows). Likewise, the common stock of a firm has value to an investor because it can generate cash inflows to the investor in the form of dividends and cash proceeds on sale of the shares. If the sales price exceeds the investor's cost, the investor has a capital gain. When the cost exceeds the sales price, the investor has a capital loss. Dividends and capital gains or losses result from the future profitability and cash flows of a firm.

One valuation approach projects the net amount of cash flows a firm will generate for the common shareholders over some number of future years. Cash flow for the common shareholders equals cash flow from operating, investing, and financing activities (other than cash transactions with common shareholders). The analyst then discounts the net amount for each year at an appropriate discount rate to find the present value of these future cash flows. (The appendix to this book discusses the procedure for discounting future

| | **EXHIBIT 5.18** | HORRIGAN CORPORATION
Financial Statement Ratio Analysis |

	Actual			**Pro Forma**
	Year 2	Year 3	Year 4	Year 5
Rate of Return on Assets	6.0%	8.9%	12.2%	15.4%
Profit Margin (before interest expense and related tax effects)	9.3%	13.2%	15.0%	15.8%
Total Assets Turnover	0.65	0.67	0.81	0.97
Cost of Goods Sold/Sales	56.7%	57.7%	58.9%	60.0%
Selling Expenses/Sales	17.1%	13.6%	11.2%	10.0%
Administrative Expenses/Sales	7.1%	5.5%	4.6%	4.5%
Depreciation Expenses/Sales	5.7%	4.5%	3.8%	3.1%
Interest Expense/Sales	2.4%	3.2%	3.4%	2.8%
Income Tax Expense/Sales	3.3%	4.5%	5.5%	5.9%
Accounts Receivable Turnover	6.8	7.6	7.8	8.0
Inventory Turnover	5.4	4.7	4.3	4.1
Fixed Asset Turnover	0.8	0.8	1.1	1.3
Rate of Return on Common Shareholders' Equity	7.0%	10.3%	15.6%	22.0%
Profit Margin Ratio (after interest and preferred dividends)	7.6%	11.0%	12.6%	13.9%
Leverage Ratio	1.4	1.4	1.5	1.6
Current Ratio	1.60	1.67	1.90	1.88
Quick Ratio	1.00	0.90	0.98	0.85
Cash Flow from Operations to Current Liabilities	26.7%	58.2%	54.7%	78.9%
Accounts Payable Turnover	4.3	5.5	7.5	8.1
Long-term Debt Ratio	14.3%	21.7%	26.8%	28.9%
Debt-Equity Ratio	25.0%	30.8%	36.9%	39.6%
Cash Flow from Operations to Total Liabilities	12.6%	24.6%	20.5%	29.8%
Interest Coverage Ratio	5.6	5.8	6.4	8.1

cash flows to their equivalent present value.) Corporate finance text discuss whether the appropriate discount rate should be the desired rate of return by the common shareholders, as in this case, or a weighted average cost of both debt and equity capital.

Refer to the pro forma statement of cash flows for Horrigan Corporation for Year 5 in Exhibit 5.17. Cash inflow from operations totals $84 million, cash outflow for investing totals $127 million, and cash inflow from new nonowner financing is $50. Thus, this firm projects a positive net cash inflow for the common shareholders of $7 million (= $84 − $127 + $50). This net cash flow is positive only because Horrigan Corporation borrowed during the year. This pattern is not unusual for a rapidly growing firm. The valuation of a firm using the present value of future cash flows rests critically on assumptions about future growth.

Assume for purposes of illustration that pro forma financial statements for Horrigan Corporation revealed the amounts in columns (**2**) through (**5**) in the table below. Column (**6**) shows the present value of the excess cash flow when discounted at 20 percent, the assumed rate of return desired by the common shareholders. The analyst expects excess cash flow after Year 9 to increase 12 percent each year. The $1,147.8 million represents the present value at the end of Year 4 of this excess cash flow after Year 9. Based on the 16 million shares of common stock outstanding (see Exhibit 5.2), the analyst estimates a market value of $83.54 per share (= $1,336.7 million/16 million shares).

Year (1)	Cash Flow from Operations (2)	Cash Flow from Investing (3)	Cash Flow from Nonowner Financing (4)	Excess Cash Flow to Common Shareholders (5)	Present Value of Cash Flows to Common Shareholders (6)
5	$ 84	$(127)	$50	$ 7	$ 5.8
6	129	(155)	50	24	16.7
7	194	(189)	50	55	31.8
8	290	(231)	50	109	52.6
9	435	(281)	50	204	82.0
After Year 9					1,147.8[a]
Total Present Value					$1,336.7

Note: Column (5) = Column (2) + Column (3) + Column (4).

[a]Assumes a growth rate in excess cash flow of 12 percent per year and a discount rate of 20 percent. See problem 43 in the appendix.

Market Multiples

A second valuation approach relies on market multiples of certain financial statement items for similar firms in the market. Identifying similar firms requires the analyst to consider such factors as the type of business, growth characteristics, and size.

Price Earnings Ratios

One common valuation approach relates market prices to multiples of earnings. The chain of logic runs as follows:

$$
\begin{aligned}
\text{Market Price} &= \frac{\text{Cash Flows from Stream of Dividends and Residual Value}}{\downarrow} \times \text{Appropriate Discount Factors} \\[2ex]
&= \text{Future Cash Flows of a Firm for All Years} \downarrow \times \text{Appropriate Discount Factors} \\[2ex]
&= \text{Future One-Year Earnings of a Firm} \downarrow \times \text{Appropriate Market Multiple} \\[2ex]
&= \text{Current One-Year Earnings of a Firm} \times \text{Appropriate Market Multiple}
\end{aligned}
$$

The analyst uses current earnings as a surrogate for future earnings and cash flows (recall from Chapter 3 that over sufficiently long periods, net income equals cash inflows minus cash outflows from operating, investing, and nonowner financing activities). Future cash flows of the firm provide the source of cash flows to the investor. The market multiple serves the function of a discount rate in present value calculation.[11]

---

[11]Actually, the discount rate and the market multiple for a no-growth firm have a reciprocal relation. Refer to the discussion of perpetuities in this book's compound interest appendix. There you will see that the current value of an indefinite stream of constant payments, say $1 per period, is $1/r when the interest (or discount) rate is r per period. Thus if the discount rate is 10 percent per period, the stream has a current value of $10 (= $1/.10), a multiple of 10, but if the discount rate is 20 percent per period, then the stream has a current value of only $5 (= $1/.20), a multiple of 5. Market multipliers for growing firms are larger than $1/r because of the need to value the growth in cash flows and earnings. See Exhibit 12.1 and the discussion of valuation in Chapter 12.

Assume that firms similar to Horrigan Corporation sell at 20 times Year 4 earnings from continuing operations. Based on the earnings of Horrigan Corporation for Year 4 of $60 million, a market multiple of 20 yields a total market value of $1,200 million, or $75.00 (= $1,200/16 shares) per share.

Market-to-Book-Value Ratios

Another valuation approach relates market values to the book values of common shareholders' equity of similar firms. Book values tend to exhibit less variability over time than earnings and provide perhaps less ambiguous indications of market values.

Assume that firms similar to Horrigan Corporation have average market-to-book-value ratios of 3.0 at the end of Year 4. The common shareholders' equity of Horrigan Corporation is $410 million at the end of Year 4, suggesting a total market value of $1,230 million, or $76.88 (= $1,230 million/16 million) per share. In Chapter 2, Problems **39** and **40** show market-to-book-value ratios for several actual firms.

Summary of Valuation Approaches

These valuation approaches yielded market values for Horrigan Corporation of approximately $75 to $84 per share. We constructed the examples so that the values fell within a narrow range. Analysis of real data will likely show a wider range of market values, so the analyst must exercise judgment in choosing an approach to provide a reasonable estimate.

SOLUTIONS TO SELF-STUDY PROBLEMS

SUGGESTED SOLUTION TO PROBLEM 5.1 FOR SELF-STUDY

(Abbott Corporation; analyzing the rate of return on assets.)

a. The declining rate of return on assets results from a decreasing total assets turnover. The profit margin ratio (before interest expense and related tax effects) was stable. The declining total assets turnover results primarily from a decreasing fixed assets turnover. Abbott Corporation has probably added productive capacity in recent years, anticipating higher sales in the future, which caused the fixed asset turnover to decline.

b. Abbott Corporation has probably implemented more effective inventory control systems, resulting in an increasing inventory turnover ratio. The more rapid inventory turnover results in fewer writedowns of inventory items for product obsolescence and physical deterioration, thereby decreasing the cost of goods sold to sales percentage.

SUGGESTED SOLUTION TO PROBLEM 5.2 FOR SELF-STUDY

(Abbott Corporation; analyzing the rate of return on common shareholders' equity.)

a. The increasing rate of return on common shareholders' equity results from an increasing proportion of debt in the capital structure. Although the rate of return on assets declined, the increase in the leverage ratio more than offset the declining operating profitability.

b. The rate of return on common shareholders' equity exceeds the rate of return on assets, suggesting that the firm's earnings on assets financed by creditors were greater than the cost of creditors' capital. The excess return benefited the common shareholders.

SUGGESTED SOLUTION TO PROBLEM 5.3 FOR SELF-STUDY

(Abbott Corporation; analyzing short-term liquidity risk.)

a. Inventories are the principal asset appearing in the current ratio but not in the quick ratio. The declining current ratio indicates that inventories are not growing as rapidly as the overall level of operations. Note the decrease in the number of days inventory items are held, suggesting that the firm exerts more effective control over the level of inventories.

b. Abbott Corporation experienced a slight increase in the number of days receivables are outstanding, which tends to decrease cash flow from operations. The decrease in the number of days a firm holds inventories increases cash flow from operations and more than offsets the effect of accounts receivable on cash flow from operations. The stable accounts payable turnover also indicates that an acceleration or delay in paying accounts payable does not explain the decline in the cash flow from operations to current liabilities ratio. Most likely, declining profitability, which results in operations throwing off less cash with each revolution of the operating cycle, caused the decline. Note that the profit margin ratio excluding financing costs remained stable over the three years (see Problem 5.1 for Self-Study), whereas the profit margin ratio including financing costs declined (see Problem 5.2 for Self-Study). Thus, the declining profitability results from increased financing costs, probably related to the level of debt in the capital structure.

c. Abbott Corporation's cash flow from operations to current liabilities ratio is marginally less than the 40 percent level considered desirable for a healthy firm. Its declining current ratio results from more effective inventory control systems, reducing short-term liquidity risk. A quick ratio around 1.0 indicates that the most liquid current assets are sufficient to pay current liabilities. These signals suggest a satisfactory level of short-term liquidity risk.

SUGGESTED SOLUTION TO PROBLEM 5.4 FOR SELF-STUDY

(Abbott Corporation; analyzing long-term liquidity risk.)

a. The response to question **b** in Problem 5.3 for Self-Study indicates that declining profitability helps explain the decrease in the cash flow from operations to total liabilities ratio. So does the increase in borrowing. This increased borrowing is both short-term and long-term, as the two debt ratios indicate.

b. The declining interest coverage ratio results primarily from increased interest expense on the increased debt loads. (Note from Problem 5.1 for Self-Study that the profit margin ratio excluding financing costs was stable during the last three years.)

c. The cash flow from operations to total liabilities ratio falls below the 20 percent level considered desirable for a healthy firm. Its interest coverage ratio remains four times earnings before interest and taxes. The growth in debt appears related to increases in fixed assets (see the response to question **a** in Problem 5.1 for Self-Study). If Abbott Corporation experienced difficulty servicing its debt, it could perhaps sell some of these fixed assets to obtain funds. Thus, the overall long-term liquidity risk level appears reasonable.

SUGGESTED SOLUTION TO PROBLEM 5.5 FOR SELF-STUDY

(Cox Corporation; computing profitability and risk ratios.)

a. Rate of return on assets $= \dfrac{\$3{,}000 + (1 - .30)(\$700)}{.5(\$20{,}000 + \$24{,}000)} = 15.9$ percent

b. Profit margin ratio $= \dfrac{\$3{,}000 + (1 - .30)(\$700)}{\$30{,}000} = 11.6$ percent

c. Cost of goods sold to sales percentage $= \dfrac{\$18{,}000}{\$30{,}000} = 60.0$ percent

d. Selling expense to sales percentage $= \dfrac{\$4{,}500}{\$30{,}000} = 15.0$ percent

e. Total assets turnover $= \dfrac{\$30{,}000}{.5(\$20{,}000 + \$24{,}000)} = 1.4$ times per year

f. Accounts receivable turnover $= \dfrac{\$30{,}000}{.5(\$3{,}600 + \$4{,}300)} = 7.6$ times per year

g. Inventory turnover $= \dfrac{\$18{,}000}{.5(\$5{,}600 + \$7{,}900)} = 2.7$ times per year

h. Fixed asset turnover $= \dfrac{\$30{,}000}{.5(\$9{,}900 + \$10{,}670)} = 2.9$ times per year

i. Rate of return on common shareholders' equity $= \dfrac{\$3{,}000 - \$100}{.5(\$8{,}000 + \$11{,}000)}$
$= 30.5$ percent

j. Profit margin ratio (after interest) $= \dfrac{\$3{,}000 - \$100}{\$30{,}000} = 9.7$ percent

k. Leverage ratio $= \dfrac{.5(\$20{,}000 + \$24{,}000)}{.5(\$8{,}000 + \$11{,}000)} = 2.3$ percent

l. Current ratio

December 31, Year 1: $= \dfrac{\$10{,}100}{\$7{,}000} = 1.4:1$

December 31, Year 2: $= \dfrac{\$13{,}300}{\$9{,}200} = 1.4:1$

m. Quick ratio

December 31, Year 1: $= \dfrac{\$4{,}200}{\$7{,}000} = .6:1$

December 31, Year 2: $= \dfrac{\$5{,}050}{\$9{,}200} = .5:1$

n. Cash flow from operations to current liabilities ratio $= \dfrac{\$3{,}300}{.5(\$7{,}000 + \$9{,}200)}$
$= 40.7$ percent

o. Accounts payable turnover $= \dfrac{\$18{,}000 + \$7{,}900 - \$5{,}600}{.5(\$3{,}500 + \$3{,}300)} = 6.0$ times per year

p. Long-term debt ratio

December 31, Year 1: $= \dfrac{\$4{,}000}{\$13{,}000} = 30.8$ percent

December 31, Year 2: $= \dfrac{\$2{,}800}{\$14{,}800} = 18.9$ percent

q. Debt-equity ratio

December 31, Year 1: $= \dfrac{\$11{,}000}{\$20{,}000} = 55.0$ percent

December 31, Year 2: $= \dfrac{\$12{,}000}{\$24{,}000} = 50.0$ percent

r. Cash flow from operations to total liabilities ratio $= \dfrac{\$3{,}300}{.5(\$11{,}000 + \$12{,}000)}$
$= 28.7$ percent

s. Interest coverage ratio $= \dfrac{\$3{,}000 + \$1{,}300 + \$700}{\$700} = 7.1$ times

KEY TERMS AND CONCEPTS

Return and risk
Time-series analysis
Cross-section analysis
Profitability
Rate of return on assets (ROA)
Profit margin ratio
Total assets turnover ratio
Accounts receivable turnover ratio
Inventory turnover ratio
Fixed asset turnover ratio
Rate of return on common shareholders'
  equity (ROCE)
Financial leverage
Leverage ratio
Earnings per share

Basic and fully diluted earnings per share
Short-term liquidity risk
Current ratio
Quick ratio or acid test ratio
Cash flow from operations to current
  liabilities ratio
Accounts payable turnover ratio
Long-term liquidity risk
Long-term debt ratio
Debt-equity ratio
Cash flow from operations to total
  liabilities ratio
Interest coverage ratio
Pro forma financial statements

QUESTIONS, EXERCISES, PROBLEMS, AND CASES

QUESTIONS

1. Review the meaning of the terms and concepts listed above in Key Terms and Concepts.
2. Describe several factors that might limit the comparability of a firm's financial statement ratios over several periods.

3. Describe several factors that might limit the comparability of one firm's financial statement ratios with those of another firm in the same industry.

4. "I can understand why the analyst adds back interest expense to net income in the numerator of the rate of return on assets, but I don't see why an adjustment is made for income taxes." Provide an explanation.

5. One company president stated, "The operations of our company are such that we must turn inventory over once every four weeks." Another company president in a similar industry stated, "The operations of our company are such that we can live comfortably with a turnover of four times each year." Explain what these two company presidents probably had in mind.

6. Some have argued that for any given firm at a particular time, there is an optimal inventory turnover ratio. Explain.

7. Under what circumstances will the rate of return on common shareholders' equity exceed the rate of return on assets? Under what circumstances will it be less?

8. A company president recently stated, "The operations of our company are such that we can effectively use only a small amount of financial leverage." Explain.

9. Define *financial leverage*. As long as a firm's rate of return on assets exceeds its aftertax cost of borrowing, why doesn't the firm increase borrowing to as close to 100 percent of financing as possible?

10. Illustrate with amounts how a decrease in working capital can accompany an increase in the current ratio.

EXERCISES

11. **Calculating and disaggregating rate of return on assets.** Recent annual reports of Cracker Barrel Old Country Store (Cracker Barrel) and Outback Steakhouse (Outback) reveal the following for Year 8 (in thousands):

	Cracker Barrel	Outback
Revenues	$1,317,104	$1,151,637
Interest Expense	3,026	2,489
Net Income	104,136	91,273
Average Total Assets	910,407	531,312

Cracker Barrel operates a chain of restaurants featuring value-priced country meals. Its restaurants are open for all meals every day. Each restaurant also sells craft items with a country theme. Outback operates a chain of restaurants featuring steaks. Each restaurant carries an Australian theme and serves primarily the dinner meal. Outback tends to locate its restaurants in buildings that were formerly restaurants that went out of business. The income tax rate for Year 8 is 35 percent.

a. Calculate the rate of return on assets for each company.

b. Disaggregate the rate of return on assets in part **a** into profit margin and total assets turnover components.

c. Comment on the relative profitability of the two companies for Year 8.

12. **Profitability analysis for two types of retailers.** Information taken from recent annual reports of two retailers appears as follows (amounts in thousands). One of these companies is TJX, a discount store chain featuring name-brand clothing, and the other is The Gap, a specialty retailer of apparel. The income tax rate is 35 percent. Indicate which of these companies is TJX and which is The Gap. Explain your reasoning using appropriate financial ratios.

	Company A	Company B
Sales	$6,507,825	$7,389,069
Interest Expense	—	4,502
Net Income	533,901	306,592
Average Total Assets	2,982,215	2,585,422

13. **Analyzing accounts receivable for two companies.** The annual reports of Gateway 2000 and Sun Microsystems, two manufacturers of computers, reveal the information below for the current year (amounts in thousands). Gateway 2000 sells custom-order personal computers, primarily to individuals. Sun Microsystems sells higher-end computers and Internet software, primarily to businesses.

	Gateway 2000	Sun Microsystems
Sales	$7,866,656	$9,790,840
Accounts Receivable, January 1	562,154	1,666,523
Accounts Receivable, December 31	638,349	1,845,765

   a. Compute the accounts receivable turnover for each company.

   b. Compute the average number of days that accounts receivable are outstanding for each company.

   c. Why do the accounts receivable turnovers of these two companies differ?

14. **Analyzing inventories over three years.** The following information relates to the activities of Kellogg, a manufacturer of breakfast cereals (amounts in millions):

	Year 6	Year 7	Year 8
Sales	$7,004	$6,677	$6,830
Cost of Goods Sold	3,178	3,123	3,270
Average Inventory	387	401	430

   a. Compute the inventory turnover for each year.

   b. Compute the average number of days that inventories are held each year.

   c. Compute the cost of goods sold to sales percentage for each year.

   d. How well has Kellogg managed its inventories over the three years?

15. **Analyzing fixed asset turnover over three years.** The following information relates to Anheuser-Busch, a brewer of beer and operator of entertainment theme parks (amounts in millions):

	Year 3	Year 4	Year 5
Sales	$10,345	$10,884	$11,066
Average Fixed Assets	6,629	6,986	7,479
Expenditures on Fixed Assets	953	968	1,199

   a. Compute the fixed asset turnover for each year.

   b. How well has Anheuser Busch managed its investment in fixed assets over the three years?

16. **Calculating and disaggregating rate of return on common shareholders' equity.** Information taken from the annual reports of Circuit City, an electronic superstore retailer selling name-brand products, for three recent years appears below (amounts in millions):

	Year 4	Year 5	Year 6
Revenues	$7,029	$7,664	$8,871
Net Income	179	136	104
Average Total Assets	2,265	2,804	3,156
Average Common Shareholders' Equity	971	1,339	1,672

   a. Compute the rate of return on common shareholders' equity for each year.
   b. Disaggregate the rate of return on common shareholders' equity into profit margin, total assets turnover, and leverage ratio components.
   c. How has the profitability of Circuit City changed over the three years?

17. **Profitability analyses for three companies.** The following data show five items from the financial statements of three companies for a recent year (amounts in millions):

	Company A	Company B	Company C
For Year			
Revenues	$1,308	$1,763	$3,817
Income before Interest and Related Taxes[a]	69	174	359
Net Income to Common Shareholders[b]	68	174	318
Average during Year			
Total Assets	925	1,449	3,985
Common Shareholders' Equity	664	745	1,829

[a]Net Income + [Interest Expense × (1 − Tax Rate)]
[b]Net Income − Preferred Stock Dividends

   a. Compute the rate of return on assets for each company. Disaggregate the rate of return on assets into profit margin and total assets turnover components.
   b. Compute the rate of return on common shareholders' equity for each company. Disaggregate the rate of return on common shareholders' equity into profit margin, total assets turnover, and leverage ratio components.
   c. The three companies are Harley Davidson (manufacturer of brand-name motorcycles), Southwest Airlines (provider of airline services), and Starbucks (operator of specialty retail coffee shops). Which of the companies corresponds to A, B, and C? What clues did you use in reaching your conclusions?

18. **Profitability analysis for three companies.** The following data show six items from the financial statements of three companies for a recent year (amounts in millions):

	Company A	Company B	Company C
For Year			
Revenues	$12,504	$19,139	$22,976
Income before Interest and Related Taxes[a]	2,213	449	2,254
Net Income to Common Shareholders[b]	2,213	299	1,850

(continued)

	Company A	Company B	Company C
Average during Year			
Total Assets	15,002	8,209	39,938
Common Shareholders' Equity	7,444	2,422	18,337
Long-term Debt/Assets	4.8%	37.5%	20.2%

[a]Net Income + [Interest Expense × (1 − Tax Rate)]
[b]Net Income − Preferred Stock Dividends

The three companies are American Stores (grocery store chain), Disney (film and theme park entertainment), and Pfizer (pharmaceutical products). Which of the companies corresponds to A, B, and C? What clues did you use in reaching your conclusions?

19. **Relating profitability to financial leverage.**
    a. Compute the rate of return on common shareholders' equity in each of the following independent cases.

Case	Average Total Assets	Average Interest-Bearing Debt	Average Common Share-holders' Equity	Rate of Return on Assets	Aftertax Cost of Interest-Bearing Debt
A	$200	$100	$100	6%	6%
B	200	100	100	8%	6%
C	200	120	80	8%	6%
D	200	100	100	4%	6%
E	200	50	100	6%	6%
F	200	50	100	5%	6%

    b. In which cases is leverage working to the advantage of the common shareholders?

20. **Interpreting changes in earnings per share.** Company A and Company B both start Year 1 with $1 million of shareholders' equity and 100,000 shares of common stock outstanding. During Year 1, both companies earn net income of $100,000, a rate of return of 10 percent on common shareholders' equity at the beginning of Year 1. Company A declares and pays $100,000 of dividends to common shareholders at the end of Year 1, whereas Company B retains all its earnings and declares no dividends. During Year 2, both companies earn net income equal to 10 percent of shareholders' equity at the beginning of Year 2.
    a. Compute earnings per share for Company A and for Company B for Year 1 and for Year 2.
    b. Compute the rate of growth in earnings per share for Company A and Company B, comparing earnings per share in Year 2 with earnings per share in Year 1.
    c. Using the rate of growth in earnings per share as the criterion, which company's management appears to be doing a better job for its shareholders? Comment on this result.

21. **Calculating and interpreting short-term liquidity ratios.** Data taken from the financial statements of Nike, a designer and manufacturer of athletic footwear and apparel, appear as follows (amounts in millions):

For the Year	Year 6	Year 7	Year 8
Revenues	$6,471	$9,187	$9,153
Cost of Goods Sold	3,907	5,503	6,066
Net Income	553	796	498
Cash Flow from Operations	340	323	518

On December 31	Year 5	Year 6	Year 7	Year 8
Cash and Marketable Securities	$ 216	$ 262	$ 445	$ 109
Accounts Receivable	1,053	1,346	1,754	1,674
Inventories	630	931	1,339	1,397
Prepayments	147	188	293	353
Total Current Assets	$2,046	$2,727	$3,831	$3,533
Accounts Payable	$ 298	$ 455	$ 687	$ 585
Bank Loans	397	445	553	480
Other Current Liabilities	412	567	627	639
Total Current Liabilities	$1,107	$1,467	$1,867	$1,704

a. Compute the current and quick ratios on December 31 of each year.

b. Compute the cash flow from operations to current liabilities ratio and the accounts receivable, inventory, and accounts payable turnover ratios for Year 6, Year 7, and Year 8.

c. How has the short-term liquidity risk of Nike changed during the three-year period?

22. Calculating and interpreting short-term liquidity ratios. Data taken from the financial statements of International Paper Company, a forest products firm, appear as follows (amount in millions):

For the Year	Year 3	Year 4	Year 5
Revenues	$13,598	$13,685	$14,966
Cost of Goods Sold	10,987	11,089	12,028
Net Income	401	289	432
Cash Flow from Operations	1,078	929	1,275

On December 31	Year 2	Year 3	Year 4	Year 5
Cash and Marketable Securities	$ 238	$ 225	$ 242	$ 270
Accounts Receivable	1,841	1,861	1,856	2,241
Inventories	1,780	1,938	2,024	2,075
Prepayments	272	342	279	244
Total Current Assets	$4,131	$4,366	$4,401	$4,830
Accounts Payable	$1,110	$1,259	$1,089	$1,204
Bank Loans	1,699	2,356	2,089	2,083
Other Current Liabilities	918	916	831	747
Total Current Liabilities	$3,727	$4,531	$4,009	$4,034

a. Compute the current and quick ratios on December 31 of each year.

b. Compute the cash flow from operations to current liabilities ratio and the accounts receivable, inventory, and accounts payable turnover ratios for Year 3, Year 4, and Year 5.

c. How has the short-term liquidity risk of International Paper Company changed during the three-year period?

23. **Calculating and interpreting long-term liquidity ratios.** Data taken from the financial statement of Hasbro, a toy manufacturer, appear below (amounts in millions). Hasbro acquired Tonka, also a toy company, in Year 2.

For the Year	Year 2	Year 3	Year 4
Net Income before Interest and Income Taxes	$248	$328	$370
Cost of Goods Sold	120	230	217
Interest Expense	43	36	30

On December 31	Year 1	Year 2	Year 3	Year 4
Long-term Debt	$ 57	$380	$ 206	$ 200
Total Liabilities	418	995	977	1,016
Total Shareholders' Equity	867	955	1,106	1,277

a. Compute the long-term debt ratio and the debt-equity ratio at the end of Year 2, Year 3, and Year 4.
b. Compute the cash flow from operations to total liabilities ratio and the interest coverage ratio for Year 2 through Year 4.
c. How has the long-term liquidity risk of Hasbro changed over this three-year period?

24. **Calculating and interpreting long-term liquidity ratios.** Data taken from the financial statements of American Airlines appear below (amounts in millions):

For the Year	Year 5	Year 6	Year 7
Net Income before Interest Expense and Income Taxes	$1,086	$1,331	$1,447
Cash Flow from Operations	1,996	2,139	2,266
Interest Expense	273	203	194

On December 31	Year 4	Year 5	Year 6	Year 7
Long-term Debt	$ 3,482	$ 3,095	$ 2,503	$ 2,319
Total Liabilities	14,090	13,983	13,034	12,399
Total Shareholders' Equity	3,233	3,646	4,528	5,354

a. Compute the long-term debt ratio and the debt-equity ratio at the end of each year.
b. Compute the cash flow from operations to total liabilities ratio and the interest coverage ratio for Year 5 through Year 7.
c. How has the long-term liquidity risk of American Airlines changed over this three-year period?

25. **Effect of various transactions on financial statement ratios.** Indicate the immediate effects (increase, decrease, no effect) of each of the following independent transactions on (1) the rate of return on common shareholders' equity, (2) the current ratio, and (3) the debt-equity ratio. State any necessary assumptions.
a. A firm purchases, on account, merchandise inventory costing $205,000.
b. A firm sells for $150,000, on account, merchandise inventory costing $120,000.

c. A firm collects $100,000 from customers on accounts receivable.

d. A firm pays $160,000 to suppliers on accounts payable.

e. A firm sells for $10,000 a machine costing $40,000 and with accumulated depreciation of $30,000.

f. A firm declares dividends of $80,000. It will pay the dividends during the next accounting period.

g. A firm issues common stock for $75,000.

h. A firm acquires a machine costing $60,000. It gives $10,000 cash and signs a note for $50,000 payable five years from now for the balance of the purchase price.

26. Effect of various transactions on financial statement ratios. Indicate the effects (increase, decrease, no effect) of the following independent transactions on (1) earnings per share, (2) working capital, and (3) the quick ratio, where accounts receivable are *included* but merchandise inventory is *excluded* from quick assets. State any necessary assumptions.

a. A firm sells for $300,000, on account, merchandise inventory costing $240,000.

b. A firm declares dividends of $160,000. It will pay the dividends during the next accounting period.

c. A firm purchases, on account, merchandise inventory costing $410,000.

d. A firm sells for $20,000 a machine costing $80,000 and with accumulated depreciation of $60,000.

e. Because of defects, a firm returns to the supplier merchandise inventory purchased for $7,000 cash. The firm receives a cash reimbursement.

f. A firm issues 10,000 shares of $10-par value common stock on the last day of the accounting period for $15 per share. It uses the proceeds to acquire the assets of another firm composed of the following: accounts receivable, $30,000; merchandise inventory, $60,000; plant and equipment, $100,000. The acquiring firm also agrees to assume current liabilities of $40,000 of the acquired company.

PROBLEMS AND CASES

27. Calculating and interpreting profitability and risk ratios. Wal-Mart Stores, Inc., is the largest retailing company in the United States. It maintains a chain of discount stores and warehouse clubs in many parts of the United States. In recent years, it has expanded operations into superstores that offer a combination of traditional discount store products and grocery products. It has also expanded internationally by acquiring established discount chains in other countries. As an extension of warehousing and distributing products for its own stores, it offers similar services to other retail stores. Exhibit 5.19 presents segment profitability ratios, Exhibit 5.20 presents comparative balance sheets, Exhibit 5.21 presents comparative income statements, and Exhibit 5.22 presents comparative statements of cash flows for Wal-Mart Stores for three recent years. Exhibit 5.23 presents a financial statement ratio analysis for Wal-Mart Stores for Year 6 and Year 7. The income tax rate is 35 percent.

a. Compute the amounts of the ratios listed in Exhibit 5.23 for Year 8.

b. What are the likely reasons for the changes in Wal-Mart's rate of return on assets during the three-year period? Analyze the financial ratios to the maximum depth possible.

c. What are the likely reasons for the changes in Wal-Mart's rate of return on common shareholders' equity during the three-year period?

d. How has the short-term liquidity risk of Wal-Mart changed during the three-year period?

e. How has the long-term liquidity risk of Wal-Mart changed during the three-year period?

EXHIBIT 5.19	WAL-MART STORES, INC. Segment Profitability Analysis (Problem 27)		

	Year 6	Year 7	Year 8
SALES MIX			
Wal-Mart Discount Stores and Supercenters	70.8%	71.3%	71.1%
Sam's Club	20.3	18.9	17.5
International	4.0	4.8	6.4
Distribution	4.9	5.0	5.0
	100.0%	100.0%	100.0%
WAL-MART DISCOUNT STORES AND SUPERCENTERS			
Profit Margin	6.9%	6.7%	7.0%
Total Assets Turnover	3.4	3.6	3.8
Rate of Return on Assets	23.6%	24.1%	26.5%
SAM'S CLUBS			
Profit Margin	2.5%	2.8%	3.0%
Total Assets Turnover	4.9	5.0	5.3
Rate of Return on Assets	12.4%	14.2%	15.9%
INTERNATIONAL			
Profit Margin	(.4%)	.5%	3.5%
Total Assets Turnover	1.6	1.7	1.0
Rate of Return on Assets	(.7%)	.8	3.5%
DISTRIBUTION			
Profit Margin	4.8%	2.1%	(3.5%)
Total Assets Turnover	.4	.4	.5
Rate of Return on Assets	1.8%	.9%	(1.7%)

28. **Calculating and interpreting profitability and risk ratios.** Nike and Reebok maintain dominant market shares in the athletic footwear market. Nike places somewhat greater emphasis on the performance characteristics of its footwear, whereas Reebok places somewhat greater emphasis on the fashion characteristics of its footwear. Exhibit 5.24 presents comparative balance sheets for Nike and Reebok at the end of Year 10 and Year 11. Exhibit 5.25 presents an income statement for each firm for Year 11. Cash flows from operations for Year 11 were $255 million for Nike and $173 million for Reebok. The income tax rate is 35 percent. On the basis of this information and appropriate financial statement ratios, which company is
a. more profitable?
b. less risky in terms of short-term liquidity?
c. less risky in terms of long-term solvency?

29. **Detective analysis—identify company.** In this problem, you become a financial analyst/detective. Exhibit 5.26 expresses condensed financial statements for 13 companies on a percentage basis. In all cases, total sales revenues appear as 100.00%. All other numbers were divided by sales revenue for the year. The 13 companies (all corporations except for the accounting firm) shown here represent the following industries:
  (1) Advertising agency
  (2) Computer manufacturer

EXHIBIT 5.20	WAL-MART STORES, INC. Comparative Balance Sheets (amounts in millions) (Problem 27)

	January 31			
	Year 5	Year 6	Year 7	Year 8
ASSETS				
Cash	$ 45	$ 83	$ 883	$ 1,447
Accounts Receivable	900	853	845	976
Inventories	14,064	15,989	15,897	16,497
Prepayments	329	406	368	432
Total Current Assets	$15,338	$17,331	$17,993	$19,352
Property, Plant, and Equipment (net)	18,485	21,497	22,904	26,344
Other Assets	1,607	1,316	1,287	2,426
Total Assets	$35,430	$40,144	$42,184	$48,122
LIABILITIES AND SHAREHOLDERS' EQUITY				
Accounts Payable	$ 5,907	$ 6,442	$ 7,628	$ 9,126
Notes Payable	1,795	2,458	—	—
Current Portion of Long-term Debt	87	340	618	1,141
Other Current Liabilities	2,184	2,214	2,711	4,193
Total Current Liabilities	$ 9,973	$11,454	$10,957	$14,460
Long-term Debt	12,320	13,203	12,596	12,412
Other Noncurrent Liabilities	411	731	1,488	2,747
Total Liabilities	$22,704	$25,388	$25,041	$29,619
Common Stock	$ 230	$ 229	$ 228	$ 224
Additional Paid-in Capital	539	545	547	585
Retained Earnings	11,957	13,982	16,368	17,694
Total Shareholders' Equity	$12,726	$14,756	$17,143	$18,503
Total Liabilities and Shareholders' Equity	$35,430	$40,144	$42,184	$48,122

EXHIBIT 5.21	WAL-MART STORES, INC. Comparative Income Statements (amounts in millions) (Problem 27)

	Year 6	Year 7	Year 8
Sales Revenue	$94,749	$106,146	$119,299
Expenses:			
Cost of Goods Sold	$74,564	$ 83,663	$ 93,438
Marketing and Administrative	14,951	16,788	19,436
Interest	888	845	784
Income Taxes	1,606	1,794	2,115
Total Expenses	$92,009	$103,090	$115,773
Net Income	$ 2,740	$ 3,056	$ 3,526

(3) Department store chain (that carries its own receivables)
(4) Distiller of hard liquor
(5) Electric utility
(6) Finance company (lends money to consumers)
(7) Grocery store chain
(8) Insurance company
(9) Pharmaceutical company
(10) Public accounting (CPA) partnership
(11) Soft-drink company
(12) Steel manufacturer
(13) Tobacco products company

Use whatever clues you can to match the companies in Exhibit 5.26 with the industries listed above. You may find it useful to refer to average industry ratios

EXHIBIT 5.22	WAL-MART STORES, INC. Comparative Statements of Cash Flows (amounts in millions) (Problem 27)		
	Year 6	**Year 7**	**Year 8**
OPERATIONS			
Net Income	$ 2,740	$ 3,056	$ 3,526
Depreciation	1,304	1,463	1,634
(Increase) in Accounts Receivable	(61)	(58)	(78)
(Increase) in Inventories	(1,850)	99	(365)
(Increase) in Prepayments	(80)	38	(64)
Increase in Accounts Payable	448	1,208	1,048
Increase in Other Current Liabilities	(118)	124	1,422
Cash Flow from Operations	$ 2,383	$ 5,930	$ 7,123
INVESTING			
Acquisition of Property, Plant, and Equipment	$(3,566)	$(2,643)	$(2,636)
Other	234	575	(1,785)
Cash Flow from Investing	$(3,332)	$(2,068)	$(4,421)
FINANCING			
Increase (Decrease) in Short-term Borrowing	$ 660	$(2,458)	—
Increase in Long-term Borrowing	1,004	632	$ 547
Increase in Common Stock	—	—	—
Decrease in Long-term Borrowing	(207)	(615)	(648)
Acquisition of Common Stock	(105)	(208)	(1,569)
Dividends	(458)	(481)	(611)
Other	93	68	143
Cash Flow from Financing	$ 987	$(3,062)	$(2,138)
Change in Cash	$ 38	$ 800	$564
Cash, Beginning of Year	45	83	883
Cash, End of Year	$ 83	$ 883	$ 1,447

EXHIBIT 5.23	WAL-MART STORES, INC. Financial Ratio Analysis (Problem 27)		
	Year 6	**Year 7**	**Year 8**
Rate of Return on Assets	8.8%	8.8%	
Profit Margin for Rate of Return on Assets	3.5%	3.4%	
Total Assets Turnover	2.51	2.58	
Cost of Goods Sold/Sales	78.7%	78.8%	
Marketing and Administrative Expenses/Sales	15.8%	15.8%	
Interest Expense/Sales	0.9%	0.8%	
Income Tax Expense/Sales	1.7%	1.7%	
Accounts Receivable Turnover Ratio	108.10	125.02	
Inventory Turnover Ratio	4.96	5.25	
Fixed Assets Turnover Ratio	4.74	4.78	
Rate of Return on Common Shareholders' Equity	19.9%	19.2%	
Profit Margin for Rate of Return on Common Shareholders' Equity	2.9%	2.9%	
Leverage Ratio	2.75	2.58	
Current Ratio	1.51	1.64	
Quick Ratio	0.08	0.16	
Cash Flow from Operations to Current Liabilities Ratio	22.2%	52.9%	
Accounts Payable Turnover Ratio	12.39	11.88	
Long-term Debt Ratio	47.2%	42.4%	
Debt-Equity Ratio	63.2%	59.4%	
Cash Flow from Operations to Total Liabilities Ratio	9.9%	23.5%	
Interest Coverage Ratio	5.89	6.74	

compiled by Dun & Bradstreet, Prentice-Hall, Robert Morris Associates, and the Federal Trade Commission. Most libraries carry copies of these documents.

30. **Interpreting profitability and risk ratios.** International Paper Company is the largest integrated paper company in the world. It grows timber in its forests, processes the harvested timber into various commodity and specialty papers in its capital-intensive plants, and distributes various paper products through wholesale and retail outlets. Its average sales mix in recent years is as follows:

Forest Products	12%
Commodity Papers	50
Specialty Papers	16
Distribution	22
	100%

   Exhibit 5.27 presents financial statement ratios for International Paper for Year 8, Year 9, and Year 10. Respond to each of the following questions.

   a. What are the likely reasons for the decrease in the cost of goods sold to sales percentage from 80.0 percent in Year 8 to 75.4 percent in Year 9?

EXHIBIT 5.24	NIKE AND REEBOK Comparative Balance Sheets (amounts in millions) (Problem 28)

	Nike		Reebok	
	Year 10	Year 11	Year 10	Year 11
ASSETS				
Cash	$ 519	$ 216	$ 79	$ 84
Accounts Receivable	703	1,053	457	532
Inventories	470	630	514	625
Prepayments	78	147	77	96
Total Current Assets	$1,770	$2,046	$1,127	$1,337
Property, Plant, and Equipment (net)	406	555	131	165
Other Assets	198	542	134	147
Total Assets	$2,374	$3,143	$1,392	$1,649
LIABILITIES AND SHAREHOLDERS' EQUITY				
Accounts Payable	$ 211	$ 298	$ 282	$ 171
Bank Loans	131	429	27	69
Other Current Liabilities	220	381	87	266
Total Current Liabilities	$ 562	$1,108	$ 396	$ 506
Long-term Debt	12	10	134	132
Other Noncurrent Liabilities	59	60	15	21
Total Liabilities	$ 633	$1,178	$ 545	$ 659
Common Stock	$ 3	$ 4	$ 1	$ 1
Additional Paid-in Capital	108	122	267	168
Retained Earnings	1,630	1,839	1,182	1,424
Treasury Stock	—	—	(603)	(603)
Total Shareholders' Equity	$1,741	$1,965	$ 847	$ 990
Total Liabilities and Shareholders' Equity	$2,374	$3,143	$1,392	$1,649

EXHIBIT 5.25	NIKE AND REEBOK Comparative Income Statements (amounts in millions) (Problem 28)

	For Year 11	
	Nike	Reebok
Sales Revenue	$4,761	$3,280
Expenses:		
Cost of Goods Sold	$2,865	$1,966
Selling and Administrative	1,222	889
Interest	24	17
Income Taxes	250	154
Total Expenses	$4,361	$3,026
Net Income	$ 400	$ 254

b. What are the likely reasons for the decrease in the plant asset turnover from 1.67 in Year 9 to 1.33 in Year 10?

c. Did financial leverage work to the advantage of the common shareholders in Year 10? Explain in such a way that indicates your understanding of the concept of financial leverage.

d. What are the likely reasons for the decrease in the current ratio from 1.21 in Year 9 to 1.02 in Year 10?

e. What are the likely reasons for the decrease in the cash flow from operations to total liabilities ratio from 16.3 percent in Year 9 to 9.9 percent in Year 10?

31. **Interpreting profitability and risk ratios.** The Limited operates specialty retail stores in shopping malls throughout the United States. Exhibit 5.28 presents financial ratios for The Limited for Year 6, Year 7, and Year 8. During Year 6, The Limited carried the accounts receivable from its credit cards on its books. During Year 7 and Year 8, The Limited sold the accounts receivable arising from its credit cards to another company in return for cash soon after the sale on account. Selected additional data appear in Exhibit 5.29.

a. What are the likely reasons for the decrease in the cost of goods sold to sales percentage from 69.5 percent in Year 6 to 66.2 percent in Year 8?

b. What are the likely reasons for the increase in the selling and administrative expenses to sales percentage from 18.7 percent in Year 6 to 23.1 percent in Year 8?

c. What are the likely reasons for the increase in the accounts receivable turnover from 11.5 times in Year 6 to 120.9 times in Year 8?

d. What are the likely reasons for the increase in the fixed asset turnover from 1.4 in Year 6 to 1.7 in Year 8?

e. Did financial leverage work to the benefit of the common shareholders in each year? Explain.

f. The proportion of debt in the capital structure increased during the three years whereas interest expense (net of taxes) as a percentage of sales decreased. Suggest reasons for this seeming inconsistency.

g. What are the likely reasons for the increases in the cash flow from operations to liabilities ratios between Year 6 and Year 7?

32. **Preparing pro forma financial statements (requires Appendix 5.1).** Problem **27** presents financial statements for Wal-Mart Stores, Inc., for Year 6, Year 7, and Year 8, as well as financial statement ratios.

a. Prepare a set of pro forma financial statements for Wal-Mart Stores, Inc., for Year 9 through Year 12 using the following assumptions:

Income Statement

1. Sales will grow 12 percent.
2. Cost of goods sold will equal 78.5 percent of sales.
3. Marketing and administrative expenses will equal 16.5 percent of sales.
4. Interest expense will equal 7 percent of average interest-bearing debt.
5. Income tax expense will equal 37 percent of income before income taxes.

Balance Sheet

6. Cash will equal the amount necessary to equate total assets with total liabilities plus shareholders' equity.
7. Accounts receivable will increase at the growth rate in sales.
8. Inventory will increase at the growth rate in sales.
9. Prepayments will increase at the growth rate in sales.
10. Plant assets (net) will grow at 14.0 percent per year.
11. Other assets will increase at the growth rate in sales.
12. Accounts payable will turn over 11.0 times per year.

EXHIBIT 5.26	Data for Ratio Detective Exercise (Problem 29)

	Company Numbers						
	(1)	**(2)**	**(3)**	**(4)**	**(5)**	**(6)**	**(7)**
Balance Sheet at End of Year							
Current Receivables	1.20%	29.11%	15.80%	13.70%	22.65%	14.11%	8.38%
Inventories	9.18	0.00	6.87	23.19	16.40	14.02	8.54
Net Plant and Equipment[a]	5.12	9.63	10.77	16.01	29.68	17.62	24.97
All Other Assets	3.64	7.02	37.91	25.63	13.49	38.18	46.45
Total Assets	19.14%	45.76%	71.35%	78.53%	82.22%	83.93%	88.34%
Current Liabilities	7.87%	9.82%	21.87%	14.09%	14.34%	22.39%	35.58%
Long-term Liabilities	2.06	7.96	12.30	16.07	41.56	39.38	14.51
Owners' Equity	9.21	27.98	37.18	48.37	26.32	22.16	38.25
Total Equities	19.14%	45.76%	71.35%	78.53%	82.22%	83.93%	88.34%
Income Statement for Year							
Revenues	100.00%	100.00%	100.00%	100.00%	100.00%	100.00%	100.00%
Cost of Goods Sold (excluding depreciation) or Operating Expenses[b]	77.17%	53.77%	53.93%	33.99%	69.14%	45.37%	40.17%
Depreciation	1.23	1.39	7.55	1.95	3.01	2.65	2.26
Interest Expense	2.44	0.52	2.88	.91	2.98	2.92	1.66
Advertising Expense	.89	0.00	0.00	1.38	2.53	4.29	8.54
Research and Development Expense	0.00	1.00	10.95	0.00	0.00	0.70	0.00
Income Taxes	1.08	0.53	2.88	5.09	2.65	5.39	6.61
All Other Items (net)	15.29	18.87	15.98	47.05	14.84	31.72	26.78
Total Expenses	98.10%	76.08%	94.17%	90.37%	95.15%	93.04%	86.02%
Net Income	1.90%	23.92%	5.83%	9.63%	4.85%	6.96%	13.98%

[a]Cost of Plant and Equipment (gross): (1) 17.71%, (2) 14.80%, (3) 21.50%, (4) 29.47%, (5) 42.79%, (6) 27.07%, (7) 38.41%.

[b]Represents operating expenses for the following companies: advertising agency, insurance company, finance company, and the public accounting partnership.

13. Current maturities of long-term debt on January 31 of each year are as follows: Year 8: $1,141; Year 9: $1,039; Year 10: $815; Year 11: $2,018; Year 12: $52.

14. Other current liabilities will grow at the growth rate in sales.

15. Long-term debt will decrease by the amount of long-term debt reclassified as a current liability, and the remaining amount will grow at the growth rate in property, plant, and equipment.

16. Other noncurrent liabilities will increase at the growth rate in sales.

17. Common stock and additional paid-in capital will not change.

18. Dividends will increase at a 20 percent growth rate.

	Company Numbers					
	(8)	**(9)**	**(10)**	**(11)**	**(12)**	**(13)**
Balance Sheet at End of Year						
Current Receivables	9.22%	14.58%	6.89%	113.30%	48.15%	295.65%
Inventories	7.81	13.92	7.72	0.00	0.00	0.00
Net Plant and Equipment[a]	55.55	66.06	152.60	13.07	8.97	10.95
All Other Assets	18.71	50.38	18.99	62.50	241.21	647.73
Total Assets	91.29%	144.94%	186.20%	188.87%	298.33%	954.33%
Current Liabilities	15.96%	39.68%	16.73%	129.32%	228.94%	515.13%
Long-term Liabilities	37.18	18.53	79.94	22.30	11.19	320.34
Owners' Equity	38.15	86.73	89.53	37.25	58.20	118.86
Total Equities	91.29%	144.94%	186.20%	188.87%	298.33%	954.33%
Income Statement for Year						
Revenues	100.00%	100.00%	100.00%	100.00%	100.00%	100.00%
Cost of Goods Sold (excluding depreciation) or Operating Expenses[b]	83.78%	28.89%	75.03%	87.69%	87.78%	26.86%
Depreciation	6.20	5.23	5.97	2.02	0.08	0.00
Interest Expense	1.23	.70	4.45	1.38	0.00	55.18
Advertising Expense	0.00	.37	0.00	0.00	0.00	0.00
Research and Development Expense	.55	13.39	0.00	0.00	0.00	0.00
Income Taxes	.23	9.86	5.04	5.23	2.83	7.82
All Other Items (net)	3.33	18.60	(.45)	(2.17)	0.00	(2.01)
Total Expenses	95.32%	77.04%	90.04%	94.15%	90.69%	88.15%
Net Income	4.68%	22.96%	9.96%	5.85%	9.31%	11.85%

[a]Cost of Plant and Equipment (gross): (8) 146.54%, (9) 92.26%, (10) 207.74%, (11) 17.81%, (12) 15.12%, (13) 12.21%.

[b]Represents operating expenses for the following companies: advertising agency, insurance company, finance company, and the public accounting partnership.

Statement of Cash Flows

19. Depreciation expense will increase at the growth rate in property, plant, and equipment.
20. The change in Other Noncurrent Assets is an investing activity.
21. The change in Other Noncurrent Liabilities is an operating activity.

b. Describe actions that Wal-Mart Stores, Inc., might take to deal with the shortage of cash projected in part a.

33. **Case analysis of bankruptcy.** On October 2, 1975, W. T. Grant Company (Grant) filed for bankruptcy protection under Chapter XI of the Bankruptcy Act. At that time, assets totaled $1.02 billion, and liabilities totaled $1.03 billion. The company

EXHIBIT 5.27	INTERNATIONAL PAPER Financial Ratios (Problem 30)

	Year 8	Year 9	Year 10
Profit Margin Ratio (before interest effects)	4.7%	8.2%	4.7%
Total Assets Turnover Ratio	.87	.95	.77
Rate of Return on Assets	4.1%	7.8%	3.6%
Profit Margin (after interest effects)	2.9%	5.8%	2.2%
Leverage Ratio	2.71	2.92	3.05
Rate of Return on Common Shareholders' Equity	6.8%	16.1%	5.1%
Cost of Goods Sold/Sales	80.0%	75.4%	79.9%
Selling & Administrative Expense/Sales	12.9%	11.9%	13.0%
Interest Expense/Sales	2.3%	2.5%	2.6%
Income Tax Expense/Sales	3.2%	5.4%	3.2%
Accounts Receivable Turnover	7.31	8.23	7.86
Inventory Turnover	5.84	6.14	5.72
Plant Asset Turnover	1.53	1.67	1.33
Current Ratio	1.20	1.21	1.02
Quick Ratio	.62	.59	.49
Cash Flow from Operations to Current Liabilities	30.9%	50.5%	32.3%
Days Accounts Receivable Outstanding	50	44	46
Days Inventories Held	62	59	64
Days Accounts Payable Outstanding	50	44	46
Long-term Debt Ratio	40.7%	45.1%	43.3%
Debt-Equity Ratio	63.5%	67.5%	66.9%
Cash Flow from Operations to Total Liabilities	11.4%	16.3%	9.9%
Interest Coverage Ratio	3.05	5.11	2.68
Growth Rate in Sales	9.4%	32.3%	1.7%
Growth Rate in Cash	11.6%	15.6%	12.8%
Growth Rate in Capital Expenditures	34.6%	69.3%	16.7%

operated at a profit for most years before 1974 but reported an operating loss of $177 million for its fiscal year January 31, 1974, to January 31, 1975. A large portion of this loss resulted from a $155.7 million provision of uncollectible accounts receivable. This case uses tools of financial statement analysis to identify the causes of W. T. Grant's bankruptcy.

Grant operated a chain of discount retail stores, similar to Wal-Mart and Kmart today. Prior to the mid-1960s, Grant located most of its stores in urban centers. With the movement to the suburbs, Grant began a rapid expansion into suburban shopping centers. It added furniture and appliances to its product line to serve the needs of new suburban homeowners. It also offered a credit card to assist customers in financing their purchases.

EXHIBIT 5.28	THE LIMITED Financial Ratios (Problem 31)		

	Year 6	Year 7	Year 8
Profit Margin for Rate of Return on Assets	7.5%	7.1%	6.9%
Assets Turnover	.9	1.0	1.1
Rate of Return on Assets	6.7%	7.3%	8.0%
Cost of Goods Sold ÷ Sales	69.5%	67.6%	66.2%
Selling and Administrative Expenses ÷ Sales	18.7%	21.4%	23.1%
Income Tax Expense (excluding tax effects of Interest expense) ÷ Sales	4.6%	4.4%	4.2%
Interest Expense (net of tax savings) ÷ Sales	3.2%	2.8%	2.5%
Accounts Receivable Turnover	11.5	118.4	120.9
Inventory Turnover	6.0	5.9	6.1
Fixed Asset Turnover	1.4	1.6	1.7
Profit Margin for Rate of Return on Common Shareholders' Equity	4.0%	3.7%	3.8%
Leverage Ratio	2.9	3.3	4.0
Rate of Return on Common Shareholders' Equity	10.5%	12.6%	17.5%
Current Ratio	3.9	1.7	1.9
Quick Ratio	2.4	.4	.8
Days Accounts Payable	18	18	18
Cash Flow from Operations ÷ Average Current Liabilities	47.2%	87.7%	59.0%
Long-term Debt Ratio	57.9%	68.9%	69.2%
Debt-Equity Ratio	64.5%	75.1%	75.2%
Cash Flow from Operations ÷ Average Total Liabilities	6.2%	12.2%	9.8%
Interest Coverage Ratio	2.4	2.5	2.7
Sales (Year 5 = 100)	126.1	153.7	171.6
Net Income (Year 5 = 100)	152.2	161.7	195.0
Assets (Year 5 = 100)	124.5	141.2	162.2
Capital Expenditures (Year 5 = 100)	127.4	175.1	186.0

Exhibits 5.30 through 5.33 contain the following kinds of information:

1. Balance sheets, income statements, and statements of cash flows for W. T. Grant Company for the 1971 through 1975 fiscal periods.
2. Additional financial information about W. T. Grant Company, the retail industry, and the economy for the same period.

Prepare an analysis that explains the major causes of Grant's collapse. Assume an income tax rate of 48 percent.

EXHIBIT 5.29	Selected Data for The Limited (Problem 31)

	Sales Mix			Operating Income Mix		
	Year 6	Year 7	Year 8	Year 6	Year 7	Year 8
Women's Brands	54%	49%	43%	9%	10%	(10%)
Intimate Brands	32	35	39	63	72	81
Emerging Brands	11	12	12	24	11	17
Men's Brands	3	4	6	4	7	12
	100%	100%	100%	100%	100%	100%

	Operating Income/Sales		
	Year 6	Year 7	Year 8
Women's Brands	2.0%	2.3%	(2.6%)
Intimate Brands	23.7	23.6	23.0
Emerging Brands	26.2	10.5	15.7
Men's Brands	16.1	20.0	22.0

	Year 6	Year 7	Year 8
Sales per Square Foot	$272	$285	$295
Sales per Employee (000)	$ 76	$ 70	$ 70

EXHIBIT 5.30	W. T. GRANT COMPANY Comparative Balance Sheets (Problem 33)

	January 31				
	1971	**1972**	**1973**	**1974**	**1975**
ASSETS					
Cash and Marketable Securities	$ 34,009	$ 49,851	$ 30,943	$ 45,951	$ 79,642
Accounts Receivable	419,731	477,324	542,751	598,799	431,201
Inventories	260,492	298,676	399,533	450,637	407,357
Other Current Assets	5,246	5,378	6,649	7,299	6,581
Total Current Assets	$719,478	$831,229	$ 979,876	$1,102,686	$ 924,781
Investments	23,936	32,367	35,581	45,451	49,764
Property, Plant, and Equipment (net)	61,832	77,173	91,420	100,984	101,932
Other Assets	2,382	3,901	3,821	3,862	5,790
Total Assets	$807,628	$944,670	$1,110,698	$1,252,983	$1,082,267
LIABILITIES AND SHAREHOLDERS' EQUITY					
Short-term Debt	$246,420	$237,741	$ 390,034	$ 453,097	$ 600,695
Accounts Payable	118,091	124,990	112,896	103,910	147,211
Current Deferred Taxes	94,489	112,846	130,137	133,057	2,000
Total Current Liabilities	$459,000	$475,577	$ 633,067	$ 690,064	$ 749,906
Long-term Debt	32,301	128,432	126,672	220,336	216,341
Noncurrent Deferred Taxes	8,518	9,664	11,926	14,649	—
Other Long-term Liabilities	5,773	5,252	4,694	4,195	2,183
Total Liabilities	$505,592	$618,925	$ 776,359	$ 929,244	$ 968,430
Preferred Stock	$ 9,600	$ 9,053	$ 8,600	$ 7,465	$ 7,465
Common Stock	18,180	18,529	18,588	18,599	18,599
Additional Paid-in Capital	78,116	85,195	86,146	85,910	83,914
Retained Earnings	230,435	244,508	261,154	248,461	37,674
Total	$336,331	$357,285	$ 374,488	$ 360,435	$ 147,652
Less Cost of Treasury Stock	(34,295)	(31,540)	(40,149)	(36,696)	(33,815)
Total Shareholders' Equity	$302,036	$325,745	$ 334,339	$ 323,739	$ 113,837
Total Liabilities and Shareholders' Equity .	$807,628	$944,670	$1,110,698	$1,252,983	$ 1,082,26

EXHIBIT 5.31	W. T. GRANT COMPANY Statement of Income and Retained Earnings (Problem 33)

	Years Ended January 31				
	1971	**1972**	**1973**	**1974**	**1975**
Sales	$1,254,131	$1,374,811	$1,644,747	$1,849,802	$1,761,952
Concessions	4,986	3,439	3,753	3,971	4,238
Equity in Earnings	2,777	2,383	5,116	4,651	3,086
Other Income	2,874	3,102	1,188	3,063	3,376
Total Revenues	$1,264,768	$1,383,735	$1,654,804	$1,861,487	$1,772,652
Cost of Goods Sold	$ 843,192	$ 931,237	$1,125,261	$1,282,945	$1,303,267
Selling, General, and					
Administration	329,768	373,816	444,377	491,287	654,112
Interest	18,874	16,452	21,127	78,040	86,079
Taxes: Current	21,140	13,487	9,588	(6,021)	(19,439)
Deferred	11,660	13,013	16,162	6,807	(98,027)
Other Expenses	557	518	502	—	24,000
Total Expenses	$1,225,191	$1,348,523	$1,617,017	$1,853,058	$1,949,992
Net Income	$ 39,577	$ 35,212	$ 37,787	$ 8,429	$ (177,340)
Dividends	(20,821)	(21,139)	(21,141)	(21,122)	(4,457)
Other	—	—	—	—	(28,990)
Change in Retained Earnings	$ 18,756	$ 14,073	$ 16,646	$ (12,693)	$ (210,787)
Retained Earnings— Beg. of Period	211,679	230,435	244,508	261,154	248,461
Retained Earnings— End of Period	$ 230,435	$ 244,508	$ 261,154	$ 248,461	$ 37,674

EXHIBIT 5.32	W. T. GRANT COMPANY Statement of Cash Flows (Problem 33)

	Years Ended January 31				
	1971	**1972**	**1973**	**1974**	**1975**
OPERATIONS					
Net Income	$ 39,577	$ 35,212	$ 37,787	$ 8,429	($177,340)
Additions: ◄					
Depreciation and Other	9,619	10,577	12,004	13,579	14,587
Decrease in Accounts Receivable	—	—	—	—	121,351
Decrease in Inventories	—	—	—	—	43,280
Increase in Accounts Payable	13,947	6,900	—	—	42,028
Increase in Deferred Taxes	14,046	18,357	17,291	2,920	—
Subtractions:					
Equity in Earnings and Other	(2,470)	(1,758)	(1,699)	(1,344)	(16,993)
Increase in Accounts Receivable	(51,464)	(57,593)	(65,427)	(56,047)	—
Increase in Inventories	(38,365)	(38,184)	(100,857)	(51,104)	—
Increase in Prepayments	(209)	(428)	(1,271)	(651)	(11,032)
Decrease in Accounts Payable	—	—	(12,093)	(8,987)	—
Decrease in Deferred Taxes	—	—	—	—	(101,078)
Cash Flow from Operations	($ 15,319)	($ 26,917)	($114,265)	($ 93,205)	($ 85,197)
INVESTING					
Noncurrent Assets:					
Property, Plant, and Equipment	($ 16,141)	($ 25,918)	($ 26,250)	($ 23,143)	($ 15,535)
Investments in Securities	(436)	(5,951)	(2,040)	(5,700)	(5,182)
Cash Flow from Investing	($ 16,577)	($ 31,869)	($ 28,290)	($ 28,843)	($ 20,717)
FINANCING					
New Financing:					
Short-term Bank Borrowing	$ 64,288	—	$152,293	$ 63,063	$147,898
Issue of Long-term Debt	—	$ 100,000	—	100,000	—
Sale of Common Stock:					
To Employees	5,218	7,715	3,492	2,584	886
On Open Market	—	2,229	174	260	—
Reduction in Financing:					
Repayment of Short-term Borrowing (net)	—	(8,680)	—	—	—
Retirement of Long-term Debt	(1,538)	(5,143)	(1,760)	(6,336)	(3,995)
Reacquisition of Preferred Stock	(948)	(308)	(252)	(618)	—
Reacquisition of Common Stock	(13,224)	—	(11,466)	(133)	—
Dividends	(20,821)	(21,138)	(21,141)	(21,122)	(4,457)
Cash Flow from Financing	$ 32,975	$ 74,675	$121,340	$137,698	$140,332
Other	$ (47)	$ (47)	$ 2,307	$ (642)	$ (727)
Net Change in Cash	$ 1,032	$ 15,842	($ 18,908)	$ 15,008	$ 33,691
Cash, Beginning of Year	32,977	34,009	49,851	30,943	45,951
Cash, End of Year	$ 34,009	$ 49,851	$ 30,943	$ 45,951	$ 79,642

| EXHIBIT 5.33 | W. T. GRANT COMPANY
Additional Information
(Problem 33) |

	Fiscal Years Ending January 31				
	1971	1972	1973	1974	1975
PROFITABILITY RATIOS					
Profit Margin for Rate of Return on Assets	3.9%	3.2%	3.0%	2.6%	(7.5%)
Total Assets Turnover	1.7	1.6	1.6	1.6	1.5
Rate of Return on Assets	6.5%	5.0%	4.7%	4.1%	(11.4%)
Profit Margin for Rate of Return on Common Shareholders' Equity	3.1%	2.5%	2.3%	.5%	(10.0%)
Leverage Ratio	2.6	2.8	3.1	3.6	5.3
Rate of Return on Common Shareholders' Equity	13.7%	11.4%	11.7%	2.5%	(84.1%)
Cost of Goods Sold/Sales	67.2%	67.7%	68.4%	69.4%	74.0%
Selling and Administrative Expenses/Revenues	26.1%	27.0%	26.9%	26.4%	36.9%
Accounts Receivable Turnover	3.2	3.1	3.2	3.2	3.4
Inventory Turnover	3.5	3.3	3.2	3.0	3.0
Fixed Asset Turnover	21.4	19.8	10.5	19.2	17.4
RISK RATIOS					
Current Ratio	1.57:1	1.75:1	1.55:1	1.60:1	1.23:1
Quick Ratio	.99:1	1.11:1	.91:1	.93:1	.68:1
Accounts Payable Turnover	7.9	8.0	10.3	12.3	10.0
Long-term Debt Ratio	9.7%	28.3%	27.5%	40.5%	65.5%
Debt Equity Ratio	62.6%	65.5%	70.0%	74.2%	89.5%
Interest Coverage Ratio	4.8	4.8	4.0	3.6	5.3
DATA FOR W.T. GRANT COMPANY					
Range of Stock Price, Dollar per Share[a]	$41\frac{7}{8}$–$70\frac{5}{8}$	$34\frac{3}{4}$–$48\frac{3}{4}$	$9\frac{7}{8}$–$44\frac{3}{8}$	$9\frac{5}{8}$–41	$1\frac{1}{2}$–12
Earnings per Share in Dollars	$ 2.64	$ 2.25	$ 2.49	$ 0.76	$(12.74)
Dividends per Share in Dollars	$ 1.50	$ 1.50	$ 1.50	$ 1.50	$ 0.30
Number of Stores	1,116	1,168	1,208	1,189	1,152
Total Store Area, Thousands of Square Feet	38,157	44,718	50,619	53,719	54,770
Sales per Square Foot	$32.87	$30.74	$32.49	$34.43	$ 32.17
Average Size of Stores (in thousands of square feet)	34.19	38.29	41.90	45.18	47.54

	Calendar Year Ending December 31				
	1970	1971	1972	1973	1974
Data for Retail Industry[b]					
Total Chain Store Industry Sales in Millions of Dollars	$6,969	$6,972	$7,498	$8,212	$8,714

	Calendar Year Ending December 31				
	1970	1971	1972	1973	1974
Data for Aggregate Economy[c]					
Gross National Product in Billions of Dollars	$1,075.3	$1,107.5	$1,171.1	$1,233.4	$1,210
Bank Short-term Lending Rate	8.48%	6.32%	5.82%	8.30%	11.28%

[a]Source: *Standard & Poor's Stock Reports*
[b]Source: *Standard Industry Surveys*
[c]Source: *Survey of Current Business*

PART THREE

MEASURING AND REPORTING ASSETS

AND EQUITIES USING GENERALLY

ACCEPTED ACCOUNTING PRINCIPLES

RECEIVABLES AND
REVENUE RECOGNITION

1. Develop an introductory understanding of (a) the economic consequences of accounting and (b) the quality of earnings as concepts for evaluating generally accepted accounting principles discussed in Chapters 6 to 12.
2. Understand why the allowance method for uncollectible accounts matches bad debts with revenues better than the direct write-off method.
3. Apply the allowance method for uncollectible accounts.
4. Develop a sensitivity to issues in recognizing and measuring revenues and expenses for various types of businesses.
5. Cement an understanding of the concept that net income over sufficiently long periods equals cash inflows minus cash outflows other than transactions with owners (a measurement issue), regardless of when firms recognize the revenues and expenses (a timing issue).

Parts One and Two (Chapters 1 through 5) introduced most of the basic concepts of financial accounting, its purpose, its theoretical framework, some of its procedures, and tools for analyzing financial statements. Part Three (Chapters 6 through 12) discusses **generally accepted accounting principles (GAAP).** Chapter 1 described GAAP as the methods that firms use to apply the general principles of the accrual basis of accounting in measuring income for a period and financial position at the end of a period. Standard-setting bodies within each country currently set GAAP, after receiving comments from various preparers and users of financial statements. The International Accounting Standards Committee (IASC) has assumed an increasing role in recent years in promoting the establishment of uniform accounting methods worldwide. The discussion in Chapters 6 to 12 considers GAAP in the United States and indicates where standards recommended by the IASC differ from U.S. GAAP.

The discussion in Part Three proceeds in approximate balance sheet order:

Chapter 6: receivables and revenue recognition

Chapter 7: inventories and cost of goods sold

INTRODUCTION TO ECONOMIC CONSEQUENCES

Do consequences result from the amounts that firms report in their financial statements? Do the financial statements affect decisions by firms, investors, regulators, and others? Do financial statements really matter? We address these questions as we begin our study of specific GAAP by considering the economic consequences of financial accounting. The term *economic consequences* has no generally accepted meaning but refers to several kinds of impacts that accounting has on wealth or behavior:

- Impacts on lenders and investors; caused by financial results reported in financial statements
- Impacts on reporting entities, their management, and users of financial statements; caused by firms' choices of accounting principles
- Impacts on reporting entities and standard setters; caused by standard setters' decisions in setting accounting standards

Chapter 1 introduced the processes that set accounting principles, that firms use to choose among acceptable accounting principles, and that readers use to interpret the resulting financial statements. Chapters 6 through 14 address the notion of economic consequences of financial accounting by discussing the impact of accounting on wealth and behavior. We define **economic consequences** of accounting as the difference between benefits and costs for managers, preparers, auditors, users, and standard setters, resulting from setting, changing, or implementing accounting standards. Members of each of these groups must assess the economic benefits and costs to them of a particular accounting standard.

Effect of Financial Results Reported in Financial Statements

IBM reports that its earnings for the quarter will be half the amounts investors had expected. The total value of IBM's shares traded on the New York Stock Exchange declines by several billion dollars.

The announcement of financial accounting numbers has economic consequences for shareholders.

Effect of Firms' Choices of Accounting Principles   When General Motors changed its methods of accounting for inventories (discussed later, in Chapter 7), management had to consider that as a result, GM would henceforth report lower accounting earnings and lower asset totals. GM's choice for inventories has consequences for reported earnings. At the same time, GM expects that changing its method of accounting for inventories will result in increased cash flow because GM will be able to defer income tax expense and reduce current cash outlays for income taxes.

We might wonder if this choice has economic consequences for shareholders—negative because of the decline in reported earnings or positive because of the increased cash flow.

We also might wonder if this choice has economic consequences for GM's top management, whose pay and bonus packages depend in part on reported accounting income.

Effect on Reporting Entities of Standard Setters' Decisions in Setting Accounting Standards The Financial Accounting Standards Board (FASB) enacts *Statement of Financial Accounting Standards (SFAS) No. 2* requiring firms to expense costs of research and development rather than capitalize them with subsequent amortization to expense. It considers requiring firms to expense advertising costs rather than capitalize them.

We might wonder if the FASB rule has economic consequences for firms, inducing them to curtail research investments they might otherwise make. Do the results of *SFAS No. 2,* enacted in 1974, affect the FASB's decisions about accounting for intellectual property in 2001 or 2002, with attendant consequences for firms?

Effect on Standard Setters of Their Decisions in Setting Accounting Standards The FASB is a private organization supported in part by the voluntary monetary contributions of companies subject to its rules. The FASB proposes accounting standards, discussed in Chapter 12, requiring firms to report expense for the value of stock options granted to managers as a form of compensation. Many executives fear the results that this rule will have on their own compensation and the depressing effect on reported earnings, which might then depress stock market valuations. As a result executives, through their trade associations, threaten to withhold financial support from the FASB.

We might wonder if the FASB considers the effects on its own future when setting accounting principles. If so, it faces the economic consequences of its own decisions.

The remaining chapters alert the reader to the consequences of the standards used to account for particular business transactions.

QUALITY OF EARNINGS

Although measuring the economic benefits and costs of a particular accounting standard can prove difficult, there can be little doubt that accounting has economic consequences. The managers of firms have incentives to report information in the financial statements to increase economic benefits for themselves (for example, to increase their bonuses or to enhance their job security). To the extent that financial statements contain bias in presenting the operating performance and financial position of a firm, investors and other users of financial statements might make unwise economic decisions. Audits by independent accountants and oversight by regulatory bodies partially inhibit such opportunistic behavior by managers. When users of financial statements have sufficient knowledge of accounting to identify situations where managers can bias reports of a firm's performance, users can then adjust the reported amounts as they deem appropriate before using them in decisions.

The phrase **quality of earnings** refers to the ability managers have to use discretion in measuring and reporting earnings. Some who use the phrase suspect that managers will usually make choices that enhance current earnings and present the firm in the best light. Analysts use the phrase in various other ways, described in the glossary; see *quality of earnings.* This discretion can involve any of the following:

- Selecting accounting principles or standards when GAAP allow a choice
- Making estimates in the application of accounting principles
- Timing transactions to allow recognizing nonrecurring items in earnings

Example 1   Construction contractors build office buildings, which usually take more than one year to complete. In many cases, such a contractor will have the choice of accounting for the profits for a specific building either over time as the contractor builds it or all at once at the end when the contractor has completed construction. Insofar as managers choose accounting principles that delay *(accelerate)* the reporting of income, analysts will label the resulting reported income as having a higher *(lower)* quality of earnings. In other examples, management can choose which items a firm will sell when it has more goods available for sale than it sells in a given period (choice of cost flow assumption for inventories and cost of goods sold in Chapter 7) and can choose how much expense a firm will report when it grants stock options to its employees (Chapter 12). Analysts will then judge the quality of earnings.

Example 2   In measuring revenue and expenses, managers and accountants must make estimates. Already, in Chapter 3, you have seen one such item. Refer to transaction **(15)** on page 124 and note there that in computing depreciation expense, the firm estimated that the items of equipment, which originally cost $125,000, have an average service life of six years and salvage value of $5,000. It computed depreciation expense as $20,000, equal to the cost of $125,000 less the estimated salvage value of $5,000 divided by the estimated life of six years: ($125,000 − $5,000)/6 = $20,000. Had the firm estimated a longer service life or a higher salvage value, it would have computed a smaller depreciation expense (with larger income for the year). Had the firm estimated a shorter service life or lower salvage value, it would have computed a larger depreciation expense (with smaller income for the year). In this and the following chapters, you will encounter several estimates that managers must make to measure income: the portion of sales on account that the firm will never collect (Chapter 6), service life and salvage value of long-term assets (Chapter 8), acquisition costs of assets acquired as a group, sometimes called a *basket purchase* (Chapter 8). In each case, managers have some discretion in making the estimate. Insofar as managers choose estimates that lead to lower current income, analysts refer to the resulting reported earnings as *higher quality.* If the estimates lead to higher current income, then analysts refer to the resulting reported earnings as *lower quality.*

Example 3   An unexpected recession in East Asia resulted in decreased earnings for a manufacturer of semiconductors. To increase net income to the level initially anticipated for the year, the firm sold a parcel of land that it did not currently need in operations. The land had a market value larger than its book value, so selling it generated a realized gain to be reported in income for the year. This component of net income is *low quality* because the firm will not likely report similar gains on sales of land on a recurring basis.

Throughout the chapters composing Part Three you will encounter managers' choices—of accounting principles, of estimates, and of the timing of asset sales—that will affect the year-to-year reported income. To the extent managers make choices enhancing currently reported income, analysts will say the firm has a lower earnings quality. The analyst can then either adjust the reported earnings to remove any perceived bias or compensate for the bias in some other way (for example, by applying a lower multiple to earnings in arriving at an acceptable stock price). We shall say time and again, however, that *over long-enough time spans, reported income will equal the sum of cash flows in less the sum of cash flows out, other than cash flows resulting from transactions with owners.* All the management choices that affect the quality of earnings affect *when* the firm reports its income, not its total *amount,* summed over time.

REVIEW OF INCOME RECOGNITION PRINCIPLES

Let's review the principles of income recognition under the accrual basis of accounting from Chapter 3. Figure 6.1 shows the flow of operating activities for a typical manufacturing firm. A manufacturing firm

(1) acquires production facilities to permit it to engage in manufacturing and acquires raw materials for use in producing products;
(2) uses labor and other services to transform the raw materials into a salable product;
(3) identifies a customer, agrees to a selling price, and delivers the product to customers;
(4) awaits collection of cash from customers, in the meantime holding an accounts receivable;
(5) collects cash from customers; and
(6) refunds cash for products returned by customers or spends cash and other assets to fulfill promises under warranty. The firm must match the costs of returns and warranties against the associated revenues in measuring net income.

The *amount* of income from these operating activities is the difference between the cash received at point (5) and the cash paid to suppliers of goods and services at times (1), (2), (3), and (4) as well as the cash or other assets spent during (6). Because the cash inflow from customers—point (5)—can occur in an accounting period different from the one during which the firm pays cash out to various suppliers—times (1) through (4) and (6)—accrual accounting attempts to match expense as closely as possible with revenues. In this way earnings match inputs with outputs, efforts with accomplishments.

The *matching principle*—that is, reporting expenses in the same period as recognizing revenue—drives the recognition of expenses. Still we have the question of when the firm should recognize the revenue against which it matches expenses. Firms could conceivably recognize revenue at any one or more than one of the six times in Figure 6.1. To answer the revenue recognition timing question, GAAP set two hurdles. As soon as a firm clears the following two hurdles for a particular operating activity, GAAP permit it to recognize revenue for that activity:

1. A firm has performed all, or a substantial portion of, the services it expects to provide or, in the case of product warranties, can forecast with reasonable precision the cost of providing the future services.

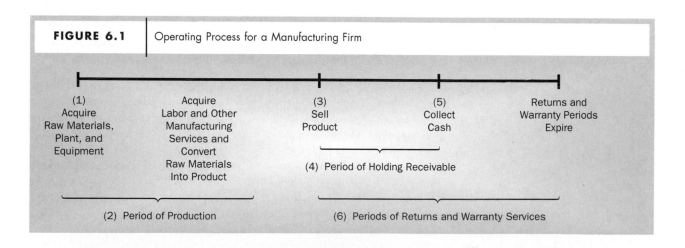

| **FIGURE 6.1** | Operating Process for a Manufacturing Firm |

(1) Acquire Raw Materials, Plant, and Equipment

Acquire Labor and Other Manufacturing Services and Convert Raw Materials Into Product

(3) Sell Product

(5) Collect Cash

Returns and Warranty Periods Expire

(4) Period of Holding Receivable

(2) Period of Production

(6) Periods of Returns and Warranty Services

2. The firm has received cash, a receivable, or some other asset capable of reasonably precise measurement or, if the firm has offered to let the customer return the product for a refund, the firm can estimate the returns with reasonable precision.

Chapter 3 points out that most firms satisfy these criteria at the time of sale or delivery of goods and services: point (3). Firms have manufactured a product or created a service, identified a customer, delivered the product or service to the customer, and either received cash immediately or assessed the credit standing of customers and concluded that customers will likely pay the amount owed. The firm can estimate the amount of product returns and the cost of warranty repairs.

The operating activities of some firms satisfy the revenue recognition criteria earlier than the time of sale: during (2). Other firms might not meet the criteria until they receive cash from customers: time (5). Still other firms, particularly those dealing with new, untested products, cannot measure the amount of net cash they will collect until the returns and warranty periods expire: at the end of (6).

This chapter explores the principles of revenue recognition in greater depth than the introductory discussion in Chapter 3. We first consider issues in measuring income at the time of sale. We then examine revenue recognition at times different from the time of sale.

REVENUE RECOGNITION AT TIME OF SALE

Although a firm may satisfy the criteria for revenue recognition at the time of sale, it still must estimate the effect of events that occur after the time of sale—that is, during times (4), (5), and (6) in Figure 6.1. Suppose, for example, that some customers do not pay the amounts owed to the firm. Or, suppose that some customers return products because they are defective or simply don't meet customers' expectations. Recognizing revenue at the time of sale and properly matching expenses with revenues requires firms to estimate the cost of uncollectible accounts, returns, and similar items and recognize them as expenses at the time of sale. This section discusses the accounting for such items.

First, we examine problems of revenue and expense recognition for firms that recognize revenue at the time of sale but grant credit to their customers and so collect some, maybe most, of their cash after sale. Accounts receivable, sometimes called *trade accounts receivable,* typically arise when a firm sells goods or services on account. The journal entry is as follows:

Accounts Receivable	250	
Sales Revenue		250

Receivables sometimes arise from transactions other than sales. For example, a firm may give advances to officers or employees or make deposits to guarantee performance or cover potential damages. The firm classifies these receivables as either current assets or investments, depending on the expected collection date. This section focuses on trade accounts receivable, considering both their valuation and their management.

A firm initially records individual accounts receivable at the amount each customer owes. The record appears either in a subsidiary ledger (manual accounting system) or in a separate computer data file. The Accounts Receivable account records the total of the amounts in individual customers' accounts.

The net amount for accounts receivable appearing on the balance sheet is the amount in the master account for Accounts Receivable, that is, the sum of all individual customers' balances, reduced by the amounts of estimated uncollectible accounts, sale discounts, and sales returns and allowances. The reporting objective is to state accounts receivable at the net amount a firm expects to collect in cash.[1] The charge against income for expected uncollectible amounts, sales discounts, and sales returns and allowances preferably occurs in the period in which the sales occur. In this way, revenue and net income for a period will reflect the amounts expected to be collected for services rendered during that period.

UNCOLLECTIBLE ACCOUNTS

Whenever a firm extends credit to customers, it will almost certainly never collect from some of its customers. Most businesses should prefer to have some customers who do not pay their bills; for most firms, the optimal amount of uncollectibles is not zero. If a firm is to have no uncollectible accounts, it must screen credit customers carefully, which is costly. Furthermore, the firm would deny credit to many customers who would pay their bills even though they could not pass a credit check designed to weed out all potential uncollectibles. Some of the customers, when the firm denies credit, will take their business elsewhere, and the firm will lose sales. As long as the amount collected from credit sales to a given group of customers exceeds the cost of goods sold and the other costs of serving that group of customers, the firm will be better off selling to that group than losing the sales. The rational firm should prefer granting credit to a group of customers who have a high probability of paying their bills rather than losing their business, even though some of them will not pay and the firm will, as a result, have some uncollectible accounts.

For example, assume that gross margin—selling price less cost of goods sold—on credit sales to a new group of customers, such as college sophomores, is 40 percent of credit sales. A firm could then afford uncollectible accounts of up to 40 percent of the credit sales to the new customers and still show increased net income, as long as all other costs of serving customers remain constant.

This does not suggest, of course, that a firm should grant credit indiscriminately or ignore collection efforts aimed at those who have not paid their bills. A cost-benefit analysis of credit policy should dictate a strategy that results in uncollectible accounts of an amount that is reasonably predictable before the firm makes any sales.

The principal accounting issue related to uncollected accounts concerns when firms should recognize the loss from uncollectibles. The following example illustrates the nature of the issue.

Example 4 Howarth's Home Center provides customer financing for sales of its appliances, furniture, and electronic equipment. Customers typically make monthly cash payments of a portion of the purchase price over 24 to 36 months. Despite efforts to collect amounts due and to repossess merchandise when customers fail to pay, Howarth's Home Center experiences losses from uncollectible accounts of 2 percent of total sales in the year of sale, 6 percent in the next year, and 4 percent in the third year. Thus the firm

---

[1] To be precise, the net amount shows the present value of the amounts the firm expects to collect. Chapters 9 and 10 discuss the present value computations.

expects that it will ultimately not collect 12 (= .02 + .06 + .04) percent of sales made in any particular year. A summary of its recent experience appears below:

| | Sales | Accounts Deemed Uncollectible in Year | | | | | Total |
Year	During Year	2	3	4	5	6	Uncollectibles
2	$ 800,000	$16,000	$48,000	$ 32,000			$ 96,000
3	1,200,000		24,000	72,000	$ 48,000		144,000
4	1,500,000			30,000	90,000	$60,000	180,000
		$16,000	$72,000	$134,000	$138,000	$60,000	

The accounting issue is,

- should the firm use the direct write-off method and recognize the loss from uncollectibles in the year it deems particular accounts to be uncollectible ($16,000 in Year 2, $72,000 in Year 3, $134,000 in Year 4, $138,000 in Year 5, and $60,000 in Year 6), or

- should the firm use the allowance method and recognize the total expected losses related to a particular year's sales in the year of the sale ($96,000 in Year 2, $144,000 in Year 3, and $180,000 in Year 4)?

Direct Write-Off Method   The **direct write-off method** recognizes losses from uncollectible accounts in the period when a firm decides that specific customers' accounts are uncollectible. For example, Howarth's Home Center decides in Year 4 that specific customers' accounts totaling $134,000 have become uncollectible. It makes the following entry using the direct write-off method:

Bad Debt Expense	134,000	
Accounts Receivable		134,000
To record losses from known uncollectible accounts.		

The direct write-off method has three important shortcomings. First, it does not usually recognize the loss from uncollectible accounts in the period in which the sale occurs and the firm recognizes revenue. For example, Howarth recognizes bad debt expense of only $16,000 in Year 2 under the direct write-off method, even though it ultimately expects not to collect $96,000 of receivables from Year 2 sales. The remaining $80,000 (= $48,000 + $32,000) appears in bad debt expense in Year 3 and Year 4, clumsily matched against those periods' sales. Based on its own expectations of collectibility of accounts, the firm recognizes too little expense in the year of sale and too much in the period of write-off.

Second, the direct write-off method provides firms with an opportunity to manipulate earnings each period by deciding when particular customers' accounts become uncollectible. Establishing the uncollectible status of customers' accounts requires judgment of the customers' willingness and ability to pay and the intensity of the firm's collection efforts. Firms desiring to increase (decrease) earnings for a particular period can delay (accelerate) the write-off of specific customer accounts.

Third, the amount of accounts receivable on the balance sheet under the direct write-off method does not reflect the amount a firm expects to collect in cash. Returning to **Example 4,** assume that Howarth's Home Center collects $200,000 of the $800,000 from sales on account during Year 2. Accounts receivable at the end of Year 2 under the direct write-off method are as follows:

Total Sales on Account during Year 2	$800,000
Collections from Customers during Year 2	(200,000)
Specific Customers' Accounts Written Off as Uncollectible	(16,000)
Accounts Receivable at End of Year 2	$584,000

Howarth's Home Center expects to collect only $504,000 (= $584,000 − $48,000 − $32,000) of its accounts receivable outstanding at the end of Year 2. The $584,000 amount for accounts receivable on the balance sheet overstates the amount the firm expects to collect in cash.

Consequently, GAAP do not allow firms to use the direct write-off method for financial reporting when they have significant amounts of expected uncollectible accounts and when the selling firm, such as a retail store, can reasonably predict them. Such firms must use the allowance method, explained below.

Firms must, however, use the direct write-off method for income tax reporting. Income tax laws permit firms to claim a deduction for bad debts only when a firm can demonstrate that particular customers will not pay. This is the first instance we have seen in this book of a firm's use of different accounting principles for financial statement and for income tax reporting. This particular instance is mandatory—GAAP require one treatment and the tax law another. Chapter 10 discusses the accounting issues raised by such differences, called *temporary differences,* whether voluntary or mandatory.

Allowance Method   When a firm can estimate with reasonable precision the amounts of uncollectibles, GAAP require an alternative procedure, the **allowance method,** for uncollectibles. The allowance method involves the following:

1. Estimate the amount of uncollectible accounts that will occur over time in connection with the sales of each period.
2. Make an adjusting entry reducing income of the period to provide for the estimated uncollectible amount. This entry typically involves a debit to an expense account. (Accounting sometimes uses the term *provision for uncollectibles* to refer to the debit of this entry.) Match this debit with a credit to the amount of accounts receivable so that the balance sheet figure reports the amount expected to be collected. The account credited is typically a separate asset contra account, Allowance for Uncollectible Accounts, which is contra to Accounts Receivable.

Alternatively, the allowance method involves the following, equivalent, series of steps:

1. Estimate the net amount of receivables the firm expects to collect.
2. Adjust the balance sheet amount of accounts receivable, with an entry to a balance sheet contra account, to reflect that expected net amount. Typically, the adjustment involves a credit to the asset contra account. Match this credit with a debit to the Bad Debt Expense or Provision for Uncollectibles account.

The following discussion explains the two different methods of implementing the allowance method. Refer to **Example 4** for Howarth's Home Center, which estimates, based on past experience, that it will not collect $96,000 of the $800,000 sales on accounts during Year 2. At the end of Year 2, the firm makes the following adjusting entry.

End of Year 2
Bad Debt Expense   96,000
    Allowance for Uncollectible Accounts   96,000
To provide for estimated uncollectible accounts relating to Year 2 sales.

Recognizing bad debt expense of $96,000 results in matching against Year 2 sales the amount the firm does not expect to collect in cash from Year 2 sales. The credit in the adjusting entry is not to Accounts Receivable because the firm is not writing off specific customers' accounts at this time. Instead, the credit account is Allowance for Uncollectible Accounts, a contra account to Accounts Receivable. Recall that Accounts Receivable is a control account—summing the amounts in individual customer's accounts. At the time the firm reduces the gross amount of receivables to its expected net amount, the firm still does not know which specific customers will not pay, so it cannot write off any particular customer's account. Thus, it cannot credit any of the individual accounts whose sums appear in Accounts Receivable. It must credit a separate contra account, which shows the subtraction from gross receivables to derive expected net receivables.

CONCEPTUAL NOTE

Views differ as to the type of account—expense or revenue contra—debited in the entry above. Some debit Bad Debt Expense and others debit a revenue contra account when providing for estimated uncollectibles. Net income remains unchanged regardless of the type of account debited. Most firms debit Bad Debt Expense and include its amount among total expenses on the income statement. They reason that generating revenues implies a certain amount of bad debts. On the other hand, using a revenue contra account permits net sales to appear at the amount of cash the firm expects to collect. When a firm debits the provision to an expense account and includes it among total expenses on the income statement, net sales will overstate the amount of cash the firm expects to receive. Advocates of using a revenue contra account point out that uncollectible accounts cannot theoretically be an expense. An expense is a gone asset. Accounts that the firm did not expect to collect at the time of recording were never assets to begin with. Although we find the arguments for using a revenue contra account persuasive, we debit Bad Debt Expense in this book because most firms debit an expense, not a revenue contra, account.

When a firm judges particular customers' accounts to be uncollectible, it writes off the account (credit) and debits Allowance for Uncollectible Accounts. For example, Howarth's makes the following adjusting entry at the end of Year 2 to write off specific customers' accounts totaling $16,000.

End of Year 2
Allowance for Uncollectible Accounts   16,000
    Accounts Receivable   16,000
To write off specific customers' accounts.

Firms sometimes write off specific customers' accounts during an accounting period as information about their uncollectible status becomes known. Such firms generally wait until the end of the accounting period to recognize bad debt expense for the period. Thus, before making the provision for bad debts for the period, the firm may experience a debit balance in the Allowance for Uncollectible Accounts account. This account always has a credit balance after the adjusting entry. This occurs because customers often fail to pay or often pay less than they owe, but they almost never pay more than they owe. Recall that the firm will not prepare a balance sheet until after it makes adjusting and closing entries, so the debit balance in the Allowance account will never appear on the balance sheet. Still, the accountant may encounter a debit balance in the Allowance account before adjusting entries and should not let this debit balance cause confusion.

The firm makes entries similar to the one above in Year 3 and Year 4 as it judges other accounts arising from Year 2 sales to be uncollectible. Note that the write-off of specific customers' accounts using the allowance method does not affect income. The income effect occurs in the year of sale, when the firm provides for estimated uncollectible accounts. Note also that the write-off of specific customers' accounts has no effect on accounts receivable net of the allowance for uncollectible accounts. Accounts Receivable decreases but so does the amount in the contra account for uncollectibles, which the accountant subtracts in reaching the balance sheet net amount for receivables.

The allowance method for uncollectible accounts overcomes the three shortcomings, discussed earlier, of the direct write-off method. First, during each period, the allowance method matches against sales revenue the amount the firm does not expect to collect in cash arising from that period's sales. The allowance method provides a better matching of revenues and expenses not only in the period of sale but also in subsequent periods. Losses from uncollectible accounts of $48,000 in Year 3 and $32,000 in Year 4 from Year 2 sales are expenses of Year 2, not Year 3 or Year 4 as with the direct write-off method.

Second, the allowance method reduces management's opportunity to manipulate earnings through the timing of write-offs. The write-off of specific customers' accounts does not affect earnings or total assets.

Third, the allowance method results in reporting accounts receivable net of the allowance for uncollectible accounts on the balance sheet at the amount the firm expects to collect in cash in future periods. For example, Howarth's Home Center reports accounts receivable on the balance sheet at the end of Year 2 as follows:

Accounts Receivable—Gross ($800,000 − $200,000 − $16,000)	$584,000
Less Allowance for Uncollectible Accounts ($96,000 − $16,000)	(80,000)
Accounts Receivable—Net	$504,000

The allowance method requires firms to estimate the amount of uncollectibles before the time when actual uncollectible accounts occur, which provides management with opportunities to manipulate earnings. Firms desiring to increase (decrease) earnings can underestimate (overestimate) bad debt expense. Such misestimates may not become evident for several accounting periods. Even then, management might attribute the misestimate to unexpected changes in economic conditions rather than earnings manipulation. Thus, quality-of-earnings issues arise under both the direct write-off method and the allowance method.

Estimating the Amount of Uncollectible Accounts
Accountants use two basic methods for calculating the amount of the adjustment for uncollectible accounts under the allowance method: the percentage-of-sales method and the aging of-accounts-

receivable method. The first requires fewer computations than the second, but the second method provides a useful check on the first. Over time the two methods, correctly used, will give the same cumulative income and asset totals.

Percentage-of-Sales Method   One easy method multiplies the total sales on account during the period by an appropriate percentage (the **percentage-of-sales method for estimating uncollectibles**) because it seems reasonable to assume that uncollectible account amounts will vary directly with the volume of credit business. The firm estimates the appropriate percentage by studying its own experience or by inquiring into the experience of similar firms. These rates generally fall within the range of 1/4 percent to 2 percent of credit sales.

For example, sales on account at Howarth's Home Center during Year 2 totaled $800,000. Experience indicates that 12 percent of sales become uncollectible. The relatively high percentage reflects the age and financial condition of most of the firm's customers. The adjusting entry is as follows:

Bad Debt Expense	96,000	
Allowance for Uncollectible Accounts		96,000
To provide for estimate of uncollectibles computed as a percentage of sales.		

If cash sales occur in a relatively constant proportion to credit sales, the accountant can apply the estimated uncollectibles percentage, proportionately reduced, to the total sales for the period.

Aging-of-Accounts-Receivable Method   Another method for calculating the amount of the adjustment estimates the amount of receivables the firm expects not to collect and from that amount estimates the amount it does expect to collect. This is the **aging-of-accounts-receivable method for estimating uncollectibles.** This method classifies each customer's account as to the length of time the account has been uncollected. One set of intervals for classifying individual accounts receivable is as follows:

1. Not yet due
2. Past due 30 days or fewer
3. Past due 31 to 60 days
4. Past due 61 to 180 days
5. Past due more than 180 days

The accountant presumes that the balance in the Allowance for Uncollectible Accounts is large enough to cover substantially all accounts receivable past due for more than, say, six months and smaller portions of the more recent accounts. A firm estimates the actual portions from experience.

As an example of the adjustments to be made, assume that the balance in accounts receivable of Howarth's Home Center at the end of Year 2, before providing for estimated uncollectible accounts, is $600,000 (= $800,000 from sales on account during Year 2 minus $200,000 of cash collections). Exhibit 6.1 presents an aging of these accounts receivable. Estimated uncollectible accounts total $98,000. The adjusting entry at the end of Year 2, assuming that Howarth's Home Center uses aging of receivables instead of percentage of sales to estimate uncollectible accounts, is as follows:

EXHIBIT 6.1	Illustration of Aging Accounts Receivable

	Amount	Estimated Uncollectible Percentage	Estimated Uncollectible Amounts
CLASSIFICATION OF ACCOUNTS			
Not yet due	$444,000	8.1	$36,000
1—30 days past due	75,000	20.0	15,000
31—60 days past due	40,000	40.0	16,000
61—180 days past due	25,000	60.0	15,000
More than 180 days past due	16,000	100.0	16,000
	$600,000		$98,000

End of Year 2

Bad Debt Expense	98,000	
Allowance for Uncollectible Accounts		98,000

To adjust the balance in the Allowance for Uncollectible Accounts to $98,000.

Before this entry, the Allowance account had a zero balance, so the amount debited to expense and credited to the allowance is the full amount of uncollectibles estimated by the aging analysis. In reality, the Allowance account will have some balance just before this entry—perhaps a debit balance. Then, the amounts in the debit and credit of this entry will be the plug amounts necessary to bring the balance to the estimated amount—$98,000. If, for example, the Allowance account had a $10,000 debit balance just before the adjusting entry, the amounts would be $108,000 (= $10,000 + $98,000). If the Allowance account had a $23,000 credit balance just before the adjusting entry, the amounts would be $75,000 (= $98,000 − $23,000). The second year's adjusting entry in Exhibit 6.2, discussed next, illustrates the adjusting entry when the Allowance account has a debit balance just before adjustment.

Even when a firm uses the percentage-of-sales method, it must age the accounts periodically to check on the accuracy of the percentage it uses. If the aging analysis shows that the balance in the Allowance for Uncollectible Accounts is apparently too large (or too small), the firm can lower (or raise) the percentage of sales it charges to the Bad Debt Expense account.

Comparing Percentage-of-Sales and Aging Methods When the firm uses the percentage-of-sales method, the periodic provision for uncollectible accounts (for example, $96,000) increases (credits) the amounts provided in previous periods (zero in this case) in the account Allowance for Uncollectible Accounts. When the firm uses the aging method, it adjusts the balance in the account Allowance for Uncollectible Accounts (in this example, $98,000) to reflect the desired ending balance. If the percentage used under the percentage-of-sales method reasonably reflects collection experience, the balance in the allowance account should be approximately the same at the end of each period under both of these methods of estimating uncollectible accounts.

EXHIBIT 6.2	Review of the Allowance Method of Accounting for Uncollectible Accounts

Transactions in the First Period

(1) Sales are $1,000,000.

(2) The firm collects cash of $937,000 from customers in payment of their accounts.

(3) At the end of the first period, the firm estimates that uncollectibles will be 2 percent of sales; .02 × $1,000,000 = $20,000.

(4) The firm writes off specific accounts totaling $7,000 as uncollectible.

(5) The firm closes the revenue and expense accounts.

Transactions in the Second Period

(6) Sales are $1,200,000.

(7) The firm writes off specific accounts totaling $22,000 during the period as information on their uncollectibility becomes known. The debit balance of $9,000 will remain in the Allowance account until the adjusting entry is made at the end of the period; see **(9)**.

(8) The firm collects cash of $1,100,000 from customers in payment of their accounts.

(9) An aging of the accounts receivable shows that the amount in the Allowance account should be $16,000. The amount of the adjustment is $25,000. It is the difference between the desired $16,000 credit balance and the current $9,000 debit balance in the Allowance account.

(10) The firm closes the revenue and expense accounts.

Cash		**Accounts Receivable**		**Allowance for Uncollectible Accounts**	
(2) 937,000		**(1)** 1,000,000			20,000 **(3)**
			937,000 **(2)**		
			7,000 **(4)**	**(4)** 7,000	
Bal. ?		Bal. 56,000			13,000 Bal.
		(6) 1,200,000			
			22,000 **(7)**	**(7)** 22,000	
(8) 1,100,000			1,100,000 **(8)**		25,000 **(9)**
Bal. ?		Bal. 134,000			16,000 Bal.

Bad Debt Expense		**Sales Revenue**	
(3) 20,000			1,000,000 **(1)**
	Closed **(5)**	**(5)** Closed	
(9) 25,000			1,200,000 **(6)**
	Closed **(10)**	**(10)** Closed	

Exhibit 6.2 illustrates the operation of the allowance method for uncollectibles over two periods. In the first period the firm uses the percentage-of-sales method. In the second period it uses the aging method. Normally, a firm would use the same method in all periods.

Summary of Accounting for Uncollectible Accounts
The accounting for uncollectible accounts using the allowance method involves four transactions or events.

(1) Sale of Goods on Account

Accounts Receivable	Selling Price
Sales Revenue	Selling Price

(2) Collection of Cash from Customers

Cash	Amount Collected
Accounts Receivable	Amount Collected

(3) Estimate of Expected Uncollectible Accounts

Bad Debt Expense	Estimated Uncollectible Amount
Allowance for Uncollectible Accounts	Estimated Uncollectible Amount

The percentage-of-sales method computes directly the amount of the debit, with the credit being a plug. The aging-of-accounts-receivable method computes directly the amount of the credit, with the debit being a plug.

(4) Write off of Actual Uncollectible Accounts using the Allowance Method

Allowance for Uncollectible Accounts	Actual Uncollectible Amount
Accounts Receivable	Actual Uncollectible Amount

Entries such as this can occur during the period, as the firm identifies specific uncollectible accounts, or at the end of the period, when the firm writes off a group of specific uncollectibles all at once, or both.

When a firm uses the direct write-off method, it makes the same entries for **(1)** and **(2)**. It does not make entry **(3)**. Entry **(4)** is as follows:

(4) Write-off of Actual Uncollectible Accounts using Direct Write-off Method

Bad Debt Expense	Actual Uncollectible Amount
Accounts Receivable	Actual Uncollectible Amount

---

P R O B L E M   6 . 1   F O R   S E L F - S T U D Y

Accounting for uncollectible accounts. Dee's Department Store opened for business on January 2, Year 4. Sales on account during Year 4 are $5,000,000. The firm estimates that uncollectible accounts will total 2 percent of sales. Dee's writes off

$40,000 of accounts as uncollectible at the end of Year 4. Collections on account during Year 4 totaled $3,500,000.

a. Present the adjusting entry on December 31, Year 4, to apply the direct write-off method for uncollectible accounts.

b. Present the adjusting entries on December 31, Year 4, to apply the allowance method for uncollectible accounts.

c. Sales on account during Year 5 totaled $6,000,000. Dee's writes off $110,000 of accounts as uncollectible on December 31, Year 5. Prepare the adjusting entry on December 31, Year 5, to apply the direct write-off method for Year 5.

d. Refer to part **c.** Prepare the adjusting entries on December 31, Year 5, to apply the allowance method for Year 5.

e. Dee's ages its accounts receivable on December 31, Year 5, and discovers that it needs a balance in its Allowance for Uncollectible Accounts of $75,000 at the end of Year 5. Give the additional adjusting entries on December 31, Year 5, beyond that in part **d** above, to apply the allowance method for Year 5.

THE ALLOWANCE METHOD APPLIES TO MANY TRANSACTIONS IN ACCOUNTING

We have just introduced the allowance method for uncollectibles. Accountants use the allowance method when the firm knows that at the time of sale, it will suffer some reduction in future cash flows (in this case for uncollected accounts) but can only estimate the amount at the time of sale. The allowance method attempts to reduce reported earnings to the amount of the expected net cash collections.

A similar phenomenon occurs often in business transactions:

■ The customer has the right to return the product for a refund. and the firm can only estimate the amount of returns at the time of sale, or

■ the customer has the right to repairs or replacement under warranty if the purchased product is defective, and the firm can only estimate the amount of warranty costs at the time of sale.

In these cases, the firm will use a method analogous to the allowance method for uncollectibles. Chapter 9 illustrates the allowance method for product warranties. You should master the concepts underlying the allowance method, which means mastering its procedures and journal entries to cement your understanding of the concepts, so that you can apply these concepts in other, similar transactions.

SALES DISCOUNTS

Often the seller of merchandise offers a reduction from the invoice price for prompt payment. Such reductions, called **sales discounts** or cash discounts, indicate that goods may have two prices: a lower cash price and a higher price if the seller grants credit.[2] The seller offers a cash discount not only to provide an interest allowance on funds paid

---

[2]See the glossary at the back of the book for the definition of a *discount* and a summary of the various contexts in which accountants use this word.

before the bill is due—the implied interest rate typically exceeds normal lending rates—but also to induce prompt payment so it can avoid additional bookkeeping and collection costs. The amount of sales discounts made available to customers appears as an adjustment in measuring net sales revenue.

SALES RETURNS AND ALLOWANCES

When a customer returns merchandise, the return cancels the sale. The firm could make an entry to reverse the sale. In analyzing sales activities, however, management may be interested in the amount of goods returned. If so, it uses a sales revenue contra account, Sales Returns, to accumulate the amount of **sales returns** for a particular period. When the firm has significant amounts of returns and can reasonably estimate their amounts, it should use an allowance method for returns. The selling firm debits a revenue contra during the period of sale for expected returns so as to report correctly the amount of cash it expects to collect from each period's sales. GAAP do not allow a firm to recognize revenue from sales when the customers have the right to return goods unless the firm can reasonably estimate the amount of returns and does so, using an allowance method.[3]

Sales allowances reduce the price charged to a customer, usually after the firm has delivered the goods and the customer has found them to be unsatisfactory or damaged. The sales allowance reduces sales revenue, but the firm may desire to accumulate the amount of such adjustments in a separate sales revenue contra account. It can use an account, Sales Allowances, for this purpose.

TURNING RECEIVABLES INTO CASH

A firm may find itself temporarily short of cash and unable to borrow from its usual sources. In such instances, it can convert accounts receivable into cash in various ways. A firm may **assign** its accounts receivable to a bank or a finance company to obtain a loan. The assigning (borrowing) company physically maintains control of the accounts receivable, collects amounts remitted by customers, and then forwards the proceeds to the lending institution. Alternatively, the firm may **pledge** its accounts receivable to the lending agency as collateral for a loan. If the borrowing firm cannot make loan repayments when due, the lending agency has the right to sell the accounts receivable to obtain payment. Finally, firms may **factor** (sell) the accounts receivable to a bank or a finance company to obtain cash. In this case, the firm sells accounts receivable to the lending institution, which physically controls the receivables and collects payments from customers. If the firm has pledged accounts receivable, a footnote to the financial statements should indicate this fact: the collection of such accounts receivable will not increase the liquid resources available to the firm to pay general trade creditors. Accounts receivable that the firm has factored or assigned do not appear on the balance sheet because the firm has sold them. Chapter 10 discusses the difficulties in ascertaining whether a transfer of receivables is a sale (no liability appears on the balance sheet) or a collateralized loan (liability appears on the balance sheet).

ILLUSTRATION OF BALANCE SHEET PRESENTATION

The balance sheet accounts presented so far in this chapter are Accounts Receivable and the Allowance for Uncollectible Accounts. Exhibit 6.3 shows how transactions affecting

---

[3]Financial Accounting Standards Board, *Statement of Financial Accounting Standards No. 48,* "Revenue Recognition When Right of Return Exists," 1981.

EXHIBIT 6.3	ALEXIS COMPANY Income Statement Illustration of Sales and Sales Adjustments Partial Income Statement for the Year Ended June 30, Year 2	

REVENUES		
Sales—Gross		$515,200
Less Sales Adjustments:		
Discounts Taken	$23,600	
Allowances	11,000	
Estimated Uncollectibles[a]	10,300	
Returns	8,600	
Total Sales Adjustments		53,500
Net Sales		$461,700

[a]Most companies call this account Bad Debt Expense and list it among the expenses.

these accounts appear in the income statement of Alexis Company. Exhibit 6.4 illustrates the presentation of these items in the balance sheet, which includes all of the current assets for Alexis Company as of June 30, Year 1 and Year 2.

Accounts receivable appear on the balance sheet at the net amount the firm expects to collect. Firms use the allowance method to reduce the gross receivables to their expected collectible amount. The accounting involves a debit to Bad Debt Expense and a credit to an Allowance (asset contra) account in the period of sale. When the firm identifies a specific account receivable as uncollectible, it credits the specific account receivable to write it off and debits the Allowance account. Periodically, the firm uses an aging-of-accounts-receivable balance to test the adequacy of the amounts debited to Bad Debt Expense.

INCOME RECOGNITION AT TIMES DIFFERENT FROM SALE

Many firms clear the hurdles mentioned earlier for revenue recognition at times other than the time of sale. Next we provide examples of such firms and discuss some of the accounting issues they present.

INCOME RECOGNITION BEFORE THE SALE

Firms sometimes recognize revenues and expenses before the sale or delivery of a product—time **(2)** in Figure 6.1. In these cases, the firm has typically contracted with a particular customer, agreed on a selling price, and performed substantial work to create the product.

Long-term Contractors   The operating process for a long-term contractor (for example, building construction, shipbuilding) differs from that for a manufacturing firm (depicted in Figure 6.1) in three important respects:

1. The period of construction (production) may span several accounting periods.

EXHIBIT 6.4	ALEXIS COMPANY Illustration of Current Assets Balance Sheet (Excerpts) June 30, Year 1 and Year 2			

	June 30, Year 1		June 30, Year 2	
CURRENT ASSETS				
Cash and Certificates of Deposit		$ 56,200		$ 63,000
Accounts Receivable, Gross	$57,200		$58,100	
Less Allowance for Uncollectible Accounts	(3,500)		(3,600)	
Accounts Receivable, Net		53,700		54,500
Merchandise Inventory[a]		67,000		72,000
Prepayments		4,300		4,800
Total Current Assets		$181,200		$194,300

[a]Additional required disclosures for this item do not appear here. See Chapter 7.

2. The firm identifies a customer and agrees on a contract price in advance (or at least in the early stages of construction). The seller has little doubt about the ability of the customer to make the agreed-on payments.
3. The buyer often makes periodic payments of the contract price as work progresses.

The activities of contractors often meet the criteria for recognizing revenue from long-term contracts during the period of construction. The existence of a contract indicates that the contractor has identified a buyer and agreed on a price. Occasionally, the contractor collects cash in advance. More often, the contractor assesses the customer's credit and reasonably expects that the customer will pay the contract price in cash as construction progresses or afterward. Although future services required on these long-term construction contracts can be substantial at any given time, the contractor can estimate, with reasonable precision, the costs to be incurred in providing these services. In agreeing to a contract price, the firm must have some confidence in its estimates of the total costs it will incur on the contract.

Percentage-of-Completion Method When a firm's construction activities meet the criteria for revenue recognition as construction progresses, the firm usually recognizes revenue during the construction period using the **percentage-of-completion method.** The percentage-of-completion method recognizes a portion of the contract price as revenue during each accounting period of construction. It bases the amount of revenue, expense, and income on the proportion of total work performed during the accounting period. It measures the proportion of total work carried out during the accounting period either from engineers' estimates of the degree of completion or from the ratio of costs incurred to date to the total costs expected for the entire contract.

The actual schedule of cash collections does not affect the revenue recognition process. Even if the contract specifies that the contractor will receive the entire contract price only on completing construction, the contractor may use the percentage-of-completion method so long as it can reasonably estimate the amount of cash it will receive and the remaining costs it expects to incur in completing the job.

As the contractor recognizes portions of the contract price as revenue, it recognizes equal portions of the total estimated contract costs as expenses. Thus, the percentage-of-completion method follows the accrual basis of accounting because the method matches expenses with related revenues.

To illustrate the percentage-of-completion method, we will assume that a firm agrees to construct a bridge for $5,000,000. The firm estimates the total cost at $4,000,000, to occur as follows: Year 1, $1,500,000; Year 2, $2,000,000; and Year 3, $500,000. Thus the firm expects a total profit of $1,000,000 (= $5,000,000 − $1,500,000 − $2,000,000 − $500,000).

Assume that the firm measures the percentage of completion by using the percentage of total costs incurred and that it incurs costs as anticipated. It recognizes revenue and expense from the contract as follows:

Year	Degree of Completion	Revenue	Expense	Profit
1	$1,500,000/$4,000,000 = 37.5%	$1,875,000	$1,500,000	$ 375,000
2	$2,000,000/$4,000,000 = 50.0%	2,500,000	2,000,000	500,000
3	$ 500,000/$4,000,000 = 12.5%	625,000	500,000	125,000
		$5,000,000	$4,000,000	$1,000,000

Completed Contract Method Some firms involved with construction contracts postpone revenue recognition until they complete the construction project and its sale. Construction contractors call this method of recognizing revenue the **completed contract method.** This is the same as the **completed sale method,** a term accountants use for the usual method of recognizing revenue when a retailing or manufacturing firm makes its sales. A firm using the completed contract method in the previous example recognizes no revenue or expense from the contract during Year 1 or Year 2. In Year 3, it recognizes contract revenue of $5,000,000 and contract expenses of $4,000,000 in measuring net income. Note that total income, or profit, is $1,000,000 under both the percentage-of-completion and the completed contract methods, equal to cash inflows of $5,000,000 less cash outflows of $4,000,000.

In some cases, firms use the completed contract method because the contracts take such a short time to complete (such as a few months) that earnings reported with the percentage-of-completion method and the completed contract method do not differ significantly. In these cases, firms use the completed contract method because they find it generally easier to implement. Firms also use the completed contract method in situations when they have not found a specific buyer while construction progresses, as sometimes happens in the construction of residential housing. These situations require future marketing effort. Moreover, substantial uncertainty may exist regarding the price that the contractor will ultimately ask and the amount of cash it will collect.

If uncertainty obscures the total costs the contractor will incur in carrying out the project, it will not use the percentage-of-completion method—even when it has a contract with a specified price. If a contractor cannot reasonably estimate total costs, it cannot estimate the percentage of total costs incurred by a given date (until the end), and it cannot measure the percentage of services already rendered. Thus, it cannot measure revenue. In parallel, the contractor cannot use the percentage-of-completion method when it cannot estimate the fraction of the work done in each period, even if it can measure total costs for the job.

Quality of Earnings Issues for Long-Term Contractors The percentage-of-completion method provides information on the profitability of a contractor as construction progresses. The completed contract method, in contrast, lumps all of the income from contracts into the period of completion. Because of the more timely reporting of operating performance in the percentage-of-completion method, GAAP require the use of this method whenever firms can make reasonable estimates of revenues and expenses.[4] Managers can either underestimate total expenses or overestimate the degree of completion to accelerate the recognition of income. Recognizing too much income during the early years of a contract means recognizing too little in later years. The need to make estimates under the percentage-of-completion method provides management with opportunities to manage reported earnings. Most analysts thus view earnings reported under the percentage-of-completion method as having lower quality than earnings reported under the completed contract method.

Forest Products Companies   The operating process for a forest products company involves a multiyear growing process for trees. This operating process takes longer and requires relatively smaller annual expenditures (primarily on maintenance and pruning of trees) than occurs for a long-term contractor. Trees grow and thereby increase in value with little additional effort by the forest products company. A similar situation arises for other products requiring aging, such as liquor and tobacco.

Firms whose products require aging seldom satisfy the criteria for revenue recognition during the aging process. Uncertainties exist regarding the amount of cash such firms will ultimately receive at the time of sale. This amount depends not only on the quality of the aged product but also on market conditions at the time of completion of the aging process. Awaiting the completion of aging to recognize revenue reduces these uncertainties. A proper matching of expenses with revenues requires that these firms capitalize, as part of the cost of the aging assets, all expenditures made (maintenance, storage) during the aging process. (To *capitalize* an expenditure means to debit the amount to an asset account rather than to an expense account.) Such costs become expenses at the time of sale, when the firm recognizes revenues.

Recognizing income before the sale requires sufficient certainty regarding the amount of cash inflows and outflows to permit a reasonably precise measurement of the total revenues and expenses.

INCOME RECOGNITION AFTER THE SALE

The operating process for some firms requires substantial performance after the time of sale. For other firms, it involves considerable uncertainty regarding the future amounts of cash inflows, cash outflows, or both. In these cases, recognizing income after the time of sale—at times **(4)**, **(5)**, or **(6)** in Figure 6.1—is appropriate.

Insurance Companies   The operating process for an insurance company involves the following steps:

1. The insurance company sells insurance policies to customers, promising to provide insurance coverage (life, health, property, liability) in the future.
2. The insurance company collects cash (premiums) from policyholders during the periods of insurance coverage.
3. The insurance company invests the cash received from policyholders in stocks, bonds, real estate, and other investments, periodically receiving interest, dividends, and other revenues.
4. Policyholders make claims on their insurance policies, requiring the insurance company to disburse cash.

---

[4]Financial Accounting Standards Board, *Statement of Financial Accounting Standards No. 111,* "Rescission of FASB Statement Number 32 and Technical Corrections," 1997.

The insurance contract requires the insurance company to provide substantial future services after the sale of the contract. Also, the insurance company cannot estimate the amount of cash it will receive from investments. The uncertainty in these steps causes the accountant to delay the recognizing of income from the time of sale to some time after the company sells the insurance.

One alternative recognizes income at the end of the period of insurance coverage (for example, at the death of the insured in the case of life insurance). At that time, the insurance company can measure with certainty the cash it received from premiums and from investments and the amount of cash it disbursed for claims. Also, the insurance company has provided the services required by the insurance contract. Such an approach, however, may inappropriately delay the recognition of income. Most policyholders pay their insurance premiums as required by the insurance contract. Insurance companies generally receive cash each period for interest and dividends from their investments. Life insurance actuaries can usually estimate the amount and timing of insurance claims. Awaiting completion of the insurance coverage period provides insufficient signals regarding the operating performance of the insurance company while it is providing the insurance coverage.

Most insurance companies therefore recognize revenues and expenses during each period of insurance coverage: time **(6)** in Figure 6.1. The receipt of cash from policyholders and from investments creates a relatively high degree of certainty regarding the amount of revenue. Insurance companies must, however, match against this revenue each period a portion of the ultimate cash outflow to satisfy claims. Because this cash outflow may occur several or even many years later, measuring expenses requires estimates. Actuaries study demographic and other data to estimate the likely amount and timing of policyholder claims. Accountants use this information to measure expenses each period. The income recognition process for an insurance company illustrates cash inflows occurring at a time different from that of cash outflows, requiring estimates in measuring income.

Franchisors Companies (franchisors) such as McDonald's, Pizza Hut, and Taco Bell typically sell franchise rights to individuals (franchisees) in particular locales. These franchise rights permit the franchisee to use the franchisor's name, as well as advertising, consulting, and other services provided by the franchisor. The franchisee agrees to pay an initial franchise fee of $50,000 or even more. Most franchisees do not have the funds to pay this initial fee at the time they acquire the franchise rights. Instead, they sign a note agreeing to pay the fee over five or more years.

Franchisors usually provide most of the services required by the franchise arrangement by the time the franchisee opens for business (for example, selecting a location and constructing buildings and equipment). Substantial uncertainty often exists, however, regarding the portion of the initial franchise fee that the franchisor will ultimately collect from its customer, the francishee. New small businesses often fail. Franchisees can usually stop making payments and walk away from the franchise arrangement. A similar situation exists for other businesses, such as land-development companies, that sell products or services with delayed payment arrangements.

When substantial uncertainty exists at the time of sale regarding the amount (or timing or both) of cash or the cash equivalent value of other assets that a firm will ultimately receive from customers, the firm delays the recognition of revenues and expenses until it receives cash: point **(5)** in Figure 6.1. Such sellers recognize revenue at the time of cash collection using either the installment method or the cost-recovery-first method. Unlike the cash method of accounting, however, these methods attempt to match expenses with revenues.

Installment Method   The **installment method** recognizes revenue as the seller collects parts of the selling price in cash. In parallel, this method recognizes as expenses each period the same portion of the cost of the good or service sold as the portion of total revenue recognized.

Example 5   Assume that a firm sells for $100 merchandise costing $60. Income from the transaction is $40 (= $100 − $60), cash inflow less cash outflow. The buyer agrees to pay (ignoring interest) $20, one-fifth of the total revenue, per month for five months. The installment method recognizes revenue of $20 each month as the seller receives cash. The cost of goods sold is $12 [= ($20/$100) × $60] each month, with expenses measured as the same proportion of total expenses as the cash collection represents of its total, one-fifth in the example. By the end of five months, the income recognized totals $40 [= 5 × ($20 − $12)].

Cost-Recovery-First Method   When the seller has substantial uncertainty about the amount of cash it will collect, it can also use the **cost-recovery-first method** of income recognition. This method matches the costs of generating revenues dollar for dollar with cash receipts until the seller recovers all such costs. Expenses equal (match) revenues in each period until the seller recovers all costs. Only when cumulative cash receipts exceed total costs will profit (that is, revenue without any matching expenses) appear in the income statement.

   To illustrate the cost-recovery-first method, we use information from the previous example.

Example 6   Assume the sale for $100 of merchandise costing $60, with the seller expecting to collect $20 each month for five months. During each of the first three months, the seller recognizes revenue of $20 and expenses of $20. By the end of the third month, cumulative cash receipts of $60 exactly equal the cost of the merchandise sold. During the fourth and fifth months, the seller recognizes revenue of $20 per month without an offsetting expense. For the five months as a whole, the seller recognizes total income of $40 but in a different pattern from that exhibited in the installment method.

Example 7   Assume instead that the seller eventually collects only four, not five, of the expected monthly payments of $20 each. Under the cost-recovery-first method, the seller will recognize no profit in the first three months, $20 in the fourth month, and $20 in total. Under the installment method, the seller would recognize $8 (= $20 − $12) each month for four months, $32 in total. Then, when the seller learns in month five that it will collect no more cash, it will have to recognize a loss of $12 (= $32 − $20) to report correctly the total profit of only $20.

Use of Installment and Cost-Recovery-First Methods   GAAP permit the seller to use the installment and the cost-recovery-first methods only when the seller cannot make reasonably certain estimates of cash collection. For most sales of goods and services, past experience and an assessment of customers' credit standings provide a sufficient basis for estimating the amount of cash the seller will receive. If the seller can reasonably estimate the amount of cash it will receive, the seller may not use the installment method or the cost-recovery-first method for financial reporting and must recognize revenue no later than the time of sale.[5] When cash collection is sufficiently

---

[5]Accounting Principles Board, *Opinion No. 10,* "Omnibus Opinion—1966," par. 12, footnote 8.

uncertain that GAAP allow either of these methods, then the cost-recovery-first method seems to reflect more accurately the substance of the uncertainty. The installment method assumes that the seller will eventually receive all cash or, if not, that when payments cease, the seller can repossess the goods, and, at that time, the goods still retain sufficient market value to cover the seller's as-yet-uncollected costs.

SUMMARY ILLUSTRATION OF INCOME RECOGNITION METHODS

Exhibit 6.5 illustrates the various methods of income recognition discussed here and in Chapter 3. The illustration involves a contract for the construction of a bridge for $12 million. The expected and actual patterns of cash receipts and disbursements under the contract appear below.

Period	Expected and Actual Cash Receipts	Expected and Actual Cash Expenditures
1	$ 1,000,000	$1,600,000
2	1,000,000	4,000,000
3	2,000,000	4,000,000
4	4,000,000	—
5	4,000,000	—
Total	$12,000,000	$9,600,000

The contractor completed the bridge in Period 3. Exhibit 6.5 indicates the contractor's periodic revenues, expenses, and income recognized during each period under the contract using the following methods:

The cash basis of accounting

The percentage-of-completion method

The completed contract (completed sale) method

The installment method

The cost-recovery-first method

No single firm could simultaneously justify all of the five methods of income recognition for financial reporting; we present them for illustrative purposes. Note that the total revenues, expenses, and income recognized for the five years are the same for all methods. Over sufficiently long time periods, total income equals cash inflows less cash outflows other than transactions with owners. The amount of income recognized each period differs, however, depending on the accounting method used.

<hr>

PROBLEM 6.2 FOR SELF-STUDY

Income recognition for contractor. Blount Construction Company contracted on May 15, Year 2, to build a bridge for the city for $4,500,000. Blount estimated that the cost of constructing the bridge would be $3,600,000. Blount incurred $1,200,000

EXHIBIT 6.5	Comprehensive Illustration of Revenue and Expense Recognition (all dollar amounts in thousands)

Cash Basis of Accounting[a]

Period	Revenue	Expense	Income
1	$ 1,000	$1,600	$ (600)
2	1,000	4,000	(3,000)
3	2,000	4,000	(2,000)
4	4,000	—	4,000
5	4,000	—	4,000
Total	$12,000	$9,600	$2,400

Period	Percentage-of-Completion Method			Completed Contract Method		
	Revenue	Expense	Income	Revenue	Expense	Income
1	$ 2,000[d]	$1,600	$ 400	$ —	$ —	$ —
2	5,000[e]	4,000	1,000	—	—	—
3	5,000[e]	4,000	1,000	12,000	9,600	2,400
4	—	—	—	—	—	—
5	—	—	—	—	—	—
Total	$12,000	$9,600	$2,400	$12,000	$9,600	$2,400

Period	Installment Method[b]			Cost-Recovery-First Method[c]		
	Revenue	Expense	Income	Revenue	Expense	Income
1	$ 1,000	$ 800[f]	$ 200	$ 1,000	$1,000	$ 0
2	1,000	800[f]	200	1,000	1,000	0
3	2,000	1,600[g]	400	2,000	2,000	0
4	4,000	3,200[h]	800	4,000	4,000	0
5	4,000	3,200[h]	800	4,000	1,600	2,400
Total	$12,000	$9,600	$2,400	$12,000	$9,600	$2,400

[a]The cash basis is not allowed for tax or financial reporting if inventories are a material factor in generating income.

[b]The installment method is allowed for financial reporting only if extreme uncertainty exists as to the amount of cash to be collected from customers. Its use for tax purposes is independent of the collectibility of cash.

[c]The cost-recovery-first method is allowed for financial reporting only if extreme uncertainty exists as to the amount of cash to be collected from customers. It is sometimes used for tax purposes.

[d]$1,600/$9,600 × $12,000.

[e]$4,000/$9,600 × $12,000.

[f]$1,000/$12,000 × $9,600.

[g]$2,000/$12,000 × $9,600.

[h]$4,000/$12,000 × $9,600.

in construction costs during Year 2, $2,000,000 during Year 3, and $400,000 during Year 4 in completing the bridge. The city paid $1,000,000 during Year 2, $1,500,000 during Year 3, and the remaining $2,000,000 of the contract price at the time the bridge was completed and approved in Year 4.

a. Calculate Blount's net income (revenue less expenses) on the contract during Year 2, Year 3, and Year 4, assuming that it uses the percentage-of-completion method.
b. Repeat part **a,** assuming that it uses the completed contract method.
c. Repeat part **a,** assuming that it uses the installment method.
d. Repeat part **a,** assuming that it uses the cost-recovery-first method.

FORMAT AND CLASSIFICATION WITHIN THE INCOME STATEMENT

Financial statement users study a firm's income statement to evaluate its past profitability and to project its likely future profitability. When assessing profitability, the analyst makes two types of distinctions regarding the nature of various income items:

1. Does the income item result from a firm's primary operating activity (creating and selling a good or service for customers) or from an activity incidental or peripheral to the primary operating activity (for example, periodic sales of equipment previously used by the firm in manufacturing)?
2. Does the income item result from an activity in which a firm will likely continue its involvement, or does the income item result from an unusual transaction or event that is unlikely to recur regularly?

Figure 6.2 depicts these distinctions, with examples of each.

A financial statement user who wants to evaluate a firm's ongoing operating profitability will likely focus on income items in the upper left cell. A financial statement user who wants to project net income of prior periods into the future would likely focus on the two "recurring income" cells. Income items in the nonrecurring cells should not affect ongoing assessments of profitability. This section considers the reporting of each type of income item.

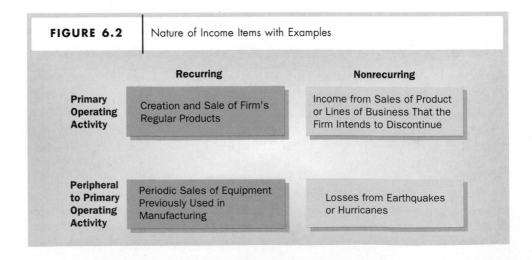

FIGURE 6.2 | Nature of Income Items with Examples

	Recurring	**Nonrecurring**
Primary Operating Activity	Creation and Sale of Firm's Regular Products	Income from Sales of Product or Lines of Business That the Firm Intends to Discontinue
Peripheral to Primary Operating Activity	Periodic Sales of Equipment Previously Used in Manufacturing	Losses from Earthquakes or Hurricanes

DISTINGUISHING REVENUE FROM GAINS AND EXPENSES FROM LOSSES

Accountants distinguish between revenues and expenses on the one hand and gains and losses on the other. Revenues and expenses result from the recurring, primary operating activities of a business (upper left cell in Figure 6.2). Income items discussed thus far in this book fall into this first category. Gains and losses result from either peripheral activities (lower left cell) or nonrecurring activities (upper and lower right cells). A second distinction is that revenues and expenses are gross concepts, whereas gains and losses are net concepts. The following examples illustrate this distinction.

Example 8   IBM sells a computer to a customer for $400,000. The computer cost IBM $300,000 to manufacture. IBM records this sale as follows:

Cash	400,000	
Sales Revenue		400,000
To record sale.		
Cost of Goods Sold	300,000	
Finished Goods Inventory		300,000
To record the cost of goods sold.		

This transaction fits into the upper left cell of Figure 6.2 (primary/recurring). The income statement reports both sales revenue and cost of goods sold, providing information to the financial statement user regarding both the manufacturing cost of the computer and IBM's ability to mark up this cost in setting selling prices. After preparing the income statement, the accountant closes both the Sales Revenue and Cost of Goods Sold accounts, increasing Retained Earnings by $100,000.

Example 9   The Gap, a retail clothing chain, sells computers previously used for processing data in its stores. This sale relates only peripherally to The Gap's primary operating activity, which is to sell casual clothes. Assume that the computers originally cost $500,000 and have $200,000 of accumulated depreciation at the time of sale. Thus, the computers have a net book value of $300,000. The sale of these computers for $400,000 results in the following journal entry on The Gap's books:

Cash	400,000	
Accumulated Depreciation	200,000	
Equipment		500,000
Gain on Sale of Equipment		100,000
Disposal of computers for $100,000 more than book value.		

This transaction fits into the lower left cell of Figure 6.2 (peripheral/recurring). Illustrating **net versus gross reporting of income items,** the income statement reports only the $100,000 gain on the sale, not the selling price of $400,000 and the book value of $300,000. The income statement reports gains and losses at net instead of gross amounts because, presumably, financial statement users do not need information on the components of either peripheral or nonrecurring income items. After preparing the income statement, the accountant closes the account, Gain on Sale of Equipment, to Retained Earnings.

Note that both revenues and gains appear as credits in journal entries and ultimately increase Retained Earnings. Both expenses and losses appear as debits in journal entries and ultimately reduce Retained Earnings. To repeat, revenues and expenses are *gross* concepts; gains and losses are *net* concepts.

AN   INTERNATIONAL   PERSPECTIVE

The IASC says that a firm should recognize revenue when

1. the seller has transferred significant risks and rewards of ownership to the buyer;
2. managerial involvement and control has passed from the seller to the buyer;
3. the seller can reliably measure the amount of revenue;
4. it is probable that the seller will receive economic benefits; and
5. the seller can reliably measure the costs (including future costs) of the transaction.[6]

You can see that these criteria do not use the same words that we have used, but the concepts do not differ from those we discuss in this chapter. The IASC explicitly states that it prefers

- the allowance method for uncollectibles when the firm recognizes the revenue,
- the percentage-of-completion method when the seller provides services, and
- the matching principles for timing of expense recognition.[7]

For construction contracts, the IASC prefers the percentage-of-completion method when the firm can "measure or reliably estimate . . . total revenue, past and future costs, and the stage of completion." If the firm cannot measure the outcome reliably, then the firm should use the cost-recovery-first method.[8]

SUMMARY

Chapter 5 points out that financial analysts care about the operating profitability of a firm. Chapters 3 and 6 discuss the underlying concepts, accounting procedures, and uses of the income statement. The most important underlying concepts involve the measurement of revenues and expenses following the principles of the accrual basis of accounting. The accrual basis provides operating performance measures superior to those

---

[6]International Accounting Standards Committee, *Statement No. 18,* "Revenue," 1984, revised and reissued 1995.
[7]Ibid.
[8]International Accounting Standards Committee, *Statement No. 11,* "Construction Contracts," 1980.

provided by the cash basis because the accrual basis matches revenues (the results of the firm's outputs) with expenses (its inputs). Imprecision in this matching occurs when the timing of cash receipts and disbursements deviates from the timing of revenue and expense recognition. Additional interpretative issues arise when a firm's income statement includes unusual or nonrecurring income items. The financial statement user must give adequate consideration to the recurring or nonrecurring nature of various income items in both assessing a firm's past operating performance and predicting its likely future performance.

APPENDIX 6.1: EFFECTS ON THE STATEMENT OF CASH FLOWS OF TRANSACTIONS INVOLVING ACCOUNTS RECEIVABLE

From this point forward, most chapters contain an appendix describing the effects that the accounting treatments of this chapter have on the statement of cash flows. In describing effects in the derivation of cash from operations, we focus most attention on the indirect method. That method begins the derivation of cash flow from operations with net income and then adjusts net income for noncash revenues and expenses.

ACCOUNTS RECEIVABLE

Transactions changing accounts receivable are operating activities. The accountant subtracts an increase in accounts receivable from net income in deriving cash flow from operations. Decreases in accounts receivable result in additions to net income to compute cash flow from operations.

Most firms report the change in accounts receivable net of the allowance for uncollectible accounts as a single item in the Operations section of the statement of cash flows. Such firms need make no further adjustment in the Operations section for uncollectible accounts to compute cash flow from operations.

Firms with significant uncollectible accounts may separately disclose transactions involving uncollectible accounts. If such firms report the gross change in accounts receivable in the Operations section, they must make an addback to net income for bad debt expense.

SOLUTIONS TO SELF-STUDY PROBLEMS

SUGGESTED SOLUTION TO PROBLEM 6.1 FOR SELF-STUDY

(Dee's Department Store; accounting for uncollectible accounts.)

a.	Bad Debt Expense	40,000	
	Accounts Receivable		40,000
	To write off uncollectible accounts using the direct write-off method for Year 4.		
b.	Bad Debt Expense	100,000	
	Allowance for Uncollectible Accounts.		100,000
	To provide for estimated uncollectible accounts using the allowance method for Year 4; .02 × $5,000,000 = $100,000.		

(continued)

Allowance for Uncollectible Accounts	40,000	
Accounts Receivable		40,000

To write off uncollectible accounts using the allowance method for Year 4.

c.

Bad Debt Expense	110,000	
Accounts Receivable		110,000

To write off uncollectible accounts using the direct write-off method for Year 5.

d.

Bad Debt Expense	120,000	
Allowance for Uncollectible Accounts		120,000

To provide for estimated uncollectible accounts using the allowance method for Year 5; .02 × $6,000,000 = $120,000.

Allowance for Uncollectible Accounts	110,000	
Accounts Receivable		110,000

To write off uncollectible accounts using the allowance method for Year 5.

e.

Bad Debt Expense	5,000	
Allowance for Uncollectible Accounts		5,000

To adjust the Allowance for Uncollectible Accounts to the desired ending balance of $75,000. The balance in the Allowance for Uncollectible Accounts after the entries in parts **b** and **d** is $70,000 (= $100,000 − $40,000 + $120,000 − $110,000).

Note: Most firms would likely combine the provision for bad debts in part **d** ($120,000) and part **e** ($5,000) into a single entry.

SUGGESTED SOLUTION TO PROBLEM 6.2 FOR SELF-STUDY

(Blount Construction Company; income recognition for contractor.)

a. Percentage-of-completion method:

Year	Incremental Percentage Complete	Revenue Recognized	Expenses Recognized	Net Income
2	12/36 (.333)	$1,500,000	$1,200,000	$300,000
3	20/36 (.556)	2,500,000	2,000,000	500,000
4	4/36 (.111)	500,000	400,000	100,000
Total	36/36 (1.000)	$4,500,000	$3,600,000	$900,000

b. Completed contract method:

Year	Revenue Recognized	Expenses Recognized	Net Income
2	$ 0	$ 0	$ 0
3	0	0	0
4	4,500,000	3,600,000	900,000
Total	$4,500,000	$3,600,000	$900,000

c. Installment method:

Year	Cash Collected (= revenue)	Fraction of Cash Collected	Expenses (= fraction × total cost)	Net Income
2	$1,000,000	1.0/4.5	$ 800,000	$200,000
3	1,500,000	1.5/4.5	1,200,000	300,000
4	2,000,000	2.0/4.5	1,600,000	400,000
Total	$4,500,000	1.0	$3,600,000	$900,000

d. Cost-recovery-first method:

Year	Cash Collected (= revenue)	Expenses Recognized	Net Income
2	$1,000,000	$1,000,000	$ 0
3	1,500,000	1,500,000	0
4	2,000,000	1,100,000	900,000
Total	$4,500,000	$3,600,000	$900,000

KEY TERMS AND CONCEPTS

Generally accepted accounting principles (GAAP)
Economic consequences
Quality of earnings
Direct write-off method
Allowance method
Percentage-of-sales method for estimating uncollectibles
Aging-of-accounts-receivable method for estimating uncollectibles
Sales discounts
Sales returns

Sales allowances
Assigning accounts receivable
Pledging accounts receivable
Factoring accounts receivable
Percentage-of-completion method
Completed contract, or completed sale, method
Installment method
Cost-recovery-first method
Net versus gross reporting of income items

QUESTIONS, EXERCISES, PROBLEMS, AND CASES

QUESTIONS

1. Review the meaning of the terms and concepts listed above in Key Terms and Concepts.
2. Which of the two methods for treating uncollectible accounts (direct write-off or allowance) implies recognizing income reductions earlier rather than later? Explain.
3. The direct write-off and the allowance method for uncollectible accounts both involve matching. How does this matching differ between the two methods?

4. **a.** Under what conditions will the direct write-off method and the allowance method result in approximately the same bad debt expense each period?
   b. Under what conditions will the direct write-off method and the allowance method result in approximately the same amount for accounts receivable (net) on the balance sheet?
5. **a.** An old wisdom in tennis holds that if your first serves are always good, you are not hitting them hard enough. An analogous statement in business might be that if you have no uncollectible accounts, you probably are not selling enough on credit. Comment on the validity and parallelism of these statements.
   b. When are more uncollectible accounts better than few uncollectible accounts?
   c. When is a higher percentage of uncollectible accounts better than a lower percentage?
6. Under what circumstances will the Allowance for Uncollectible Accounts have a debit balance during the accounting period? The balance sheet figure for the Allowance for Uncollectible Accounts at the end of the period should never show a debit balance. Why?
7. Construction companies often use the percentage-of-completion method. Why doesn't a typical manufacturing firm use this method of income recognition?
8. Both the installment method and the cost-recovery-first method recognize revenue when a firm collects cash. Why, then, does the pattern of income (that is, revenues minus expenses) over time differ under these two methods?
9. Compare and contrast the installment method and the cash basis of financial accounting.
10. "When the total amount of cash that a firm expects to collect from a customer is highly uncertain, the cost-recovery-first method seems more appropriate than the installment method." Explain.
11. Economists typically define income as an increase in value, or wealth, while a firm holds assets. Accountants typically recognize income when the criteria for revenue recognition are satisfied. Why does the accountants' approach to income recognition differ from that of the economists?
12. "The usefulness of the income statement declines as the quality of earnings declines." Do you agree? Why or why not?

EXERCISES

13. **Journal entries for the allowance method.** Data related to sales on account of Kesler Company appear below:

| | | Accounts Written Off as Uncollectible in Year | | | | | |
Year	Sales on Account	6	7	8	9	10	Total
6	$ 420,000	$1,200	$5,500	$1,700	—	—	$ 8,400
7	480,000	—	1,500	6,100	$2,100	—	9,700
8	550,000	—	—	1,900	7,500	$1,300	10,700
	$1,450,000	$1,200	$7,000	$9,700	$9,600	$1,300	$28,800

Kesler Company estimates that 2 percent of sales on account will become uncollectible.
   a. Prepare journal entries to recognize bad debt expense and to write off uncollectible accounts for Year 6, Year 7, and Year 8 using the allowance method.

b. Does 2 percent of sales on account appear to be a reasonable rate for estimating uncollectibles?

14. **Journal entries for the allowance method.** Data related to sales on account of Emmons Corporation appear below:

Year	Sales on Account	Accounts Written Off as Uncollectible in Year					
		1	2	3	4	5	Total
1 ..	$1,500,000	$2,300	$18,600	$ 9,000	—	—	$ 29,900
2 ..	1,800,000	—	3,500	24,900	$ 7,800	—	36,200
3 ..	2,400,000	—	—	4,100	31,900	$11,700	47,700
	$5,700,000	$2,300	$22,100	$38,000	$39,700	$11,700	$113,800

Emmons Corporation estimates that 3.0 percent of sales on account will become uncollectible.

a. Prepare journal entries to recognize bad debt expense and to write off uncollectible accounts for Year 1, Year 2, and Year 3 using the allowance method.

b. Does 3.0 percent of sales on account appear to be a reasonable rate for estimating uncollectibles?

15. **Allowance method: reconstructing journal entry from events.**

a. (From a problem by S.A. Zeff.) During Year 6, Pandora Company wrote off $2,200 of accounts receivable as uncollectible. During the year, the company received $800 cash from customers whose accounts it had previously written off as uncollectible. The balance in the Allowance for Uncollectibles began Year 6 at $3,500, and the balance at the end of the year, on the balance sheet after all adjusting and closing entries, was $5,000. Present the journal entry that the company made to provide for uncollectibles during Year 6.

b. The balance sheets of Milton Corporation on December 31, Year 1 and Year 2, showed gross accounts receivable of $15,200,000 and $17,600,000, respectively. The balances in the Allowance for Uncollectible Accounts account at the beginning and end of Year 2, after closing entries, were credits of $1,400,000 and $1,550,000, respectively. The income statement for Year 2 shows that the expense for estimated uncollectible accounts was $750,000, which was 1 percent of sales. The firm makes all sales on account. There were no recoveries during Year 2 of accounts written off in previous years. Give all the journal entries made during Year 2 that have an effect on Accounts Receivable and Allowance for Uncollectible Accounts.

16. **Reconstructing events when using the allowance method.** Selected data from the accounts of Seward Company after adjusting entries but before closing entries appear below.

	January 1	December 31
Accounts Receivable	$82,900 Dr.	$ 87,300 Dr.
Allowance for Uncollectible Accounts	8,700 Cr.	9,100 Cr.
Bad Debt Expense	—	4,800 Dr.
Sales	—	240,000 Cr.

The firm makes all sales on account. There were no recoveries during the year of accounts written off in previous years.

Set up T-accounts for each of the four accounts above and enter the balances on January 1 and December 31. Enter in the T-accounts the entries that Seward Corporation made during the year for the following:
a. Sales on account
b. Provision for estimated uncollectible accounts
c. Write-off of actual uncollectible accounts
d. Collection of cash from customers from sales on account

17. **Reconstructing events when using the allowance method.** Selected data from the accounts of Logue Corporation before adjusting and closing entries appear below:

	January 1	December 31
Accounts Receivable	$115,900 Dr.	$122,700 Dr.
Allowance for Uncollectible Accounts	18,200 Cr.	2,900 Dr.
Bad Debt Expense	—	—
Sales	—	450,000 Cr.

Logue Corporation estimates that 6 percent of sales, which are all on account, will become uncollectible. There were no recoveries during the year of accounts written off in previous years.

Set up T-accounts for each of the four accounts above and enter the balances on January 1 and December 31. Enter in the T-accounts the entries that Logue Corporation made *during the year* for the following:
a. Sales on account
b. Write-off of actual uncollectible accounts
c. Collection of cash from customers from sales on account
Enter in the T-accounts the adjusting entry on December 31 to provide for estimated uncollectible accounts.

18. **Aging accounts receivable.** Dove Company's accounts receivable show the following balances by age:

Age of Accounts	Balance Receivable
0–30 Days	$400,000
31–60 Days	90,000
61–120 Days	40,000
More than 120 Days	20,000

The credit balance in the Allowance for Uncollectible Accounts is now $17,200.

Dove Company's independent auditors suggest that the following percentages be used to compute the estimates of amounts that will eventually prove uncollectible: 0–30 days, 0.5 of 1.0 percent; 31–60 days, 1.0 percent; 61–120 days, 10 percent; and more than 120 days, 70 percent. Prepare a journal entry that will carry out the auditors' suggestion.

19. **Aging accounts receivable.** Rorke Company's accounts receivable show the following balances:

Age of Accounts	Balance Receivable
0–30 Days	$700,000
31–60 Days	225,000
61–120 Days	90,000
More than 120 Days	50,000

Rorke Company has already made an adjusting entry based on the percentage-of-sales method for the period. The credit balance in the Allowance for Uncollectible Accounts is now $36,000. The Bad Debt Expense account has a balance of $28,700.

Analysis of recent collection experience suggests that the following percentages be used to compute the estimates of amounts that will eventually prove uncollectible: 0–30 days, 0.5 of 1.0 percent; 31–60 days, 1.0 percent; 61–120 days, 10 percent; and more than 120 days, 30 percent. Prepare the indicated adjusting entry.

20. **Reconstructing events from journal entries.** Give the likely transaction or event that would result in making each of the independent journal entries that follow.

a. Bad Debt Expense	2,300	
Allowance for Uncollectible Accounts		2,300
b. Allowance for Uncollectible Accounts	450	
Accounts Receivable		450
c. Bad Debt Expense	495	
Accounts Receivable		495

21. **Effects, on cash flows, of transactions involving suppliers and customers.** Refer to the trial balance excerpts for Home and Office Depot in Exhibit 6.6. These are the post-closing trial balance at the beginning of the year and the adjusted, preclosing trial balance at the end of the year. This means that the firm has made all year-end adjusting entries but has not closed its income statement accounts to retained earnings. Home and Office Depot deals with

- many retail customers, some of whom have paid for special orders not yet delivered and some of whom have not yet paid for goods they have purchased, and
- many suppliers of goods, some of whom the firm has paid for orders not yet received and some of whom have delivered goods for which the firm has not yet paid.

Home and Office Depot settles all its accounts with customers and suppliers with cash, never with noncash assets.
   a. Calculate the amount of cash the firm received from its customers during the year.
   b. Calculate the amount of cash the firm paid to its suppliers of retail merchandise during the year.

	EXHIBIT 6.6	HOME AND OFFICE DEPOT Selected Details from Trial Balances (Exercise 6.21)

	Post-Closing Trial Balance Beginning of Year		Adjusted, Preclosing Trial Balance End of Year	
	Debits	**Credits**	**Debits**	**Credits**
Accounts Receivable from Retail Customers	$ 8,000		$ 8,600	
Allowance for Uncollectible Retail Receivables		$ 700		$ 750
Accounts Payable to Suppliers of Retail Merchandise		7,000		7,500
Advances to Suppliers of Retail Merchandise	10,000		10,400	
Inventory of Retail Merchandise	11,000		11,200	
Sales Revenue from Retail Customers				130,000
Bad Debt Expense			2,000	
Cost of Retail Merchandise Sold			85,000	
All Other Accounts (Net)		21,300	21,050	
Totals	$29,000	$29,000	$138,250	$138,250

22. **Percentage-of-completion and completed contract methods of income recognition.** The Bechtel Construction Company agreed to build a warehouse for $4,000,000. Expected and actual costs to construct the warehouse were as follows: Year 1, $800,000; Year 2, $1,920,000; and Year 3, $480,000. The firm completed the warehouse in Year 3.

    Compute revenue, expense, and net income for Year 1, Year 2, and Year 3 using the percentage-of-completion method and the completed contract method.

23. **Installment and cost-recovery-first methods of income recognition.** JMB Realty Partners sold a tract of land costing $60,000 to a manufacturing firm for $100,000. The manufacturing firm agreed to pay $25,000 per year for four years (plus interest).

    Compute revenue, expense, and net income for each of the four years using the installment method and the cost-recovery-first method. Ignore interest.

24. **Revenue recognition for various types of businesses.** Discuss when each of the following types of businesses is likely to recognize revenue:
    a. A shoe store
    b. A shipbuilding firm constructing an aircraft carrier under a government contract
    c. A real estate developer selling lots on long-term contracts with small down payments required
    d. A barbershop
    e. A citrus-growing firm
    f. A producer of television movies working under the condition that the rights to the movies are sold to a television network for the first three years and all rights thereafter revert to the producer
    g. A residential real estate developer who constructs only "speculative" houses and later sells the houses to buyers
    h. A producer of fine whiskey that is aged from 6 to 12 years before sale

    i. A savings and loan association lending money for home mortgages

    j. A travel agency that sells tickets in one period and has customers take trips or return tickets in the next period

    k. A printer who prints only custom-order stationery

    l. A seller to food stores of trading stamps redeemable by food store customers for various household products

    m. A wholesale food distributor

    n. A livestock rancher

    o. A shipping company that loads cargo in one accounting period, carries cargo across the ocean in a second accounting period, and unloads the cargo in a third period; the shipping is all done under contract, and cash collection of shipping charges is relatively certain

PROBLEMS AND CASES

25. Analyzing changes in accounts receivable. Selected data from the financial statements of Whirlpool Corporation appear below (amounts in millions):

Balance Sheet	Year 4	Year 5	Year 6	Year 7
Accounts Receivable, net of allowance for uncollectible accounts of $2.4 at the end Year 4, $2.6 at the end of Year 5, $3.3 at the end of Year 6, and $4.4 at the end of Year 7	$ 247.0	$ 260.9	$ 323.4	$ 419.5
Income Statement				
Sales on Account	$3,987.6	$4,008.7	$4,179.0	$4,314.5
Statement of Cash Flows Addback to Net Income in Deriving Cash Flow from Operations:				
Bad Debt Expense	$ 5.4	$ 6.0	$ 17.7	$ 11.5

    a. Prepare journal entries for Year 5, Year 6, and Year 7 for the following events:

        (1) Sales on account

        (2) Provision for estimated uncollectible accounts

        (3) Write-off of actual bad debts

        (4) Collection of cash from customers

    b. Compute the amount of the following ratios:

        (1) Bad debt expense divided by sales on account for Year 5, Year 6, and Year 7

        (2) Allowance for uncollectible accounts divided by accounts receivable (gross) at the end of Year 5, Year 6, and Year 7

    c. What do the ratios computed in part **b** suggest about the manner in which Whirlpool Corporation provides for estimated uncollectible accounts?

26. **Analyzing changes in accounts receivable.** The financial statements and notes for May Department Stores reveal the following for four recent years (amounts in millions):

	Year 9	Year 10	Year 11	Year 12
Total Sales	$8,330	$9,456	$10,035	$10,615
Credit Sales/Total Sales	62.2%	64.9%	66.9%	68.7%
Bad Debt Expense	$57	$64	$82	$96

			End of Year		
	Year 8	Year 9	Year 10	Year 11	Year 12
Accounts Receivable, Gross ...	$1,592	$2,099	$2,223	$2,456	$2,607
Less Allowance for Uncollectible Accounts	(47)	(61)	(66)	(84)	(99)
Accounts Receivable, Net	$1,545	$2,038	$2,157	$2,372	$2,508

   a. Compute the amount of accounts written off as uncollectible during Year 9, Year 10, Year 11, and Year 12.
   b. Compute the amount of cash collections from credit customers during Year 9, Year 10, Year 11, and Year 12.
   c. Calculate the accounts receivable turnover ratio for Year 9, Year 10, Year 11, and Year 12 using total sales in the numerator and average accounts receivable (net) in the denominator.
   d. Repeat part **c** but use credit sales in the numerator.
   e. What are the likely reasons for the different trends in the two measures of the accounts receivable turnover ratio in parts **c** and **d?**

27. **Reconstructing transactions affecting accounts receivable and uncollectible accounts.** The sales, all on account, of Pins Company in Year 10, its first year of operations, were $700,000. Collections totaled $500,000. On December 31, Year 10, Pins Company estimated that 2 percent of all sales would probably be uncollectible. On that date, Pins Company wrote off specific accounts in the amount of $8,000.

   Pins Company's *unadjusted* trial balance (after all nonadjusting entries and after all write-offs of specific accounts receivable identified during Year 11 as being uncollectible) on December 31, Year 11, includes the following accounts and balances:

Accounts Receivable (Dr.)	300,000	
Allowance for Uncollectible Accounts (Dr.)	10,000	
Bad Debt Expense	—	—
Sales (Cr.)		800,000

   On December 31, Year 11, Pins Company carried out an aging of its accounts receivable balances and estimated that the Year 11 ending balance of accounts receivable contained $11,000 of probable uncollectibles. That is, the allowance account should have an $11,000 ending credit balance. It made adjusting entries appropriate for this estimate. Some of the $800,000 sales during Year 11 were for cash and some were on account; we purposefully do not give the amounts.

    a. What was the balance in the Accounts Receivable (gross) account at the end of *Year 10?* Give the amount and whether it was a debit or a credit.

    b. What was the balance in the Allowance for Uncollectible Accounts account at the end of *Year 10?* Give the amount and whether it was a debit or a credit.

    c. What was bad debt expense for *Year 11?*

    d. What was the amount of specific accounts receivable written off as being uncollectible during *Year 11?*

    e. What were total cash collections in *Year 11* from customers (for cash sales and collections from customers who had purchased on account in either Year 10 or Year 11)?

    f. What was the net balance of accounts receivable included in the balance sheet asset total for December 31, *Year 11?*

28. **Decision to extend credit to a new class of customers.** The Nordstrom Department Store near the University of Washington campus has a gross margin on credit sales of 30 percent; that is, cost of goods sold on account is 70 percent of sales on account. Uncollectible accounts amount to 2 percent of credit sales. If the firm extends credit to a group of new student customers, credit sales will increase by $10,000, 7 percent of the new credit sales will be uncollectible, and all other costs, including interest to finance extra inventories, will increase by $1,100.

    a. Would Nordstrom be better or worse off if it extended credit to the new class of customers, and by how much?

    b. How would your answer to part **a** differ if $3,000 of the $10,000 increase in credit sales had been made anyway as sales for cash? (Assume that the uncollectible amount on new credit sales is $800 and the cash sales alone generate $300 of "all other costs.")

29. **Decision to extend credit: working backward to uncollectible rate.** Hanrahan Company has credit sales of $250,000 and a gross margin on those sales of 20 percent, with 2 percent of the credit sales uncollectible. If the firm extends credit to a new class of customers, credit sales will increase by $20,000, other expenses will increase by $300, and uncollectibles will be 3 percent of *all* credit sales. Verify that Hanrahan Company will be $600 better off if it extends credit to the new customers. What percentage of the new credit sales is uncollectible?

30. **Effect of errors involving accounts receivable on financial statement ratios.** Indicate—using O/S (overstated), U/S (understated), or NO (no effect)—the pre-tax effect of each of the following errors on (1) the rate of return on assets, (2) the cash flow from operations to average current liabilities ratio, and (3) the debt equity ratio. Each of these ratios is less than 100 percent before discovering the error.

    a. A firm using the allowance method neglected to provide for estimated uncollectible accounts at the end of the year.

    b. A firm using the allowance method neglected to write off specific accounts as uncollectible at the end of the year.

    c. A firm credited a check received from a customer to Advances from Customers even though the customer was paying for purchases previously made on account.

31. **Income recognition for a nuclear generator manufacturer.** General Electric Company agreed on June 15, Year 2, to construct a nuclear generator for Consolidated Edison Company. The contract price of $200 million is to be paid as follows: at the time of signing, $20 million; on December 31, Year 3, $100 million; and at completion on June 30, Year 4, $80 million. General Electric Company incurred the following costs in constructing the generator: Year 2, $42 million; Year 3, $54 million; and Year 4, $24 million. These amounts conformed to original expectations.

a. Calculate the amount of revenue, expense, and net income for Year 2, Year 3, and Year 4 under each of the following revenue recognition methods:
   (1) Percentage-of-completion method
   (2) Completed contract method
   (3) Installment method
   (4) Cost-recovery-first method
b. Which method do you believe provides the best measure of General Electric Company's performance under the contract? Why?

32. **Income recognition for a contractor.** On March 15, Year 1, Clinton Construction Company contracted to build a shopping center at a contract price of $120 million. The schedule of expected and actual cash collections and contract costs is as follows:

Year	Cash Collections from Customers	Estimated and Actual Cost Incurred
1	$ 24,000,000	$ 20,000,000
2	30,000,000	30,000,000
3	30,000,000	35,000,000
4	36,000,000	15,000,000
	$120,000,000	$100,000,000

a. Calculate the amount of revenue, expense, and net income for each of the four years under the following revenue recognition methods:
   (1) Percentage-of-completion method
   (2) Completed contract method
   (3) Installment method
   (4) Cost-recovery-first method
b. Which method do you believe provides the best measure of Clinton Construction Company's performance under the contract? Why?

33. **Point-of-sale versus installment method of income recognition.** The J. C. Spangle catalog division began business on January 1, Year 8. Activities of the company for the first two years are as follows:

	Year 8	Year 9
Sales, All on Account	$200,000	$300,000
Collections from Customers:		
On Year 8 Sales	90,000	110,000
On Year 9 Sales	—	120,000
Purchase of Merchandise	180,000	240,000
Inventory of Merchandise at 12/31	60,000	114,000
All Expenses Other Than Merchandise, Paid in Cash	32,000	44,000

a. Prepare income statements for Year 8 and Year 9, assuming that the company uses the accrual basis of accounting and recognizes revenue at the time of sale.
b. Prepare income statements for Year 8 and Year 9, assuming that the company uses the accrual basis of accounting and recognizes revenue at the time of cash collection following the installment method of accounting. "All Expenses Other Than Merchandise, Paid in Cash" are period expenses.

34. **Revenue recognition for a franchise.** Pickin Chicken, Inc., and Country Delight, Inc., both sell franchises for their chicken restaurants. The franchisee receives the

right to use the franchisor's products and to benefit from national training and advertising programs. The franchisee agrees to pay $50,000 for exclusive franchise rights in a particular city. Of this amount, the franchisee pays $20,000 on signing the franchise agreement and promises to pay the remainder in five equal annual installments of $6,000 each.

Pickin Chicken, Inc., recognizes franchise revenue as it signs agreements, whereas Country Delight, Inc., recognizes franchise revenue on an installment basis. In Year 2, both companies sold eight franchises. In Year 3, they both sold five franchises. In Year 4, neither company sold a franchise.

a. Calculate the amount of revenue recognized by each company during Year 2, Year 3, Year 4, Year 5, Year 6, Year 7, and Year 8.

b. When do you think a franchiser should recognize franchise revenue? Why?

35. **Income recognition for various types of business.** Most business firms recognize revenues at the time of sale or delivery of goods and services and, following the principles of the accrual basis of accounting, match expenses either with associated revenues or with the period when they consume resources in operations. Users of financial statements should maintain a questioning attitude as to the appropriateness of recognizing revenues at the time of sale and as to the timing of expense recognition. Exhibit 6.7 presents common-size income statements for seven firms for a recent year, with all amounts expressed as a percentage of total revenues. Exhibit 6.7 also indicates the revenues generated by each firm for each dollar of assets in use on average during the year. A brief description of the activities of each firm follows.

Amgen Amgen engages in the development, manufacturing, and marketing of biotechnology products. Developing and obtaining approval of biotechnology products takes 10 or more years. Amgen has two principal products that it manufactures and markets and several more products in the development pipeline.

Brown-Forman Brown-Forman is a distiller of hard liquors. After combining the ingredients, the company ages the liquors for five or more years before sale.

Deere Deere manufactures farm equipment. It sells this equipment to a network of independent distributors, who in turn sell the equipment to final consumers. Deere provides financing and insurance services both to its distributors and to final consumers.

Fluor Fluor engages in construction services on multiyear construction projects. It subcontracts most of the actual construction work and receives a fee for its services.

Golden West Golden West is a savings and loan company. It takes deposits from customers and lends funds, primarily to individuals for home mortgages. Customers typically pay a fee (called "points") at the time of loan origination based on the amount borrowed. Their monthly mortgage payments include interest on the outstanding loan balance and a partial repayment of the principal of the loan.

Merrill Lynch Merrill Lynch engages in the securities business. It obtains funds primarily from short-term capital market sources and invests the funds primarily in short-term, readily marketable financial instruments. It attempts to generate an excess of investment returns over the cost of the funds invested. Merrill Lynch also offers fee-based services, such as financial consulting, buying and selling securities for customers, securities underwriting, and investment management.

Rockwell Rockwell is a technology-based electronics and aerospace company. It engages in research and development on behalf of its customers, which include the U.S. government (space shuttle program, defense electronics) and private-sector entities. Its contracts tend to run for many years on a constantly renewed basis.

EXHIBIT 6.7 | Common-Size Income Statements for Selected Companies (Problem 35)

	Amgen	Brown-Forman	Deere	Fluor	Golden West	Merrill Lynch	Rockwell
Revenues							
Sales of Goods	98.7%	99.9%	83.6%	—	—	—	99.3%
Sales of Services	—	—	—	99.7%	2.0%	47.5%	—
Interest on Investments	1.3	.1	16.4	.3	98.0	52.5	.7
Total Revenues	100.0%	100.0%	100.0%	100.0%	100.0%	100.0%	100.0%
Expenses							
Cost of Goods or Services Sold	(14.3)	(35.5)	(69.4)	(95.6)	—	(43.3)	(77.4)
Selling and Administrative	(23.4)	(33.1)	(11.4)	(.6)	(15.9)	—	(12.6)
Other Operating[a]	(26.4)	(15.4)	(3.5)	—	(3.3)	—	—
Interest	(.7)	(1.3)	(11.0)	(.2)	(60.4)	(47.2)	(.9)
Income before Income Taxes	35.2%	14.7%	4.7%	3.6%	20.4%	9.5%	9.1%
Income Tax Expense	(16.1)	(5.9)	(1.6)	(1.3)	(8.4)	(3.9)	(3.5)
Net Income	19.1%	8.8%	3.1%	2.3%	12.0%	5.6%	5.6%
Revenues/Average Total Assets	.9	1.3	.7	3.1	.1	.1	1.2

[a]Represents research and development costs for Amgen and Deere, excise taxes for Brown-Forman, and a provision for loan losses by Golden West.

a. When should each of these companies recognize revenue? What unique issues does each company face in the recognition of expenses?

b. Suggest possible reasons for differences in the net income to revenues percentages for these companies.

36. **Analyzing Revenue Recognition from Franchising—Franchise Fees, Lease Rentals, Software Sales.** Boston Chicken, Inc., franchises and operates retail food-service stores under the name *Boston Market*. These stores specialize in fresh, convenient meals featuring home-style entrees of chicken, turkey, ham, and meat loaf, as well as a variety of freshly prepared vegetables, salads, and other side dishes. Its product line also includes sandwiches, soups, and holiday home-replacement meals. The total number of stores in the Boston Market system increased from 83 on December 27, Year 12, to 829 on December 31, Year 15. Gross systemwide store revenues increased from $42.7 million during the Year 12 fiscal year to $792.9 million during the Year 15 fiscal year. Franchisees owned and operated all but three of the Boston Market stores open at the end of Year 15. The company retains ownership of three stores to test-market new entrees, assess new operating procedures, and train employees.

Area Developers The company relies on area developers to achieve rapid penetration of targeted markets. Area developers are independently owned companies to which Boston Market grants an exclusive franchise in a particular geographical area to develop and operate Boston Market stores. An experienced retail food-service veteran with substantial invested equity capital heads each firm that is an area developer. The company currently has 22 area developers. There are 829 stores open at the end of Year 15. The area developers have committed to opening an additional 934 stores within the next several years. These area developers have incurred substantial net losses during the recent rapid expansion of stores ($51.3 million in Year 14 and $148.3 million in Year 15), and most have negative net worth. The company believes that the area developers will recover such losses as the rate of expansion moderates by reduction or elimination of development costs, increased operational efficiencies as a result of postexpansion operational focus, greater economies of scale, increased advertising efficiencies, and increased store revenue. The company anticipates that its current area developers will undertake domestic expansion of the Boston Market concept. The Company does not, therefore, seek additional domestic area developers or franchisees.

Development Agreements Development agreements provide for the development of a specified number of stores within a defined geographic territory in accordance with a schedule of dates. The development schedule generally covers two to five years and typically has store operation benchmarks for the number of stores to be open and in operation at six-month intervals. Area developers currently pay a nonrefundable development fee of $5,000 per store to be developed and make a deposit of $5,000 per store to be developed toward the store's initial franchise fee (discussed below). Failure to meet development schedules or other breaches of the area development agreement may lead to termination of the exclusivity provided by the agreement.

Franchise Agreements Once the company and the area developer execute an acceptable lease for an approved store site, they enter into a franchise agreement under which the area developer becomes the franchisee for the specific store to be developed at the site. The company assists the area developer with site selection and construction coordination, for which it receives a real estate fee. Current franchise agreements typically provide for payment of a $35,000-per-store initial franchise fee (less the $5,000 deposit), a 5 percent royalty on gross store revenue, and a $10,000 minimum grand-opening expenditure. In addition, the franchise agreement provides that the company may specify computer software for use in the stores; the franchisee pays an upfront license fee plus an ongoing maintenance fee for this software. Integrated hardware and software permit the company to closely monitor the operations of each store as well as communicate new developments. The company may own a particular store's equipment, for which it receives periodic lease revenue from franchisees.

Area Developer Financing The company believes that the development and operation of stores in a targeted market is enhanced when the area developer does not have to spend time raising capital. Accordingly, the company extends secured debt financing to area developers to partially finance store development and working capital needs in maximum amounts equal to three to four times the area developer's paid-in capital. As of the end of Year 15, the company had agreements to provide secured financing to 17 of its area developers. Such commitments aggregated $621.5 million, of which $471.0 million was outstanding. The company's loan agreement with its area developers generally requires the area developer to expend at least 75 percent of its contributed capital toward developing stores before drawing on its revolving loan. The draw period is approximately two to three years. On expiration of the draw period, the loan converts to an amortizing term loan payable over four to five years in periodic installments, generally with a final balloon payment.[9] The borrower pays interest each period at a rate set at 1 percent over the applicable "reference rate" of the Bank of America Illinois as established from time to time. A pledge of substantially all of the assets of the area developer secures the loan. Some loans have a conversion feature in which the company may convert unpaid amounts of the loan into an equity interest in the area developer. The company can exercise the conversion feature only after a moratorium period has elapsed (generally two years after execution of the loan) or after the area developer defaults on the loan. The conversion price is set at a 12 percent to 15 percent premium over the per-unit equity price paid by the area developer for its equity interest in the area development entity.

Marketing The company markets through television, radio, newspapers, and other print media, direct mail, and in-store point-of-purchase displays. Franchisees pay a national advertising fee of 2 percent of gross store revenues and a local advertising fee of 4 percent of gross store revenues.

Financial Statements and Notes Exhibit 6.8 presents balance sheets, Exhibit 6.9 presents income statements, and Exhibit 6.10 presents statements of cash flows for Boston Chicken, Inc., for the Year 13 through Year 15 fiscal years. Selected notes to these financial statements appear below.

Revenue Recognition Revenue from company-operated stores is recognized in the period for which related food and beverage products are sold. Royalties are recognized in the same period in which related franchise store revenue is generated. Revenue derived from initial franchise fees and area development fees is recognized when the franchise store opens. Interest, real estate services, and software maintenance fees are recognized as earned. Lease income is recognized over the life of the lease on a straight-line basis. Software license income is recognized as the software is placed in service.

Accounts Receivable Accounts receivable includes amounts currently due from area developers and franchisees other than for loans (see discussion of notes receivable, below). The amounts appearing in Exhibit 6.8 are net of an allowance for un-

---

[9]The term *amortizing term loan* means that the borrower makes payments each period for interest and for principal. The principal payments are large enough in this case that the borrower pays off the entire loan in five years or less. The fact that the loan involves a *final balloon payment* means that the last payment is larger, usually much larger, than the preceding payments.

| EXHIBIT 6.8 | BOSTON CHICKEN, INC.
Balance Sheets (amounts in thousands)
(Problem 36) |

	December 27, Year 12	December 26, Year 13	December 25, Year 14	December 31, Year 15
ASSETS				
Cash	$ 9,709	$ 4,537	$ 25,304	$ 310,436
Accounts Receivable (net)	859	5,202	13,002	23,059
Notes Receivable	83	1,512	16,906	5,462
Other Current Assets	364	1,843	4,117	4,858
Total Current Assets	$11,015	$ 13,094	$ 59,329	$ 343,815
Property, Plant, & Equipment (net)	9,934	51,331	163,314	258,550
Notes Receivable—Noncurrent	690	44,204	185,594	450,572
Other Assets	1,031	1,435	18,745	20,940
Total Assets	$22,670	$110,064	$426,982	$1,073,877
LIABILITIES AND SHAREHOLDERS' EQUITY				
Accounts Payable	$ 1,383	$ 6,216	$ 15,188	$ 12,292
Accrued Liabilities	835	1,835	6,587	9,095
Deferred Franchise Revenue	981	2,255	5,505	8,945
Total Current Liabilities	$ 3,199	$ 10,306	$ 27,280	$ 30,332
Long-term Debt	—	—	130,000	307,178
Deferred Franchise Revenue	1,177	3,139	5,815	2,072
Deferred Income Taxes	—	—	3,011	16,631
Other Noncurrent Liabilities	1,257	1,713	1,061	833
Total Liabilities	$ 5,633	$ 15,158	$167,167	$ 357,046
Common Stock	$ 112	$ 347	$ 447	$ 591
Additional Paid-in Capital	27,675	103,662	252,298	675,611
Retained Earnings	(10,750)	(9,103)	7,070	40,629
Total Shareholders' Equity	$17,037	$ 94,906	$259,815	$ 716,831
Total Liabilities and Shareholders' Equity	$22,670	$110,064	$426,982	$1,073,877

collectible accounts of $77,000 on December 27, Year 12, $323,000 on December 26, Year 13, $246,000 on December 25, Year 14, and $1,043,000 on December 31, Year 15. Bad debt expense was $321,000 for Year 13, $187,000 for Year 14, and $797,000 for Year 15.

Notes Receivable Notes receivable include amounts payable by area developers and franchisees under multiyear lending arrangements (see discussion of area developer financing, above). The company maintains an allowance for loan losses at a level that in management's judgment is adequate to provide for estimated possible loan losses. The company bases the amount of the allowance on management's review of each area developer's use of loan proceeds, adherence to its store development schedule, store performance trends, type and amount of collateral securing the loan, prevailing economic conditions, and other factors that management deems

EXHIBIT 6.9	BOSTON CHICKEN, INC. Income Statement (amounts in thousands) (Problem 36)

	Year 13		Year 14		Year 15	
REVENUES						
Royalties	$ 5,464	12.8%	$ 17,421	18.1%	$ 34,841	21.8%
Initial Development & Franchisee Fees	5,230	12.3	13,057	13.6	13,712	8.6
Interest on Area Developer Financing	1,130	2.7	11,632	12.1	33,251	20.9
Real Estate and Lease Services	253	.6	5,361	5.6	17,939	11.3
Software Fees	—	—	6,480	6.7	7,723	4.8
Other	604	1.4	1,284	1.3	447	.3
Total from Developers and Franchisees	$ 12,681	29.8%	$ 55,235	57.4%	$107,913	67.7%
Company-Owned Stores	29,849	70.2	40,916	42.6	51,566	32.3
Total Revenues	$ 42,530	100.0%	$ 96,151	100.0%	$159,479	100.0%
EXPENSES						
Cost of Goods Sold	$(11,287)	(26.5)	$(15,876)	(16.5)	$ (19,737)	(12.4)
Salaries & Benefits	(15,437)	(36.3)	(22,637)	(23.5)	(31,137)	(19.5)
Administrative	(13,879)	(32.6)	(27,930)	(29.1)	(41,367)	(25.9)
Interest	(640)	(1.5)	(5,827)	(6.1)	(15,352)	(9.6)
Income Taxes	—		(4,277)	(4.4)	(20,814)	(13.1)
Provision for Relocation	—		(5,097)	(5.3)	—	—
Other (net)	360	.8	1,666	1.7	2,487	1.5
Net Income	$ 1,647	3.9%	$ 16,173	16.8%	$ 33,559	21.0%

relevant at the time. Based on this review and analysis, no allowance was required at the end of the Year 12, Year 13, Year 14, or Year 15 fiscal year.

National and Local Advertising Funds The company administers a National Advertising Fund, to which company-operated stores and franchisees make contributions based on individual franchise agreements (generally 2 percent of store revenues). Collected amounts are spent primarily on developing marketing and advertising materials for use systemwide. The National Advertising Fund is accounted for separately and is not included in the financial statements of the company. The company also maintains Local Advertising Funds, which provide comprehensive advertising and sales promotion support for the Boston Market stores in particular markets. Periodic contributions by company-owned stores and franchisees (generally 4 percent of store revenues) finance local advertising and promotion expenditures. The Local Advertising Funds are accounted for separately and are not included in the financial statements of the company. Actual expenditures on national and local advertising as of December 31, Year 15, have exceeded the amounts collected from franchisees by $9.6 million. The company includes this excess amount in accounts receivable on its balance sheet.

Related Party Transactions The company and certain area developers have entered into secured loan and area development agreements in which certain directors

	Year 13	Year 14	Year 15
OPERATIONS			
Net Income	$ 1,647	$ 16,173	$ 33,559
Depreciation	1,970	6,074	11,442
Deferred Income Taxes	—	4,277	12,133
Deferred Franchise Revenue	3,236	5,926	(303)
Interest on Zero Coupon Borrowing	—	—	8,075
Loss (Gain) on Sale of Assets	(150)	(368)	231
(Increase) Decrease in Accounts Receivable	(4,343)	(7,800)	(10,057)
(Increase) Decrease in Other Current Assets	(1,479)	(2,274)	(741)
Increase (Decrease) in Accounts Payable	4,833	8,972	(2,896)
Increase (Decrease) in Accrued Liabilities	1,000	4,752	2,508
Other	1,332	186	1,525
Cash Flow from Operations	$ 8,046	$ 35,918	$ 55,476
INVESTING			
Sale of Assets	$ 6,161	$ 62,342	$ 80,910
Purchase of Property, Plant, and Equipment	(49,151)	(163,622)	(145,756)
Issuance of Notes Receivable	(45,690)	(225,282)	(661,033)
Repayment of Notes Receivable	747	68,498	407,499
Acquisition of Other Assets	(1,093)	(12,790)	(9,788)
Cash Flow from Investing	$(89,026)	$(270,854)	$(328,168)
FINANCING			
Borrowing under Credit Facility	$ 32,275	$ 96,130	$ 229,240
Increase in Long-term Debt	9,658	130,000	172,464
Issuance of Common Stock	66,150	125,703	385,360
Repayments under Credit Facility	(32,275)	(96,130)	(229,240)
Cash Flow from Financing	$ 75,808	$ 255,703	$ 557,824
Change in Cash	$ (5,172)	$ 20,767	$ 285,132
Cash—Beginning of Year	9,709	4,537	25,304
Cash—End of Year	$ 4,537	$ 25,304	$ 310,436

EXHIBIT 6.10 BOSTON CHICKEN, INC. Statement of Cash Flows (amounts in thousands) (Problem 36)

and certain current and former officers of the company and members of their families have a direct or indirect equity interest. The company has received from these entities in Year 13, Year 14, and Year 15 approximately $6.6 million, $30.9 million, and $46.0 million, respectively, in development, franchise, royalty, software license, software maintenance, accounting and other miscellaneous fees, rent, and interest on their loans with the company. In addition, these entities have paid approximately $3.5 million, $11.3 million, and $20.0 million in national and local advertising contributions during the same periods. The company has also sold to certain of these entities Boston Market stores, inventory, equipment, and other miscellaneous assets, including reimbursement of the company's general and administrative costs and expenses of operating the stores, for which it received $5.0 million, $47.1 million, and $14.6 million in Year 13, Year 14, and Year 15, respectively. The company believes that the terms of these agreements are as favorable to the company as are those of agreements with other area developers. The company has paid to one of these area developers $146,000 in Year 14 and $100,000 in Year 15 for various services. During Year 13, the company's chief executive officer received from the company $107,066 as reimbursement for payments he made to Bowana Aviation, Inc., for the company's use of an aircraft owned by Bowana. During Year 14 and Year 15, the company paid $527,744 and $661,960, respectively, to Bowana for the use of aircraft. The company's chief executive officer and a relative own Bowana. The company believes that the amounts charged are at rates comparable to those charged by third parties.

Relocation In September Year 14, the company consolidated its four Chicago-based support-center facilities into a single facility and relocated to Golden, Colorado. The cost of the relocation, including moving personnel and facilities, making severance payments, and writing off vacated leasehold improvements, was $5.1 million.

a. Discuss the appropriateness of the timing of revenue recognition by Boston Chicken for each of the following:

   (1) Development franchise fee

   (2) Initial franchise fee

   (3) Royalties

   (4) Interest on loans to area developers

   (5) Real estate service and leasing fees

   (6) Software license and maintenance fees

   (*Hint:* Analyze the changes in the allowance for uncollectible accounts for Year 13, Year 14, and Year 15 to assess the collectibility of outstanding accounts and notes receivable.)

b. Suggest possible reasons why Boston Chicken might choose to develop and operate its stores through nonowned area developers and franchisees instead of through outright ownership.

c. Suggest possible reasons why Boston Chicken might choose to structure its marketing activities using the National Advertising Fund and the Local Advertising Funds.

d. Exhibit 6.11 presents selected operating data and financial statement ratios for Boston Chicken (in addition to the common-size income statement in Exhibit 6.9). Analyze the changes in the profitability and risk of Boston Chicken between Year 13 and Year 15.

EXHIBIT 6.11	BOSTON CHICKEN, INC. Selected Data (Problem 36)		

	Year 13	Year 14	Year 15
Systemwide Revenues of All Boston Market Stores (000's)	$152,056	$383,691	$792,948
Number of Stores in Operation at Year-End:			
Company-Operated	38	41	3
Financed Area Developers	78	314	712
Nonfinanced Area Developers	101	179	114
Total	217	534	829
Profit Margin for ROA	4.9%	20.8%	27.3%
Assets Turnover	.6	.4	.2
Rate of Return on Assets	3.1%	7.4%	5.8%
Leverage Ratio	1.0	1.5	1.5
Rate of Return on Common Shareholders' Equity	2.9%	9.1%	6.9%
Current Ratio	1.3	2.2	11.3
Quick Ratio	.5	2.0	11.2
Cash Flow from Operations/Average Current Liabilities	119.4%	191.1%	192.6%
Liabilities/Assets	13.8%	39.2%	33.2%
Long-term Debt/Assets	—	30.4%	28.0%
Cash Flow from Operations/Average Total Liabilities	77.5%	39.4%	21.2%
Interest Coverage Ratio	3.6	4.5	4.5
Cash Flow from Operations/Capital Expenditures	.2	.2	.4

CHAPTER 7

INVENTORIES: THE SOURCE
OF OPERATING PROFITS

LEARNING OBJECTIVES

1. Apply to inventory items, both purchased and manufactured, the principles of cost inclusions for assets.
2. Learn how to apply the accrual basis of accounting to manufacturing firms, mastering both accrual concepts and recording procedures.
3. Understand the effect—on balance sheet and income statement amounts—of different valuation bases for inventory: acquisition cost, current cost, lower of cost or market.
4. Understand the difference between periodic and perpetual inventory systems for tracing costs and the conditions under which each system provides the better benefit/cost tradeoffs.
5. Understand why most firms either must make, or prefer to make, a cost flow assumption for inventories and cost of goods sold.
6. Develop the skills to compute cost of goods sold and ending inventory using a first-in, first-out (FIFO), a last-in, first-out (LIFO), and a weighted-average cost flow assumption.
7. Understand the effect—on balance sheet and income statement amounts—of using FIFO, LIFO, and weighted-average cost flow assumptions.
8. Develop the skills to convert balance sheet and income statement amounts under a LIFO cost flow assumption to a FIFO cost flow assumption.
9. Develop the skills to calculate operating margins, realized holding gains and losses, and unrealized holding gains and losses for inventory.

In the last 30 years, many major U.S. corporations changed their accounting for inventories and cost of goods sold. As a result, these corporations reported net income that was hundreds of millions of dollars smaller than would have been reported without the change. Paradoxically, perhaps, these firms made themselves better off by changing. This chapter explains how income tax effects can make a firm better off when it reports smaller, rather than larger, net income.

This chapter introduces the choices that a firm must make in accounting for inventories and shows the impact of these decisions on reported expenses and net income for the period. The choices made in accounting for inventories can make two companies that are otherwise alike appear to be different.

Example 1 Wal-Mart Stores reported cost of goods sold of $93,438 million and net income of $3,526 million in a recent year. The ratio of cost of goods sold to net income for Wal-Mart is 26.5 to 1 (= 93,438/$3,526). Assume that Wal-Mart must make inventory choices (discussed in this chapter) that would reduce its cost of goods sold by, say, 2 percent. A 2 percent reduction in cost of goods sold results in a $1,869 (= .02 × $93,438) million decrease in cost of goods sold and a corresponding increase in income before taxes. Assuming an income tax rate of 35 percent, net income would increase by $1,215 [= (1.00 − .35) × $1,869] million to $4,741 (= $3,526 + $1,215) million. A 2 percent decrease in cost of goods sold increases net income by 34.4 percent (= $1,215/$3,526). Thus, a seemingly small change in cost of goods sold can significantly affect net income.

INVENTORY TERMINOLOGY

The term **inventory** means a stock of goods or other items that a firm owns and holds for sale or for further processing as part of ordinary business operations. Tools, for example, are inventory of a tool manufacturer or of a hardware store but not of a carpenter. Marketable securities are inventory of a securities dealer but not of a manufacturer. *Merchandise inventory* denotes goods held for sale by a retail or wholesale business; *finished goods inventory* denotes goods held for sale by a manufacturing concern. The inventories of manufacturing firms also include *raw materials* (materials being stored that will become part of goods to be produced) and work-in-process (partially completed products in the factory). The balance sheet may also include inventories of supplies for use in administrative, selling, and manufacturing operations.

As a verb, to *inventory* a stock of goods means to prepare a list of the items on hand at some specified date, to assign a unit cost to each item, and to calculate the total cost of the goods.

SIGNIFICANCE OF ACCOUNTING FOR INVENTORIES

Accounting for inventories affects income measurement by assigning the acquisition cost of inventories to various accounting periods as expenses. Accountants must allocate the total cost of goods available for sale during a period between the current period's use (cost of goods sold, an expense now) and the amounts carried forward to future periods (end-of-period inventory, an asset now but an expense later).

INVENTORY EQUATION

The **inventory equation** helps one understand accounting for inventory. The following equation measures all quantities in physical units:

Beginning Inventory + Additions − Withdrawals = Ending Inventory

Goods Available for Use or Sale

If we begin a period with 2,000 pounds of sugar (beginning inventory) and purchase (add) 4,500 pounds during the period, then there are 6,500 (= 2,000 + 4,500) pounds available for use or sale. If we use (withdraw) 5,300 pounds during the period, 1,200 pounds of sugar should remain at the end of the period (ending inventory).

The inventory equation can also appear as follows:

$$\underbrace{\text{Beginning Inventory} + \text{Additions}}_{\text{Goods Available for Use or Sale}} - \text{Ending Inventory} = \text{Withdrawals}$$

If we begin the period with 2,000 pounds of sugar, purchase 4,500 pounds during the period, and observe 1,200 pounds on hand at the end of the period, then we know the firm used 5,300 (= 2,000 + 4,500 − 1,200) pounds of sugar during the period. The term *goods available for use or sale* denotes the sum of Beginning Inventory plus Additions. In this example, 6,500 pounds of sugar are available for use.

Financial statements report dollar amounts, not physical units such as pounds or cubic feet. The accountant must transform physical quantities for beginning inventory, additions, withdrawals, and ending inventory into dollar amounts in order to measure income for the period as well as the financial position at the beginning and end of the period. When acquisition costs of inventory items remain constant, inventory accounting problems are minor because all items carry the same per-unit cost; physical quantities and dollar valuations change together. Any variation in the values of inventories results only from changes in quantities. The major problems in inventory accounting arise because the per-unit acquisition costs of inventory items change over time.

Example 2   Suppose that an appliance store has a beginning inventory of one television set, TV set 1, which costs $250. Suppose further that it purchases two TV sets during the period, TV set 2 for $290 and TV set 3 later in the period for $300, and that it sells one TV set for $550. The three TV sets are physically identical; the firm acquired them at different times as costs changed, so only their costs differ.

We can write the inventory equation as follows, measuring all quantities in dollars of cost:

$$\underbrace{\begin{array}{ccc} \text{Beginning} & & \text{Net} \\ \text{Inventory} & + & \text{Purchases} \\ \$250 & + & \$590 \end{array}}_{\substack{\text{Cost of Goods} \\ \text{Available for Sale} \\ = \$840}} - \begin{array}{c} \text{Ending} \\ \text{Inventory} \\ ? \end{array} = \begin{array}{c} \text{Cost of} \\ \text{Goods Sold} \\ ? \end{array}$$

If the firm identifies which TV set it sold and which two TV sets remain on hand at the end of the period, the measurement of cost of goods sold and ending inventory presents no difficulties. The physical similarity of some products, however, creates difficulties in identifying the products sold and the products in ending inventory. Even when technology (such as product bar codes) allows the firm to keep track of every single item in inventory, it may prefer not to incur the costs to do so.

If the firm is to prepare financial statements with amounts measured in dollar terms, it must make some assumption about which TV set it sold. It can make at least four assumptions in applying the inventory equation to compute the Cost of Goods Sold expense for the income statement and the ending inventory for the balance sheet. Exhibit 7.1 shows these four possibilities. As the inventory equation and the TV set example both show, the higher the Cost of Goods Sold, the lower is the Ending Inventory. Which particular pair of numbers appears—one in the income statement and one in the balance

| EXHIBIT 7.1 | Assumptions for Inventory Illustrations |

Assumed Item Sold	Cost of Goods Available for Sale (beginning Inventory plus purchases)[a]	= Cost of Goods Sold (for income statement)	+ Ending Inventory (for balance sheet)
TV Set 1	$840	$250	$590
TV Set 2	840	290	550
TV Set 3	840	300	540
Average TV Set	840	280[b]	560[b]

[a]Cost of goods available for sale = Cost of (TV set 1 + TV set 2 + TV set 3) = ($250 + $290 + $300) = $840.

[b]Average cost of a TV set = $840/3 = $280.

sheet—reflects the cost flow assumption, a major accounting issue discussed later in the chapter.

ISSUES OF INVENTORY ACCOUNTING

The remainder of this chapter discusses five issues of inventory accounting:

1. The costs included in the acquisition cost of purchased inventory
2. The costs included in the acquisition cost of manufactured inventory
3. The cost (or valuation) basis used for items in inventory
4. The frequency of carrying out inventory computations—periodically or perpetually
5. The cost flow assumption used to trace the movement of costs into and out of inventory, an assumption that need not parallel the actual physical movement of the goods

Because income tax laws affect some of a firm's choices in accounting for inventories, this chapter discusses income taxes at appropriate places.

ISSUE 1: COSTS INCLUDED IN PURCHASED INVENTORY

The guiding principle for cost inclusions is that the balance sheet amount for inventory should include all costs incurred to acquire goods and prepare them for sale. For a merchandising firm, such costs should include purchasing, transporting, receiving, unpacking, inspecting, and shelving, as well as any costs for bookkeeping and for recording purchases. The example on page 48 (in Chapter 2), applying this cost-inclusion principle to equipment, applies to inventory as well.

THE PURCHASE TRANSACTION

The purchase transaction includes ordering goods, receiving them, inspecting them, and recording the purchase. Legally, a firm should record **purchases** in the formal accounting records when legal title to the goods passes from seller to buyer. Determining just *when* title passes often involves technicalities in the contract between the purchaser and the seller. Law students can spend months mastering the answers to the question, "When does title pass?" Managers, accountants, and economists can think of the issue as, "When do the risks and rewards of ownership pass to the customer?" or, "If the goods, while uninsured, are destroyed or stolen, who bears the loss?" For convenience, the accountant usually recognizes purchases only after a firm receives the invoice and inspects the goods. The accountant can adjust the amounts at the end of the accounting period to reflect the legal formalities for goods in transit that belong to the purchaser and for goods on hand that still belong to the seller.

MERCHANDISE PURCHASES ADJUSTMENTS

The invoice price of goods purchased seldom measures their total acquisition cost. A firm incurs additional costs in transporting and handling the goods. Cash discounts, returned goods, and other adjustments of the invoice price may require deductions from the invoiced amounts. The accountant could debit or credit all of these adjustments to the Merchandise Inventory account. Frequently, however, the accountant uses a number of adjunct and contra accounts for these adjustments to provide a more complete analysis of the cost of purchases. An adjunct account accumulates additions to another account. A contra account accumulates subtractions from another account. Purchase Discounts, Freight-in, Purchase Returns, and Purchase Allowances accounts provide the needed detail. The accounting for purchase adjustments closely parallels the accounting for sales adjustments discussed in Chapter 6. Throughout this book, we assume that firms include all purchases and purchase adjustments in the Merchandise Inventory account.

The largest adjustment to the invoice price of merchandise is likely to be that for **purchase discounts.** Sellers often offer a discount from the invoice price for prompt payment. For example, the terms of sale "2/10, net/30" mean that the seller offers a 2 percent discount from invoice price if the buyer makes payment within 10 days, with the full invoice price due within 30 days. The annual interest rate implied in these terms of sale is about 45 percent; that is, a purchaser who does not take such a discount borrows money from the seller at an interest rate of about 45 percent per year. Most purchasers find it advantageous to take such discounts and to borrow elsewhere at lower rates.

Although practice varies, we treat purchase discounts as a reduction in the purchase price of inventory items.

ISSUE 2: COSTS INCLUDED IN MANUFACTURED INVENTORY

For a manufacturing firm, inventory costs include direct materials, direct labor, and manufacturing overhead. A manufacturing firm initially debits *all* costs of production to either Raw Material Inventory or Work-in-Process Inventory accounts and later allocates those costs to individual items transferred to the Finished Goods Inventory account. This section illustrates the accumulation of costs and their flow through the inventory accounts, but not the allocation of accumulated costs to individual inventory items, which is a topic of cost accounting. The procedure followed in accumulating inventory costs in the accounts is known as **full absorption costing,** and both external financial reporting and income tax reporting require it. Next, we provide the conceptual basis for full absorption costing and then illustrate it for manufactured inventories.

ACCRUAL BASIS FOR MANUFACTURERS

The discussion in Chapter 3 points out that over sufficiently long time periods, net income equals the amount of cash inflows minus cash outflows other than transactions with owners. Chapter 6 pointed out that most merchandising firms recognize revenue in the period when they sell goods. They then match expenses either directly with the revenue or with the period when the firm consumes goods or services. A manufacturing firm incurs costs in changing the physical form of the goods it produces. Figure 6.1 depicts the operating process for a typical manufacturing firm. See page 307. Such a firm

- acquires productive facilities (plant and equipment) to provide capacity to manufacture goods;
- acquires raw materials for use in production; and
- converts raw materials into a salable product and, in doing so, consumes labor and other manufacturing services (for example, utilities, insurance, taxes, and depreciation on production facilities) during the period of production.

The firm holds the finished product in inventory until it sells the goods. When it sells the goods, the firm either collects cash or obtains a receivable from the customer.

Most manufacturing firms recognize revenue at the time they sell goods. At this time the manufacturing firm has completed the production activity, identified a customer, and agreed on a selling price. An assessment of the customer's credit standing provides a reasonable basis for estimating the present value of the amount of cash the firm will collect. The manufacturing firm matches against this revenue the expense for the manufacturing cost of the items sold.

ACCOUNTING FOR MANUFACTURING COSTS

The accounting for manufacturing costs differs from the accounting for inventory costs by a merchandising firm. As Chapter 3 noted, a merchandising firm acquires inventory items in finished form, ready for sale. The acquisition cost of these items remains in the asset account, Merchandise Inventory, until the firm sells the units. At the time of sale, the firm recognizes revenue and transfers the cost of the items sold from the asset account, Merchandise Inventory, to the expense account, Cost of Goods Sold.

A manufacturing firm, in contrast, incurs three types of costs to convert raw materials into finished products. These costs include direct material (or raw material), direct labor, and manufacturing overhead.

- The manufacturer can trace (or match) **direct material** and **direct labor** costs to the units of product it manufactures.
- **Manufacturing overhead** includes a variety of indirect costs (depreciation, insurance, and taxes on manufacturing facilities, supervisory labor, and supplies for factory equipment) that do not match specific products but provide a firm with productive capacity.

Until the firm sells the units and recognizes revenue, it treats manufacturing costs as **product costs**—which are assets—and accumulates them in various inventory accounts.

A manufacturing firm, like a merchandising firm, also incurs various marketing costs (commissions for the sales staff, depreciation, insurance and taxes on the sales staff's automobiles) and administrative costs (salary of the chief executive officer, depreciation on computer facilities used in administration). Both merchandising and manufacturing firms treat selling and administrative costs as **period expenses.** Figure 7.1 summarizes the nature and **flow of costs** for a manufacturing firm.

A manufacturing firm maintains separate inventory accounts to accumulate the product costs that it incurs at various stages of completion. The **Raw Materials Inventory** account includes (with debits) the cost of raw materials purchased but not yet transferred to production. The balance in the Raw Materials Inventory account indicates the cost of

| FIGURE 7.1 | Diagram of Cost Flows |

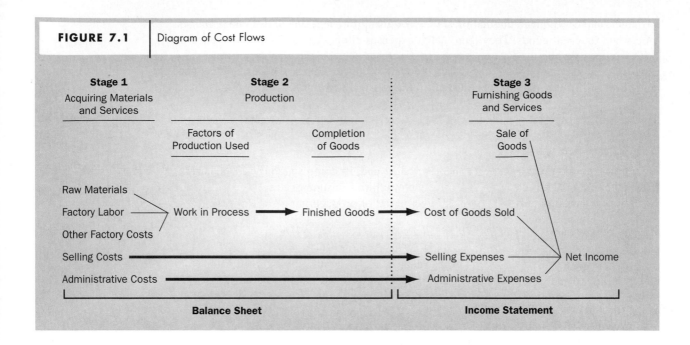

raw materials on hand in the raw materials storeroom or warehouse. When the manufacturer begins to use raw materials in production departments, it transfers the cost of the materials from the Raw Materials Inventory account (with credits) to the Work-in-Process Inventory account (with debits).

The **Work-in-Process Inventory** account accumulates the costs incurred in producing units during the period. The Work-in-Process Inventory account accumulates (with debits) the cost of raw materials transferred from the raw materials storeroom, the cost of direct labor services used, and the manufacturing overhead costs incurred. When the firm completes manufacturing, it transfers the completed units to the finished goods storeroom. It reduces (with credits) the balance in the Work-in-Process account and increases (with debits) the balance in the Finished Goods Inventory account. The balance in the Work-in-Process Inventory account indicates the product costs incurred thus far for units not yet finished as of the date of the balance sheet.

The **Finished Goods Inventory** account includes the total manufacturing cost of units completed but not yet sold. The sale of manufactured goods to customers results in a transfer of their cost from the Finished Goods Inventory account (with credits) to the expense account Cost of Goods Sold (with debits).

Figure 7.2 shows the flow of manufacturing costs through the various inventory and other accounts. Compare the movement of amounts through the accounts in Figure 7.2 with the parallel physical movement of inventory in Figure 7.1.

ILLUSTRATION OF THE ACCOUNTING PROCESS FOR A MANUFACTURING FIRM

This section illustrates the accounting process for a manufacturing firm using information about the operations of Moon Manufacturing Company. The company began operations on January 1 by issuing 10,000 shares of $10-par value common stock for $30 per share. Transactions during January and the appropriate journal entries follow:

(1) The firm acquires a building costing $200,000 and equipment costing $50,000 for cash.

(1) Building (A)	200,000	
Equipment (A)	50,000	
Cash (A)		250,000

(2) The firm purchases raw materials costing $25,000 on account.

(2) Raw Materials Inventory (A)	25,000	
Accounts Payable (L)		25,000

(3) It issues, to producing departments, raw materials costing $20,000.

(3) Work-in-Process Inventory (A)	20,000	
Raw Materials Inventory (A)		20,000

(4) The total payroll for January is $60,000: $40,000 paid to factory workers and $20,000 paid to marketing and administrative personnel.

(4) Work-in-Process Inventory (A)	40,000	
Salaries Expense (SE)	20,000	
Cash (A)		60,000

Recall that a manufacturing firm records nonmanufacturing costs as expenses of the period when the firm consumes the services because these costs rarely create assets with future benefits. Journal entry **(4)**, as well as entries **(5)** and **(6)**, which follow, illustrates the difference between the recording of a product cost and the recording of a period expense. The debits may, on first glance, look similar, but note that the first increases an asset account and the second increases an expense account.

(5) The expenditures for utilities during January are $1,200. Of this amount, $1,000 is for manufacturing and the remaining $200 is for marketing and administrative activities.

(5) Work-in-Process Inventory (A)	1,000	
Utilities Expense (SE)	200	
Cash (A)		1,200

These debits also split the expenditure between asset (product cost) and expense for the period.

(6) Depreciation on building and equipment during January is as follows: factory, $8,000; marketing and administrative, $2,000.

(6) Work-in-Process Inventory (A)	8,000	
Depreciation Expense (SE)	2,000	
Accumulated Depreciation (XA)		10,000

FIGURE 7.2 Flow of Manufacturing Costs through the Accounts

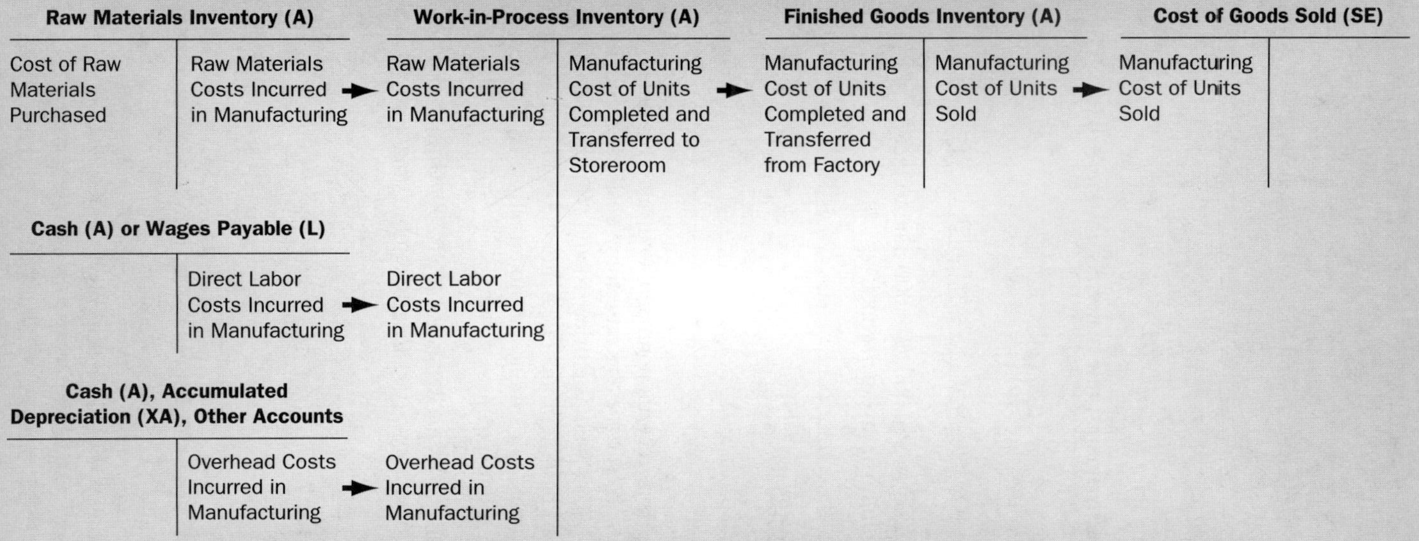

A = Asset; L = Liability; SE = Shareholders' Equity; XA = Contra Asset

Note the split of the depreciation charge between product cost Work-in-Process (asset) and period expense. The credit, to an asset contra account, enables the original cost of the equipment to remain, unreduced, in the accounts.

(7) Units completed during January and transferred to the finished goods storeroom have a manufacturing cost of $48,500.

(7) Finished Goods Inventory (A)	48,500	
Work-in-Process Inventory (A)		48,500

(8) Sales during January total $75,000, of which $25,000 is on account.

(8) Cash (A)	50,000	
Accounts Receivable (A)	25,000	
Sales Revenue (SE)		75,000

(9) The cost of the goods sold during January is $42,600.

(9) Cost of Goods Sold (SE)	42,600	
Finished Goods Inventory (A)		42,600

Exhibit 7.2 shows how the various manufacturing and other costs incurred by Moon Manufacturing Company flow through the accounts. Exhibit 7.3 presents an income statement for the firm for January.

SUMMARY OF THE ACCOUNTING FOR MANUFACTURING OPERATIONS

The accounting procedures for the marketing and administrative costs of manufacturing firms resemble those for merchandising firms. The firm expenses these costs in the same period that it consumes the services. The accounting procedures for a manufacturing firm differ from those for a merchandising firm primarily in the treatment of inventories. A manufacturing firm incurs costs in transforming raw materials into finished products. Until the manufacturing firm sells the units produced, it accumulates manufacturing costs in inventory accounts—the Raw Materials Inventory account, the Work-in-Process Inventory account, or the Finished Goods Inventory account—depending on the stage of completion of each inventory item. The firm therefore debits product costs to inventory (asset) accounts until it sells the units produced.

FULL ABSORPTION COSTING OR VARIABLE COSTING: A MANAGERIAL ACCOUNTING ISSUE

The procedure illustrated above is called *full absorption costing* because the inventory accounts absorb—include—all the costs incurred in manufacturing (that is, the process debits all manufacturing costs to inventory accounts). The conceptual basis for full absorption costing stems from the accountant's belief that an asset's acquisition cost should include all costs necessary to prepare the asset for its intended use. A manufactured good requires raw material, direct labor services to transform the raw materials into a finished good, and manufacturing facilities in which to perform the transformation. Generally accepted accounting principles (GAAP) and income tax laws require firms to use full

EXHIBIT 7.2	MOON MANUFACTURING COMPANY T-Accounts Showing Transactions during January

Raw Materials Inventory (A)

(2)	25,000	20,000	**(3)**
Bal. 1/31	5,000		

Work-in-Process Inventory (A)

(3)	20,000	48,500	**(7)**
(4)	40,000		
(5)	1,000		
(6)	8,000		
Bal. 1/31	20,500		

Finished Goods Inventory (A)

(7)	48,500	42,600	**(9)**
Bal. 1/31	5,900		

Cost of Goods Sold (SE)

(9)	42,600		
Bal. 1/31	42,600		

Cash (A)

Bal. 1/1	300,000	250,000	**(1)**
(8)	50,000	60,000	**(4)**
		1,200	**(5)**
Bal. 1/31	38,800		

Accounts Receivable (A)

(8)	25,000		
Bal. 1/31	25,000		

Building (A)

(1)	200,000		
Bal. 1/31	200,000		

Equipment (A)

(1)	50,000		
Bal. 1/31	50,000		

Accumulated Depreciation (XA)

		10,000	**(6)**
		10,000	**Bal. 1/31**

Salaries Expense (SE)

(4)	20,000		
Bal. 1/31	20,000		

Sales Revenue (SE)

		75,000	**(8)**
		75,000	**Bal. 1/31**

Accounts Payable (L)

		25,000	**(2)**
		25,000	**Bal. 1/31**

Utilities Expense (SE)

(5)	200		
Bal. 1/31	200		

Depreciation Expense (SE)

(6)	2,000		
Bal. 1/31	2,000		

absorption costing for financial and tax reporting. Under full absorption costing, the unit costs of products manufactured tend to vary inversely with the total number of units produced. This results from the fact that the procedure allocates fixed manufacturing costs (those that tend to be relatively unaffected in the short run by the number of units produced, such as depreciation on manufacturing facilities) to the units produced. The larger the number of units produced, the smaller is the per-unit cost. The variations in unit costs

EXHIBIT 7.3	MOON MANUFACTURING COMPANY Income Statement for the Month of January

Sales Revenue		$75,000
Less Expenses:		
Cost of Goods Sold	$42,600	
Salaries Expense	20,000	
Utilities Expense	200	
Depreciation Expense	2,000	
Total Expenses		64,800
Net Income		$10,200

in one period versus another, depending on the number of units produced, can sometimes lead managers to make unwise product and pricing decisions. An alternative procedure, known as **variable (direct) costing,** may provide superior information for internal management purposes. The variable costing procedure classifies product costs into variable manufacturing costs (those that tend to vary with output) and fixed manufacturing costs (those that tend not to vary with output). The procedure treats fixed manufacturing costs in the same way as selling and administrative costs—as expenses assigned to the period of incurrence rather than as costs assigned to the product produced. The procedure charges all fixed manufacturing costs against revenues in calculating net income for the period. The conceptual basis for variable costing is that fixed manufacturing costs are not incremental costs to manufacturing; firms incur these costs each period even if they produce no units. Fixed manufacturing costs under variable costing are period expenses, not product costs. Managerial accounting courses discuss the criticisms of full absorption costing and the suggested benefits of variable costing for internal management uses. We use full absorption costing throughout this book.

PROBLEM 7.1 FOR SELF-STUDY

Flow of manufacturing costs through the accounts. The following data relate to the manufacturing activities of Haskell Corporation during March:

	March 1	March 31
Raw Materials Inventory	$42,400	$ 46,900
Work-in-Process Inventory	75,800	63,200
Finished Goods Inventory	44,200	46,300
Factory Costs Incurred during the Month		
Raw Materials Purchased		$ 60,700
Labor Services Received		137,900
Heat, Light, and Power		1,260
Rent		4,100

(continued)

Expirations of Previous Factory Acquisitions and Prepayments	
Depreciation of Factory Equipment	$ 1,800
Prepaid Insurance Expired	1,440
Other Data Relating to the Month	
Sales	$400,000
Selling and Administrative Expenses	125,000

a. Calculate the cost of raw materials used during March.
b. Calculate the cost of units completed during March and transferred to the finished goods storeroom.
c. Calculate the cost of units sold during March.
d. Calculate income before taxes for March.

ISSUE 3: COST BASIS FOR INVENTORY

The basis for valuing inventory—the rule for assigning a cost to a physical unit—affects both periodic net income and the amount at which inventories appear on the balance sheet. Accounting uses at least five valuation bases for various purposes: acquisition cost, current cost measured by replacement cost, current cost measured by net realizable value, lower of (acquisition) cost or market, and standard cost. GAAP require the use of the lower-of-cost-or-market basis for most purposes. Some of the following discussion reviews fundamentals from Chapter 2.

ACQUISITION COST BASIS

The **acquisition cost basis** values units in inventory at their historical cost until sold. In accounting, the terms *acquisition cost* and *historical cost* mean the same thing. Independent accountants verify acquisition cost amounts by examining purchase invoices, canceled checks, and similar documents underlying the purchase transaction.

Using acquisition costs implies using the **realization convention:** gains (or losses) caused by increases (or decreases) in the market value of assets do not appear in income until a firm sells the particular assets. When a firm uses the acquisition cost basis, any changes in the value of inventory items occurring during the time span between acquisition and sale do not appear in the financial statements until the time of sale. The balance sheet amount for inventory becomes out-of-date to the extent that purchase prices have changed since the firm acquired the items. The longer the period of time since the firm acquired inventory, the more likely the current value of the inventory is to differ from its acquisition cost.

CURRENT COST BASIS

A current cost basis values units in inventory at a current market price. Two current cost bases are (1) current entry value, often called *replacement cost,* and (2) current exit value, often called *net realizable value.*

Replacement Cost (Entry Value)   The **replacement cost** of an item at a given time is the amount a firm would have to pay to acquire the item at that time. In computing replacement cost, one assumes a fair market (or arm's-length) transaction between a willing buyer and a willing seller. One also assumes that the firm purchases inventory in the customary fashion in the customary quantities. Replacement cost envisions normal transactions, not forced purchases of inventory by a frantic buyer from a hoarding seller (which implies a premium price). It assumes purchases of normal quantities, not of abnormally large ones (which often can be bought at a lower-than-normal price) or of abnormally small quantities (which usually cost more per unit to acquire).

Net Realizable Value (Exit Value) **Net realizable value** represents the amount that a firm could realize as a willing seller (not a distressed seller) in an arm's-length transaction with a willing buyer in the ordinary course of business. The measurement of net realizable value can present problems for inventory items not yet ready for sale (for example, partially complete inventory in a manufacturing firm). The firm will incur additional manufacturing costs before it can sell the items. Also, the firm will likely incur a sales commission and other selling costs, such as packaging and freight costs. In these cases, net realizable value is the estimated final selling price of the inventory minus the estimated costs necessary to prepare the items for sale and to sell them. As examples, consider agricultural products and precious metals on hand at the close of an accounting period. A farmer measuring the cost of a bushel of apples harvested from an orchard will likely find estimating its market price less selling costs easier than measuring its historical cost.

When a firm states inventories at current cost, it revalues inventory items at the end of each period to current cost. Assume a particular inventory item has an acquisition cost of $100 and a current cost of $120 at the end of the period. Reporting inventory at current cost requires the accountant to debit inventory for $20 at period-end to recognize the increase in current cost. To keep the balance sheet in balance, the accountant must credit some shareholders' equity account for $20 as well. The firm might treat the $20 increase as an unrealized holding gain reported as part of net income for the period. Alternatively, the firm might include the $20 increase in a separate shareholders' equity account and await the final sale to customers to include the full realized gain in net income.

Contrast acquisition cost for inventory, which shows objective, verifiable information that may be out-of-date, with current cost, which shows up-to-date information that is potentially more useful but requires additional, harder-to-audit measurements. GAAP do not allow a current cost basis for inventories in external financial reports when current cost exceeds acquisition cost. GAAP require current cost valuations when acquisition cost exceeds current cost, as the next section discusses.

LOWER-OF-COST-OR-MARKET BASIS

The **lower-of-cost-or-market basis** is the smaller of the two amounts—acquisition cost or market value, with the latter generally measured as replacement cost. The definition of *market value* in the computation of lower of cost or market is more complex than mere replacement cost; see the glossary definition of *lower of cost or market*. Some accountants use the acronym *LOCOM*.

The accountant can recognize a decline of $5,000 in the market value of inventory with the following entry:

Loss from Decline in Value of Inventory	5,000	
Inventory		5,000

The account debited can appear on the income statement on a separate line. Some firms do not explicitly record the previous entry; instead, they include the unrealized holding loss as part of a higher cost of goods sold. Consider, for example, the calculations in

	Cost Basis	Lower-of-Cost-or-Market Basis

EXHIBIT 7.4 Calculating Cost of Goods Sold Using Different Bases of Inventory Valuation

	Cost Basis	Lower-of-Cost-or-Market Basis
Beginning Inventory	$ 19,000	$ 19,000
Purchases	100,000	100,000
Goods Available for Sale	$119,000	$119,000
Less Ending Inventory	(25,000)	(20,000)
Cost of Goods Sold	$ 94,000	$ 99,000

Exhibit 7.4 of cost of goods sold when beginning inventory is $19,000, purchases are $100,000, and ending inventory has a cost of $25,000 but has a market value of $20,000. Note that cost of goods sold is $5,000 larger when the firm values ending inventory at lower of cost or market than when it uses the acquisition cost basis for ending inventory. The loss of $5,000 does not appear separately, but income will be $5,000 smaller than when the firm uses the acquisition cost basis. To avoid misleading readers of the financial statements, the accountant should disclose in the notes the existence of large write-downs included in cost of goods sold.

The lower-of-cost-or-market basis for inventory valuation is a conservative accounting policy. Conservatism in accounting tends to result in a higher quality of earnings figures (1) because it recognizes losses from decreases in market value before the firm sells goods but it does not record gains from increases in market value before a sale takes place and (2) because inventory figures on the balance sheet are never greater, but may be less, than acquisition cost.[1] In other words, the lower-of-cost-or-market basis results in reporting *unrealized holding losses* on inventory items currently in the financial statements through lower net income amounts but delays reporting *unrealized holding gains* until the firm sells the goods.

Over sufficiently long time spans, however, income equals cash inflows minus cash outflows (other than transactions with owners). For any one unit, there is only one total gain or loss figure: the difference between its selling price and its acquisition cost. The valuation rule determines when this gain or loss appears in the financial statements over the accounting periods between acquisition and final disposition. When a firm uses the lower-of-cost-or-market basis, the net income for the period of an inventory write-down will be lower than if the firm had used the acquisition cost basis, but if so, the net income of a later period, when the firm sells the unit, will be higher.

STANDARD COST

Standard cost is a predetermined estimate of what items of manufactured inventory *should* cost. Studies of past and estimated future cost data provide the basis for standard costs. Manufacturing firms frequently use standard cost systems for internal performance

[1]Consult the glossary for the definition of *conservatism* in accounting. Conservative accounting policies result in both lower asset totals and lower retained earnings totals, thus implying lower cumulative net income totals. Conservatism does not mean reporting lower income in every period. Over long-enough time spans, income will be cash-in less cash-out, other than transactions with owners. If a given accounting policy results in reporting lower income in earlier periods, it must report higher income in some subsequent periods. The conservative accounting policy results in lower income in the *early* periods. See Exercise **28** at the end of this chapter.

measurement and control. Managerial and cost accounting texts discuss these uses and how the accounting system reconciles the *should* of standard costs with the *actual* costs that the firm incurs.

GENERALLY ACCEPTED ACCOUNTING BASIS FOR INVENTORY VALUATION

Accounting uses an acquisition cost basis for most assets. The market value of some inventory items can drop significantly below their acquisition cost, either because purchase prices change for this kind of inventory in general or because the particular items in an inventory deteriorate physically. GAAP require lower of cost or market for inventory, which implies that accounting uses market values when inventory has fallen below cost.[2] Computing market value requires both replacement cost and net realizable value amounts. Thus GAAP for inventory valuation and measurement of cost of goods sold require a combination of three valuation bases: acquisition cost, replacement cost, and net realizable value. In a period of rising prices, replacement cost and net realizable value will likely exceed acquisition cost, so valuations at acquisition cost and at the lower of cost or market are usually the same.

ISSUE 4: TIMING OF COMPUTATIONS

Two principal approaches to calculating the physical quantity and the dollar amount of an inventory are the *periodic* inventory system and the *perpetual* inventory system.

PERIODIC INVENTORY SYSTEM

In a **periodic inventory system,** the ending inventory figure results from the firm's making a physical count of units on hand at the end of an accounting period and multiplying the quantity on hand by the cost per unit. The firm then uses the inventory equation to calculate the withdrawals that represent the cost of goods sold, an expense. (The examples and problems in this book have all used the periodic inventory system until now.) The following form of the inventory equation computes the cost of goods sold under a periodic system:

$$
\underbrace{\begin{matrix} \text{Beginning} \\ \text{Inventory} \\ \text{(known)} \end{matrix} + \begin{matrix} \text{Purchases} \\ \text{(known)} \end{matrix}}_{\begin{matrix}\text{Goods Available} \\ \text{for Use or Sale}\end{matrix}} - \begin{matrix} \text{Ending} \\ \text{Inventory} \\ \text{(counted} \\ \text{and costed)} \end{matrix} = \begin{matrix} \text{Cost of} \\ \text{Goods Sold} \\ \text{(solved for)} \end{matrix}
$$

When a firm uses the periodic system, it makes no entry for withdrawals (cost of goods sold) until it counts and costs the inventory on hand at the end of the accounting period.

---

[2]AICPA, Committee on Accounting Procedure, *Accounting Research Bulletin No. 43,* "Inventory Pricing," 1953: Chapter 4, Statements 5 and 6.

To understand the periodic system, assume that sales during a year amounted to $165,000. The entries made to record sales during the year have the combined effect of the following entry:

Cash and Accounts Receivable	165,000	
Sales		165,000
Sales recorded throughout the year.		

At the end of the year, the firm physically counts and assigns costs to ending inventory. Refer to Exhibit 7.4. Physically counting and assigning costs to ending inventory using a lower-of-cost-or-market basis results in an ending inventory of $20,000. Subtracting this amount from the $119,000 cost of goods available for sale yields cost of goods sold of $99,000. The firm recognizes cost of goods sold in a single entry:

Cost of Goods Sold	99,000	
Merchandise Inventory		99,000
Cost of goods sold recognized under a periodic inventory system.		

A periodic inventory system treats all goods not in the physical ending inventory count as used or sold. Any losses from **shrinkage** (the general name for losses due to breakage, theft, evaporation, and waste) appear in the cost of goods sold amount. A periodic inventory system generates no separate information to aid in controlling losses from shrinkage.

In addition, a periodic inventory system disrupts operations by requiring physical counts of the inventory at the end of the accounting period. Some firms using the periodic inventory system even close down and engage a large staff to physically count the items on hand. Preparing income statements more frequently than once a year is expensive when the inventory figures result only from physically counting the inventories.

PERPETUAL INVENTORY SYSTEM

A **perpetual (continuous) inventory system** calculates and records cost of goods sold whenever a firm takes an item from inventory. A perpetual inventory system requires a constant tracing of costs as items move into and out of inventory. The firm makes such entries as the following from day to day:

Accounts Receivable	800	
Sales		800
Cost of Goods Sold	475	
Merchandise Inventory		475
To record the $475 cost of goods withdrawn from inventory and sold for $800.		

After the accountant completes all postings for a period, updating the inventory accounts for the reductions as in the entry above, the balance in the Merchandise Inventory account shows the cost of the goods that *should* be on hand. The accountant can prepare statements without physically counting the inventory. In a perpetual inventory system, the following form of the inventory equation computes goods *expected* to be remaining in the ending inventory after each acquisition or withdrawal:

$$\underbrace{\underset{\text{(known)}}{\text{Beginning Inventory}} + \underset{\text{(known)}}{\text{Purchases}}}_{\text{Goods Available for Use or Sale}} - \underset{\text{(recorded)}}{\text{Withdrawals}} = \underset{\text{(solved for)}}{\text{Ending Inventory}}$$

Using a perpetual inventory system does not eliminate the need to take a physical inventory in which the firm counts and costs the items of inventory on hand. A physical count and the assignment of costs to remaining items enable measurement of any loss from shrinkage. The loss is the difference between the amounts in the ending Inventory account and the cost of the goods actually on hand. For example, assume that the accounting records show ending inventory of $10,000, whereas the physical count reveals the inventory on hand as costing $9,200. The entry to record the shrinkage is as follows:

Loss from Inventory Shrinkage	800	
Merchandise Inventory		800
To write down ending inventory from book amount of $10,000 to actual amount of $9,200.		

The credit reduces the recorded amount for ending inventory, $10,000, to the correct amount, $9,200. The debit is to a loss account or, if immaterial, to Cost of Goods Sold. In either case, it reduces net income for the current period.

Some firms using a perpetual system make a complete physical count at the end of the accounting period, in the same way as do firms using a periodic inventory system, but other firms use a more effective procedure. Rather than take the inventory of all items at one time, firms may stagger the count throughout the period. For example, a college bookstore may check actual physical amounts of textbooks with the inventory account amounts at the end of the school year, but it might compare actual beachwear with recorded beachwear in November. The firm should count all items at least once during every year but need not count all items at the same time. It should schedule the count of a particular item for a time when it holds a relatively small physical stock of that item.

CHOOSING BETWEEN PERIODIC AND PERPETUAL INVENTORY SYSTEMS

The periodic inventory system costs less to use than the perpetual system because it involves fewer accounting computations, but the perpetual inventory system provides useful information not provided by the periodic system.

A perpetual inventory system helps maintain up-to-date information on quantities actually on hand. When a firm finds that being "out of stock" leads to costly consequences, such as customer dissatisfaction or the need to shut down production lines, it should use the perpetual system. In such cases, a perpetual inventory system might keep track of the physical quantities of inventory but not the dollar amounts. Controlling losses is easier under a perpetual system because inventory records always indicate the goods that should remain. Although a periodic inventory system usually costs less than a perpetual inventory system, the periodic system provides no data on shrinkages.

To make the choice, a firm should compare costs with benefits. A periodic inventory system is likely to be cost-effective when being out of stock is not extremely costly, when there is a large volume of items with a small value per unit, or when items are hard to steal or pilfer. Perpetual inventory systems are cost-effective when there is a small volume of high-value items or when running out of stock is costly.

As the cost of record-keeping with computer-based readers of product bar codes declines, the cost of perpetual inventory systems declines. Their use, therefore, increases over time. For example, nearly all supermarkets now use perpetual inventory systems for their thousands of different items held for sale. Tracing every single item sold would have been prohibitively costly even 10 years ago.

ISSUE 5: COST FLOW ASSUMPTIONS

SPECIFIC IDENTIFICATION AND THE NEED FOR A COST FLOW ASSUMPTION

The inventory costing problem arises because of two unknowns in the inventory equation:

Beginning Inventory (known)	+	Net Purchases (known)	=	Cost of Goods Sold (unknown)	+	Ending Inventory (unknown)

Goods Available for Use or Sale

We know the costs of the beginning inventory and the net purchases, but we do not know either the amount for cost of goods sold or the amount for ending inventory. Do we compute amounts for the units in ending inventory using the most recent costs, the oldest costs, the average cost, or some other choice? Or we could ask how to compute amounts for the cost of goods sold. Once we place an amount on one unknown quantity, the inventory equation automatically determines the amount for the other. The sum of the two unknowns, Cost of Goods Sold and Ending Inventory, must equal the cost of goods available for sale (= Beginning Inventory + Net Purchases). The higher the cost we assign to one unknown, the lower must be the cost we assign to the other.

A firm can sometimes physically match individual units sold with a specific purchase. If so, no special problems arise in ascertaining the acquisition cost of the units withdrawn from inventory and the cost of the units still on hand. For example, cost can appear on the unit or on its container, or the firm can trace the unit back to its purchase invoice or cost record. An automobile dealer or a dealer in diamonds or fur coats might compute the cost of ending inventory and cost of goods sold using **specific identification.** However, the inventory items of some firms are sufficiently similar that the firm cannot feasibly use specific identification costs. Even if a firm finds specific identification feasible, it may choose to make a cost flow assumption to achieve a desired financial or tax reporting result.

When purchase prices change, no acquisition cost-based accounting method for costing ending inventory and cost of goods sold allows the accountant to show up-to-date costs on both the income statement and the balance sheet. For example, consider a period of rising prices. If measurements of cost of goods sold for the income statement use recent, higher acquisition prices, then older, lower acquisition prices must appear in costs of the ending inventory for the balance sheet. As long as accounting bases cost of goods sold and ending inventory on acquisition costs, financial statements can present current cost amounts in the income statement or the balance sheet but not in both.

If a firm has more goods available for sale than it uses or sells, and if it finds specific identification not feasible or desirable, it must make some assumption about the flow of costs. The accountant computes the acquisition cost applicable to the units sold and to the units remaining in inventory using one of the following **cost flow assumptions:**

1. First-in, first out (FIFO)
2. Last-in, first-out (LIFO)
3. Weighted average

The following demonstrations of each of these methods use the TV set example introduced earlier and repeated at the top of Exhibit 7.5. The example of the three TV sets illustrates most of the important points about the cost flow assumption required in accounting for inventories and cost of goods sold.

FIRST-IN, FIRST-OUT

The **first-in, first-out (FIFO)** cost flow assumption assigns the costs of the earliest units acquired to the withdrawals and assigns the costs of the most recent acquisitions to the ending inventory. This cost flow assumes that the firm uses the oldest materials and goods first. This cost flow assumption conforms to good business practice in managing physical flows, especially in the case of items that deteriorate or become obsolete. Column (1) of Exhibit 7.5 illustrates FIFO. FIFO assumes that the firm sells TV set 1 while TV sets 2 and 3 remain in inventory. The designation "FIFO" refers to the cost flow of the units sold. A parallel description for ending inventory is last-in, still-here, or LISH.

EXHIBIT 7.5	Comparison of Cost Flow Assumptions, Historical Cost Basis

Assumed Data

Beginning Inventory: TV Set 1 Cost	....	$250
Purchases:	TV Set 2 Cost	290
	TV Set 3 Cost	300
Cost of Goods Available for Sale	....	$840
Sales: One TV set	....	$550

	Cost Flow Assumption		
	FIFO	**Weighted Average**	**LIFO**
Financial Statements	**(1)**	**(2)**	**(3)**
Sales	$550	$550	$550
Cost of Goods Sold	250[a]	280[b]	300[c]
Gross Margin on Sales	$300	$270	$250
Ending Inventory	$590[d]	$560[e]	$540[f]

[a]TV set 1 costs $250.
[b]Average TV sets costs $280 (= $840/3).
[c]TV set 3 costs $300.
[d]TV sets 2 and 3 cost $290 + $300 = $590.
[e]Two average TV sets cost 2 × $280 = $560.
[f]TV sets 1 and 2 cost $250 + $290 = $540.

LAST-IN, FIRST-OUT

The **last-in, first out (LIFO)** cost flow assumption assigns the costs of the latest units acquired to the withdrawals and assigns the costs of the oldest units to the ending inventory. Some theorists argue that LIFO matches current costs to current revenues and, therefore, that LIFO better measures income. Column (3) of Exhibit 7.5 illustrates LIFO. LIFO assumes that the firm sells TV set 3 costing $300 while the costs of TV sets 1 and 2 remain in inventory. The designation "LIFO" refers to the cost flow for the units sold. A parallel description for ending inventory is first-in, still-here, or FISH.

Firms have increasingly used LIFO since it first became acceptable for income tax reporting in 1939. In a period of consistently rising purchase prices, LIFO results in a higher cost of goods sold, a lower reported periodic income, and lower current income taxes than either the FIFO or the weighted-average cost flow assumption. You might be tempted to conclude, therefore, that LIFO always provides a higher quality of earnings. Such a conclusion is incorrect, however, as we discuss later, in the context of "dips into LIFO layers."

LIFO usually does not reflect physical flows, but firms use it because it produces a cost-of-goods-sold figure based on more up-to-date purchase prices. In a period of rising acquisition costs, LIFO's higher (than FIFO's) cost-of-goods-sold figure reduces reported income and income taxes. A later section discusses income tax factors.

WEIGHTED AVERAGE

Under the **weighted-average** cost flow assumption, the firm calculates the average of the costs of all goods available for sale (or use) during the accounting period, including the cost applicable to the beginning inventory.[3] The weighted-average cost applies to the units sold during the period and to units on hand at the end of the period. Column (2) in Exhibit 7.5 illustrates the weighted-average cost flow assumption. The weighted-average cost of TV sets available for sale during the period is $280 [= 1/3 × ($250 + $290 + $300)]. Cost of Goods Sold is thus $280, and ending inventory is $560 (= 2 × $280).

COMPARISON OF COST FLOW ASSUMPTIONS

Of the three cost flow assumptions, FIFO results in balance sheet figures that are the closest to current cost because the latest purchases dominate the ending inventory amounts. Remember LISH: last-in, still-here. The Cost of Goods Sold expense tends to be out-of-date, however, because FIFO assumes that the earlier purchase prices of the beginning inventory and the earliest purchases during the period become expenses. When purchase prices rise, FIFO usually leads to the highest reported net income of the three methods, and when purchase prices fall, it leads to the smallest.

LIFO ending inventory can contain costs of items acquired many years previously. When purchase prices have been rising and inventory amounts increasing, LIFO produces balance sheet figures usually much lower than current costs. LIFO's cost-of-goods-sold figure closely approximates current costs. Exhibit 7.6 summarizes the differences between FIFO and LIFO. Of the cost flow assumptions (LIFO, FIFO, weighted average), LIFO usually results in the smallest net income when purchase prices are rising (highest

---

[3]This description applies only when the firm uses a periodic inventory system. This book does not illustrate the weighted-average cost flow assumption in a perpetual inventory system.

EXHIBIT 7.6	Age of Information about Inventory Items

Cost Flow Assumption	Income Statement	Balance Sheet	Inventory-on-Hand Assumption
FIFO	Old Purchase Prices	Current Purchase Prices	LISH
LIFO	Current Purchase Prices	VERY[a] Old Purchase Prices	FISH

[a]The oldest purchase prices on the FIFO income statement are just over one year old in nearly all cases, and the average purchase price on the FIFO income statement (for a year) is slightly more than one-half year old. The larger the rate of inventory turnover, the closer the average age on the income statement is to one-half year. LIFO balance sheet items are generally much older than FIFO income statement items, with some costs from the 1940s in many cases.

cost of goods sold) and the largest when purchase prices are falling (lowest cost of goods sold). Also, LIFO results in the least fluctuation in reported income in businesses in which selling prices tend to change as purchase prices of inventory items change.

The weighted-average cost flow assumption falls between the other two in its effects, but it resembles FIFO more than LIFO in its effects on the financial statements. When inventory turns over rapidly, the weighted-average inventory cost flow provides amounts virtually identical to FIFO's amounts. The remaining discussion treats FIFO and weighted average similarly.

Differences in cost of goods sold and inventories under the cost flow assumptions relate in part to the rate of change in the acquisition costs of inventory items. Using older purchase prices for inventories under LIFO or using older purchase prices for cost of goods sold under FIFO has little impact if prices have been stable for several years. As the rate of price change increases, the effect of using older versus more recent prices increases, resulting in larger differences in cost of goods sold and inventories between FIFO and LIFO.

Differences in cost of goods sold also relate in part to the rate of inventory turnover. As the rate of inventory turnover increases, purchases during the period make up an increasing proportion of the cost of goods available for sale. Because purchases are the same regardless of the cost flow assumption, cost of goods sold amounts will not vary as much with the choice of cost flow assumption. Consider the impact of a choice of cost flow assumption for a florist (small effect because of fast turnover) versus that for a distiller of liquor that requires aging (large effect because of slow turnover). Even with a rapid inventory turnover, inventory amounts on the balance sheet can still differ significantly depending on the cost flow assumption. The longer a firm uses LIFO, the larger will be the likely difference between inventories on a FIFO and a LIFO cost flow assumption.

PROBLEM 7.2 FOR SELF-STUDY

Computing cost of goods sold and ending inventory under various cost flow assumptions. Exhibit 7.7 presents data on beginning inventory, purchases, withdrawals, and ending inventory for June and July.

EXHIBIT 7.7	Data for Inventory Calculations (Problem 7.2 for Self-Study)			

		Units	Unit Cost	Total Cost
ITEM X				
Beginning Inventory, June 1		—	—	—
Purchases, June 1		100	$10.00	$1,000
Purchases, June 7		400	11.00	4,400
Purchases, June 18		100	12.50	1,250
Total Goods Available for Sale		600		$6,650
Withdrawals during June		(495)		?
Ending Inventory (June 30) and				
Beginning Inventory (July 1)		105		$?
Purchases, July 5		300	13.00	3,900
Purchases, July 15		200	13.50	2,700
Purchases, July 23		250	14.00	3,500
Total Goods Available for Sale		855		$?
Withdrawals during July		(620)		?
Ending Inventory (July 31)		235		$?

a. Compute the cost of goods sold and the ending inventory for June using (1) FIFO, (2) LIFO, and (3) weighted-average cost flow assumptions.

b. Compute the cost of goods sold and the ending inventory for July using (1) FIFO, (2) LIFO, and (3) weighted-average cost flow assumptions.

A CLOSER LOOK AT LIFO'S EFFECTS ON FINANCIAL STATEMENTS

LIFO usually presents a cost-of-goods-sold figure that reflects current costs. It also generally has the practical advantage of deferring income taxes. If a firm uses a LIFO assumption in its income tax return, it must also use LIFO in its financial reports to shareholders. This "LIFO conformity rule" results from the restrictions placed by the Internal Revenue Service on firms using LIFO for income tax reporting.

In the last 30 years, many firms, including duPont, General Motors, Eastman Kodak, and Sears, have switched from FIFO to LIFO. Given the rapid rate of purchase price increases in the past, the switch from FIFO to LIFO has resulted in substantially lower cash payments for income taxes. For example, when duPont and General Motors switched from FIFO to LIFO, they each lowered current income taxes by about $150 million. At the same time, these firms reported lower net income to shareholders than they would have reported if they had still used FIFO, which explains the apparent paradox in the introduction to this chapter.

LIFO Layers   In any year when purchases exceed sales, the quantity of units in inventory increases. The amount added to inventory for that year is called a **LIFO inventory layer.** For example, assume that a firm acquires 100 TV sets each year and sells 98 TV sets each year for four years. Its inventory at the end of the fourth year contains 8 units. The cost of the 8 units under LIFO is the cost of sets numbered 1 and 2 (from the first year), 101 and 102 (from the second year), 201 and 202 (from the third year), and 301 and 302 (from the fourth year). Common terminology would say that this firm has four LIFO layers, each labeled with its year of acquisition. The physical units on hand would almost certainly be the units most recently acquired in Year 4, units numbered 393 through 400, but they would appear on the balance sheet at costs incurred for purchases during each of the four years.

To take another example, the data in Exhibit 7.8 illustrate four LIFO inventory layers, one for each of the years shown.

Dipping into LIFO Layers   A firm using LIFO must worry about dipping into old LIFO layers. LIFO reduces current taxes in periods of rising purchase prices and rising inventory quantities. If inventory quantities decline, however, the opposite effect occurs in the year of the decline: older, lower costs per unit of prior years' LIFO layers leave the balance sheet and become expenses.

If a firm must for some reason reduce end-of-period physical inventory quantities below the beginning-of-period quantities, cost of goods sold will reflect the current period's purchases plus a portion of the older and lower costs in the beginning inventory. Such a firm will have lower cost of goods sold as well as larger reported income and larger income taxes in that period than if the firm had been able to maintain its ending inventory at beginning-of-period levels. Because firms often control whether inventory quantities increase or decrease through their purchase or production decisions, LIFO affords firms an opportunity to manage their earnings in a particular year. Analysts view firms that dip into LIFO layers to manage their earnings as having a lower quality of earnings than firms that use FIFO.

Example 3   Assume that LIFO inventory at the beginning of Year 5 comprises 460 units with a total cost of $34,200, as in Exhibit 7.8. Assume that the cost at the end of Year 5 is $120 per unit and that the income tax rate is 40 percent. If, for some reason, Year 5 ending inventory drops to 100 units, all 360 units purchased in Years 2 through Year 4 will enter cost of goods sold. These 360 units cost $29,200 (= $6,600 + $9,600 + $13,000), but the current cost of comparable units is $43,200 (= 360 units × $120 per unit). Cost of goods sold will be $14,000 smaller (= $43,200 − $29,200) than if quantities had not declined because the firm dipped into old LIFO layers. Income subject to income taxes will be $14,000 larger than if the firm had purchased inventory so that

EXHIBIT 7.8	Data for Illustration of LIFO Layers (Inventory at January 1, Year 5)			
LIFO Layers			**Cost**	
Year Purchased		Number of Units	Per Unit	Total Cost
1	....	100	$ 50	$ 5,000
2	....	110	60	6,600
3	....	120	80	9,600
4	....	130	100	13,000
		460		$34,200

quantities had not declined from 460 to 100 units. LIFO permits firms to defer taxes as long as they do not dip into LIFO layers.

Annual Report Disclosure   Many firms using LIFO have inventory cost layers built up since the 1940s, and the costs of the early units are often as little as 10 percent of the current cost. For these firms, a dip into old layers will substantially increase income. A footnote from an earlier annual report of USX Corporation (formerly U.S. Steel) illustrates this phenomenon:

> Because of the continuing high demand throughout the year, inventories of many steel-making materials and steel products were unavoidably reduced and could not be replaced during the year. Under the LIFO system of accounting, used for many years by U.S. Steel, the net effect of all the inventory changes [reductions] was to increase income for the year by about $16 million [about 5 percent].

In later years, USX shortened its explanation; for example, in a year when it reported a loss of $36 million, it said:

> Cost of sales has been reduced and income from all operations increased by $621 million . . . from the liquidations of LIFO inventories.

PROBLEM 7.3 FOR SELF-STUDY

Assessing the impact of a LIFO layer liquidation.   Refer to the data in Problem 7.2 for Self-Study. During August the firm purchased 600 units for $15 each and sold 725 units.

a. Compute the cost of goods sold and the ending inventory for August using (1) FIFO, (2) LIFO, and (3) weighted-average cost flow assumptions.
b. Calculate the effect of the LIFO liquidation on net income before income taxes for the year.

LIFO's Effects on Purchasing Behavior   Consider the quandary faced by a purchasing manager of a LIFO firm nearing the end of a year when the quantity sold has exceeded the quantity purchased so far during the year. If the year ends with units sold exceeding units purchased, the firm will dip into old LIFO layers and will have to pay increased taxes. Assume that the purchasing manager thinks current purchase prices for the goods are abnormally high and prefers to delay making purchases until prices drop, presumably in the next year. Waiting implies dipping into old LIFO layers during this period and paying higher taxes. Buying now may entail higher inventory and carrying costs.

Example 4   Refer to the data in Exhibit 7.8. Assume that the cost per unit at the end of Year 5 has risen to $120 per unit and that the inventory on hand at the end of Year 5 is 460 units, with costs as in Exhibit 7.8. The purchasing manager thinks the price will drop back to $105 per unit early in Year 6. An order of 50 new units arrives, which the firm will fill. The firm has two strategies:

1. The purchasing manager can refuse to acquire 50 more units for $120. Then, the 50 units sold will carry costs of $100 each (from the Year 4 layer). Taxable income will be $1,000 larger [= 50 units × ($120 − $100)] than if the firm acquires units at the end of Year 5 for $120 each.

2. The firm can acquire 50 more units for $120. Then, the firm will have paid $750 more [= 50 units × ($120 − $105)] for inventory than if it had waited until the beginning of Year 6 to acquire inventory. In this example, so long as income tax rates are less than 75 percent, the firm will probably prefer the first strategy. If the income tax rate is 40 percent, for example, the cost of the first strategy is $400 (= .40 × $1,000) in extra taxes, whereas the second strategy incurs extra costs of $750 to buy sooner rather than later. In reality, of course, the purchasing manager can seldom be sure about future prices and will have to make estimates for computations such as those above.

LIFO can induce firms to manage LIFO layers and cost of goods sold in a way that would be unwise in the absence of tax effects. LIFO also gives management the opportunity to manipulate income: under LIFO, end-of-year purchases, which the firm can manipulate, affect net income for the year.

LIFO Balance Sheet LIFO usually leads to a balance sheet amount for inventory so much less than current costs that it may mislead readers of financial statements. For example, in recent years various manufacturers of steel products have reported that the cost of their ending inventory based on LIFO is about one-half of what it would have been had FIFO been used. Inventory on the balance sheet, reported assuming LIFO cost flow, makes up about 10 percent of total assets. Using FIFO cost flow, inventory would be about 20 percent of total assets.

Consider the current ratio (= current assets ÷ current liabilities). Financial statement analysts use the current ratio to assess the short-term liquidity of a company. If a firm uses LIFO in periods of rising prices while inventory quantities increase, the amount of inventory included in the numerator will be much smaller than it would be if the firm valued inventory at more current costs using FIFO. Hence, the unwary reader may underestimate the liquidity of a company that uses a LIFO cost flow assumption.

Similarly, the use of LIFO can affect the calculation of inventory turnover (= cost of goods sold ÷ average inventory during the period). The inventory turnover ratio measures how quickly a firm sells its inventory. Again referring to the example of steel companies, the inventory turnover ratio from the financial statements constructed assuming LIFO cost flow is about twice as large as would result under the FIFO cost flow assumption.

P R O B L E M   7 . 4   F O R   S E L F - S T U D Y

Effect of cost flow assumptions on financial ratios. Refer to the data in Problems 7.2 and 7.3 for Self-Study. Assume the following:

	June 30	July 31	August 31
Current Assets Excluding Inventories	$1,650	$3,480	$3,230
Current Liabilities	2,290	4,820	3,750

a. Compute the current ratio for June 30, July 31, and August 31 using (1) FIFO, (2) LIFO, and (3) weighted-average cost flow assumptions for inventories. Assume for this part that there are no differences in income taxes payable related to the three cost flow assumptions.

b. Compute the inventory turnover ratio (= cost of goods sold ÷ average inventory) for July and August using (1) FIFO, (2) LIFO, and (3) weighted-average cost flow assumptions.

THE IMPACT OF FIFO VERSUS LIFO ON FINANCIAL STATEMENTS: AN ILLUSTRATION

No accounting method for inventories based on historical cost can simultaneously report current data in both the income statement and the balance sheet. If a firm reports current costs in the income statement under LIFO, its balance sheet amount for ending inventory contains some *very* old costs. The Securities and Exchange Commission (SEC) has worried that this out-of-date information might mislead the readers of financial statements. As a result, the SEC requires firms using LIFO to disclose, in notes to the financial statements, the amounts at which LIFO inventories would appear if the firm had used FIFO or current cost.

MISLEADING TERMINOLOGY

Some managers refer to the excess of FIFO or current cost over LIFO cost of inventories as the *LIFO reserve*. For reasons discussed in the glossary at the back of the book, the term *reserve* is objectionable because it misleads some readers. Some firms nevertheless continue to use it. A term such as inventory valuation allowance is as descriptive as *LIFO reserve* and is less likely to mislead financial statement readers.

From the SEC-required disclosure and the inventory equation, we can compute what a LIFO firm's income would have been if it had instead used FIFO. The analyst can make the financial statements of firms using LIFO more comparable to the financial statements of firms using FIFO. To understand this concept, consider a note to the financial statements of General Electric Company. It says, in part: "If the FIFO method of inventory accounting had been used to value all inventories, they would have been $2,240 [million] higher than reported at [year-end] and $1,950 [million] higher at [the beginning of the year]."

General Electric's beginning inventories under LIFO amounted to $3,161 million, its ending inventory amounted to $3,343 million, and its cost of goods sold totaled $17,751 million. Exhibit 7.9 demonstrates the calculation of cost of goods sold on a FIFO basis. Recall the inventory equation:

$$\frac{\text{Beginning}}{\text{Inventory}} + \text{Purchases} - \frac{\text{Ending}}{\text{Inventory}} = \frac{\text{Cost of}}{\text{Goods Sold}}$$

FIFO's higher beginning inventory increases the reported cost of goods available for sale and the cost of goods sold by $1,950 million, relative to LIFO. FIFO's higher ending inventory decreases cost of goods sold by $2,240 million, relative to LIFO. Hence, the cost of goods sold is $2,240 million minus $1,950 million, or $290 million, less under FIFO than it would be under LIFO. General Electric's pretax income would be $290 million more under FIFO than under the LIFO flow assumption actually used.

The choice of cost flow assumption can significantly affect financial statements and their interpretation. During periods of substantial price change, no other choice among GAAP affects financial statements for most companies as much as the cost flow assumption for inventory.

EXHIBIT 7.9	Derivation of FIFO Income Data for LIFO Company, Inventory Data from Financial Statements and Footnotes of General Electric Company (all dollar amounts in millions)

(Amounts shown in **boldface** appear in GE's financial statements. We derive other amounts as indicated.)

	LIFO Cost Flow Assumption (actually used)	+	Excess of FIFO over LIFO Amount	=	FIFO Cost Flow Assumption (hypothetical)
Beginning Inventory	**$ 3,161**		**$1,950**		$ 5,111
Purchases	17,933[a]		0		17,933
Cost of Goods Available for Sale	$21,094		**$1,950**		$23,044
Less Ending Inventory	**3,343**		**2,240**		5,583
Cost of Goods Sold	**$17,751**		$ (290)		$17,461
Sales	**$24,959**		0		**$24,959**
Less Cost of Goods Sold	**17,751**		$ (290)		17,461
Gross Margin on Sales	$ 7,208		$ 290		$ 7,498

[a]Computation of Purchases not presented in financial statements:

Purchases = Cost of Goods Sold + Ending Inventory − Beginning Inventory

$17,933 = **$17,751** + **$3,343** − **$3,161**

IDENTIFYING OPERATING MARGIN AND HOLDING GAINS

In general, the reported net income under FIFO exceeds that under LIFO during periods of rising purchase prices. This higher reported net income results from including a larger realized holding gain in reported net income under FIFO than under LIFO. This section illustrates the significance of holding gains in the calculation of net income under FIFO and LIFO.

The conventionally reported gross margin (sales minus cost of goods sold) comprises (1) an operating margin and (2) a realized holding gain (or loss). The term **operating margin** denotes the difference between the selling price of an item and its replacement cost at the time of sale. This operating margin gives some indication of a particular firm's relative advantage, such as a reputation for quality or service, in the market for its goods. The term **realized holding gain** denotes the difference between the current replacement cost of an item at the time of sale and its acquisition cost. It reflects the change in cost of an item during the period the firm holds the inventory item. Holding gains indicate increasing purchase prices and the skill (or luck) of the purchasing department in timing acquisitions.

Holding inventory generates costs. The costs are both explicit, such as for storage, and implicit, such as for the earnings forgone because the firm invests cash to acquire the inventory. Even when a firm experiences holding gains, the amount of the gain need not be sufficient to compensate the firm for its costs to hold inventory. Management should want to know about both the costs of holding inventory and the benefits.

To understand the calculation of the operating margin and the holding gain, consider the TV set example discussed in this chapter. The acquisition cost of the three items available for sale during the period is $840. Assume that the firm sells one TV set for $550. The replacement cost of the TV set at the time of sale is $320. The current replacement cost at the end of the period for each item in ending inventory is $350. The top portion of Exhibit 7.10 separates the conventionally reported gross margin into the operating margin and the realized holding gain.

The operating margin is the difference between the $550 selling price and the $320 replacement cost at the time of sale. The operating margin of $230 is, by definition, the same under both the FIFO and the LIFO cost flow assumptions. The realized holding gain is the difference between cost of goods sold based on replacement cost and cost of goods sold based on acquisition cost. The realized holding gain under FIFO exceeds that under LIFO because FIFO charges the earlier purchases at lower costs to cost of goods sold. The larger realized holding gain explains why net income under FIFO typically exceeds that under LIFO during periods of rising prices. The smaller realized holding gains and losses under LIFO explain why earnings under LIFO tend to fluctuate less over time than under FIFO (except when a firm dips into LIFO layers). In conventional financial statements, the realized holding gain does *not* appear separately, as in Exhibit 7.10. The term **inventory profit** sometimes denotes the realized holding gain on inventory. The amount of inventory profit varies from period to period as the rate of change in the purchase prices of inventories varies. The larger the inventory profit, the less sustainable are earnings and therefore the lower is the quality of earnings.

The calculation of an unrealized holding gain on units in ending inventory also appears in Exhibit 7.10. The **unrealized holding gain** shows the difference between the current

EXHIBIT 7.10	Reporting of Operating Margins and Holding Gains for TV Sets Using the Periodic Inventory Method			

| | | **Cost Flow Assumption** | | |
		FIFO		**LIFO**
Sales Revenue		$550		$550
Less Replacement Cost of Goods Sold		320		320
Operating Margin on Sales			$230		$230
Realized Holding Gain on TV Sets				
Replacement Cost (at time of sale) of Goods Sold		$320		$320
Less Acquisition Cost of Goods Sold (FIFO—TV set 1; LIFO—TV set 3)		250		300
Realized Holding Gain on TV Sets (inventory profit)			70		20
Conventionally Reported Gross Margin[a]			$300		$250
Unrealized Holding Gain				
Replacement Cost of Ending Inventory (2 × $350)		$700		$700
Less Acquisition Cost of Ending Inventory (FIFO—TV sets 2 and 3; LIFO—TV sets 1 and 2)		590		540
Unrealized Holding Gain on TV Sets			110		160
Economic Profit on Sales and Holding Inventory of TV Sets (not reported in financial statements)			$410		$410

[a]Note that Exhibit 7.5 stops here.

replacement cost of the ending inventory and its acquisition cost.[4] This unrealized holding gain on ending inventory does not appear in the firm's income statement as presently prepared under GAAP. The unrealized holding gain under LIFO exceeds that under FIFO because earlier purchases with lower costs remain in ending inventory under LIFO. The sum of the operating margin plus all holding gains (both realized and unrealized), labeled "Economic Profit" in Exhibit 7.10, is the same under FIFO and LIFO. FIFO recognizes most of the holding gain (that is, the realized portion) in computing net income each period. LIFO does not recognize most of the holding gain (that is, the unrealized portion) in the income statement. Instead, under LIFO, the unrealized holding gain remains unreported as long as the older acquisition costs appear on the balance sheet as ending inventory.

The total increase in wealth for a period includes both realized and unrealized holding gains. That total increase, $410 in the example, does not depend on the cost flow assumption and does not appear in financial statements under currently accepted accounting principles.

PROBLEM 7.5 FOR SELF-STUDY

Identifying operating margins and holding gains. Refer to the data in Problem 7.2 for Self-Study. Sales revenue during June was $7,500. The average replacement cost at the time of sale was $12 per unit. The replacement cost on June 30 is $12.60 per unit.

a. Calculate the operating margin, the realized holding gain, and the unrealized holding gain during June using (1) FIFO, (2) LIFO, and (3) weighted-average cost flow assumptions. Refer to Exhibit 7.10 for the desired format for this analysis.

b. "A firm's cost flow assumption does not affect the operating margin." Explain.

c. "The FIFO cost flow assumption typically includes most of the holding gain in net income, whereas the LIFO cost flow assumption implicitly includes more of the holding gain in the balance sheet." Explain.

AN INTERNATIONAL PERSPECTIVE

Statement No. 2 of the International Accounting Standards Committee supports the use of the lower-of-cost-or-market method for the valuation of inventories, with market value based on net realizable values.[5] All major industrialized countries require the lower-of-cost-or-market method in the valuation of inventories, although the definition of *market value* varies across countries. *Statement No. 2* states a preference for the FIFO and

---

[4]The unrealized holding gain for a given year on items on hand both at the beginning and at the end of the year is the difference between year-end current cost and beginning-of-year current cost. The examples in this chapter do not illustrate this complication; all items on hand at the end of the year are purchased during the year. See the glossary definition of *inventory profit* for an illustration of the computation of holding gain for a year in which the beginning inventory includes unrealized holding gains from preceding periods.

[5]International Accounting Standards Committee, *Statement No. 2:* "Inventories," 1993.

weighted-average cost flow assumptions. LIFO is an acceptable alternative, but firms should disclose how LIFO inventories differ from those valued under the lower-of-cost-or-market method. Few countries, except the United States and Japan, allow LIFO. Even in Japan, few firms use LIFO. Firms in most countries use FIFO and weighted-average cost flow assumptions.

SUMMARY

Inventory measurements affect both the cost of goods sold on the income statement for the period and the amount shown for inventory on the balance sheet at the end of the period. The sum of the two must equal the beginning inventory plus the cost of purchases, at least in accounting based on acquisition costs and market transactions. The allocation between expense and asset depends primarily on the valuation basis and the cost flow assumption used.

Common business terminology often inhibits clear thinking about inventory accounting. Business people often use the term *inventory method.* For example, a student may read the terms *absorption costing method, acquisition cost method, perpetual method,* and *LIFO method,* but these are not alternatives to one another. An inventory method results from a combination of choices, one from each of the following:

1. Inclusion: absorption or variable costing, but GAAP do not allow the use of variable costing
2. Basis: acquisition cost, lower of cost or market, current cost, or standard cost, among others, but GAAP do not allow the use of current cost when current cost exceeds acquisition cost
3. Frequency of computations: periodic or perpetual
4. Specific identification or a cost flow assumption: FIFO, LIFO, or weighted average

Most analysts would say that LIFO, coupled with lower of cost or market, provides the highest quality of earnings. Such analysts recognize, however, that LIFO earnings are not high quality during periods of dips into old LIFO layers.

APPENDIX 7.1: EFFECTS ON THE STATEMENT OF CASH FLOWS OF TRANSACTIONS INVOLVING INVENTORY

All transactions involving inventory affect the Operations section of the statement of cash flows. None of the inventory transactions discussed in this chapter require special adjustments in deriving cash flow from operations.

Consider, for example, the adjusting entry to recognize cost of goods sold in a periodic inventory system:

Cost of Goods Sold	12,000	
Inventory		12,000

Although this entry recognizes an expense that does not use cash, it does reduce the net balance in the Inventory account. Reductions in Inventory, like other reductions in current assets, appear in the Operations section of the statement of cash flows as an addition to net income in deriving cash flow from operations. Refer to Exhibit 4.16. The expense reduces income and cash from operations; the reduction in Inventory increases cash from operations. The total leaves cash provided from operations unchanged, which is correct because cash did not change.

Or, consider the entry recognizing the acquisition of inventory on account:

Inventory	140,000	
Accounts Payable		140,000

The current asset for Inventory increases, absorbing cash from operations, but the current liability for Accounts Payable also increases, providing cash from operations. The net effect is that cash provided by operations does not change. Later, when the firm makes payment, the entry is as follows:

Accounts Payable	140,000	
Cash		140,000

The current liability Accounts Payable declines, absorbing cash from operations.

Firms that write down their inventories to reflect a lower-of-cost-or-market valuation debit either the Cost of Goods Sold account or a loss account for the amount of the write-down while crediting the Inventory account. The write-down reduces income but not cash. The Operations section shows the credit to the Inventory account as an addback to net income, so that the loss has no effect on cash flow from operations. The statement of cash flows does not show a specific addback for this loss because the loss resulted from a decline in the valuation of a current asset.

SOLUTIONS TO SELF-STUDY PROBLEMS

SUGGESTED SOLUTION TO PROBLEM 7.1 FOR SELF-STUDY

(Haskell Corporation; flow of manufacturing costs through the accounts.) The transactions and events relating to manufacturing activities appear in the appropriate T-accounts in Exhibit 7.11.
a. The cost of raw materials used is $56,200.
b. The cost of units completed during March is $215,300.
c. The cost of units sold during March is $213,200.
d. Income before taxes is $61,800 (= $400,000 − $213,200 − $125,000).

SUGGESTED SOLUTION TO PROBLEM 7.2 FOR SELF-STUDY

(Computing cost of goods sold and ending inventory under various cost flow assumptions.)
a. See Exhibit 7.12.
b. See Exhibit 7.13.

EXHIBIT 7.11	HASKELL CORPORATION T-Accounts and Transactions (Problem 7.1 for Self-Study)

Raw Materials Inventory

Bal.	42,400		
(1)	60,700	56,200	**(2)**[a]
Bal.	46,900		

Finished Goods Inventory

Bal.	44,200		
(8)	215,300	213,200	**(9)**[a]
Bal.	46,300		

Cash or Various Liabilities

	60,700	**(1)**
	137,900	**(3)**
	1,260	**(4)**
	4,100	**(5)**

Work-in-Process Inventory

Bal.	75,800		
(2)	56,200	215,300	**(8)**[a]
(3)	137,900		
(4)	1,260		
(5)	4,100		
(6)	1,800		
(7)	1,440		
Bal.	63,200		

Cost of Goods Sold

(9)	213,200	

Prepaid Insurance

	1,440	**(7)**

Accumulated Depreciation

	1,800	**(6)**

[a]Amounts calculated by plugging.

EXHIBIT 7.12	(Suggested Solution to Problem 7.2 for Self-Study, part **a**)

	Units	Unit Cost	Total Cost FIFO	Total Cost LIFO	Total Cost Weighted Average
Beginning Inventory	—	—	—	—	
Purchases, June 1	100	$10.00	$1,000	$1,000	$1,000
Purchases, June 7	400	11.00	4,400	4,400	4,400
Purchases, June 18	100	12.50	1,250	1,250	1,250
Total Goods Available for Sale	600		$6,650	$6,650	$6,650
Withdrawals during June	(495)		(5,345)[a]	(5,595)[c]	(5,486)[e]
Ending Inventory	105		$1,305[b]	$1,055[d]	$1,164[f]

[a](100 × $10.00) + (395 × $11.00) = $5,345.
[b](100 × $12.50) + (5 × $11.00) = $1,305.
[c](100 × $12.50) + (395 × $11.00) = $5,595.
[d](100 × $10.00) + (5 × $11.00) = $1,055.
[e]495 × ($6,650/600) = $5,486.
[f]105 × ($6,650/600) = $1,164.

EXHIBIT 7.13	(Suggested Solution to Problem 7.2 for Self-Study, part **b**)

	Units	Unit Cost	Total Cost FIFO	Total Cost LIFO	Total Cost Weighted Average
Beginning Inventory, July 1	105	See Exhibit 7.12	$ 1,305	$ 1,055	$ 1,164
Purchases, July 5	300	$13.00	3,900	3,900	3,900
Purchases, July 15	200	13.50	2,700	2,700	2,700
Purchases, July 23	250	14.00	3,500	3,500	3,500
Total Goods Available for Sale	855		$11,405	$11,155	$11,264
Withdrawals during July	(620)		(8,115)[a]	(8,410)[c]	(8,168)[e]
Ending Inventory	235		$ 3,290[b]	$ 2,745[d]	$ 3,096[f]

[a]$1,305 + (300 × $13.00) + (200 × $13.50) + (15 × $14.00) = $8,115.

[b](235 × $14.00) = $3,290.

[c](250 × $14.00) + (200 × $13.50) + (170 × $13.00) = $8,410.

[d]$1,055 + (130 × $13.00) = $2,745.

[e]620 × ($11,264/855) = $8,168.

[f]235 × ($11,264/855) = $3,096.

SUGGESTED SOLUTION TO PROBLEM 7.3 FOR SELF-STUDY

(Assessing the impact of a LIFO layer liquidation.)
a. See Exhibit 7.14.
b. 125 × ($15 − $13) = $250.

SUGGESTED SOLUTION TO PROBLEM 7.4 FOR SELF-STUDY

(Effect of cost flow assumptions on financial ratios.)

a. JUNE 30	FIFO	LIFO	Weighted Average
($1,650 + $1,305)/$2,290	1.29		
($1,650 + $1,055)/$2,290		1.18	
($1,650 + $1,164)/$2,290			1.23
JULY 31			
($3,480 + $3,290)/$4,820	1.40		
($3,480 + $2,745)/$4,820		1.29	
($3,480 + $3,096)/$4,820			1.36

(continued)

EXHIBIT 7.14	(Suggested Solution to Problem 7.3 for Self-Study, part **a**)

| | | | Total Cost | | |
	Units	Unit Cost	FIFO	LIFO	Weighted Average
Beginning Inventory	235	See Exhibit 7.13	$ 3,290	$ 2,745	$ 3,096
Purchases during August	600	$15	9,000	9,000	9,000
Total Goods Available for Sale	835		$12,290	$11,745	$12,096
Withdrawals during August	(725)		(10,640)[a]	(10,625)[c]	(10,503)[e]
Ending Inventory	110		$ 1,650[b]	$ 1,120[d]	$ 1,593[f]

[a]$3,290 + (490 × $15) = $10,640.
[b](110 × $15) = $1,650.
[c](600 × $15) + (125 × $13) = $10,625.
[d]$1,055 + (5 × $13) = $1,120.
[e]($12,096/835) × 725 = $10,503.
[f]($12,096/835) × 110 = $1,593.

AUGUST 31	FIFO	LIFO	Weighted Average
($3,230 + $1,650)/$3,750	1.30		
($3,230 + $1,120)/$3,750		1.16	
($3,230 + $1,593)/$3,750			1.29
b. JULY			
$8,115/.5($1,305 + $3,290)	3.53		
$8,410/.5($1,055 + $2,745)		4.43	
$8,168/.5($1,164 + $3,096)			3.83
AUGUST			
$10,640/.5($3,290 + $1,650)	4.31		
$10,625/.5($2,745 + $1,120)		5.50	
$10,503/.5($3,096 + $1,593)			4.48

SUGGESTED SOLUTION TO PROBLEM 7.5 FOR SELF-STUDY

(Identifying operating margins and holding gains.)
a. See Exhibit 7.15.
b. The operating margin relates sales to the replacement cost of goods sold. The replacement cost at the time of sale depends on prices for the items at that time (even though the firm purchased no items then) and not on the prices that the firm, earlier, actually paid. In contrast, in historical cost accounting, when the firm makes a cost flow assumption, it matches one of the earlier prices with the sales revenue at the time of sale.
c. The holding gain arises because the replacement costs of inventory items increase while firms hold them. The length of the assumed holding period *for goods sold* under a FIFO cost flow assumption exceeds the assumed holding period under LIFO (unless a firm dips into LIFO layers of earlier years). Thus, FIFO typically reports a larger realized

EXHIBIT 7.15	(Suggested Solution to Problem 7.5 for Self-Study, part **a**)

| | **Cost Flow Assumption** | | |
	FIFO	**LIFO**	**Weighted Average**
OPERATING MARGIN			
Sales Revenue	$7,500	$7,500	$7,500
Less Replacement Cost of Goods Sold (495 × $12)	(5,940)	(5,940)	(5,940)
Operating Margin	$1,560	$1,560	$1,560
REALIZED HOLDING GAIN			
Replacement Cost of Goods Sold	$5,940	$5,940	$5,940
Acquisition Cost of Goods Sold	(5,345)	(5,595)	(5,486)
Realized Holding Gain	$ 595	$ 345	$ 454
Conventionally Reported Gross Margin	$2,155	$1,905	$2,014
UNREALIZED HOLDING GAIN			
Replacement Cost of Ending Inventory (105 × $12.60)	$1,323	$1,323	$1,323
Acquisition Cost of Ending Inventory	(1,305)	(1,055)	(1,164)
Unrealized Holding Gain	$ 18	$ 268	$ 159
Economic Profit	$2,173	$2,173	$2,173

holding gain as part of net income. The length of the assumed holding period *for goods in ending inventory* under a LIFO cost flow assumption exceeds the assumed holding period under FIFO. Thus, LIFO's inventory valuation on the balance sheet reflects a larger unrealized holding gain.

KEY TERMS AND CONCEPTS

Inventory
Inventory equation
Purchases
Purchase discounts
Full absorption costing
Direct material
Direct labor
Manufacturing overhead
Product cost
Period expense
Flow of costs
Raw Materials Inventory
Work-in-Process Inventory
Finished Goods Inventory
Variable (direct) costing
Acquisition cost basis
Realization convention
Replacement cost

Net realizable value
Lower-of-cost-or-market basis
Standard cost
Periodic inventory system
Shrinkages
Perpetual (continuous) inventory system
Specific identification
Cost flow assumption
First-in, first-out (FIFO)
Last-in, first-out (LIFO)
Weighted average
LIFO inventory layer
Inventory valuation allowance
Operating margin
Realized holding gain
Inventory profit
Unrealized holding gain

QUESTIONS, EXERCISES, PROBLEMS, AND CASES

QUESTIONS

1. Review the meaning of the terms and concepts listed above in Key Terms and Concepts.
2. Identify the underlying accounting principle that guides the measurement of the acquisition cost of inventories, equipment, buildings, and other assets. What is the rationale for this accounting principle?
3. "Firms may treat depreciation on equipment either as a product cost or as a period expense, depending on the type of equipment." Explain.
4. Compare and contrast the Merchandise Inventory account of a merchandising firm and the Finished Goods Inventory account of a manufacturing firm.
5. "The total income from an inventory item is the difference between the cash received from selling the item and the cash paid to acquire it. The inventory valuation method (acquisition cost, current cost, lower of cost or market) is therefore largely irrelevant." Do you agree? Why or why not?
6. Assume that a firm changes its cost basis for inventory from acquisition cost to current cost, that current costs exceed acquisition costs at the end of the year of change, and that the firm sells all year-end inventory during the following year. Ignore income tax effects. What will be the impact of the change on net income for the year of change? on income for the following year? on total income over the two years?
7. Explain each of the following statements:
   a. A periodic inventory system provides no information to control shrinkages.
   b. A perpetual inventory system requires elements of a periodic inventory system to be effective.
   c. The choice between a periodic and a perpetual inventory system depends in part on the quantity and the value of individual inventory items.
   d. The choice between a periodic and a perpetual inventory system depends in part on the cost of being "out of stock" of an inventory item.
8. Would you expect to find a periodic or a perpetual inventory system used in each of the following situations?
   a. The greeting card department of a retail store
   b. The fur coat department of a retail store
   c. Supplies storeroom for an automated production line
   d. Automobile dealership
   e. Wholesale dealer in bulk salad oil
   f. Grocery store
   g. College bookstore
   h. Diamond ring department of a jewelry store
   i. Ballpoint pen department of a jewelry store
9. "Inventory computations require cost flow assumptions only because specific identification of items sold is costly. Specific identification is theoretically superior to any cost flow assumption and eliminates the possibility of income manipulation available with some cost flow assumptions." Comment.
10. Assume no changes in physical quantities during the period. During a period of rising purchase prices, will a FIFO or a LIFO cost flow assumption result in the higher ending inventory amount? the lower amount? Which cost flow assumption will result in the higher ending inventory amount during a period of declining purchase prices? the lower inventory amount?

11. **a.** During a period of rising purchase prices, will a FIFO or a LIFO cost flow assumption result in the higher cost of goods sold? the lower cost of goods sold? Assume no changes in physical quantities during the period.

    b. Which cost flow assumption, LIFO or FIFO, will result in the higher cost of goods sold during a period of declining purchase prices? the lower cost of goods sold?

12. "LIFO provides a more meaningful income statement than FIFO, even though it provides a less meaningful balance sheet." Does it ever? Does it always?

13. Explain each of the following statements:

    a. Differences between the effects of FIFO and LIFO on the financial statements increase as the rate of change in the cost of inventory items increases.

    b. Differences between the effects of FIFO and LIFO on cost of goods sold decrease as the rate of inventory turnover increases.

    c. Differences between FIFO and LIFO amounts for inventories on the balance sheet do not decrease as the rate of inventory turnover increases.

14. Assume that a steel manufacturer and a retailing firm have identical sales and income and that the costs of their purchased inputs of goods and services increase at the same rate. The steel company has inventory turnover (= cost of goods sold ÷ average inventory) of about four times per year, whereas the retailer has inventory turnover of about ten times per year. Which of the two firms is likely to benefit more by switching from FIFO to LIFO? Explain.

15. Identify the reasons a firm might dip into an old LIFO layer.

16. "A firm that changes its selling prices when the acquisition costs of its inventory items change will report smoother gross margins over time under LIFO than under FIFO." Explain this statement using the concepts of operating margins and realized holding gains.

17. Suggest reasons a firm would choose a FIFO instead of a LIFO cost flow assumption for financial reporting.

18. "A firm that dips into its LIFO layers and pays additional taxes in a particular year is still better off than if had used FIFO all along." Explain. Under what circumstances will the firm be worse off?

EXERCISES

19. **Identifying inventory cost inclusions.** Trembly Department Store commenced operations on January 2. It engaged in the following transactions during January. Identify the amount that the firm should include in the valuation of merchandise inventory.

    a. Purchases of merchandise on account during January totaled $300,000.

    b. The freight cost to transport merchandise to Trembly's warehouse was $13,800.

    c. The salary of the purchasing manager was $3,000.

    d. Depreciation, taxes, insurance, and utilities for the warehouse totaled $27,300.

    e. The salary of the warehouse manager was $2,200.

    f. The cost of merchandise that Trembly purchased in part **a** and that was returned to the supplier was $18,500.

    g. Cash discounts taken by Trembly from purchases on account in part **a** totaled $4,900.

20. **Identifying product costs and period expenses.** Indicate whether each of the following types of wages and salaries is (1) a product cost or (2) a period expense:

    a. Cutting-machine operators

    b. Delivery labor

    c. Factory janitors

    d. Factory payroll clerks

    e. Factory superintendent

    f. General office secretaries

    g. Guards at a factory gate

    h. Inspectors in a factory

    i. Maintenance workers who service factory machinery

    j. Security guards at the factory

    k. General office clerks

    l. Operator of a lift truck in the shipping room

    m. President of the firm

    n. Sales manager

    o. Raw materials receiving-room workers

    p. Sweepers who clean a retail store

    q. Traveling salespeople

21. **Identifying product costs, period expenses, and assets.** Indicate whether each of the following costs is (1) a period expense, (2) a product cost, or (3) some balance sheet account other than those for product costs:

    a. Office supplies used

    b. Salary of the factory supervisor

    c. Purchase of a fire insurance policy on the store building for the three-year period beginning next month

    d. Expiration of one month's protection of the insurance in part **c**

    e. Property taxes for the current year on the factory building

    f. Wages of truck drivers who deliver finished goods to customers

    g. Wages of factory workers who install a new machine

    h. Wages of mechanics who repair and service factory machines

    i. Salary of the president of the company

    j. Depreciation of office equipment

    k. Factory supplies used

22. **Raw materials inventory transactions.** Transactions related to raw materials inventory for a particular company over a four-year period appear below:

	Year 2	Year 3	Year 4	Year 5
Raw Materials Inventory, Jan. 1	$19,500	?	$28,700	?
Purchases of Raw Materials	87,600	$93,700	?	$98,200
Raw Materials Used	84,300	?	87,600	91,600
Raw Materials Inventory, Dec. 31	?	28,700	36,000	?

    a. Compute the missing items for each year.

    b. Suggest possible reasons for the changes observed in the Raw Materials Inventory account during the four-year period.

23. **Work-in-process inventory transactions.** Transactions related to work-in-process inventory for a particular company over a four-year period appear below:

	Year 4	Year 5	Year 6	Year 7
Work-in-process Inventory, Jan. 1	$ 67,900	?	$ 72,615	?
Raw Materials Used	247,800	$260,190	156,115	?
Direct Labor Costs	242,600	254,730	?	$275,110

(continued)

	Year 4	Year 5	Year 6	Year 7
Manufacturing Overhead Costs	87,100	91,455	87,600	96,100
Cost of Units Completed	575,200	?	426,670	607,340
Work-in-Process Inventory, Dec. 31	?	72,615	42,500	77,000

a. Compute the missing items for each year.
b. Suggest possible reasons for the pattern of changes observed in the Work-in-Process Inventory account over the four-year period.

24. **Finished goods inventory transactions.** Transactions related to finished goods inventory for a particular company over a four-year period appear below:

	Year 6	Year 7	Year 8	Year 9
Finished Goods Inventory, Jan. 1	$ 48,900	?	?	?
Cost of Units Completed	460,700	$515,980	?	$664,690
Cost of Units Sold	455,200	?	$560,800	634,000
Finished Goods Inventory, Dec. 31	?	69,660	91,920	?

a. Compute the missing items for each year.
b. Suggest possible reasons for the pattern of changes observed in the Finished Goods Inventory account over the four-year period.

25. **Income computation for a manufacturing firm.** The following data relate to the Procter & Gamble Company for a single year (amounts in millions):

Sales	$33,434
Cost of Units Completed	19,937
Cost of Units Sold	19,600
Marketing and Administrative Expenses	9,655
Income Tax Rate	35%

Compute net income for the period.

26. **Income computation for a manufacturing firm.** The following data relate to Rockwell International Corporation for a single year (amounts in millions):

	October 1	September 30
Raw Materials Inventory	$492	$473
Work-in-Process Inventory ..	850	920
Finished Goods Inventory ...	330	356

The company incurred manufacturing costs (direct material used, direct labor, and manufacturing overhead) during the year totaling $8,771. Sales revenue was $11,123, marketing and administrative expenses were $1,409, and interest expenses were $100. The income tax rate is 35 percent. Compute net income for the year.

27. **Effect of inventory valuation basis on net income.** Colt Real Estate Development Corporation acquired two parcels of land, Parcel A and Parcel B, for $9,000 each on April 15, Year 6. The firm sold Parcel A on August 20, Year 7, for $24,600 and

Parcel B on March 16, Year 8, for $19,700. The net realizable values of the two parcels on various dates appear below:

	Parcel A	Parcel B
December 31, Year 6	$16,700	$ 8,500
December 31, Year 7		14,400

The firm uses the calendar year as its accounting period.

a. Compute the amount of income from these two parcels of land for Year 6, Year 7, and Year 8, assuming the firm reports land inventory on its balance sheet using (1) acquisition cost, (2) current cost (net realizable value), and (3) lower of cost or market.

b. Compare the income for Year 6, Year 7, and Year 8 and for the three years combined under the three inventory valuation bases.

28. **Over sufficiently long time spans, income is cash-in less cash-out; cost basis for inventory.** Duggan Company began business on January 1, Year 1. Information concerning merchandise inventories, purchases, and sales for the first three years of operations follows:

	Year 1	Year 2	Year 3
Sales	$200,000	$300,000	$400,000
Purchases	210,000	271,000	352,000
Inventories, Dec. 31:			
At cost	60,000	80,000	115,000
At market	50,000	65,000	120,000

a. Compute the gross margin on sales (sales minus cost of goods sold) for each year, using the lower-of-cost-or-market basis in valuing inventories.

b. Compute the gross margin on sales (sales minus cost of goods sold) for each year, using the acquisition cost basis in valuing inventories.

c. Indicate your conclusion about whether the lower-of-cost-or-market basis of valuing inventories is conservative.

29. **When goods available for sale exceed sales, firms can manipulate income even when they use specific identification.** Cypres, a discounter of consumer electronics, has 300 identical computers available for sale during December. It acquired these computers as follows: 100 in June for $300 each, 100 in August for $400 each, and 100 in November for $350 each. Assume that sales for December are 200 units at $600 each.

a. Compute gross margin for December assuming FIFO.

b. Compute gross margin for December assuming specific identification of computers sold to minimize reported income for tax purposes.

c. Compute gross margin for December assuming specific identification of computers sold to maximize reported income for the purpose of increasing the store manager's profit-sharing bonus for the year.

30. **Computations involving different cost flow assumptions.** Harris Company's raw material purchases during September, its first month of operations, were as follows:

	Quantity	Cost per Pound	Total Costs
9/1 Purchased	1,500 pounds	$4.50	$ 6,750
9/5 Purchased	4,000 pounds	4.60	18,400
9/14 Purchased	2,500 pounds	4.90	12,250
9/27 Purchased	3,500 pounds	5.15	18,025
9/29 Purchased	2,000 pounds	5.25	10,500
Total Goods Available for Sale	13,500 pounds		$65,925

The inventory at September 30 was 2,500 pounds. Assume a periodic inventory system. Compute the cost of the inventory on September 30 and the cost of goods sold for September under each of the following cost flow assumptions:

a. FIFO
b. Weighted average
c. LIFO

31. **Computations involving different cost flow assumptions.** Moon Company's raw materials purchases during June, its first month of operations, were as follows:

	Quantity	Cost per Unit	Total Costs
6/1 Purchased	8,600	$3.25	$ 27,950
6/8 Purchased	12,300	3.20	39,360
6/17 Purchased	10,900	3.10	33,790
6/26 Purchased	9,200	3.00	27,600
Totals	41,000		$128,700

The inventory on June 30 was 12,500 units. Assume a periodic inventory system. Compute the cost of the inventory on June 30 and the cost of goods sold for June under each of the following cost flow assumptions:

a. FIFO
b. Weighted average
c. LIFO

32. **Over sufficiently long time spans, income equals cash inflows minus cash outflows; cost flow assumptions.** Benton Company has been in business for four years. Its purchases and sales during that four-year period appear below.

	Purchases		Sales	
	Units	Unit Cost	Units	Unit Price
Year 1	15,000	$20	7,000	$25
Year 2	12,000	22	10,000	28
Year 3	10,000	24	12,000	30
Year 4	7,000	26	15,000	33
Totals	44,000		44,000	

Ignore income taxes.

a. Compute income for each of the four years assuming FIFO cost flow.

  b. Compute income for each of the four years assuming LIFO cost flow.

  c. Compare total income over the four-year period. Does the cost flow assumption matter?

33. **Effect of LIFO on financial statements over several periods.** Barnard Corporation commenced operations on January 2, Year 3. Its purchases and sales for its first five years of operations appear below.

	Purchases		Sales	
	Units	Unit Cost	Units	Unit Price
Year 3	8,000	$4.00	6,000	$5.00
Year 4	11,000	4.40	8,200	5.50
Year 5	12,000	4.75	10,800	5.94
Year 6	15,000	5.32	17,200	6.65
Year 7	20,000	5.85	18,300	7.32

  Barnard Corporation uses a LIFO cost flow assumption. Ignore income taxes.

  a. Compute the ending inventory for each of the five years.

  b. Compute income for each of the five years.

  c. Compute the ratio of income divided by sales for each of the five years.

  d. Interpret the pattern of income-to-sales percentages computed in part **c.**

34. **Reconstructing financial statement data from information on effects of liquidations of LIFO layers.** The inventory footnote to the annual report of Chan Company reads in part as follows:

  > Because of continuing high demand throughout the year, inventories were unavoidably reduced and could not be replaced. Under the LIFO system of accounting, used for many years by Chan Company, the net effect of all the inventory changes was to increase pretax income by $900,000 over what it would have been had inventories been maintained at their physical levels at the start of the year.

  The price of Chan Company's merchandise purchases was $26 per unit during the year, after having risen erratically over past years. Chan Company uses a periodic inventory method. Its inventory positions at the beginning and the end of the year appear below.

Date	Physical Count of Inventory	LIFO Cost of Inventory
January 1	200,000 units	$?
December 31	150,000 units	$600,000

  a. What was the average cost per unit of the 50,000 units removed from the January 1 LIFO inventory?

  b. What was the January 1 LIFO cost of inventory?

35. **LIFO provides opportunity for income manipulation.** EKG Company, a manufacturer of medical supplies, began the year with 10,000 units of product that cost $8 each. During the year, it produced another 60,000 units at a cost of $15 each. Sales for the year were expected to total 70,000 units. During November the company needs to plan production for the remainder of the year. The company might produce no additional units beyond the 60,000 units already produced. On the other hand, the company could

produce up to 100,000 additional units; the cost would be $22 per unit regardless of the quantity produced. The company uses a periodic LIFO inventory. Assume that sales are 70,000 units for the year at an average price of $30 per unit.

a. What production level for the remainder of the year gives the largest cost of goods sold for the year? What is that cost of goods sold?

b. What production level for the remainder of the year gives the smallest cost of goods sold for the year? What is that cost of goods sold?

c. Compare the gross margins implied by the two production plans devised in the preceding parts.

36. **Analysis of annual report; usage of LIFO.** The notes to the financial statements in an annual report of Sears, Roebuck, and Company contained the following statement: "If the physical quantity of goods in inventory at [year-end and the beginning of the year] . . . were to be replaced, the estimated expenditures of funds required would exceed the amounts reported by approximately $670 million and $440 million, respectively." Sears uses LIFO.

a. How much higher or lower would Sears's pretax reported income have been if it had valued inventories at current costs rather than with a LIFO cost flow assumption?

b. Sears reported $606 million net income for the year. Assume tax expense equal to 34 percent of pretax income. By what percentage would Sears's net income have increased if a FIFO flow assumption had been used?

37. **Identifying quantity and price changes.** The financial statements of Boise Cascade Corporation revealed the following for three years (amounts in millions):

	Year 9	Year 10	Year 11
Inventories at Current Costs	$483	$538	$540
Less Excess of Current Costs over LIFO Cost	(59)	(53)	(61)
Inventories at LIFO Cost	$424	$485	$479

a. Did inventory quantities and replacement costs for inventory items increase or decrease during Year 10? Explain.

b. Did inventory quantities and replacement costs for inventory items increase or decrease during Year 11? Explain.

38. **Separating operating margin from holding gains.** On January 1, the merchandise inventory of Giles Computer Store comprised 200 units acquired for $300 each. During the year, the firm acquired 2,500 additional units at an average price of $400 each and sold 2,300 units for $800 each. The replacement cost of these units at the time they were sold averaged $400 during the year. The replacement cost of units on December 31 was $500 per unit.

a. Calculate cost of goods sold under both FIFO and LIFO cost flow assumptions.

b. Prepare partial income statements showing gross margin on sales as revenues less cost of goods sold under both FIFO and LIFO cost flow assumptions.

c. Prepare partial income statements, separating the gross margin on sales into operating margins and realized holding gains, under both FIFO and LIFO.

d. Append to the bottom of the statements prepared in part c a statement showing the amount of unrealized holding gains and the total of realized income plus unrealized holding gains.

e. If you did the previous steps correctly, the totals in part d are the same for both FIFO and LIFO. Is this equality a coincidence? Why or why not?

39. **Effect of inventory errors.** On December 30, Year 1, Warren Company received merchandise costing $1,000 and counted it in the December 31 listing of all items on hand. The firm received an invoice on January 4, Year 2, when it recorded the acquisition as a Year 2 acquisition. It should have recorded the acquisition for Year 1. Assume that the firm never discovered the error. Warren Company uses a periodic inventory system. Indicate the effect (overstatement, understatement, none) on each of the following amounts (ignore income taxes):

   a. Inventory, 12/31/Year 1
   b. Inventory, 12/31/Year 2
   c. Cost of goods sold, Year 1
   d. Cost of goods sold, Year 2
   e. Net income, Year 1
   f. Net income, Year 2
   g. Accounts payable, 12/31/Year 1
   h. Accounts payable, 12/31/Year 2
   i. Retained earnings, 12/31/Year 2

PROBLEMS AND CASES

40. **Preparation of journal entries and income statement for a manufacturing firm.** Soft Touch, Inc., a glove manufacturer, showed the following amounts in its inventory accounts on January 1:

Raw Materials Inventory	$ 20,000
Work-in-Process Inventory	105,000
Finished Goods Inventory	38,000

Soft Touch engaged in the following transactions during January:

(1) Acquired raw materials costing $66,700 on account.
(2) Issued, to producing departments, raw materials costing $63,900.
(3) Paid salaries and wages during January for services received during the month as follows:

Factory Workers	$175,770
Sales Personnel	19,200
Administrative Officers	22,500

(4) Calculated depreciation on buildings and equipment during January as follows:

Manufacturing Facilities	$16,200
Selling Facilities	3,100
Administrative Facilities	2,200

(5) Incurred and paid other operating costs in cash as follows:

Manufacturing	$18,300
Selling	5,600
Administrative	4,100

(6) The cost of goods manufactured and transferred to the finished goods storeroom totaled $270,870.

(7) Sales on account during January totaled $350,000.

(8) A physical inventory taken on January 31 revealed a finished goods inventory of $40,200.

a. Present journal entries to record the transactions and events that occurred during January.

b. Prepare an income statement for Soft Touch, Inc., for January.

41. Preparation of journal entries and an income statement for a manufacturing firm. Famous Horse Garment Factory manufactures jeans for Guess and Jordache in Hong Kong. It showed the following amounts in Hong Kong dollars in its inventory accounts on January 1:

Raw Materials Inventory	$ 80,000
Work-in-Process Inventory	192,000
Finished Goods Inventory	146,000

The firm engaged in the following transactions during January:

(1) Acquired raw materials costing $245,400 on account.

(2) Issued, to production, raw materials costing $238,400.

(3) Paid salaries and wages during January for services received during the month as follows:

Factory Workers	$175,200
Sales Personnel	37,800
Administrative Personnel	54,800

(4) Calculated depreciation on buildings and equipment during January as follows:

Manufacturing Facilities	$29,400
Selling Facilities	4,800
Administrative Facilities	5,800

(5) Incurred and paid other operating costs in cash as follows:

Manufacturing	$36,400
Selling	14,600
Administrative	8,800

(6) The cost of goods completed and transferred to the finished goods storeroom totaled $468,000.

(7) Sales on account during January totaled $650,000.

(8) A physical inventory taken on January 31 revealed a finished goods inventory of $140,000.

a. Present journal entries to record the transactions and events that occurred during January.

b. Prepare an income statement for Famous Horse Garment Factory for January.

42. **Flow of manufacturing costs through the accounts.** The following data relate to the manufacturing activities of Parkhurst Company during July:

	July 1	July 31
Raw Materials Inventory	$53,900	$48,600
Factory Supplies Inventory	8,700	9,200
Work-in-Process Inventory	73,200	74,800
Finished Goods Inventory	49,200	45,700

It incurred factory costs during the month as follows:

Raw Materials Purchased	$397,400
Supplies Purchased	26,100
Labor Services Received	294,900
Heat, Light, and Power	12,200
Insurance	3,600

It experienced expirations of previous factory acquisitions and prepayments as follows:

Depreciation on Factory Equipment	$47,300
Prepaid Rent Expired	4,800

a. Calculate the cost of raw materials and factory supplies used during July.

b. Calculate the cost of units completed during July and transferred to the finished goods storeroom.

c. Calculate the cost of goods sold during July.

43. **Flow of manufacturing costs through the accounts.** The following data relate to the activities of Oak Ridge Industries during April:

	April 1	April 30
Raw Materials Inventory	$25,300	$27,200
Work-in-Process Inventory	78,100	76,900
Finished Goods Inventory	38,400	39,700

It incurred factory costs during the month as follows:

Raw Materials Purchased	$91,300
Labor Services Received	72,400
Heat, Light, and Power	3,100
Depreciation	17,600

Other data relating to the month included the following:

Sales	$250,000
Selling and Administrative Expenses	41,300

a. Calculate the cost of raw materials used during April.

b. Calculate the cost of units completed during April and transferred to the finished goods storcroom.

c. Calculate net income for April.

44. **Preparing T-account entries, income statement, and balance sheet for a manufacturing firm.** Wilmington Chemical Company commenced operations on October 1. The trial balance at that date was as follows:

Cash	$580,800	
Raw Materials Inventory	28,800	
Factory Equipment	204,000	
Accounts Payable		$ 33,600
Capital Stock		780,000
	$813,600	$813,600

The following data relate only to the manufacturing operations of the firm during October:

(1) Purchased materials on account for $242,400.

(2) Received labor services from factory employees totaling $222,000 and paid $168,630 of this amount; see **(5)** below.

(3) Requisitioned and put into process during the month raw materials costing $253,200.

(4) Acquired equipment during the month at a cost of $168,000. The firm made a down payment of $60,000 and signed an equipment contract payable in eight equal monthly installments for the remainder.

(5) Paid the following in cash:

Raw Materials Suppliers	$210,000
Payroll for Labor Services	168,630
Building Rent	9,000
Utilities	4,380
Insurance Premiums (for 1 year from October 1)	14,400
Miscellaneous Factory Costs	39,600
	$446,010

(6) Received invoices for the following (not paid as of October 31):

City Water Department	$ 180
Hoster Machine Supply Company (for additional equipment)	3,600

(7) Computed depreciation on equipment for the month of $1,800.
(8) Recorded one month's insurance expiration.
(9) The cost of parts finished during October was $422,625.
In addition to these manufacturing activities, the following transactions relating to selling and administrative activities occurred during October:
(10) Made sales, on account, totaling $510,900.
(11) Collected cash from customers from sales on account, $495,000.
(12) Selling and office employees earned salaries during the month as follows: sales, $46,200; office $46,800.
(13) Paid the following in cash:

Sales Salaries	$ 41,445
Office Salaries	41,325
Advertising during October	10,800
Rent of Office and Office Equipment for October	3,300
Office Supplies	2,400
Miscellaneous Office Costs	2,100
Miscellaneous Selling Costs	4,200
Total	$105,570

(14) The inventory of office supplies on October 31 was $1,200.
(15) The inventory of finished goods on October 31 was $88,500.
a. Open T-accounts and enter the amounts from the opening trial balance.
b. Record the transactions during the month in the T-accounts, opening additional accounts as needed.
c. Enter closing entries in the T-accounts, using an Income Summary account.
d. Prepare a combined statement of income and retained earnings for the month.
e. Prepare a balance sheet as of October 31.
45. **Detailed comparison of various choices for inventory accounting.** Hartison Corporation commenced retailing operations on January 1, Year 1. It made purchases of merchandise inventory during Year 1 and Year 2 as follows:

	Quantity Purchased	Unit Price	Acquisition Cost
1/10/Year 1	1,200	$10	$12,000
6/30/Year 1	700	12	8,400
10/20/Year 1	400	13	5,200
Total Year 1	2,300		$25,600

(continued)

	Quantity Purchased	Unit Price	Acquisition Cost
2/18/Year 2	600	$15	$ 9,000
7/15/Year 2	1,200	16	19,200
12/15/Year 2	800	18	14,400
Total Year 2	2,600		$42,600

Hartison Corporation sold 1,800 units during Year 1 and 2,800 units during Year 2. The firm uses a periodic inventory system.

a. Calculate the cost of goods sold for Year 1 using a FIFO cost flow assumption.

b. Calculate the cost of goods sold for Year 1 using a LIFO cost flow assumption.

c. Calculate the cost of goods sold for Year 1 using a weighted-average cost flow assumption.

d. Calculate the cost of goods sold for Year 2 using a FIFO cost flow assumption.

e. Calculate the cost of goods sold for Year 2 using a LIFO cost flow assumption.

f. Calculate the cost of goods sold for Year 2 using a weighted-average cost flow assumption.

g. For the two years taken as a whole, will FIFO or LIFO result in reporting the larger net income? What is the difference in net income for the two-year period under FIFO as compared with LIFO? Assume an income tax rate of 40 percent for both years.

h. Which method, LIFO or FIFO, should Hartison Corporation probably prefer and why?

46. **Continuation of preceding problem introducing current cost concepts.** (Do not attempt this problem until you have worked Problem **45.**) Assume the same data for Hartison Corporation as given in the previous problem. In addition, assume the following:

Selling Price per Unit

Year 1	$18
Year 2	24

Average Current Replacement Cost

Year 1	$12
Year 2	16

Current Replacement Cost

December 31, Year 1	$14
December 31, Year 2	18

a. Prepare an analysis for Year 1 that identifies operating margins, realized holding gains and losses, and unrealized holding gains and losses for the FIFO, LIFO, and weighted-average cost flow assumptions.

b. Repeat part **a** for Year 2.

c. Demonstrate that over the two-year period, income plus holding gains before taxes of Hartison Corporation are independent of the cost flow assumption.

47. **Detailed comparison of various choices for inventory accounting.** Burton Corporation commenced retailing operations on January 1, Year 1. Purchases of merchandise inventory during Year 1 and Year 2 appear below:

	Quantity Purchased	Unit Price	Acquisition Cost
1/10/Year 1	600	$10	$ 6,000
6/30/Year 1	200	12	2,400
10/20/Year 1	400	15	6,000
Total Year 1	1,200		$14,400

	Quantity Purchased	Unit Price	Acquisition Cost
2/18/Year 2	500	$14	$ 7,000
7/15/Year 2	500	12	6,000
12/15/Year 2	800	10	8,000
Total Year 2	1,800		$21,000

Burton Corporation sold 1,000 units during Year 1 and 1,500 units during Year 2. It uses a periodic inventory system.

a. Calculate the cost of goods sold for Year 1 using a FIFO cost flow assumption.

b. Calculate the cost of goods sold for Year 1 using a LIFO cost flow assumption.

c. Calculate the cost of goods sold for Year 1 using a weighted-average cost flow assumption.

d. Calculate the cost of goods sold for Year 2 using a FIFO cost flow assumption.

e. Calculate the cost of goods sold for Year 2 using a LIFO cost flow assumption.

f. Calculate the cost of goods sold for Year 2 using a weighted-average cost flow assumption.

g. Will FIFO or LIFO result in reporting the larger net income for Year 1? Explain.

h. Will FIFO or LIFO result in reporting the larger net income for Year 2? Explain.

48. **Continuation of preceding problem introducing current cost concepts.** (Do not attempt this problem until you have worked Problem **47.**) Assume the same data for Burton Corporation as given in the previous problem. In addition, assume the following:

Selling Price per Unit

Year 1	$25
Year 2	22

Average Current Replacement Cost

Year 1	$14
Year 2	12

Current Replacement Cost

December 31, Year 1	$16
December 31, Year 2	10

a. Prepare an analysis for Year 1 that identifies operating margins, realized holding gains and losses, and unrealized holding gains and losses for the FIFO, LIFO, and weighted-average cost flow assumptions.

b. Repeat part **a** for Year 2.

c. Demonstrate that over the two-year period, income plus holding gains before taxes of Burton Corporation are independent of the cost flow assumption.

49. **Effect of FIFO and LIFO on gross margin over several periods.** Whitmore Corporation commenced operations on January 2, Year 5. Its purchases and sales for the first four years appear below:

	Purchases		Sales	
	Units	Unit Cost	Units	Unit Price
Year 5	4,000	$10.00	3,600	$15.00
Year 6	9,000	12.00	8,000	18.00
Year 7	6,000	11.00	5,500	16.50
Year 8	9,000	10.00	10,000	15.00

Ignore income taxes.

a. Compute the gross margin (sales minus cost of goods sold) for each year using a FIFO cost flow assumption.

b. Compute the gross margin for each year using a LIFO cost flow assumption.

c. Compute the percentage change in the gross margin and the percentage change in sales each year (Year 6 relative to Year 5; Year 7 relative to Year 6; Year 8 relative to Year 7) for FIFO and for LIFO.

d. Why are the percentage changes in the gross margin each year less under LIFO than under FIFO?

50. **Dealing with LIFO inventory layers.** (Adapted from a problem by S. A. Zeff.) The Back Store has been using a LIFO cost flow assumption for several decades. On December 31, Year 30, the company's inventory comprised the following layers:

Year 10 Layer	60,000 units at $3.00 =	$180,000
Year 22 Layer	20,000 units at 6.00 =	120,000
Year 30 Layer	10,000 units at 9.00 =	90,000
	90,000 units	$390,000

During Year 30, the company had bought 200,000 units at $9 each. At the end of the year, the replacement cost of units was $8. During Year 31, the company bought 250,000 units at $10 per unit, which was the average costs of units for the entire year. The company sold 300,000 units at $15 each during Year 31. At the end of the year, the replacement cost of units was $11.

a. How many units did the company sell during Year 30?

b. What was the operating margin on sales, that is, the replacement cost gross margin, for Year 31?

c. What was the gross margin conventionally reported for Year 30 assuming LIFO?

d. What was the economic profit, that is, realized margin plus all holding gains, for Year 31?

e. If the company had used FIFO for both Year 30 and Year 31, what would have been the conventionally reported gross margin for Year 31?

51. **Reconstructing underlying events from ending inventory amounts.** (Adapted from CPA examination.) Burch Corporation began a merchandising business on January 1, Year 1. It acquired merchandise costing $100,000 in Year 1, $125,000 in Year 2, and $135,000 in Year 3. Information about Burch Corporation's inventory as it would appear on the balance sheet under different inventory methods appears below:

December 31	LIFO Cost	FIFO Cost	Lower of FIFO Cost or Market
Year 1	$40,200	$40,000	$37,000
Year 2	36,400	36,000	34,000
Year 3	41,800	44,000	44,000

In answering each of the following questions, indicate how you deduced the answer. You may assume that in any one year, prices moved only up or down but not both.
a. Did prices go up or down in Year 1?
b. Did prices go up or down in Year 3?
c. Which inventory method would show the highest income for Year 1?
d. Which inventory method would show the highest income for Year 2?
e. Which inventory method would show the highest income for Year 3?
f. Which inventory method would show the lowest income for all three years considered as a single period?
g. For Year 3, how much higher or lower would income be on the FIFO cost basis than on the lower-of-cost-or-market basis?

52. **LIFO layers influence purchasing behavior and provide opportunity for income manipulation.** Wilson Company sells chemical compounds made from expensium. The company has used a LIFO inventory flow assumption for many years. The inventory of expensium on December 31, Year 10, comprised 4,000 pounds from Year 1 through Year 10 at prices ranging from $30 to $52 per pound. Exhibit 7.16 shows the layers of Year 10 ending inventory.

Expensium costs $62 per pound during Year 11, but the purchasing agent expects its price to fall back to $52 per pound in Year 12. Sales for Year 11 require 7,000 pounds of expensium. Wilson Company wants to carry a stock of 4,000 pounds of

EXHIBIT 7.16	WILSON COMPANY Layers of Year 10 Year-End Inventory (Problem 52)

		Year 10 Year-End Inventory	
Year Acquired	Purchase Price per Pound	Pounds	Cost
Year 1	$30	2,000	$ 60,000
Year 6	46	200	9,200
Year 7	48	400	19,200
Year 10	52	1,400	72,800
		4,000	$161,200

inventory. The purchasing agent suggests that the firm decrease the inventory of expensium from 4,000 to 600 pounds by the end of Year 11 and replenish it to the desired level of 4,000 pounds early in Year 12.

The controller argues that such a policy would be foolish. If the firm allows inventories to decrease to 600 pounds, the cost of goods sold will be extraordinarily low (because Wilson will consume older LIFO layers) and income taxes will be extraordinarily high. The controller suggests that the firm plan Year 11 purchases to maintain an end-of-year inventory of 4,000 pounds.

Assume that sales for Year 11 do require 7,000 pounds of expensium, that the prices for Year 11 and Year 12 are as forecast, and that the income tax rate for Wilson Company is 40 percent.

a. Calculate the cost of goods sold and the end-of-year LIFO inventory for Year 11, assuming that the firm follows the controller's advice and that inventory at the end of Year 11 is 4,000 pounds.

b. Calculate the cost of goods sold and the end-of-year LIFO inventory for Year 11, assuming that the firm follows the purchasing agent's advice and that inventory at the end of Year 11 is 600 pounds.

c. Assume the firm follows the controller's, not the purchasing agent's, advice. Calculate the tax savings for Year 11 and the extra cash costs for inventory.

d. What should Wilson Company do?

e. Management of Wilson Company wants to know what discretion it has to vary income for Year 11 by planning its purchases of expensium. If the firm follows the controller's policy, aftertax income for Year 11 will be $50,000. What is the range, after taxes, of income that the firm can achieve by the purposeful management of expensium purchases?

53. **Interpreting disclosures relating to LIFO inventories.** A note to the financial statements of Deere & Company reveals the following:

> Substantially all inventories owned by Deere & Company and its United States subsidiaries are valued at cost on the "last-in, first-out" (LIFO) method.
>
> During the fourth quarter, Deere & Company's inventories declined due to a lower level of production. As a result, lower costs which prevailed in prior years were matched against current year's revenues, the effect of which was to increase net income by $20.8 million or 28 cents per share.
>
> If all the company's inventories had been valued on a current cost basis, which approximates FIFO, inventories at year-end were estimated to be $1,885 million compared with approximately $1,941 million at the beginning of the year.

The balance sheet reported inventories of $760.9 million at the end of the year and $872.0 million at the beginning of the year. Assume an income tax rate of 34 percent for the current year and all prior years.

a. The second paragraph refers to inventory declines caused by lower production levels. By how much did the costs of the older inventories "matched against current year's revenues" differ from current costs? Give the amount and indicate whether it was larger or smaller.

b. How much did the dip into old LIFO layers, referred to in the second paragraph, cost Deere in extra income tax payments?

c. How much did Deere save in income taxes for the current year by using LIFO instead of FIFO? (*Note:* Deere would have saved even more if it had not dipped into old LIFO layers.)

d. How much has Deere reduced its income taxes payable since it adopted LIFO?

54. Comparing gross margins using FIFO and LIFO cost flow assumptions. Sankyo, a leading pharmaceutical company in Japan, uses a weighted-average cost flow assumption for inventories. Eli Lilly, a leading pharmaceutical company in the United States, uses a LIFO cost flow assumption. Selected data for the same year from the financial statements of the two firms appear below (in millions of yen or dollars):

	Sankyo	Eli Lilly
Beginning Inventories	¥ 79,186	$ 938.4
Ending Inventories	86,347	1,103.0
Sales	516,750	6,452.4
Cost of Goods Sold	260,225	1,959.0
Excess of FIFO over LIFO:		
Beginning Inventories	—	88.9
Ending Inventories	—	110.7

a. Compute the gross margin percentage (= gross margin ÷ sales) for each firm based on its reported amounts.

b. Compute the gross margin percentage for Eli Lilly assuming that it had used a FIFO cost flow assumption.

c. How does the cost flow assumption affect your conclusions regarding the relative profitability of these two firms for the current year?

d. Compute the inventory turnover ratio for each firm based on its reported amounts.

e. Compute the inventory turnover ratio for Eli Lilly assuming that it had used a FIFO cost flow assumption.

f. How does the cost flow assumption affect your conclusions regarding the inventory turnovers of these two firms for the current year?

55. Analysis of disclosures from published financial reports on effects of changing from average cost to LIFO. Various disclosures from the annual reports of E. I. duPont de Nemours & Company in the year it switched from average cost to LIFO for most of its inventories, as well as in the two following years, appear below. Assume an income tax rate of 34 percent.

Year 1 During the year, duPont changed its cost flow assumption for most of its inventories from average cost to LIFO to achieve a better matching of current costs with revenues. Net income declined by $249.6 million, 27 percent, for the year.

Year 2 During the year, the firm reduced inventory quantities from the abnormally high levels at the start of the year. This resulted in liquidation of LIFO inventory quantities carried at costs lower than those prevailing during the year. Net income increased by approximately $40.4 million.

Year 3 If the firm had valued inventory at current cost, rather than at historical cost using a LIFO cost flow assumption, the amounts on the balance sheet would have exceeded the amounts reported by $490 million at the end of the year and by $410 million at the beginning of the year.

a. By how much did LIFO cost of goods sold in Year 1 differ from the amount computed with an average-cost cost flow assumption?

b. Why does a liquidation of LIFO layers, such as in Year 2, increase net income?

c. By how much did cost of goods sold for Year 2 differ from the amount that would have been reported had the layers not been liquidated? Give the amount and indicate whether this represents an increase or a decrease in cost of goods sold.

    d. Why might the company not have reverted to average cost for Year 2?

    e. Assume that an average-cost cost flow assumption gives ending inventory amounts that are approximately the same as current costs. Compute the Year 3 tax savings that resulted from duPont's using LIFO rather than average cost.

    f. Why might duPont choose an inventory cost flow assumption that reduces reported income?

56. **Assessing the effect of LIFO versus FIFO on the financial statements.** Exhibit 7.17 summarizes data taken from the financial statements and notes for Bethlehem Steel Company for three years (in millions):

    a. Compute the amount of cost of goods sold for Year 9, Year 10, and Year 11, assuming that Bethlehem Steel Company had used a FIFO instead of a LIFO cost flow assumption.

    b. Compute the cost of goods sold divided by sales percentages for Year 9, Year 10, and Year 11, using both LIFO and FIFO cost flow assumptions.

    c. Refer to part **b.** Explain the rank-ordering of the cost of goods sold percentages for each year—that is, why does the LIFO percentage exceed the FIFO percentage or vice versa? (*Hint:* attempt to ascertain the direction of the change in inventory quantities and manufacturing costs each year.)

    d. Compute the inventory turnover ratios (cost of goods sold divided by average inventories) for Year 9, Year 10, and Year 11, using both a LIFO and a FIFO cost flow assumption.

    e. Which inventory turnover ratio in part **d** more accurately measures the actual inventory turnover rate? Explain your reasoning.

    f. Compute the current ratio (current assets divided by current liabilities) at the end of each year using both LIFO and FIFO cost flow assumptions. Assume that the extra income taxes paid if the firm had used FIFO result in a reduction in cash.

EXHIBIT 7.17	BETHLEHEM STEEL COMPANY Financial Data (Problem 56)

	For the Year Ended December 31		
	Year 9	**Year 10**	**Year 11**
Sales	$5,250.9	$4,899.2	$4,317.9
Cost of Goods Sold (LIFO)	$4,399.1	$4,327.2	$4,059.7
Net Income (Loss)	$ 245.7	$ (463.5)	$ (767.0)
Income Tax Rate	34%	34%	34%

	December 31			
	Year 8	**Year 9**	**Year 10**	**Year 11**
Inventories at FIFO Cost	$ 899.1	$ 972.8	$ 967.4	$958.3
Excess of FIFO Cost over LIFO Values	(530.1)	(562.5)	(499.1)	(504.9)
Inventories at LIFO Cost	$ 369.0	$ 410.3	$ 468.3	$453.4
Current Assets (LIFO)	$1,439.8	$1,435.2	$1,203.2	$957.8
Current Liabilities	$ 870.1	$ 838.0	$ 831.4	$931.0

(*Hint:* the adjustment for income taxes must reflect the *cumulative* income tax effect between the date that Bethlehem Steel Company adopted LIFO and each year-end, not just the additional taxes payable each year.)

g. Assess the short-term liquidity risk of Bethlehem Steel Company to the extent permitted by the information presented in this problem.

57. **Analysis of financial statement ratios affected by cost flow assumptions.** An annual report of General Motors Corporation contained the following in the section "Financial Review: Management's Discussion and Analysis." (Dates have been changed for convenience.)

General Motors' liquidity can be measured by its current ratio (ratio of current assets to current liabilities). For the years ended December 31, Year 2 and Year 1, the current ratio, based on LIFO inventories, was 1.13 and 1.09, respectively. The LIFO method, while improving Corporate cash flow, adversely affects the current ratio. . . . If inventories were valued at FIFO, the current ratio would be 1.21 and 1.18, at the ends of Year 2 and Year 1, respectively.

Assume an income tax rate of 34 percent. Also assume that current assets were $14,043 million and $13,714 million at the end of Year 2 and Year 1, respectively.

a. Compute the difference between FIFO and LIFO inventories at the ends of Year 2 and Year 1.

b. How did the use of LIFO affect cash flow for Year 2?

c. By how much has the use of LIFO improved cash flow since the time it was adopted?

58. **Calculating operating margins and realized holding gains.** British Petroleum Company (BP) uses a FIFO cost flow assumption. Data from BP's financial statements for four years appear below (in million of British pounds).

	Year 8	Year 9	Year 10	Year 11
Sales	£ 25,922	£ 29,641	£ 33,039	£ 32,613
Cost of Goods Sold Based on:				
Acquisition Cost	19,562	21,705	24,178	25,746
Current Replacement Cost	19,330	22,095	24,655	25,117

a. Compute the amount of the operating margin, the realized holding gain, and the gross margin for each of the four years.

b. Compute the operating margin to sales percentage and the gross margin to sales percentage for each of the four years.

c. Why might BP voluntarily disclose information about the current replacement cost of goods sold?

59. **Interpreting inventory disclosures.** Olin Corporation is a diversified chemicals, metals, and aerospace company. Its annual report discloses inventories under LIFO of $320 million at the beginning of the year and $329 at the end of the year and cost of goods sold of $2,161 for the year. If the firm had used a FIFO cost flow assumption, its beginning inventory would have been $501 million and its ending inventory would have been $474 million. Sales for the year totaled $2,423 million.

a. Compute the amount for cost of goods sold for the year assuming Olin Corporation had used a FIFO instead of a LIFO cost flow assumption.

b. Did the quantities of items in inventory increase or decrease during the year? Explain.

    c. Did the cost of items in inventory increase or decrease during the year? Explain.

    d. Compute the inventory turnover ratio for Olin Corporation under both LIFO and FIFO for the year.

    e. Why does the inventory turnover ratio under LIFO exceed that under FIFO?

    f. "The choice of inventory cost flow assumption affects the inventory turnover ratio but should not normally affect the accounts payable turnover ratio." Explain.

CHAPTER 8

PLANT, EQUIPMENT, AND INTANGIBLE ASSETS: THE SOURCE OF OPERATING CAPACITY

1. Understand and apply the concepts distinguishing expenditures that accountants capitalize as assets, and subsequently amortize, from expenditures that accountants expense in the period incurred.
2. Understand depreciation as a process of cost allocation, not one of valuation.
3. Develop the skills to compute depreciation under various commonly used depreciation methods.
4. Develop the skills to re-compute depreciation for changes in estimates of depreciable lives and salvage values.
5. Develop the skills to compute an impairment loss on plant, equipment, and intangible assets.
6. Develop the skills to record the retirement of assets at various selling prices.
7. Understand the capitalization/amortization process for intangible assets and related issues of earnings quality.

Assets are future benefits, short-lived or long-lived. A business acquires a short-lived asset, such as insurance coverage, in one period and uses up its benefits within a year. To reap the benefits of a long-lived asset, the owner uses it for several years. In this case, the accountant allocates the cost of the asset over the several accounting periods of benefit. The term **amortization** denotes this general process. Depreciation refers to amortization of **plant assets,** which include the fixtures, machinery, equipment, and physical structures of a business.

In addition to plant assets, companies such as Exxon and Santa Fe Industries own natural resources, called *wasting assets*. Firms eventually use up oil wells, coal mines, uranium deposits, and other natural resources. The term *depletion* denotes the amortization of the cost of these wasting assets.

Businesses may also acquire intangible assets. Several well-known examples are Coca-Cola, Kleenex, and Xerox, all famous trademarks. A firm may purchase a McDonald's or KFC (Kentucky Fried Chicken) franchise. Other intangible assets are goodwill, copyrights, and patents. Although such intangibles may have indefinite economic lives, the accountant generally amortizes their costs over the periods of benefit. There is no specific name for the amortization of intangibles; the general name *amortization* refers to the process of writing off the cost of all intangibles.

Most of this chapter discusses depreciation because plant assets are the most common long-lived assets and because depreciation problems illustrate almost all other amortization problems.

TERMINOLOGY NOTE

Business practice often uses the terms *plant assets* and *fixed assets* interchangeably. They both refer to long-lived assets used in the operations of trading, service, and manufacturing enterprises and include land, buildings, machinery, and equipment. The ordinary usage of the terms *plant assets* and *fixed assets* often does not adequately encompass the class of long-lived assets that includes all land, buildings, machinery, and equipment. *Plant assets* means more than items in a factory or plant. *Fixed assets* means more than immovable items such as land and buildings. Sometimes, business terminology refers to costs associated with plant assets as *fixed costs*, which does not means "fixed" in the sense of "nonvariable." Many costs associated with plant assets, repairs for example, vary with usage of the plant assets.

The problems of plant asset valuation and depreciation measurement conveniently divide into the consideration of four separate events:

1. Recording the acquisition of the asset
2. Recording its use over time
3. Recording adjustments for changes in capacity or efficiency and for repairs or improvements
4. Recording the asset's retirement or other disposal

ACQUISITION OF PLANT ASSETS

The cost of a plant asset includes all charges necessary to prepare it for rendering services. The cost of a piece of equipment will be the sum of the entries to recognize the invoice price (less any discounts), transportation costs, installation charges, and any other costs incurred before the equipment is ready for use. See the example on page 48. Also consider the following, more complex, example.

Example 1   A firm incurs the following costs in searching for and acquiring a new property:

1. Purchase price of land with an existing building, $1,000,000
2. Fees paid to lawyer in handling purchase contracts, $10,000
3. Transfer taxes paid to local real estate taxing authorities, $2,000
4. Salaries earned by management personnel during the search for the site and the negotiation of its purchase, $8,000
5. Operating expenditures for company automobiles used during the search, $75
6. Depreciation charges for company automobiles used during the search, $65
7. Fees paid to consulting engineer for a report on the structural soundness of the building, its current value, and the estimated cost of making needed repairs, $15,000

8. Uninsured costs to repair automobiles damaged in a multivehicle accident during the search, $3,000
9. Profits lost on sales the company failed to make because management was distracted from serving a potential new customer during the search, $20,000

The first six cost items relate to the search for, and acquisition of, the land and building. The firm should accumulate these items in a temporary Land and Building account. Some firms would treat items **5** and **6** as expenses of the period because of their immaterial amount, but strict application of accounting theory suggests capitalization of these costs as an asset. After completing the acquisition of the land and building, the firm should allocate the accumulated costs of $1,020,140 (= $1,000,000 + $10,000 + $2,000 + $8,000 + $75 + $65) between these two assets. (Accounting requires such division of costs, or allocation, because the firm will depreciate the building but not the land.) The allocation uses the relative market values of the land and building. For example, if the engineer in item **7** estimates the current value of the existing building to be $250,000, then the firm might allocate 25 percent (= $250,000/$1,000,000) of the combined costs of $1,020,140 to the building and 75 percent to the land.

Item **7** relates to the building only, so the accountant includes the cost of the engineer's report in the cost of the building.

Accountants would not agree on the treatment of item **8**, repair costs for the accident. Some would think it part of the cost of the site, to be allocated to the land and the building. Others would report it as an expense of the period. Probably all practicing accountants would classify it as expense for financial reporting so that the firm could bolster its argument for calling it a current tax deduction in computing taxable income.

Item **9**, forgone profits, does not result from an expenditure. The firm did not incur this cost in an arm's-length transaction with outsiders. Historical cost accounting would not record this cost, sometimes called an *opportunity cost,* in any account.

SELF-CONSTRUCTED ASSET

When a firm constructs its own buildings or equipment, it will record many entries in these asset accounts for the labor, material, and overhead costs incurred. Generally accepted accounting principles (GAAP) require the firm to include (capitalize) **interest paid during construction** as part of the cost of the asset being constructed.[1] Accounting's capitalization of interest results from reasoning that financing costs are as necessary a cost for self-constructing an asset as are labor and material costs. The accountant computes the amount of financing costs from the entity's actual borrowings and interest payments. The amount represents the interest cost that the firm incurred during periods of asset acquisition and that in principle the firm could have avoided if it had not acquired the assets. The inclusion of interest stops after the firm has finished constructing the asset.

CONCEPTUAL NOTE

The Financial Accounting Standards Board (FASB) did not explain why it measures financing costs from interest on borrowings and not from the firm's overall cost of capital, including shareholders' equity as well as borrowings. The brief discussion in the FASB *Statement of Financial Accounting Standards No. 34* refers to measurement problems but gives little further explanation.

---

[1]Financial Accounting Standards Board, *Statement of Financial Accounting Standards No. 34,* "Capitalization of Interest Cost," 1979.

If the firm borrows new funds in connection with the asset being constructed, it will use the interest rate on that borrowing. If the expenditures on construction exceed such new borrowings, then the interest rate applied to the excess is the weighted-average rate the firm pays for its other borrowings. The total amount of interest capitalized cannot exceed total interest costs for the period. The capitalization of interest into plant assets during construction reduces otherwise reportable interest expense and thereby increases income during periods of construction. In later periods, the plant will have higher depreciation charges, reducing income.

Example 2   Assume the following long-term debt structure:

Construction Loan at 15 Percent on Building under Construction	$1,000,000
Other Borrowings at 12 Percent Average Rate	3,600,000
Total Long-Term Debt	$4,600,000

The account Building under Construction has an average balance during the year of $3,000,000. The firm bases the amount of interest to be capitalized on all of the new construction-related borrowings ($1,000,000) and enough of the older borrowings ($2,000,000) to bring the total to $3,000,000. The firm computes interest capitalized as follows:

$1,000,000 × .15	$150,000
$2,000,000 × .12	240,000
$3,000,000	$390,000

The entries to record interest and to capitalize the required amounts might be as follows:

Interest Expense	582,000	
Interest Payable		582,000

To record all interest as expense: $582,000 = (.15 × $1,000,000) + (.12 × $3,600,000) = $150,000 + $432,000.

Building under Construction	390,000	
Interest Expense		390,000

The amount capitalized reduces interest expense and increases the recorded cost of the building.

The firm might combine the preceding two entries into one as follows:

Interest Expense	192,000	
Building under Construction	390,000	
Interest Payable		582,000

The amount for Interest Expense is a plug.

The firm must disclose, in notes to the financial statements, both total interest for the year, $582,000, and the amount capitalized, $390,000. The income statement will report interest expense, $192,000 in this example. Interest capitalization in earlier years will cause the depreciation of the building in future years to exceed its amount without capitalization. Over the life of the asset, from construction through retirement, capitalizing interest does not change total income because larger depreciation charges later exactly offset the increased income that lower interest charges cause during the construction period. Over sufficiently long time spans, total expenses incurred for using plant assets must equal total cash expenditures made to acquire them.

PROBLEM 8.1 FOR SELF-STUDY

Calculating the acquisition cost of fixed assets.   Jensen Company purchased land with a building as the site for a new plant it planned to construct. The company received bids from several independent contractors for demolition of the old building and construction of the new one. It rejected all bids and undertook demolition and construction using company labor, facilities, and equipment.

It debited or credited amounts for all transactions relating to these properties to a single account, Real Estate. Descriptions of various items in the Real Estate account appear below. Jensen Company will close the Real Estate account at the completion of construction. It will remove all amounts in it and reclassify them into the following accounts:

1. Land account
2. Building account
3. Revenue, gain, expense, or loss account
4. Some balance sheet account other than Land or Building

Reclassify the amounts of the following transactions into one or more of these accounts. If you use **4** (some other balance sheet account), indicate the nature of the account.

a. Cost of land, including old building
b. Legal fees paid to bring about purchase of land and to transfer its title
c. Invoice cost of materials and supplies used in construction
d. Direct labor and materials costs incurred in demolishing old building
e. Direct costs of excavating raw land to prepare it for the foundation of the new building
f. Discounts earned for prompt payment of item **c**
g. Interest for the year on notes issued to finance construction
h. Amounts equivalent to interest on Jensen Company's own funds that it used in construction but that it would have invested in marketable securities if it had used an independent contractor; it debited the amount to Real Estate and credited Interest Revenue so that the cost of the real estate would be comparable to the cost if it had purchased the building from an independent contractor
i. Depreciation during the construction period on trucks used both in construction and in regular company operations
j. Proceeds of sale of materials salvaged from the old buildings; the firm had debited these to Cash and credited Real Estate
k. Cost of building permits
l. Salaries of certain corporate engineering executives; these represent costs for both Salary Expense and Real Estate, with the portion debited to Real Estate representing an estimate of the portion of the time spent during the year on planning and construction activities for the new building

m. Payments for property taxes on the plant site (its former owner owed these taxes but Jensen Company assumed responsibility to pay them)

n. Payments for property taxes on plant site during construction period

o. Insurance premiums to cover workers engaged in demolition and construction activities; the insurance policy contains various deductible clauses, requiring the company to pay the first $5,000 of damages from any accident

p. Cost of injury claims for $2,000 paid by the company because the amount was less than the deductible amount in the policy

q. Costs of new machinery to be installed in the building

r. Installation costs for the machinery in item **q**

s. Profit on construction of the new building (computed as the difference between the lowest independent contractor's bid and the actual construction cost); the firm debited this to Real Estate and credited Construction Revenue

DEPRECIATION: FUNDAMENTAL CONCEPTS

PURPOSE OF DEPRECIATION

The firm can keep most plant assets intact and in usable operating condition for more than a year but will eventually retire them from service (with the exception of land). **Depreciation** systematically allocates the cost of these assets to the periods of their use.

Allocation of Cost The cost of a depreciating asset is the price paid for a series of future services. The asset is a prepayment, similar to prepaid rent or insurance—a payment in advance for services the firm will receive. As the firm uses the asset in each accounting period, it treats a portion of the cost of the asset as the cost of the service received and recognizes the cost as an expense of the period or as part of the cost of goods produced during the period. Accountants must decide how to allocate the cost of the asset: to the periods when the firm uses the asset or to the products the firm makes with the asset.

Depreciation *Is* a Process of Cost Allocation This chapter discusses the problems of allocating assets' costs to the periods of benefit. A depreciation problem will exist whenever (1) the firm invests funds in future services provided by a plant asset and (2) at some future date, the firm retires the asset from service with a residual value less than its acquisition cost.

Accounting cannot compute a uniquely correct amount for the periodic charge for depreciation. The plant asset benefits several accounting periods. Accountants and economists call such an asset a **joint cost** of the several benefited periods because each of the periods of the asset's use benefits from its services. There is usually no single correct way to allocate a joint cost, so the process, although systematic, is to a degree arbitrary.

Return of Capital A firm attempts to earn both a return of capital and a return on capital. Before a firm can earn a return on capital (as measured by accounting profits), it must recover all costs. Depreciation charges the cost of plant assets against revenues. In historical cost accounting, the process allows for a return of the cost of the asset, no more and no less. But the depreciation charges occur over the asset's entire life, not just in the first few periods of its life.

CONCEPTUAL NOTE

Because prices of the services provided by plant assets generally increase over time, accountants increasingly recognize that basing depreciation charges on acquisition costs will not, in most cases, expense amounts sufficiently large to maintain the productive capacity of the business. Basing depreciation on acquisition costs will enable a business to expense an amount equal to its initial cash investment but will not necessarily provide expense equal to the cost of replacing the physical productive capacity initially purchased with the cash.

Depreciation *Is Not* a Decline in Value   Depreciation is a process of cost allocation; depreciation is not a process of valuation. In ordinary conversation (and in economics), *depreciation* frequently does mean a decline in **value.** Over the entire service life of a plant asset, the asset's value declines from acquisition until the firm retires it from service. The charge made to the operations of each accounting period does not measure the decline in value during that period but rather represents a process of cost allocation—a systematic process, but one in which the firm has some freedom to choose. If, in a given period, an asset increases in value, the firm will still record depreciation during that period. There have been two partially offsetting processes: (1) a holding gain on the asset, which historical cost-based accounting does not usually recognize, and (2) an allocation of the asset's historical cost to the period of benefit, which accounting does recognize.

THE CAUSES OF THE PROCESS REQUIRING DEPRECIATION

The causes of the process requiring depreciation are the same causes that make an asset's service potential decline. Unless the asset's service potential declines, its owner records no depreciation. The decline in service potential results from either physical or functional causes.

The physical factors include such things as ordinary wear and tear from use, chemical action such as rust, and the effects of wind and rain. The most important functional (nonphysical) cause is obsolescence. Inventions, for example, may result in new processes that reduce the unit cost of production to the point where the firm finds continued operation of old equipment uneconomical, even though the equipment may be relatively unimpaired physically. Computers may work as well as ever, but firms replace them because new, smaller computers occupy less space and compute faster. Although display cases and storefronts may not have worn out, retail stores replace them to make the store look better. Changed economic conditions may also cause depreciation. Consider a city that finds an old airport inadequate, abandons it, and builds a new, larger one to meet the requirements of heavier traffic. Or consider how an increase in the cost of gasoline reduces demand for automobile products, which reduces the scale of operations in automobile manufacturing, causing the manufacturing equipment, undiminished physically, to have smaller service potential.

Measuring depreciation does not require identifying its specific causes. Almost every physical asset loses service potential, and the firm may retire an asset before it has deteriorated physically. Understanding the specific causes can, nevertheless, help in estimating an asset's useful life.

The three principal accounting issues in allocating the cost of an asset over time are as follows:

1. Measuring the depreciable basis of the asset
2. Estimating its useful service life
3. Deciding on the pattern of expiration of asset cost over the useful service life

Depreciation is a process of allocating an asset's cost, less salvage value, to the periods of benefit. Because of the estimates involved, we can say that the process is systematic, based on rational judgments, but gives the firm some freedom to choose. The following discussion shows how accounting applies rational judgments in devising the process.

DEPRECIABLE BASIS OF PLANT ASSETS: COST LESS SALVAGE VALUE

Historical cost accounting bases depreciation charges on the acquisition cost of the asset less the estimated residual value—the amount the firm will receive when it retires the asset from service. Because the firm will recover the residual value at retirement, it need not depreciate that amount.

Estimating Salvage Value Accounting bases depreciation charges on the difference between acquisition cost and the asset's estimated salvage value or net residual value. The terms **salvage value** and **net residual value** refer to estimated proceeds on the disposition of an asset less all removal and selling costs. At any time before the firm retires an asset, it can only estimate the salvage value. Hence, before retirement, the terms *salvage value* and *estimated salvage value* are synonyms.

For buildings, common practice assumes a zero salvage value. This treatment rests on the assumption that the cost to be incurred in tearing down the building will approximate the sales value of the scrap materials recovered. Other assets, however, have substantial salvage value, so the accountant should take this into account in making the periodic depreciation charge. For example, a car-rental firm will replace its automobiles at a time when other owners can use the cars for several years more. The rental firm will be able to recover a substantial part of acquisition cost from selling used cars. Past experience usually forms the best basis for estimating salvage value. (Salvage value can be negative. Consider the cost of dismantling a nuclear electricity-generating plant.) Estimates of salvage value are necessarily subjective. Disputes over estimated salvage value have led to many disagreements between Internal Revenue Service agents and taxpayers. Partly to reduce such controversy, the Internal Revenue Code provides that a firm may ignore salvage value entirely in calculating depreciation for tax reporting. When calculating depreciation in problems in this text, take the entire salvage value into account unless the problem gives explicit contrary instructions, such as for declining-balance depreciation methods.

Unit of Account Whenever feasible, a firm should compute depreciation for individual items such as a single building, machine, or automobile. When the firm uses many similar items, each one with relatively small cost, individual calculations become impracticable, and the firm computes the depreciation charge for the group as a whole. Furniture and fixtures, tools, and telephone poles exemplify assets that firms usually depreciate in groups.

ESTIMATING SERVICE LIFE

The depreciation calculation requires an estimate of the economic **service life,** or **depreciable life,** of the asset. In making the estimate, the accountant must consider both the physical and the functional causes of depreciation. Experience with similar assets, corrected for differences in the planned intensity of use or alterations in maintenance policy, usually provides the best guide for this estimate.

Despite abundant data from experience, estimating service lives for financial reporting presents the most difficult task in the depreciation calculation. Because obsolescence typically results from forces outside the firm, accountants have difficulty anticipating obsolescence well enough to be confident of their accounting for it. For this reason, accountants reconsider assets' estimated service lives every few years. Income tax laws allow a firm to use a life shorter than estimated service life in computing depreciation for tax reporting, but the firm must use the estimated service life, not the shorter tax life, for financial reporting.

The shorter depreciable lives for tax reporting have their basis in congressional legislation called the **Modified Accelerated Cost Recovery System (MACRS).** Taxpayers use MACRS lives for tax reporting, understanding that the IRS will not challenge these lives even when they are shorter than economic service lives. MACRS groups almost all assets into one of seven classes as follows:

Class	Examples
3-year	Some racehorses; almost no others
5-year	Cars, trucks, some manufacturing equipment, research and development property
7-year	Office equipment, railroad cars, locomotives
10-year	Vessels, barges, and land improvements
20-year	Municipal sewers
27.5-year	Residential rental property
39-year	Nonresidential buildings acquired after 1993; otherwise 31.5 years

PATTERN OF EXPIRATION OF COSTS

After measuring the asset's cost and estimating both its salvage value and its service life, the firm has fixed the total of depreciation charges and the time span over which to charge those costs. If the firm estimates salvage value of zero, it will depreciate the entire cost. The firm must select the pattern for allocating those charges to the specific years of the life. Depreciation based on the passage of time follows one of five basic patterns. These appear as lines E, A, S, D, and N in Figures 8.1 and 8.2. Figure 8.1 traces the net book value (on the balance sheet) over the asset's life. Figure 8.2 shows the periodic depreciation charge over the asset's life.

The next section discusses the patterns in more detail. The patterns represent depreciation timing as follows:

Pattern A	Accelerated depreciation
Pattern S	Straight-line depreciation
Pattern D	Decelerated depreciation
Pattern E	Expense immediately
Pattern N	No depreciation

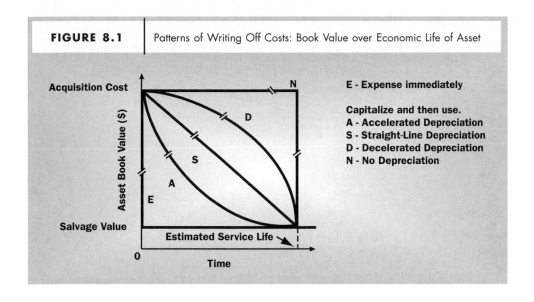

FIGURE 8.1 | Patterns of Writing Off Costs: Book Value over Economic Life of Asset

You can more easily understand the terms accelerated and decelerated if you compare the depreciation charges in the early years with straight-line depreciation. See Figure 8.2. GAAP do not allow pattern D in financial reporting; managerial accounting texts sometimes discuss this method because of its useful managerial accounting applications. Pattern E represents immediate expensing of the item. The section on intangibles discusses this pattern. Pattern N represents the situation, such as for land, in which there are no periodic amortization charges. The asset appears on the books at acquisition cost until the firm sells or otherwise retires it.

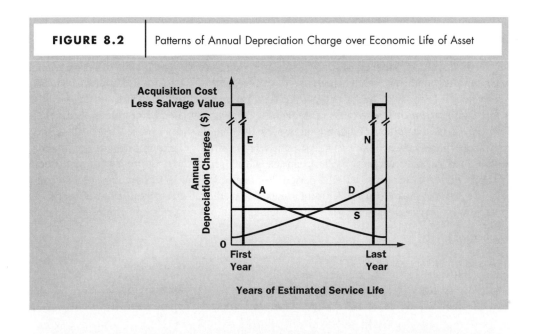

FIGURE 8.2 | Patterns of Annual Depreciation Charge over Economic Life of Asset

DEPRECIATION METHODS

All depreciation methods systematically allocate the cost of the asset minus its estimated salvage value to the periods when the firm uses the asset. The methods discussed here are as follows:

1. Straight-line (time) method (pattern S)
2. Production or use (straight-line use) method
3. Accelerated depreciation (pattern A)
   a. Declining-balance methods
   b. Sum-of-the-years'-digits methods
   c. Modified Accelerated Cost Recovery System for income tax reporting

When acquiring or retiring a depreciable asset during an accounting period, the firm should calculate depreciation only for that portion of the period during which it uses the asset.

THE STRAIGHT-LINE (TIME) METHOD

Financial reporting most commonly uses the **straight-line (time) method.** The straight-line method divides the cost of the asset, less any estimated salvage value, by the number of years of its expected life, to arrive at the annual depreciation.

$$\text{Annual Depreciation} = \frac{\text{Cost Less Estimated Salvage Value}}{\text{Estimated Life in Years}}$$

For example, if a machine costs $50,000, has an estimated salvage value of $5,000, and has an expected useful life of five years, the annual depreciation will be $9,000 [= ($50,000 − $5,000)/5]. Occasionally, instead of a positive salvage value, the cost of removal exceeds the gross proceeds on disposition. Add this excess of removal costs over gross proceeds to the cost of the asset in making the calculation. Thus, if a firm constructs a building for $3,500,000 and estimates a cost of $500,000 to remove it at the end of 25 years, the annual depreciation will be $160,000 [= ($3,500,000 + $500,000)/25].

PRODUCTION OR USE (STRAIGHT-LINE USE) METHOD

Firms do not use all assets uniformly over time. Manufacturing plants often have seasonal variations in operation, so that they use certain machines 24 hours a day at one time of the year and 8 hours or less a day at another time of the year. Trucks do not receive the same amount of use in each year of their lives. The straight-line (time) method of depreciation may result in depreciation patterns unrelated to usage patterns.

When the rate of usage varies over periods and when the firm can estimate the total usage of an asset over its life, the firm can use a **straight-line (use) method** based on actual production or usage during the period. For example, the firm could base depreciation of a truck for a period on the ratio of miles driven during the period to total miles expected to be driven over the truck's life. The depreciation cost per unit (mile) of use is as follows:

$$\text{Depreciation Cost per Unit} = \frac{\text{Cost Less Estimated Salvage Value}}{\text{Estimated Number of Units}}$$

Assume that a truck costs $54,000, has an estimated salvage value of $4,000, and will provide 200,000 miles of use before its retirement. The depreciation per mile is $.25

[= ($54,000 − $4,000)/200,000]. If the truck operates 2,000 miles in a given month, the depreciation charge for the month is 2,000 × $.25 = $500.

ACCELERATED DEPRECIATION

The earning power of some plant assets declines as they grow older. Cutting tools lose some of their precision; printing presses require more frequent shutdowns for repairs; rent receipts from an old office building fall below those from a new one. Some assets provide more and better services in the early years of their lives and require increasing amounts of maintenance as they grow older. These cases justify accelerated depreciation methods, which recognize larger depreciation charges in early years and smaller depreciation charges later. The term *accelerated depreciation* results from recognizing larger depreciation charges in the early years of the asset's life than in later years. Accelerated depreciation leads to a pattern such as A in Figures 8.1 and 8.2. Accounting does not require a firm to use an accelerated method even when the firm suspects asset usage will be accelerated. A firm can almost always use a straight-line method.

Even when a firm computes depreciation charges for a year on an accelerated method, it allocates amounts within a year on a straight-line basis. Thus depreciation charges for a month are 1/12 the annual amount.

Declining-Balance Methods   Under **declining-balance methods,** the depreciation charge results from multiplying a fixed rate times the net book value of the asset (cost less accumulated deprecation but without subtracting salvage value) at the start of each period. Even though the method does not subtract salvage value from cost, the depreciation stops when net book value reaches salvage value. Because the net book value declines from period to period, the result is a declining periodic charge for depreciation throughout the life of the asset.

Arithmetic Difficulty Leads to Rules of Thumb   The algebra underlying declining-balance methods sets a fixed depreciation rate designed to write off the cost less salvage value of the asset over its service life. The formula for computing the rate is as follows:

$$\text{Depreciation Rate} = 1 - \sqrt[n]{\frac{s}{c}} = 1 - \left(\frac{s}{c}\right)^{1/n}$$

In this formula, n = estimated periods of service life, s = estimated salvage value, and c = cost.

Estimates of salvage value affect the rate. Unless the computation assumes a positive salvage value, the rate is 100 percent—that is, all depreciation charges occur in the first period. For an asset costing $10,000 with an estimated life of five years, the depreciation rate is 40 percent per period if salvage value is $778, but it is 60 percent if salvage value is $102. The large effect on the rate of small changes in salvage value and the arithmetic difficulty of the formula have led accountants to use approximations, or rules of thumb, rather than the formula itself.

The arithmetic of declining-balance methods would never fully depreciate an asset's cost. A firm using a declining-balance method must switch to straight-line at some point in the asset's life. Because declining-balance methods first became prominent in tax reporting, firms chose to switch so as to maximize the tax deduction for depreciation. This practice has evolved into financial reporting computations as well.

Firms sometimes use the 200-percent (or double) declining-balance method. This method depreciates an asset with an estimated 10-year life at a rate of 20 percent

EXHIBIT 8.1

200 Percent Declining-Balance Depreciation with Switch to Straight-Line as Appropriate, Asset Costing $5,000 with Five-Year Life and $200 Salvage Value (Asset is retired at start of Year 6, when book value = $200.)

Start of Year	Acquisition Cost (1)	Accumulated Depreciation as of Jan. 1 (2)	Net Book Value as of Jan. 1 (3)	Double Declining-Balance Depreciation Rate (4)	Double Declining-Balance Depreciation Charge for the Year (5)	Net Book Value as of Jan. 1 Less Salvage Value of $200 (6)	Straight-Line Depreciation for Year (7)	Depreciation Charge for Year (8)
1	$5,000	$ 0	$5,000	40%	$2,000	$4,800	$960	$2,000
2	5,000	2,000	3,000	40	1,200	2,800	700	1,200
3	5,000	3,200	1,800	40	720	1,600	533	720
4	5,000	3,920	1,080	40	432	880	440	440[a]
5	5,000	4,360	640	40	256	440	440	440
6	5,000	4,800	200					$4,800

Column (1), given.

Column (2) = column (2), previous period + column (8), previous period.

Column (3) = column (1) − column (2).

Column (4) = 2/life of asset in years = 2/5.

Column (5) = column (3) × column (4).

Column (6) = column (3) − salvage value, $200.

Column (7) = column (6)/remaining life in years: 5 for first row; 4 for second row; 3 for third row; 2 for fourth row; 1 for fifth row. This is the charge resulting from using straight-line for the first time in this year.

Column (8) = larger of column (5) and column (7).

[a]Firm switches to straight-line method in fourth year, when straight-line depreciation charges first exceed double declining-balance depreciation charges.

(= 2 × 1/10) per year of book value at the start of the year. Under declining-balance methods, the firm switches to straight-line depreciation of the remaining book value, usually when straight-line provides higher depreciation charges. Assume a firm purchases a machine costing $5,000 on January 1, Year 1, estimates it to have a five-year life with a $200 salvage value, and uses double declining-balance depreciation. It would use a 40 percent (= 2 × 1/5) rate for three years and then switch to straight-line depreciation. Exhibit 8.1 shows the depreciation charges.

Sum-of-the-Years'-Digits Method   Under the **sum-of-the-years'-digits method,** the depreciation charge results from applying a fraction, which decreases from year to year, to the cost less estimated salvage value of the asset. The fraction has numerator and denominator as follows:

- Numerator—the number of years of remaining life at the beginning of the year of the depreciation calculation
- Denominator—the sum of all such numbers, one for each year of estimated service life

If the service life is n years, the denominator for the sum-of-the-years'-digits method is $1 + 2 + \ldots + n$. Consider an asset costing $5,000, purchased on January 1, Year 1, with an estimated service life of five years and an estimated salvage value of $200. The sum of the years' digits[2] is 15 (= 1 + 2 + 3 + 4 + 5). The depreciation charges appear in Exhibit 8.2.

Modified Accelerated Cost Recovery System for Income Tax Reporting   For income tax reporting, firms generally use the Modified Accelerated Cost Recovery System (MACRS). The term *modified* results from the change in the tax law from an earlier version called the *Accelerated Cost Recovery System (ACRS)*. MACRS results in depreciation charges accelerated in three distinct ways.

EXHIBIT 8.2	Sum-of-the-Years'-Digits Depreciation, Asset with Five-Year Life, $5,000 Cost, and $200 Estimated Salvage Value

Year	Acquisition Cost Less Salvage Value (1)	Remaining Life in Years (2)	Fraction =(2)/15 (3)	Depreciation Charge for the Year =(3)×(1) (4)
1	$4,800	5	5/15	$1,600
2	4,800	4	4/15	1,280
3	4,800	3	3/15	960
4	4,800	2	2/15	640
5	4,800	1	1/15	320
				$4,800

---

[2] A formula useful for summing the numbers 1 through n is $1 + 2 + \ldots + n = n(n+1)/2$. According to this formula, $1 + 2 + 3 + 4 + 5 = 5(5 + 1)/2 = 15$.

	Modified Accelerated Cost Recovery System
EXHIBIT 8.3	Percentage of Depreciable Cost Allowed by Year of Asset's Life

Recovery Year	Property Class			
	3-Year	**5-Year**	**7-Year**	**10-Year**
1[a]	33.3%	20.0%	14.3%	10.0%
2	44.4	32.0	24.5	18.0
3	14.8	19.2	17.5	14.4
4	7.5	11.5	12.5	11.5
5		11.5	8.9	9.2
6		5.8	8.9	7.4
7			8.9	6.6
8			4.5	6.6
9				6.6
10				6.6
11				3.1
Total	100.0%	100.0%	100.0%	100.0%

[a]The method assumes asset acquisition occurs at midpoint of the first year, independent of the actual acquisition date. In the first year, MACRS allows only a half-year of depreciation. So, for example, the first-year charge for an asset in the 5-year is 20 percent = 1/2 (for first half-year) × 2 (for 200-percent declining balance) × 1/5 (for 5-year life).

■ First, MACRS uses depreciable lives shorter than economic lives. (Straight-line depreciation for a shorter period will produce depreciation charges accelerated when compared with straight-line over a longer period.)

■ Second, for assets other than buildings, MACRS provides for depreciation over the specified life based on the 150-percent and 200-percent declining-balance depreciation methods, which are more rapid than straight-line. MACRS assumes, however, that the taxpayer acquires each asset at midyear of the year of acquisition, so the first-year percentage represents only a half-year of depreciation.

■ Third, MACRS allows the taxpayer to write off the entire depreciation basis over the depreciation period; it ignores salvage value.

Assets in the 3-year, 5-year, 7-year, and 10-year classes use the 200-percent declining-balance method. Assets in the 15-year and 20-year classes use the 150-percent declining-balance method. Assets in the 27.5-year and 39-year classes must use the straight-line basis. Exhibit 8.3 shows the percentage of an asset's cost to be depreciated under MACRS for tax reporting for 200-percent declining-balance classes of property.

An automobile with a 7-year estimated service life for financial reporting is in the 5-year property class for MACRS. If it costs $20,000 and has $2,500 estimated salvage value, the MACRS deductions for the tax return would be as follows:

$4,000 (= .200 × $20,000) in the first year, when MACRS charges only one-half year of accelerated depreciation

$6,400 (= .320 × $20,000) in the second year

$3,840 (= .192 × $20,000) in the third year
$2,300 (= .115 × $20,000) in the fourth and fifth years
$1,160 (= .058 × $20,000) in the sixth year, which contains the last half-year of the asset's life

Note that MACRS ignores salvage value, so if the taxpayer retires the asset for $2,500, a taxable gain on retirement of $2,500 will result. A firm would rarely judge MACRS appropriate for financial reporting. For financial reporting under the straight-line method, this automobile would have depreciation charges of $2,500 [= ($20,000 − $2,500)/7] per year for seven years and would have a book value of $2,500 at the end of the seventh year.

PROBLEM 8.2 FOR SELF-STUDY

Calculating periodic depreciation. Markam Corporation acquires a new machine costing $20,000 on January 2, Year 3. The firm expects

- to use the machine for five years,
- to operate it for 24,000 hours during that time, and
- to recoup an estimated salvage value of $2,000 at the end of five years.

Calculate the depreciation charge for each of the five years using the following:

a. The straight-line (time) method
b. The sum-of-the-years'-digits method
c. The double declining-balance method, switching to the straight-line method in the fourth year
d. The units-of-production method; expected operating times are 5,000 hours each year for four years and 4,000 hours in the fifth year

FACTORS IN CHOOSING THE DEPRECIATION METHOD

Depreciation affects both income reported in the financial statements and taxable income on tax returns. A firm will likely choose different depreciation methods for financial and tax reporting purposes. If so, the difference between depreciation in the financial statements and on the tax return leads to an issue in accounting for income taxes, discussed in Chapter 10.

Tax Reporting In selecting depreciation methods for tax reporting, the firm should try to maximize the present value of the reductions in tax payments from claiming depreciation. When tax rates stay constant over time, earlier deductions have greater value than later ones because a dollar saved today has greater value than a dollar saved tomorrow. Congress has presented business firms with several permissible alternatives under MACRS to follow in computing the amount of depreciation to deduct each year. A firm will generally choose the alternative that meets the general goal of allowing it to pay the least amount of tax, as late as possible, within the law. Accountants call this goal the *least and latest rule.*

Financial Reporting Financial reporting for long-lived assets seeks an income statement that realistically measures the expiration of the assets' benefits and provides a reasonable pattern of cost allocation. No one knows, however, just how much service potential of a long-lived asset expires in any one period. The cost of the plant asset jointly benefits all the periods of use, and accountants have found no single correct way to allocate such joint costs. Financial statements should report depreciation charges based on reasonable estimates of asset expirations. Most U.S. firms use the straight-line method for financial reporting. Chapter 14 discusses more fully a firm's selection of alternative accounting methods, including the choice of depreciation methods. Analysts understand that accelerated methods provide higher-quality earnings measures than do straight-line methods, but the differences are minor. Analysts will not likely downgrade a company because it uses straight-line depreciation methods.

ACCOUNTING FOR PERIODIC DEPRECIATION

In recording periodic depreciation, the accountant debits either an expense account or a product cost account. The cost for depreciation of factory buildings and equipment in manufacturing operations, a product cost, becomes part of the cost of work-in-process and finished goods. The cost for depreciation on sales equipment becomes a selling expense. The cost for depreciation of office equipment becomes a general or administrative expense.

In recording depreciation, the accountant could, in principle, record the matching credit directly in the asset account, such as Buildings or Equipment. In practice, most firms credit a contra-asset account, Accumulated Depreciation. This leaves the acquisition cost of the asset undisturbed and permits the analyst to compute both the amount written off through depreciation and the undepreciated original cost. If the firm credited the asset account directly, an analysis of the accounts would disclose only the second of these. (Question **6** at the end of this chapter shows how the analyst can use this information to make useful inferences.) Whether the firm uses a contra-asset account does not affect net assets.

The entry to record periodic depreciation of office facilities, a period expense first illustrated in Chapter 3, is as follows:

Depreciation Expense	1,500	
Accumulated Depreciation		1,500

The entry to record periodic depreciation of manufacturing facilities, a product cost first illustrated in Chapter 7, is as follows:

Work-in-Process Inventory	1,500	
Accumulated Depreciation		1,500

As a part of the regular closing-entry procedure, the accountant closes the Depreciation Expense account at the end of the accounting period. The Work-in-Process Inventory account is an asset. Product costs, such as depreciation on manufacturing facilities, accumulate in the Work-in-Process Inventory account until the firm completes goods produced and transfers them to Finished Goods Inventory. The Accumulated Depreciation account remains open at the end of the period and appears on the balance sheet as a deduction from the asset account to which it is contra. The balance in the Accumulated Depreciation account usually represents the total charges in all accounting periods up through the balance sheet date for the depreciation on assets currently in use. The terms *book value* and *net book value* of an asset refer to the difference between the balance of an asset account and the balance of its accumulated depreciation account.

CHANGES IN PERIODIC DEPRECIATION

The original depreciation schedule for a particular asset usually requires changing. A firm periodically re-estimates useful life and salvage value. The accuracy of the estimates improves as retirement approaches. If changing from the old to the new estimates would have a material impact, the firm must change the depreciation schedule. The generally accepted procedure makes no adjustment for the past misestimate but spreads the remaining undepreciated balance less the new estimate of salvage value over the new estimate of the remaining service life of the asset.

The rationale for adjusting current and future depreciation charges instead of correcting past depreciation charges rests on the nature and role of estimates in accounting. The accountant makes estimates for depreciable lives and salvage values, uncollectible accounts, warranty costs, and similar items based on the available information at the time of the estimate. These changes in estimates occur regularly. Requiring firms to restate previously issued financial statements each year might confuse users and undermine the credibility of the statements. Retroactive restatement might also provide management with an opportunity to inflate earnings of earlier periods, knowing that any adjustment will not affect future earnings. Chapter 12 discusses these issues more fully.

To understand the **treatment of changes in periodic depreciation,** assume the following facts, illustrated in Figure 8.3. A firm

- purchases an office machine on January 1, Year 1, for $9,200,
- estimates that it will use the machine for 15 years, and
- estimates a salvage value of $200.

The depreciation charge recorded for each of the years from Year 1 through Year 5 under the straight-line method has been $600 [= ($9,200 − $200)/15]. On December 31, Year 6, before closing the books for the year, the firm decides that

- the machine will have a total useful life of only 10 years, and
- the salvage estimate of $200 remains reasonable.

The accepted procedure for recognizing this substantial decrease in service life revises the future depreciation so that the correct total will accumulate in the Accumulated Depreciation account at the end of the revised service life. The firm makes no adjustments of amounts previously recorded. In our example, the total amount of acquisition cost yet to be depreciated before the Year 6 change is $6,000 [= ($9,200 − $200) − (5 × $600)]. The new estimate of the remaining life is five years (the year just ended plus the next four), so the new annual depreciation charge is $1,200 (= $6,000/5). The accounting changes the amount recorded for annual depreciation in the current and future years, to $1,200 from $600. The depreciation entry on December 31, Year 6, and each year thereafter would be as follows:

Depreciation Expense	1,200	
Accumulated Depreciation		1,200
To record depreciation for Year 6 based on revised estimates.		

Figure 8.3 illustrates the revised depreciation path.

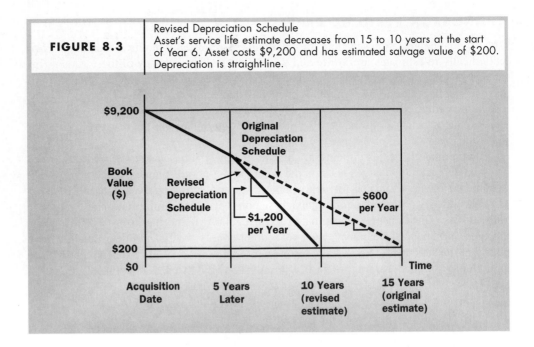

FIGURE 8.3

Revised Depreciation Schedule
Asset's service life estimate decreases from 15 to 10 years at the start of Year 6. Asset costs $9,200 and has estimated salvage value of $200. Depreciation is straight-line.

PROBLEM 8.3 FOR SELF-STUDY

Adjustments for changes in estimates. Central States Electric Company constructs a nuclear power-generating plant at a cost of $200 million. It expects the plant to last 50 years before retiring the plant from service. The company estimates that at the time it retires the plant from service, it will incur $20 million in "decommissioning" costs (costs to dismantle the plant and dispose of the radioactive materials). The firm computes and charges straight-line depreciation once per year, at year-end.

During the company's 11th year of operating the plant, Congress enacts new regulations governing nuclear waste disposal. The estimated decommissioning costs increase from $20 million to $24 million. During the 31st year of operation, the firm revises the life of the plant. It will last 60 years in total, not 50 years.

a. What is the depreciation charge for the first year?
b. What is the depreciation charge for the 11th year?
c. What is the depreciation charge for the 31st year?

REPAIRS AND IMPROVEMENTS

A firm can spend cash throughout an asset's life for various reasons, including

1. to acquire it,
2. to repair it,

3. to maintain it,
4. to improve it, and, perhaps,
5. to dispose of it.

All these expenditures will become expenses, and accrual accounting asks, "When?" (Over sufficiently long time spans, expense equals cash expenditures.) The process of debiting an asset account for the acquisition cost and amortizing that cost (less salvage value) over the service life eventually charges the entire acquisition cost (less salvage value) to expense. During an asset's life, the firm will spend cash for repairs, maintenance, and improvements. Distinguishing among these purposes affects reported periodic income because the firm will immediately expense expenditures for repairs and maintenance but will debit expenditures for improvements to an asset account and, then, amortize those amounts in future periods.

REPAIRS AND MAINTENANCE

A firm repairs and services an asset to maintain its expected operating condition. **Repairs** include the costs of restoring an asset's service potential after breakdowns or other damage. **Maintenance** includes routine costs such as for cleaning and adjusting. Expenditures for these items do not extend the estimated service life or otherwise increase productive capacity beyond the firm's original expectations for the asset. Because these expenditures restore future benefits to originally estimated levels, accounting treats such expenditures as expenses of the period when the firm makes the expenditure. In practice, to distinguish repairs from maintenance is difficult. Because expenditures for both become immediate expenses, accountants need not devote energy to distinguishing between them.

The repair policy a firm adopts will affect the depreciation rate for its assets. If, for example, a firm checks and repairs its assets often, the assets are likely to last longer than otherwise, and the depreciation rate will be lower.

IMPROVEMENTS

Expenditures for **improvements,** sometimes called *betterments* or *capital expenditures,* make an asset perform better than before. Such expenditures may increase the asset's life or reduce its operating cost or increase its rate of output. Because the expenditure improves the asset's service potential, accounting treats such an expenditure as an asset acquisition. The firm has acquired new future benefits. When the firm makes the expenditure, it can debit a new asset account or the existing asset account. Subsequent depreciation charges will increase.

Example 3   Assume a firm suffers loss to its building in a fire. The firm spends $200,000 to replace the loss. It judges that $160,000 of the expenditure replaces assets lost in the fire, and $40,000 represents improvements to the building. It could make the following single journal entry.

Building	40,000	
Loss from Fire	160,000	
Cash		200,000
To record loss and subsequent expenditure.		

The following two entries are equivalent and may be easier to understand:

Loss from Fire	160,000	
Building		160,000
To record loss from fire.		
Building	200,000	
Cash		200,000
To record expenditures on building.		

DISTINGUISHING REPAIRS FROM IMPROVEMENTS

Accountants must distinguish repairs from improvements because of the effect on periodic income. Some expenditures may both repair and improve. Consider expenditures to replace a roof damaged in a hurricane. The firm installs a new roof purposefully designed to be stronger than the old one so that it will support air conditioning equipment that the firm plans to install. Clearly, part of the expenditure represents repair and part, improvement.

The accountant must make judgments and allocate costs between repairs and improvements. When in doubt, the accountant tends to call the expenditure a repair because of conservatism. The firm may also believe that expensing the item for financial reporting will support its immediate deduction for income tax reporting.

Asset Composites   Some asset accounts comprise composites of assets. To understand this point, consider a truck costing $48,000 that comprises three separate components: a chassis with allocated cost of $37,800, an engine with allocated cost of $9,000, and tires with allocated cost of $1,200. The chassis lasts six years before the user must retire it; the engine, three years; and the tires, two years. Refer to the data in Exhibit 8.4, which shows expenditure data, including $800 to repair windows broken by vandals.

Until this point of the book, you would depreciate the truck over a six-year life. Expenditures of $1,200 at the end of the second and fourth year for tires become maintenance expense. Expenditures for a new engine of $9,000 at the end of the third year and repairs of windows broken by vandals in the fifth year costing $800 also become immediate expenses. See the top panel of Exhibit 8.4.

But accounting allows another treatment: setting up separate asset accounts for

1. the chassis, depreciated over six years,
2. the engine, depreciated over three years, and
3. the tires, depreciated over two years.

This accounting recognizes new asset acquisitions for a new engine, costing $9,000, at the end of the third year, and for new tires, costing $1,200, at the end of the second and fourth years. Then, the firm will depreciate each of the separate assets over their useful lives. The firm will expense the window repair, costing $800, in the fifth year. See the lower panel of Exhibit 8.4.

Note that over the six-year period, total expense equals total expenditures of $60,200 under both treatments. Over sufficiently long time spans, expense equals expenditure.

<table>
<tr><td>EXHIBIT 8.4</td><td>Unit of Account Influences Depreciation Charges and Distinguishes Maintenance or Repairs from Improvements</td></tr>
</table>

Truck: Cost $48,000, Six-Year Life
Components of Truck:
   Chassis: Cost $37,800, Six-Year Life
   Engine: Cost $9,000, Three-Year Life
   Tires: Cost $1,200, Two-Year Life
Window Repair: Cost $800 in Year 5
(straight-line depreciation)

	Depreciation of			Maintenance and Repairs	Total Expense
	Truck	**Engine**	**Tires**		
SINGLE ASSET ACCOUNT					
Year 1	$ 8,000[a]	—	—	—	$ 8,000
Year 2	8,000	—	—	$ 1,200[b]	9,200
Year 3	8,000	—	—	9,000[c]	17,000
Year 4	8,000	—	—	1,200[b]	9,200
Year 5	8,000	—	—	800[d]	8,800
Year 6	8,000	—	—	—	8,000
	$48,000			$12,200	$60,200
SEPARATE ASSET ACCOUNTS					
Year 1	$6,300[e]	$ 3,000[f]	$ 600[g]	—	$ 9,900
Year 2	6,300	3,000	600	—	9,900
Year 3	6,300	3,000	600[g]	—	9,900
Year 4	6,300	3,000[f]	600	—	9,900
Year 5	6,300	3,000	600[g]	$ 800[d]	10,700
Year 6	6,300	3,000	600	—	9,900
	$37,800	$18,000	$3,600	$ 800	$60,200

[a] $48,000/6.
[b] Tires.
[c] Engine.
[d] Window Repair.
[e] Chassis: ($48,000 − $9,000 − $1,200)/6.
[f] Engine: $9,000/3.
[g] Tires: $1,200/2.

Distinguishing repairs from improvements. Purdy Company acquired two used trucks from Foster Company. Although the trucks were not identical, they both cost $15,000. Purdy knew when it negotiated the purchase price that the first truck required extensive engine repair, expected to cost about $4,000. The repair was made the week after acquisition and actually cost $4,200. Purdy Company thought the second truck was in normal operating condition when it negotiated the purchase price but discovered, after taking possession of the truck, that it required new bearings. The firm made this repair, costing $4,200, during the week after acquisition.

a. What costs should Purdy Company record in the accounts for the two trucks?
b. If the amounts recorded in part a are different, distinguish between the two repairs.

IMPAIRMENT OF ASSETS

A firm acquires assets for their future benefits. The world changes, and expected future benefits change, sometimes increasing and sometimes decreasing in value. Accounting does not permit assets whose values have declined substantially to remain on the balance sheet at amortized acquisition cost. When the firm has information indicating that its assets have declined in market value or will provide a smaller future benefit than originally anticipated, it tests to see if the decline in value is so drastic that the expected future cash flows from the asset have declined below book value. If then-current book value exceeds the sum of expected undiscounted cash flows, an asset **impairment** has occurred. At the time the firm judges that an impairment has occurred, the firm writes down the book value of the asset to its then-current fair value. That fair value is the market value of the asset or, if the firm cannot assess the market value, the expected net present value of the future cash flows.[3]

CONCEPTUAL NOTE

The FASB uses the word *impairment* only when the book value exceeds the sum of the expected undiscounted future cash flows. When a smaller decline in an asset's value occurs but the expected undiscounted future cash flows nevertheless exceed then-current book value, the firm has suffered an economic loss, but the technical term *impairment* does not apply.

We illustrate the application of the impairment test and the subsequent revaluations with examples.

BASIC IMPAIRMENT EXAMPLE

Miller Company owns an apartment building that originally cost $20 million and by the end of the current period has accumulated depreciation of $5 million, with net book value of $15 (= $20 − $5) million. Miller Company had originally expected to collect $50 million over 30 years of expected rentals before selling the building for $8 million. Unanticipated placement of a new shopping center has caused Miller Company to reassess the future rentals. Miller Company expects the building to provide rentals for only 15 more years before Miller will sell it. Miller Company uses a discount rate of 12 percent per year in discounting expected rentals from the building.

Case A Miller expects to receive annual rentals of $1.35 million per year for 15 years and to sell the building for $5 million after 15 years, which, discounted at 12 percent per year, has present value of $10.1 million. The building has market value of $10 million today.

---

[3]Financial Accounting Standards Board, *Statement of Financial Accounting Standards No. 121,* "Accounting for the Impairment of Long-Lived Assets and for Long-Lived Assets to Be Disposed Of," 1995.

Miller decides that no impairment has occurred because the expected undiscounted future cash flows of $25.25 [= ($1.35 × 15) + $5] million exceed the book value of $15 million. The firm has suffered an economic loss but will not recognize any loss in its accounts.

Case B Miller expects to receive annual rentals of $600,000 per year for 15 years and to sell the building for $3 million after 15 years, which, discounted at 12 percent per year, has present value of $4.6 million. The building has market value of $4 million today.

Miller decides that an asset impairment has occurred because the book value of $15 million exceeds the expected undiscounted future cash flows of $12.0 [= ($0.6 × 15) + $3] million. Miller accounts for the impairment by removing the building's original cost and the accumulated depreciation from the accounts and establishing a new asset cost equal to then-current fair value, which is market value because the firm can estimate that amount. The journal entries (with amounts in millions) could be as follows:

Accumulated Depreciation	5.0	
Apartment Building (New Valuation)	4.0	
Loss on Impairment	11.0	
Apartment Building (Original Cost)		20.0

The loss appears on the income statement. The $11 million loss equals the excess of old net book value of $15 million over current market value of $4 million. The firm uses undiscounted amounts to decide there is impairment but uses discounted present values to measure the loss.

Case C As in the preceding case, Miller expects to receive annual rentals of $600,000 per year for 15 years and to sell the building for $3 million after 15 years, which, discounted at 12 percent per year, has present value of $4.6 million. Because of new housing code regulations, Miller Company cannot readily find a buyer or anyone who will quote a market value. FASB *Statement of Financial Accounting Standards No. 121* says that in such a case, fair value is present value of future cash flows, or $4.6 million.

An asset impairment has occurred because book value of $15 million exceeds the expected undiscounted future cash flows of $12.0 [= ($0.6 × 15) + $3] million. Miller Company accounts for the impairment by removing the building's original cost and the accumulated depreciation from the accounts. It establishes a new asset cost equal to then-current fair value, which is present value of expected cash flows because the firm cannot estimate market value. The journal entries (with amounts in millions) could be as follows:

Accumulated Depreciation	5.0	
Apartment Building (New Valuation)	4.6	
Loss on Impairment	10.4	
Apartment Building (Original Cost)		20.0

The loss appears on the income statement. The $10.4 million loss equals the excess of old net book value of $15 million over current fair value of $4.6 million.

We will illustrate another application of asset impairment later in this chapter, after we discuss accounting for goodwill.

RETIREMENT OF ASSETS

Now consider the accounting when a firm retires a long-lived asset, which it may retire through sale to another entity. Before making the entry to write off the asset and its accumulated depreciation, the firm records an entry to bring the depreciation up to date. That is, the firm records the depreciation that has occurred between the start of the current accounting period and the date of disposition. When a firm retires an asset from service, it removes the cost of the asset and the related amount of accumulated depreciation from the books. As part of this entry, the firm records the amount received from the sale, a debit, and the amount of net book value removed from the books, a net credit (that is, a credit to the asset account and a smaller debit to the accumulated depreciation account). Typically, these two—debit for retirement proceeds and net credit to remove the asset from the accounts—differ from each other. The excess of the proceeds received on retirement over the book value is a gain (if positive) or a loss (if negative, that is, if net book value exceeds proceeds).

To understand the retirement of an asset, assume sales equipment costs $5,000, has an expected life of four years, and has an estimated salvage value of $200. The firm has depreciated this asset on a straight-line basis at $1,200 [= ($5,000 − $200)/4] per year. The firm has recorded depreciation for two years and sells the equipment at midyear in the third year. The firm records the depreciation from the start of the accounting period to the date of sale: $600 [= ½ × ($5,000 − $200)/4].

Depreciation Expense	600	
Accumulated Depreciation		600
To record depreciation charges up to the date of sale.		

The book value of the asset is now its cost less 2½ years of straight-line depreciation of $1,200 per year or $2,000 (= $5,000 − 2½ × $1,200 = $5,000 − $3,000). The entry to record the retirement of the asset depends on the amount of the selling price.

1. Suppose the firm sells the equipment for cash at its book value of $2,000. The entry to record the sale would be as follows:

Cash	2,000	
Accumulated Depreciation	3,000	
Equipment		5,000

2. Suppose the firm sells the equipment for $2,300 cash, more than its book value. The entry to record the sale would be as follows:

Cash	2,300	
Accumulated Depreciation	3,000	
Equipment		5,000
Gain on Retirement of Equipment		300

The gain on retirement recognizes that past depreciation charges have been too large, given information now available. The gain appears on the income statement and, after closing entries, increases Retained Earnings. The gain restores to Retained Earnings the excess depreciation charged in the past.

3. Suppose the firm sells the equipment for $1,500 cash, less than its book value. The entry to record the sale would be as follows:

Cash	1,500	
Accumulated Depreciation	3,000	
Loss on Retirement of Equipment	500	
Equipment		5,000

The loss on retirement recognizes that past depreciation charges have been too small, given information now available. The loss appears on the income statement and, after closing entries, decreases Retained Earnings. The loss reduces Retained Earnings for the shortfall in depreciation charged in the past, in effect increasing depreciation charges all at once.

TRADE-IN TRANSACTIONS

Instead of selling an asset to retire it from service, the firm may trade it in on a new asset. This is common practice for automobiles. Think of a trade-in transaction as a sale of the old asset followed by a purchase of the new asset. The accounting for trade-in transactions determines simultaneously the gain or loss on disposal of the old asset and the acquisition cost recorded for the new asset. The procedures depend on the data available about the market value of the asset traded in and the cash equivalent cost of the new asset. Intermediate accounting texts explain the various procedures. See also the Glossary entry for *trade-in transaction.*

NATURAL RESOURCE ASSETS AND DEPLETION

Accounting includes (capitalizes) in an asset account the costs of finding natural resources and of preparing to extract them from the earth. Whether the firm should capitalize into the asset accounts all costs of exploration or only the costs of the successful explorations remains an open accounting question. GAAP allow two treatments. *Full costing* capitalizes the costs of all explorations (both successful and unsuccessful) so long as the expected benefits from the successful explorations will more than cover the cost of all explorations. *Successful efforts costing* capitalizes the costs of only the successful efforts; the costs of unsuccessful exploration efforts become expenses of the period when the fact becomes apparent that the efforts will not result in productive sites.[4]

Example 4   Shell Oil has extensive experience drilling for oil. In a certain type of terrain, it has found, from experience, that one in eight exploratory wells leads to a producing property. It undertakes to drill eight new wells at a cost of $1 million each in hopes of finding at least one well with recoverable crude oil having net realizable value (that is, fair market value less cost to lift and sell the crude oil) of $15 million. It spends

---

[4]Financial Accounting Standards Board, *Statement of Financial Accounting Standards No. 25,* "Suspension of Certain Accounting Requirements for Oil and Gas Producing Companies," 1979.

$8.8 million, drills eight wells, and finds one well with recoverable crude having net realizable value of $13 million. Shell will credit cash (and other assets) for the $8.8 million drilling expenditure. Under successful efforts costing, Shell would debit an expense for the $7.7 million cost of the dry holes and would debit an asset for the $1.1 million cost of the successful well. Under full costing, which Shell does not use, it would debit the entire $8.8 million to the asset account for the producing well.

Amortization of natural resources, sometimes called **wasting assets,** has a special name: **depletion.** Firms most often use the **units-of-production depletion method.**

Example 5   Assume that a firm incurs $4.5 million in costs to discover an oil field that contains an estimated 1.5 million barrels of oil. Then, the firm would amortize (deplete) the costs of $4.5 million at the rate of $3 (= $4,500,000/1,500,000) for each barrel of oil removed from the field.

The major accounting problem of extractive industries stems from uncertainty about the eventual total number of units that will result from exploratory efforts.

INTANGIBLE ASSETS AND AMORTIZATION

Assets can provide future benefits without having physical form. Accountants call such assets **intangibles.** Examples are research costs, advertising costs, patents, trade secrets, know-how, trademarks, and copyrights. The first issue involving intangibles involves the future benefits, if any, produced by expeditures:

■ Have the expenditures made to acquire or develop intangibles generated sufficient future benefits that the firm should **capitalize** them (treat them as assets) and amortize them over time, or

■ have the expenditures produced no future benefits, or future benefits hard to quantify, so that the firm should charge the costs to expense for the period in which the firm incurs the costs?

The immediate expensing of the asset's cost appears as pattern E in Figures 8.1 and 8.2. The second problem, arising for capitalized costs only, is how to amortize the capitalized costs—the life and the pattern. One can only estimate the service life and adjust the estimates to new information as time passes. Firms usually use the straight-line method for amortizing capitalized intangibles, but they may use other methods if appropriate. This section discusses some common intangibles and the issues involved in deciding whether to expense or to capitalize their costs. GAAP require all intangible assets acquired after 1970 to be amortized over a period no longer than 40 years.[5]

RESEARCH AND DEVELOPMENT

Successful firms often make expenditures for **research and development (R&D).** Firms incur such costs for various reasons. Perhaps the firm seeks to develop a technological or marketing advance in order to gain an edge on competition. Or, it might wish to explore possible applications of existing technology to design a new product or improve an old

---

[5]Accounting Principles Board, *Opinion No. 17,* "Intangible Assets," 1970.

one. It may undertake other research in responding to a government contract, in preparing for bids on potential contracts, or in making advances in basic research, with no specific product in mind. Whatever the reason, practically all research costs will yield their benefits, if any, in future periods. Herein lies the accounting issue: should the firm treat research and development costs as expenses immediately as incurred, or should it capitalize them as assets and amortize them over future periods?

GAAP require immediate expensing of research and development costs.[6] The FASB requires this treatment because, it said, the future benefits from most R&D efforts are too uncertain to warrant capitalization, and writing them off as soon as possible is more conservative.

CONCEPTUAL NOTE

We find this logic uncompelling. Many physical assets—which the FASB allows on the balance sheet as assets, such as special-purpose machine tools for experimental, unproven products—have future benefits at least as uncertain as those embodied in some intangibles for which the FASB requires expensing. Second, writing off assets is always more conservative, by definition. So these arguments do not distinguish R&D expenditures from others that are not expensed by the FASB rule. We suspect the requirement stems from the standard setters' (and auditors') preference for physical assets over intangible assets.

Some accountants believe that there must be future benefits in many cases or firms would not pursue R&D efforts. They think that accounting should match R&D costs with the benefits produced by the R&D expenditures through the capitalization procedure, with amortization over the benefited periods. GAAP do not allow this procedure. A firm with substantial R&D assets, such as Microsoft or Merck, will have high accounting rates of return on assets, hard to comprehend until the analyst realizes that its major assets do not appear on the balance sheet.

PATENTS

A patent is a right granted by the federal government to exclude others from the benefits of an invention. The legal life of patent protection can extend for 20 years, although it may have a shorter economic life. The accounting for patent costs depends on whether the firm purchased the patent from another party or developed it internally. If the firm purchased the patent, it capitalizes the cost. If the firm developed the patent internally, it expenses the total cost of product development, as required for all R&D costs. The FASB has not given reasoning to justify this distinction in accounting treatments of purchased versus developed patents. The firm will amortize the cost of a purchased patent over a period equal to the shorter of (1) the remaining legal life or (2) its estimated economic life. If for some reason the patent suffers impairment in value, the firm treats it like other long-lived, but impaired, assets.

---

[6]Financial Accounting Standards Board, *Statement of Financial Accounting Standards No. 2*, "Accounting for Research and Development Costs," 1974.

ADVERTISING

Firms spend cash for advertising to increase sales, currently and in the future, but time passes between the incurrence of these costs and their impact. The effect of advertising probably extends into subsequent periods. Even so, GAAP require immediately expensing almost all advertising costs, regardless of the timing of their impact (see pattern E in Figures 8.1 and 8.2).[7] Those supporting this practice make the following arguments:

1. Expensing advertising costs is more conservative than capitalizing them.
2. Accountants find it difficult to quantify the future effects and timing of benefits derived from these costs; auditors find it equally difficult to attest to the estimates.
3. When these costs remain stable from year to year, the capitalization policy (that is, whether to expense immediately or to capitalize and amortize) does not result in different income effects after the first few years.

Some accountants support the capitalization treatment because doing so will better report assets and match costs with resulting benefits. Firms with substantial advertising assets, such as Coca-Cola Company, will have accounting rates of return on assets misleadingly high until the analyst realizes that the major assets of such firms do not appear on the balance sheet.

Many companies that market branded products to consumers own major economic assets that do not appear on their balance sheets. Rates of return computed from accounting data for firms with substantial economic benefits in the form of intangibles, not recognized as accounting assets, can mislead the unwary analyst.

Example 6   Procter & Gamble Corporation (P&G) owns well-known brand names such as Tide and Crest. In recent years, P&G's net income has been about $3.8 billion, and its total accounting assets have been on the order of $30 billion. Thus, its accounting rate of return (= net income/total assets) has been approximately 13 percent (= $3.8/$30). In recent years, P&G has spent about $3.5 billion per year on advertising. If P&G had capitalized its advertising costs and amortized them over three years on a straight-line basis, charging one-half year of amortization in the first and fourth years, its assets would be about $5.25 (= 5/6 × $3.5 + 3/6 × $3.5 + 1/6 × $3.5 = 9/6 × $3.5) billion larger and its accounting rate of return would be about 11 percent (= $3.8/$35.25).

BASKET PURCHASES AND GOODWILL

Goodwill can arise when one company purchases another company or an operating unit from another company. Terminology often refers to such a purchase as a **basket purchase** because the acquiring firm acquires many assets (and liabilities) in a single transaction. Imagine checking out of a grocery store with a basketful of groceries but getting only a bill with a single grand total, not an itemized cash register receipt. The acquiring company has some idea of the market values of the individual items in the basket it has acquired, but it did not pay separately for these items. The acquiring firm must put each of the acquired assets and liabilities onto its balance sheet at the fair market value of the items acquired on the date of acquisition. The acquired asset, such as a patent or a trade-

---

[7]American Institute of Certified Public Accountants, *Statement of Procedure 93-7*, "Reporting on Advertising Costs," 1993. The exceptions involve some direct-mail advertising costs.

mark developed earlier by the acquired firm, will appear on the new balance sheet even though it may not appear on the balance sheet of the firm being acquired. Immediately after the acquisition, the acquiring firm must write off the newly recorded value of R&D assets it has just acquired, referred to as *in-process technology* (or **R&D In Process**), unless those R&D assets have already provided commercially feasible results, such as a patent.[8]

Accounting measures **goodwill** as the difference between the amount paid for the acquired company (or operating unit) as a whole and the sum of the current values of its identifiable net assets. Goodwill will equal the sum of fair values of individual assets net of the fair value of its liabilities, whether or not they appear on the acquired unit's balance sheet. Goodwill will appear in the financial statements of the company making the acquisition. Present practice amortizes goodwill (and other intangibles) acquired after October 1970 over a time period not longer than 40 years.[9] As this book goes to press, the FASB is considering reducing the amortization period for goodwill to 20 years.

PROBLEM 8.5 FOR SELF-STUDY

Recording costs in basket purchase. On January 1, Year 1, Large Co. pays cash to buy Small Co. when Small Co.'s assets and liabilities have book and market values as in Exhibit 8.5. At the time of the purchase, Small Co. has recorded book value of

EXHIBIT 8.5	SMALL CO. PURCHASED BY LARGE CO. Book and Market Values of Assets and Liabilities at Time of Purchase (dollar amounts in thousands) (Problem 8.5 For Self-Study)

	Book Values on Small's Balance Sheet (1)	Market Values at Time of Purchase by Large Co. (2)
Cash	$15,000	$ 15,000
Inventories	30,000	37,500
Land, Buildings, Equipment	50,000	65,000
Patents Developed by Small	—	70,000
Patents Purchased by Small	35,000	38,500
R & D In Process	—	55,000
Brand Names and Trademarks	—	45,000
Less:		
Current Liabilities	(20,000)	(20,000)
Long-term Debt	(40,000)	(47,000)
Totals	$70,000	$259,000

---

[8]Financial Accounting Standards Board, *Interpretation No. 4,* "Applicability of FASB Statement No. 2 to Business Combinations Accounted for by the Purchase Method," 1975.

[9]Accounting Principles Board, *Opinion No. 17,* 1970.

shareholders' equity of $70 million and market value of shareholders' equity of $259 million. Assume that Large Co. amortizes goodwill, if any, over 20 years.

a. Indicate the new asset and liability valuations on Large Co.'s balance sheet if it pays $259 million for Small Co. What assets, if any, will Large Co. write off after recording these items? Give the journal entry. What will be the annual charge, if any, for amortization of goodwill?

b. Indicate the new asset and liability valuations on Large Co.'s balance sheet if it pays $270 million for Small Co. What assets, if any, will Large Co. write off immediately after recording these items? Give the journal entry. What will be the annual charge, if any, for amortization of goodwill?

c. Now assume that Large Co. values R&D In Process at $66 million, not $55 million, and pays $270 million for Small Co. What assets, if any, will Large Co. write off immediately after recording these items? What will be the annual charge, if any, for amortization of goodwill? Compare Large Co.'s annual earnings before taxes for Year 1 through Year 20 in this part with the earnings in part **b**.

Goodwill and Other Components of a Basket Purchase: A Quality-of-Earnings Issue   The interaction between the accounting rules (illustrated in Problem 8.5 for Self-Study) for goodwill and purchased R&D In Process have caused some firms to use accounting procedures to manipulate their quality of earnings. The Securities and Exchange Commission (SEC) has discouraged such practices. Here, we introduce the issue. Recall that analysts prefer that firms have high recurring earnings—recurring earnings are higher quality than one-shot earnings. All else being equal, the higher the recurring earnings, the higher will be valuation placed on a firm. A corollary applies to a firm that must report either one-time losses or continuing expenses: all else equal, analysts will give to the firm with a one-time charge a higher valuation than they will give to a firm that reports an expense that continues year to year. This occurs even though the total amounts debited against earnings are the same in the two cases. So some companies prefer to allocate the cost of purchased firms to R&D In Process, which they immediately write off, rather than to goodwill, which they would amortize over many years.

Example 7   During the last decade, WorldCom bought MCI for about $37 billion. Both are telephone companies. WorldCom proposed to allocate about $7 billion of the purchase price to R&D In Process, which it would then write off in a single, one-time loss of $7 billion in the year of acquisition (as in part **c** of Problem 8.5 for Self-Study). The SEC questioned this allocation, suggesting that $3 billion was a more reasonable valuation. WorldCom then allocated the other $4 billion to goodwill. Amortizing that goodwill over 40 years will decrease income by about $1 billion per year (as in part **b** of Problem 8.5 for Self-Study). WorldCom preferred the one-time charge of the large amount over the continuing charge of the smaller amount. The SEC found that questionable.

Goodwill and Asset Impairment   The accounting rules for impairment, discussed earlier, apply to intangibles, including purchased goodwill.

Example 8   Burns, Philp and Company Limited (B-P), a food ingredients company, spent $100 million to acquire the plant assets and brand names of Tone's Spices. B-P intended to sell Tone's Spices in warehouse stores like Sam's Clubs and Price/Costco warehouses. B-P allocated $15 million to plant assets, $35 million to brand names, and the remaining $50 million to goodwill. Within days of the acquisition, market pressure from competitor McCormick Spices forced B-P to offer higher-than-anticipated cash discounts and slotting fees (for the rights to put spices into the club stores and warehouses) to its large customers. B-P judged that the expected undiscounted future cash flows from the Tone operations had declined to only $90 million and the market value of the Tone operations had dropped to $60 million.

An asset impairment has occurred because book value of the acquisition of $100 million exceeds expected future cash flows of $90 million. B-P writes down the assets acquired by $40 million, from $100 million, to their fair value of $60 million. Assume that B-P judges the plant assets have retained their fair value of $15 million, so that the brand names and goodwill together have total book value of only $45 (= $60 − $15) million. FASB *Statement of Financial Accounting Standards No. 121* requires that B-P allocate the decline in market value of $40 entirely to goodwill before writing down specific intangibles such as the brand names. Thus, B-P will allocate the entire impairment loss to the goodwill acquired along with the plant assets and brand names. The brand names will retain their original $35 million valuation, at least until B-P begins to amortize them. The journal entries could be as follows (with amounts in millions), with the first one made at the time of acquisition and the second on discovery of the impairment:

Plant Assets	15.0	
Brand Names	35.0	
Goodwill on Acquisition of Tone Spices	50.0	
Cash		100.0
To record the acquisition of Tone Spices for $100 million cash.		
Loss on Impairment	40.0	
Goodwill on Acquisition of Tone Spices		40.0

The loss appears on the income statement. The loss equals the excess of old net book value of $100 million over current fair value of $60 million. Assets remain with book value of $60 = $15 for plant + $35 for brand names + $10 for goodwill.

FINANCIAL STATEMENT PRESENTATION

This section discusses the presentation of plant-related items in the balance sheet and income statement. Appendix 8.1 discusses their presentation in the statement of cash flows.

BALANCE SHEET

The balance sheet separates noncurrent from current assets. Property, plant, and equipment accounts appear in the balance sheet among the noncurrent assets. Firms generally disclose the assets' cost and accumulated depreciation in one of the three ways illustrated with the following data from a recent annual report of the General Electric Company (with dollar amounts in millions):

1. All information is listed in the balance sheet (the style used by Walt Disney Company).

Property, Plant, and Equipment	
Acquisition Cost	$25,168
Less Accumulated Depreciation	(11,557)
Property, Plant, and Equipment—Net	$13,611

2. Acquisition cost is omitted from the balance sheet (the style used by USX Corporation).

Property, Plant, and Equipment, less	
Accumulated Depreciation of $11,557	$13,611

3. Acquisition cost and accumulated depreciation are omitted from the balance sheet but are detailed in the notes (the style used by General Electric).

Property, Plant, and Equipment—Net	$13,611

With the second disclosure format, the reader can deduce the missing quantity—acquisition cost—by adding together the two disclosed quantities. With the third format, the reader must consult the notes to learn the acquisition cost and the accumulated depreciation.

INCOME STATEMENT

Depreciation expense appears in the income statement, sometimes disclosed separately and sometimes, particularly for manufacturing firms, as part of cost of goods sold expense. USX Corporation lists depreciation expense separately from other costs of goods sold, explicitly noting that cost of goods sold excludes depreciation. General Electric includes depreciation expense in cost of goods sold and separately discloses the amount of depreciation in the notes. Gain or loss on retirement of plant assets appears on the income statement, but often the amounts are so small that some "Other" caption includes them.

AN INTERNATIONAL PERSPECTIVE

The accounting for plant assets in most developed countries closely parallels that in the United States. Firms commonly value plant assets at acquisition, or historical, cost. France permits periodic revaluations of plant assets to current market values. Few firms perform these revaluations, however, because the French immediately tax the unrealized gains. As a result of the book-tax conformity requirement in France, few firms choose to revalue their plant assets for financial reporting. Firms in Great Britain also periodically revalue their plant assets to current market value. Unlike in France, in Great Britain the revaluations do not result in immediate taxation. Refer to Exhibit 2.8, a balance sheet for Ranks Hovis McDougall PLC. This firm revalued its tangible assets during Year 8 (it also purchased additional tangible assets). The offsetting credit for the revaluation is to the account Revaluation Reserve, shown among Capital and Reserves on the balance sheet.

Depreciation accounting in developed countries also closely parallels that in the United States. Firms use both straight-line and accelerated depreciation methods. In countries where financial and tax reporting closely conform (such as Japan and Germany), firms tend to use accelerated depreciation methods for both financial and tax reporting. When firms in Great Britain recognize depreciation on revalued plant assets, they charge the depreciation on the revalued amount above historical cost to the Revaluation Reserve account. Thus, neither the initial unrealized holding gain nor depreciation of this unrealized gain flows through the income statement. The income statement includes depreciation based on historical cost amounts only.

The International Accounting Standards Committee (IASC) has specified accounting procedures for impairments similar to the procedures used in the United States.[10] The IASC has specified accounting principles for intangibles different from those used in the United States. For expenditures on development—the "D" of R&D, the stage following research, where the firm has found something with commercial value—the IASC suggests that the firm capitalize those costs into an asset account if the future economic benefits will flow from the expenditures and the firm can reliably measure the costs.[11]

VALUING BRAND NAMES

In Great Britain firms can place a valuation on their **brand names** and include this item among assets on the balance sheet. These firms must generally hire independent appraisers to obtain the needed valuations. Appraisers might base their valuations on premium prices charged customers for a branded over a nonbranded product, on the promotion and other costs likely to be incurred in launching a new branded product, or on the price paid in recent mergers and acquisitions for branded product firms.

Relief from Royalty Method   Some firms use the *relief from royalty* method to value trademarks, tradenames, brand names, and technological assets. In this method, the firm estimates the royalties that other firms pay for use of similar assets to measure its savings inherent in owning its own intangibles. Burns, Philp and Company Limited owns the rights to the following brand names: Fleischmann's yeast, Spice Islands spices, and Durkee's dressing, among others. It shows the acquisition cost of its intangible assets in a recent annual report at A$850 million (Australian dollars). In a note, it shows the market value of these intangibles at A$1.5 billion, valued by independent consultants who used the relief from royalty method. A recent annual report says:

> The selection of appropriate royalty rates to be applied to the individual projected revenue streams varied according to the nature of each individual trademark, tradename, brand name, and technological asset, but all fell within the range of 1% to 15%, with the majority in the range of 2% to 5%. Discount rates were then applied to each royalty stream to take into

---

[10]International Accounting Standards Committee, *Statement No. 36,* "Impairment of Assets," 1998.

[11]International Accounting Standards Committee, *Statement No. 38,* "Intangible Assets," 1998.

account the time value of money and the risks inherent in the projections. The discount rates averaged 10%.

The disclosure goes on to give the names of both the firm doing the independent valuations and the individual doing the work. A discount rate of only 10 percent would seem low to us for use in parallel U.S. valuations, but we have no reason to question the amount for Australian valuations. See Example **17** in the appendix at the back of the book for an illustration of the relief from royalty method.

Present Value of Brand Name Cash Flows   Another sensible way to place a valuation on a brand name uses accounting methods to find the value of the cash flows that the brand—in contrast to the firm's other assets—produces.

Exhibit 8.6 illustrates how one might value the Tootsie Roll family of brands (Tootsie Roll, Charms, and Junior Mints, among others) at more than $200 million based on the present value of the cash flows it generates. The method involves four steps, each labeled in the exhibit; all but one typically involves subjective judgment. The interaction of these judgments produces a range of final estimates, which shows the imprecision of the process. This imprecision makes U.S. accountants reluctant to audit and attest to such valuations.

1. The first step attempts to measure the cash flow that the brand, in this example Tootsie Roll, generates. The computation shows brand revenues less brand operating expenses, all of which ultimately result in cash flows. A more precise computation adjusts revenues and expenses for changes in receivables and payables, but Exhibit 8.6 does not illustrate this substep. Brand revenues in excess of operating expenses for the year are $64.1 million.
2. The next step computes the cost of the physical capital—such as land, factories, inventories, and other components of working capital, assets for distributing the branded product—used to produce the cash flow. Tootsie Roll devotes about $188 million of assets to the production and distribution of Tootsie Roll products. (Computing this amount may require estimates and approximations.) Exhibit 8.6 assumes that Tootsie Roll expects to earn 12 percent per year, before taxes, on its assets. Thus, Tootsie Roll

EXHIBIT 8.6	Illustration of Steps to Estimate the Value of a Brand Name Using Present Value of Discounted Cash Flows Caused by the Tootsie Roll Family of Brands (all dollar amounts in millions)

Worldwide Sales	$312.7
Cost of Goods Sold and Operating Expenses	(248.6)
[1] Operating Margin (20 percent)	$ 64.1
Employed Physical Capital	$188.1
Subtract Pretax Profit on Physical Capital Required at 12 Percent	(22.6)
[2] Profit Generated by Brand	$ 41.5
Subtract Income Taxes at 37 Percent	(15.3)
[3] Net Brand Profits	$ 26.2
Multiply by Aftertax Capitalization Factor	× 8.0
[4] Estimated Brand Value	$209.6

must earn $22.6 (= .12 × $188) million from the Tootsie Roll family of products just to pay the cost of the physical capital devoted to the production of products carrying the Tootsie Roll brand. That leaves $41.5 (= $64.1 − $22.6) million of pretax profits attributable to the nonphysical assets, in this case the brands themselves. We base this calculation on the historical cost of the physical assets, but one might more logically use some measure of their current cost.

3. Exhibit 8.6 assumes that Tootsie Roll must pay income taxes at the rate of 37 percent of taxable income, so that after taxes, the brands generate $26.2 [= (1.00 − .37) × $41.5] million of aftertax cash flows for the year.

4. Now comes the toughest part of the estimation: how long does the analyst expect the cash flows from the brand to last, and how risky are they? If the analyst expected the brand-generated cash flow, $26.2 million per year, to persist for just one year, the analyst would value the brand at the amount of those cash flows—$26.2 million. If the analyst expected the brand values to last indefinitely and used an aftertax discount rate of 10 percent per year, then the analysis would result in a brand valuation of $262 million (= $26.2 million × 1/.10). (See the discussion of the valuation of perpetuities in the appendix at the back of the book, at Examples **15** and following.) Exhibit 8.6 shows a multiplier (like a price/earnings ratio) of 8, which suggests that the brand is worth about $209 million (= 8 × $26.2 million).[12]

PROBLEM 8.6 FOR SELF-STUDY

Sensitivity of brand valuation to estimates. Refer to the computations of brand value for Tootsie Roll in Exhibit 8.6 and observe the sensitivity of the final valuation to these estimates.

a. Recompute the brand value assuming a pretax charge for physical capital of 10 percent per year and a multiplier for brand cash flows of 10.

b. Recompute the brand value assuming a pretax charge for physical capital of 20 percent per year and a multiplier for brand cash flows of 6.

[12]Examine Table 4 at the back of the book. Notice that a multiplier of 8 implies a discount rate of 8 percent for cash flows lasting 13 years or 10 percent for cash flows lasting 17 years or 12.5 percent for cash flows lasting forever (in perpetuity). The appendix at the back of the book explains Table 4 and how to use it. A comprehensive discussion of brand valuation from an accounting perspective appears in Patrick Barwise, Christopher Higson, Andrew Likierman, and Paul Marsh, *Accounting for Brands* (London: London Business School and The Institute of Chartered Accountants of England and Wales, 1989). See Carol J. Simon and Mary W. Sullivan, "The Measurement and Determinants of Brand Equity: A Financial Approach," *Marketing Science* 12, no. 1 (Winter 1993): 28–52, for the classic study of the economics of brand valuation. Simon and Sullivan find that of all the food-product brand names they examined, Tootsie Roll had the highest ratio of brand value to other asset value.

SUMMARY

Long-lived operating assets include plant assets, wasting assets (nonrenewable natural resources), and intangibles. Each class presents the same accounting problems:

1. Calculating the cost of the asset to be capitalized as an asset
2. Estimating the total period of benefit or the amount of expected benefits
3. Assigning, in a systematic and reasonable fashion, the amortizable cost to the benefited periods or units produced

The chapter emphasized depreciable plant assets and their depreciation. The total cost the firm will charge for amortization over the life of the asset equals acquisition cost reduced by any salvage value. The firm estimates the period (or number of units) of benefit from experience or, for tax reporting, from guidelines set by the Internal Revenue Service. Most firms use straight-line depreciation for financial reporting.

If the firm finds that the expected undiscounted future cash flows from the asset have declined since acquisition, it will test to see if that impairment of future benefits warrants a write-down of then-current book value to the present value of the remaining cash flows.

If the firm retires the asset before the end of the estimated service life for an amount different from its book value, a gain or loss will result. This gain or loss appears on the income statement. Intangibles such as trademarks, copyrights, patents, and computer programs are the most valuable resources owned by some firms. Firms account for intangibles purchased from others just as they account for tangible assets. For most intangibles developed within a firm, accounting requires the immediate expensing of the development costs.

APPENDIX 8.1: EFFECTS ON THE STATEMENT OF CASH FLOWS OF TRANSACTIONS INVOLVING PLANT AND INTANGIBLE ASSETS

The statement of cash flows reports as investing activities both the cash used for acquisition of plant or intangible assets and the cash provided by their retirement. It usually shows adjustments for depreciation and amortization in deriving cash from operations when the firm uses the indirect method.

RETIREMENT ENTRIES IN THE STATEMENT OF CASH FLOWS

When the firm sells a plant or intangible asset for cash, it reports that cash in the Investing section as a nonoperating source, Proceeds from Disposition of Noncurrent Assets. Usually, the firm sells a plant or intangible asset for an amount different from its book value at the time of sale. Thus, the retirement generates a loss (proceeds less than book value) or a gain (proceeds greater than book value).

Loss on Retirement

The Investing section of the statement shows all the proceeds from selling the plant or intangible asset. None of that cash results from operations. In the indirect format for operating cash flow, the statement of cash flows begins with net income, which includes the loss on sale. Because the sale is a (dis)investing—not an operating—activity, the presentation must add back the amount of the loss in deriving operating cash flows. The addback presentation resembles the addback for depreciation expense.

Gain on Retirement

The gain on retirement increases net income, but the cash from retirement produces (dis)investing, not operating, cash flow. When the statement of cash flows presents cash from operations using the indirect format, it must subtract the amount of the gain from net income so that operating cash flow will exclude the cash from retirement, properly classified among investing activities.

DEPRECIATION AND AMORTIZATION CHARGES

Whether or not depreciation and amortization charges appear in the statement of cash flows depends on whether the firm chooses to use the direct method or the indirect method for reporting cash generated by operations. A firm using the direct method reports only receipts minus expenditures for operating activities. A firm using the indirect method reports net income—revenues minus expenses—along with various addbacks and subtractions to convert the amount into receipts minus expenditures. Because depreciation and amortization expenses reduce income but use no cash currently, an addback for depreciation and amortization expenses appears in the derivation of cash from operations. Most firms use the indirect method and show such an addback.

Depreciation Charges for a Manufacturing Firm

Chapter 7 introduced the notion, repeated in this chapter, that manufacturing firms typically do not debit all depreciation charges to depreciation expense. Rather, such firms debit depreciation on manufacturing facilities to the Work-in-Process Inventory account. The firm transfers the depreciation costs from Work-in-Process to Finished Goods Inventory at the same time that it transfers the goods from the production line to the finished goods warehouse. Then, the depreciation charges remain in Finished Goods Inventory until the firm sells the goods embodying the depreciation. Only then do the depreciation charges become expense—part of the Cost of Goods Sold expense account. Conventionally, however, a manufacturing firm adds back all depreciation charges for a given period in its derivation of cash from operations for the same period in which the firm incurred those charges.

- If the firm has sold the goods embodying the depreciation, the addback cancels the depreciation included in Cost of Goods Sold.
- If the firm has not yet sold the inventory embodying the depreciation, then the current asset Inventories will increase by the amount of any depreciation embodied in the Work-in-Process accounts. Recall that in the indirect method, the firm subtracts the increase in inventory accounts in deriving cash flows from operations. (Refer to Exhibit 4.16. Note that the addback on line 2 and the subtraction on line 3 increase by the same amount.)

Thus, whether the firm sells or keeps in inventory the manufactured goods embodying the depreciation charges, it will add back all depreciation charges, manufacturing and other, to net income in deriving operating cash flows. If the firm has not sold the goods, the subtraction for the increase in inventory will cancel just the right part—the depreciation charges in ending inventory—of the addback.

NONCASH ACQUISITIONS OF PLANT AND INTANGIBLE ASSETS

Firms often borrow funds from a lender to acquire plant and intangible assets from a third party. A firm, for example, might borrow $5 million from an insurance company and use the cash to acquire a building from a developer. The loan appears on the statement of cash flows as a financing activity, and the acquisition of the building appears as an investing activity.

Firms sometimes give consideration other than cash to the seller (the developer in the above example) in acquiring plant and intangible assets. The consideration might be a mortgage note or the firm's shares. Because these investing and financing transactions involve a bartering that does not use cash, they do not appear on the statement of cash flows. The firm must report such transactions in a supplementary schedule or note.

SOLUTIONS TO SELF-STUDY PROBLEMS

SUGGESTED SOLUTION TO PROBLEM 8.1 FOR SELF-STUDY

(Jensen Company; calculating the acquisition cost of fixed assets.)

(1) a, b, d, j, l, m, o, p

(2) c, e, f, g, i, k, l, n, o, p

(3) h, i, p, s

(4) i, q, r

Comments and Explanations

d. Removing the old building makes the land ready to accept the new one. These costs apply to the land, not to the new building. For tax purposes, the firm might prefer to allocate this cost to the building because it can depreciate the building, but not the land.

f. The reduction in cost of materials and supplies will reduce the cost of the building. The actual accounting entries depend on the method used to record the potential discount. This book does not discuss these issues.

h. Although one capitalizes explicit interest, one may not capitalize opportunity-cost interest or interest imputed on one's own funds used. The adjusting entry credits Real Estate and debits Interest Revenue. The debit reduces income, removing the revenue that had been recognized by the company.

i. Computation of the amounts to be allocated requires an estimate. Once the firm estimates amounts, it debits them to Building or to Depreciation Expense and Work-in-Process Inventory, as appropriate, for the regular company operations.

j. Credit to Land account, reducing its cost.

l. Allocate to Land and Building, based on an estimate of how time was spent. Given the description, most of these costs are probably for the building.

m. Include as part of the cost of the land.

n. Capitalize as part of the Building account for the same reasons that a firm capitalizes interest during construction. Some accountants would treat this item as expense. In any case, the firm can treat this item as an expense for tax reporting.

o. Allocate the costs for insuring workers to the same accounts as the wages for those workers.

p. Most accountants would treat this as an expense or loss for the period. Others would capitalize as part of the cost of the building for the same reason that they capitalized the explicit insurance cost. If, however, the company was irrational in acquiring insurance policies with deductible clauses, this item would be an expense or loss. Accounting usually assumes that most managements make rational decisions most of the time. In any case, one can treat this item as an expense or loss for tax reporting.

q. Debit to Machine and Equipment account, an asset account separate from Building.

r. Treat the same as the preceding item; installation costs are part of the cost of the asset; see Chapter 2.

s. Recognizing revenue is incorrect. Credit the Real Estate account and debit the Construction Revenue account.

SUGGESTED SOLUTION TO PROBLEM 8.2 FOR SELF-STUDY

(Markam Corporation; calculating periodic depreciation.)
a. Straight-Line Method:

Years 3-7: ($20,000 − $2,000)/5 = $3,600 each year
Total: $3,600 × 5 = $18,000

b. Sum-of-the-Years'-Digits Method:

Year 3: 5/15 × ($20,000 − $2,000) = $ 6,000
Year 4: 4/15 × ($20,000 − $2,000) =   4,800
Year 5: 3/15 × ($20,000 − $2,000) =   3,600
Year 6: 2/15 × ($20,000 − $2,000) =   2,400
Year 7: 1/15 × ($20,000 − $2,000) =   1,200
    Total $18,000

c. Double Declining-Balance Method:

Year 3: 2/5 × $20,000 = $ 8,000
Year 4: 2/5 × ($20,000 − $8,000) =   4,800
Year 5: 2/5 × ($20,000 − $8,000 − $4,800) =   2,880
Year 6: 1/2 × ($4,320[a] − $2,000) =   1,160
Year 7: 1/2 × ($4,320 − $2,000) =   1,160
    Total $18,000

[a]$20,000 − $8,000 − $4,800 − $2,880 = $4,320

d. Units-of-Production Method:

Years 3–6: 5,000 × $.75[a] = $3,750 per year
Year 7: 4,000 × $.75[a] = 3,000
    Total [($3,750 × 4) + $3,000] = $18,000

[a]($20,000 − $2,000)/24,000 = $.75 per hour

SUGGESTED SOLUTION TO PROBLEM 8.3 FOR SELF-STUDY

(Central States Electric Company; adjustments for changes in estimates.)
(All dollar amounts in millions.)
a. $4.4 per year = ($200 + $20)/50 years
b. $4.5 per year = [$200 + $20 + $4 − ($4.4 per year × 10 years)]/40 years remaining
            life
        = ($224 − $44)/40
        = $180/40

c. $3.0 per year $= [\$180 - (\$4.5 \times 20 \text{ years})]/30$ years remaining life
$$= (\$180 - \$90)/30$$
$$= \$90/30$$

SUGGESTED SOLUTION TO PROBLEM 8.4 FOR SELF-STUDY

(Purdy Company; distinguishing repairs from improvements.)
a. Record the first truck at $19,200. Record the second truck at $15,000; debit $4,200 to expense or loss.
b. When Purdy Company acquired the first truck, it knew it would have to make the "repair," which is an improvement. The purchase price was lower because of the known cost to be incurred. At the time of acquisition, the firm anticipated the cost as required to produce the expected service potential of the asset. The fact that the cost was $4,200, rather than "about $4,000," does not seem to violate Purdy Company's expectations at the time it acquired the truck. If the repair had cost significantly more than $4,000—say, $7,000—then the excess could be loss or expense.

Purdy Company believed that the second truck was operable when it agreed on the purchase price. Purdy Company incurred the cost of the repair to achieve the level of service potential it thought it had acquired. There are no more future benefits after the repair than it had anticipated at the time of acquisition. Therefore, the $4,200 is expense or loss.

SUGGESTED SOLUTION TO PROBLEM 8.5 FOR SELF-STUDY

(Large Co. buys Small Co.; recording costs in basket purchase.)
a. The assets and liabilities will appear on Large Co.'s balance sheet at the exact amounts appearing in Column (2) of Exhibit 8.5. Large Co. will write off the asset for R&D In Process with an entry such as the following:

Loss on Acquisition of R&D In Process	55,000,000	
R&D In Process		55,000,000

There will be no goodwill nor, hence, any future amortization charges for goodwill.
b. The assets and liabilities will appear on Large Co.'s balance sheet at the amounts appearing in Column (2) of Exhibit 8.5 along with a new asset Goodwill in the amount of $11 [= $270 − $259] million. Large Co. will write off $55 million of R&D In Process, with the same journal entry as above in a. Amortization charges for goodwill will be $1.1 [=$11/10 years] million per year.
c. The assets and liabilities will appear on Large Co.'s balance sheet at the amounts appearing in Column (2) of Exhibit 8.5 except that R&D In Process will first appear at $76 million. There will be no Goodwill. Immediately thereafter, Large Co. will write off $76 million of R&D In Process and will have no future amortization charges for Goodwill. During the first year, Year 1, Large Co's income before taxes will be smaller by about $19.9 [= $21.00 − $1.1] million than in part b. After that, for years 2 through 20, Large Co.'s income will be $1.1 million larger than in part b. These differences result because Large Co. allocated more dollars of the basket purchase's cost to R&D In Process and hence less to Goodwill. Because it must immediately expense the R&D In Process, it will have no future amortization charges for those amounts.

SUGGESTED SOLUTION TO PROBLEM 8.6 FOR SELF-STUDY

(Tootsie Roll; sensitivity of brand valuations to estimates)

TOOTSIE ROLL
Illustration of Steps to Estimate the Value of a Brand Name Using Present Value of Discounted Cash Flows Caused by the Tootsie Roll Family of Brands with Variations in Assumptions
(all dollar amounts in millions)

	Part a	Part b
Worldwide Sales	$312.7	$312.7
Operating Expenses	(248.6)	(248.6)
[1] Operating Margin (28 percent)	$ 64.1	$ 64.1
Employed Physical Capital $188.1		
Subtract Pretax Profit on Physical Capital Required at 10 (part **a**) or 20 (part **b**) Percent	(18.8)	(37.6)
[2] Profit Generated by Brand	$ 45.3	$ 26.5
Subtract Income Taxes at 37 Percent	(16.8)	(9.8)
[3] Net Brand Profits	$ 28.5	$ 16.7
Multiply by Aftertax Capitalization Factor	× 10.0	× 6.0
[4] Estimated Brand Value	$285.0	$100.2

KEY TERMS AND CONCEPTS

Amortization
Plant assets
Interest paid during construction
Depreciation
Joint cost
Value
Salvage or net residual value
Service or depreciable life
Modified Accelerated Cost Recovery System (MACRS)
Straight-line (time and use) methods
Declining-balance methods
Sum-of-the-years'-digits method
Treatment of changes in periodic depreciation (estimates of useful lives and residual values of long-lived assets)

Repairs
Maintenance
Improvements
Impairments
Wasting assets
Depletion
Units-of-production depletion method
Intangibles
Capitalize
Research and development (R&D)
Basket purchase
R&D In Process
Goodwill
Brand name

QUESTIONS, EXERCISES, PROBLEMS, AND CASES

QUESTIONS

1. Review the meaning of the terms and concepts listed above in Key Terms and Concepts.
2. A particular firm's property department maintains buildings and equipment used in manufacturing, selling, and administrative activities. The salaries of personnel in the property department during the current period may appear as an expense during the

current period, as an expense next period, or as an expense during several future periods. Explain.

3. A manufacturing firm receives a bid from a local construction company to build a warehouse for $300,000. The firm decides to build the warehouse itself and does so at a cost of $250,000. Why is it that GAAP do not permit the firm to record the warehouse at $300,000 and recognize revenue of $50,000? How will net income differ if the firm follows the generally accepted procedure versus recording the warehouse at $300,000?

4. **a.** What is the effect of capitalizing interest on reported net income summed over all the periods of the life of a given self-constructed asset, from building through use until eventual retirement? Contrast with a policy of expensing interest as incurred.

   b. Consider a company engaging in increasing dollar amounts of self-construction activity each period during periods when interest rates do not decline. What is the effect on reported income each year of capitalizing interest in contrast to expensing interest as incurred?

5. **a.** "Accounting for depreciating assets would be greatly simplified if accounting periods were only long enough or assets' lives short enough." What is the point of the quotation?

   b. "The major purpose of depreciation accounting is to provide funds for the replacement of assets as they wear out." Do you agree? Explain.

6. "Showing both acquisition cost and accumulated depreciation amounts separately provides a rough indication of the relative age of the firm's long-lived assets."

   a. Assume that the Dickens Company acquired an asset with a depreciable cost of $100,000 and no salvage value several years ago. Accumulated depreciation as of December 31, recorded on a straight-line basis, is $60,000. The depreciation charge for the year is $10,000. What is the asset's depreciable life? How old is the asset?

   b. Assume straight-line depreciation. Devise a formula that, given the depreciation charge for the year and the asset's accumulated depreciation, you can use to estimate the age of the asset.

7. Some critics of the required accounting for changes in estimates of service lives of depreciable assets characterize it as the "always wrong" method. Why do you think these critics use this characterization?

8. "Applying the accounting for repairs versus betterments often comes down to a matter of materiality." Explain.

9. A firm expects to use a delivery truck for five years. At the end of three years, the transmission wears out and requires replacement at a cost of $4,000. The firm argues that it should capitalize this expenditure because without it the useful life is zero and with it the useful life will be another three years. Comment on the firm's reasoning relative to GAAP.

10. A firm sold for $10,000 a machine that originally cost $30,000 and had accumulated depreciation of $24,000 (book value = $6,000). Why does accounting include a gain on sale of machine of $4,000 in the income statement instead of showing sales revenue of $10,000 and cost of machine sold of $6,000?

11. "Over sufficiently long time periods, full costing and successful efforts costing for mineral resources produce identical total expenses." Explain.

12. Suggest reasons why generally accepted accounting procedures permit successful efforts costings for mineral exploration costs but not for the research and development costs of a pharmaceutical company.

13. A firm that incurs research and development costs to develop a patented product must expense these costs as incurred. A firm that purchases that same patent from its creator, however, capitalizes the expenditure as an asset and amortizes it. What is the rationale for this different treatment of the patent?

EXERCISES

14. **Classifying expenditure as asset or expense.** For each of the following expenditures or acquisitions, indicate the type of account debited. Classify the account as asset other than product cost, product cost (Work-in-Process Inventory), or expense. If the account debited is an asset account, specify whether it is current or noncurrent.
    a. $150 for repairs of office machines
    b. $1,500 for emergency repairs to an office machine
    c. $250 for maintenance of delivery trucks
    d. $5,000 for a machine acquired in return for a three-year note
    e. $4,200 for research and development staff salaries
    f. $3,100 for newspaper ads
    g. $6,400 for wages of factory workers engaged in production
    h. $3,500 for wages of factory workers engaged in installing equipment the firm has purchased
    i. $2,500 for salaries of the office work force
    j. $1,000 for legal fees incurred in acquiring an ore deposit
    k. $1,200 for a one-year insurance policy beginning next month
    l. $1,800 for U.S. Treasury notes, to be sold to pay the next installment due on income taxes
    m. $4,000 for royalty payment on a patent used in manufacturing
    n. $10,000 for purchase of a trademark
    o. $100 filing fee for copyright-registration application

15. **Cost of self-constructed assets.** Assume that Bolton Company purchased a plot of land for $90,000 as a plant site. A small office building sits on the plot, conservatively appraised at $20,000. The company plans to use the office building after making some modifications and renovations. The company had plans drawn for a factory and received bids for its construction. It rejected all bids and decided to construct the plant itself. Management believes that plant asset accounts should include the following additional items:

(1) Materials and Supplies	$200,000
(2) Excavation	12,000
(3) Labor on Construction	140,000
(4) Cost of Remodeling Old Building into Office Building	13,000
(5) Interest Paid on Cash Borrowed by Bolton[a]	6,000
(6) Interest Forgone on Bolton's Own Cash Used	9,000
(7) Cash Discounts on Materials Purchased	7,000
(8) Supervision by Management	10,000
(9) Workers' Compensation Insurance Premiums	8,000
(10) Payment of Claims for Injuries Not Covered by Insurance	3,000
(11) Clerical and Other Expenses of Construction	8,000
(12) Paving of Streets and Sidewalks	5,000
(13) Architect's Plans and Specifications	4,000
(14) Legal Costs of Conveying Land	2,000
(15) Legal Costs of Injury Claim	1,000
(16) Income Credited to Retained Earnings Account (the difference between the Forgone cost and the lowest contractor's bid)	11,000

[a]This interest is the entire amount of interest paid during the construction period.

Show in detail the items Bolton should include in the following accounts: Land, Factory Building, Office Building, and Site Improvements. Explain the reason for excluding any of these items from the four accounts.

16. **Cost of self-developed product.** New Hampshire Wood Stove Company incurs various costs in developing a new, cleaner-burning wood stove. Indicate the accounting treatment of each of the following expenditures.

(1) Salaries of company engineers to design wood stove $40,000
(2) Cost of prototype of wood stove built by external contractor 3,000
(3) Cost of supplies and salaries of personnel to test prototype 6,500
(4) Fees paid to Environmental Protection Agency to test emissions of new wood stove 1,500
(5) Legal fees incurred to register and establish a patent on the wood stove 2,500
(6) Cost of castings, or molds, for metal parts of new wood stove 16,000

17. **Amount of interest capitalized during construction.** Samson Chemical Company builds some of its own chemical-processing plants. At the start of the year the Construction-in-Process account had a balance of $4 million. Construction activity occurred uniformly throughout the year. At the end of the year the balance was $60 million. The borrowings of the company during the year were as follows:

New Construction Loans at 10 Percent per Year .... $ 30,000,000
Old Bond Issues Maturing at Various Times, Averaging 8 Percent Rate 70,000,000
Total Interest-Bearing Debt $100,000,000

a. Compute the amount of interest capitalized in the Construction-in-Process account for the year.
b. Present journal entries for interest for the year.
c. Early in Year 3, Samson completed the plant and put it to work. Average Construction-in-Process for Year 3 was $10 million. Present journal entries for Year 3 related to interest expense and interest capitalization.

18. **Capitalizing interest during construction.** Nebok Company recently constructed a new headquarters building. Its Construction-in-Process account showed a balance of $23,186,000 on May 31, Year 9, and $68,797,000 on May 31, Year 10. Construction activity occurred evenly throughout the year. Nebok Company completed construction during Year 11. Nebok Company's note on long-term debt revealed the following (in thousands):

	May 31	
	Year 9	Year 10
8.5% unsecured term loan	$25,000	$25,000
12.5% loan secured by real estate	15,600	15,100
14.0% loan secured by real estate	10,900	9,600
Total	$51,500	$49,700

None of this debt relates specifically to construction of the headquarters building. Interest expense before capitalization of interest for the year ending May 31, Year 10, is $5,480,000.

a. Compute the amount of interest capitalized in the Construction-in-Process account for the year.

b. Present journal entries for interest for the year.

c. Nebok Company's net income before interest expense and income taxes for the year is $16,300,000. Nebok Company is subject to a 34 percent income tax rate. Compute net income for the year ending May 31, Year 10.

d. Compute the interest coverage ratio (equals net income before interest expense and income taxes divided by interest expense) using the amounts computed in part **c**.

e. Repeat part **d** using the interest expense before capitalization of interest of $5,480,000 in the denominator.

f. Which measure of the interest coverage ratio provides a more appropriate measure for assessing risk?

19. **Calculations for various depreciation methods.** Assume that Gateway Motors acquires a machine for $29,600. It expects the machine to last six years and to operate for 30,000 hours during that time. Estimated salvage value is $2,600 at the end of the machine's useful life. Calculate the depreciation charge for each of the first three years using each of the following methods:

a. The straight-line (time) method

b. The sum-of-the-years'-digits method

c. The declining-balance method using a 33 percent rate

d. The units-of-production method, with the following operating times: first year, 4,500 hours; second year, 5,000 hours; third year, 5,500 hours

20. **Calculations for various depreciation methods.** On January 1, Year 8, assume that Luck Delivery Company acquired a new truck for $30,000. It estimated the truck to have a useful life of five years and no salvage value. The company closes its books annually on December 31. Indicate the amount of the depreciation charge for each year of the asset's life under the following methods:

a. The straight-line method

b. The declining-balance method at twice the straight-line rate, with a switch to straight-line in Year 11

c. The sum-of-the-years'-digits method

d. MACRS depreciation, assuming that the truck belongs to the five-year property class (*Hint:* charge depreciation for each of six calendar years)

e. Assume now that the firm acquired the truck on April 1, Year 8. Indicate the amount of the depreciation charge for each of the years from Year 8 to Year 13, using the sum-of-the-years'-digits method. (*Hint:* the firm allocates depreciation charges for a year, regardless of the depreciation method, on a straight-line basis to periods within a year.)

21. **Calculations for various depreciation methods.** Calculate the depreciation charge for the first and second years of the asset's life in each of the following cases.

Asset	Cost	Estimated Salvage Value	Life (Years)	Depreciation Method
a. Warehouse	$450,000	$50,000	40	Straight-Line
b. Cutting Machine	$220,000	$40,000	20	Double Declining-Balance (use twice the straight-line rate)
c. Computer	$ 80,000	$20,000	5	Sum-of-the-Years'-Digits
d. Cleaning Machine	$125,000	$25,000	10	150% Declining-Balance
e. Delivery Truck	$ 24,000	$ 4,000	6	Straight-Line
f. Delivery Truck	$ 24,000	$ 4,000	5	Modified Accelerated Cost Recovery System

22. **Production or use depreciation.** Assume that United Express purchased a new panel truck in May, Year 6. The truck cost $22,600. United expected that it would drive the truck for 100,000 miles before trading the truck in and that the salvage value at that time would be $2,600. Odometer readings were as follows:

December 31, Year 6	14,000
December 31, Year 7	48,000
December 31, Year 8	80,000
June 16, Year 9	98,000

On June 16, Year 9, the firm sold the truck for $2,600.
   a. Compute the depreciation charges for each year through Year 8, using a "production or use" method.
   b. Record the entry on June 16, Year 9, to sell the truck.
23. **Revision of estimated service life changes depreciation schedule.** Fast Pace Shipping Company buys a new machine for $40,000 on January 1, Year 7. It estimates that the machine will last 10 years and have a salvage value of $4,000. Early in Year 9, it discovers that the machine will last only an additional six years, or eight years total (with no change in estimated salvage value). The company closes its books on December 31. Present a table showing the depreciation charges for each year from Year 7 to Year 10, using each of the following methods:
   a. The straight-line method
   b. The sum-of-the-years'-digits method
24. **Journal entries for revising estimate of life.** Give the journal entries for the following selected transactions of Fort Manufacturing Corporation. The company uses the straight-line method of calculating depreciation and closes its books annually on December 31.
   a. The firm purchases a polishing machine on November 1, Year 9, for $45,000. It estimates that the machine will have a useful life of 12 years and a salvage value of $1,800 at the end of that time. Give the journal entry for the depreciation at December 31, Year 9.
   b. Record the depreciation for the year ending December 31, Year 10.
   c. In August, Year 15, the firm estimates that the machine will probably have a total useful life of 14 years and a $960 salvage value. Record the depreciation for the year ending December 31, Year 15.

d. The firm sells the machine for $10,000 on March 31, Year 20. Record the entries of that date, assuming that the firm records depreciation as indicated in part **c.**

25. **Retirement of plant assets.** Suppose that Neptune Equipment Corporation acquires a new machine for $9,600 on July 1, Year 4. It estimates that the machine will have a useful life of four years and a salvage value of $1,600. The company closes its books annually on June 30.

   a. Compute the depreciation charges for each year of the asset's life assuming the straight-line method.

   b. The firm sells the machine for $2,700 on September 30, Year 7. Give the journal entries on this date.

   c. Repeat part **b,** but assume that the firm sells the machine for $2,700 on December 31, Year 7.

26. **Working backward to derive proceeds from disposition of plant assets.** The balance sheets of Wilcox Corporation at the beginning and end of the year contained the following data:

	Beginning of Year	End of Year
Property, Plant, and Equipment (at cost)	$400,000	$550,000
Accumulated Depreciation	180,000	160,000
Net Book Value	$220,000	$390,000

During the year, Wilcox Corporation sold machinery and equipment at a gain of $4,000. It purchased new machinery and equipment at a cost of $230,000. Depreciation charges on machinery and equipment for the year amounted to $50,000. Calculate the proceeds Wilcox Corporation received from the sale of the machinery and equipment.

27. **Use of a single asset account or separate asset accounts affects classification of expenditures as repairs or improvements.** Assume that Checker's Pizza Company purchased a delivery truck for $18,000 at the start of Year 1. It expected the truck to last for four years, but the engine requires replacement at the end of Year 2 at a cost of $5,000. Checker's must choose between depreciating the truck as a single unit or as two separate assets—the engine and the rest of the truck. The company uses straight-line depreciation for financial reporting.

   a. Compute total expense for each of the four years of the truck's life, depreciating the entire cost of $18,000 in a single asset account.

   b. Compute total expense for each year of the truck's life, depreciating the engine and the rest of the truck in separate asset accounts.

28. **Journal entries to correct accounting errors.** Give correcting entries for the following situations. In each case, the firm uses the straight-line method of depreciation and closes its books annually on December 31. Recognize all gains and losses currently.

   a. A firm purchased a computer for $3,000 on January 1, Year 3. It depreciated the computer at a rate of 25 percent of original cost per year. On June 30, Year 5, it sold the computer for $800 and acquired a new computer for $4,000. The book-keeper made the following entry to record the transaction:

Equipment	3,200	
Cash		3,200

b. A firm purchased a used truck for $7,000. Its cost, when new, was $12,000. The bookkeeper made the following entry to record the purchase:

Truck	12,000	
Accumulated Depreciation		5,000
Cash		7,000

c. A firm purchased a testing mechanism on April 1, Year 6, for $1,200. It depreciated the testing mechanism at a 10 percent annual rate. A burglar stole the testing mechanism on June 30, Year 8. The firm had not insured against this theft. The bookkeeper made the following entry:

Theft Loss	1,200	
Testing Mechanism		1,200

29. **Journal entries for depreciable asset transactions.** Assume that on March 31, Year 6, Boston Can Corporation acquired a new machine for $16,000. The seller agreed to accept in payment $10,000 in cash and a 10 percent, one-year note for $6,000. Boston Can Corporation estimated the new machine to have a service life of ten years and a salvage value of $1,000.

Boston Can Corporation had purchased a similar old machine on January 1, Year 1, for $12,000. The firm estimated that the old machine would have a useful life of eight years, after which it would have a salvage value of $800. It sold the old machine for $4,000 on April 30, Year 6.

Prepare dated journal entries to record all transactions through December 31, Year 8, including year-end adjustments but excluding closing entries.

30. **Effect of transaction on statement of cash flows.** (Requires coverage of Appendix 8.1.) Refer to the simplified statement of cash flows in Exhibit 4.16. Numbers appear on nine of the lines in the statement. Ignore the unnumbered lines in responding to the questions that follow.

Assume that the accounting cycle is complete for the period and that the firm has prepared all of the financial statements. It then discovers that it has overlooked a transaction. It records that transaction in the accounts and corrects all of the financial statements. For each of the following transactions, indicate which of the numbered lines of the statement of cash flows change and the amount and direction of the change. Ignore income tax effects.

a. A firm sells for $3,000 cash a machine that cost $10,000 and that has $6,000 of accumulated depreciation.

b. A firm sells for $5,000 cash a machine that cost $10,000 and that has $6,000 of accumulated depreciation.

c. A firm trades in on a new machine an old machine that cost $10,000 and that has $6,000 of accumulated depreciation. The new machine has a cash price of $9,000. The firm receives a trade-in allowance for the old machine of $5,000 and pays $4,000. Following GAAP, the firm records no gain or loss on trade-in but records the new machine at $8,000.

d. A fire destroys a warehouse. The loss is uninsured. The warehouse cost $90,000 and at the time of the fire had accumulated depreciation of $40,000.

e. Refer to the facts of part **d.** The fire also destroyed inventory costing $60,000. The loss is uninsured. Record the effects of only these new facts.

PROBLEMS AND CASES

31. **Allocation of cost in basket purchases.** In each of the following situations, compute the amounts of gain or loss appearing on the income statement for the year, as well as the amount of asset appearing on the balance sheet as of the end of the year. Show the journal entry or entries required, and provide reasons for your decisions.

   a. A company wants to acquire a five-acre site for a new warehouse. The land it wants is part of a 10-acre site that the owner insists must be purchased as a whole for $24,000. The company purchases the land, spends $3,000 in legal fees for rights to divide the site into two five-acre plots, and immediately offers half of the land for resale. The two best offers it receives are as follows:

   (1) $18,000 for the east half
   (2) $12,000 for the west half
   The company sells the east half for $18,000.

   b. Assume the same data as in part **a,** except the two best offers are as follows:

   (1) $10,000 for the east half
   (2) $15,000 for the west half
   The company sells the west half for $15,000.

32. **Basket purchases and R&D In Process.** When Intellicorp Inc., a business software firm, purchased ICS Deloitte Management's interface technology for $6.6 million, it allocated $4.8 million to R&D In Process. Assume it allocated the rest of the purchase price to land.

   ■ In the year of the purchase, Intellicorp's net income before accounting for the costs of this purchase was $1.7 million.

   ■ The SEC challenged the allocation of $4.8 million to R&D In Process, and Intellicorp decreased the charge for the quarter of purchase for R&D In Process to $2.7 million. Intellicorp then allocated the $2.1 (= $4.8 − $2.7) million to goodwill.

   ■ Intellicorp will amortize goodwill arising as a result of the SEC's challenge over 10 years and will charge a full year of amortization against earnings for the year of acquisition.

   ■ Assume Intellicorp's earnings before costs relating to this purchase increase to $2.6 million per year as a result of the purchase.

   ■ Ignore income tax effects of this purchase in analyzing the following questions.

   a. What was Intellicorp's net earnings for the year of the purchase when it allocated $4.8 million to R&D In Process? What will be the earnings in subsequent years?

   b. What was Intellicorp's net earnings for the year of the purchase when it allocated $2.7 million to R&D In Process? What will be the earnings in subsequent years?

   c. If an analyst projects Intellicorp's value at 15 times annual earnings, how does the SEC's ruling that Intellicorp must change its accounting for R&D In Process affect the analyst's valuation of the company?

33. **Depreciation calculations affect net income; working backward to derive depreciable assets' cost.** The third-quarter report of Deutsch Lufthansa AG for a recent year reported a change in the airline's depreciation policies. The following was reported in the *Wall Street Journal:*

   BONN—Using new accounting methods for depreciation [Lufthansa] was able to limit its pretax losses in the first nine months . . . to 262 million marks. The pretax loss of 262 million marks in the first nine months represented an accomplishment for the company, which announced first-half pretax losses (for this year) of 542 million marks. . . . The reason the pretax loss for the first nine months narrowed from the level of the first half is because of [*sic*] accounting practices. The German state-owned air carrier said in September that it would change the way it does its accounts with a new policy of writing off its fleet of aircraft over a 12-year period to 15 percent of their (cost). The previous policy had called for planes to be written off over 10 years to 5 percent of their cost. . . . One analyst said that the entire improvement in Lufthansa's third quarter results was attributable to (restating depreciation for the first nine months of the year for the) new accounting principles, rather than fundamentals.

Use these details to deduce the cost in marks of Lufthansa's fleet of aircraft.

34. **Effect on net income of changes in estimates for depreciable assets.** American Airlines has $3 billion of assets, including airplanes costing $2.5 billion with net book value of $1.6 billion. It earns net income equal to approximately 6 percent of total assets. American Airlines depreciates its airplanes for financial reporting purposes on a straight-line basis over 10-year lives to a salvage value equal to 10 percent of original cost. American announces a change in depreciation policy; it will use 14-year lives and salvage values equal to 12 percent of original cost. The airplanes are all four years old. Assume an income tax rate of 34 percent.

Calculate the approximate impact on net income of the change in depreciation policy. Compute both dollar and percentage effects.

35. **Composite depreciation versus individual-item depreciation.** Cord Manufacturing acquired three used machine tools for a total price of $68,000. Costs to transport the machine tools from the seller to Cord's factory were $4,000. Cord renovated, installed, and put the machine tools to use in manufacturing the firm's products. The costs of renovation and installation were as follows:

	Machine Tool A	Machine Tool B	Machine Tool C
Renovation Costs	$1,100	$1,800	$1,700
Installation Costs	400	600	300

The machine tools have the following estimated remaining lives: tool A, six years; tool B, eight years; tool C, four years.

a. Assume that Cord capitalizes each machine tool in a separate asset account and uses the remaining life of each machine tool as the basis for allocating the joint costs of acquisition. Compute the depreciable cost of each of the three machine tools.

b. Present journal entries to record depreciation charges for years 1, 5, and 8, given the assumption in part **a.** Use the straight-line method.

c. Assume that Cord treats the three machine tools as one composite asset in the accounts. If management decides to depreciate the entire cost of the composite asset on a straight-line basis over eight years, what is the depreciation charge for each year?

d. Which treatment, **a** or **c,** should management of Cord Manufacturing probably prefer for tax purposes and why?

36. **Interpreting disclosures regarding plant assets.** Mead Corporation reports the following information in its financial statements and notes for a recent year (amounts in millions):

	December 31	
	Year 7	**Year 8**
Property, Plant, and Equipment (at cost)	$3,824.0	$3,938.5
Accumulated Depreciation	(1,803.7)	(1,849.3)
Property, Plant, and Equipment (net)	$2,020.3	$2,089.2

	For Year 8
Depreciation Expense	$ 188.1
Expenditures on Property, Plant, and Equipment	315.6
Proceeds from Sales of Property, Plant, and Equipment	38.7
Sales	4,557.5

a. Give the journal entries for the transactions and events that account for the changes in the Property, Plant, and Equipment account and the Accumulated Depreciation account for Year 8.

b. Mead Corporation uses the straight-line depreciation method for financial reporting. Estimate the average *total* life of property, plant, and equipment in use during Year 8.

c. Refer to part **b.** Estimate the average age to date of property, plant, and equipment in use during Year 8.

d. Compute the plant asset turnover for Year 8.

e. Mead Corporation uses accelerated depreciation for income tax purposes. From information in the financial statement note on income taxes (discussed in Chapter 10), the balance in the accumulated depreciation account using accelerated depreciation would have been $2,810.2 million on December 31, Year 7, and $2,830.5 million on December 31, Year 8. Compute the plant asset turnover ratio using accelerated depreciation.

37. Interpreting disclosures regarding plant assets. PepsiCo reports the following information in its financial statements and notes in a recent year (amounts in millions):

	December 31	
	Year 6	**Year 7**
Property, Plant, and Equipment (at cost)	$14,250.0	$16,130.1
Accumulated Depreciation	(5,394.4)	(6,247.3)
Property, Plant, and Equipment (net)	$ 8,855.6	$ 9,882.8

	For Year 7
Sales	$28,472.4
Depreciation Expense	1,200.0
Expenditures on Property, Plant, and Equipment	2,253.2
Proceeds from Sales of Property, Plant, and Equipment	55.3

a. Give the journal entries for the transactions and events that account for the changes in the Property, Plant, and Equipment account and the Accumulated Depreciation account during Year 7.

b. PepsiCo uses the straight-line depreciation method for financial reporting. Estimate the average *total* life of property, plant, and equipment in use during Year 7.

c. Refer to part **b.** Estimate the average age to date of property, plant, and equipment in use during Year 7.

d. Compute the plant asset turnover for Year 7.

e. PepsiCo uses accelerated depreciation for income tax purposes. From information in the financial statement note on income taxes (discussed in Chapter 10), the balance in the accumulated depreciation account using accelerated depreciation would have been $7,018.8 on December 31, Year 6, and $7,736.7 on December 31, Year 7. Compute the plant asset turnover ratio using accelerated depreciation.

38. **Accounting for plant asset revaluations.** Grand Met, a consumer products company in Great Britain, purchased office equipment for £50,000 on January 1, Year 3. It estimated that the machine would have a five-year useful life and zero salvage value. Grand Met uses the straight-line depreciation method.

   On January 1, Year 6, Grand Met revalues this machine to £25,000. The firm still expects the machine to last for a total life of five years with zero salvage value.

   a. Give the journal entries to record depreciation for Year 3, Year 4, and Year 5.

   b. Give the journal entry to record the revaluation on January 1, Year 6, assuming that the firm credits a shareholders' equity account titled Revaluation Allowance.

   c. Give the journal entries to record depreciation for Years 6 and 7 assuming that Grand Met charges depreciation on the revaluation against the Revaluation Allowance account. The firm made no further revaluation during the remaining life of the office equipment.

   d. What effect did the revaluation have on net income of Year 6 and Year 7?

39. **Capitalizing versus expensing advertising costs: effects on financial statements and rate of return.** Consumer Products Company has $300,000 of total assets. The company has historically earned $45,000 per year and generated $45,000 per year of cash flow from operations. Each year Consumer Products Company distributes its earnings by paying $45,000 cash to owners. Management believes that a new advertising campaign now will lead to increased sales over the next four years. The company anticipates incremental net cash flows of the campaign as follows:

Beginning of Year	Net Cash Inflow (Outflow)
1	($24,000)
2, 3, and 4	10,000 each year

Assume that the company undertakes the advertising campaign, that cash flows occur as forecast, and that Consumer Products Company makes payments to owners of $45,000 at the end of the first year and $47,000 at the end of each of the next three years. Assume that there are no interest expenses in any year. Ignore any income tax effects.

   a. Compute net income and the rate of return on assets (= net income/assets) of Consumer Products Company for each of the four years, assuming that the company expenses advertising expenditures as they occur. Use the year-end balance of total assets in the denominator of the rate-of-return calculation.

   b. Compute net income and the rate of return on assets of Consumer Products Company for each year of the project, assuming that the company capitalizes advertising costs and then amortizes them on a straight-line basis over the last three years. Use the year-end balance of total assets in the denominator of the rate of return on assets.

c. How well has the management of Consumer Products Company carried out its responsibility to its owners? On what basis do you make this judgment? Which method of accounting seems to reflect performance more adequately?

40. **Expensing versus capitalizing advertising costs for firm advertising every year.** General Mills plans to spend $90,000 at the beginning of each of the next several years advertising the company's brand names. As a result of the advertising expenditure for a given year, it expects aftertax income (not counting advertising expense) to increase by $36,000 a year for three years, including the year of the expenditure itself. General Mills has other aftertax income of $30,000 per year. The controller of General Mills is curious about the effect on the financial statements of following one of two accounting policies with respect to advertising expenditures:

    (1) Expensing the advertising costs in the year of expenditure

    (2) Capitalizing the advertising costs and amortizing them over three years, including the year of the expenditure itself

    Assume that the company does spend $90,000 at the beginning of each of four years and that the planned increase in income occurs. Ignore income tax effects.

    a. Prepare a four-year condensed summary of net income, assuming that General Mills follows policy **(1)** and expenses advertising costs as incurred.

    b. Prepare a four-year condensed summary of net income, assuming that General Mills follows policy **(2)** and capitalizes advertising costs, then amortizes them over three years. Also compute the amount of Deferred Advertising Costs (asset) appearing on the balance sheet at the end of each of the four years.

    c. In what sense is policy **(1)** a conservative policy?

    d. Ascertain the effect on net income and on the balance sheet if General Mills continues to spend $90,000 each year and the aftertax income effects continue as in the first four years.

41. **Valuation of the brand name.** Ross Laboratories sells various formulations of infant baby food around the world under the brand name Similac. In a recent year, worldwide sales less operating expenses were $600 million. Ross Laboratories employed $500 million of physical capital to produce and sell this food. Estimate the value of the Similac brand assuming the following:

    a. Ross Laboratories charges 10 percent, before taxes, for physical capital, pays income taxes at the rate of 40 percent of pretax income, and uses a price/earnings ratio (capitalization factor) of 12.

    b. Ross Laboratories charges 20 percent, before taxes, for physical capital, pays income taxes at the rate of 40 percent of pretax income, and uses a price-earnings ratio (capitalization factor) of 8.

42. **Improvements versus repairs or maintenance.** The balance sheet of May Department Stores includes a building with an original cost of $800,000 and accumulated depreciation of $660,000. The firm depreciates the building on a straight-line basis over 40 years. The remaining service life of the building and its depreciable life are both seven years. On January 2 of the current year, the firm makes an expenditure of $28,000 on the entrance ramps and stairs of the store. Indicate the accounting for the current year if May Department Stores made the expenditure of $28,000 under each of the following circumstances. Consider each of these cases independently, except where noted. Ignore income tax effects.

    a. Management decided that improved entrances would make the store more attractive and that new customers would come. The ramps and stairs are a worthwhile investment.

    b. A flood on New Year's Day ruined the entrance ramps and stairs previously installed. The firm carried no insurance coverage for this sort of destruction. The new ramps and stairs are physically identical to the old ones. The old ones had a book value of $28,000 at the time of the flood.

c. Vandals destroyed the ramps and stairs on New Year's Eve. May carried no insurance for this sort of destruction. The ramps and stairs installed are physically identical to the old ones, which had a book value of $28,000 at the time of the destruction.

d. The old entrances were not handicapped-accessible. Management had previously considered replacing its old entrances with new, handicapped-accessible ones but had decided that there was zero benefit to the firm in doing so. It installed new entrance ramps and stairs because a new law required that all stores have such ramps and stairs on the street level. The alternative to installing the new ramps was to shut down the store. In responding to this part, assume *zero* benefits result from the new ramps. Part **e** considers the more realistic case of some benefits.

e. Management had previously considered replacing its old entrances with new ones but had decided that the handicapped-accessible ramps and stairs were worth only $7,000 (that is, would produce future benefits of only $7,000) and so were not a worthwhile investment. The new law (see part **d**), however, now requires the store to do so (or else shut down), and management installs the new entrance facilities.

43. **Accounting for intangibles.** In Year 1, Epstein Company acquired the assets of Falk Company, which included various intangibles. Discuss the accounting for the acquisition in Year 1, and in later years, for each of the following items.

a. Registration of the trademark Thyrom® for thyristors expires in three years. Epstein Company believes that the trademark has a fair market value of $100,000. It expects to continue making and selling Thyrom thyristors indefinitely.

b. The design patent covering the ornamentation of the containers for displaying Thyrom thyristors expires in five years. Epstein Company thinks that the design patent has a fair market value of $30,000 and expects to continue making the containers indefinitely.

c. Epstein Company views an unpatented trade secret on a special material used in manufacturing thyristors as having a fair market value of $200,000.

d. Refer to the trade secret in part **c.** Suppose that in Year 2 a competitor discovers the trade secret but does not disclose the secret to other competitors. How should Epstein Company change its accounting policies?

e. During Year 1, Epstein Company produced a sales promotion film, *Using Thyristors for Fun and Profit,* at a cost of $45,000. It licensed the film to purchasers of thyristors for use in training their employees and customers. Epstein has copyrighted the film.

44. **Capitalizing versus expensing; if capitalized, what amortization period?** In each of the following situations, compute the amounts of revenue, gain, expense, and loss appearing on the income statement for the year and the amount of asset appearing on the balance sheet as of the end of the year. Show the journal entry or entries required, and provide reasons for your decisions. The firm uses straight-line amortization. The reporting period is the calendar year. Consider each of the situations independently, except where noted.

a. Because of a new fire code, MCB Upholstery Shop must install an additional fire escape on its building. Management previously considered installing the additional fire escape. It rejected the idea because it had already installed a modern sprinkler system, which was even more cost-effective. The new code gives management no alternative except to close the store. MCB acquires the fire escape for $28,000 cash on January 1. It expects to demolish the building seven years from the date it installs the fire escape.

b. Many years ago, a firm acquired shares of stock in General Electric Company for $100,000. On December 31, the firm acquired a building with an appraised value of $1 million. The company paid for the building by giving up its shares in General Electric Company at a time when equivalent shares traded on the New York Stock Exchange for $1,050,000.

c. Same data as in part **b,** except that the shares of stock represent ownership in Small Timers, Inc., whose shares trade on a regional stock exchange. The last transaction in shares of Small Timers, Inc., occurred on December 27. Using the prices of the most recent trades, the shares of stock of Small Timers, Inc., given in exchange for the building have a market value of $1,050,000.

d. Oberweis Dairy decides that it can save $3,500 a year for 10 years by switching from small panel trucks to larger delivery vans. To do so requires remodeling costs of $18,000 for various garages. The first fleet of delivery vans will last for five years, and the garages will last for 20 years. Oberweis remodeled the garages on January 1.

e. Woods Petroleum drills for oil. It sinks 10 holes during the year at a cost of $1 million each. Nine of the holes are dry, but the tenth is a gusher. By the end of the year, the oil known to be recoverable from the gusher has a net realizable value of $40 million, and Amoco has offered to buy the field for $40 million. Woods extracted no oil during the year.

f. A company manufactures aircraft. During the current year, it made all sales to the government under defense contracts. The company spent $400,000 on institutional advertising to keep its name before the business community. It expects to resume sales of small jet planes to corporate buyers in two years.

g. AT&T runs a large laboratory that has, over the years, found marketable ideas and products worth tens of millions of dollars. On average, the successful products have a life of 10 years. Assume that expenditures for the laboratory this year were $1,500,000.

h. A textile manufacturer gives $250,000 to the Textile Engineering Department at Georgia Tech for basic research in fibers. The results of the research, if any, will belong to the general public.

i. On January 1, assume that Mazda incurs costs of $6 million for specialized machine tools necessary to produce a new-model automobile. Such tools last for six years, on average, but Mazda expects to produce the new model automobile for only three years.

j. On January 1, assume that USAir purchased a fleet of airplanes for $100 million cash. USAir expects the airplanes to have a useful life of 10 years and zero salvage value. At the same time the airline purchased for cash $20 million of spare parts for use with those airplanes. The spare parts have no use, now or in the future, other than replacing broken or worn-out airplane parts. During the first year of operation, USAir used no spare parts.

k. Refer to the data in **j.** In the second year of operation, USAir used $1 million of spare parts.

45. **Recognizing and measuring impairment losses.** Give the journal entry to recognize an impairment loss, if appropriate, in each of the following cases. If a loss does not qualify as an impairment loss, explain the reason, and indicate the appropriate accounting.

a. Commercial Realty Corporation leases office space to tenants in Boston. One of its office buildings originally cost $80 million and has accumulated depreciation of $20 million. The city of Boston has announced its intention to construct an exit ramp from a nearby expressway on one side of the office building. Rental rates in the building will likely decrease as a result. The expected future undiscounted cash flows from rentals and from disposal of the building decreased from $120 million before the announcement to $50 million afterward. The market value of the building decreased from $85 million before the announcement to $32 million afterward.

b. Refer to part **a.** Assume that the undiscounted cash flows totaled $70 million and that the market value totaled $44 million after the announcement.

c. Medical Services Corporation plans, and then builds, its own office building and clinic. It originally anticipated that the building would cost $15 million. The physicians in charge of overseeing construction had medical practices so busy that they did not closely track costs, which ultimately reached $25 million. The expected future cash flows from using the building total $22 million, and the market value of the building totals $16 million.

d. Medco Pharmaceuticals acquired New Start Biotechnology two years ago for $40 million. Medco allocated $25 million to a patent held by New Start and $15 million to goodwill. By the end of the current period, Medco has written down the book value of both the patent and the goodwill, the patent to $20 million and the goodwill to $14 million. A competitor recently received approval for a biotechnology drug that will reduce the value of the patent that Medco acquired from New Start. The expected future undiscounted cash flows from sales of the patented drug total $18 million, and the market value of the patent is $12 million.

e. Chicken Franchisees, Inc., acquires franchise rights in the Atlanta area for Chicken Delight Restaurants, a national restaurant chain. The franchise rights originally cost $15 million; since acquisition, Chicken Franchisees has written down the book value to $10 million. Chicken Delight Restaurants recently received negative publicity because the chickens it delivered to its franchisees contained potentially harmful pesticides. As a result, business has declined. Chicken Franshisees estimates that the future undiscounted cash flows associated with the Chicken Delight name total $6 million and that the franchise rights have market value of $3 million.

46. **Preparing statement of cash flows.** (Adapted from a problem by S. Baiman.) (Requires coverage of Appendix 8.1.) Exhibit 8.7 shows comparative balance sheets, an income statement for Year 2, and supplementary notes of Ormes Company.

    Prepare the Year 2 statement of cash flows, with funds defined as cash.

47. **Analysis of financial statement disclosure of effects of depreciation policy.** A recent annual report of Caterpillar Tractor Company contained the following statement of depreciation policy:

    > Depreciation is computed principally using accelerated methods for both income tax and financial reporting purposes. These methods result in a larger allocation of the cost of buildings, machinery, and equipment to operations in the early years of the lives of assets than does the straight-line method.

    Then Caterpillar disclosed the amounts for "Buildings, Machinery, and Equipment—Net" as they would appear if the straight-line method had always been used. Exhibit 8.8 shows these amounts and other data from the financial statements for three recent years.

    a. What amounts would be reported for depreciation expense for Years 2 and 3 if the straight-line method had always been used?

    b. Now assume a 40 percent tax rate. Assume also that straight-line depreciation had always been used for both income tax and financial reporting purposes and that Buildings, Machinery, and Equipment—Net on the balance sheet amounted to $4,020 at the end of Year 3. What other items on the balance sheet for the end of Year 3 would probably change and by how much?

EXHIBIT 8.7	ORMES COMPANY Comparative Balance Sheets and Income Statement (Problem 46)

| | December 31 | |
	Year 1	Year 2
BALANCE SHEETS		
Cash	$ 25,700	$ 31,500
Accounts Receivable	120,000	130,000
Less Allowance for Uncollectibles	(2,400)	(3,200)
Inventory	175,000	200,000
Property, Plant, and Equipment	247,300	300,200
Accumulated Depreciation	(78,000)	(95,000)
Patents	—	75,000
Accumulated Amortization	—	(15,000)
Total Assets	$487,600	$ 623,500
Accounts Payable	$155,000	$ 182,000
Common Stock	100,000	173,900
Retained Earnings	232,600	267,600
Total Equities	$487,600	$ 623,500
YEAR 2 INCOME STATEMENT		
Net Sales		$1,000,000
Gain on Sale of Patent		125,000
		$1,125,000
Cost of Goods Sold		$ 750,000
Selling and Administrative Expense		203,000
Bad Debt Expense		20,000
Depreciation Expense		39,000
Amortization Expense		15,000
Loss on Sale of Equipment		8,000
Income Tax Expense		30,000
Total Expenses		$1,065,000
Net Income		$ 60,000

Notes: (1) During Year 2, Ormes acquired property, plant, and equipment as follows:

For Cash	$62,900
By Issuing Common Stock	30,000

(2) During Year 2, Ormes sold a patent on a device developed internally by its research staff for $125,000 and purchased a patent for cash totaling $75,000.

EXHIBIT 8.8	CATERPILLAR TRACTOR COMPANY Excerpts from Annual Report (all dollar amounts in millions) (Problem 47)		
	Year 3	**Year 2**	**Year 1**
Buildings, Machinery, and Equipment—Net:			
As Reported	$3,339	$3,300	$2,928
If Straight-Line Depreciation Were Used	4,020	3,894	3,431
Depreciation Expense Reported	505	448	370

48. **Straight-line depreciation is probably too conservative; it usually writes off an asset's cost faster than future benefits disappear.** (Requires coverage of the appendix.) Firms acquire assets for the assets' future benefits—the future cash flows they produce, either cash inflows or savings of cash outflows. As the firm receives the near-term cash flows, the value of the future benefits declines, but the remaining future cash flows come closer to payoff time, increasing in value. The present value of future cash flows may, in total, increase or decrease during any one year. This problem explores changes in the present value of future cash flows with the passage of time and illustrates the phenomenon that, for many business projects, the present value of future benefits (that is, future cash flows) declines at a rate much slower than implied by straight-line depreciation.

Pasteur Company plans to acquire an asset that will have a 10-year life and that promises to generate cash flows of $10,000 per year at the end of each of the 10 years of its life. Given the risk of the project that uses the asset, Pasteur Company judges that a 12 percent rate is appropriate for discounting its future cash flows. Using a 12 percent discount rate, the present value of $1 received at the end of each of the next 10 years is $5.65022 (see Table 4 at the back of the book: 10-period row, 12 percent column). Because the firm expects the project to generate $10,000 per year, the present value of the cash flows is $56,502 (= $10,000 × 5.65022). Assume that Pasteur Company purchases the asset for exactly $56,502 at the beginning of Year 1. Exhibit 8.9 shows for each year the present value of the cash flows remaining at the beginning of each year of the asset's life. The numbers in column (3) result from multiplying $10,000 by the number appearing in Table 4, 12 percent column, for the number of periods remaining in the asset's life. Column (4) shows the percentage of the asset's present value of the cash flows remaining, and column (5) shows the percentage loss in present value of cash flows during the preceding year.

Column (6) shows the percentage write-off in cost each year using straight-line depreciation—10 percent per year. Note that the decline in present value of cash flows is less than straight-line in the first five years but greater in the last four years.

a. Construct an exhibit similar to Exhibit 8.9 for an asset with a five-year life promising $10,000 of cash flows at the end of each year. Use a discount rate of 15 percent per year. The asset costs $33,522. Compare the resulting decline in present value with straight-line depreciation.

b. Now consider another asset with a five-year life with risk appropriate for a 15 percent discount rate. This asset also has net present value of cash flows of $33,522, but the expected cash flows are $11,733 at the end of the first year, $10,767 at the end of the second year, $9,722 at the end of the third year, $8,716 at the end of the fourth year, and $7,710 at the the end of the fifth year. Construct an exhibit

		Pattern of Expiration of Future Benefits Measured as the Net
EXHIBIT 8.9		Present Value of Future Cash Flows
		(Problem 48)

Asset Costs $56,502 and Has 10-Year Life.
Asset Yields $10,000 per Year of Cash Inflow.
Discount Rate = 12 Percent per Year.

Beginning of Year (1)	Years Remaining (2)	Present Value of Remaining Cash Flows (3)	Percentage of Present Value of Cash Flows Remaining (4)	Percentage of Loss in Value during Preceding Year (5)	Straight-Line Depreciation for Preceding Year (6)
1	10	$56,502	100%		
2	9	53,282	94	6%	10%
3	8	49,676	88	6	10
4	7	45,638	81	7	10
5	6	41,114	73	8	10
6	5	36,048	64	9	10
7	4	30,373	54	10	10
8	3	24,018	43	11	10
9	2	16,901	30	13	10
10	1	8,929	16	14	10
11	0	0	0	16	10
Total				100%	100%

Column (3) derived from Table 4 (at back of book), 12 percent column, row corresponding to number in column (2) here, multiplied by $10,000.

Column (4) = number in column (3)/$56,502.

Column (5) = column (4) preceding year − column (4) this year.

similar to Exhibit 8.9 for this asset. You should find that the present value of future cash flows disappears at the rate of 20 percent of $33,522 per year, the initial present value.

c. Using the results of your work, comment on the nature of conservatism of straight-line depreciation.

49. **Analysis of financial statements to compute the change in property and plant assets required to sustain sales growth.** (Developed from a suggestion by Katherine Schipper). Exhibit 8.10 shows data from several years for General Electric Company (GE). Assume that analysis of GE's markets indicates that GE can sustain sales growth of 10 percent per year for the next several years. The corporate treasurer must plan ways to raise the new funds that will be required to finance the expansion of assets needed to support such increased sales. Assume that GE's financial policy calls for financing new property and plant with long-term financing, owners' equity (including earnings and retentions), and long-term borrowings. Financing for current assets, such as receivables and inventory, can be generated with current liabilities, such as increases in payables and short-term bank borrowings.

Past relations appear in Exhibit 8.10; note the computation of the fixed asset turnover ratio and the total asset turnover ratio. These ratios show the average amount of sales per dollar of investment in plant and equipment and the average amount of sales per dollar of investment in total assets. The total asset turnover ratio averages

EXHIBIT 8.10

GENERAL ELECTRIC COMPANY
Data on Sales, Plant/Equipment, and Total Assets (dollar amounts in millions)
(Problem 49)

Year (1)	Sales (2)	Dollar Change from Preceding Year (3)	Plant and Equipment — Balance Sheet Total Net of Accumulated Depreciation December 31 (4)	Dollar Change from Preceding Year (5)	New Acquisitions for Year (6)	Total Assets — Balance Sheet Total December 31 (7)	Dollar Change from Preceding Year (8)	Turnover Ratios — Fixed Assets (9)	Total Assets (10)
12	$27,240	$2,281	$6,844	$1,064	$2,025	$20,942	$2,431	4.32	1.38
11	24,959	2,498	5,780	1,167	1,948	18,511	1,867	4.80	1.42
10	22,461	2,807	4,613	590	1,262	16,644	1,608	5.20	1.42
9	19,654	2,135	4,023	439	1,055	15,036	1,339	5.17	1.37
8	17,519	1,822	3,584	228	823	13,697	1,647	5.05	1.36
7	15,697	1,592	3,356	175	740	12,050	1,309	4.80	1.38
6	14,105	187	3,181	565	588	10,741	1,372	4.87	1.40
5	13,918	1,973	2,616	255	813	9,369	1,045	5.59	1.57
4	11,945	1,471	2,361	224	735	8,324	922	5.31	1.52
3	10,474	917	2,137	111	501	7,402	514	5.03	1.47
2	9,557	723	2,026	277	711	6,888	689	5.06	1.46
1	8,834		1,749		685	6,199			
Weighted average								4.94	1.42

Columns (2), (4), (6), (7): taken from annual reports.

Columns (3), (5), (8): amount for a given year computed by subtracting amount for preceding year from amount for given year, using data in preceding column.

$$\text{Column (9)} = \frac{\text{Column (2)}}{.5 \times [\text{Column (4)} + \text{Column (4), Preceding Year}]}$$

$$\text{Column (10)} = \frac{\text{Column (2)}}{.5 \times [\text{Column (7)} + \text{Column (7), Preceding Year}]}$$

1.42, indicating that $1.42 of sales requires about $1.00 of total assets. Putting it another way, about $.70 (= $1/1.42) of assets is required for each dollar of sales. The average fixed asset turnover ratio of 4.94 indicates that about $1 of net property and plant is required for $4.94 of sales, or that $1 of sales requires about $.20 (= $1/4.94) of property and plant. From these data, management has tentatively concluded that to increase sales by $1 will require about $.70 of new assets, of which about $.20 will be invested in new property and plant, with the remaining $.50 being invested in current assests such as receivables and inventories. Thus to increase sales by 10 percent, or $2.7 billion, will require about $1.9 (= .70 × $2.7) billion of new funds, with about $540 million (= .20 × $2.7 billion) required from long-term sources.

Can you sharpen and improve this analysis? Consider the *incremental* sales achieved by past incremental investments in both property/plant and total assets. Consider that turnover ratios deal with average relations, whereas the questions at issue require analysis of incremental relations—how much additional investment is required for additional sales.

50. **Effect of capitalizing versus expensing on reported income.** America Online, Inc. (AOL), offers the largest consumer on-line service in the United States. Subscribers to its on-line service receive e-mail, on-line conferences, entertainment, software, computing support, an extensive newsstand of electronic magazines and newspapers, and seamless access to the Internet. Acquisitions in Year 5 and Year 6 permit it to offer a vertically integrated product and service line for users of the Internet.

The company aggressively attracts new subscribers to its on-line service through independent marketing programs, such as direct mail, disk inserts and inserts in publications, and advertising. It has also entered into co-marketing agreements with numerous personal computer hardware, software, and peripheral production companies. These companies bundle AOL software with their products, thus facilitating easy trial use of the company's services. The company has also entered into co-marketing agreements with certain of its media partners to market directly to specific audiences. AOL uses specialized retention programs designed to increase customer loyalty and satisfaction and to maximize customer subscription life. These retention programs include regularly scheduled on-line events and conferences, the regular addition of new content, services, and software programs, and on-line promotions of upcoming on-line events. The company also provides a variety of support mechanisms such as telephone customer-support services.

Exhibit 8.11 presents comparative balance sheets, Exhibit 8.12 presents comparative income statements, and Exhibit 8.13 presents comparative statements of cash flows for AOL for the Year 3 through Year 6 fiscal years. Selected notes to the financial statements appear below part **g.**

a. Describe the rationale that the company would likely make to its independent auditors to justify its practice of deferring and subsequently amortizing subscriber acquisition costs.

b. Prepare an analysis that accounts for the change in the Deferred Subscriber Acquisition Costs account on the balance sheet for each of the Year 3 through Year 6 fiscal years.

c. FASB *Statement of Financial Accounting Standards No. 86* requires firms to expense when incurred all costs of developing computer software until such time as the technological feasibility of the software has been established. Firms must capitalize and subsequently amortize software development and production costs incurred after establishing technological feasibility. FASB *Statement of Financial Accounting Standards No. 2* requires firms to expense research and development

EXHIBIT 8.11	AMERICA ONLINE Comparative Balance Sheets (amounts in thousands) (Problem 50)

| | June 30 | | | |
	Year 3	Year 4	Year 5	Year 6
ASSETS				
Cash	$ 9,224	$ 43,891	$ 45,378	$118,421
Short-term Investments	5,105	24,052	18,672	10,712
Accounts Receivable	2,861	10,583	43,279	72,613
Other Current Assets	1,723	5,753	25,527	68,832
Total Current Assets	$18,913	$ 84,279	$132,856	$270,578
Property, Plant, and Equipment (net)	2,402	20,306	70,466	101,277
Product Development Costs (net)	3,915	7,912	18,914	44,295
Deferred Subscriber Acquisition Costs (net)	6,890	26,392	77,229	314,181
Goodwill	—	—	54,356	51,691
Other Assets	282	15,695	52,643	176,732
Total Assets	$32,402	$154,584	$406,464	$958,754
LIABILITIES AND SHAREHOLDERS' EQUITY				
Accounts Payable	$ 3,766	$ 15,642	$84,639	$105,904
Short-term Debt	—	2,287	2,314	2,435
Other Current Liabilities	4,851	18,460	46,359	181,567
Total Current Liabilities	$ 8,617	$ 36,389	$133,312	$289,906
Long-Term Debt	—	7,015	19,496	19,306
Other Noncurrent Liabilities	—	12,883	35,712	137,040
Total Liabilities	$ 8,617	$ 56,287	$188,520	$446,252
Common Stock	$ 59	$ 308	$ 375	$ 926
Additional Paid-in Capital	22,652	98,836	251,539	519,342
Accumulated Deficit	1,074	(847)	(33,970)	(7,766)
Total Shareholders' Equity	$23,785	$ 98,297	$217,944	$512,502
Total Liabilities and Shareholders' Equity	$32,402	$154,584	$406,464	$958,754

costs in the year incurred regardless of the subsequent success of the research efforts. What justification can you see for these treatments of the costs of developing new technologies?

d. Prepare an analysis that accounts for the change in the Product Development Costs account on the balance sheet for each of the Year 3 through Year 6 fiscal years.

e. FASB *Interpretation No. 4* requires firms to expense in the year of a corporate acquisition any portion of the purchase price allocated to technologies that have not reached a stage of commercial feasibility as of the time of the acquisition (referred to as *in-process technologies*). In contrast, firms must capitalize and subsequently amortize any amounts allocated to commercially feasible technologies (for example, a patent). What rationale can you see for this different accounting treatment?

EXHIBIT 8.12	AMERICA ONLINE Comparative Income Statements (amounts in thousands) (Problem 50)

	Year Ended June 30			
	Year 3	Year 4	Year 5	Year 6
Revenues	$51,984	$115,722	$394,290	$1,093,854
Cost of Revenues	(28,820)	(69,043)	(229,724)	(627,372)
Marketing Expenses	(9,745)	(23,548)	(77,064)	(212,710)
Product Development Expenses	(2,913)	(4,961)	(12,842)	(53,817)
Administrative Expenses	(8,581)	(13,562)	(41,966)	(110,653)
Acquired Research & Development ..	—	—	(50,335)	(16,981)
Amortization of Goodwill	—	—	(1,653)	(7,078)
Operating Income	$ 1,925	$ 4,608	$ (19,294)	$ 65,243
Other Income (net)	371	1,774	3,023	(2,056)
Merger Expenses	—	—	(2,207)	(848)
Income before Income Taxes	$ 2,296	$ 6,382	$ (18,478)	$ 62,339
Income Tax Expense	(764)	(3,832)	(15,169)	(32,523)
Net Income	$ 1,532	$ 2,550	$ (33,647)	$ 29,816

f. Refer to the income statements for AOL in Exhibit 8.12. Recompute the operating income for each of the Year 3 through Year 6 fiscal years assuming that

- AOL expensed subscription acquisition costs and product development costs in the year incurred instead of capitalizing and amortizing them, and
- excludes from operating income the charge for acquired research and development costs because of its materiality and nonrecurring nature.

g. Identify the likely reasons for the changes in the operating profitability of AOL between the Year 3 and Year 6 fiscal years. (*Hint:* Using both originally reported amounts and the amounts restated in part **f**, express operating expenses and operating income as a percentage of revenues.) AOL reports the following information to aid your assessment of profitability.

June 30	Number of Subscribers (000's)
Year 3	303
Year 4	903
Year 5	3,005
Year 6	6,198

Fiscal Year	Average Online Revenues per Subscriber
Year 4	$174.00
Year 5	$195.36
Year 6	$215.52

EXHIBIT 8.13	AMERICA ONLINE Comparative Statements of Cash Flows (amounts in thousands)

	Year Ended June 30			
	Year 3	Year 4	Year 5	Year 6
OPERATIONS				
Net Income (loss)	$ 1,532	$ 2,550	$(33,647)	$ 29,816
Depreciation and Amortization	1,957	2,965	11,136	33,366
Amortization of Subscriber Acquisition Costs	7,038	17,922	60,924	126,072
Loss/(Gain) on Sale of Fixed Assets	(39)	5	37	44
Charge for Acquired Research & Development	—	—	50,335	16,981
Changes in Assets and Liabilities:				
Accounts Receivable	(1,902)	(4,947)	(23,430)	(28,728)
Other Current Assets	(1,494)	(2,867)	(19,641)	(43,305)
Deferred Subscriber Acquisition Costs	(10,685)	(37,424)	(111,761)	(363,024)
Accounts Payable	2,119	10,204	60,824	21,150
Other Current Liabilities	3,209	12,215	14,739	135,316
Other Assets and Liabilities	470	1,261	6,375	5,585
Cash Flow from Operations	$ 2,205	$ 1,884	$ 15,891	$ (66,727)
INVESTING				
Sale of Fixed Assets	$ 62	$ 95	$ 180	—
Acquisition of Fixed Assets	(2,041)	(17,886)	(57,751)	$ (50,262)
Product Development Costs	(1,831)	(5,132)	(13,011)	(32,631)
Short-term Investments	(5,105)	(18,947)	5,380	7,960
Acquired Businesses	—	—	(20,523)	(4,133)
Cash Flow from Investing	$ (8,915)	$(41,870)	$(85,725)	$ (79,066)
FINANCING				
Issuances of Common Stock	$ 609	$ 67,372	$ 61,253	$217,674
Increase in Borrowings	7,187	14,200	13,741	3,000
Decrease in Borrowings	(7,036)	(7,858)	(3,673)	(2,337)
Cash Flow from Financing	$ 760	$ 73,714	$ 71,321	$218,337
Change in Cash	$ (5,950)	$ 33,728	$1,487	$ 72,544
Cash, Beginning of Year	16,113	10,163	43,891	45,378
Cash, End of Year	$10,163	$ 43,891	$ 45,378	$117,922

Notes to the AOL Financial Statements

Revenue Recognition The Company recognizes on-line service revenue in the period that it provides services.

Deferred Subscriber Acquisition Costs The Company defers subscriber acquisition costs and amortizes them as a charge to operations over a period determined by calculating the ratio of current revenues related to direct response advertising versus the total expected revenues related to this advertising, or twenty-four months (straight-line), whichever is shorter. The amortization begins the month after incurring such costs. These costs, which relate directly to subscriber solicitations, principally include printing, production and shipping of starter kits and the costs of obtaining qualified prospects by various targeting direct marketing programs (for example, direct marketing response cards, mailing lists) and from third parties. Subscriber acquisition costs include no indirect costs. To date, all subscriber acquisition costs relate to the solicitation of specific identifiable prospects. The Company expenses when incurred all marketing costs that are not targeted at specific identifiable prospects for the Company's services. The Company reports Deferred Subscriber Costs in the noncurrent assets section of its balance sheet as follows (amounts in thousands):

June 30, Year 2	$ 3,243
June 30, Year 3	$ 6,890
June 30, Year 4	$ 26,392
June 30, Year 5	$ 77,229
June 30, Year 6	$314,181

Product Development Costs The Company capitalizes costs incurred for the production of computer software used in the sale of its services. Costs capitalized include direct labor and related overhead for software produced by the Company and the costs of software purchased from third parties. All costs in the software development process that is classified as research and development are expensed when incurred until technological feasibility has been established. Once technological feasibility has been established, such costs are capitalized until the software is commercially available. The Company amortizes capitalized software development costs on a product-by-product basis, using the greater of the straight-line method or current year revenue as a percent of total revenue estimates for the related software product not to exceed five years, commencing with the month after the date of product release.

Deferred product development costs appear on the balance sheet as a noncurrent asset as follows (amounts in thousands):

June 30, Year 2	$ 2,876
June 30, Year 3	$ 3,915
June 30, Year 4	$ 7,912
June 30, Year 5	$18,914
June 30, Year 6	$44,295

Product development expenses on the income statement include the following:

	Fiscal Year Ended June 30			
	Year 3	Year 4	Year 5	Year 6
Amortization of Capitalized Costs	$ 792	$1,135	$ 2,009	$ 7,250
Research and Development Costs	1,542	2,776	3,856	16,449
Other Product Development Costs	579	1,050	6,977	30,118
Total	$2,913	$4,961	$12,842	$53,817

Business Acquisitions The Company made several corporate acquisitions during the Year 5 and Year 6 fiscal years, using a combination of cash and shares of the Company's common stock. The aggregate purchase price exceeded the market value of the net assets acquired. The Company allocated a portion of the excess purchase price to in-process research and development of the acquired companies. Generally accepted accounting principles require the Company to expense in the year of the acquisition all amounts allocated to in-process research and development. The Company allocated any remaining excess purchase price in these acquisitions to goodwill, which the Company amortizes over ten years.

Income Taxes The Company treats subscriber acquisition costs and product development costs as an expense in computing taxable income in the year that it incurs such costs. Income tax expense in the income statement includes a provision for income taxes that the Company saves in the year that it claims such tax deductions but must pay in later years as it amortizes such costs for financial reporting. The income tax law does not permit the Company to deduct expenditures for in-process research and development acquired in corporate acquisitions or merger expenses in computing taxable income.

CHAPTER 9

LIABILITIES: INTRODUCTION

LEARNING OBJECTIVES

1. Understand and apply the concept of an accounting liability to obligations whose certainty of payment dates and whose amounts vary.
2. Develop the skills to compute the issue price, book value, and current market value of various debt obligations in an amount equal to the present value of the future cash flows.
3. Understand and apply the concept of debt amortization using the same effective interest method for various long-term debt obligations.
4. Understand the accounting procedures for debt retirements, whether at or before maturity, and the reporting of any gain or loss on retirement.

Chapters 9, 10, and 12 examine the accounting concepts and procedures for the right-hand side of the balance sheet, which shows the sources of a firm's financing. The funds used to acquire assets come from two sources: owners and nonowners. Chapter 12 discusses shareholders' equity. This chapter and Chapter 10 discuss obligations incurred by a business as a result of raising funds from nonowners. Banks and creditors providing debt on a long-term basis understand their role as providers of funds. Suppliers and employees who do not require immediate cash payment for goods provided or services rendered usually do not think of themselves as contributing to a firm's funds, but they do. Likewise, customers who advance cash to a firm before delivery of a good or service provide funds to the firm. The obligations of a business to these nonowners who contribute funds are liabilities.

A thorough understanding of liabilities requires knowledge of compound interest and present value computations. These computations allow valid comparisons between payments made at different times by taking into account the interest that cash can earn over time. The appendix at the back of the book describes and illustrates compound interest and present value. Understanding all the material in this chapter requires that you master the material in the appendix. Without such mastery, you will have to accept on faith some of the computations in this chapter.

BASIC CONCEPTS OF LIABILITIES

LIABILITY RECOGNITION

Nearly all liabilities are obligations, but not all obligations are liabilities. According to the Financial Accounting Standards Board (FASB), accounting generally recognizes an entity's obligation as a **liability** if the obligation meets three criteria.[1]

1. The obligation involves a probable future sacrifice of resources—a future transfer of cash, goods, or services or the foregoing of a future cash receipt—at a specified or determinable date. The firm can measure, with reasonable precision, the cash equivalent value of resources needed to satisfy the obligation.
2. The firm has little or no discretion to avoid the transfer.
3. The transaction or event giving rise to the entity's obligation has already occurred. (We suggest to our students that they understand this third FASB criterion by saying that for an obligation to be a liability, it must arise from something other than an executory contract, that is, the obligation arises from something other than a mere exchange of promises.)

Example 1   General Electric has borrowed $75 million by issuing bonds that require it to pay interest of 4 percent every six months for 20 years and to repay the $75 million at the end of 20 years. This borrowing arrangement obligates General Electric to make definite cash payments in the future at specified times and is a liability, titled Bonds Payable.

Example 2   Avon Products' employees have earned wages and salaries that Avon will not pay until the next payday, two weeks after the end of the current accounting period. Avon owes suppliers substantial amounts for goods sold to Avon, but these debts do not come due for 10 to 30 days after the end of the period. Avon owes the federal and state governments for taxes, but the payments are not due until next month. Although the payment dates are not necessarily fixed, Avon can estimate those dates with reasonable precision. Each of these items therefore meets the three criteria for a liability. The items appear as liabilities under titles such as Wages Payable, Salaries Payable, Accounts Payable, and Taxes Payable.

Example 3   When Sony USA sells television sets, it gives a warranty to repair or replace any faulty parts or faulty sets within one year after sale. This obligation meets the three criteria of a liability. Because some television sets will surely need repair, the future sacrifice of resources is probable. Sony has the obligation to make repairs. The transaction giving rise to the obligation, the sale of the television set, has already occurred. Sony does not know the amount with certainty, but Sony's experience with its television sets permits a reasonably precise estimate of the expected costs of repairs or replacements. The repairs or replacements will occur within a time span that Sony estimates with reasonable precision. Sony USA will thus show Estimated Warranty Liability on its balance sheet.

Example 4   The Boston Red Sox receive $240,000 from the sale of tickets for the upcoming baseball season. *Sports Illustrated* receives $175,000 for the sale of magazine subscriptions for the next three years. The American Automobile Association receives

---

[1]Financial Accounting Standards Board, *Statement of Financial Accounting Concepts No. 6*, "Elements of Financial Statements," 1985, par. 36.

$140,000 from the sale of memberships for the next two years. These advances from customers obligate the firms to provide services in the future. The amount of the cash advance serves as a measure of the liability until the firms provide the services. Accounting refers to these obligations as **partially executed contracts.**

Example 5 Columbia Pictures has signed a binding contract to supply films to Cineplex Odeon, a chain of movie theaters, within the next six months. In this case, there is an obligation, definite time, and definite amount (of goods, if not cash), but no past or current transaction has occurred. Chapter 2 pointed out that accounting does not recognize assets or liabilities for **executory contracts**—the mere exchange of promises with no mutual performance. Without some mutual performance, there is no current or past benefit. Thus no accounting liability arises in this case.

Example 6 Online Corporation has signed a contract promising to employ its president for the next five years and to pay the president a salary of $750,000 per year. The salary will increase in future years at the same rate of increase as the Consumer Price Index, published by the U.S. government. Online Corporation has an obligation to make payments (although the president may quit at any time without penalty). The payments are of reasonably certain amounts and will occur at definite times. At the time Online signs the contract, no mutual performance has occurred; the contract is purely executory. Because no exchange has occurred, no liability appears on the balance sheet. A liability will, of course, arise as the president performs services over time and earns the salary.

Example 7 Chevron Corporation has signed a contract with Tenneco Oil Pipeline Company to ship at least 10,000 barrels of crude oil per month for the next three years. Chevron must pay for the shipping services, even if it does not ship the oil. An arrangement such as this, called a *throughput contract,* does not qualify as an accounting liability because accounting views actual shipment, which has not yet occurred, as the event causing a liability. Chevron will disclose the obligation in notes. Similarly, obligations for take-or-pay contracts, in which the purchaser must pay for certain quantities of goods whether or not the purchaser actually takes delivery of the goods, are not formal liabilities. Firms obligating themselves with take-or-pay contracts must disclose them.[2] Accounting views both throughput and take-or-pay contracts as executory.

Example 8 Smokers have sued Philip Morris in a lawsuit alleging damages of $6 billion. The smokers claim that the company knowingly withheld information about the harmful effects of smoking and that misleading advertising about Marlboro cigarettes injured them. Shook, Hardy & Bacon, lawyers from Kansas City retained by the corporation, think that Philip Morris can mount an adequate defense to the charges. Because Philip Morris has no obligation to make a payment at a reasonably definite time, it has no liability. The notes to the financial statements will disclose the existence of the lawsuit, but normally no liability will appear on the balance sheet.

Example 9 Citibank extends $800 million in lines of credit to its customers, agreeing to make loans up to this amount as customers need funds. Because the line of credit is an executory contract (a mere exchange of promises), accounting does not

---

[2]Financial Accounting Standards Board, *Statement of Financial Accounting Standards No. 47,* "Disclosure of Long-Term Obligations," 1981.

EXHIBIT 9.1	Classifications of Accounting Liabilities by Degree of Certainty

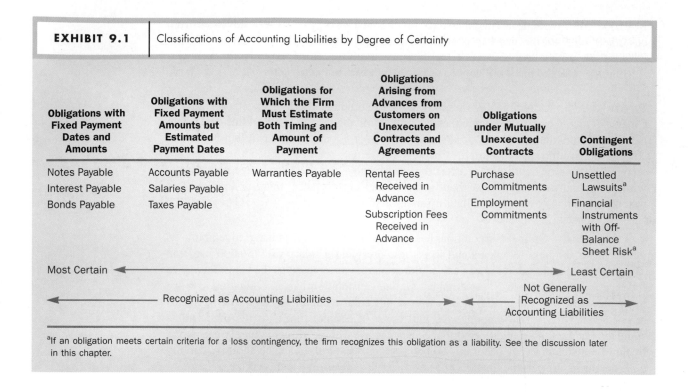

Obligations with Fixed Payment Dates and Amounts	Obligations with Fixed Payment Amounts but Estimated Payment Dates	Obligations for Which the Firm Must Estimate Both Timing and Amount of Payment	Obligations Arising from Advances from Customers on Unexecuted Contracts and Agreements	Obligations under Mutually Unexecuted Contracts	Contingent Obligations
Notes Payable	Accounts Payable	Warranties Payable	Rental Fees Received in Advance	Purchase Commitments	Unsettled Lawsuits[a]
Interest Payable	Salaries Payable		Subscription Fees Received in Advance	Employment Commitments	Financial Instruments with Off-Balance Sheet Risk[a]
Bonds Payable	Taxes Payable				

Most Certain ⟵——————————————————————————⟶ Least Certain

⟵————— Recognized as Accounting Liabilities —————⟶   ⟵— Not Generally Recognized as —⟶ Accounting Liabilities

[a]If an obligation meets certain criteria for a loss contingency, the firm recognizes this obligation as a liability. See the discussion later in this chapter.

recognize it as a liability. Citibank discloses the amount of such lending commitments in the notes to its financial statements.

Summary of Liability Recognition   Exhibit 9.1 classifies obligations into six groups based on the degree to which they satisfy the criteria for liability recognition. Accounting recognizes obligations in the first four groups as liabilities. As the examples above illustrate, accounting typically does not recognize as liabilities obligations under mutually unexecuted contracts. The exclusion of executory contracts from liabilities has created controversy in accounting. Chapter 10 discusses commitments arising from a long-term noncancelable lease, an executory contract that accounting recognizes as a liability if the lease agreement satisfies certain conditions.

CONTINGENCIES: POTENTIAL OBLIGATIONS

The question of whether to recognize contingent, or potential, obligations as liabilities causes controversy. One criterion for deciding whether an obligation qualifies as a liability is that the firm will make a probable future sacrifice of resources. The world of business and law contains many uncertainties. At any given time a firm may find itself potentially liable for events that have occurred in the past. Accounting does not recognize contingencies of this nature as liabilities. They are potential future obligations rather than current obligations. The potential obligations arise from events that occurred in the past but whose outcome remains uncertain. Whether an item becomes a liability—and, if it does, the size of the liability—depend on a future event, such as the outcome of a lawsuit.

Suppose that an employee sues Mattel, the toy manufacturer, in a formal court proceeding for damages from an accident. The court has scheduled a trial sometime after the end of this accounting period. If Mattel's lawyers and auditors agree that the court will likely find for Mattel (or that any adverse settlement will be small), then Mattel will not recognize a liability on its balance sheet. The notes to the financial statements, however, must disclose significant contingencies.

Both the FASB and the International Accounting Standards Committee (IASC) have said that a firm should recognize an estimated loss from a contingency in the accounts only if the contingency meets both of the following conditions: (a) information available before issuance of the financial statements indicates that it is probable that an asset has been impaired or that a liability has been incurred and (b) the amount of the loss can be reasonably estimated.[3]

When information indicates that events have probably impaired an asset or led to a liability and when the firm has estimated the amount but the amount is a range, then the firm should use the lower end of the range. For example, if Mattel estimates the loss in a range from $1 million to $5 million, it must use the $1 million amount.

TERMINOLOGY NOTE

In stating the conditions, quoted above, for the firm to record a liability, the FASB has said that the loss must be *probable,* but the FASB has not defined what it means by *probable.* In recent years, the FASB has discussed whether *probable* means "more likely than not"—any probability above 50 percent—or something larger, such as 80 to 85 percent. Currently, most accountants and auditors appear to use *probable* to mean 80 to 85 percent or larger. The FASB has used the phrase *more likely than not* when it means a probability greater than 50 percent. In contrast, the IASC has defined *probable* to mean "more likely than not."[4] The difference in meanings of the word *probable* can matter in applying accounting principles, and we expect the two standard-setting bodies to reconcile this difference within the next few years.

Example 10   A toy manufacturer, such as Mattel, has sold products for which the Consumer Protection Agency has discovered a safety hazard. The toy manufacturer thinks it probable that it has incurred a liability. This potential obligation meets condition **b** if the firm's experience or other information enable it to make a reasonable estimate of the loss. The journal entry would be as follows:

Loss from Damage Claim	1,000,000	
Estimated Liability for Damages		1,000,000
To recognize estimated liability for expected damage arising from safety hazard on toys sold.		

This entry debits a loss account (presented among Other Expenses on the income statement) and credits an **estimated liability,** which should appear on the balance sheet as a current liability, similar to the Estimated Warranty Liability account. In practice, an

---

[3]Financial Accounting Standards Board, *Statement of Financial Accounting Standards No. 5*, "Accounting for Contingencies," 1975; International Accounting Standards Committee, *Statement No. 37*, "Provisions, Contingent Liabilities, and Contingent Assets," 1998.

[4]IASC, *Statement No. 37*.

account with the title Estimated Liability for Damages would seldom, if ever, appear in published financial statements because firms fear that a court or jury might perceive it as an admission of guilt. Such an admission would likely affect the outcome of the lawsuit. Most firms would combine the liability account with others for financial statement presentation.

Contingency Disclosure   Accounting uses the term *contingency,* or sometimes **contingent liability,** only when it recognizes the item not in the accounts but rather in the notes. A recent annual report of General Motors illustrates the disclosure of contingencies as follows:

> Note 21. Commitments and Contingent Liabilities. .   . . The Corporation and its subsidiaries are subject to potential liability under government regulations and various claims and legal actions which are pending or may be asserted against them. Some of the pending actions purport to be class actions. The aggregate ultimate liability of the Corporation and its subsidiaries under these government regulations, and under these claims and actions, was not determinable at [year-end]. In the opinion of management, such liability is not expected to have a material adverse effect on the Corporation's consolidated operations or financial position.

CONSTRUCTIVE LIABILITIES

As this book goes to press, the FASB is struggling with a new concept, that of *constructive liability,* and whether firms should record them. You can understand the definition of constructive liability here, but you need to master some of the material in Chapter 12 on recurring and nonrecurring income before you can understand why constructive liabilities have become an issue. Firms have discovered that by recording constructive liabilities, they give themselves more wiggle room, more flexibility, in reporting income and, more important, patterns of reported income over time. Refer to Problem **45** at the end of Chapter 12 for more details, an actual example, and a presentation of the issues.

A **constructive liability** arises not from an obligation but from management intent. Assume management has decided it will close a plant and knows that it will reduce the labor force, laying off current employees and making severance payments in amounts yet to be determined. It can recognize an expense, often euphemistically called *Restructuring Charges,* with a journal entry such as:

Restructuring Charges	1,000	
Liability for Severance Pay to Employees		1,000

Now the firm has established a liability. Later, when it discharges workers and makes a $200 cash payment for severance benefits, it can record the following entry:

Liability for Severance Pay to Employees	200	
Cash		200

No controversy arises from the above, conservative accounting. Issues arise from different circumstances. Assume management decides that the initial $1,000 charge for estimated severance payments was $300 too large, that the charge should have been only $700. At the later time when it decides the initial charge was too large, it will make the following entry to reverse part of the initial charge:

Liability for Severance Pay to Employees 300
    Reversal of Restructuring Charges 300
    Reversal of prior charge; reversal appears in income for the current year.

Management reduced income in the year of initial charge by $1,000 and then increased income in the reversal year by $300. The FASB suspects that firms are using this ability to record initial intent with later reversals as a way to manipulate income. Analysts say that the mere ability of firms to reduce income and then later increase income based on its own intent, without obligation, reduces the quality of income.

LIABILITY VALUATION

In historical cost accounting, liabilities appear on the balance sheet at the present value of payments that a firm expects to make in the future. The interest rate a firm uses in computing the present value amount throughout the life of a liability is the interest rate appropriate for the specific borrower at the time it initially incurred the liability. That is, the firm uses the historical interest rate.

As Chapter 2 mentions, most current liabilities appear at the undiscounted amount payable because of the immaterially small difference between the amount ultimately payable and its present value.

LIABILITY CLASSIFICATION

The balance sheet generally classifies liabilities as current or noncurrent. Firms separate current from noncurrent liabilities based on the length of time that will elapse before the borrower must make payment. Current liabilities fall due within the operating cycle, usually one year, and noncurrent liabilities fall due later.

CURRENT LIABILITIES

Current liabilities, those due within the current operating cycle, normally one year, include accounts payable to creditors, short-term notes payable, payroll accruals, taxes payable, and a few others. A firm continually discharges current liabilities and replaces them with new ones in the course of business operations.

The firm will not pay these obligations for several weeks or months after the current balance sheet date. They have present value less than the amount to be paid. Even so, accountants show these items at the full amount owed because, considering the small difference between the amount owed and its present value, a separate accounting for this difference as interest expense would not be cost-effective.

ACCOUNTS PAYABLE TO CREDITORS

A firm seldom pays for goods and services as received. It defers payment until it receives a bill from the supplier. Then it may not pay the bill immediately but instead accumulate it with other bills until a specified time of the month when it pays all bills. Because these accounts do not accrue explicit interest, management tries to obtain as much funding as possible from its creditors by delaying payment as long as possible. Failure to keep scheduled promises to creditors can lead to poor credit ratings and to restrictions on future credit. The Marmon Group, a Chicago-based conglomerate, has instructed its purchasing agents to negotiate as much delay as they can for paying bills but instructs the controllers always to pay bills by the due date.

SHORT-TERM NOTES AND INTEREST PAYABLE

Firms obtain interim financing for less than a year from banks or other creditors in return for a short-term note called a *note payable*. The borrower records a liability. As time passes, the borrower makes entries, usually adjusting entries, debiting Interest Expense and crediting Interest Payable. When the borrower makes payments, the entry credits Cash and debits Interest Payable and, perhaps, Notes Payable. Payment amounts go first to reduce the liability for Interest Payable and then, if the amount exceeds the balance in the Interest Payable account, to reduce the principal for Notes Payable.

WAGES, SALARIES, AND OTHER PAYROLL ITEMS

When employees earn wages, they owe part of their earnings to governments for income and other taxes. They may also owe other amounts for union dues and insurance plans. Although these amounts form part of the employer's wage expense, the employer does not pay them directly to employees but pays them, on employees' behalf, to the governments, unions, and insurance companies.

In addition, the employer must pay various payroll taxes and may have agreed to pay for other fringe benefits because employees earned wages. Employers owe federal Social Security and Medicare taxes (called **FICA taxes,** for Federal Insurance Contributions Act) for each employee, as well as both federal and state unemployment compensation taxes (called **FUTA taxes,** for Federal Unemployment Tax Act).

Employers often provide paid vacations to employees who have worked for a specified period, such as six months or one year. The employer must accrue the costs of the earned but unused vacations (including the payroll taxes and fringe benefits on them) at the time the employees earn them, not at the later time when employees take vacations and receive their wages. This treatment results in charging each quarter of the year with a portion of the cost of vacations rather than allocating all costs to the summer, when most employees take the majority of their vacation days.

Example 11   Assume that the Sacramento Radio Shack's employees earn $100,000, that the employees' withholding rates for federal income taxes average 20 percent, that the employees' withholding rates for state income taxes average 8 percent, and that employees owe 10 percent of their wages for Social Security and Medicare taxes. In addition, employees in aggregate owe $500 for union dues to be withheld by the employer and $3,000 for health insurance plans.

Radio Shack must pay FICA taxes of 10 percent of gross wages and FUTA taxes of 3.5 percent on the first $40,000 of gross wages. Radio Shack must pay part (2.7 percent) of the FUTA tax to the California state government and part (0.8 percent) to the federal government. The employer owes $4,500 to Fireman's Fund for payments to provide life and health insurance coverage. Employees have earned vacation pay estimated to be $4,000; Radio Shack estimates employer payroll taxes and fringe benefits to be 18 percent of the gross amount.

The journal entries that follow record these wages. If production workers had earned some of the wages, the firm would debit some of the amounts to Work-in-Process Inventory rather than to Wages and Salaries Expense. Although we show three journal entries (one for payments to employees, one for employer payroll taxes, and one for the accrual for estimated vacation pay), in practice Radio Shack might prepare 11 separate entries or even a single entry.

Wages and Salaries Expense	100,000	
U.S. Withholding Taxes Payable		20,000
State Withholding Taxes Payable		8,000
FICA Taxes Payable		10,000
Withheld Dues Payable to Union		500
Insurance Premiums Payable		3,000
Wages and Salaries Payable		58,500
To record wage expense; plug for $58,500 actually payable to employees.		
Wages and Salaries Expense	15,900	
FICA Taxes Payable		10,000
FUTA Taxes Payable to U.S. Government		320
FUTA Taxes Payable to State Government		1,080
Insurance Premiums Payable		4,500
To record employer's expense for amounts not payable directly to employees. The debit is a plug.		
Wages and Salaries Expense	4,720	
Estimated Vacation Wage and Fringes Payable		4,720
To record estimate of vacation pay and fringes thereon earned during the current period: .18 × $4,000 = $720.		

On payday Radio Shack pays $58,500 to employees, discharging the direct liability to them. It writes checks at various times to the federal government, the state government, the union, and the insurance companies. It may send such checks as often as twice a week (for withheld income and FICA taxes when the amounts are sufficiently large) or as seldom as once or twice per year (for life insurance). It might pay for the insurance in advance, debiting Prepaid Insurance; if so, the credits when the firm records wages will be to the Prepaid Insurance account. When the employees take vacations, the firm debits the amounts paid to the liability account Estimated Vacation Wages and Fringes Payable, not to an expense account.

Most employers also provide pension, health care, and other benefits to retired employees. The employer recognizes the cost of these retirement plans as an expense during the years while the employee works instead of when the employee receives amounts during retirement.

INCOME TAXES PAYABLE

Businesses organized as corporations must pay federal income taxes based on their taxable income from business activities. In contrast, businesses organized as partnerships or sole proprietorships do not pay income taxes. Instead the Internal Revenue Service taxes the income of the business entity as income of the individual partners or the sole proprietor. Each partner or sole proprietor adds his or her share of business income to income from all other (nonbusiness) sources in preparing an individual income tax return.

The rules for computing the income tax on corporations change. The rates and schedules of payments mentioned here do not indicate the exact procedure in force at any particular time but do suggest the type of accounting procedures involved.

Corporations must estimate the amount of taxes that will be due for the year and make quarterly payments equal to one-fourth of the estimated tax as the year passes. Accountants frequently describe this as "pay-as-you-go" taxation. A corporation on a calendar-year basis must pay 25 percent of the estimated tax by April 15, 50 percent by June 15, 75 percent by September 15, and the entire estimated tax by December 15. If these dates fall on a weekend, the firm owes its taxes on the following Monday.

The estimated income, and hence the estimated tax, can change as the year passes. The corporation must report such changed estimates quarterly. It revises the amount of the quarterly payment to reflect the new estimated tax and takes into account the cumulative payments made during previous quarters of the year. The corporation must file its final income tax return for the year by March 15 of the next year. It must pay any difference between the actual tax liability for the year and the cumulative tax payments by March 15 of the next year. The law provides for penalties if the firm substantially underestimates the actual tax liability.

A corporation might prepare income statements more often than quarterly or not have the end of its reporting periods coinciding with the tax payment period. Such a corporation must estimate the income tax for the reporting period so that it can report a more accurate measurement of the net income for the period. Firms usually cannot make dependable monthly (or other short-period) estimates of the tax because of various special provisions in the tax law. During the early quarters of the year, a corporation will not know which of the special provisions it can ultimately use. The firm makes a reasonable estimate of tax in light of the earnings for the year to date and the prospects for the remainder of the year.

Illustration of Income Tax Computations   Exhibit 9.2 illustrates the income tax computations over several quarterly payments. The illustration assumes an income tax rate of 40 percent. The related journal entries are of two types, as follows:

Income Tax Expense	100,000	
Income Taxes Payable		100,000
To accrue quarterly payment.		
Income Taxes Payable	100,000	
Cash		100,000
To make payment.		

DEFERRED PERFORMANCE LIABILITIES: ADVANCES FROM CUSTOMERS

Another current liability arises when a firm receives cash from customers for goods or services it will deliver in the future. It discharges this liability, unlike the preceding ones, by delivering goods or services rather than by paying cash. When the firm discharges the liability it will recognize revenue. Some, therefore, label this liability as *unearned revenue.*

An example of this type of liability is the Houston Rockets' advance sale of basketball game tickets for, say, $200,000. At the time of the sale, the Rockets record the following entry:

Cash	200,000	
Advances from Customers		200,000

The Rockets sell tickets for cash but earn no revenue until the organization renders the service when the team plays. These deferred performance obligations qualify as liabilities. The firm credits an account such as Advances from Customers or Liability for Advance

| | EXHIBIT 9.2 | Estimating Quarterly Income Tax Payments and Calculating Final Payments of Actual Taxes |

Date	Estimates of Taxable Income for Year 1	Amounts Payable for Income Taxes in Year 1
Year 1		
April 15	$1,000,000	$100,000[a]
June 15	1,000,000	100,000[b]
September 15	1,000,000	100,000[c]
December 15	1,000,000	100,000[d]
Year 2		
March 15	1,100,000[e]	40,000[f]

[a].25 × (.40 × [$1,000,000]).
[b].50 × (.40 × [$1,000,000]) − $100,000.
[c].75 × (.40 × [$1,000,000]) − $200,000.
[d]1.00 × (.40 × [$1,000,000]) − $300,000.
[e]Actual income for Year 1 was $1,100,000.
[f](.40 × $1,100,000) − $400,000.

Sales. After a game, the firm has discharged its obligation so it recognizes (credits) revenue and reduces (debits) the liability.

| Advances from Customers .... | 200,000 | |
| Performance Revenue .... | | 200,000 |

Deferred performance liabilities arise also in connection with the sale of magazine subscriptions, airline tickets, and service contracts.

DEFERRED PERFORMANCE LIABILITIES: PRODUCT WARRANTIES

A similar deferred performance liability arises when a firm provides a warranty for service or repairs for some period after a sale. At the time of the sale, the firm can only estimate the likely amount of warranty liability.

Example 12 J&R Music World makes sales of $280,000 during the accounting period and estimates that it will eventually use an amount equal to 4 percent of the sales revenue to satisfy warranty claims. It will make the following entry:

Accounts Receivable	280,000	
Warranty Expense	11,200	
Sales		280,000
Estimated Warranty Liability		11,200
To record sales and estimated liability for warranties on items sold.		

Note that this entry recognizes the warranty expense in the period when the firm recognizes revenue, even though it will make the repairs in a later period. The accounting matches warranty expense with associated revenue. Because it recognizes the expense, it creates the liability. In this case, the firm knows neither the amount nor the due date of the liability for sure, but it can estimate both with reasonable precision. FASB *Statement of Financial Accounting Standards No. 5,* "Accounting for Contingencies," requires the accrual of the expense and the related warranty liability when the firm can "reasonably estimate" the amount.

As J&R makes expenditures of, say, $1,750 in the next period for repairs under the warranty, the entry is as follows:

Estimated Warranty Liability	1,750	
Cash (or other assets consumed for repairs)		1,750
To record repairs made. Recognize no expense now; the firm recognized all expense in the period of sale.		

Note that *actual* expenditures to satisfy warranty claims do not affect net income. The net income effect occurs in the year of sale when the firm estimates the *expected* amount of expenditures that it will make in all future periods to satisfy warranty claims arising from products sold in a particular year. With experience, the firm will adjust the percentage of sales that it charges to Warranty Expense. It attempts to maintain the Estimated Warranty Liability account at each balance sheet date with a credit balance that reasonably estimates the actual cost of repairs to be made under warranties outstanding at that time. The accounting for warranties resembles the allowance method for uncollectibles discussed in Chapter 6.

A firm may not use the allowance method of accounting for warranties (or for bad debts) in tax reporting. In tax reporting, taxpayers recognize expense in the period when they use cash or other assets to discharge the obligation.

PROBLEM 9.1 FOR SELF-STUDY

Journal entries for transactions involving current liabilities. Prepare journal entries for each of the following transactions of Ashton Corporation during January, the first month of operations. The firm closes its books monthly.

a. January 2: The firm borrows $10,000 on a 9 percent, 90-day note from First National Bank.

b. January 3: The firm acquires merchandise costing $8,000 from suppliers on account.

c. January 10: The firm receives $1,500 from a customer as a deposit on merchandise that Ashton Corporation expects to deliver in February.

d. Month of January: The firm sells merchandise costing $6,000 to customers on account for $12,000.

e. Month of January: The firm pays suppliers $8,000 of the amount owed for purchases of merchandise on account and collects $7,000 of amounts owed by customers.

f. January 31: Products sold during January include a two-year warranty. Ashton Corporation estimates that warranty claims will equal 8 percent of sales. No customer made warranty claims during January.

g. January 31: Employees earned wages of $4,000 for the month of January. The firm must withhold for federal taxes from the amounts it pays to employees, as follows: 20 percent for income taxes, 10 percent for Social Security taxes, and $200 for union dues. The employer must pay Social Security taxes of 10 percent and unemployment taxes of 3.5 percent. These wages and taxes remain unpaid at the end of January.

h. January 31: The firm accrues interest expense on the bank loan (see transaction **a**).

i. January 31: The firm accrues income tax expense at a rate of 40 percent on net income during January. The firm must make the first installment payment for income taxes in April.

j. February 1: Ashton Corporation pays employees their January wages net of withholdings.

k. February 10: The firm delivers merchandise costing $800 to the customer in transaction **c** in full satisfaction of its order.

l. February 15: The firm remits payroll taxes and union dues to government and union authorities.

m. February 20: A customer who purchased merchandise during January returns goods for warranty repairs. The repairs, paid for in cash, cost $220.

LONG-TERM LIABILITIES

The principal long-term liabilities are mortgages, notes, bonds, and leases. Borrowers usually pay interest on long-term liabilities at regular intervals during the life of a long-term obligation, whereas they pay interest on short-term debt in a lump sum at maturity. Borrowers often repay the principal of long-term obligations in installments or accumulate special funds for retiring long-term liabilities.

Accounting for all long-term liabilities generally follows the same procedures. We outline these procedures next and illustrate them throughout the rest of this chapter and Chapter 10.

PROCEDURES FOR RECORDING LONG-TERM LIABILITIES

In return for promising to make future payments, the borrower receives cash (or cash equivalents). The borrower initially records a long-term liability for that amount. By definition, the book value of the borrowing at any time equals the present value of all the then-remaining promised payments using the historical market interest rate applicable at the time the firm originally incurred the liability.

Sometimes a borrower knows the amount of cash received from a loan, the market interest rate, and the various future times when it must pay. In this case, it uses the interest rate and the elapsed time between payments to compute the amounts due at the various future dates.

More often, however, a borrower knows the amount of cash received as well as the amounts and due dates of cash repayments, but the loan does not explicitly state the market interest rate or, perhaps, states it incorrectly. Finding the market interest rate implied by the receipt of a given amount of cash now in return for a series of promised future repayments requires a process called "finding the internal rate of return." The *internal rate of return* is the interest rate that discounts a series of future cash flows to its present value. The appendix at the end of the book illustrates the process of finding the internal rate of return.

The borrower uses the original market interest rate, either specified or computed at the time the borrower receives the loan, throughout the life of the loan to compute interest expense. When the borrower makes a cash payment, a portion (perhaps all) of the payment represents interest. Any excess of cash payment over interest expense reduces the borrower's liability for the principal amount. If a given payment is too small to cover all the interest expense accrued since the last payment date, then the liability principal increases by the excess of interest expense over cash payment.

Borrowers can retire long-term liabilities in several ways, but the accounting process is the same for all. The borrower debits the liability account for its current book value, credits cash, and recognizes any difference as a gain (when book value exceeds cash disbursement, a credit) or a loss (when cash disbursement exceeds book value, a debit) on retirement of debt.

MORTGAGES AND NOTES

In a **mortgage** contract, the lender (such as a bank) takes legal title to certain property of the borrower, with the provision that the title reverts to the borrower when the borrower repays the loan in full. (In a few states, the lender merely acquires a lien on the borrower's property rather than legal title to it.) The mortgaged property is **collateral** for the loan. The customary terminology designates the lender as the **mortgagee** and the borrower as the **mortgagor.**

TERMINOLOGY NOTE

Accountants generally use the word *collateral,* rather than *security,* in this context. Whether the loan is secured requires legal judgment; moreover, accountants do not want to imply that the value of the collateral will be sufficient to satisfy the debt, as the word *secured* might imply. When you borrow money to finance a home purchase, you give the bank a mortgage, and the bank accepts the mortgage and lends you cash.

As long as the mortgagor (borrower) makes the payments required by the mortgage agreement, the mortgagee (lender) does not have the ordinary rights of an owner to possess and use the property. If the mortgagor defaults by failing to make the periodic payments, the mortgagee can usually arrange to sell the property for its benefit through a process called *foreclosure.* The mortgagee has first rights to the proceeds from the foreclosure sale for satisfying any unpaid claim. If funds remain, the mortgagee pays them to the mortgagor. If the proceeds are too small to pay the remaining loan, the lender becomes an unsecured creditor of the borrower for the unpaid balance.

A note payable resembles a mortgage payable except that the borrower does not pledge property as collateral.

Accounting for Mortgages and Notes Some of the more common problems in accounting for mortgages appear in the following illustration. On October 1, Year 1, Western Company borrows $125,000 for five years from the Home Savings and Finance Company to obtain funds for additional working capital. As collateral, Western Company pledges to Home Savings and Finance Company several parcels of land that it owns and that are on its books at a cost of $50,000. The mortgage specifies that interest will accrue on the unpaid balance of the loan principal at a rate of 12 percent per year compounded semiannually (that is, 6 percent interest will accrue every six months). The borrower must make payments on April 1 and October 1 of each year. Western agrees to make 10 payments over the five years of the mortgage so that when it makes the last payment on October 1, Year 6, it will have paid the loan and all interest. The contract calls for the first nine payments to be $17,000 each. The tenth payment will discharge the balance of the loan. Western Company closes its books annually on December 31. (The derivation of the semiannual payment of $17,000 appears in Example **11** in the Appendix at the end of the book.)

The entries from the time Western issues the mortgage through December 31, Year 2, follow:

10/1/Year 1	Cash	125,000	
	Mortgage Payable		125,000
	To record loan obtained from Home Savings and Finance Company for five years at 12 percent compounded semiannually.		

As Example 11 in the appendix shows, $125,000 approximately equals the present value of 10 semiannual cash payments of $17,000, each discounted at 12 percent compounded semiannually.

12/31/Year 1	Interest Expense	3,750	
	Interest Payable		3,750
	To record adjusting entry: interest expense on mortgage from 10/1/Year 1 to 12/31/Year 1.		

Interest expense on the loan for the first six months is $7,500 (= .12 × $125,000 × 6/12). To simplify the calculations, accounting typically assumes that the interest accrues evenly over the six-month period. Thus interest expense for the three-month period (October, November, and December) equals one-half of the $7,500, or $3,750.

4/1/Year 2	Interest Expense	3,750	
	Interest Payable	3,750	
	Mortgage Payable	9,500	
	Cash		17,000
	To record cash payment made: interest expense on mortgage from 1/1/Year 2 to 4/1/Year 2, payment of six months' interest, and reduction of loan by the difference, $17,000 − $7,500 = $9,500.		

After the cash payment on April 1, Year 2, the unpaid principal of the loan is $115,500 (= $125,000 − $9,500). Interest expense during the second six-month period accrues on this unpaid principal amount.

10/1/Year 2	Interest Expense	6,930	
	Mortgage Payable	10,070	
	Cash		17,000

To record cash payment made: interest expense for the period 4/1/Year 2 to 10/1/Year 2 is $6,930 [= .12 × ($125,000 − $9,500) × 6/12]; the loan balance declines by the difference, $17,000 − $6,930 = $10,070.

12/31/Year 2	Interest Expense	3,163	
	Interest Payable		3,163

To record adjusting entry: interest expense from 10/1/Year 2 to 12/31/Year 2 = [.12 × ($125,000 − $9,500 − $10,070) × 3/12].

Amortization Schedule Exhibit 9.3 presents an amortization schedule for this mortgage. For each period it shows the balance at the beginning of the period, the interest for the period, the payment for the period, the reduction in principal for the period, and

---

EXHIBIT 9.3	Amortization Schedule for $125,000 Mortgage (or Note), Repaid in 10 Semiannual Installments of $17,000, Interest Rate of 12 Percent, Compounded Semiannually (6 percent compounded each six months)

Semiannual Journal Entry

Dr. Interest Expense .... Amount in Column **(3)**

Dr. Mortgage (or Note) Payable .... Amount in Column **(5)**

    Cr. Cash .... Amount in Column **(4)**

6-Month Period (1)	Loan Balance Start of Period (2)	Interest Expense for Period (3)	Payment (4)	Portion of Payment Reducing Principal (5)	Loan Balance End of Period (6)
0					$125,000
1	$125,000	$7,500	$17,000	$ 9,500	115,500
2	115,500	6,930	17,000	10,070	105,430
3	105,430	6,326	17,000	10,674	94,756
4	94,756	5,685	17,000	11,315	83,441
5	83,441	5,006	17,000	11,994	71,447
6	71,447	4,287	17,000	12,713	58,734
7	58,734	3,524	17,000	13,476	45,258
8	45,258	2,715	17,000	14,285	30,973
9	30,973	1,858	17,000	15,142	15,831
10	15,831	950	16,781	15,831	0

Note: In preparing this table, we rounded calculations to the nearest dollar.

Column (2) = column (6) from previous period.

Column (3) = .06 × column (2).

Column (4) is given, except row 10, where it is the amount such that column (4) = column (2) + column (3).

Column (5) = column (4) − column (3).

Column (6) = column (2) − column (5).

the balance at the end of the period. (The last payment, $16,781 in this case, often differs slightly from the others because of the cumulative effect of rounding errors.) All long-term liabilities have analogous amortization schedules, which aid in understanding the timing of payments to discharge the liability. Amortization schedules for various long-term liabilities appear throughout this chapter and the next.

PROBLEM 9.2 FOR SELF-STUDY

Accounting for an interest-bearing note. Avner Company receives cash of $112,434 in return for a three-year, $100,000 note, promising to pay $15,000 at the end of one year, $15,000 at the end of two years, and $115,000 at the end of three years. The market interest rate on the original issue date of the note is 10 percent.

a. Prepare an amortization schedule similar to Exhibit 9.3 for the life of the note.
b. Prepare journal entries that would be made on three dates: the date of issue, six months after the date of issue (assuming Avner closes the books then), and one year after the date of issue (assuming Avner makes a cash payment then).

CONTRACTS AND LONG-TERM NOTES: INTEREST IMPUTATION

Firms often finance the acquisition of buildings, equipment, and other fixed assets using interest-bearing notes, which the previous section discussed. Some borrowing arrangements do not state an explicit interest rate. Instead, the purchase price includes carrying charges, and the buyer pays the total over a certain number of months. The contract does not mention the specific charge for interest. The principal on the note in this case includes **implicit interest.**

Generally accepted accounting principles (GAAP) require that all long-term monetary liabilities, including those carrying no explicit interest, appear on the balance sheet at the present value of the future cash payments. To compute a present value requires an interest rate, sometimes in this context called a *discount rate.* In historical cost accounting, the discounting process uses the historical (or original) interest rate appropriate for the particular borrower at the time it incurred the obligation. That rate will have depended on the amount and terms of the borrowing arrangement as well as on the borrower's risk of defaulting on its obligations. The rate is known as the **imputed (inherent) interest rate.** The excess of the par, or face, value of the liability over its present value represents interest to be recognized over the period of the loan. The next two sections discuss two acceptable ways to compute the present value of the liability and the amount of imputed interest.

The first approach uses the market value of the asset acquired as a basis for computing the present value of the liability.

Example 13 Hixon Saab can purchase a piece of equipment for $10,500 cash. The firm purchases the equipment in return for a single-payment note with a face amount of $16,000 payable in three years. The implied interest rate is about 15 percent per year; that is, $10,500 grows at 15 percent in one year to $12,075 (= $10,500 × 1.15), in two years to about $13,900 (= $12,075 × 1.15), and in three years to about $16,000 (= $13,900 × 1.15). The journal entry using this approach would be as follows:

Equipment	10,500	
Note Payable		10,500
To record purchase of equipment using the known cash price. The firm infers the amount for the note from the known cash price of the equipment.		

At the end of each accounting period that intervenes between the acquisition of the equipment and repayment of the note, Hixon Saab makes journal entries for depreciation of the equipment. We do not show these here. The firm must also make journal entries to recognize interest expense. Assume that Hixon Saab issued the note at the beginning of a year. The entries for the three years would be as follows:

(1) Interest Expense	1,575	
Note Payable		1,575
Entry made one year after issuance of note.		

Interest is .15 × $10,500. The firm does not pay $1,575 in cash but adds it to the principal amount of the liability.

(2) Interest Expense	1,811	
Note Payable		1,811
Entry made one year after entry **(1)**, two years after issuance of note.		

Interest is .15 × ($10,500 + $1,575).

(3) Interest Expense	2,114	
Note Payable		2,114
Entry made one year after entry **(2)**, at maturity of note to increase liability to its maturity amount, $16,000.		

Interest = $16,000 − ($10,500 + $1,575 + $1,811), which is approximately equal to .15 × ($10,500 + $1,575 + $1,811); the difference represents the accumulated rounding error caused by using 15 percent as the implicit interest rate rather than the exact rate, which is 15.074 percent.

(4) Note Payable	16,000	
Cash		16,000
To repay note at maturity.		

Of the $16,000 paid at maturity, $5,500 represents interest accumulated on the note since its issue.

Use of Market Interest Rate to Establish Market Value of Asset and Present Value of Note

If the firm purchased used equipment with the same three-year note, it might be unable to establish a reliable estimate of the current market value of the asset acquired. To find the present value of the note, the firm would discount the payments using the interest rate it would have to pay for a similar loan in the open market at the time that it acquired the equipment. The firm would continue to use this rate throughout the life of the note. GAAP allow this second method for quantifying the amount of the liability and computing the imputed interest.

Example 14 Refer to the data in Example 13. When Hixon Saab borrows using single-payment notes with maturity of three years, it pays interest of 12 percent compounded annually, rather than 15 percent. The present value at 12 percent per year of the $16,000 note due in three years is $11,388 (= $16,000 × .71178; see Appendix Table 2 at the back of the book, 3-period row, 12-percent column). The entry to record the purchase of used equipment paid for with the note would be as follows:

Equipment	11,388	
Note Payable		11,388

To record purchase of equipment. The firm infers the cost of equipment from known interest rate.

The firm would make entries at the end of each period to recognize interest expense (using the 12 percent borrowing rate) and to increase the principal amount of the liability. After the third period, the principal amount of the liability would be $16,000.

Total Expense Is Independent of Interest Rate

In Example 13, the buyer records the equipment of $10,500 and recognizes $5,500 of imputed interest. In Example 14, the buyer records the equipment at $11,388 and recognizes $4,612 of imputed interest. The expense over the combined lives of the note and the equipment—interest plus depreciation plus gain or loss on sale—will total the same amount, $16,000, no matter which interest rate the buyer uses. Over sufficiently long time periods, total expense equals total cash expenditure; accrual accounting affects only the timing of the expense recognition.

Long-Term Notes Held as Receivables

A borrower's long-term note payable is the lender's long-term asset, note receivable. GAAP require the lender to show the asset in the Long-Term Note Receivable account at its present value. The rate at which the lender discounts the note should, in theory, equal the rate the borrower uses. In practice, the two rates sometimes differ because the lender and the borrower reach different conclusions regarding the borrower's credit risk. The lender's accounting mirrors the borrower's: the lender has interest revenue, whereas the borrower has interest expense.

Accounting for note with imputed interest rate. Chang Company purchased a truck from Guttman's Auto Agency. The truck had a list price of $25,000, but sellers often offer discounts of 8 to 20 percent from list prices for purchases of this sort. Chang Company paid for the truck by giving a noninterest-bearing note due two years from the date of purchase. The note had a maturity value of $28,730. The rate of interest that Chang Company paid to borrow on secured two-year loans ranged from 10 percent to 15 percent during the period when the purchase occurred.

a. Record the acquisition of the truck on Chang Company's books, computing the fair market value of the truck using a 10 percent discount from list price.

b. What imputed interest rate will Chang use for computing interest expense throughout the loan if it records the acquisition as in part **a?**

c. Record the acquisition of the truck on Chang Company's books, assuming that the estimated interest rate Chang Company must pay to borrow is reliable and is 12 percent per year.

d. Record the acquisition of the truck on Chang Company's books, assuming that the interest rate Chang Company must pay to borrow is 1 percent per month.

e. Prepare journal entries to record the loan and to record interest over two years, assuming that Chang records the truck at $23,744 and that the interest rate implicit in the loan is 10 percent per year.

f. Throughout, this book has stressed that over sufficiently long time periods, total expense is equal to total cash outflow. In what sense is the total expense for this transaction the same, independent of the interest rate (and, therefore, the interest expense)?

BONDS

When a firm can borrow funds from one lender, the firm usually issues mortgages or notes. When it needs larger amounts, the firm may have to borrow from the general investing public with a bond issue. Corporations and governmental units are the usual issuers. Bond issues have the following features:

1. A firm or its investment banker writes a **bond indenture,** or agreement, which gives the terms of the loan and the rights and duties of the borrower and other parties to the contract. To provide some protection to bondholders, bond indentures typically limit the borrower's right to declare dividends and to make other distributions to owners.

2. The borrower can prepare engraved bond certificates. Each one represents a portion of the total loan. The usual minimum denomination in business practice is $1,000. The federal government issues some bonds in denominations as small as $50.

3. If the borrower pledges property as collateral for the loan (such as in a mortgage bond), the indenture names a trustee to hold title to the property serving as collateral. The trustee, usually a bank, acts as the representative of the bondholders.

4. The borrower or trustee appoints an agent, usually a bank, to act as *registrar* and *disbursing agent.* The borrower deposits interest and principal payments with the disbursing agent, who distributes the funds to the bondholders.

5. Some bonds are **coupon bonds.** Coupons attached to the bond certificate represent promises to make periodic payments throughout the life of the bond. When a coupon comes due, the bondholder cuts it off and deposits it with a bank. The bank sends the coupon through the bank clearing system to the disbursing agent, who deposits the payment in the bondholder's account at the bank. In recent years, most bonds are registered, which means that the borrower records the name and address of the bond-holder and sends the periodic payments to the registered owner, who need not clip coupons and redeem them.

6. The borrower usually issues the entire loan to an investment banking firm or to a group of investment bankers known as a *syndicate,* which takes over the responsibility for selling the bonds to the investing public. Members of the syndicate usually bear the risks and rewards of interest rate fluctuations during the period while they are selling the bonds to the public.

Types of Bonds   Mortgage bonds carry a mortgage on real estate as collateral for the repayment of the loan. Issuers of *collateral trust bonds* usually hand over stocks and bonds of other corporations to the trustee. The most common type of corporate bond, except in the railroad and public utility industries, is the **debenture bond.** This type carries no special collateral; instead, the borrower issues it on the general credit of the business. For added protection to the bondholders, the bond indenture usually includes provisions that limit the dividends that the borrower can declare or the amount of subsequent long-term debt that it can incur. **Convertible bonds** are debentures that the holder (lender) can exchange, possibly after some specific period of time has elapsed, for a specific number of shares of common stock or, perhaps, of preferred stock of the borrower.

From the viewpoint of the issuer (borrower), all bonds require future cash outflows in return for a current or previous cash inflow. The pattern of future cash outflows varies across bonds depending on the provisions in the bond indenture.

Example 15   Ford Motor Company issues $250 million of 10 percent, semiannual, 20-year bonds. The bond indenture requires Ford to pay interest of $12.5 million each six months for 20 years and to repay the $250 million principal at the end of 20 years.

Example 16   DaimlerChrysler Corporation issues $180 million of 15-year bonds. The bond indenture requires DaimlerChrysler to pay $13.1 million each six months for 15 years. Each periodic payment includes interest plus repayment of a portion of the principal. (Common terminology refers to such bonds as **serial bonds.**)

Example 17   General Motors Corporation (GM) issues bonds that do not require a periodic cash payment (common terminology refers to such bonds as **zero coupon bonds**), but it promises a single payment of $300 million at the end of 10 years. The $300 million paid after 10 years includes both interest and principal.

COMPUTATIONAL NOTE

By the time you have completed the appendix to this book, you should be able to work out the implicit interest rate in this GM bond issue, given the amount of initial issue proceeds. To take an example, assume GM receives $140 million for this issue. Then the implicit interest rate is just under 8 percent per year. See Table 2 at the back of the book, 10-period column and 8-percent row. Multiply that factor by $300, and notice that you get slightly less than $140, which indicates that 8 percent slightly overstates the implicit rate, which is 7.92 percent. Later in this section, we show the derivation of proceeds for this note assuming a 10 percent rate. Over the life of the bond issue, GM will record $160 million of interest expense, which it will pay all at maturity along with the $140 million originally borrowed.

The bond indenture indicates the par value or face value of a bond. The par value is usually an even amount (for example, $250 million in Example 15, $180 million in Example 16, and $300 million in Example 17). Bonds requiring periodic payments (called *coupon* payments if the bonds have coupons) use the par value as the base for computing the amount of the cash payment. For example, the Ford Motor Company bonds in Example 15 require the payment of 10 percent of the par amount each year, payable in two installments. The semiannual payment is $12.5 million (= .10 × $250 million × .5).

TERMINOLOGY NOTE

Almost everyone in business refers to the periodic payments as *interest payments*. This term causes confusion because, as you will soon see, the amount of interest expense for a period almost never equals the amount of these payments for that same period. The periodic payment will always include some amount to pay interest to the lender. If sufficiently large, the payment will discharge some of the principal amount. Both payment of interest and payment of principal serve to reduce the debt, so one all-purpose term used for the payments is *debt service payments*. We urge you not to think of them as interest payments until you have understood why they do not equal interest expense.

PROCEEDS OF A BOND ISSUE

The price at which a firm issues bonds on the market depends on two factors: the future cash payments that the bond indenture requires the firm to make; and the discount rate that the market deems appropriate given the risk of the borrower, the general level of interest rates in the economy, and other factors. The issuing price equals the present value of the required cash flows discounted at the appropriate market interest rate.

Example 18   Refer to Example 15. Assume that the market charges Ford an interest rate of 10 percent, compounded semiannually. Ford will receive $250 million for its bond issue, computed as follows:

Required Cash Flows	Present Value Factor for 10 Percent Interest Rate Compounded Semiannually for 20 Years	Present Value of Required Cash Flows
$250.0 million at end of 20 years	.14205[a]	$ 35.5
$12.5 million every six months for 20 Years	17.15909[b]	214.5
Issue Price		$250.0

[a]Table 2, 5-percent column and 40-period row.
[b]Table 4, 5-percent column and 40-period row.

Example 19   Refer to Example 16. Assume that the market deems that an appropriate interest rate for DaimlerChrysler's bonds on the date of issue is also 10 percent, compounded semiannually. The issue price of DaimlerChrysler's bonds is $201.4 million, computed as follows:

Required Cash Flows	Present Value Factor for 10 Percent Interest Rate Compounded Semiannually for 15 Years	Present Value of Required Cash Flows
$13.1 million every six months for 15 years	15.37245[a]	$201.4
Issue Price		$201.4

[a]Table 4, 5-percent column and 30-period row.

Example 20 Refer to Example 17. Assume that the market deems that 10 percent, compounded semiannually, is an appropriate interest rate on the date of issue for GM bonds. The issue price is $113.1 million, computed as follows:

Required Cash Flows	Present Value Factor for 10 Percent Interest Rate Compounded Semiannually for 10 Years	Present Value of Required Cash Flows
$300 million at end of 10 years	.37689[a]	$113.1
Issue Price		$113.1

[a]Table 2, 5-percent column and 20-period row.

The issue price will usually differ from the par value of the bonds. (The Ford example above, where the price and the value equal each other, is the exceptional case, and we include it for learning purposes.) The difference arises because the coupon interest rate stated in the bond indenture differs from the interest rate that the market charges the issuer to borrow.

If the market-required rate exceeds the coupon rate, the bonds will sell for less than par value. The difference between the par value and the selling price is known as the *discount* on the bonds. The zero coupon bonds of GM in Example 20 have a par value of $300 million and an issue price of $113.1 million. The 10 percent rate required by the lenders before they will purchase these bonds exceeds the bonds' promised periodic payment rate, zero in this case. Purchasing the GM bonds for $113.1 million and receiving $300 million 10 years later yields the purchasers a return of 10 percent compounded semiannually. That is, $300 million is the future value of $113.1 million invested to yield 10 percent compounded semiannually for 10 years.

If the coupon rate exceeds the market-required rate, the bonds will sell for more than par value. The difference between the selling price and the par value is known as the *premium* on the bond. The DaimlerChrysler bonds in Example 19 have an issue price of $201.4 million and a par value of $180 million. Purchasing the DaimlerChrysler bonds for $201.4 million and receiving $13.1 million every six months for 15 years yields the lenders a return of 10 percent compounded semiannually.

If the coupon rate equals the market-required rate, a rare occurrence, the bonds will sell for par value. The Ford Motor Company bonds in Example 18 have a coupon rate and a market-required rate of 10 percent compounded semiannually. The issue price of $250 million equals the par value of the bonds. Purchasing these bonds for $250 million and receiving $12.5 million every six months for 20 years and $250 million at the end of 20 years yields the purchaser 10 percent compounded semiannually.

The presence of a discount or premium by itself indicates nothing about the credit standing of the borrower. A solid firm, such as General Electric, with a credit standing that would enable it to borrow funds at 8 percent, might issue 7 percent bonds that would sell at a discount. In contrast, an untested firm with a lower credit standing that requires it to pay 12 percent on loans might issue 15 percent bonds that would sell at a premium.

Issued at Par

The Macaulay Corporation issues $100,000 face value of 12 percent semiannual coupon debenture bonds on July 1, Year 1. Macaulay must repay the principal amount five years later, on July 1, Year 6. Macaulay owes periodic payments (coupons) on January 1 and July 1 of each year. The coupon payments promised at each payment date total $6,000. Figure 9.1 presents a time line for the two sets of cash flows associated with this bond. Assume that the market rate of interest for Macaulay on July 1, Year 1, exactly equals 12 percent compounded semiannually. Then, the calculation of the loan proceeds would be as follows (the appendix at the back of the book explains the present value calculations):

(a) Present Value of $100,000 to Be Paid at the End of Five Years . . . . $ 55,839

(Table 2 at the back of the book shows the present value of $1 to be paid in 10 periods at 6 percent per period to be $.55839; $100,000 × .55839 = $55,839.)

(b) Present Value of $6,000 to Be Paid Each Six Months for Five Years   44,161

(Table 4 shows the present value of an ordinary annuity of $1 per period for 10 periods discounted at 6 percent to be $7.36009; $6,000 × 7.36009 = $44,161.)

Total Proceeds $100,000

Common terminology quotes bond prices as a percentage of par value. The issue price of these bonds is 100.0 (that is, 100 percent of par), which implies that the market interest rate is 12 percent, compounded semiannually, the same as the coupon rate.

Issued at Less Than Par

Assume that Macaulay Corporation issued these same bonds at a price to yield 14 percent compounded semiannually. The cash flows promised after July 1, Year 1, associated with these bonds (periodic payments plus repayment of principal) equal those in the time line in Figure 9.1. The market discounts these future cash flows to their present value using a 14 percent discount rate compounded semiannually. The calculation of the issue proceeds (that is, initial market price) follows:

(a) Present Value of $100,000 to Be Paid at the End of Five Years $50,835

(Present value of $1 to be paid in 10 periods at 7 percent per period is $.50835; $100,000 × .50835 = $50,835.)

(b) Present Value of $6,000 to Be Paid Each Six Months for
Five Years   42,141

(Present value of an ordinary annuity of $1 per period for 10 periods discounted at 7 percent per period = $7.02358; $6,000 × 7.02358 = $42,141.)

Total Proceeds $92,976

Assume Macaulay issues these bonds at 92.98 for $92,980. This implies a market yield of slightly less than 14 percent compounded semiannually.

Issued at More than Par

Assume that Macaulay Corporation issued the bonds at a price to yield 10 percent compounded semiannually. The cash flows promised after July 1, Year 1, again equal those in Figure 9.1. The market discounts these future cash flows at 10 percent compounded semiannually. The calculation of the proceeds follows:

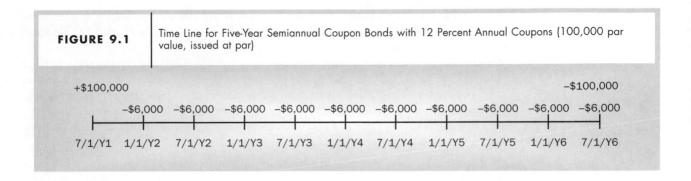

FIGURE 9.1	Time Line for Five-Year Semiannual Coupon Bonds with 12 Percent Annual Coupons (100,000 par value, issued at par)

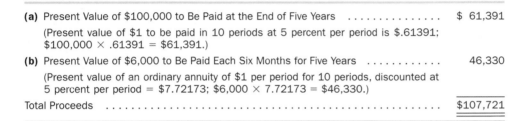

(a) Present Value of $100,000 to Be Paid at the End of Five Years . . . . $ 61,391

 (Present value of $1 to be paid in 10 periods at 5 percent per period is $.61391; $100,000 × .61391 = $61,391.)

(b) Present Value of $6,000 to Be Paid Each Six Months for Five Years   46,330

 (Present value of an ordinary annuity of $1 per period for 10 periods, discounted at 5 percent per period = $7.72173; $6,000 × 7.72173 = $46,330.)

Total Proceeds $107,721

Assume Macaulay issues these bonds at 107.72 (that is, 107.72 percent of par) for $107,720. The price would imply a market yield of slightly more than 10 percent compounded semiannually.

Bond Tables   One need not make these tedious calculations every time one analyzes a bond issue. **Bond tables** show the results of calculations like those just described. Tables 5 and 6 at the back of the book illustrate such tables. Table 5 shows the price for 10 percent semiannual coupon bonds as a percent of par for various market interest rates (yields) and years to maturity. Table 6 shows market rates and implied prices for 12 percent semiannual coupon bonds. (Most calculators make the calculations represented by these tables in a few seconds.)

The percentages of par shown in these tables represent the present value of the bond indicated. Because the tables give factors as a percent of par, the user must multiply them by 10 to find the price of a $1,000 bond. If you have never used bond tables before now, turn to Table 6 after the appendix at the back of the book, and find in the 5-year row the three different prices for the three different market yields used in the preceding examples. Notice further that a bond will sell at par if and only if it has a market yield equal to its coupon rate.

These tables apply both when a corporation issues a bond and when an investor later resells it. Computing the market price will be the same in either case. The following generalizations describe bond prices:

1. When the market interest rate equals the coupon rate, the market price will equal par.
2. When the market interest rate exceeds the coupon rate, the market price will be less than par.
3. When the market interest rate is less than the coupon rate, the market price will be greater than par.

Calculating the issue price of bonds. Dryden Corporation intends to issue $1,000,000 face-value bonds on January 2, Year 1. The bonds carry a 10 percent coupon rate, payable in two installments on June 30 and December 31 each year. The bonds mature on December 31, Year 10.

Compute the issue price of these bonds assuming that the market requires the following yields:

a. 8 percent compounded semiannually
b. 10 percent compounded semiannually
c. 12 percent compounded semiannually

Accounting for Bonds Issued at Par   The following illustrates bonds issued at par. We use the data presented in the previous sections for the Macaulay Corporation bonds issued at par, and we assume that the firm closes its books semiannually on June 30 and December 31. The entry at the time of issue follows:

7/1/Year 1	Cash	100,000	
	Debenture Bonds Payable		100,000
	$100,000 of 12 percent, five-year bonds issued at par.		

The borrower would make entries for interest at the end of the accounting period and on the payment dates. Entries through January 1, Year 2, would be as follows:

12/31/Year 1	Interest Expense	6,000	
	Interest Payable		6,000
1/1/Year 2	Interest Payable	6,000	
	Cash		6,000
	To record payment of six months' interest.		

Bond Issued between Payment Dates   The actual date when a firm issues a bond seldom coincides with one of the periodic payment dates. Assuming that Macaulay brought these same bonds to market on September 1, rather than July 1, at par, the borrower would expect the purchasers of the bonds to pay for two months' of periodic payments in advance. After all, on the first coupon, Macaulay Corporation promises a full $6,000 for six months' debt service, but it would have had the use of the borrowed funds for only four months. The purchasers of the bonds would pay $100,000 plus two months' interest of $2,000 (= .12 × $100,000 × 2/12) and would get the $2,000 back when Macaulay redeemed the first coupons. The journal entry made by Macaulay Corporation, the issuer, would be as follows:

9/1/Year 1	Cash	102,000	
	Bonds Payable		100,000
	Interest Payable		2,000
	To record issue of bonds at par between payment dates.		

The purchasers pay an amount equal to interest for the first two months but will get it back when the borrower pays for the first coupons.

Accounting for Bonds Issued at Less than Par   The following illustrates bonds issued at less than par. Assume the data presented above where the Macaulay Corporation issued 12 percent, $100,000-par value, five-year bonds to yield 14 percent compounded semiannually. Earlier, we derived the issue price to be $92,976. The journal entry at issue would be as follows:

7/1/Year 1	Cash	92,976	
	Debenture Bonds Payable		92,976

The issuance of these bonds for $92,976, instead of for the $100,000 par value, indicates that lenders demand more than 12 percent from Macaulay Corporation, the borrower. If purchasers of these bonds paid the $100,000 par value, they would earn only 12 percent compounded semiannually, the coupon rate. Purchasers desiring a rate of return of 14 percent will postpone their purchases until the market price drops to $92,976. At this price, purchasers of the bonds will earn the 14 percent return they require. The return will comprise 10 coupon payments of $6,000 each over the next five years plus $7,024 (= $100,000 − $92,976) as part of the payment at maturity.

For Macaulay Corporation, the total interest expense over the life of the bonds will equal $67,024 (= periodic payments totaling $60,000 plus $7,024 paid at maturity). The accounting for these payments allocates the total interest expense of $67,024 to the periods of the loan using the effective interest method, explained next. Following the next discussion may be easier if you refer to Exhibit 9.4.

Interest Expense under the Effective Interest Method   Under the **effective interest method,** interest expense each period equals the market interest rate at the time the firm initially issued the bonds (14 percent compounded semiannually, which is 7 percent per six months, in this example) multiplied by the book value of the liability at the beginning of the interest period. For example, interest expense for the period from July 1, Year 1, to December 31, Year 1, the first six-month period, is $6,508 (= .07 × $92,976). The bond indenture provides that the borrower repay only $6,000 (= .06 × $100,000) on January 1, Year 2. This amount equals the coupon rate times the par value of the bonds. The difference between the interest expense of $6,508 and the interest then payable of $6,000 increases the book value of the bond. The borrower will pay this amount as part of the principal payment at maturity. The journal entry made on December 31, Year 1, to recognize interest for the last six months of Year 1 follows:

12/31/Year 1	Interest Expense	6,508	
	Interest Payable		6,000
	Debenture Bonds Payable		508
	To recognize interest expense for six months.		

The Interest Payable account will appear as a current liability on the balance sheet at the end of Year 1. Debenture Bonds Payable of $93,484 (= $92,976 + $508) will appear on the balance sheet as a noncurrent liability.

On January 1, Year 2, the borrower makes the first periodic cash payment.

1/1/Year 2	Interest Payable	6,000	
	Cash		6,000
	To record payment of interest for six months.		

Interest expense for the second six months (from January 1, Year 2, through June 30, Year 2) is $6,544 (= .07 × $93,484). It exceeds the $6,508 for the first six months because the recorded book value of the liability at the beginning of the second six months has grown. The journal entry on June 30, Year 2, to record interest expense follows:

6/30/Year 2	Interest Expense	6,544	
	Interest Payable		6,000
	Debenture Bonds Payable		544
	To recognize interest expense for six months.		

EXHIBIT 9.4

Effective Interest Amortization Schedule for $100,000 of 12 Percent Semiannual Coupon, Five-Year Bonds Issued for 92.976 Percent of Par to Yield 14 Percent, Interest Compounded Semiannually

Semiannual Journal Entry

Dr. Interest Expense . . . .　　　Amount in Column **(3)**
　　Cr. Cash . . . .　　　　　　　　Amount in Column **(4)**
　　Cr. Debenture Bonds Payable . . . .　　　　　　　Amount in Column **(5)**

Period (6-Month Intervals) (1)	Liability at Start of Period (2)	Effective Interest: 7 Percent per Period (3)	Coupon Rate: 6 Percent of Par (4)	Increase in Recorded Book Value of Liability (5)	Liability at End of Period (6)
0					$ 92,976
1	$92,976	$ 6,508	$6,000	$ 508	93,484
2	93,484	6,544	6,000	544	94,028
3	94,028	6,582	6,000	582	94,610
4	94,610	6,623	6,000	623	95,233
5	95,233	6,666	6,000	666	95,899
6	95,899	6,713	6,000	713	96,612
7	96,612	6,763	6,000	763	97,375
8	97,375	6,816	6,000	816	98,191
9	98,191	6,873	6,000	873	99,064
10	99,064	6,936	6,000	936	100,000
Total		$67,024	$60,000	$7,024	

Note: In preparing this table, we rounded calculations to the nearest cent. Then, for presentation, we rounded results to the nearest dollar.

Column (2) = column (6) from previous period.

Column (3) = .07 × column (2).

Column (4) is given.

Column (5) = column (3) − column (4).

Column (6) = column (2) + column (5).

An amortization schedule for these bonds over their five-year life appears in Exhibit 9.4. Column (3) shows the periodic interest expense, and column (6) shows the book value that appears on the balance sheet at the end of each period.

The effective interest method of recognizing interest expense on a bond has the following financial statement effects:

1. Interest expense on the income statement will equal a constant percentage of the recorded liability at the beginning of each interest period. This percentage will equal the market interest rate for these bonds when the borrower issued them. When the borrower issues bonds for less than par value, the dollar amount of interest expense will increase each period as the recorded book value amount increases.
2. On the balance sheet at the end of each period, the bonds will appear at the present value of the remaining cash outflows discounted at the market interest rate when the borrower initially issued the bonds. For example, on July 1, Year 2, just after the borrower has made a coupon payment, the remaining cash payments have present value computed as follows:

(a) Present Value of $100,000 to Be Paid at the End of Four Years	$58,201
(Table 2 shows the present value of $1 to be paid at the end of eight periods discounted at 7 percent to be $.58201; $100,000 × .58201 = $58,201.)	
(b) Present Value of Eight Remaining Semiannual Interest Payments Discounted at 14 Percent Compounded Semiannually	35,827
(Table 4 shows the present value of an ordinary annuity of $1 per period for eight periods discounted at 7 percent to be $5.97130; $6,000 × 5.97130 = $35,827.)	
Total Present Value	$94,028

The amount $94,028 appears in column (6) of Exhibit 9.4 for the liability at the end of the second six-month period.

Discount on Bonds Payable Account The preceding description of the recording of bonds issued below par value shows the balance sheet book value of the bonds directly in the Bonds Payable account. Some accountants prefer to show Bonds Payable at par value with a liability contra account, titled Discount on Bonds Payable, carrying the amount by which par value must be reduced to equal book value. Using the Discount on Bonds Payable account, the balance sheet on June 30, Year 2, after two semiannual interest periods, would show the following:

Bonds Payable—Par Value	$100,000
Less Discount on Bonds Payable	5,972
Bonds Payable—Net Book Value	$ 94,028

Accounting for Bonds Issued at More than Par The following discussion illustrates bonds issued at more than par. Assume the data presented where the Macaulay Corporation issued 12 percent, $100,000-par value, five-year bonds to yield approximately 10 percent compounded semiannually. The issue price, derived previously, was $107,721. The journal entry at the time of issue follows:

7/1/Year 1	Cash	107,721	
	Debenture Bonds Payable		107,721

The firm borrows $107,721. The issuance of these bonds for $107,721, instead of the $100,000 par value, indicates that 12 percent exceeds the interest rate the purchasers (lenders) demand. If purchasers of these bonds paid the $100,000 par value, they would earn 12 percent compounded semiannually, the coupon rate. Purchasers requiring a rate of return of only 10 percent will bid up the market price to $107,721. At this price, purchasers of the bonds will earn only the 10 percent return they demand. Their return comprises 10 coupon payments of $6,000 each over the next five years reduced by the $7,721 (= $107,721 − $100,000) lent but not repaid at maturity.

For Macaulay Corporation, the total interest expense over the life of the bonds equals $52,279 (= periodic payments totaling $60,000 less $7,721 received at the time of original issue but not repaid at maturity). Following the next discussion may be easier if you refer to Exhibit 9.5.

Interest Expense under the Effective Interest Method   Under the effective interest method, interest expense each period equals the market interest rate at the time the firm initially issued the bonds (10 percent compounded semiannually, equals 5 percent per six months, in this example), multiplied by the recorded book value of the

EXHIBIT 9.5	Effective Interest Amortization Schedule for $100,000 of 12 Percent, Semiannual Coupon, Five-Year Bonds Issued for 107.721 Percent of Par to Yield 10 Percent, Compounded Semiannually

Semiannual Journal Entry

Dr. Interest Expense . . . .   Amount in Column **(3)**
Dr. Debenture Bonds Payable . . . .   Amount in Column **(5)**
  Cr. Cash . . . .   Amount in Column **(4)**

Period (6-Month Intervals) (1)	Liability at Start of Period (2)	Effective Interest: 5 Percent per Period (3)	Coupon Rate: 6 Percent of Par (4)	Decrease in Recorded Book Value of Liability (5)	Liability at End of Period (6)
0					$107,721
1	$107,721	$ 5,386	$ 6,000	$ 614	107,107
2	107,107	5,355	6,000	645	106,462
3	106,462	5,323	6,000	677	105,785
4	105,785	5,289	6,000	711	105,074
5	105,074	5,245	6,000	746	104,328
6	104,328	5,216	6,000	784	103,544
7	103,544	5,177	6,000	823	102,721
8	102,721	5,136	6,000	864	101,857
9	101,857	5,093	6,000	907	100,950
10	100,950	5,050	6,000	950	100,000
Total		$52,279	$60,000	$7,721	

Column (2) = column (6) from previous period.
Column (3) = .05 + column (2).
Column (4) is given.
Column (5) = column (4) − column (3).
Column (6) = column (2) − column (5).

liability at the beginning of the interest period. For example, interest expense for the period from July 1, Year 1, to December 31, Year 1, the first six-month period, is $5,386 (= .05 × $107,721). The bond indenture requires the borrower to pay $6,000 (= .06 × $100,000) on January 1, Year 2. This amount equals the coupon rate times the face value of the bonds. The difference between the payment of $6,000 and the interest expense of $5,386 reduces the amount of the liability. The journal entry made on December 31, Year 1, to recognize interest for the last six months of Year 1 follows:

12/31/Year 1	Interest Expense	5,386	
	Debenture Bonds Payable	614	
	Interest Payable		6,000
	To recognize interest expense for six months.		

The Interest Payable account appears as a current liability on the balance sheet at the end of Year 1. Debenture Bonds Payable has a new balance of $107,107 (= $107,721 − $614), which appears as a noncurrent liability.

On January 1, Year 2, the borrower makes the first periodic cash payment and the following entry:

1/1/Year 2	Interest Payable	6,000	
	Cash		6,000
	To record payment of interest for six months.		

Interest expense for the second six months (from January 1, Year 2, through June 30, Year 2) equals $5,355 (= .05 × $107,107). Because the amount of the liability has declined from the beginning of the preceding period to the beginning of the current period, the amount of interest expense for the period declines from $5,386 for the first six months, and the borrower records it as follows:

6/30/Year 2	Interest Expense	5,355	
	Debenture Bonds Payable	645	
	Interest Payable		6,000
	To recognize interest expense for six months.		

An amortization schedule for these bonds over their five-year life appears in Exhibit 9.5. Column (3) shows the periodic interest expense, and column (6) shows the book value that appears on the balance sheet at the end of the period.

The effective interest method of recognizing interest expense on a bond has the following financial statement effects:

1. Interest expense on the income statement equals a constant percentage of the recorded liability at the beginning of each interest period. This percentage equals the market interest rate when the borrower first issued the bonds. When the borrower issues bonds for more than par value, the dollar amount of interest expense will decrease each period as the unpaid liability decreases to the amount to be paid at maturity.
2. On the balance sheet at the end of each period, the bonds will appear at the present value of the remaining cash flows discounted at the market interest rate when the borrower initially issued the bonds. For example, on July 1, Year 2, just after the borrower

has made the coupon payment, the remaining cash payments have present value computed as follows:

(a) Present Value of $100,000 to Be Paid at the End of Four Years	$ 67,684
(Table 2 shows the present value of $1 to be paid at the end of eight periods discounted at 5 percent to be $.67684; $100,000 × .67684 = $67,684.)	
(b) Present Value of Eight Remaining Semiannual Interest Payments Discounted at 10 Percent, Compounded Semiannually	38,779
(Table 4 shows the present value of an ordinary annuity of $1 per period for eight periods discounted at 5 percent to be $6.46321; $6,000 × 6.46321 = $38,779.)	
Total Present Value	$106,463

The amount $106,462, different because of rounding effects, appears in column (6) of Exhibit 9.5 for the liability at the end of the second six-month period.

Premium on Bonds Payable Account The preceding description of the recording of bonds issued above par value shows the book value of the bonds directly in the Bonds Payable account. Some accountants prefer to show Bonds Payable at par value with a liability adjunct account, titled Premium on Bonds Payable, carrying the amount added to par value to show book value. (An *adjunct account* accumulates additions to another account; contrast this with a contra account, which accumulates subtractions from another account.)

Using the Premium on Bonds Payable account, the balance sheet on June 30, Year 2, after two semiannual interest periods, would show:

Bonds Payable—Par Value	$100,000
Plus Premium on Bonds Payable	6,462
Bonds Payable—Net Book Value	$106,462

P R O B L E M   9 . 5   F O R   S E L F - S T U D Y

Preparing journal entries to account for bonds. Refer to Problem 9.4 for Self-Study. Prepare the journal entries on January 1, June 30, and December 31, Year 1, to account for the bonds, assuming each of the following market-required interest rates:

a. 8 percent compounded semiannually
b. 10 percent compounded semiannually
c. 12 percent compounded semiannually

Bond Retirement Many bonds remain outstanding until the stated maturity date. Refer to Exhibit 9.4, where Macaulay Corporation issued the 12 percent coupon bonds to yield 14 percent. The company pays the final coupon, $6,000, and the face amount, $100,000, on the stated maturity date. The entries are as follows:

7/1/Year 6	Interest Expense	6,936	
	Cash		6,000
	Debenture Bonds Payable		936
	See row 10 of Exhibit 9.4.		
	Debenture Bonds Payable	100,000	
	Cash		100,000
	To record retirement at maturity of bonds.		

Retirement before Maturity A firm sometimes purchases its own bonds on the open market before maturity. Because market interest rates constantly change, the purchase price will seldom equal the recorded book value of the bonds. Assume that Macaulay Corporation originally issued its 12 percent coupon bonds to yield 14 percent compounded semiannually. Assume that three years later, on July 1, Year 4, interest rates in the marketplace have increased so that the market currently requires Macaulay Corporation to pay a 15 percent interest rate. Refer to Table 6 in the appendix at the back of the book, 2-year row, 15-percent column; there you see that 12 percent bonds with two years until maturity sell in the marketplace for 94.9760 percent of par when the current interest rate is 15 percent compounded semiannually.

The principles of historical cost accounting do not constrain the pricing of bonds in the marketplace. Even though Macaulay Corporation shows Debenture Bonds Payable on the balance sheet at $96,612 (see row 6 of Exhibit 9.4), the marketplace puts a price of only $94,976 on the entire bond issue. From the point of view of the marketplace, these bonds are the same as two-year bonds issued on July 1, Year 4, at an effective yield of 15 percent, so they carry a discount of $5,024 (= $100,000 − $94,976).

If on July 1, Year 4, Macaulay Corporation purchased $10,000 of par value of its own bonds, it would have to pay only $9,498 (= .94976 × $10,000) for those bonds, which have a book value of $9,661. Macaulay would make the following journal entries at the time of purchase:

7/1/Year 4	Interest Expense	6,713	
	Interest Payable		6,000
	Debenture Bonds Payable		713
	See row for Period 6 of Exhibit 9.4.		
	Interest Payable	6,000	
	Cash		6,000
	To record payment of coupons, as usual.		
	Debenture Bonds Payable	9,661	
	Cash		9,498
	Gain on Retirement of Bonds		163
	To record purchase of bonds for less than the current amount shown in the accounting records.		

Historical cost accounting calls the entry to make debits equal credits in recording the retirement a *gain*. This gain arises because the firm can retire a liability recorded at one amount, $9,661, for a smaller cash payment, $9,498. The borrower earned this gain as interest rates increased between Year 1 and Year 4. Historical cost accounting reports the gain in the period when the borrower realizes it—that is, in the period when the borrower retires the bonds. This phenomenon parallels the economic events that occur when a firm invests in land, holds the land as its value increases, sells the land in a subsequent year, and reports all the gain in the year of sale. The phenomenon results from the historical cost accounting convention of recording amounts at historical cost and not recording increases in wealth until the firm realizes those increases in arm's-length transactions with outsiders.

A Quality-of-Earnings Issue During the 1980s, interest rates jumped upward from their levels in the 1960s. Many companies had issued bonds in the 1960s at prices near par, with coupon rates of only 3 or 4 percent per year. When interest rates in the 1980s jumped to 10 or 12 percent per year, these bonds traded in the market for substantial discounts from face value. Many companies repurchased their own bonds, recording substantial gains in the process. (In one year Pan American World Airlines reported profits after seven consecutive years of losses. Pan Am had gains on bond retirement that year in excess of the entire amount of reported net income and later went bankrupt.) Such gains do not form part of high-quality earnings.

Historical cost accounting provides no alternative to showing a gain (or loss) on bond retirement (the debits must equal the credits). The FASB does not want companies to manage their own reported income by timing the repurchase of bonds. The FASB, therefore, generally requires firms to report gains and losses on bond retirements as extraordinary items on the income statement.[5] Net income includes such items but lists them in a section separate from that reporting income from continuing operations. (See the discussion in Chapter 12.)

Serial Bonds The bond indenture may require the issuing firm to make a provision for partial early retirement of the bond issue. Such requirements generally take one of two forms. One, for serial bonds, provides that stated portions of the principal amount will come due on a series of maturity dates. The DaimlerChrysler Corporation bonds in Example 16 are serial bonds.

Sinking Fund Bonds The other major type of partial early retirement provision in bond indentures requires the firm to accumulate a fund of cash or other assets to use to pay the bonds when the maturity date arrives or to reacquire and retire portions of the bond issue. Financial terminology refers to these funds as **sinking funds,** although *bond retirement funds* would be more descriptive.[6] The trustee of the bond issue usually holds the assets of the sinking fund. The fund appears on the balance sheet of the borrower as a noncurrent asset in the Investments section.

Refunded Bonds Most bond indentures make no provision for **bond refunding,** that is, for making serial repayments or for accumulating sinking funds for bond retirement. The market judges these bonds to be protected with property held by trustees as collateral or with the high credit standing of the issuer. In such cases, the borrower may pay the entire bond liability at maturity out of cash in the bank at that time. Quite commonly, however, the firm refunds the bond issue. It issues a new set of bonds to obtain the funds to retire the old ones when they come due.

[5]Financial Accounting Standards Board, *Statement of Financial Accounting Standards No. 4,* "Reporting Gains and Losses from Extinguishment of Debt," 1975. The next footnote describes an exception.

[6]Gain or loss on bond retirement resulting from sinking fund provisions appears as part of ordinary income; see *SFAS No. 4.* The gain or loss, like the gain or loss on voluntary bond retirement, does not produce or use cash from operations. Thus, in the statement of cash flows, deriving cash from operations using the indirect method requires a subtraction from net income for the amount of the gain.

Callable Bonds A common provision gives the issuing company the right to retire portions of the bond issue before maturity if it so desires, but the provision does not require the company to do so. To facilitate such reacquisition and retirement of the bonds, the bond indenture provides that the bonds be *callable*. That is, the issuing company has the right, but not the obligation, to reacquire its bonds before stated maturity at prices specified in the bond indenture. When the borrower calls the bonds, the trustee will not immediately pay a subsequent coupon presented for redemption. Rather, the trustee will notify the holder to present all remaining coupons and the bond principal for payments equal to the call price plus accrued interest.

The indenture usually sets the **call price** initially higher than the par value and provides a declining schedule for the call price as the maturity date approaches. Because the borrower may exercise the call provision at a time when the coupon rate exceeds the market interest rate, the market usually prices callable bonds at something less than the price of otherwise similar but noncallable bonds.

Assume, for example, that a firm issued 12 percent semiannual coupon bonds at a discount, implying a borrowing rate higher than 12 percent. Later, market interest rates and the firm's credit standing allow it to borrow at 10 percent. Assume the borrower has recorded all accrued interest expense and the bonds have a current book value of $98,000, including accrued interest. If the borrower calls $100,000 of par value of these bonds at 105 percent of par, the entry would be as follows:

Debenture Bonds Payable	98,000	
Loss on Retirement of Bonds	7,000	
Cash		105,000
To record bonds called and retired.		

The loss is an extraordinary item unless the retirement results from a sinking fund provision. The loss recognized on bond retirement, like the analogous gain, generally appears as an extraordinary item in the income statement. (Chapter 12 discusses extraordinary items and other subdivisions of the income statement.)

The market rate of interest that a firm must pay to borrow depends on two factors: the general level of interest rates and its own creditworthiness. If the market rate of interest has risen since the borrower issued the bonds (or if the firm's credit rating has declined), the bonds will sell in the market at less than issue price. A firm that wanted to retire such bonds would not call them because the call price would typically exceed the face value. Instead the firm would probably purchase its bonds on the open market and realize a gain on the bonds' retirement.

UNIFYING PRINCIPLES OF ACCOUNTING FOR LONG-TERM LIABILITIES

Long-term liabilities obligate the borrowing firm to pay specified amounts at definite times more than one year in the future. We now state a single set of principles to describe the balance sheet presentation of all long-term liabilities and a single procedure for computing that amount and the amount of interest expense. First, we describe the amounts on the balance sheet, a "state description" (like a blueprint). Then, we describe the process for computing the amounts, a "process description" (like a recipe).

State Description All long-term liabilities appear on the balance sheet at the present value of the remaining future payments. The present value computations use the historical rate of interest—the market interest rate on the date the borrower incurred the obligation.

Process Description The methods of computing balance sheet amounts for all long-term liabilities and their related expenses embody identical concepts and follow the same procedures:

1. Record the liability at the cash (or cash equivalent) value received. This amount equals the present value of the future contractual payments discounted using the market interest rate for the borrower on the date the loan begins. (Sometimes the borrower must compute the original-issue market interest rate by finding the internal rate of return. See the appendix at the back of the book.)
2. At any subsequent time when the firm makes a cash payment or an adjusting entry for interest, it computes interest expense as the book value of the liability accounts (including any interest added in prior periods) multiplied by the historical interest rate. The accountant debits this amount to Interest Expense and credits it to the liability accounts. If the firm makes a cash payment, the accountant debits the liability accounts and credits Cash.

The effect will increase or decrease the book value of the liabilities for the start of the next period. If the accountant follows these procedures, the liabilities on the balance sheet will always satisfy the state description above. The liabilities will have book value equal to the present value of the remaining future payments discounted at the historical market interest rate.

Amortization schedules, such as in Exhibits 9.3, 9.4, 9.5, 9.6, and, in Chapter 10, 10.1, illustrate this unchanging procedure for a variety of long-term liabilities. The next problem for self-study focuses on the procedure.

PROBLEM 9.6 FOR SELF-STUDY

Unifying principles of accounting for long-term liabilities. This problem illustrates the unifying principles of accounting for long-term liabilities described just above. Assume that a firm closes its books once per year, making adjusting entries once per year. On the date the firm borrows, the market requires it to pay interest at the rate of 10 percent per year, compounded annually for all loans spanning a two-year period. Note the following steps:

1. Compute the initial issue proceeds received by the firm issuing the obligation (that is, borrowing the cash) on the date of issue.
2. Give the journal entry for issue of the liability and receipt of cash.
3. Show the journal entry or entries for interest accrual and cash payment, if any, at the end of the first year, and recompute the book value of all liabilities related to the borrowing at the end of the first year. Combine the liability accounts for the main borrowing and accrued interest into a single account called Monetary Liability.
4. Show the journal entry or entries for interest accrual and cash payment at the end of the second year, and recompute the book value of all liabilities related to the borrowing at the end of the second year.

Perform the above steps for each of the following borrowings:

a. The firm issues a single-payment note on the first day of the first year, promising to pay $1,000 on the last day of the second year.

b. The firm issues a 10 percent annual coupon bond, promising to pay $100 on the last day of the first year and $1,100 (= $1,000 + $100) on the last day of the second year.

c. The firm issues an 8 percent annual coupon bond, promising to pay $80 on the last day of the first year and $1,080 (= $1,000 + $80) on the last day of the second year.

d. The firm issues a 12 percent annual coupon bond, promising to pay $120 on the last day of the first year and $1,120 (= $1,000 + $120) on the last day of the second year.

e. The firm issues a level-payment note (like a mortgage or installment note), promising to pay $576.19 on the last day of the first year and another $576.19 on the last day of the second year.

SUMMARY

A liability obligates a firm to make a (probable) future sacrifice of resources. The firm can estimate the amount of the obligation and its timing with reasonable certainty. The transaction causing the obligation has already occurred; in other words, the obligation arises from other than an executory contract.

Accounting initially records long-term liabilities at the cash-equivalent value the borrower receives (which equals the present value of the future cash flows the borrower promises, discounted at the market interest rate for that borrower). As the maturity date of the liability draws near, the book value of the liability approaches the amount of the final cash payment. To compute interest expense throughout the accounting life of the liability, historical cost accounting uses the borrower's market interest rate on the date the borrower incurred the liability. Interest expense for any period is the book value of the liability at the start of the period multiplied by the historical interest rate.

Borrowers retire liabilities in different ways. In each case the borrower debits the liability retired for its book value, credits the asset given up, and recognizes gain or loss on retirement. In most circumstances, the gain or loss on bond retirement appears on the income statement as an extraordinary item.

APPENDIX 9.1: EFFECTS ON THE STATEMENT OF CASH FLOWS OF TRANSACTIONS INVOLVING LONG-TERM LIABILITIES

INTEREST ON BONDS ISSUED FOR LESS THAN PAR

Recognizing interest expense on bonds issued at less than par may require special treatment in computing cash flow from operations in the statement of cash flows. Refer to Exhibit 9.4. Interest expense reported for the first six months is $6,508 (= $6,000 in coupon payments and $508 in increased principal amount). Notice that the borrower used only $6,000 of cash for the expense. Liabilities increased by $6,508. A cash payment of $6,000 followed. The remainder of the interest expense, $508, increased the noncurrent liability Debenture Bonds Payable. Consequently, when the firm uses the indirect method of deriving cash flow from operations, the accountant must add back to net income the remainder of the expense, $508, which did not use cash.

BONDS ISSUED AT A PREMIUM

The periodic cash payments for bonds originally issued at amounts above par exceed periodic interest expense. Because the amount of cash disbursed exceeds interest expense, the accountant must subtract the excess in deriving cash flow from operations when the statement follows the indirect format. The amount subtracted equals the excess of cash disbursed over interest expense.

GAIN OR LOSS ON BOND RETIREMENT

When a firm retires a bond for cash, it reports the cash in the Financing section as a non-operating use, Cash Used to Reduce Debt. In most cases the amount of cash the firm uses to retire a liability differs from the book value of the liability at the time of retirement. Thus, the retirement generates a gain (when book value exceeds cash used) or a loss (when cash used exceeds book value).

The Financing section of the statement shows all the cash used to retire the liability; that use of cash had nothing to do with operations. When the statement of cash flows presents cash from operations with the indirect format, the computation starts with net income. That figure includes the gain or loss on the repurchase of the liability. Because the repurchase is financing, not operating, the accountant subtracts the amount of the gain or adds back the amount of the loss in deriving operating cash flows. See lines (3) and (2) of Exhibit 4.16.

SOLUTIONS TO SELF-STUDY PROBLEMS

SUGGESTED SOLUTION TO PROBLEM 9.1 FOR SELF-STUDY

(Ashton Corporation; journal entries for transactions involving current liabilities.)

a. January 2

Cash	10,000	
Note Payable		10,000

To record 90-day, 9 percent bank loan.

b. January 3

Merchandise Inventory	8,000	
Accounts Payable		8,000

To record purchases of merchandise on account.

c. January 10

Cash	1,500	
Advance from Customer		1,500

To record advance from customer on merchandise scheduled for delivery in February.

d. Month of January

Accounts Receivable	12,000	
Sales Revenue		12,000

To record sales on account during January.

Cost of Goods Sold	6,000	
Merchandise Inventory		6,000

To record the cost of merchandise sold.

e. Month of January

Accounts Payable	8,000	
Cash		8,000

To record payments to suppliers for purchases on account.

Cash	7,000	
Accounts Receivable		7,000

To record collections from customers for sales on account.

f. January 31

Warranty Expense	960	
Estimated Warranty Liability		960

To record estimated warranty cost for goods sold during January; .08 × \$12,000 = \$960.

g. January 31

Wages Expense	4,000	
U.S. Withholding Taxes Payable		800
FICA Taxes Payable		400
Withheld Union Dues Payable		200
Wages Payable		2,600

To record January wages net of taxes and union dues withheld.

Wages Expense	540	
FICA Taxes Payable		400
FUTA Taxes Payable		140

To record employer's share of payroll taxes.

h. January 31

Interest Expense	75	
Interest Payable		75

To record interest expense on notes payable for January; \$10,000 × .09 × 30/360 = \$75.

i. January 31

Income Tax Expense	170	
Income Tax Payable		170

To accrue income taxes payable for January: .40 × (\$12,000 − \$6,000 − \$960 − \$4,000 \$540 − \$75) = \$170.

j. February 1

Wages Payable	2,600	
Cash		2,600

To pay employees their January wages net of withholdings.

k. February 10

Advance from Customer	1,500	
Sales Revenue		1,500

To record the sale of merchandise to customer.

Cost of Goods Sold	800	
Merchandise Inventory		800

To record the cost of merchandise sold.

l. February 15

U.S. Withholding Taxes Payable	800	
FICA Taxes Payable	800	
FUTA Taxes Payable	140	
Withheld Union Dues Payable	200	
Cash		1,940

To record payment of payroll taxes and union dues.

m. February 20

Estimated Warranty Liability	220	
Cash		220

To record the cost of warranty repairs on products sold during January.

EXHIBIT 9.6	Amortization Schedule for Note with Face Value of $100,000 Issued for $112,434, Bearing Interest at the Rate of 15 Percent of Face Value per Year, Issued to Yield 10 Percent (Problem 9.2 for Self-Study)

Yearly Periods (1)	Loan Balance Start of Period (2)	Interest Expense for Period (3)	Payment (4)	Portion of Payment Reducing Book Value of Liability (5)	Loan Balance End of Period (6)
0					$112,434
1	$112,434	$11,243	$ 15,000	$ 3,757	108,677
2	108,677	10,868	15,000	4,132	104,545
3	104,545	10,455	115,000	104,545	0

Column (2) = column (6) from previous period.
Column (3) = .10 × column (2).
Column (4) is given.
Column (5) = column (4) − column (3).
Column (6) = column (2) − column (5).

SUGGESTED SOLUTION TO PROBLEM 9.2 FOR SELF-STUDY

(Avner Company; accounting for an interest-bearing note.)
a. See Exhibit 9.6.

b. **Date of Issue**

Cash	112,434	
Note Payable		112,434

Proceeds of issue of note.

Six Months after Issue

Interest Expense	5,622	
Interest Payable		5,622

See Exhibit 9.6; accrual of six months' interest = $11,243/2.

One Year after Issue

Interest Expense	5,621	
Interest Payable	5,622	
Notes Payable	3,757	
Cash		15,000

Interest expense for the remainder of the first year and cash payment made. Excess of cash payment over interest expense reduces note principal.

SUGGESTED SOLUTION TO PROBLEM 9.3 FOR SELF-STUDY

(Chang Company; accounting for note with imputed interest rate.)

a.

Truck	22,500	
Note Payable		22,500

.90 × $25,000 = $22,500.

b. $28,730/$22,500 = 1.27689$. The truck has fair market value of $22,500 (= .90 \times$ $25,000)$; $(1 + r)^2 = 1.27689$, which implies that $r = \sqrt{1.27689} - 1 = .13$, or 13 percent per year. In other words, $22,500 grows to $28,730 in two years when the interest rate is 13 percent per period.

c.

Truck	22,903	
Note Payable		22,903
$(1.12)^{-2} = .79719$; $.79719 \times 28,730 = $22,903$.		

d. $(1.01)^{-24} = .78757$. (See Table 2 at the end of the book, 24-period row, 1-percent column.) $.78757 \times $28,730 = $22,627$.

Truck	22,627	
Note Payable		22,627

e.

Truck	23,744	
Note Payable		23,744
Year 1:		
Interest Expense (= .10 \times $23,744)	2,374	
Note Payable		2,374
Year 2:		
Interest Expense [= .10 \times ($23,744 + $2,374)] . . .	2,612	
Note Payable		2,612
Balance in Note Payable Account at End of Year 2		$28,730

f. Total expense equals interest expense on the note plus depreciation on the truck. Interest expense is $28,730 less the amount at which the firm records the truck. Depreciation expense is equal to the amount at which Chang records the truck less estimated salvage value. Thus, over the life of the truck or two years, whichever is longer, the total expense equals $28,730 less the salvage value of the truck.

SUGGESTED SOLUTION TO PROBLEM 9.4 FOR SELF-STUDY

(Dryden Corporation; calculating the issue price of bonds.)

a.

Required Cash Flows	Present Value Factor for 8 Percent Interest Rate Compounded Semiannually for 10 Years	Present Value of Required Cash Flows
$1,000,000 at end of 10 years	.45639[a]	$ 456,390
$50,000 every six months for 10 years	13.59033[b]	679,516
Issue Price		$1,135,906

[a]Table 2, 4-percent column and 20-period row.
[b]Table 4, 4-percent column and 20-period row.

b.

Required Cash Flows	Present Value Factor for 10 Percent Interest Rate Compounded Semiannually for 10 Years	Present Value of Required Cash Flows
$1,000,000 at end of 10 years	.37689[a]	$376,890
$50,000 every six months for 10 years	12.46221[b]	623,110
Issue Price		$1,000,000

[a]Table 2, 5-percent column and 20-period row.
[b]Table 4, 5-percent column and 20-period row.

c.

Required Cash Flows	Present Value Factor for 12 Percent Interest Rate Compounded Semiannually for 10 Years	Present Value of Required Cash Flows
$1,000,000 at end of 10 years	.31180[a]	$311,800
$50,000 every six months for 10 years	11.46992[b]	573,496
Issue Price		$885,296

[a]Table 2, 6-percent column and 20-period row.
[b]Table 4, 6-percent column and 20-period row.

SUGGESTED SOLUTION TO PROBLEM 9.5 FOR SELF-STUDY

(Dryden Corporation; preparing journal entries to account for bonds.)

a. January 1

Cash	1,135,906	
Bonds Payable		1,135,906

To record issue of $1,000,000-par value, 10 percent semiannual coupon bonds priced to yield 8 percent compounded semiannually.

June 30

Interest Expense (.04 × 1,135,906)	45,436	
Bonds Payable	4,564	
Cash (.05 × $1,000,000)		50,000

To record interest expense and amount payable for first six months.

December 31

Interest Expense [.04 × ($1,135,906 − $4,564)]	45,254	
Bonds Payable	4,746	
Cash (.05 × $1,000,000)		50,000

To record interest expense and amount payable for second six months.

b. January 1

Cash	1,000,000	
Bonds Payable		1,000,000

To record issue of $1,000,000-par value, 10 percent semiannual coupon bonds priced to yield 10 percent compounded semiannually.

June 30

Interest Expense (.05 × $1,000,000)	50,000	
Cash (.05 × $1,000,000)		50,000

To record interest expense and amount payable for first six months.

December 31

Interest Expense (.05 × $1,000,000)	50,000	
Cash (.05 × $1,000,000)		50,000

To record interest expense and amount payable for second six months.

c. January 1

Cash	885,296	
Bonds Payable		885,296

To record issue of $1,000,000-par value, 10 percent semiannual coupon bonds priced to yield 12 percent compounded semiannually.

June 30

Interest Expense (.06 × $885,296)	53,118	
Cash (.05 × $1,000,000)		50,000
Bonds Payable		3,118

To record interest expense and amount payable for first six months.

December 31

Interest Expense [.06 × ($885,296 + $3,118)]	53,305	
Cash (.05 × $1,000,000)		50,000
Bonds Payable		3,305

To record interest expense and amount payable for second six months.

SUGGESTED SOLUTION TO PROBLEM 9.6 FOR SELF-STUDY

(Unifying principles of accounting for long-term liabilities.)
Exhibit 9.7 shows the accounting for five types of long-term monetary liabilities stated at the present value of future cash flows. The accounting for each of these monetary liabilities follows a common procedure.

1. Compute the initial amount of cash received by the borrower as well as the historical interest rate. Sometimes you will know both of these. Sometimes you will know the cash received and you must calculate the interest rate. Sometimes, as Exhibit 9.7 illustrates in all five cases, you will know the interest rate and must compute the initial cash received.
   a. To compute the initial amount of cash received, given the contractual payments and the market interest rate, multiply each of the contractual payments by the present value factor (as from Table 2 at the back of the book) for a single payment of $1 to be received in the future. Exhibit 9.7 shows the present value factors at 10 percent interest for payments to be received in 1 year (.90909) and in 2 years (.82645).
   b. Computing the market interest rate, given the initial cash proceeds and the series of contractual payments, requires finding the *internal rate of return* of the series of cash flows. The appendix at the back of the book illustrates this process. Exhibit 9.7 shows that only the 10 percent coupon bond and the level-payment note have initial cash proceeds equal to $1,000. The difference in amounts arises because each

	a. Single-Payment Note of $1,000 Maturing in Two Years			b. Two-Year Annual Coupon Bond—10 Percent ($100) Coupons		
	Amount	Dr.	Cr.	Amount	Dr.	Cr.
(1) Compute Present Value of Future Contractual Payments Using Historical Interest Rate on Day Monetary Liability is First Recorded. Rate is 10.0 Percent.						
(a) 1 Year Hence	$ 0			$ 100.00		
(b) 2 Years Hence	$1,000.00			$1,100.00		
Multiply Payment by Present Value Factors (Table 2).						
.90909 × (a)	$ 0			$ 90.91		
.82645 × (b)	826.45			909.09		
(c) Total Present Value	$ 826.45			$1,000.00		
(2) Record Initial Liability and Cash or Other Assets Received from Step 1.						
Dr. Cash or Other Assets		826.45			1,000.00	
Cr. Monetary Liability			826.45			1,000.00
(3) First Recording (payment date or end of period): End of First Year						
(a) Compute Interest Expense as Monetary Liability × Historical Interest Rate.						
Amount on Line 1(c) × .10	$ 82.64			$ 100.00		
(b) Record Interest Expense.						
Dr. Interest Expense		82.64			100.00	
Cr. Monetary Liability			82.64			100.00
(c) Record Cash Payment (if any).						
Dr. Monetary Liability		—			100.00	
Cr. Cash			—			100.00
(d) Compute Book Value of Monetary Liability.						
Beginning Balance	$ 826.45			$1,000.00		
Add Interest Expense	82.64			100.00		
Subtotal	$ 909.09			$1,100.00		
Subtract Cash Payment (if any) . .	—			(100.00)		
= Ending Balance	$ 909.09			$1,000.00		
(4) Second Recording: End of Second Year						
(a) Compute Interest Expense as Monetary Liability × Historical Interest Rate.						
Amount on Line 3(d) × .10	$ 90.91			$ 100.00		
(b) Record Interest Expense.						
Dr. Interest Expense.		90.91			100.00	
Cr. Monetary Liability			90.91			100.00
(c) Record Cash Payment (if any).						
Dr. Monetary Liability		1,000.00			1,100.00	
Cr. Cash			1,000.00			1,100.00
(d) Compute Book Value of Monetary Liability.						
Beginning Balance	$ 909.09			$1,000.00		
Add Interest Expense	90.91			100.00		
Subtotal	$1,000.00			$1,100.00		
Subtract Cash Payment (if any) . .	(1,000.00)			(1,100.00)		
= Ending Balance	$ 0			$ 0		

	c. Two-Year Annual Coupon Bond—8 Percent ($80) Coupons			d. Two-Year Annual Coupon Bond—12 Percent ($120) Coupons			e. Two-Year Level-Payment Note— Annual Payments of $576.19		
	Amount	Dr.	Cr.	Amount	Dr.	Cr.	Amount	Dr.	Cr.
	$ 80.00			$ 120.00			$ 576.19		
	$1,080.00			$1,120.00			$ 576.19		
	$ 72.73			$ 109.09			$ 523.81		
	892.57			925.62			476.19		
	$ 965.30			$1,034.71			$1,000.00		
		965.30			1,034.71			1,000.00	
			965.30			1,034.71			1,000.00
	$ 96.53			$ 103.47			$ 100.00		
		96.53			103.47			100.00	
			96.53			103.47			100.00
		80.00			120.00			576.19	
			80.00			120.00			576.19
	$ 965.30			$1,034.71			$1,000.00		
	96.53			103.47			100.00		
	$1,061.83			$1,138.18			$1,100.00		
	(80.00)			(120.00)			(576.19)		
	$ 981.83			$1,018.18			$ 523.81		
	$ 98.18			$ 101.82			$ 52.38		
		98.18			101.82			52.38	
			96.18			101.82			52.38
		1,080.00			1,120.00			576.19	
			1,080.00			1,120.00			576.19
	$ 981.83			$1,018.18			$ 523.81		
	98.18			101.82			52.38		
	$1,080.01			1,120.00			$ 576.19		
	(1,080.00)			(1,120.00)			(576.19)		
	$ 0[a]			$ 0			$ 0		

[a]Rounding error of $.01.

of the items has a different present value, in spite of the fact that some people might, loosely speaking, call each a "$1,000 liability."

2. Record a journal entry debiting cash and crediting the monetary liability with the amount of cash received. This presentation showing the common theme uses the generic account title Monetary Liability, although in practice a firm would use more descriptive titles.

3. At every contractual payment date and at the end of an accounting period, compute interest expense as the book value of the liability at the beginning of the period (which includes the principal liability account and the Interest Payable account if the firm keeps these amounts in separate accounts) multiplied by the historical interest rate. Debit the computed amount to interest expense and credit the liability account.

   If the borrower makes a cash payment, credit cash and debit the liability. The book value of the liability is now equal to the beginning balance plus interest expense recorded less cash payments made, if any.

   Exhibit 9.7 does not illustrate this fact directly, but if you were to return to step **1** at this point and compute the present value of the remaining contractual payments using the historical interest rate (10 percent in the examples), that present value would equal the book value computed after step **3.**

4. At each payment date, or at each period-end closing date, repeat step **3.** Eventually, when the borrower makes the final payment (as illustrated at the bottom of Exhibit 9.7), it will have discharged the entire amount of the liability plus interest. The remaining liability is zero.

KEY TERMS AND CONCEPTS

Liability	Imputed (inherent) interest rate
Partially executed contract	Bond indenture
Executory contract	Coupon bond
Estimated liability	Debenture bonds
Contingent liability	Convertible bonds
Constructive liability	Serial bond
FICA taxes	Zero coupon bond
FUTA taxes	Bond tables
Mortgage	Effective interest method
Collateral	Sinking fund
Mortgagee, mortgagor	Bond refunding
Implicit interest	Call price

QUESTIONS, EXERCISES, PROBLEMS, AND CASES

QUESTIONS

1. Review the meaning of the terms and concepts listed above in Key Terms and Concepts.
2. For each of the following items, indicate whether the item meets all of the criteria of a liability. If so, how does the firm value it?
   a. Interest accrued but not paid on a note
   b. Advances from customers for goods and services to be delivered later
   c. Confirmed orders from customers for goods and services to be delivered later

  d. Bonds payable

  e. Product warranties

  f. Damages the company must pay if it loses a pending lawsuit

  g. Future costs of restoring strip-mining sites after completing mining operations

  h. Contractual promises to purchase natural gas for each of the next 10 years

  i. Promises by an airline to provide free flights in the future if customers accumulate a certain number of miles at regular fares

  3. While shopping in a store on July 5, Year 6, a customer slips on the floor and sustains back injuries. On January 15, Year 7, the customer sues the store for $1 million. The case comes to trial on April 30, Year 7. The jury renders its verdict on June 15, Year 7, and finds the store liable for negligence. The jury grants a damage award of $400,000 to the customer. The store, on June 25, Year 7, appeals the decision to a higher court on the grounds that the lower court failed to admit certain evidence. The higher court rules on November 1, Year 7, that the trial court should have admitted the evidence. The trial court rehears the case beginning on March 21, Year 8. Another jury, on April 20, Year 8, again finds the store liable for negligence and awards $500,000. On May 15, Year 8, the store pays the $500,000 judgment. When should the store recognize a loss from these events? Explain your reasoning.

  4. What is the amount of the liability recognized in each of the independent cases below?

  a. A plaintiff files a lawsuit against a company. The probability is 90 percent that the company will lose. If it loses, the amount of the loss will most likely be $100,000.

  b. A cereal company issues redeemable coupons for "free" boxes of cereal. Now, it issues one million coupons that promise the retailer who redeems the coupons $1 per coupon. The probability of redemption of any one coupon is 9 percent.

  5. "Firms should obtain as much financing as possible from suppliers through accounts payable because it is a free source of capital." Do you agree? Why or why not?

  6. The Francis W. Parker School, a private academy, has a reporting year ending June 30. It hires teachers for a 10-month period: September of one year through June of the following year. It contracts to pay teachers in 12 monthly installments over the period September of one year through August of the next year. For the current academic year, suppose that the total contractual salaries to be paid to teachers is $360,000. How should the school account for this amount in the financial statements issued June 30, at the end of the academic year?

  7. A magazine publisher offers a reduced annual subscription fee if customers pay for three years in advance. Under this subscription program, the magazine publisher receives from customers $45,000, which it credits to the account Advances from Customers. The estimated cost of publishing magazines for these customers is $32,000. Why does accounting report a liability of $45,000 instead of $32,000?

  8. A noted accountant once remarked that the optimal number of faulty TV sets for Sony to sell is "not zero," even if Sony promises to repair all faulty Sony sets that break down, for whatever reason, within two years of purchase. Why could the optimal number be "not zero"?

  9. Describe the similarities and differences between the allowance method for uncollectibles (see Chapter 6) and the allowance method for estimated warranty costs.

10. What factors determine the amount of money a firm actually receives when it offers a bond issue to the market?

11. Distinguish between the following sets of terms for bonds. Under what circumstances will they be the same? Under what circumstances will they differ?

  a. Par value and face value

  b. Par value and book value

  c. Book value and current market value

12. "Using the market interest rate at the time of issue to account for bonds in subsequent periods provides a book value for bonds that is consistent with using historical, or acquisition, cost valuations for assets." Explain.

13. "The effective interest method results in a constant percentage of interest expense but not necessarily a constant amount." Explain.

14. If the Deer Valley Ski Association borrows $1,000,000 by issuing, at par, 20-year, 10 percent bonds with semiannual coupons, the total interest expense over the life of the issue is $2,000,000 (= 20 × .10 × $1,000,000). If Deer Valley undertakes a 20-year mortgage or note with an implicit borrowing rate of 10 percent, the annual payments are $1,000,000/8.51356 = $117,460. (See Table 4 at the end of the book, 20-period row, 10-percent column.) The total mortgage payments are $2,349,200 (= 20 × $117,460), and the total interest expense over the life of the note or mortgage is $1,349,200 (= $2,349,200 − $1,000,000).

Why are the amounts of interest expense different for these two types of borrowing for the same length of time at identical interest rates?

15. Define *zero coupon bonds*. What are the advantages of a zero coupon bond to the issuer and to the investor?

16. A call premium is the difference between the call price of a bond and its par (face) value. What is the purpose of such a premium?

17. Critics of historical cost accounting for long-term debt argue that the procedures give management unreasonable opportunity to "manage" income with the timing of bond retirements. What phenomenon do these critics have in mind?

EXERCISES

18. **Journal entries for payroll.** During the current period, suppose that McGee Associates' office employees earned wages of $700,000. McGee withheld 18 percent of this amount for payments for federal income taxes, 5 percent for state income taxes, and 6 percent for Social Security taxes. McGee must pay 6 percent of gross wages for Social Security taxes, 2 percent for state FUTA taxes, and 1 percent for federal FUTA taxes. McGee has promised to contribute 4 percent of gross wages to a profit-sharing fund, which workers will share as they retire. Employees earned vacation pay estimated to be $14,000; estimated fringe benefits are 20 percent of that amount.
    a. Prepare journal entries for these wage-related items.
    b. What is total wage and salary expense?

19. **Computations and journal entries for income taxes payable.** PepsiCo files its income tax returns on a calendar-year basis and issues financial statements quarterly as of March 31, June 30, and so on. It estimates and pays income taxes at the rate of 35 percent of taxable income. Suppose that the following data are applicable to the company's income tax for Year 1:

Year 1

Mar. 31	The firm estimates that total taxable income for Year 1 will be about $1,900 million. It prepares the first quarter's financial statements.
April 15	It makes the first payment on estimated taxes.
June 15	The firm now estimates that total taxable income for the year will be about $2,010 million. It makes the second payment on estimated taxes.
June 30	It prepares the second quarter's financial statements.
Sept. 15	The firm now estimates that total taxable income for the year will be about $1,940 million. It makes the third payment on estimated taxes.
Dec. 15	The firm now estimates that total taxable income for the year will be about $1,950 million. It makes the fourth payment on estimated taxes.

Dec. 31   Income for the year is $2,000 million. The firm prepares financial statements for the year.

Year 2

Mar. 15   The firm pays the balance of taxes for Year 1.

---

a. Prepare schedules showing the following:
  (1) For tax returns: estimated taxes for year, cumulative payments due, and payment made on each payment date.
  (2) For financial statements: tax expenses for the quarterly reports and annual report.
b. Record the transactions related to Year 1 income taxes in journal entry form.
c. Present the T-accounts for Cash, Prepaid Income Taxes (if necessary), Income Taxes Payable, and Income Tax Expense.

20. **Journal entries for coupons.** Morrison's Cafeteria sells coupons that customers may use later to purchase meals. Each coupon book sells for $25 and has a face value of $30; that is, the customer can use the book to purchase meals with menu prices of $30. On January 1, redeemable unused coupons with a face value of $4,000 were outstanding. Cash inflows during the next three months appear below:

	January	February	March
Cash-paying Customers	$48,000	$48,500	$50,000
Sale of Coupon Books	2,100	2,200	2,400
Total Cash Receipts	$50,100	$50,700	$52,400

Customers returned coupons with a face value for meals as follows: January, $1,600; February, $2,300; March $2,100.
a. Prepare journal entries for January, February, and March to reflect the above information.
b. What effect, if any, do the coupon sales and redemptions have on the liabilities on the March 31 balance sheet?

21. **Journal entries for service contracts.** Abson Corporation began business on January 1. Abson sells copiers to business firms. It also sells service contracts to maintain and repair copiers for $600 per year. When a customer signs a contract, Abson collects the $600 fee and credits Service Contract Fees Received in Advance. Abson recognizes revenues on a quarterly basis during the year in which the coverage is in effect. For purposes of computing revenue, Abson assumes that all sales of service contracts occur midway through each quarter. Sales of contracts and service expenses for its first year of operations appear below:

	Sales of Contracts	Service Expenses
First Quarter	$180,000 (300 contracts)	$ 32,000
Second Quarter	300,000 (500 contracts)	71,000
Third Quarter	240,000 (400 contracts)	105,000
Fourth Quarter	120,000 (200 contracts)	130,000

a. Prepare journal entries for the first three quarters of the year for Abson Corporation. Assume that the firm prepares quarterly reports on March 31, June 30, and September 30.
b. What is the balance in the Service Contract Fees Received in Advance account on December 31?

22. **Journal entries for estimated warranty liabilities and subsequent expenditures.** A new appliance introduced by Maypool Corporation carries a two-year warranty against defects. The firm *estimates* that the total cost of warranty claims over the two-year period on appliances sold in a particular year (for example, Year 1) will equal 4 percent of sales revenue in the year of sale (that is, Year 1). The firm will incur *actual* warranty costs over the two-year period following the time of sale. Sales (all on account) and actual warranty expenditures (all paid in cash) for the first two years of the appliance's life were as follows:

	Sales	Actual Warranty Expenditures
Year 1	$1,200,000	$12,000
Year 2	1,500,000	50,000

   a. Prepare journal entries for the events of Year 1 and Year 2. Closing entries are not required.
   b. What is the balance in the Estimated Warranty Liability account at the end of Year 2?

23. **Journal entries for estimated warranty liabilities and subsequent expenditures.** Global Motors Corporation offers three-year warranties against defects on the sales of its automobiles. The firm *estimates* that the total cost of warranty claims over the three-year warranty period on automobiles sold in a particular year (for example, Year 1) will equal 6 percent of sales revenue in the year of sale (that is, Year 1). The firm will incur *actual* warranty costs over the three-year period following the time of sale. Sales (all for cash) and actual warranty costs incurred on automobiles under warranty (60 percent in cash and 40 percent in parts) appear below:

	Sales	Actual Warranty Costs Incurred during Year on Automobiles under Warranty
Year 1	$ 800,000	$22,000
Year 2	1,200,000	55,000
Year 3	900,000	52,000

   a. Prepare journal entries for the events of Year 1, Year 2, and Year 3. Closing entries are not required.
   b. What is the balance in the Estimated Warranty Liability account at the end of Year 3?

24. **Journal entry for short-term note payable.** On December 1, Sung Company obtained a 60-day loan for $50,000 from the City State Bank at an annual interest rate of 6 percent. On the maturity date, the bank renewed the note for another 30 days, and Sung Company issued a check to the bank for the accrued interest. Sung Company closes its books annually at December 31.

   a. Present entries on the books of Sung Company to record the issue of the note, the year-end adjustment, the renewal of the note, and the payment of cash at maturity of the renewed note.
   b. Present entries at the maturity date of Sung Company's original note for the following variations in the settlement of the note.
      (1) Sung pays the original note at maturity.
      (2) Sung Company renews the note for 30 days; the new note bears interest at 9 percent per annum. Sung did not pay interest on the old note at maturity.

25. **Amortization schedule for note where explicit interest differs from market rate of interest.** Blaydon Company acquires a computer from Orange Computer

Company. The cash price (fair market value) of the computer is $36,157. Blaydon Company gives a three-year, interest-bearing note with maturity value of $40,000. The note requires annual interest payments of 8 percent of face value, or $3,200 per year. The interest rate implicit in the note is 12 percent per year.

a. Prepare an amortization schedule for the note.

b. Prepare journal entries for Blaydon Company over the life of the note.

26. **Computing the issue price of bonds.** Skinner Corporation issues $10,000,000-par value, 8 percent semiannual coupon bonds due in 10 years. Compute the issue price of these bonds assuming the following market-required interest rates on the date of issue:

a. 6 percent compounded semiannually

b. 8 percent compounded semiannually

c. 10 percent compounded semiannually

27. **Computing the issue price of bonds.** Compute the issue price of each of the following bonds:

a. $1,000,000-par value, 12 percent semiannual coupon bonds, with interest payable each six months and the principal due in 15 years, priced on the market to yield 10 percent compounded semiannually

b. $1,000,000-par value serial bonds repayable in equal semiannual installments of $75,000 for 15 years, priced on the market to yield 8 percent compounded semiannually

c. $1,000,000-par value zero coupon bonds due in 15 years, priced on the market to yield 12 percent compounded semiannually

28. **Computing the issue price of bonds and interest expense.** O'Brien Corporation issues $8,000,000-par value, 8 percent semiannual coupon bonds maturing in 20 years. The market initially prices these bonds to yield 6 percent compounded semiannually.

a. Compute the issue price of these bonds.

b. Compute interest expense for the first six-month period.

c. Compute interest expense for the second six-month period.

d. Compute the book value of the bonds after the second six-month period.

e. Use present value computations to verify the book value of the bonds after the second six-month period as computed in part **d** above.

29. **Computing the issue price of bonds and interest expense.** Robinson Company issues $5,000,000-par value, 8 percent semiannual coupon bonds maturing in 10 years. The market initially prices these bonds to yield 10 percent compounded semiannually.

a. Compute the issue price of these bonds.

b. Compute interest expense for the first six-month period.

c. Compute interest expense for the second six-month period.

d. Compute the book value of the bonds after the second six-month period.

e. Use present value computations to verify the book value of the bonds after the second six-month period as computed in part **d** above.

30. **Using bond tables; computing interest expense.** Refer to Table 5 at the back of the book for 10 percent semiannual coupon bonds. On January 1, Year 1, assume that Florida Edison Company issued $1 million face value, 10 percent semiannual coupon bonds maturing in 10 years (on December 31, Year 10) at a price to yield 12 percent per year, compounded semiannually. Use the effective interest method of computing interest expense.

a. What were the proceeds of the original issue?

b. What was the interest expense for the first half of Year 1?

c. What was the interest expense for the second half of Year 1?

d. What was the book value of the bonds on January 1, Year 6 (when the bonds have five years until maturity)?

e. What was the interest expense for the first half of Year 6?

31. **Using bond tables.** Refer to Table 6 for 12 percent semiannual coupon bonds issued to yield 11 percent per year compounded semiannually. All of the questions that follow refer to the $1 million face value of such bonds issued by Centrix Company.
    a. What are the initial issue proceeds for bonds issued to mature in 25 years?
    b. What is the book value of those bonds after five years?
    c. What is the book value of the bonds when they have 15 years until maturity?
    d. What are the initial issue proceeds for bonds issued to mature in 15 years? (Compare your answer to part **c**.)
    e. Write an expression for interest expense for the last six months before maturity.
    f. If the market rate of interest on the bonds is 13 percent compounded semiannually, what is the market value of the bonds when they have 15 years to maturity?
    g. When the bonds have 10 years until maturity, they trade in the market for 112.46 percent of par. What is the effective market rate at that time?

32. **Journal entries for bond coupon payments and retirement.** (Adpated from a problem by S. Zeff.) On December 31, Year 7, at the close of Mendoza Corporation's fiscal year, the company has outstanding $1 million face value of 12 percent semiannual coupon bonds, with payments due on July 1 and December 31 each year through the bonds' maturity date of December 31, Year 16. The company issued the bonds at a market yield (interest rate) of 10 percent, compounded semiannually. On December 31, Year 7, the market interest rate for similar bonds is 14 percent, compounded semiannually. The company uses the effective interest method of accounting for these bonds, rounds computations to the nearest dollar, and closes its books once per year, on December 31.
    a. Give the journal entries to record the company's interest expense for both the first and the second payments during Year 7.
    b. Suppose the firm repurchases one-half of the bonds for cash in the open market on December 31, Year 7, at the price implied by the market interest rate of 14 percent compounded semiannually on that date. Give the journal entry, ignoring income taxes.
    c. How would the gain or loss in **b** appear on the income statement?

33. **Amortization schedule for bonds.** Womack Company issues 10 percent semiannual coupon bonds maturing five years from the date of issue. Interest of 5 percent of the face value of $100,000 is payable January 1 and July 1. The firm issues the bonds to yield 8 percent, compounded semiannually.
    a. What are the initial issue proceeds received by Womack Company?
    b. Construct an amortization schedule, similar to that in Exhibit 9.4, for this bond issue.
    c. Assume that at the end of the third year of the bond's life, Womack Company reacquires $10,000 face value of bonds for 103 percent of par and retires them. Give the journal entry to record the retirement.

34. **Amortization schedule for bonds.** Seward Corporation issues on January 2, Year 1, 8 percent semiannual coupon bonds maturing three years from the date of issue. Interest of 4 percent of the face value of $100,000 is payable on January 1 and July 1. The firm issues the bonds to yield 10 percent, compounded semiannually.
    a. What are the issue proceeds received by Seward Corporation?
    b. Construct an amortization schedule, similar to that in Exhibit 9.4, for this bond issue.
    c. Give the journal entries relating to these bonds for the first year. Seward Corporation uses a calendar year for its accounting period.
    d. Assume that on January 2, Year 3, Seward Corporation reacquires $20,000 face value of these bonds for 102 percent of par and retires them. Give the journal entry to record the retirement.

35. **Journal entries to account for bonds.** Brooks Corporation issues $100,000 face value, 10-year bonds on January 2, Year 2. The bonds bear interest at 8 percent per year, payable in semiannual installments on June 30 and December 31 of each year. The market initially prices the bonds to yield 6 percent compounded semiannually.
   a. Compute the issue price of the bonds.
   b. Give the journal entries to account for these bonds during Year 2.
   c. Brooks Corporation reacquires these bonds on the open market on January 2, Year 3, at a time when the market prices the bonds to yield 10 percent compounded semiannually. Give the journal entry to record the reacquisition.

PROBLEMS AND CASES

36. **Allowance method for warranties; reconstructing transactions.** Assume that Central Appliance sells appliances, all for cash. It debits all acquisitions of appliances during a year to the Merchandise Inventory account. The company provides warranties on all its products, guaranteeing to make required repairs, within one year of the date of sale, for any of its appliances that break down. The company has many years of experience with its products and warranties.

   The schedule shown in Exhibit 9.8 contains summary trial balances for Central Appliance at the end of Year 1 and Year 2. The trial balances for the end of Year 1 are the Adjusted Preclosing Trial Balance (after making all adjusting entries) and

EXHIBIT 9.8	CENTRAL APPLIANCE (Problem 36)

Trial Balances—End of Year 1	Adjusted Preclosing		Post-Closing	
	Dr.	Cr.	Dr.	Cr.
Estimated Liability for Warranty Repairs		$ 6,000		$ 6,000
Merchandise Inventory	$ 100,000		$100,000	
Sales		800,000		
Warranty Expense	18,000			
All Other Accounts	882,000	194,000	110,000	204,000
Totals	$1,000,000	$1,000,000	$210,000	$210,000

Trial Balance—End of Year 2			Unadjusted Trial Balance	
			Dr.	Cr.
Estimated Liability for Warranty Repairs			$ 15,000	
Merchandise Inventory			820,000	
Sales				$1,000,000
Warranty Expense			—	—
All Other Accounts			265,000	100,000
Totals			$1,100,000	$1,100,000

the final Post-Closing Trial Balance. The trial balance shown for the end of Year 2 is taken before any adjusting entries of any kind, although the firm made entries to the Estimated Liability for Warranty Repairs account during Year 2 as it made repairs. Central Appliance closes its books once each year.

At the end of Year 2, the management of Central Appliance analyzes the appliances sold within the preceding 12 months. It classifies all appliances still covered by warranty as follows: those sold on or before June 30 (more than six months old), those sold after June 30 but on or before November 30 (more than one month but less than six months old), and those sold on or after December 1. Assume that it estimates that one-half of 1 percent of the appliances sold more than six months ago will require repair, 5 percent of the appliances sold one to six months before the end of the year will require repair, and 8 percent of the appliances sold within the last month will require repair. From this analysis, management estimates that $5,000 of repairs will still have to be made in Year 3 on the appliances sold in Year 2. Ending inventory on December 31, Year 2, is $120,000.

a. What were the total acquisitions of merchandise inventory during Year 2?

b. What was the cost of goods sold for Year 2?

c. What was the dollar amount of repairs made during Year 2?

d. What was the warranty expense for Year 2?

e. Give journal entries for repairs made during Year 2, for the warranty expense for Year 2, and for cost of goods sold for Year 2.

37. **Accounting for zero-coupon debt.** Early in the 1990s, Time Warner, Inc., announced its intention to borrow about $500 million by issuing 20-year zero coupon (single-payment) notes. *The Wall Street Journal* reported the following:

> NEW YORK—Time Warner Inc. announced an offering of debt that could yield the company as much as $500 million. . . . The media and entertainment giant said that it would offer $1.55 billion principal amount of zero-coupon . . . notes due [in 20 years] . . . through Merrill Lynch. . . . Zero-coupon debt is priced at a steep discount to principal, [which] is fully paid at maturity. . . . A preliminary prospectus . . . didn't include the issue price and yield of the notes.[7]

Assume Time Warner borrows funds at the beginning of Year 1 and pays $1.55 billion in a single payment at the end of Year 20.

a. Assume the yield of the notes is 6 percent per year, compounded annually. What initial issue proceeds will Time Warner, Inc., realize from issuing these notes? That is, how much cash will Time Warner receive on issuing the notes?

b. Assume the initial issue proceeds from these notes is $500 million. What is the annual yield on these notes?

c. Assume the initial issue proceeds from these notes is $400 million and their annual yield is 7 percent compounded annually. What interest expense will Time Warner record for Year 1, the first year the notes are outstanding?

d. Assume the initial issue proceeds from these notes is $400 million and their annual yield is 7 percent compounded annually. What interest expense will Time Warner record for Year 20, the last year the notes are outstanding?

38. **Accounting for long-term bonds.** The notes to the financial statements of Aggarwal Corporation for Year 4 reveal the following information with respect to long-term debt. *All interest rates in this problem assume semiannual compounding and the effective interest method of amortization.*

[7]*The Wall Street Journal,* December 8, 1992, p. A6.

	December 31, Year 3	December 31, Year 4
$800,000 zero coupon notes due December 31, Year 13, initially priced to yield 10 percent	$301,512	?
$1,000,000, 7 percent bonds due December 31, Year 8. Interest is payable on June 30 and December 31. The bonds were initially priced to yield 8 percent	?	$966,336
$1,000,000, 9 percent bonds due December 31, Year 19. Interest is payable on June 30 and December 31. The bonds were initially priced to yield 6 percent	$1,305,832	?

a. Compute the book value of the zero coupon notes on December 31, Year 4. A zero coupon note requires no periodic cash payments; only the face value is payable at maturity. Do not overlook the italicized sentence on the preceding page.

b. Compute the amount of interest expense for Year 4 on the 7 percent bonds.

c. On July 1, Year 4, Aggarwal Corporation acquires half of the 9 percent bonds ($500,000 face value) in the market for $526,720 and retires them. Give the journal entry to record this retirement.

d. Compute the amount of interest expense on the 9 percent bonds for the second half of Year 4.

39. Accounting for long-term bonds. The notes to the financial statements of Wal-Mart Stores reveal the following information with respect to long-term debt. *All interest rates in this problem assume semiannual compounding and the effective interest method of amortization.*

	January 31	
	Year 11	Year 12
$100,000,000-par value of 9 percent debenture bonds due January 31, Year 20, initially priced on the market to yield 12 percent	$ 83,758,595	?
? par value zero coupon bonds due July 31, Year 16, initially priced on the market to yield 8 percent	$162,395,233	$175,646,684
$400,000,000 face value 9.25 percent notes due January 31, Year 20, initially priced on the market to yield ? percent	$400,000,000	$400,000,000

a. Compute the amount of interest expense on the 9 percent coupon bonds for fiscal year Year 12. Do not overlook the italicized sentence above.

b. Compute the book value of the 9 percent bonds on January 31, Year 12.

c. Compute the par value of the zero coupon bonds.

d. Compute the initial market yield on the $400,000,000 notes.

40. Comparison of straight-line and effective interest methods of amortizing debt discount. IBM established IBM Credit Corporation (IBMCC) on May 1, Year 1. On July 1, Year 1, IBMCC issued $150 million of zero coupon notes due July 1, Year 8. These notes promise to pay a single amount of $150 million at maturity, seven years after issue date. IBMCC marketed these notes to yield 14 percent compounded semiannually. IBMCC may at any time redeem these notes, in part or in whole, for 100 percent of the principal amount.

IBMCC computes interest expense for financial reporting using the effective interest method but amortizes original-issue discount on the notes in equal semiannual amounts for tax reporting. That is, if IBMCC issued the $150 million face value of notes for $66 million, the original-issue discount is $84 (= $150 − $66) million and the semiannual interest expense each period is $6 [= $84/(7 years × 2 periods per year)] million per year. Assume an income tax rate of 40 percent. The financial statements of IBMCC present the following data about long-term debt on December 31, Year 1:

(all dollar amounts in thousands)	
14 3/8 Percent Notes Due July, Year 6	$100,000
Zero Coupon Notes Due July, Year 8	150,000
	$250,000
Less Unamortized Discount, Related Principally to the Zero Coupon Notes	87,762
	$162,238

a. Calculate the proceeds to IBMCC from issuing the zero coupon notes.

b. Compute the amount of interest expense reported on the income statement for these notes for the six-month period ending December 31, Year 1.

c. Compute the amount of the interest deduction on the tax return for Year 1 resulting from these notes. Assuming IBMCC can fully deduct this amount on its income tax return, how much does this reduce the income taxes payable that IBMCC would otherwise compute?

d. What was the amount of "Unamortized Discount" that relates only to the zero coupon notes on the balance sheet at the end of Year 1?

e. A news story in Year 2 reported the following:

> [T]he Treasury wants to plug a tax loophole that has enabled companies to borrow billions of dollars cheaply. . . . At issue is a tax break granted to companies issuing . . . "zero-coupon" bonds . . . and other deeply discounted debt instruments, which pay very low interest rates.

Describe the advantages to issuers and purchasers of zero coupon bonds. Give your interpretation of the tax loophole alleged by the U.S. Treasury. Be specific in your response by indicating the dollar amount of the "loophole" that IBMCC used in Year 1. What tax policy with respect to interest on zero coupon notes would you recommend?

41. **Managing income and the debt-equity ratio through bond retirement.** Suppose that Quaker Oats Company issued $40 million of 5 percent semiannual coupon bonds many years ago at par. The bonds now have 20 years until scheduled maturity. Because market interest rates have risen to 9 percent, the market value of the bonds has dropped to 63 percent of par. Quaker Oats has $5 million of current liabilities and $35 million of shareholders' equity in addition to the $40 million of long-term debt in its financial structure. The debt-equity ratio (= total liabilities/ total liabilities plus shareholders' equity) is 56 percent [= ($40 + $5)/($5 + $40 + $35)]. (Shareholders' equity includes an estimate of the current year's income.) The president of Quaker Oats is concerned about boosting reported income for the year, which is about $8 million in the absence of any other actions. Also, the debt-equity ratio appears to be larger than that of other firms in the industry. The president

wonders what the impact on net income and the debt-equity ratio would be if the company issues at par new 9 percent semiannual coupon bonds to mature in 20 years and uses the proceeds to retire the outstanding bond issue. Assume that such action is taken and that any gain on bond retirement is taxable immediately, at the rate of 40 percent.

a. Prepare the journal entries for the issue of new bonds in the amount required to raise funds to retire the old bonds, for the retirement of the old bonds, and for the income tax effects.

b. What is the effect on income for the year? Give both dollar and percentage amounts.

c. What is the debt-equity ratio after the transaction?

42. **Accounting for bonds in a troubled debt restructuring.** On January 1, 1985, First National Bank (FNB) acquired $10 million of face value bonds issued on that date by Occidental Oceanic Power Systems (OOPS). The bonds carried 12 percent semi-annual coupons and were to mature 20 years from the issue date. OOPS issued the bonds at par.

By 1990, OOPS was in severe financial difficulty and threatened to default on the bonds. After much negotiation with FNB (and other creditors), it agreed to repay the bond issue but only on less burdensome terms. OOPS agreed to pay 5 percent per year, semiannually, for 25 years and to repay the principal on January 1, 2015, or 25 years after the negotiation. FNB will receive $250,000 every six months starting July 1, 1990, and $10 million on January 1, 2015. By January 1, 1990, OOPS was being charged 20 percent per year, compounded semiannually, for its new long-term borrowings.

a. What is the value of the bonds that FNB holds? In other words, what is the present value of the newly promised cash payments when discounted at OOPS's current borrowing rate of 20 percent per year, compounded semiannually?

b. Repeat part **a,** but use the market interest rate at the time of initial issue, 12 percent, compounded semiannually, to calculate the present value of the newly promised cash payments.

c. Consider three accounting treatments for this negotiation (called a "troubled debt restructuring" by the FASB in its *Statement of Financial Accounting Standards No. 114*).

(1) Write down the bonds to the value computed in part **a,** and base future interest revenue computations on that new book value and the new historical interest rate of 20 percent per year, compounded semiannually.

(2) Write down the bonds to the value computed in part **b,** and base future interest revenue computations on that new book value and the old historical interest rate of 12 percent per year, compounded semiannually.

(3) Make no entry to record the negotiation, and record interest revenue as the amount of cash, $250,000, that FNB receives semiannually.

Over the new life of the bond issue, how will total income vary as a function of the method chosen?

d. Which of the three methods listed in **c** would you recommend? Why?

43. **Discounting warranty obligations.** GAAP require long-term monetary liabilities to appear at the present value of the future cash flows discounted at the market rate of interest appropriate to the monetary items at the time the firm initially recorded them. The Accounting Principles Board *Opinion No. 21* specifically excludes from present value valuation those obligations that arise from warranties. The *Opinion* requires that warranties, being nonmonetary liabilities, be stated at the estimated cost of providing warranty goods and services in the future.

Assume that the estimated future costs of a three-year warranty plan on products sold during Year 1 are as follows:

Year of Expected Expenditure	Expected Cost
2	$ 500,000
3	600,000
4	900,000
Total	$2,000,000

Actual costs coincided with expectations as to both timing and amount.

a. Prepare the journal entries for each of the years 1 through 4 for this warranty plan following current GAAP.

b. Now assume that GAAP allow these liabilities to appear at their present value. Prepare the journal entries for each of the years 1 through 4 for this warranty plan, assuming that the firm states warranty liability at the present value of the future costs discounted at 10 percent. To simplify the calculations, assume that the firm incurs all warranty costs on December 31 of each year.

c. What theoretical arguments can you offer for the valuation basis in part **b?**

44. **Effects on statement of cash flows.** Exhibit 4.16 in Chapter 4 provides a simplified statement of cash flows with numbered lines. For each of the transactions that follow, indicate the number(s) of the line(s) affected by the transaction and state the amount and direction (increase or decrease) of the effect. If the transaction affects net income on line (1) or cash on line (9), be sure to indicate if it increases or decreases the line. Ignore income tax effects.

a. The firm issues bonds for $100,000 cash.

b. The firm issues a note with a fair market value of $100,000 for a building.

c. The firm retires, for $90,000 cash, bonds with a book value of $100,000.

d. The firm calls for $105,000 and retires bonds with a book value of $100,000.

e. The firm records interest expense and expenditures for the first half of a year on bonds. The bonds have a face value of $100,000 and a book value at the beginning of the year of $90,000. The coupon rate is 10 percent, paid semiannually in arrears, and the bonds were originally issued to yield 12 percent, compounded semiannually.

f. The firm records interest expense and expenditures for the first half of a year on bonds. The bonds have a face value of $100,000 and a book value at the beginning of the year of $105,000. The coupon rate is 12 percent, paid semiannually in arrears, and the bonds were originally issued to yield 10 percent, compounded semiannually.

45. **Preparing a statement of cash flows.** (Adapted from a problem by S. Baiman.) Exhibit 9.9 shows comparative balance sheets, an income statement, and supplementary notes for Rhodes Company for Year 2. Prepare a statement of cash flows for Year 2.

EXHIBIT 9.9	RHODES COMPANY Comparative Balance Sheets and Income Statement (Problem 45)

	December 31	
	Year 1	**Year 2**
Balance Sheets		
Cash	$ 47,000	$ 42,800
Accounts Receivable	80,000	87,000
Less Allowance for Uncollectibles	(1,200)	(1,300)
Inventory	110,000	122,000
Property, Plant, and Equipment	474,000	482,200
Accumulated Depreciation	(189,800)	(192,700)
Total Assets	$520,000	$540,000
Accounts Payable	$ 70,000	$ 81,000
Bonds Payable	195,000	170,000
Common Stock	100,000	111,000
Retained Earnings	155,000	178,000
Total Equities	$520,000	$540,000
Year 2 Income Statement		
Net Sales		$1,000,000
Gain on Sale of Equipment		4,900
Total Revenues		$1,004,900
Cost of Goods Sold		$ 700,000
Selling and Administrative Expense		153,100
Bad Debt Expense		9,000
Depreciation Expense		48,000
Interest Expense		10,000
Income Tax Expense		28,800
Total Expenses		$ 948,900
Income before Extraordinary Items		$ 56,000
Extraordinary Loss on Bond Retirement		(3,000)
Net Income		$ 53,000

Notes:

(1) During Year 2, Rhodes sold equipment originally costing $60,100.

(2) The firm issued $11,000 of common stock during Year 2 to acquire a machine.

(3) The firm retired bonds on January 1, Year 2, with a face value of $75,000 and a book value of $70,000. The firm paid $73,000 to retire the bonds (assume the transaction has no income tax effects).

(4) The firm issued $50,000 face value of bonds on December 31, Year 2, for $50,000.

(5) The remaining bonds outstanding carry coupon interest rates that exceeded the market interest rate at the time of issue. Coupon payments on these bonds exceeded the interest expense during Year 2 by $5,000.

CHAPTER 10

LIABILITIES: OFF-BALANCE SHEET FINANCING, LEASES, DEFERRED INCOME TAXES, RETIREMENT BENEFITS, AND DERIVATIVES

LEARNING OBJECTIVES

1. Understand (a) why firms attempt to structure debt financing to keep debt off the balance sheet and (b) how standard-setters have refined the concept of an accounting liability to reduce off-balance sheet financing abuses.
2. Distinguish between the economic characteristics and accounting criteria for an operating lease and a capital lease and the financial statement effects of each type of lease.
3. Understand why firms may recognize revenues and expenses for financial reporting in a period different from that used for tax reporting and the effect of such differences on the measurement of income tax amounts on the income statement and the balance sheet.
4. Understand the accounting issues related to retiree benefit plans (such as pensions and health-care benefits).
5. Learn the basics about derivative instruments and hedging: how firms use derivatives to hedge financial risks and the related accounting issues.

Chapter 9 discussed the concept of an accounting liability and illustrated its application to current liabilities and long-term debt. This chapter explores liabilities further by considering five controversial accounting topics of the past decade: off-balance sheet financing, leases, deferred taxes, retirement benefits, and derivative instruments.

OFF-BALANCE SHEET FINANCING

In 1980, *Forbes* magazine noted, "The basic needs of humans are simple: to get enough food, to find shelter, and to keep debt off the balance sheet." This section discusses the rationale for off-balance sheet financing and illustrates several financing arrangements to keep debt off the balance sheet.

RATIONALE FOR OFF-BALANCE SHEET FINANCING

Firms often attempt to structure their financing to keep debt off the balance sheet (that is, to obtain funds without crediting a liability account). They hope to show fewer liabilities on the balance sheet and thereby to improve the debt ratios that analysts use to assess the financial risk of a firm. Reasons frequently cited for **off-balance sheet financing** include the following:

1. It lowers the cost of borrowing. Unwary lenders may ignore off-balance sheet financing and set lower interest rates for loans than the underlying risk levels warrant.
2. It avoids violating debt covenants. Covenants in existing debt contracts may prevent a firm from increasing debt ratios above defined levels. Structuring an off-balance sheet financing arrangement permits the firm to obtain needed funds without affecting the debt ratios. It also provides a cushion in the event that the firm must engage in on-balance sheet financing in the future.

The first rationale above for off-balance sheet financing assumes that some lenders, credit-rating agencies, and others who assess financial risks do not possess the knowledge, skills, or information needed to identify and deal appropriately with such financing arrangements. Even though firms have little evidence that financial statement users systematically ignore these obligations, firms often structure their financings as though they believe that assumption. Standard-setting bodies have required increased disclosures of off-balance sheet financings in recent years to alert financial statement users.

STRUCTURING OFF-BALANCE SHEET FINANCING

Off-balance sheet financings generally fall into one of the two categories of obligations that accounting does not recognize as liabilities: executory contracts and contingent obligations (see Exhibit 9.1).

Executory Contracts   Firms frequently sign contracts promising to pay defined amounts in the future in return for future benefits. To recognize an accounting liability, a firm must incur an obligation for a past or current benefit received—the event or transaction must already have happened. If the firm will receive the benefit in the future, accounting treats the obligation as an executory contract and typically does not recognize a liability.

Example 1   Delta Airlines needs additional aircraft to expand internationally. Delta could borrow the needed funds and purchase the aircraft. This arrangement places additional debt on the balance sheet. Instead, Delta signs a lease agreeing to pay the owner of the aircraft certain amounts each year for 12 years. Delta paints its name on the aircraft, uses them in operations, and makes the required lease payments. The usual accounting assumes that Delta receives benefits when it uses the aircraft, not when it initially signs the lease. Thus, Delta obtains financing for its flight equipment without showing a liability on the balance sheet.

Example 2   Boise Cascade and Georgia-Pacific Corporation (forest products companies) need additional pulp-processing capacity. Each firm could borrow the needed funds and build its own manufacturing plant. Instead, they form a joint venture to build a pulp-processing plant suitable for their joint needs. Each firm agrees to use one-half of the new plant's capacity each year for 20 years and to pay half of all operating and debt-service costs. The joint venture uses the purchase commitments of Boise Cascade and Georgia-Pacific to obtain a loan to build the facility. Accounting views the purchase commitments as executory contracts—all benefits occur in the future—and therefore does not recognize a liability. Thus, each firm obtains financing for the plant without showing a liability on its balance sheet.

Contingent Obligations As an alternative to borrowing funds and using a particular asset as collateral, a firm might obtain funds by "selling" the asset with the understanding that the firm will give cash back to the "purchaser" under stated conditions. Such sales usually provide that the selling firm must repay cash to the purchaser in the future if, for example, the asset sold generates less cash for the purchaser than anticipated at the time of "sale." If such payments do not meet the criteria for a loss contingency, as discussed in Chapter 9, then the firm treats the transaction as a sale, keeping debt off the balance sheet, instead of as a loan collateralized by the asset.

Example 3 Sears extends credit to its customers to purchase appliances, furniture, and other goods. Sears could borrow from banks using its accounts receivable as collateral, thereby placing debt on the balance sheet. Sears would use collections from customers to repay the bank loans with interest. Instead, Sears "sells" the accounts receivable to the banks. The amount Sears expects to collect from receivables sold exceeds the amount of cash Sears receives from the banks. This excess provides the banks with their expected return, or interest income on their "loan" to Sears. Sears agrees to collect the receivables from customers and remit the cash to the banks. Sears will probably treat this transaction as a sale and thus avoid placing debt on the balance sheet.

Example 4 Seagram Company, a distiller of liquors, ages its whiskeys for approximately 10 years. The firm must pay the costs to produce the whiskey and to store it during aging. Using the whiskey as collateral, Seagram could borrow the necessary funds; however, this would lead to increased liabilities. Instead, it "sells" the whiskey to the banks. Seagram oversees the aging process on behalf of the banks. At the completion of the aging, Seagram arranges for others to purchase the whiskey and remits the proceeds to the banks. If the sales proceeds fall below specified levels, Seagram must pay the difference to the banks. Seagram will probably treat this transaction as a sale and thereby avoid placing debt on the balance sheet.

The Financial Accounting Standards Board (FASB) has dealt with various off-balance sheet financing arrangements on a case-by-case basis. A unifying theme appears in the FASB rules:

- First, the accountant identifies the party that enjoys the economic benefits of the item in each transaction and that bears the economic risks of holding it.
- Then, the accountant identifies the party that *needs* financing.

When the party *needing* financing controls the benefits and risks, the transaction usually leads to recognizing a liability on the balance sheet of the controlling party. When the party *providing* the financing controls the benefits and risks, the debt does not appear as a liability on the balance sheet of the firm needing financing.

Example 5 Refer to Example 1, but assume that Delta signs a lease for 20 years. Also assume that the aircraft Delta is leasing have a useful life of approximately 20 years and that the required lease payments compensate the owner of the aircraft (that is, the lessor) for the cost of the aircraft plus a reasonable return for the level of risk incurred. Then Delta has rights to use nearly all the economic benefits of the aircraft and incurs the risks of technological obsolescence, overcapacity during economic downturns, and similar factors. Because Delta controls the enjoyment of economic benefits and incurs the economic risks, it will, following FASB rules discussed later, likely report its lease commitment as a liability. If, as in Example 1, the lease spans a period substantially shorter than the expected useful life of the aircraft and if the economics of the transaction virtually require that the lessor either sell the aircraft at the end of the lease period or release them to another airline, then the lessor incurs the benefits and risks of ownership. In this case, the lease commitment will not appear as a liability on Delta's balance sheet. The next section of this chapter more fully discusses the accounting for leases.

Example 6 Refer to Example 2. Suppose that the lender requires Boise Cascade to guarantee payment of the loan in case the joint venture defaults. Suppose also that Georgia-Pacific Corporation experiences severe financial difficulties and fails to pay its share of operating and debt-service costs. Boise Cascade bears most of the economic risk of this joint venture and should probably recognize a liability. If the lender relies solely on the joint venture to repay the loan and does not require either Boise Cascade or Georgia-Pacific Corporation to guarantee the loan, then the debt will probably not appear on the balance sheet of either company. The loan would appear as a liability on the books of the joint venture.

Example 7 Refer to Example 3. Assume that Sears must transfer additional uncollected receivables to the lender/purchaser banks for any receivables judged uncollectible. Assume further that Sears must transfer additional uncollected receivables to the banks if interest rates rise above a specified level. In this case, Sears bears credit and interest rate risks and treats the transfer of receivables as a loan and not as a sale, with debt appearing on its balance sheet. If instead the banks bear credit and interest rate risks, Sears records the transfer of receivables as a sale; no debt related to the transaction appears on its balance sheet.

Example 8 Refer to Example 4. Assume that Seagram's guarantees an ultimate selling price that provides the lender with both a return of the original "purchase price" and coverage of storage and interest costs. Seagram's bears the economic risks and must show a liability on its balance sheet. Assume, in contrast, that the lender does not require Seagram's to guarantee a minimum selling price for the whiskey (for example, the lender might conclude that the quality of Seagram's whiskey and a favorable market outlook for whiskey make such a guarantee unnecessary). Then Seagram's will likely record the transaction as a sale and not a loan.

Firms continue to create innovative financing schemes to keep debt off the balance sheet. The FASB continues to consider the appropriate accounting for each transaction as it arises. Some accountants think that there will never be a satisfactory solution until accounting requires the recording of a liability whenever a firm has an obligation to pay a reasonably definite amount at a reasonably definite time, independent of the executory nature of the contract.

Attempting off-balance sheet financing. Assume that International Paper Company (IP) needs $75 million of additional financing but, because of restrictions in existing debt covenants, cannot put any more debt on its balance sheet. To obtain the needed funds, it plans to transfer cutting rights to a mature timber tract to a newly created trust as of January 1 of the current year. The trust will use the cutting rights to obtain a $75 million, five-year bank loan, with interest at 14 percent, due in five equal installments on December 31 of each year.

The trust will harvest and sell timber each year to obtain funds to service the loan and pay operating costs. At current prices, the standing wood available has value 10 percent greater than the trust will need to service the loan and to pay the ongoing operating costs (including wind, fire, and erosion insurance) of the tract. The future selling price of timber will determine the trust's actions, as follows:

- If the selling price of timber declines in the future, the trust will harvest more timber and sell it to service the debt and to pay other operating costs.

- If the selling price of timber increases in the future, the trust will harvest timber at the level originally planned but will invest any cash left over after debt service and coverage of operating costs, to provide a cushion for possible future price decreases. At the end of five years, the trust will distribute the value of any cash or uncut timber to IP.

IP will not guarantee the debt. The bank, however, has the right to inspect the tract at any time and to replace IP's forest-management personnel with managers of its own choosing if it feels that IP is mismanaging the tract.

a. Identify IP's economic returns and risks in this arrangement.
b. Identify the economic returns and risks in this arrangement for the bank lending the funds.
c. Should IP treat this transaction as a loan (a liability will appear on IP's balance sheet) or as a sale (no liability will appear on IPs balance sheet)? Explain your reasoning.

LEASES

Many firms acquire rights to use assets through long-term noncancelable leases. Examples 1 and 5 above, in which Delta Airlines signed leases to acquire the use of airplanes, illustrate such financing arrangements. A company seeking office space might agree to lease a floor of a building for 5 years or an entire building for 40 years, promising to pay a fixed periodic fee for the duration of the lease. Promising to make an irrevocable series of lease payments commits the firm just as surely as a bond indenture or mortgage and, often, results in similar accounting. This section examines two methods of accounting for long-term leases: the operating lease method and the capital lease method.

To understand these two methods, suppose that Food Barn wants to acquire a computer that has a three-year life and costs $45,000. Assume that Food Barn must pay 15 percent per year to borrow funds for three years. The computer manufacturer will sell the equipment for $45,000 or lease it for three years. Food Barn must pay for property taxes, maintenance, and repairs of the computer whether it purchases or leases. Food Barn signs the lease on January 1, Year 1, and promises to make payments on the lease on December 31, Year 1, Year 2, and Year 3. In practice, a lessee (the "buyer" or "tenant") usually makes payments in advance, but assuming the payments occur at year-end makes the computations simpler in these illustrations. Compound interest computations show that each lease payment must be $19,709.[1]

OPERATING LEASE METHOD

In an **operating lease,** the owner, or lessor (the "landlord"), transfers only the rights to use the property to the lessee for specified periods of time. At the end of the lease period, the lessee (the user or "tenant") returns the property to the lessor. For example, car rental companies lease cars by the day or week on an operating basis. If Food Barn can cancel its lease, stop making payments, and return the computer at any time, accounting considers the lease to be an executory contract and treats it as an operating lease. Food Barn would make no entry on January 1, Year 1, when it signs the lease. It makes the following entry on December 31, Year 1, Year 2, and Year 3:

Rent Expense	19,709	
Cash		19,709
To recognize annual expense of leasing computer.		

CAPITAL LEASE METHOD

If Food Barn may not cancel the lease, accounting views the arrangement as an executed contract—a form of borrowing to purchase the computer. Food Barn must account for it as a **capital lease.**[2] This treatment recognizes the signing of the lease as the simultaneous acquisition of a long-term asset, called a *leasehold,* and the incurring of a long-term liability for lease payments. At the time Food Barn signs the lease, it records both the leasehold asset and the liability at the asset's present value, $45,000 in the example. The entry at the time Food Barn signed its three-year noncancelable lease would be as follows:

Asset—Computer Leasehold	45,000	
Liability—Present Value of Lease Obligation		45,000
To recognize acquisition of the asset and the related liability.		

At the end of the year, Food Barn must make two separate entries—one related to the asset and one to the liability. First, it must amortize the leasehold, a long-term asset, over its useful life. The first entry made at the end of each year records this amortization.

---

[1]The present value of $1 paid at the end of this year and each of the next two years equals $2.28323 when discounted at an annual rate of 15 percent. See Table 4 at the end of the book, 15-percent column, 3-period row. Because the lease payments must have a present value of $45,000, each payment must equal $45,000/2.28323 = $19,709.

[2]Financial Accounting Standards Board, *Statement of Financial Accounting Standards No. 13,* "Accounting for Leases," 1976, reissued and reinterpreted 1980.

Assuming that Food Barn uses straight-line amortization of its leasehold, it makes the following entries at the end of Year 1, Year 2, and Year 3:

Amortization Expense (on Computer Leasehold)	15,000	
Asset—Computer Leasehold		15,000

An alternative treatment credits a contra-asset account, Accumulated Amortization of Computer Leasehold. The second entry made at the end of each year recognizes that the debt-service payment—the lease payment—pays interest and, in part, reduces the liability itself. The entries made at the end of each of the three years, based on the amortization schedule in Exhibit 10.1, would be as follows:

December 31, Year 1:

Interest Expense	6,750	
Liability—Present Value of Lease Obligation	12,959	
Cash		19,709

To recognize lease payment, interest on liability for the year (.15 × $45,000 = $6,750), and the plug for reduction in the liability. The present value of the liability after this entry is $32,041 = $45,000 − $12,959.

December 31, Year 2:

Interest Expense	4,806	
Liability—Present Value of Lease Obligation	14,903	
Cash		19,709

To recognize lease payment, interest on liability for the year (.15 × $32,041 = $4,806), and the plug for reduction in the liability. The present value of the liability after this entry is $17,138 = $32,041 − $14,903.

December 31, Year 3:

Interest Expense	2,571	
Liability—Present Value of Lease Obligation	17,138	
Cash		19,709

To recognize lease payment, interest on liability for the year (.15 × $17,138 = $2,571), and the plug for reduction in the liability. The present value of the liability after this entry is zero (= $17,138 − $17,138).

Exhibit 10.1 shows the amortization schedule for this lease. Note that it has the same form as the mortgage amortization schedule in Exhibit 9.3.

ACCOUNTING METHOD DETERMINES TIMING, BUT NOT AMOUNT, OF TOTAL EXPENSE

In the capital lease method, the expense over the three years totals $59,127, comprising $45,000 (= $15,000 + $15,000 + $15,000) for amortization expense and $14,127 (= $6,750 + $4,806 + $2,571) for interest expense. This exactly equals the total expense of $59,127 recognized under the operating lease method described previously ($19,709 × 3 = $59,127). The capital lease method recognizes expense sooner than does the operating lease method, as Exhibit 10.2 summarizes. But over sufficiently long time periods, expense equals cash expenditure. The operating lease method and the capital lease method differ in the *timing*, but not in the total *amount*, of expense. The capital lease method

EXHIBIT 10.1	Amortization Schedule for $45,000 Lease Liability, Accounted for as a Capital Lease, Repaid in Three Annual Installments of $19,709 Each, Interest Rate 15 percent, Compounded Annually

Annual Journal Entry

Dr. Interest Expense	Amount in Column (3)
Dr. Liability—Present Value of Lease	
Obligation	Amount in Column (5)
Cr. Cash	Amount in Column (4)

Year (1)	Lease Liability, Start of Year (2)	Interest Expense for Year (3)	Payment (4)	Portion of Payment Reducing Lease Liability (5)	Lease Liability, End of Year (6)
0					$45,000
1	$45,000	$6,750	$19,709	$12,959	32,041
2	32,041	4,806	19,709	14,903	17,138
3	17,138	2,571	19,709	17,138	0

Column (2) = column (6), previous period.

Column (3) = .15 × column (2).

Column (4) is given.

Column (5) = column (4) − column (3).

Column (6) = column (2) − column (5).

EXHIBIT 10.2	Comparison of Expense Recognized under Operating and Capital Lease Methods

	Expense Recognized Each Year Under	
Year	Operating Lease Method	Capital Lease Method
1	$19,709	$21,750 (= $15,000 + $ 6,750)
2	19,709	19,806 (= 15,000 + 4,806)
3	19,709	17,571 (= 15,000 + 2,571)
Total	$59,127[a]	$59,127 (= $45,000[b] + $14,127[c])

[a]Rent expense

[b]Amortization expense

[c]Interest expense

recognizes both the asset (leasehold) and the liability on the balance sheet, whereas the operating lease recognizes neither.

CHOOSING THE ACCOUNTING METHOD

When a journal entry debits an asset account and credits a liability account, the debt-equity ratio (= total liabilities divided by total equities) increases, making the company appear more risky. Thus, given a choice, most managers prefer not to show an asset and a related liability on the balance sheet. Because both installment purchases and capital leases record assets and liabilities on the balance sheet, increasing debt ratios, these managers prefer operating leases for acquiring asset services. Many managers would also prefer to recognize expenses later rather than sooner for financial reporting. These preferences have led managers to structure asset acquisitions so that the financing takes the form of an operating lease. Meanwhile, the FASB has tried to specify rules for curtailing the use of the operating lease accounting treatment. Most analysts think that the capital lease method provides higher quality measures of financial position.

Conditions Requiring Capital Lease Accounting   The FASB has provided rules for classifying long-term noncancelable leases.[3] A firm must account for a lease as a capital lease if the lease meets *any one* of four conditions:

1. It transfers ownership to the lessee at the end of the lease term.
2. Transfer of ownership at the end of the lease term seems likely because the lessee (user) has a "bargain purchase" option. (A "bargain purchase" option gives the lessee the right to purchase the asset at a specified future time for a price less than the currently predicted fair market value of the asset at the future time.)
3. The lease extends for at least 75 percent of the asset's life.
4. The present value of the minimum contractual lease payments equals or exceeds 90 percent of the fair market value of the asset at the time the lessee signs the lease. The present value computation uses a discount rate appropriate for the creditworthiness of the lessee.

These criteria attempt to identify who enjoys the economic benefits and bears the economic risks of the leased asset. The FASB's rules reflect the concepts that when the lessor bears the risks of a lease, it is an operating lease, but that when the lessee bears the risks, it is a capital lease. If the leased asset, either automatically or for a bargain price, becomes the property of the lessee at the end of the lease period, then the lessee enjoys all of the economic benefits of the asset and incurs all risks of ownership. If the life of the lease extends for most of the expected useful life of the asset (the FASB specifies 75 percent or more), then the lessee enjoys most of the economic benefits of the asset and incurs most of the risk of technological obsolescence.

Lessees who want to treat a lease as an operating lease, rather than a capital lease, can usually avoid the first three conditions but not the fourth. The fourth compares the present value of the lessee's contractual minimum lease payments with the fair market value of the asset at the time the lessee signs the lease. The present value of the minimum lease payments has the economic character of a purchase price in that the lessee has committed to make payments just as it would commit to make payments in an installment purchase. The FASB says, in effect, that if this present value (purchase price) exceeds

---

[3]Ibid., par. 7.

90 percent of the asset's value, then the lessee has effectively purchased the asset and must account for the asset as though it had.

Note on the Risks of the Leasing Business What is the major long-term asset of Hertz or of Avis? Used cars: Hertz and Avis must deal on a daily basis with an inventory of used cars and will bear the loss should government regulations make obsolete the current stock of used cars because, for example, they consume too much gasoline or do not have passenger-side airbags. Hertz and Avis price their car rentals to compensate for the obsolescence risks they bear. A manufacturer of airplanes such as Boeing may find the new-airplane business sufficiently risky that it does not want to bear the additional risks of being in the used-airplane business, so Boeing might require its lease customers to sign long-term noncancelable leases.

Consequence of Lessors' Desire to Avoid Used-Asset Risk Lessors of assets, such as airplanes and computers, do not want to lease an asset under conditions in which they have more than 10 percent of the asset's original market value at risk. When the lessee returns the asset to the lessor, the lessor must re-lease it or sell it in order to capture the benefits originally expected from the asset and to realize all the profit inherent in its original manufacture. Many lessors will not accept such risks without additional payment from the lessee. A lease that meets the fourth condition above has transferred the risks and rewards of ownership from the lessor to the lessee. In economic substance, the lessee has acquired an asset and has agreed to pay for it under a long-term installment-payment contract. Accounting recognizes that contract as the lessee's long-term liability.

Effects on Lessor The lessor (landlord) generally uses the same criteria as does the lessee (tenant) for classifying a lease as a capital lease or an operating lease. When the lessor and lessee sign a capital lease, the lessor recognizes revenue in an amount equal to the present value of all future lease payments and recognizes expense (analogous to cost of goods sold) in an amount equal to the book value of the leased asset. The difference between the revenue and the expense is the lessor's income on the "sale" of the asset. The lessor records the lease receivable like any other long-term receivable—at the present value of the future cash flows. It recognizes interest revenue over the collection period of the payments with entries that are mirror images of those of the lessee. The entries made by the lessor of the computer to Food Barn appear below. These entries assume that the lessor manufactured the computer at a cost of $39,000.

Operating Lease Method by Lessor

January 1, Year 1

Equipment (Computer Leased to Customers)	39,000	
Inventory		39,000

To record the transfer of product from inventory to equipment (in hands of lessee).

December 31 of each year

Cash	19,709	
Rent Revenue		19,709

To recognize annual revenue from renting computer.

Depreciation Expense	13,000	
Accumulated Depreciation on Computer Leased		
to Customers		13,000

To recognize depreciation on rented computer ($13,000 = $39,000/3).

(continued)

Capital Lease Method by Lessor

January 1, Year 1

Lease Receivable	45,000	
Sales Revenue		45,000

To recognize the "sale" of a computer for a series of future cash flows with a present value of $45,000.

Cost of Goods Sold	39,000	
Inventory		39,000

To record the cost of the computer "sold" as an expense.

December 31, Year 1

Cash	19,709	
Interest Revenue		6,750
Lease Receivable		12,959

To recognize lease receipt, interest on receivable, and reduction in receivable for Year 1. See supporting calculations in the lessee's journal entries and in Exhibit 10.1.

December 31, Year 2

Cash	19,709	
Interest Revenue		4,806
Lease Receivable		14,903

To recognize lease amounts for Year 2.

December 31, Year 3

Cash	19,709	
Interest Revenue		2,571
Lease Receivable		17,138

To recognize lease amounts for Year 3.

Lessors tend to prefer capital lease accounting for financial reporting because it enables them to recognize all income from the sale of the asset on the date the parties sign the lease while spreading the interest revenue over the life of the lease. The operating lease method recognizes all lease revenue—which implicitly includes manufacturing profit and interest—gradually over time as the lessor receives lease payments.

Income Tax Consideration in Lease Arrangements Leasing has become an industry separate from manufacturing. That is, companies such as General Electric Capital Services buy computers from, say, IBM and lease them to end-users. The leasing industry developed in part because the users of computers, airplanes, and other depreciable assets did not have sufficient taxable income to take advantage of accelerated depreciation deductions. A tax deduction has value only to the extent the taxpayer has taxable income against which to offset the deduction, reducing taxes otherwise payable. A taxpayer without taxable income cannot "take advantage" of a deduction, such as for depreciation. Other entities, such as financial institutions or manufacturers of leased equipment, have sufficient taxable income to benefit from these deductions. These parties structure leases as operating leases for income tax purposes so that the lessors claim depreciation deductions and save taxes. Lessees attempt to negotiate lower lease payments with the lessors, implicitly sharing a portion of the benefits of reduced taxes.

The rules for classifying a lease as operating or capital for income tax purposes differ from the FASB rules discussed here for financial reporting. Thus, leases sometimes appear as operating leases for tax purposes and capital leases for financial reporting, or vice versa.

PROBLEM 10.2 FOR SELF-STUDY

Operating and capital lease methods for lessee and lessor. On January 2, Year 1, Holt Book Store will acquire a delivery van that a local automobile dealer sells for $25,000. The dealer offers Holt Book Store the option of leasing the van for four years, with rentals of $8,231 due on December 31 of each year. Holt Book Store must return the van at the end of four years, although the automobile dealer anticipates that the resale value of the van after four years will be negligible. The automobile dealer acquired the van from the manufacturer for $23,500. The automobile dealer considers 12 percent an appropriate interest rate to charge Holt Book Store to finance the acquisition.

   a. Does this lease qualify as an operating lease or as a capital lease for financial reporting according to the four criteria specified by the FASB? Explain.
   b. Assume for this part that the lease qualifies as an operating lease. Give the journal entries made by Holt Book Store over the first two years of the life of the lease.
   c. Repeat part **b** for the automobile dealership. Use straight-line depreciation and zero estimated salvage value.
   d. Assume for this part that the lease qualifies as a capital lease. Give the journal entries made by Holt Book Store over the first two years of the life of the lease.
   e. Repeat part **d** for the automobile dealership.
   f. Compute the amount of expenses that Holt Book Store recognizes during each of the four years under the operating lease method and the capital lease method.
   g. Compute the amount of revenues and expenses that the automobile dealership recognizes during each of the four years under the operating lease method and the capital lease method.
   h. Why are the lessee's total expenses the same under the operating and the capital lease methods? Why is the lessor's total revenue, or income, the same under the operating and the capital lease methods?
   i. Why do the total expenses of the lessee differ from the total income of the lessor?

INCOME TAX ACCOUNTING AND DEFERRED INCOME TAXES

The amount that a firm reports as income before income taxes for financial reporting usually differs from the amount of taxable income that appears on its income tax return.

TERMINOLOGY NOTE

We find the correct term *income before income taxes for financial reporting* too cumbersome to use throughout this section. Instead, we use *book income* to refer to income before income taxes reported in the financial statements, and we use *taxable income* to refer to the amount reported in the income tax return. Similarly, the terms *book purposes* and *tax purposes* distinguish the financial statements from the tax return. We use the term *pre-tax income* to refer to an item on the financial statements and the term *taxable income* to refer to an item on the tax return. You will be less likely to

EXHIBIT 10.3

BURNS CORPORATION
Computation of Income Taxes over Six-Year Life of Equipment
Equipment Costs $120,000 and Has Six-Year Life

Information from (or Based on) Tax Returns

Year	Income before Depreciation and Taxes [1]	Depreciation Deduction on Tax Return [2]	Taxable Income [3]	Income Taxes Payable [4]
1	$100,000	$ 24,000	$ 76,000	$ 30,400
2	100,000	38,400	61,600	24,640
3	100,000	22,800	77,200	30,880
4	100,000	14,400	85,600	34,240
5	100,000	13,200	86,800	34,720
6	100,000	7,200	92,800	37,120
Totals		$120,000	$480,000	$192,000

Information from (or Based on) Financial Statements

				Not Allowed by GAAP		**Accounting Required by GAAP**	
Year	Income before Depreciation and Taxes [5]	Depreciation Expense [6]	Pre-Tax Income = $100,000 − $20,000 [7]	Pre-Tax Income Less Income Taxes Payable [8]	Percentage Change in Column [8] [9]	Pre-Tax Income Less Income Taxes at 40% of Pre-Tax Income [10]	Percentage Change in Column [10] [11]
1	$100,000	$ 20,000	$ 80,000	$ 49,600		$ 48,000	
2	100,000	20,000	80,000	55,360	11.6%	48,000	—
3	100,000	20,000	80,000	49,120	−11.3%	48,000	—
4	100,000	20,000	80,000	45,760	−6.8%	48,000	—
5	100,000	20,000	80,000	45,280	−1.0%	48,000	—
6	100,000	20,000	80,000	42,880	−5.3%	48,000	—
Totals		$120,000	$480,000	$288,000		$288,000	

[1] = Given   [3] = [1] − [2]   [5] = Given   [7] = [5] − [6]   [9] = ([8] this year/[8] last year) − 1

[2] = Given   [4] = .40 × [3]   [6] = $120,000/6   [8] = [7] − [4]   [10] = (1.00 − .40) × [7]

confuse yourself and others if you also use these terms this way. The term **book basis** means the amortized cost—that is, original cost less accumulated depreciation from the financial statements—and **tax basis** means the cost for tax purposes less the sum of prior depreciation deductions on the tax return.

The difference between book and taxable income arises from two factors:

1. **Permanent differences**—book income includes revenues (such as interest revenue on municipal bonds) or expenses (such as amortization of goodwill purchased before 1993) that taxable income never includes.
2. **Temporary differences**—book income includes revenues or expenses (such as depreciation on plant assets and bad debt expense) in one accounting period whereas taxable income includes them in a different period.

Firms compute **income tax payable** for a particular period using taxable income as the base. Taxable income excludes permanent differences and uses the accounting methods that a firm selects for income tax purposes.

A more controversial issue concerns the appropriate base for computing **income tax expense,** which appears on the income statement. Should income tax expense equal the income taxes actually payable each period based on taxable income, or should income tax expense equal income taxes actually payable each period plus (minus) the income taxes a firm expects to pay (save) in the future when temporary differences reverse?

Advocates of setting income tax expense equal to income taxes currently payable view income taxes similar to other taxes (such as property taxes, sales taxes, or payroll taxes). Government entities define the tax base (for example, assessed value of property, sales, or payroll costs) and apply a tax rate to this tax base to measure the taxes due each period. Some accountants want to follow the same procedure for income taxes by reporting income tax expense equal to income taxes payable currently.

Advocates of setting income tax expense equal to income taxes currently payable plus (minus) income taxes payable (saved) in the future when temporary differences reverse use the *matching convention* to support their position. (Permanent differences never reverse, never affect cash outflows for income taxes, and therefore should not affect income tax expense.) The current period's book income includes revenues and expenses that ultimately affect cash outflows for income taxes. Proponents argue that proper matching of income tax expense with pretax book income requires firms to include the future income tax effects of temporary differences in measuring income tax expense each period. Moreover, they say, assets provide future benefits; plant assets provide a future benefit in the form of reduced taxes payable caused by taking depreciation deductions on the tax return. If the firm uses some extra benefits in early years, it ought to show the liability for greater taxes in later years.

Example 9   Exhibit 10.3 shows data for Burns Corporation for a six-year period. This exhibit shows why accounting for income taxes presents a problem for firms with temporary differences. Burns Corporation acquires a plant asset that costs $120,000 and that has a six-year life with no expected salvage value. Columns [1] and [5] show Burns Corporation's income—*before depreciation expense and income tax expense*—of $100,000 for each of the six years of the asset's life.

Columns [1] through [4] show data from Burns Corporation's income tax return for each of the six years: Column [2] shows the (accelerated) depreciation deductions, column [3] (= [1] − [2]) shows taxable income, and column [4] shows income taxes payable computed as 40 percent of taxable income from column [3].

The data in columns [5] through [7] come from the financial statements. Column [6] shows the (straight-line) depreciation expense, and column [7] shows pre-tax income equal to column [5] minus column [6].

Assume, *contrary* to generally accepted accounting principles (GAAP), that firms report income tax expense equal to income tax payable. In the Burns example, this means that income tax expense equals the amounts in column [4], resulting in the hypothetical net income numbers in column [8]. The caption on column [8] does not say *Net Income* because GAAP do not report net income this way. Column [8] represents pre-tax financial statement income less income taxes payable.

Note the time series of income numbers in column [8]: up about 11.6 percent from Year 1 to Year 2, down 11.3 percent from Year 2 to Year 3, and down in each of the next three years by varying amounts. Recall, from Chapter 3, that the income statement intends to help the reader understand *why* income behaves over time as it does. When operations remain the same year after year and tax rates do not change, the reader will expect net income not to change. Looking at the amounts in column [8] (if they were net income figures), the reader of Burns Corporation's income statements will wonder, "What's going on with this company?" The answer is: nothing unusual. Burns does the same thing for six years, and its performance remains constant over the six-year period. Yet if the accountant sets income tax expense equal to income taxes payable, reported earnings vary from year to year. Reported income behaves strangely over time because of temporary differences: in each year the depreciation deduction on the tax return differs from depreciation expense in the financial statements.

GAAP require firms to base income tax expense on pre-tax income in the financial statements. Thus, when pre-tax income remains the same, $80,000 (= $100,000 − $20,000) in this example, income tax expense also remains the same, $32,000 (= .40 × $80,000). Net income is $48,000 (= $80,000 − $32,000) each year, as column [10] shows. This paragraph assumes there are no permanent differences.

RECORDING INCOME TAX EXPENSE

Exhibit 10.3 illustrates that income tax expense differs from income tax payable each year. The accountant debits or credits this difference to a deferred income tax liability account. The journal entry to record income taxes for Year 1 is as follows:

Year 1		
Income Tax Expense	32,000	
Income Tax Payable		30,400
Deferred Tax Liability		1,600

The credit to the Deferred Tax Liability account equals the 40 percent tax rate times the difference between the depreciation deduction of $24,000 on the tax return and the depreciation expense of $20,000 on the financial statements. The **deferred tax liability,** $1,600 in this example for Burns, represents the income taxes that the taxpayer will pay in future years when the temporary difference reverses.

Burns will make similar entries during Year 2 and Year 3, adding $7,360 [= .40 × ($38,400 − $20,000)] to the Deferred Tax Liability account in Year 2 and $1,120 [= .40 × ($22,800 − $20,000)] in Year 3. See Exhibit 10.4, which tracks the Deferred Tax Liability account over the six years of this example. The balance in the Deferred Tax Liability account at the end of Year 3 is $10,080 (= $1,600 + $7,360 + $1,120). This amount equals the 40 percent income tax rate times the cumulative difference between tax depreciation

EXHIBIT 10.4	BURNS CORPORATION Deferred Income Tax Liability Account over 6-Year Period (Amounts with Check Mark [√] Appear on Balance Sheet)

Deferred Tax Liability

Entry	Debit	Credit	
		0 √	Balance at Beginning of Year 1
		1,600 [1]	Entry for Year 1
		1,600 √	Balance at End of Year 1
		7,360 [2]	Entry for Year 2
		8,960 √	Balance at End of Year 2
		1,120 [3]	Entry for Year 3
		10,080 √	Balance at End of Year 3
Entry for Year 4 [4]	2,240		
		7,840 √	Balance at End of Year 4
Entry for Year 5 [5]	2,720		
		5,120 √	Balance at End of Year 5
Entry for Year 6 [6]	5,120		
		0 √	Balance at End of Year 6

of $85,200 (= $24,000 + $38,400 + $22,800) and book depreciation of $60,000 (= $20,000 × 3); note that the deferred tax liability equals $10,080 [= .40 × ($85,200 − $60,000)].

The temporary differences for depreciation begin to reverse in Year 4. The journal entry to recognize income tax expense for Year 4 is as follows:

Year 4		
Income Tax Expense	32,000	
Deferred Tax Liability	2,240	
Income Tax Payable		34,240

Depreciation expense recognized for financial reporting, $20,000, exceeds the depreciation deduction for tax purposes, $14,400. The income taxes currently payable because the temporary difference reversed are $2,240 [= .40 × ($20,000 − 14,400)].

Burns will make entries similar to the above in Year 5, reducing the Deferred Tax Liability by $2,720 [= .40 × ($20,000 − $13,200)], and in Year 6, reducing the Deferred Tax Liability account by $5,120 [= .40 × ($20,000 − $7,200)]. The reductions in the Deferred Tax Liability account during these three years total $10,080 (= $2,240 + $2,720 + $5,120). The balance in this account at the end of Year 6 is zero. The zero balance indicates that total, lifetime, depreciation amounts on the equipment both for financial reporting and for income tax reporting are the same: $120,000.

P R O B L E M   1 0 . 3   F O R   S E L F - S T U D Y

Computing income tax expense.   Wade Corporation acquires a machine on January 1, Year 1, costing $80,000 and having a four-year useful life and zero salvage value. Wade uses accelerated depreciation on its income tax return. For taxes, it deducts the following:

- 33 percent of the cost of the machine in Year 1
- 44 percent in Year 2
- 15 percent in Year 3
- 8 percent in Year 4

The firm uses the straight-line depreciation method for financial reporting. Income before depreciation and income taxes is $100,000, and the income tax rate is 40 percent.

a. Compute the amount of income taxes currently payable for each year.
b. Compute the amount of income tax expense for each year.
c. Give the journal entries for income taxes for each year.

A FURTHER LOOK AT GAAP FOR INCOME TAXES

The illustration for Burns Corporation in the previous section showed that income tax expense each period equaled pre-tax income for financial reporting multiplied by the income tax rate; in each year, income tax expense was $32,000 (= .40 × $80,000). Income tax expense also equaled income taxes currently payable plus the change in the Deferred Tax Liability account. For example, income tax expense for Year 1 equals income taxes currently payable of $30,400 plus the increase in the Deferred Tax Liability account of $1,600, and income tax expense for Year 4 equals income taxes currently payable of $34,240 reduced by the $2,240 amount by which the Deferred Tax Liability account decreased. The Deferred Tax Liability account changed each year in the amount of the tax effect of the temporary differences between depreciation in the financial statements and on the tax return.

The FASB requires a more complex accounting for income taxes than given in this simple illustration for Burns Corporation, for the following reasons:

1. The income tax rate that firms will have to pay in the future might change, and if so, the amount in the Deferred Tax Liability account will not represent the amount of taxes that the firm must pay later.
2. Temporary differences might create **deferred tax assets** instead of deferred tax liabilities. A deferred tax asset arises when a firm recognizes an expense earlier for financial reporting than for tax reporting. For example, for financial reporting, a firm provides for estimated warranty costs in the year it sells the warranted product but claims a tax deduction later, when it makes actual expenditures for warranty repairs. Similarly, for financial reporting, a firm reports Bad Debt Expense in the year it makes a credit sale but claims a tax deduction only later, when it writes off specific uncollectible accounts. These temporary differences create deferred tax assets.

3. GAAP require firms to recognize a **deferred tax asset valuation allowance** (similar in concept to an allowance for uncollectible accounts) to reduce the balance in the Deferred Tax Asset account to the amount the firm expects to realize in tax savings in the future.

Thus, the Deferred Tax Asset or Deferred Tax Liability accounts on the balance sheet can change each period because of temporary differences originating or reversing during the current period, changes in income tax rates expected to apply in future periods when temporary differences reverse, and changes in the valuation allowance for Deferred Tax Assets.

The illustration for Burns Corporation in Exhibit 10.3 assumed that only the first of the three factors affected deferred income taxes each year. In such cases, we can measure income tax expense using pre-tax income amounts from the financial statements and plug the difference between income tax expense and income tax payable to deferred asset or liability accounts on the balance sheet.

Because the second and third factors often occur, GAAP require firms to measure income tax expense with a procedure more complex than the one we illustrate here.[4] The International Accounting Standards Committee has issued rules virtually the same as the FASB rules illustrated here.[5]

PROBLEM 10.4 FOR SELF-STUDY

Working backward to components of book and tax income. Dominiak Company reports the following information about its financial statements and tax return for a year:

Depreciation Expense from Financial Statements	$270,000
Financial Statement Pretax Income	160,000
Income Tax Expense from Financial Statements	36,000
Income Taxes Payable from Tax Returns	24,000

The federal and state governments combine to tax taxable income at a rate of 40 percent. Permanent differences result from municipal bond interest that appears as revenue in the financial statements but is exempt from income taxes. Temporary differences result from the use of accelerated depreciation for tax returns and straight-line depreciation for financial reporting.

Reconstruct the income statement for financial reporting and for tax reporting for the year, identifying temporary differences and permanent differences.

---

[4]We discuss and illustrate this more general but more complex procedure on the Web Site that the publisher has made available for this book. To view this material, go to the publisher's Web Site (refer to the book's preface for a description of the site) or (1) go to http://www.harcourtcollege.com; (2) go to the pull-down menu for disciplines and select "accounting"; (3) select the icon for *Financial Accounting* by Stickney & Weil; (4) select "Student"; (5) select "Additional Topics"; (6) select "Deferred Taxes."

[5]International Accounting Standards Committee, *International Accounting Standards No. 12,* "Income Taxes," revised 1996.

DISCLOSURE OF INCOME TAXES IN FINANCIAL STATEMENTS

Notes to the financial statements provide additional information regarding a firm's income tax expense. Exhibit 10.5 illustrates these disclosures for General Products Company. Firms report four items of information:

1. *Components of Income before Income Taxes.* This section indicates the amount of book income before income taxes that a firm derives from both its domestic and its foreign operations.
2. *Components of Income Tax Expense.* This section indicates the amount of income taxes currently payable and the amount deferred because of temporary differences. It also separates the total taxes currently payable into the portions payable to U.S. and foreign government entities.
3. *Reconciliation from Statutory to Effective Income Tax Rates.* The **effective tax rate** equals (book) income tax expense divided by book income before income taxes. The effective tax rate of 29.9 percent for Year 4 equals $902 million income tax expense divided by $3,012 million income before income taxes. This section of the income tax note explains why the effective tax rate differs from the **statutory tax rate** of 35 percent. The differences result primarily from differences in tax rate (for example, General Products operates in countries whose average tax rate is less than the U.S. rate of 35 percent) and from permanent differences. Examples of permanent differences are the exclusion from taxable income of interest from state and municipal bonds and a portion of the dividend received from intercorporate investments. The U.S. system taxes income at the corporate level and again, after the corporation pays dividends to shareholders, at the personal level. To keep from taxing corporate income every time one corporation pays dividends to another, the system provides an exemption from taxes for part of the dividends that one corporation pays to another. See *double taxation* in the glossary.
4. *Components of Deferred Tax Assets and Liabilities.* This section discloses the types of temporary differences that result in the deferred tax asset and the deferred tax liability on the balance sheet each period. The change in these deferred tax accounts on the balance sheet equals the deferred portion of income tax expense each period. The journal entries to record income tax expense for General Products Company each year are as follows:

Year 2		
Income Tax Expense	869	
Deferred Tax Asset (= $141 − $107)	34	
Deferred Tax Liability (= $172 − $151)		21
Cash or Income Tax Payable (= $716 + $166)		882
Year 3		
Income Tax Expense	962	
Deferred Tax Asset (= $186 − $141)	45	
Deferred Tax Liability (= $196 − $172)		24
Cash or Income Tax Payable (= $762 + $221)		983
Year 4		
Income Tax Expense	902	
Deferred Tax Asset (= $236 − $186)	50	
Deferred Tax Liability (= $260 − $196)		64
Cash or Income Tax Payable (= $711 + $177)		888

EXHIBIT 10.5	GENERAL PRODUCTS COMPANY Illustrative Disclosure in Notes about Income Taxes Excerpts from Financial Statements[a] (all dollar amounts in millions)

	Year 2	Year 3	Year 4
INCOME BEFORE INCOME TAXES			
Domestic	$2,158	$2,208	$2,262
Foreign	612	747	750
Total	$2,770	$2,955	$3,012
COMPONENTS OF INCOME TAX EXPENSE			
Income Taxes Currently Payable:			
Domestic	$716	$762	$711
Foreign	166	221	177
Income Taxes Deferred	(13)	(21)	14
Income Tax Expense	$869	$962	$902
RECONCILIATION FROM STATUTORY TO EFFECTIVE INCOME TAX RATES			
U.S. Federal Statutory Rate	35.0%	35.0%	35.0%
Reduction in Taxes Resulting from:			
Income from Tax-Exempt Investments	(1.6)	(1.2)	(1.7)
Exclusion of 80% of Intercorporate Dividends Received	(0.5)	(0.1)	(0.8)
Foreign Income Taxed at Rate Lower than 35%	(1.5)	(1.1)	(2.6)
Effective Income Tax Rate[b]	31.4%	32.6%	29.9%

COMPONENTS OF DEFERRED TAX ASSETS AND LIABILITIES	End of Year			
	Year 1	Year 2	Year 3	Year 4
DEFERRED TAX ASSETS				
Uncollectible Accounts Receivable[c]	$ 45	$ 55	$ 72	$ 90
Warranty Liability[d]	67	93	126	161
Valuation Allowance[e]	(5)	(7)	(12)	(15)
Total Deferred Tax Assets	$107	$141	$186	$236
DEFERRED TAX LIABILITIES				
Depreciable Assets[f]	$126	$142	$155	$213
Installment Accounts Receivable[g]	25	30	41	47
Total Deferred Tax Liabilities	$151	$172	$196	$260

Authors' Notes (Notes such as these do not usually appear in published financial statements):

[a]Adapted from disclosures of General Electric and Sears, Roebuck.

[b]Income Tax Expense/Income before Income Tax Expense.

[c]General Products Company uses the allowance method for book purposes and, as required, the direct write-off method for tax purposes.

[d]For book purposes, General Products Company recognizes estimated warranty expense (and the related liability) at the time of sale, but, as required, it takes a tax deduction for warranty costs only when repairs and replacements under warranty are actually made.

[e]Adjustment to reflect the amount of deferred tax assets General Products expects to realize.

[f]General Products uses accelerated depreciation for tax purposes and straight-line depreciation for book purposes.

[g]General Products sells certain products on an installment-payment plan, for which it recognizes revenue for book purposes when it makes the sale and for tax purposes when it collects cash from customers using the installment method.

CRITICISMS OF DEFERRED TAX ACCOUNTING

Some accountants have criticized the accounting for deferred income taxes, for several reasons.

Benefits and Costs Ignored Requiring firms to record income tax expense currently on temporary differences for which the income tax law permits firms to delay payment conceals the economic benefit realized. Likewise, permitting firms to exclude from income tax expense currently the tax effects of temporary differences that require an immediate cash outflow, such as those created by bad debt expense, conceals the economic cost incurred.

Not an Asset or an Obligation An asset is a resource that provides future benefits. A liability is an obligation that requires a future sacrifice of resources, usually cash. A growing firm finds that its deferred tax asset and its deferred tax liability grow continually. For example, the book amount for warranty expense based on the current period's sales exceeds the tax amount for warranty expense based on warranty expenditures. The depreciation deduction on the income tax return using an accelerated depreciation method exceeds depreciation expense on the financial statements using the straight-line method. The continual growth in the deferred tax asset suggests that the firm never receives the benefits of future tax deductions. The continual growth in the deferred tax liability suggests that the firm never pays these income taxes.

Proponents of deferred tax accounting argue that individual temporary differences do reverse but that new temporary differences of larger amounts replace them. Thus, firms do realize the benefits of deferred tax assets and must pay deferred tax liabilities. These proponents argue that the deferred tax accounts on the balance sheet do not differ from accounts receivable and accounts payable. New accounts continually replace old accounts, but these accounts still represent assets and liabilities. Critics of deferred tax accounting counter that governmental entities impose income taxes on aggregate taxable income, not on individual temporary differences.

Undiscounted Amount Deferred tax liabilities appear at undiscounted amounts on the balance sheet. Other long-term liabilities, such as bonds and capitalized leases, appear at the present value of future cash flows discounted at an interest rate appropriate to the obligation on the date the firm first records the obligation. When the FASB issued *Statement No. 109,* "Accounting for Income Taxes," in 1992, it indicated its desire to defer consideration of the discounting of deferred taxes for several reasons, including the complexity of the process and the FASB's wish to consider discounting in a broad context as it applies to several accounting issues.

DEFERRED COMPENSATION: PENSION BENEFITS AND OTHER DEFERRED COMPENSATION

Most employers provide retirement benefits to their employees. Typical benefits include pensions, health insurance, and life insurance. Some employers set aside cash during the employees' working years to ensure the availability of funds to pay these retirement benefits later. Other firms use a pay-as-you-go system, paying for retirement benefits as retired employees receive them.

The employer must count as expense the cost of these retirement benefits in measuring net income. The accounting question arises whether firms should recognize the expense during the years while employees render services or later, when the firm pays the benefits during the employees' retirement. The matching convention of accrual accounting requires that firms recognize the expense during employees' working years because the labor services of those years generate revenues. The cost of **deferred compensation** does not differ from the cost of current compensation (that is, salaries and wages). Employees agree to render services currently for a package of compensation, some of which the employees receive immediately and some of which the employees receive later. Delaying the recognition of deferred compensation costs until employees retire results in an expense without a matching revenue from those employees' services and overstates income of the period when the firm earned the revenue.

This section discusses the accounting issues for pension benefit plans. The accounting for other retirement benefits follows similar principles. Under a *pension plan,* an employer promises to make payments to employees after they retire. Private pension plan systems have grown in number and size over the last several decades. For many individuals, the present value of their pension benefits is their major financial asset, and for many firms, the present value of their pension promises forms a significant obligation. The variety of details about pension plans can hide their basic structure, which we discuss next.

PENSION PLAN STRUCTURE AND DEFINITIONS

Employer This section discusses the structure of a pension plan from the viewpoint of the employer.

1. The employer sets up a pension plan specifying the eligibility of employees, the types of promises made to employees, the method of funding, and the pension plan administrator. Some employers promise to contribute a certain amount to the pension plan each period for each employee (usually based on an employee's salary), without specifying the benefits the employee will receive during retirement. The amounts employees eventually receive depend on the investment performance of the pension plan. Common terminology refers to such plans as **defined contribution pension plans.** Other employers specify the benefit that employees will receive during retirement. The employer must contribute sufficient amounts to the pension plan so that those contributions plus earnings from investments made with those contributions will be sufficient to pay the specified benefit. Common terminology refers to such plans as **defined benefit pension plans.**

2. The employer computes pension expense each period. Pension expense under a defined contribution plan equals the amount contributed for the period. The FASB prescribes the measurement of pension expense for a defined benefit plan, but we do not discuss these details in this book.[6] The employer debits Pension Expense and credits Pension Liability, following a process called *expensing pension obligations.*

3. The employer transfers cash to a separate pension fund each period according to some formula. The employer debits Pension Liability and credits Cash, following a process called *funding pension obligations.*

4. If cumulative pension expenses exceed cumulative pension funding, a pension liability appears on the employer's balance sheet. If cumulative pension funding exceeds cumulative pension expenses, a pension asset appears on the employer's balance sheet. In addition, the FASB requires firms to report a pension liability on the balance sheet if the present value of pension commitments to employees exceeds the assets in the pension fund.

---

[6]Financial Accounting Standards Board, *Statement of Financial Accounting Standards No. 87,* "Employer's Accounting for Pensions," 1985.

Pension Plan   The pension plan carries out the following steps.

1. The plan receives cash each period from the employer. The plan invests this cash in bonds, capital stock, real estate, and other investments to generate income. The plan pays cash to retired employees each period. The assets in the pension plan change each period as follows:

> Assets at Beginning of the Period
> ± Actual Earnings on Pension Plan Investments
> + Contributions Received from the Employer
> − Payments to Retirees
> = Assets at End of the Period

The assets in the pension fund do not appear on the balance sheet of the employer.

2. The pension plan computes the amount of the pension liability each period. The liability of a defined contribution plan just equals the assets in the pension fund. The computation of the pension liability for a defined benefit plan uses the pension benefit formula underlying the pension plan and depends on assumptions about employee turnover, mortality, interest rates, and other factors. The liability of the pension plan equals the present value of the expected amounts payable to employees.

The typical benefit formula takes into account the employee's length of service and some measure of average earnings. For example, the employer might promise to pay each employee during retirement an annual pension equal to a stated percentage of the average annual salary during the five highest-paid working years for that employee. The percentage might increase by 2 percentage points for each year of service, so that an employee with 40 years of service receives an annual pension equal to 80 percent of that employee's average salary during the five highest-paid working years.[7]

DEFERRED COMPENSATION: HEALTH CARE AND OTHER BENEFITS

Health care, insurance, and other benefits resemble, in concept, pension benefits. Employers promise to provide benefits to employees during retirement. The present value of these commitments, called **health-care benefits obligation,** represents an economic obligation of the employer. Until the FASB issued its rules in the early 1990s, few firms had either recognized an expense for these obligations or set aside cash to fund them. The FASB requires firms to recognize expenses for employees' health care and similar benefits and to recognize liabilities for the firms' underfunded obligations to pay for these benefits.[8] Firms may recognize the full liability in one year or recognize it piecemeal over several years.

DERIVATIVE INSTRUMENTS

Firms face risks in carrying out their business operations. Examples include the following: the risk that customers will stop buying a firm's products and services; the risk that

[7]We discuss and illustrate more of the accounting concepts and methods for pensions and pension plans on the Web Site that the publisher has made available for this book. To view this material, which includes problems for self-study as well as exercises and other problems, go to the publisher's Web Site (refer to the book's preface for a description of the site) or (1) go to http://www.harcourtcollege.com; (2) go to the pull-down menu for disciplines and select "accounting"; (3) select the icon for *Financial Accounting* by Stickney & Weil; (4) select "Student"; (5) select "Additional Topics"; (6) select "Pensions."

[8]Financial Accounting Standards Board, *Statement of Financial Accounting Standards No. 106,* "Employers' Accounting for Postretirement Benefits Other Than Pensions," 1990.

raw material used in production will increase in cost after the firm has committed to a fixed selling price for the final product; the risk that dollars eventually collected from sales to a customer who has agreed to pay in euros will fall short of the amount anticipated at the time the customer agreed to the euro sales price; the risk that interest rates will rise, forcing the firm, which has borrowed using variable-rate (often called *floating-rate*) debt, to pay more cash; and the risk that employees will decide to quit or retire in larger-than-expected numbers.

Firms can purchase financial instruments to mitigate some business risks (for example, all but the first and last of those listed). A **derivative instrument** (sometimes called a *financial derivative* or merely a *derivative*) is a financial instrument designed to help firms cope with various kinds of risk. The technical definition of a *derivative* appears in the glossary; mastering the technical details of derivatives and the accounting for them goes beyond the scope of this book. A derivative can be an asset or a liability. We include the discussion of derivatives in this chapter on liabilities, but we could just as well have included it in the next chapter on holdings of marketable securities and investments. The FASB requires that firms show all derivatives on the balance sheet at their fair market value at the end of the period.[9] GAAP require firms to report the changes in derivatives' market value in earnings in some situations, noted below, but not in all. Chapter 12 introduces the new GAAP concept, "Other Comprehensive Income," which includes the market value changes that firms do not include in reported earnings.

The following examples illustrate some of the risk-reduction purposes and processes that firms attempt by using derivatives.

Example 10   Rhodes Company, a manufacturer of gold jewelry, holds an inventory of gold, which it purchased at a low price. Rhodes Company can use the gold to manufacture jewelry over the next eight months or it can sell the gold now for a profit. It decides to keep the gold to use in manufacturing operations. It worries, however, that gold prices will decline over the next eight months and it will lose the profit from its purchase. If gold prices rise further, it will profit further because it will be able to charge higher prices for its manufactured jewelry. So, Rhodes Company sells a forward contract promising to deliver gold eight months hence. If gold prices decline, it will profit from this contract. If gold prices rise, the contract will lose, but the gain in the value of its gold inventory will offset the loss. The forward contract is a financial instrument—a derivative—and Rhodes Company has hedged its gold position. The FASB calls this a **fair-value hedge.**

Example 11   Rhodes Company has borrowed $1 million short term (one-year maturity), using variable-rate commercial paper, knowing that changes in short-term interest rates will change the interest amount it pays each month. Rhodes Company would prefer to pay a fixed interest rate over the next year. It can buy an **interest-rate swap,** from a **counterparty** such as Bear Stearns. The swap is a financial instrument that promises to pay to Rhodes Company each month the interest on a short-term loan whose interest rate resets each month. In return, Rhodes Company agrees to pay each month to Bear Stearns a fixed amount, based on the one-year borrowing rate. If Rhodes Company buys such a swap, it will have achieved its goal of paying, each month, a fixed amount. It pays Bear Stearns the fixed amount; it receives the variable interest-based payment from Bear Stearns each month; and it pays a variable interest amount to its own lenders, that is, the purchasers of the commercial paper. Rhodes Company's receipt of the variable

[9]Financial Accounting Standards Board, *Statement of Financial Accounting Standards No. 133,* "Accounting for Derivative Instruments and Hedging Activities," 1998. The source for the other FASB references in the remainder of this section come from *Statement No. 133.*

payments from Bear Stearns just offsets its payments to its lenders. Rhodes Company's total, overall payment is the fixed amount it pays each month to Bear Stearns. Rhodes Company has converted a **variable-rate debt** into fixed-rate debt by using an interest-rate swap. As we have described this transaction, Rhodes Company and Bear Stearns exchange payments with each other each month. In practice, only one counterparty pays the other and pays only the net amount. The FASB calls this a **cash-flow hedge**; the interest-rate swap itself is a *derivative instrument*.

Fair-Value Hedge and Cash-Flow Hedge

Sometimes, as in Example 10, the firm faces uncertainty about market values of liabilities or assets. In Example 10, the firm owns gold, an asset whose market value fluctuates. Other times, as in Example 11, the firm faces uncertainty about future streams of cash flow amounts. When the firm acquires a derivative and attempts to reduce risk involving fluctuations in a market value, the FASB classifies the transaction as a *fair-value hedge*. When the firm acquires a derivative and attempts to reduce the risk in future streams of cash flows (inflows or outflows), the FASB classifies the transaction as a *cash-flow hedge*.

The derivative appears on the balance sheet at fair value. The FASB requires the firm to show in income each period the change in the fair value of a derivative that qualifies as a fair-value hedge. The firm will also record at fair value the asset or liability it is hedging, so under most circumstances the net effect on both net assets and net income will be zero.

A cash-flow hedge does not match an explicit asset or liability on the balance sheet but hedges some future cash flows. The firm will show the cash-flow hedge at its fair value on the balance sheet but will not report the matching gain or loss in net earnings of the period. The gain or loss will appear as part of comprehensive income (discussed in Chapter 12) and will appear on the balance sheet in owners' equity but does not affect retained earnings.

Rationale for Different Treatment of Fair-Value and Cash-Flow Hedges

The logic for the FASB's different treatment of gains and losses from changes in fair values of financial instruments results from applying the matching principle. In a fair-value hedge, both the hedged asset (or liability) and its related derivative appear on the balance sheet. The firm revalues both the hedged asset (or liability) and its derivative to fair value each period and reports the gain or loss on the hedged asset (or liability) and the related loss or gain on the derivative in earnings. To the degree the firm has acquired an effective hedge, these amounts cancel each other out. If the attempt does not achieve a perfect hedge, the firm will report in income the net cost of the unsuccessful hedge or the net benefit of the oversuccessful hedge. In a cash-flow hedge, the hedged cash flow commitment does not appear on the balance sheet. The related derivative does appear on the balance sheet. Including the gain or loss on changes in the fair value of the derivative each period but awaiting settlement of the cash flow commitment to recognize the offsetting loss or gain would result in poor matching. GAAP require that the unrealized gain or loss on the cash-flow hedge remain on the balance sheet in a separate shareholders' equity account to later match against any loss or gain on the cash-flow commitment when it settles.

If the firm acquires a derivative instrument but does not use it to hedge some fair value or cash flow, then it must report changes in the market value of that derivative in net income. Such derivatives do not attempt to hedge some other asset, liability, or future cash flow, so there is no current or future economic event to match against. Thus, gains or losses on derivatives that do not attempt to hedge appear in income as they occur.

Example 12 Tennille Company plans to borrow $10 million nine months from now. It finds current borrowing rates attractive, but it does not need to borrow the funds for nine months and it worries that interest rates will increase during the next nine months. So, Tennille Company purchases a derivative—it could use an interest-rate option or a forward contract—to lock in today's rate. This is a cash-flow hedge.

Example 13 Merck, a large international pharmaceuticals firm, expects to sell 1 billion deutsche marks (DM) of its products in Germany during the next period. It has not made those sales yet but has confidence in its sales projections. It knows its costs in dollars to produce the drugs it will sell in Germany. Although Merck is confident of the future DM receipts, it is unsure how many dollars it will receive in, say, one year when it converts DM to dollars to send back to the United States. So, today, Merck buys a foreign-exchange forward contract that fixes the rate at which Merck can exchange approximately 1 billion DM into dollars. That contract, a financial instrument, fluctuates in value as the exchange rate between the dollar and the DM changes. Merck has little concern about that fluctuation because it will use the DM it receives one year hence from its sales to fulfill its obligation under the foreign-exchange contract. It is confident of its future receipt in DM and has used the contract to ensure a certain exchange rate into dollars. The FASB calls this a cash-flow hedge.

Coca-Cola has a similar problem with its purchases of a major raw material: sugar in its various forms. Coke can be confident of future sales of soft drinks but is less confident about the price of sugar. Coke can enter into a derivative contract today guaranteeing its price for a stated quantity of sugar to be received one year hence. Under some conditions, the FASB calls this too a cash-flow hedge.

Example 14 Linderman Company has borrowed $1 million long term via a noncallable bond with substantial prepayment penalties requiring fixed debt-service payments each period. The company prefers to pay short-term rates, renegotiated each month. It can engage in the mirror-image transaction of the one described in Example 11, converting fixed-rate debt into variable-rate debt using an interest-rate swap. The FASB calls this a fair-value hedge. Linderman Company has a fixed-rate liability on its balance sheet. As interest rates change, so does the market value of its outstanding debt.

Example 15 Linderman Company believes that the shares of FurnitureOnLine.com are about to rise dramatically in price on the NASDAQ, so it purchases options to acquire 10,000 shares of FurnitureOnLine.com. Although these options are derivatives, Linderman Company did not acquire them to hedge any of its assets or liabilities, or its cash flows. Hence, the company will report the changes in market value of these options in periodic income. They are *marketable securities,* as well as being derivatives, and Linderman Company will account for them using the methods described in Chapter 11.

JOURNAL ENTRIES OF DERIVATIVE INSTRUMENTS USED AS A FAIR-VALUE HEDGE

Lacey Corporation issued 8 percent, fixed-rate, semiannual coupon bonds on January 1 at par for $100 million. It simultaneously entered into an interest-rate swap with National Bank, the counterparty. Lacey will pay the bank at the end of each six-month period if interest rates exceed 8 percent, and the bank will pay Lacey if interest rates are below 8 percent. If the market rate is r on the date of the payment, then the bank will pay Lacey an amount equal to $\frac{1}{2} \times (.08 - r) \times \$100,000,000$; the one-half factor results from the semiannual timing of the payments. Lacey's interest expense will therefore vary with the changes in the interest rate. The interest-rate swap represents a fair-value hedge The interest-rate swap has a zero market value on January 1, since the interest rate is 8 percent on this date.

Lacey would record the issuance of the bonds as follows (dollar amounts in millions):

January 1		
Cash	100	
Bonds Payable		100

By June 30, six months after Lacey issued the bonds, interest rates have decreased to 6 percent. Lacey makes the following entries on June 30 for interest:

June 30		
Interest Expense ($\frac{1}{2} \times .08 \times \$100$)	4	
Cash		4
Cash [$\frac{1}{2} \times (.08 - .06) \times \$100$]	1	
Interest Expense		1

Lacey will report interest expense of $3, which equals the six-month portion of the annual variable interest rate of 6 percent. Lacey will also have to revalue the bonds on its books. The decrease in interest rate will increase the market value of its bonds by, say, $8. Recall that an increase in the book value of a liability results in a loss to the issuer of the liability. Lacey will make the following entry in its accounts:

June 30		
Loss on Revaluation of Bonds	8	
Bonds Payable		8

Accountants historically have not revalued bonds for changes in market value. The FASB requires firms to revalue bonds when the firm hedges them with a fair-value hedge. Lacey will also have to report the derivative financial instrument (that is, the swap) at its market value on June 30. Assume that the change in the value of the derivative exactly mirrors the change in the market value of the bond. Lacey will make the following entry:

June 30		
Derivative Financial Asset	8	
Gain on Derivative Asset		8

Both the loss on the revaluation of the bond and the gain on the revaluation of the derivative asset appear in net income for the period. If the derivative serves as a perfect hedge, the loss and the gain exactly offset each other.

JOURNAL ENTRIES FOR CASH-FLOW HEDGE

Assume, now, that on January 1 when interest rates are 8 percent per year, Lacey Corporation issues at par $100 million of variable-rate bonds, with semiannual interest payments based on the interest rate at the end of each six-month period. The firm also enters into an interest-rate swap with National Bank; it agrees to pay the bank each six months the difference between 8 percent interest and any variable interest rate below 8 percent. In return, the bank agrees to pay Lacey for any difference between the variable rate and 8 percent when the variable rate exceeds 8 percent. In this way, Lacey converts its variable-rate debt into 8 percent fixed-rate debt and has achieved a cash-flow hedge.

For the issuance of the bonds on January 1, Lacey makes the same entry as shown above.

January 1

Cash	100	
Bonds Payable		100

By June 30, the variable rate has decreased to 6 percent. The entries on June 30 are as follows:

June 30

Interest Expense ($\frac{1}{2} \times .06 \times \$100$)	3	
Cash		3
Interest Expense [$\frac{1}{2} \times (.08 - .06) \times \$100$]	1	
Cash		1

Lacey will also have to recognize a liability for the decline in market value of the derivative because of the decrease in interest rates. The entry, assuming that the derivative declines in value by $8, is as follows:

Other Equity Adjustment (Comprehensive Income)	8	
Derivative Liability		8

Chapter 12 discusses the debit entry above. That debit represents the loss in the value of the derivative, but it does not affect net income immediately. It reduces comprehensive income (see Chapter 12), and Lacey debits this amount directly to a separate line in the shareholders' equity section of the balance sheet labeled Accumulated Comprehensive Income or Other Nonowner Equity Adjustments. Over the life of the derivative contract, the market value of the interest-rate swap agreement will change as interest rates change. At the end of the contract term, the market value of the contract will be zero and the cumulative amount in comprehensive income will net to zero.

AN INTERNATIONAL PERSPECTIVE

LEASES

Most industrialized countries maintain a distinction between operating leases and capital leases (often called *financing leases*). The criteria for a capital lease in Japan, Germany, and France follow income tax laws, whereas standard-setting bodies set the criteria in the

United States, Canada, and the United Kingdom. The criteria in each case attempt to identify the entity enjoying the rewards and bearing the risk of the asset.

INCOME TAX ACCOUNTING

Countries that permit firms to select different methods of accounting for financial and tax reporting (such as the United States, Canada, and Great Britain) require deferred tax accounting. Firms provide deferred taxes for all temporary differences in the United States and Canada, whereas firms in Great Britain provide deferred taxes only when a firm expects that a liability for deferred taxes will materialize. The book/tax conformity requirement in France, Japan, and Germany largely eliminates the need for deferred tax accounting in these countries.

RETIREMENT BENEFITS

The types of retirement benefits that employers provide for employees vary across industrialized countries. The law in Germany, France, and most socialized countries guarantees employees their rights to retirement benefits. Japan has historically provided a severance benefit, although pension benefits have increased in use. Disclosures about retirement benefits in most countries contain less detail than in the United States.

SUMMARY

Analyzing a firm's risk involves an assessment of the adequacy of a firm's assets and cash flows to pay liabilities as they come due. This chapter discusses commitments and obligations that accounting may not recognize as liabilities (certain asset sales with recourse provisions or operating leases), may partially recognize (some pension, health care, and other retirement benefits), or may recognize in an amount larger than the expected cash outflow (deferred tax liability). Effective analysis of risk requires an understanding of the accounting for each of these obligations and commitments. Firms can use derivative instruments to hedge some of the risks of their business operations. These derivatives appear on the balance sheet at fair value, and changes in those values will not affect net income when the firm has successfully used the derivatives to hedge the specific risks it faces.

APPENDIX 10.1: EFFECTS ON THE STATEMENT OF CASH FLOWS OF TRANSACTIONS INVOLVING LIABILITIES

LEASES

When firms account for leases as operating leases, the amount reported as rent revenue (by the lessor) or rent expense (by the lessee) usually equals the lessee's cash payment to the lessor. Thus, the accountant makes no adjustment to net income to compute cash flow from operations under the indirect method.

Assume that the lessee either prepays or delays payment of the rental fee. Then the accountant includes the change in the lessee's account Prepaid Rent (Rental Fees Received in Advance, for the lessor) or the lessee's account Rent Payable (Rent Receivable, for the lessor) as an addition to, or subtraction from, net income to compute cash flow from operations.

At the time that a lessee signs a lease accounted for as a capital lease, it debits an asset account for the leased asset and credits a lease liability account. The signing of a capital lease is an investing and a financing activity that does not affect cash. Lessees must report such transactions in a supplementary schedule or notes to the financial statements.

During the lease period, the lessee depreciates the leased asset. The accountant adds back depreciation expense to net income when computing cash flow from operations. The lessee treats lease payments partially as interest expense and partially as a repayment of the lease liability. Refer to the example for Food Barn in the chapter. The firm made the following entry on December 31, Year 1:

Interest Expense	6,750	
Liability—Present Value of Lease Obligation	12,959	
Cash		19,709

The portion of the cash payment representing interest expense requires no adjustment when converting net income to cash flow from operations under the indirect method. The portion of the cash payment representing repayment of the lease liability requires the following entry on the worksheet used to construct the statement of cash flows (but not in the journal):

Liability—Present Value of Lease Obligation	12,959	
Cash (Financing—Repayment of Lease Liability)		12,959

DEFERRED INCOME TAXES

Refer to Example **9,** Exhibit 10.3, for Burns Corporation. In the first year, income tax expense of $32,000 exceeds income taxes payable of $30,400 by $1,600. That $1,600 of tax expense did not use cash. The statement of cash flows requires an addback to net income in deriving cash flow from operations when the firm uses the indirect format. The $1,600 of expense increases the noncurrent liability for deferred income taxes. Income tax expense exceeds income taxes payable in the second and third years, requiring addbacks in those years as well.

In the fourth, fifth, and sixth years, the firm uses more cash than the amount of the expense. For the sixth year, for example, the firm uses $37,120 cash to pay taxes but reports income tax expense of only $32,000 in the income statement. Consequently, it must subtract $5,120 (= $37,120 − $32,000) in the statement of cash flows to derive cash flow from operations when the firm uses the indirect format.

The statement of cash flows for Ellwood Corporation in Exhibit 13.3 illustrates on line (5) the addback to net income for deferred taxes in arriving at cash flow from operations.

PENSIONS

When a firm records pension expense, income decreases and a liability for pensions increases. When a firm funds pension liabilities, it reduces both cash and liabilities. Thus, when pension funding in a period equals pension expense for that period, the accountant need make no pension-related adjustments to net income in deriving cash flow from operations. If pension expense is more than (less than) pension funding, deriving cash flow from operations requires an addback (subtraction) of the excess (shortfall) when the firm uses the indirect format. (When pension expense differs from pension funding, other issues arise that go beyond the scope of this discussion.)

DERIVATIVES

When a firm records changes in the market value of a derivative, this sometimes affects net income without affecting cash flow. These gains or losses not matching cash flows require adjustments to net income in deriving cash from operations when the firm uses the indirect method, but such adjustments go beyond the scope of this book.

SOLUTIONS TO SELF-STUDY PROBLEMS

SUGGESTED SOLUTION TO PROBLEM 10.1 FOR SELF-STUDY

(International Paper Company; attempting off-balance sheet financing.)

a. IP receives an immediate benefit of $75 million cash on January 1. IP retains a residual interest in the cash and uncut timber at the end of five years. IP's principal risk is that the bank will replace IP's forest-management personnel with managers of its own choosing who might mismanage the property. For example, to control operating costs, the new managers might not remove stumpage from harvested trees or might not replant new seedlings.

b. The bank has rights to an uncertain future revenue stream of 14 percent of the unpaid balance of the loan. Factors affecting this uncertainty include

- the absence of a loan guarantee by IP,
- the adequacy of 10 percent excess timber to cover interest, operating costs, and decreases in selling prices, and
- a fixed yield on the loan regardless of changes in interest rates.

c. Timber and pulp prices vary significantly each year depending on economic conditions, availability and usage of heavily capital-intensive pulp-processing plants, and foreign competition. A key factor affecting the treatment of this transaction is the adequacy of the 10 percent excess timber to compensate for timber price decreases. If the amount of timber transferred to the trust is sufficient to assure the bank of repayment of its loan with interest, then the bank bears little risk and IP would recognize a liability. If the amount of timber transferred creates considerable uncertainty that the bank will receive the loan repayment with interest, then IP will treat the transaction as a sale (no liability recognized). If the 10 percent "protection" parameter is 30 percent, then IP surely would recognize a liability. If the factor is only 5 percent, International need not recognize a liability.

SUGGESTED SOLUTION TO PROBLEM 10.2 FOR SELF-STUDY

(Holt Book Store and automobile dealer; operating and capital lease methods for lessee and lessor.)

a. Application of the four criteria is as follows:

(1) Ownership transferred to lessee at end of lease term: not satisfied.

(2) Lease contains a bargain purchase option for lessee: not satisfied.

(3) Lease period extends for at least 75 percent of asset's life: satisfied.

(4) Present value of contractual lease payments equals or exceeds 90 percent of fair market value of the asset at the time lessee signs the lease: satisfied. The present value of the lease payments when discounted at 12 percent is $25,000 (= $8,231 × 3.03735), which equals the $25,000 market value of the asset on January 2, Year 1. The lease is therefore a capital lease.

b. December 31 of each year:

Rent Expense	8,231	
Cash		8,231
To recognize annual expense of renting delivery van.		

c. December 31 of each year:

Equipment (delivery van)	23,500	
Merchandise Inventory		23,500
To record transfer of delivery van from inventory to equipment.		
Cash	8,231	
Rent Revenue		8,231
To recognize annual revenue from renting delivery van.		

December 31 of each year:

Depreciation Expense	5,875	
Accumulated Depreciation		5,875
To recognize depreciation on leased van; $5,875 = $23,500/4.		

d. January 2, Year 1:

Asset—Delivery Van	25,000	
Liability—Present Value of Lease Obligation		25,000
To recognize acquisition of delivery van and the related liability.		

December 31, Year 1:

Interest Expense (.12 × $25,000)	3,000	
Liability—Present Value of Lease Obligation	5,231	
Cash		8,231
To record first lease payment. The book value of the lease liability after this entry is $19,769 (= $25,000 − $5,231).		

December 31, Year 1:

Depreciation Expense ($25,000/4)	6,250	
Accumulated Depreciation		6,250
To record depreciation expense for Year 1.		

December 31, Year 2:

Interest Expense (.12 × $19,769)	2,372	
Liability—Present Value of Lease Obligation	5,859	
Cash		8,231
To record second lease payment. The book value of the lease liability after this entry is $13,910 (= $19,769 − $5,859).		

December 31, Year 2:

Depreciation Expense	6,250	
Accumulated Depreciation		6,250
To record depreciation expense for Year 2.		

e. January 2, Year 1:

Lease Receivable	25,000	
Sales Revenue		25,000
To record sale of delivery van.		

January 2, Year 1:

Cost of Goods Sold	23,500	
Merchandise Inventory		23,500
To record cost of delivery van sold.		

December 31, Year 1:

Cash	8,231	
Interest Revenue		3,000
Lease Receivable		5,231
To record lease receipt for Year 1; amounts mirror those for lessee.		

December 31, Year 2:

Cash	8,231	
Interest Revenue		2,372
Lease Receivable		5,859
To record lease receipt for Year 2; amounts mirror those for lessee.		

f.

	Operating Lease Method	Capital Lease Method		
Year	Rent Expense	Interest Expense	Depreciation Expense	Total
1	$ 8,231	$ 3,000	$ 6,250	$ 9,250
2	8,231	2,372	6,250	8,622
3	8,231	1,669[a]	6,250	7,919
4	8,231	883[b]	6,250	7,133
	$32,924	$ 7,924	$25,000	$32,924

[a].12 × $13,910 = $1,669. Book value of lease liability after this entry is $7,348 [= $13,910 − ($8,231 − $1,669)].

[b].12 × $7,348 = $882, which differs from $883 due to rounding.

g.

	Operating Lease Method			Capital Lease Method		
Year	Rent Revenue	Depreciation Expense	Total	Gain from Sale	Interest Revenue	Total
1	$ 8,231	$ 5,875	$2,356	$1,500	$3,000	$4,500
2	8,231	5,875	2,356	—	2,372	2,372
3	8,231	5,875	2,356	—	1,669	1,669
4	8,231	5,875	2,356	—	883	883
	$32,924	$23,500	$9,424	$1,500	$7,924	$9,424

h. The lessee's total expenses equal cash outflows, and the lessor's total revenue, or income, equals cash inflows minus cash outflows. The operating and the capital lease methods recognize the revenues and expenses associated with these cash flows in different periods.

i. The lessee's total expenses equal its total cash outflows of $32,924 (= $8,231 × 4). The lessor's total income equals cash inflows of $32,924 (= $8,231 × 4) minus cash outflows of $23,500. Although the lessor's receipts equal the lessee's payments, the lessor must pay for the goods, which reduces its income with a subtraction for cost of goods sold. This cost of goods sold accounts for the difference between the lessee's expense and the lessor's income.

SUGGESTED SOLUTION TO PROBLEM 10.3 FOR SELF-STUDY

(Wade Corporation; computing income tax expense.)

a.

Year	Income before Depreciation and Income Taxes [1]	Deduction on Tax Return [2]	Taxable Income [3]	Income Tax Payable [4]
1	$100,000	$26,400	$ 73,600	$ 29,440
2	$100,000	35,200	64,800	25,920
3	$100,000	12,000	88,000	35,200
4	$100,000	6,400	93,600	37,440
Totals	$400,000	$80,000	$320,000	$128,000

Column [1] is given.
Column [2] = $80,000 × .33 for Year 1, .44 for Year 2, .15 for Year 3, and .08 for Year 4.
Column [3] = [1] − [2].
Column [4] = .40 × [3].

b.

Year	Income before Depreciation and Income Taxes [1]	Depreciation Expense [2]	Income before Income Taxes [3]	Income Tax Expense [4]
1	$100,000	$20,000	$ 80,000	$ 32,000
2	100,000	20,000	80,000	32,000
3	100,000	20,000	80,000	32,000
4	100,000	20,000	80,000	32,000
Totals	$400,000	$80,000	$320,000	$128,000

Column [1] is given.

Column [2] = $80,000/4 = $20,000.

Column [3] = [1] − [2].

Column [4] = .40 × [3].

c.   *Year 1*

Income Tax Expense	32,000	
Income Tax Payable...........................		29,440
Deferred Tax Liability		2,560

Year 2

Income Tax Expense	32,000	
Income Tax Payable		25,920
Deferred Tax Liability		6,080

Year 3

Income Tax Expense	32,000	
Deferred Tax Liability	3,200	
Income Tax Payable		35,200

Year 4

Income Tax Expense	32,000	
Deferred Tax Liability	5,440	
Income Tax Payable		37,440

SUGGESTED SOLUTION TO PROBLEM 10.4 FOR SELF-STUDY

(Dominiak Company; working backward to components of book and tax income.) See Exhibit 10.6.

EXHIBIT 10.6	DOMINIAK COMPANY Illustration of Temporary Differences and Permanent Differences (Suggested Solution to Problem 10.4 for Self-Study)

	Financial Statements	Type of Difference	Income Tax Return
Operating Income except Depreciation	$360,000 (6)	—	$360,000 (4)
Depreciation	(270,000) (g)	Temporary	(300,000) (3)
Municipal Bond Interest	70,000 (5)	Permanent	—
Taxable Income			$ 60,000 (2)
Pretax Income	$160,000 (g)		
Income Taxes Payable at 40 Percent			$ 24,000 (g)

Income Tax Expense at 40 Percent
  of $90,000 = $160,000 −
  $70,000, Which Is Book Income
  Excluding Permanent
  Differences ....
	(36,000) (g)		

Net Income	$124,000 (1)		

Order and derivation of computations:

(g) Given.

(1) $124,000 = $160,000 − $36,000.

(2) $60,000 = $24,000/.40.

(3) Temporary difference for depreciation is ($36,000 − $24,000)/.40 = $30,000. Because income taxes payable are less than income tax expense, we know that depreciation deducted on tax return exceeds depreciation expense on financial statements. Thus the depreciation deduction on the tax return is $300,000 = $270,000 + $30,000.

(4) $360,000 = $300,000 + $60,000.

(5) Financial statement Income before taxes, excluding permanent differences, is $90,000 = $36,000/.40. Financial statement income before taxes, including permanent differences, is $160,000. Hence permanent differences are $160,000 − $90,000 = $70,000.

(6) $160,000 + $270,000 − $70,000 = $360,000. See also (4), for check.

KEY TERMS AND CONCEPTS

Off-balance sheet financing
Operating lease
Capital lease
Book basis
Tax basis
Permanent differences
Temporary differences
Income tax payable
Income tax expense
Deferred tax liabilities
Deferred tax assets
Deferred tax asset valuation allowance

Effective tax rate
Statutory tax rate
Deferred compensation
Defined contribution pension plan
Defined benefit pension plan
Health-care benefits obligation
Derivative instrument
Fair-value hedge
Interest-rate swap
Counterparty
Variable-rate debt
Cash-flow hedge

QUESTIONS, EXERCISES, PROBLEMS, AND CASES

QUESTIONS

1. Review the meaning of the terms and concepts listed in Key Terms and Concepts.
2. "The concern with off-balance sheet financing is overstated. As long as the notes to the financial statements provide information about the transaction, the analyst can incorporate the financing into debt ratios as appropriate." Do you agree or disagree? Explain.
3. Compare and contrast the financial statement effects of achieving off-balance sheet financing through an executory contract versus an asset sale with recourse.
4. Explain why the following question is important for lease accounting: "Who enjoys the potential rewards and bears the risks of an asset?"
5. In what ways is the economic substance of a lessee's capital lease similar to, and different from, that of an installment purchase?
6. Distinguish between the lessee's accounting for a capital lease and for an installment purchase.
7. In what sense is the total expense from a lease independent of the lessee's method of accounting for it?
8. "The lessor recognizes the same amount of income (revenue minus expenses) over the term of a lease as the lessee recognizes expenses." Do you agree or disagree? Explain.
9. "The rationale for deferred tax accounting rests on the matching convention." Explain.
10. "One might view deferred income taxes as an interest-free loan from the government." Do you agree? Why or why not?
11. You have been called to testify before a congressional committee on income taxation. One committee member states: "My staff has added up the amounts shown for Deferred Tax Liability on the balance sheets of the 500 largest U.S. corporations. If we collected these amounts immediately, we could reduce the national deficit by billions of dollars. After all, I have to pay my taxes as they become due each year. Why shouldn't corporations have to do the same?" How would you respond?
12. How should an analyst wanting to study the debt-equity ratio (= total liabilities/total equities) of a business treat the deferred income tax liability?
13. Under what circumstances will a firm report a deferred tax asset on the balance sheet? Under what circumstances will a firm report a deferred tax liability on the balance sheet?
14. Most firms report income tax expense at a percentage of pretax book income that differs from the statutory federal income tax rate. What might cause this difference?
15. "The principal accounting issues involving deferred compensation plans relate to the matching convention in accounting." Explain.
16. Suggest reasons why the assets and liabilities of a pension plan do not appear on the employer's balance sheet.
17. What are the economic and accounting differences between a defined-benefit pension plan and a defined-contribution plan?
18. Under what circumstances will a firm report a pension fund asset on its balance sheet? a pension fund liability?
19. When is a derivative also a hedge? When is it not also a hedge?
20. Distinguish between a fair-value hedge and a cash-flow hedge.

21. When will a firm not show in income the periodic gain or loss caused by the change in fair value of a derivative?

EXERCISES

22. Using accounts receivable to achieve off–balance sheet financing. Cypres Appliance Store has $100,000 of accounts receivable on its books on January 2, Year 2. These receivables are due on December 31, Year 2. The firm desires to use these accounts receivables to obtain financing.
   a. Prepare journal entries during Year 2 for the transactions in parts (**i**) and (**ii**) below:
      (**i**) The firm borrows $89,286 from its bank, using the accounts receivable as collateral. The loan is repayable on December 31, Year 2, with interest at 12 percent.
      (**ii**) The firm sells the accounts receivable to the bank for $89,286. It collects amounts due from customers on these accounts and remits the cash to the bank.
   b. Compare and contrast the income statement and balance sheet effects of these two transactions.
   c. How should Cypres Appliance Store attempt to structure this transaction to ensure that it qualifies as a sale instead of a collateralized loan?
23. Using inventory to achieve off-balance sheet financing. P. J. Lorimar Company grows and ages tobacco. On January 2, Year 5, the firm has aging tobacco with a cost of $200,000 and a current market value of $300,000. P. J. Lorimar Company wants to use this tobacco to obtain financing. The firm uses a December 31 year-end.
   a. Prepare journal entries during Year 5 and Year 6 for the transactions in parts (**i**) and (**ii**) below:
      (**i**) The firm borrows $300,000 from its bank, using the tobacco inventory as collateral. The loan is repayable on December 31, Year 6, with interest at 10 percent per year compounded annually. Assume zero storage costs. The firm expects to sell the tobacco on December 31, Year 6, for $363,000.
      (**ii**) The firm sells the tobacco inventory to the bank for $300,000. It promises to sell the inventory on behalf of the bank at the end of two years and remit the proceeds to the bank.
   b. Compare and contrast the income statement and balance sheet effects of these two transactions.
   c. How should P. J. Lorimar Company attempt to structure this transaction to ensure that it qualifies as a sale instead of a collateralized loan?
24. Applying the capital lease criteria. Boeing manufactures a jet aircraft at a cost of $50 million. The usual selling price for this aircraft is $60 million, and its typical useful life is 25 years. American Airlines desires to lease this aircraft from Boeing. The parties contemplate the following alternatives for structuring the lease. Indicate whether each arrangement qualifies as an operating lease or a capital lease. Assume that all cash flows occur at the end of each year.
   a. American will lease the aircraft for 20 years at an annual rental of $6 million. At the end of 20 years, American will return the aircraft to Boeing. The interest rate appropriate to a 20-year collateralized loan for American is 10 percent.
   b. American will lease the aircraft for 15 years at an annual rental of $7.2 million. At the end of 15 years, American will return the aircraft to Boeing. The interest rate appropriate for a 15-year collateralized loan for American is 10 percent.

   c. American will lease the aircraft for 10 years at an annual rental of $5.5 million. At the end of 10 years, American has the option of returning the aircraft to Boeing or purchasing it for $55 million. The interest rate appropriate for a 10-year collateralized loan for American is 8 percent.

   d. American will lease the aircraft for 18 years at an annual rental of $6.2 million. In addition, American will pay a fee of $1,500 per hour for each hour over 5,000 hours per year that American flies the aircraft. American's average usage of its aircraft is currently 6,200 hours per year. The interest rate appropriate for an 18-year collateralized loan for American is 10 percent.

25. **Preparing lessee's journal entries for an operating lease and a capital lease.** General Motors Corporation (GM) sells a luxury minivan for $24,000. FedUp Delivery Services agrees to lease a minivan for a monthly rental of $750 for three years. FedUp Delivery Services will return the minivan to GM at the end of the lease period. GM then expects to lease the minivan to Rent-a-Wreck for the remaining two years of its useful life. The appropriate interest rate for a three-year collateralized loan for FedUp Delivery Services is 12 percent compounded monthly. Assume that FedUp Delivery Services makes all rental payments at the end of each month.

   a. Is the lease with FedUp Delivery Services an operating lease or a capital lease?

   b. Assume that this lease is an operating lease. Give the journal entries for FedUp Delivery Services at the time it signs the lease and at the end of each of the first two months of the lease period.

   c. Repeat part **b** assuming that the lease is a capital lease. FedUp Delivery Services uses the straight-line depreciation method and records depreciation monthly.

26. **Preparing lessee's journal entries for an operating lease and a capital lease.** On January 2, Year 6, Baldwin Products, as lessee, leases a machine used in its operations. The annual lease payment of $10,000 is due on December 31 of Year 6, Year 7, and Year 8. The machine reverts to the lessor at the end of three years. The lessor can either sell the machine or lease it to another firm for the remainder of its expected total useful life of five years. Baldwin Products could borrow on a three-year collateralized loan at 12 percent. The market value of the machine at the inception of the lease is $30,000.

   a. Is this lease an operating lease or a capital lease?

   b. Assume that this lease qualifies as an operating lease. Give the journal entries for Baldwin Products over the three-year lease period.

   c. Assume that this lease qualifies as a capital lease. Repeat part **b.**

   d. Compute the total expenses for the three-year period under the operating and capital lease methods.

27. **Preparing lessor's journal entries for an operating lease and a capital lease.** Sun Microsystems manufactures an engineering workstation for $7,200 and sells it for $12,000. Although the workstation has a physical life of approximately 10 years, rapid technological change limits its expected useful life to three years. Sun leases a workstation to Design Consultants for the three-year period beginning January 2, Year 2. The annual rental payments of $4,386.70 are due at the beginning of each year for that year. The interest rate appropriate for discounting cash flows is 10 percent. Sun uses a calendar year as its reporting period.

   a. Does this lease qualify as an operating lease or a capital lease?

   b. Assume that this lease qualifies as an operating lease. Give the journal entries for Sun over the three-year lease period.

   c. Repeat part **b** assuming that the lease qualifies as a capital lease.

28. Preparing journal entries for income tax expense. The income tax note to the financial statements of Ingersoll-Rand for three recent years shows the following (amounts in millions):

	Year 9	Year 10	Year 11
Components of Income Tax Expense			
Currently Payable	$110,975	$105,537	$104,615
Deferred	(43,575)	(15,537)	14,185
Total Income Tax Expense	$ 67,400	$ 90,000	$118,800

Assume that all deferred taxes relate to the use of accelerated depreciation for income tax purposes and the straight-line method for financial reporting.

a. Give the journal entry to record income tax expense for Year 9, Year 10, and Year 11.

b. Describe the likely reasons for the pattern of currently payable and deferred income taxes for each of the three years.

29. Preparing journal entries for income tax expense. The income tax note to the financial statements of L.A. Gear for three recent years reveals the following (amounts in thousands):

	Year 4	Year 5	Year 6
Components of Income Tax Expense			
Currently Payable	$37,919	$12,884	$(17,184)
Deferred	(3,555)	(3,492)	(5,543)
Total Income Tax Expense	$34,364	$ 9,392	$(22,727)

The deferred taxes relate to uncollectible accounts. Assume that L.A. Gear has only deferred tax assets, no deferred tax liabilities.

a. Give the journal entry to record income tax expense for Year 4, Year 5, and Year 6.

b. Describe the likely reasons for the pattern of currently payable and deferred income taxes for each of the three years.

30. Computations and journal entries for income taxes with both temporary and permanent differences. Sung Company reported the following amounts for book and tax purposes for its first three years of operations:

	Year 1	Year 2	Year 3
Pretax Book Income	$560,000	$500,000	$620,000
Taxable Income	600,000	450,000	560,000

The differences between book income and taxable income result from different depreciation methods. The income tax rate was 40 percent during all years.

a. Give the journal entry to record income tax expense for each year.

b. Assume for this part that the firm included $10,000 of interest on state and municipal bonds in the pretax book income amounts shown above for each year but properly excluded these amounts from taxable income. Give the journal entry to record income tax expense for each year.

31. **Deriving permanent and temporary differences from financial statement disclosures.** Beneish Company reports the following information for a year:

Book Income before Income Taxes	$159,000
Income Tax Expense	78,000
Income Taxes Payable for This Year	24,000
Income Tax Rate on Taxable Income	40 percent

The company has both permanent and temporary differences between book income and taxable income. The permanent difference relates to goodwill, and the temporary difference relates to depreciation. Assume an income tax rate at 40 percent.

a. What is the amount of temporary differences for the year? Give the amount, and indicate whether the effect is to make book income larger or smaller than taxable income.

b. What is the amount of permanent differences for the year? Give the amount, and indicate whether the effect is to make book income larger or smaller than taxable income.

32. **Effect of temporary differences on income taxes.** Woodward Corporation purchases a new machine for $50,000 on January 1, Year 1. The machine has a four-year estimated service life and an estimated salvage value of zero. After paying the cost of running and maintaining the machine, the firm enjoys a $25,000-per-year excess of revenues over expenses (except depreciation and taxes). In addition to the $25,000 from the machine, other pretax income each year is $35,000. Woodward uses straight-line depreciation for financial reporting and MACRS for tax reporting. The MACRS depreciation percentages for this machine are 33 percent in the first year, 44 percent in the second, 15 percent in the third, and 8 percent in the fourth. Depreciation is Woodward's only temporary difference. Woodward pays combined federal and local income taxes at a rate of 40 percent of taxable income.

a. Compute the amount of income taxes currently payable for each of the four years.

b. Compute the book value of the machine for financial reporting and the tax basis of the machine for tax reporting at the end of each of the four years. The tax basis is the amortized cost for income tax purposes.

c. Compute the amount of income tax expense for each of the four years.

d. Give the components of the journal entries to record income tax expense and income tax payable for Year 1 through Year 4.

33. **Reconstructing information about income taxes.** Lilly Company reports the following information about its financial statements and tax return for a year:

Depreciation Expense from Financial Statements	$322,800
Financial Statement Pretax Income	190,800
Income Tax Expense from Financial Statements	42,000
Income Taxes Payable from Tax Returns	27,600

The federal and state governments combine to tax taxable income at a rate of 40 percent. Permanent differences result from municipal bond interest that appears as revenue in the financial statements but is exempt from income taxes. Temporary differences result from the use of accelerated depreciation for tax returns and straight-line depreciation for financial reporting.

Reconstruct the income statement for financial reporting and for tax reporting for the year, identifying temporary differences and permanent differences.

34. **Interpreting hedging transaction.** Mascagni Company manufactures and sells pasta products. The cost of pasta products depends primarily on the cost of the commodities the company uses as ingredients. On January 1, Year 4, Mascagni Company had excess inventories of commodities that it had acquired at a cost of $100,000. The company can use those commodities later to produce pasta products, or it can sell the commodities now to others. To hedge against the possible decline in price of the commodities, Mascagni Company sold commodity futures, obligating the company to deliver the commodities at the end of February for a price to be received then of $120,000.

    Is this hedge a cash-flow hedge or a fair-value hedge? Explain your answer.

35. **Interpreting derivatives and hedging disclosures.** A recent report of the Daimler-Chrysler Corporation contained the following note:

    > DaimlerChrysler manages risk arising from fluctuations in interest rates and currency exchange rates by using derivative financial instruments. DaimlerChrysler manages exposure to counterparty credit risk by entering into derivative financial instruments with highly rated institutions that can be expected to fully perform under the terms of such agreements. *DaimlerChrysler does not use derivative financial instruments for trading purposes.* . . . When DaimlerChrysler sells vehicles outside the United States or purchases components from suppliers outside of the United States, transactions are frequently denominated in currencies other than U.S. dollars. Periodically, DaimlerChrysler initiates hedging activities by entering into currency exchange agreements, consisting principally of currency forward contracts and purchases options, to minimize revenue and cost variation which could result from fluctuations in currency exchange rates. These instruments, consistent with the underlying purchase or sale commitments, typically mature within three years of origination. Fees paid for purchased currency options are deferred and included in other assets. The currency exchange agreements are treated as off-balance-sheet financial instruments, with the deferred fees and related gains and losses recognized in earnings upon the settlement of the underlying transactions.

    a. What is "counterparty credit risk"?
    b. Does DaimlerChrysler acquire derivatives in order to speculate in securities markets? How can you tell?
    c. When DaimlerChrysler hedges to minimize revenue and cost variations, are these fair-value hedges or cash-flow hedges? How can you tell?
    d. What justification can you give for DaimlerChrysler's policy of deferring fees paid to acquire purchased currency options?

36. **Journal entries for hedging transactions.** Fixed Issue Company issued 9 percent, fixed-rate, semiannual coupon bonds on January 1 at par for $10 million. It simultaneously entered into an interest-rate swap with Counterparty Bank: Fixed will pay the bank at the end of each six-month period if interest rates exceed 9 percent; and the bank will pay Fixed if interest rates are below 9 percent. If the market rate is r on the date of the payment, then the bank will pay Fixed an amount equal to $1/2 \times (.09 - r) \times \$10,000,000$. The market interest rate is 9 percent at the time of issue. Interest rates decrease to 6 percent by the end of the first six-month period, increasing the market value of the bonds to $14 million and increasing the market value of the interest-rate swap by $3.8 million. By the end of the year, interest rates rise to 7 percent and the market value of the bonds decreases to $12.75 million. The market value of the interest-rate swap decreases by $1.1 million during the period from July 1 through December 31.

    a. Record journal entries for the following dates: January 1, at the time of bond issue; June 30, at the time of the first debt-service payments; and December 31, at the time of the second debt-service payments.

b. Is this a fair-value hedge or a cash-flow hedge? Has the hedge fulfilled its purpose?

37. **Journal entries for hedging transactions.** On January 1, when the interest rate is 9 percent per year, Floating Issue Company issued at par $10 million of variable-rate bonds, with semiannual interest payments based on the market interest rate at the beginning of each six-month period. It simultaneously entered into an interest-rate swap with Counterparty Bank: it agrees to pay the bank each six months the difference between 9 percent interest and any variable interest rate below 9 percent; the bank agrees to pay Floating for any difference between the variable rate and 9 percent when the variable rate exceeds 9 percent. If the market rate is r on the date of the payment, then Floating will pay the bank an amount equal to $\frac{1}{2} \times$ $(.09 - r) \times \$10,000,000$. The market interest rate is 9 percent at the time of issue. Interest rates decrease to 6 percent by the end of the first six-month period. Floating will pay interest at the rate of 9 percent for the first six-month period and at the rate of 6 percent for the second six-month period. The market value of the variable-rate bonds does not change. The market value of the interest-rate swap decreases by $3.8 million during the first six-month period. By the end of the year, interest rates rise to 7 percent. The market value of the variable-rate bonds continues not to change, but the market value of the interest-rate swap increases by $1.1 million.

   a. Record journal entries for the following dates: January 1, at the time of bond issue; June 30, at the time of the first debt-service payments; December 31, at the time of the second debt-service payments.

   b. Is this a fair-value hedge or a cash-flow hedge? Can you tell how effectively the hedge has fulfilled its purpose?

38. **Effects of leases on statement of cash flows.** Refer to the simplified statement of cash flows in Exhibit 4.16. Nine of the lines in the statement are numbered. Ignore the unnumbered lines in considering the transactions below.

   Assume that the accounting cycle is complete for the period and that a firm has prepared all of its financial statements. It then discovers that it has overlooked a transaction. It records that transaction in the accounts and corrects all of the financial statements. For each of the following transactions, indicate which of the numbered lines of the statement of cash flows change and the amount and direction (increase or decrease) of the change. Ignore income tax effects except when the problem explicitly mentions taxes.

   For the following transactions, assume that the leased asset has an economic life of 10 years, costs $100,000, and requires lease payments of $19,925 per year, payable at the end of each year.

   a. The lessor, using the operating lease method, records depreciation for the year.

   b. The lessor, using the operating lease method, records receipt of a cash payment for the year. The lessor has not previously recognized revenue.

   c. The lessee, using the operating lease method, records payment of cash for the year. The lessee has not previously recognized expense.

   d. The lessee records the signing of a capital lease. The present value of the future cash payment when discounted at 15 percent is $100,000.

   e. The lessee, using the capital lease method, records payment of cash for the first year and uses an interest rate of 15 percent per year. Interest is $15,000, and $4,925 is a payment of principal.

39. **Effects of income taxes on statement of cash flows.** Refer to the instructions in the preceding exercise. For each of the following transactions, indicate which of the

numbered lines of the statement of cash flows change and by how much. Assume an income tax rate of 40 percent of taxable income.

a. Pretax financial statement income is $200,000. Depreciation claimed on the tax return exceeds depreciation expense on the financial statements by $50,000. The firm makes an entry to record income tax expense and accrual of amounts payable because it has made no previous entry.

b. Pretax financial statement income is $300,000. Warranty deductions allowed on the tax return are less than warranty expense on the financial statements by $40,000. The firm makes an entry to record income tax expense and payment of amounts payable because it has made no previous entry for taxes.

c. Pretax financial statement income is $300,000. Bad debt expense on the financial statements exceeds deductions for bad debts allowed on the tax return by $40,000. The firm makes an entry to record income tax expense and payment of amounts payable because it has made no previous entry for taxes.

d. A firm records nontaxable municipal bond interest revenue of $10,000. It has made no previous entry for this interest. The firm records all effects of this transaction, including income tax effects (if any).

PROBLEMS AND CASES

40. Financial statement effects of operating and capital leases. The notes to the financial statements of Wal-Mart Stores for the year ending January 31, Year 9, appear below (amounts in millions).

Long-term Lease Obligations. The company and certain of its subsidiaries maintain long-term leases for stores and equipment. Aggregate minimum annual rentals at January 31, Year 9, under leases appear below. Assume that Wal-Mart makes lease payments at the end of each fiscal year.

Fiscal Year Ending January 31:	Capital Leases	Operating Leases
Year 10	$ 204.7	$ 249.3
Year 11	205.2	238.2
Year 12	204.6	229.6
Year 13	204.8	220.7
Year 14	204.7	224.1
After Year 14	2,859.7	2,409.6
Total	$3,883.7	$3,571.5
Less Interest at 11 Percent	(2,189.5)	
Capital Lease Liability	$1,694.2	

a. Prepare the journal entry to record cash payments under capital leases during fiscal Year 10.

b. Prepare the journal entry to record cash payments under operating leases during fiscal Year 10.

c. Assume that the present value of Wal-Mart's *operating* lease commitments when discounted at 12 percent is $1,586.5 million on January 31, Year 9, and that these leases have a remaining life of 15 years. Give the journal entries to convert these operating leases into capital leases as of January 31, Year 9, and to account for them as capital leases for the year ending January 31, Year 10.

41. **Financial statement effects of operating and capital leases.** The notes to the financial statements of American Airlines for a recent year reveal the following (amounts in millions):

	December 31	
	Year 10	**Year 11**
Asset—Leasehold (net of accumulated depreciation)	$1,716	$1,878
Liability—Present Value of Lease Obligation.	$2,233	$2,403

Future minimum commitments under noncancelable leases with lease periods extending beyond one year appear below.

	Capital Leases		**Operating Leases**	
Year	**December 31, Year 10**	**December 31, Year 11**	**December 31, Year 10**	**December 31, Year 11**
11	$ 268	—	$ 946	—
12	281	$ 273	924	$ 982
13	268	300	920	967
14	250	280	931	939
15	245	276	912	954
16	240	270	915	961
Later Years	2,164	2,440	14,463	16,420
	$3,716	$3,839	$20,011	$21,223
Interest Portion (8%)	(1,483)	(1,436)		
Capitalized Lease Obligation	$2,233	$2,403		

a. Assume that American Airlines makes all lease payments at the end of each year. Prepare an analysis that explains how the liability for capital leases increased from $2,233 million on December 31, Year 10, to $2,403 million on December 31, Year 11.

b. Prepare an analysis that explains how the leasehold asset increased from $1,716 million on December 31, Year 10, to $1,878 million on December 31, Year 11.

c. Give the journal entries to account for capital leases during Year 11.

d. Give the journal entries to account for operating leases during Year 11.

e. The present value at 10 percent of American's *operating* lease commitments is $7,793 million on December 31, Year 10, and $8,164 million on December 31, Year 11. The leases have an average remaining useful life of 22 years on each date. Prepare the journal entries to convert these operating leases into capital leases as of December 31, Year 10, and to account for the leases as capital leases during Year 11.

42. **Comparison of borrow/buy with operating and capital leases.** Carom Sports Collectibles Shop plans to acquire, as of January 1, Year 1, a computerized cash register system that costs $100,000 and has a five-year life and no salvage value. The company is considering two plans for acquiring the system:

(1) *Outright purchase.* To finance the purchase, the firm will issue $100,000 of par-value, 10 percent semiannual coupon bonds issued January 1, Year 1, at par. The bonds mature in five years.

(2) *Lease.* The lease requires five annual payments on December 31, Year 1, Year 2, Year 3, Year 4, and Year 5. The lease payments are such that they have a present value of $100,000 on January 1, Year 1, when discounted at 10 percent per year. The firm will use straight-line amortization methods for all depreciation and amortization computations for assets.

a. Verify that the amount of the required lease payment is $26,380 by constructing an amortization schedule for the five payments. Note that there will be a $2 rounding error in the fifth year. Nevertheless, you may treat each payment as being $26,380 in the rest of the problem.

b. What balance sheet accounts are affected if the firm selects plan **(1)?** What if the firm uses plan **(2)**, the lease is cancelable, and the firm uses the operating lease treatment? What if the firm selects plan **(2)**, the lease is noncancelable, and it uses the capital lease treatment?

c. What is the total depreciation and interest expense for the five years under plan **(1)?**

d. What is the total expense for the five years under plan **(2)** if the firm was able to account for the lease as an operating lease? as a capital lease?

e. Why are the answers in part **d** the same? Why do the answers in part **c** differ from those in part **d**?

f. What is the total expense for Year 1 under plan **(1)?** under plan **(2)** accounted for as an operating lease? under plan **(2)** accounted for as a capital lease?

g. Repeat part **f** for Year 5.

43. **Financial statement effects of capitalizing operating leases.** Selected data (in millions) for three U.S. airlines appear below.

	American	Delta	United
Long-term Debt on Balance Sheet, End of Year	$7,878	$3,121	$3,617
Shareholders' Equity (Deficit), End of Year	3,380	1,827	(267)
Net Income (Loss), for Year	228	408	77
Present Value of Operating Lease Commitments, End of Year	8,164	7,307	10,645

a. Compute the ratio of long-term debt/(long-term debt plus shareholders' equity) for the three airlines using amounts reported on the balance sheet.

b. Repeat part **a** but include the present value of operating lease commitments in long-term debt.

c. Suggest reasons why these airlines prefer to treat these leases as operating leases.

d. Suggest how these airlines might have structured their leases to qualify as operating leases.

e. Suggest reasons why airlines tend to lease rather than purchase their aircraft.

44. **Interpreting income tax disclosures.** Deere & Company manufactures agricultural and industrial equipment, which it sells through independent distributors. Deere recognizes revenue for financial reporting at the time it ships equipment to its independent distributors. It recognizes revenue for tax purposes using the installment method. Distributors have no rights to return unsold equipment, unless it is faulty. Deere rebates a portion of the selling price to distributors if they sell a certain volume of products each year. Deere also provides financing services to retail customers for Deere products sold by its independent distributors.

EXHIBIT 10.7	DEERE & COMPANY Income Tax Disclosures (Problem 44)

	Year 10	Year 11
Income before Income Taxes	$588	$ (26)
Income Tax Expense		
Current	$124	$ 95
Deferred	58	(100)
Total	$182	$ (5)
Income Taxes on Income before Income Taxes at the Statutory Tax Rate of 35%	$206	$ (9)
Tax Exempt Interest	(30)	(3)
Goodwill Amortization	6	7
Income Tax Expense (credit)	$182	$ (5)

	September 30		
	Year 9	Year 10	Year 11
COMPONENTS OF DEFERRED TAXES			
Deferred Tax Assets			
Uncollectible Accounts	$ 36	$ 44	$ 70
Sales Rebates and Allowances	22	37	58
Pensions	41	35	44
Valuation Allowance	(22)	(34)	(23)
Net Deferred Tax Assets	$ 77	$ 82	$149
Deferred Tax Liabilities			
Installment Sales Receivable	$126	$167	$127
Depreciable Assets	186	208	215
Deferred Tax Liability	$312	$375	$342

The income tax note for Deere for Year 10 and Year 11 appears in Exhibit 10.7 (amounts in millions).

a. Give the journal entry to record income tax expense for Year 10.

b. Was book income before income taxes larger or smaller than taxable income for Year 10? Explain.

c. Give the journal entry to record income tax expense for Year 11.

d. Was book income before income taxes larger or smaller than taxable income for Year 11? Explain.

e. What is the likely reason for the direction of change in the deferred asset relating to installment sales between Year 10 and Year 11?

f. Assume that the income tax rate applicable to Year 11 and future years did not change during Year 11. Depreciation expense for book purposes was $209 million during Year 11. Compute the amount of depreciation expense Deere recognized for tax purposes for Year 11.

g. What is the likely reason that the goodwill amortization item in the income tax reconciliation carries a positive sign?

| | EXHIBIT 10.8 | SUN MICROSYSTEMS
Income Tax Disclosures
(Problem 45) | | |

	Year 5	Year 6	Year 7
INCOME (LOSS) BEFORE TAXES			
Domestic	$130	$ 49	$250
International	94	235	274
	$224	$284	$524

	Year 5	Year 6	Year 7
TAXES ON INCOME			
Current —Federal	$ 38	$ 28	$123
Foreign	38	60	57
State and Local	6	4	10
Deferred—Federal	(14)	(5)	(17)
Foreign	3	(5)	(11)
State and Local	(4)	6	5
	$ 67	$ 88	$167
EFFECTIVE TAX RATE			
Federal Tax Rate	35%	35%	35%
State and Local Taxes	2	2	1
Nontaxable Interest Revenue	(3)	(2)	(1)
Foreign Tax Rates	(4)	(5)	(6)
Other	—	1	3
	30%	31%	32%

	December 31			
	Year 4	Year 5	Year 6	Year 7
COMPONENTS OF DEFERRED TAXES				
Deferred Tax Assets				
Pension	$ 68	$ 73	$ 85	$101
Inventories	74	77	89	94
Deferred Tax Assets	$142	$150	$174	$195
Deferred Tax Liabilities				
Depreciation	$ 14	$ 7	$ 27	$ 25
Deferred Tax Liabilities	$ 14	$ 7	$ 27	$ 25

45. **Interpreting income tax disclosures.** Exhibit 10.8 presents data from the income tax note for Sun Microsystems for Year 5, Year 6, and Year 7 (amounts in millions). No changes occurred in the income tax rates applicable to Years 5 through 7 or to future years.

　a. Give the journal entry to record income tax expense for Year 5. You may combine federal, foreign, state, and local taxes.

　b. Was book income before income taxes larger or smaller than taxable income for Year 5? Explain.

　c. Repeat part a for Year 6.

    d. Repeat part **b** for Year 6.

    e. Repeat part **a** for Year 7.

    f. Repeat part **b** for Year 7.

    g. What was the likely direction of change in expenditures on depreciable assets between Year 6 and Year 7? Explain.

46. **Interpreting income tax disclosures.** Refer to the income tax note for General Products Company in Exhibit 10.5 in this chapter. The income tax rate applicable to Year 1 through Year 4 and future years did not change.

    a. Was book income before income taxes larger or smaller than taxable income during Year 3? Explain.

    b. Was book income before income taxes larger or smaller than taxable income during Year 4? Explain.

    c. What is the likely interpretation of the increasing deferred tax asset for both uncollectible accounts receivable and warranty liability?

    d. By how much did depreciation claimed on the tax return for Year 4 exceed book depreciation?

47. **Behavior of deferred income tax account when a firm acquires new assets every year.** Equilibrium Company has adopted a program of purchasing a new machine each year. It uses MACRS on its income tax return and straight-line depreciation on its financial statements. Each machine costs $12,000 installed, has an economic life of six years for financial reporting, and is in the five-year property class for MACRS. MACRS deductions are 20, 32, 19, 12, 11, and 6 percent of cost in each of the first six years, respectively.

    a. Calculate the total depreciation deduction on the tax return for each of the first seven years in accordance with MACRS.

    b. Calculate depreciation for each year using the straight-line method of depreciation.

    c. Calculate the annual difference in depreciation charges using the results from parts **a** and **b**.

    d. Calculate the annual increase in the Deferred Tax Liability account for the balance sheet by multiplying the tax rate, 40 percent, by the amount found in the preceding part.

    e. Calculate year-end balances for the Deferred Tax Liability account on the balance sheet.

    f. If Equilibrium Company continues to follow its policy of buying a new machine every year for $12,000, what will happen to the balance in the Deferred Tax Liability account on the balance sheet?

48. **Attempts to achieve off-balance sheet financing.** (Adapted from materials by R. Dieter, D. Landsittel, J. Stewart, and A. Wyatt.) Shiraz Company wants to raise $50 million cash but, for various reasons, does not want to do so in a way that results in a newly recorded liability. It is sufficiently solvent and profitable that its bank is willing to lend up to $50 million at the prime interest rate. Shiraz Company's financial executives have devised six different plans, described in the following sections.

    Plan 1: Transfer of Receivables with Recourse. Shiraz Company will transfer to Credit Company its long-term accounts receivable, which call for payments over the next two years. Credit Company will pay an amount equal to the present value of the receivables less an allowance for uncollectibles as well as a discount because it is paying now but will collect cash later. Shiraz Company must repurchase from Credit Company at face value any receivables that become uncollectible in excess of the allowance. In addition, Shiraz Company may repurchase any of the receivables not yet due at face value less a discount specified by formula and based on the prime rate at the time of the initial transfer. (This option permits Shiraz Company to benefit if an unexpected drop in interest rates occurs after the transfer.) The accounting issue is whether the transfer is a sale (Shiraz Company debits Cash, credits Accounts Receivable, and debits an expense or loss on transfer) or whether the transfer is merely a loan collateralized by the receivables (Shiraz Company debits Cash and credits Notes Payable at the time of transfer).

Plan 2: Product Financing Arrangement. Shiraz Company will transfer inventory to Credit Company, who will store the inventory in a public warehouse. Credit Company may use the inventory as collateral for its own borrowings, whose proceeds will be used to pay Shiraz Company. Shiraz Company will pay storage costs and will repurchase all the inventory within the next four years at contractually fixed prices plus interest accrued for the time elapsed between the transfer and later repurchase. The accounting issue is whether Shiraz has sold the inventory to Credit Company, with later repurchases treated as new acquisitions for Shiraz's inventory, or whether Shiraz has merely borrowed from Credit Company, with the inventory remaining on Shiraz's balance sheet.

Plan 3: Throughput Contract. Shiraz Company wants a branch line of a railroad built from the main rail line to carry raw material directly to its own plant. It could, of course, borrow the funds and build the branch line itself. Instead, it will sign an agreement with the railroad to ship specified amounts of material each month for 10 years. Even if it does not ship the specified amounts of material, it will pay the agreed shipping costs. The railroad will take the contract to its bank and, using it as collateral, borrow the funds to build the branch line. The accounting issue is whether Shiraz Company should debit an asset for future rail services and credit a liability for payments to the railroad. The alternative is to make no accounting entry except when Shiraz makes payments to the railroad.

Plan 4: Construction Joint Venture. Shiraz Company and Mission Company will jointly build a plant to manufacture chemicals that both companies need in their production processes. Each will contribute $5 million to the project, called Chemical. Chemical will borrow another $40 million from a bank, with Shiraz, only, guaranteeing the debt. Shiraz and Mission are each to contribute equally to future operating expenses and debt-service payments of Chemical, but in return for guaranteeing the debt, Shiraz will have an option to purchase Mission's interest for $20 million four years later. The accounting issue is whether Shiraz Company, which will ultimately be responsible for all debt-service payments, should recognize a liability for the funds that Chemical borrowed. Alternatively, the debt guarantee is merely a commitment that Shiraz Company must disclose in notes to its financial statements.

Plan 5: Research and Development Partnership. Shiraz Company will contribute a laboratory and preliminary finding about a potentially profitable gene-splicing discovery to a partnership, called Venture. Venture will raise funds by selling the remaining interest in the partnership to outside investors for $2 million and by borrowing $48 million from a bank, with Shiraz Company guaranteeing the debt. Although Venture will operate under the management of Shiraz Company, it will be free to sell the results of its further discoveries and development efforts to anyone, including Shiraz Company. Shiraz Company has no obligation to purchase any of Venture's output. The accounting issue is whether Shiraz Company should recognize the liability. (Would it make any difference if Shiraz Company did not guarantee the loan but had either the option to purchase or an obligation to purchase the results of Venture's work?)

Plan 6: Hotel Financing. Shiraz Company owns and operates a profitable hotel. It could use the hotel as collateral for a conventional mortgage loan. Instead, it considers selling the hotel to a partnership for $50 million cash. The partnership will sell ownership interests to outside investors for $5 million and borrow $45 million from a bank on a conventional mortgage loan, using the hotel as collateral. Shiraz Company guarantees the debt. The accounting issue is whether Shiraz Company should record the liability for the guaranteed debt of the partnership.

Discuss whether Shiraz Company should recognize any of these obligations or commitments as a liability on its balance sheet.

CHAPTER 11

MARKETABLE SECURITIES

AND INVESTMENTS

1. Understand why firms acquire securities and other financial instruments.
2. Understand why firms invest in other firms and how the purpose of the investment governs the method of accounting for that investment.
3. Develop skills to apply the market value method to minority, passive investments.
4. Develop skills to apply the equity method to minority, active investments, contrasting its financial statement effects with those of the market value method.
5. Understand the concepts underlying consolidated financial statements for majority active investments, contrasting the financial statement effects of consolidation with those of the equity method.
6. Develop the necessary skills to prepare consolidated financial statements (Appendix 11.1).
7. Develop an understanding of the financial statement effects of using the purchase method and the pooling-of-interests (sometimes called *uniting-of-interests*) method to account for a corporate acquisition (Appendix 11.2).

For a variety of reasons, corporations often acquire the **marketable securities** (bonds and capital stock) of other corporations. For example, a corporation may temporarily hold excess cash that it does not need for operations. Rather than have the cash remain idle in its bank account, the corporation can acquire the bonds or capital stock of another corporation. Relatively short-term holdings of corporate securities will usually appear as "Marketable Securities" in the Current Assets section of the balance sheet. Firms often acquire other financial instruments—derivative instruments—to hedge risks or, occasionally, for speculation.

A corporation may acquire another corporation's capital stock for some long-term purpose. For example, a firm may acquire shares of common stock of a major raw materials supplier to help ensure the continued availability of raw materials. Or a firm may want to diversify its operations by acquiring a controlling interest in an established firm in some new area of business. When Hewlett-Packard announced its acquisition of Apollo

Computer, Hewlett-Packard indicated its continuing interest in Apollo's developing technology. Long-term investments in corporate securities typically appear on the asset side of the balance sheet in a separate section, "Investments." Industrial firms seldom acquire bonds of other corporations as long-term investments

TYPES OF INVESTMENTS

The accounting for investments depends on the purpose of the investment and on the percentage of voting stock that one corporation owns of another. Refer to Figure 11.1, which identifies three types of investments.

1. In **minority, passive investments,** an investor views acquiring shares of capital stock of another corporation as a worthwhile expenditure and acquires them for the dividends and capital gains (increases in the market price of the shares) anticipated from owning them. The acquiring company owns such a small percentage of the other corporation's shares that it cannot control or exert **significant influence** over the other company. Occasionally, an owner of a small percentage of the shares has the contractual right to elect one or more members of the board of directors. If so, the acquiring company, even though a small percentage holder, could exercise significant influence. Generally accepted accounting principles (GAAP) view investments of less than 20 percent of the voting stock of another company as minority, passive investments in most cases.[1] The owner may intend to hold these shares for relatively short time spans and classify them as current assets, called *marketable securities,* or for an indefinite time and classify them as investments.

2. In **minority, active investments,** an investor acquires shares of another corporation so that it can exert significant influence over the other company's activities. The investor might seek broad policy-making influence through representation on the other corporation's board of directors. Many different entities own the shares of most publicly held corporations, and most of these do not collaborate in voting their shares. Therefore, an owner can exert significant influence over another corporation with ownership of less than a majority of the voting stock. GAAP view investments of between 20 and 50 percent of the voting stock of another company as minority, active investments "unless evidence indicates that significant influence cannot be exercised."[2]

3. In **majority, active investments,** an investor acquires shares of another corporation so that it can control the other company both at the broad policy-making level and at the day-to-day operational level. Walt Disney acquired ABC/Capital Cities to add television broadcasting to its entertainment capabilities. GAAP view ownership of more than 50 percent of the voting stock of another company as implying an ability to control, unless there is evidence to the contrary.[3] Appendix 11.2 discusses the accounting for the acquisition—the distinction between purchase accounting and pooling (or uniting) of interests.

---

[1] Accounting Principles Board, *Opinion No. 18,* "The Equity Method of Accounting for Investments in Common Stock," 1971.

[2] Ibid.; Financial Accounting Standards Board, *Interpretation No. 35,* "Criteria for Applying the Equity Method of Accounting for Investments in Common Stock," 1981.

[3] As this book goes to press, the FASB is proposing to change the rules so that when a firm controls another, it will account for that investment as described for these majority investments even when it owns less than 50 percent of the shares. An investor cannot exercise control over a corporation, despite owning a majority of the voting stock, if a court effectively controls the corporation in bankruptcy proceedings or if the investor owns shares in a foreign company whose government restricts the withdrawal of assets from the country.

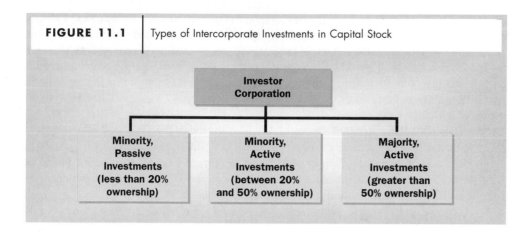

FIGURE 11.1 | Types of Intercorporate Investments in Capital Stock

Investor Corporation

- Minority, Passive Investments (less than 20% ownership)
- Minority, Active Investments (between 20% and 50% ownership)
- Majority, Active Investments (greater than 50% ownership)

Throughout our discussion of the three types of investments, we will designate the acquiring corporation as P, for purchaser or for parent, depending on the context, and the acquired corporation as S, for seller or for subsidiary.

TERMINOLOGY NOTE

Although we and others often use the phrase *short-term investment*, the preferred usage reserves the word *investment* for a holding with a long-term purpose.

MARKETABLE SECURITIES: CURRENT ASSETS

A business may find itself with more cash than it needs for current and near-term business purposes. Rather than allow cash to remain unproductive, the business may invest some of its currently excess cash in income-yielding securities, such as U.S. government bonds or stocks or bonds of other companies. Such liquid assets appear under the caption Marketable Securities in the Current Assets section of the balance sheet.

A business may also acquire securities that it intends to hold for a longer period. Accounting treats such securities as long-term Investments in Securities. This section considers the classification and valuation of securities held either as current assests (held temporarily) or as long-term investments.

CLASSIFICATION OF SECURITIES

Securities appear as Marketable Securities among current assets as long as the firm can readily convert them into cash *and* intends to do so when it needs cash, usually within one year of the date of the balance sheet. Securities that do not meet both of these criteria appear under Investments in Securities, a noncurrent asset, on the balance sheet.

Example 1 The New York Times Company invested $150,000 of temporarily excess funds in U.S. Treasury notes. The notes mature in three months. The firm includes this investment in Marketable Securities because it intends to sell the notes when it needs cash.

Example 2 The New York Times Company acquired 20-year bonds of the General Electric Company, in addition to U.S. Treasury notes. It had the same intention as in the preceding example: the investment of temporarily excess cash to earn a return. The firm includes these bonds in Marketable Securities. If the New York Times Company intends to hold these bonds to maturity, the securities will appear as long-term Investments in Securities on the balance sheet.

Example 3 IBM acquired shares of Intel on the open market. IBM plans to hold these shares as a long-term investment. Even though IBM can readily sell its shares in Intel, IBM does not include them in Marketable Securities because it does not intend to turn the securities into cash within a reasonably short period. These securities appear as long-term Investments in Securities on IBM's balance sheet.

In published financial statements, all Marketable Securities appear together on a single line on the balance sheet as a current asset. All Investments in Securities appear on a single line of the balance sheet, typically between Current Assets and Property, Plant, and Equipment. The accounting for securities depends both on the type of security (debt versus equity) and on the firm's purpose for holding the security, which later sections discuss.

VALUATION OF SECURITIES AT ACQUISITION

A firm initially records the acquisition of securities at acquisition cost, which includes the purchase price plus any commissions, taxes, and other costs incurred. For example, if a firm acquires securities classified as Marketable Securities for $10,000 plus $300 for commissions and taxes, the entry is as follows:

Marketable Securities	10,300	
Cash		10,300

Dividends on equity securities become revenue when declared. Interest on debt securities becomes revenue when earned. Assume that a firm holds equity securities earning $250 through dividend declarations and debt securities earning $300 from interest earned and that it has not yet received these amounts in cash. The entry is as follows:

Dividends and Interest Receivable	550	
Dividend Revenue		250
Interest Revenue		300

The valuation of marketable securities at the date of acquisition or the recording of dividends and interest presents no new issues. Valuing marketable securities after acquisition, however, departs from acquisition cost accounting.

VALUATION OF SECURITIES AFTER ACQUISITION

The Financial Accounting Standards Board (FASB) *Statement of Financial Accounting Standards No. 115* requires firms to classify securities into three categories:

1. Debt securities for which a firm has both the positive intent and the ability to hold to maturity—shown on the balance sheet at an amount based on acquisition cost

2. Debt and equity securities held as trading securities—shown on the balance sheet at market value, with changes in market value of securities held at the end of the accounting period reported each period in income
3. Debt and equity securities held as securities available for sale—shown on the balance sheet at market value, with changes in market value of securities held at the end of the accounting period not affecting reported income until the firm sells the securities[4]

This three-way classification resulted from one of the most contentious battles ever to occupy the attention of accounting standard-setters, including the FASB and several of its predecessor organizations. We discuss the controversy at the end of this section.

Debt Securities Held to Maturity   Firms sometimes acquire debt securities with the intention of holding these securities until maturity, as in the next example.

Example 4   Consolidated Edison, an electric utility, has $100 million of bonds payable outstanding that mature in five years. The utility acquires U.S. government securities whose periodic interest payments and maturity value exactly equal those on the utility's outstanding bonds. The firm intends to use the cash received from the government bonds to make required interest and principal payments on its own bonds.

A Practice of Corporate Finance   Some students ask why a business would use a cash fund to buy bonds and the cash throwoff from those bonds to make debt-service payments rather than directly use the cash fund to retire the bonds. After firms issue bonds, the broad investing public holds these securities. The subsequent transaction costs the firm would incur if it were to attempt to contact all of the holders and then persuade them to turn in their bonds for cash make the effort too expensive to be cost-effective. Instead the firm uses the cash to acquire other bonds whose cash throwoffs approximately match the cash needs for debt service. Corporate finance courses treat transactions such as these. Here, the presentation emphasizes the accounting for the transaction, not why the firm enters into it.

Accounting for Debt Held to Maturity   Debt securities for which a firm has a positive intent and ability to hold to maturity appear in the balance sheet at amortized acquisition cost. A firm initially records these debt securities at acquisition cost. This acquisition cost may differ from the maturity value of the debt for reasons discussed in Chapter 9. The firm must amortize any difference between acquisition cost and maturity value over the life of the debt as an adjustment to interest revenue. The amortization procedure involves the same compound interest computation that Chapter 9 introduced for the issuer of the bonds.

The holder of the debt records interest revenue each period at an amount equal to the book value of the investment in debt at the start of the period multiplied by the market rate of interest applicable to that debt on the day the firm acquired it. It credits Interest Revenue and debits the Investment account. Then, if it receives cash, it debits Cash and credits the Investment account. The result of this process is a new book value (called the *amortized cost*) for use in the computations during the next period. See Exhibit 9.7. The holder of the debt securities in those illustrations makes the same entries, with reversed debits and credits.

---

[4]Financial Accounting Standards Board, *Statement of Financial Accounting Standards No. 115,* "Accounting for Certain Investments in Debt and Equity Securities," 1993.

PROBLEM 11.1 FOR SELF-STUDY

Accounting for an interest-bearing note receivable. (Compare with Problem 9.2 for Self-Study.) General Electric Capital Services (GECS) lends $112,434 to Avner Company. GECS lends the cash of $112,434 in return for a three-year, $100,000 note, in which Avner Company promises to pay $15,000 after one year, $15,000 after two years, and $115,000 after three years. The market interest rate on the original issue date of the note is 10 percent.

a. Prepare an amortization schedule, similar to that in Exhibit 9.3, for the life of the note. Change the column headings as follows: Column (2) is Note Receivable Balance Start of Period; Column (3) is Interest Revenue for Period; Column (6) is Note Receivable Balance End of Period.

b. Prepare journal entries that GECS would make on three dates: the date of issue, six months after the date of issue (assuming GECS closes the books then), and one year after the date of issue (assuming GECS receives a cash payment from Avner then).

Trading Securities   Firms sometimes purchase and sell debt and equity securities for the short-term profit potential—some would say *for speculation*. The term *trading* implies active and frequent buying and selling with the objective of generating profits from short-term differences in market prices. Commercial banks, for example, often trade securities in different capital markets worldwide to take advantage of temporary differences in market prices. Other financial firms such as thrift institutions, insurance companies, and brokerage firms also trade securities. Manufacturers, retailers, and other nonfinancial firms occasionally invest funds for trading purposes, but such situations are unusual. Firms account for derivatives that are not hedges (see Chapter 10) the same as trading securities. Firms include trading securities in Marketable Securities in the Current Assets section of the balance sheet.

FASB *Statement No. 115* requires firms to report trading securities at *market value* on the balance sheet. The FASB justifies this departure from acquisition cost accounting on two factors: (1) active securities markets provide objective measures of market values, and (2) market values provide financial statement users with the most relevant information for assessing the success of a firm's trading activities over time.

The income statement reports the debit (loss) for decreases in the market value and the credit (gain) for increases in the market value of trading securities in the account with a title such as *Unrealized Holding Loss (or Gain or Gains and Losses, net,) on Valuation of Trading Securities.*

Example 5   First Insurance acquired shares of Sun Microsystems' common stock on December 28, Year 3, for $400,000. The market value of these securities on December 31, Year 3, was $435,000. First Insurance sold these shares on January 3, Year 4, for $480,000. The journal entries to record these transactions appear below.

December 28, Year 3

Marketable Securities	400,000	
Cash		400,000

To record acquisition of trading securities.

December 31, Year 3

Marketable Securities	35,000	
Unrealized Holding Gain on Trading Securities (IncSt)		35,000

To revalue trading securities to market value and recognize an unrealized holding gain in income. We use the designation *IncSt* to remind the reader that this account appears in income before closing to the Retained Earnings account.

January 3, Year 4

Cash	480,000	
Marketable Securities		435,000
Realized Gain on Sale of Trading Securities (IncSt)		45,000

To record the sale of trading securities at a gain. Again, the designation *IncSt* reminds the reader that this account appears in the income statement before closing to Retained Earnings.

The total income from the purchase and sale of these securities is $80,000 (equals cash inflows of $480,000 minus cash outflows of $400,000). The required accounting allocates $35,000 to Year 3, the change in market value during that year, and $45,000 to Year 4, the change in market value during that year.

Example 6 See Example **15** in Chapter 10. Linderman Company believes that the shares of FurnitureOnLine.com are about to rise dramatically in price on the NASDAQ, so it purchases options to acquire 10,000 shares of FurnitureOnLine.com. The options expire in three months. Although these options are derivatives, Linderman Company did not acquire them to hedge any of its assets or liabilities, or its cash flows. Hence, the company will report the changes in market value of these options in periodic income. They are *trading (marketable) securities,* as well as being derivatives.

Securities Available for Sale FASB *Statement No. 115* classifies securities that are neither debt securities held to maturity nor trading securities as *securities available for sale.* The FASB requires firms to report these securities at market value on the balance sheet. Securities in this category often trade in active securities markets and therefore have easily measurable market values. Firms typically acquire these securities for an operating purpose rather than for their short-term profit potential. Securities that a firm intends to sell within one year appear in Marketable Securities in the Current Assets section of the balance sheet. All others appear in Investments in Securities.

Example 7 JCPenney receives $2.5 million from customers during the Christmas holiday season. The firm will use a large portion of this figure to pay amounts due to employees and suppliers in early January. JCPenney acquires $2.5 million of U.S. Treasury notes on December 26 with the intention of selling them early in January. These securities appear in Marketable Securities as a security available for sale.

Example 8 Hewlett-Packard Company has ¥100 million of Japanese-yen bonds payable outstanding that mature in four years. To protect against exchange-rate changes, the Company invests in four-year Japanese corporate bonds with a maturity value of ¥100 million. The firm plans to use the proceeds from the corporate bonds to repay its own bonds. Hewlett-Packard would sell the corporate bonds, however, if the credit standing of the issuer deteriorated or if interest rates changed in a manner that made it attractive for Hewlett-Packard to retire its bonds before maturity. Because market interest rates prior to maturity might affect Hewlett-Packard's decision to hold the corporate bonds until maturity, these bonds fall in the category of securities available for sale, not debt held to maturity. These bonds appear in Investments in Securities on the balance sheet.

Example 9 Nike, an athletic footwear company, has temporarily excess cash and acquires common stock of Merck, a pharmaceutical company. Nike intends to sell the shares within the next eight months. These securities appear in Marketable Securities as a security available for sale.

Example 10 Boise Cascade, a forest products company, acquires common stock of the *Washington Post* to develop a long-term relation with this major customer for its newsprint products. These securities appear in Investments in Securities as a security available for sale.

FASB *Statement No. 115* requires firms to report securities available for sale at market value on the balance sheet. *The unrealized holding gain or holding loss each period does not affect income immediately, as is the case with trading securities, but instead increases or decreases a separate shareholders' equity account and appears in comprehensive income,* discussed in Chapter 12. Holding gains and losses on securities available for sale affect net income only when the firm sells these securities. The FASB's reasoning for delaying the recognition of holding gains and losses in earnings is that firms do not acquire securities classified as available for sale for the short-term returns, as with trading securities, but for support of an operating activity. Also, including unrealized gains and losses in earnings might result in significant earnings changes that could easily reverse during future periods.

Example 11 Refer to Example 9. Nike acquires the common stock of Merck for $400,000 on November 1, Year 3. The market value of these shares is $435,000 on December 31, Year 3. Nike sells these shares on August 15, Year 4, for $480,000. The journal entries to record these transactions are as follows:

November 1, Year 3		
Marketable Securities	400,000	
Cash		400,000
To record acquisition of securities available for sale.		
December 31, Year 3		
Marketable Securities	35,000	
Unrealized Holding Gain on Securities Available for Sale		
(SE/CompY)		35,000
To revalue securities available for sale to market value and record an unrealized gain. We show the designation *SE/CompY* to emphasize that this account appears directly in the Shareholders' Equity section and in comprehensive income, but not in net income.		

TERMINOLOGY NOTE

Economists use the letter *Y*, almost always capitalized, to represent income, in part because the letter *I* sometimes represents interest and sometimes, investment. We use this convention in abbreviating comprehensive income as *CompY.*

August 15, Year 4

Cash	480,000	
Marketable Securities		400,000
Realized Gain on Sale of Securities Available for Sale (IncSt)		80,000

To record the sale of securities available for sale at a gain based on original cost. The designation *IncSt* reminds the reader that this account appears in income before closing to the Retained Earnings account.

The total income from the purchase and sale of these securities is $80,000 (equals cash inflow of $480,000 minus cash outflow of $400,000). The required accounting allocates the full gain to the year of sale, even though the balance sheet reports changes in market value of the assets as they occur. At the time of sale, or later in the period when the firm makes adjusting entries, it must make the following entry:

August 15, Year 4 (or later, at time of adjusting entries)

Unrealized Holding Gain on Securities Available for Sale (SE/CompY)	35,000	
Marketable Securities		35,000

To eliminate the previously recorded effects of changes in market values of securities available for sale.

The credit in this entry reduces the asset valuation: the firm no longer holds the security, so the accounting must remove from the balance sheet not only the asset's original cost—as in the first August 15 entry above—but also the increases in market value included in the asset's valuation. The debit removes the unrealized gain from shareholders' equity. Total shareholders' equity has increased by $80,000 while this firm held the securities, and the Gain on Sale account shows all that gain, which will increase Retained Earnings after closing entries.

We can summarize the effects as follows:

- In the year of purchase, asset valuation and shareholders' equity both increased by $35,000 from the increase in market value, but the increase has no effect on income or Retained Earnings.

- In the next year, asset valuation and shareholders' equity increased another $45,000. Retained Earnings increases by $80,000—the full gain on holding the securities. The shareholders' equity account for Unrealized Gain must decrease by $35,000 (= $80,000 − $45,000), just equal to the amounts of the market gain increase that the firm recorded in periods before the firm sold the security and realized the gain.

Summary of Accounting for Marketable Securities Available for Sale
The accounting for marketable securities available for sale involves three transactions or events.

1. Acquisition of Marketable Securities

Marketable Securities	Acquisition Cost	
Cash		Acquisition Cost

---

2. Revaluation to Market Value at End of Each Accounting Period

---

Marketable Securities . . . .   Increase in Market Value
                                       above Book Value

     Unrealized Holding Gain on Securities
         Available for Sale (SE/CompY) . . . .   Increase in Market Value
                                                   above Book Value

Unrealized Holding Loss on Securities
     Available for Sale (SE/CompY) . . . .   Decrease in Market Value
                                               below Book Value

     Marketable Securities . . . .   Decrease in Market Value
                                                     below Book Value

---

The unrealized holding gain and loss accounts are shareholders' equity accounts, not income statement accounts. The accountant can make separate entries for each security held or a single, combined entry for the portfolio of securities.

3. Sale of Marketable Securities

Cash . . . .   Proceeds of Sale

     Marketable Securities . . . .   Acquisition Cost

     Realized Gain on Sale of Securities
         Available for Sale (IncSt) . . . .   Plug Amount

Securities sold for amount larger than acquisition cost.

Cash . . . .   Proceeds of Sale

Realized Loss on Sale of Securities Available
     for Sale (IncSt) . . . .   Plug Amount

     Marketable Securities . . . .   Acquisition Cost

Securities sold for amount smaller than acquisition cost.

The realized gain or loss accounts appear in the income statement before closing to Retained Earnings. Once the firm has sold the securities, it no longer has an unrealized gain or loss from holding these securities. The final step in the accounting eliminates from the balance sheet the recording of the unrealized holding gain or loss. The next entry eliminates the difference between the book value of the securities sold and their original acquisition cost.

Unrealized Holding Gain on Securities
     Available for Sale (SE/CompY) . . . .   Excess of Book Value over
                                                 Acquisition Cost

     Marketable Securities . . . .   Excess of Book Value
                                                 over Acquisition Cost

---

These securities had risen in value between the time of acquisition and the time of sale. The firm had recorded an unrealized holding gain and an increase in the value of the securities. Now it eliminates both the unrealized holding gain and the marketable securities themselves.

When the firm sells securities, it records the gain (or loss) as the difference between sales price and original cost. It reduces the carrying amount of Marketable Securities by the amount of original cost in the entry recognizing the gain (or loss). The above entry reduces the carrying amount of Marketable Securities for the increases recorded since acquisition. After this entry, the balance in the Marketable Securities account for the securities sold is zero because the firm no longer holds these specific securities. The accountant can make this entry at the time of sale of an individual security or at the end of the period as part of the revaluation of the portfolio of securities.

If the firm had recorded unrealized holding losses on the securities before it sold them, the final entry, made at time of sale or the end of the period, would be:

Marketable Securities	Excess of Acquisition Cost over Book Value

Unrealized Holding Loss on
    Securities Available
    For Sale (SE/CompY)	

	Excess of Acquisition Cost over Book Value

When the firm sells securities, it records the loss as the difference between sales price and original cost. It reduces the carrying amount of Marketable Securities by the amount of original cost in the entry recognizing the loss, which creates a credit balance in the Marketable Securities account for the security sold. This entry restores the balance in that account to zero. The accountant can make this entry at the time of sale of an individual security or at the end of the period as part of the revaluation of the portfolio of securities.

PROBLEM 11.2 FOR SELF-STUDY

Accounting for securities available for sale. Transactions involving Conlin Corporation's marketable securities available for sale appear in Exhibit 11.1.

a. Give the journal entries to account for these securities during Year 2 and Year 3.

b. How would the journal entries in part **a** differ if Conlin Corporation classified these securities as trading securities?

EXHIBIT 11.1	CONLIN CORPORATION (Problem 11.2 for Self-Study)

					Market Value	
Security	**Date Acquired**	**Acquisition Cost**	**Date Sold**	**Selling Price**	**Dec. 31, Year 2**	**Dec. 31, Year 3**
A	2/3/Year 2	$ 40,000	—	—	$ 38,000	$ 33,000
B	7/15/Year 2	75,000	9/6/Year 3	$78,000	79,000	—
C	11/27/Year 2	90,000	—	—	93,000	94,000
		$205,000			$210,000	$127,000

RECLASSIFICATION OF SECURITIES

The firm's purpose for holding certain securities may change, requiring it to transfer securities from one of the three categories to another one. The firm transfers the security at its market value at the time of the transfer. FASB *Statement No. 115* prescribes the accounting for any unrealized gain or loss at the time of the transfer, a topic discussed in intermediate accounting principles textbooks.

DISCLOSURES ABOUT SECURITIES

FASB *Statement No. 115* requires the following disclosures each period:

1. The aggregate market value, gross unrealized holding gains, gross unrealized holding losses, and amortized cost for debt securities held to maturity and debt and equity securities available for sale
2. The proceeds from sales of securities available for sale and the gross realized gains and gross realized losses on those sales
3. The change during the period in the net unrealized holding gain or loss on securities available for sale included in a separate shareholders' equity account
4. The change during the period in the net unrealized holding gain or loss on trading securities included in earnings

In addition, firms often show the gross gains and gross losses included in earnings from transfers of securities from the available-for-sale category. Exhibit 11.2, expanded from Exhibit 6.4, illustrates these disclosures.

CONTROVERSY SURROUNDING THE ACCOUNTING FOR MARKETABLE SECURITIES

The accounting for marketable securities has been controversial. We try to give the flavor of the controversy without the details. The accounting issues are as follows:

- Whether to report these instruments at historical cost (or some method based on historical cost) or at market value on the balance sheet date
- If reported at market value, whether to report the changes in market value from period to period as part of that period's income or await the period when the firm sells or otherwise disposes of the instrument to record the gain or loss in income

Nonfinancial Firms For nonfinancial firms, the primary controversy surrounds the treatment of the financial derivatives that these firms use in reducing, that is, *hedging,* their risks of exposure to fluctuations in interest rates or in prices of raw materials that the firm will need to acquire later. Chapter 10 discussed the accounting treatment for such cash-flow hedges. Before the FASB *Statement of Financial Accounting Standards No. 133,* "Accounting for Derivative Instruments and Hedging Activities," in 1998, nonfinancial firms engaging in cash-flow hedges of anticipated transactions feared that the FASB would require them to show the gains and losses in income each period. The FASB had proposed such treatment; however, under pressure from nonfinancial firms, it ruled that such gains and losses need not appear in net income but only in comprehensive income, until subsequent events unfolded.

EXHIBIT 11.2	ALEXIS COMPANY Detailed Illustration of Current Assets Balance Sheet (Excerpts) June 30, Year 1 and Year 2

		June 30, Year 1	June 30, Year 2
Current Assets			
Cash in Change and Petty Cash Funds		$ 800	$ 1,000
Cash in Bank		11,000	13,000
Cash Held as Compensating Balances		1,500	1,500
Certificates of Deposit		7,500	8,000
Marketable Securities at Market Value (see Note A)		25,000	27,000
Notes Receivable (see Note B)		10,000	12,000
Interest and Dividends Receivable		400	500
Accounts Receivable, Gross	$57,200		$58,100
Less Allowance for Uncollectible Accounts	(3,500)		(3,600)
Accounts Receivable, Net		53,700	54,500
Merchandise Inventory[a]		67,000	72,00
Prepayments		4,300	4,800
Total Current Assets		$181,200	$194,300

Note A. Gross unrealized holding gains and gross unrealized holding losses on Marketable Securities are as follows:

	June 30, Year 1	June 30, Year 2
Gross Unrealized Holding Gains	$ 7,000	$ 7,000
Gross Unrealized Holding Losses	(1,000)	(10,000)
Net Unrealized Holding Gain (Loss)	$ 6,000	($ 3,000)

The net unrealized holding gain (loss) changed during the year as follows:

Net Unrealized Holding Gain, June 30, Year 1	$ 6,000
Unrealized Holding Gain on Securities Sold	1,000
Unrealized Holding Loss for Year Ending June 30, Year 2	(10,000)
Net Unrealized Holding Loss, June 30, Year 2	($ 3,000)

Note B. The amount shown for Notes Receivable does not include notes with a face amount of $2,000 that have been discounted with recourse at The First National Bank. The company is contingently liable for these notes, should the makers not honor them at maturity. The estimated amount of the company's liability is zero.

[a]Additional required disclosures for this item do not appear here. See Chapter 7.

Before 1993, firms reported on their portfolios of securities as a whole and reported the amount for the entire portfolio on the balance sheet at the lower of cost or market. This enabled firms to hide (or at least not disclose) the losses on some of their holdings if gains on other holdings offset those losses. In addition, firms had some ability to *gains trade,* that is, to sell securities that had appreciated in value since acquisition, reporting that gain in net income, while not reporting some of the unrealized holding losses on securities remaining in the portfolio. FASB *Statement No. 115* removed much of the opportunity for offsetting losses against gains and for gains trading. Managements of firms benefiting from the old rules resisted the enactment of the new ones. Most analysts believe that the current rules lead to higher-quality measures of financial position because the balance sheet reports marketable securities at current market values.

Financial Firms Financial firms have more concern with balance sheet effects of changes in market value of financial instruments than with income statement effects. The increased concern results from financial firms' having higher, usually much higher, debt/equity ratios than do nonfinancial firms and from the attention that regulators pay to this ratio. To understand how the accounting interacts with the regulations to make financial firms, particularly banks, sensitive to market value accounting, refer to Problem **56** at the end of this chapter.

MINORITY, PASSIVE INVESTMENTS

When a firm owns 50 percent or less of another firm's shares, the owning firm has a minority investment. When the firm does not, or cannot, influence the operations and financial decisions of the owned company, the investment is passive. GAAP presume that when the investor owns less than 20 percent of the shares, the investor has a passive investment. The facts of a particular case may indicate that an investor, even though owning less than 20 percent, has an active (that is, nonpassive) purpose in owning the shares. On the other hand, an investor can own 20 percent or more and still have a passive purpose (1) because, for example, the investor has agreed with the Justice Department not to vote its shares or (2) because, perhaps, another investor owns more than 50 percent of the shares and makes all important decisions.

Thus the facts of the particular case, not the presumption of GAAP, determine the accounting. The owner of a passive minority investment must account for the investment using the **market value method,** described earlier in this chapter. These securities are typically *securities available for sale,* not *trading securities.* The following summarizes the accounting, under the market value method, for passive investments:

1. The investor records the initial investment at acquisition cost, including costs of acquisition, such as brokerage fees and commissions. The investor uses the account title Investment in Securities account, not Marketable Securities, to designate the long-term purpose of the investment.
2. The investor records dividends declared by the owned firm as dividend revenue. (Some investors will not make an entry until they receive the dividends, but this is an expedient, not the proper accrual accounting treatment.)
3. At the end of each period, the investor adjusts the book value of each investment to its market value. The offsetting debit or credit is to an Unrealized Holding Loss or Unrealized Holding Gain on Investments in Securities account. This account appears in comprehensive income, not net income, and in the Shareholders' Equity section of the balance sheet, typically between Additional Paid-in Capital and Retained Earnings.
4. When the investor sells a particular investment, it recognizes the difference between the selling price and the acquisition cost of the investment as a realized gain or loss in calculating net income. Either at the time of sale or at the end of the period, the firm eliminates the balance in the Unrealized Holding Loss account related to these securities. Thus, the net effect of all changes in market value between the time a firm acquires an investment and the time it later sells that investment appears in net income in the period of sale.

EXHIBIT 11.3	INVESTOR CORPORATION (Problem 11.3 for Self-Study)

Security	Date Acquired	Acquisition Cost	Date Sold	Selling Price	Market Value Dec. 31, Year 2	Market Value Dec. 31, Year 3
A	1/10/Year 1	$ 60,000			$ 63,000	$65,000
B	3/20/Year 1	80,000	6/19/Year 2	$65,000	72,000	—
C	10/2/Year 1	40,000			42,000	33,000
		$180,000			$177,000	$98,000

P R O B L E M   1 1 . 3   F O R   S E L F - S T U D Y

Journal entries to apply the market value method for long-term investments in securities. Exhibit 11.3 summarizes data about Investor Corporation's minority, passive investments in securities for its first two years of operations.

Investor Corporation received dividends of $2,000 on December 31, Year 1, and $2,200 on December 31, Year 2, from Security A. Neither Security B or Security C declared or paid dividends.

Prepare journal entries for the following:

a. Record the acquisitions of the three securities during Year 1.
b. Record the dividend received from Security A on December 31, Year 1.
c. Apply the market value method on December 31, Year 1.
d. Record the sale of Security B on June 19, Year 2.
e. Record the dividend received from Security A on December 31, Year 2.
f. Apply the market value method on December 31, Year 2.

MINORITY, ACTIVE INVESTMENTS

When an investor owns less than a majority of the voting stock of another corporation, the accountant must judge when the investor can exert significant influence. For the sake of uniformity, GAAP presume that one company can significantly influence another company when the investor company owns 20 percent or more of the voting stock of the other company. An investor can exert significant influence even when owning less than 20 percent, but then its management must convince the independent accountants that the company can do so. Analysts become suspicious when they see an investor changing its ownership from just below 20 percent to just above, or vice versa. They suspect that the investor is trying to manipulate earnings by changing its accounting techniques to suit the circumstances.

Minority, active investments, generally those where the investor owns between 20 and 50 percent, require the **equity method** of accounting. Under the equity method, the investor firm recognizes as revenue (expense) each period its share of the net income (loss) of the other firm. The investor does not recognize dividends received from S as income but as a return of investment. In the discussion that follows, we designate the investor firm as P and the firm whose shares it owns as S.

EQUITY METHOD: RATIONALE

To understand why GAAP require the equity method for minority, active investments, review the financial statement effects of using the market value method for such investments. Under the market value method for securities available for sale, P recognizes income statement effects only when it receives a dividend (revenue) or sells some of the investment (gain or loss). Suppose, as often happens, that S follows a policy of financing its own growing operations through retaining earnings, consistently declaring dividends less than its net income. The market price of S's shares will probably increase to reflect this retention of assets. Under the market value method, P reports income only from the dividends it receives. Because P, by assumption, exerts significant influence over S, it can affect S's dividend policy, which in turn affects P's income. When P can so easily manipulate its own income (via dividends from S), the market value method will not reasonably reflect P's earnings from investing in S. The equity method better measures a firm's earnings from its investment when, because of its ownership interest, it can exert significant influence over the operations and dividend policy of the investee firm.

EQUITY METHOD: PROCEDURES

The equity method records the initial purchase of an investment at acquisition cost, just as is done under the market value method. Each period, Company P treats as revenue its proportionate share of the periodic earnings, not the dividends, of Company S. Company P treats dividends declared by S as a reduction in P's Investment in S account.

Suppose that P acquires 30 percent of the outstanding shares of S for $600,000. The entry to record the acquisition is as follows:

(1) Investment in Stock of S	600,000	
Cash		600,000
Investment made in 30 percent of Company S.		

Between the time of the acquisition and the end of P's next accounting period, S reports income of $80,000. P, using the equity method, records the following:

(2) Investment in Stock of S	24,000	
Equity in Earnings of Affiliate		24,000
To record 30 percent of income earned by investee, accounted for using the equity method.		

The account Equity in Earnings of Affiliate is a revenue account. If S declares and pays a dividend of $30,000 to holders of common stock, P receives $9,000 and records the following:

(3) Cash	9,000	
Investment in Stock of S		9,000
To record dividends received from investee, accounted for using the equity method, and the resulting reduction in the Investment account.		

Notice the credit to the Investment in S account. P records income earned by S as an increase in investment. The dividend returns part of the investment and decreases the Investment account.

Hint: students often have difficulty understanding journal entry **(3)**, particularly the credit by the investor when the investee company pays a dividend. The transactions and entries resemble those for an individual's ordinary savings account at a local bank. Assume that you put $600,000 in a savings account, that later the bank adds interest of 4 percent (or $24,000) to the account, and that still later you withdraw $9,000 from the savings account. You can record journal entries **(1)** through **(3)** for these three events, with slight changes in the account titles: Investment in S changes to Savings Account, and Equity in Earnings of Affiliate changes to Interest Revenue. The cash withdrawal reduces the amount invested in the savings account. Similarly, the payment of a cash dividend by an investee company accounted for with the equity method reduces the investor's investment in the company. The investor, Company P, owns a sufficiently large percentage of the voting shares that it can "require" Company S to pay a dividend, just as you can require the savings bank to remit cash to you almost whenever you choose.

Suppose that S subsequently reports earnings of $100,000 and also pays dividends of $40,000. P's entries are as follows:

(4) Investment in Stock of S	30,000	
Equity in Earnings of Affiliate		30,000
(5) Cash	12,000	
Investment in Stock of S		12,000
To record revenue and dividends from investee, accounted for using the equity method.		

P's Investment in S account now has a balance of $633,000 as follows:

Investment in Stock of S

(1)	600,000	9,000	**(3)**	
(2)	24,000	12,000	**(5)**	
(4)	30,000			
Bal.	633,000			

If P now sells one-fourth of its shares for $165,000, P's entry to record the sale is as follows:

Cash	165,000	
Investment in Stock of S		158,250
Gain on Sale of Investment in S		6,750
Cost of investments sold is $158,250 = 1/4 × $633,000.		

Goodwill on Acquisition of Equity Method Investment One complication arises when P pays more for its investment than its proportion of the book value of the net assets (= assets − liabilities), or shareholders' equity, of S at the date of acquisition. For example, assume that P acquires 25 percent of the stock of S for $400,000 when S has total shareholders' equity of $1 million. P's cost exceeds book value acquired by $150,000 [= $400,000 − (.25 × $1,000,000)]. The equity method requires the amortization of this excess acquisition cost over a period that has not been allowed to exceed 40 years. By the time you read this, the FASB is likely to have changed that maximum.[5] P records amortization expense each year of $7,500 (= $150,000/20) if it uses a 20-year life. The journal entry is as follows:

Amortization Expense	7,500	
Investment in Stock of S		7,500
To record amortization of excess acquisition cost over 20 years.		

At the end of the amortization period, the amount in the Investment in S account will equal P's proportionate interest in the book value of the net assets of S.

Summary of Equity Method   On the balance sheet, an investment accounted for with the equity method appears in the Investments section. The amount shown generally equals the acquisition cost of the shares plus P's share of S's undistributed earnings since the date P acquired the shares. On the income statement, P shows its share of S's income as a revenue each period. The accounting method used by the investor, P, does not affect the financial statements of the investee, S.

PROBLEM 11.4 FOR SELF-STUDY

Journal entries to apply the equity method for long-term investments in securities.   Exhibit 11.4 summarizes data about the minority, active investments of Equity Investing Group.

Equity Investing Group amortizes any excess acquisition cost over 10 years. Prepare the journal entries to do the following:

a. Record the acquisition of these securities on January 1, Year 1.
b. Apply the equity method for Year 1.
c. Apply the equity method for Year 2.
d. Record the sale of Security E on January 2, Year 3, for $190,000.

MAJORITY, ACTIVE INVESTMENTS

When one firm, P, owns more than 50 percent of the voting stock of another company such as S, P can control the activities of S. P can control both broad policy-making and day-to-day operations. Common usage refers to the majority investor as the **parent** and to the majority-owned company as the **subsidiary.** GAAP require the parent to combine the financial statements of majority-owned companies with those of the parent, in **consolidated financial statements.**[6]

---

[5]Accounting Principles Board, *Opinion No. 17,* "Intangible Assets," 1970. As this book goes to press, the FASB is proposing to reduce the amortization period to 20 years.

[6]Financial Accounting Standards Board, *Statement of Financial Accounting Standards No. 94,* "Consolidation of All Majority-Owned Subsidiaries," 1987. As this book goes to press, the FASB is proposing to require this consolidation treatment whenever the parent controls the subsidiary, independent of the percentage ownership.

				Book Value of	Earnings (Loss)		Dividends	
Security	Date Acquired	Acquisition Cost	Ownership Percentage	Net Assets on January 1, Year 1	Year 1	Year 2	Year 1	Year 2
D	1/1/Year 1	$ 80,000	40%	$200,000	$ 40,000	$ 50,000	$10,000	$12,000
E	1/1/Year 1	190,000	30	500,000	120,000	(40,000)	30,000	—
F	1/1/Year 1	200,000	20	800,000	200,000	50,000	60,000	60,000

EXHIBIT 11.4 — EQUITY INVESTING GROUP (Problem 11.4 for Self-Study)

REASONS FOR LEGALLY SEPARATE CORPORATIONS

Business firms have several reasons for preferring to operate as a group of legally separate corporations rather than as a single entity. From the standpoint of the parent company, the more important reasons for maintaining legally separate subsidiary companies include the following:

1. To reduce the parent's risk. Separate corporations may mine raw materials, transport them to a manufacturing plant, produce the product, and sell the finished product to the public. If any one part of the total process proves to be unprofitable or inefficient, losses from insolvency will fall only on the owners and creditors of the one subsidiary corporation. (Some drug firms acquire subsidiaries to make and market medical products in the hope that if something goes wrong in future years, the parent firm will not be liable for losses of the customers of the subsidiary. Individuals who believe the subsidiary's products have harmed them often sue the parent and sometimes succeed in "piercing the corporate veil.")
2. To meet more effectively the requirements of state corporation laws and tax legislation. If an organization does business in a number of states, it often faces overlapping and inconsistent taxation, regulations, and requirements. Organizing separate corporations to conduct operations in the various states can sometimes reduce administrative costs.
3. To expand or diversify with a minimum of capital investment. A firm may absorb another company by acquiring a controlling interest in its voting stock. (When Silicon Graphics first proposed to acquire Cray Computer, it suggested it would acquire a majority, but not all, of the shares in order to reduce the cost of acquiring control.) The firm may accomplish this result with a substantially smaller capital investment, as well as with less difficulty, inconvenience, and risk, than if it constructs a new plant or starts a new line of business. (General Mills' acquisitions of Eddie Bauer and Kenner Toys appear to have had these motives.)
4. To sell an unwanted operation with a minimum of administrative, legal, and other costs. Firms generally save costs if they sell the common stock of a subsidiary rather than trying to sell each of its assets and transfer all known and, perhaps, unknown liabilities to a buyer.

PURPOSE OF CONSOLIDATED STATEMENTS

For a variety of reasons, then, a single economic entity may exist in the form of a parent and several legally separate subsidiaries. (General Electric Company, for example, comprises about 150 legally separate companies.) A consolidation of the financial statements of the parent and each of its subsidiaries presents the results of operations, financial position, and cash flows of an affiliated group of companies under the control of a parent as if the group of companies composed a single entity. The parent and each subsidiary are legally separate entities, but they operate as one centrally controlled **economic entity.** Consolidated financial statements generally provide more useful information to the shareholders of the parent corporation than do separate financial statements for the parent and each subsidiary.

Consolidated financial statements also generally provide more helpful information than does the equity method. The parent, because of its voting interest, can effectively control the use of all of the subsidiary's assets. Consolidation of the individual assets, liabilities, revenues, and expenses of both the parent and the subsidiary provides a more realistic picture of the operations and financial position of the single economic entity.

In a legal sense, consolidated statements merely supplement, and do not replace, the separate statements of the individual corporations, although common practice presents only the consolidated statements in published annual reports.

Example 12 General Motors, General Electric, and IBM, among others, have wholly-owned finance subsidiaries. These subsidiaries make a portion of their loans to customers who want to purchase the products of the parent company. The parent company consolidates the financial statements of these subsidiaries. These subsidiaries have billions of dollars of assets, mostly receivables. Statement readers may misunderstand the relative liquidity of firms preparing consolidated statements, which combine the parent's assets—largely noncurrent manufacturing plant and equipment—with the more liquid assets of the finance subsidiary. This suggests preparing separate statements for the manufacturing parent and for the financial subsidiary. The counterargument suggests that these entities operate as a single integrated unit, so that consolidated financial statements more accurately depict the nature of their operating relations. For many years, General Electric has shown the separate financial statements of its finance subsidiaries in addition to the consolidated statements.

Example 13 A major mining corporation owns a mining subsidiary in South America. The government of the country enforces stringent control over cash payments outside the country. The company cannot control the use of all the assets, despite owning a majority of the voting shares. Therefore, it does not prepare consolidated statements with the subsidiary. The parent company will probably carry the investment on its books at cost.

DISCLOSURE OF CONSOLIDATION POLICY

The summary of significant accounting principles, a required part of the financial statement notes, must include a statement about the **consolidation policy** of the parent. If an investor does not consolidate a significant majority-owned subsidiary, the notes will disclose that fact. A recent annual report of American Home Products Corporation contained the following (bracketed remarks do not appear in the original):

Notes to Consolidated Financial Statements

1. *Summary of Significant Accounting Policies:* . . . Principles of Consolidation: The accompanying consolidated financial statements include the accounts of the Company and its subsidiaries with the exception of those subsidiaries described in Note 3 which are accounted for on a cash basis. . . .

3. *Provision for Impairment of Investment in Certain Foreign Locations:* [During the preceding year], the Corporation recorded a charge of $50,000,000 recognizing the impairment of its investment in its subsidiaries in South America, except for its investment in Brazil. The provision was made after determining that the continued imposition of constraints such as

dividend restrictions, exchange controls, price controls, and import restrictions in these countries so severely impede management's control of the economic performance of the businesses that continued inclusion of these subsidiaries in the consolidated financial statements is inappropriate. The Company is continuing to operate these businesses, which for the most part are self-sufficient; however, the investments have been deconsolidated and earnings are recorded on a cash [similar to the market value method] basis. Net sales from these operations aggregated $97,790,000, $95,084,000, and $100,045,000 [in the last three years]. . . . Net income included in the consolidated statements of income was approximately $2,200,000 . . . and $2,000,000 [for the last two years].

UNDERSTANDING CONSOLIDATED STATEMENTS

This section discusses three concepts essential for understanding consolidated financial statements:

1. The need for intercompany eliminations
2. The meaning of consolidated net income
3. The nature of the external minority interest

We illustrate the concepts for understanding consolidated statements with the data in Exhibit 11.5 for Company P and Company S.

- Column (1) shows the balance sheet and income statement for Company P.
- Column (2) shows the balance sheet and income statement for Company S.
- Column (3) sums the amounts from columns (1) and (2), but these amounts do not represent the correct amounts for the consolidated statements.
- Column (4) presents the correct consolidated financial statements.

The following discussion explains why the correct amounts in column (4) differ from the sums in column (3).

Appendix 11.1 presents the accounting procedures for deriving the consolidated financial statements from the information about Company P and Company S. You can refer to Exhibit 11.9 now and as you read the next several pages, although you will be able to understand the nature of consolidated financial statements without mastering Appendix 11.1. Here, as elsewhere in this book, mastering the accounting procedures will cement your understanding of the statements derived with them.

Need for Intercompany Eliminations State corporation laws typically require each legally separate corporation to maintain its own accounting records. Thus, during the accounting period, each corporation will record transactions of that entity with all other entities (both affiliated and nonaffiliated). At the end of the period, each corporation will prepare its own financial statements. The consolidation, or combining, of these financial statements basically involves summing the amounts for various financial statement items across the separate company statements. The accountant must adjust the amounts resulting from the summation, however, to eliminate double-counting resulting from **intercompany transactions.**

The guiding principle is that consolidated financial statements will reflect the results that the affiliated group would report if it were a single company. Consolidated financial statements reflect the transactions between the consolidated group of entities and others outside the entity. Thus, to take a simple example, if one affiliate company sells goods to another, the consolidation must remove from the financial statements the effects of this intercompany transaction.

EXHIBIT 11.5	Illustrative Data for Preparation of Consolidated Financial Statements

| | Single-Company Statements | | | Consolidated (See Exhibit 11.9) |
	Company P (1)	Company S (2)	Combined (3) = (1) + (2)	(4)
CONDENSED BALANCE SHEETS ON DECEMBER 31, YEAR 4				
Assets				
Accounts Receivable	$ 200,000	$ 25,000	$ 225,000	$ 213,000
Investment in Stock of Company S (using equity method)	705,000	—	705,000	—
Other Assets	2,150,000	975,000	3,125,000	3,125,000
Total Assets	$3,055,000	$1,000,000	$4,055,000	$3,338,000
Equities				
Accounts Payable	$ 75,000	$ 15,000	$ 90,000	$ 78,000
Other Liabilities	70,000	280,000	350,000	350,000
Common Stock	2,500,000	500,000	3,000,000	2,500,000
Retained Earnings	410,000	205,000	615,000	410,000
Total Equities	$3,055,000	$1,000,000	$4,055,000	$3,338,000
CONDENSED INCOME STATEMENTS FOR YEAR 4				
Revenues				
Sales	$ 900,000	$ 250,000	$1,150,000	$1,110,000
Equity in Earnings of Company S	48,000	—	48,000	—
Total Revenues	$ 948,000	$ 250,000	$1,198,000	$1,110,000
Expenses				
Cost of Goods Sold (excluding depreciation)	$ 440,000	$ 80,000	$ 520,000	$ 480,000
Depreciation Expense	120,000	50,000	170,000	170,000
Administrative Expense	80,000	40,000	120,000	120,000
Income Tax Expense	104,000	32,000	136,000	136,000
Total Expenses	$ 744,000	$ 202,000	$ 946,000	$ 906,000
Net Income	$ 204,000	$ 48,000	$ 252,000	$ 204,000
Dividends Declared	50,000	13,000	63,000	50,000
Increase in Retained Earnings for the Year	$ 154,000	$ 35,000	$ 189,000	$ 154,000

The consolidated entity does not have its own set of journals and ledgers. The eliminations to remove intercompany transactions typically appear on a consolidation work sheet, not in the records of any of the companies in the consolidated entity. The accountant prepares the consolidated financial statements directly from the work sheet. Exhibit 11.9, in Appendix 11.1, presents such a work sheet.

Eliminating Double-Counting of Intercompany Payables   Separate company records indicate that $12,000 of Company S's accounts receivable represent amounts receivable from Company P. Column (3) counts the current assets underlying this transaction twice: once as part of Accounts Receivable on Company S's books and a second time as Cash (Other Assets) on Company P's books. Also, the liability shown on Company P's books appears in the combined amount for Accounts Payable in column (3).

The consolidated group does not owe this $12,000 to an outsider. To eliminate double-counting on the asset side and to report Accounts Payable at the amount payable to outsiders, the consolidation process must eliminate $12,000 from the amounts for Accounts Receivable and Accounts Payable in column (3). In column (4), the consolidated Accounts Receivable and Accounts Payable both total $12,000 less than their sum in column (3).

If either company holds bonds or long-term notes of the other, the consolidation process will eliminate the investment and related liability in the consolidated balance sheet. It will also eliminate the "borrower's" interest expense and the "lender's" interest revenue from the consolidated income statement.

Eliminating Double-Counting of Investment   Company P's balance sheet shows an asset, Investment in Stock of Company S, which represents P's investment in S's net assets. The subsidiary's balance sheet shows its individual assets. When column (3) adds the two balance sheets, the sum shows both Company P's investment in Company S's assets and S's assets themselves. The consolidation process must eliminate Company P's account, Investment in Stock of Company S, $705,000, from the sum of the balance sheets. Because the consolidated balance sheet must maintain the accounting equation, the process must make corresponding eliminations of $705,000 from the equities.

To understand the eliminations from the equities in the balance sheet, recall that the right-hand side shows the *sources* of the firm's financing. Financing for Company S comes from creditors (liabilities of $295,000) and from owners (shareholders' equity of $705,000). Company P owns 100 percent of Company S's voting shares. Thus the financing for the assets of the consolidated entity comes from the creditors of both companies and from Company P's shareholders. In other words, the equities of the consolidated entity are the liabilities of both companies plus the shareholders' equity of Company P alone. Column (3) adds the shareholders' equity accounts of Company S to those of Company P. It counts the financing from Company P's shareholders twice (once on the parent's books and once on the subsidiary's books). Hence, when the consolidation process eliminates Company P's investment account ($705,000) from the sum of the two companies' assets, it eliminates the shareholders' equity accounts of Company S ($500,000 of common stock and $205,000 of retained earnings). See column (4).

Learning Aid   When we prepare a consolidated balance sheet for two entities, we must deal with two sets of assets, two sets of liabilities, and two sets of owners' equity accounts. Which assets, liabilities, and owners' equity accounts provide a better understanding of the entity operating as one economic whole? The parent's balance sheet shows on one line, Investment in Subsidiary, the net assets of the subsidiary, whose individual amounts appear on the subsidiary's balance sheet. The individual components of net assets of the subsidiary provide more helpful information than does the single asset, Investment in Subsidiary. Thus, we eliminate the Investment in Subsidiary account and replace it with the individual assets and liabilities of the subsidiary. The shareholders' equity of the parent financed the subsidiary's shareholders' equity. Thus, we eliminate the subsidiary's shareholders' equity when we eliminate the parent's investment account. As a result, a consolidated balance sheet reports the individual assets of the parent and the subsidiary, except the Investment in Subsidiary account, the individual liabilities of both entities, and the shareholders' equity of the parent.

Back to Basics   By now, you should understand that Retained Earnings represents a source of financing for assets, not a pool of assets. Owners of P provide the financing to the consolidated group, so the consolidation process eliminates the retained earnings of S.

Some students cannot understand what happens to S's retained earnings, which apparently disappear in consolidation. The difficulty stems from confusing Retained Earnings with assets, rather than understanding it as a source of assets, a component of shareholders' equity.

Eliminating Intercompany Sales   The consolidation process must eliminate intercompany transactions from the sum of the income statements so that the consolidated income statement will present only the consolidated entity's transactions with outsiders. Consider intercompany sales. Separate company records indicate that Company S sold merchandise at its cost of $40,000 to Company P for $40,000 during the year. None of this inventory remains in Company P's inventory on December 31. Therefore, the merchandise inventory items sold appear in Sales Revenue both on Company S's books (sale to Company P) and on Company P's books (sale to outsiders). Thus column (3) overstates sales of the consolidated entity to outsiders. Likewise, Cost of Goods Sold of both companies in column (3) counts twice the cost of the goods sold, first by Company S to Company P and then by Company P to outsiders. The consolidation process eliminates the effects of the intercompany sale from Company S to Company P. See column (4) for Sales and Cost of Goods Sold.

A Realistic Complication   We simplified the above example by having Company S sell the goods to Company P at cost, $40,000, so that you can easily see that the consolidation process reduces both sales and cost of goods sold by $40,000. Often S sells the goods to P for a price larger than S's cost. Assume, now, that S sold goods costing $30,000 to P for $40,000, goods that P later sold to outsiders for $45,000. The consolidation process still eliminates $40,000 from both combined sales and combined cost of goods sold. The transactions remaining in the consolidated income statement will be P's sales to outsiders for $45,000 and S's cost of $30,000, just as if they were a single company selling, for $45,000, goods that cost $30,000.

Eliminating Double-Counting of Income   Company P's accounts show Equity in Earnings of Company S of $48,000. Company S's records show individual revenues and expenses that net to $48,000. When column (3) sums the revenues and expenses of the two companies, it counts that income twice. The consolidation process must eliminate the account Equity in Earnings of Company S. See column (4) for Equity in Earnings

Consolidated Income   The amount of consolidated net income for a period exactly equals the amount that the parent would show on its separate company books if it used the equity method for all its subsidiaries. That is, consolidated net income is as follows:

Parent Company's Net Income from Its Own Activities	+	Parent Company's Share of Subsidiaries' Net Income	−	Profit (or + Loss) on Intercompany Transactions

A consolidated income statement differs from an income statement using the equity method only in the components presented. The equity method for an unconsolidated subsidiary shows the parent's share of the subsidiary's net income minus gain (or plus loss) on intercompany transactions on a single line, Equity in Earnings of Unconsolidated Subsidiary. A consolidated income statement combines the individual revenues and expenses of the subsidiary (less intercompany adjustments) with those of the parent. The consolidation process eliminates the account Equity in Earnings of Unconsolidated Subsidiary.

TERMINOLOGY NOTE

Accountants sometimes refer to the equity method as a *one-line consolidation* because the revenues less the expenses of the subsidiary appear in the one account Equity in Earnings of Unconsolidated Subsidiary. Applying the equity method in realistic situations sometimes presents ambiguities. The guiding principle: treat the items in such a way that the parent's net income equals the same amount that it would show if it consolidated the investment rather than used the equity method for it.

External Minority Interest in Consolidated Subsidiary Often, the parent does not own 100 percent of the voting stock of a consolidated subsidiary. The parent refers to the owners of the remaining shares of voting stock as the external minority shareholders or the **minority interest.** These shareholders have provided a portion or fraction of the subsidiary's financing and have a claim to this same fraction of its net assets (= total assets − total liabilities) shown on the subsidiary's separate corporate records. They also have a claim to the same fraction of the earnings of the subsidiary. Do not confuse this minority interest in a consolidated subsidiary with a firm's own minority investments, discussed earlier. The minority interest represents ownership by others outside the parent and its economic entity. The parent's minority investments represent its ownership of shares of other companies in which the parent owns less than 50 percent of the shares.

The Minority Interest in Net Assets in the Consolidated Balance Sheet Assume now that the parent owns less than 100 percent of the subsidiary's shares—80 percent to be concrete. The minority shareholders own 20 percent of the subsidiary. Should the parent's consolidated statements show (1) only its 80 percent fraction of each of the assets and liabilities of the subsidiary or (2) all of the subsidiary's assets and liabilities?

The parent, with its controlling voting interest, can direct the use of *all* the subsidiary's assets and liabilities, not merely the 80 percent it owns claim to. The generally accepted accounting principle, therefore, shows all of the assets and liabilities of the subsidiary. The consolidated balance sheet and income statement will disclose the interest of the minority shareholders in the consolidated, but less-than-wholly-owned subsidiary.

The amount of the minority interest appearing in the balance sheet generally results from multiplying the common shareholders' equity of the subsidiary by the minority's percentage of ownership. For example, if the common shareholders' equity (= assets − liabilities) of a consolidated subsidiary totals $500,000, and the minority owns 20 percent of the common stock, the minority interest will appear on the consolidated balance sheet as $100,000 (= .20 × $500,000). The minority interest typically appears among the equities on the consolidated balance sheet, between the liabilities and shareholders' equity.

The parent's consolidated income statement shows all the subsidiary's revenues less all the subsidiary's expenses and so includes all of the subsidiary's income even though that amount does not appear with a separate caption. The minority shareholders claim part of this income, typically an amount equal to the subsidiary's net income multiplied by the minority's percentage of ownership. The consolidated income statement subtracts the minority's share of the subsidiary's income in calculating consolidated net income, which shows the parent's shareholders' claim on the income of the entire group of companies.[7]

LIMITATIONS OF CONSOLIDATED STATEMENTS

The consolidated statements, provided for the parent's shareholders, do not replace the statements of individual corporations.

- Creditors must rely on the resources of the one corporation to which they loaned funds. They may misunderstand the protection for their loans if they use only a consolidated statement combining the data of a company that is sound with the data of one that is verging on insolvency.
- A corporation can declare dividends only against its own retained earnings.
- When the parent company does not own all of the shares of the subsidiary, the minority shareholders can judge the dividend constraints, both legal and financial, only by inspecting the subsidiary's statements.

PROBLEM 11.5 FOR SELF-STUDY

Understanding consolidation concepts. Exhibit 11.6 presents income statement data and Exhibit 11.7 presents balance sheet data for Parent and its 80-percent-owned Sub. The first two columns in each exhibit show amounts taken from the separate-company accounting records of each firm. The third column sums the amounts in the first two columns. The fourth column shows consolidated amounts for Parent and Sub after making intercompany eliminations.

a. Does the account Investment in Sub (equity method) on the Parent's books include any unamortized excess acquisition cost relative to the book value of the shareholders' equity of Sub?

b. Suggest four ways in which the data in Exhibits 11.6 and 11.7 confirm that Parent owns 80 percent of Sub.

c. Why does the amount for accounts receivable in column (3) of Exhibit 11.7 differ from the amount in column (4)?

d. Explain why the account Investment in Sub does not appear on the consolidated balance sheet.

e. Why does the total shareholders' equity of $692 on the consolidated balance sheet equal the shareholders' equity on Parent's separate-company books?

f. Compute the amount of intercompany sales during Year 1.

g. Explain why the $80 for Equity in Earnings of Sub does not appear on the consolidated income statement.

h. Why does the account Minority Interest in Earnings of Sub appear on the consolidated income statement but not on the income statements of either Parent or Sub?

---

[7]We discuss and illustrate more of the accounting procedures for minority interest on the Web Site that the publisher has made available for this book. To view this material, which includes problems for self-study as well as other problems, go to the publisher's Web Site (refer to the book's preface for a description of the site) or (1) go to http://www.harcourtcollege.com; (2) go to the pull-down menu for disciplines and select "accounting"; (3) select the icon for *Financial Accounting* by Stickney & Weil; (4) select "Student"; (5) select "Additional Topics"; (6) select "Minority Interest."

| | EXHIBIT 11.6 | PARENT AND SUB
Income Statement Data for Year 1
(Problem 11.5 for Self-Study) |

| | Separate Company Books | | | |
	Parent (1)	Sub (2)	Combined (3) = (1) + (2)	Consolidated (4)
Sales	$4,000	$2,000	$6,000	$5,500
Equity in Earnings of Sub	80	—	80	—
Cost of Goods Sold	(2,690)	(1,350)	(4,040)	(3,540)
Selling and Administrative Expenses	(1,080)	(480)	(1,560)	(1,560)
Interest Expense	(30)	(20)	(50)	(50)
Income Tax Expense	(70)	(50)	(120)	(120)
Minority Interest in Earnings of Sub	—	—	—	(20)
Net Income	$ 210	$ 100	$ 310	$ 210

| | EXHIBIT 11.7 | PARENT AND SUB
Balance Sheet Data, December 31, Year 1
(Problem 11.5 for Self-Study) |

| | Separate Company Books | | | |
	Parent (1)	Sub (2)	Combined (3) = (1) + (2)	Consolidated (4)
ASSETS				
Cash	$ 125	$ 60	$ 185	$ 185
Accounts Receivable	550	270	820	795
Inventories	460	210	670	670
Investment in Sub (equity method)	192	—	192	—
Property, Plant, and Equipment (net)	680	380	1,060	1,060
Total Assets	$2,007	$920	$2,927	$2,710
LIABILITIES AND SHAREHOLDERS' EQUITY				
Accounts Payable	$ 370	$170	$ 540	$ 515
Notes Payable	400	250	650	650
Other Current Liabilities	245	60	305	305
Long-term Debt	300	200	500	500
Total Liabilities	$1,315	$680	$1,995	$1,970
Minority Interest Net Assets of Sub	—	—	—	$ 48
Common Stock	$ 200	$ 50	$ 250	$ 200
Retained Earnings	492	190	682	492
Total Shareholders' Equity	$ 692	$240	$ 932	$ 692
Total Liabilities and Shareholders' Equity	$2,007	$920	$2,927	$2,710

AN INTERNATIONAL PERSPECTIVE

Most countries outside of the United States require that the accounting for minority, passive investments use the lower-of-cost-or-market method, not the market value method. The accounting for minority and majority, active investments closely parallels practices in the United States: the equity method for minority, active investments and consolidation for majority investments. Practices for these active investments have become similar, however, only in recent years. Countries such as Germany and Japan have historically followed a strict legal definition of the corporate entity, with all intercorporate investments reported at acquisition cost and dividends received reported as the only revenues from these investments. The movement toward the use of the equity method and consolidation reflects increasing recognition that the economic entity likely differs from the legal entity and that financial statements based on the economic entity provide more useful information to users. The International Accounting Standards Committee (IASC) requires the equity method for investments where the holder exerts significant influence and has no plans to sell its investment in the near future.[8] The IASC expresses a preference for the consolidation of controlled entities, even if the investor owns less than 50 percent of the shares, and allows the cost method, the lower-of-cost-or-market method, the market value method, and the equity method for noncontrolling investments.[9]

SUMMARY

Marketable securities appear in current or noncurrent asset accounts on the balance sheet. Except for certain financial institutions, most firms classify their securities as securities available for sale. Firms report these securities at market values each period. Changes in market value during the period appear in a separate shareholders' equity account. The income statement includes gains and losses from these securities only when firms sell them. Firms report gains and losses in market value on trading securities in current income. The firm reports on debt securities at amortized cost when it has both the ability and the intent to hold the securities to maturity.

Businesses acquire stock in other businesses for a variety of reasons and in a variety of ways. The investor records the acquisition of stock of another company as a long-term investment as follows:

Investment in S	X
Cash or Other Consideration Given	X

---

[8]International Accounting Standards Committee, *International Accounting Standard No. 28,* "Investments in Associates," 1989, revised in 1998.

[9]International Accounting Standards Committee, *International Accounting Standard No. 27,* "Consolidated Financial Statements," 1989.

The investor records in the investment account the amount of cash given or the market value of other consideration exchanged.

The accounting for the investment subsequent to acquisition depends on the ownership percentage:

- The market value method generally applies when the parent owns less than 20 percent; most long-term investments are securities available for sale.

- The equity method generally applies when the parent owns at least 20 percent but not more than 50 percent of the stock of another company.

- The equity method applies also when the investor company can exercise significant influence even though it owns less than 20 percent.

- The investor generally prepares consolidated statements when it owns more than 50 percent of the voting shares of another company, but the FASB proposes to require consolidated statements whenever the investor controls the other company.

Figure 11.2 summarizes the structure of accounting for holdings of securities, and Exhibit 11.8 summarizes the accounting for investments subsequent to acquisition.

The market value method for investments recognizes income only when the investor becomes entitled to receive dividends or when it sells the securities.

Consolidated statements and the equity method have the same effect on net income. The parent shows as income its proportional share of the acquired firm's periodic income after acquisition. In the equity method, this share appears on a single line of the income statement. Income statement amounts of revenues and expenses are larger in consolidation because the consolidated income statement combines the revenues and expenses of

---

EXHIBIT 11.8 | Effects of Various Methods of Accounting for Long-term Investments in Corporate Securities

Method of Accounting	Balance Sheet	Income Statement	Statement of Cash Flows
Market value method (generally used when ownership percentage is less than 20 percent)	Investment account appears at current market value as a noncurrent asset. Unrealized holding gains and losses appear in a separate shareholders' equity account.	Dividends declared by investee appear as revenue of investor. Gains and losses (from acquisition cost) are reported in income only when realized in arm's-length transactions with outsiders.	Dividends received from investee are included in cash provided by operations of investor.
Equity method (generally used when ownership percentage is at least 20 percent but not more than 50 percent)	Investment account appears at acquisition cost plus share of investee's net income less share of investee's dividends since acquisition.	Equity in investee's net income is part of revenue in the period that investee earns income.	Deduct equity in investee's undistributed earnings from net income to derive cash provided by operations of investor. Cash from operations thus increases only by the amount of dividend received.
Consolidation (generally used when ownership percentage exceeds 50 percent)	Eliminate investment account and replace it with individual assets and liabilities of subsidiary. Show minority interest in subsidiary's net assets among equities.	Combine individual revenues and expenses of subsidiary with those of parent. Subtract minority interest in subsidiary's net income.	Combine individual sources and uses of cash of subsidiary with those of parent. Add minority interest in net income to obtain cash provided by operations.

FIGURE 11.2 Roadmap to Investments

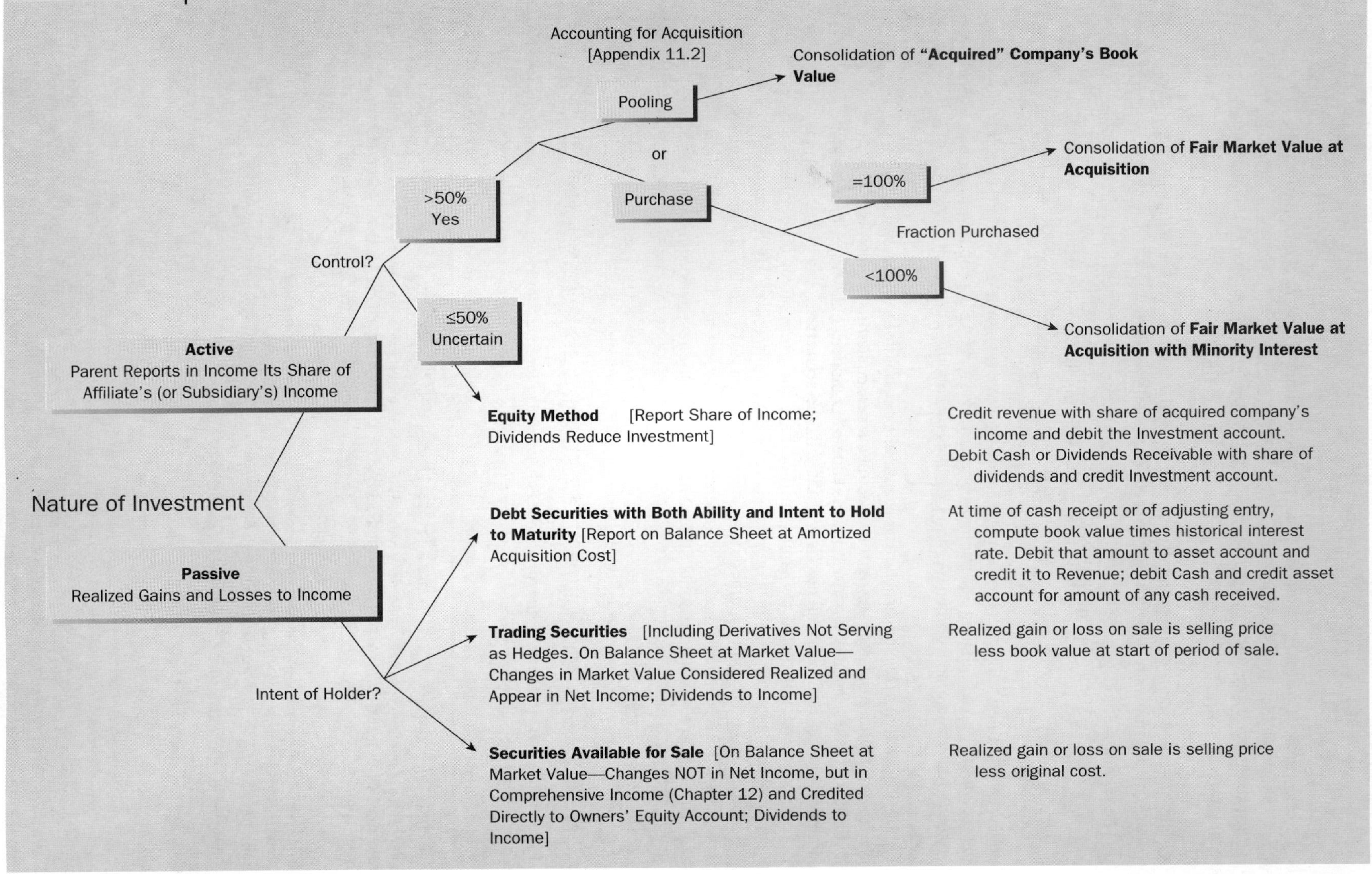

Nature of Investment

Active
Parent Reports in Income Its Share of Affiliate's (or Subsidiary's) Income

Control?

>50%
Yes

≤50%
Uncertain

Equity Method [Report Share of Income; Dividends Reduce Investment]

At time of cash receipt or of adjusting entry, compute book value times historical interest rate. Debit that amount to asset account and credit it to Revenue; debit Cash and credit asset account for amount of any cash received.

Accounting for Acquisition [Appendix 11.2]

Pooling

or

Purchase

Consolidation of "Acquired" Company's Book Value

Fraction Purchased

=100%

<100%

Consolidation of **Fair Market Value at Acquisition**

Consolidation of **Fair Market Value at Acquisition with Minority Interest**

Credit revenue with share of acquired company's income and debit the Investment account. Debit Cash or Dividends Receivable with share of dividends and credit Investment account.

Passive
Realized Gains and Losses to Income

Intent of Holder?

Debt Securities with Both Ability and Intent to Hold to Maturity [Report on Balance Sheet at Amortized Acquisition Cost]

Realized gain or loss on sale is selling price less book value at start of period of sale.

Trading Securities [Including Derivatives Not Serving as Hedges. On Balance Sheet at Market Value—Changes in Market Value Considered Realized and Appear in Net Income; Dividends to Income]

Securities Available for Sale [On Balance Sheet at Market Value—Changes NOT in Net Income, but in Comprehensive Income (Chapter 12) and Credited Directly to Owners' Equity Account; Dividends to Income]

Realized gain or loss on sale is selling price less original cost.

the acquired company with those of the parent. Balance sheet components under the consolidation method will exceed those under the equity method; the consolidated balance sheet substitutes the individual assets and liabilities of the acquired company for the parent company's investment in the subsidiary.

APPENDIX 11.1: PREPARING CONSOLIDATED FINANCIAL STATEMENTS

This appendix illustrates the preparation of consolidated financial statements for Company P and Company S. Learning how to interpret and to analyze consolidated financial statements does not require knowing how to construct them, but such knowledge helps.

DATA FOR THE ILLUSTRATION

The single-company financial statements of Company P and Company S appear in Exhibit 11.5. The following additional information affects the preparation of the consolidated financial statements.

1. Company P acquired 100 percent of the outstanding shares of Company S for $650,000 cash on January 1, Year 1. At the time of acquisition, the book value of the shareholders' equity of Company S was $650,000, comprising the following account balances:

COMPANY S, JANUARY 1, YEAR 1

Common Stock	$500,000
Retained Earnings	150,000
Total Shareholders' Equity	$650,000

Company P made the following journal entry on its books at the time of acquisition:

Investment in Stock of Company S	650,000	
Cash		650,000

---

2. Company P records its investment in the shares of Company S using the equity method. The Retained Earnings of Company S have increased since January 1, Year 1, the date of acquisition, by $55,000 (= $205,000 − $150,000). This increase appears in the Investment in Company S account on Company P's books: $705,000 = $650,000 + $55,000.
3. At December 31, Year 4, $12,000 of Company S's accounts receivable represent amounts payable by Company P.
4. During Year 4, Company S sold merchandise to Company P for $40,000. None of that merchandise remains in Company P's inventory as of December 31, Year 4.

WORK SHEET PREPARATION

Preparing consolidated statements for Company P and Company S requires the following steps, characteristic of the consolidation procedure:

1. Eliminating the parent company's investment account
2. Eliminating intercompany receivables and payables
3. Eliminating intercompany sales and purchases

EXHIBIT 11.9 | COMPANY P and COMPANY S
Work Sheet to Derive Consolidated Financial Statements Based on Data from Preclosing Trial Balances for Year 4

	Company P		Company S		Adjustments and Eliminations		P and S Consolidated	
	Debit	Credit	Debit	Credit	Debit	Credit	Debit	Credit
Trial Balance Accounts								
Accounts Receivable	$ 200,000		$ 25,000			(2) $ 12,000	$ 213,000	
Investment in Stock of Company S	705,000		—			(1) 705,000	—	
Other Assets	2,150,000		975,000				3,125,000	
Accounts Payable		$ 75,000		$ 15,000	(2) $ 12,000			$ 78,000
Other Liabilities		70,000		280,000				350,000
Common Stock		2,500,000		500,000	(1) 500,000			2,500,000
Retained Earnings, Company P		206,000						206,000
Company S				157,000	(1) 157,000			
Sales		900,000		250,000	(3) 40,000			1,110,000
Equity in Earnings of Company S		48,000		—	(1) 48,000			
Cost of Goods Sold	440,000		80,000			(3) 40,000	480,000	
Depreciation Expense	120,000		50,000				170,000	
Administrative Expense	80,000		40,000				120,000	
Income Tax Expense	104,000		32,000				136,000	
Totals	$ 3,799,000	$ 3,799,000	$ 1,202,000	$ 1,202,000	$ 757,000	$ 757,000	$ 4,244,000	$ 4,244,000

This illustration starts with the information in single-company, preclosing trial balances. In Exhibit 11.9, these data appear in the first two pairs of columns, which contain the same information as the first two columns of Exhibit 11.5. Note that the amounts shown for Retained Earnings are the balances as of December 31, Year 4, before closing revenue and expense accounts but after subtracting dividend declarations for Year 4. The fourth pair of columns in Exhibit 11.9 shows the amounts on a consolidated basis for Company P and Company S. The amounts in the last pair of columns horizontally sum the amounts in the other columns: Company P items, Company S items, plus adjustments and eliminations. These adjustments and eliminations, discussed in the sections that follow, appear only on a work sheet to prepare consolidated statements, not in the accounting records of either company.

1. *Elimination of Parent Company's Investment Account.* Company P acquired the shares of Company S for a price equal to their book value, $650,000. Since acquisition, Company P has used the equity method and has recorded the increase in Retained Earnings of Company S, $55,000, in its investment account. To avoid double-counting the net assets of Company S (the assets themselves on Company S's balance sheet and Company P's investment in them on Company P's balance sheet), the accountant must use the consolidation process to eliminate the investment account. The elimination is as follows:

(1) Common Stock (Company S)	500,000	
Retained Earnings (Company S)	157,000	
Equity in Earnings of Company S (Company P)	48,000	
Investment in Stock of Company S (Company P)		705,000

Except for the minority interest, if any, the shareholders of the parent provide the shareholders' equity of the consolidated entity. This example does not have minority interest. Thus the shareholders' equity of the subsidiary comes entirely from the parent's financing. If the consolidation process merely added together the shareholders' equity of the parent and of the subsidiary, it would double-count equities. When the consolidation process eliminates Company P's investment account to avoid double-counting of net assets, it eliminates the subsidiary's shareholders' equity accounts— corresponding to the parent's investment—to avoid double-counting the equities. The total amount eliminated equals the balance in the investment account, $705,000. This amount also equals the total shareholders' equity of Company S on December 31, Year 4, $705,000 (= $500,000 + $205,000); see Exhibit 11.5. Because the elimination applies to a preclosing trial balance, the revenue and expense accounts of Company S remain open, not yet closed to Company S's Retained Earnings.

In addition to eliminating the common stock of Company S, $500,000, the consolidation process eliminates the balances in Retained Earnings of Company S, $157,000, and the Equity in Earnings of Company S for Year 4, $48,000. The balance in the income statement account Equity in Earnings of Company S equals Company S's net income for the year. The consolidation process eliminates this account and replaces it with the individual revenues less expenses of Company S (whose difference is also Company S's net income) in the consolidated income statement.

2. *Elimination of Intercompany Receivables and Payables.* A parent may sell goods on account to (or buy goods on account from) a subsidiary and treat the resulting obligation as an account receivable (or an account payable). The subsidiary will treat the obligation as an account payable (or an account receivable). A parent often makes loans to

subsidiaries; these loans appear among the parent's assets as Notes Receivable, Investment in Bonds, or Advances to Subsidiary. The subsidiary would show Notes Payable, Bonds Payable, or Advances from Parent among its liabilities. A single company would not show Accounts Receivable and Accounts Payable for departments within the company. The consolidation process eliminates these transactions from the consolidated balance sheet so that the resulting statement appears like that of a single company.

In the illustration, Company S's accounts receivable include $12,000 due to it from Company P. The entry to record the elimination of the intercompany receivables and payables in Exhibit 11.9 is as follows:

(2) Accounts Payable	12,000	
Accounts Receivable		12,000
To eliminate intercompany payables and receivables.		

3. *Elimination of Intercompany Sales and Purchases.* A consolidated income statement will not report sales between consolidated companies for the same reason that an income statement for a single company will not report transfers from Work-in-Process Inventory to Finished Goods Inventory as sales. During Year 4, Company P acquired $40,000 of merchandise inventory from Company S. Eliminating intercompany sales requires a debit to Sales (of the selling corporation) and a credit to Inventories or to Cost of Goods Sold (of the purchasing corporation), depending on whether it has yet computed Cost of Goods Sold. In this illustration, Company P has already computed its cost of goods sold from the inventory equation:

$$\text{Cost of Goods Sold} = \text{Beginning Inventory} + \text{Purchases} - \text{Ending Inventory}$$
$$= \text{Goods Available for Sale} - \text{Ending Inventory}$$

Therefore, the offsetting credit to eliminate intercompany sales must be to the Cost of Goods Sold account:

(3) Sales	40,000	
Cost of Goods Sold		40,000
To eliminate intercompany sales and purchases.		

Company S sold goods to Company P, and Company P sold the goods to outsiders. Not to eliminate the intercompany sales forces the income statement to count them twice, but it also counts cost of good sold twice, so gross profit appears correctly. To see that profits appear properly, even without the elimination, assume that the goods cost Company S $30,000 and that Company P sold them for $45,000. In the single-company income statements, Company S's profits are $10,000 (= $40,000 − $30,000) as a result of the sale to Company P. Company P's profits are $5,000 (= $45,000 − $40,000) as a result of its sales to others. Total profits of the consolidated group from these transactions are $15,000, or Company P's revenue of $45,000 less Company S's cost of $30,000. The elimination of intercompany sales does not change the consolidated sales to outsiders, the consolidated cost of goods sold to outsiders, or consolidated profit.

STATEMENT PREPARATION

After completing the consolidation work sheet, the accountant prepares the consolidated statements. Column (4) of Exhibit 11.5 presents a consolidated balance sheet on December 31, Year 4, and a consolidated income statement for Year 4 for Company P and

Company S. Compare the results of using the equity method for an unconsolidated subsidiary, as in Column (1), with consolidating that subsidiary, as in Column (4):

1. When a parent does not consolidate the subsidiary, the parent's balance sheet shows the investment in the subsidiary's net assets in a single investment account. When it consolidates the subsidiary, the individual assets and liabilities of the subsidiary replace the investment account.
2. After the parent consolidates a subsidiary, consolidated retained earnings equals the same amount as when the parent uses the equity method for the subsidiary.
3. When a parent does not consolidate a subsidiary, the parent's interest in the earnings of the subsidiary appears on the single line Equity in Earnings of Company S on the parent's income statement. When it does consolidate the subsidiary, the individual revenues and expenses of the subsidiary replace the Equity in Earnings of Company S account.
4. After the parent consolidates a subsidiary, consolidated net income equals the same amount as when the parent uses the equity method for the subsidiary.

ACQUISITION PRICE EXCEEDS BOOK VALUE ACQUIRED

The parent company may acquire a subsidiary for an amount that exceeds the book value of the subsidiary's net assets. Suppose, for example, that Company P had paid $700,000, rather than $650,000, for its 100 percent investment in Company S. The $50,000 difference in purchase price represents the amount paid for Company S's assets in excess of their book value, for goodwill, or for both. Recall that goodwill equals the excess of purchase price paid for an acquisition over the fair market value of the identifiable net assets acquired. Assume that on the date of acquisition, January 1, Year 1, the book value of Company S's recorded assets and liabilities equaled their market values, and Company S has no unrecorded, separately identifiable assets (as it would if it had developed its own patents).

The fact that Company P was willing to pay $700,000 for identifiable assets having book values and market values equal to $650,000 means that Company S must have had unidentifiable assets of $50,000 on January 1, Year 1. The $50,000 of unidentifiable assets represents **goodwill.** GAAP require an owner to amortize goodwill over a period, which the FASB has allowed to be as long as 40 years but which it will soon restrict to a period of no longer than 20 years.[10] Assume that Company P chooses a 10-year amortization period. On its separate company books, Company P makes the following entry during each of the years 1 through 4:

Amortization Expense	5,000	
Investment in Stock of Company S		5,000
To amortize goodwill: $5,000 = ($700,000 − $650,000)/10.		

Assume, now, that Company P is preparing the consolidation work sheet at the end of Year 4. Entry (1) is the same as that shown in Exhibit 11.9. After entry (1), the Investment in Stock of Company S still has a debit balance of $30,000 [= $50,000 − (4 × $5,000)]. This amount represents the unamortized goodwill arising from P's acquisition of S. To

---

[10]Accounting Principles Board, *Opinion No. 17*. As this book goes to press, the FASB is proposing to shorten the maximum amortization period to 20 years.

continue the consolidation procedure, make a work sheet entry to reclassify this amount from the investment account to goodwill. The entry is as follows:

Goodwill	30,000	
Investment in Stock of Company S		30,000
To reclassify the remaining investment as goodwill.		

The consolidated balance sheet on December 31, Year 4, will show goodwill of $30,000 [= $50,000 − (4 × $5,000)]. Consolidated net income for Year 4 will now be $199,000 (= $204,000 − $5,000) to reflect amortization expense for Year 4. Consolidated retained earnings will be $390,000 [= $410,000 − (4 × $5,000)].

PROBLEM 11.6 FOR SELF-STUDY

Preparing consolidation work sheet adjustment and elimination entries.
Exhibit 11.10 presents preclosing trial balance data for P Company and S Company for Year 6. P Company acquired all of the common stock of S Company on January 1, Year 6, for $430. During Year 6, P Company sold merchandise on account costing $600 to S Company for $1,000. S Company sold all of this merchandise to its customers by the end of Year 6. On December 31, Year 6, S Company still owes P Company $200 related to these intercompany merchandise transactions.

EXHIBIT 11.10	P COMPANY AND S COMPANY Trial Balance Data for Year 6 (Problem 11.6 for Self-Study)

	P Company		S Company	
	Debit	**Credit**	**Debit**	**Credit**
Cash	$ 220		$ 90	
Accounts Receivable	790		420	
Inventories	640		390	
Investment in S Company	530		—	
Property, Plant, and Equipment (net)	970		640	
Accounts Payable		$ 730		$ 450
Other Current Liabilities		520		260
Long-term Debt		600		300
Common Stock		300		100
Retained Earnings (Preclosing)		800		330
Sales		4,000		3,000
Equity in Earnings of S Company		100		—
Cost of Goods Sold	2,800		2,200	
Selling and Administrative Expenses ...	940		640	
Interest Expense	60		25	
Income Tax Expense	100		35	
	$7,050	$7,050	$4,440	$4,440

a. Prepare the work sheet adjustment and elimination entries to consolidate P Company and S Company for Year 6.

b. Assume for this part that P Company paid $510 for all of the common stock of S Company on January 1, Year 6. The common shareholders' equity of S Company was $430 on this date (= common stock of $100 + retained earnings of $330). P Company attributes any excess of the acquisition cost over the book value of the net assets acquired to goodwill. P Company amortizes the excess over 10 years.

(1) Compute the balance in the account Investment in S Company on P Company's books on December 31, Year 6, assuming P Company uses the equity method.

(2) Prepare the work sheet adjustment and elimination entries to consolidate P Company and S Company for Year 6.

APPENDIX 11.2: ACCOUNTING FOR CORPORATE ACQUISITIONS

In a corporate acquisition, one corporation acquires all, or substantially all, of another corporation's common shares. GAAP require firms to use one of two methods to account for corporate acquisitions: the **purchase method** or the **pooling-of-interests method.** After the acquisition, the results reported for the combined company differ substantially as a result of the accounting for the acquisition, so acquiring companies care about the methods they must use. As this book goes to press, the FASB is proposing to eliminate (or curtail) the pooling-of-interests method. Even if it does eliminate the pooling-of-interests method, the IASC allows approximately the same method of accounting for an acquisition that meets stringent tests. The IASC calls its method **uniting of interests.** This appendix presents the issues behind acquisition accounting and introduces the methods of applying the two methods. If you master the concepts here, you will better understand the controversy sure to rage over the elimination of the pooling-of-interests method and the subsequent pressure from affected companies to allow them to use the uniting-of-interests method.

The method of accounting for the acquisition affects the *amounts* in the entries on the consolidation work sheet but not the accounting *procedures.*

PURCHASE METHOD

The purchase method uses acquisition cost accounting. The parent initially records the Investment in Subsidiary account at the amount of cash or the market value of other consideration given in the exchange. The consolidation process allocates any difference between the amount in the investment account on the date of acquisition and the book value of the net assets acquired to individual assets less liabilities. The guiding principle: the consolidated balance sheet on the date of the acquisition shows all assets and liabilities of the acquired company at their fair market values on the date of acquisition.

Any excess of the purchase price over the market values of the individual assets less liabilities becomes goodwill. Thus, the purchase method reports the assets less liabilities of the acquired company at their market values in the consolidated balance sheet at the date of acquisition. The consolidated income statement in subsequent periods will show expenses (depreciation and amortization) based on these market values, which typically exceed their former book values in the acquired company's records. The illustration of the consolidation procedures in Appendix 11.1 follows the purchase method of accounting.

POOLING-OF-INTERESTS METHOD

The pooling-of-interests method treats the corporate acquisition as the uniting of owner-ship interests of two companies by exchange of equity (common stock) securities. Ac-counting views the exchange of equity interests as a change in form, not in substance; that is, the shareholders of the predecessor companies become shareholders in the new, combined enterprise. Each of the predecessor companies continues carrying out its operations as be-fore. Because the substance of neither the ownership interest nor the nature of the activities of the enterprises changes, no new basis of accountability arises, which means old book val-ues for assets and liabilities remain unchanged in the new entity's records. We agree with the FASB (and other academics) that this rationale lacks logic and the weight of substance.

CONCEPTUAL NOTE

We, like the FASB, think most business combinations are purchases, not uniting of ownership interests. Most combinations result from the actions of one firm to take over or acquire another. Managements of acquired firms rarely stay intact. We think most firms structure their acquisitions to qualify for pooling because of the accounting effects, not because of interests that have become united.

In a pooling, the book values of the assets and liabilities of the predecessor companies carry over to the new combined, or consolidated, enterprise. The guiding principle: the consolidated balance sheet on the date of the acquisition shows all assets and liabilities of the acquired company at their book values on the date of acquisition.

In the purchase method, assets appear at their market values, typically higher than book values, whereas in the pooling-of-interests method, assets appear at their—typically lower—book values at the date of acquisition on the consolidated balance sheet. As a re-sult of these—typically lower—old valuations, the pooling method reports subsequent ex-penses at lower amounts than occur under purchase accounting.

ILLUSTRATION OF PURCHASE AND POOLING-OF-INTERESTS METHODS

Refer to the illustration in Exhibit 11.11, which contrasts the effects of using the purchase and the pooling-of-interests methods. Assume that Company P and Company S decide to combine operations. Management estimates that the combination will save $50,000 a year in expenses. Columns (1) and (2) in Exhibit 11.11 show abbreviated, single-company fi-nancial statements for Company P and Company S before combination. Company S has 20,000 shares of stock outstanding that sell for $84 per share in the market. Company S, as a going concern, has a market value of $1,680,000 (= $84 × 20,000). Company S has been in business for several years, and the market value of its long-term assets exceeds their book value by $400,000. In addition Company S has intangibles, such as loyal employees (and loyal customers) who voluntarily return to work (or to buy). The market apparently values these intangibles at $830,000. After P acquires S, it will call these intan-gibles *goodwill.* As column (3) shows, S's shareholders have $1,230,000 (= $400,000 + $830,000) of equity not recorded on the books.

Company P has 100,000 shares outstanding, which have a $5 par value and sell for $42 each in the market. The illustration ignores income taxes.

Purchase Method

To carry out the acquisition, P issues (sells) 40,000 additional shares on the market for $42 each, or $1,680,000 in total, and uses the proceeds to purchase all shares of S for $84 each. P has acquired 100 percent of the shares of S and now owns S.

| **EXHIBIT 11.11** | Consolidated Statements Comparing Purchase and Pooling-of-Interests Methods |

| | Historical Cost | | S Shown at Current Values | Companies P and S Consolidated at Date of Acquisition | |
	P (1)	S (2)	(3)	Purchase (4)	Pooling of Interests (5)
BALANCE SHEETS					
Assets					
Current Assets	$1,500,000	$600,000	$ 600,000	$1,950,000	$2,100,000
Long-term Assets less Accumulated Depreciation	1,700,000	300,000	700,000	2,550,000	2,000,000
Goodwill	—	—	830,000	830,000	—
Total Assets	$3,200,000	$900,000	$2,130,000	$5,330,000	$4,100,000
Equities					
Liabilities	$1,300,000	$450,000	$ 450,000	$1,750,000	$1,750,000
Common Stock ($5 par)	500,000	100,000	100,000	700,000[a]	700,000[a]
Additional Paid-in Capital	200,000	150,000	150,000	1,680,000[b]	250,000[c]
Retained Earnings	1,200,000	200,000	200,000	1,200,000[d]	1,400,000[e]
Unrecorded Equity at Current Valuation	—	—	1,230,000	—	—
Total Liabilities and Shareholders' Equity	$3,200,000	$900,000	$2,130,000	$5,330,000	$4,100,000
INCOME STATEMENTS (IGNORING INCOME TAXES)[h]					
Precombination Income	$ 300,000	$160,000		$ 460,000	$ 460,000
From Combination:					
Cost Savings (projected)	—	—		50,000	50,000
Extra Depreciation Expense	—	—		(80,000)[f]	—
Amortization of Goodwill	—	—		(83,000)[g]	—
Net Income	$ 300,000	$160,000		$ 347,000[h]	$ 510,000[h]
Number of Common Shares Outstanding	100,000	20,000		140,000	140,000
Earnings per Share	$3.00	$8.00		$2.48	$3.64
RATE-OF-RETURN RATIOS					
Rate on Assets (Net Income/Total Assets)	9.4%	17.8%		6.5%	12.4%
Return on Common Shareholders' Equity (Net Income/Shareholders' Equity)	15.8%	35.6%		9.7%	21.7%

Assumptions: (1) Company S has 20,000 shares outstanding that sell for $84 each in the market.

(2) Company P's shares sell for $42 each in the market. Company P issues 40,000 shares for the purpose of acquiring Company S.

[a]P's 100,000 original shares plus 40,000 new shares at $5 par.

[b]P's $200,000 original additional paid-in capital plus 40,000 shares × ($42 − $5) per share.

[c]Plug to equate pooled shareholders' equity to the sum of all shareholders' equity accounts of the combining companies before combination; cannot derive this number until after deriving the number $1,400,000, below.

[d]P's retained earnings.

[e]Sum of P's and S's retained earnings.

[f]1/5 × ($850,000 − $300,000) = $110,000.

[g]1/10 × $830,000 = $83,000.

[h]As projected.

Under these conditions, P must use the purchase method to account for the acquisition of S. P chooses to amortize the revalued long-term asset costs of $400,000 over five years and the goodwill of $830,000 over 10 years. Consolidated financial reports under the purchase method appear in Exhibit 11.11 in column (4). The consolidated balance sheet sums columns (1) and (3), except for the shareholders' equity section. Since P issued 40,000 new shares for $42 each, the Common Stock account shows 140,000 shares of $5 par value. The Additional Paid-in Capital account shows former Additional Paid-in Capital plus the addition arising from the new stock issue: $200,000 + [40,000 × ($42 − $5)] = $1,680,000. The retained earnings of the consolidated enterprise equals P's retained earnings. Now that P has purchased S, P's shareholders supply all the financing for S, including that supplied as retained earnings.

The consolidated income statement starts with the combined incomes before consolidation. The cost savings of $50,000 resulting from the more efficient operations of the combination increases net income. The additional expense arising from amortizing both the higher, fair-market asset valuations and the goodwill reduces net income.

The projected consolidated net income is $347,000. Note that the sum of the separate net income figures before acquisition, $460,000, exceeds this consolidated total resulting from purchase accounting. Managers of acquiring companies do not like to report lower income than prior managers reported, so they have sought to find another way—pooling—that will combine operations without leading to the lower income.

The consolidated balance sheet after the acquisition will report net assets at market value at the time of acquisition for a purchase. Exhibit 11.12 summarizes these effects for the example in this appendix.

Pooling of Interests

Now examine the accounting for the acquisition in column (5) of Exhibit 11.11, assuming that it qualifies for the pooling-of-interests method. Under GAAP (from 1970 at least through press time for this book), P can qualify the acquisition for pooling treatment by issuing the 40,000 shares of stock directly to the owners of S in return for their shares. The owners of S each get two shares of P for each share of S they owned. The balance sheet items, except for the individual shareholders' equity accounts, sum the single-company amounts from columns (1) and (2). The shareholders' equity after pooling must then equal total shareholders' equity before pooling.

Construct the pooled shareholders' equity accounts with the following steps:

1. The common stock of the pooled enterprise must equal the par value of the shares outstanding after pooling. After pooling, the new enterprise has 140,000 shares outstanding with a par value of $700,000.
2. Generally, the pooled retained earnings balance equals the sum of the retained earnings accounts before pooling. The example illustrates the general rule.
3. The total contributed capital (par value plus additional paid-in capital) after pooling will generally equal the sum of the contributed capital accounts of the firms before pooling. Generally, then, the additional paid-in capital of the pooled firm is the plug to equate the pooled contributed capital with the sum of the contributed capital accounts before pooling. (If this plug requires a negative number, then an exception operates at step **2,** which forces additional paid-in capital to zero and plugs for the required retained earnings amount.)

The income statement resulting from a pooling of interests shows the same revenues and cost savings as shown in the income statement following a purchase. Pooling accounting does not require increased asset valuations or goodwill recognition, so that it

EXHIBIT 11.12	Effect on Consolidated Balance Sheet Contrasting Purchase and Pooling-of-Interests Methods Based on Example in Exhibit 11.11, where Company P Acquires (Purchase) or Unites with (Pooling) Company S Income Statement

(When Company P and Company S remain separate entities, these effects occur only in the process of constructing the consolidated balance sheet. When Company S formally merges with Company P, the journal entry at acquisition records these items into Company P's accounts.)

Purchase Method (Consolidated Statements Report Current Market Values for Company S)

Effects on Consolidated Net Asset Accounts:

Current Assets	$ 600,000
Long-term Assets (net)	700,000
Goodwill	830,000
Less Liabilities	(450,000)
Net Assets Acquired	$1,680.000

Effects on Consolidated Shareholders' Equity Accounts:

Common Stock ($5 Par)	$ 200,000
Additional Paid-in Capital	1,480,000
Net Assets Acquired	$1,680,000

Pooling-of-Interests Method (Consolidated Statements Report Book Values at Acquisition of Company S)

Effects on Consolidated Net Asset Accounts:

Current Assets	$ 600,000
Long-term Assets (net)	300,000
Less Liabilities	(450,000)
Net Assets Acquired	$ 450,000

Effects on Consolidated Shareholders' Equity Accounts:

Common Stock ($5 Par)	$ 200,000
Additional Paid-in Capital	50,000
Retained Earnings	200,000
Net Assets Acquired	$ 450,000

Note: Only when Company S formally merges with Company P will Company P record journal entries derived from the numbers above to combine the accounts of Company S and Company P. Otherwise, Company P will record its Investment in Company S as the net assets acquired—$1,680,000 in the Purchase example and $450,000 in the Pooling example.

does not report extra depreciation and amortization expenses. Consequently, the pooled enterprise reports net income of $510,000 and shareholders' equity of $2,350,000, whereas the identical acquisition accounted for using the purchase method reports smaller income of $347,000 and larger shareholders' equity of $3,580,000. Notice that the earnings-per-share figure under the pooling-of-interest method exceeds that under the purchase method by almost 50 percent. Pooling results in a rate of return on common shareholders' equity of 21.7 percent, more than twice as large as the 9.7 percent resulting from purchase accounting.

This example understates, if anything, the difference between post-acquisition results from the purchase and the pooling methods. Notice that S's market value before the merger, $1,680,000, exceeds its book value of $450,000 by less than a factor of four to one: $1,680,000/$450,000 = 3.7. In practice, pooling of interests has occurred when the market value exceeds the book value by a factor of ten to one. Thus the amortization charges of the purchased subsidiary's assets often exceed the amortization of the pooled subsidiary's assets by an even larger ratio than in this example.

The consolidated balance sheet after the acquisition will report net assets at book value from Company S's books at the time of acquisition for a pooling of interests. Exhibit 11.12 summarizes these effects for the example in this appendix.

MANAGING EARNINGS

Pooling of interests not only keeps earnings from declining after the merger but also allows the management of the pooled companies to manipulate the reported earnings.

Example 14

Company P merges with an old, established firm, Company F, which produces commercial movie films. Company F amortized its films made in the 1960s and 1970s, so that by now these films have book value of nearly zero. But these films have substantial market value because television stations and cable networks will rent these films to show their audiences. If Company P purchases Company F, the old films will appear on the consolidated balance sheet at the films' current market value. If Company P merges with Company F using the pooling-of-interests method, the films will appear on the consolidated balance sheet at their near-zero book values. Then, when Company P wants to boost reported earnings for the year, it can sell some old films to a television network and report a large gain. Actually, of course, the owners of Company F enjoyed this gain when they exchanged their shares with Company P at current values rather than at the obsolete book values.

In Defense of Pooling

Those who defend pooling-of-interests accounting argue that the management of the pooled enterprise has no more opportunity to manage earnings than did the management of Company F before the pooling. Management of Company F can sell old films any time it chooses and report handsome gains. The historical cost basis of accounting causes the problem. It recognizes gains only after a market transaction between, in this example, Company F and some entity outside Company F. Defenders of pooling prefer not to penalize the management of a merged company relative to the management of an established company with assets undervalued on its books. Opponents of pooling reply, using the designations of this example, that management of Company F earned the holding gains, whereas pooling allows management of Company P to report them.

In summary, purchase accounting typically reduces the reported income of the combined enterprise because of additional depreciation and amortization expenses. The extra depreciation and amortization expenses result from recognizing increased asset valuations and, perhaps, goodwill. Pooling-of-interests accounting typically reports larger income for the consolidated enterprise than does purchase accounting.

PROBLEM 11.7 FOR SELF-STUDY

Financial statement effects of the purchase method and the pooling-of-interests method. Exhibit 11.13 presents balance sheet data for Powell Corporation and Steele Corporation as of January 1, Year 8. On this date, Powell Corporation exchanges 2,700 shares of its common stock, selling for $20 per share, for all of the common stock of Steele Corporation.

EXHIBIT 11.13	POWELL CORPORATION AND STEELE CORPORATION Financial Statement Data for January 1, Year 8 (Problem 11.7 for Self-Study)			

	Historical Cost		Current Market Value
	Powell Corp.	**Steele Corp.**	**Steele Corporation**
ASSETS			
Current Assets	$10,000	$ 7,000	$ 7,000
Property, Plant, and Equipment (net)	30,000	18,000	23,000
Goodwill	—	—	40,000
Total Assets	$40,000	$25,000	$70,000
EQUITIES			
Liabilities	$25,000	$16,000	$16,000
Common Stock ($1 par value)	1,000	1,000	1,000
Additional Paid-in Capital	9,000	5,000	5,000
Retained Earnings	5,000	3,000	3,000
Unrecorded Excess of Market Value over Historical Costs	—	—	45,000
Total Equities	$40,000	$25,000	$70,000

a. Prepare a consolidated balance sheet for Powell Corporation and Steele Corporation on January 1, Year 8, using (1) the purchase method and (2) the pooling-of-interests method.

b. Projected net income for Year 8 before considering the effects of the corporate acquisition is $4,000 for Powell Corporation and $3,000 for Steele Corporation. The firms amortize any excess acquisition cost allocated to property, plant, and equipment straight-line over five years and any excess acquisition cost allocated to goodwill over 10 years. Compute the amount of consolidated net income and earnings per share for Powell Corporation and Steele Corporation for Year 8 using (1) the purchase method and (2) the pooling-of-interests method.

APPENDIX 11.3: EFFECTS ON THE STATEMENT OF CASH FLOWS OF INVESTMENTS IN SECURITIES

MARKET VALUE METHOD

When Company P uses the market value method to account for its investment in Company S, all dividend revenues recognized in computing net income also generally produce cash. Therefore, calculating cash flow from operations normally requires no adjustment to net income for this component of income.

Changes in the Investments account and in the account for Unrealized Holding Gains or Losses, which arise in the market value method, do not appear in the statement of cash flows for Securities Available for Sale. In contrast, holding gains and losses on trading securities do appear in income but do not affect cash flow, so they do require an adjustment to net income in deriving cash flow from operations if the firm uses the indirect method.

The firm will disclose material changes in market value in a supplementary schedule or note.

EQUITY METHOD

Accounting for investments using the equity method requires an adjustment to net income to compute cash flow from operations if the firm uses the indirect method in its statement of cash flows. Suppose that Company P prepares its financial statements at the end of a year during which occurred transactions **(1)** through **(5)** described in the section "Equity Method: Procedures" on pages 602–603. P reported revenue from its investment in S of $54,000. This amount results from summing the revenue recognized in transactions **(2)** and **(4).** P's income (ignoring income tax effects) increased $54,000 because of its investment. However, P's cash increased by only $21,000—transactions **(3)** and **(5)**—as a result of S's dividends. Consequently, in computing cash flow from operations, P must subtract from net income an amount equal to the excess of revenue over cash flow, or $33,000 (= $54,000 − $21,000), to show that cash did not increase by as much as the amount of revenue recognized under the equity method.

In preparing Ps statement of cash flows with the indirect format, the accountant needs to explain the following change in a noncurrent asset account.

Investment in Stock of S

Bal. 0	
Bal. 633,000	

The entries that appear on the work sheet to prepare the statement of cash flows and that explain this debit change of $633,000 are as follows:

Investment in Stock of S	600,000	
Cash (Investing—Acquisition of Investment)		600,000
To recognize use of cash for an investment in a noncurrent asset.		
Investment in Stock of S	33,000	
Cash (Operations: Subtraction—Undistributed		
Income under Equity Method)		33,000
To recognize that cash did not increase by the full amount of revenue recognized under the equity method.		

If a firm acquires an investment for an amount that exceeds the book value of the underlying net assets, the firm must amortize the excess purchase price. The amortization expense does not use cash and requires an addback to net income when computing cash flow operations under the indirect method.

CONSOLIDATION

The accountant prepares a consolidated statement of cash flows from the consolidated balance sheet and income statement. Advanced accounting texts discuss the adjustments unique to a consolidated statement of cash flows, such as for a minority interest in a consolidated subsidiary. You should be able to recognize, however, that the minority interest subtracted on the consolidated income statement generally differs from the dividends paid by the subsidiary to the minority shareholders, so that the consolidated cash flow from operations, when presented in the indirect format, requires such adjustments.

SOLUTIONS TO SELF-STUDY PROBLEMS

SUGGESTED SOLUTION TO PROBLEM 11.1 FOR SELF-STUDY

(General Electric Capital Services and Avner Company; accounting for an interest-bearing note receivable.)

a. See Exhibit 9.6; the numbers remain the same; only the column captions change.

b. *Date of Issue*

Note Receivable	112,434	
Cash		112,434

GECS lends cash to Avner and receives note.

Six Months after Issue

Interest Receivable	5,622	
Interest Revenue		5,622

See Exhibit 9.6; accrual of six months' interest = $11,243/2.

One Year after Issue

Cash	15,000	
Interest Receivable		5,622
Interest Revenue		5,621
Notes Receivable		3,757

Interest revenue for the remainder of the first year and cash received. Excess of cash payment over interest expense reduces note principal.

SUGGESTED SOLUTION TO PROBLEM 11.2 FOR SELF-STUDY

(Conlin Corporation; accounting for securities available for sale.)

a. **(1)** *February 3, Year 2*

Marketable Securities (A)	40,000	
Cash		40,000

To record acquisition of Security A.

(2) *July 15, Year 2*

Marketable Securities (B)	75,000	
Cash		75,000

To record acquisition of Security B.

(3) *November 27, Year 2*

Marketable Securities (C)	90,000	
Cash		90,000

To record acquisition of Security C.

(4) *December 31, Year 2*

Unrealized Holding Loss on Security A Available for Sale (SE/CompY)	2,000	
Marketable Securities (A)		2,000

To revalue Security A to market value. *Continued*

(5) *December 31, Year 2*

Marketable Securities (B) 4,000

   Unrealized Holding Gain on Security B Available for
     Sale (SE/CompY) 4,000

To revalue Security B to market value.

(6) *December 31, Year 2*

Marketable Securities (C) 3,000

   Unrealized Holding Gain on Security C Available for
     Sale (SE/CompY) 3,000

To revalue Security C to market value.

Note: The accountant could combine entries **(4)**, **(5)**, and **(6)** above as follows:

December 31, Year 2

Marketable Securities 5,000

   Unrealized Holding Gain (net) on Securities Available for
     Sale (SE/CompY) 5,000

To revalue the *portfolio* of marketable securities available for sale
to market value.

(7) *September 6, Year 3*

Cash 78,000

   Marketable Securities (B) 75,000

   Realized Gain on Sale of Security B Available for Sale
     (IncSt) 3,000

To record sale of Security B at a gain equal to the difference between selling price and acquisition cost and include the realized gain in net income.

(8) *September 6, Year 3, or December 31, Year 3*

Unrealized Holding Gain on Security B Available for Sale
   (SE/CompY) 4,000

   Marketable Securities (B) 4,000

To eliminate the effects of changes previously recorded in the market values of securities available for sale.

(9) *December 31, Year 3*

Unrealized Holding Loss on Security A Available for
   Sale (SE/CompY) 5,000

   Marketable Securities (A) 5,000

To revalue Security A to market value.

(10) *December 31, Year 3*

Marketable Securities (C) 1,000

   Unrealized Holding Gain on Security C Available for
     Sale (SE/CompY) 1,000

To revalue Security C to market value.

Note: The accountant could combine entries **(8)**, **(9)**, and **(10)** above as follows:

December 31, Year 3

Unrealized Holding Gain (net) on Securities Available for
   Sale (SE/CompY) 8,000

   Marketable Securities (SE/CompY) 8,000

To revalue the *portfolio* of marketable securities available for sale
to market value.

b. The first three journal entries are identical. The unrealized holding gain or loss accounts in entries **(4)**, **(5)**, **(6)**, **(9)**, and **(10)** are income statement accounts when the firm classifies the securities as trading securities. Entry **(7)** is as follows:

September 6, Year 3		
Cash	78,000	
Realized Loss from Sale of Trading Security B (IncSt)	1,000	
Marketable Securities (B)		79,000
To record sale of trading security for less than its book value at the time of sale.		

Entry **(8)** would not be made if the security was a trading security.

SUGGESTED SOLUTION TO PROBLEM 11.3 SELF-STUDY

(Investor Corporation; journal entries to apply the market value method for long-term investments in securities.)

a.	*January 10, Year 1*		
	Investment in Securities (A)	60,000	
	Cash		60,000
	March 20, Year 1		
	Investment in Securities (B)	80,000	
	Cash		80,000
	October 2, Year 1		
	Investment in Securities (C)	40,000	
	Cash		40,000
b.	*December 31, Year 1*		
	Cash	2,000	
	Dividend Revenue		2,000
c.	*December 31, Year 1*		
	Investment in Securities (A)	3,000	
	Investment in Securities (C)	2,000	
	Unrealized Holding Gain on Investments in Securities (SE/CompY)		5,000
	December 31, Year 1		
	Unrealized Holding Loss on Investments in Securities (SE/CompY)	8,000	
	Investment in Securities (B)		8,000
d.	*June 19, Year 2*		
	Cash	65,000	
	Realized Loss on Sale of Investments (IncSt)	15,000	
	Investment in Securities (B)		80,000
	June 19, Year 2, or December 31, Year 2		
	Investment in Securities (B)	8,000	
	Unrealized Holding Loss on Investments in Securities (SE/CompY)		8,000

e. *December 31, Year 2*

Cash 2,200

    Dividend Revenue   2,200

f. *December 31, Year 2*

Investment in Securities (A) 2,000

    Unrealized Holding Gain on Investments in Securities
    (SE/CompY)   2,000

December 31, Year 2

Unrealized Holding Gain on Investments in Securities
(SE/CompY) 2,000

Unrealized Holding Loss on Investments in Securities
(SE/CompY) 7,000

    Investments in Securities (C)   9,000

SUGGESTED SOLUTION TO PROBLEM 11.4 FOR SELF-STUDY

(Equity Investing Group; journal entries to apply the equity method for long-term investments in securities.)

a.

Investment in Securities (D) 80,000

Investment in Securities (E) 190,000

Investment in Securities (F) 200,000

    Cash   470,000

b.

Investment in Securities (D) (.40 × $40,000) 16,000

Investment in Securities (E) (.30 × $120,000) 36,000

Investment in Securities (F) (.20 × $200,000) 40,000

    Equity in Earnings of Affiliates   92,000

Cash 25,000

    Investment in Securities (D) (.40 × $10,000)   4,000

    Investment in Securities (E) (.30 × $30,000)   9,000

    Investment in Securities (F) (.20 × $60,000)   12,000

Amortization Expense 8,000

    Investment in Securities (E)   4,000

    Investment in Securities (F)   4,000

Security	Book Value of Investee on January 1, Year 1	Ownership Percentage	Share of Book Value Acquired	Acquisition Cost of Investment	Excess Acquisition Cost	Annual Amortization for 10 Years
D	$200,000	40%	$ 80,000	$ 80,000	—	—
E	500,000	30%	150,000	190,000	$40,000	$4,000
F	800,000	20%	160,000	200,000	40,000	4,000

c.

Investment in Securities (D) (.40 × $50,000) 20,000

Investment in Securities (F) (.20 × $50,000) 10,000

    Investment in Securities (E) (.30 × $40,000)   12,000

    Equity in (Net) Earnings of Affiliates   18,000

Cash	16,800	
Investment in Securities (D) (.40 × $12,000)		4,800
Investment in Securities (F) (.20 × $60,000)		12,000
Amortization Expense	8,000	
Investment in Securities (E)		4,000
Investment in Securities (F)		4,000

d.

Cash	190,000	
Loss on Sale of Investment in Securities	7,000	
Investment in Securities (E)		197,000

$197,000 = $190,000 + $36,000 − $9,000 − $4,000 − $12,000 − $4,000.

SUGGESTED SOLUTION TO PROBLEM 11.5 FOR SELF-STUDY

(Parent and Sub; understanding consolidation concepts.)

a. No. The investment account shows a balance of $192, which equals 80 percent of Sub's shareholders' equity ($192 = .80 × $240).

b. **(1)** The account Investment in Sub has a balance of $192, which equals 80 percent of the shareholders' equity of Sub. This clue supports the 80 percent ownership only because no unamortized excess acquisition cost exists (see the response to question **a**).

(2) The minority interest in the net assets of Sub is $48, which equals 20 percent of the shareholders' equity of Sub ($48 = .20 × $240).

(3) The account Equity in Earnings of Sub on Parent's books has a balance of $80 for Year 1, which equals 80 percent of the net income of Sub for Year 1 ($80 = .80 × $100).

(4) The account Minority Interest in Earnings of Sub has a balance of $20 for Year 1 ($20 = .20 × $100).

c. Parent and Sub have intercompany accounts receivable and accounts payable. Combined accounts receivable exceed consolidated accounts receivable by $25 (= $820 − $795), the same as the excess of combined accounts payable over consolidated accounts payable ($25 = $540 − $515).

d. Double-counting results if both the investment account and the individual assets and liabilities of Sub appear on the consolidated balance sheet.

e. The $240 of Sub's shareholders' equity disappears in consolidation as follows:

Elimination of Investment in Sub	$192
Recognition of Minority Interest in Net Assets of Sub	48
Total	$240

f. $500 (= $6,000 − $5,500 or $4,040 − $3,540).

g. Consolidated amounts include individual revenues, expenses, and minority interest in earnings, which net to $80. Double-counting this earnings results if the accountant does not eliminate the equity in earnings account.

h. The separate-company income statements report the total revenues and expenses of each entity without regard to who owns the common stock of each company. The consolidated income statement shows the earnings allocable to the shareholders of the parent company. These shareholders have a claim on all of the earnings of Parent but on only 80 percent of the earnings of Sub. Consolidated revenues and expenses included the combined amounts for both companies, adjusted for intercompany transactions.

The minority interest in net income of Sub shows the portion of Sub's net income not subject to a claim by Parent's shareholders.

SUGGESTED SOLUTION TO PROBLEM 11.6 FOR SELF-STUDY

(P Company and S Company; preparing consolidation work sheet adjustment and elimination entries.)

a.

Common Stock (S Company)	100	
Retained Earnings (S Company)	330	
Equity in Earnings of S Company (P Company)	100	
Investment in S Company (P Company)		530
To eliminate investment account and subsidiary's shareholders' equity accounts.		
Sales Revenue	1,000	
Cost of Goods Sold		1,000
To eliminate intercompany sales of merchandise.		
Accounts Payable	200	
Accounts Receivable		200
To eliminate intercompany receivables and payables.		

b. (1)

Acquisition Cost of Investment in S Company	$510	
Plus Equity in Earnings of S Company, Year 6	100	
Less Amortization of Excess Acquisition Cost for Year 6: ($510 − $430)/10	(8)	
Investment Account, December 31, Year 6	$602	

(2)

Common Stock (S Company)	100	
Retained Earnings (S Company)	330	
Equity in Earnings of S Company (P Company)	100	
Goodwill	72	
Investment in S Company (P Company)		602
Sales Revenue	1,000	
Cost of Goods Sold		1,000
Accounts Payable	200	
Accounts Receivable		200

SUGGESTED SOLUTION TO PROBLEM 11.7 FOR SELF-STUDY

(Powell Corporation and Steele Corporation; financial statement effects of the purchase method and the pooling-of-interests method.)

a. Exhibit 11.14 presents the consolidated balance sheet of January 1, Year 8, using (1) the purchase method and (2) the pooling-of-interests method.

b.

	(1) Purchase Method	(2) Pooling-of-Interests Method
Precombination Projected Net Income	$7,000	$7,000
Additional Depreciation: $5,000/5	(1,000)	—
Goodwill Amortization: $40,000/10	(4,000)	—
Revised Net Income	$2,000	$7,000
Number of Common Shares Outstanding	3,700	3,700
Earnings Per Share	$.54	$1.89

EXHIBIT 11.14	POWELL CORPORATION AND STEELE CORPORATION Consolidated Balance Sheet, January 1, Year 8 (Problem 11.7 for Self-Study)	

	(1) Purchase Method	(2) Pooling-of-Interests Method
ASSETS		
Current Assets	$ 17,000	$17,000
Property, Plant, and Equipment (net)	53,000	48,000
Goodwill	40,000	—
Total Assets	$110,000	$65,000
EQUITIES		
Liabilities	$ 41,000	$41,000
Common Stock	3,700[a]	3,700[a]
Additional Paid-in Capital	60,300[b]	12,300[c]
Retained Earnings	5,000	8,000
Total Equities	$110,000	$65,000

[a]$3,700 = $1,000 + (2,700 \times $1)$.
[b]$60,300 = $9,000 + (2,700 \times 19)$.
[c]$1,000 + $9,000 + $1,000 + $5,000 = $16,000; $16,000 - (3,700 \times $1) = $12,300$.

KEY TERMS AND CONCEPTS

Marketable securities
Minority, passive investments
Significant influence
Minority, active investments
Majority, active investments
Market value method
Equity method
Parent
Subsidiary

Consolidated financial statements
Economic entity
Consolidation policy
Intercompany transactions
Minority interest
Goodwill
Purchase method
Pooling-of-interests method
Uniting of interests

QUESTIONS, EXERCISES, PROBLEMS, AND CASES

QUESTIONS

1. Review the meaning of the terms and concepts listed above in Key Terms and Concepts.
2. "The classification of securities on the balance sheet as a current asset (Marketable Securities) or as a noncurrent asset (Investment in Securities) depends on a firm's intent." Explain.
3. Distinguish between the following pairs of terms:
   a. Debt securities classified as "held to maturity" versus "available for sale"
   b. Equity securities classified as "trading securities" versus "available for sale"
   c. Amortized acquisition cost versus market value of debt securities

    d. Unrealized holding gain or loss on trading securities versus on securities available for sale

    e. Realized gain or loss on trading securities versus on securities available for sale

4. What is the GAAP justification for including unrealized holding gains and losses on trading securities in income but reporting unrealized holding gains and losses on securities available for sale in a separate shareholders' equity account?

5. "The realized gain or loss from the sale of a particular security classified as available for sale will likely differ in amount from the realized gain or loss if the firm had classified that same security as a trading security." Explain.

6. "Reporting marketable securities available for sale at market values on the balance sheet but not including the unrealized holding gains and losses in income is inconsistent." Do you agree? Why or why not?

7. Refer to Example **6** in the chapter. Assume that Linderman Company is a conventional, walk-in-and-see-it furniture store and is worried that Web-based furniture stores will put it out of business. It has bought the options on FurnitureOnLine.com to hedge the risks that it may have to go out of business if its traditional business becomes unprofitable. Would this transaction qualify as either a fair-value hedge or a cash-flow hedge? How would Linderman Company classify the options for accounting purposes?

8. Compare and contrast each of the following pairs of accounts:

    a. Unrealized Holding Gain or Loss on Marketable Equity Securities, and Unrealized Holding Gain or Loss on Investments in Securities

    b. Dividend Revenue, and Equity in Earnings of Unconsolidated Affiliates

    c. Equity in Earnings of Unconsolidated Affiliate, and Minority Interest in Earnings of Consolidated Subsidiary

    d. Minority Interest in Earnings of Consolidated Subsidiary, and Minority Interest in Net Assets of Consolidated Subsidiary

9. "Dividends received or receivable from another company are either a revenue in calculating net income or a return of investment, depending on the method of accounting the investor uses." Explain.

10. Why is the equity method sometimes described as a *one-line consolidation*? Consider both the balance sheet and the income statement in your response.

11. Distinguish between minority investments in other companies and the minority interest in a consolidated subsidiary.

12. "Accounting for an investment in a subsidiary using the equity method and not consolidating it yields the same net income as consolidating the subsidiary. Total assets will differ, however, depending on whether or not the investor consolidates the subsidiary." Explain.

EXERCISES

13. **Classifying securities.** Firms must classify securities along two dimensions:

    ■ Purpose of investment: debt securities held to maturity, trading securities, or securities available for sale

    ■ Length of expected holding period: current asset (Marketable Securities) or noncurrent asset (Investment in Securities)

    Classify each of the securities below along each of these two dimensions.

    a. A forest products company plans to construct a pulp-processing plant beginning in April of next year. It issues common stock for $200 million on December 10 of this year to help finance construction. The company invests this $200 million in U.S. government debt securities to generate income until it needs the cash for construction.

b. An electric utility has bonds payable outstanding for $100 million that mature in five years. The electric utility acquires U.S. government bonds that have a maturity value of $100 million in five years. The firm plans to use the proceeds from the government bonds to repay its own outstanding bonds.

c. A commercial bank acquires bonds of the state of New York to generate tax-exempt interest revenue. The bank plans to sell the bonds when it needs cash for loans and other ongoing operating needs.

d. A pharmaceutical company acquires common stock of a biogenetic engineering company that conducts research in human growth hormones. The pharmaceutical company hopes the investment will lead to strategic alliances or joint ventures in the future.

e. A commercial bank maintains a department that regularly purchases and sells securities on stock exchanges around the world. This department acquires common stock of Toyota on the New York Stock Exchange because it thinks the market price does not fully reflect favorable news about Toyota.

f. A U.S. computer company has bonds payable outstanding that are denominated in French francs. The bonds mature in installments during the next five years. The computer company purchases a French winery's bonds, denominated in French francs, that mature in seven years. The computer company will sell a portion of the bonds of the French winery each year to obtain the French francs needed to repay its franc-denominated bonds.

14. Journal entries for holdings of marketable equity securities. Events related to Vermont Company's investment in the common stock of Texas Instruments appear below. Vermont Company closes its books on December 31 of each year.

8/21 Vermont Company purchases 1,000 shares of Texas Instruments' common stock for $45 per share as an investment of temporarily excess cash (classified as Securities Available for Sale).

9/13 The stockbroker for Vermont Company calls to report that the shares of Texas Instruments closed on the preceding day at $48 per share.

9/30 Texas Instruments declares a dividend of $.50 per share.

10/25 Vermont Company receives a dividend check from Texas Instruments for $500.

12/31 The stockbroker calls Vermont Company to report that Texas Instruments' shares closed the year at $51 per share. Vermont Company closes its books for the year.

1/20 Vermont Company sells 600 shares for $55 per share, the closing price for the day.

Prepare dated journal entries as required by these events. Ignore income taxes.

15. Journal entries for holdings of marketable equity securities. Events related to Elston Corporation's investments of temporarily excess cash appear below. The firm classifies these investments as Securities Available for Sale.

			Market Value on December 31			
Security	**Date Acquired**	**Acquisition Cost**	**Year 4**	**Year 5**	**Date Sold**	**Selling Price**
A	10/15/Year 4	$28,000	$25,000	—	2/10/Year 5	$24,000
B	11/2/Year 4	$49,000	$55,000	$53,000	7/15/Year 6	$57,000

Elston received no dividends on Security A. It received dividends from Security B of $1,000 on December 31, Year 4, and $1,200 on December 31, Year 5. Prepare dated journal entries for the events related to these investments, assuming that the accounting period is the calendar year.

a. Acquisition of securities
b. Receipt of dividends
c. Revaluation on December 31
d. Sale of securities

16. **Journal entries for holdings of marketable equity securities.** Events related to Simmons Corporation's investments of temporarily excess cash appear below. The firm classifies these investments as Securities Available for Sale.

Security	Date Acquired	Acquisition Cost	Year 6	Year 7	Date Sold	Selling Price
					Market Value on December 31	
S	6/13/Year 6	$12,000	$13,500	$15,200	2/15/Year 8	$14,900
T	6/13/Year 6	$29,000	$26,200	$31,700	8/22/Year 8	$28,500
U	6/13/Year 6	$43,000	—	—	10/11/Year 6	$39,000

None of these three securities paid dividends. Prepare dated journal entries for the events related to these investments, assuming that the accounting period is the calendar year.

a. Acquisition of securities.
b. Revaluation on December 31.
c. Sale of securities.

17. **Working backward from data on marketable securities transaction.** (Adapted from a problem by S. A. Zeff.) During Year 3, Fischer/Black Co. purchased equity securities. On May 22, Year 4, the company recorded the following correct journal entry to record the sale of the equity securities:

Cash	15,000	
Realized Loss	5,000	
Unrealized Holding Loss		3,000
Marketable Securities		17,000

a. What was the original cost of these securities in Year 3?
b. What was the market value of these securities at the end of Year 3?
c. What is the total amount of securities gain or loss that Fischer/Black reports on the income statement for Year 4?

18. **Working backward from data on marketable securities transaction.** (Adapted from a problem by S. A. Zeff.) On December 12, Year 2, Canning had purchased 2,000 shares of Werther. By December 31, the market price of these shares had dropped to $12,000. On March 2, Year 3, Canning sold the 2,000 shares for $17,000 and reported a realized gain on the transaction of $4,000.

a. What was the original cost of these securities if Canning had accounted for them as trading securities?

b. What was the original cost of these securities if Canning had accounted for them as securities available for sale?

19. **Reconstructing events from journal entries.** Give the likely transaction or event that would result in making each of the independent journal entries that follow:

a.

Unrealized Loss on Securities Available for Sale	4,000	
Marketable Securities		4,000

b.

Cash	1,200	
Realized Loss on Sale of Securities Available for Sale	100	
Marketable Securities		1,300

c.

Marketable Securities	750	
Unrealized Holding Gain on Securities Available for Sale		750

d.

Cash	1,800	
Marketable Securities		1,700
Realized Gain on Sale of Securities Available for Sale		100

20. **Amount of income recognized under various methods of accounting for investments.** On January 1, Apollo Corporation acquired common stock of Venus Corporation. At the time of acquisition, the book value and the fair market value of Venus Corporation's net assets were $500 million. During the year, Venus Corporation earned $80 million and declared dividends of $20 million. The market value of shares increased by 10 percent during the year. How much income would Apollo Corporation report for the year related to its investment under the assumption that it took the following actions?
   a. Paid $75 million for 15 percent of the common stock and uses the market value method to account for its investment in Venus Corporation.
   b. Paid $115 million for 15 percent of the common stock and uses the market value method to account for its investment in Venus Corporation.
   c. Paid $150 million for 30 percent of the common stock and uses the equity method to account for its investment in Venus Corporation..
   d. Paid $230 million for 30 percent of the common stock and uses the equity method to account for its investment in Venus Corporation. Amortize goodwill over ten years.

21. **Balance sheet and income effects of alternative methods of accounting for investments.** On January 1, Trusco acquired common stock of USP Company. At the time of acquisition, the book value and the market value of USP's net assets were $400 million. During the current year, USP earned $50 million and declared dividends of $20 million. Indicate the amount shown for Investment in USP on the balance sheet on December 31 and the amount of income Trusco would

report for the year related to its investment under the assumption that Trusco did the following:

a. Paid $40 million for a 10 percent interest in USP and uses the market value method. The market value of USP on December 31 was $400 million.

b. Same as part **a** except that the market value of USP on December 31 was $390 million.

c. Paid $45 million for a 10 percent interest in USP and uses the market value method. The market value of USP on December 31 was $450 million.

d. Paid $120 million for a 30 percent interest in USP and uses the equity method.

e. Paid $160 million for a 30 percent interest in USP and uses the equity method. Trusco amortizes goodwill over 10 years.

22. **Journal entries to apply the market value method for long-term investments in securities.** The following information summarizes data about the minority, passive investments in securities of Randle Company for its first two years of operations.

| | | | | | Market Value | |
Security	Date Acquired	Acquisition Cost	Date Sold	Selling Price	Dec. 31, Year 1	Dec. 31, Year 2
M	4/10/Year 1	$ 37,000	10/15/Year 2	$43,000	$ 35,000	$ —
N	7/11/Year 1	31,000			38,000	45,000
O	9/29/Year 1	94,000			87,000	89,000
		$162,000			$160,000	$134,000

Randle Company received dividends on December 31 of each year as follows:

Security	Year 1	Year 2
M	$1,500	—
N	1,400	$1,600
O	5,000	4,000

Prepare journal entries to account for these investments in securities during Year 1 and Year 2 using the market value method.

23. **Journal entries to apply the market value method for long-term investments in securities.** The following information summarizes data about minority, passive investments in securities of Blake Company.

| | | | | | Market Value | |
Security	Date Acquired	Acquisition Cost	Date Sold	Selling Price	Dec. 31, Year 4	Dec. 31, Year 5
F	7/9/Year 3	$93,700	10/29/Year 4	$89,700	—	—
G	7/2/Year 4	42,800			$38,300	$36,900
H	10/19/Year 4	29,600	9/17/Year 5	32,300	31,600	—
I	2/9/Year 5	18,100			—	20,700

The market value of the investment in Security F totaled $91,200 on December 31, Year 3. Assume that none of the investees paid dividends during Year 4 or Year 5. Prepare journal entries to account for these investments in securities during Year 4 and Year 5 using the market value method.

24. **Journal entries to apply the equity method of accounting for investments in securities.** Wood Corporation made three long-term intercorporate investments on January 2. Data relating to these investments for the year appear below.

Company	Percentage Acquired	Book Value and Market Value of Net Assets on January 2	Acquisition Cost	Net Income (Loss) for the Year	Dividends Declared during the Year
Knox Corporation	50%	$700,000	$350,000	$70,000	$30,000
Vachi Corporation	30	520,000	196,000	40,000	16,000
Snow Corporation	20	400,000	100,000	(24,000)	—

Give the journal entries to record the acquisition of these investments and to apply the equity method during the year. Wood amortizes goodwill over 20 years.

25. **Journal entries to apply the equity method of accounting for investments in securities.** The following information summarizes data about the minority, active investments of Stebbins Corporation.

Security	Date Acquired	Acquisition Cost	Ownership Percentage	Book Value of Net Assets on January 1, Year 1	Earnings (Loss) Year 1	Earnings (Loss) Year 2	Dividends Year 1	Dividends Year 2
R	1/1/Year 1	$250,000	25%	$800,000	$200,000	$225,000	$125,000	$130,000
S	1/1/Year 1	325,000	40	750,000	120,000	75,000	80,000	80,000
T	1/1/Year 1	475,000	50	950,000	(150,000)	50,000	—	—

Stebbins Corporation amortizes any excess acquisition cost over 20 years.

a. Give the journal entries to record the acquisition of these investments and to apply the equity method during Year 1 and Year 2.

b. Stebbins Corporation sells Security S on January 1, Year 3, for $330,000. Give the journal entry to record the sale.

26. **Journal entries under various methods of accounting for investments.** Mulherin Corporation made three long-term investments on January 2. Data relating to these investments appear below.

Company	Percentage Acquired	Book Value and Market Value of Net Assets on January 2	Acquisition Cost	Net Income for Year	Dividends Declared during the Year	Market Value of Shares Held on December 31
Hanson	15%	$2,000,000	$ 320,000	$200,000	$ 40,000	$ 305,000
Maloney	30	2,000,000	680,000	500,000	180,000	700,000
Quinn	100	2,000,000	2,800,000	600,000	310,000	1,950,000

Assume that these were the only intercorporate investments of Mulherin Corporation. Mulherin amortizes goodwill over 20 years.

a. Give the journal entries on Mulherin Corporation's books to record these acquisitions of common stock and to account for the intercorporate investments under GAAP. Mulherin Corporation accounts for its investment in Quinn Corporation using the equity method on its separate-company books.

b. (Requires coverage of Appendix 11.1.) Give the work sheet entry to consolidate Mulherin Corporation and Quinn Corporation. The preclosing trial balance of Quinn Corporation shows the following:

Common Stock	$200,000
Additional Paid-in Capital	800,000
Retained Earnings (preclosing)	690,000
Net Income for Year	600,000

27. **Consolidation policy and principal consolidation concepts.** CAR Corporation manufactures computers in the United States. It owns 75 percent of the voting stock of Charles Electronics, 80 percent of the voting stock of Alexandre du France Software Systems (in France), and 90 percent of the voting stock of R Credit Corporation (a finance company). CAR Corporation prepares consolidated financial statements consolidating Charles Electronics, uses the equity method for R Credit Corporation, and treats its investment in Alexandre du France Software Systems as securities available for sale. Data from the annual reports of these companies appear below.

	Percentage Owned	Net Income	Dividends	Accounting Method
CAR Corporation Consolidated	—	$1,200,000	$ 84,000	—
Charles Electronics	75%	120,000	48,000	Consolidated
Alexandre du France Software Systems[a]	80	96,000	60,000	Market Value
R Credit Corporation	90	144,000	120,000	Equity

[a]Market value of shares exceeds cost.

a. Which, if any, of the companies does CAR incorrectly account for according to GAAP?

Assuming the accounting for the three subsidiaries shown above is correct, answer the following questions:

b. How much of the net income reported by CAR Corporation Consolidated results from the operations of the three subsidiaries?

c. What is the amount of the minority interest now shown on the income statement, and how does it affect net income of CAR Corporation Consolidated?

d. If CAR had consolidated all three subsidiaries, what would have been the net income of CAR Corporation Consolidated?

e. If CAR had consolidated all three subsidiaries, what minority interest would appear on the income statement?

28. **Equity method and consolidation elimination entries.** Clinton Corporation acquired control of Dole Computer Company on January 2 by purchasing 100 percent of its outstanding stock for $500 million. Clinton attributes the entire excess of cost

over book value acquired to goodwill, which it amortizes over 10 years. The shareholders' equity accounts of Dole Computer Company appeared as follows on January 2 and December 31 of the current year (amounts in millions):

	Jan. 2	Dec. 31
Common Stock	$300	$300
Retained Earnings	120	190

Dole Computer had earnings of $100 million and declared dividends of $30 million during the year. The accounts receivable of Clinton Corporation at December 31 included $3 million due from Dole Computer. Clinton Corporation accounts for its investment in Dole Computer on its single-company books using the equity method.

a. Give the journal entries to record the acquisition of the shares of Dole Computer and to apply the equity method during the year on the books of Clinton Corporation.

b. (Requires coverage of Appendix 11.1.) Give the required elimination entries for a consolidation work sheet at the end of the year, assuming that the work sheet uses preclosing trial balance data.

29. **Equity method and consolidation elimination entries.** Hanna Company purchased 100 percent of the common stock of Denver Company on January 2 for $550,000. The common stock of Denver Company at this date was $200,000, and the retained earnings balance was $350,000. During the year, net income of Denver Company was $120,000; dividends declared were $40,000. Hanna Company uses the equity method to account for the investment.

a. Give the journal entry made by Hanna Company during the year to account for its investment in Denver Company.

b. (Requires coverage of Appendix 11.1.) Give the elimination entry for the investment account, assuming that the consolidation work sheet uses preclosing trial balance data.

30. **Equity method and consolidation work sheet entries.** Vogel Company is a subsidiary of Joyce Company. Joyce Company accounts for its investment in Vogel Company using the equity method on its single-company books.

a. Present journal entries for the following selected transactions. Record the set of entries on the books of Vogel Company separately from the set of entries on the books of Joyce Company.

(1) On January 2, Joyce Company acquired on the market, for cash, 100 percent of the common stock of Vogel Company. The outlay was $420,000. The total contributed capital of Vogel Company's stock outstanding was $300,000; the retained earnings balance was $80,000. Joyce attributes the excess of cost over book value acquired to goodwill and amortizes it over 10 years.

(2) Vogel Company purchased materials for $29,000 from Joyce Company on account at the latter's cost.

(3) Vogel Company obtained an advance of $6,000 from Joyce Company. Vogel Company deposited the funds in the bank.

(4) Vogel Company paid $16,000 on the purchases in **(2)**.

(5) Vogel Company repaid $4,000 of the loan received from Joyce Company in **(3)**.

(6) Vogel Company declared and paid a dividend of $20,000 during the year.

(7) The net income of Vogel Company for the year was $30,000.

b. (Requires coverage of Appendix 11.1.) Prepare the necessary adjustment and elimination entries on December 31 for a consolidated balance sheet, recognizing the effects of only the previously listed transactions. Assume that the work sheet uses preclosing financial statement data.

31. **Working backward to consolidation relations.** Laesch Company, as parent, owns shares in one other company. It has owned them since it formed the other company. Laesch Company has retained earnings from its own operations independent of intercorporate investments of $100,000. The consolidated balance sheet shows no goodwill and shows retained earnings of $156,000. Consider each of the following questions independently of the others:
    a. If the parent owns 70 percent of its consolidated subsidiary, what are the retained earnings of the subsidiary?
    b. If the subsidiary has retained earnings of $77,000, what fraction of the subsidiary does the parent own?
    c. If the parent had not consolidated the subsidiary but instead had accounted for it using the equity method, how much revenue in excess of dividends received would the parent company have recognized from the investment?

32. **Working backward from consolidated income statements.** Dealco Corporation published a consolidated income statement for the year, shown in Exhibit 11.15. The unconsolidated affiliate retained 20 percent of its earnings of $140 million during the year, having paid out the rest as dividends. The consolidated subsidiary earned $280 million during the year and declared no dividends.
    a. What percentage of the unconsolidated affiliate does Dealco Corporation own?
    b. What dividends did Dealco Corporation receive from the unconsolidated affiliate during the year?
    c. What percentage of the consolidated subsidiary does Dealco Corporation own?

EXHIBIT 11.15	DEALCO CORPORATION Consolidated Income Statement (Exercise 32)

REVENUES		
Sales		$ 1,400,000
Equity in Earnings of Unconsolidated Affiliate		56,000
Total Revenues		$ 1,456,000
EXPENSES		
Cost of Goods Sold (excluding depreciation)		$ 910,000
Administrative Expense		140,000
Depreciation Expense		161,000
Amortization of Goodwill		7,000
Income Tax Expenses:		
Currently Payable	$ 58,800	
Deferred	14,000	72,800
Total Expenses		$ 1,290,800
Income of the Consolidated Group		$ 165,200
Less Minority Interest in Earnings of Consolidated Subsidiary		42,000
Net Income to Shareholders		$ 123,200

33. **Eliminating intercompany transactions.** (Requires Appendix 11.1; adapted from a problem by S. A. Zeff.) Alpha owns 100 percent of Omega and consolidates Omega in an entity called Alpha/Omega. Beginning in Year 2, Alpha sold merchandise to Omega at a price 50 percent larger than Alpha's costs. Omega sold some, but not all, of these goods to customers at a further markup. Excerpts from the single-company statements of Alpha and Omega and from the consolidated financial statements of Alpha/Omega appear below.

	Single-Company Statements		Consolidated Financial Statements
	Alpha	**Omega**	
Sales Revenue	$450,000	$250,000	$610,000
Cost of Goods Sold	300,000	210,000	430,000
Merchandise Inventory	60,000	50,000	100,000

   a. What was the total sales price at which Alpha sold goods to Omega during Year 2?
   b. What was Omega's cost of the goods it had purchased from Alpha but has not yet sold by the end of Year 2? What was Alpha's cost of those goods? Which of those two numbers appears in the total Merchandise Inventory on the consolidated balance sheet?

34. **Working backward from purchase data to reconstruct pooling.** (Requires Appendix 11.2; adapted from a problem by S. A. Zeff.) On May 1, Year 1, Homer acquired the assets and agreed to pay the liabilities of Tonga in exchange for 10,000 of Homer's common shares. On the date of acquisition Tonga's book value of depreciable assets exceeded Homer's estimate of their market value, but Homer judged all other items on Tonga's books to reflect market value on that date. On the date of the acquisition, Tonga's shareholders' equity of $980,000 comprised $160,000 of par value of common shares, $420,000 of additional paid-in capital, and $400,000 of retained earnings.
   Homer made the following journal entry to record the acquisition:

Current Assets	210,000	
Depreciable Assets (net)	700,000	
Goodwill	130,000	
Liabilities		90,000
Common Stock—Par		150,000
Additional Paid-in Capital		800,000

   a. What was the book value on Tonga's books of its total assets just before the acquisition?
   b. What journal entry would Homer have made for the acquisition if it had qualified for a pooling of interests?

35. **Financial statement effects of purchase and pooling-of-interests methods.** (Requires coverage of Appendix 11.2.) Exhibit 11.16 presents condensed balance sheet data for Water Company and Soluble Company on January 2, Year 5. On this date, Water Company exchanges common stock with a market value of $280 for all of the outstanding common stock of Soluble Company.

	Historical Cost		Current Market Value
	Water Company	Soluble Company	Soluble Company
ASSETS			
Current Assets	$200	$150	$150
Property, Plant, and Equipment (net)	400	200	250
Goodwill	—	—	100
Total Assets	$600	$350	$500
EQUITIES			
Liabilities	$350	$220	$220
Common Stock	100	50	50
Retained Earnings	150	80	80
Unrecorded Equity at Current Valuation	—	—	150
Total Equities	$600	$350	$500

EXHIBIT 11.16 WATER COMPANY AND SOLUBLE COMPANY Balance Sheet Data for January 2, Year 5 (Exercise 35)

a. Prepare a consolidated balance sheet for Water Company and Soluble Company as of January 2, Year 5, using (1) the purchase method and (2) the pooling-of-interests method.

b. Projected net income for Year 5 before consideration of the corporate acquisition was $60 for Water Company and $20 for Soluble Company. These firms intend to amortize any excess acquisition cost allocated to property, plant, and equipment over five years and any excess allocated to goodwill over 20 years. Compute the amount of consolidated net income projected for Year 5 assuming that these firms account for the corporate acquisition using (1) the purchase method and (2) the pooling-of-interests method.

36. **Financial statement effects of purchase and pooling-of-interests methods.** (Requires coverage of Appendix 11.2.) Bristol-Myers Corporation and Squibb, both pharmaceutical companies, agreed to merge as of January 2, Year 10. Bristol-Myers exchanged 234 million shares of its common stock for the outstanding shares of Squibb. The shares of Bristol-Myers sold for $55 per share on the merger date, resulting in a transaction with a market value of $12.87 billion. Condensed balance sheet data on January 2, Year 10, appear below (amounts in millions).

	Bristol-Myers	Squibb
Assets	$5,190	$3,083
Liabilities	1,643	1,682
Shareholders' Equity	3,547	1,401
	$5,190	$3,083

a. Prepare a condensed consolidated balance sheet on the date of the merger assuming that the firms accounted for the merger using (1) the purchase method and (2) the pooling-of-interests method. Assume that any excess acquisition cost over the book value of Squibb's net assets relates to goodwill, which the firms amortize over 10 years.

b. Projected net income for Year 10 before considering the effects of the merger are $1,225 for Bristol-Myers and $523 for Squibb. Compute the amount of consolidated net income projected for Year 10 for Bristol-Myers and Squibb using (1) the purchase method and (2) the pooling-of-interests method.

c. Which method of accounting will these firms likely prefer to account for the merger? Explain.

37. **Effect of transactions on the statement of cash flows.** (Requires coverage of Appendix 11.3.) Refer to the simplified statement of cash flows in Exhibit 4.16. Numbers appear on nine of the lines in the statement. Ignore the unnumbered lines in considering the transactions below. Assume that the accounting cycle is complete for the period and that the firm has prepared all of its financial statements. It then discovers that it has overlooked a transaction. It records the transaction in the accounts and corrects all of the financial statements. For each of the following transactions or events, indicate which of the numbered lines of the statement of cash flows change and the amount and direction of the change (increase or decrease). Ignore income tax effects.

a. A firm purchased marketable securities costing $59,700 during the period. The firm classifies these as Securities Available for Sale.

b. A firm sold for $47,900 marketable securities available for sale originally costing $42,200 and with a book value of $44,000 at the time of sale.

c. A firm sold for $18,700 marketable securities available for sale originally costing $25,100 and with a book value of $19,600 at the time of sale.

d. A particular marketable equity security purchased during the period for $220,500 had a market value of $201,500 at the end of the accounting period. The firm classifies the security as a Security Available for Sale.

e. Assume the same information as in part **d** except that the market value of the security at the end of the accounting period is $226,900.

f. The firm receives a dividend of $7,000 on shares held as an *investment* available for sale and accounted for using the market value method.

g. The firm writes down, from $10,000 to $8,000, securities available for sale accounted for with the market value method.

h. A 40-percent-owned affiliate accounted for using the equity method earns $25,000 and pays dividends of $10,000.

i. A 40-percent-owned affiliate accounted for using the equity method reports a loss for the year of $12,500.

j. The firm amortizes $2,000 of the excess of the purchase price over the book value of the underlying net assets in a 40-percent-owned affiliate.

38. **Effect of errors involving marketable securities and accounts receivable on financial statement ratios.** Indicate using O/S (overstated), U/S (understated), or NO (no effect) the pre-tax effect of each of the following errors on (1) the rate of return on assets, (2) the cash flow from operations to average current liabilities ratio, and (3) the debt-equity ratio. Each of these ratios is less than 100 percent before discovering the error.

a. A firm holding marketable securities classified as available for sale neglected to write down the securities to market value at the end of the year.

b. A firm using the allowance method neglected to provide for estimated uncollectible accounts at the end of the year.

c. A firm using the allowance method neglected to write off specific accounts as uncollectible at the end of the year.

d. A firm credited a check received from a customer to Advances from Customers even though the customer was paying for purchases previously made on account.

e. A firm neglected to accrue interest receivable on a note at the end of the year.

39. Effect of errors on financial statements. Using the notation O/S (overstated), U/S (understated), or No (no effect), indicate the effects on assets, liabilities, shareholders' equity, and net income of each of the independent errors that follow. Ignore income tax effects.

a. In applying the market value method to minority, passive investments in securities, a firm incorrectly credits dividends received to the investment account.

b. The market value of minority, passive investments in securities at the end of a firm's first year of operations was $5,000 less than cost. The firm neglected to make the required journal entry in applying the market value method.

c. In applying the equity method, P correctly accrues its share of S's net income for the year. However, when receiving a dividend, P credits Dividend Revenue.

d. P acquired 30 percent of S on January 1 of the current year for an amount in excess of the market value of S's net assets. P correctly accounted for its share of S's net income and dividends for the year but neglected to amortize any of the excess purchase price.

e. During the current year, P sold inventory items to S, its wholly-owned subsidiary, at a profit. S sold these inventory items, and S paid P for them before the end of the year. The firms made no elimination entry for this intercompany sale on the consolidation work sheet.

f. Refer to part **e.** Assume that S owes P $10,000 for intercompany purchases at year-end. The firm made no elimination entry for this intercompany debt.

g. P owns 90 percent of S. P treats the minority interest in consolidated subsidiaries as part of shareholders' equity. In preparing a consolidated work sheet, the firms made no entry to accrue the minority interest's share of S's net income or of S's net assets.

PROBLEMS AND CASES

40. Journal entries and financial statement presentation of marketable equity securities. The following information summarizes data about Dostal Corporation's marketable securities held as current assets and as securities available for sale.

Security	Date Acquired	Acquisition Cost	Date Sold	Selling Price	Market Value Dec. 31, Year 1	Market Value Dec. 31, Year 2
A	2/5/Year 1	$60,000	6/5/Year 2	$72,000	$66,000	—
B	8/12/Year 1	25,000	—	—	20,000	$23,000
C	1/22/Year 2	82,000	—	—	—	79,000
D	2/25/Year 2	42,000	6/5/Year 2	39,000	—	—
E	3/25/Year 2	75,000	—	—	—	80,000

a. Give all journal entries relating to these marketable equity securities during Year 1 and Year 2, assuming that the accounting period is the calendar year.

b. Demonstrate the presentation of marketable securities in the balance sheet and related notes on December 31, Year 1.

c. Demonstrate the presentation of marketable securities in the balance sheet and related notes on December 31, Year 2.

41. **Journal entries and financial statement presentation of marketable equity securities.** The following information summarizes data about Rice Corporation's marketable equity securities held as current assets and as securities available for sale.

Security	Date Acquired	Acquisition Cost	Date Sold	Selling Price	Market Value Dec. 31, Year 1	Market Value Dec. 31, Year 2
A	3/5/Year 1	$40,000	10/5/Year 2	$52,000	$45,000	—
B	5/12/Year 1	80,000	—	—	70,000	$83,000
C	3/22/Year 2	32,000	—	—	—	27,000
D	5/25/Year 2	17,000	10/5/Year 2	15,000	—	—
E	5/25/Year 2	63,000	—	—	—	67,000

a. Give all journal entries relating to these marketable equity securities during Year 1 and Year 2, assuming that the accounting period is the calendar year.

b. Demonstrate the presentation of marketable securities in the balance sheet and related notes on December 31, Year 1.

c. Demonstrate the presentation of marketable securities in the balance sheet and related notes on December 31, Year 2.

42. **Reconstructing transactions involving marketable securities.** The financial statements of Zeff Corporation reveal the following information with respect to securities available for sale:

	December 31	
	Year 1	Year 2
Balance Sheet		
Marketable Securities at Market Value	$187,000	$195,000
Net Unrealized Holding Gain on Securities Available for Sale	12,000	10,000
Income Statement		**Year 2**
Realized Gain on Sale of Securities Available for Sale		$4,000

During Year 2, Zeff Corporation sold securities for $14,000 that had a book value at the time of sale of $13,000.

Set up T-accounts for each of the three accounts above and enter the balances on December 31, Year 1 and Year 2, before making the closing entries for Year 2. Enter in the T-accounts the entries that Zeff Corporation made during Year 2 for the following:

a. Sale of marketable securities

b. Revaluation of marketable securities to market value on December 31, Year 2.

c. Purchase of marketable securities during Year 2.

43. **Analysis of financial statement disclosures for marketable equity securities.** Exhibit 11.17 reproduces data about the marketable equity securities held as securities available for sale for Sunshine Mining Company for a recent year, with dates changed

EXHIBIT 11.17	SUNSHINE MINING COMPANY Data on Marketable Equity Securities (all dollar amounts in thousands) (Problem 43)

Marketable Equity Securities	Acquisition Cost	Market Value
At December 31, Year 2:		
Current Marketable Securities	$ 7,067	$ 4,601
Noncurrent Marketable Securities	$ 6,158	$ 8,807
At December 31, Year 1:		
Noncurrent Marketable Securities	$21,685	$11,418

for convenience. Assume that Sunshine held no current marketable securities at the end of Year 1, sold no current marketable securities during Year 2, purchased no non-current marketable securities during Year 2, and transferred no noncurrent marketable securities to the current portfolio during Year 2. The income statement for Year 2 shows a realized loss on sale of noncurrent marketable securities of $3,068,000.

   a. What amount of net unrealized holding gain or loss on noncurrent marketable securities appears on the balance sheet for the end of Year 1?

   b. What amount of net unrealized gain or loss on noncurrent marketable securities appears on the balance sheet for the end of Year 2?

   c. What were the proceeds of the sale of noncurrent marketable securities sold during Year 2?

   d. What amount of unrealized holding gain or loss on marketable securities appears on the income statement for Year 2?

44. Effect of various methods of accounting for marketable equity securities. Information related to marketable equity securities of Callahan Corporation appears below.

Security	Acquisition Cost in Year 1	Dividends Received during Year 1	Market Value on Dec. 31, Year 1	Selling Price in Year 2	Dividends Received during Year 2	Market Value on Dec. 31, Year 2
G	$18,000	$ 800	$16,000	$14,500	$ 200	—
H	25,000	1,500	24,000	26,000	500	—
I	12,000	1,000	14,000	—	1,500	$15,000
	$55,000	$3,300	$54,000	$40,500	$2,200	$15,000

   a. Assume that these securities represent trading securities. Indicate the nature and amount of income recognized during Year 1 and Year 2 and the presentation of information about these securities on the balance sheet on December 31, Year 1 and Year 2.

   b. Repeat part **a** assuming that these securities represent temporary investments of excess cash by Callahan Corporation.

   c. Repeat part **a** assuming that these securities represent long-term investments by Callahan Corporation.

   d. Compute the combined income for Year 1 and Year 2 under each of the three treatments of these securities in parts **a, b,** and **c.** Why do the combined income amounts differ? Will total shareholders' equity differ? Why or why not?

45. Analysis of financial statement disclosures related to marketable securities. Citibank reports the following information relating to its marketable securities classified as Securities Available for Sale for a recent year (amounts in millions):

	December 31	
	Year 10	Year 11
Marketable Securities at Acquisition Cost	$14,075	$13,968
Gross Unrealized Holding Gains	957	1,445
Gross Unrealized Holding Losses	(510)	(218)
Marketable Securities at Market Value	$14,522	$15,195

Cash proceeds from sales and maturities of marketable securities totaled $37,600 million in Year 11. Gross realized gains totaled $443 million and gross realized losses totaled $113 million during Year 11. The book value of marketable securities sold or matured totaled $37,008 million. Interest and dividend revenue during Year 11 totaled $1,081 million. Purchases of marketable securities totaled $37,163 million during Year 11.

a. Give the journal entries to record the sale of marketable securities during Year 11.

b. Analyze the change in the net unrealized holding gain from $447 million on December 31, Year 10, to $1,227 million on December 31, Year 11.

c. Compute the total income (both realized and unrealized) *occurring during Year 11* on Citibank's investments in securities.

d. How might the judicious selection of marketable securities sold during Year 11 permit Citibank to report an even larger net realized gain?

46. Using contra and adjunct accounts for securities available for sale. Exhibit 11.18 illustrates the effects on the T-accounts of transactions in marketable securities, accounted for first as trading securities and then as securities available for sale. The illustration covers two years. In illustrating the T-accounts for Securities Available for Sale, we use separate contra/adjunct accounts for both Marketable Securities and Owners' Equity. We designate these accounts as *X/A*: when the asset account has a debit balance, it is an adjunct; when it has a credit balance it is a contra account. When the equity account has a debit balance, it is a contra account; when it has a credit balance, it is an adjunct account. An adjunct account accumulated additions to another account, whereas a contra account accumulated subtractions from another account. You do not have to use these contra/adjunct accounts in working problems, but some students find it easier to do so.

a. Explain how using the contra/adjunct accounts for Securities Available for Sale can facilitate solving problems involving holding gains and losses.

b. Use the following facts in preparing the journal entries for Year 1 and Year 2, using a contra/adjunct account. In Year 1, the firm purchased a portfolio of marketable securities for $1,000, which it holds as securities available for sale, current assets. At the end of Year 1, the portfolio had a market value of $1,200. During Year 2, the firm sold some of the securities, for $120, that had originally cost $100 but that had a market value of $105 at the end of Year 1. At the end of Year 2, the remaining securities had a market value of $750. Record the journal entries from the end of both Year 1 and Year 2.

47. Journal entries and consolidation work sheet entries for various methods of accounting for intercorporate investments. Rockwell Corporation acquired, as long-term investments, shares of common stock of Company R, Company S, and

EXHIBIT 11.18 Accounting for Securities Available for Sale (SAS) and Trading Securities (TS)

The Events

(BB) Start with $100 of Cash and $100 of Retained Earnings.

(1) Buy Marketable Securities for $100.

(2) At end of Year 1, securities have market value of $110.

(3) At end of Year 2, securities have market value of $92.

(4) During Year 3, sell securities for $97.

(5) At time of Year 3 sale or at end of Year 3, get rid of X/A balance for SAS only.

(EB) End with $97 of Cash and $97 of Retained Earnings.

Trading Securities—Balance Sheet

Cash

(BB)	100	100	(1)
(4)	97		
(EB)	97		

Marketable Securities

(1)	100		
(2) √	10	18	(3)
	110	92	(4)
√√	92		
(EB)	0		

Retained Earnings

		100	(BB)
(3c)	18	10	(2c) √
		110	
		92	√√
		5	(4c)
		97	(EB)

Income Statements for Trading Securities Company

Year 1	$ 10
Year 2	(18)
Year 3	5
Total	($ 3)

(2) closed from here to balance sheet.
(3) closed from here to balance sheet.
(4) closed from here to balance sheet.

Securities Available for Sale—Balance Sheet

Cash

(BB)	100	100	(1)
(4)	97		
(EB)	97		

Marketable Securities

(1)	100	100	(4)
√ √√			
(EB)	0		

Marketable Securities X/A

(2) √	10	18	(3)
(5)	8	8	√√
(EB)	0		

Retained Earnings

		100	(BB) √ √√
			[closed here from Income Statement]
(4c)	3		
		97	(EB)

Owners' Equity X/A

		10	(2)
		10	√
(3)	18		
√√	8	8	(5)
		0	(EB)

Income Statements for Securities Available for Sale Company

Year 1	$ 0
Year 2	0
Year 3	(3)
Total	($ 3)

Total Loss Realized over Three Years is $3.

TS report gains and losses in all periods.
SAS report all loss recognized in 3rd period.

X/A Means an Account That Can Be Either Contra or Adjunct.

TS means Trading Securities.
SAS means Securities Available for Sale.

Notes.
BB means Beginning Balance.
EB means Ending Balance.

√ Means balance at end of Year 1.
√√ Means balance at end of Year 2.

Company T on January 2. These are the only long-term investments in securities that Rockwell Corporation holds. Data relating to the acquisitions follow. Amortize any goodwill arising from the acquisitions over 10 years.

Company	Percentage Acquired	Book Value and Market Value of Total Net Assets on January 2	Acquisition Cost	Net Income for Year	Dividends Declared for Year	Market Value of Shares Owned on December 31
R	10%	$6,000,000	$ 648,000	$1,200,000	$480,000	$ 624,000
S	30	6,000,000	2,040,000	1,200,000	480,000	2,052,000
T	100	6,000,000	6,000,000	1,200,000	480,000	6,240,000

a. Give the journal entries made to acquire the shares of Company R and to account for the investment during the year, using the market value method.

b. Give the journal entries made to acquire the shares of Company S and to account for the investment during the year, using the equity method.

c. Give the journal entries made to acquire the shares of Company T and to account for the investment during the year, using the equity method.

(Parts **d** through **g** require coverage of Appendix 11.1.)

d. Give the consolidation work sheet entry to eliminate the Investment in Stock of Company T account at the end of the year, assuming that Rockwell uses the equity method and that the work sheet starts with preclosing trial balance amounts. Company T had $2,400,000 in its Common Stock account throughout the year and a zero balance in Additional Paid-in Capital.

e. Repeat part **d,** but assume that the work sheet starts with postclosing trial balance amounts.

f. Assume that Rockwell Corporation had acquired the shares of Company T for $6,600,000 instead of $6,000,000. Give the journal entries made during the year to acquire the shares of Company T and to account for the investment using the equity method. Rockwell Corporation treats any excess of acquisition cost over book value as goodwill and amortizes it over 10 years.

g. Refer to part **f.** Give the consolidation work sheet entry to eliminate the Investment in Stock of Company T account, assuming the work sheet uses preclosing trial balance data.

48. Preparing a consolidation work sheet. (Requires coverage of Appendix 11.1.) The trial balances of Peak Company and Valley Company on December 31 of the current year appear in Exhibit 11.19.

Peak Company acquired all of the common stock of Valley Company on January 1 of this year for $50,000. The shareholders' equity of Valley Company on January 1 comprised $5,000 of common stock and $45,000 of retained earnings. Valley Company earned $10,000, then declared and paid dividends of $4,000 during the current year. The preclosing trial balances on December 31 contain advances from Peak Company to Valley Company totaling $8,000; Peak includes the advances in its Accounts Receivable; Valley shows the advances in its Accounts Payable.

a. Prepare a consolidation work sheet for Peak Company and Valley Company for the current year. The adjustments and elimination columns should contain entries to (1) eliminate the investment account and (2) eliminate intercompany receivables and payables.

EXHIBIT 11.19	PEAK COMPANY AND VALLEY COMPANY Preclosing Trial Balances (Problem 48)

	Peak Company	Valley Company
DEBITS		
Cash	$ 13,000	$ 6,000
Accounts Receivable	42,000	20,000
Investment in Stock of Valley Company (using equity method)	56,000	—
Other Assets	143,000	85,000
Cost of Goods Sold	320,000	90,000
Selling and Administrative Expenses	44,000	20,000
Income Tax Expense	12,000	5,000
Totals	$630,000	$226,000
CREDITS		
Accounts Payable	$ 80,000	$ 25,000
Bonds Payable	50,000	30,000
Common Stock	10,000	5,000
Retained Earnings	80,000	41,000
Sales Revenue	400,000	125,000
Equity in Earnings of Valley Company	10,000	—
Totals	$630,000	$226,000

b. Assume for this part that Peak Company paid $70,000, instead of $50,000, for all of the common stock of Valley Company. The market values of Valley Company's recorded assets and liabilities equaled their book values. Peak Company amortizes goodwill over 10 years. The Investment in Stock of Valley Company account showed a balance of $74,000 on December 31. (You should be able to derive this $74,000 balance in the Investment account. Try doing so before peeking at the footnote below, which shows the derivation.)[11] Give the consolidation work sheet entry to eliminate the investment account.

49. **Preparing a consolidation work sheet.** (Requires coverage of Appendix 11.1.) The preclosing trial balances of Company P and Company S on December 31, Year 2, appear in Exhibit 11.20. Company P acquired 100 percent of the common stock of Company S on January 2, Year 2, for $240,000. The shareholders' equity accounts of Company S on this date appear below:

Common Shares	$ 80,000
Retained Earnings	160,000
Total	$240,000

---

[11]$74,000 = $70,000 initial investment + $10,000 earnings for year − $4,000 dividends − $2,000 amortization of goodwill.

EXHIBIT 11.20	COMPANY P AND COMPANY S Preclosing Trial Balances (Problem 49)

	Company P	Company S
DEBITS		
Receivables	$ 60,000	$ 40,000
Investment in Stock of Company S (using equity method)	272,000	—
Other Assets	496,000	352,000
Cost of Goods Sold	1,160,000	496,000
Other Expenses	280,000	112,000
Totals	$2,268,000	$1,000,000
CREDITS		
Accounts Payable	$ 72,000	$ 48,000
Other Liabilities	88,000	72,000
Common Stock	160,000	80,000
Retained Earnings	316,000	160,000
Sales Revenue	1,600,000	640,000
Equity in Earnings of Company S	32,000	—
Totals	$2,268,000	$1,000,000

During Year 2, Company P sold merchandise costing $32,000, on account, to Company S for $40,000. Of the amount, $12,000 remains unpaid at year-end. Company S sold all of the merchandise during Year 2. Company P declared and paid $40,000 of dividends during Year 2. Company S did not declare or pay a dividend during Year 2.

a. Prepare a consolidation work sheet for Company P and Company S for Year 2. The adjustments and eliminations columns should contain entries to (1) eliminate the investment account, (2) eliminate intercompany sales, and (3) eliminate intercompany receivables and payables.

b. Prepare a consolidated statement of income and retained earnings for Year 2 and a consolidated balance sheet as of December 31, Year 2.

50. **Preparing a consolidation work sheet.** (Requires coverage of Appendix 11.1.) The condensed balance sheets of Ely Company and Sims Company at December 31 appear in Exhibit 11.21. The receivables of Ely Company and the liabilities of Sims Company contain an advance from Ely Company to Sims Company of $7,500. Ely Company acquired 100 percent of the capital stock of Sims Company on the market at January 2 of this year for $70,000. At that date, the balance in the Retained Earnings account of Sims Company was $40,000. Amortize goodwill, if any, over 10 years.

Prepare a consolidation work sheet for Ely Company and Sims Company. The adjustment and elimination columns should contain entries to (1) eliminate the Investment in the Sims Company account and (2) eliminate intercompany obligations.

51. **Preparing a consolidation work sheet subsequent to year of acquisition.** (Requires coverage of Appendix 11.1.) The condensed balance sheets of Companies S and J on December 31, Year 2, appear in Exhibit 11.22.

Company S owns 100 percent of the common stock of Company J. It acquired the stock of Company J on January 1, Year 1, when Company J's retained earnings

	Ely Company	Sims Company
EXHIBIT 11.21 ELY COMPANY AND SIMS COMPANY Balance Sheet Data (Problem 50)		
ASSETS		
Cash	$ 12,000	$ 5,000
Receivables	25,000	15,000
Investment in Sims Company (using equity method)	78,000	—
Other Assets	85,000	80,000
	$200,000	$100,000
LIABILITIES AND SHAREHOLDERS' EQUITY		
Current Liabilities	$ 45,000	$ 40,000
Common Stock	50,000	10,000
Retained Earnings	105,000	50,000
	$200,000	$100,000

amounted to $40,000. Company S holds a note issued by Company J in the amount of $16,400. Company S attributes any excess of cost over book value acquired to goodwill and amortizes it over 10 years.

Prepare a work sheet for a consolidation balance sheet.

52. **Effect of purchase and pooling-of-interests methods on financial statements.** (Requires coverage of Appendix 11.2.) Hatfield Corporation and McCoy Corporation agree to merge on January 1, Year 8, when the balance sheets of the two companies appear as follows (amounts in thousands):

	Hatfield Corporation	McCoy Corporation
Assets	$2,000	$1,500
Liabilities	$ 800	$ 700
Common Stock ($1 par)	100	100
Additional Paid-in Capital	400	300
Retained Earnings	700	400
Total Equities	$2,000	$1,500

Hatfield issues 50,000 shares of its common stock with a market value of $1,400,000 to the owners of McCoy in return for their 100,000 shares of McCoy Corporation common stock. The recorded assets of McCoy Corporation have a market value in excess of book value of $400,000.

a. Prepare a consolidated balance sheet for Hatfield Corporation and McCoy Corporation on January 1, Year 8, using (1) the purchase method and (2) the pooling-of-interests method.

b. Projected partial income statements for Hatfield Corporation and McCoy Corporation for Year 8 before considering the effects of the merger appear below.

EXHIBIT 11.22	COMPANY S AND COMPANY J Balance Sheet Data December 31, Year 2 (Problem 51)

	Company S	Company J
ASSETS		
Cash	$ 36,000	$ 26,000
Accounts and Notes Receivable	180,000	50,000
Inventories	440,000	250,000
Investment in Stock of Company J (using equity method)	726,000	—
Plant Assets	600,000	424,000
Total Assets	$1,982,000	$750,000
LIABILITIES AND SHAREHOLDERS' EQUITY		
Accounts and Notes Payable	$ 110,000	$ 59,000
Other Liabilities	286,000	22,000
Common Stock	1,200,000	500,000
Capital Contributed in Excess of Stated Value	—	100,000
Retained Earnings	386,000	69,000
Total Liabilities and Shareholders' Equity	$1,982,000	$750,000

	Hatfield Corporation	McCoy Corporation
Sales	$8,000,000	$6,000,000
Other Revenues	100,000	25,000
Total Revenues	$8,100,000	$6,025,000
Expenses Other Than Income Taxes	(6,300,000)	(4,825,000)
Pretax Income	$1,800,000	$1,200,000
Income Tax Expense	(720,000)	(480,000)
Net Income	$1,080,000	$ 720,000

Make the following assumptions:
(1) The income tax rate for the consolidated firm is 40 percent.
(2) Where necessary, Hatfield Corporation amortizes the extra asset costs over five years and the goodwill over 10 years in the consolidated statements.
(3) In calculations for tax returns, Hatfield Corporation cannot deduct, from taxable income, amortization of asset costs and goodwill arising from the purchase.
(4) McCoy Corporation declared no dividends.

Prepare consolidated income statements and consolidated earnings per share for the first year following the merger. Assume that the merger is treated as (1) a purchase and (2) a pooling of interests.

53. Effect of intercorporate investment policies on financial statements. Coca-Cola Company (Coke) and PepsiCo (Pepsi) dominate the soft drink industry in the United States and maintain leading market positions in many other countries. Coke has followed a policy of holding a 49 percent ownership interest in its bottlers, whereas

	COKE and PEPSI Financial Statement Data for Year 11 (amounts in millions) (Problem 53)			
EXHIBIT 11.23				

	Coke As Reported (1)	Coke's Bottlers (2)	Coke As Consolidated with Bottlers (3)	Pepsi As Reported (4)
ASSETS				
Current Assets	$4,143	$ 2,153	$ 6,296	$ 4,081
Investment in Bottlers	2,025	—	—	—
Property, Plant, and Equipment	3,112	8,957	12,069	5,711
Goodwill	—	—	310	5,845
Total Assets	$9,280	$11,110	$18,675	$15,637
LIABILITIES AND SHAREHOLLDERS' EQUITY				
Current Liability	$4,296	$ 2,752	$ 7,048	$ 3,264
Long-term Liabilities	1,133	4,858	5,991	7,469
External Interest in Bottlers	—	—	1,785	—
Shareholders' Equity	3,851	3,500	3,851	4,904
Total Liabilities and Shareholders' Equity	$9,280	$11,110	$18,675	$15,637
Net Income for Year 11	$1,364	$ 290	$ 1,364	$ 1,091
Interest Expense for Year 11	$ 231	$ 452	$ 683	$ 689

Pepsi wholly owns its bottling operations. Exhibit 11.23 presents selected balance sheet data for Coke and Pepsi for Year 11.

The first column shows amounts for Coke as reported, with Coke using the equity method to account for investments in its bottlers. The second column shows amounts for Coke's bottlers as reflected in a note to Coke's financial statements. The third column shows consolidated amounts for Coke and its bottlers. The 51 percent external interest in these bottlers appears on a line between liabilities and shareholders' equity. The fourth column shows amounts for Pepsi as reported, with its bottlers consolidated.

a. Compute the rate of return on assets for Year 11 under each of the four treatments in Exhibit 11.23. Assume an income tax rate of 34 percent. Also assume that the amounts shown for total assets in Exhibit 11.23 approximate the average assets for Year 11.

b. Compute the ratio of total liabilities to total assets at the end of Year 11 under each of the four treatments in Exhibit 11.23.

c. Evaluate the operating profitability and risk of Coke versus Pepsi using the ratios computed in questions **a** and **b**.

d. Suggest reasons why Coke might choose to own 49 percent of its bottlers whereas Pepsi holds 100 percent of its bottlers.

54. **Preparing a statement of cash flows.** Exhibit 11.24 presents comparative balance sheets and Exhibit 11.25 represents an income statement for Agee Electronics for Year 5. The notes to these financial statements appear below.

Note 1: All marketable securities are classified as "available for sale." Marketable securities sold during the year had an original acquisition cost of $115 and a book value at the time of sale of $120.

EXHIBIT 11.24	AGEE ELECTRONICS Balance Sheet (Problem 54)		

	December 31	
	Year 4	**Year 5**
ASSETS		
Cash	$ 130	$ 185
Marketable Securities (Note 1)	270	290
Accounts Receivable—Net (Note 2)	730	920
Inventories	620	570
Prepayments	120	170
Total Current Assets	$1,870	$2,135
Investments in Securities (Note 3)	$ 460	$ 380
Property, Plant, and Equipment:		
At Cost (Note 4)	$2,840	$3,310
Less Accumulated Depreciation	(1,210)	(1,450)
Net	$1,630	$1,860
Total Assets	$3,960	$4,375
LIABILITIES AND SHAREHOLDERS' EQUITY		
Accounts Payable	$ 490	$ 460
Bank Loans Payable	820	880
Dividends Payable	60	80
Other Current Liabilities	90	200
Total Current Liabilities	$1,460	$1,620
Long-term Debt (Note 4)	510	650
Total Liabilities	$1,970	$2,270
Common Stock	$ 100	$ 150
Additional Paid-in Capital	460	470
Unrealized Holding Gain on Marketable Securities	40	50
Unrealized Holding Loss on Investment in Securities	(120)	(90)
Retained Earnings	1,510	1,525
Total Shareholders' Equity	$1,990	$2,105
Total Liabilities and Shareholders' Equity	$3,960	$4,375

Note 2: Accounts receivable appear net of an allowance for uncollectible accounts of $40 on December 31, Year 4, and $50 on December 31, Year 5. Agee Electronics wrote off accounts totaling $35 as uncollectible during Year 5.

Note 3: All investments in securities are classified as "available for sale." During the year, Agee Electronics sold investments in securities that had an original acquisition cost of $110 and a book value at the time of sale of $70.

Note 4: Agee Electronics acquired equipment costing $140 during Year 5 by issuing a long-term note. It sold equipment originally costing $150 and with accumulated depreciation of $110 at the time of sale.

Prepare a statement of cash flows for Agee Electronics for Year 5. Support this statement of cash flows with a T-account worksheet.

EXHIBIT 11.25	AGEE ELECTRONICS Income Statement (Problem 54)

REVENUES

Sales	$5,200
Interest and Dividend Revenues	70
Gain on Sale of Equipment (Note 4)	40
Gain on Sale of Marketable Securities (Note 1)	30
Total Revenues	$5,340

EXPENSES

Cost of Goods Sold	$3,120
Marketing and Administrative	1,635
Interest	15
Loss on Sale of Investments in Securities (Note 3)	40
Income Taxes	210
Total Expenses	$5,020
Net Income	$ 320

55. **Preparing a statement of cash flows.** (Adapted from a problem by S. Baiman.) Exhibit 11.26 presents a comparative balance sheet for Cherry Corporation for Year 5 and Year 6. Additional information follows:

(1) For the year ended December 31, Year 6, Cherry reported net income of $496,000.

(2) Cherry wrote off uncollectible accounts receivable of $4,500 as a result of defaults.

(3) Cherry estimates bad debt expense on Year 6 sales on account to be $5,000.

(4) On January 3, Year 6, Cherry acquired 45 percent of the outstanding common stock of Zuber Co. To consummate this transaction, Cherry paid $72,000 cash and issued 3,500 shares of its preferred stock and 2,400 shares of its common stock. The market price of Cherry's preferred stock on January 3, Year 6, was $3 a share, and the market price of its common stock was $12 a share. The market value of the cash and stock given up by Cherry was equal to its share of Zuber's net book value. Cherry accounts for its investment in Zuber using the equity method. For the year ended December 31, Year 6, Zuber Co. reported $320,000 of net income and declared and paid cash dividends of $20,000.

(5) Cherry invested in the common stock of Roy Co. on December 31, Year 5, purchasing a 3 percent interest. On January 31, Year 6, Cherry sold this investment for $46,000. In addition, Cherry acquired new plant assets at a cost of $81,000. Cherry sold for $3,200 plant assets with a cost of $22,000 and with accumulated depreciation of $17,600. The remaining increase in plant assets resulted from major improvements that Cherry treated properly as capital expenditures.

(6) Amortization of patents for Year 6 was $3,000. Cherry acquired a new patent for cash.

(7) On January 2, Year 6 (before the purchase of Zuber), Cherry declared and issued a 4 percent stock dividend on its common stock. The market price of the common stock on that date was $12 a share. On December 31, Year 6, Cherry

EXHIBIT 11.26	CHERRY CORPORATION Comparative Balance Sheets (Problem 55)

	December 31	
	Year 5	Year 6
ASSETS		
Current Assets:		
Cash	$ 287,000	$ 450,000
Accounts Receivable (net of allowance for doubtful accounts)	550,000	645,000
Inventories	298,000	460,000
Total Current Assets	$ 1,135,000	$ 1,555,000
Investments:		
Common Stock of Roy Co. (3 percent)	39,000	0
Common Stock of Zuber Co. (45 percent)	0	246,300
Plant Assets	381,000	455,000
Less Accumulated Depreciation	(144,000)	(193,000)
Patents (net)	19,000	26,000
Total Assets	$ 1,430,000	$ 2,089,300
LIABILITIES AND SHAREHOLDERS' EQUITY		
Current Liabilities:		
Dividends Payable	$ 0	$ 181,000
Accounts Payable	70,000	170,000
Accrued Liabilities	41,800	24,800
Total Current Liabilities	$ 111,800	$ 375,800
Long-term Bonds Payable	133,000	174,000
Total Liabilities	$ 244,800	$ 549,800
Preferred Stock at Par ($2)	$ 53,000	$ 60,000
Additional Paid-in Capital—Preferred	2,500	6,000
Common Stock at Par ($10)	700,000	752,000
Additional Paid-in Capital—Common	9,600	20,000
Retained Earnings	420,100	701,500
Total Shareholders' Equity	$ 1,185,200	$ 1,539,500
Total Liabilities and Shareholders' Equity	$ 1,430,000	$ 2,089,300

declared cash dividends of $145,000 on the common stock and $36,000 on the preferred stock.

(8) During Year 6, Cherry repurchased for $17,000 bonds with a face value of $20,000 and a book value of $17,000. During Year 6 interest expense exceeded the coupon cash payment on bonds by $4,000.

a. Prepare a T-account work sheet for a statement of cash flows.

b. Prepare a statement of cash flows for Cherry Corporation for Year 6.

56. **Interaction of regulation and accounting rules for financial institutions, particularly banks.** Exhibit 11.27 illustrates the key features of a banking or thrift institution. Because regulators and investors view the banking business—borrowing funds

and lending them to others at higher rates—as less risky than most other businesses, they allow banks and thrifts to carry smaller shareholders' equity as a percentage of total equities than do most nonfinancial firms. That is, banks have, with the blessing of regulators, higher financial leverage than nonfinancial firms.

Exhibit 11.27 illustrates a thrift institution that regulators allow to have shareholders' equity equal to only 8 percent of assets. (The effects illustrated here would be even more dramatic with a capital ratio of 5 percent or less, which many banks use.) Other realistic assumptions, used for illustration, are as follows:

- Liabilities can be 11.5 times as large as owners' equity; this follows from the assumption that owners' equity is 8 percent of total equities, so that liabilities can be 92 percent of total equities.
- Liabilities cost 5.5 percent (interest expense) each year.
- Assets earn 7.0 percent (interest revenues) each year.
- Variable operating expenses are 0.4 percent of total assets.
- Fixed operating expenses are 0.1 percent of the bank's starting asset position of $1,000.
- There are no income taxes.

Key features of a bank are that (1) they tend to borrow funds for short terms, such as through accepting cash into checking and savings accounts or by issuing short-term certificates of deposits, while (2) they lend funds for longer terms, such as for home mortgages or customers' auto purchases.

The top panel of Exhibit 11.27 shows the balance sheet for the bank as it starts in business. The firm starts with contributed capital of $80; it borrows $920, giving it $1,000 of equities and funds available for lending. It lends $1,000, earning 7 percent on those assets. It pays interest on its $920 of borrowings, pays its operating expenses, and reports income of $14.4.

Now, let the market value of the bank's financial assets—loans—increase by 5 percent, or $50, as shown in the second panel. Show this increase on the balance sheet. The transactions are as follows:

(1) Assets increase in value by $50, so Retained Earnings increase by $50.

(2) The bank uses the extra owners' equity of $50 to borrow an additional $575 (= 11.5 × $50), which it lends to new customers, increasing total assets by $575.

The income statement shows more revenues and more expenses, but rates of return change little from those of the original bank. Note, however, the effect on the bank's size: a 5 percent increase in market value allows the bank to increase its assets and size by 62.5 percent, from $1,000 in assets to $1,625 in assets. This creates no problem for the bank. Bank managers are happy because their compensation often depends on bank size, not just bank profitability.

Now, go back to the original bank and let the market value of the bank's financial assets decrease by 5 percent, or $50, as shown in the third panel. Observe this decrease on the balance sheet. The transactions are as follows:

(3) Assets decrease in value by $50, so Retained Earnings decrease by $50.

(4) The bank's decrease in owners' equity requires it to reduce borrowings by $575 (= 11.5 × $50). In order to pay back its creditors and to reduce assets, it must reduce its lendings by $575.

The income statement shows smaller revenues and smaller expenses, but rates of return change little from those of the original bank. Note, however, the effect on the bank's size: a 5 percent decrease in market value has forced the bank to

EXHIBIT 11.27 | Effects of Changing Market Value of Assets on a Bank's Activities

Step [1]: Market Value of Assets Increases, Also Increasing Owners' Equity.
Step [2]: Bank Increases Lending to Maintain Capital (Leverage) Ratio at 8 Percent.
Step [3]: Market Value of Original Bank Decreases, Decreasing Owners' Equity.
Step [4]: Bank Decreases Lending to Maintain Capital (Leverage) Ratio at 8 Percent.
Operating Income Excludes Gains and Losses in Market Value of Assets Held.

Balance Sheet		Partial Income Statement		Rate of Return On:	
Original Bank, before Market Value Changes					
Assets	Equities	Revenues as % of Assets			
	Liabilities:				
$1,000 Original	Borrowings $920	7.0%	$70.0		
		Interest Expense as % of Borrowing			
		5.5%	(50.6)		
	Owners' Equity	Operating Expense % of Assets			
	Contributed Capital . . . 80	0.4%	(4.0)		
	Retained Earnings. . . . 0	Fixed costs	(1.0)	Assets[a] 1.4%	
	Total Owners' Equity . . $80			Owners'	
$1,000	Totals $1,000	Operating Income . . . $14.4		Equity 18.0%	
Market Value of Assets Increases 5.0%					
Assets	Equities	Revenues as % of Assets			
	Liabilities:				
$1,000 Original	Original Borrowings . . .$920	7.0%	$113.8		
		Interest Expense as % of Borrowing			
		5.5%	(82.2)		
[1] 50 Market Value Increase		Operating Expense			
[2] 575 New Lending	[2] New Borrowings 575	% of Assets			
		0.4%	(6.5)		
	Owners' Equity	Fixed costs	(1.0)		
	Contributed Capital . . . 80				
	[1] Retained Earnings. . . . 50				
	Total Owners' Equity . .$130			Assets[a] 1.5%	
				Owners'	
$1,625	Totals $1,625	Operating Income . . . $24.1		Equity 18.5%	
Market Value of Assets Decreases −5.0%					
Assets	Equities	Revenues as % of Assets			
	Liabilities:				
$1,000 Original	Original Borrowings . . .$920	7.0%	$26.3		
		Interest Expense as % of Borrowing			
[3] (50) Market Value Decline		5.5%	(19.0)		
[4] (575) Reduce Lending	[4] Reduce Borrowings . . .(575)	Operating Expense % of Assets			
	Owners' Equity	0.4%	(1.5)		
	Contributed Capital . . . 80	Fixed costs	(1.0)		
	[3] Retained Earnings. . . . (50)				
	Total Owners' Equity . . $30			Assets[a] 1.3%	
				Owners'	
$375	Totals $375	Operating Income $4.8		Equity 16.0%	

[a]Banks do not add back interest expense when computing the rate of return on assets.

reduce its size by 62.5 percent, from $1,000 in assets to $375 in assets. This creates a major problem for the bank. The problem arises because the bank must shrink in size, by a lot and quickly. The bank's assets comprise loans it has made to customers, typically long-term loans. The bank cannot easily recall those loans without incurring significant cost. (The typical loan gives the bank's customer the right to prepay the loan whenever the customer wants but does not allow the bank to call in the loan at the bank's whim.) Perhaps the bank will have to sell its assets to others, at a loss, to raise cash to reduce its own borrowings and its size.

Whatever it does, the bank has a problem. This problem arises because the bank shows the losses on its balance sheet and must reduce owners' equity because of this loss. Bankers understand this feature of market value accounting for assets, and they have, historically, been the most vocal opponents of such accounting for financial assets. For many years, bankers have prevailed in keeping the changes in market values of their assets off the balance sheet.

Many banks' assets are not marketable securities but are loans, which do not trade in the marketplace. The FASB does not require the marking to market value of nonmarketable financial assets. For such assets, banks use the amortized cost method, illustrated in Problem 11.1 for Self-Study. For marketable debt securities, the bank will use market value accounting for trading securities or the amortized cost method (debt held to maturity), depending on its holding intention and ability. So long as the bank can show that it has both the ability and the intent to hold a loan until it matures, the bank need not show changes in that loan's market value on the balance sheet.

Repeat the analysis in Exhibit 11.27, using a capital ratio of 5 percent instead of 8 percent, and set the changes in market value of assets first to an increase of 4 percent and then to a decrease of 4 percent.

REPORTING EARNINGS, COMPREHENSIVE INCOME, AND SHAREHOLDERS' EQUITY

CHAPTER 12

LEARNING OBJECTIVES

1. Understand why the format for reporting income matters and master the concept that different kinds of income require different formats.
2. Understand the distinction between *earnings* and *comprehensive income.*
3. Understand the different priority claims of common and preferred shareholders on the assets of a firm and the disclosure of those claims in the shareholders' section of the balance sheet.
4. Understand the underlying concepts, and apply the accounting procedures, for the issuance of capital stock, particularly with respect to capital stock issued under various option arrangements for security holders.
5. Understand the underlying concepts, and apply the accounting procedures, for the acquisition and reissue of treasury stock.
6. Understand the underlying concepts, and apply the accounting procedures, for cash, property, and stock dividends and other changes in retained earnings.
7. Develop the skills to interpret disclosures about changes in shareholders' equity accounts.

Chapters 6 to 11 discussed generally accepted accounting principles (GAAP) for various assets and liabilities. Changes in assets and liabilities often cause shareholders' equity to change. Changes in shareholders' equity result from two types of transactions:

1. *Capital Transactions.* Firms can issue additional common or preferred stock, repurchase shares of outstanding common or preferred stock, and declare and pay dividends. Analysts use information about capital transactions to measure the claims of common and preferred shareholders on the net assets of a firm and the changes in voting interest of any particular class of shares, changes that occur when a firm issues or repurchases shares of its capital stock.
2. *Operating Transactions.* Firms use assets provided by creditors and owners to generate earnings. Analysts use information about past earnings to project future earnings

and often use projected earnings to value the firm, particularly when they use price-earnings ratios.

This chapter discusses GAAP for capital transactions and operating transactions. We begin with operating transactions because they have been a primary focus of previous chapters. Thus far we have concentrated on measuring the results of operating transactions. Now, we focus on *reporting,* or *disclosing,* operating transactions in the financial statements.

REPORTING OPERATING TRANSACTIONS

To understand the issues involved in reporting operating transactions, consider the earnings data for Bernard Company in Exhibit 12.1. To simplify the illustration, we assume that revenues result in immediate cash receipts and that expenses require immediate cash expenditures. Thus, income flows equal cash flows.

Suppose that an analyst wanted to value Bernard Company using the present value of the cash flows of its individual activities—some recurring, some not. Think of the cash flows as being aftertax. Assume the discount rate appropriate for finding the present value of Bernard Company's cash flows is 10 percent per year. Corporate finance classes discuss the issues related to choosing the discount rate, and the appendix to this book introduces the techniques of present-value analysis. To understand this problem, you need not have studied the appendix if you will take on faith the derivation of the numbers in the right-hand column of Exhibit 12.1.

Bernard Company engages in six activities, numbered 1 through 6, shown in Exhibit 12.1.

Activity 1. The first activity generates $100 per year, with the cash flow at the end of the year, indefinitely. The present value of this activity is $1,000 (= $100/.10). See Example **18** in the appendix. Investors sometimes call this process of deriving market value from a series of future cash flows *capitalizing earnings.* The analyst might say that the earnings of $100 have a *price/earnings ratio* of 10 or that the earnings "deserve [or carry] a multiple of 10."

Activity 2. The second activity generates $30 at the end of the first year and a cash flow that grows by 6 percent per year thereafter. The present value of this activity is $750 [= $30/(.10 − .06)]. See Example **19** in the appendix. The price/earnings ratio (or multiple) for these cash flows is 25 because of their growth. Management interested in higher market prices for its firm's shares want investors to think of the company as a growth stock, because investors put higher values on growing-earnings companies than on stable-earnings companies.

Activity 3. The third activity is cyclic, generating $115 per year at the end of each odd-numbered year. The present value of this activity is $602.38. See Example **20** in the appendix.

Activity 4. The fourth activity is nonrecurring, generating a single cash flow of $120 at the end of the first year, with present value of $109.09 (= $120/1.10) at the start of the first year.

Activity 5. The fifth activity, an expenditure (outflow), uses $40 of cash each year, at the end of each year. The present value of this activity is −$400 (= −$40/.10).

Activity 6. The sixth activity, a single expenditure (outflow), uses $70 cash at the end of the first year and has present value of −$63.64 (= −$70/1.10).

EXHIBIT 12.1

BERNARD COMPANY
Measurement of Firm's Market Value from Cash Flow Data

Activities of the Firm	Cash Flows Occur at the End of Each Period — Period Number								Present Value of Activity Using Discount Rate of 10%
	1	**2**	**3**	**4**	**5**	**6**	**7**	**8**	
1. Recurring	$100	$100	$100	$100	$100	$100	$100	$100	$1,000.00
2. Recurring, but Growing at 6% per Year	30	32	34	36	38	40	43	45	750.00
3. Cyclic	115	0	115	0	115	0	115	0	602.38
4. Nonrecurring	120	0	0	0	0	0	0	0	109.09
5. Recurring	(40)	(40)	(40)	(40)	(40)	(40)	(40)	(40)	(400.00)
6. Nonrecurring	(70)	0	0	0	0	0	0	0	(63.64)
Income for Year 1	$255								
Present Value [= Fair Market Value] of Entire Firm									$1,997.83

The value of the firm is the sum of the present values of its individual activities, $1,998 in Exhibit 12.1. In this example, most of the value of this firm comes from the recurring activities. In deriving firm values, investors generally care about recurring activities more than nonrecurring ones because recurring activities add value each year whereas nonrecurring activities, by their very nature, happen only once.

Exhibit 12.1 shows the net earnings for Year 1 of $255. How can analysts and investors deduce the value of the company from this one year's earnings statement? They can't. This firm is too complex for even a sophisticated user to derive the value from a single column of data, without further information. Some investors and analysts want to know about the components of a firm's earnings so that they can estimate the market value of the firm. Analysts feel more confident estimating the value of firms with recurring activities than with nonrecurring activities. Analysts may also want to include changes in the market value of a firm's assets and liabilities in their valuation of a company even though GAAP may not include these market value changes in earnings.

GAAP require firms to report operating transactions in ways that aid the analyst and other users in projecting future earnings. We examine the reporting of three types of operating transactions:

1. Recurring versus nonrecurring
2. Central versus peripheral
3. Unrealized gains and losses from changes in the market values of assets and liabilities

The issues discussed affect the quality of earnings. Firms have incentives to report good earnings news in ways that make such news appear recurring and central but to report bad earnings news as nonrecurring and peripheral. Analysts must sort through the various components of earnings, recognizing possible biases injected by management, and must apply appropriate multiples to the earnings components in valuing firms. GAAP attempt to aid this process by requiring firms to classify operating transactions in particular ways in the financial statements.

REPORTING RECURRING/NONRECURRING AND CENTRAL/PERIPHERAL ACTIVITIES

An analyst likely asks two questions when using a firm's past profitability to project its likely future profitability:

1. Does the earnings item result from an activity in which a firm will likely continue its involvement, or does the earnings item result from an unusual transaction or event that is unlikely to recur regularly?
2. Does the earnings item result from a firm's primary operating activity (creating and selling a good or service for customers) or from an activity incidental or peripheral to the primary operating activity (for example, periodic sales of equipment previously used by the firm in manufacturing)?

Figure 12.1 depicts these distinctions, with examples of each.

A financial statement user who wants to evaluate a firm's ongoing operating profitability will likely focus on earnings items in the upper left cell. A financial statement user who wants to project earnings of prior periods into the future would likely focus on the two *recurring earnings* cells. Earnings items in the nonrecurring cells should not affect ongoing assessments of profitability. This section considers the reporting of each type of earnings item.

MEASUREMENT OF EARNINGS EFFECT

Accountants distinguish between revenues and expenses on the one hand and gains and losses on the other. Revenues and expenses result from the recurring, primary operating activities of a business (upper left cell in Figure 12.1). Earnings items in this first category are the ordinary, recurring operating activities of the firm. Gains and losses result from either peripheral activities (lower left cell) or nonrecurring activities (upper and lower right cells). A second distinction is that revenues and expenses are gross concepts, whereas gains and losses are net concepts. The following examples illustrate this distinction.

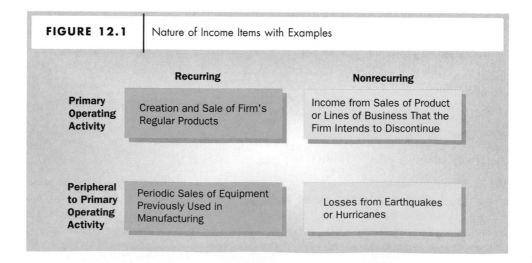

FIGURE 12.1 Nature of Income Items with Examples

	Recurring	Nonrecurring
Primary Operating Activity	Creation and Sale of Firm's Regular Products	Income from Sales of Product or Lines of Business That the Firm Intends to Discontinue
Peripheral to Primary Operating Activity	Periodic Sales of Equipment Previously Used in Manufacturing	Losses from Earthquakes or Hurricanes

Example 1   IBM sells a computer to a customer for $400,000. The computer cost IBM $300,000 to manufacture. IBM records this sale as follows:

Cash	400,000	
Sales Revenue		400,000
To record sale.		
Cost of Goods Sold	300,000	
Finished Goods Inventory		300,000
To record the cost of goods sold.		

This transaction fits into the upper left cell of Figure 12.1 (primary/recurring). The income statement reports both sales revenue and cost of goods sold, providing information to the financial statement user regarding both the manufacturing cost of the computer and IBM's ability to mark up this cost in setting selling prices. After preparing the income statement, the accountant closes both the Sales Revenue and the Cost of Goods Sold accounts, increasing Retained Earnings by $100,000.

Example 2   The Gap, a retail clothing chain, sells computers previously used for processing data in its stores. This sale relates only peripherally to The Gap's primary operating activity, which is to sell casual clothes. Assume that the computers originally cost $500,000 and have $200,000 of accumulated depreciation at the time of sale. Thus, the computers have a net book value of $300,000. The sale of these computers for $400,000 results in the following journal entry on The Gap's books:

Cash	400,000	
Accumulated Depreciation	200,000	
Equipment		500,000
Gain on Sale of Equipment		100,000
Disposal of computers for $100,000 more than book value.		

This transaction fits into the lower left cell of Figure 12.1 (peripheral/recurring). The income statement reports only the $100,000 gain on the sale, not the selling price of $400,000 and the book value of $300,000. The income statement reports gains and losses at net, instead of gross, amounts because, presumably, financial statement users do not care about information on the individual components composing the peripheral or nonrecurring earnings items. After preparing the income statement, the accountant closes the account, Gain on Sale of Equipment, to Retained Earnings.

Note that both revenues and gains appear as credits in journal entries and ultimately increase Retained Earnings. Both expenses and losses appear as debits in journal entries and ultimately reduce Retained Earnings. To repeat, revenues and expenses are gross concepts about operating or central items; gains and losses are net concepts about nonrecurring or peripheral items.

CLASSIFICATIONS IN THE INCOME STATEMENT

Income statements contain some or all of the following sections or categories, depending on the nature of a firm's earnings for the period:

1. Earnings from continuing operations
2. Earnings, gains, and losses from discontinued operations

3. Extraordinary gains and losses

4. Adjustments for changes in accounting principles

The majority of income statements include only the first section. Exhibit 12.2 presents Hypothetical Company's income statement, which includes all four sections.

Earnings from Continuing Operations   Revenues, gains, expenses, and losses from the continuing areas of business activity of a firm appear in the first section of the income statement, Earnings from Continuing Operations. This section includes earnings derived from a firm's primary business activities as well as from activities peripherally related to operations. The key distinction is that the firm expects these sources of earnings to continue. Firms without the nonrecurring categories of earnings for a particular year (discussed next) need not use the title Earnings from Continuing Operations

EXHIBIT 12.2	HYPOTHETICAL COMPANY Income Statement (amounts in millions)		
	Year 4	**Year 5**	**Year 6**
INCOME FROM CONTINUING OPERATIONS			
Sales	$ 240	$ 265	$ 295
Cost of Goods Sold	(144)	(154)	(165)
Selling and Administrative Expenses	(50)	(58)	(67)
Operating Income	$ 46	$ 53	$ 63
Interest Revenue	4	5	7
Interest Expense	(15)	(19)	(22)
Gain on Sale of Equipment	4	9	3
Income from Continuing Operations before Taxes	$ 39	$ 48	$ 51
Income Taxes	(13)	(16)	(17)
Income from Continuing Operations	$ 26	$ 32	$ 34
INCOME, GAINS, AND LOSSES FROM DISCONTINUED OPERATIONS			
Income (Loss) from Operations of Business Sold in Year 6 (net of income taxes)	$16	$ (4)	$ 2
Gain on Sale of Division (net of income taxes)	—	—	40
Income from Discontinued Operations	$16	$ (4)	$ 42
EXTRAORDINARY GAINS AND LOSSES			
Gain on Retirement of Bonds (net of income taxes)	—	$ 12	—
ADJUSTMENTS FOR CHANGES IN ACCOUNTING PRINCIPLES			
Effect of Change in Accounting for Income Taxes	$ 8	—	—
Net Income	$ 50	$ 40	$ 76
EARNINGS PER COMMON SHARE			
Continuing Operations	$2.60	$3.05	$3.09
Discontinued Operations	1.60	(.38)	3.82
Extraordinary Items	—	1.14	—
Changes in Accounting Principles	.80	—	—
Net Income	$5.00	$3.81	$6.91

in their income statements. In this case, the absence of nonrecurring types of earnings implies that all reported revenues, gains, expenses, and losses relate to continuing operations. Chapter 3 indicates that firms often report a subtotal within the Continuing Operations section of the income statement. This subtotal, labeled *operating income,* reports the revenues and expenses from the firm's primary business activity of creating and selling a good or service. Revenues from marketable securities and investments in securities, interest expense on borrowings, and gains and losses from peripheral activities appear separately as *nonoperating income* in the Continuing Operations section of the income statement.

Earnings, Gains, and Losses from Discontinued Operations

Sometimes a firm sells a major division or segment of its business during the year or contemplates its sale within a foreseeable time after the end of the accounting period. If so, it must disclose separately any earnings, gains, and losses related to that segment. The separate disclosure appears in the next section of the income statement, Earnings, Gains, and Losses from Discontinued Operations, so that the financial statement reader will know that the firm does not expect this source of earnings to continue.[1] Firms typically report the earnings, gain, or loss on a single line, net of income tax effects. This section follows the section presenting Earnings from Continuing Operations.

Extraordinary Gains and Losses

A separate section of the income statement presents Extraordinary Gains and Losses. For an item to be extraordinary, it must generally meet both of the following conditions:

1. Unusual in nature
2. Infrequent in occurrence[2]

An example of an item likely to be extraordinary for most firms is a loss from an earthquake or the confiscation of assets by a foreign government. Firms report extraordinary items net of their tax effects.

Adjustments for Changes in Accounting Principles

A firm that changes its principles (or methods) of accounting during the period must in some cases disclose the effects that the changes had on the net earnings of current and previous years.[3] This information appears in a separate section of the income statement, Adjustments for Changes in Accounting Principles.

UNREALIZED GAINS AND LOSSES FROM CHANGES IN MARKET VALUES OF ASSETS AND LIABILITIES

The Financial Accounting Standards Board (FASB) has increasingly required firms to report certain assets and liabilities at their current market values at the end of each period instead of their historical, or acquisition, costs. Examples discussed in previous chapters include:

1. Valuation of inventories at lower of cost of market (Chapter 7)
2. Valuation of plant assets and intangibles at current market value when evidence indicates that an asset impairment has occurred (Chapter 8)

---

[1] Accounting Principles Board, *Opinion No. 30,* "Reporting the Results of Operations," 1973.

[2] Ibid.

[3] Accounting Principles Board, *Opinion No. 20,* "Accounting Changes," 1971.

3. Valuation of financial instruments, including derivatives used to hedge risk, at market value (Chapter 10)
4. Valuation of marketable equity securities at market value (Chapter 11)

When a firm writes assets and liabilities down or up to market value, the question arises as to how it should treat the offsetting debit (loss) or credit (gain). At the time of the revaluation, the firm has not yet realized gains or losses. That is, the firm has not yet sold the asset or settled the liability and realized the gain or loss. In some cases, GAAP require firms to include the gains and losses, even though not yet realized, in earnings in the period of the revaluation. Firms include losses from the write-down of inventories, plant assets, and intangibles in computing earnings in the period of the revaluation. Firms include gains and losses from the revaluation of financial instruments classified as fair-value hedges in earnings each period as the market values of the hedged financial instrument and its derivative change.

The FASB has been reluctant, however, to require firms to include all unrealized gains and losses from the revaluation of assets and liabilities in earnings. We suspect the reason has to do with the volatility of some unrealized gains and losses. Including all unrealized gains and losses on marketable equity securities in earnings each period, for example, will cause reported earnings to fluctuate (in response to fluctuations in market prices) more than they would otherwise.

Many, probably most, managers prefer to report stable earnings in contrast to fluctuating earnings. All else being equal, the less risky the earnings stream—that is, the less volatile the reported earnings—the higher will be the market price of the firm's shares. Financial institutions in particular do not like fluctuations in net income; see Problem **56** at the end of Chapter 11 for a discussion of why. Managers have succeeded over the years in lobbying the FASB to keep many fluctuating components of income out of reported earnings. Unrealized gains and losses have typically appeared on a separate line in the shareholders' equity section of the balance sheet.

The FASB has become increasingly concerned that users of financial statements might overlook these value changes if the changes appear on the comparative balance sheet only and not in the income statement. As a consequence, the FASB requires firms to disclose unrealized gains and losses, which have historically bypassed the income statement, in a new category called **Other Comprehensive Income.**[4]

Other Comprehensive Income includes changes in the market value of marketable equity securities and changes in the market value of derivatives used as cash-flow hedges. Other Comprehensive Income also includes unrealized translation gains and losses from translating the financial statements of foreign units into U.S. dollars and certain changes in pension liabilities, topics covered in advanced financial accounting courses.

Firms can report Other Comprehensive Income in several ways. They can

1. include it in a combined statement of earnings and other comprehensive income, in effect appending it to the bottom of the traditional income statement,
2. include it in a separate statement of other comprehensive income, or
3. include it in a statement of changes in shareholders' equity.

Exhibit 12.3 shows the required disclosure of comprehensive income in the first two of the allowed formats—as part of a combined earnings and comprehensive income statement

---

[4]Financial Accounting Standards Board, *Statement of Financial Accounting Standards No. 130,* "Reporting Comprehensive Income," 1997.

EXHIBIT 12.3	Reporting Comprehensive Income, Two Allowed Formats

ONE-STATEMENT APPROACH

Statement of Income (Earnings) and Comprehensive Income

Revenues		$100,000
Expenses		(25,000)
Gain on Sale of Securities		2,000
Other Gains and Losses		8,000
Earnings from Continuing Operations before Income Tax		$ 85,000
Income Tax Expense		(21,250)
Earnings before Discontinued Operations and Extraordinary Items		$ 63,750
Discontinued Operations, Net of Tax		30,000
Extraordinary Items, Net of Tax		(28,000)
Income before Cumulative Effect of Accounting Change		$ 65,750
Cumulative Effect of Accounting Change, Net of Tax		(2,500)
Net Income (Earnings)		**$ 63,250**
Other Comprehensive Income, Net of Tax:		
Foreign Currency Translation Adjustments		$ 7,000
Unrealized Gains and Losses on Securities:		
Unrealized Holding Gains Arising during Period	$13,000	
Less: Reclassification Adjustment for Gain Included in Net Income (Earnings)	(1,500)	11,500
Minimum Pension Liability Adjustment		(2,500)
Other Comprehensive Income (Loss)		**$ 16,000**
Comprehensive Income (Loss)		**$ 79,250**

TWO-STATEMENT APPROACH

Statement of Income (Earnings)

Revenues		$100,000
Expenses		(25,000)
Gain on Sale of Securities		2,000
Other Gains and Losses		8,000
Earnings from Continuing Operations before Income Tax		$ 85,000
Income Tax Expense		(21,250)
Earnings before Discontinued Operations and Extraordinary Items		$ 63,750
Discontinued Operations, Net of Tax		30,000
Extraordinary Items, Net of Tax		(28,000)
Income before Cumulative Effect of Accounting Change		$ 65,750
Cumulative Effect of Accounting Change, Net of Tax		(2,500)
Net Income (Earnings)		**$ 63,250**

STATEMENT OF COMPREHENSIVE INCOME

Net Income (Earnings)		**$ 63,250**
Other Comprehensive Income, Net of Tax:		
Foreign Currency Translation Adjustments		$ 7,000
Unrealized Gains and Losses on Securities:		
Unrealized Holding Gains Arising during Period	$13,000	
Less: Reclassification Adjustment for Gain Included in Net Income (Earnings)	(1,500)	11,500
Minimmum Pension Liability Adjustment		(2,500)
Other Comprehensive Income (Loss)		**$ 16,000**
Comprehensive Income (Loss)		**$ 79,250**

and as part of a separate statement of comprehensive income. We illustrate the third format, as part of a statement explaining the reasons for changes in shareholders' equity accounts, later in this chapter, in Exhibit 12.7. The required disclosures include also the effects of accounting adjustments related to prior periods, discussed later in this chapter.

TERMINOLOGY NOTE

The FASB faced an issue in naming the amount that we call *net income* **in the traditional income statement. Use of the term** *net* **implies that it is a bottom-line number. Yet firms that append other comprehensive income to the bottom of their income statements need a label to differentiate traditional net income from the combined amounts of traditional net income plus other comprehensive income. The FASB expressed a preference to eliminate the term** *net income* **altogether, to label traditional net income as** *earnings,* **and to label the combined amounts of earnings and other comprehensive income as** *comprehensive income.* **The FASB gave firms wide latitude not only in their choice of reporting formats but also in their choice of terminology. Most firms choose to follow the third reporting format above, leaving the traditional income statement unchanged. Thus, we will continue to use** *net income* **to designate the bottom line of the traditional income statement.**

AN INTERNATIONAL PERSPECTIVE

Firms in all industrialized countries and in most developing countries around the world prepare financial statements based on the accrual, rather than the cash, basis of accounting. The particular measurement rules used in applying the accrual basis differ among countries.

The format and classification of earnings items within the earnings statement also vary across countries. The general measurement and disclosure principles discussed in this book should permit the reader of the financial statements to understand and interpret various earnings statement formats. Refer to the earnings statement for Wellcome PLC, a British pharmaceutical company, in Exhibit 12.4. Although this financial statement uses terminology different from that used in this book, the reader should be able to infer the nature of various items.

Title Used in Exhibit 12.4	Title Used in This Book
Group Profit and Loss Account	Income Statement
Turnover	Sales Revenue
Trading Profit	Operating Earnings
Profit on Ordinary Activities	Earnings from Continuing Operations

EXHIBIT 12.4	WELLCOME PLC Group Profit and Loss Account (amounts in millions)		
		Year 7	**Year 8**
Turnover		£1,147.4	£1,272.2
Operating Costs:			
Raw Materials and Consumables		(246.9)	(245.4)
Other External Charges		(401.5)	(424.4)
Staff Costs		(309.1)	(337.4)
Depreciation		(38.8)	(44.1)
Change in Stocks of Finished Goods and Work in Progress		36.5	18.7
Other Operating Charges		(10.3)	(6.7)
Trading Profit		£ 177.3	£ 232.9
Net Interest Payable		(8.2)	(11.7)
Profit on Ordinary Activities before Taxation		£ 169.1	£ 221.2
Tax on Profit from Ordinary Activities		(71.4)	(89.4)
Profit on Ordinary Activities Attributable to Shareholders		£ 97.7	£ 131.8

Wellcome's statement in Exhibit 12.4 classifies operating costs according to their nature (for example, raw materials, labor, depreciation) instead of according to functional activity (for example, cost of goods sold, marketing expenses, administrative expenses). European companies often classify expenses by nature. One item seldom seen in annual reports of U.S. companies is "Change in Stocks of Finished Goods and Work in Process." Wellcome reports among its operating costs on the income statement actual raw materials, labor, and overhead costs incurred during the year. It assigns a portion of these costs to units in the Work-in-Process Inventory and Finished Goods Inventory accounts at the end of the period. For example, at the end of Year 8, £18.7 million of costs included in various operating cost items in the income statement actually apply to units in process or in finished goods at the end of Year 8 and not to units sold. Netting this £18.7 million against the actual total cost results in the proper matching of costs against revenues.

FINANCING A CORPORATION

Both creditors and owners provide the funds to finance a corporation's assets and therefore have a claim on those assets. Thus,

Assets = Liabilities + Shareholders' Equity

Assets = Financing of Assets

Assets = Claims on Assets

If a firm declares bankruptcy, creditors' claims on the assets of a firm are generally senior to those of shareholders. In recent years firms have, however, issued securities that blur the distinction between liabilities and shareholders' equity. Furthermore, firms have issued various capital stock classes that differ in their priority ranking in bankruptcy proceedings. Also, accounting standard-setting bodies have issued pronouncements that create new shareholders' equity accounts. An effective analysis of the profitability and risk of a firm requires an understanding of the accounting for shareholders' equity.

This chapter focuses on the shareholders' equity of **corporations**. The corporate form has at least three advantages:

1. The corporate form provides the owner (shareholder) with limited liability; that is, should the corporation become insolvent, creditors can claim the assets of the corporate entity only. The corporation's creditors cannot claim the assets of the individual owners. On the other hand, to settle debts of partnerships and sole proprietorships, creditors have a claim on both the owners' business and the owners' personal assets.
2. The corporate form allows the firm to raise funds by issuing shares. The general public can acquire the shares in varying amounts. Individual investments can range from a few dollars to billions of dollars.
3. The corporate form makes transfer of ownership interests relatively easy because owners can sell individual shares to others without interfering with the ongoing operations of the business. Ongoing changes in ownership do not affect the continuity of the management and of operations.

The corporation has legal status separate from its owners. Individuals or other entities make capital contributions under a contract between themselves and the corporation. Because those who contribute funds receive certificates for shares of stock, business usage calls them *stockholders or shareholders.*

TERMINOLOGY NOTE

In accounting for owners' equity, the term *contribution* almost never means a gift; for capital given to the corporation as a gift, use the term *donated capital*. Because *stock* means inventory in the United Kingdom, those who attempt to provide clarity to U.K. readers use *share*, rather than *stock*, in the context of ownership.

Various laws and contracts govern the rights and obligations of a shareholder:

1. The corporation laws of the state in which incorporation takes place
2. The articles of incorporation or the **corporate charter** (this contract sets out the agreement between the firm and the state in which the business incorporates; the state grants to the firm the privileges of operating as a corporation for certain stated purposes and of obtaining its capital through the issue of shares of stock)
3. The **corporate bylaws** (the board of directors adopts bylaws, which are the rules and regulations governing the internal affairs of the corporation)
4. The **capital stock contract** (each type of **capital stock** has its own provisions on matters such as voting, sharing in earnings, distributing assets generated by earnings, and sharing in assets in case of dissolution)

DISCLOSURE OF SHAREHOLDERS' EQUITY

Exhibit 12.5 illustrates typical disclosures of the shareholders' equity section of the balance sheet. The shareholders' equity section distinguishes between the equity of preferred shareholders and that of common shareholders.

PREFERRED SHAREHOLDERS' EQUITY

Owners of **preferred stock** generally have a senior claim on the assets of a firm in the event of bankruptcy relative to common shareholders. Preferred shares also carry special rights. Although these rights vary from issue to issue, a preferred share usually entitles its holder to dividends at a certain rate, which the firm must pay before it can pay dividends to common shareholders. For example, the Series A preferred stock in Exhibit 12.5 has rights to a $5 annual dividend, the Series B preferred stock has rights to a $3 annual dividend, and the Series C preferred stock has rights to an $8 dividend. Firms may sometimes postpone or omit preferred dividends. Most preferred shares, however, have **cumulative dividend rights,** which means that a firm must pay all current and previously postponed preferred dividends before it can pay any dividends on common shares.

In recent years, corporations have made many of their preferred share issues callable; see, for example, the Series A preferred stock in Exhibit 12.5. The corporation can reacquire **callable preferred shares** at a specified price, which may vary according to a preset time schedule. If financing becomes available at a cost lower than the rate fixed for the

EXHIBIT 12.5	Disclosure of Shareholders' Equity

	December 31	
	Year 4	Year 5
Preferred Stock		
Series A: $100 par value, 50,000 shares issued and outstanding, subject to $5 dividends and callable at par on December 31, Year 10	$ 5,000,000	$ 5,000,000
Series B: $50 par value, 80,000 issued and outstanding, subject to $3 dividends and convertible into two shares of common stock for each preferred share	4,000,000	4,000,000
Series C: $100 par value, 30,000 issued and outstanding, subject to $8 dividend	3,000,000	3,000,000
Common Stock: $10 par value, 1,000,000 and 1,025,000 issued respectively	10,000,000	10,250,000
Additional Paid-in Capital	25,000,000	28,000,000
Accumulated Other Comprehensive Income		
Unrealized Loss on Valuation of Investments in Securities	(14,500)	(20,600)
Foreign Exchange Adjustment	46,700	(28,300)
Retained Earnings	87,300,000	112,775,000
Total	$134,332,200	$162,976,100
Less Cost of Treasury Stock	(283,900)	(327,900)
Total Shareholders' Equity	$134,048,300	$162,648,200

preferred shares, the issuing firm may want to reduce its financing costs by issuing some new securities and then exercising its option to reacquire the callable shares at a fixed price. Some naive critics think callability benefits only the firm issuing callable shares. The callability option provides a valuable alternative to the issuing firm but makes the shares less attractive to potential owners of the shares. Other things being equal, a firm will be able to issue noncallable shares at a price higher than that for callable shares. The purchaser of the callable shares benefits from acquiring the callable shares at the lower price.

Firms sometimes issue preferred shares with a conversion feature. The Series B preferred stock in Exhibit 12.5 contains a conversion right. **Convertible preferred shares** give their holder the option to convert them into a specified number of common shares at a specified time. The conversion option may appear advantageous to both the individual shareholder and the corporation. The preferred shareholders enjoy the security of a relatively ensured dividend as long as they hold the shares. The shareholders also have the option to realize capital appreciation by converting the shares into common stock if the market price of the common shares rises sufficiently. Because of this option, changes in the market price of the convertible preferred shares will often parallel changes in the market price of the common shares. The firm may also benefit from the conversion option. By including it in the issue, the firm is usually able to specify a lower dividend rate on the preferred stock than otherwise would have been required to issue the shares for a given price.

Some preferred share issues carry mandatory redemption features; that is, the issuing firm must repurchase the shares from their holders, paying a specified dollar amount at a specified future time. Because such **redeemable preferred shares** have some of the characteristics of debt, the Securities and Exchange Commission requires disclosure of them separately from the shareholders' equity section of the balance sheet.[5] The firm may not include them with other shareholders' equity issues in a sum with a caption indicating shareholders' equity total or subtotal. Still, firms continue to issue mandatorily redeemable preferred shares in attempts to keep debt off the balance sheet. Wendy's International created a subsidiary that issued such shares and used the shares to acquire Wendy's debt. These transactions had the combined effect of keeping the debt from appearing on Wendy's balance sheet; refer to Problem **44** at the end of the chapter.

COMMON SHAREHOLDERS' EQUITY

Firms need not issue preferred stock. All firms, however, must issue **common stock.** Common shareholders have a claim on the assets of a firm after creditors and preferred shareholders have received amounts promised to them. Frequently, corporations grant voting rights only to common shares, giving their holders the right to elect members of the board of directors and decide certain broad corporate policies (spelled out in the stock contract).

Accountants disclose the common shareholders' equity of a firm in various accounts on the balance sheet:

1. *Capital Contributions.* Shares of common stock usually have either a **par** or a **stated value.** The articles of incorporation specify the amount, which appears on the face of the stock certificate. The par value of common stock once had legal significance, but

---

[5]Securities and Exchange Commission, *Accounting Series Release No. 268,* "Presentation in Financial Statements of 'Redeemable Preferred Stock,'" 1979. Reissued in Section 211 of *Codification of Financial Reporting Policies.* See also Financial Accounting Standards Board, *Statement of Financial Accounting Standards No. 47,* "Disclosure of Long-Term Obligation," 1981.

it has little economic substance. The issue price of a share of common stock depends on its market value, not its par value. For outdated legal reasons, but for no logical or conceptual reason, accountants separate receipts from the issuance of common stock between amounts that equal the par value and amounts that exceed the par value. The latter amount appears in the **Additional Paid-in Capital account.** No economic, logical, or conceptual reason underlies this practice, which persists out of custom. Firms sometimes issue common shares without a par value. These firms give the no-par-value shares a stated value, which serves the same function as a par value.

HISTORICAL NOTE

Par value of common stock formerly represented an investment that a corporation had to maintain for the protection of creditors. The par value investment amount represented the *legal* or *statutory* or *stated* capital, and many states prohibited corporations from debiting dividends against such capital. In the modern corporation, creditors have found more effective ways to protect themselves, such as through specific limitations, in debt contracts, on corporate financing behavior. Such practices have rendered par value obsolete, but some state laws still require a par value, and many corporations, even when not required, use par-value shares, mostly reflecting inertia on the part of the firms.

2. *Earnings and Dividends.* The assets that a firm generates from earnings in excess of amounts payable to creditors and preferred shareholders belong to the common shareholders. Net income allocable to the common shareholders therefore increases the Retained Earnings account each period. When a firm distributes assets to shareholders for dividends, it reduces the Retained Earnings account.
3. *Accumulated Other Comprehensive Income.* Standard-setting bodies have ruled that even though some operating transactions affect the economic value of a firm, they should not affect net income or retained earnings until a future period. Firms include such items in Accumulated Other Comprehensive Income, a component of shareholders' equity distinct from capital contributions and retained earnings (see the disclosures in Exhibit 12.7, discussed later). Accumulated Other Comprehensive Income includes unrealized gains on losses from investments in securities held for sale and a few other items, as discussed earlier in this chapter.
4. *Treasury Share Transactions.* Firms sometimes reacquire shares of their outstanding common stock for various corporate purposes (discussed later). Common terminology refers to such reacquired shares as *treasury shares.* Firms will often reissue these shares at a later time. Because repurchased common shares reduce the owners' claims on the firm's assets, the cost of treasury shares appears as a subtraction from total shareholders' equity.

Total common shareholders' equity results from the operating activities of generating both earnings and other comprehensive income and from the financing activities of receiving capital contributions, declaring dividends (which reduces equity), and issuing or repurchasing treasury stock (which can reduce or increase equity). Firms often report the

book value per share of common stock—total common shareholders' equity divided by the number of common shares outstanding—in their annual reports. Security analysts sometimes apply a multiple to a firm's book value of common stock to ascertain a reasonable market price (see the discussion of valuation in Appendix 5.1).

The sections that follow discuss the accounting for capital contributions, treasury stock transactions, and retained earnings.

CAPITAL CONTRIBUTIONS

Firms may issue capital stock (preferred or common) for cash, for noncash assets, or under various option arrangements.

ISSUE FOR CASH

Firms usually issue shares for cash at the time of their initial incorporation and at periodic intervals as they need additional shareholder capital. New firms often issue shares to employees instead of cash for partial payment of wages. The issue price for preferred stock usually approximates its par value. Firms generally issue common shares for amounts greater than par (or stated) value. Typically, individuals who purchase newly issued shares from a seasoned corporation pay a price larger than that paid by the original owners. The larger price compensates current shareholders for the additional assets accumulated through the retention of earnings, as well as for increases in the market values of assets over their book values. The firm credits the excess of issue proceeds over par (or stated) value to the Additional Paid-in Capital account.

If a firm issues par-value shares, the credit to the Additional Paid-in Capital account always equals the difference between the amount received and the par value of the shares issued. Thus the entry to record the issue of 1,000 common shares with a par value of $10 per share for $100,000 is as follows:

Cash	100,000	
Common Stock—$10 Par Value		10,000
Additional Paid-in Capital		90,000

To record the issue of common shares for cash in an amount greater than par value.

ISSUE FOR NONCASH ASSETS

Firms occasionally issue common stock for assets other than cash. For example, a firm might want to acquire the assets of another firm in an effort to expand or diversify its operations. The firm records the shares issued at an amount equal to the market value of the assets received or, if the firm cannot make a reasonable estimate, at the market value of the shares issued.[6]

Assume that a firm issues 1,000 shares of its common stock with a par value of $10 per share in the acquisition of another firm's assets having the following market values:

---

[6]Accounting Principles Board, *Opinion No. 29,* "Accounting for Nonmonetary Transactions," 1973.

accounts receivable, $6,000; inventories, $12,000; land, $10,000; building, $62,000; and equipment, $10,000. The journal entry to record the exchange is as follows:

Accounts Receivable	6,000	
Inventories	12,000	
Land	10,000	
Building	62,000	
Equipment	10,000	
Common Stock—$10 Par Value		10,000
Additional Paid-in Capital		90,000
To record the issue of common shares for noncash assets in an amount greater than par value.		

If the firm issues 100 shares with $10 par value to employees for $10,000 of wages, instead of paying cash, the entry would be as follows:

Wage Expense	10,000	
Common Stock—$10 Par Value		1,000
Additional Paid-in Capital		9,000
To record the issue of common shares instead of cash for wages of $10,000 paid to employees.		

ISSUE UNDER OPTION ARRANGEMENTS

Corporations often give various individuals or entities the right, or option, to acquire shares of common stock at a price that is less than the market price of the shares at the time they exercise the option.

Example 3 Ford, IBM, and other corporations with publicly traded common shares give **stock options** to their managerial employees each period as an element of their compensation. The stock options permit the employees to purchase shares of common stock at a price usually set equal to the market price of the stock at the time the firm grants the stock option. Employees exercise these stock options at a later time, after the stock price has increased. Firms adopt stock-option plans to motivate employees to take actions that will increase the market value of a firm's common shares. Some firms issue employee stock options as a way to conserve cash. Likewise, firms issue **stock rights** to current shareholders.

Example 4 Firms sometimes issue bonds with **stock warrants** attached. The bond contract gives the holder the right to receive periodic interest payments and the principal amount at maturity. The stock warrant permits the holder to exchange the warrant and a specified amount of cash for shares of the firm's common stock. Attaching a stock warrant permits the firm to issue bonds at a lower interest cost than would be required for bonds without such a warrant attached.

Example 5 Firms sometimes issue bonds or shares of preferred stock that are convertible into shares of common stock (for example, Series B preferred stock in Exhibit 12.5). The holders receive periodic interest or preferred dividend payments before conversion and usually maintain a senior claim on the firm's assets relative to the common shareholders. The conversion into common stock usually does not require any additional cash investment at the time of conversion. Including the conversion option in a debt or preferred stock issue permits the firm to pay a lower interest or preferred dividend rate than it would have to pay without the conversion option.

Each of these options has economic value. As the sections below discuss, however, accounting generally does not recognize the value of the options at the time firms grant them. Some accountants argue that measuring the value of the option requires too much subjectivity to justify recognition in the accounts. Recent research in finance demonstrates valuation approaches that seem to meet accountants' standards for objective measurement. Standard-setting bodies are ready to move toward explicit measurement of the value of at least some of these options. During the early 1990s, when the FASB discussed charging earnings for the value of employee stock options, management lobbied vigorously against the idea. Managers who criticized charges for option value focused on the uncertainty of valuation but seemed more upset that a valuable form of compensation would become more costly, in an accounting sense, to the issuing firm. See Problem **47** at the end of this chapter.

Employee Stock Option Plans   An understanding of the accounting for stock options requires several definitions. The *grant date* is the date a firm gives a stock option to employees. The *exercise date* is the date employees exchange the option and cash for shares of common stock. The *exercise price* is the price specified in the stock-option contract for purchasing the common stock. Firms usually structure stock-option plans so that a period of time elapses between the grant date and the exercise date. Firms may either preclude employees from exercising the option for one or more years or set an exercise price sufficiently high that the employee would not desire to exercise the option until the stock price increases.

If firms set the exercise price equal to the market value of the common stock on the grant date, as is typically the case, then GAAP make no entry for the granting of stock options.[7] Under some circumstances, if the market price on the exercise date exceeds the exercise price, the firm may have to recognize compensation expense for the difference. For example, suppose that a firm awards options to employees to acquire 1,000 shares of common stock at an exercise price of $35 per share. If the market price of the shares on the date of the grant is $35, the accountant makes no entry to record the awarding of the stock options. When the employees exercise their options, the accountant records the transaction as the issue of shares at the option price.

Cash	35,000	
Common Shares—Par Value		5,000
Additional Paid-in Capital		30,000
To record the issue of 1,000 shares of $5-par value stock at exercise of options and the receipt of $35,000 cash.		

The employees receive an economic benefit from purchasing, for $35, shares that likely sell on the market for a price greater than $35. The firm forgoes the opportunity to issue shares at the higher market price. GAAP currently give no recognition to this economic sacrifice or cost to the firm.

---

[7]Accounting Principles Board, *Opinion No. 25,* "Accounting for Stock Issued to Employees," 1972.

Option Valuation The value of a stock option results from two elements: the benefit realized on the exercise date because the market price of the stock exceeds the exercise price, and the length of the period during which the holder can exercise the option. One cannot know the amount of the benefit element before the exercise date. (The value of an option to buy one share of stock can never exceed the current market price of that share—if it did, the holder would always prefer to buy the share than to buy an option to acquire the share.) In general, stock options with exercise prices less than the current market price of the stock (described as *in the money*) have a higher value than stock options with exercise prices exceeding the current market price of the stock (described as *out of the money*). The second element of an option's value results from the protection it provides its holder from increases in the market price of the stock during the exercise period. An option provides the holder with the right to enjoy the benefits of market price increases for the stock. This second element of an option will have more value the longer the exercise period and the more volatile the market price of the stock. Note that a stock option may have an exercise price that exceeds the current market price (zero value for the first element) but still have a value because of the possibility that the market price will exceed the exercise price on the exercise date (positive value for the second element). As the expiration date of the option approaches, the value of the second element approaches zero.[8]

An alternative treatment, not currently required, recognizes as compensation expense the cost to the issuing firm on the date of granting the stock options. For example, assume that the stock options discussed above have a market value of $7,000 on the grant date. The entry to record the awarding of the options is as follows:

Compensation Expense	7,000	
Common Stock Options		7,000

To record the issue of stock options for 1,000 shares valued at $7,000. The accountant would include the Common Stock Options account in Additional Paid-in Capital.

The entry to record the later issue of shares for $35 a share is as follows:

Cash	35,000	
Common Stock Options	7,000	
Common Stock—Par Value		5,000
Additional Paid-in Capital		37,000

To record the issue of 1,000 shares of $5-par value stock at exercise of options valued at $7,000 and $35,000 cash.

Both the accounting that does not record compensation expense and the allowed (but seldom, to date, seen) alternative, which does measure expense, result in the same total for common shareholders' equity. The alternative treatment results in smaller net income and retained earnings and larger contributed capital relative to the standard treatment. The FASB requires firms to disclose results from accounting for stock options in a manner

---

[8]For an elaboration on the theory of option pricing, see Fischer Black and Myron Scholes, "The Pricing of Options and Corporate Liabilities," *Journal of Political Economy* (May-June 1973), pp. 637–54.

similar to this alternative treatment. It encourages the alternative treatment for income measurement but does not require this treatment.[9]

Political Pressure on Standard-Setters The FASB originally proposed to require a form of this alternative treatment, but the business community lobbied various congressional interests sufficiently vigorously that some senators brought pressure on the FASB to withdraw its original proposal. The FASB proposal would have required including among expenses on the date of grant the cost of the options on that date. This would have reduced reported earnings for an estimate of the wage cost embodied in the options. The FASB has substituted a requirement for increased disclosure about the market value of employee stock options. No sooner had the FASB allowed the disclosure alternative than corporate interests began lobbying to water down those disclosures. We cannot forecast the outcome. We prefer the accounting represented by the withdrawn FASB proposal, in which firms must show as compensation expense the cost of the employee options it grants.

GAAP require that the terms of options granted, outstanding, and exercised during a period be disclosed in notes to the financial statements. Exhibit 12.6, a schedule presented by General Electric Company, illustrates the typical disclosure on stock options.

Stock Rights Like stock options, stock rights give their holder the right to acquire shares of stock at a specified price. The major differences between stock options and stock rights are as follows:

- Firms grant stock options to employees. Employees receive them as a form of compensation and may not transfer or sell them to others.
- Firms grant stock rights to current shareholders. The rights usually trade in public markets.

EXHIBIT 12.6	GENERAL ELECTRIC COMPANY Disclosure of Employee Stock Options		
Stock Options	**Shares Subject to Option**	**Average per Share**	
		Option Price	**Market Price**
Balance at December 31, Year 1	2,388,931	$45	$72
Options Granted	475,286	77	77
Options Exercised	(297,244)	42	76
Options Terminated	(90,062)	45	—
Balance at December 31, Year 2	2,476,911	50	83
Options Granted	554,965	75	75
Options Exercised	(273,569)	42	74
Options Terminated	(58,307)	52	—
Balance at December 31, Year 3	2,700,000	54	77

---

[9]Financial Accounting Standards Board, *Statement of Financial Accounting Standards No. 123,* "Accounting for Stock-Based Compensation," 1995.

Firms issue stock rights to raise new capital from current shareholders. The granting of stock rights to current shareholders requires no accounting entries. When holders exercise the rights, the firm records the issue of shares at the price paid just as it records the issue of new shares for cash.

Stock Warrants   Firms issue stock warrants to the general investing public for cash. Assume that a corporation issues warrants for $15,000 cash. The warrants allow holders to purchase 10,000 shares for $20 each. The entry is as follows:

Cash	15,000	
Common Stock Warrants		15,000

To record the issue of warrants to the public. The accountant normally includes the Common Stock Warrants account with Additional Paid-in Capital for balance sheet presentation.

When warrant holders exercise their rights, the firm issues 10,000 shares of $5-par value common stock in exchange for the warrants plus $200,000 and records the following entry:

Cash	200,000	
Common Stock Warrants	15,000	
Common Stock—$5 Par Value		50,000
Additional Paid-in Capital		165,000

To record the issue of 10,000 shares for $200,000 cash and the redemption of warrants. (The amount originally received for the warrants transfers to Additional Paid-in Capital.)

If the warrants expire before the holders exercise them, the firm records the following entry:

Common Stock Warrants	15,000	
Additional Paid-in Capital		15,000

To record the expiration of common stock warrants and the transfer to permanent contributed capital.

Firms sometimes attach to a bond or preferred stock common stock warrants that the holder can detach and redeem separately from the bond or preferred stock. The holder receives periodic interest or preferred dividends and holds an option to purchase common shares. When the accountant can objectively measure the value of the stock warrants separately from the value of the associated bond or preferred stock, the accounting allocates the issue price between the two securities.

To illustrate, assume that a firm issues 20-year, $1,000,000 bonds with 7 percent semi-annual coupons. The bonds contain stock warrants that their holders can either sell on the open market or exercise to acquire 10,000 shares of common stock for $200,000. The issue price for the bonds and warrants is $1,050,000. Immediately after issue, the bonds sell on the market for $1,035,000 and the warrants sell for $15,000. The accountant records the issue of the bonds as follows:

Cash	1,050,000	
Bonds Payable		1,035,000
Common Stock Warrants		15,000

The subsequent accounting for the bonds follows the procedures discussed in Chapter 9 for bonds issued above or below par value. The accounting for the warrants follows the procedures illustrated above for warrants issued for cash.

If the accountant cannot objectively measure the value of the stock warrants separately from the value of the bond or preferred stock, the accounting credits the full issue price to the bond or preferred stock and none of the price to the common stock warrants.

Convertible Bonds and Convertible Preferred Stock

Convertible bonds and convertible preferred stock permit an owner either to hold the security as a bond or preferred stock or to convert the security into shares of common stock. The market value of the conversion option does not trade independently of the bond or preferred stock, as was the case above for bonds or preferred stock issued with a separable stock warrant. Thus, the accountant has greater difficulty allocating the issue price of a convertible bond or convertible preferred stock between its debt or preferred stock attributes and its conversion feature.

The required accounting allocates the full issue price to the bonds or preferred stock and none of the price to the conversion feature. Suppose, for example, that Johnson Company's credit rating would allow it to issue $100,000 of ordinary 10-year, 14 percent semiannual coupon bonds at par. The firm prefers to issue convertible bonds with a lower coupon rate. Assume that Johnson Company issues at par $100,000 of 10-year, 10 percent semiannual coupon bonds but that the holder of each $1,000 bond can convert it into 50 shares of Johnson Company $5-par value common stock. (Holders in aggregate can convert the entire issue into 5,000 shares.) Accounting requires the following entry:

Cash	100,000	
Convertible Bonds Payable		100,000
To record the issue of convertible bonds at par.		

This entry effectively treats convertible bonds just like ordinary, nonconvertible bonds, and it records the value of the conversion feature at zero.

An alternative treatment, but one not currently permitted, allocates a portion of the issue price to the conversion feature. Appendix Table 5 (for 10 percent coupon bonds) indicates that 10 percent, 10-year semiannual (nonconvertible) coupon bonds sell for about 79 percent of par for an issuer with a market borrowing rate of 14 percent. Thus, if the firm can issue 10 percent convertible bonds at par, the conversion feature must be worth about 21 (= 100 − 79) percent of par. This indicates that the bond buyers have paid 21 percent of the proceeds from the bond issue as a capital contribution for the right to acquire common stock later. If GAAP allowed the accountant to record the substance of the issue of these 10 percent convertible bonds at par, the entry would be as follows:

Cash	100,000	
Convertible Bonds Payable		79,000
Additional Paid-in Capital		21,000
To record the issue of 10 percent semiannual coupon convertible bonds at a time when ordinary 10 percent bonds could be issued for 79 percent of par. GAAP do not allow this entry.		

Notice that the calculation of the amounts for this entry requires knowing the proceeds of an issue of nonconvertible bonds with other features similar to the convertible bonds.

Because auditors often believe that they are unable to estimate this information reasonably objectively, GAAP do not allow the previous journal entry. The entry under GAAP simply debits Cash and credits Convertible Bonds Payable for $100,000.

The usual entry to record the conversion of bonds into shares ignores current market prices in the interest of simplicity and merely shows the swap of shares for bonds at their book value. For example, assume that the common stock of Johnson Company increases in the market to $30 a share, so that the holder of one $1,000 bond, convertible into 50 shares, can convert it into shares with a market value of $1,500. If holders convert all the convertible issue into common shares at this time, the firm would issue 5,000 shares of $5-par value stock on conversion and make the following journal entry:

Convertible Bonds Payable	100,000	
Common Shares—$5 Par		25,000
Additional Paid-in Capital		75,000
To record the conversion of 100 convertible bonds with book value of $100,000 into 5,000 shares of $5-par value stock.		

An allowable alternative treatment recognizes that market prices provide information useful in quantifying the market value of the shares issued. Under the alternative treatment, with $30 market price per share and $150,000 fair market value of the 5,000 shares issued on conversion, the journal entry would be as follows:

Convertible Bonds Payable	100,000	
Loss on Conversion of Bonds	50,000	
Common Shares—$5 Par		25,000
Additional Paid-in Capital		125,000
To record the conversion of 100 convertible bonds into 5,000 shares of $5-par value stock at a time when the market price is $30 per share.		

The alternative entry results in the same total shareholders' equity, with smaller retained earnings (because the Loss on Conversion of Bonds will reduce current net income and thus the Retained Earnings account) but with larger contributed capital. It results from treating the conversion as the following two separate transactions:

Cash	150,000	
Common Shares—$5 Par		25,000
Additional Paid-in Capital		125,000
To record issue of 5,000 shares of $5-par value stock at $30 per share.		
Convertible Bonds Payable	100,000	
Loss on Retirement of Bonds	50,000	
Cash		150,000
To retire, by purchase for $150,000, 100 convertible bonds carried on the books at $100,000.		

PROBLEM 12.1 FOR SELF-STUDY

Journal entries for capital contributions. Prepare the journal entries to record the following transactions for Healy Corporation during Year 1.

a. Issued 100,000 of $10-par value common stock for $14 per share on January 2.
b. Issued 10,000 shares of common stock on January 2 in the acquisition of a patent. The firm has no separate information about the fair value of the patent.
c. Issued 2,000 shares of $100 convertible preferred stock on March 1 for $100 per share. Holders may convert each share of preferred stock into four shares of common stock.
d. Sold 10,000 common warrants on the open market on June 1 for $5 per warrant. Holders can exchange each warrant and $24 in cash for a share of common stock.
e. Holders of 600 shares of convertible preferred stock (see **c**) exchanged their shares for common stock on September 15. The market price of the common stock on this date was $26 per share. Record the conversion using the book values.
f. Holders of 4,000 common stock warrants exchanged their warrants (see **d**) and $96,000 in cash for common stock on November 20. The market price of the common stock on this date was $32 per share.
g. Granted rights to employees to purchase 5,000 shares of common stock for $35 per share on December 31. The market price per share on this date was $35.

TREASURY SHARES

When the issuing corporation reacquires previously issued shares, accounting calls these **treasury stock** or **treasury shares.** Reasons for reacquiring outstanding common stock include the following:

1. To use in various option arrangements. When holders of stock options, stock rights, stock warrants, and convertible securities exercise their options, firms usually receive less cash (or market value of other consideration) than the market value of the common stock at the time.
2. To serve as a worthwhile investment of excess cash. Some firms believe that their own shares provide a good investment. Evidence supports the notion that share prices increase after news becomes public that a firm intends to or has reacquired its own shares. Such shares do not receive dividends, nor do they have voting rights, because corporation laws do not consider them to be outstanding shares for these purposes. Firms can resell the treasury shares when they need cash.
3. To defend against an unfriendly takeover bid. Many firms have received unfriendly takeover bids in recent years. To defend against takeover attempts, firms use available cash to repurchase shares of common stock on the market. Two different motives appear to be at work here:

   ■ This action reduces the amount of common shareholders' equity and increases the proportion of debt in the capital structure, making the firm more risky and therefore less attractive to an unfriendly bidder. Some firms even borrow cash to repurchase shares, an action that affects the debt ratio even more than using already available cash to reacquire shares.

■ The acquisition of shares uses available cash and thereby reduces the attractiveness of the company to outsiders who believe the available cash makes the company an attractive target.

4. To distribute cash to shareholders in a tax-advantaged way. Rather than pay dividends to all shareholders, many of whom will owe personal income taxes on the entire dividend amount, the firm can buy back shares from those who want to raise cash. Many shareholders will have lower tax rates on receipts from sales of shares than on dividend receipts.

ACCOUNTING FOR TREASURY SHARES

Accounting for treasury shares follows from the fundamental principle that a corporation does not report profit or loss on transactions involving its own shares. Even though the firm may sell (technically, reissue) the shares for more than their acquisition cost, the accounting does not report the "gain" in income. Similarly, the firm may subsequently reissue shares for less than their acquisition cost, but even so, the "loss" will not reduce net income. The required accounting views treasury stock purchases and sales as capital, not operating, transactions and therefore debits ("loss") or credits ("gain") the contributed capital accounts for the adjustments for reissue of treasury shares. The amounts bypass the income statement, comprehensive income, and generally, the Retained Earnings account.

When a firm reacquires common shares, it debits a Treasury Shares—Common account (a shareholders' equity contra account) with the total amount paid to reacquire the shares.

Treasury Shares—Common	11,000	
Cash		11,000

To record $11,000 paid to reacquire 1,000 common shares. Treasury Shares—Common is a contra account to shareholders' equity.

If the firm later reissues treasury shares for cash, it debits Cash with the amount received and credits the Treasury Shares—Common account with the cost of the shares. If it reissues treasury shares at the conversion of bonds or preferred stock into common stock, it debits the convertible bonds or preferred stock instead of debiting cash. The reissue price will usually differ from the amount paid to acquire the treasury shares. If the reissue price exceeds the acquisition price, the credit to make the entry balance is to the Additional Paid-in Capital account. Assuming that the above firm reissued for $14,000 the 1,000 shares reacquired previously, the entry would be as follows:

Cash	14,000	
Treasury Shares—Common		11,000
Additional Paid-in Capital		3,000

To reissue 1,000 shares of treasury stock at a price greater than acquisition cost. The $3,000 "gain" does not appear on the income statement.

If the amount paid for the treasury shares exceeds the reissue price, the firm debits the balance to Additional Paid-in Capital, so long as that account has a sufficiently large credit balance. To the extent that the required debit exceeds the credit balance in the Additional Paid-in Capital account, the firm reduces that account to zero and debits the excess to retained earnings. This debit to the Retained Earnings account resembles a dividend; it does not appear as an expense or a loss reported on the income statement.

The Treasury Shares account appears as a subtraction from total shareholders' equity on the balance sheet; see Exhibit 12.5.

PROBLEM 12.2 FOR SELF-STUDY

Journal entries for treasury stock transactions.   Prepare journal entries for the following transactions of Crissie Corporation.

a. Reacquired 2,000 shares of $10-par value common stock on January 15 for $45 per share.
b. Issued 1,200 shares of treasury stock to employees upon the exercise of stock options at a price of $48 per share on April 26.
c. Reacquired 3,000 shares of $10-par value common stock for $52 per share on August 15.
d. Issued 1,600 shares of treasury stock to holders of 800 shares of convertible preferred stock, which had a book value of $80,000 on November 24. Crissie Corporation uses a first-in, first-out assumption on reissues of treasury stock and uses book values to record conversions of preferred stock.
e. Sold 1,500 shares of treasury stock on the open market for $47 per share on December 20.

RETAINED EARNINGS

The Retained Earnings account increases (decreases) each period by the amount of net income (net loss) and decreases for dividends declared. The first section of this chapter discussed the disclosure of various earnings components in the income statement and in other comprehensive income. This section discusses some issues in accounting for earnings and dividend transactions.

REPORTING EARNINGS TRANSACTIONS

What purpose does the income statement serve? We argue that it is *not* "to show earnings for the period." The reader of the financial statements can generally ascertain earnings by subtracting the beginning balance of the Retained Earnings account from its ending balance and adding dividends. Accountants provide an income statement so that managers and investors can see the *causes* of earnings. Then a reader can compare a company's performance with that of other companies (cross-section analysis) or with that of the company itself over time (time-series analysis), to make more informed projections about the future.

Earnings Statements and Cash Flow Statements Explain Balance Sheet Changes   We can make parallel statements about the statement of cash flows. The purpose of the statement of cash flows is *not* "to report the change in cash for the period." You can deduce this change by subtracting the balance in the Cash account at the start of the period from the balance at the end of the period. The purpose is to report the *causes* of the changes in the Cash account. That the purpose of the income statement (or statement of cash flows) is not to report the earnings (or cash) amount comes as a surprise to most. Understanding this fact helps you understand why and how managers use discretion to design the structure and captions of the income statement (and the cash flow statement).

Insofar as the income statement attempts to help readers understand the past in hopes of predicting the future, reporting on these transactions in the income statement without noting their special nature makes this task more difficult. Consider the following examples:

1. General Motors (GM) discontinues automobile manufacturing at a plant in Texas. It sells the plant facilities at a loss of $40 million.
2. Disney World incurs $15 million of uninsured losses from a hurricane in Florida.
3. Dell Computer Corporation discovers that it neglected to count $250,000 of inventory items stored in a warehouse in Texas at the end of last year. In consequence, Dell understated its earnings last period.
4. American Airlines depreciates its aircraft over a 20-year life. More fuel-efficient aircraft now available on the market cause American Airlines to begin slowly replacing its existing aircraft with the new aircraft. American Airlines reduces the depreciable life of its existing aircraft, thus increasing current and future depreciation charges relative to the recent past.
5. The Internal Revenue Service audits the income tax returns of Georgia-Pacific Corporation and assesses the firm $25 million in additional taxes on its return filed five years previously.

Each of these five examples requires the accountant to decide whether to include the items in the income statement for the current period or to debit or credit them directly to retained earnings, thereby bypassing the income statement.

Advocates of including these items in the income statement argue that each item has an earnings effect. All earnings items should appear in the income statement of some period before their transfer to retained earnings. In this way, the cumulative series of income statements includes all earnings items. The financial statement reader will be less likely to overlook the items if they appear in the income statement than if firms record the amounts directly in retained earnings. Adequate disclosure of the nature of each item in the income statement will permit the financial statement user to assess its importance when evaluating the firm's profitability. Probably with good reason, some on this side of the argument suggest that if managers have the discretion to leave such items out of the income statement, many of them will find ways to justify excluding from earnings the bad news (such as GM's loss on the plant closing or Disney's hurricane loss) and including in earnings only the good news (such as Dell's overlooked inventory). Virtually all theorists agree that giving managers the discretion to report good news and bad news as they see fit will lead to less-useful financial statements unless auditors become more critical of their clients' accounting than they have been historically.

Advocates of reporting these items directly in retained earnings argue that the items should not affect assessments of a firm's ongoing profitability. The items either are peripheral or nonrecurring relative to operations of the current period or relate to activities of the prior period. An income statement based on only the usual, recurring transactions of the current period provides the financial statement reader with more useful information for assessing a firm's profitability.

GAAP usually adopt the first view, requiring the disclosure of all earnings items in the earnings statement before their transfer to retained earnings.

Reporting Correction of Errors   Errors result from such actions as miscounting inventories, miscalculating figures, and misapplying accounting principles. The accountant makes a **correction of errors,** if material, with direct debits or credits to the Retained Earnings account.[10] Assume, for example, that a firm discovers that its merchandise inventory was $10,000 less than it reported at the end of the previous period and that it understated cost of goods sold last period using a periodic inventory method, as follows:

$$\frac{\text{Cost of}}{\text{Goods Sold}} = \frac{\text{Beginning}}{\text{Inventory}} + \text{Purchases} - \frac{\text{Ending}}{\text{Inventory}}$$

The firm makes the following entry (ignoring income tax effects) this period:

Retained Earnings	10,000	
Merchandise Inventory		10,000

To correct inventory error. The firm understated last period's cost of goods sold and overstated earnings.

Reporting Changes in Estimates   As time passes, new information becomes available that sharpens the estimates required to apply accounting principles. Examples include the amount of uncollectible accounts and the useful lives of depreciable assets. Earlier chapters have pointed out that accountants do not correct revenues and expenses of previous periods to incorporate new information. Instead, the accountant allows the effect of the change in estimate to affect earnings of current and future periods.[11] Refer, for example, to Figure 8.3, which illustrates the effect of a change in depreciable life on depreciation expense. Rather than correct Retained Earnings directly, the firm adjusts current and future depreciation charges, but no past ones, to take into account both the book value at the time the new information arrives and the new information itself.

Accrual accounting requires frequent, ongoing changes in estimates. Restating the financial statements of previous years each time a firm changes an estimate (which would require changing the opening balance of retained earnings for the period of the change) might reduce the credibility of financial reporting. This approach would also provide management with methods for boosting earnings of current and future periods by lowering the already reported earnings of previous periods.

Changes in estimates do not always relate to recurring accrual accounting measurements, such as depreciable lives. Some changes in estimates concern unusual or nonrecurring events. Consider, for example, the following:

- A court this period finds a firm responsible for an act that occurred several years previously and caused injury. The damage award differs from the amount, if any, that the firm previously recognized with a debit to a loss and a credit to a liability.

- The Internal Revenue Service assesses additional income taxes on a firm's taxable income of previous years. The amount previously recognized as income tax expense for those years understates the final amount payable.

[10]Accounting Principles Board, *Opinion No. 20,* "Accounting Changes," 1971.
[11]Ibid.

Prior-Period Adjustments   These events provide new information regarding measurements made in previous periods. Even though the events do not recur, GAAP treat them similarly to changes in estimates for recurring items. The earnings effect of these items appears in the earnings statement of the current period, appropriately disclosed, and not in retained earnings as a direct adjustment. Direct adjustments of retained earnings, called **prior-period adjustments,** almost never appear in financial statements.[12]

CORPORATE DIVIDEND POLICIES

Retained earnings represent a firm's total lifetime earnings less its total lifetime dividends. After a new business has become established and profitable, it usually generates additional shareholders' equity from earnings exceeding dividends. These undistributed earnings represent the net assets accumulated by a firm that does not distribute all its earnings. Retaining the earnings increases shareholders' equity, and the firm can use the assets retained to replace old assets or to expand.

Most publicly held firms use a portion of the assets generated by earnings to distribute as a dividend to shareholders. The board of directors declares these dividends periodically. The directors, in considering whether to declare cash dividends, must conclude that declaring a dividend is both legal (under law and contract) and financially expedient.

Legal Limits on Dividends—Statutory (by Law)   State corporation laws limit directors' freedom to declare dividends. These limitations attempt to protect a firm's creditors. Without these limits, directors might dissipate the firm's assets for the benefit of shareholders, harming the creditors. Neither directors nor shareholders are liable for the corporation's debts.

Generally, the laws provide that the board may not declare dividends "out of capital," that is, debited against the Contributed Capital account, which results from capital transactions, but must declare them "out of earnings," by debiting against the Retained Earnings account, which results from operating transactions. The wording and the interpretation of this rule vary among states. "Capital" usually means the total amount paid by shareholders. Some states allow corporations to declare dividends out of the earnings of the current period even though the Retained Earnings account has a debit (negative) balance because of accumulated losses from previous periods.

For most companies, statutory limits do not influence the accounting for shareholders' equity and dividends. A balance sheet does not provide all the legal details of amounts available for dividends, but it should disclose the information necessary for the user to apply the legal rules of the corporation's state of incorporation. For example, state statutes can provide that the corporation "may acquire treasury shares only in amounts less than retained earnings." In other words, dividends cannot exceed the amount of retained earnings reduced by the cost of currently held treasury shares. If a firm acquires treasury shares under these constraints, the amount of future dividends it might otherwise declare declines. The firm must disclose this fact in a footnote to the balance sheet.[13]

The firm can meet the statutory requirements for declaring dividends by building up a balance in retained earnings. Such a balance does not mean that the firm has a fund of cash available for the dividends. Some readers of financial statements mistakenly

---

[12]Financial Accounting Standards Board, *Statement of Financial Accounting Standards No. 16,* "Prior Period Adjustments," 1977, par. 10.

[13]Accounting Principles Board, *Opinion No. 6,* "Status of Accounting Research Bulletins," 1965.

believe that retained earnings represent cash available for dividends. This error often results from the confusion of assets (such as cash) with sources of assets (such as retained earnings). Retained earnings represent increased net assets but not necessarily, or even usually, cash.

Managing cash requires the techniques of corporate finance; a firm must anticipate cash needs for dividends just as it anticipates cash needs for the purchase of equipment, the retirement of debts, and so on. A prudent firm might borrow from the bank to pay the regular dividend if its financial condition justifies the resulting increase in liabilities.

Legal Limits on Dividends—Contractual   Contracts with bondholders, other lenders, and preferred shareholders often limit dividend payments and thereby compel the retention of earnings. A bond contract may require the retirement of the debt to be made "out of earnings." Such a provision involves curtailing dividends so that the necessary debt-service payments, plus any dividends, do not exceed the amount of earnings for the period. This provision forces the shareholders to increase their investment in the business by limiting the amount of dividends that the board might otherwise declare for them. Financial statement notes must disclose significant limitations on dividend declarations.

The notes to a financial statement of Sears, Roebuck and Co. contain the following disclosure:

> Dividend payments are restricted by several statutory and contractual factors, including: Certain indentures relating to the long-term debt of Sears, Roebuck and Co., which represent the most restrictive contractual limitation on the payment of dividends, provide that the company cannot take specified actions, including the declaration of cash dividends, which would cause its consolidated unencumbered assets, as defined [in the indentures, not in the annual report], to fall below 150 percent of its consolidated liabilities, as defined. At . . . [year-end], $11.2 billion in retained income [of a total of $12.7 billion of retained earnings] could be paid in dividends to shareholders under the most restrictive indentures. [Sears declared dividends for the year of approximately $700 million.]

Dividends and Corporate Financial Policy   Directors usually declare dividends that are less than the legal maximum. The directors may allow retained earnings to increase as a matter of corporate financial policy for several reasons:

1. Available cash did not increase by as much as the amount of earnings, so maximum dividends would require raising more cash.
2. Restricting dividends in prosperous years may permit level or steadily growing dividend payments in poor years.
3. The firm may need funds for expansion of working capital or plant and equipment.
4. Reducing the amount of borrowings, rather than paying dividends, may seem prudent.

Even when the board wants to distribute cash to owners, it may authorize stock buy-back programs rather than pay dividends. Such programs often have income tax advantages for shareholders. The statement of cash flows helps the reader understand how the firm has used cash provided by operations and other sources.

ACCOUNTING FOR DIVIDENDS

A firm may pay dividends in cash, other assets, or shares of its common stock.

Cash Dividends When the board declares a **cash dividend,** the entry is as follows:

Retained Earnings	150,000	
Dividends Payable		150,000

To record declaration of dividends. (Sometimes the firm debits an account called Dividends or Dividends Declared. The Dividends account is a temporary account, and the accountant closes it with a debit to the Retained Earnings account at the end of the period.)

Once the board of directors declares a dividend, the dividend becomes a legal liability of the corporation. Dividends Payable appears as a current liability on the balance sheet if the firm has not yet paid the dividends at the end of the accounting period. When the firm pays the dividends, the entry is as follows:

Dividends Payable	150,000	
Cash		150,000

Property Dividends Corporations sometimes distribute assets other than cash when paying a dividend; such a dividend is known as a *dividend in kind* or a **property dividend.** The accounting for such dividends resembles that for cash dividends, except that when the firm pays the dividend, it credits the asset given up, rather than cash. The amount debited to Retained Earnings equals the fair market value of the assets distributed. When this market value differs from the book value of the asset distributed, a gain or loss arises. The firm reports any gain or loss as part of earnings for the period.

Stock Dividends The retention of earnings may lead to a substantial increase in shareholders' equity, which represents a relatively permanent commitment by shareholders to the business. The permanency results from the firm's having invested the net assets generated by the earnings process in operating assets such as inventories and plant. (You may have realized by now that even though individual items of inventory come and go regularly, many successful firms have a permanent investment in inventories.) To indicate such a permanent commitment of assets generated by reinvested earnings, the board of directors may declare a **stock dividend.** The accounting involves a debit to the Retained Earnings account and a credit to the contributed capital accounts. The stock dividend has no effect on total shareholders' equity. It reallocates amounts from Retained Earnings to the contributed capital accounts. When the firm declares a stock dividend, shareholders receive additional shares of stock in proportion to their existing holdings. If the firm issues a 5 percent stock dividend, each shareholder receives one additional share for every 20 shares held before the dividend.

GAAP require firms to record the value of the newly issued shares based on the market value of the shares issued. For example, the directors of a corporation may decide to declare a stock dividend of 10,000 additional shares of common stock with a par value of $10 per share at a time when the market price of a share is $40. The entry would be as follows:

Retained Earnings	400,000	
Common Stock—$10 Par		100,000
Additional Paid-in Capital		300,000

To declare a stock dividend, recorded using market price of shares to quantify the amounts: $40 × 10,000 shares = $400,000.

The stock dividend relabels, as a more permanent form of shareholders' equity, a portion of the retained earnings that had been legally available for dividend declarations. A stock dividend formalizes the fact that the firm has used some funds represented by past earnings to expand plant facilities, to replace assets at increased prices, or to retire bonds. The firm does not have this cash available for cash dividends. The stock dividend does not affect the availability of cash that the firm has already invested; the stock dividend signals this event, perhaps more clearly than before, to readers of the balance sheet.

Stock dividends have little economic substance for shareholders. More pieces of paper represent the same ownership. If the shareholders receive the same type of shares that they already own, each shareholder's proportionate interest in the capital of the corporation and each one's proportionate voting power do not change. Although the book value per common share (total common shareholders' equity divided by number of common shares outstanding) decreases, the shareholder has a proportionately larger number of shares, so the total book value of each shareholder's interest remains unchanged. The market value per share should decline, but all else being equal, the total market value of an individual's shares will not change. To describe such a distribution of shares as a "dividend"—meaning a distribution of assets generated by earnings—may mislead some readers, but the terminology is generally accepted.

STOCK SPLITS

Stock splits (or, more technically, splitups) are similar to stock dividends. The corporation issues additional shares of stock to shareholders in proportion to their existing holdings. The firm receives no additional assets. A stock split reduces the par value of all the stock in the issued class. A corporation may, for example, have 1,000 shares of $10-par value stock outstanding and, by a stock split, exchange those shares for 2,000 shares of $5-par value stock (a two-for-one split) or for 4,000 shares of $2.50-par value stock (a four-for-one split) or for any number of shares of no-par stock. If the shares outstanding have no par value, the shareholders keep the existing certificates and receive the new ones.

A stock split generally does not require a journal entry. The amount of retained earnings does not decline. The amount shown in the Capital Stock account represents a larger number of shares. Of course the firm must record, in the subsidiary capital stock records, the additional number of shares held by each shareholder. Sometimes the firm accounts for stock splits as stock dividends with a transfer from the Retained Earnings account to the Contributed Capital account. If so, the amounts reflect the market value of the shares on the date of the split. There is no easy way to distinguish stock splits from stock dividends. Usually firms treat small-percentage distributions as stock dividends and larger ones as stock splits.

A stock split (or a stock dividend) usually reduces the market value per share, all else remaining equal, in inverse proportion to the split (or dividend). Thus a two-for-one split could be expected to result in a 50 percent reduction in the market price per share. Therefore, management has used stock splits to keep the market price per share from rising to a level unacceptable to management. For example, the board of directors might think that a market price of $60 to $80 is an effective trading range for its stock. (This subjective judgment almost never has supporting evidence. Warren Buffet, chairman of Berkshire Hathaway, has refused to split the common shares of his company, even though the Class A shares sell in the marketplace for over $70,000 per share. Buffet appears not to believe that his company's share price suffers as a result.) If the share price has risen to $150 in the market, the board of directors may declare a two-for-one split. Certainly, stock splits and dividends result in increased record-keeping costs. Corporations that plan to begin public trading of their shares in a public market often split their stocks.

Journal entries for earnings and retained earnings transactions. The share-holders' equity section of the balance sheet of Baker Corporation on January 1, Year 5, appears below:

Shareholders' Equity

Common Stock ($10 par value, 25,000 shares issued and outstanding)	$250,000
Additional Paid-in Capital	50,000
Retained Earnings	150,000
Total	$450,000

Prepare journal entries for each of the following transactions of Baker Corporation for Year 5. Ignore income taxes.

a. January 15: As a result of a computer software error the preceding December, the firm failed to record a total of $35,000 in depreciation on office facilities.

b. March 20: An earthquake in California causes an uninsured loss of $70,000 to a ware-house.

c. March 31: The board of directors declares a cash dividend of $.50 per share. The firm will pay the dividend on April 15.

d. April 15: The firm pays the dividend declared on March 31.

e. June 30: The board of directors declares and distributes a 10 percent stock dividend. The market price per share on this date is $15.

f. December 31: The firm acquired its office building six years before December 31, Year 5. The building cost $400,000, had zero estimated salvage value, and had a 40-year life. The firm uses the straight-line depreciation method. Baker Corporation now esti-mates that the building will have a total useful life of 30 years instead of 40 years. Record depreciation expense on the building for Year 5 and any required adjustment to depreciation of previous years.

g. The board of directors declares a 2-for-1 stock split and changes the par value of the common shares from $10 to $5.

EARNINGS PER SHARE

Publicly held firms must show earnings-per-share data in the body of the income state-ment.[14] **Earnings per common share** result from dividing net earnings minus preferred stock dividends by the average number of outstanding common shares during the ac-counting period. Firms reporting more than one of the four categories of earnings items must disclose earnings per common share for each reported category.

The issues involved in calculating earnings per common share go beyond the scope of this book. Problem **46** at the end of this chapter illustrates some of the calculations.

---

[14]Financial Accounting Standards Board, *Statement of Financial Accounting Standards No. 128,* "Earnings per Share," 1997.

EXHIBIT 12.7 | MICHIGAN COMPANY (adapted from Ford Motor Company)
Consolidated Statement of Shareholders' Equity
(all dollar amounts in millions)

Line Number[a]		Shares	Amount	Additional Paid-in Capital	Retained Earnings	Accumulated Other Comprehensive Income	Treasury Shares	Total Shareholders' Equity
	Balance, January 1, Year 1	101.5	$253.7	$379.5	$5,328.1	$137.7	$(56.5)	$6,042.5
(1)	Net Income				906.5			906.5
(2)	Unrealized Gain (Loss) on Securities Available for Sale					46.2		46.2
(3)	Cash Dividends				(317.1)			(317.1)
(4)	Common Stock Issued under Certain Employee Stock Plans	0.2	0.5	9.9				10.4
(5)	Conversion of Debentures			0.6			10.2	10.8
(6)	Common Stock Retired	(2.5)	(6.2)	(9.5)	(140.9)			(156.6)
	Balance, December 31, Year 1	99.2	$248.0	$380.5	$5,776.6	$183.9	$(46.3)	$6,542.7
(1)	Net Income				360.9			360.9
(2)	Unrealized Gain (Loss) on Securities Available for Sale					(53.7)		(53.7)
(3)	Cash Dividends				(298.1)			(298.1)
(4)	Common Stock Issued under Certain Employee Stock Plans	0.1	0.2	1.8				2.0
(5)	Conversion of Debentures			1.4			30.6	32.0
(6)	Common Stock Retired	(5.7)	(14.2)	(21.8)	(194.0)			(230.0)
	Balance, December 31, Year 2	93.6	$234.0	$361.9	$5,645.4	$130.2	$(15.7)	$6,355.8

[a]This caption and the line numbers do not appear on the original statement. The line numbers correspond to the journal entries in Exhibit 12.8.

EXHIBIT 12.8	MICHIGAN COMPANY (adapted from Ford Motor Company) Journal Entries Illustrating Transactions Involving Shareholders' Equity, Years 1 and 2 (all dollar amounts in millions)

Entry and Explanation	Year 1		Year 2	
(1) Income Summary	906.5		360.9	
Retained Earnings		906.5		360.9
Net income for the year, recorded assuming that the firm used an Income Summary account. This entry in effect closes all temporary revenue and expense accounts, with the credit balance reported as net income for the year.				
(2) Marketable Security Investments Available for Sale	46.2			
Unrealized Holding Gain (Loss) on Securities Available for Sale		46.2		
Unrealized Holding Gain (Loss) on Securities Available for Sale			53.7	
Marketable Security Investments Available for Sale				53.7
To record increase in market value in Year 1 (decrease in market value in Year 2) with increase in asset account in Year 1 (decrease in asset account in Year 2) matching credit in Year 1 (debit in Year 2) to Accumulated Other Comprehensive Income, a shareholders' equity account, bypassing the income statement.				
(3) Retained Earnings	317.1		298.1	
Cash (or Dividends Payable)		317.1		298.1
Cash dividends declared.				
(4) Cash	10.4		2.0	
Common Stock		0.5		0.2
Additional Paid-in Capital		9.9		1.8
Common stock issued under certain employee stock plans.				
(5) Convertible Debentures (Bonds)	10.8		32.0	
Treasury Stock		10.2		30.6
Additional Paid-in Capital		0.6		1.4
Common stock issued on conversion of convertible debentures (bonds). The shares "issued" on conversion were shares reissued from a block of treasury shares that had cost $10.2 (for Year 1) and $30.6 (for Year 2).				
(6) Common Stock	6.2		14.2	
Additional Paid-in Capital	9.5		21.8	
Retained Earnings	140.9		194.0	
Cash		156.6		230.0
Retirement of common stock acquired for cash. When a firm acquires shares for the treasury, it usually debits a Treasury Stock account, shown as a contra to all of shareholders' equity. In this case, the firm "retires" the shares, so the journal entry identifies the specific amounts for Additional Paid-in Capital and Retained Earnings corresponding to these shares. The debits are to these accounts instead of to a single contra account.				

DISCLOSURE OF CHANGES IN SHAREHOLDERS' EQUITY

The annual reports to shareholders must explain the changes in all shareholders' equity accounts.[15] The reconciliation of retained earnings may appear in the balance sheet, in a statement of earnings and retained earnings, or in a separate statement. The reconciliation of Other Comprehensive Income may also appear in a separate statement.

Exhibit 12.7 shows the consolidated statement of shareholders' equity for Michigan Company (information adapted from the annual report of Ford Motor Company). The two-year comparative statement shows separate columns for common stock at par, additional paid-in capital, retained earnings, accumulated other comprehensive income, treasury shares, and total shareholders' equity. The statement shows opening balances, net income, unrealized gain (loss) on securities available for sale, cash dividends, stock issued under employee option plans, common stock issued on conversion of convertible bonds, and common stock retired.

The FASB has suggested that firms use a reporting format reconciling beginning balance of other comprehensive income, its components for a year, and the ending balance in a format such as the one below, which uses data for the General Electric Company (GE) for a recent year (dollar amounts in millions):

Accumulated Other Comprehensive Income, Beginning of Year	$1,340
Components of Other Comprehensive Income for Year	324
Accumulated Other Comprehensive Income, End of Year	$1,664

Some firms find this reporting distasteful because, we suspect, they do not want to point to any total other than net income as deserving the title *income*. Hence, they find various ways to re-label both the balance sheet beginning and ending balances as well as the components of other comprehensive income for the year. GE, for example, shows just under the income statement a separate Statement of Changes in Share Owners' Equity, which has the following components (dollar amounts in millions). The information in brackets *does not appear* in the GE report; we add this information here for clarity.:

Changes in Share Owners' Equity

Balance [of Share Owners' Equity], January 1		$34,438
Dividends and other transactions [treasury share acquisitions and dispositions] with share owners		(5,178)
Changes other than transactions with share owners		
Increases attributable to net earnings [that is, net income less dividends]	$9,296	
Unrealized gains (losses) on investment securities	264	
Currency translation adjustments [another component of other comprehensive income]	60	
Total changes other than transactions with share owners		9,620
Balance at December 31		$38,880

What is other comprehensive income for the year? It is $324 (= $264 + $60), but unsophisticated readers of financial statements will likely not know this because of the methods of disclosure. GE shows the beginning and ending balances of Other Comprehensive Income, which it calls *Nonowner changes other than earnings,* in the note reconciling all of the changes in the components of shareholders' equity.

JOURNAL ENTRIES FOR CHANGES IN SHAREHOLDERS' EQUITY

Exhibit 12.8 reconstructs the journal entries of Michigan Company for Year 1 and Year 2. The amounts in the entries in Exhibit 12.8 represent millions of dollars, and the numbers of the journal entries correspond to the lines in Exhibit 12.7.

---

[15]Accounting Principles Board, *Opinion No. 12,* "Omnibus Opinion—1967," 1967.

AN INTERNATIONAL PERSPECTIVE

The accounting for shareholders' equity in most developed countries closely parallels that in the United States.

- Contributed capital accounts increase when firms issue shares of common or preferred stock.
- Revenues, gains, expenses, and losses affect the measurement of periodic earnings, and then the closing process transfers them to the Retained Earnings account.
- Dividends reduce retained earnings and either reduce corporate assets (cash dividends or dividends in kind) or increase other shareholders' equity accounts (stock dividends).

Accounting in many other countries, unlike in the United States, uses **shareholders' equity reserve accounts.** Reserve accounts generally have credit balances and appear in the shareholders' equity section of the balance sheet. Foreign firms often use a reserve account to disclose to financial statement readers that the firm will not declare dividends against a portion of retained earnings. Firms in the United States can achieve the same result by declaring a stock dividend.

TERMINOLOGY NOTE

GAAP in the United States discourage the use of the word *reserve.* Here's why. Think about the word *reserve* as used in ordinary English. Do you think it refers to something in accounting with a debit balance or a credit balance? When we ask this question, almost all students respond, "Debit," thinking of things like oil reserves and cash set aside for a rainy day. In accounting, the word *reserve* always means an account with a credit balance: Reserve for Depreciation means Accumulated Depreciation, not cash set aside to acquire new equipment; Reserve for Bad Debts means the Allowance for Uncollectible Accounts, not cash set aside in case customers do not pay their bills; Reserve for Warranties means the Estimated Liability for Warranties, not cash set aside to pay for warranty repairs. Since the word *reserve* causes so much confusion, most accountants in the United States do not use it. (We still encounter accountants, even young ones, who use the term, but we do not understand why anyone interested in clarity would use this word in accounting.)

Example 6 Japanese accounting standards require that firms declaring dividends transfer from Retained Earnings to a Legal Capital Reserve account a specified percentage of the dividend each period. Japanese firms make this entry in addition to the usual entry for dividends. To illustrate, Oji Paper Company declared and paid a ¥10 million dividend during a recent year and made the following entry (amounts in millions):

Retained Earnings	10	
Cash		10
To record declaration and payment of cash dividend.		

The firm also made the following entry:

Retained Earnings	3	
Legal Capital Reserve		3
To reclassify 30 percent of dividends out of retained earnings and into a permanent capital account.		

The second entry effectively marks a portion of retained earnings as unavailable to support dividend declarations. Including the ¥3 million in a capital account indicates to the reader of the financial statements that the firm cannot declare dividends up to the full amount of retained earnings.

Example 7 French accounting standards permit firms to reclassify a portion of retained earnings to a reserve account to indicate that the firm cannot declare dividends up to the full amount of retained earnings, at least temporarily. An annual report of Société National Elf Acquitaine revealed the following:

Reserves:	
Legal	Fr 100
Long-term Capital Gains	3,885
Operating Costs	7,300
Unappropriated	5,227

This disclosure indicates that the firm may declare dividends against Fr5,227 of retained earnings but not against retained earnings Fr11,285 (= Fr100 + Fr3,885 + Fr7,300), which represent net assets permanently or temporarily not available for payment as dividends. For example, suppose a customer is suing the firm for Fr20,000. Although the firm feels that it has an adequate defense, it might lose. The firm could make the following entry when the customer files the suit:

Retained Earnings (unappropriated)	20,000	
Operating Risk Reserve		20,000
To reclassify a portion of retained earnings into an operating risk reserve.		

Assume now that the firm loses the suit and incurs an uninsured liability of Fr12,000. The entry, assuming immediate cash payment, is as follows:

Loss from Damage Suit (income statement account)	12,000	
Cash		12,000

Because the firm has now settled the lawsuit, it reclassifies the operating risk reserve back to retained earnings with the following entry:

Operating Risk Reserve	20,000	
Retained Earnings		20,000

A second use of reserve accounts relates to revaluations of assets. Accounting regulations in Great Britain and France permit firms to revalue periodically their plant and other assets.

Example 8   Refer to Exhibit 2.8, which shows the balance sheet of Ranks Hovis McDougall PLC, a British company. During the current year, this firm revalued its fixed assets and recognized its brand names as assets, with debits. It credited a revaluation reserve account. The firm will charge (debit) future depreciation and amortization of these revalued amounts to the revaluation reserve account, not to the earnings statement. Neither the initial revaluation nor the subsequent depreciation or amortization enters the earnings statement.

The reader of financial statements issued by firms outside of the United States will frequently encounter, in the shareholders' equity section of the balance sheet, various accounts containing the word *reserve*. The reader must be wary of these accounts for the following reasons:

1. Firms rarely set aside assets in the amount of the reserve for the purpose indicated by the title of the reserve (for example, "reserve for plant replacement," "reserve for business risks"). Because of the balance sheet equality of assets and equities, one can conclude only that there are assets in some form (for example, equipment or goodwill) equal to the amount of the reserve. But the assets would be there even if the amounts remained in the Retained Earnings account, without the firm's re-labeling them as reserves.
2. Firms increase and decrease reserves for a variety of purposes (such as reclassifying retained earnings and revaluing assets). The reader should understand the nature of each reserve and the events that cause its amounts to change.

SUMMARY

The shareholders' equity section of the balance sheet reports the preferred and common shareholders' equity, or interests, in the net assets of a firm. The equity of the preferred shareholders usually approximates the par value of the preferred shares. The remaining shareholders' equity accounts relate to the equity of the common shareholders. The equity of the common shareholders equals the sum of the amounts appearing in the Common Stock, Additional Paid-in Capital, Retained Earnings, Accumulated Other Comprehensive Income, Treasury Stock, and other common-share equity accounts. The user of the financial statements gains insight into capital contributions, earnings, other comprehensive income, dividends, and treasury stock transactions only by studying changes in the individual accounts.

APPENDIX 12.1: EFFECTS ON THE STATEMENT OF CASH FLOWS OF TRANSACTIONS INVOLVING SHAREHOLDERS' EQUITY

With the exception of earnings, most transactions affecting shareholders' equity accounts appear in the statement of cash flows as financing transactions.

CAPITAL CONTRIBUTIONS

Firms that issue preferred or common stock for cash report the transaction as a financing activity. If the firm receives an asset other than cash (for example, building, equipment, or patent), it does not report the transaction as investing and financing activities that involve cash. The firm discloses the transaction in a supplementary schedule or note to the financial statements.

STOCK OPTIONS, RIGHTS, AND WARRANTS

The firm reports the cash received from the issuance of stock under options, rights, or warrants arrangements as a financing activity. If the firm recognized compensation expense at the time it issued stock options to employees, it must add back the expense to earnings when computing cash flow from operations.

CONVERSIONS OF BONDS OR PREFERRED STOCK

The firm does not report the conversion of convertible bonds or convertible preferred stock into common stock as a financing activity that involves cash. The firm discloses this transaction in a supplementary schedule or note to the financial statements.

TREASURY STOCK TRANSACTIONS

Reacquisitions and reissuances of a firm's capital stock (that is, treasury stock) appear as financing activities in the statement of cash flows.

DIVIDENDS

Dividends that a firm declares and pays in cash during a period appear as financing activities. If a portion of the dividend paid during the current period relates to dividends declared during the previous period or if the firm does not pay all dividends declared during the current period by the end of the period, then the amount in the Dividends Payable account will change. The change in the Dividends Payable account, a current liability, appears in the Financing section of the statement of cash flows as an adjustment to the amount of dividends declared. The adjustment converts dividends declared during the period to the amount of dividends paid in cash. Until this point of the book, all changes in current assets and liabilities, other than cash, marketable securities, and short-term borrowings, appeared as adjustments to net earnings in deriving cash provided by operations when the firm uses the indirect method in the statement of cash flows. Because all dividend activities are financing, the change in the Dividends Payable account must appear in the Financing section.

Firms sometimes issue property dividends (that is, dividends payable in inventory, equipment, or some other asset). Such dividends do not use cash and therefore appear in a supplementary schedule or note to the financial statements. If the firm recognized a gain or loss at the time that it distributed the property dividend, it subtracts the gain or adds back the loss to earnings when computing cash flow from operations under the indirect method.

Stock dividends, likewise, do not involve cash and therefore do not appear in the statement of cash flows. Nor do such dividends appear in a supplementary schedule or note because they do not usually change the equity ownership of the firm.

SOLUTIONS TO SELF-STUDY PROBLEMS

SUGGESTED SOLUTION TO PROBLEM 12.1 FOR SELF-STUDY

(Healy Corporation; journal entries for capital contributions.)

a. *January 2, Year 1*

Cash	1,400,000	
Common Stock—$10 Par		1,000,000
Additional Paid-in Capital		400,000

Issue of 100,000 shares of $10-par value common stock for $14 per share.

b. *January 2, Year 1*

Patent	140,000	
Common Stock—$10 Par		100,000
Additional Paid-in Capital		40,000

Issue of 10,000 shares of $10-par value common stock in exchange for a patent. The value of the patent is not easily determinable, so we use the issue price of $14 per share from part **a.**

c. *March 1, Year 1*

Cash	200,000	
Preferred Stock		200,000

Issue of 2,000 shares of convertible preferred stock at par value.

d. *June 1, Year 1*

Cash	50,000	
Common Stock Warrants		50,000

Issue of 10,000 common stock warrants for $5 per warrant.

e. *September 15, Year 1*

Preferred Stock	60,000	
Common Stock—$10 Par		24,000
Additional Paid-in Capital		36,000

To record the conversion of 600 preferred shares into 2,400 common shares at book value.

f. *November 20, Year 1*

Cash	96,000	
Common Stock Warrants	20,000	
Common Stock—Par Value		40,000
Additional Paid-in Capital		76,000

Issue of 4,000 shares of common stock in exchange for 4,000 stock warrants and $96,000 cash.

g. No entry.

SUGGESTED SOLUTION TO PROBLEM 12.2 FOR SELF-STUDY

(Crissie Corporation; journal entries for treasury stock transactions.)

a. *January 15*

Treasury Shares—Common	90,000	
Cash		90,000

Paid $90,000 to reacquire 2,000 common shares at $45 per share.

b. *April 26*

Cash	57,600	
Treasury Shares—Common		54,000
Additional Paid-in Capital		3,600

Reissue of 1,200 shares of treasury stock costing $45 per share; treasury shares reissued to employees under stock option plan with an exercise price of $48 per share.

c. *August 15*

Treasury Shares—Common	156,000	
Cash		156,000

Paid $156,000 to reacquire 3,000 common shares at $52 per share.

d. *November 24*

Preferred Stock	80,000	
Treasury Stock		77,600
Additional Paid-in Capital		2,400

Reissue of 1,600 shares of treasury stock with a cost of $77,600 [= (800 × $45) + (800 × $52)] in exchange for convertible preferred stock with a book value of $80,000.

e. *December 20*

Cash	70,500	
Additional Paid-in Capital	7,500	
Treasury Stock		78,000

Reissue of 1,500 shares of treasury stock costing $52 per share; treasury shares sold on the open market for $47 per share.

SUGGESTED SOLUTION TO PROBLEM 12.3 FOR SELF-STUDY

(Baker Corporation; journal entries for earnings and retained earnings transactions.)

a. *January 15*

Retained Earnings	35,000	
Accumulated Depreciation		35,000

To correct error in prior year's depreciation.

b. *March 20*

Loss from Earthquake	70,000	
Building		70,000

To record loss from earthquake.

c. *March 31*

Retained Earnings	12,500	
Dividends Payable		12,500

To record declaration of cash dividend of $.50 per share on 25,000 shares.

d. *April 15*

Dividends Payable	12,500	
Cash		12,500

To pay cash dividend declared on March 31.

e. *June 30*

Retained Earnings	37,500	
Common Stock		25,000
Additional Paid-in Capital		12,500

To record issuance of 10 percent stock dividend: $.10 \times 25,000 = 2,500$ shares; $2,500 \times \$15 = \$37,500$.

f. *December 31*

Depreciation Expense	14,000	
Accumulated Depreciation		14,000

Original depreciation: $\$400,000/40 = \$10,000$ per year. Book value on January 1, Year 5, is $350,000 [= \$400,000 - (\$10,000 \times 5)]$. Depreciation for Year 5 is $14,000 (= \$350,000/25)$.

g.

Common Stock, $10 par value	275,000	
Common Stock, $5 par value		275,000

To record 2-for-1 stock split. Alternatively, the firm might make no formal entry in the accounting records.

KEY TERMS AND CONCEPTS

Other comprehensive income
Corporation
Corporate charter
Corporate bylaws
Capital stock contract
Capital stock
Preferred stock
Cumulative dividend rights
Callable preferred shares
Convertible preferred shares
Redeemable preferred shares
Common stock
Par or stated value
Additional Paid-in Capital account
Book value per share

Stock options
Stock rights
Stock warrants
Convertible bonds
Treasury shares, treasury stock
Correction of error
Changes in estimates
Prior-period adjustment
Cash dividend
Property dividend
Stock dividend
Stock split
Earnings per common share
Shareholders' equity reserve accounts

QUESTIONS, EXERCISES, PROBLEMS, AND CASES

QUESTIONS

1. Review the meaning of the terms listed in Key Terms and Concepts.

2. Why should GAAP exclude from earnings Other Comprehensive Income items such as holding gains and losses on securities available for sale?

3. The chapter states that the amount in various common shareholders' equity accounts represents the common shareholders' equity in the net assets of a firm. If a bankrupt firm sold its assets and used the proceeds to pay creditors, preferred shareholders, and common shareholders, would these common shareholders likely receive an amount equal to the amount in the common shareholders' equity accounts on the balance sheet? Explain.

4. A construction corporation is attempting to borrow money on a note secured by some of its property. A bank agrees to accept the note, provided the president personally guarantees its payment. What is the point of this requirement? Why would the bank not likely require such a guarantee if the construction company were a partnership?

5. A security analyst states: "The classification of accounts in the right-hand side of the balance sheets as liabilities or shareholders' equity no longer makes sense." What did the security analyst have in mind when making this statement? Suggest an alternative classification scheme.

6. Under what circumstances would you expect a firm to issue par-value common stock at a price in excess of par?

7. "Par value of preferred stock is usually a significant figure, but par value of common stock possesses little significance." Explain.

8. A firm contemplates issuing 10,000 shares of $100-par value preferred stock. The preferred stock promises a $4-per-share annual dividend. The firm considers making this preferred stock callable, convertible, or subject to mandatory redemption. Will the issue price be the same in each of these three cases? Explain.

9. "The option elements included in stock options and convertible bonds have economic value that accountants should recognize in the accounts." Do you agree? Why or why not?

10. Compare and contrast a stock option, a stock right, and a stock warrant. How does the accounting for these three differ?

11. A firm that sells inventory for more than its acquisition cost realizes an economic gain that accountants include in earnings, but a firm that sells treasury stock for more than its acquisition cost realizes an economic gain that accountants exclude from earnings. What is the rationale for the difference in treatment of these economic gains?

12. Accounting reports the acquisition cost of treasury stock as a subtraction from total shareholders' equity. This accounting has the same effect on total shareholders' equity as retiring the stock with debits to common stock, additional paid-in capital, and retained earnings for the acquisition cost. Suggest reasons why firms typically do not account for treasury stock as retired stock.

13. Alexander Corporation retained almost all of its earnings, only rarely paying a cash dividend. When some of the shareholders objected, the president replied: "Why do you want cash dividends? You would just have to go to the trouble of reinvesting them. Where can you possibly find a better investment than our own company?" Comment.

14. At the annual shareholders' meeting, the president of the Lilly Corporation made the following statement: "The earnings for the year, after taxes, was $1,096,000. The

directors have decided that the corporation can afford to distribute only $500,000 as a cash dividend." Are the two sentences of this statement compatible?

15. Why is the amount in the Retained Earnings account for a profitable, growing company that has been in business for several decades unlikely to be of much value for predicting future dividend declarations?

16. Compare the position of a shareholder who receives a cash dividend with that of one who receives a stock dividend.

17. Distinguish between the nature of, and accounting for, a correction of an error in previously issued financial statements and the adjustment for a change in an accounting estimate made in preparing previously issued financial statements.

18. What are prior-period adjustments? Why do some accountants think that GAAP should only rarely allow them?

19. Distinguish among the following three terms: *comprehensive income, other comprehensive income,* and *accumulated other comprehensive income.* What would the term *accumulated comprehensive income,* not mentioned in the text, mean?

EXERCISES

20. **Journal entries to record the issuance of capital stock.** Prepare journal entries to record the issuance of capital stock in each of the independent cases below. You may omit explanations for the journal entries. A firm does the following:
    a. Issues 25,000 shares of $10-par value common stock for $25 per share.
    b. Issues 10,000 shares of $100-par value convertible, callable preferred stock at par.
    c. Issues 12,000 shares of common stock ($1 stated value) in the acquisition of land. The shares trade on the market for $15 per share. The assessed value of the land is $140,000. The owners of the land listed it for sale at $190,000.
    d. Grants 5,000 stock options to employees to purchase shares of the firm's common stock ($10 par value) for $60 per share, the market price on the date of the grant.
    e. Refer to part **d.** Holders of 3,000 stock options exercise their options.
    f. Issues 10,000 shares of par-value common stock ($10 par value) in exchange for convertible bonds with a book value of $300,000. The shares sell on the market for $35 per share. Use the book value method to record the conversion.
    g. Refer to part **f.** Record the conversion using the market value method.

21. **Journal entries for the issuance of capital stock.** Prepare journal entries to record the issuance of capital stock in each of the independent cases below. You may omit explanations for the journal entries. A firm does the following:
    a. Issues 40,000 shares of $15-par value common stock in the acquisition of inventory with a market value of $250,000, land valued at $160,000, a building valued at $1,200,000, and equipment valued at $390,000.
    b. Issues 10,000 shares of $50-par value preferred stock at par. The preferred stock is subject to mandatory redemption in five years.
    c. Issues 20,000 shares of $1-par value common stock upon the exercise of stock warrants. The firm had issued the stock warrants several years previously for $2 per share and properly recorded the sale of the warrants in the accounts. The exercise price is $18 plus one warrant for each share of common stock.
    d. Issues 50,000 shares of $10-par value common stock upon the conversion of 20,000 shares of $100-par value convertible preferred stock originally issued for par. Record the conversion using book values.

22. **Journal entries for employee stock options.** Vertovec Corporation grants 20,000 stock options to its managerial employees on December 31, Year 3, to purchase 20,000 shares of its common stock ($10 par value) for $25 per share. A financial consulting

firm estimates that the market value of these options on the grant date is $100,000. On October 15, Year 5, holders of 15,000 options exercise their option at a time when the market price of the stock is $30 per share. On November 30, Year 6, holders of the remaining options exercise them at a time when the market price of the stock is $34 per share.

   a. Present journal entries to record these transactions, under GAAP, on December 31, Year 3; October 15, Year 5; and November 30, Year 6.

   b. Repeat part **a** following the currently allowable, but infrequently used, procedure of recording compensation on the grant date.

23. **Journal entries for stock warrants.** Haskins Corporation sells 40,000 common stock warrants for $3 each on February 26, Year 6. Each warrant permits its holder to purchase a share of the firm's $5-par value common stock for $40 per share at any time during the next two years. The market price of the common shares was $30 per share on February 21, Year 6. Holders of 30,000 warrants exercised their warrants on June 6, Year 7, at a time when the market price of the stock was $48 per share. Haskins Corporation experienced a major uninsured loss from a fire late in Year 7, and its market price fell immediately to $32 per share. The market price remained around $32 until the stock warrants expired on February 26, Year 8. Present journal entries relating to these stock warrants on February 26, Year 6; June 6, Year 7; and February 26, Year 8.

24. **Journal entries for convertible bonds.** Higgins Corporation issues $1 million of 20-year, $1,000 face value, 10 percent semiannual coupon bonds at par on January 2, Year 1. Each $1,000 bond is convertible into 40 shares of $1-par value common stock. Assume that Higgins Corporation's credit rating is such that it could issue 15 percent semiannual, nonconvertible bonds at par. On January 2, Year 5, holders convert their bonds into common stock. The common stock has a market price of $45 per share on January 2, Year 5.

   a. Present the journal entries made under GAAP on January 2, Year 1 and Year 5, to record the issue and conversion of these bonds. Use the book value method to record the conversion.

   b. Repeat part **a** but record the issuance of the bonds in a manner that allocates a portion of the issue price on January 2, Year 1, to the conversion option. (GAAP do not allow this treatment.)

25. **Journal entries for treasury stock transactions.** Prepare journal entries to record the following treasury stock transactions of Huerta Corporation.

   a. Purchases 8,000 shares of $10-par value common stock for $30 per share.

   b. Issues 3,000 treasury shares to employees under stock-option plans. The exercise price is $32 per share. Assume that the market price of the common stock on the exercise date will be $35 per share.

   c. Purchases 5,000 shares of common stock for $38 per share.

   d. Issues 6,000 shares of common stock in the acquisition of land valued at $200,000. Huerta Corporation uses a FIFO assumption for reissues of treasury stock.

   e. Sells the remaining shares of treasury stock for $36 per share.

26. **Journal entries for treasury stock transactions.** Prepare journal entries to record the following treasury stock transactions of Melissa Corporation.

   a. Purchases 10,000 shares of $5-par value common stock for $12 per share.

   b. Issues 6,000 treasury shares upon the conversion of bonds with a book value of $72,000. Melissa Corporation records bond conversions using the book value method.

   c. Purchases 20,000 shares of common stock for $15 per share.

   d. Issues 24,000 treasury shares and 6,000 newly issued shares of common stock in the acquisition of land with a market value of $540,000.

27. Journal entries to correct errors and adjust for changes in estimates. Prepare journal entries to record each of the following items for Uncertainty Corporation for Year 13. Ignore income tax effects.

   a. Discovers on January 15, Year 13, that it neglected to amortize a patent during Year 12 in the amount of $12,000.

   b. Discovers on January 20, Year 13, that it recorded the sale of a machine on December 30, Year 12, for $16,000 with the following journal entry:

Cash	6,000	
Loss on Sale of Machine	4,000	
Machine (acquisition cost)		10,000

   The machine had accumulated depreciation of $7,000 on the date of the sale.

   c. Changes the depreciable life of a building as of December 31, Year 13, from a total useful life of 30 years to a total of 42 years. The building has an acquisition cost of $2,400,000 and is 11 years old as of December 31, Year 13. The firm has not recorded depreciation for Year 13. It uses the straight-line method and zero estimated salvage value.

   d. The firm has used 2 percent of sales as its estimate of uncollectible accounts for several years. Its actual losses have averaged only 1.50 percent of sales. As a consequence, the Allowance for Estimated Uncollectibles account has a credit balance of $25,000 at the end of Year 13 before making the provision for bad debt expense (see the glossary at *provision*) for Year 13. An aging of customers' accounts suggests that the firm needs $35,000 in the allowance account at the end of Year 3 to cover estimated uncollectibles. Sales for Year 3 are $1,000,000.

28. Journal entries for cash dividends. Journalize the following transactions:

   a. A firm declares a cash dividend of $2 a share on the outstanding preferred stock. There are 6,000 shares authorized, 2,500 shares issued, and 200 shares reacquired and held in the treasury.

   b. The firm declares a cash dividend of $3 a share on the no-par common stock, of which there are 20,000 shares authorized, 12,000 shares issued, and 2,000 shares reacquired and held in the treasury.

   c. The firm pays the dividend on the preferred stock.

   d. The firm pays the dividend on the common stock.

29. Journal entries for dividends. Give journal entries, if required, for the following transactions, which are unrelated unless otherwise specified:

   a. A firm declares the regular quarterly dividend on its 10 percent, $100-par value preferred stock. There are 10,000 shares authorized and 8,000 shares issued, of which the firm has previously reacquired 1,600 shares, which it holds in the treasury.

   b. The firm pays the dividend on the preferred stock in part **a.**

   c. A company declares and issues a stock dividend of $250,000 of no-par common stock to its common shareholders.

   d. The shares of no-par stock of a corporation sell on the market for $300 a share. To bring the market value down to a more popular price and thereby broaden the distribution of its stockholdings, the board of directors votes to issue four extra shares to shareholders for each share they already hold. The corporation issues the shares.

30. **Journal entries for dividends.** Prepare journal entries for the following transactions of Watt Corporation. The firm has 20,000 shares of $15-par value common stock outstanding on January 1, Year 6. The balance in the Additional Paid-in Capital account on this date is $200,000. The firm does the following:
   a. Declares a dividend of $.50 per share on March 31, Year 6.
   b. Pays the dividend in part **a** on April 15, Year 6.
   c. Declares and distributes a 10 percent stock dividend on June 30, Year 6. The market price of the stock is $20 on this date.
   d. Declares a $.50 per share dividend on September 30, Year 6.
   e. Pays the dividend in part **d** on October 15, Year 6.
   f. Declares a 3-for-2 stock split on December 31, Year 6, but does not alter the par value.

31. **Effects on statement of cash flows.** Refer to the simplified statement of cash flows in Exhibit 4.16. Numbers appear on nine of the lines in the statement. Ignore the unnumbered lines in considering the following transactions. Assume that a firm has completed the accounting cycle for the period and prepared all of the financial statements. It then discovers that it has overlooked a transaction. It records the transaction in the accounts and corrects all of the financial statements. For each of the following transactions, indicate which of the numbered lines of the statement of cash flows changes and by how much. Ignore income tax effects.
   a. The firm issues common shares for $200,000.
   b. The firm repurchases for $75,000 common shares originally issued for $50,000 and retires them.
   c. Holders of convertible bonds with a book value of $100,000 and a market value of $240,000 convert them into common shares with a par value of $10,000 and a market value of $240,000.
   d. The firm issues for $15,000 treasury shares that have been previously acquired for $20,000.
   e. The directors declare a stock dividend. The par value of the shares issued is $1,000, and their market value is $300,000.
   f. The directors declare a cash dividend of $70,000, but the firm has not yet paid it.
   g. The firm pays a previously declared cash dividend of $70,000.
   h. Holders of stock rights exercise them. The shares issued have a par value of $1,000 and a market value of $35,000 on the date of exercise. The firm receives the exercise price of $20,000 in cash.

PROBLEMS AND CASES

32. **Transactions to incorporate and run a business.** The following events relate to shareholders' equity transactions of Wilson Supply Company during the first year of its existence. Present journal entries for each of the transactions.
   a. January 2. The firm files articles of incorporation with the State Corporation Commission. The authorized capital stock consists of 5,000 shares of $100-par value preferred stock that offers an 8 percent annual dividend and 50,000 shares of no-par common stock. The original incorporators acquire 300 shares of common stock at $30 per share; the firm collects cash for the shares. It assigns a stated value of $30 per share to the common stock.
   b. January 6. The firm issues 2,000 shares of common stock for cash at $30 per share.
   c. January 8. It issues 4,000 shares of preferred stock at par.
   d. January 9. The firm issues certificates for the shares of preferred stock.

e. January 12. The firm acquires the tangible assets and goodwill of Richardson Supply, a partnership, in exchange for 1,000 shares of preferred stock and 12,000 shares of common stock. It values the tangible assets acquired as follows: inventories, $50,000; land, $80,000; buildings, $210,000; and equipment, $120,000.

f. July 3. The directors declare the semiannual dividend on preferred stock outstanding, payable July 25, to shareholders of record on July 12.

g. July 5. The firm operated profitably for the first six months, and it decides to expand. The company issues 25,000 shares of common stock for cash at $33 per share.

h. July 25. It pays the preferred stock dividend declared on July 3.

i. October 2. The directors declare a dividend of $1 per share on the common stock, payable October 25, to shareholders of record on October 12.

j. October 25. The firm pays the common stock dividend declared on October 2.

33. **Transactions to incorporate and run a business.** The following events relate to shareholders' equity transactions of Hutchins Company. Present journal entries for these transactions.

a. July 5, Year 1. The company files articles of incorporation with the secretary of state. The authorized capital stock consists of 5,000 shares of 4 percent preferred stock with a par value of $100 per share and 50,000 shares of no-par common stock.

b. July 8, Year 1. The company issues 6,000 shares of common stock for cash at $40 per share.

c. July 9, Year 1. The company issues 4,000 shares of common stock for the assets of the partnership of Hutchins and Hutchins. The company values the assets received as follows: accounts receivable, $20,000; inventories, $30,000; land, $40,000; buildings, $50,000; and equipment, $20,000.

d. July 13, Year 1. The company issues 800 shares of preferred stock at par for cash.

e. December 31, Year 1. The balance in the Income Summary account, after closing all expense and revenue accounts, is a $75,000 credit. Close the account to the Retained Earnings account.

f. January 4, Year 2. The directors declare the regular semiannual dividend on the preferred stock and a dividend of $3 per share on the common stock. The dividends are payable on February 1.

g. February 1, Year 2. The company pays the dividends declared on January 4.

h. July 2, Year 2. The directors declare the regular semiannual dividend on the preferred stock. The dividend is payable on August 1.

i. August 1, Year 2. The company pays the dividend declared on July 2.

34. **Reconstructing transactions involving shareholders' equity.** Conrad Company began business on January 1. Its balance sheet on December 31 contained the shareholders' equity section in Exhibit 12.9.

During the year, Conrad Company engaged in the following transactions:

(1) Issued shares for $15 each.

(2) Acquired, in a single transaction, a block of 300 shares for the treasury.

(3) Reissued some of the treasury shares.

(4) Sold for $5,000 securities available for sale with original cost of $3,000. At the end of the year, securities available for sale had original cost of $6,000 and market value of $7,000.

Assuming that these were all of the common stock transactions during the year, answer the following questions:

a. How many shares did Conrad Company issue for $15?

b. What was the price at which it acquired the treasury shares?

EXHIBIT 12.9	CONRAD COMPANY Shareholders' Equity as of December 31 (Problem 34)

Common Stock ($10 par value)	$30,000
Additional Paid-in Capital	15,720
Retained Earnings	6,000
Less 180 Shares Held in Treasury	(3,600)
Total Shareholders' Equity	$48,120

    c. How many shares did it reissue from the block of treasury shares?
    d. What was the price at which it reissued the treasury shares?
    e. What journal entries did it make during the year?
    f. In which statement or statements will Conrad Company report the various gains and losses on its holdings of securities available for sale?

35. **Reconstructing transactions involving shareholders' equity.** Shea Company began business on January 1. Its balance sheet on December 31 contained the shareholders' equity section shown in Exhibit 12.10.

    During the year, Shea Company engaged in the following transactions:
    (1) Issued shares for $30 each.
    (2) Acquired, in a single transaction, a block of 2,000 shares for the treasury.
    (3) Reissued some of the treasury shares.
    (4) Sold for $12,000 securities available for sale for which had originally cost $14,000. At the end of the year, securities available for sale, still on hand, which had originally cost $25,000 had market value of $18,000.

Assuming that these were the only common stock transactions during the year, answer the following questions:
    a. How many shares did Shea Company issue for $30 each?
    b. What was the price at which it acquired the treasury shares?
    c. How many shares did it reissue from the block of treasury shares?
    d. What was the price at which it reissued the treasury shares?
    e. What journal entries did it make during the year?
    f. In which statement or statements will Shea Company report the various gains and losses on its holdings of securities available for sale?

EXHIBIT 12.10	SHEA COMPANY Shareholders' Equity as of December 31 (Problem 35)

Common Stock ($5 par value)	$100,000
Additional Paid-in Capital	509,600
Retained Earnings	50,000
Less 1,200 Shares Held in Treasury	(33,600)
Total Shareholders' Equity	$626,000

36. **Dilutive effects of stock options.** Refer to the schedule in Exhibit 12.6, which shows employee stock option data for General Electric Company (GE). At December 31, Year 3, employees held 2.7 million options giving them the right to purchase shares at an average of $54 per share. Total shareholders' equity at December 31, Year 3, was about $2.5 billion.

    a. If GE were to issue 2.7 million shares in a public offering at the market price per share on December 31, Year 3, what would be the proceeds of the issue?

    b. If GE were to issue 2.7 million shares to employees who exercised all outstanding stock options, what would be the proceeds of the issue?

    c. Are GE's shareholders better off under **a** or under **b?**

    d. The text accompanying the stock option data in the GE annual report reads, in part, as follows:

    > Option price under these plans is the full market value of General Electric common stock on date of grant. Therefore, participants in the plans do not benefit unless the stock's market price rises, thus benefiting all share owners.

    GE seems to be saying that these options do not harm shareholders, whereas your answers to parts **a** and **b** show that shareholders are worse off when holders exercise options than when the firm issues shares to the public. Attempt to reconcile GE's statement with your own analysis in parts **a** and **b.**

37. **Accounting for detachable warrants.** After several years of rapid expansion, Jastern Company approached the State National Bank for a $1 million, five-year loan. The bank was willing to lend the money at an interest rate of 12 percent per year. Jastern Company then approached an individual investor who was willing to provide the same funds for only 8 percent per year payable annually, provided that Jastern Company gave the investor an option to purchase 20,000 shares of Jastern Company $5-par value common stock for $20 per share at any time within five years of the initial date of the loan.

    Jastern weighed both opportunities and decided to borrow from the investor. At the time of the loan, the common shares had a market price of $15 per share. Five years after the initial date of the loan, the investor exercised the option and purchased 20,000 shares for $20 each. At that time, the market price of the common shares was $45 each.

    a. Did the use of the detachable warrants (the technical name for the option granted to the investor) reduce Jastern Company's cost of borrowing?

    b. How should Jastern Company record the loan and the annual interest payments of $80,000 in its books to reflect the economic reality of the transaction?

    c. How might Jastern Company record the exercise of the warrants (and the purchase of the 20,000 shares)?

    d. Did the exercise of the option dilute the shareholders' equity of the other shareholders on the date the option was exercised?

    e. What disclosures during the life of the loan do you think are appropriate? Why?

38. **Comprehensive review of accounting for shareholders' equity.** The shareholders' equity section of the balance sheet of Alex Corporation at December 31 appears on page 719.

    a. Calculate the total book value and the book value per common share as of December 31.

    b. For each of the following transactions or events, give the appropriate journal entry and compute the total book value and the book value per common share of

EXHIBIT 12.11

NESLIN COMPANY
Statement of Changes in Shareholders' Equity Accounts for Year 2
(Problem 39)

	Market Value per Share[a]	Number of Shares	Par Value	Additional Paid-in Capital	Retained Earnings	Accumulated Other Comprehensive Income	Treasury Stock	Total Shareholders' Equity
Balances, Dec. 31, Year 1	$50	100,000	$1,000,000	$5,400,000	$ 9,600,000	$1,200,000		$17,200,000
Events Causing Changes								
(1)	52	20,000	200,000	840,000	—			1,040,000
(2)	55	4,000	—	—	—		$(220,000)	(220,000)
(3)	48	(3,000)	—	(21,000)	—		165,000	144,000
(4)	60	(1,000)	—	5,000	—		55,000	60,000
(5)	62	—	—	—	2,400,000		—	2,400,000
(6)	63	—	—	—	—	(150,000)	—	(150,000)
(7)	63	—	—	—	(1,200,000)	—	—	(1,200,000)
Balances, Dec. 31, Year 2		120,000	$1,200,000	$6,224,000	$10,800,000	$1,050,000	$ —	$19,274,000

[a]Before event.

Alex Corporation after the transaction. The transactions and events are independent of one another, except where noted.

Shareholders' Equity

Common Stock—$10 Par Value (250,000 Shares Authorized and 50,000 Shares Outstanding)	$ 500,000
Additional Paid-in Capital	250,000
Retained Earnings	1,500,000
Total Shareholders' Equity	$2,250,000

(1) Declares a 10 percent stock dividend when the market price of Alex Corporation's common stock is $30 per share.

(2) Declares a 2-for-1 stock split and reduces the par value of the common stock from $10 to $5 per share. The firm issues the new shares immediately.

(3) Purchases 5,000 shares of Alex Corporation's common stock on the open market for $25 per share and holds the shares as treasury stock.

(4) Purchases 5,000 shares of Alex Corporation's common stock on the open market for $15 per share and holds the shares as treasury stock.

(5) Sells, for $35 per share, the shares acquired in (3).

(6) Sells, for $20 per share, the shares acquired in (3).

(7) Sells, for $15 per share, the shares acquired in (3).

(8) Officers exercise options to acquire 5,000 shares of Alex Corporation stock for $15 per share.

(9) Same as (8), except that the exercise price is $50 per share.

(10) Holders of convertible bonds with a book value of $150,000 and a market value of $170,000 exchange them for 10,000 shares of common stock with a market value of $17 per share. The firm recognizes no gain or loss on the conversion of bonds.

(11) Same as (10), except that the firm recognizes gain or loss on the conversion of bonds into stock. Ignore income tax effects.

c. Using the results from part **b,** summarize the transactions and events that result in a reduction in (1) total book value and (2) book value per share.

39. **Reconstructing events affecting shareholders' equity.** Exhibit 12.11 reproduces the statement of changes in shareholders' equity accounts for Neslin Company for Year 2.

a. Identify the most likely events or transactions for each of the events numbered (1) to (6) in the exhibit. The events are not independent of one another.

b. Prepare journal entries for each of these events or transactions.

40. **Journal entries for changes in shareholders' equity.** Exhibit 12.12 presents a statement of changes in shareholders' equity for Wal-Mart Stores for Year 11. Prepare journal entries for each of these transactions or events. The corporate acquisition involved an investment in the common stock of another entity.

41. **Journal entries for changes in shareholders' equity.** Exhibit 12.13 presents a statement of changes in shareholders' equity for Wellington Company for Year 7. Prepare journal entries for each of these transactions or events.

42. **Preparing a statement of cash flows.** Exhibit 12.14 presents comparative balance sheets, an earnings statement, and supplementary information for Baiman Corporation for Year 2.

a. Prepare a T-account worksheet for a statement of cash flows.

b. Prepare a statement of cash flows for Baiman Corporation for Year 2.

EXHIBIT 12.12

WAL-MART STORES
Statement of Changes in Shareholders' Equity Accounts for Year 11
(Problem 40) (amounts in thousands)

	Number of Shares	Common Stock	Additional Paid-in Capital	Retained Earnings	Accumulated Other Comprehensive Income	Treasury Stock	Total
Balance, January 31, Year 10	566,135	$ 56,613	$180,465	$3,728,482	$763,488		$4,729,048
(1) Net Income				1,291,024			1,291,024
(2) Cash Dividends				(158,889)			(158,889)
(3) Exercise of Stock Options	662	66	3,754				3,820
(4) Two-for-One Stock Split	568,797	56,680	(56,680)				—
(5) Shares Issued in Corporate Acquisition	10,366	1,037	273,659				274,696
(6) Purchase of Shares						$(25,826)	(25,826)
(7) Mark Securities to Market					(57,086)		(57,086)
Balance, January 31, Year 11	1,145,960	$114,396	$401,198	$4,860,617	$706,402	$(25,826)	$6,056,787

EXHIBIT 12.13	WELLINGTON COMPANY Statement of Changes in Shareholders' Equity Accounts for Year 7 (Problem 41)

	Common Stock	Additional Paid-in Capital	Retained Earnings	Accumulated Other Comprehensive Income	Treasury Stock	Total
Balance, January 1, Year 7	$49,700	$287,600	$437,400	$(76,330)		$698,370
(1) Net Income			210,500			210,500
(2) Cash Dividends			(120,000)			(120,000)
(3) Conversion of Bonds	6,270	63,730				70,000
(4) Issue of Stock under Stock Options	73	877				950
(5) Stock Dividend	5,604	57,206	(62,810)			
(6) Purchase of Stock					$(48,600)	(48,600)
(7) Resale of Treasury Stock		—			42,700	42,700
(8) Increase Recorded Valuation of Securities Available for Sale		—		44,400	—	44,400
Balance, December 31, Year 7	$61,647	$409,413	$465,090	$(31,930)	$ (5,900)	$898,320

43. **Treasury shares and their effects on performance ratios.** Exhibit 12.15 presents the changes in common shareholders' equity of Merck for Year 3 through Year 5. Merck regularly purchases shares of its common stock and reissues them in connection with stock option plans. It will usually issue a small number of new common shares when it requires fractional shares to complete a stock-option transaction. Earnings per common share were $2.70 in Year 3, $3.20 in Year 4, and $3.83 in Year 5.

   a. Give the journal entries for Year 5 to record (1) the issue of common shares in connection with stock-option plans and (2) the purchase of treasury stock.

   b. Compute the percentage change in net income and in earnings per share between Year 3 and Year 4 and between Year 4 and Year 5. Why do the percentage changes in earnings per share exceed the percentage changes in net income in both Year 4 and Year 5?

   c. Compute the book value per outstanding common share at the end of Year 3, Year 4, and Year 5 and the percentage change in book value per share between Year 3 and Year 4 and between Year 4 and Year 5. Why are the percentage changes in book value per common share less than the percentage changes in both net income and earnings per share?

   d. Compute the rate of return on common shareholders' equity for Year 3, Year 4, and Year 5.

   e. Do the treasury stock purchases appear to be motivated primarily by the need to satisfy commitments under stock option plans? Explain.

44. **Mandatorily redeemable preferred shares.** (Adapted from an idea and materials provided by Katherine Schipper.) Exhibit 12.16 reproduces excerpts from the financial statements of Wendy's International for Years 5 and 6. The statement of cash flows indicates that Wendy's does not generate from operations sufficient cash to support its investing activities. In Year 5, Wendy's issued $284 million of long-term debt.

EXHIBIT 12.14	BAIMAN CORPORATION Comparative Balance Sheets and Income Statement (Problem 42)

	December 31	
	Year 1	Year 2
BALANCE SHEETS		
Cash	$ 45,000	$ 54,000
Accounts Receivable (net)	160,000	175,000
Inventory	115,000	135,000
Property, Plant, and Equipment	265,000	300,000
Accumulated Depreciation	(120,000)	(130,000)
Total Assets	$ 465,000	$ 534,000
Accounts Payable	$ 105,000	$ 106,000
Dividends Payable	10,000	14,000
Bonds Payable (nonconvertible)	90,000	93,000
Convertible Bonds Payable	50,000	—
Deferred Income Tax Liability	20,000	27,000
Total Liabilities	$ 275,000	$ 240,000
Preferred Stock	$ 60,000	$ 60,000
Common Stock (par)	25,000	47,000
Additional Paid-in Capital	65,000	153,000
Retained Earnings	55,000	64,000
Total	$ 205,000	$ 324,000
Cost of Treasury Stock	(15,000)	(30,000)
Total Shareholders' Equity	$ 190,000	$ 294,000
Total Liabilities and Shareholders' Equity	$ 465,000	$ 534,000
INCOME STATEMENT		
Sales		$1,000,000
Cost of Goods Sold		750,000
Selling and Administrative Expenses		136,000
Depreciation Expense		28,000
Loss on Sale of Equipment		4,000
Interest Expense		9,000
Income Tax Expense		25,000
Total Expenses		$ 952,000
Net Income		$ 48,000

Notes:

(1) Baiman Corporation acquired a machine during the period with a market value of $20,000. It issued shares of its common stock with a par value of $4,000 to acquire the machine.

(2) The firm sold equipment originally costing $30,000 during Year 2.

(3) Interest expense on the nonconvertible bonds payable exceeded the coupon cash payments by $3,000 during Year 2.

(4) Holders of the firm's convertible bonds exercised their conversion option on January 1, Year 2. The common shares issued had a par value of $10,000.

(5) Dividends declared during the year were $3,000 on preferred stock and $36,000 on common stock.

(6) The firm reissued for $12,000 treasury stock that originally cost $10,000.

EXHIBIT 12.15	MERCK & CO. Analysis of Changes in Common Shareholders' Equity (amounts in millions) (Problem 43)

	Common Stock[a]			Treasury Stock		
	Shares	Amount	Retained Earnings	Shares	Amount	Total
December 31, Year 2	1,483.168	$4,667.8	$10,942.0	(235.342)	$(4,470.8)	$11,139.0
Net Income			3,376.6			3,376.6
Dividends			(1,578.0)			(1,578.0)
Stock Options Exercised	.295	74.7		14.104	294.3	369.0
Treasury Stock Purchased				(33.377)	(1,570.9)	(1,570.9)
December 31, Year 3	1,483.463	$4,742.5	$12,740.6	(254.615)	$(5,747.4)	$11,735.7
Net Income			3,870.5			3,870.5
Dividends			(1,793.4)			(1,793.4)
Stock Options Exercised	.156	225.0		15.982	426.0	651.0
Treasury Stock Purchased				(38.384)	(2,493.3)	(2,493.3)
December 31, Year 4	1,483.619	$4,967.5	$14,817.7	(277.017)	$(7,814.7)	$11,970.5
Net Income			4,596.5			4,596.5
Dividends			(2,094.8)			(2,094.8)
Stock Options Exercised	.307	286.5		14.183	427.6	714.1
Treasury Stock Purchased				(27.444)	(2,572.8)	(2,572.8)
December 31, Year 5	1,483.926	$5,254.0	$17,319.4	(290.278)	$(9,959.9)	$12,613.5

[a]Includes Additional Paid-in Capital.

It needed still more funds in Year 6 but did not want its balance sheet to show more debt. It undertook the following series of transactions:

(1) Formed a subsidiary, Wendy's Financing I (Financing), wholly owned, to issue preferred equity and to use the proceeds to acquire a single asset, bonds issued by Wendy's

(2) Caused the subsidiary to issue to the public $200 million of preferred shares, which Wendy's guaranteed just as though this were Wendy's debt issue

(3) Issued $202 million of its own debt to Financing in return for the cash that Financing had just raised from the preferred issue

After this series of transactions, the public holds preferred shares with Wendy's guarantee, which means that the market will price those shares much as it would Wendy's debt with similar guarantees. Wendy's describes the results of this series of transactions as follows, taken from its notes:

Note 3. Company-Obligated Mandatorily Redeemable Preferred Securities
In September, Year 6, Wendy's Financing I (the trust) issued $200,000,000 of $2.50 Term Convertible Securities, Series A (the trust preferred securities). Wendy's Financing

EXHIBIT 12.16	WENDY'S INTERNATIONAL Excerpts from Financial Statements for Years 5 and 6 (dollar amounts in millions) (Problem 44)

	Statement of Cash Flows for	
	Year 6	Year 5
Cash Flow from Operations	$ 189.9	$ 164.9
Cash Used in Investing Activities	(262.0)	(187.7)
Proceeds of Issue of Long-term Debt	—	284.4
Proceeds from Issue of Trust Preferred Securities	200.0	—
Net Cash Used in Other Financing Transactions (Dividends and Debt Service Payments)	(115.0)	(175.5)
Increase in Cash and Cash Equivalents	$ 12.9	$ 86.1

	Balance Sheet at End of	
	Year 6	Year 5
Total Assets	$1,781.4	$1,509.2
Current Liabilities	$ 207.8	$ 295.9
Long-term Liabilities	253.9	346.6
Deferred Income Taxes	63.0	47.9
Company-obligated Mandatorily Redeemable Preferred Securities of Subsidiary Wendy's Financing I Holding Solely Wendy's Convertible Securities	200.0	—
Total Shareholders' Equity	1,056.7	818.8
Total Equities	$1,781.4	$1,509.2

I, a statutory business trust, is a wholly-owned consolidated subsidiary of the company with its sole asset being $202 million aggregate principal amount of 5% Convertible Subordinated Debentures due September 15, Year 26, of Wendy's (the trust debenture).

The trust preferred securities are non-voting (except in limited circumstances), pay quarterly distributions at an annual rate of 5%, carry a liquidation value of $50 per share and are convertible into the company's common shares at any time prior to the close of business on September 15, Year 26, at the option of the holder. The trust preferred securities are convertible into common shares. . . . The company [that is, Wendy's] has executed a guarantee with regard to the trust preferred securities. The guarantee, when taken together with the company's obligations under the trust indenture, the indenture pursuant to which the trust indenture was issued, and the applicable trust document, provides a full and an unconditional guarantee of the trust's obligations under the trust preferred securities.

In thinking about and responding to the questions below, you may ignore income taxes. Firms pay careful attention to the income tax treatment of securities such as the ones in this case, but you do not need to worry about such issues here.

a. Explain why Wendy's might prefer following this course of action rather than directly issuing its debt in the market.

b. Why does the debt issued by Wendy's not appear on Wendy's balance sheet?

c. Compute Wendy's debt-equity ratio for the end of Year 5 and Year 6. For Year 6, make two calculations, one assuming the mandatorily preferred shares are debt and the other assuming they are shareholders' equity. Treat Deferred Income Taxes as shareholders' equity in all calculations.

45. **Analysis of nonrecurring transactions; introduction to constructive liabilities.** (Adapted from an idea and materials provided by Katherine Schipper.) Exhibit 12.17 reproduces excerpts from the income statement and notes for Kellogg's (Kellogg Company and Subsidiaries) for Years 2, 3, and 4. Notes include the following:

Note 3. Non-recurring charges
Operating profit for [each of the years] includes non-recurring charges [amounts appear in Exhibit 12.17] comprising . . . streamlining initiatives and . . . asset impairment losses. . . .
Streamlining initiatives
From Year 2 to the present, management has commenced major productivity and operational streamlining initiatives in an effort to optimize the Company's cost structure and move toward a global business model. The incremental costs of these programs . . . [appear] as non-recurring charges.

[Kellogg's then gives details of the components of the streamlining initiatives in the United States, Australia, Latvia, Denmark, and Italy.] Total cash outlays during Year 4 for streamlining initiatives were $85 million, . . . [during Year 3] approximately $120 million, . . . and [during Year 2 approximately] $40 million. . . . The components of the streamlining charges as well as the reserve balances [that is, credit balances in balance sheet liability accounts at the end of each year, also appear in Exhibit 12.17].

TERMINOLOGY NOTE

Kellogg's uses the term *reserve* to mean the estimated liability for future charges relating, in this case, to streamlining. Reversing a reserve (see footnote b in Exhibit 12.17) means debiting the liability and crediting cash if there is a cash disbursement or crediting the asset accounts if Kellogg's is writing down, or writing off, assets already on hand.

In thinking about and responding to the questions below, ignore income taxes.
a. Give the journal entries made during Years 2, 3, and 4 for streamlining charges, cash payments, and asset write-downs and write-offs. Rather than use the word *reserve* in your account titles, however, use the title Liability for Streamlining Costs.
b. If you did part **a** correctly, you already included the effect of the information about Year 3 from footnote **b** in Exhibit 12.17. That is, Kellogg's already includes, in the numbers in the schedule, the effects reported by that footnote. Assume now that Kellogg's first recorded its journal entry for Year 3 using the gross streamlining charge for that year, $144.1 (= $23.0 + $121.1) million, and then recorded the information about the reversal. Give the two implied journal entries to recognize the expense and the reversal. What was the effect on net income for Year 3 of this reversal? That is, without it, would income for Year 3 have been larger or smaller and by how much?
c. Assume that Kellogg's had known in Year 2 what it learned in Year 3 about the actual costs of the streamlining charges in Year 2. That is, assume Kellogg's made streamlining charges in Year 2 just large enough that it did not need to make any reversals in Year 3. What would have been the effect on net income for Year 2 and Year 3 of this reversal? That is, without the need for the reversal, changing the charges for Years 2 and 3, what would be the effect on income for both Year 2 and

EXHIBIT 12.17	KELLOGG'S Excerpts from Financial Statements for Years 2, 3, and 4 (dollar amounts in millions) (Problem 45)

From Income Statement	Year 4	Year 3	Year 2
Operating Profit	$1,009.1	$958.9	$837.5
Net Earnings	$ 546.0	$531.0	$490.3

From Notes on Non-Recurring Charges	Employee Retirement & Severance Benefits[a]	Asset Write-offs	Other Costs	Total
Year 2 Streamlining Charges	$ 183.6	$106.5	$ 57.9	$348.0
Amounts Used during Year 2	(126.1)	(106.5)	(21.4)	(254.0)
Remaining Reserve at December 31, Year 2	$ 57.5	$ —	$ 36.5	$94.0
Year 3 Streamlining Charges	31.4	37.5	52.2	121.1
Amounts Used during Year 3[b]	(65.0)	(37.5)	(58.3)	(160.8)
Remaining Reserve at December 31, Year 3	$ 23.9	$ —	30.4	$ 54.3
Year 4 Streamlining Charges	22.4	78.1	60.6	161.1
Amounts Used during Year 4	(22.7)	(78.1)	(62.7)	(163.5)
Remaining Reserve at December 31, Year 4	$ 23.6	$ —	$ 28.3	$ 51.9

[a]Includes approximately $105 of pension and other post-retirement health costs.

[b]Includes $23 of reversals of prior-year reserves due to lower-than-expected employee severance payments and other favorable factors.

Year 3? Would income be larger or smaller and by how much? What would have been the income for each of the three years?

d. Compare the pattern of income you derive in part **c** with the pattern that Kellogg's actually reported. Would an investor or analyst likely give a higher valuation if using the data from Kellogg's report of the actual income or if using the data that Kellogg would have reported under the assumptions of part **c?** Comment on the qualify of earnings provided by the streamlining charges, the opportunity for income manipulation, and Kellogg's use (or not) of that opportunity.

e. Chapter 9 introduced the FASB's new concept of *constructive liability*—a cost that management has no obligation to incur but expects to incur, one that it can measure with reasonable precision and that may require a future cash outlay. Using your analysis above, explain why some standard-setters and many analysts fear that if the FASB allows firms to record constructive liabilities, the quality of earnings will decline. What is the smallest extra charge for Year 2, reversed in Year 3, that would enable Kellogg's to report income rising from year to year, without any dips, as compared with the base case in part **c?**

46. Earnings-per-share calculations for a complex capital structure. Layton Ball Corporation has a relatively complicated capital structure—that is, it raises funds using a variety of financing devices. In addition to common shares, it has issued stock options, warrants, and convertible bonds. Exhibit 12.18 summarizes some pertinent information about these items. Net income for the year is $9,500, and the income tax rate used in computing income tax expense is 40 percent of pretax income.

a. First, ignore all items of capital except for the common shares. Calculate earnings per common share.

b. In past years, employees have been issued options to purchase shares of stock. Exhibit 12.18 indicates that the price of the common stock throughout the current year has remained steady at $25 but that holders of the stock options could exercise them at any time for $15 per share. That is, the option allows the holder to surrender it, along with $15 cash, and receive one share in return. Thus the number of shares would increase, which would decrease the earnings-per-share figure. The company would, however, have more cash. Assume that the holders of options tender them, along with $15 each, to purchase shares. Assume that the company uses the cash to purchase shares for its own treasury at a price of $25 each. Compute a new earnings-per-share figure. The firm does not count shares in its own treasury in the denominator of the earnings-per-share calculation.

c. Exhibit 12.18 indicates that there were also warrants outstanding in the hands of the public. The warrant allows the holder to turn in that warrant, along with $30 cash, to purchase one share of stock. If holders exercised the warrants, the number of outstanding shares would increase, which would reduce earnings per share. However, the company would have more cash, which it could use to purchase shares for the treasury, reducing the number of shares outstanding. Assume that all holders of warrants exercise them. Assume that the company uses the cash to purchase outstanding shares for the treasury. Compute a new earnings-per-share figure. Ignore the information about options and the calculations in part **b** at this point. Note that rational warrant holders would not exercise the warrants for $30 when they could purchase a share for $25.

d. The firm also has convertible bonds outstanding. Each convertible bond entitles the holder to trade in that bond for 10 shares. If holders convert the bonds, the number of shares would increase, which would tend to reduce earnings per share. On the other hand, the company would not have to pay interest and thus would have no interest expense on the bond because it would no longer be outstanding.

EXHIBIT 12.18	LAYTON BALL CORPORATION Information on Capital Structure for Earnings-per-Share Calculations (Problem 46)

Assume the following data about the capital structure and earnings for Layton Ball Corporation for the year:

Number of Common Shares Outstanding throughout the Year	2,500 shares
Market Price per Common Share throughout the Year	$25
Options Outstanding during the Year:	
Number of Shares Issuable on Exercise of Options	1,000 shares
Exercise Price per Share	$15
Warrants Outstanding during the Year:	
Number of Shares Issuable on Exercise of Warrants	2,000 shares
Exercise Price per Share	$30
Convertible Bonds Outstanding:	
Number (issued 15 years ago)	100 bonds
Proceeds per Bond at Time of Issue (= par value)	$1,000
Shares of Common Issuable on Conversion (per bond)	10 shares
Coupon Rate (per year)	$4\frac{1}{6}$ percent

This would tend to increase income and earnings per share. Assume that all holders of convertible bonds convert their bonds into shares. Compute a new net income figure (do not forget income tax effects on the income produced by the interest saved) and a new earnings-per-share figure. Ignore the information about options and warrants and the calculations in parts **b** and **c** at this point.

e. Now consider all the previous calculations. Which sets of assumptions from parts **b, c,** and **d** lead to the lowest possible earnings per share when they are all made simultaneously? Compute a new earnings per share under the most restrictive set of assumptions about reductions in earnings per share.

f. Accountants publish several earnings-per-share figures for companies with complicated capital structures and complicated events during the year. The *Wall Street Journal,* however, publishes only one figure in its daily columns (where it reports the price-earnings ratio—the price of a share of stock divided by its earnings per share). Which of the figures computed previously for earnings per share do you think the *Wall Street Journal* should report as the earnings-per-share figure? Why?

47. **Case for discussion: value of stock options.** (The text does not give an explicit answer to this question but provides a sufficient basis to enable students to discuss the question.) Below is an excerpt from an article published in the *San Francisco Examiner,* a leading Silicon Valley newspaper. The article appeared at the height of the controversy over the accounting for employee stock options.

> For example, if StartUp Inc. recruits the brilliant software designer Joe Bithead . . . by offering him the option to buy 10,000 shares of StartUp's stock at its current [publicly traded market] price of a penny a share, what's the value of Joe's grant? If StartUp goes belly up, as 80 percent of new high-tech firms do, the grant is worthless. . . . If, on the other hand, after five years of struggle, StartUp manages to create a successful product and outperforms its competitors, the company's stock might sell for $10 a share. . . . For a penny each, Joe can buy the 10,000 shares. . . . He unloads them in the market for a $100,000 profit.

The accounting question is, What cost, if any, does StartUp incur on the day it grants Bithead the option to acquire 10,000 shares five years hence for $.01 per share? Because the word *cost* has so many meanings (see *cost terminology* in the Glossary), you should make this question operational and specific by considering the following.

Imagine that you are the financial executive of StartUp and that Goldman-Sachs offers to relieve you of the obligation to deliver the shares to Bithead. That is, Goldman will take a payment from you today and will deliver the shares to Bithead if he exercises the options but will do nothing otherwise, except keep your cash. How much are you willing to pay Goldman *today* to relieve you of your obligation to Bithead? That is, you pay Goldman now, and Goldman later delivers shares to Bithead if he exercises his options. No one can be sure of the exact answer, given the sketchy data, but which of the following ranges do you think you would be most willing to pay?

a. $0 to $10
b. $10 to $100
c. $100 to $1,000
d. $1,000 to $10,000
e. $10,000 to $100,000
f. Some other answer (indicate answer)

CHAPTER 13

STATEMENT OF CASH FLOWS:
ANOTHER LOOK

LEARNING OBJECTIVES

1. Review the T-account procedure for preparing the statement of cash flows introduced in Chapter 4.

2. Cement an understanding of the effect on the statement of cash flows of various transactions studied in Chapters 6 through 12.

3. Develop more effective skills in analyzing and interpreting the statement of cash flows.

Chapter 4 introduced the statement of cash flows, discussing its rationale and illustrating a T-account approach for preparing this financial statement. Subsequent chapters briefly described the impact that various transactions have on the statement of cash flows. This chapter synthesizes these chapter-by-chapter discussions by providing a comprehensive example of a statement of cash flows.

REVIEW OF T-ACCOUNT PROCEDURE FOR PREPARING THE STATEMENT OF CASH FLOWS

The accountant prepares the statement of cash flows after completing the balance sheet and the income statement. Chapter 4 describes and illustrates a procedure for preparing the statement of cash flows using a T-account work sheet. A summary of the procedure follows:

Step 1 Obtain a balance sheet for the beginning and the end of the period spanned by the statement of cash flows.

Step 2 Prepare a T-account work sheet. A master T-account for cash appears at the top of the work sheet. This master T-account has three sections, labeled Operations, Investing, and Financing. Enter the beginning and the ending balances in cash and cash equivalents in the master T-account. *Cash equivalents* represent short-term, highly liquid investments in which a firm has temporarily placed excess cash. Generally only

729

investments with maturities of three months or less qualify as cash equivalents. We use the term *cash flows* to refer to changes in cash and cash equivalents. Complete the T-account work sheet by preparing a T-account for each balance sheet account other than cash and cash equivalents and enter the beginning and the ending balances.

Step 3   Explain the change in the master cash account between the beginning and the end of the period by explaining, or accounting for, the changes in the other balance sheet accounts. Do this by reconstructing the entries originally made in the accounts during the period and entering them in appropriate T-accounts on the work sheet. By explaining the changes in balance sheet accounts other than cash, this process also explains the change in cash and cash equivalents. The cash change equation serves as the basis for this step:

$$\Delta C = \Delta L + \Delta SE - \Delta N\$A$$

where:

$$\Delta C = \text{change in cash}$$
$$\Delta L = \text{change in liabilities}$$
$$\Delta SE = \text{change in shareholders' equity}$$
$$\Delta N\$A = \text{change in noncash assets}$$

Step 4   Prepare a statement of cash flows using information in the T-account work sheet.

COMPREHENSIVE ILLUSTRATION OF THE STATEMENT OF CASH FLOWS

The comprehensive illustration that follows uses data for Ellwood Corporation for Year 2. Exhibit 13.1 presents an income statement for Year 2; Exhibit 13.2 presents a comparative balance sheet for December 31, Year 1 and Year 2; and Exhibit 13.3 presents a statement of cash flows. The calculation of cash flow from operations follows the indirect method; we adjust net income for revenues that do not provide cash and expenses that do not use cash to derive cash flow from operations. The sections that follow explain each of the line items in Exhibit 13.3.

LINE 1: NET INCOME

The income statement indicates net income for the period of $1,000. The work sheet entry presumes that cash provisionally increases by the amount of net income.

(1a) Cash (Operations—Net Income)	1,000	
Retained Earnings		1,000

The effect of net income on the cash change equation is as follows:

$$\Delta C \qquad = \Delta L + \Delta SE \qquad - \Delta N\$A$$
$$\text{Operations} + \$1,000 \text{ (1a)} = \$0 + \$1,000 \text{ (1a)} - \$0$$

LINE 2: DEPRECIATION OF BUILDINGS AND EQUIPMENT

Internal records indicate that depreciation on manufacturing facilities totaled $500 and on selling and administrative facilities totaled $200 during the year. The firm included these

EXHIBIT 13.1	ELLWOOD CORPORATION Consolidated Income Statement for Year 2

REVENUES

Sales	$10,500
Interest and Dividends	320
Equity in Earnings of Affiliate	480
Gain on Sale of Equipment	30
Total Revenues	$11,330

EXPENSES

Cost of Goods Sold	$ 6,000
Selling and Administration	3,550
Loss on Sale of Marketable Equity Securities	30
Interest	450
Income Taxes	300
Total Expenses	$10,330
Net Income	$ 1,000

amounts in cost of goods sold and selling and administrative expenses respectively in the income statement in Exhibit 13.1. None of this $700 of depreciation required an operating cash flow during Year 2. The firm reported cash expenditures for these assets as investing activities in the earlier periods when it acquired them. Thus the work sheet adds back depreciation to net income in deriving cash flow from operations.

(2a) Cash (Operations—Depreciation Expense Addback)	700	
Accumulated Depreciation		700

Thus,

$$
\begin{array}{rlll}
& \Delta C & = \Delta L + \quad \Delta SE & - \quad \Delta N\$A \\
\text{Operations} & -\$700 \text{ (1a)} = \$0 + -\$700 \text{ (1a)} & - \quad \$ \quad 0 \\
\text{Operations} & +700 \text{ (2a)} = \underline{\quad 0} + \underline{\quad\quad 0} & - \quad \underline{-700} \text{ (2a)} \\
\text{Net} & \underline{\underline{\$ \quad 0}} \quad = \underline{\underline{\$0}} + \underline{\underline{-\$700}} & - \quad \underline{\underline{-\$700}}
\end{array}
$$

Addback for Depreciation as a Product Cost   The addback for the $500 of depreciation on manufacturing facilities requires elaboration. Chapter 7 explains that accountants count such depreciation charges as a product cost, not a period expense. The accountant debits Work-in-Process Inventory for this $500. If, during the period, the firm sells all the goods it produces, cost of goods sold includes this $500. Because cost of goods sold includes an amount that does not use cash, the addback to net income cancels the depreciation included in cost of goods sold.

Suppose, however, that the firm does not sell all the goods it produces during the period. The ending inventory of Work-in-Process Inventory or Finished Goods Inventory includes a portion of the $500 depreciation charge. Assume, for example, that the firm sold 80 percent of the units produced during the period. Cost of goods sold includes $400 of the depreciation, and inventory accounts include the remaining $100. The statement of cash flows adds back to net income the entire $500 of depreciation on manufacturing

EXHIBIT 13.2	ELLWOOD CORPORATION Consolidated Balance Sheet		

		December 31	
		Year 1	Year 2
ASSETS			
Current Assets			
Cash		$ 1,150	$ 1,050
Certificate of Deposit		1,520	790
Marketable Equity Securities		280	190
Accounts Receivable (net)		3,400	4,300
Inventories		1,500	2,350
Prepayments		800	600
Total Current Assets		$ 8,650	$ 9,280
Investments			
Investment in Company A (15%)		$ 1,250	$ 1,270
Investment in Company B (40%)		2,100	2,420
Total Investments		$ 3,350	$ 3,690
Property, Plant, and Equipment			
Land		$ 1,000	$ 1,000
Buildings		8,600	8,900
Equipment		10,840	11,540
Less Accumulated Depreciation		(6,240)	(6,490)
Total Property, Plant, and Equipment		$14,200	$14,950
Intangible Assets			
Patent		$ 2,550	$ 2,550
Less Accumulated Amortization		(600)	(750)
Total Intangible Assets		$ 1,950	$ 1,800
Total Assets		$28,150	$29,720

(continued)

facilities for the period. The $100 of depreciation included in the cost of units not sold caused the inventory accounts to increase. Under the indirect method of computing cash flow from operations, the accountant subtracts this increase in inventories in computing cash flow from operations. The $500 addition for depreciation less the $100 subtraction for the increase in inventories nets to a $400 addition to income. Because cost of goods sold includes only $400 of depreciation, the addition required to cancel the depreciation included in cost of goods sold equals $400. Thus, the worksheet entry **2a** shows an add-back for the full amount of depreciation for the period (both as a product cost and as a period expense), not just the amount included in cost of goods sold; then, line 13 of the statement of cash flows includes a subtraction for the $100 increase in inventories caused by adding depreciation to work in process.

LINE 3: AMORTIZATION OF PATENT

The effect of patent amortization on cash flow is conceptually identical to that of depreciation. Company records indicate that cost of goods sold for Year 2 includes patent amortization of $150. The work sheet entry is as follows:

		December 31	
EXHIBIT 13.2 *(continued)*	ELLWOOD CORPORATION Consolidated Balance Sheet		
		Year 1	Year 2
LIABILITIES AND SHAREHOLDERS' EQUITY			
Current Liabilities			
Bank Notes Payable		$ 2,000	$ 2,750
Accounts Payable (for inventory)		2,450	3,230
Warranties Payable		1,200	1,000
Advances from Customers		600	900
Total Current Liabilities		$ 6,250	$ 7,880
Noncurrent Liabilities			
Bonds Payable		$ 2,820	$ 1,370
Capitalized Lease Obligation		1,800	2,100
Deferred Income Taxes		550	650
Total Noncurrent Liabilities		$ 5,170	$ 4,120
Shareholders' Equity			
Preferred Stock		$ 1,000	$ 1,200
Common Stock		2,000	2,100
Additional Paid-in Capital		4,000	4,200
Accumulated Other Comprehensive Income			
Unrealized Holding Loss on Marketable Securities		(30)	(40)
Unrealized Holding Gain on Investments In Securities		50	70
Retained Earnings		9,960	10,570
Total		$16,980	$18,100
Less Cost of Treasury Stock		(250)	(380)
Total Shareholders' Equity		$16,730	$17,720
Total Liabilities and Shareholders' Equity		$28,150	$29,720

(3a) Cash (Operations—Amortization Expense Addback) 150

            Accumulated Amortization   150

Thus,

$$
\begin{array}{rlll}
\Delta C & = \Delta L + & \Delta SE & - & \Delta N\$A \\
\text{Operations} - \$150 \ (1a) = \$0 + & -\$150 \ (1a) & - & \$ \ \ 0 \\
\text{Operations} + 150 \ (3a) = \underline{\quad} + & \underline{\qquad} & - & -150 \ (3a) \\
\text{Net} \quad \underline{\$ \ \ 0} \quad = \$0 + & -\$150 & - & -\$150
\end{array}
$$

LINE 4: LOSS ON SALE OF MARKETABLE EQUITY SECURITIES

The accounting records indicate that Ellwood Corporation sold marketable equity securities held as a short-term investment during Year 2. Ellwood Corporation acquired these securities for $80 during Year 1, wrote them down to their market value of $70 at the end

EXHIBIT 13.3	ELLWOOD CORPORATION Consolidated Statement of Cash Flows for Year 2

OPERATIONS

(1) Net Income	$1,000

Noncash Revenues, Expenses, Gains, and Losses Included in Income:

(2) Depreciation of Buildings and Equipment	700
(3) Amortization of Patent	150
(4) Loss on Sale of Marketable Equity Securities	30
(5) Deferred Income Taxes	100
(6) Excess of Coupon Payments over Interest Expense	(50)
(7) Gain on Sale of Equipment	(30)
(8) Equity in Undistributed Earnings of Affiliate	(320)
(9) Decrease in Prepayments	200
(10) Increase in Accounts Payable (for inventory)	780
(11) Increase in Advances from Customers	300
(12) Increase in Accounts Receivable (net)	(900)
(13) Increase in Inventories	(850)
(14) Decrease in Warranties Payable	(200)
Cash Flow from Operations	$ 910

INVESTING

(15) Sale of Marketable Equity Securities	$ 50	
(16) Sale of Equipment	180	
(17) Acquisition of Equipment	(1,300)	
Cash Flow from Investing		(1,070)

FINANCING

(18) Short-Term Bank Borrowing	$ 750	
(19) Long-Term Bonds Issued	400	
(20) Preferred Stock Issued	200	
(21) Retirement of Long-term Debt at Maturity	(1,500)	
(22) Acquisition of Common Stock	(130)	
(23) Dividends	(390)	
Cash Flow from Financing		(670)
Net Change in Cash		$ (830)
Cash, Beginning of Year 2		2,670
Cash, End of Year 2		$1,840

of Year 1, and sold them during Year 2 for $50. The firm made the following entries in the accounting records to record this sale:

(4) Cash	50	
Realized Loss on Sale of Marketable Equity Securities (IncSt)	30	
Marketable Equity Securities		80
Marketable Equity Securities	10	
Unrealized Holding Loss on Marketable Equity Securities (SE)		10

The work sheet entries to reflect this transaction are the following:

(4a) Cash (Investing—Sale of Marketable Equity Securities)	50	
Cash (Operations—Loss on Sale of Marketable Equity Securities Addback)	30	
Marketable Equity Securities		80
(4b) Marketable Equity Securities	10	
Unrealized Holding Loss on Marketable Equity Securities (SE)		10

   The statement of cash flows classifies all $50 cash proceeds as an investing activity on Line 15 and none as an operating activity. Net income on Line 1 in Exhibit 13.3 includes a subtraction for the loss on the sale of marketable equity securities. To avoid understating the amount of cash flow from operations, the accountant adds back the loss to net income. This addback offsets the loss included in the calculation of net income and eliminates its effect on cash flow from operations. Line 15 shows the cash proceeds from the sale as an investing activity. The analyst might reasonably view purchases and sales of marketable equity securities as operating activities because these transactions involve the use of temporarily excess cash. Most, but not all, firms consider these transactions sufficiently peripheral to the firms' principal operating activity—selling goods and services to customers—that they classify such purchases and sales as investing activities.
   Thus,

$$
\begin{array}{lrcccccl}
 & \Delta C & = & \Delta L & + & \Delta SE & - & \Delta N\$A \\
\text{Operations} & -\$30\ (1a) & = & \$0 & + & -\$30\ (1a) & - & \$\ 0 \\
\text{Investing} & +50\ (4a) & = & 0 & + & 0 & - & -80\ (4a) \\
\text{Operations} & \underline{+30\ (4a)} & = & 0 & + & 0 & - & 0 \\
 & & & & + & \underline{10\ (4b)} & - & \underline{10\ (4b)} \\
\text{Net} & \underline{\underline{+\$50}} & = & \underline{\underline{\$0}} & + & \underline{\underline{-\$20}} & - & \underline{\underline{-\$70}}
\end{array}
$$

LINE 5: DEFERRED INCOME TAXES

Notes to the financial statements of Ellwood Corporation indicate that income tax expense of $300 comprises $200 currently payable taxes and $100 deferred to future periods. Ellwood Corporation made the following entry during the year to recognize income tax expense.

(5) Income Tax Expense	300	
Cash		200
Deferred Income Taxes		100

The $100 of deferred income taxes reduced net income but did not require a cash outflow during Year 2. The work sheet must, therefore, add back deferred income taxes to net income to derive cash flow from operations.

(5a) Cash (Operations—Deferred Tax Addback)	100	
Deferred Income Taxes		100

Thus,

	ΔC	=	ΔL	+	ΔSE	−	$\Delta N\$A$
Operations	−$300 (1a) =		$ 0	+	−$300 (1a)	−	$0
Operations	+100 (5a) =		100 (5a)	+	0	−	0
Net	−$200	=	+$100	+	−$300	−	$0

LINE 6: EXCESS OF COUPON PAYMENTS OVER INTEREST EXPENSE

Bonds Payable on the balance sheet includes one series of bonds initially issued at a premium (that is, the coupon rate exceeded the required market rate of interest when Ellwood Corporation issued the bonds, so that initial issue proceeds exceeded face value). The amortization of bond premium makes interest expense over the life of the bonds less than the periodic debt service payments for coupons. The entry made in the accounting records for interest expense during the period was as follows:

(6) Interest Expense	450	
Bonds Payable	50	
Cash		500

The firm spent $500 of cash even though it subtracted only $450 of interest expense in computing net income. The work sheet subtracts an additional $50 from net income to derive cash flow from operations.

(6a) Bonds Payable	50	
Cash (Operations—Excess Coupon Payments Subtraction)		50

The statement of cash flows classifies cash used for interest expense as an operating activity because it views interest as a cost of carrying out operations. Some security analysts suggest that this $50 use of cash for principal repayment is a financing activity for debt service, not an operating activity, and would place it in the Financing section. The Financial Accounting Standards Board *Statement of Financial Accounting Standards No. 95*, however, classifies the $50 cash outflow as an operating activity.

Thus,

	ΔC	=	ΔL	+	ΔSE	−	$\Delta N\$A$
Operations	−$450 (1a) =		$ 0	+	−$450 (1a)	−	$0
Operations	−50 (6a) =		−50 (6a)	+	0	−	0
Net	−$500	=	−$50	+	−$450	−	$0

LINE 7: GAIN ON SALE OF EQUIPMENT

The accounting records indicate that the firm sold for $180 during Year 2 a machine originally costing $600, with accumulated depreciation of $450. The journal entry made to record this sale was as follows:

(7) Cash		180	
Accumulated Depreciation		450	
Equipment			600
Gain on Sale of Equipment			30

Line 16 shows all the cash proceeds of $180 as an increase in cash from an investing activity. Line 1 includes the $30 gain on sale. To avoid overstating the amount of cash derived from this sale, the accountant subtracts the $30 gain from net income in computing cash flow from operations.

(7a) Cash (Investing—Sale of Equipment)		180	
Accumulated Depreciation		450	
Equipment			600
Cash (Operations—Gain on Sale of Equipment Subtraction)			30

The statement of cash flows classifies all cash proceeds as investing activities and none as operating activities. Most firms acquire and sell fixed assets with the objective of providing a capacity to carry out operations rather than as a means of generating operating income.

Thus,

	ΔC	$= \Delta L +$	ΔSE	$- \Delta N\$A$
Operations	$+\$\ 30$ (1a)	$= \$0 +$	$\$30$ (1a)	$- \$\ \ 0$
Investing	$+180$ (7a)	$= \ \ 0 +$	0	$- +450$ (7a)
Operations	-30 (7a)	$= \ \ 0 +$	0	$- -600$ (7a)
Net	$+\$180$	$= \$0 +$	$\$30$	$- -\$150$

Fixed assets sold at a loss instead of a gain require an addback to net income in deriving cash flow from operations. The work sheet entry, assuming the data of the preceding entry except that Ellwood Corporation sells the equipment for $110, would be as follows:

Cash (Investing—Sale of Equipment)		110	
Accumulated Depreciation		450	
Cash (Operations—Loss on Sale of Equipment Addback)		40	
Equipment			600

LINE 8: EQUITY IN UNDISTRIBUTED EARNINGS OF AFFILIATE

The balance sheet indicates that Ellwood Corporation owns 40 percent of the common stock of Company B. During Year 2, Company B earned $1,200 and paid $400 of dividends. Ellwood Corporation made the following entries on its books during the year.

(8) Investment in Company B	480	
Equity in Earnings of Affiliate		480
Records equity in earnings of $480 = .40 × $1,200.		
Cash	160	
Investment in Company B		160
Records dividends received of $160 = .40 × $400.		

Net income of Ellwood Corporation on Line 1 of Exhibit 13.3 includes $480 of equity income. It received only $160 of cash. Thus, the work sheet subtracts $320 (= $480 − $160) from net income in deriving cash from operations.

(8a) Investment in Company B	320	
Cash (Operations—Equity in Undistributed Earnings Subtraction)		320

Thus,

$$
\begin{array}{rcccl}
 & \Delta C & = \Delta L\ + & \Delta SE & -\ \Delta N\$A \\
\text{Operations} & +\$480\ \text{(1a)} & = \$0\ + & \$480\ \text{(1a)} & -\ \$\ \ 0 \\
\text{Operations} & -320\ \text{(8a)} & = \underline{\ \ 0}\ + & \underline{\ \ \ \ \ 0} & -\ \underline{\ \ 320}\ \text{(8a)} \\
\text{Net} & +\$160 & = \underline{\underline{\$0}}\ + & \underline{\underline{\$480}} & -\ \underline{\underline{\$320}}
\end{array}
$$

LINE 9: DECREASE IN PREPAYMENTS

Because prepayments decreased by $200 during Year 2, the firm expended less cash during Year 2 for new prepayments than it expensed prepayments of earlier years. Assume that all prepayments relate to selling and administrative activities. The journal entries that Ellwood Corporation made in the accounting records during the year had the following combined effect:

(9a) Selling and Administrative Expenses	3,550	
Cash		3,350
Prepayments		200

The work sheet adds back $200 to net income for the credit change in an operating current asset account so that cash flow from operations reports expenditures, not expenses.

(9a) Cash (Operations—Decrease in Prepayments)	200	
Prepayments		200

Thus,

$$
\begin{array}{rcccl}
 & \Delta C & = \Delta L\ + & \Delta SE & -\ \Delta N\$A \\
\text{Operations} & -\$3,550\ \text{(1a)} & = \$0\ + & -\$3,550\ \text{(1a)} & -\ \$\ \ 0 \\
\text{Operations} & +200\ \text{(9a)} & = \underline{\ \ 0}\ + & \underline{\ \ \ \ \ \ \ 0} & -\ \underline{-200}\ \text{(9a)} \\
\text{Net} & -\$3,350 & = \underline{\underline{\$0}}\ + & \underline{\underline{-\$3,550}} & -\ \underline{\underline{-\$200}}
\end{array}
$$

LINE 10: INCREASE IN ACCOUNTS PAYABLE

An increase in accounts payable indicates that new purchases on account during Year 2 exceeded payments during Year 2 for previous purchases on account. This increase in accounts payable, a credit change in an operating current liability account, implicitly provides cash. If you think of this source of cash as financing, you have the right idea. Suppliers have provided financing so that Ellwood Corporation can acquire goods on account. You might think of it this way. Imagine a firm borrows from a supplier, debiting Cash and crediting Notes Payable. Then the firm uses the cash to acquire inventory or other items. You can see that the supplier has provided cash, and the firm increases a current liability account. A firm buying on account has achieved the same result, except that it credits Accounts Payable, not Notes Payable. Because the supplier ties the financing to the purchase of goods used in operations, accounting classifies this source of cash in the operating, not financing, section of the statement of cash flows.

(10a) Cash (Operations—Increase in Accounts Payable)	780	
Accounts Payable (for inventory)		780

We will explore the effect that the adjustment for the change in accounts payable has on the equation for the change in cash when we discuss the adjustment for inventory.

LINE 11: INCREASE IN ADVANCES FROM CUSTOMERS

The $300 increase in customer advances means that the firm received $300 more cash during Year 2 than it recognized as revenue. The work sheet adds this excess to net income in deriving cash flow from operations.

(11a) Cash (Operations—Increase in Advances from Customers)	300	
Advances from Customers		300

We will consider the effect that the adjustment for advances for customers has on the equation for the change in cash next, when we discuss the adjustment for accounts receivable.

LINE 12: INCREASE IN ACCOUNTS RECEIVABLE

The increase in accounts receivable indicates that the firm collected less cash from customers than the amount shown for sales on account. The work sheet subtracts the increase in accounts receivable, a debit change in an operating current asset account, in deriving cash flow from operations.

(12a) Accounts Receivable (net)	900	
Cash (Operations—Increase in Accounts Receivable)		900

Note that this entry automatically incorporates the effect of any change in the Allowance for Uncollectible Accounts. The work sheet could make separate work sheet entries for the change in gross accounts receivable and the change in allowance for uncollectible accounts.

We can now summarize the effect that changes in accounts receivable and advances from customers have on the equation for changes in cash. Ellwood Corporation made entries during the year with the following combined effect:

Cash	9,900	
Accounts Receivable (net)	900	
Advances from Customers		300
Sales Revenue		10,500

Thus,

	ΔC		$= \Delta L$		$+ \Delta SE$		$- \Delta N\$A$
Operations	$+\$10,500$ (1a)	=	$\$\ 0$	+	$\$10,500$ (1a)	−	$\$\ 0$
Operations	$+300$ (11a)	=	300 (11a)	+	0	−	0
Operations	-900 (12a)	=	0	+	0	−	900 (12a)
Net	$+\$\ 9,900$	=	$\$300$	+	$\$10,500$	−	$\$900$

LINE 13: INCREASE IN INVENTORIES

The increase in inventories indicates the firm purchased more merchandise than it sold during Year 2. The work sheet subtracts this debit change in inventory in deriving cash flow from operations.

(13a) Inventories	850	
Cash (Operations—Increase in Inventories)		850

We can now consider the effect on cash of the change in inventories and the change in accounts payable. Ellwood Corporation made entries during the year that had the following combined effect:

Cost of Goods Sold	6,000	
Inventories	850	
Accounts Payable (for inventory)		780
Cash		6,070

Thus,

	ΔC		$= \Delta L$		$+ \Delta SE$		$- \Delta N\$A$
Operations	$-\$6,000$ (1a)	=	$\$\ 0$	+	$-\$6,000$ (1a)	−	$\$\ 0$
Operations	$+780$ (10a)	=	780 (10a)	+	0	−	0
Operations	-850 (13a)	=	0	+	0	−	$+850$ (13a)
Net	$-\$6,070$	=	$+\$780$	+	$-\$6,000$	−	$+\$850$

LINE 14: DECREASE IN WARRANTIES PAYABLE

Recall that firms estimate future warranty costs on current sales using the allowance method for warranties. The Warranties Payable account increases for the estimated cost of future warranty services on products sold during the period and decreases by the actual cost of warranty services performed. During Year 2, the firm paid $200 more in warranty claims than it reported as expenses on the income statement. Ellwood Corporation includes estimated warranty expense of $920 in selling and administrative expenses in its income statement in Exhibit 13.3. The firm made entries during the year with the following combined effect:

(9a) Selling and Administrative Expenses	920	
Warranties Payable	200	
Cash		1,120

The work sheet subtracts this decrease in Warranties Payable, a debit change in an operating current liability account so that cash flow from operations reports cash expenditures, not expenses.

(14a) Warranties Payable	200	
Cash (Operations—Decrease in Warranties Payable)		200

Thus,

$$\Delta C = \Delta L + \Delta SE - \Delta N\$A$$

$$\text{Operations } -\$\ 920 \text{ (1a)} = \$\ \ 0 + -\$920 \text{ (1a)} - \$0$$

$$\text{Operations } \underline{-200} \text{ (14a)} = \underline{-200} \text{ (14a)} + \underline{\ \ \ \ 0} - \underline{\ \ 0}$$

$$\text{Net } \underline{\underline{-\$1,120}} = \underline{\underline{-\$200}} + \underline{\underline{-\$920}} - \underline{\underline{\$0}}$$

Cash flow from operations is $910 for Year 2.

LINES 15 AND 16

See the discussion for Lines 4 and 7.

LINE 17: ACQUISITION OF EQUIPMENT

The firm acquired equipment costing $1,300 during Year 2. The analytic entry for this investing activity is as follows:

(17a) Equipment	1,300	
Cash (Investing—Acquisition of Equipment)		1,300

The effect of the acquisition of equipment on the cash change equation is as follows:

$$\Delta C = \Delta L + \Delta SE - \Delta N\$A$$

$$\text{Investing } -\$1,300 \text{ (17a)} = \$0 + \$0 - \$1,300 \text{ (17a)}$$

Cash flow from investing for Year 2 is a net outflow of $1,070.

LINE 18: SHORT-TERM BANK BORROWING

Ellwood Corporation borrowed $750 during Year 2 from its bank under a short-term borrowing arrangement. Even though this loan is short-term, the statement of cash flows classifies it as a financing instead of an operating activity. The analytic entry on the work sheet is as follows:

(18a) Cash (Financing—Short-Term Bank Borrowing)	750	
Bank Note Payable		750

The effect on the cash change equation is as follows:

$$\Delta C \qquad = \Delta L \qquad + \Delta SE - \Delta N\$A$$

$$\text{Financing} +\$750 \ (18a) = \$750 \ (18a) + \$0 \ - \$0$$

LINE 19: LONG-TERM BONDS ISSUED

The firm issued long-term bonds totaling $400 during Year 2.

(19a) Cash (Financing—Long-Term Bonds Issued)	400	
Bonds Payable		400

This transaction has the following effect on the cash change equation:

$$\Delta C \qquad = \Delta L \qquad + \Delta SE - \Delta N\$A$$

$$\text{Financing} +\$400 \ (19a) = \$400 \ (19a) + \$0 \ - \$0$$

LINE 20: PREFERRED STOCK ISSUED

The firm issued preferred stock totaling $200 during the year.

(20a) Cash (Financing—Preferred Stock Issued)	200	
Preferred Stock		200

The effect on the cash change equation is as follows:

$$\Delta C \qquad = \Delta L + \Delta SE \qquad - \Delta N\$A$$

$$\text{Financing} +\$200 \ (20a) = \$0 + \$200 \ (20a) - \$0$$

LINE 21: RETIREMENT OF LONG-TERM DEBT AT MATURITY

Ellwood Corporation retired $1,500 of long-term debt at maturity. The income statement in Exhibit 13.1 shows no gain or loss on retirement of debt. Thus, Ellwood Corporation must have retired the debt at its book value. We make the following work sheet entry:

(21a) Bonds Payable	1,500	
Cash (Financing—Retirement of Long-Term Debt)		1,500

The effect on the cash change equation is as follows:

$$\Delta C \qquad = \Delta L \qquad + \Delta SE - \Delta N\$A$$
$$\text{Financing} -\$1,500 \ (21a) = -\$1,500 \ (21a) + \$0 \quad - \$0$$

If the firm had retired the debt prior to maturity, the firm would likely have recognized a gain or loss. The work sheet would eliminate the gain or loss from net income in computing cash flow from operations and classify as a financing activity the full amount of cash used to retire the debt.

LINE 22: ACQUISITION OF COMMON STOCK

The firm acquired common stock costing $130 during Year 2.

(22a) Treasury Stock 130
         Cash (Financing—Acquisition of Common Stock) 130

The treasury stock acquisition has the following effect on the cash change equation:

$$\Delta C \qquad = \Delta L + \quad \Delta SE \qquad - \Delta N\$A$$
$$\text{Financing} -\$130 \ (22a) = \$0 + -\$130 \ (22a) - \$0$$

LINE 23: DIVIDENDS

Ellwood Corporation declared and paid $390 of dividends to its shareholders during Year 2. The analytic entry is as follows:

(23a) Retained Earnings 390
         Cash (Financing—Dividends) 390

The dividend affects the cash change equation as follows:

$$\Delta C \qquad = \Delta L + \quad \Delta SE \qquad - \Delta N\$A$$
$$\text{Financing} -\$390 \ (23a) = \$0 + -\$390 \ (23a) - \$0$$

Net cash outflow for financing totaled $670 during the year.

NONCASH INVESTING AND FINANCING TRANSACTIONS

Some investing and financing transactions do not involve cash and therefore do not appear on the statement of cash flows. These transactions nevertheless help explain changes in balance sheet accounts. The accountant must enter these transactions in the T-account worksheet to account fully for all balance sheet changes and compute correctly the portion of the changes affecting cash.

Write-Down of Marketable Equity Securities   During Year 2, Ellwood Corporation wrote down marketable equity securities to their market value. The journal entry made for this write-down is as follows:

---

(24) Unrealized Holding Loss on Marketable Equity Securities (SE)   20
         Marketable Equity Securities   20

This entry does not affect cash and therefore does not appear in the statement of cash flows. It does, however, help explain the change during the year in the two marketable equity securities accounts above and requires the following entry in the T-account work sheet:

(24a) Unrealized Holding Loss on Marketable Equity Securities   20
         Marketable Equity Securities   20

The effect on the cash change equation is as follows:

$$\Delta C = \Delta L +\quad \Delta SE \qquad -\quad \Delta N\$A$$
$$\$0 = \$0 + -\$20 \text{ (24a)} - -\$20 \text{ (24a)}$$

Write-Up of Investment in Securities   During Year 2, Ellwood Corporation also wrote up its Investment in Company A to reflect market value. The journal entry for the write-up is as follows:

---

(25) Investment in Company A   20
         Unrealized Holding Gain on Investment in Securities (SE)   20

This entry does not affect cash flows but explains the change during the year in the two investment in securities accounts above and requires the following entry in the T-account work sheet:

(25a) Investment in Company A   20
         Unrealized Holding Gain on Investment in Securities   20

The effect on the cash change equation is as follows:

$$\Delta C = \Delta L + \Delta SE \qquad - \Delta N\$A$$
$$\$0 = \$0 + \$20 \text{ (25a)} - \$20 \text{ (25a)}$$

Capitalization of Leases   During Year 2, Ellwood Corporation signed a long-term lease for a building. It classified the lease as a capital lease and recorded it in the accounts as follows:

(26) Building	300	
Capitalized Lease Obligation		300

Note that this entry does not affect cash. It does affect the investing and financing activities of Ellwood Corporation and requires disclosure in a supplementary schedule or notes to the financial statements. The accountant makes the following entry in the T-account work sheet:

(26a) Building	300	
Capitalized Lease Obligation		300

The effect that capitalizing these leases has on the cash change equation is as follows:

$$\Delta C = \Delta L \quad + \Delta SE - \Delta N\$A$$
$$\$0 = \$300 \ (26a) + \$0 \quad - \$300 \ (26a)$$

Conversion of Debt into Equity   During Year 2, investors in bonds of Ellwood Corporation exercised their option to convert their debt securities into shares of common stock. The entry made in the accounting records to record the conversion is as follows:

(27) Bonds Payable	300	
Common Stock		100
Additional Paid-In Capital		200

The accountant reflects this financing transaction on the T-account work sheet by making the following entry:

(27a) Bonds Payable	300	
Common Stock		100
Additional Paid-in Capital		200

The effect on the cash change equation is as follows:

$$\Delta C = \quad \Delta L \qquad + \Delta SE \qquad - \Delta N\$A$$
$$\$0 = -\$300 \ (27a) + \$300 \ (27a) - \$0$$

Exhibit 13.4 presents a T-account work sheet for Ellwood Corporation for Year 2.

EXHIBIT 13.4 ELLWOOD CORPORATION
T-Account Work Sheet

Cash

√	2,670	

Operations

Net Income	**(1a)**	1,000	50	**(6a)**	Excess Coupon Payments
Depreciation Expense	**(2a)**	700	30	**(7a)**	Gain on Sale of Equipment
Amortization Expense	**(3a)**	150	320	**(8a)**	Equity in Undistributed Earnings
Loss on Sale of Marketable Securities	**(4a)**	30	900	**(12a)**	Increase in Accounts Receivable (net)
Deferred Income Taxes	**(5a)**	100	850	**(13a)**	Increase in Inventories
Decrease in Prepayments	**(9a)**	200	200	**(14a)**	Decrease in Warranties Payable
Increase in Accounts Payable	**(10a)**	780			
Increase in Advances from Customers	**(11a)**	300			

Investing

Sale of Marketable Securities	**(4a)**	50	1,300	**(17a)**	Acquisition of Equipment
Sale of Equipment	**(7a)**	180			

Financing

Short-term Borrowing	**(18a)**	750	1,500	**(21a)**	Retirement of Long-term Debt
Long-term Bonds Issued	**(19a)**	400	130	**(22a)**	Acquisition of Common Stock
Preferred Stock Issued	**(20a)**	200	390	**(23a)**	Dividends

√	1,840	

Marketable Equity Securities				**Accounts Receivable (net)**			**Inventories**		
√	280			√	3,400		√	1,500	
		70	**(4a)**	**(12a)**	900		**(13a)**	850	
		20	**(24a)**				√	2,350	
√	190			√	4,300				

Prepayments				**Investment in Company A**			**Investment in Company B**		
√	800			√	1,250		√	2,100	
		200	**(9a)**	**(25a)**	20		**(8a)**	320	
√	600			√	1,270		√	2,420	

Land			**Buildings**			**Equipment**			
√	1,000		√	8,600		√	10,840		
			(26a)	300		**(17a)**	1,300	600	**(7a)**
√	1,000		√	8,900		√	11,540		

(continued)

EXHIBIT 13.4 *(continued)*	ELLWOOD CORPORATION T-Account Work Sheet

Accumulated Depreciation

		6,240	√
(7a)	450	700	**(2a)**
		6,490	√

Patent

√	2,550	
√	2,550	

Accumulated Amortization

		600	√
		150	**(3a)**
		750	√

Bank Notes Payable

	2,000	√
	750	**(18a)**
	2,750	√

Accounts Payable (for inventory)

	2,450	√
	780	**(10a)**
	3,230	√

Warranties Payable

		1,200	√
(14a)	200		
		1,000	√

Advances from Customers

	600	√
	300	**(11a)**
	900	√

Bonds Payable

		2,820	√
(6a)	50	400	**(19a)**
(21a)	1,500		
(27a)	300		
		1,370	√

Capitalized Lease Obligation

		1,800	√
		300	**(26a)**
		2,100	√

Deferred Income Taxes

	550	√
	100	**(5a)**
	650	√

Preferred Stock

		1,000	√
		200	**(20a)**
		1,200	√

Common Stock

		2,000	√
		100	**(27a)**
		2,100	√

Additional Paid-in Capital

		4,000	√
		200	**(27a)**
		4,200	√

Unrealized Holding Loss on Marketable Securities

√	30		
(24a)	20	10	**(4a)**
√	40		

Unrealized Holding Gain on Investments in Securities

		50	√
		20	**(25a)**
		70	√

Retained Earnings

		9,960	√
(23a)	390	1,000	**(1a)**
		10,570	√

Treasury Stock

√	250		
(22a)	130		
√	380		

PROBLEM 13.1 FOR SELF-STUDY

Effects of transactions on the statement of cash flows.   Exhibit 4.16 in Chapter 4 presents a simplified statement of cash flows. For each of the transactions that follow, indicate the number(s) of the line(s) in Exhibit 4.16 affected by the transaction and indicate the amount and direction (increase or decrease) of the effect. If the transaction affects net income, be sure to indicate whether it increases or decreases. Ignore income tax effects.

a. A firm sells for $12,000 equipment that originally cost $30,000 and has accumulated depreciation of $16,000 at the time of sale.

b. A firm owns 25 percent of the common stock of an investee acquired several years ago at book value and uses the equity method. The investee had net income of $80,000 and paid dividends of $20,000 during the period.

c. A firm, as lessee (tenant), records lease payments of $50,000 on capital leases for the period, of which $35,000 represents interest expense.

d. Income tax expense for the period totals $120,000, of which the firm pays $90,000 immediately and defers the remaining $30,000 because of temporary differences between the accounting principles used for financial reporting and those used for tax reporting.

e. A firm owns 10 percent of the common stock of an investee acquired at its book value several years ago and accounts for it at market value as a long-term investment. The investee had net income of $100,000 and paid dividends of $40,000 during the period. The market value at the end of the period equaled the market value at the beginning of the period.

INTERPRETING THE STATEMENT OF CASH FLOWS

Chapter 4 points out that the proper interpretation of information in the statement of cash flows requires

- an understanding of the economic characteristics of the industries in which a firm conducts operations, and
- a multiperiod view.

This section discusses the interpretation of the statement of cash flows more fully.

RELATION BETWEEN NET INCOME AND CASH FLOW FROM OPERATIONS

Net income and cash flow from operations differ for two principal reasons:

1. Changes in noncurrent assets and noncurrent liabilities
2. Changes in operating working capital accounts

Changes in Noncurrent Assets and Noncurrent Liabilities   The extent to which a firm adjusts net income for changes in noncurrent assets and noncurrent liabilities in deriving cash flow from operations depends on the nature of its operations. Capital-intensive firms will likely show a substantial addback to net income for depreciation expense, whereas service firms will show a smaller amount. Firms heavily engaged in acquisition activity will often show an addback for goodwill amortization. Rapidly growing firms usually show an addback for deferred tax expense, whereas firms that stop growing or that shrink show a subtraction. Firms that grow or diversify by acquiring minority ownership positions in other businesses will often show a subtraction from net income for equity in undistributed earnings. Firms that decrease in size will usually show additions or subtractions for losses and gains on the disposal of assets.

Changes in Operating Working Capital Accounts   The adjustment for changes in operating working capital accounts depends in part on a firm's rate of growth. Rapidly growing firms usually experience significant increases in accounts receivable and inventories. Some firms use suppliers or other creditors to finance these working capital needs (classified as operating activities), whereas other firms use short- or long-term borrowing or equity financing (classified as financing activities).

RELATIONS BETWEEN CASH FLOWS FROM OPERATING, INVESTING, AND FINANCING ACTIVITIES

The product life-cycle concept from microeconomics and marketing provides useful insights into the relations between cash flows from operating, investing, and financing activities.

During the introduction phase, cash outflow exceeds cash inflow from operations because operations are not yet earning profits while the firm must invest in accounts receivable and inventories. Investing activities result in a net cash outflow to build productive capacity. Firms must rely on external financing during this phase to overcome the negative cash flow from operations and investing.

The growth phase portrays cash flow characteristics similar to the introduction phase. The growth phase reflects sales of successful products, and net income turns positive. A growing firm makes more sales, but it also needs to acquire more goods to sell. Because it usually must pay for the goods it acquires before it collects for the goods it sells, the growing firm finds itself ever short of cash from operations. The faster it grows (even though profitable), the more cash it needs. Banks do not like to lend for such needs. They view such needs (even though for current assets) as a permanent part of the firm's financing needs. Thus banks want firms to use shareholders' equity or long-term debt to finance growth in nonseasonal inventories and receivables.

The maturing of a product alters these cash flow relations. Net income usually reaches a peak, and working capital stops growing. Operations generate positive cash flow, enough to finance expenditures on property, plant, and equipment. Capital expenditures usually maintain, rather than increase, productive capacity. Firms use the excess cash flow to repay borrowing from the introduction and growth phases and to begin paying dividends to shareholders.

Weakening profitability—from reduced sales or reduced profit margins on existing sales—signals the beginning of the decline phase, but ever-declining accounts receivable and inventories can produce positive cash flow from operations. In addition, sales of unneeded property, plant, and equipment can result in positive cash flow from investing activities. Firms can use the excess cash flow to repay remaining debt or diversify into other areas of business.

Biotechnology and Internet firms are in their growth phase, consumer foods companies are in their mature phase, and steel manufacturers are in the late maturity or, perhaps, the early decline phase.

SOLUTION TO SELF-STUDY PROBLEM

SUGGESTED SOLUTION TO PROBLEM 13.1 FOR SELF-STUDY

(Effects of transactions on the statement of cash flows.)

a. The journal entry to record this transaction is as follows:

Cash	12,000	
Accumulated Depreciation	16,000	
Loss on Sale of Equipment	2,000	
Equipment		30,000

The debit to the Cash account results in an increase on Line (9) of $12,000. Selling equipment is an investing transaction, so Line (4) increases by $12,000. The loss on the sale reduces net income, so Line (1) decreases by $2,000. Because the loss does not use cash, Line (2) increases by $2,000 to add back the loss to net income when computing cash flow from operations.

b. The journal entry to record this transaction is as follows:

Cash	5,000	
Investment in Securities	15,000	
Equity in Earnings of Affiliate		20,000

The debit to the Cash account results in an increase on Line (9) of $5,000. Line (1) increases by $20,000 for the equity in earnings. Because the firm receives only $5,000 in cash, Line (3) must increase by $15,000 to subtract from earnings the excess of equity in earnings over the dividends received.

c. The journal entry to record this transaction is as follows:

Interest Expense	35,000	
Capitalized Lease Obligation	15,000	
Cash		50,000

The credit to the Cash account reduces Line (9) by $50,000. The recognition of interest expense reduces net income on Line (1) by $35,000. This amount represents an operating use of cash and therefore requires no addback or subtraction in computing cash flow from operations. The remaining cash payment of $15,000 is a financing use of cash, so Line (7) increases by $15,000.

d. The journal entry to record this transaction is as follows:

Income Tax Expense	120,000	
Deferred Tax Liability		30,000
Cash		90,000

The credit to the Cash account results in a reduction on Line (9) of $90,000. The recognition of income tax expense reduces net income on Line (1) by $120,000. Because the firm used only $90,000 in cash for income taxes this period, Line (2) increases by $30,000 for the portion of the expense that did not use cash.

e. The journal entry to record this transaction is as follows:

Cash	4,000	
Dividend Revenue		4,000

The debit to the Cash account results in an increase on Line (9) of $4,000. The recognition of dividend revenue increases net income on Line (1) by $4,000. Because dividends received from investments in securities are operating transactions and the amount of the dividends revenue equals the amount of cash received, the accountant makes no adjustment to net income when computing cash flow from operations.

PROBLEMS AND CASES

1. **Effects of transactions on statement of cash flows.** Exhibit 4.16 in Chapter 4 provides a simplified statement of cash flows. For each of the transactions that follow, indicate the number(s) of the line(s) in Exhibit 4.16 affected by the transaction and the amount and direction (increase or decrease) of the effect. If the transaction affects net income on line (1) or cash on line (9), be sure to indicate if it increases or decreases the line. Ignore income tax effects.

   a. A firm declares cash dividends of $15,000, of which it pays $12,000 immediately to its shareholders; it will pay the remaining $3,000 early in the next accounting period.

   b. A firm borrows $75,000 from its bank.

   c. A firm sells for $20,000 machinery originally costing $40,000 and with accumulated depreciation of $35,000.

   d. A firm as lessee records lease payments on operating leases of $28,000 for the period.

   e. A firm acquires, with temporarily excess cash, marketable equity securities costing $39,000.

   f. A firm writes off a fully depreciated truck originally costing $14,000.

   g. A marketable equity security (available for sale) acquired during the current period for $90,000 has a market value of $82,000 at the end of the period. Indicate the effect of any year-end adjusting entry to apply the market value method.

   h. A firm records interest expense of $15,000 for the period on bonds issued several years ago at a discount, comprising a $14,500 cash payment and a $500 addition to Bonds Payable.

   i. A firm records amortization of $22,000 for the period on goodwill arising from the acquisition several years ago of an 80 percent investment in a subsidiary.

   j. A firm acquires a building costing $400,000, paying $40,000 cash and signing a promissory note to the seller for $360,000.

   k. A firm using the allowance method records $32,000 of bad debt expense for the period.

   l. A firm using the allowance method writes off accounts totaling $28,000 as uncollectible.

   m. A firm owns 30 percent of the common stock of an investee acquired several years ago at book value. The investee had net income of $40,000 and paid dividends of $50,000 during the period.

   n. A firm sells for $22,000 marketable equity securities (available for sale) originally costing $25,000 and with a book value of $23,000 at the time of sale.

o. Holders of a firm's preferred stock with a book value of $10,000 convert their preferred shares into common stock with a par value of $2,000. Use the book value method.

p. A firm gives land with an acquisition cost and market value of $5,000 in settlement of the annual legal fees of its corporate attorney.

q. A firm reduces the liability account Rental Fees Received in Advance for $8,000 when it provides rental services.

r. A firm reclassifies long-term debt of $30,000, maturing within the next year, as a current liability.

s. A firm using the percentage-of-completion method for long-term contracts recognizes $15,000 of revenue for the period.

t. A local government donates land with a market value of $50,000 to a firm as an inducement to locate manufacturing facilities in the area.

u. A firm writes down long-term investments in securities by $8,000 to reflect the market value method.

v. A firm records $60,000 depreciation on manufacturing facilities for the period. The firm has sold all goods it manufactured this period.

w. A firm using the allowance method recognizes $35,000 as warranty expense for the period.

x. A firm using the allowance method makes expenditures totaling $28,000 to provide warranty services during the period.

y. A firm recognizes income tax expense of $80,000 for the period, comprising $100,000 paid currently and a $20,000 reduction in the Deferred Income Tax Liability account.

z. A firm writes down inventories by $18,000 to reflect the lower-of-cost-or-market valuation.

2. **Effect of transactions on cash changes equation.** Indicate the effect of each of the transactions in problem **1** on the cash change equation: $\Delta C = \Delta L + \Delta SE - \Delta N\$A$, where ΔC = change in cash, ΔL = change in liabilities, ΔSE = change in shareholders' equity, and $\Delta N\$A$ = change in noncash assets. If the transaction affects the income statement, indicate the effect on net income first and then indicate any adjustment made to net income to compute cash flow from operations using the indirect method. For example, the sale of land, originally costing $100, for $120 in cash affects the cash change equation as follows:

$$\Delta C \quad = \Delta L + \Delta SE - \Delta N\$A$$

Operations	+$ 20	= $0 +	$20	−	$0
Investing	+120	= 0 +	0	−	−100
Operations	−20				
Net	+$120	= $0 +	$20	−	−$100

3. **Working backward from the statement of cash flows.** Exhibit 13.5 presents a statement of cash flows for Alcoa for Year 9. Give the entry made on the T-account work sheet for each of the numbered line items. For example, the work sheet entry for Line (1) is as follows (amounts in millions):

Cash (Operations—Net Income)	$1,367.4	
Retained Earnings		$1,367.4

EXHIBIT 13.5	ALCOA Statement of Cash Flows for Year 9 (amounts in millions) (Problem 3)

OPERATIONS

(1) Net Income	$1,367.4
Adjustments for Noncash Transactions:	
(2) Depreciation	664.0
(3) Increase in Deferred Tax Liability	82.0
(4) Equity in Undistributed Earnings of Affiliates	(47.1)
(5) Gain from Sale of Marketable Securities	(20.8)
(6) (Increase) Decrease in Accounts Receivable	74.6
(7) (Increase) Decrease in Inventories	(198.9)
(8) (Increase) Decrease in Prepayments	(40.3)
(9) Increase (Decrease) in Accounts Payable	33.9
(10) Increase (Decrease) in Other Current Liabilities	(110.8)
Cash Flow from Operations	$1,804.0

INVESTING

(11) Sale of Marketable Securities	$ 49.8
(12) Acquisition of Marketable Securities	(73.2)
(13) Acquisition of Property, Plant, and Equipment	(875.7)
(14) Acquisition of Subsidiaries	(44.5)
Cash Flow from Investing	$ (943.6)

FINANCING

(15) Common Stock Issued to Employees	$ 34.4
(16) Repurchase of Common Stock	(100.9)
(17) Dividends Paid to Shareholders	(242.9)
(18) Additions to Short-term Borrowing	127.6
(19) Additions to Long-term Debt	121.6
(20) Payments on Long-term Dent	(476.4)
Cash Flow from Financing	$ (536.6)
Change in Cash	$ 323.8
Cash, Beginning of Year	506.8
Cash, End of Year	$ 830.6

SUPPLEMENTARY INFORMATION
Acquisition of Property, Plant, and Equipment by:

(21) Mortgaged Borrowing	$76.9
(22) Capital Leases	98.2
(23) Conversion of Debt into Common Stock	47.8

4. **Working backward from the statement of cash flows.** Exhibit 13.6 presents a statement of cash flows from Ingersoll-Rand for Year 5. Give the entry made on the T-account work sheet for each of the numbered line items. For example, the work sheet entry for Line (1) is as follows (amounts in millions):

Cash (Operations—Net income)	$270.3	
Retained Earnings		$270.3

EXHIBIT 13.6	INGERSOLL-RAND Statement of Cash Flows for Year 5 (amounts in millions) (Problem 4)

OPERATIONS

(1) Net Income	$ 270.3
Adjustments for Noncash Transactions:	
(2) Depreciation	179.4
(3) Gain on Sale of Property, Plant, and Equipment	(3.6)
(4) Equity in Earnings of Affiliates	(41.5)
(5) Deferred Income Taxes	15.1
(6) (Increase) Decrease in Accounts Receivable	50.9
(7) (Increase) Decrease in Inventories	(15.2)
(8) (Increase) Decrease in Other Current Assets	(33.1)
(9) Increase (Decrease) in Accounts Payable	(37.9)
(10) Increase (Decrease) in Other Current Liabilities	19.2
Cash Flow from Operations	$ 403.6

INVESTING

(11) Capital Expenditures	$(211.7)
(12) Proceeds from Sale of Property, Plant, and Equipment	26.5
(13) (Increase) Decrease in Marketable Securities	(4.6)
(14) Advances from Equity Companies	18.4
Cash Flow from Investing	$(171.4)

FINANCING

(15) Decrease in Short-term Borrowing	$ (81.5)
(16) Issue of Long-term Debt	147.6
(17) Payment of Long-term Debt	(129.7)
(18) Proceeds from Exercise of Stock Options	47.9
(19) Proceeds from Sale of Treasury Stock	59.3
(20) Dividends Paid	(78.5)
Cash Flow from Financing	$ (34.9)
Change in Cash	$ 197.3
Cash, Beginning of Year	48.3
Cash, End of Year	$ 245.6

SUPPLEMENTARY INFORMATON

(21) New Capital Leases Signed	$147.9
(22) Conversion of Preferred Stock into Common Stock	62.0
(23) Issue of Common Stock to Acquire Investments in Securities	94.3

5. Work Problem **46** in Chapter 8.
6. Work Problem **45** in Chapter 9.
7. Work Problem **55** in Chapter 11.
8. Work Problem **42** in Chapter 12.
9. **Preparing a statement of cash flows.** (Adapted from CPA examination.) The management of Warren Corporation, concerned over a decrease in cash, provides you with the comparative analysis of changes in account balances between December 31, Year 4, and December 31, Year 5, appearing in Exhibit 13.7.

EXHIBIT 13.7	WARREN CORPORATION Changes in Account Balances between December 31, Year 4, and December 31, Year 5 (Problem 9)

	December 31	
	Year 4	Year 5
DEBIT BALANCES		
Cash	$ 223,200	$ 174,000
Accounts Receivable	327,600	306,000
Inventories	645,600	579,600
Securities Held for Plant Expansion Purposes	—	180,000
Machinery and Equipment	776,400	1,112,400
Leasehold Improvements	104,400	104,400
Patents	36,000	33,360
Totals	$2,113,200	$2,489,760
CREDIT BALANCES		
Allowance for Uncollectible Accounts	$ 20,400	$ 19,200
Accumulated Depreciation of Machinery and Equipment	446,400	499,200
Allowance for Amortization of Leasehold Improvements	58,800	69,600
Accounts Payable	126,000	279,360
Cash Dividends Payable	—	48,000
Current Portion of 6 Percent Serial Bonds Payable	60,000	60,000
6 Percent Serial Bonds Payable (noncurrent portion)	360,000	300,000
Preferred Stock	120,000	108,000
Common Stock	600,000	600,000
Retained Earnings	321,600	506,400
Totals	$2,113,200	$2,489,760

During Year 5, Warren Corporation engaged in the following transactions:

(1) Purchased new machinery for $463,200. In addition, it sold certain obsolete machinery, having a book value of $73,200, for $57,600. It made no other entries in Machinery and Equipment or related accounts other than provisions for depreciation.

(2) Paid $2,400 of legal costs in a successful defense of a new patent, which it correctly debited to the Patents account. It recorded patent amortization amounting to $5,040 during Year 5.

(3) Purchased 120 shares of preferred stock, par value $100, at $110 and subsequently canceled it. Warren Corporation debited the premium paid to Retained Earnings.

(4) On December 10, Year 5, the board of directors declared a cash dividend of $.24 per share, payable to holders of common stock on January 10, Year 6.

(5) The following presents a comparative analysis of retained earnings as of December 31, Year 4 and Year 5:

	December 31	
	Year 4	**Year 5**
Balance, January 1	$157,200	$321,600
Net Income	206,400	234,000
	$363,600	$555,600
Dividends Declared	(42,000)	(48,000)
Premium on Preferred Stock Repurchased	—	(1,200)
Balance, December 31	$321,600	$506,400

(6) Warren Corporation wrote off accounts totaling $3,600 as uncollectible during Year 5.

   a. Prepare a T-account work sheet for the preparation of a statement of cash flows.

   b. Prepare a formal statement of cash flows for Warren Corporation for the year ending December 31, Year 5.

10. **Preparing a statement of cash flows.** (Adapted from CPA examination.) Roth Company has prepared its financial statements for the year ended December 31, Year 6, and for the three months ended March 31, Year 7. You have been asked to prepare a statement of cash flows for the three months ended March 31, Year 7. Exhibit 13.8 presents the company's balance sheet at December 31, Year 6, and March 31, Year 7, and Exhibit 13.9 presents its income statement for the three months ended March 31, Year 7. You are satisfied that the amounts presented are correct.

   Your discussion with the company's controller and a review of the financial records reveal the following information:

   (1) On January 8, Year 7, the company sold marketable securities for cash. The firm had purchased these securities on December 31, Year 6. The firm purchased no marketable securities during Year 7.

   (2) The company's preferred stock is convertible into common stock at a rate of one share of preferred for two shares of common. The preferred stock and common stock have par values of $2 and $2, respectively.

   (3) On January 17, Year 7, the local government condemned three acres of land. Roth Company received an award of $48,000 in cash on March 22, Year 7. It does not expect to purchase additional land as a replacement.

   (4) On March 25, Year 7, the company purchased equipment for cash.

   (5) Interest expense on bonds payable exceeded the cash coupon payments by $225 during the three-month period. On March 29, Year 7, the company issued bonds payable for cash.

   (6) The investment in the 30-percent-owned company includes an amount attributable to goodwill of $4,830 at December 31, Year 6. Roth Company amortizes goodwill at an annual rate of $720.

   (7) Roth Company declared $12,000 in dividends during the three months.

   a. Prepare a T-account work sheet for the preparation of a statement of cash flows, defining funds as cash and cash equivalents.

   b. Prepare a formal statement of cash flows for Roth Company for the three months ending March 31, Year 7.

11. **Preparing a statement of cash flows.** (Adapted from CPA examination.) Exhibit13.10 presents a comparative statement of financial position for Biddle Corporation

	Dec. 31, Year 6	Mar. 31, Year 7
EXHIBIT 13.8 ROTH COMPANY Balance Sheet (Problem 10)		

	Dec. 31, Year 6	Mar. 31, Year 7
Cash	$ 37,950	$131,100
Marketable Securities	24,000	10,200
Accounts Receivable (net)	36,480	73,980
Inventory	46,635	72,885
Total Current Assets	$145,065	$288,165
Land	60,000	28,050
Building	375,000	375,000
Equipment	—	122,250
Accumulated Depreciation	(22,500)	(24,375)
Investment in 30-Percent-Owned Company (using equity method)	91,830	100,470
Other Assets	22,650	22,650
Total Assets	$672,045	$912,210
Accounts Payable	$ 31,830	$ 25,995
Dividend Payable	—	12,000
Income Taxes Payable	—	51,924
Total Current Liabilities	$ 31,830	$ 89,919
Other Liabilities	279,000	279,000
Bonds Payable	71,550	169,275
Deferred Income Tax	765	1,269
Preferred Stock	45,000	—
Common Stock	120,000	165,000
Unrealized Holding Loss on Marketable Securities	(750)	(750)
Retained Earnings	124,650	208,497
Total Equities	$672,045	$912,210

EXHIBIT 13.9 ROTH COMPANY
Income Statement Data for the Three Months Ended March 31, Year 7
(Problem 10)

Sales	$364,212
Gain on Sale of Marketable Securities	3,600
Equity in Earnings of 30-Percent-Owned Company	8,820
Gain on Condemnation of Land	16,050
Total Revenues	$392,682
Cost of Sales	$207,612
General and Administration Expenses	33,195
Depreciation	1,875
Interest Expense	1,725
Income Taxes	52,428
Total Expenses	$296,835
Net Income	$ 95,847

as of December 31, Year 1 and Year 2. Exhibit 13.11 presents an income statement for Year 2. Additional information follows:

(1) On February 2, Year 2, Biddle issued a 10 percent stock dividend to shareholders of record on January 15, Year 2. The market price per share of the common stock on February 2, Year 2, was $15.

(2) On March 1, Year 2, Biddle issued 1,900 shares of common stock for land. The common stock and land had current market values of approximately $20,000 on March 1, Year 2.

(3) On April 15, Year 2, Biddle repurchased long-term bonds with a face and book value of $25,000. It reported the gain of $11,000 as an extraordinary item on the income statement.

(4) On June 30, Year 2, Biddle sold equipment costing $26,500, with a book value of $11,500, for $9,500 cash.

EXHIBIT 13.10	BIDDLE CORPORATION Statement of Financial Position (Problem 11)

	December 31	
	Year 1	**Year 2**
ASSETS		
Cash	$ 45,000	$ 50,000
Accounts Receivable (net of allowance for doubtful accounts of $10,000 and $8,000, respectively)	70,000	105,000
Inventories	110,000	130,000
Total Current Assets	$225,000	$285,000
Land	100,000	162,500
Plant and Equipment	316,500	290,000
Less Accumulated Depreciation	(50,000)	(45,000)
Patents	16,500	15,000
Total Assets	$608,000	$707,500
LIABILITIES AND SHAREHOLDERS' EQUITY		
Liabilities		
Accounts Payable	$100,000	$130,000
Accrued Liabilities	105,000	100,000
Total Current Liabilities	$205,000	$230,000
Deferred Income Taxes	50,000	70,000
Long-term Bonds (due December 15, Year 13)	90,000	65,000
Total Liabilities	$345,000	$365,000
Shareholders' Equity		
Common Stock, Par Value $5, Authorized 50,000 Shares, Issued and Outstanding 21,000 and 25,000 Shares, Respectively	$105,000	$125,000
Additional Paid-in Capital	85,000	116,500
Retained Earnings	73,000	101,000
Total Shareholders' Equity	$263,000	$342,500
Total Liabilities and Shareholders' Equity	$608,000	$707,500

EXHIBIT 13.11	BIDDLE CORPORATION Income Statement for the Year Ended December 31, Year 2 (Problem 11)

Sales	$500,000
Expenses:	
Cost of Goods Sold	$280,000
Salary and Wages	95,000
Depreciation	10,000
Patent Amortization	1,500
Loss on Sale of Equipment	2,000
Interest	8,000
Miscellaneous	4,000
Total Expenses	$400,500
Income before Income Taxes and Extraordinary Item	$ 99,500
Income Taxes	
Current	$ 25,000
Deferred	20,000
Provision for Income Taxes	$ 45,000
Income before Extraordinary Item	$ 54,500
Extraordinary Item—Gain on Repurchase of Long-term Bonds (net of $5,000 income tax)	6,000
Net Income	$ 60,500
Earnings per Share:	
Income before Extraordinary Item	$2.21
Extraordinary Item	0.24
Net Income	$2.45

(5) On September 30, Year 2, Biddle declared and paid a $.04 per share cash dividend to shareholders of record on August 1, Year 2.

(6) On October 10, Year 2, Biddle purchased land for $42,500 cash.

(7) Deferred income taxes represent timing differences relating to the use of different depreciation methods for income tax and financial statement reporting.

    a. Prepare a T-account work sheet for the preparation of a statement of cash flows.

    b. Prepare a formal statement of cash flows for Biddle Corporation for the year ended December 31, Year 2.

12. **Preparing a statement of cash flows.** (Adapted from CPA examination.) Exhibit 13.12 presents the comparative balance sheets for Plainview Corporation for Year 4 and Year 5.

    The following additional information relates to Year 5 activities:

    (1) The Retained Earnings account changed as follows:

Retained Earnings, December 31, Year 4		$758,200
Add Net Income after Extraordinary Items (loss of $3,000)		236,580
Subtotal		$994,780
Deduct:		
Cash Dividends	$130,000	
Loss on Reissue of Treasury Stock	3,000	
Stock Dividend	100,200	233,200
Retained Earnings, December 31, Year 5		$761,580

EXHIBIT 13.12	PLAINVIEW CORPORATION Comparative Balance Sheets December 31, Year 4 and Year 5 (Problem 12)

	Year 4	Year 5
ASSETS		
Cash	$ 165,300	$ 142,100
Marketable Securities (at market value)	129,200	122,600
Accounts Receivable (net)	371,200	312,200
Inventories	124,100	255,200
Prepayments	22,000	23,400
Bond Sinking Fund	63,000	—
Investment in Subsidiary (at equity)	152,000	134,080
Plant and Equipment (net)	1,534,600	1,443,700
Total Assets	$2,561,400	$2,433,280
EQUITIES		
Accounts Payable	$ 213,300	$ 238,100
Notes Payable—Current	145,000	—
Accrued Payables	18,000	16,500
Income Taxes Payable	31,000	97,500
Deferred Income Taxes (noncurrent)	128,400	127,900
6 Percent Mortgage Bonds Payable (due Year 17)	310,000	—
8 Percent Debentures Payable (due Year 25)	—	125,000
Common Stock, $10 Par Value	950,000	1,033,500
Additional Paid-in Capital	51,000	67,700
Accumulated Other Comprehensive Income		
Unrealized Holding Gain on Marketable Securities	2,500	2,500
Retained Earnings	755,700	759,080
Treasury Stock—at Cost of $3 per Share	(43,500)	(34,500)
Total Equities	$2,561,400	$2,433,280

(2) On January 2, Year 5, Plainview Corporation sold for $127,000 marketable securities with an acquisition cost and a book value of $110,000. The firm used the proceeds from this sale, the funds in the bond sinking fund, and the amount received from the issuance of the 8 percent debentures to retire the 6 percent mortgage bonds. The firm accrues income taxes on any gain or loss on retirement at 40 percent.

(3) The firm reissued treasury stock on February 28, Year 5. It treats "losses" on the reissue of treasury stock as a charge to Retained Earnings.

(4) The firm declared a stock dividend on October 31, Year 5, when the market price of Plainview Corporation's stock was $12 per share.

(5) On April 30, Year 5, a fire destroyed a warehouse that cost $100,000 and on which depreciation of $65,000 had accumulated. The loss was not insured. Plainview Corporation properly included the loss in the Continuing Operations section of the income statement.

(6) Plant and equipment transactions consisted of the sale of a building at its book value of $4,000 and the purchase of machinery for $28,000.

(7) The firm wrote off accounts receivable as uncollectible totaling $16,300 in Year 4 and $18,500 in Year 5. It recognized expired insurance of $4,100 in Year 4 and $3,900 in Year 5.

(8) The subsidiary, which is 40 percent owned, reported a loss of $44,800 for Year 5.

   a. Prepare a T-account work sheet for Plainview Corporation for Year 5, defining funds as cash and cash equivalents.

   b. Prepare a formal statement of cash flows for the year ending December 31, Year 5.

13. **Preparing and interpreting the statement of cash flows.** UAL Corporation is the parent company for United Airlines. Exhibit 13.13 presents a comparative balance sheet,

EXHIBIT 13.13	UAL CORPORATION Comparative Balance Sheet (amounts in millions) (Problem 13)		

	December 31		
	Year 8	Year 9	Year 10
ASSETS			
Cash	$1,087	$ 465	$ 221
Marketable Securities	—	1,042	1,066
Accounts Receivable (net)	741	888	913
Inventories	210	249	323
Prepayments	112	179	209
Total Current Assets	$2,150	$2,823	$2,732
Property, Plant, and Equipment	7,710	7,704	8,587
Accumulated Depreciation	(3,769)	(3,805)	(3,838)
Other Assets	610	570	605
Total Assets	$6,701	$7,292	$8,086
LIABILITIES AND SHAREHOLDERS' EQUITY			
Accounts Payable	$ 540	$ 596	$ 552
Short-term Borrowing	121	446	447
Current Portion of Long-term Debt	110	84	89
Advances from Customers	619	661	843
Other Current Liabilities	1,485	1,436	1,826
Total Current Liabilities	$2,875	$3,223	$3,757
Long-term Debt	1,418	1,334	1,475
Deferred Tax Liability	352	364	368
Other Noncurrent Liabilities	715	719	721
Total Liabilities	$5,360	$5,640	$6,321
Common Stock	$ 119	$ 119	$ 120
Additional Paid-in Capital	48	48	52
Accumulated Other Comprehensive Income			
Unrealized Holding Gain on Marketable Securities	—	85	92
Retained Earnings	1,188	1,512	1,613
Treasury Stock	(14)	(112)	(112)
Total Shareholders' Equity	$1,341	$1,652	$1,765
Total Liabilities and Shareholders' Equity	$6,701	$7,292	$8,086

EXHIBIT 13.14	UAL CORPORATION Comparative Income Statement (amounts in millions) (Problem 13)

	Year 9	Year 10
REVENUES		
Sales	$ 9,794	$11,037
Interest Revenue	121	123
Gains on Dispositions of Property, Plant, and Equipment	106	286
Total Revenues	$10,021	$11,446
EXPENSES		
Compensation	$ 3,158	$ 3,550
Fuel	1,353	1,811
Commissions	1,336	1,719
Depreciation	517	560
Other Operating Costs	2,950	3,514
Interest	169	121
Income Taxes	214	70
Total Expenses	$ 9,697	$11,345
Net Income	$ 324	$ 101

and Exhibit 13.14 presents a comparative income statement for UAL Corporation for Year 9 and Year 10. Expenditures on new property, plant, and equipment were $1,568 million in Year 9 and $2,821 million in Year 10. Changes in other noncurrent assets are investing activities, and changes in other noncurrent liabilities are financing activities.

   a. Prepare T-account work sheets for Year 9 and Year 10 for a statement of cash flows.
   b. Prepare a comparative statement of cash flows for Year 9 and Year 10.
   c. Comment on the relations between cash flows from operating, investing, and financing activities for Year 9 and Year 10.

14. **Preparing and interpreting the statement of cash flows.** Irish Paper Company (Irish) manufactures and markets various paper products around the world. Paper manufacturing is a capital-intensive activity. A firm that does not adequately use its manufacturing capacity will experience poor operating performance. Sales of paper products tend to be cyclical with general economic conditions, although consumer paper products are less cyclical than business paper products.

   Exhibit 13.15 presents comparative income statements, and Exhibit 13.16 presents comparative balance sheets for Irish Paper Company for Year 9, Year 10, and Year 11. Additional information appears below (amounts in millions).

(1) **Cash Flow Information**	Year 9	Year 10	Year 11
Investments in Affiliates[a]	$ (92)	$ 86	$ (13)
Expenditures on Property, Plant, and Equipment	(775)	(931)	(315)
Long-term Debt Issued	449	890	36

[a]Excludes earnings and dividends.

EXHIBIT 13.15	IRISH PAPER COMPANY Comparative Income Statements (amounts in millions) (Problem 14)

	Year 9	Year 10	Year 11
Sales	$5,066	$5,356	$4,976
Equity in Earnings of Affiliates	31	38	30
Interest Income	34	23	60
Gain (Loss) on Sale of Property, Plant, and Equipment	221	19	(34)
Total Revenues	$5,352	$5,436	$5,032
Cost of Goods Sold	$3,493	$3,721	$3,388
Selling Expenses	857	925	1,005
Administrative Expenses	303	414	581
Interest Expense	158	199	221
Income Tax Expense	165	8	(21)
Total Expenses	$4,976	$5,267	$5,174
Net Income	$ 376	$ 169	$ (142)

(2) Depreciation expense was $306 million in Year 9, $346 million in Year 10, and $353 million in Year 11.

(3) During Year 9, Irish purchased outstanding stock warrants for $201 million. It recorded the transaction by debiting the Common Stock account.

(4) During Year 9, Irish sold timberlands at a gain. It received cash of $5 million and a long-term note receivable for $220 million, which it includes in Other Assets on the balance sheet.

(5) In addition to the cash expenditures presented above, Irish acquired property, plant, and equipment during Year 10 costing $221 million by assuming a long-term mortgage payable.

(6) During Year 11, Irish resold treasury stock for an amount greater than its cost.

(7) Changes in Other Assets are investing activities.

    a. Prepare T-account work sheets for a statement of cash flows for Irish for Year 9, Year 10, and Year 11.

    b. Prepare a comparative statement of cash flows for Irish for Year 9, Year 10, and Year 11.

    c. Comment on the pattern of cash flows from operating, investing, and financing activities for each of the three years.

15. **Preparing a statement of cash flows.** (Adapted from a problem prepared by Stephen A. Zeff.) Selected information from the accounting records of Breda Enterprises Inc. appears below. The firm uses a calendar year as its reporting period. You are asked to prepare a statement of cash flows for Breda Enterprises Inc. for Year 6. Key all figures in the statement of cash flows to the numbered items below.

(1) Net income for Year 6 is $90,000.

EXHIBIT 13.16	IRISH PAPER COMPANY Comparative Balance Sheets (amounts in millions) (Problem 14)

	Year 8	Year 9	Year 10	Year 11
ASSETS				
Cash	$ 374	$ 49	$ 114	$ 184
Accounts Receivable (net)	611	723	829	670
Inventories	522	581	735	571
Prepayments	108	54	54	56
Total Current Assets	$1,615	$1,407	$1,732	$1,481
Investments in Affiliates	254	375	322	333
Property, Plant, and Equipment	5,272	5,969	7,079	7,172
Accumulated Depreciation	(2,160)	(2,392)	(2,698)	(2,977)
Other Assets	175	387	465	484
Total Assets	$5,156	$5,746	$6,900	$6,493
LIABILITIES AND SHAREHOLDERS' EQUITY				
Accounts Payable	$ 920	$ 992	$1,178	$1,314
Current Portion of Long-term Debt	129	221	334	158
Other Current Liabilities	98	93	83	38
Total Current Liabilities	$1,147	$1,306	$1,595	$1,510
Long-term Debt	1,450	1,678	2,455	2,333
Deferred Income Taxes	607	694	668	661
Total Liabilities	$3,204	$3,678	$4,718	$4,504
Preferred Stock	$ 7	$ 7	$ 7	$ 7
Common Stock	629	428	432	439
Retained Earnings	1,331	1,648	1,758	1,557
Treasury Stock	(15)	(15)	(15)	(14)
Total Shareholders' Equity	$1,952	$2,068	$2,182	$1,989
Total Liabilities and Shareholders' Equity	$5,156	$5,746	$6,900	$6,493

(2) Beginning and ending balances in three accounts relating to the firm's customers were as follows:

	December 31, Year 5	December 31, Year 6
Accounts Receivable (gross)	$41,000	$53,000
Allowance for Uncollectible Accounts	$ 1,800	$ 3,200
Advances from Customers	$ 3,700	$ 1,000

On November 1, Year 6, a customer gave the firm a six-month, 8 percent, $15,000 note in satisfaction of an account receivable of $15,000. Interest is payable at maturity. This was the only note receivable held by the company during Year 6.

(3) The balances in Merchandise Inventory and Accounts Payable were as follows:

	December 31, Year 5	December 31, Year 6
Merchandise Inventory	$47,000	$43,000
Accounts Payable	$27,000	$39,000

(4) During Year 6 the firm sold, for $25,000 cash, equipment with a book value of $38,000. The firm also purchased equipment for cash. Depreciation expense for Year 6 was $42,000. The balance in the Equipment account at acquisition cost decreased $26,000 between the beginning and end of Year 6. The balance in the Accumulated Depreciation account increased $11,000 between the beginning and end of Year 6.

(5) The balances in the Leasehold Asset and Lease Liability accounts were as follows on various dates:

	December 31, Year 4	December 31, Year 5	December 31, Year 6
Leasehold Asset (net)	$0	$76,000	$71,000
Lease Liability	$0	$76,000	$73,600

On December 31, Year 5, the firm signed a long-term lease which, by its terms, qualified as a capital lease. The firm made a payment under the lease of $10,000 on December 31, Year 6.

(6) The firm declared cash dividends during Year 6 of $26,000, of which $10,000 remains unpaid on December 31, Year 6. During Year 6, the firm paid $8,000 cash for dividends declared during Year 5.

(7) The firm classifies all marketable securities as available for sale. It purchased no marketable securities during Year 6 but sold marketable equity securities that had originally cost $4,500 for $9,100 cash in November, Year 6. The market and book values of marketable equity securities were $4,000 on December 31, Year 5, and $10,500 on December 31, Year 6.

(8) Investors in $100,000 face value of convertible bonds of Breda Enterprises Inc. converted them into 8,000 shares of the firm's $12-par value common stock during Year 6. The common stock had a market value of $15 per share on the conversion date. Breda Enterprises Inc. had originally issued the bonds at a premium. Their book value on the date of the conversion was $105,000. The firm chose the generally accepted (alternative) accounting principle of recording the issuance of the common stock at market value and recognizing a loss of $15,000. The loss is not classified as an extraordinary item. The firm amortized $1,500 of the bond premium between January 1, Year 6, and the date of the conversion.

16. **Interpreting the statement of cash flows.** Exhibit 13.17 presents a statement of cash flows for L.A. Gear, manufacturer of athletic shoes and sportswear, for three recent years.

    a. What is the likely reason for the negative cash flow from operations?

    b. How did L.A. Gear finance the negative cash flow from operations during each of the three years? Suggest reasons for L.A. Gear's choice of financing source for each year.

	L.A. GEAR		
EXHIBIT 13.17	Statement of Cash Flows (amounts in thousands) (Problem 16)		

	December 31		
	Year 8	**Year 9**	**Year 10**
OPERATIONS			
Net Income	$ 4,371	$ 22,030	$ 55,059
Depreciation	133	446	1,199
Noncash Compensation to Employees	—	—	558
Increase in Accounts Receivable	(12,410)	(34,378)	(51,223)
Increase in Inventories	(1,990)	(50,743)	(72,960)
Increase in Prepayments	(599)	(2,432)	(8,624)
Increase in Accounts Payable	1,656	7,197	17,871
Increase (Decrease) in Other Current Liabilities	(537)	11,193	10,587
Cash Flow from Operations	$(9,376)	$(46,687)	$(47,533)
INVESTING			
Sale of Marketable Securities	$ 5,661	—	—
Acquisition of Property, Plant, and Equipment	(874)	$ (2,546)	$ (6,168)
Acquisition of Other Noncurrent Assets	(241)	(406)	(246)
Cash Flow from Investing	$ 4,546	$ (2,952)	$ (6,414)
FINANCING			
Increase (Decrease) in Short-term Borrowing	$ 4,566	$ 50,104	$(19,830)
Issue of Common Stock	—	495	69,925
Cash Flow from Financing	$ 4,566	$ 50,599	$ 50,095
Change in Cash	$ (264)	$ 960	$ (3,852)
Cash, Beginning of Year	3,509	3,245	4,205
Cash, End of Year	$ 3,245	$ 4,205	$ 353

c. Expenditures on property, plant, and equipment substantially exceeded the add-back for depreciation expense each year. What is the likely explanation for this difference in amounts?

d. The addback for depreciation expense is a relatively small proportion of net income. What is the likely explanation for this situation?

e. L.A. Gear had no long-term debt in its capital structure during Year 7 through Year 9. What is the likely explanation for such a financial structure?

17. **Interpreting the statement of cash flows.** Exhibit 13.18 presents a statement of cash flows for Campbell Soup Company for three recent years. Campbell Soup Company is in the consumer foods industry, a relatively mature industry in the United States.

a. Cash flow from operations each year approximately equals net income plus add-backs for depreciation, deferred taxes, and other. What is the likely explanation for this relation?

b. In the Investing section of Campbell's statement of cash flow, what are the indications that the company is in a relatively mature industry?

c. In the Financing section of Campbell's statement of cash flows, what are the indications that the company is in a relatively mature industry?

EXHIBIT 13.18	CAMPBELL SOUP COMPANY Statement of Cash Flows (amounts in millions) (Problem 17)

	Year 6	Year 7	Year 8
OPERATIONS			
Net Income	$ 223	$ 247	$ 274
Depreciation	127	145	171
Deferred Income Taxes	29	46	31
Other Addbacks	21	34	11
(Increase) in Accounts Receivable	(19)	(40)	(55)
(Increase) Decrease in Inventories	13	(13)	6
(Increase) in Prepayments	(7)	(11)	(40)
Increase in Accounts Payable	27	53	72
Increase (Decrease) in Other Current Liabilities	29	2	(1)
Cash Flow from Operations	$ 443	$ 463	$ 469
INVESTING			
Sale of Property, Plant, and Equipment	$ 30	$ 21	$ 41
Sale of Marketable Securities	328	535	319
Acquisition of Property, Plant, and Equipment	(275)	(250)	(245)
Acquisition of Marketable Securities	(472)	(680)	(70)
Acquisition of Investments in Securities	—	—	(472)
Other Investing Transactions	(5)	(34)	(48)
Cash Flow from Investing	$(394)	$(408)	$(475)
FINANCING			
Increase in Short-term Borrowing	—	$ 5	$ 86
Increase in Long-term Borrowing	$ 220	29	103
Issue of Common Stock	4	2	—
Decrease in Short-term Borrowing	(3)	—	(5)
Decrease in Long-term Borrowing	(168)	(27)	(106)
Acquisition of Common Stock	—	—	(28)
Dividends	(84)	(92)	(103)
Cash Flow from Financing	$ (31)	$ (83)	$ (53)
Change in Cash	$ 18	$ (28)	$ (59)
Cash, Beginning of Year	155	173	145
Cash, End of Year	$ 173	$ 145	$ 86

PART FOUR

SYNTHESIS

4

SIGNIFICANCE AND IMPLICATIONS OF ALTERNATIVE ACCOUNTING PRINCIPLES

1. Review the process through which standard-setting bodies establish acceptable accounting principles.
2. Review the generally accepted accounting principles discussed in previous chapters, emphasizing the effects of alternative principles on the financial statements.
3. Consider the effects of alternative accounting principles on investment decisions and market values of firms.
4. Understand the factors that firms consider in choosing their accounting principles from the set of acceptable principles.

The independent accountant expresses an unqualified opinion on a firm's financial statements by noting that the statements follow generally accepted accounting principles (GAAP). Previous chapters described and illustrated the important accounting principles that firms currently use in preparing their financial statements. This chapter focuses on the following questions:

1. How do standard-setting bodies select the set of GAAP from the universe of possible principles?
2. How do alternative accounting principles affect the financial statements?
3. How do alternative accounting principles affect investment decisions and the market prices of a firm's debt and equity securities?
4. What criteria should a firm use to select its accounting principles from those that the accounting profession considers generally acceptable?

Refer to Figure 14.1. Circle A indicates the universe of possible accounting principles. The dashed line represents the difficulty of defining the relative size, or boundaries, of possible accounting principles. Circle B represents the set of accounting principles designated as generally acceptable by standard-setting bodies. Circle C represents an individual firm's selection of accounting principles. This chapter discusses the narrowing from

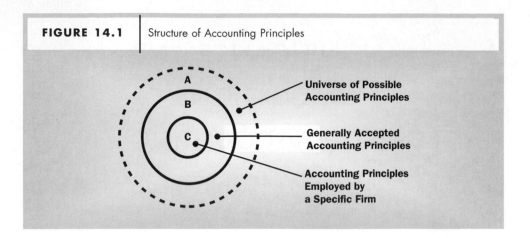

FIGURE 14.1 | Structure of Accounting Principles

Circle A to Circle C. Anyone who understands the significance and implications of alternative GAAP can read and interpret published financial statements more effectively. This chapter uses the terms *accounting principles, standards,* and *methods* interchangeably.

ESTABLISHING ACCEPTABLE ACCOUNTING PRINCIPLES

A standard-setting body within each country typically has authority to select the accounting principles that firms must follow in preparing financial statements within that country. Chapter 1 discussed several issues regarding the selection and operation of this standard-setting body:

1. Should a governmental body or a private-sector body set acceptable accounting principles?
2. Should standard-setting bodies require uniform accounting principles for all firms, or should they allow firms a degree of flexibility to choose the accounting methods that most effectively measure the economic effects of their activities?
3. Should standard-setting bodies require firms to use the same accounting principles for both financial reporting and income tax reporting?
4. Should standard-setting bodies select acceptable accounting principles by establishing a broad theoretical framework and then deducing the accounting methods most consistent with this theoretical framework? Alternatively, should standard-setting bodies follow a democratic process and choose those accounting principles most favored by preparers, users, and others involved with financial accounting reports?

STANDARD SETTING IN THE UNITED STATES

Congress has the ultimate authority to specify acceptable accounting principles in the United States. It has delegated its authority in almost all cases to the **Securities and Exchange Commission (SEC),** an agency of the federal government. The SEC has indicated that it will generally accept pronouncements of the **Financial Accounting Standards Board (FASB)** as constituting acceptable accounting principles. Although this delegation of authority suggests that the standard-setting process resides primarily in the private sector in the United States, in reality the SEC and the FASB communicate continually as reporting issues arise. The FASB, at the SEC's urging, formed the

Emerging Issues Task Force (EITF) to deal with new reporting issues when the FASB has not yet issued statements.

Firms in the United States have varying degrees of flexibility in choosing their accounting principles. In some instances, the specific conditions associated with a transaction or event dictate the accounting method used. For example, the method of accounting for investments in common stock of other firms depends primarily on the ownership percentage. In other instances, firms have wider flexibility in choosing among alternative methods, such as in selecting a cost flow assumption for inventories and cost of goods sold and in selecting depreciation methods. One might characterize the range of acceptable accounting principles in the United States as one of constrained flexibility.

The delegation of authority to the SEC and the FASB to set accounting principles in part recognizes that the information needs of users of financial accounting reports differ from the government's need to raise tax revenues. Thus, with the exception of the LIFO cost flow assumption for inventories, firms need not use the same methods of accounting for financial reporting and for tax reporting.

In selecting accounting principles, the FASB follows a process that incorporates both deduction from a broad theoretical framework and induction from the information needs and preferences of its various constituencies. Figure 1.4 in Chapter 1 summarizes the FASB's **conceptual framework.** Chapters 2 through 4 discuss more fully the concepts of assets, liabilities, revenues, expenses, and cash flows. The FASB uses this conceptual framework in guiding its selection of acceptable accounting principles.

The conceptual framework does not always give the FASB clear guidance when it considers alternative methods to account for a particular transaction or event. The conceptual framework includes broad financial reporting objectives and general concepts. Standard-setters often logically deduce more than one accounting method from such a framework. Furthermore, preparers and users of financial accounting reports often lobby for other methods to account for a transaction or event. They sometimes argue that they cannot cost-effectively apply accounting methods under consideration by the FASB or that the methods will seriously disrupt firms' decisions or capital markets. Refer, for example, to the discussion in Chapter 12 on the accounting for employee stock options. The FASB proposed an accounting method that would have required firms to recognize additional expenses, thereby lowering net income. Intense lobbying against the proposed accounting standard bombarded the FASB. The FASB settled on a standard that allows firms to disclose the earnings effects of stock options in notes to the financial statements instead of in the income statement. Such lobbying shows the political nature of the standard-setting process and illustrates the difficulties that standard-setting bodies encounter when moving from Circle A to Circle B of Figure 14.1.

STANDARD-SETTING IN OTHER COUNTRIES

Until recently, the standard-setting process varied widely across countries. Governmental agencies played a major role in establishing acceptable accounting principles in some countries. Examples include Germany, France, and Japan. The methods of accounting that firms used for financial reporting closely conformed to the methods of accounting used in preparing income tax returns. Ownership of common stock in these countries typically resided in a few wealthy families and in large corporations and financial institutions. These shareholders closely monitored the activities of the businesses that they owned. Thus, there was less need to use financial statements as a source of information for assessing operating performance and financial position. The need to raise income taxes in an efficient manner and the desire to use the income tax system to achieve certain public policy goals had a major influence on establishing acceptable accounting principles.

Other countries followed a standard-setting process similar to that of the United States: a private-sector body set acceptable accounting principles. Examples include the United Kingdom, Canada, and Australia. Broad public ownership characterizes stock ownership in these countries. Financial statements serve as a major source of information for shareholders to monitor the activities of firms in which they invest funds. The accounting principles that firms use for financial reporting often differ from the methods used for income tax purposes.

These different approaches to setting accounting standards resulted in different accounting principles across countries and a lack of comparability of financial statement information. The **International Accounting Standards Committee (IASC),** an entity comprising representatives from most industrialized countries of the world, has endeavored since the early 1970s to achieve greater uniformity in accounting principles. The IASC has no legal authority to set accounting principles within individual countries. Its process has been to encourage IASC representatives to obtain their countries' acceptance of pronouncements of the IASC.

Until the mid-1990s, the progress in reducing worldwide diversity in accounting principles was slow. The rapid growth of global business, cross-border mergers and acquisitions, and capital market integration during the last several years have fostered greater realization of the need for comparable financial statement information across firms and across countries. In 1995 the International Organization of Securities Commissions (IOSCO) challenged the IASC to develop by 1998 a set of core accounting principles acceptable to that association. Members of that association, including the SEC in the United States, would then push for legislation within their countries to allow any firm whose financial statements conform to IASC accounting principles to list their shares of common stock on stock exchanges within that country. The financial statements of the listed firms would not need to conform to accounting principles established by standard-setting bodies within the country as long as they were consistent with IASC pronouncements. The accounting principles developed by the IASC are similar, with a few exceptions, to those discussed in this book.

As this book goes to press, the process described above is well under way. However, it has not progressed to the point where IASC pronouncements carry the full weight of accounting principles set within individual countries. The pressures for greater comparability in worldwide financial reporting have never been greater. Thus, one can expect even more rapid progress in the program set forth by the International Organization of Securities Commissions.

REVIEW OF GENERALLY ACCEPTED ACCOUNTING PRINCIPLES

This section summarizes the major currently acceptable accounting principles in the United States and as set forth by the IASC. Previous chapters have discussed these GAAP.

REVENUE RECOGNITION

A firm may recognize revenue

1. at the time it sells goods or renders services (typical under the accrual basis of accounting),
2. at the time it collects cash (installment method or cost-recovery-first method),
3. as it engages in production or construction (percentage-of-completion method for long-term contracts), or

4. perhaps not until the customer no longer has the right to return goods for a refund (such as when a firm gives customers the right to return goods for a specified time after purchase).

Recognizing revenue at the time of production or construction reports the largest cumulative income statement earnings and balance sheet assets. Recognition at the time of sale reports the next-largest cumulative income and assets, followed by recognition at the time of cash collection or at the time the refund period expires. However, the revenue recognition method that produces the largest earnings for any particular accounting period depends on the growth characteristics of a firm. Growing firms generally report the largest earnings each period when they recognize revenue at the time of production or construction. Declining firms generally report the largest earnings each period when they recognize revenue at the time of cash collection. When firms neither grow nor decline, the income recognition methods usually report similar earnings amounts each period. To repeat a theme of this book, over long time periods, cumulative income must equal cash inflows minus cash outflows other than transactions with owners. Different revenue recognition methods, and different accounting methods generally, affect only the timing of recognition, not the amount of revenue.

To recognize revenue, a firm must have

1. performed all, or most, of the services it expects to provide and
2. received cash or some other asset, such as a receivable, susceptible to reasonably precise measurement.

The generality of these criteria provides firms with flexibility in choosing their revenue recognition method. Most firms recognize revenue at the time they sell (deliver) goods or render services. Firms that conduct operations using multiyear contracts, such as construction companies, generally recognize revenue throughout the contract period using the percentage-of-completion method.

UNCOLLECTIBLE ACCOUNTS

A firm may recognize an expense for uncollectible accounts in the period when it recognizes revenue (allowance method) or, if it cannot reasonably predict the amount of uncollectibles, in the period when it discovers that it cannot collect specific accounts (direct write-off method). The allowance method results in the smallest cumulative earnings and assets on the balance sheet because it recognizes bad debt expense earlier than the direct write-off method. The method that produces the largest earnings for any particular period depends on the growth characteristics of the firm and on the amounts judged uncollectible during the period.

GAAP require firms with predictable uncollectible amounts to use the allowance method in financial reporting. Income tax laws require U.S. firms to use the direct write-off method for tax reporting under all circumstances.

INVENTORIES

A firm records its inventories using one of several bases: acquisition cost, lower of acquisition cost or market, standard cost, and in the case of some by-products and precious minerals, net realizable value. When the firm cannot (or chooses not to) specifically identify which goods it sold, the firm makes a cost flow assumption. Allowable cost flow assumptions include FIFO, LIFO, and weighted average, although the IASC expresses a preference for FIFO or weighted average. FIFO generally provides the largest earnings and assets valuations when acquisition costs increase and the lowest earnings and assets valuations when acquisition costs decline. LIFO usually provides the smallest earnings and assets valuations when acquisitions costs increase and the highest when they decline. The weighted-average cost flow assumption provides earnings amounts between those for FIFO and LIFO but with expense, income, and asset valuation amounts similar to those under FIFO.

The extent to which net income and assets differ under FIFO, LIFO, and weighted-average cost flow assumptions depends on three factors: the relative magnitude of acquisition cost changes, the rate of inventory turnover, and the presence or absence of a LIFO layer liquidation. Relatively small changes in acquisition costs cause minor differences in earnings and asset valuations, whereas larger changes magnify the differences. A rapid rate of inventory turnover reduces the difference in effects of the three cost flow assumptions, whereas a slower rate magnifies the differences. If a firm must dip into old LIFO layers priced at acquisition costs significantly higher or lower than current costs, generalizations about the effect of LIFO on earnings and assets will not usually hold.

Firms have some latitude in selecting a cost flow assumption for financial and tax reporting. A U.S. firm must, however, use LIFO for financial reporting if it uses LIFO in tax reporting.

INVESTMENTS IN SECURITIES

A U.S. firm accounts for investments in the common stock securities of other firms using the market value method or the equity method, or it prepares consolidated statements, depending on its ownership percentage. IASC standards also permit the use of the lower-of-cost-or-market method. These four accounting methods provide different financial statement effects as follows:

Accounting Method	Income Statement	Balance Sheet
Market Value	Dividends received or receivable and realized holding gains and losses	Market value
Lower of Cost or Market	Dividends received or receivable, unrealized holding losses, realized holding gains and losses	Lower of cost or market
Equity	Share of investee's earnings	Acquisition cost plus share of investee's earnings minus dividends received
Consolidation	Subsidiary's revenues and expenses minus minority interest in net income of subsidiary	Subsidiary's assets and liabilities minus minority interest in net assets of subsidiary

Net income reported by the equity method equals that reported in consolidated statements, although individual revenue and expense amounts differ. Total assets and total liabilities in consolidated statements usually exceed those under the equity method, but total shareholders' equity is the same under the two methods.

The accounting method used for financial reporting depends primarily on the owner's ability to significantly influence the investee company, with presumption of influence based on the percentage of outstanding shares held. U.S. firms holding less than 20 percent of another firm's outstanding shares generally use the market value method. Firms in most other countries use the lower-of-cost-or-market method. The equity method applies to holdings between 20 percent and 50 percent. Generally, firms must prepare consolidated financial statements when the ownership percentage exceeds 50 percent. Firms must use the equity method when owning less than 20 percent if they can exert significant influence over an investee and must not use it, even when owning more than 20 percent, if they cannot exert significant influence. Firms do not consolidate a majority-owned subsidiary if they control it only temporarily. For example, a firm would not consolidate a subsidiary if it intends to dispose of its controlling interest soon. A firm would also not consolidate a subsidiary if it cannot exercise majority control. For example, a parent company would not consolidate a subsidiary in bankruptcy, and therefore under the control of the courts, or a subsidiary in a foreign country that does not allow the parent to withdraw cash or other assets from the subsidiary.

MACHINERY, EQUIPMENT, AND OTHER DEPRECIABLE ASSETS

Firms may depreciate fixed assets using the straight-line, declining-balance, sum-of-the-years'-digits, or units-of-production methods. In countries where tax reporting historically played a major role in establishing acceptable accounting principles, such as Germany, France, and Japan, firms tend to use accelerated depreciation methods for financial reporting. In countries with a history of using different methods of accounting for financial and tax reporting, such as the United States and the United Kingdom, firms tend to use the straight-line method.

The straight-line method usually provides the largest cumulative earnings and asset valuations, followed by the sum-of-the-years'-digits method and then the declining-balance methods. The financial statement effects of the units-of-production method depend on the intensity of use of the asset. The straight-line method usually results in the largest earnings for any period when a firm increases its depreciable assets and the smallest earnings when a firm decreases depreciable assets. When acquisition costs of depreciable assets remain stable and firms maintain their level of investment in such assets, the depreciation methods produce similar earnings and balance sheet effects.

Firms can choose any of these depreciation methods for financial reporting. Firms will frequently use different estimates of service lives for similar assets, partly as a function of the intended intensity of use and the maintenance or repair policy. Income tax laws specify the depreciation methods and service lives for various types of depreciable assets. The depreciation rates incorporate declining-balance depreciation methods. Income tax laws in most countries do not require conformity between financial and tax reporting for depreciable assets, but there are exceptions.

CORPORATE ACQUISITIONS

Firms account for the acquisition of another firm using either the purchase method or the pooling-of-interests method. The purchase method results in reporting the assets and liabilities of the acquired company at the market value of the consideration given to execute the acquisition. When the acquisition price exceeds the market value of identifiable assets and liabilities, goodwill appears as an asset on the post-acquisition consolidated balance sheet. The pooling-of-interests method reports the assets and liabilities of the acquired company at their book values at the time of the acquisition, with no recognition given to the market value of the consideration given in the transaction. As this book goes to press, the FASB is considering eliminating the pooling-of-interests method as an allowable accounting method for corporate acquisitions.

The market value of the consideration given in most acquisitions exceeds the book values of the assets and liabilities of the acquired firm. The purchase method will report lower future earnings because future expenses derive from the initially higher asset valuations. Firms that account for an acquisition using the purchase method must amortize goodwill over some number of future years. The amortization period ranges from 5 years in Japan to 40 years in the United States. The IASC sets forth 20 years as the maximum amortization period unless a firm can justify a longer period. As this book goes to press, the FASB is considering reducing the maximum amortization period to 20 years, with the presumption of no more than 10 years unless a firm can justify a longer period.

The structure of a corporate acquisition determines if the firm will use the purchase method or the pooling-of-interests method. The pooling-of-interests method envisions a merging of shareholder groups by an exchange of common stock for common stock. The IASC standard, which uses the term *uniting of interests* instead of *pooling of interests,* envisions two firms of approximately equal market value. The U.S. standard does not contain a criterion regarding the relative size of the two firms. Accounting standards specify the conditions that a firm must meet to use the pooling method. If a firm does not meet these criteria, it must use the purchase method for financial reporting. Firms account for corporate acquisitions for income tax purposes using methods that parallel those described above. Because the criteria for financial and tax reporting differ, the accounting methods used for corporate acquisitions in these two sets of reports can differ.

LEASES

A firm using property rights acquired under lease may record the lease as an asset and subsequently amortize it (the capital, or finance, lease method) or the firm may recognize the lease transaction only as the company makes the lease payments each period (the operating lease method). Likewise, the lessor (the provider of the property rights under lease) can set up the rights to receive future lease payments as a receivable at the inception of the lease (the capital, or finance, lease method) or can recognize the lease only when the lessor becomes entitled to receive rental payments each period (the operating lease method).

From the lessee's perspective, total expenses over the life of a lease do not depend on the accounting method. Remember: total expense ultimately equals total cash outflow. Depreciation and interest expenses under the capital lease method usually exceed rent expense under the operating lease method during the early years of a lease. The operating lease method reports higher total expenses during the later years of a lease. By the end of the lease term, expense totals will equalize. Lessees with growing lease activity will likely show higher expenses each year using the capital lease method than they would show using the operating lease method because more of their leases are in the early years of the lease period. Firms with a declining level of leases should experience earnings effects just the opposite of those for a firm with a growing level of leases. The choice of accounting method for leases causes major differences in balance sheet amounts. The capital lease method includes the leased asset and the lease liability on the balance sheet, whereas the operating lease method does not. Because of the lessee's increased debt-equity ratio under the capital lease method, many managers prefer operating lease accounting.

From the lessor's perspective, total revenues over the life of the lease do not depend on the accounting method. Remember: total revenue ultimately equals total cash inflow. Because lessors often recognize a gain at the inception of a capital lease (equivalent to gross margin in a sales transaction), cumulative earnings for the lessor using the capital lease method generally exceed those of the lessor using the operating lease method until the final year of the lease. Lessors tend to report slightly higher asset valuations under the capital lease method.

- Under the capital lease method, the balance sheet shows the lease receivable, which declines as the lessor receives cash.
- Under the operating method, the balance sheet shows the asset itself, which declines in amount as the asset depreciates.

Whether a firm uses the capital or the operating lease method for financial reporting depends on which firm, the lessor or the lessee, bears the risks of the leased asset. Risks include uncertain residual values of the leased asset at the end of the lease period, due either to excessive use or obsolescence, changes in interest rates, changes in the demand for goods produced or services rendered with the leased asset, and similar factors. Comparing the life of the lease to the life of the leased asset and the present value of the lease payments to the market value of the leased property at the inception of the lease determines which entity bears the risks. The capital lease method is appropriate when the lessee bears most of the risks, and the operating lease method is appropriate when the lessor bears the risks. The facts of each lease agreement determine the appropriate method. The lessor and the lessee generally use the same method for a given lease because they apply the same capital-versus-operating lease criteria. There is, however, no requirement that they coordinate their decision about the accounting method. The criteria for a capital versus an operating lease for tax purposes differ somewhat from those used for financial reporting. Thus, firms may account for the same lease using different methods for financial and tax reporting.

EMPLOYEE STOCK OPTIONS

A U.S. firm compensating its employees by granting them options to purchase its shares

- may merely disclose the cost of those grants in the notes, or
- may charge that cost as an expense for the period when it makes the grant.

The "merely disclosing" company will never report expense for the cost of the options on the grant date. Thus, the two accounting principles lead to different total cumulative expenses. Retained earnings will also differ, but the additional paid-in capital accounts will differ by offsetting amounts, so that total shareholders' equity is the same whichever treatment the firm uses. The firm makes no cash expenditure for the grant, and this fact leads some theorists to suggest that the firm should not record a cost for the grant. Others, including us, believe that the firm should account for the grant as though the firm issued the options in the open market for cash and paid the cash to the employees. This issue remains controversial.

SUMMARY

The preceding discussion does not list all of the alternative GAAP in the United States and as provided by the IASC. Advanced courses in financial accounting consider additional reporting areas involving differences in accounting principles. Firms must disclose their accounting principles in a note to the financial statements.[1]

---

[1]Accounting Principles Board, *Opinion No. 22,* "Disclosure of Accounting Policies," 1972.

Firms enjoy considerable latitude in applying GAAP for a particular item. For example, firms using the allowance method for uncollectible accounts base their periodic provisions on judgments of the amount of bad debts. Firms using the straight-line depreciation method base their depreciation calculations on judgments of useful life and salvage value. Firms amortize goodwill arising from a purchase-method corporate acquisition over a number of years up to a maximum set by the FASB. Thus, uniformity in the accounting principles used by two firms does not necessarily result in comparable earnings and asset valuations for these firms. Firms seldom disclose sufficient information about their application of particular accounting principles to permit financial statement users to assess the degree of comparability between firms.

Firms can also control their reported earnings by timing their expenditures. Recall from earlier chapters that firms must generally expense, as incurred, expenditures on research and development, advertising, and maintenance of depreciable assets. Firms can accelerate or defer their expenditures, however, to achieve higher or lower earnings for a particular period.

Thus, an assessment of the effects of alternative accounting principles must consider not only the principles themselves but how firms apply those principles.

AN ILLUSTRATION OF THE EFFECTS OF ALTERNATIVE ACCOUNTING PRINCIPLES ON A SET OF FINANCIAL STATEMENTS

This section illustrates the effects that the use of different accounting principles can have on a set of financial statements. We constructed the illustration so that the accounting principles used create significant differences in the financial statements. Therefore, do not try to infer from this example the usual magnitude of the effects of alternative methods.

THE SCENARIO

On January 1, two identical corporations establish merchandising businesses. The two firms carry out identical operations and differ only in their methods of accounting. Conservative Company chooses the accounting principles that will minimize its reported net income. High Flyer Company chooses the accounting principles that will maximize its reported net income. The following events occur during the year.

1. Both corporations issue two million shares of $10-par value stock on January 1, for $20 million cash.
2. Both firms acquire equipment on January 1 for $14 million cash. The firms estimate the equipment to have a 10-year life and zero salvage value.
3. Both firms make the following purchases of merchandise inventory:

Date	Units Purchased	Unit Price	Cost of Purchases
January 1	170,000	@$60	$10,200,000
May 1	190,000	@$63	11,970,000
September 1	200,000	@$66	13,200,000
Total	560,000		$35,370,000

4. During the year, both firms sell 420,000 units at an average price of $100 each. The firms make all sales for cash.

5. During the year, both firms have selling, general, and administrative expenses, excluding depreciation, of $2.7 million.
6. The income tax rate is 35 percent.

ACCOUNTING PRINCIPLES USED

The following sections describe the methods of accounting used by each firm and the effects that each choice has on the financial statements.

Inventory Cost Flow Assumption   Conservative Company makes a LIFO cost flow assumption, whereas High Flyer Company makes a FIFO assumption. Each firm uses its chosen method for both financial reports and income tax returns. Because the beginning inventory is zero, the cost of goods available for sale by each firm equals the purchases during the year of $35,370,000. Both firms have 140,000 units in ending inventory. Conservative Company therefore reports a cost of goods sold of $26,970,000 [= $35,370,000 − (140,000 × $60)], whereas High Flyer Company reports a cost of goods sold of $26,130,000 [= $35,370,000 − (140,000 × $66)]. Income tax regulations in the United States require a firm to use LIFO in its financial reports if it uses LIFO for its tax return. High Flyer company does not want to use LIFO in its financial reports and therefore forgoes the tax savings opportunities from using LIFO for tax purposes.

Depreciation   Conservative Company decides to depreciate its equipment using the double (200 percent) declining-balance method in its financial statements, whereas High Flyer Company decides to use the straight-line method. Conservative Company therefore reports depreciation expense of $2.8 million (= 2 × 1/10 × $14,000,000), whereas High Flyer Company reports depreciation expense of $1.4 million (= 1/10 × $14,000,000) to shareholders. Both companies compute depreciation for tax purposes using a seven-year life, the double declining-balance depreciation method, and the initial half-year depreciation convention. Depreciation on both tax returns equals $2.0 million for the year.

COMPARATIVE INCOME STATEMENTS

Exhibit 14.1 presents comparative income statements for Conservative Company and High Flyer Company for the year ending December 31. For each company, the revenues and expenses (except for depreciation) reported in the financial statements equal those in the income tax return.

   Conservative Company reports $800,000 (= $2,800,000 − $2,000,000) more depreciation in the financial statements than in the tax return. The $800,000 difference causes taxable income to exceed income before income taxes for financial reporting. Income tax expense of $3,335,500 equals the income tax rate of 35 percent times income before income taxes. Income taxes currently payable equal the income tax rate of 35 percent times taxable income. The difference between income tax expense of $3,335,500 and the income tax payable of $3,615,500 results in a deferred tax asset of $280,000 on the balance sheet. This account reports the future tax savings that Conservative Company will realize when it deducts the $800,000 additional depreciation for income tax purposes in later years.

   High Flyer Company reports $600,000 (= $1,400,000 − $2,000,000) less depreciation in the financial statements than in the tax return. Income before income taxes exceeds taxable income; therefore, income tax expense exceeds income tax currently payable. The firm recognizes a deferred tax liability for the future taxes payable of $210,000 (= .35 × $600,000). Note in this illustration that High Flyer Company reports significantly larger

EXHIBIT 14.1	Comparative Income Statements Based on Different Accounting Principles for the Year Ending December 31 (all dollar amounts in thousands, except for per-share amounts)

	Conservative Company		High Flyer Company	
	Financial Statement	Tax Return	Financial Statement	Tax Return
Sales Revenue	$42,000.0	$42,000.0	$42,000.0	$42,000.0
Expenses:				
Cost of Goods Sold	$26,970.0	$26,970.0	$26,130.0	$26,130.0
Depreciation on Equipment	2,800.0	2,000.0	1,400.0	2,000.0
Other Selling, General, and Administrative	2,700.0	2,700.0	2,700.0	2,700.0
Expenses before Income Taxes	$32,470.0	$31,670.0	$30,230.0	$30,830.0
Net Income before Income Taxes	$ 9,530.0	$10,330.0	$11,770.0	$11,170.0
Income Tax Expense[a]	3,335.5		4,119.5	
Net Income	$ 6,194.5		$ 7,650.5	
Earnings per Share (2,000,000 shares outstanding)	$3.10		$3.83	

[a]Computation of Income Taxes:

Credits to Income Taxes Currently Payable on Balance Sheet		
0.35 × $10,330.0	$3,615.5	
0.35 × $11,170.0		$3,909.5
Credits (Debits) to Deferred Income Taxes on Balance Sheet		
Dr. = .35 × $800	(280.0)	
Cr. = .35 × $600		210.0
Total Debit to Income Tax Expense on Income Statement	$3,335.5	$4,119.5

net income and earnings per share than Conservative Company. Other management choices could magnify the difference. If both firms had issued stock options to employees as compensation in lieu of cash, with Conservative Company expensing them and High Flyer merely disclosing them, then Conservative Company's income would decline by the cost of the options and High Flyer's income would not change.

COMPARATIVE BALANCE SHEETS

Exhibit 14.2 presents comparative balance sheets for Conservative Company and High Flyer Company as of December 31. Merchandise inventory and equipment (net) as well as total assets of Conservative Company have lower valuations than those of High Flyer Company. Cash represents the only real difference between the economic positions of the two companies. The difference in the amount of cash results from the payment of different amounts of income taxes by the two firms. Note that Conservative Company's higher cash results from paying smaller amounts of income taxes. Some analysts, including us, believe that Conservative Company has a stronger financial position than does High Flyer Company.

EXHIBIT 14.2	Comparative Balance Sheets Based on Different Accounting Principles, December 31 (all dollar amounts in thousands)	
	Conservative Company	**High Flyer Company**
ASSETS		
Cash	$ 6,314.5	$ 6,020.5
Merchandise Inventory	8,400.0	9,240.0
Equipment (at acquisition cost)	14,000.0	14,000.0
Less Accumulated Depreciation	(2,800.0)	(1,400.0)
Deferred Tax Asset	280.0	—
Total Assets	$26,194.5	$27,860.5
EQUITIES		
Deferred Tax Liability	—	$ 210.0
Common Stock	$20,000.0	20,000.0
Retained Earnings	6,194.5	7,650.5
Total Equities	$26,194.5	$27,860.5

The differences in the amounts for merchandise inventory and equipment (net) result from the different accounting methods used by the two companies. Conservative Company reports smaller amounts than High Flyer Company because Conservative Company recognizes a larger portion of the costs incurred during the period as an expense. Conservative Company also shows a Deferred Tax Asset of $280,000 arising from temporary differences in depreciation for financial and tax reporting, whereas High Flyer Company reports a Deferred Tax Liability relating to the same temporary differences.

Note the effect that the use of alternative accounting principles has on the rate of return on total assets, a measure of a firm's operating profitability. Conservative Company reports a smaller amount of net income but also a smaller amount of total assets. One may expect the rate of return on total assets of the two firms to approximate each other more closely than either net income or total assets individually. One still observes significant differences in the ratios for the two firms in this illustration, however. The rate of return on total assets for Conservative Company is as follows:

$$26.8 \text{ percent} = \$6,194,500/[(\$20,000,000 + \$26,194,500)/2]$$

For High Flyer Company the rate is as follows:

$$32.0 \text{ percent} = \$7,650,500/[(\$20,000,000 + \$27,860,500)/2]$$

Note that neither firm uses debt financing, so there is no need to add back interest expense net of tax saving in the numerator of the rate of return on assets.

Exhibit 14.3 presents comparative statements of cash flows for Conservative Company and High Flyer Company. The amount of cash flow from operations for Conservative Company exceeds that for High Flyer Company. The difference of $294.0 million (= $314.5 million − $20.5 million) results from the difference in the amount of income taxes paid. These companies paid different amounts of income taxes because they used

EXHIBIT 14.3	Comparative Statements of Cash Flows for the Year Ending December 31 (all dollar amounts in thousands)		

	Conservative Company	High Flyer Company
OPERATIONS		
Net Income	$6,194.5	$7,650.5
Additions:		
Depreciation Expense	2,800.0	1,400.0
Increase in Deferred Tax Liability	—	210.0
Subtractions:		
Increase in Deferred Tax Asset	(280.0)	
Increase in Merchandise Inventory	(8,400.0)	(9,240.0)
Cash Flow from Operations	$ 314.5	$ 20.5
INVESTING		
Acquisition of Equipment	(14,000.0)	(14,000.0)
FINANCING		
Issue of Common Stock	20,000.0	20,000.0
Net Change in Cash	$ 6,314.5	$ 6,020.5
Cash, January 1	—	—
Cash, December 31	$ 6,314.5	$ 6,020.5

different cost flow assumptions for inventories on their tax returns. The following schedule shows the cause of the difference in cash flow:

Conservative Company: LIFO Cost of Goods Sold	$26,970
High Flyer Company: FIFO Cost of Goods Sold	26,130
Difference in Cost of Goods Sold and Taxable Income	$ 840
Multiply by Tax Rate	× 35%
Difference in Cash Flow (= $6,314.5 − $6,020.5)	$ 294

Note that the use of different depreciation methods by these firms *on their financial statements* has no effect on the statement of cash flows. As long as both firms use the same depreciation method on their tax returns (double declining-balance method in this case), cash flows related to depreciation will not differ.

MORAL OF THE ILLUSTRATION

Effective interpretation of published financial statements requires sensitivity to the particular accounting principles that firms select. Comparing the reports of several companies may necessitate adjusting the amounts for different accounting methods. Previous chapters illustrated the techniques for making some of these adjustments (for example, LIFO to FIFO cost flow assumption). The notes to financial statements disclose the accounting methods used but not necessarily the data needed to make the appropriate adjustments.

ASSESSING THE EFFECTS OF ALTERNATIVE ACCOUNTING PRINCIPLES ON INVESTMENT DECISIONS

Previous sections of this chapter emphasized the flexibility that firms have in selecting and applying their accounting principles and the effects that the use of different accounting principles has on the financial statements. We now examine two related and important questions:

- Do investors accept financial statement information as presented, without noticing the differences in accounting methods that underlie the statements?
- Or, do they somehow filter out all or most of the financial statement variances that result from differences in the selection and application of accounting methods?

Suppose that investors accept financial statement information as presented, without adjustments for the methods of accounting used. Then, two firms that are otherwise identical except for their accounting principles might raise capital at different costs or raise unequal amounts of capital. Then, the use of alternative accounting principles leads to a misallocation of resources in the economy. The managers of a firm might have an incentive to select those accounting principles that place the firm and its managers in the most favorable light rather than to select those accounting principles that most accurately measure the economic effects of transactions and events.

Those who believe that alternative accounting principles can mislead investors make the following arguments.

1. Most investors do not understand accounting well enough to make adjustments for differences in accounting principles.
2. Financial statements and related notes do not provide sufficient information to permit the user to understand how firms applied the accounting methods selected, much less provide sufficient information to allow the user to adjust for alternative accounting principles.
3. The financial press frequently reports on firms whose market prices fall dramatically when reports about their misuse of specific accounting methods hit the market.

Those who believe that alternative accounting principles rarely mislead investors make the following arguments.

1. Capital market prices adjust quickly and appropriately to new information. Sophisticated security analysts, who dominate the pricing of securities through their buy and sell recommendations, have the necessary skills to make adjustments for alternative accounting principles.
2. The financial statement effects of differences in accounting principles can be sufficiently small that adjusting for them does not justify the effort. For example, the financial statement effects of using FIFO versus LIFO cost flow assumptions for inventories and cost of goods sold are small when prices do not change significantly and inventory turns over rapidly. Differences in depreciation methods do not cause serious financial statement distortions when acquisition costs remain relatively stable and firms do not grow rapidly.

Both of these positions have support in empirical evidence. Most of the evidence for the position that alternative accounting principles mislead investors relates to individual firms. Most of the evidence for the position that alternative accounting principles do not mislead investors relates to aggregate market effects. Thus, evidence that capital markets in general react appropriately to financial disclosures by firms does not preclude the possibility that the market may react inappropriately to the financial disclosures of particular firms for a particular period. Research regarding the effects of alternative accounting principles on investment decisions continues to progress but has not yet reached a consensus.[2]

QUALITY OF EARNINGS REVISITED

Security analysts examine a firm's **quality of earnings** when using earnings information in valuing the firm. Assessments of a firm's quality of earnings involve examining the choices a firm makes in

1. selecting its accounting principles from among alternative GAAP,
2. applying the accounting principles selected, and
3. timing business transactions to temporarily increase or decrease earnings.

Throughout, this book emphasizes that net income over sufficiently long time periods equals cash inflows minus cash outflows other than transactions with owners. Firms, however, measure earnings for shorter, discrete time periods. Revenue recognition often precedes the receipt of cash from customers. Firms must therefore estimate at the time of sale the amount of uncollectible accounts and sales returns to measure earnings. Expense recognition often follows the cash outflows for goods and services acquired, sometimes by many years, as in the case of fixed assets. Expense recognition may also precede cash outflows, as occurs with warranty services. The longer the time that elapses between revenue recognition and cash receipts and between expense recognition and cash expenditures, the more opportunity a firm has to bias its reported earnings and therefore lower its quality of earnings.

A concept related to quality of earnings is **quality of financial position.** The choices a firm makes in reporting revenues and expenses also affect assets and liabilities on the balance sheet. Analysts use balance sheet amounts in assessing a firm's profitability (for example, balance sheet amounts affect rates of return on assets and shareholders' equity and asset turnovers) and its risk (balance sheet amounts affect current, quick and debt ratios).

The next section reviews the impact of various financial reporting topics on assessments of the quality of earnings and the quality of financial position. Although we examine each reporting topic separately, assessments of quality must consider the net effect of all areas in which firms make reporting choices.

Revenue Recognition and Receivables
Most firms recognize revenues at the time of sale, or delivery, of goods and services. Firms that collect cash from customers at the time of sale (for example, fast-food restaurants, movie theaters) have a higher quality of earnings, at least with respect to revenues, than firms that must estimate the amount of uncollectible accounts. Firms that sell to many customers, have historical data on the collectibility of receivables, and collect cash within one to three months after the sale (for example, department stores with their own credit cards) generally have higher-quality earnings than firms that sell to just a few customers, have

---

[2]For a review of these studies, see Ray Ball and George Foster, "Corporate Financial Reporting: A Methodological Review of Empirical Research," *Studies in Current Methodologies in Accounting: A Critical Evaluation,* supplement to *Journal of Accounting Research* 20 (1982): 117–48, and Baruch Lev and James A. Ohlson, "Market-Based Empirical Research: A Review, Interpretation, and Extension," ibid., 249–332.

limited historical data on collectibility, and permit customers to stretch out payments over many months or even years (for example, sellers of restaurant franchises, sellers of undeveloped residential real estate). Firms that provide customers with liberal rights to return products (for examples, sellers of products by mail or over the Internet) or that sell products requiring additional services before customer acceptance (for example, new computer software) must estimate the likely amount of returns in order to measure earnings, thereby affecting earnings quality. Each of these choices that affect the measurement of revenue simultaneously affects the measurement of accounts receivable on the balance sheet.

Firms that recognize revenue on multiperiod contracts as work progresses, such as construction companies, must estimate the degree of completion and the expected amount of total revenues and total expenses in order to measure earnings each period. The need to make such estimates before completion of the construction work affects the quality of earnings and the valuation of Contracts in Process on the balance sheet.

Cost of Goods Sold and Inventories

Most firms choose either a FIFO, LIFO, or weighted-average cost flow assumption for inventories and cost of goods sold. LIFO generally matches more current cost with revenues than does FIFO and leads to higher-quality, sustainable earnings. Firms that dip into LIFO layers, however, match some older acquisition costs with revenues and negatively influence the quality of earnings. Whether a firm dips into LIFO layers is partially at the discretion of management. During periods of rising acquisition costs, dipping into LIFO layers can increase net income. LIFO provides, for inventories, balance sheet amounts that may reflect acquisitions costs of many years ago, when the firm created the LIFO layers. FIFO provides balance sheet amounts more closely reflecting current costs and therefore results in higher-quality measures of financial position. Thus, accounting methods that increase earnings quality may provide lower-quality measures of financial position.

Depreciation and Fixed Assets

Firms with a high proportion of depreciable assets, such as manufacturing firms, have a lower quality of earnings, at least with respect to the measurement of depreciation expense, than firms with lower proportions of fixed assets, such as service and retail firms. Firms with depreciable assets must estimate the length of the period during which depreciable assets will provide services and the residual value at the end of that period. Such firms must also choose a depreciation method. These choices provide firms with opportunities to bias earnings in their favor.

Firms can measure depreciation using the straight-line method or an accelerated method. Because analysts often suspect that firms overstate rather than understate earnings, they view accelerated depreciation as providing higher-quality earnings. The vast majority of U.S. firms use the straight-line depreciation method. The depreciation method choice is therefore not an important source of difference in earnings quality between U.S. firms. Firms in countries such as Germany, France, and Japan frequently use accelerated depreciation methods for financial reporting. Thus, the depreciation method choice does affect assessments of earnings quality in cross-national comparisons.

Most countries require acquisition cost valuations for fixed assets. The longer the time period a firm holds fixed assets, the more out-of-date these acquisition cost valuations become. When the market values of fixed assets decline below their book values, GAAP require firms to recognize an impairment loss. Thus, the book values after recognizing the impairment loss will equal the market values of the assets and provide high-quality measures of financial position. When the market values of fixed assets increase above book values, GAAP in most countries do not permit firms to write up the assets. Thus, the reported amounts for fixed assets will understate the financial position of the firm.

Amortization and Intangible Assets Firms that acquire intangibles in external market transactions must capitalize their costs as assets and subsequently amortize them. Firms that develop intangibles internally must generally expense their costs in the year incurred. The immediate expensing leads to more conservative measures of earnings and, in the view of most analysts, a higher quality of earnings. Immediate expensing also eliminates the need to estimate the expected life and to choose an amortization method, actions required of firms acquiring intangibles in external market transactions. Firms that develop intangibles internally, however, have discretion regarding when they expend resources and therefore can bias earnings in their favor in a particular year by delaying or accelerating expenditures.

Corporate Acquisitions The purchase method of accounting for a corporate acquisition reports assets and liabilities of an acquired company at the acquirer's acquisition cost, which equals the market value at the time of the acquisition. Subsequent expenses reflect these relatively up-to-date asset and liability valuations. The pooling-of-interests method ignores the market value of the acquired company and carries over its older book values subsequent to the acquisition. Thus, the pooling-of-interests method reports more out-of-date assets, liabilities, revenues, and expenses. Most analysts view the purchase method as providing higher-quality measures of earnings and financial position than the pooling-of-interests method. Firms using the purchase method must allocate the aggregate purchase price among each of the assets and liabilities acquired and then subsequently amortize them. The initial allocation and subsequent amortization present management with opportunities to bias balance sheet and earnings amounts. Thus, the analyst must consider the possible impact of the purchase method on quality assessments.

Warranties Firms that promise to provide future warranty services on products sold must estimate the expected costs of warranty claims and recognize that amount as an expense in the year it sells the products. When the warranty period is short, such as one year, and the firm has historical data on warranty claim costs for similar products, opportunities to bias earnings and measures of the warranty liability are more limited than when the warranty period extends for many years and historical data on similar products are lacking.

The earnings and balance sheet amounts for insurance companies present quality issues similar to warranties. Insurance companies recognize revenues each period from insurance premiums and investments. They must recognize an expense for the expected costs of claims arising from insurance in force during each period. The claim period may be relatively short, as in the case of damage to automobile and buildings, or much longer, as in the case of liability or life insurance coverage. Insurance companies encounter difficulties estimating the timing and amount of claims, particularly from events that do not occur in predictable patterns (such as hurricanes) and events for which insurance companies do not have historical data (such as Year 2000 computer problems).

Leases Lessees usually prefer the operating lease method because it permits them to keep the lease liability off the balance sheet. The operating lease method provides lower-quality measures of financial position than the capital lease method because the lease obligation is, in economic substance, similar to reported liabilities. The operating lease method also keeps the leased asset off the books and understates the resources under the control and responsibility of management.

Employee Stock Options   Firms that choose to merely disclose in the notes the cost of employee stock options have lower-quality earnings than firms that recognize the cost as an expense. Fortunately, the required disclosure of the cost of the options permits the analyst to adjust reported earnings easily.

Investments in Securities   Firms might vary their ownership percentage in other companies to achieve a desired income statement or balance sheet result. Firms that invest in start-up companies may keep their ownership percentage below 20 percent to avoid having to accrue a share of the net losses expected during the early years. Firms investing in companies with high proportions of debt in their capital structures may keep the ownership percentage below 50 percent to avoid having to consolidate the debt into their balance sheet. Analysts must assess whether legitimate business reasons explain the ownership percentages or whether firms are gaming GAAP to their advantage. Ownership percentages of 19.9 percent and 49.9 percent arouse suspicion.

Timing of Transactions and Events   Perhaps the aspect of earnings quality most difficult for the analyst to assess is the impact of the discretionary timing of transactions and events. A firm may reduce expenditures for maintenance in a particular year, for example, stating that facilities were in less need of repair than in prior years. The analyst must assess whether the firm can sustain the increased earnings in future years. Firms may increase the depreciable lives of buildings and equipment, explaining that they were too conservative in their original estimates. Analysts must assess whether the longer lives seem reasonable, given the depreciable lives used by other firms in the industry, or whether a firm may have changed the depreciable lives to boost current earnings. Firms may experience decreased earnings in a particular year because of a weak economy. Because capital markets expect lower earnings, firms might take advantage of that expectation by writing down or writing off assets, a phenomenon frequently referred to as the *big bath*. The recognition of losses from asset impairments, for example, may fall in an otherwise weak earnings year. Firms hope that investors will view the charge as nonrecurring and will ignore or deemphasize it. By writing down or writing off assets, the firm will report larger earnings in future periods. Firms hope that investors will forget that part of the reason for increased earnings is the earlier write-down of assets that would otherwise now be part of expenses.

Summary of Earnings Quality   Assessing the quality of earnings and the quality of financial position is among the most important and yet the most difficult tasks of the analyst. This assessment requires the analyst to ask:

1. Does the firm have valid business reasons for the choices it makes, or does enhancing reported earnings or financial position appear to be the chief aim?
2. Which areas of choice have the largest impact on a particular firm's income statement and balance sheet? A firm's choice of accounting principles may appear conservative, for example choosing LIFO or accelerated depreciation in measuring cost of goods sold and depreciation expense. Yet if the firm is not growing rapidly and acquisition costs are not changing significantly, these choices have relatively little impact on earnings. Delaying maintenance, advertising, or research and development expenses might have a much larger effect and should be the focus of the analyst's energies.
3. Do the firm's choices enhance the quality of earnings at the expense of the quality of financial position, or vice versa? Firms using LIFO or accelerated depreciation may

enhance their quality of earnings but may provide, for inventories and fixed assets, balance sheet amounts that significantly understate their current values.

4. Does the firm disclose sufficient information to permit the analyst to restate reported amounts, or must the analyst inject an intolerable level of subjectivity in order to improve the quality of earnings or balance sheet information?

THE FIRM'S SELECTION OF ALTERNATIVE ACCOUNTING PRINCIPLES

We next address the following questions:

1. Which accounting principles from among those prescribed as generally accepted should a firm choose in preparing its financial statements (that is, how should a firm move from Circle B to Circle C in Figure 14.1)?
2. Which accounting principles should it select for income tax purposes?

FINANCIAL REPORTING PURPOSES

A firm's reporting strategy or objective might guide its selection of accounting principles for financial reporting. This section considers four possible strategies or objectives: (1) accurate presentation, (2) conservatism, (3) profit maximization, and (4) income smoothing.

Accurate Presentation One might judge the usefulness of accounting information by assessing whether it provides an **accurate presentation** of the underlying events and transactions. A firm could base its selection of accounting principles on accuracy of presentation. For example, previous chapters define assets as resources having future service potential and define expenses as the cost of services consumed during the period. In applying the accuracy basis, firms would select the inventory cost flow assumption and the depreciation method that most accurately measure the pattern of services consumed during the period and the amount of services still available at the end of the period.

This approach has at least one serious limitation as a basis for selecting accounting methods. The accountant can seldom directly observe the services consumed and the service potential remaining. Without this information, the accountant cannot ascertain which accounting principles lead to the most accurate presentation of the underlying events. Accuracy of presentation serves primarily as a normative guide for firms to use in selecting their accounting principles.

Conservatism In choosing among alternative generally acceptable methods, firms might select the set that provides the most conservative measure of net income and assets. Considering the uncertainties involved in measuring benefits received as revenues and services consumed as expenses, some accountants suggest providing a conservative measure of earnings, thereby reducing the possibility of unwarranted optimism by financial statement users. As a criterion for selecting accounting principles, **conservatism** implies selecting methods that minimize asset totals and cumulative reported earnings. That is, firms should recognize expenses as quickly as possible and postpone the recognition of revenues as long as possible. This reporting objective generally leads to selecting the double declining-balance or the sum-of-the-years'-digits depreciation method and the LIFO cost flow assumption if a firm anticipates periods of rising prices.

Many accountants and financial statement users challenge the rationale for conservatism as a reporting objective. Over the life of the firm, income equals cash receipts minus cash expenditures other than transactions with owners. Thus, to the extent that conservatism reduces net income of earlier periods, it increases earnings of later periods. The "later" periods of larger income may, however, be many periods later, sometimes even the last period of the firm's existence. Also, earnings reports based on conservative reporting principles may mislead some statement users. Consider, for example, investors who sell shares because they believe that a firm does not operate in a sufficiently profitable manner with the resources available, whereas less conservatively reported earnings would not have induced them to sell. Or consider the potential lenders who will not provide financing because the published conservative statement of earnings misleads them.

Profit Maximization   **Profit maximization,** a reporting objective having an effect just the opposite of that of conservatism, suggests selecting accounting methods that maximize asset totals and cumulative reported earnings. That is, a firm should recognize revenues as quickly as possible and postpone the recognition of expenses as long as possible. For example, a firm would use the straight-line method of depreciation and the FIFO cost flow assumption when it anticipates periods of rising prices. Using profit maximization as a reporting objective extends the notion that a firm attempts to generate profits and that it should present as favorable a report on performance as possible within currently acceptable accounting methods. Some firms' managers, whose compensation depends in part on reported earnings, prefer larger reported earnings to smaller. Compared with other accounting principles, profit-maximizing principles result in reporting income earlier, which means reporting smaller income in some later period. Note that profit maximization as a financial reporting objective differs from the profit maximization dictum of microeconomics.

Income Smoothing   **Income smoothing** guides some firms' choices of accounting principles. This criterion suggests selecting accounting methods that result in the smoothest earnings trend over time. Empirical research has shown a relation between changes in stock prices and changes in earnings.[3] Advocates of income smoothing suggest that if a firm minimizes fluctuations in earnings, it will reduce the perceived risk of investing in its shares of stock and, all else being equal, obtain a higher stock price. It will be able to raise capital at a lower cost. Note that this reporting criterion suggests smoothing net income, not revenues and expenses individually. As a result, a firm must consider the total pattern of its operations before selecting the appropriate accounting methods. For example, straight-line depreciation provides the smoothest amount of depreciation expense on a machine over its life. If, however, the productivity of the machine declines with age so that revenues decrease in later years, the straight-line method may not provide the smoothest net income stream.

Summary   We summarize this discussion of the strategies that firms consider in selecting their accounting principles for financial reporting by presenting a series of questions for you to ponder:

1. Do business firms have a moral obligation to select the accounting principle that most accurately measures the economic effects of a transaction or event (if such a principle exists), or do firms satisfy any moral obligation by selecting their accounting principles from the set of principles deemed acceptable by standard-setting bodies?

---

[3]For a review of these studies, see Baruch Lev, "On the Usefulness of Earnings and Earnings Reasearch: Lessons and Directions from Two Decades of Empirical Research," *Studies on the Information Content of Accounting Earnings,* supplement to *Journal of Accounting Research* 27 (1989): 153–92.

2. Should firms, in selecting their accounting principles, pursue a particular reporting strategy to take advantage of market inefficiencies that may exist in the pricing of their debt or equity securities?

3. Should firms select the same accounting principles as their principal competitors, to provide apparently more comparable financial statements? If so, should they apply these accounting principles differently than do their competitors, to achieve particular reporting objectives? For example, a firm might choose the straight-line depreciation for its plant assets, the same method used by its competitors, but use longer depreciable lives than competitors to appear more profitable.

4. Should firms disclose only the minimum information required by GAAP, requiring the analyst to estimate the impact of other accounting alternatives, or should firms adopt a policy of more complete disclosure to aid the analyst in making adjustments?

INCOME TAX REPORTING PURPOSES

For income tax purposes, firms should select accounting procedures that minimize the present value of the stream of income tax payments. This guide, sometimes called the **least and latest rule,** suggests that a firm pay the least amount of taxes as late as possible within the law. The least and latest rule generally translates into a policy of recognizing expenses as quickly as possible and postponing the recognition of revenues as long as possible. Expected changes in income tax rates or the availability of operating loss carryforwards to offset taxable income of the current year might alter the strategy in implementing the least and latest rule.

Recognizing expenses as soon as possible suggests adopting the LIFO inventory cost flow assumption, accelerated depreciation, and immediate expensing of research and development, advertising, and similar costs. Using the installment basis of recognizing revenue, where permitted by the Internal Revenue Code and Regulations, will benefit a firm because it postpones revenue recognition and the resulting income tax payments until a firm collects cash.

SUMMARY

This chapter summarizes the accounting principles discussed in Chapters 6 through 12 and serves (along with Problem 14.1 for Self-Study) as a review of the more technical aspects of alternative accounting principles and their implications for earnings quality. This chapter also revisits questions, raised in Chapter 1, regarding the standard-setting process and the desired degree of uniformity versus flexibility in accounting principles. These latter issues remain open to debate as researchers continue to study the effects of alternative accounting principles.

PROBLEM 14.1 FOR SELF-STUDY

Review of Chapters 1–14. A set of financial statements for Kaplan Corporation follows, including a consolidated income statement (Exhibit 14.4), a comparative consolidated balance sheet on December 31, Year 1 and Year 2 (Exhibit 14.5), and a consolidated statement of cash flows (Exhibit 14.6). A series of notes provides additional information on certain items in the financial statements.

Compute the results required on page 797, using information from the financial statements and notes. We suggest that you study the statements and notes carefully before attempting to respond to the questions.

Note 1: Kaplan Corporation selected the accounting policies in the following list:

- *Basis of consolidation.* Kaplan Corporation consolidates its financial statements with those of Heimann Corporation, an 80-percent-owned subsidiary acquired on January 2, Year 1.
- *Marketable securities.* Marketable securities appear at market value.
- *Accounts Receivable.* Kaplan Corporation uses the allowance method for uncollectible accounts.
- *Inventories.* Kaplan Corporation uses a last-in, first-out (LIFO) cost flow assumption for inventories and cost of goods sold.
- *Investments.* Kaplan Corporation uses the market value method for investments of less than 20 percent of the outstanding common stock of other companies and the equity method for investments of 20 to 50 percent of the outstanding common stock of unconsolidated affiliates.
- *Buildings and equipment.* Kaplan Corporation uses the straight-line method of depreciation for financial reporting and uses accelerated depreciation for tax reporting.
- *Goodwill.* The corporation amortizes goodwill over a period of 10 years.
- *Interest on long-term debt.* The calculation of interest expense on bonds payable uses the effective interest method.
- *Deferred income taxes.* The corporation provides deferred income taxes for temporary differences between book income and taxable income.

EXHIBIT 14.4	KAPLAN CORPORATION Consolidated Income Statement for Year 2 (all dollar amounts in thousands) (Problem 14.1 for Self-Study)

Revenues and Gains

Sales	$12,000
Equity in Earnings of Unconsolidated Affiliates	300
Dividend Revenue	20
Gain on Sale of Marketable Securities	30
Total Revenues and Gains	$12,350

Expenses and Losses

Cost of Goods Sold	$ 7,200
Selling and Administrative	2,709
Loss on Sale of Equipment	80
Interest (Notes 7 and 8)	561
Total Expenses and Losses	$10,550
Net Income before Income Taxes	$ 1,800
Income Tax Expense	540
Net Income	$ 1,260

Note 2: Marketable securities appear at market values that are less than their acquisition cost by $50,000 on December 31, Year 1, and by $70,000 on December 31, Year 2.

Note 3: Accounts receivable appear net of an allowance for uncollectible accounts of $200,000 on December 31, Year 1, and $250,000 on December 31, Year 2. Selling and administrative expenses include bad debt expense of $120,000.

Note 4: Inventories comprise the following:

	December 31, Year 1	December 31, Year 2
Raw Materials	$ 330,000	$ 380,000
Work-in-Process	460,000	530,000
Finished Goods	1,800,000	2,200,000
Total	$2,590,000	$3,110,000

EXHIBIT 14.5	KAPLAN CORPORATION Consolidated Balance Sheets December 31, Year 1 and Year 2 (all dollar amounts in thousands) (Problem 14.1 for Self-Study)

	December 31, Year 1	December 31, Year 2
ASSETS		
Current Assets		
Cash	$ 1,470	$ 2,919
Marketable Securities (Note 2)	450	550
Accounts Receivable (net; Note 3)	2,300	2,850
Inventories (Note 4)	2,590	3,110
Prepayments	800	970
Total Current Assets	$ 7,610	$10,399
Investments (Note 5)		
Investment in Maher Corporation (10 percent)	$ 200	$ 185
Investment in Johnson Corporation (30 percent)	310	410
Investment in Burton Corporation (40 percent)	800	930
Total Investments	$ 1,310	$ 1,525
Property, Plant, and Equipment		
Land	$ 400	$ 500
Buildings	800	940
Equipment	3,300	3,800
Total Cost	$ 4,500	$ 5,240
Less Accumulated Depreciation	(1,200)	(930)
Net Property, Plant, and Equipment	$ 3,300	$ 4,310
Goodwill (Note 6)	$ 90	$ 80
Total Assets	$12,310	$16,314

The current cost of inventories exceeded the amounts computed on a LIFO basis by $420,000 on December 31, Year 1, and $730,000 on December 31, Year 2.

Note 5: Burton Corporation had a net income of $400,000 and paid dividends of $75,000 in Year 2.

Note 6: On January 2, Year 1, Kaplan Corporation acquired 80 percent of the outstanding common shares of Heimann Corporation by issuing 20,000 shares of Kaplan Corporation common stock. The Kaplan Corporation shares had a market value on January 2, Year 1, of $40 per share. Kaplan Corporation treats any difference between the acquisition price and the book value of the identifiable net assets acquired as goodwill and amortizes it over a period of 10 years from the date of acquisition.

Note 7: Current liabilities include a one-year note payable due on January 2, Year 3. The note requires annual interest payments on December 31 of each year.

EXHIBIT 14.5 *(continued)*	KAPLAN CORPORATION Consolidated Balance Sheets December 31, Year 1 and Year 2 (all dollar amounts in thousands) (Problem 14.1 for Self-Study)

	December 31, Year 1	December 31, Year 2
LIABILITIES AND SHAREHOLDERS' EQUITY		
Current Liabilities		
Note Payable (Note 7)	$ —	$ 2,000
Accounts Payable	1,070	1,425
Salaries Payable	800	600
Interest Payable	300	400
Income Taxes Payable	250	375
Total Current Liabilities	$ 2,420	$ 4,800
Long-term Liabilities		
Bonds Payable (Note 8)	$ 6,209	$ 6,209
Deferred Tax Liability	820	940
Total Long-term Liabilities	$ 7,029	$ 7,149
Shareholders' Equity		
Common Shares ($10 par value)	$ 500	$ 600
Additional Paid-in Capital	800	1,205
Unrealized Holding Loss on Marketable Securities.	(50)	(70)
Unrealized Holding Loss on Investments in Securities	(25)	(40)
Retained Earnings	1,666	2,690
Total	$ 2,891	$ 4,385
Less Treasury Shares (at cost)	(30)	(20)
Total Shareholders' Equity	$ 2,861	$ 4,365
Total Liabilities and Shareholders' Equity	$12,310	$16,314

EXHIBIT 14.6	KAPLAN CORPORATION Consolidated Statement of Cash Flows for Year 2 (all dollar amounts in thousands) (Problem 14.1 for Self-Study)

OPERATIONS

Net Income	$1,260	
Additions:		
Depreciation	560	
Deferred Taxes	120	
Loss on Sale of Equipment	80	
Excess of Interest Expense over Coupon Payments	28	
Amortization of Goodwill	10	
Increase in Accounts Payable	355	
Increase in Interest Payable	100	
Increase in Income Taxes Payable	125	
Subtractions:		
Gain on Sale of Marketable Securities	(30)	
Equity in Earnings of Affiliates in Excess of Dividends Received	(180)	
Amortization of Premium on Bonds	(28)	
Increase in Accounts Receivable	(550)	
Increase in Inventories	(520)	
Increase in Prepayments	(170)	
Decrease in Salaries Payable	(200)	
Cash Flow from Operations		$ 960

INVESTING

Sale of Marketable Securities	$ 210	
Sale of Equipment	150	
Investment in Johnson Corporation	(50)	
Purchase of Marketable Securities	(300)	
Acquisition of:		
Land	(100)	
Building	(300)	
Equipment	(1,400)	
Cash Flow from Investing		(1,790)

FINANCING

Increase in Notes Payable	$2,000	
Common Stock Issued	500	
Treasury Stock Sold	15	
Dividends	(236)	
Cash Flow from Financing		2,279
Net Change in Cash		$1,449
Cash, January 1		1,470
Cash, December 31		$2,919

Note 8: Bonds payable are as follows:

	December 31, Year 1	December 31, Year 2
4 Percent, $2,000,000 Bonds Due Dec. 31, Year 7, with Interest Payable Semiannually	$1,800,920	$1,829,390
10 Percent, $3,000,000 Bonds Due Dec. 31, Year 11, with Interest Payable Semiannually	3,407,720	3,379,790
8 Percent, $1,000,000 Bonds Due Dec. 31, Year 17, with Interest Payable Semiannually	1,000,000	1,000,000
Total	$6,208,640	$6,209,180

a. Kaplan Corporation sold marketable securities originally costing $180,000 during Year 2. Ascertain the price at which it sold these securities.

b. Refer to part **a.** Compute the cost of marketable securities purchased during Year 2.

c. What was the amount of specific customers' accounts that Kaplan Corporation wrote off as uncollectible during Year 2?

d. Compute the amount of cash collected from customers during the year.

e. Compute the cost of units completed and transferred to the finished goods inventory during Year 2.

f. Direct labor and overhead costs incurred in manufacturing during the year totaled $4,500,000. Compute the cost of raw materials purchased during Year 2.

g. Assume that the amounts disclosed in Note 4 for the current cost of inventories represent the amounts that would result from using a first-in, first-out (FIFO) cost flow assumption. Compute the cost of goods sold if the firm had used FIFO rather than LIFO.

h. Prepare an analysis that explains the causes of the changes in each of the three intercorporate investment accounts.

i. Prepare an analysis that explains the change in each of the four following accounts during Year 2: Land; Building; Equipment; and Accumulated Depreciation.

j. Give the journal entry made on Kaplan Corporation's books on January 2, Year 1, when it acquired Heimann Corporation.

k. Compute the book value of the net assets of Heimann Corporation on January 2, Year 1.

l. Kaplan Corporation initially priced the 4 percent bonds payable to yield 6 percent compounded semiannually. The firm initially priced the 10 percent bonds to yield 8 percent compounded semiannually. Use the appropriate present value tables at the back of the book to show that $1,800,920 and $3,407,720 (see Note 8) are the correct book values for these two bond issues on December 31, Year 1.

m. Calculate the amount of interest expense and any change in the book value of the bond liability for Year 2 on each of the three long-term bond issues (see Note 8).

n. Compute the amount of income taxes actually paid during Year 2.

o. On July 1, Year 2, Kaplan Corporation issued 10,000 shares of its common stock on the open market for $50 per share. Prepare an analysis explaining the change during Year 2 in each of the following accounts: Common Shares; Additional Paid-in Capital; Retained Earnings; and Treasury Shares.

SOLUTION TO SELF-STUDY PROBLEM

SUGGESTED SOLUTION TO PROBLEM 14.1 FOR SELF-STUDY

(Kaplan Corporation; review of chapters 1–14.)

a. Cost of Marketable Securities Sold	$180,000
Gain on Sale (from Income Statement)	30,000
Selling Price	$210,000

The statement of cash flows shows the $210,000 cash proceeds from the sale as an investing activity. The accountant must subtract the gain on sale of marketable securities from net income in the operations section to avoid overstating the amount of cash inflow from the transaction.

b. Marketable Securities at Market Value on December 31, Year 1	$450,000
Plus Cost of Marketable Securities Purchased	?
Less Cost of Marketable Securities Sold	(180,000)
Less Increase in Unrealized Holding Loss	(20,000)
Marketable Securities at Market Value on December 31, Year 2	$550,000

The cost of marketable securities purchased during Year 2 was $300,000. The statement of cash flows reports these purchases as an investing activity. The recognition of an unrealized holding loss of $20,000 from price declines of marketable securities did not reduce net income or use cash. Thus, the accountant need not make an adjustment to net income when computing cash flow from operations.

c. Allowance for Uncollectible Accounts, December 31, Year 1	$200,000
Plus Provision for Uncollectible Accounts during Year 2	120,000
Less Specific Customers' Accounts Written Off as Uncollectible during Year 2	?
Allowance for Uncollectible Accounts, December 31, Year 2	$250,000

Specific customers' accounts written off as uncollectible during Year 2 totaled $70,000.

d. Gross Accounts Receivable, December 31, Year 1[a]	$ 2,500,000
Plus Sales during the Year	12,000,000
Less Gross Accounts Receivable, December 31, Year 2[b]	(3,100,000)
Accounts Collected or Written Off	$11,400,000
Less Write-Offs	(70,000)
Cash Collected during the Year	$11,330,000

[a]$2,300,000 + $200,000.
[b]$2,850,000 + $250,000.

Kaplan Corporation generated $11,330,000 cash from credit customers during Year 2. Net income includes $11,880,000 from credit sales (= sales revenue of $12,000,000 − bad debt expense of $120,000). The accountant subtracts the $550,000 difference (= $11,880,000 − $11,330,000) from net income when computing cash flow from operations. This $550,000 amount equals the increase in accounts receivable (net) during Year 2 (= $2,850,000 − $2,300,000).

e.

Finished Goods Inventory, December 31, Year 1	$1,800,000
Plus Cost of Units Completed during the Year	?
Less Cost of Units Sold during the Year	(7,200,000)
Finished Goods Inventory, December 31, Year 2	$2,200,000

The cost of units completed was $7,600,000.

f.

Work-in-Process Inventory, December 31, Year 1	$ 460,000
Plus Cost of Raw Materials Used	?
Plus Direct Labor and Manufacturing Overhead Costs Incurred	4,500,000
Less Cost of Units Completed	(7,600,000)
Work-in-Process Inventory, December 31, Year 2	$ 530,000

The cost of raw materials used during Year 2 was $3,170,000.

Raw Materials Inventory, December 31, Year 1	$ 330,000
Plus Cost of Raw Materials Purchased	?
Less Cost of Raw Materials Used	(3,170,000)
Raw Materials Inventory, December 31, Year 2	$ 380,000

The cost of raw materials purchased was $3,220,000.

g.

	LIFO	Difference	FIFO
Inventory, December 31, Year 1	$ 2,590,000	$ 420,000	$ 3,010,000
Purchases plus Costs Incurred	7,720,000	—	7,720,000
Goods Available	$10,310,000	$ 420,000	$10,730,000
Less Inventory, December 31, Year 2	3,110,000	730,000	3,840,000
Cost of Goods Sold	$ 7,200,000	$(310,000)	$ 6,890,000

Cost of goods sold under FIFO would have been $6,890,000. Note that cost of goods sold under LIFO of $7,200,000 is less than the cost of purchases plus costs incurred of $7,720,000. The accountant subtracts the difference of $520,000 (= $7,720,000 − $7,200,000), which equals the increase in inventories during Year 2 (= $3,110,000 − $2,590,000), when converting net income to cash flow from operations. To compute cash flow from operations, the accountant also adds to net income the increase in accounts payable of $355,000 because Kaplan Corporation did not make cash expenditures for the full amount of the increase in inventories.

h. **Investment in Maher Corporation (market value method)**

Balance, December 31, Year 1	$200,000
Plus Additional Investments	0
Less Sale of Investments	0
Less Increase in Unrealized Holding Loss on Investments in Securities	15,000
Balance, December 31, Year 2	$185,000

Investment in Johnson Corporation (equity method)

Balance, December 31, Year 1	$310,000
Plus Additional Investments	50,000
Plus Equity in Earnings (total equity in earnings of $300,000 from income statement minus equity in Earnings of Burton Corporation of $160,000)	140,000
Less Sale of Investments	0
Less Dividend Received (plug)	(90,000)
Balance, December 31, Year 2	$410,000

Investment in Burton Corporation (equity method)

Balance, December 31, Year 1	$800,000
Plus Additional Investments	0
Plus Equity in Earnings (.40 × $400,000)	160,000
Less Sale of Investments	0
Less Dividends Received (.40 × $75,000)	(30,000)
Balance, December 31, Year 2	$930,000

Kaplan Corporation recognized a total of $300,000 (= $140,000 + $160,000) equity in earnings, yet received dividends of $120,000 (= $90,000 + $30,000). The statement of cash flows shows a subtraction from net income of $180,000 (=$300,000 − $120,000) for the excess of revenues over dividends from investments when computing cash flow from operations. The statement of cash flows reports the additional investment in Johnson Corporation as an investing activity.

i. **Land**

Balance, December 31, Year 1	$ 400,000
Plus Acquisitions	100,000
Less Disposals	0
Balance, December 31, Year 2	$ 500,000

Building

Balance, December 31, Year 1	$ 800,000
Plus Acquisitions	300,000
Less Retirements (plug)	(160,000)
Balance, December 31, Year 2	$ 940,000

Equipment

Balance, December 31, Year 1	$3,300,000
Plus Acquisitions	1,400,000
Less Disposals (plug)	(900,000)
Balance, December 31, Year 2	$3,800,000

Accumulated Depreciation

Balance, December 31, Year 1	$1,200,000
Plus Depreciation for Year 2	560,000
Less Accumulated Depreciation on Building Retired (plug)	(160,000)
Less Accumulated Depreciation on Equipment Sold (see below)	(670,000)
Balance, December 31, Year 2	$ 930,000
Selling Price of Equipment Sold	$ 150,000
Loss on Sale of Equipment	80,000
Book Value of Equipment Sold	$ 230,000
Cost of Equipment Sold (from above)	$ 900,000
Less Accumulated Depreciation on Equipment Sold (plug)	(670,000)
Book Value of Equipment Sold	$ 230,000

The statement of cash flows shows the acquisitions of land, building, and equipment as investing activities. The cash proceeds from the sale of equipment of $150,000 appears as an investing activity. The statement of cash flows shows an addback to net income of $80,000 for the loss on sale of equipment to avoid understating the amount of cash generated from the sale. Depreciation expense for Year 2 of $560,000 appears as an addback to net income because this expense does not use cash.

j.

Investment in Heimann Corporation	800,000	
Common Stock (20,000 × $10)		200,000
Additional Paid-in Capital (20,000 × $30)		600,000

k.

Cost of Investment in Heimann Corporation	$800,000
Goodwill, $80,000 + (2 × $10,000)	(100,000)
Book Value of Net Assets Acquired	$700,000

l. 4 Percent Bond Issue

$40,000 × 9.9540	$ 398,160
$2,000,000 × .70138	1,402,760
Total	$1,800,920

10 Percent Bond Issue

$150,000 × 13.59033	$2,038,550
$3,000,000 × .45639	1,369,170
Total	$3,407,720

	Liability, Beginning of the Period	Market Interest Rate	Interest Expense	Amount Payable	Addition to (or Reduction in) Liability	Liability, End of the Period
m. 4 Percent Bond Issue						
January 1, Year 2	$1,800,920	0.03	$ 54,028	$ 40,000	$ 14,028	$1,814,948
July 1, Year 2	1,814,948	0.03	54,448	40,000	14,448	1,829,396
Total			$108,476	$ 80,000	$ 28,476	
10 Percent Bond Issue						
January 1, Year 2	$3,407,720	0.04	$136,309	$150,000	$(13,691)	$3,394,029
July 1, Year 2	3,394,029	0.04	135,761	150,000	(14,239)	3,379,790
Total			$272,070	$300,000	$(27,930)	
8 Percent Bond Issue						
January 1, Year 2	$1,000,000	0.04	$ 40,000	$ 40,000	$ 0	$1,000,000
July 1, Year 2	1,000,000	0.04	40,000	40,000	0	1,000,000
Total			$ 80,000	$ 80,000	$ 0	

Interest expense on the 4 percent bonds of $108,476 exceeds the amount payable of $80,000. The statement of cash flows shows an addback to net income for the difference, the amortization of discount on these bonds. Interest expense on the 10 percent bonds of $272,070 is less than the amount payable of $300,000. The statement of cash flows shows a subtraction from net income for the difference, the amortization of premium on these bonds. The statement of cash flows also shows an addition to net income for the increase in interest payable of $100,000, indicating that cash expenditures for interest were less than the amounts accrued as payable for Year 2.

n. Income Taxes Payable, December 31, Year 1		$250,000
Plus Current Income Tax Expense for Year 2 (see below)		420,000
Less Cash Payment during Year 2		?
Income Taxes Payable, December 31, Year 2		$375,000
Total Income Tax Expense		$540,000
Less Increase in Deferred Income Taxes		(120,000)
Current Income Tax Expense		$420,000

Cash payments for income taxes totaled $295,000 during Year 2. The statement of cash flows should show an addback to net income of $120,000 for the portion of income tax expense that does not require a current expenditure (that is, the increase in the Deferred Tax Liability account). The statement of cash flows also shows an addition to net income for the increase in income taxes payable of $125,000, indicating that cash expenditures for income taxes were less than the amount accrued as payable for Year 2.

	Common Shares		Additional Paid-in Capital	Retained Earnings	Treasury Shares
	Number of Shares	Amount			
0. Balance, December 31, Year 1	50,000	$500,000	$ 800,000	$1,666,000	$30,000
Common Stock Issued on the Open Market	10,000	100,000	400,000	—	—
Treasury Stock Sold	—	—	5,000	—	(10,000)
Net Income.	—	—	—	1,260,000	—
Dividends (plug)[a]	—	—	—	(236,000)	—
Balance, December 31, Year 2	60,000	$600,000	$1,205,000	$2,690,000	$20,000

[a]Or, see statement of cash flows.

The $500,000 proceeds from issuing common stock appears as a financing activity on the statement of cash flows. The $15,000 cash proceeds from reissuing treasury stock (= $10,000 + $5,000) also appears as a financing activity. Note that the excess of the $15,000 reissue price over the $10,000 cost of the treasury stock increases additional paid-in capital, not net income.

KEY TERMS AND CONCEPTS

Generally accepted accounting principles (GAAP)
Securities and Exchange Commission (SEC)
Financial Accounting Standards Board (FASB)
Conceptual framework
International Accounting Standards Committee (IASC)

Quality of earnings
Quality of financial position
Accurate presentation
Conservatism
Profit maximization
Income smoothing
Least and latest rule

QUESTIONS, EXERCISES, PROBLEMS, AND CASES

QUESTIONS

1. Review the terms and concepts listed above in Key Terms and Concepts.
2. Reconcile the following two positions:
   (1) "Standard-setting bodies need a conceptual framework to guide their selection of alternative accounting principles if the principles are to have a sound foundation and exhibit consistency over time."
   (2) "Standard-setting bodies must continually interact with various preparers and users of financial statements to be sure that alternative accounting principles are generally acceptable."
3. A critic of accounting stated: "The financial statements are virtually useless because firms have too much latitude in selecting from among generally accepted accounting

methods." Another critic of accounting reacted: "I agree that the financial statements are useless, but it is because firms have too little latitude in the way they account for certain transactions under generally accepted accounting principles." Respond to these statements.

4. "The controversy over alternative generally accepted accounting principles disappears if we require all firms to use the same methods of accounting in both their financial statements and their tax return." Respond to this proposal.

5. If net income over sufficiently long time periods equals cash inflows minus cash outflows other than transactions with owners, why not allow the timing of cash flows to dictate the timing of revenue and expense recognition and eliminate alternative GAAP?

6. "The total reported net income over sufficiently long time periods is the same regardless of whether a firm follows a conservative strategy or a profit-maximizing strategy in selecting its accounting methods." Explain.

7. "The direction of the cumulative effect of two alternative accounting principles on earnings may differ from the direction of the current year's effect." Explain.

8. "Alternative accounting principles have less of an effect on the statement of cash flows than on the balance sheet and income statement." Explain.

9. If capital markets react quickly and in an unbiased manner to the release of information, including information contained in the financial statements, what is the benefit of analyzing a set of financial statements?

EXERCISES

10. **Identifying generally accepted accounting principles.** Indicate the generally accepted accounting principle or method described in each of the following statements. Explain your reasoning.

   a. This inventory cost flow assumption results in reporting the largest net income during periods of rising prices.

   b. This method of accounting for uncollectible accounts recognizes the implied income reduction in the period of sale.

   c. This method of accounting for long-term investments in the securities of other corporations usually requires an adjustment to net income to calculate cash flow from operations in the statement of cash flows.

   d. This method of accounting for long-term leases by the lessee gives rise to a non-current liability.

   e. This inventory cost flow assumption results in approximately the same balance sheet amount as is produced under the FIFO flow assumption.

   f. This method of recognizing interest expense on bonds provides a uniform annual rate of interest expense over the life of the bond.

   g. During periods of rising prices, this inventory valuation basis produces approximately the same results as does the acquisition cost valuation basis.

   h. When a firm deems specific customers' accounts uncollectible and writes them off, this method of accounting results in a decrease in the current ratio.

   i. This method of depreciation generally provides the largest amounts of depreciation expense during the first several years of an asset's life.

   j. This method of accounting for intercorporate investments in securities can result in a decrease in the investor's total shareholders' equity without affecting the Retained Earnings account.

   k. This method of recognizing income from long-term contracts generally results in the least amount of fluctuation in earnings over several periods.

l. When a firm identifies specific customers' accounts as uncollectible and writes them off, this method of accounting results in no change in working capital (equals current assets minus current liabilities).

m. When a firm uses this inventory cost flow assumption in calculating taxable income, it generally must use it in calculating net income reported to shareholders.

n. This method of accounting for long-term leases of equipment by the lessor shows on the income statement an amount for depreciation expense.

o. This inventory cost flow assumption results in inventory balance sheet amounts closest to current replacement cost.

p. This method of accounting for long-term investments in securities results in recognizing revenue for dividends received or receivable.

q. This method of depreciation generally results in the largest amounts for depreciable assets on the balance sheet during the first several years of an asset's life.

r. This inventory cost flow assumption results in reporting the smallest net income during periods of falling prices.

s. The method of accounting for long-term leases of equipment by the lessee results in showing an amount for rent expense on the income statement.

t. This inventory cost flow assumption results in inventory balance sheet amounts that may differ significantly from current replacement cost.

u. This method of accounting for long-term leases of equipment by the lessor results in showing revenue at the time of signing a lease.

v. This inventory cost flow assumption can result in substantial changes in the relation between cost of goods sold and sales if inventory quantities decrease during a period.

11. Identifying generally accepted accounting principles. Indicate the accounting principle or procedure apparently being used to record each of the following independent transactions. Also describe the transaction or event being recorded.

a. Bad Debt Expense	X	
Accounts Receivable		X
b. Cash	X	
Dividend Revenue		X
c. Unrealized Holding Loss on Marketable Securities Available for Sale	X	
Marketable Securities		X
d. Cash	X	
Investment in Affiliated Company		X
Dividend declared and received from affiliate company.		
e. Bad Debt Expense	X	
Allowance for Uncollectible Accounts		X
f. Rent Expense (for lease contract)	X	
Cash		X
g. Investment in Affiliated Company	X	
Equity in Earnings of Affiliated Company		X
h. Allowance for Uncollectible Accounts	X	
Accounts Receivable		X
I. Loss from Price Decline for Inventories	X	
Merchandise Inventories		X
j. Liability under Long-Term Lease	X	
Interest Expense	X	
Cash		X

12. **Identifying effects of generally accepted accounting principles on reported income.** Indicate the accounting principle that provides the smallest amount of *cumulative* earnings in each of the following cases:

   a. The valuation of inventories at acquisition cost or lower of cost or market

   b. FIFO, LIFO, or weighted-average cost flow assumption for inventories during periods of rising prices

   c. FIFO, LIFO, or weighted-average cost flow assumption for inventories during periods of declining prices

   d. Market value method or equity method of accounting for long-term investments in securities when the investee declares dividends less than its earnings

   e. Market value method or equity method of accounting for long-term investments in the securities of unconsolidated subsidiaries when the investee realizes net losses and does not pay dividends

   f. Sum-of-the-years'-digits or straight-line depreciation method during the first one-third of an asset's life

   g. Sum-of-the-years'-digits or straight-line depreciation method during the last one-third of an asset's life

   h. The operating lease method or the capital lease method for the lessee during the first several years of the life of a lease

   i. The operating lease method or the capital lease method for the lessor during the last several years of the life of a lease

PROBLEMS AND CASES

13. **Impact of capitalizing and amortizing versus expensing when incurred.** West Company, a U.S. company, and East Company, a Japanese company, incur $100 million of research and development (R&D) costs each year. West Company must expense these costs immediately, whereas East Company capitalizes the costs and amortizes them over five years.

   a. For each of the first six years, compute the amount of R&D expense that each firm would report on the income statement and the amount of deferred R&D costs that each firm would report on the balance sheet.

   b. For this part, assume that the amount of R&D costs incurred by each firm increases by $20,000 each year. Repeat part **a.**

   c. Comment on the differences noted in parts **a** and **b.**

14. **Impact of alternative accounting principles on two firms.** On January 1, Year 1, two corporations establish merchandising businesses. The firms are alike in all respects except for their methods of accounting. Humble Company chooses the accounting principles that minimize its reported net income. Huff Company chooses the accounting principles that maximize its reported net income but, where permitted, uses accounting methods that minimize its taxable income. The following events occur during Year 1.

   (1) Both firms issue 500,000 shares of $1-par value common shares for $8 per share on January 1, Year 1.

   (2) Both firms acquire equipment on January 2, Year 1, for $2,750,000 cash. The firms estimate the equipment to have a 10-year life and zero salvage value.

   (3) Both firms engage in extensive sales promotion activities during Year 1, incurring costs of $375,000.

   (4) The two firms make the following purchases of merchandise inventory, on account.

Date	Units Purchased	Unit Price	Cost of Purchase
January 2	30,000	$8.00	$ 240,000
April 1	80,000	8.10	648,000
August 15	20,000	8.25	165,000
November 30	70,000	8.40	588,000
Total	200,000		$1,641,000

On December 31, Year 1, purchases of inventory on account totaling $310,000 remain unpaid.

(5) During the year, both firms sell 150,000 units at an average price of $18 each.

(6) Selling, general, and administrative expenses, other than advertising, total $150,000 during the year.

Humble Company uses the following accounting methods (for both book and tax purposes): LIFO inventory cost flow assumption, accelerated depreciation, and immediate expensing of the costs of sales promotion. It uses the sum-of-the-years'-digits depreciation method for financial reporting and the allowable accelerated depreciation method for tax purposes. For tax purposes, depreciation on this equipment is $293,700 for Year 1.

Huff Company uses the following accounting methods: FIFO inventory cost flow assumption for both book and tax purposes, the straight-line depreciation method for book and the allowable accelerated depreciation method for tax purposes, and capitalization and amortization of the costs of the sales promotion campaign over four years for book and immediate expensing for tax purposes.

a. Prepare comparative income statements for the two firms for Year 1. Include separate computations of income tax expense. The income tax rate is 30 percent.

b. Prepare comparative balance sheets for the two firms as of December 31, Year 1. Both firms have $1,300,000 of outstanding accounts receivable on this date. Each firm has a current liability for unpaid income taxes equal to one-fifth of the taxes payable on the current year's taxable income.

c. Prepare comparative statements of cash flows for the two firms for Year 1, defining funds as cash.

d. Prepare an analysis that explains the difference in the cash of Humble Company and that of Huff Company on December 31, Year 1.

15. Impact of two sets of alternative accounting principles on net income and cash flows. Brown Corporation commences operations on January 2, Year 1, with the issuance at par of 100,000 shares of $10-par value common stock for cash. During Year 1, the following transactions occur.

(1) Brown Corporation acquires the assets of Joan's Department Store on January 2, Year 1, for $600,000 cash. The market values of Joan's identifiable assets are as follows: accounts receivable, $150,000; merchandise inventory, $300,000 (150,000 units); store equipment, $112,500; and goodwill, $37,500.

(2) During the year, the firm sells 157,500 units at an average price of $3.20.

(3) The firm offers extensive training programs during the year to acquaint previous employees of Joan's Department Store with the merchandising policies and procedures of Brown Corporation. The costs incurred in the training programs total $37,500.

(4) Selling, general, and administrative costs incurred and recognized as an expense during Year 1 are $60,000.

(5) Brown Corporation purchases, on account, merchandise inventory during Year 1 as follows:

Date	Units Purchased	Unit Price	Cost of Purchase
April 1	22,500	$2.10	$47,250
August 1	15,000	2.20	33,000
October 1	37,500	2.40	90,000
Total	75,000		$170,250

On December 31, Year 1, Brown Corporation owes $30,200 for purchases on account.

(6) Brown Corporation estimates the store equipment to have a 10-year useful life and zero salvage value.

(7) The income tax rate is 30 percent. The goodwill arising from this corporate acquisition is not deductible in computing taxable income, and the difference is a permanent difference, not a timing difference. (Some tax jurisdictions allow deductions for goodwill amortization, so some tax/book differences for goodwill are temporary.)

The management of Brown Corporation is uncertain about the accounting methods that it should use in preparing its financial statements. It narrows the choice to two sets of accounting methods and asks you to calculate net income for Year 1 using each set.

Set A consists of the following accounting methods (for book and tax purposes): LIFO inventory cost flow assumption, accelerated depreciation, immediate expensing of the costs of the training program, and amortization of goodwill (for book) over 10 years. Set A computes depreciation using the double declining-balance method for book purposes (10-year useful life and zero estimated salvage value). Accelerated depreciation for tax purposes is $16,073.

Set B consists of the following accounting methods: FIFO inventory cost flow assumption, straight-line depreciation for book purposes (10-year life and zero estimated salvage value), capitalization and amortization of the costs of the training program over five years for book and immediate expensing for tax purposes, and amortization of goodwill (for book) over 20 years. Accelerated depreciation for tax purposes is $16,073.

a. Calculate the net income for Year 1 under each set of accounting methods.

b. Calculate cash flow from operations under each set of accounting methods. Assume that accounts receivable total $120,000 and accounts payable total $30,200 at year-end. Also assume that one-fourth of the income taxes payable on the current year's taxable income remains unpaid at year-end.

c. Prepare an analysis that explains the difference in cash flow from operations under Set A and Set B.

16. **Comprehensive review problem.** Exhibits 14.7 and 14.8 present a partial set of financial statements of Chicago Corporation for Year 2, including a consolidated statement of income and retained earnings for Year 2 and consolidated comparative balance sheets at December 31, Year 1 and Year 2. A series of questions relating to the financial statements of Chicago Corporation follows these financial statements. You should study the financial statements before responding to these questions and problems. Additional information is as follows:

(1) During Year 2, Chicago Corporation sold, for cash, machinery and equipment costing $1,000,000 and with a book value of $200,000.

(2) The only transaction affecting common or preferred stocks during Year 2 was the sale of treasury stock.

(3) The bonds payable have a maturity value of $4 million.

    a. Compute the amount of specific customers' accounts that Chicago Corporation wrote off as uncollectible during Year 2, assuming that it made no recoveries during Year 2 on accounts written off in years prior to Year 2.

    b. Chicago Corporation uses the LIFO cost flow assumption in computing its cost of goods sold and its beginning and ending merchandise inventory amounts. If it had used a FIFO cost flow assumption, the beginning inventory would have been $1,800,000 and the ending inventory would have been $1,700,000. Compute the actual gross profit (net sales less cost of goods sold)

EXHIBIT 14.7	CHICAGO CORPORATION Consolidated Statement of Income and Retained Earnings for Year 2 (Problem 16)

Revenues

Sales		$13,920,000
Gain on Sale of Machinery and Equipment		200,000
Equity in Earnings of Affiliates:		
Chicago Finance Corporation.	$1,800,000	
Rosenwald Company.	125,000	
Hutchinson Company	75,000	2,000,000
Total Revenues		$16,120,000

Expenses

Cost of Goods Sold	$ 5,000,000
Employee Payroll	3,000,000
Depreciation of Plant and Equipment and Amortization of Leased Property Rights	1,000,000
Amortization of Intangibles	200,000
Bad Debt Expense	120,000
Interest	455,000
General Corporate	345,000
Income Taxes—Current	1,430,000
Income Taxes—Deferred	170,000
Total Expenses	$11,720,000
Net Income	$ 4,400,000
Less: Dividends on Preferred Shares	(120,000)
Dividends on Common Shares	(2,080,000)
Increase in Retained Earnings	$ 2,200,000
Retained Earnings, January 1, Year 2	2,800,000
Retained Earnings, December 31, Year 2	$ 5,000,000
Basic Earnings per Common Share (based on 1,600,000 average shares outstanding)	$2.675
Fully Diluted Earnings per Share (assuming conversion of preferred stock)	$2.20

EXHIBIT 14.8	CHICAGO CORPORATION Consolidated Balance Sheets December 31 (Problem 16)

	Year 1	Year 2
ASSETS		
Current Assets		
Cash	$ 200,000	$ 100,000
Certificate of Deposit	—	300,000
Accounts Receivable (net of estimated uncollectibles of $100,000 in Year 1 and $160,000 in Year 2)	500,000	600,000
Merchandise Inventory	1,500,000	1,800,000
Prepayments	200,000	200,000
Total Current Assets	$ 2,400,000	$ 3,000,000
Investments (at equity)		
Chicago Finance Corporation (40 percent owned)	$ 2,200,000	$ 4,000,000
Rosenwald Company (50 percent owned)	900,000	1,025,000
Hutchinson Company (25 percent owned)	100,000	175,000
Total Investments	$ 3,200,000	$ 5,200,000
Property, Plant, and Equipment		
Land	$ 400,000	$ 500,000
Building	4,000,000	4,000,000
Machinery and Equipment	7,300,000	8,000,000
Property Rights Acquired under Lease	1,500,000	1,500,000
Total	$ 13,200,000	$14,000,000
Less Accumulated Depreciation and Amortization	(3,800,000)	(4,000,000)
Total Property, Plant, and Equipment	$ 9,400,000	$10,000,000
Intangibles (at net book value)		
Patent	$ 875,000	$ 750,000
Goodwill	1,125,000	1,050,000
Total Intangibles	$ 2,000,000	$ 1,800,000
Total Assets	$ 17,000,000	$20,000,000

of Chicago Corporation for Year 2 under LIFO and the corresponding amount of gross profit if FIFO had been used (ignore income tax effects). Chicago Corporation used the periodic inventory method.

c. Refer to part **b.** Did the quantity and acquisition costs of merchandise inventory increase or decrease between the beginning and the end of Year 2? Explain.

d. Chicago Corporation accounts for its three intercorporate investments in unconsolidated affiliates using the equity method. It acquired the shares in each of these companies at book value at the time of acquisition. How much did each of these three companies declare in dividends during Year 2? How can you tell?

e. Chicago Corporation accounts for its three intercorporate investments in unconsolidated affiliates using the equity method. It acquired the shares in each

	Year 1	Year 2
LIABILITIES AND SHAREHOLDERS' EQUITY		
Current Liabilities		
Accounts Payable	$ 400,000	$ 550,000
Advances from Customers	660,000	640,000
Salaries Payable	240,000	300,000
Income Taxes Payable	300,000	430,000
Rent Received in Advance	—	50,000
Other Current Liabilities	200,000	460,000
Total Current Liabilities	$ 1,800,000	$ 2,430,000
Long-term Debt		
Bonds Payable	$ 3,600,000	$ 3,648,000
Equipment Mortgage Indebtedness	1,300,000	332,000
Capitalized Lease Obligation	1,100,000	1,020,000
Total Long-term Debt	$ 6,000,000	$ 5,000,000
Deferred Tax Liability	$ 1,400,000	$ 1,570,000
Shareholders' Equity		
Convertible Preferred Stock	$ 2,000,000	$ 2,000,000
Common Stock	2,000,000	2,000,000
Additional Paid-in Capital	2,400,000	3,000,000
Retained Earnings	2,800,000	5,000,000
Total	$ 9,200,000	$12,000,000
Less Cost of Treasury Shares	(1,400,000)	(1,000,000)
Total Shareholders' Equity	$ 7,800,000	$11,000,000
Total Liabilities and Shareholders' Equity	$17,000,000	$20,000,000

of these companies at book value at the time of acquisition. Give the journal entry (entries) made during Year 2 to apply the equity method.

f. Chicago Corporation acquired its only building on January 1, Year 1. It estimated the building to have a 40-year useful life and zero salvage value at that time. Calculate the amount of depreciation expense on this building for Year 2, assuming that the firm uses the double declining-balance method.

g. Chicago Corporation sold machinery and equipment costing $1,000,000, with a book value of $200,000, for cash during Year 2. Give the journal entry to record the disposition.

h. The bonds payable carry 6 percent annual coupons and require the payment of interest on December 31 of each year. Give the journal entry made on

December 31, Year 2, to recognize interest expense for Year 2, assuming that Chicago Corporation uses the effective interest method.

i. Refer to part **h.** What was the effective or market interest rate on these bonds on the date they were issued? Explain.

j. The $170,000 deferred portion of income tax expense for Year 2 includes $150,000 relating to the use of different depreciation methods for financial and tax reporting. If the income tax rate was 30 percent, calculate the difference between the depreciation deduction reported on the tax return and the depreciation expense reported on the income statement.

k. Give the journal entry that explains the change in the treasury shares account assuming that no other transactions affected the common or preferred shares during Year 2.

l. If the original acquisition cost of the patent is $1,250,000, and the firm amortizes the patent on a straight-line basis, how long before December 31, Year 2, did the firm acquire the patent?

m. Chicago Corporation acquired the stock of Hutchinson Company on December 31, Year 1. If it held the same amount of stock during the year, but the amount represented only a 15 percent ownership of the Hutchinson Company, how would the financial statements have differed? Disregard income tax effects, and assume the market price of the shares exceeds their acquisition cost by $25,000 on December 31, Year 2.

n. During Year 2, Chicago Corporation paid $170,000 to the lessor of property represented on the balance sheet by "Property Rights Acquired under Lease." Property rights acquired under lease have a 10-year life, and Chicago Corporation amortizes them on a straight-line basis. What was the total expense reported by Chicago Corporation during Year 2 from using the leased property?

o. How would the financial statements differ if Chicago Corporation accounted for inventories on the lower-of-cost-or-market basis and if the market value of these inventories had been $1,600,000 at the end of Year 2? Disregard income tax effects.

p. Refer to the earnings-per-share amounts in the income statement of Chicago Corporation. How many shares of common stock would the firm issue if holders of the outstanding shares of preferred stock converted them into common stock?

q. Prepare a T-account work sheet for a statement of cash flows for Chicago Corporation for Year 2. The certificate of deposit is a cash equivalent.

r. The treasurer of Chicago Corporation recently remarked, "The value or worth of our company on December 31, Year 2, is $11,000,000, as measured by total shareholders' equity." Describe briefly at least three reasons why the difference between recorded total assets and recorded total liabilities on the balance sheet does not represent the firm's value or worth.

s. Some financial statement users criticize the accounting profession for permitting several GAAP for the same or similar transactions. What are the major arguments for (1) narrowing the range of acceptable methods or (2) continuing the present system of permitting business firms some degree of flexibility in selecting their accounting methods?

17. Comprehensive review problem. Exhibit 14.9 presents a consolidated statement of income and retained earnings for Year 22, and Exhibit 14.10 presents a consolidated balance sheet for Tuck Corporation as of December 31, Year 21 and Year 22. A statement of accounting policies and a set of notes to the financial statements appear below. After studying these financial statements and notes, respond to each of the following questions and calculation requirements.

EXHIBIT 14.9	TUCK CORPORATION Consolidated Statement of Income and Retained Earnings for Year 22 (Problem 17)	

Revenues and Gains

Sales	$4,000,000	
Gain on Sale of Equipment	3,000	
Rental Revenue	240,000	
Dividend Revenue	8,000	
Equity in Earnings of Unconsolidated Affiliates	102,000	
Total Revenues and Gains		$4,353,000

Expenses, Losses, and Deductions

Cost of Goods Sold (including depreciation and amortization)	$2,580,000	
Selling and Administration Expenses (including depreciation and amortization)	1,102,205	
Warranty Expense	46,800	
Interest Expense	165,995	
Loss on Sale of Marketable Equity Securities	8,000	
Income Tax Expense	150,000	
Total Expenses, Losses, and Deductions		4,053,000
Consolidated Net Income		$ 300,000
Less Dividends Declared		(119,500)
Increase in Retained Earnings for Year 22		$ 180,500
Retained Earnings, December 31, Year 21		277,000
Retained Earnings, December 31, Year 22		$ 457,500

a. Prepare an analysis that explains the change in the Marketable Equity Securities account during Year 22.
b. Calculate the proceeds from sales of marketable equity securities classified as current assets during Year 22.
c. Calculate the amount of the estimated uncollectible accounts provision made during Year 22.
d. Calculate the amount of cost of goods sold assuming Tuck Corporation used a FIFO cost flow assumption.
e. Give the journal entry(s) to account for the change in the Investment in Thayer Corporation account during Year 22.
f. Calculate the amount of income or loss from the Investment in Thayer Corporation during Year 22.
g. Give the journal entry(s) to account for the change in the Investment in Davis Corporation account during Year 22.
h. Refer to Note 5. Give the journal entry to record the sale of equipment during Year 22.
i. Refer to Note 9. Demonstrate that the $106,036 is the correct amount of the leasehold asset at the beginning of the lease term.
j. Calculate the amount of cash received during Year 22 for rental fees.
k. Calculate the actual cost of goods and services required to service customers' warranties during Year 22.

EXHIBIT 14.10	TUCK CORPORATION Consolidated Comparative Balance Sheet (Problem 17)

	December 31, Year 21	December 31, Year 22
ASSETS		
Current Assets		
Cash	$ 240,000	$ 280,000
Marketable Securities (Note 1)	125,000	141,000
Accounts Receivable—Net (Note 2)	1,431,200	1,509,600
Inventories (Note 3)	1,257,261	1,525,315
Prepayments	28,000	32,000
Total Current Assets	$3,081,461	$3,487,915
Investments (Note 4)		
Investment in Thayer Corporation (15 percent owned)	$ 92,000	$ 87,000
Investment in Hitchcock Corporation (30 percent owned)	120,000	135,000
Investment in Davis Corporation (40 percent owned)	215,000	298,000
Total Investments	$ 427,000	$ 520,000
Property, Plant, and Equipment (Note 5)		
Land	$ 82,000	$ 82,000
Building	843,000	843,000
Equipment	497,818	1,848,418
Leasehold	106,036	106,036
Total Plant Assets at Cost	$1,528,854	$2,879,454
Less Accumulated Depreciation and Amortization	(383,854)	(420,854)
Total Plant Assets—Net	$1,145,000	$2,458,600
Intangibles		
Goodwill—Net	$ 36,000	$ 34,000
Total Assets	$4,689,461	$6,500,515

	December 31, Year 21	December 31, Year 22
LIABILITIES AND SHAREHOLDERS' EQUITY		
Current Liabilities		
Note Payable (Note 6)	$ 100,000	$ 200,000
Accounts Payable	666,100	723,700
Rental Fees Received in Advance	46,000	58,000
Estimated Warranty Liability	75,200	78,600
Interest Payable on Notes	1,500	2,000
Dividends Payable	25,000	30,000
Income Taxes Payable—Current	140,000	160,000
Mortgage Payable—Current Portion	37,383	37,383
Capitalized Lease Obligation—Current Portion	10,000	10,000
Total Current Liabilities	$1,101,183	$1,299,683
Noncurrent Liabilities		
Bonds Payable (Note 7)	$1,104,650	$1,931,143
Mortgage Payable (Note 8)	262,564	243,560
Capitalized Lease Obligation (Note 9)	52,064	46,229
Deferred Tax Liability	130,000	145,000
Total Noncurrent Liabilities	$1,549,278	$2,365,932
Total Liabilities	$2,650,461	$3,665,615
Shareholders' Equity		
Convertible Preferred Stock, $100 par Value (Note 10)	$ 700,000	$ 200,000
Common Stock, $10 par Value (Note 11)	1,000,000	1,650,000
Additional Paid-in Capital—Common	130,000	583,600
Accumulated Other Comprehensive Income: Unrealized Holding Loss on Marketable Securities	(25,000)	(21,000)
Unrealized Holding Loss on Investments in Securities	(16,000)	(21,000)
Retained Earnings	277,000	457,500
Total	$2,066,000	$2,849,100
Less Cost of Treasury Stock (Note 12)	(27,000)	(14,200)
Total Shareholders' Equity	$2,039,000	$2,834,900
Total Liabilities and Shareholders' Equity	$4,689,461	$6,500,515

l. Refer to Note 7. Calculate the amount of interest expense on the $1 million, 6 percent bonds for Year 22.

m. Give the journal entry(s) for the change in the Mortgage Payable accounts during Year 22. Be sure to consider the current portion.

n. Verify that the book value of the combined current and noncurrent portions of the Capitalized Lease Obligation on December 31, Year 21, should be $62,064.

o. Prepare an analysis that explains the change in the book value of the combined current and noncurrent portions of the Capitalized Lease Obligation during Year 22.

p. Give the journal entry to record income tax expense for Year 22.

q. Compute the amount of cash payments for income taxes during Year 22.

r. The income tax rate is 30 percent. Assume that during Year 22, Tuck Corporation recognized $12,000 of deferred tax expense related to differences in depreciation methods. Calculate the difference between the amount of depreciation recognized for financial reporting purposes and the amount recognized for tax purposes.

s. Give the journal entry made on July 1, Year 22, upon conversion of the preferred stock.

t. Give the journal entry(s) to account for the change in the Treasury Stock account during Year 22.

u. Prepare a T-account work sheet for the preparation of a statement of cash flows, defining funds as cash.

STATEMENT OF ACCOUNTING POLICIES

- *Basis of consolidation.* Tuck Corporation consolidates its financial statements with those of Harvard Corporation, a 100-percent-owned subsidiary acquired on January 2, Year 20.

- *Marketable equity securities.* The firm reports marketable securities at market value.

- *Accounts receivable.* The firm accounts for customers' uncollectible accounts using the allowance method.

- *Inventories.* Tuck Corporation uses a last-in, first-out (LIFO) cost flow assumption for inventories.

- *Investments.* The firm accounts for investments of less than 20 percent of the outstanding common stock of other companies using the market value method. It accounts for investments of 20 to 50 percent of the outstanding common stock of affiliates using the equity method.

- *Building, equipment, and leaseholds.* Tuck Corporation calculates depreciation for financial reporting purposes using the straight-line method and for income tax reporting using MACRS depreciation.

- *Goodwill.* The firm amortizes goodwill arising from investments in Harvard Corporation over a period of 20 years.

- *Interest expense on long-term debt.* The firm measures interest expense on long-term debt using the effective interest method.

- *Deferred income taxes.* Tuck Corporation provides deferred income taxes for temporary differences between book and taxable income.

NOTES TO THE FINANCIAL STATEMENTS

- *Note 1:* The balance sheet presents marketable equity securities at market value, which is less than acquisition cost by $25,000 on December 31, Year 21, and

$21,000 on December 31, Year 22. Tuck Corporation sold marketable equity securities costing $35,000 during Year 22. It received no dividends from marketable equity securities during Year 22.

- *Note 2:* The balance sheet presents accounts receivable net of an allowance for uncollectible accounts of $128,800 on December 31, Year 21, and $210,400 on December 31, Year 22. Tuck Corporation wrote off a total of $63,000 of accounts receivable as uncollectible during Year 22.

- *Note 3:* The valuation of inventories on a FIFO basis exceeded the amounts on a LIFO basis by $430,000 on December 31, Year 21, and by $410,000 on December 31, Year 22.

- *Note 4:* Davis Corporation reported net income for Year 22 of $217,500 and declared and paid dividends totaling $60,000 during the year. Tuck Corporation invested an additional $20,000 in Davis Corporation during Year 22, but its ownership percentage remained at 40 percent.

- *Note 5:* Tuck Corporation sold equipment with a cost of $23,000 and a book value of $4,000 during Year 22. This was the only disposition of property, plant, or equipment during the year.

- *Note 6:* Tuck Corporation paid at maturity a 90-day, 9 percent note with a face amount of $100,000 with interest on January 30, Year 22. On December 1, Year 22, Tuck Corporation borrowed $200,000 from its local bank, promising to repay the principal plus interest at 12 percent in six months.

- *Note 7:* Bonds Payable on the balance sheet comprises the following:

	December 31, Year 21	December 31, Year 22
$1,000,000, 6 Percent, 20-Year Semiannual Coupon Bonds, Due Dec. 31, Year 36, Priced at $1,125,510 to Yield 5 Percent, Compounded Semiannually, at the Time of Issue	$1,104,650	$1,099,823
$1,000,000, 8 Percent, 20-Year Semiannual Coupon Bonds, Due Dec. 31, Year 41, Priced at $828,409 to Yield 10 Percent, Compounded Semiannually, at the Time of Issue	—	831,320
Total	$1,104,650	$1,931,143

- *Note 8:* Mortgage Payable represents a building mortgage requiring equal installment payments of $40,000 on December 31 of each year. The loan underlying the mortgage bears interest of 7 percent, compounded annually. The final installment payment is due on December 31, Year 32.

- *Note 9:* The Capitalized Lease Obligation represents a 20-year, noncancelable lease on certain equipment. The lease requires annual payments, in advance, of $10,000 on January 2 of each year. The last lease payment will be made on January 2, Year 29. Tuck Corporation capitalizes the lease at the lessee's borrowing rate (at the inception of the lease) of 8 percent.

- *Note 10:* Each share of preferred stock is convertible into five shares of common stock. On July 1, Year 22, holders of 5,000 shares of preferred stock exercised their options. Tuck Corporation recorded the conversion using book values.

- *Note 11:* On October 1, Year 22, Tuck Corporation issued 40,000 shares of common stock on the open market for $15 per share.

■ *Note 12:* Treasury Stock comprises the following:

Dec. 31, Year 21: 2,250 Shares at $12 per Share	$27,000
Dec. 31, Year 22: 450 Shares at $12 per Share	$ 5,400
550 Shares at $16 per Share	8,800
	$14,200

During Year 22, Tuck Corporation sold 1,800 shares of treasury stock and acquired 550 shares.

18. **Selecting accounting methods.** Champion Clothiers, Inc., owns and operates 80 New England retailing establishments that specialize in quality men's and women's clothing. James Champion established the company many years ago, and members of the Champion family have run the company ever since. Currently, Ronald Champion, grandson of the founder, is president and chief executive officer. Members of the Champion family hold all of the company's shares.

The setting for this case is March 2000. Ronald Champion and the company's accountant, Tom Morrissey, engage in the following conversation.

Champion (president): "Tom, you said on the telephone that the financial statements for 1999 are now complete. How much did we earn in 1999?"

Morrissey (accountant): "Net income was $800,000, with earnings per share at $1.60. With the $1.20 per share earned in 1997 and $1.38 earned in 1998, we have maintained our 15 percent growth rate in profits."

Champion: "That sounds great! Tom, at our board meeting next week I am going to announce that the Champion family will take the company public. We will be issuing shares equal to a 40 percent stake in the company early in 2001. It is important that our earnings for 2000 continue to reflect the growth rate we have been experiencing. By my calculations, we need an earnings per share for 2000 in the neighborhood of $1.84. Does this seem likely?"

Morrissey: "I'm afraid not. Our current projections indicate an earnings per share around $1.65 for this year. Major unexpected style changes earlier this year left us with obsolete inventory that will have to be written off. In addition, increased competition in several of our major markets is putting a squeeze on margins. Even the acquisition of Green Trucking Company in June of this year will not help earnings that much."

Champion: "I know you accountants have all kinds of games you can play to doctor up the numbers. There must be something we can do to increase earnings to the desired level. What about our use of LIFO for inventories?"

Morrissey: "We have used LIFO in the past because it reduces income and saves taxes during a period of rising prices. The more recent, higher acquisition costs of inventory items enter into the computation of cost of goods sold in the income statement. The older, lower acquisition prices form the basis for the valuation of inventory on the balance sheet. We could switch to FIFO for 2000. That would add about $.21 to earnings per share. However, we would probably have to use FIFO for tax purposes as well, increasing our taxes for the year by about $50,000."

Champion: "I don't like paying more taxes, but FIFO certainly more closely approximates the physical flow of our goods. If we decide to stay on LIFO, is there anything we can do in applying the LIFO method to prop up earnings?"

Morrissey: "We now classify our inventory very broadly into two LIFO groups, or pools: one for men's clothing and one for women's clothing. We do this to minimize the possibility of dipping into an old LIFO layer. As you will recall, if we sell more than we purchase during a given period, we dip into an old LIFO layer. These LIFO layers use acquisition costs of the year the layer was added as the basis for their valuation. Some of these layers reflect costs of the mid-1950s. When we dip into one of these layers, we have to use these old, lower costs in figuring cost of goods sold and net income. By defining our LIFO pools broadly to include our dollar investment in men's clothing and our dollar investment in women's clothing, we minimize the probability of liquidating an old LIFO layer. We could define our LIFO pools more narrowly to increase the possibility of dipping. We could then let the inventory of particular items run down at the end of the year, dip into the LIFO layer to increase earnings, and then rebuild the inventory early in the next year. I suspect we could add about $.02 a share to 2000 earnings if we used narrower pools."

Champion: "We own all of our store buildings and display counters. Is there anything we can do with depreciation expense?"

Morrissey: "We now depreciate these items using the shortest lives allowed and the fastest write-off permitted by tax law. However, whereas we have to use LIFO for financial reporting if we use it for tax reporting, we do not have to calculate depreciation for financial reporting in the same way as we do for tax reporting. We could depreciate these items over the expected economic life of each asset, which would be longer than the tax life. That should add about $.04 to earnings per share for 2000. We could also use the straight-line depreciation method for financial reporting. Although our depreciable assets probably decrease in value faster than the straight-line method indicates, we would be using the depreciation method that most of our competitors use for financial reporting. The use of straight-line depreciation would add another $.08."

Champion: "Now you're talking. What else can we do?"

Morrissey: "There are some possibilities with respect to the acquisition of Green Trucking later this year. We currently plan to account for this acquisition using the purchase method. Under the purchase method, we will record the assets (and liabilities) of Green Trucking on our books at their market value on the date of acquisition. Since we expect to pay a price higher than the market value of Green's identifiable assets, we will also record some goodwill."

Champion: "How does the acquisition affect earnings for 2000?"

Morrissey: "On the plus side, we will include the earnings of Green Trucking from the date of acquisition in June until the end of the year. However, we must base cost of goods sold and depreciation expense on the higher current market values recorded on our books for Green's assets rather than on the lower amounts recorded on Green's books. In addition, we will have to amortize the goodwill. I expect to pick up $.08 per share in earnings for 2000 from the Green acquisition, but this is already reflected in my $1.65 estimate for the year."

Champion: "Can we account for the acquisition any differently?"

Morrissey: "If we can qualify, we may be able to use the pooling-of-interests method. Under the pooling method, we would record Green's assets (and liabilities) on our books at the amounts at which they are stated on Green's books; that is, the older, lower book values would carry over. This means that cost of goods sold and depreciation expense will be lower this year and in the future than if we used the purchase method. In addition, we would not recognize goodwill and therefore no goodwill amortization in 2000 and future years. Also, we would reflect in our earnings for 2000 the earnings of Green Trucking for all of 2000, not just that portion after June. Under the pooling method, earnings per share should be $.10 more than if we used the purchase method."

Champion: "That sounds great, but what do we have to do to qualify?"

Morrissey: "To justify carrying over the old book values of Green Trucking, we have to show that we are merely combining the predecessor companies *and their shareholders.* The shareholders of Green Trucking must receive common stock of Champion Clothiers in exchange for their shares in Green Trucking. The shareholders in each of the predecessor companies then become shareholders in the new combined company (which will carry the Champion name). The Green shareholders would own 10 percent of Champion after the acquisition. Accountants view such a transaction as a change in form rather than in substance and permit the carryover of the old book values of Green."

Champion: "My family may not be too happy about this arrangement, but let's move on."

Morrissey: "Well, there is one thing we can do very easily with our pension plan to improve earnings. When we adopted the pension plan two years ago, we gave all employees credit for their service prior to adoption. This created an immediate obligation for past service. We are amortizing this obligation as a charge against earnings over a 10-year period. GAAP permit us to use 15 years instead of 10 years as the amortization period; that switch would increase earnings per share by $.05 for 2000."

Champion: "All of the things you have suggested deal with the selection or application of accounting methods. Can we do anything with the timing of expenditures to help 2000 earnings?"

Morrissey: "Well, we could postpone painting and other maintenance of our stores scheduled for the last quarter of this year until the first quarter of next year. That would add $.02 to earnings per share. In addition, we anticipate running a major advertising campaign just after Christmas. Although the advertising expenditure will be in 2000 and will reduce earnings per share by $.03, we will realize all of the benefits of the campaign by way of greater sales early in 2001."

Champion: "I hadn't realized how much flexibility we had for managing our earnings. Before we decide which choices to make, can you think of any other avenues open to us?"

Morrissey: "We could always sell off assets on which we have potential gain. For example, we hold some marketable securities that we purchased last year. Selling those securities would net us an additional $.02 in earnings per share. In addition, we own two parcels of land that we hope to use someday for new stores. We could sell these parcels at a gain of $.04 per share."

Champion: "It strikes me that these alternatives could increase earnings per share for 2000 to the $2.00-plus range. This level is a lot more appealing than the $1.65 per share anticipated for the year. Will we have to do anything to earnings per share for prior years if we adopt any of these alternatives?"

Morrissey: "I have set out in Exhibit 14.11 the impact of each of the choices on earnings per share for 2000, as well as any restatement required for prior years. This summary should help us decide on our strategy."

How much do you think Champion Clothiers should report as earnings per share for 2000? Indicate the avenues you would choose (from among those described by Tom Morrissey) to arrive at your recommended earnings per share amount, and state the justification for your choices.

19. **Identifying quality-of-earnings issues.** Petite-Marts, Inc., maintains a chain of U.S. retail clothing stores offering stylish women's clothes in petite sizes. The company offers its own credit card and charges no interest on unpaid balances of three months or less. Exhibit 14.12 presents balance sheets for January 31, Year 5, to January 31, Year 8. Exhibit 14.13 presents income statements, and Exhibit 14.14 presents

EXHIBIT 14.11	CHAMPION CLOTHIERS, INC. Alternative Strategies for Managing Earnings per Share (Problem 18)

	Impact on Earnings Per Share			
Alternative	1997[a]	1998[b]	1999[a]	2000[b]
Actual (1997–1999) or Anticipated (2000)	$1.20	$1.38	$1.60	$1.65
Adoption of FIFO	+.15	+.17	+.20	+.21
Use of Narrower LIFO Pools	+.02	+.03	+.02	+.02
Use of Longer Depreciation Lives	—	—	—	+.04
Adoption of Straight-Line Depreciation	+.05	+.06	+.07	+.08
Adoption of Pooling of Interests	+.02	+.04	+.06	+.10
Amortization of Pension Obligation over 15 Years	—	—	—	+.05
Deferral of Maintenance	—	—	—	+.02
Deferral of Advertising	—	—	—	+.03
Sale of Marketable Securities	—	—	—	+.02
Sale of Land	—	—	—	+.04

[a]Restated as required by GAAP.
[b]Projected.

statements of cash flows for the three fiscal years ending January 31, Year 6 to Year 8. Excerpts from the notes to the financial statements appear below.

Note 1: The company recognizes revenue at the time of sale to customers. Accounts receivable are net of an allowance for uncollectible accounts and sales returns of $1,438 million on January 31, Year 5, $1,785 million on January 31, Year 6, $2,010 million on January 31, Year 7, and $1,759 million on January 31, Year 8. Selling and administrative expenses include a provision for uncollectible accounts and sales returns of $994 million for fiscal Year 6, $1,010 million for fiscal Year 7, and $703 million for fiscal Year 8.

Note 2: The company uses a last-in, first-out (LIFO) cost flow assumption for inventories and cost of goods sold. The inventories on a first-in, first-out cost flow assumptions would have exceeded their LIFO amounts as follows: January 31, Year 5, $2,448 million; January 31, Year 6, $2,969 million; January 31, Year 7, $3,572 million; January 31, Year 8, $2,247 million. During fiscal Year 8 the company dipped into LIFO layers created in earlier years, increasing income before income taxes by $916 million.

Note 3: The company uses the straight-line depreciation method. It depreciates buildings over 20 years and, until fiscal Year 8, depreciated equipment over 5 years. A review of equipment usage early in fiscal Year 8 suggested that a longer depreciable life was appropriate. The company therefore revised the depreciable lives of equipment from 5 years to 8 years beginning with the Year 8 fiscal year. The change decreased depreciation expense for fiscal Year 8 by $1,583 million. During fiscal Year 7, new federal health and safety regulations led to the need to recognize a

EXHIBIT 14.12	PETITE-MARTS, INC. Comparative Balance Sheets (Problem 19)

| | January 31: | | | |
	Year 5	Year 6	Year 7	Year 8
ASSETS				
Cash	$ 929	$ 994	$ 1,064	$ 1,005
Accounts Receivable (net)	8,000	8,560	9,159	8,782
Inventories	8,160	8,731	8,927	8,202
Prepayments	420	447	1,328	1,301
Total Current Assets	$ 17,509	$ 18,732	$ 20,478	$19,290
Land	$ 345	$ 345	$ 345	$ 225
Buildings	17,960	17,960	15,462	15,462
Equipment	9,493	13,880	19,429	22,805
Construction in Progress	0	0	0	1,987
Less Accumulated Depreciation	(8,287)	(11,522)	(15,689)	(19,101)
Property, Plant, and Equipment (net)	$ 19,511	$ 20,663	$ 19,547	$21,378
Total Assets	$37,020	$39,395	$ 40,025	$40,668
LIABILITIES AND SHAREHOLDERS' EQUITY				
Accounts Payable	$ 4,149	$ 4,439	$ 4,775	$ 3,609
Notes Payable to Banks	2,550	2,739	2,931	2,810
Other Current Liabilities	4,229	4,526	4,841	4,575
Total Current Liabilities	$ 10,928	$ 11,704	$ 12,547	$10,994
Long-term Debt	12,000	12,000	12,000	12,000
Total Liabilities	$ 22,928	$ 23,704	$ 24,547	$22,994
Common Stock	$ 2,000	$ 2,000	$ 2,000	$ 2,000
Additional Paid-in Capital	6,250	6,250	6,250	6,250
Retained Earnings	5,842	7,441	7,228	9,424
Total Shareholders' Equity	$ 14,092	$ 15,691	$ 15,478	$17,674
Total Liabilities and Shareholders' Equity	$ 37,020	$ 39,395	$ 40,025	$40,668

building impairment loss totaling $2,498 million. The company commenced construction of a new home office building during fiscal Year 8. It incurred total costs of $1,987 million, including $147 million of capitalized interest.

Note 4: The company expenses advertising costs in the year the advertisement appears. Advertising expense was $1,987 million in fiscal Year 6, $2,179 million in fiscal Year 7, and $1,859 million in fiscal Year 8.

Note 5: The company is subject to an income tax rate of 34 percent.

a. Identify quality-of-earnings issues in the income statements for fiscal Year 6, Year 7, and Year 8.

b. Recompute net income for each of the three years as you think appropriate in light of the quality-of-earnings issues discussed in part a.

c. Discuss the changes in profitability of Petite-Marts, Inc., during the three-year period.

EXHIBIT 14.13	PETITE-MARTS, INC. Comparative Income Statements (Problem 19)

	For the Fiscal Year Ended:		
	Year 6	Year 7	Year 8
Sales	$49,680	$53,158	$50,234
Cost of Goods Sold	(33,782)	(36,200)	(34,260)
Depreciation Expense	(3,235)	(4,167)	(3,412)
Selling and Administrative Expenses	(7,453)	(7,814)	(7,285)
Asset Impairment Charge	0	(2,498)	0
Operating Income	$ 5,210	$ 2,479	$ 5,277
Gain on Sale of Land	0	0	708
Interest Expense	(1,172)	(1,187)	(1,042)
Income before Income Taxes	$ 4,038	$ 1,292	$ 4,943
Income Tax Expense	(1,373)	(439)	(1,681)
Net Income	$ 2,665	$ 853	$ 3,262

EXHIBIT 14.14	PETITE-MARTS, INC. Comparative Statements of Cash Flows (Problem 19)

	For the Fiscal Year Ended:		
	Year 6	Year 7	Year 8
OPERATIONS			
Net Income	$ 2,665	$ 853	$ 3,262
Depreciation Expense	3,235	4,167	3,412
Asset Impairment Charge	0	2,498	0
Gain on Sale of Land	0	0	(708)
(Increase) Decrease in Accounts Receivable	(560)	(599)	377
(Increase) Decrease in Inventories	(571)	(196)	725
(Increase) Decrease in Prepayments	(27)	(881)	27
Increase (Decrease) in Accounts Payable	290	336	(1,166)
Increase (Decrease) in Other Current Liabilities	297	315	(266)
Cash Flow from Operations	$ 5,329	$ 6,493	$ 5,663
INVESTING			
Sale of Land	$ 0	$ 0	$ 828
Acquisition of Equipment	(4,387)	(5,549)	(3,376)
Self-Construction Costs Incurred	0	0	(1,987)
Cash Flow for Investing	$(4,387)	$(5,549)	$(4,535)
FINANCING			
increase (Decrease) in Notes Payable to Bank	$ 189	$ 192	$ (121)
Dividends Paid	(1,066)	(1,066)	(1,066)
Cash Flow from Financing	$(877)	$ (874)	$(1,187)
Change in Cash	$ 65	$ 70	$ (59)
Cash, Beginning of Year	929	994	1,064
Cash, End of Year	$ 994	$ 1,064	$ 1,005

COMPOUND INTEREST: CONCEPTS AND APPLICATIONS

1. Begin to master compound interest concepts of future value, present value, present discounted value of single sums and annuities, discount rates, interest rates, and internal rates of return on cash flows.
2. Apply those concepts to problems of finding the single payment or, in the context of annuities, the amount for a series of payments required to meet a specified objective.
3. Begin using perpetuity growth models in valuation analysis.
4. Learn how to find the interest rate to satisfy a stated set of conditions, such as to make the present value of a stream of cash flows equal a specified amount.
5. Begin to learn how to construct problems, of the types described above, from a description of a business or accounting situation.

Owners of cash, like owners of other scarce resources, can permit borrowers to rent the use of their cash for a period of time. Payment for the rental of cash differs little from other rental payments, such as those made to a landlord for the use of property or to a car rental agency for the use of a car. *Interest* is payment for the use of cash. Accounting must record, for both the lender and the borrower, transactions caused by lenders' providing cash to borrowers.

Accountants and managers deal with interest calculations for other reasons. Expenditures for an asset most often precede the receipts for services produced by that asset. Cash received later has less value than cash received sooner. The difference in timing affects the amount of profit from a firm's acquiring an asset. Amounts of cash received at different times have different values. Managers use interest calculations to make valid comparisons among amounts of cash paid or received at different times. Accountants and analysts use interest-related calculations involving present values to help them estimate the values of entire divisions and firms.

Contracts involving a series of cash payments over time, such as bonds, mortgages, notes, and leases, have present values. The **present value** of a series of payments represents the single amount of cash that one would pay now to receive the entire series of cash payments in the future.

COMPOUND INTEREST CONCEPTS

Contracts typically state interest cost as a percentage of the amount borrowed per unit of time. Examples are 12 percent per year and 1 percent per month, which differ from one another. When the statement of interest cost does not explicitly state a period, then the rate applies to a year, so that "interest at the rate of 12 percent" means 12 percent per year. In some inflation-ravaged countries, such as Brazil, the standard interest quotation is for a month.

The amount borrowed or lent is the **principal.** The term **compound interest** means that the amount of interest earned during a period increases the principal, which is thus larger for the next interest period. For example, if you deposit $1,000 in a savings account that pays compound interest at the rate of 6 percent per year, you will earn $60 by the end of one year. If you do not withdraw the $60, then $1,060 will earn interest during the second year. During the second year, your principal of $1,060 will earn $63.60 in interest: $60 on the initial deposit of $1,000 and $3.60 on the $60 earned the first year. By the end of the second year, your principal will total $1,123.60.

When only the original principal earns interest during the entire life of the loan, the interest due at the time the borrower repays the loan is called **simple interest.** Simple interest calculations ignore interest on previously earned interest. If the lender may withdraw interest earned, or the borrower must make periodic payments with further interest charges for late payments, then compound interest techniques will still apply.

Simple Interest: Accounting Uses and Economic Uses
The use of simple interest calculations in accounting arises in the following way: if you borrow $10,000 at a rate of 12 percent per year but compute interest for any month as $100 (= $10,000 × .12 × 1/12), you are using a simple interest calculation. Nearly all economic calculations, however, involve compound interest. When firms use simple interest to compute amounts for periods of less than a year, some distortion of periodic numbers results, but no harm. Early periods get charged "too much" interest and later periods get charged "too little," but the distortions are minor.

Power of Compound Interest
The force, or effect, of compound interest exceeds the intuition of many people. For example, compounded annually at 8 percent, cash doubles itself in nine years. Put another way, if you invest $100 at 8 percent compounded annually, you will have $200 in nine years. If you were to invest $1 in the stock market at age 25 and leave it there for 40 years and the market increased for the next 45 years the way it has for the last 10 years, you would have over $500 by the time you reached age 70.

Problems involving compound interest generally fall into two groups with respect to time.

- First, we may want to know the future value of cash invested or loaned today, as in the two examples in the preceding paragraph.
- Second, we may want to know the present value, or today's value, of cash to be received or paid at later dates. (If I want to have $100,000 available at retirement, how much must I invest today?)

In addition, the accountant must sometimes find the interest rate implicit in specified payment streams. For example, assume a bank will lend you $1,000 in return for your promise to repay $91.70 per month for one year or $73.24 per month for 15 months. You might want to know that the implied rate of interest is 1.5 percent per month for the first offer and 1.2 percent per month for the second.

FUTURE VALUE

If you invest $1 today at 12 percent compounded annually, it will grow to $1.12000 at the end of one year, $1.25440 at the end of two years, $1.40493 at the end of three years, and so on, according to the following formula:

$$F_n = P(1 + r)^n,$$

where

F_n = accumulation or future value
P = one-time investment today
r = interest rate per period
n = number of periods from today

The amount F_n is the **future value** of the present payment, P, compounded at r percent per period for n periods. Table 1 at the back of the book on page 852 shows the future values of $P = \$1$ for various numbers of periods and for various interest rates. Extracts from that table appear here in Table A.1.

EXAMPLE PROBLEMS IN COMPUTING FUTURE VALUE

Example 1 How much will $1,000 deposited today at 8 percent compounded annually grow to in 10 years?

Refer to Table A.1, 10-period row, 8-percent column. One dollar deposited today at 8 percent will grow to $2.15892; therefore, $1,000 will grow to $1,000 $\times$ $(1.08)^{10}$ = $1,000 $\times$ 2.15892 = $2,158.92.

TABLE A.1	(Excerpt from Table 1) Future Value of $1 at 8 Percent and 12 Percent per Period $F_n = (1 + r)^n$

Number of Periods = n	Rate = r	
	8 Percent	12 Percent
1	1.08000	1.12000
2	1.16640	1.25440
3	1.25971	1.40493
10	2.15892	3.10585
20	4.66096	9.64629

Example 2 Macaulay Corporation deposits $10,000 in an expansion fund today. The fund will earn 12 percent per year. How much will the $10,000 grow to in 20 years if Macaulay leaves the entire fund and all interest earned on it on deposit in the fund?

One dollar deposited today at 12 percent will grow to $9.64629 in 20 years. Therefore, $10,000 will grow to $96,463 (= $10,000 × 9.64629) in 20 years.

PRESENT VALUE

The preceding section developed the computation of the future value, F_n, of a sum of cash, P, deposited or invested today. You know P, and you calculate F_n. This section deals with the problems of calculating how much principal, P, you must invest today in order to have a specified amount, F_n, at the end of n periods. You know the future amount, F_n, the interest rate, r, and the number of periods, n. You want to find P. In order to have $1 one year from today when deposits earn 8 percent, you must invest P of $.92593 today. That is, $F_1 = P(1.08)^1$ or $1 = $.92593 × 1.08. Because $F_n = P(1 + r)^n$, dividing both sides of the equation by $(1 + r)^n$ yields

$$\frac{F_n}{(1 + r)^n} = P,$$

or

$$P = \frac{F_n}{(1 + r)^n} = F_n(1 + r)^{-n}$$

PRESENT VALUE TERMINOLOGY

The number $(1 + r)^{-n}$ equals the present value of $1 to be received after n periods when interest accrues at r percent per period. Accountants often use the words *discount* and **discounted value** in this context as follows. The discounted present value of $1 to be received n periods in the future is $(1 + r)^{-n}$ when the discount rate is r percent per period for n periods. The number r is the **discount rate,** and the number $(1 + r)^{-n}$ is the **discount factor** for n periods. A discount factor $(1 + r)^{-n}$ is merely the reciprocal, or inverse, of a number, $(1 + r)^n$, in Table A.1. Table 2 at the back of the book shows discount factors or, equivalently, present values of $1 for various interest (or discount) rates for various numbers of periods. Portions of this table appear in Table A.2.

TABLE A.2	(Excerpt from Table 2) Present Value of $1 at 8 Percent and 12 Percent per Period $P = F_n(1 + r)^{-n}$

| **Number of Periods = n** | **Rate = r** | |
	8 Percent	**12 Percent**
1	.92593	.89286
2	.85734	.79719
3	.79383	.71178
10	.46319	.32197
20	.21455	.10367

EXAMPLE PROBLEMS IN COMPUTING PRESENT VALUES

Example 3 What is the present value of $1 due 10 years from now if the interest rate (equivalently, the discount rate) r is 8 percent per year?

From Table A.2, 8-percent column, 10-period row, the present value of $1 to be received 10 periods hence at 8 percent is $.46319.

Example 4 (This is Example **14** in Chapter 9.) You issue a single-payment note that promises to pay $16,000 three years from today in exchange for used equipment. How much is that promise worth today if the discount rate appropriate for such notes is 12 percent per period? (An accountant needs to know the answer to the question to record the acquisition cost of the used equipment just acquired.)

One dollar paid three years hence discounted at 12 percent has a present value of $.71178. Thus, the promise is worth $16,000 × .71178 = $11,388. (Record the equipment at a cost of $11,388.)

CHANGING THE COMPOUNDING PERIOD: NOMINAL AND EFFECTIVE RATES

"Twelve percent, compounded annually" states the price for a loan; this means that interest increases, or converts to, principal once a year at the rate of 12 percent. Often, however, the price for a loan states that compounding is to take place more than once a year. A savings bank may advertise that it pays 6 percent, compounded quarterly. This means that at the end of each quarter the bank credits savings accounts with interest calculated at the rate of 1.5 percent (= 6 percent ÷ 4). The investor can withdraw the interest payment or leave it on deposit to earn more interest.

The sum of $10,000 invested today at 12 percent, compounded annually, grows to a future value one year later of $11,200. If the rate of interest is 12 percent compounded semiannually, the bank adds 6 percent interest to the principal every six months. At the end of the first six months, $10,000 will have grown to $10,600; that amount will grow to $10,600 × 1.06 = $11,236 by the end of the year. Notice that 12 percent compounded semiannually is equivalent to 12.36 percent compounded annually. Suppose that the bank quotes interest as 12 percent, compounded quarterly. It will add an additional 3 percent of the principal every three months. By the end of the year, $10,000 will grow to $10,000 × $(1.03)^4$ = $10,000 × 1.12551 = $11,255. At 12 percent compounded monthly, $1 will grow to $1 × $(1.01)^{12}$ = $1.12683, and $10,000 will grow to $11,268. Thus, 12 percent compounded monthly provides the same ending amount as 12.68 percent compounded annually. Common terminology would say that *12 percent compounded monthly* has an "effective rate of 12.68 percent compounded annually" or is "equivalent to 12.68 percent compounded annually."

For a given nominal rate, such as the 12 percent in the examples above, the more often interest compounds, the higher will be the effective rate of interest paid. If a nominal rate, r, compounds m times per year, the effective rate equals $(1 + r/m)^m - 1$.

In practice, to solve problems that require computation of interest quoted at a nominal rate r percent per period compounded m times per period for n periods, use the tables for rate = r/m and periods = $m × n$. For example, 12 percent compounded quarterly for five years is equivalent to the rate found in the interest tables for r = 12/4 = 3 percent for $m × n$ = 4 × 5 = 20 periods.

Some savings banks advertise that they compound interest daily or even continuously. The mathematics of calculus provides a mechanism for finding the effective rate when the interest compounds continuously. If interest compounds continuously at nominal rate r per year, the effective annual rate is $e^r - 1$, where e is the base of the natural logarithms. Six percent per year compounded continuously is equivalent to 6.1837 percent compounded annually. Twelve percent per year compounded continuously is equivalent to 12.75 percent compounded annually. Do not confuse the compounding period with the payment period. Some banks, for example, compound interest daily but pay interest quarterly. You can be sure that these banks do not employ clerks or even computers to calculate interest every day. They derive an equivalent effective rate to apply at the end of each quarter.

EXAMPLE PROBLEMS IN CHANGING THE COMPOUNDING PERIOD

Example 5 What is the future value five years hence of $600 invested at 16 percent compounded semiannually?

Sixteen percent compounded two times per year for five years is equivalent to 8 percent per period compounded for 10 periods. Table A.1 shows the value of $F_{10} = (1.08)^{10}$ to be 2.15892. Six hundred dollars, then, would grow to $600 \times 2.15892 = \$1,295.35$.

Example 6 How much cash must you invest today at 16 percent compounded semiannually in order to yield $10,000 in 10 years from today?

Sixteen percent compounded two times a year for 10 years is equivalent to 8 percent per period compounded for 20 periods. The present value, Table A.2, of $1 received 20 periods hence at 8 percent per period is $.21455. That is, $.21455 invested today for 20 periods at an interest rate of 8 percent per period will grow to $1. To have $10,000 in 20 periods (10 years), you must invest $2,146 (= $10,000 \times $.21455) today.

Example 7 A local department store offers its customers credit and advertises its interest rate at 18 percent per year, compounded monthly at the rate of 1.5 percent per month. What is the effective annual interest rate?

One and one-half percent per month for 12 months is equivalent to $(1.015)^{12} - 1 = 19.562$ percent per year. See Table 1, 12-period row, 1.5-percent column, where the factor is 1.19562.

Under truth-in-lending legislation, lenders must disclose the effective annual interest rate, called the **APR** or annual percentage rate, to borrowers.

Example 8 If prices increased at the rate of 6 percent during each of two consecutive six-month periods, how much did prices increase during the entire year?

If a price index is 100.00 at the start of the year, it will be $100.00 \times (1.06)^2 = 112.36$ at the end of the year. The price change for the entire year is $(112.36/100.00) - 1 = 12.36$ percent.

ANNUITIES

An annuity is a series of equal payments, one per period for periods equally spaced through time. Examples of annuities include monthly rental payments, semiannual corporate bond coupon payments, and annual payments to a lessor under a lease contract. Armed with an understanding of the tables for future and present values, you can solve any annuity problem. Annuities arise so often, however, and their solution is so tedious without special tables or calculator functions, that annuity problems merit special study and the use of special tables or functions.

The common computer spreadsheet programs such as Lotus 1-2-3© and Microsoft Excel© include functions for annuity and other compound interest functions. Knowing which function to use to solve a given problem and which values for the variables to insert into the formula requires the same clear understanding that you need to use the tables. Hence, if you want to use spreadsheet functions, you must master the use of the tables in this book or gain equivalent knowledge. We recommend that you master the use and format of the printed tables to help you establish a mental map of the structures and patterns of compound interest computations.

TERMINOLOGY FOR ANNUITIES

An annuity involves *equally spaced payments of equal amounts*. If either the time between payments or the amounts of the payments vary, then the stream is not an annuity. An annuity with payments occurring at the end of each period is an **ordinary annuity (annuity in arrears).** Semiannual corporate bonds usually promise that debt service (coupon) payments will be paid in arrears or, equivalently, that the first payment will not occur until after the bond has been outstanding for six months. An annuity with payments occurring at the beginning of each period is an *annuity due* or an *annuity in advance*. Rent paid at the beginning of each month is an annuity due. In a **deferred annuity,** the first payment occurs sometime later than the end of the first period.

Annuity payments can go on forever. Such annuities are *perpetuities*. Bonds that promise payments forever are *consols*. The British and the Canadian governments have issued consols from time to time. A perpetuity can be in arrears or in advance. The only difference between the two is the timing of the first payment.

Annuities can be confusing. Studying them is easier with a time line such as the one shown below.

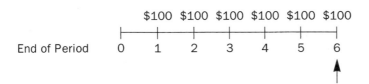

A time line marks the end of each period, numbers the period, shows the payments to be received or paid, and indicates the time in which the accountant wants to value the annuity. The time line above represents an ordinary annuity (in arrears) for six periods of $100 to be valued at the end of period 6. The end of period 0 is *now*. The first payment occurs one period from now.

ORDINARY ANNUITIES (ANNUITIES IN ARREARS)

The future values of ordinary annuities appear in Table 3 at the back of the book. Table A.3 reproduces portions of this table.

TABLE A.3	(Excerpt from Table 3) Future Value of an Ordinary Annuity of $1 per Period at 8 Percent and 12 Percent $F_A = \dfrac{[(1 + r)^n - 1]}{r}$	

| Number of Periods = n | Rate = r | |
	8 Percent	12 Percent
1	1.00000	1.00000
2	2.08000	2.12000
3	3.24640	3.37440
5	5.86660	6.35285
10	14.48656	17.54874
20	45.76196	72.05244

Consider an ordinary annuity for three periods at 12 percent. The time line for the future value of such an annuity is as follows:

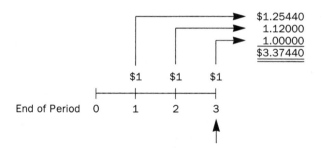

The $1 received at the end of the first period earns interest for two periods, so it grows to $1.25440 at the end of period 3 (see Table A.1). The $1 received at the end of the second period grows to $1.12000 by the end of period 3, and the $1 received at the end of period 3 is, of course, worth $1.00000 at the end of period 3. The entire annuity is worth $3.37440 at the end of period 3. This amount appears in Table A.3 for the future value of an ordinary annuity for three periods at 12 percent. Factors for the future value of an annuity for a particular number of periods sum the factors for the future value of $1 for each of the periods. The future value of an ordinary annuity is as follows:

$$\text{Future Value of Ordinary Annuity} = \text{Periodic Payment} \times \text{Factor for the Future Value of an Ordinary Annuity}$$

Thus,

$$\$3.37440 \quad = \quad \$1 \quad \times \quad 3.37440$$

Table 4 at the back of the book shows the present value of ordinary annuities. Table A.4 reproduces excerpts from Table 4.

TABLE A.4	(Excerpt from Table 4) Present Value of an Ordinary Annuity of $1 per Period at 8 Percent and 12 Percent $P_A = \dfrac{[1 - (1 + r)^{-n}]}{r}$		

Number of Periods = n		Rate = r	
		8 Percent	**12 Percent**
1	....	.92593	.89286
2	....	1.78326	1.69005
3	....	2.57710	2.40183
5	....	3.99271	3.60478
10	....	6.71008	5.65022
20	....	9.81815	7.46944

The time line for the present value of an ordinary annuity of $1 per period for three periods, discounted at 12 percent, is as follows:

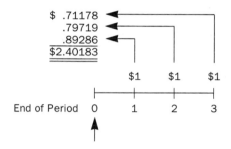

The $1 due at the end of period 1 has a present value of $.89286, the $1 due at the end of period 2 has a present value of $.79719, and the $1 due at the end of period 3 has a present value of $.71178. Each of these numbers comes from Table A.2. The present value of the annuity is the sum of these individual present values, $2.40183, shown in Table A.4.

The present value of an ordinary annuity for *n* periods is the sum of the present value of $1 received one period from now plus the present value of $1 received two periods from now, and so on until we add on the present value of $1 received *n* periods from now. The present value of an ordinary annuity is as follows:

$$\begin{matrix} \text{Present Value} \\ \text{of an} \\ \text{Ordinary Annuity} \end{matrix} = \begin{matrix} \text{Periodic} \\ \text{Payment} \end{matrix} \times \begin{matrix} \text{Factor for} \\ \text{the Present} \\ \text{Value of an} \\ \text{Ordinary Annuity} \end{matrix}$$

Thus,

$$\$2.40183 \quad = \quad \$1 \quad \times \quad 2.40183$$

EXAMPLE PROBLEMS INVOLVING ORDINARY ANNUITIES

Example 9   You plan to invest $1,000 at the end of each of the next 10 years in a savings account. The savings account accumulates interest of 8 percent compounded annually. What will be the balance in the savings account at the end of 10 years?

The time line for this problem is as follows:

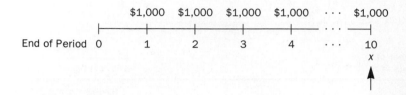

The symbol x denotes the amount you must calculate. Table A.3 indicates that the factor for the future value of an annuity at 8 percent for 10 periods is 14.48656. Thus,

$$\begin{array}{c}\text{Future Value}\\ \text{of an}\\ \text{Ordinary Annuity}\end{array} = \begin{array}{c}\text{Periodic}\\ \text{Payment}\end{array} \times \begin{array}{c}\text{Factor for}\\ \text{the Future}\\ \text{Value of an}\\ \text{Ordinary Annuity}\end{array}$$

$$x \quad = \$1{,}000 \times \quad 14.48656$$
$$x \quad = \$14{,}487$$

Example 10   You want to receive \$600 every six months, starting six months hence, for the next five years. How much must you invest today if the funds accumulate at the rate of 8 percent compounded semiannually?

The time line is as follows:

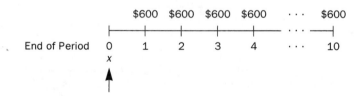

The factor from Table 4 for the present value of an annuity at 4 percent (= 8 percent per year ÷ 2 semiannual periods per year) for 10 (= 2 periods per year × 5 years) periods is 8.11090. Thus,

$$\begin{array}{c}\text{Present Value}\\ \text{of an}\\ \text{Ordinary Annuity}\end{array} = \begin{array}{c}\text{Periodic}\\ \text{Payment}\end{array} \times \begin{array}{c}\text{Factor for}\\ \text{the Present}\\ \text{Value of an}\\ \text{Ordinary Annuity}\end{array}$$

$$x \quad = \$600 \times \quad 8.11090$$
$$x \quad = \$4{,}866.54$$

If you invest \$4,866.54 today, the principal plus interest compounded on the principal will provide sufficient funds that you can withdraw \$600 every six months for the next five years.

Example 11   (This example also appears in Chapter 9 as the Western Company mortgage problem. See Exhibit 9.3.) A company borrows \$125,000 from a savings and loan association. The interest rate on the loan is 12 percent compounded semiannually.

The company agrees to repay the loan in equal semiannual installments over the next five years, with the first payment six months from now. What is the required semiannual payment?

The time line is as follows:

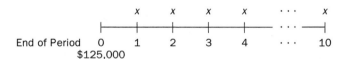

This problem resembles Example **10** because both involve periodic future payments discounted to today. Example **10** gives the amount of the periodic payment and asks for the present value. Example **11** gives the present value and asks for the amount of the periodic payment. Table 4 indicates that the present value of an annuity at 6 percent (= 12 percent per year ÷ 2 semiannual periods per year) for 10 periods (= 2 periods per year × 5 years) is 7.36009. Thus,

$$\begin{array}{ccccc} \text{Present Value} & & & & \text{Factor for} \\ \text{of an} & = & \text{Periodic} & \times & \text{the Present} \\ \text{Ordinary Annuity} & & \text{Payment} & & \text{Value of an} \\ & & & & \text{Ordinary Annuity} \end{array}$$

$$\$125{,}000 = x \times 7.36009$$

$$x = \frac{\$125{,}000}{7.36009}$$

$$x = \$16{,}983$$

To find the periodic payment, divide the present value amount of $125,000 by the present value factor. (Exhibit 9.3 presents the amortization table for this loan. That exhibit shows the amount of each semiannual payment as $17,000, rather than $16,983, and the last payment as $16,781, less than $17,000, to compensate for the extra $17 paid in each of the preceding periods and the interest on those amounts.)

Example 12 (This example also appears in Chapter 10 as the Food Barn lease problem. See Exhibit 10.1.) A company signs a lease acquiring the right to use property for three years. The company will make lease payments of $19,709 annually at the end of this and the next two years. The discount rate is 15 percent per year. What is the present value of the lease payments?

The time line is as follows:

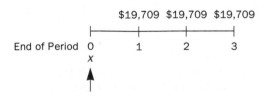

The factor from Table 4 for the present value of an annuity at 15 percent for three periods is 2.28323. Thus,

$$
\begin{array}{ccc}
\text{Present Value} & & \text{Factor for} \\
\text{of an} & = \text{Periodic} & \times \text{the Present} \\
\text{Ordinary Annuity} & \text{Payment} & \text{Value of an} \\
& & \text{Ordinary Annuity}
\end{array}
$$

$$x = \$19{,}709 \times 2.28323$$
$$x = \$45{,}000$$

The Food Barn example in Chapter 10 gives the cost of the equipment, $45,000, and we compute the periodic rental payment with an annuity factor. Thus,

$$
\begin{array}{ccc}
\text{Present Value} & & \text{Factor for} \\
\text{of an} & = \text{Periodic} & \times \text{the Present} \\
\text{Ordinary Annuity} & \text{Payment} & \text{Value of an} \\
& & \text{Ordinary Annuity}
\end{array}
$$

$$\$45{,}000 = x \times 2.28323$$
$$x = \frac{\$45{,}000}{2.28323}$$
$$x = \$19{,}709$$

Example 13   A company promises to make annual payments to a pension fund at the end of each of the next 30 years. The payments must have a present value today of $100,000. What must the annual payment be if the fund expects to earn interest at the rate of 8 percent per year?

   The time line is as follows:

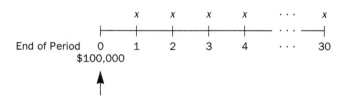

Table 4 indicates that the factor for the present value of $1 paid at the end of the next 30 periods at 8 percent per period is 11.25778. Thus,

$$
\begin{array}{ccc}
\text{Present Value} & & \text{Factor for} \\
\text{of an} & = \text{Periodic} & \times \text{the Present} \\
\text{Ordinary Annuity} & \text{Payment} & \text{Value of an} \\
& & \text{Ordinary Annuity}
\end{array}
$$

$$\$100{,}000 = x \times 11.25778$$
$$x = \frac{\$100{,}000}{11.25778}$$
$$x = \$8{,}883$$

Example 14   Mr. Mason is 62 years old. He wants to invest equal amounts on his 63rd, 64th, and 65th birthdays so that starting on his 66th birthday, he can withdraw $50,000 on each birthday for 10 years. His investments will earn 8 percent per year. How much should he invest on the 63rd through 65th birthdays?

The time line for this problem is as follows:

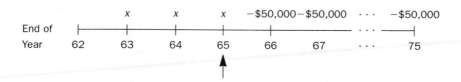

At 65, Mr. Mason needs to have accumulated a fund equal to the present value of an annuity of $50,000 per period for 10 periods, discounted at 8 percent per period. The factor from Table A.4 for 8 percent and 10 periods is 6.71008. Thus,[1]

$$
\begin{array}{ccc}
\text{Present Value} & & \text{Factor for} \\
\text{of an} & = \text{Periodic} \times & \text{the Present} \\
\text{Ordinary Annuity} & \text{Payment} & \text{Value of an} \\
& & \text{Ordinary Annuity}
\end{array}
$$

$$X = \$50,000 \times 6.71008$$
$$X = \$335,500$$

The time line now appears as follows:

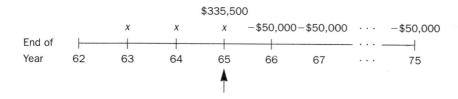

The question now becomes, how much must Mr. Mason invest on his 63rd, 64th, and 65th birthdays to accumulate to a fund of $335,500 on his 65th birthday? The factor for the future value of an annuity for three periods at 8 percent is 3.24640. Thus,

$$
\begin{array}{ccc}
\text{Future Value} & & \text{Factor for} \\
\text{of an} & = \text{Periodic} \times & \text{the Future} \\
\text{Ordinary Annuity} & \text{Payment} & \text{Value of an} \\
& & \text{Ordinary Annuity}
\end{array}
$$

$$\$335,500 = X \times 3.24640$$
$$X = \frac{\$335,500}{3.24640}$$
$$X = \$103,350$$

The solution above expresses all calculations in terms of equivalent amounts on Mr. Mason's 65th birthday. That is, the present value of an annuity of $50,000 per period for 10 periods at 8 percent equals the future value of an annuity of $103,350 per period for three periods at 8 percent, and both of these amounts equal $335,500. You could work this problem by selecting any common time period between Mr. Mason's 62nd and 75th birthdays.

One alternative expresses all calculations in terms of equivalent amounts on Mr. Mason's 62nd birthday. To solve the problem in this way, first find the present value on

---

[1]We rounded the results of this and subsequent computations to five significant digits.

Mr. Mason's 65th birthday of an annuity of $50,000 per period for 10 periods ($335,500 = $50,000 × 6.71008). Discount $335,500 back three periods using Table 2 for present value of single payments: $266,330 = $335,500 × .79383. The result is the present value of the payments measured as of Mr. Mason's 62nd birthday. Then, find the amounts that Mr. Mason must invest on his 63rd, 64th, and 65th birthdays to have a present value on his 62nd birthday equal to $266,330. The calculation is as follows:

$$
\begin{array}{ccccc}
\text{Present Value} & & & & \text{Factor for} \\
\text{of an} & = & \text{Periodic} & \times & \text{the Present} \\
\text{Ordinary Annuity} & & \text{Payment} & & \text{Value of an} \\
& & & & \text{Ordinary Annuity} \\
\$266{,}330 & = & x & \times & 2.57710 \\
x & & = \$103{,}350 & &
\end{array}
$$

We computed the same amount, $103,350, above.

PERPETUITIES

A periodic payment to be received forever is a **perpetuity.** Future values of perpetuities are undefined. One dollar to be received at the end of every period discounted at rate r percent has a present value of $1/r$. Observe what happens in the expression for the present value of an ordinary annuity of $A per payment as n, the number of payments, approaches infinity:

$$
P_A = \frac{A[1 - (1 + r)^{-n}]}{r}
$$

As n approaches infinity, $(1 + r)^{-n}$ approaches 0, so that P_A approaches $A(1/r)$. If the first payment of the perpetuity occurs now, the present value is $A[1 + 1/r]$.

EXAMPLES OF PERPETUITIES

Example 15   The Canadian government offers to pay $30 every six months forever in the form of a perpetual bond. What is that bond worth if the discount rate is 10 percent compounded semiannually?

Ten percent compounded semiannually is equivalent to 5 percent per six-month period. If the first payment occurs six months from now, the present value is $30 ÷ .05 = $600. If the first payment occurs today, the present value is $30 + $600 = $630.

Example 16   Every two years, the Bank of Tokyo gives ¥5 million (Japanese yen) to the university to provide a scholarship for an entering student in a two-year business administration course. If the university credits 6 percent per year to its investment accounts, how much must the bank give to the university to provide such a scholarship every two years forever, starting two years hence?

A perpetuity in arrears assumes one payment at the end of each period. Here, the period is two years. Six percent compounded once a year over two years is equivalent to a rate of $(1.06)^2 - 1 = .12360$ or 12.36 percent compounded once per two-year period. Consequently, the present value of the perpetuity paid in arrears every two years is ¥40.45 (= ¥5 ÷ .1236). A gift of ¥40.45 million will provide a ¥5 million scholarship forever. If the university will award the first scholarship now, the gift must be ¥45.45 (= ¥40.45 + ¥5.00) million.

Example 17 (This is an example of the relief from royalty method, introduced in Chapter 8.) Burns, Philp and Company (B-P) wants to value its trademark for Fleischmann's Yeast using the relief from royalty method. B-P estimates that sales of the product will continue at the rate of $100 million per year in perpetuity and that if it had to pay a royalty to another firm that owned the trademark, it would have to pay 4 percent of sales at the end of each year. It uses a discount rate of 10 percent per year in computing present values. What is the value of the trademark under these assumptions?

If B-P paid royalties of 4 percent of sales, these would total $4 (= .04 × $100) million per year, in perpetuity. The present value of a perpetual stream of payments of $4 million per year, discounted at 10 percent per year, is $40 (= $4 ÷ .10) million. Under these assumptions, the trademark has a value of $40 million.

B-P, more realistically, might estimate that sales will grow each year by, say, 2 percent more than the rate of inflation. When one assumes that a perpetuity's payments, which start at p per period, or $4 million in this example, will grow at a constant rate g, or 2 percent in this example, then the value of the perpetuity is $p \div (r - g) = \$4 \div (.10 - .02) = \$50$ million in this example.

The next three examples all refer to the data in Exhibit 12.1, where we evaluate the six individual activities of Bernard Company to find the value of the entire firm.

Example 18 Bernard Company's Activity 1 generates $100 per year, with the cash flow at the end of year, indefinitely. The present value of this activity is $1,000 (= $100 ÷ .10). Investors sometimes call this process of deriving market value from a series of future cash flows *capitalizing earnings*. The analyst might say that the earnings of $100 have a *price/earnings* ratio of 10 or that the earnings "deserve [or carry] a multiple of 10." The price/earnings ratio for a perpetuity is the reciprocal of the discount rate. In the example, where the discount rate is 10 percent per period, the price/earnings ratio is 10.

Example 19 Bernard Company's second activity generates $30 at the end of the first year and a cash flow that grows by 6 percent per year thereafter. The present value of this activity is $750 [= $30 ÷ (.10 − .06)]: if the cash flow starts at $1 per year and grows at rate g per year, then the present value of the growing cash flows is $\$1/(r - g)$. Analysts refer to the preceding formula in various ways. We call it the **perpetuity growth model.** This example and the formula for it assume the cash flows and growth last forever. Forever is a long time. Sometimes students derive silly results from assuming *forever*, particularly when the growth rate is large. We have seen analysts project growth rates so much larger than the growth of the U.S. economy that the analyzed company's projected sales after 50 or so years exceed the entire U.S. gross domestic product. Use these perpetuity-based, arithmetic tools to learn and to make approximations but do not expect firms to grow *forever* at high growth rates.

Example 20 Bernard Company's third activity is cyclic, generating $115 per year at the end of each odd-numbered year. The present value of this activity is $602.38, derived as follows. Think of this series of cash flows as a perpetuity with $115 per period; each period is two years long. Then, when the discount rate is 10 percent per year, the discount rate for a two-year period must be 21 percent [= (1.10 × 1.10) − 1]. The cash flows from Year 2 onward have present value of $547.62 (= $115 ÷ .21) at the start of Year 2 and present value of $497.84 (= $547.62 ÷ 1.10) at the start of Year 1. The $115 cash flow received at the end of Year 1 has present value of $104.54 (= $115 ÷ 1.10) at the start of Year 1. The entire series has present value of $602.38 (= $497.84 + $104.54) at the start of Year 1.

IMPLICIT INTEREST RATES: FINDING INTERNAL RATES OF RETURN

The preceding examples computed a future value or a present value given the interest rate and stated cash payment. Or they computed the required payments given a known future value or a known present value. In other calculations, however, you know the present or the future value and the periodic payments; you must find the implicit interest rate. For example, Chapter 9 illustrates a case in which you know that the cash price of some equipment is $10,500 and that the firm acquired the asset in exchange for a single-payment note. The note has a face value of $16,000 and matures in three years. To compute interest expense over the three-year period, you must know the **implicit interest rate (internal rate of return).** The time line for this problem is as follows:

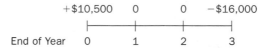

	+$10,500	0	0	−$16,000
End of Year	0	1	2	3

The implicit interest rate is *r:*

(A.1)
$$0 = \$10,500 - \frac{\$16,000}{(1 + r)^3}$$

(A.2)
$$\$10,500 = \frac{\$16,000}{(1 + r)^3}$$

That is, the present value of $16,000 discounted three periods at *r* percent per period is $10,500. The present value of all current and future cash flows discounted at *r* per period must be zero. In general, to find such an *r* requires trial and error. In cases where *r* appears only in one term, as here, you can find *r* analytically. Here $r = (\$16,000 \div \$10,500)^{1/3} - 1 = .1507 = 15.1$ percent.

The general procedure is *finding the internal rate of return of a series of cash flows.* The internal rate of return of a series of cash flows is the discount rate that makes the net present values of that series of cash flows equal to zero. The steps in finding the internal rate of return are as follows:

1. Make an educated guess, called the "trial rate," at the internal rate of return. If you have no idea what to guess, try zero.
2. Calculate the present value of all the cash flows (including the one at the end of Year 0).
3. If the present value of the cash flows is zero, stop. The current trial rate is the internal rate of return.
4. If the amount found in step **2** is less than zero, try a larger interest rate as the trial rate and go back to step **2.**
5. If the amount found in step **2** is greater than zero, try a smaller interest rate as the new trial rate and go back to step **2.**

The iterations below illustrate the process for the example in Equation A.1.

	Net Present Value:	
Iteration Number	**Trial Rate = r**	**Right-Hand Side of Equation A.1**
1	0.0%	−$5,500
2	10.0	−1,521
3	15.0	−20
4	15.5	116
5	15.2	34
6	15.1	7

With a trial rate of 15.1 percent, the right-hand side is close enough to zero that you can use 15.1 percent as the implicit interest rate in making the adjusting entries for interest expense. Continued iterations would find trial rates even closer to the true rate, which is about 15.0739 percent.

Finding the internal rate of return for a series of cash flows can be tedious; you should not attempt it unless you have at least a calculator. An exponential feature, which allows the computation of $(1 + r)$ raised to various powers, helps. Computer spreadsheets, such as Lotus 1-2-3$^©$ or Microsoft Excel$^©$, have a built-in function to find the internal rate of return.

EXAMPLE PROBLEM INVOLVING IMPLICIT INTEREST RATES

Example 21   Alexis Company acquires a machine with a cash price of $10,500. It pays for the machine by giving a note for $12,000, promising to make payments equal to 7 percent of the face value, $840 ($= .07 \times$ $12,000$), at the end of each of the next three years and a single payment of $12,000 in three years. What is the interest rate implicit in the loan?

The time line for this problem is as follows:

$10,500   −$840   −$840   −$12,840

End of Year   0   1   2   3

The implicit interest rate is r:

(A.3) $$\$10,500 = \frac{\$840}{(1 + r)} + \frac{\$840}{(1 + r)^2} + \frac{\$12,840}{(1 + r)^3}$$

Compare this formulation to that in Equation A.1. Note that the left-hand side equals 0 in Equation A.1 but not in Equation A.3. You may use any left-hand side that you find convenient for the particular context.

The iteration process finds an internal rate of return of 12.2 percent to the nearest tenth of 1 percent:

Iteration Number	**Trial Rate**	**Right-Hand Side of Equation A.3**
1	7.0%	$12,000
2	15.0	9,808
3	11.0	10,827
4	13.0	10,300
5	12.0	10,559

(continued)

6	12.5	10,428
7	12.3	10,480
8	12.2	10,506
9	12.1	10,532

SUMMARY

Accountants typically use one of four kinds of compound interest calculations: (1) the present value or (2) the future value of (3) a single payment or of (4) a series of payments. In working annuity problems, you may find a time line helpful in deciding the particular kind of annuity involved. Computer spreadsheet programs have a built-in function to perform the computations described in this appendix.

KEY TERMS AND CONCEPTS

Present value
Principal
Compound interest
Simple interest
Future value
Discounted value
Discount rate
Discount factor

APR
Ordinary annuity (annuity in arrears)
Deferred annuity
Perpetuity
Perpetuity growth model
Implicit interest rate (internal rate of
   return)

QUESTIONS, EXERCISES, PROBLEMS, AND CASES

QUESTIONS

1. Review the terms and concepts listed above in Key Terms and Concepts.
2. What is *interest?*
3. Distinguish between simple and compound interest.
4. Distinguish between the discounted present value of a stream of future payments and their net present value. If there is no distinction, then so state.
5. Distinguish between an annuity due and an ordinary annuity.
6. Describe the implicit interest rate for a series of cash flows and a procedure for finding it.
7. Does the present value of a given amount to be paid in 10 years increase or decrease if the interest rate increases? What if the amount is due in 5 years? 20 years? Does the present value of an annuity to be paid for 10 years increase or decrease if the discount rate decreases? What if the annuity is for 5 years? 20 years?
8. Rather than pay you $1,000 a month for the next 20 years, the person who injured you in an automobile accident is willing to pay a single amount now to settle your claim for injuries. Would you rather use an interest rate of 6 percent or 12 percent in computing the present value of the lump-sum settlement? Comment or explain.

EXERCISES

9. **Effective interest rate.** State the rate per period and the number of periods in the following:
   a. 12 percent per year, for 5 years, compounded annually
   b. 12 percent per year, for 5 years, compounded semiannually

c. 12 percent per year, for 5 years, compounded quarterly
d. 12 percent per year, for 5 years, compounded monthly

Exercises 10 through 26 involve calculations of present and future value for single payments and for annuities. To make the exercises more realistic, we do not give specific guidance with each individual exercise.

10. Compute the future value of the following:
    a. $100 invested for 5 years at 4 percent compounded annually
    b. $500 invested for 15 periods at 2 percent compounded once per period
    c. $200 invested for 8 years at 3 percent compounded semiannually
    d. $2,500 invested for 14 years at 8 percent compounded quarterly
    e. $600 invested for 3 years at 12 percent compounded monthly
11. Compute the present value of the following:
    a. $100 due in 30 years at 4 percent compounded annually
    b. $250 due in 8 years at 8 percent compounded quarterly
    c. $1,000 due in 2 years at 12 percent compounded monthly
12. Compute the amount (future value) of an ordinary annuity (an annuity in arrears) of the following:
    a. 13 rental payments of $100 at 1½ percent per period
    b. 8 rental payments of $850 at 6 percent per period
    c. 28 rental payments of $400 at 4 percent per period
13. Mr. Altgeldt has DM5,000 to invest. He wants to know how much it will amount to if he invests it at the following rates:
    a. 6 percent per year for 21 years
    b. 8 percent per year for 33 years
14. Mme. Barefield wants to have Fr150,000 at the end of 8 years. How much must she invest today to accomplish this purpose if the interest rate is
    a. 6 percent per year?
    b. 8 percent per year?
15. Mr. Case plans to set aside $4,000 each year, the first payment to be made on January 1, 1999, and the last on January 1, 2004. How much will he have accumulated by January 1, 2004, if the interest rate is
    a. 6 percent per year?
    b. 8 percent per year?
16. Ms. Namura wants to have ¥45 million on her 65th birthday. She asks you to tell her how much she must deposit on each birthday from her 58th to 65th, inclusive, in order to receive this amount. Assume the following interest rates:
    a. 8 percent per year
    b. 12 percent per year
17. If Mr. Enmetti invests 90,000 lira on June 1 of each year from 1991 to 2001 inclusive, how much will he have accumulated on June 1, 2002 (note that one year elapses after the last payment), if the interest rate is
    a. 5 percent per year?
    b. 10 percent per year?
18. Ms. Fleming has £145,000 with which she purchases an annuity on February 1, 2000. The annuity consists of six annual payments, the first to be made on February 1, 2001. How much will she receive in each payment? Assume the following interest rates:
    a. 8 percent per year
    b. 12 percent per year
19. In Exercises **10** through **18,** you computed a number. To do so, first you must decide on the appropriate factor from the tables, and then you use that factor in the appropriate calculation. Notice that you could omit the last step. You could write an

arithmetic expression showing the factor you want to use without actually copying down the number and doing the arithmetic. For example, the notation T(*i, p, r*) means Table *i* (1, 2, 3, or 4), row *p* (periods 1 to 20, 22, 24 . . . , 40, 45, 50, 100), and column *r* (interest rates from ½ percent up to 20 percent). Thus, *T*(3, 16, 12) would be the factor in Table 3 for 16 periods and an interest rate of 12 percent per period, which is 42.75328. Using this notation, you can write an expression for any compound interest problem. A clerk or a computer can evaluate the expression. You can check that you understand this notation by observing that the following are true statements:

$$
\begin{aligned}
\text{T(1, 20, 8)} &= 4.66096 \\
\text{T(2, 12, 5)} &= 0.55684 \\
\text{T(3, 16, 12)} &= 42.75328 \\
\text{T(4, 10, 20)} &= 4.19247
\end{aligned}
$$

In the following questions, write an expression for the answer using the notation introduced here but do not attempt to evaluate the expression.

a. Work the **a** parts of Exercises **10** through **14.**

b. Work the **b** parts of Exercises **15** through **18.**

c. How might your instructor use this notation to write examination questions on compound interest without having to supply you with tables?

20. Mr. Grady agrees to lease a certain property for 10 years, at the following annual rental, payable in advance:

> Years 1 and 2—$1,000 per year
> Years 3 to 6—$2,000 per year
> Years 7 to 10—$2,500 per year

What single immediate sum will pay all of these rents, discounted at

a. 6 percent per year?

b. 8 percent per year?

c. 10 percent per year?

21. To establish a fund that will provide a scholarship of $3,000 per year indefinitely, with the first award to occur now, how much must a donor deposit if the fund earns

a. 6 percent per period?

b. 8 percent per period?

22. Consider the scholarship fund in the preceding question. Suppose that the first scholarship award occurs one year from now and the donor wants the scholarship to grow by 2 percent per year. How much should the donor deposit if the fund earns

a. 6 percent per period?

b. 8 percent per period?

Suppose that the first scholarship award occurs five years from now but is to grow at 2 percent per year after Year 5, the time of the first $3,000 award. How much should the donor deposit if the fund earns

c. 6 percent per year?

d. 8 percent per year?

23. An old agreement obliges the state to help a rural county maintain a bridge by paying $60,000 now and every two years thereafter forever toward the expenses. The state wants to discharge its obligation by paying a single sum to the county now for the payment due and all future payments. How much should the state pay the county if the discount rate is

a. 8 percent per year?

b. 12 percent per year?

24. Find the interest rate implicit in a loan of $100,000 that the borrower discharges with two annual installments of $55,307 each, paid at the ends of Years 1 and 2.

25. A single-payment note promises to pay $140,493 in three years. The issuer exchanges the note for equipment having a fair market value of $100,000. The exchange occurs three years before the maturity date on the note. What interest rate will the accounting impute for the single-payment note?

26. A single-payment note promises $67,280 at maturity. The issuer of the note exchanges it for land with a fair market value of $50,000. The exchange occurs two years before the maturity date on the note.

    a. What interest rate will the accounting impute for this single-payment note?

    b. Using the imputed interest rate, construct an amortization schedule for the note. Show book value of the note at the start of each year, interest for each year, the amount reducing or increasing book value each year, and book value at the end of the year.

27. **Finding implicit interest rates; constructing amortization schedules.** Berman Company purchased a plot of land for possible future development. The land had fair market value of $86,000. Berman Company gave a three-year interest-bearing note. The note had face value of $100,000 and provided for interest at a stated rate of 8 percent. The note requires payments of $8,000 at the end of each of three years, the last payment coinciding with the maturity of the note's face value of $100,000.

    a. What is the interest rate implicit in the note, accurate to the nearest tenth of 1 percent?

    b. Construct an amortization schedule for the note for each year. Show the book value of the note at the start of the year, interest for the year, payment for the year, amount reducing or increasing the book value of the note for each payment, and the book value of the note at the end of each year. Use the interest rate found in part a. See Exhibit 9.3 for an example of an amortization schedule.

28. The terms of sale "2/10, net/30" mean that the buyer can take a discount of 2 percent from gross invoice price by paying the invoice within 10 days; otherwise, the buyer must pay the full amount within 30 days.

    a. Viewing the entire discount as interest for funds received sooner rather than later, write an expression for the implied annual rate of interest being offered. (Note that by not taking the discount, the buyer borrows 98 percent of the gross invoice price for 20 days.)

    b. The tables at the back of the book do not permit the exact evaluation of the expression derived in part a. The rate of interest implied is 44.59 percent per year. Use the tables to convince yourself that this astounding (to some) answer must be close to correct.

PROBLEMS AND CASES

Problems 29–35 involve using future value and present value techniques to solve a variety of realistic problems. The problems give no hints as to the specific calculation required.

29. An oil-drilling company figures that it must spend $30,000 for an initial supply of drill bits and that it must spend $10,000 every month to replace the worn-out bits. What is the present value of the cost of the bits if the company plans to be in business indefinitely and discounts payments at 1 percent per month?

30. If you promise to leave $35,000 on deposit at the Dime Savings Bank for four years, the bank will give you a new car, a GM Geo, today and your $35,000 back at the end of four years. How much are you paying today for the car, in effect, if the bank pays other customers 8 percent interest compounded quarterly (2 percent paid four times per year)?

31. When Mr. Shafer died, his estate after taxes amounted to $300,000. His will provided that Mrs. Shafer would receive $24,000 per year starting immediately from the principal of the estate and that the balance of the principal would pass to the Shafers' children upon Mrs. Shafer's death. The state law governing this estate provided for a dower option. If Mrs. Shafer elects the dower option, she renounces the will and can have one-third of the estate in cash now. The remainder will then pass immediately to their children. Mrs. Shafer wants to maximize the present value of her bequest. Should she take the annuity or elect the dower option if she will receive five payments and discounts payments at

a. 8 percent per year?

b. 12 percent per year?

(*Note:* This problem explicitly states that Mrs. Shafer will receive five payments. In reality, life expectancy is uncertain. The correct calculation combines a mortality table with the present value tables. Actuaries deal with such calculations.)

32. Mrs. Heileman occasionally drinks beer. (Guess which brand.) She consumes one case in 20 weeks. She can buy beer in disposable cans for $25.20 per case or for $24.00 per case of returnable bottles if she pays a $3.00 refundable deposit at the time of purchase. If her discount rate is ½ percent per week, how much in present value dollars does she save by buying the returnable bottles and thereby losing the use of the $3.00 deposit for 20 weeks?

33. When General Electric Company first introduced the Lucalox ceramic, screw-in light bulb, the bulb cost three and one-half times as much as an ordinary bulb but lasted five times as long. An ordinary bulb cost $1.00 and lasted about eight months. If a firm has a discount rate of 12 percent compounded three times a year, how much would it save in present value dollars by using one Lucalox bulb?

34. Dean Foods Dairy switched from delivery trucks with regular gasoline engines to ones with diesel engines. The diesel trucks cost $2,000 more than the ordinary gasoline trucks but $600 per year less to operate. Assume that Dean Foods saves the operating costs at the end of each month. If Dean Foods uses a discount rate of 1 percent per month, approximately how many months, at a minimum, must the diesel trucks remain in service for the switch to be sensible?

35. On January 1, Year 1, assume that Levi Strauss opened a new textile plant to produce synthetic fabrics. The plant is on leased land; 20 years remain on the nonrenewable lease.

The cost of the plant was $20 million. Net cash flow to be derived from the project is estimated to be $3,000,000 per year. The company does not normally invest in such projects unless the anticipated yield is at least 12 percent.

On December 31, Year 1, the company finds cash flows from the plant to be $2,800,000 for the year. On the same day, farm experts predict cotton production will be unusually low for the next two years. Levi Strauss estimates the resulting increase in demand for synthetic fabrics will boost cash flows to $3,500,000 for each of the next two years. Estimates for subsequent years remain unchanged. Ignore tax considerations.

a. Calculate the present value of the future expected cash flows from the plant when it opened.

b. What is the present value of the plant on January 1, Year 2, immediately after the reestimation of future income?

c. On January 2, Year 2, the day following the cotton production news release, a competitor announces plans to build a synthetic fabrics plant, to open in three years. Levi Strauss keeps its Year 2 to Year 4 estimates but reduces the estimated annual cash flows for subsequent years to $2,000,000. What is the value of Levi Strauss's present plant on January 1, Year 2, after the new projections?

d. On January 2, Year 2, an investor contacts Levi Strauss about purchasing a 20 percent share of the plant. If the investor expects to earn at least a 12 percent annual return on the investment, what is the maximum amount that the investor can pay? Assume that the investor and Levi Strauss both know all relevant information and use the same estimates of annual cash flows.

36. **Finding implicit interest rates (truth-in-lending laws reduce the type of deception suggested by this problem).** Friendly Loan Company advertises that it is willing to lend money for five years at the low rate of 8 percent per year. A potential borrower discovers that a five-year, $10,000 loan requires that the 8 percent interest be paid in advance, with interest deducted from the loan proceeds. The borrower will collect $6,000 [= $10,000 − (5 × .08 × $10,000)] in cash and must repay the $10,000 loan in five annual installments of $2,000, one each at the end of the next five years. Compute the effective interest rate implied by these loan terms.

37. **Deriving net present value of cash flows for a decision to dispose of an asset.** Suppose that yesterday Black & Decker Company purchased and installed a made-to-order machine tool for fabricating parts for small appliances. The machine cost $100,000. Today, Square D Company offers a machine tool that will do exactly the same work but costs only $50,000. Assume that the discount rate is 12 percent, that both machines will last for five years, that Black & Decker will depreciate both machines on a straight-line basis with no salvage value for tax purposes, that the income tax rate is and will continue to be 40 percent, and that Black & Decker earns sufficient income that it can use any loss from disposing of or depreciating the "old" machine to offset other taxable income. How much, at a minimum, must the "old" machine fetch on resale at this time to make purchasing the new machine worthwhile?

38. **Computation of present value of cash flows; untaxed acquisition, no change in tax basis of assets.** The balance sheet of Lynch Company shows net assets of $100,000 and owners' equity of $100,000. The assets are all depreciable assets with remaining lives of 20 years. The income statement for the year shows revenues of $700,000, depreciation of $50,000 (= $1,000,000 ÷ 20 years), no other expenses, income taxes of $260,000 (= 40 percent of pretax income of $650,000), and net income of $390,000.

Bages Company is considering purchasing all of the stock of Lynch Company. It is willing to pay an amount equal to the present value of the cash flows from operations for the next 20 years discounted at a rate of 10 percent per year.

The transaction will be a tax-free exchange; that is, after the purchase, the tax basis of the assets of Lynch Company will remain unchanged, so that depreciation charges will remain at $50,000 per year and income taxes will remain at $260,000 per year. Revenues will be $700,000 per year for the next 20 years.

a. Compute the annual cash flows produced by Lynch Company.

b. Compute the maximum amount Bages Company should be willing to pay.

39. **Computation of the present value of cash flows; taxable acquisition, changing tax basis of assets.** Refer to the data in the preceding problem. Assume now that the acquisition is taxable, so that the tax basis of the assets acquired changes after the purchase. If the purchase price is $V, then depreciation charges will be $V ÷ 20 per year for 20 years. Income taxes will be 40 percent of pretax income. What is the maximum Bages Company should be willing to pay for Lynch Company?

40. **Analysis of benefits of acquisition of long-term assets.** (Adapted from a problem by S. Zeff.) Lexie T. Colleton is the chief financial officer of Ragazze, and one of her duties is to give advice on investment projects. Today's date is December 31, Year 0.

Colleton requires that, to be acceptable, new investments must provide a positive net present value after discounting cash flows at 12 percent per year.

A proposed investment is the purchase of an automatic gonculator, which involves an initial cash disbursement on December 31, Year 0. The useful life of the machine is nine years, through Year 9. Colleton expects to be able to sell the machine for cash of $30,000 on December 31, Year 9. She expects commercial production to begin on December 31, Year 1. Ragazze will depreciate the machine on a straight-line basis. Ignore income taxes.

During Year 1, the break-in year, Ragazze will perform test runs in order to put the machine in proper working order. Colleton expects that the total cash outlay for this purpose will be $20,000, incurred at the end of Year 1.

Colleton expects that the cash disbursements for regular maintenance will be $60,000 at the end of each of Years 2 through 5, inclusive, and $100,000 at the end of each of Years 6 through 8, inclusive.

Colleton expects the cash receipts (net of all other operating expenses) from the sale of the product that the machine produces to be $130,000 at the end of each year from Year 2 through Year 9, inclusive.

a. What is the maximum price that Ragazze can pay for the automatic gonculator on December 31, Year 0, and still earn a positive net present value of cash flows?

b. Independent of your answer to part **a,** assume the purchase price is $250,000, which Ragazze will pay with an installment note requiring four equal annual installments starting December 31, Year 1, and an implicit interest rate of 10 percent per year. What is the amount of each payment?

41. **Valuation of intangibles with perpetuity formulas.** When the American Basketball Association (ABA) merged with the National Basketball Association (NBA), the owners of the ABA St. Louis Spirits agreed to dissolve their team and not enter the NBA. In return, the NBA promised to pay, in perpetuity, to the Spirits' owners an amount each year equal to 40 percent of the TV revenues that the NBA paid to any one of its regular teams. Currently, the owners receive $4 million per year. The NBA wants to pay a single amount to the owners now and not have to pay more in the future. Of course, the owners prefer to collect more, rather than less, but here they want to know the reasonable minimum that will make them indifferent to receiving the single payment in lieu of receiving the annual payments in perpetuity. Ignore income tax effects.

a. Assume that the owners expect the TV revenues to remain constant, so that they can expect $4 million per year in perpetuity, and that they use an interest rate of 8 percent in their discounting calculations. What minimum price should these owners be willing to accept?

b. Refer to the specifications for **a.** If the owners use a smaller interest rate for discounting, will the minimum price they are willing to accept increase, decrease, or remain unchanged?

c. The owners use an 8 percent discount rate, and they expect TV revenues to increase by 2 percent per year in perpetuity. What minimum price should the owners be willing to accept?

d. Refer to the specifications in **c.** If the owners use a smaller interest rate for discounting, will the minimum price they are willing to accept increase, decrease, or remain unchanged?

e. Refer to the specifications in **c.** If the owners assume a smaller rate for growth in future receipts from the NBA, will the minimum price they are willing to accept increase, decrease, or remain unchanged?

42. **Choosing between investment alternatives.** (Adapted from a problem by S. Zeff.) William Marsh, CEO of Gulf Coast Manufacturing, wants to know which of two strategies he has chosen for acquiring an automobile has the lower present value of cost.

Strategy L. Acquire a new Lexus, keep it for six years, then trade it in on a new car.

Strategy M. Acquire a new Mercedes-Benz, trade it in after three years on a second Mercedes-Benz, keep that for another three years, then trade it in on a new car.

Data pertinent to these choices appear below. Assume that Marsh will receive the trade-in value in cash or as a credit toward the purchase price of a new car. Ignore income taxes, and use a discount rate of 10 percent per year. Gulf Coast Manufacturing depreciates automobiles on a straight-line basis over 8 years for financial reporting, assuming zero salvage value at the end of 8 years.

a. Which strategy has the lower present value of costs?

b. What role, if any, do depreciation charges play in the analysis and why?

	Lexus	Mercedes-Benz
Initial Cost at the Start of Year 1	$60,000	$45,000
Initial Cost at the Start of Year 4		48,000
Trade-in Value		
End of Year 3		23,000
End of Year 6[a]	16,000	24,500
Estimated Annual Cash Operating Costs,		
Except Major Servicing	4,000	4,500
Estimated Cash Cost of Major Servicing		
End of Year 4	6,500	
End of Year 2 and End of Year 5		2,500

[a]At this time, the Lexus is six years old; the second Mercedes-Benz is three years old.

43. **Horrigan Corporation; Perpetuity Growth Model Derivation of Results in Chapter 5.** Refer to the discussion on page 274 in Chapter 5. There, in estimating the value of a share of common stock of Horrigan Corporation, we computed the present value of excess cash flows at the end of Year 4 to be $1,336.7 million. This exercise requires you to confirm that computation.

To compute the amount for the years after Year 9, note we assume that the excess cash flows are $204 million at the end of Year 9 and grow at the rate of 12 percent per year thereafter. That means the cash flows for the end of Year 10 are $228.48 (= 1.12 × $204) million. You can use the perpetuity growth model to verify that the present value at the end of Year 9 of that growing stream of payments is $2,856 million. That is, if a payment (in this case $228.48 million), grows at rate g (in this case, 12 percent) per period forever, the discount rate is r (in this case, 20 percent) per period, and the first payment flows at the end of the first period, then the present value of that stream is $2,856 [= $228.48/(r − g) = $228.48/(.20 − .12)] million. Then, we discount that amount to the end of Year 4 to derive $1.147.8 million.

(We do not expect that any firm's excess cash flows could increase forever at 12 percent per year. After a century, such a firm would be larger than the rest of the entire U.S. economy, combined. We use such computations to estimate values. When the discount rate (here 20 percent per year) exceeds the growth rate (here 12 percent per year) by a substantial amount (here by 8 percentage points), the present value of payments far in future, say more than 40 years out, is negligble.)

Reproduce the numbers in Column (6) on page 274 using the data from Column (5) and the appropriate present value computations.

COMPOUND INTEREST, ANNUITY, AND BOND TABLES

TABLE 1

Future Value of $1

$$F_n = P(1 + r)^n$$

r = interest rate; n = number of periods until valuation; P = \$1

Periods = n	$\frac{1}{2}\%$	1%	$1\frac{1}{2}\%$	2%	3%	4%	5%	6%	7%	8%	10%	12%	15%	20%	25%
1	1.00500	1.01000	1.01500	1.02000	1.03000	1.04000	1.05000	1.06000	1.07000	1.08000	1.10000	1.12000	1.15000	1.20000	1.25000
2	1.01003	1.02010	1.03023	1.04040	1.06090	1.08160	1.10250	1.12360	1.14490	1.16640	1.21000	1.25440	1.32250	1.44000	1.56250
3	1.01508	1.03030	1.04568	1.06121	1.09273	1.12486	1.15763	1.19102	1.22504	1.25971	1.33100	1.40493	1.52088	1.72800	1.95313
4	1.02015	1.04060	1.06136	1.08243	1.12551	1.16986	1.21551	1.26248	1.31080	1.36049	1.46410	1.57352	1.74901	2.07360	2.44141
5	1.02525	1.05101	1.07728	1.10408	1.15927	1.21665	1.27628	1.33823	1.40255	1.46933	1.61051	1.76234	2.01136	2.48832	3.05176
6	1.03038	1.06152	1.09344	1.12616	1.19405	1.26532	1.34010	1.41852	1.50073	1.58687	1.77156	1.97382	2.31306	2.98598	3.81470
7	1.03553	1.07214	1.10984	1.14869	1.22987	1.31593	1.40710	1.50363	1.60578	1.71382	1.94872	2.21068	2.66002	3.58318	4.76837
8	1.04071	1.08286	1.12649	1.17166	1.26677	1.36857	1.47746	1.59385	1.71819	1.85093	2.14359	2.47596	3.05902	4.29982	5.96046
9	1.04591	1.09369	1.14339	1.19509	1.30477	1.42331	1.55133	1.68948	1.83846	1.99900	2.35795	2.77308	3.51788	5.15978	7.45058
10	1.05114	1.10462	1.16054	1.21899	1.34392	1.48024	1.62889	1.79085	1.96715	2.15892	2.59374	3.10585	4.04556	6.19174	9.31323
11	1.05640	1.11567	1.17795	1.24337	1.38423	1.53945	1.71034	1.89830	2.10485	2.33164	2.85312	3.47855	4.65239	7.43008	11.64153
12	1.06168	1.12683	1.19562	1.26824	1.42576	1.60103	1.79586	2.01220	2.25219	2.51817	3.13843	3.89598	5.35025	8.91610	14.55192
13	1.06699	1.13809	1.21355	1.29361	1.46853	1.66507	1.88565	2.13293	2.40985	2.71962	3.45227	4.36349	6.15279	10.69932	18.18989
14	1.07232	1.14947	1.23176	1.31948	1.51259	1.73168	1.97993	2.26090	2.57853	2.93719	3.79750	4.88711	7.07571	12.83918	22.73737
15	1.07768	1.16097	1.25023	1.34587	1.55797	1.80094	2.07893	2.39656	2.75903	3.17217	4.17725	5.47357	8.13706	15.40702	28.42171
16	1.08307	1.17258	1.26899	1.37279	1.60471	1.87298	2.18287	2.54035	2.95216	3.42594	4.59497	6.13039	9.35762	18.48843	35.52714
17	1.08849	1.18430	1.28802	1.40024	1.65285	1.94790	2.29202	2.69277	3.15882	3.70002	5.05447	6.86604	10.76126	22.18611	44.40892
18	1.09393	1.19615	1.30734	1.42825	1.70243	2.02582	2.40662	2.85434	3.37993	3.99602	5.55992	7.68997	12.37545	26.62333	55.51115
19	1.09940	1.20811	1.32695	1.45681	1.75351	2.10685	2.52695	3.02560	3.61653	4.31570	6.11591	8.61276	14.23177	31.94800	69.38894
20	1.10490	1.22019	1.34686	1.48595	1.80611	2.19112	2.65330	3.20714	3.86968	4.66096	6.72750	9.64629	16.36654	38.33760	86.73617
22	1.11597	1.24472	1.38756	1.54598	1.91610	2.36992	2.92526	3.60354	4.43040	5.43654	8.14027	12.10031	21.64475	55.20614	135.5253
24	1.12716	1.26973	1.42950	1.60844	2.03279	2.56330	3.22510	4.04893	5.07237	6.34118	9.84973	15.17863	28.62518	79.49685	211.7582
26	1.13846	1.29526	1.47271	1.67342	2.15659	2.77247	3.55567	4.54938	5.80735	7.39635	11.91818	19.04007	37.85680	114.4755	330.8722
28	1.14987	1.32129	1.51722	1.74102	2.28793	2.99870	3.92013	5.11169	6.64884	8.62711	14.42099	23.88387	50.06561	164.8447	516.9879
30	1.16140	1.34785	1.56308	1.81136	2.42726	3.24340	4.32194	5.74349	7.61226	10.06266	17.44940	29.95992	66.21177	237.3763	807.7936
32	1.17304	1.37494	1.61032	1.88454	2.57508	3.50806	4.76494	6.45339	8.71527	11.73708	21.11378	37.58173	87.56507	341.8219	1262.177
34	1.18480	1.40258	1.65068	1.96068	2.73191	3.79432	5.25335	7.25103	9.97811	13.69013	25.54767	47.14252	115.80480	492.2235	1972.152
36	1.19668	1.43077	1.70914	2.03989	2.89828	4.10393	5.79182	8.14725	11.42394	15.96817	30.91268	59.13557	153.15185	708.8019	3081.488
38	1.20868	1.45953	1.76080	2.12230	3.07478	4.43881	6.38548	9.15425	13.07927	18.62528	37.40434	74.17966	202.54332	1020.675	4814.825
40	1.22079	1.48886	1.81402	2.20804	3.26204	4.80102	7.03999	10.28572	14.97446	21.72452	45.25926	93.05097	267.86355	1469.772	7523.164
45	1.25162	1.56481	1.95421	2.43785	3.78160	5.84118	8.98501	13.76461	21.00245	31.92045	72.89048	163.9876	538.76927	3657.262	22958.87
50	1.28323	1.64463	2.10524	2.69159	4.38391	7.10668	11.46740	18.42015	29.45703	46.90161	117.3909	289.0022	1083.65744	9100.438	70064.92
100	1.64667	2.70481	4.43205	7.24465	19.21863	50.50495	131.5013	339.3021	867.7163	2199.761	13780.61	83522.27	117×10^4	828×10^5	491×10^7

TABLE 2

Present Value of $1

$P = F_n(1 + r)^{-n}$

r = discount rate; n = number of periods until payment; $F_n = \$1$

Periods = n	½%	1%	1½%	2%	3%	4%	5%	6%	7%	8%	10%	12%	15%	20%	25%
1	.99502	.99010	.98522	.98039	.97087	.96154	.95238	.94340	.93458	.92593	.90909	.89286	.86957	.83333	.80000
2	.99007	.98030	.97066	.96117	.94260	.92456	.90703	.89000	.87344	.85734	.82645	.79719	.75614	.69444	.64000
3	.98515	.97059	.95632	.94232	.91514	.88900	.86384	.83962	.81630	.79383	.75131	.71178	.65752	.57870	.51200
4	.98025	.96098	.94218	.92385	.88849	.85480	.82270	.79209	.76290	.73503	.68301	.63552	.57175	.48225	.40960
5	.97537	.95147	.92826	.90573	.86261	.82193	.78353	.74726	.71299	.68058	.62092	.56743	.49718	.40188	.32768
6	.97052	.94205	.91454	.88797	.83748	.79031	.74622	.70496	.66634	.63017	.56447	.50663	.43233	.33490	.26214
7	.96569	.93272	.90103	.87056	.81309	.75992	.71068	.66506	.62275	.58349	.51316	.45235	.37594	.27908	.20972
8	.96089	.92348	.88771	.85349	.78941	.73069	.67684	.62741	.58201	.54027	.46651	.40388	.32690	.23257	.16777
9	.95610	.91434	.87459	.83676	.76642	.70259	.64461	.59190	.54393	.50025	.42410	.36061	.28426	.19381	.13422
10	.95135	.90529	.86167	.82035	.74409	.67556	.61391	.55839	.50835	.46319	.38554	.32197	.24718	.16151	.10737
11	.94661	.89632	.84893	.80426	.72242	.64958	.58468	.52679	.47509	.42888	.35049	.28748	.21494	.13459	.08590
12	.94191	.88745	.83639	.78849	.70138	.62460	.55684	.49697	.44401	.39711	.31863	.25668	.18691	.11216	.06872
13	.93722	.87866	.82403	.77303	.68095	.60057	.53032	.46884	.41496	.36770	.28966	.22917	.16253	.09346	.05498
14	.93256	.86996	.81185	.75788	.66112	.57748	.50507	.44230	.38782	.34046	.26333	.20462	.14133	.07789	.04398
15	.92792	.86135	.79985	.74301	.64186	.55526	.48102	.41727	.36245	.31524	.23939	.18270	.12289	.06491	.03518
16	.92330	.85282	.78803	.72845	.62317	.53391	.45811	.39365	.33873	.29189	.21763	.16312	.10686	.05409	.02815
17	.91871	.84438	.77639	.71416	.60502	.51337	.43630	.37136	.31657	.27027	.19784	.14564	.09293	.04507	.02252
18	.91414	.83602	.76491	.70016	.58739	.49363	.41552	.35034	.29586	.25025	.17986	.13004	.08081	.03756	.01801
19	.90959	.82774	.75361	.68643	.57029	.47464	.39573	.33051	.27651	.23171	.16351	.11611	.07027	.03130	.01441
20	.90506	.81954	.74247	.67297	.55368	.45639	.37689	.31180	.25842	.21455	.14864	.10367	.06110	.02608	.01153
22	.89608	.80340	.72069	.64684	.52189	.42196	.34185	.27751	.22571	.18394	.12285	.08264	.04620	.01811	.00738
24	.88719	.78757	.69954	.62172	.49193	.39012	.31007	.24698	.19715	.15770	.10153	.06588	.03493	.01258	.00472
26	.87838	.77205	.67902	.59758	.46369	.36069	.28124	.21981	.17220	.13520	.08391	.05252	.02642	.00874	.00302
28	.86966	.75684	.65910	.57437	.43708	.33348	.25509	.19563	.15040	.11591	.06934	.04187	.01997	.00607	.00193
30	.86103	.74192	.63976	.55207	.41199	.30832	.23138	.17411	.13137	.09938	.05731	.03338	.01510	.00421	.00124
32	.85248	.72730	.62099	.53063	.38834	.28506	.20987	.15496	.11474	.08520	.04736	.02661	.01142	.00293	.00079
34	.84402	.71297	.60277	.51003	.36604	.26355	.19035	.13791	.10022	.07305	.03914	.02121	.00864	.00203	.00051
36	.83564	.69892	.58509	.49022	.34503	.24367	.17266	.12274	.08754	.06262	.03235	.01691	.00653	.00141	.00032
38	.82735	.68515	.56792	.47119	.32523	.22529	.15661	.10924	.07646	.05369	.02673	.01348	.00494	.00098	.00021
40	.81914	.67165	.55126	.45289	.30656	.20829	.14205	.09722	.06678	.04603	.02209	.01075	.00373	.00068	.00013
45	.79896	.63905	.51171	.41020	.26444	.17120	.11130	.07265	.04761	.03133	.01372	.00610	.00186	.00027	.00004
50	.77929	.60804	.47500	.37153	.22811	.14071	.08720	.05429	.03395	.02132	.00852	.00346	.00092	.00011	.00001
100	.60729	.36971	.22563	.13803	.05203	.01980	.00760	.00295	.00115	.00045	.00007	.00001	.00000	.00000	.00000

TABLE 3

Future Value of Annuity of $1 in Arrears

$$P_F = \frac{(1+r)^n - 1}{r}$$

r = interest rate; n = number of payments

No. of Payments = n	½%	1%	1½%	2%	3%	4%	5%	6%	7%	8%	10%	12%	15%	20%	25%
1	1.00000	1.00000	1.00000	1.00000	1.00000	1.00000	1.00000	1.00000	1.00000	1.00000	1.00000	1.00000	1.00000	1.00000	1.00000
2	2.00500	2.01000	2.01500	2.02000	2.03000	2.04000	2.05000	2.06000	2.07000	2.08000	2.10000	2.12000	2.15000	2.20000	2.25000
3	3.01503	3.03010	3.04523	3.06040	3.09090	3.12160	3.15250	3.18360	3.21490	3.24640	3.31000	3.37440	3.47250	3.64000	3.81250
4	4.03010	4.06040	4.09090	4.12161	4.18363	4.24646	4.31013	4.37462	4.43994	4.50611	4.64100	4.77933	4.99338	5.36800	5.76563
5	5.05025	5.10101	5.15227	5.20404	5.30914	5.41632	5.52563	5.63709	5.75074	5.86660	6.10510	6.35285	6.74238	7.44160	8.20703
6	6.07550	6.15202	6.22955	6.30812	6.46841	6.63298	6.80191	6.97532	7.15329	7.33593	7.71561	8.11519	8.75374	9.92992	11.25879
7	7.10588	7.21354	7.32299	7.43428	7.66246	7.89829	8.14201	8.39384	8.65402	8.92280	9.48717	10.08901	11.06680	12.91590	15.07349
8	8.14141	8.28567	8.43284	8.58297	8.89234	9.21423	9.54911	9.89747	10.25980	10.63663	11.43589	12.29969	13.72682	16.49908	19.84186
9	9.18212	9.36853	9.55933	9.75463	10.15911	10.58280	11.02656	11.49132	11.97799	12.48756	13.57948	14.77566	16.78584	20.79890	25.80232
10	10.22803	10.46221	10.70272	10.94972	11.46388	12.00611	12.57789	13.18079	13.81645	14.48656	15.93742	17.54874	20.30372	25.95868	33.25290
11	11.27917	11.56683	11.86326	12.16872	12.80780	13.48635	14.20679	14.97164	15.78360	16.64549	18.53117	20.65458	24.34928	32.15042	42.56613
12	12.33556	12.68250	13.04121	13.41209	14.19203	15.02581	15.91713	16.86994	17.88845	18.97713	21.38428	24.13313	29.00167	39.58050	54.20766
13	13.39724	13.80933	14.23683	14.68033	15.61779	16.62684	17.71298	18.88214	20.14064	21.49530	24.52271	28.02911	34.35192	48.49660	68.75958
14	14.46423	14.94742	15.45038	15.97394	17.08632	18.29191	19.59863	21.01507	22.55049	24.21492	27.97498	32.39260	40.50471	59.19592	86.94947
15	15.53655	16.09690	16.68214	17.29342	18.59891	20.02359	21.57856	23.27597	25.12902	27.15211	31.77248	37.27971	47.58041	72.03511	109.6868
16	16.61423	17.25786	17.93237	18.63929	20.15688	21.82453	23.65749	25.67253	27.88805	30.32428	35.94973	42.75328	55.71747	87.44213	138.1085
17	17.69730	18.43044	19.20136	20.01207	21.76159	23.69751	25.84037	28.21288	30.84022	33.75023	40.54470	48.88367	65.07509	105.9306	173.6357
18	18.78579	19.61475	20.48938	21.41231	23.41444	25.64541	28.13238	30.90565	33.99903	37.45024	45.59917	55.74971	75.83636	128.1167	218.0446
19	19.87972	20.81090	21.79672	22.84056	25.11687	27.67123	30.53900	33.75999	37.37896	41.44626	51.15909	63.43968	88.21181	154.7400	273.5558
20	20.97912	22.01900	23.12367	24.29737	26.87037	29.77808	33.06595	36.78559	40.99549	45.76196	57.27500	72.05244	102.44358	186.6880	342.9447
22	23.19443	24.47159	25.83758	27.29898	30.53678	34.24797	38.50521	43.39229	49.00574	55.45676	71.40275	92.50258	137.63164	271.0307	538.1011
24	25.43196	26.97346	28.63352	30.42186	34.42647	39.08260	44.50200	50.81558	58.17667	66.76476	88.49733	118.15524	184.16784	392.4842	843.0329
26	27.69191	29.52563	31.51397	33.67091	38.55304	44.31174	51.11345	59.15638	68.67647	79.95442	109.18177	150.33393	245.71197	567.3773	1319.489
28	29.97452	32.12910	34.48148	37.05121	42.93092	49.96758	58.40258	68.52811	80.69769	95.33883	134.20994	190.69889	327.10408	819.2233	2063.952
30	32.28002	34.78489	37.53868	40.56808	47.57542	56.08494	66.43885	79.05819	94.46079	113.28321	164.49402	241.33268	434.74515	1181.881	3227.174
32	34.60862	37.49407	40.68829	44.22703	52.50276	62.70147	75.29883	90.88978	110.21815	134.21354	201.13777	304.84772	577.10046	1704.109	5044.710
34	36.96058	40.25770	43.93309	48.03380	57.73018	69.85791	85.06696	104.18375	128.25876	158.62667	245.47670	384.52098	765.36535	2456.118	7884.609
36	39.33610	43.07688	47.27597	51.99437	63.27594	77.59831	95.83632	119.12087	148.91346	187.10215	299.12681	484.46312	1014.34568	3539.009	12321.95
38	41.73545	45.95272	50.71989	56.11494	69.15945	85.97034	107.70955	135.90421	172.56102	220.31595	364.04343	609.83053	1343.62216	5098.373	19255.30
40	44.15885	48.88637	54.26789	60.40198	75.40126	95.02552	120.79977	154.76197	199.63511	259.05652	442.59256	767.09142	1779.09031	7343.858	30088.66
45	50.32416	56.48107	63.61420	71.89271	92.71986	121.0294	159.7002	212.7435	285.7493	386.5056	718.9048	1358.230	3585.12846	18281.31	91831.50
50	56.64516	64.46318	73.68283	84.57940	112.7969	152.6671	209.3480	290.3359	406.5289	573.7702	1163.909	2400.018	7217.71628	45497.19	280255.7
100	129.33370	170.4814	228.8030	312.2323	607.2877	1237.624	2610.025	5638.368	12381.66	27484.52	137796.1	696010.5	783×10^4	414×10^6	196×10^8

Note: To convert from this table to values of an annuity in advance, determine the annuity in arrears above for one more period and subtract 1.00000.

TABLE 4

Present Value of Annuity of $1 in Arrears

$$P_A = \frac{1-(1+r)^{-n}}{r} \times \$1.00$$

r = discount rate; n = number of payments

n Periods = Payments

Payments in Arrears

P_A (Value in Table 4) $\longrightarrow \sum \left(\begin{array}{c} \text{Individual Values} \\ \text{from Table 2} \end{array} \right)$

P_F (Value in Table 3)

No. of Payments = n	½%	1%	1½%	2%	3%	4%	5%	6%	7%	8%	10%	12%	15%	20%	25%
1	.99502	.99010	.98522	.98039	.97087	.96154	.95238	.94340	.93458	.92593	.90909	.89286	.86957	.83333	.80000
2	1.98510	1.97040	1.95588	1.94156	1.91347	1.88609	1.85941	1.83339	1.80802	1.78326	1.73554	1.69005	1.62571	1.52778	1.44000
3	2.97025	2.94099	2.91220	2.88388	2.82861	2.77509	2.72325	2.67301	2.62432	2.57710	2.48685	2.40183	2.28323	2.10648	1.95200
4	3.95050	3.90197	3.85438	3.80773	3.71710	3.62990	3.54595	3.46511	3.38721	3.31213	3.16987	3.03735	2.85498	2.58873	2.36160
5	4.92587	4.85343	4.78264	4.71346	4.57971	4.45182	4.32948	4.21236	4.10020	3.99271	3.79079	3.60478	3.35216	2.99061	2.68928
6	5.89638	5.79548	5.69719	5.60143	5.41719	5.24214	5.07569	4.91732	4.76654	4.62288	4.35526	4.11141	3.78448	3.32551	2.95142
7	6.86207	6.72819	6.59821	6.47199	6.23028	6.00205	5.78637	5.58238	5.38929	5.20637	4.86842	4.56376	4.16042	3.60459	3.16114
8	7.82296	7.65168	7.48593	7.32548	7.01969	6.73274	6.46321	6.20979	5.97130	5.74664	5.33493	4.96764	4.48732	3.83716	3.32891
9	8.77906	8.56602	8.36052	8.16224	7.78611	7.43533	7.10782	6.80169	6.51523	6.24689	5.75902	5.32825	4.77158	4.03097	3.46313
10	9.73041	9.47130	9.22218	8.98259	8.53020	8.11090	7.72173	7.36009	7.02358	6.71008	6.14457	5.65022	5.01877	4.19247	3.57050
11	10.67703	10.36763	10.07112	9.78685	9.25262	8.76048	8.30641	7.88687	7.49867	7.13896	6.49506	5.93770	5.23371	4.32706	3.65640
12	11.61893	11.25508	10.90751	10.57534	9.95400	9.38507	8.86325	8.38384	7.94269	7.53608	6.81369	6.19437	5.42062	4.43922	3.72512
13	12.55615	12.13374	11.73153	11.34837	10.63496	9.98565	9.39357	8.85268	8.35765	7.90378	7.10336	6.42355	5.58315	4.53268	3.78010
14	13.48871	13.00370	12.54338	12.10625	11.29607	10.56312	9.89864	9.29498	8.74547	8.24424	7.36669	6.62817	5.72448	4.61057	3.82408
15	14.41662	13.86505	13.34323	12.84926	11.93794	11.11839	10.37966	9.71225	9.10791	8.55948	7.60608	6.81086	5.84737	4.67547	3.85926
16	15.33993	14.71787	14.13126	13.57771	12.56110	11.65230	10.83777	10.10590	9.44665	8.85137	7.82371	6.97399	5.95423	4.72956	3.88741
17	16.25863	15.56225	14.90765	14.29187	13.16612	12.16567	11.27407	10.47726	9.76322	9.12164	8.02155	7.11963	6.04716	4.77463	3.90993
18	17.17277	16.39827	15.67256	14.99203	13.75351	12.65930	11.68959	10.82760	10.05909	9.37189	8.20141	7.24967	6.12797	4.81219	3.92794
19	18.08236	17.22601	16.42617	15.67846	14.32380	13.13394	12.08532	11.15812	10.33560	9.60360	8.36492	7.36578	6.19823	4.84350	3.94235
20	18.98742	18.04555	17.16864	16.35143	14.87747	13.59033	12.46221	11.46992	10.59401	9.81815	8.51356	7.46944	6.25933	4.86958	3.95388
22	20.78406	19.66038	18.62082	17.65805	15.93692	14.45112	13.16300	12.04158	11.06124	10.20074	8.77154	7.64465	6.35866	4.90943	3.97049
24	22.56287	21.24339	20.03041	18.91393	16.93554	15.24696	13.79864	12.55036	11.46933	10.52876	8.98474	7.78432	6.43377	4.93710	3.98111
26	24.32402	22.79520	21.39863	20.12104	17.87684	15.98277	14.37519	13.00317	11.82578	10.80998	9.16095	7.89566	6.49056	4.95632	3.98791
28	26.06769	24.31644	22.72672	21.28127	18.76411	16.66306	14.89813	13.40616	12.13711	11.05108	9.30657	7.98442	6.53351	4.96967	3.99226
30	27.79405	25.80771	24.01584	22.39646	19.60044	17.29203	15.37245	13.76483	12.40904	11.25778	9.42691	8.05518	6.56598	4.97894	3.99505
32	29.50328	27.26959	25.26714	23.46833	20.38877	17.87355	15.80268	14.08404	12.64656	11.43500	9.52638	8.11159	6.59053	4.98537	3.99683
34	31.19555	28.70267	26.48173	24.49859	21.13184	18.41120	16.19290	14.36814	12.85401	11.58693	9.60857	8.15656	6.60910	4.98984	3.99797
36	32.87102	30.10751	27.66068	25.48884	21.83225	18.90828	16.54685	14.62099	13.03521	11.71719	9.67651	8.19241	6.62314	4.99295	3.99870
38	34.52985	31.48466	28.80505	26.44064	22.49246	19.36786	16.86789	14.84602	13.19347	11.82887	9.73265	8.22099	6.63375	4.99510	3.99917
40	36.17223	32.83469	29.91585	27.35548	23.11477	19.79277	17.15909	15.04630	13.33171	11.92461	9.77905	8.24378	6.64178	4.99660	3.99947
45	40.20720	36.09451	32.55234	29.49016	24.51871	20.72004	17.77407	15.45583	13.60552	12.10840	9.86281	8.28252	6.65429	4.99863	3.99983
50	44.14279	39.19612	34.99969	31.42361	25.72976	21.48218	18.25593	15.76186	13.80075	12.23348	9.91481	8.30450	6.66051	4.99945	3.99994
100	78.54264	63.02888	51.62470	43.09835	31.59891	24.50500	19.84791	16.61755	14.26925	12.49432	9.99927	8.33323	6.66666	5.00000	4.00000

Note: To convert from this table to values of an annuity in advance, determine the annuity in arrears above for one fewer period and add 1.00000.

TABLE 5

Bond Values in Percent of Par: 10-Percent Semiannual Coupons

Bond value $= 10/r + (100 - 10/r)(1 + r/2)^{-2n}$

r = yield to maturity; n = years to maturity

Market Yield Percent per Year Compounded Semiannually

Years to Maturity	8.0	9.0	9.5	10	10.5	11.0	12.0	13.0	14.0	15.0	20.0
0.5	100.9615	100.4785	100.2387	100.0	99.7625	99.5261	99.0566	98.5915	98.1308	97.6744	95.4545
1.0	101.8861	100.9363	100.4665	100.0	99.5368	99.0768	98.1666	97.2691	96.3840	95.5111	91.3223
1.5	102.7751	101.3745	100.6840	100.0	99.3224	98.6510	97.3270	96.0273	94.7514	93.4987	87.5657
2.0	103.6299	101.7938	100.8917	100.0	99.1186	98.2474	96.5349	94.8613	93.2256	91.6267	84.1507
2.5	104.4518	102.1950	101.0899	100.0	98.9251	97.8649	95.7876	93.7665	91.7996	89.8853	81.0461
5.0	108.1109	103.9564	101.9541	100.0	98.0928	96.2312	92.6399	89.2168	85.9528	82.8398	69.2772
9.0	112.6593	106.0800	102.9803	100.0	97.1339	94.3770	89.1724	84.3513	79.8818	75.7350	58.9929
9.5	113.1339	106.2966	103.0838	100.0	97.0393	94.1962	88.8419	83.8979	79.3288	75.1023	58.1754
10.0	113.5903	106.5040	103.1827	100.0	96.9494	94.0248	88.5301	83.4722	78.8120	74.5138	57.4322
15.0	117.2920	108.1444	103.9551	100.0	96.2640	92.7331	86.2352	80.4120	75.1819	70.4740	52.8654
19.0	119.3679	109.0250	104.3608	100.0	95.9194	92.0976	85.1540	79.0312	73.6131	68.8015	51.3367
19.5	119.5845	109.1148	104.4017	100.0	95.8854	92.0357	85.0509	78.9025	73.4701	68.6525	51.2152
20.0	119.7928	109.2008	104.4408	100.0	95.8531	91.9769	84.9537	78.7817	73.3366	68.5140	51.1047
25.0	121.4822	109.8810	104.7461	100.0	95.6068	91.5342	84.2381	77.9132	72.3985	67.5630	50.4259
30.0	122.6235	110.3190	104.9381	100.0	95.4591	91.2751	83.8386	77.4506	71.9216	67.1015	50.1642
40.0	123.9154	110.7827	105.1347	100.0	95.3175	91.0345	83.4909	77.0728	71.5560	66.7690	50.0244
50.0	124.5050	110.9749	105.2124	100.0	95.2666	90.9521	83.3825	76.9656	71.4615	66.6908	50.0036

TABLE 6

Bond Values in Percent of Par:
12-Percent Semiannual Coupons

Bond value $= 12/r + (100 - 12/r)(1 + r/2)^{-2n}$

r = yield to maturity; n = years to maturity

P_0 = Par Value

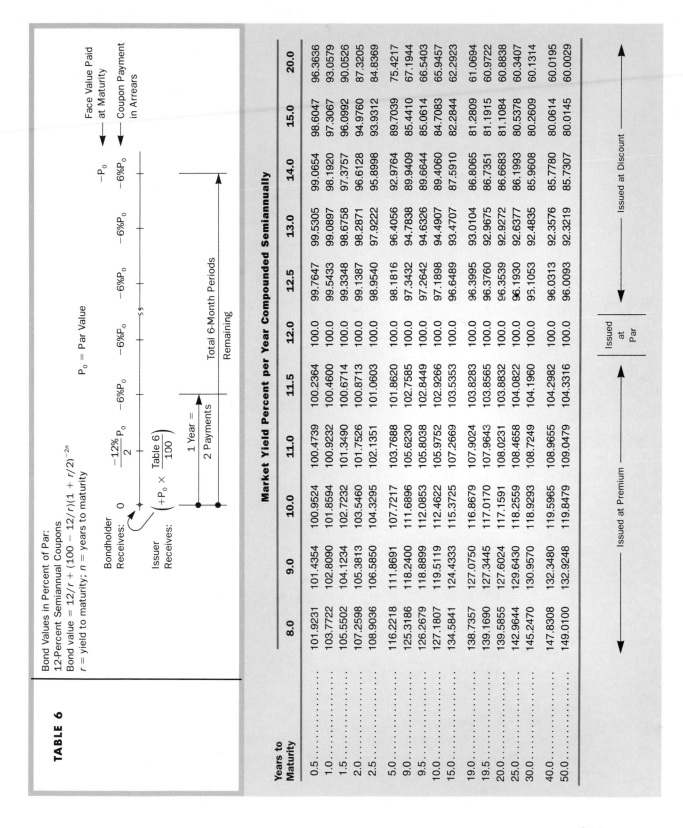

Market Yield Percent per Year Compounded Semiannually

Years to Maturity	8.0	9.0	10.0	11.0	11.5	12.0	12.5	13.0	14.0	15.0	20.0
0.5	101.9231	101.4354	100.9524	100.4739	100.2364	100.0	99.7647	99.5305	99.0654	98.6047	96.3636
1.0	103.7722	102.8090	101.8594	100.9232	100.4600	100.0	99.5433	99.0897	98.1920	97.3067	93.0579
1.5	105.5502	104.1234	102.7232	101.3490	100.6714	100.0	99.3348	98.6758	97.3757	96.0992	90.0526
2.0	107.2598	105.3813	103.5460	101.7526	100.8713	100.0	99.1387	98.2871	96.6128	94.9760	87.3205
2.5	108.9036	106.5850	104.3295	102.1351	101.0603	100.0	98.9540	97.9222	95.8998	93.9312	84.8369
5.0	116.2218	111.8691	107.7217	103.7688	101.8620	100.0	98.1816	96.4056	92.9764	89.7039	75.4217
9.0	125.3186	118.2400	111.6896	105.6230	102.7585	100.0	97.3432	94.7838	89.9409	85.4410	67.1944
9.5	126.2679	118.8899	112.0853	105.8038	102.8449	100.0	97.2642	94.6326	89.6644	85.0614	66.5403
10.0	127.1807	119.5119	112.4622	105.9752	102.9266	100.0	97.1898	94.4907	89.4060	84.7083	65.9457
15.0	134.5841	124.4333	115.3725	107.2669	103.5353	100.0	96.6489	93.4707	87.5910	82.2844	62.2923
19.0	138.7357	127.0750	116.8679	107.9024	103.8283	100.0	96.3995	93.0104	86.8065	81.2809	61.0694
19.5	139.1690	127.3445	117.0170	107.9643	103.8565	100.0	96.3760	92.9675	86.7351	81.1915	60.9722
20.0	139.5855	127.6024	117.1591	108.0231	103.8832	100.0	96.3539	92.9272	86.6683	81.1084	60.8838
25.0	142.9644	129.6430	118.2559	108.4658	104.0822	100.0	96.1930	92.6377	86.1993	80.5378	60.3407
30.0	145.2470	130.9570	118.9293	108.7249	104.1960	100.0	96.1053	92.4835	85.9608	80.2609	60.1314
40.0	147.8308	132.3480	119.5965	108.9655	104.2982	100.0	96.0313	92.3576	85.7780	80.0614	60.0195
50.0	149.0100	132.9248	119.8479	109.0479	104.3316	100.0	96.0093	92.3219	85.7307	80.0145	60.0029

Issued at Premium ⟷ Issued at Par ⟷ Issued at Discount

GLOSSARY

The definitions of many words and phrases in the glossary use other glossary terms. In a given definition, we *italicize* terms that themselves (or variants thereof) appear elsewhere under their own listings. The cross-references generally take one of two forms:

1. **absorption costing.** See *full absorption costing.*
2. **ABC.** *Activity-based costing.*

Form (1) refers you to another term for discussion of this bold-faced term. Form (2) tells you that this bold-faced term is synonymous with the *italicized* term, which you can consult for discussion if necessary.

A

AAA. *American Accounting Association.*

Abacus. A scholarly journal containing articles on theoretical aspects of accounting, published by Basil Blackwell for the Accounting Foundation of the University of Sydney.

abatement. A complete or partial cancellation of a levy imposed by a government unit.

ABC. *Activity-based costing.*

abnormal spoilage. Actual spoilage exceeding that expected when operations are normally efficient. Usual practice treats this cost as an *expense* of the period rather than as a *product cost.* Contrast with *normal spoilage.*

aboriginal cost. In public utility accounting, the *acquisition cost* of an *asset* incurred by the first *entity* devoting that asset to public use; the cost basis for most public utility regulation. If regulators used a different cost basis, then public utilities could exchange assets among themselves at ever-increasing prices in order to raise the rate base and, then, prices based on them.

absorbed overhead. *Overhead* costs allocated to individual products at some *overhead rate;* also called *applied overhead.*

absorption costing. See *full absorption costing.*

Abstracts of the EITF. See *Emerging Issues Task Force.*

accelerated cost recovery System (ACRS). A form of accelerated depreciation that Congress enacted in 1981 and amended in 1986, so that now most writers refer to it as *MACRS,* or *Modified Accelerated Cost Recovery System.* The system provides percentages of the asset's cost that a firm depreciates each year for tax purposes. The percentages derive, roughly, from 150-percent *declining-balance depreciation* methods. ACRS ignores salvage value. We do not generally use these amounts for *financial accounting.*

accelerated depreciation. In calculating *depreciation* charges, any method in which the charges become progressively smaller each period. Examples are *double declining-balance depreciation* and *sum-of-the-years'-digits depreciation* methods.

acceptance. A written promise to pay; equivalent to a *promissory note.*

account. A device for representing the amount (*balance*) for any line (or a part of a line) in the *balance sheet* or *income statement.* Because income statement accounts explain the changes in the balance sheet account Retained Earnings, the definition does not require the last three words of the preceding sentence. An account is any device for accumulating additions and subtractions relating to a single *asset, liability,* or *owners' equity* item, including *revenues* and *expenses.*

account analysis method. A method of separating *fixed costs* from *variable costs* based on the analyst's judgment of whether the cost is fixed or variable. Based on their names alone, the analyst might classify *direct labor (materials) costs* as variable and *depreciation* on a factory building as fixed. In our experience, this method results in too many fixed costs and not enough variable costs—that is, analysts have insufficient information to judge management's ability to reduce costs that appear to be fixed.

account form. The form of *balance sheet* in which *assets* appear on the left and *equities* appear on the right. Contrast with *report form.* See *T-account.*

accountability center. *Responsibility center.*

accountancy. The British word for *accounting.* In the United States, it means the theory and practice of accounting.

accountant's comments. Canada: a written communication issued by a public accountant at the conclusion of a review engagement. It consists of a description of the work performed and a statement that, under the terms of the engagement, the accountant has not performed an audit and consequently expresses no opinion. (Compare *auditor's report; denial of opinion.*)

accountant's opinion. *Auditor's report.*

accountant's report. *Auditor's report.*

accounting. A system conveying information about a specific *entity.* The information is in financial terms and will appear in accounting statements only if the accountant can measure it with reasonable precision. The *AICPA* defines accounting as a service activity whose "function is to provide quantitative information, primarily financial in nature, about economic entities that is intended to be useful in making economic decisions."

accounting adjustments. *Prior-period adjustments,* changes in accounting principles accounted for on a cumulative basis, and corrections of errors. See *accounting changes.*

The *FASB* indicates that it will tend to call these items "accounting adjustments," not "accounting changes," when it requires the reporting of *comprehensive income*.

Accounting and Tax Index. A publication that indexes, in detail, the accounting literature of the period. Published by UMI, a subsidiary of Bell & Howell.

accounting changes. As defined by *APB Opinion No. 20,* a change in (1) an *accounting principle* (such as a switch from *FIFO* to *LIFO* or from *sum-of-the-years'-digits depreciation* to *straight-line depreciation*), (2) an accounting estimate (such as estimated useful lives or salvage value of depreciable assets and estimates of *warranty* costs or *uncollectible accounts*), or (3) the reporting *entity*. The firm should disclose changes of type (1). It should include in reported earnings for the period of change the cumulative effect of the change on *retained earnings* at the start of the period during which it made the change. The firm should treat changes of type (2) as affecting only the period of change and, if necessary, future periods. The firm should disclose reasons for changes of type (3) in statements reporting on operations of the period of the change, and it should show the effect of the change on all other periods, for comparative purposes. In some cases (such as a change from *LIFO* to other inventory *flow assumptions* or a change in the method of accounting for long-term construction contracts), *GAAP* treat changes of type (1) like changes of type (3). That is, for these changes the firm should restate all statements shown for prior periods to show the effect of adopting the change for those periods as well. See *all-inclusive (income) concept* and *accounting errors.*

accounting conventions. Methods or procedures used in accounting. Writers tend to use this term when the method or procedure has not yet received official authoritative sanction by a pronouncement of a group such as the *APB, EITF, FASB,* or *SEC*. Contrast with *accounting principles.*

accounting cycle. The sequence of accounting procedures starting with *journal entries* for various transactions and events and ending with the *financial statements* or, perhaps, the *post-closing trial balance.*

accounting deficiency. Canada: a failure to adhere to generally accepted *accounting principles* or to disclose essential information in *financial statements.*

accounting entity. See *entity.*

accounting equation. *Assets = Equities; Assets = Liabilities + Owners' Equity.*

accounting errors. Arithmetic errors and misapplications of *accounting principles* in previously published financial statements. The firm corrects these during the current period with direct *debits* or *credits* to *retained earnings.* In this regard, the firm treats them like *prior-period adjustments,* but technically *APB Opinion No. 9* does not classify them as prior-period adjustments. See *accounting changes,* and contrast with changes in accounting estimates as described there.

accounting event. Any occurrence that is recorded in the accounting records.

Accounting Horizons. Quarterly journal of the *American Accounting Association.*

accounting methods. *Accounting principles;* procedures for carrying out accounting principles.

accounting period. The time period between consecutive *balance sheets;* the time period for which the firm prepares *financial statements* that measure *flows,* such as the *income statement* and the *statement of cash flows.* See *interim statements.*

accounting policies. *Accounting principles* adopted by a specific *entity.*

accounting principles. The methods or procedures used in accounting for events reported in the *financial statements.* We tend to use this term when the method or procedure has received official authoritative sanction from a pronouncement of a group such as the *APB, EITF, FASB,* or *SEC.* Contrast with *accounting conventions* and *conceptual framework.*

Accounting Principles Board. See *APB.*

accounting procedures. See *accounting principles.* However, this term usually refers to the methods for implementing accounting principles.

accounting rate of return. Income for a period divided by average investment during the period; based on income, rather than discounted cash flows, and hence a poor decision-making aid or tool. See *ratio.*

Accounting Research Bulletin (ARB). The name of the official pronouncements of the former *Committee on Accounting Procedure (CAP)* of the *AICPA.* The committee issued fifty-one bulletins between 1939 and 1959. *ARB No. 43* restated and codified the parts of the first forty-two bulletins not dealing solely with definitions.

Accounting Research Study (ARS). One of a series of studies published by the Director of Accounting Research of the *AICPA* and "designed to provide professional accountants and others interested in the development of accounting with a discussion and documentation of accounting problems." The AICPA published fifteen such studies in the period 1961–73.

Accounting Review. Scholarly publication of the *American Accounting Association.*

Accounting Series Release (ASR). See *SEC.*

accounting standards. *Accounting principles.*

Accounting Standards Executive Committee (AcSEC). The senior technical committee of the *AICPA* authorized to speak for the AICPA in the areas of *financial accounting* and reporting as well as *cost accounting.*

accounting system. The procedures for collecting and summarizing financial data in a firm.

Accounting Terminology Bulletin (ATB). One of four releases of the Committee on Terminology of the *AICPA* issued in the period 1953–57.

Accounting Trends and Techniques. An annual *AICPA* publication that surveys the reporting practices of 600 large corporations. It presents tabulations of specific practices, terminology, and disclosures along with illustrations taken from individual annual reports.

accounts payable. A *liability* representing an amount owed to a *creditor;* usually arising from the purchase of *merchandise* or materials and supplies, not necessarily due or past due; normally, a *current liability.*

accounts receivable. Claims against a *debtor;* usually arising from sales or services rendered, not necessarily due or past due; normally, a *current asset.*

accounts receivable turnover. Net sales on account divided by average accounts receivable. See *ratio.*

accretion. Occurs when a *book value* grows over time, such as a *bond* originally issued at a *discount;* the correct technical term is "accretion," not "amortization." This term also refers to an increase in economic worth through physical change caused by natural growth, usually said of a natural resource such as timber. Contrast with *appreciation.* See *amortization.*

accrual. Recognition of an *expense* (or *revenue*) and the related *liability* (or *asset*) resulting from an *accounting event,* frequently from the passage of time but not signaled by an explicit cash transaction; for example, the recognition of interest expense or revenue (or wages, salaries, or rent) at the end of a period even though the firm makes no explicit cash transaction at that time. Cash flow follows accounting recognition; contrast with *deferral.*

accrual basis of accounting. The method of recognizing *revenues* as a firm sells *goods* (or delivers them) and as it renders *services,* independent of the time when it receives cash. This system recognizes *expenses* in the period when it recognizes the related revenue, independent of the time when it pays cash. *SFAC No. 1* says, "Accrual accounting attempts to record the financial effects on an enterprise of transactions and other events and circumstances that have cash consequences for the enterprise in the periods in which those transactions, events, and circumstances occur rather than only in the periods in which cash is received or paid by the enterprise." Contrast with the *cash basis of accounting.* See *accrual* and *deferral.* We could more correctly call this "accrual/deferral" accounting.

accrue. See *accrued,* and contrast with *incur.*

accrued. Said of a *revenue (expense)* that the firm has earned (recognized) even though the related *receivable (payable)* has a future due date. We prefer not to use this adjective as part of an account title. Thus, we prefer to use Interest Receivable (Payable) as the account title rather than Accrued Interest Receivable (Payable). See *matching convention* and *accrual.* Contrast with *incur.*

accrued depreciation. An incorrect term for *accumulated depreciation.* Acquiring an asset with cash, capitalizing it, and then amortizing its cost over periods of use is a process of *deferral* and allocation, not of *accrual.*

accrued payable. A *payable* usually resulting from the passage of time. For example, *salaries* and *interest* accrue as time passes. See *accrued.*

accrued receivable. A *receivable* usually resulting from the passage of time. See *accrued.*

accumulated benefit obligation. See *projected benefit obligation* for definition and contrast.

accumulated depreciation. A preferred title for the asset *contra account* that shows the sum of *depreciation* charges on an asset since the time the firm acquired it. Other account titles are *allowance* for *depreciation* (acceptable term) and *reserve* for *depreciation* (unacceptable term).

accumulated other comprehensive income. *Balance sheet* amount in *owners' equity* showing the total of all *other comprehensive income* amounts from all prior periods.

accurate presentation. The qualitative accounting objective suggesting that information reported in financial statements should correspond as precisely as possible with the economic effects underlying transactions and events. See *fair presentation* and *full disclosure.*

acid test ratio. *Quick ratio.*

acquisition cost. Of an *asset,* the net *invoice* price plus all *expenditures* to place and ready the asset for its intended use. The other expenditures might include legal fees, transportation charges, and installation costs.

ACRS. *Accelerated Cost Recovery System.*

AcSEC. *Accounting Standards Executive Committee* of the *AICPA.*

activity accounting. *Responsibility accounting.*

activity-based costing (ABC). Method of assigning *indirect costs,* including nonmanufacturing *overhead costs,* to products and services. ABC assumes that almost all overhead costs associate with activities within the firm and vary with respect to the *drivers* of those activities. Some practitioners suggest that ABC attempts to find the drivers for all indirect costs; these people note that in the long run, all costs are *variable,* so *fixed* indirect costs do not occur. This method first assigns costs to activities and then to products based on the products' usage of the activities.

activity-based depreciation. *Production method (depreciation).*

activity-based management (ABM). Analysis and management of activities required to make a product or to produce a service. ABM focuses attention to enhance activities that add value to the customer and to reduce activities that do not. Its goal is to satisfy customer needs while making smaller demands on costly resources. Some refer to this as "activity management."

activity basis. *Costs* are *variable* or *fixed* (*incremental* or *unavoidable*) with respect to some activity, such as production of units (or the undertaking of some new project). Usage calls this activity the "activity basis."

activity center. Unit of the organization that performs a set of tasks.

activity variance. *Sales volume variance.*

actual cost (basis). *Acquisition* or *historical cost.* Also contrast with *standard cost.*

actual costing (system). Method of allocating costs to products using actual *direct materials,* actual *direct labor,* and actual *factory overhead.* Contrast with *normal costing* and *standard costing.*

actuarial. An adjective describing computations or analyses that involve both *compound interest* and probabilities, such as the computation of the *present value* of a life-contingent *annuity*. Some writers use the word even for computations involving only one of the two.

actuarial accrued liability. A 1981 report of the Joint Committee on Pension Terminology (of various actuarial societies) agreed to use this term rather than *prior service cost*.

ad valorem. A method of levying a tax or duty on goods by using their estimated value as the tax base.

additional paid-in capital. An alternative acceptable title for the *capital contributed in excess of par (or stated) value account*.

additional processing cost. *Costs* incurred in processing *joint products* after the *split-off point*.

adequate disclosure. An auditing standard that, to achieve *fair presentation* of *financial statements,* requires *disclosure* of *material* items. This *auditing standard* does not, however, require publicizing all information detrimental to a company. For example, the company may face a lawsuit, and disclosure might require a *debit* to a *loss* account and a *credit* to an *estimated liability*. But the court might view the making of this entry as an admission of liability, which could adversely affect the outcome of the suit. The firm should debit expense or loss for the expected loss, as required by *SFAS No. 5,* but need not use such accurate account titles that the court can spot an admission of liability.

adjunct account. An *account* that accumulates additions to another account. For example, Premium on Bonds Payable is adjunct to the liability Bonds Payable; the effective liability is the sum of the two account balances at a given date. Contrast with *contra account*.

adjusted acquisition (historical) cost. Sometimes said of the *book value* of a *plant asset,* that is, *acquisition cost* less *accumulated depreciation*. Also, cost adjusted to a *constant-dollar* amount to reflect *general price-level changes*.

adjusted bank balance of cash. The *balance* shown on the statement from the bank plus or minus amounts, such as for unrecorded deposits or outstanding checks, to reconcile the bank's balance with the correct cash balance. See *adjusted book balance of cash*.

adjusted basis. The *basis* used to compute gain or loss on the disposition of an *asset* for tax purposes. See also *book value*.

adjusted book balance of cash. The *balance* shown in the firm's account for cash in bank plus or minus amounts, such as for *notes* collected by the bank or bank service charges, to reconcile the account balance with the correct cash balance. See *adjusted bank balance of cash*.

adjusted trial balance. *Trial balance* taken after *adjusting entries* but before *closing entries*. Contrast with *pre-* and *post-closing trial balances*. See *unadjusted trial balance* and *post-closing trial balance*. See also *work sheet*.

adjusting entry. An entry made at the end of an *accounting period* to record a *transaction* or other *accounting event* that the firm has not yet recorded or has improperly recorded during the accounting period; an entry to update the accounts. See *work sheet*.

adjustment. An *account* change produced by an *adjusting entry*. Sometimes accountants use the term to refer to the process of restating *financial statement* amounts to *constant dollars*.

administrative costs (expenses). *Costs (expenses)* incurred for the firm as a whole, in contrast with specific functions such as manufacturing or selling; includes items such as salaries of top executives, general office rent, legal fees, and auditing fees.

admission of partner. Occurs when a new partner joins a *partnership*. Legally, the old partnership dissolves, and a new one comes into being. In practice, however, the firm may keep the old accounting records in use, and the accounting entries reflect the manner in which the new partner joined the firm. If the new partner merely purchases the interest of another partner, the accounting changes the name for one capital account. If the new partner contributes *assets* and *liabilities* to the partnership, then the firm must recognize them. See *bonus method*.

ADR. See *asset depreciation range*.

advances from (by) customers. A preferred title for the *liability* account representing *receipts* of *cash* in advance of delivering the *goods* or rendering the *service*. After the firm delivers the goods or services, it will recognize *revenue*. Some refer to this as "deferred revenue" or "deferred income," terms likely to confuse the unwary because the item is not yet *revenue* or *income*.

advances to affiliates. *Loans* by a parent company to a *subsidiary;* frequently combined with "investment in subsidiary" as "investments and advances to subsidiary" and shown as a *noncurrent asset* on the parent's *balance sheet*. The consolidation process eliminates these advances in *consolidated financial statements*.

advances to suppliers. A preferred term for the *asset* account representing *disbursements* of cash in advance of receiving *assets* or *services*.

adverse opinion. An *auditor's report* stating that the financial statements are not fair or are not in accord with *GAAP*.

affiliated company. A company controlling or controlled by another company.

after closing. Post-closing; a *trial balance* at the end of the period.

after cost. *Expenditures* to be made after *revenue* recognition. For example, *expenditures* for *repairs* under warranty are after cost. Proper recognition of after cost involves a debit to expense at the time of the sale and a credit to an *estimated liability*. When the firm discharges the liability, it debits the estimated liability and credits the assets consumed.

AG (Aktiengesellschaft). Germany: the form of a German company whose shares can trade on the stock exchange.

agency fund. An account for *assets* received by governmental units in the capacity of trustee or agent.

agency theory. A branch of economics relating the behavior of *principals* (such as owner nonmanagers or bosses) and that of their *agents* (such as nonowner managers or subordinates).

The principal assigns responsibility and authority to the agent, but the agent's own risks and preferences differ from those of the principal. The principal cannot observe all activities of the agent. Both the principal and the agent must consider the differing risks and preferences in designing incentive contracts.

agent. One authorized to transact business, including executing contracts, for another.

aging accounts receivable. The process of classifying *accounts receivable* by the time elapsed since the claim came into existence for the purpose of estimating the amount of uncollectible accounts receivable as of a given date. See *sales contra, estimated uncollectibles,* and *allowance for uncollectibles.*

aging schedule. A listing of *accounts receivable,* classified by age, used in *aging accounts receivable.*

AICPA (American Institute of Certified Public Accountants). The national organization that represents *CPAs.* See *AcSEC.* It oversees the writing and grading of the Uniform CPA Examination. Each state sets its own requirements for becoming a CPA in that state. See *certified public accountant.* Web Site: www.aicpa.org.

all-capital earnings rate. *Rate of return on assets.*

all-current method. *Foreign currency translation* in which all *financial statement* items are translated at the *current exchange rate.*

all-inclusive (income) concept. A concept that does not distinguish between *operating* and *nonoperating revenues* and *expenses.* Thus, the only entries to retained earnings are for *net income* and *dividends.* Under this concept, the *income statement* reports all *income, gains,* and *losses*; thus, net income includes events usually reported as *prior-period adjustments* and as *corrections of errors. GAAP* do not include this concept in its pure form, but *APB Opinions No. 9* and *No. 30* move far in this direction. They do permit retained earnings entries for prior-period adjustments and correction of errors.

allocate. To divide or spread a *cost* from one *account* into several accounts, to several products or activities, or to several periods.

allocation base. The systematic method that assigns *joint costs* to *cost objectives.* For example, a firm might assign the cost of a truck to periods based on miles driven during the period; the allocation base is miles. Or the firm might assign the cost of a factory supervisor to a product based on *direct labor* hours; the allocation base is direct labor hours.

allocation of income taxes. See *deferred income tax.*

allowance. A balance sheet *contra account* generally used for *receivables* and depreciable assets. See *sales* (or *purchase*) *allowance* for another use of this term.

allowance for funds used during construction. In accounting for public utilities, a *revenue* account *credited* for *implicit interest* earnings on *shareholders' equity* balances. One principle of public utility regulation and rate setting requires that customers should pay the full costs of producing the services (e.g., electricity) that they use, nothing more

and nothing less. Thus, an electric utility must capitalize into an *asset* account the full costs, but no more, of producing a new electric power-generating plant. One of the costs of building a new plant is the *interest* cost on cash tied up during construction. If *funds* are explicitly borrowed by an ordinary business, the journal entry for interest of $1,000 is typically:

Interest Expense	1,000	
Interest Payable		1,000
Interest expense for the period.		

If the firm is constructing a new plant, then another entry would be made, capitalizing interest into the plant-under-construction account:

Construction Work-in-Progress	750	
Interest Expense		750
Capitalize relevant portion of interest relating to construction work in progress into the asset account.		

The cost of the *plant asset* increases; when the firm uses the plant, it charges *depreciation.* The interest will become an expense through the depreciation process in the later periods of use, not currently as the firm pays for interest. Thus, the firm reports the full cost of the electricity generated during a given period as expense in that period. But suppose, as is common, that the electric utility does not explicitly borrow the funds but uses some of its own funds, including funds raised from equity issues as well as from debt. Even though the firm incurs no explicit interest expense or other explicit expense for capital, the funds have an *opportunity cost.* Put another way, the plant under construction will not have lower economic cost just because the firm used its own cash rather than borrowing. The public utility using its own funds, on which it would have to pay $750 of interest if it had explicitly borrowed the funds, will make the following entry:

Construction Work-in-Progress	750	
Allowance for Funds Used during Construction		750
Recognition of interest, an opportunity cost, on own funds used.		

The allowance account is a form of *revenue,* to appear on the income statement, and the firm will close it to Retained

Earnings, increasing it. On the *statement of cash flows* it is an income or revenue item not producing funds, and so the firm must subtract it from net income in deriving *cash provided by operations*. *SFAS No. 34* specifically prohibits nonutility companies from capitalizing, into plant under construction, the opportunity cost (interest) on their own funds used.

allowance for uncollectibles (accounts receivable). A *contra account* that shows the estimated *accounts receivable* amount that the firm expects not to collect. When the firm uses such an allowance, the actual write-off of specific accounts receivable (*debit* allowance, *credit* specific customer's account) does not affect *revenue* or *expense* at the time of the write-off. The firm reduces revenue when it debits *bad debt expense* (or, our preference, a revenue contra account) and credits the allowance; the firm can base the amount of the credit to the allowance on a percentage of sales on account for a period of time or compute it from *aging accounts receivable*. This contra account enables the firm to show an estimated receivables amount that it expects to collect without identifying specific uncollectible accounts. See *allowance method*.

allowance method. A method of attempting to match all *expenses* of a transaction with their associated *revenues;* usually involves a debit to expense and a credit to an *estimated liability,* such as for estimated warranty expenditures, or a debit to a revenue (*contra*) account and a credit to an asset (*contra*) account, such as in some firms' accounting for uncollectible accounts. See *allowance for uncollectibles* for further explanation. When the firm uses the allowance method for *sales discounts,* the firm records sales at gross invoice prices (not reduced by the amounts of discounts made available). The firm *debits* an estimate of the amount of discounts to be taken to a revenue contra account and *credits* an allowance account, shown contra to *accounts receivable*.

American Accounting Association (AAA). An organization primarily for academic accountants but open to all interested in accounting. It publishes the *Accounting Review* and several other journals.

American Institute of Certified Public Accountants. See *AICPA*.

American Stock Exchange (AMEX) (ASE). A public market where various corporate *securities* are traded.

AMEX. *American Stock Exchange*.

amortization. Strictly speaking, the process of liquidating or extinguishing ("bringing to death") a *debt* with a series of payments to the *creditor* (or to a *sinking fund*). From that usage has evolved a related use involving the accounting for the payments themselves: "amortization schedule" for a mortgage, which is a table showing the allocation between *interest* and *principal*. The term has come to mean writing off ("liquidating") the cost of an asset. In this context it means the general process of *allocating* the *acquisition cost* of an asset either to the periods of benefit as an *expense* or to *inventory* accounts as a *product cost*. This is

called *depreciation* for *plant assets, depletion* for *wasting assets* (natural resources), and "amortization" for *intangibles*. *SFAC No. 6* refers to amortization as "the accounting process of reducing an amount by periodic payments or write-downs." The expressions "unamortized debt discount or premium" and "to amortize debt discount or premium" relate to *accruals,* not to *deferrals*. The expressions "amortization of long-term assets" and "to amortize long-term assets" refer to deferrals, not accruals. Contrast with *accretion*.

amortized cost. A measure required by *SFAS No. 115* for *held-to-maturity securities*. This amount results from applying the method described at *effective interest method*. The firm records the security at its initial cost and computes the *effective interest rate* for the security. Whenever the firm receives cash from the issuer of the security or whenever the firm reaches the end of one of its own *accounting periods* (that is, reaches the time for its own *adjusting entries*), it takes the following steps. It multiplies the amount currently recorded on the books by the effective interest rate (which remains constant over the time the firm holds the security). It debits that amount to the debt security account and credits the amount to Interest Revenue. If the firm receives cash, it debits Cash and credits the debt security account. The firm recomputes the book value of the debt security as the book value before these entries plus the increase for the interest revenue less the decrease for the cash received. The resulting amount is the amortized cost for the end of that period.

analysis of variances. See *variance analysis*.

annual report. A report prepared once a year for shareholders and other interested parties. It includes a *balance sheet,* an *income statement,* a *statement of cash flows,* a reconciliation of changes in *owners' equity* accounts, a *summary of significant accounting principles,* other explanatory *notes,* the *auditor's report,* and comments from management about the year's events. See *10-K* and *financial statements*.

annuitant. One who receives an *annuity*.

annuity. A series of payments of equal amount, usually made at equally spaced time intervals.

annuity certain. An *annuity* payable for a definite number of periods. Contrast with *contingent annuity*.

annuity due. An *annuity* whose first payment occurs at the start of period 1 (or at the end of period 0). Contrast with *annuity in arrears*.

annuity in advance. An *annuity due*.

annuity in arrears. An *ordinary annuity* whose first payment occurs at the end of the first period.

annuity method of depreciation. See *compound interest depreciation*.

antidilutive. Said of a *potentially dilutive* security that will increase *earnings per share* if its holder *exercises* it or *converts* it into common stock. In computing *primary* and *fully diluted earnings per share,* the firm must assume that holders of antidilutive securities will not exercise their options or convert securities into common shares. The opposite assumption would lead to increased reported earnings per share in a given period.

APB. Accounting Principles Board of the *AICPA*. It set *accounting principles* from 1959 through 1973, issuing 31 *APB Opinions* and 4 *APB Statements*. The *FASB* superseded it.

APB Opinion. The name for the APB pronouncements that compose much of *generally accepted accounting principles*; the APB issued 31 *APB Opinions* from 1962 through 1973.

APB Statement. The *APB* issued four *APB Statements* between 1962 and 1970. The *Statements* were approved by at least two-thirds of the board, but they state recommendations, not requirements. For example, *Statement No. 3* (1969) suggested the publication of *constant-dollar* financial statements but did not require them.

APBs. An abbreviation used for *APB Opinions*.

applied cost. A *cost* that a firm has *allocated* to a department, product, or activity; not necessarily based on actual costs incurred.

applied overhead. *Overhead costs* charged to departments, products, or activities. Also called *absorbed overhead*.

appraisal. In valuing an *asset* or *liability*, a process that involves expert opinion rather than evaluation of explicit market transactions.

appraisal method of depreciation. The periodic *depreciation* charge that equals the difference between the beginning-of-period and the end-of-period appraised values of the *asset* if that difference is positive. If negative, there is no charge. Not based on *historical cost*, this method is thus not generally accepted.

appreciation. An increase in economic value caused by rising market prices for an *asset*. Contrast with *accretion*.

appropriated retained earnings. See *retained earnings, appropriated*.

appropriation. In governmental accounting, an *expenditure* authorized for a specified amount, purpose, and time.

appropriation account. In governmental accounting, an account set up to record specific authorizations to spend. The governmental unit credits this account with appropriation amounts. At the end of the period, the unit closes to (debits) this account all *expenditures* during the period and all *encumbrances* outstanding at the end of the period.

approximate net realizable value method. A method of assigning joint costs to *joint products* based on revenues minus *additional processing costs* of the end products.

ARB. *Accounting Research Bulletin*.

arbitrage. Strictly speaking, the simultaneous purchase in one market and sale in another of a *security* or commodity in hope of making a *profit* on price differences in the different markets. Often writers use this term loosely when a trader sells an item that is somewhat different from the item purchased; for example, the sale of shares of common stock and the simultaneous purchase of a *convertible bond* that is convertible into identical common shares. The trader hopes that the market will soon see that the similarities of the items should make them have equal market values. When the market values converge, the trader closes the positions and profits from the original difference in prices, less trading costs.

arbitrary. Having no causation basis. Accounting theorists and practitioners often, properly, say, "Some cost allocations are arbitrary." In that sense, the accountant does not mean that the allocations are capricious or haphazard but does mean that theory suggests no unique solution to the allocation problem at hand. Accountants require that arbitrary allocations be systematic, rational, and consistently followed over time.

arm's length. A transaction negotiated by unrelated parties, both acting in their own self-interests; the basis for a *fair market value* estimation or computation.

arrears. *Cumulative dividends* that the firm has not yet declared. See *annuity in arrears* for another context.

ARS. *Accounting Research Study*.

articles of incorporation. Document filed with state authorities by persons forming a corporation. When the state returns the document with a certificate of incorporation, the document becomes the corporation's *charter*.

articulate. The relation between any operating statement (for example, *income statement* or *statement of cash flows*) and comparative balance sheets, where the operating statement explains (or reconciles) the change in some major balance sheet category (for example, *retained earnings* or *working capital*).

ASE. *American Stock Exchange*.

ASR. *Accounting Series Release*.

assess. To value property for the purpose of property taxation; to levy a charge on the owner of property for improvements thereto, such as for sewers or sidewalks. The taxing authority computes the assessment.

assessed valuation. For real estate or other property, a dollar amount that a government uses as a basis for levying taxes. The amount need not have some relation to *market value*.

asset. *SFAC No. 6* defines assets as "probable future economic benefits obtained or controlled by a particular entity as a result of past transactions. . . . An asset has three essential characteristics: (a) it embodies a probable future benefit that involves a capacity, singly or in combination with other assets, to contribute directly or indirectly to future net cash inflows, (b) a particular entity can obtain the benefit and control others' access to it, and (c) the transaction or other event giving rise to the entity's right to or control of the benefit has already occurred." A footnote points out that "probable" means that which we can reasonably expect or believe but that is not certain or proved. You may understand condition (c) better if you think of it as requiring that a future benefit cannot be an asset if it arises from an *executory contract*, a mere exchange of promises. Receiving a purchase order from a customer provides a future benefit, but it is an executory contract, so the order cannot be an asset. An asset may be *tangible* or *intangible*, short-term (current) or long-term (noncurrent).

asset depreciation range (ADR). The range of *depreciable lives* allowed by the *Internal Revenue Service* for a specific depreciable *asset*.

asset turnover. Net sales divided by average assets. See *ratio*.

assignment of accounts receivable. Transfer of the legal ownership of an account receivable through its sale. Contrast with *pledging* accounts receivable, where the receivables serve as *collateral* for a *loan*.

ATB. *Accounting Terminology Bulletin*.

at par. A *bond* or *preferred shares* issued (or selling) at *face amount*.

attachment. The laying claim to the *assets* of a borrower (or debtor) by a lender (or creditor) when the borrower has failed to pay debts on time.

attest. An auditor's rendering of an *opinion* that the *financial statements* are fair. Common usage calls this procedure the "attest function" of the CPA. See *fair presentation*.

attestor. Typically independent *CPA*s, who *audit financial statements* prepared by management for the benefit of users. The *FASB* describes accounting's constituency as comprising preparers, attestors, and users.

attribute measured. The particular *cost* reported in the balance sheet. When making physical measurements, such as of a person, one needs to decide the units with which to measure, such as inches or centimeters or pounds or grams. One chooses the attribute height or weight independently of the measuring unit, English or metric. Conventional accounting uses *historical cost* as the attribute measured and *nominal dollars* as the measuring unit. Some theorists argue that accounting would better serve readers if it used *current cost* as the attribute measured. Others argue that accounting would better serve readers if it used *constant dollars* as the measuring unit. Some, including us, think accounting should change both the measuring unit and the attribute measured. One can measure the attribute historical cost in nominal dollars or in constant dollars. One can also measure the attribute current cost in nominal dollars or constant dollars. Choosing between the two attributes and the two measuring units implies four different accounting systems. Each of these four has its uses.

attribute(s) sampling. The use of sampling technique in which the observer assesses each item selected on the basis of whether it has a particular qualitative characteristic in order to ascertain the rate of occurrence of this characteristic in the population. See also *estimation sampling*. Compare *variables sampling*. Example of attributes sampling: take a sample population of people, note the fraction that is male (say, 40 percent), and then infer that the entire population contains 40 percent males. Example of variables sampling: take a sample population of people, observe the weight of each sample point, compute the mean of those sampled people's weights (say 160 pounds), and then infer that the mean weight of the entire population equals 160 pounds.

audit. Systematic inspection of accounting records involving analyses, tests, and *confirmations*. See *internal audit*.

audit committee. A committee of the board of directors of a *corporation*, usually comprising outside directors, who nominate the independent auditors and discuss the auditors'

work with them. If the auditors believe the shareholders should know about certain matters, the auditors, in principle, first bring these matters to the attention of the audit committee; in practice, the auditors may notify management before they notify the audit committee.

Audit Guides. See *Industry Audit Guides*.

audit program. The procedures followed by the *auditor* in carrying out the *audit*.

audit trail. A reference accompanying an entry, or *post*, to an underlying source record or document. Efficiently checking the accuracy of accounting entries requires an audit trail. See *cross-reference*.

Auditing Research Monograph. Publication series of the *AICPA*.

auditing standards. Standards promulgated by the *AICPA*, including general standards, standards of field work, and standards of reporting. According to the AICPA, these standards "deal with the measures of the quality of the performance and the objectives to be attained" rather than with specific auditing procedures.

Auditing Standards Board. *AICPA* operating committee that promulgates auditing rules.

auditor. Without a modifying adjective, usually refers to an external auditor—one who checks the accuracy, fairness, and general acceptability of accounting records and statements and then *attests* to them. See *internal auditor*.

auditor's opinion. *Auditor's report*.

auditor's report. The auditor's statement of the work done and an opinion of the *financial statements*. The auditor usually gives unqualified ("clean") opinions but may qualify them, or the auditor may disclaim an opinion in the report. Often called the "accountant's report." See *adverse opinion*.

AudSEC. The former Auditing Standards Executive Committee of the *AICPA*, now functioning as the *Auditing Standards Board*.

authorized capital stock. The number of *shares* of stock that a corporation can issue; specified by the *articles of incorporation*.

available for sale, securities. *Marketable securities* a firm holds that are classified as neither *trading securities* nor *held-to-maturity (debt) securities*. This classification is important in *SFAS No. 115*, which requires the owner to carry marketable equity securities on the balance sheet at market value, not at cost. Under *SFAS No. 115*, the income statement reports *holding gains and losses* on trading securities but not on securities available for sale. The required accounting *credits* (*debits*) holding gains (losses) on securities available for sale directly to an *owners' equity* account. On sale, the firm reports realized gain or loss as the difference between the selling price and the original cost, for trading securities, and as the difference between the selling price and the book value at the beginning of the period of sale, for securities available for sale and for debt securities held to maturity. By their nature, however, the firm will only rarely sell debt securities "held to maturity."

average. The arithmetic mean of a set of numbers; obtained by summing the items and dividing by the number of items.

average collection period of receivables. See *ratio.*

average-cost flow assumption. An inventory *flow assumption* in which the cost of units equals the *weighted average* cost of the *beginning inventory* and purchases. See *inventory equation.*

average tax rate. The rate found by dividing *income tax* expense by *net income* before taxes. Contrast with *marginal tax rate* and *statutory tax rate.*

avoidable cost. A *cost* that ceases if a firm discontinues an activity; an *incremental* or *variable* cost. See *programmed cost.*

B

backflush costing. A method of *allocating indirect costs* and *overhead;* used by companies that hope to have zero or small *work-in-process inventory* at the end of the period. The method *debits* all *product costs* to *cost of goods sold* (or *finished goods inventory*) during the period. To the extent that work in process actually exists at the end of the period, the method then debits work-in-process and *credits* cost of goods sold (or finished goods inventory). This method is "backflush" in the sense that costing systems ordinarily, but not in this case, allocate first to work-in-process and then forward to cost of goods sold or to finished goods. Here, the process allocates first to cost of goods sold (or finished goods) and then, later if necessary, to work-in-process.

backlog. Orders for which a firm has insufficient *inventory* on hand for current delivery and will fill in a later period.

backlog depreciation. In *current cost accounting,* a problem arising for the *accumulated depreciation* on *plant assets.* Consider an *asset* costing $10,000 with a 10-year life depreciated with the straight-line method. Assume that a similar asset has a current cost of $10,000 at the end of the first year but $12,000 at the end of the second year. Assume that the firm bases the depreciation charge on the average current cost during the year, $10,000 for the first year and $11,000 for the second. The depreciation charge for the first year is $1,000 and for the second is $1,100 (= .10 × $11,000), so the *accumulated depreciation account* is $2,100 after two years. Note that at the end of the second year, the firm has used 20 percent of the asset's future benefits, so the accounting records based on current costs must show a *net book value* of $9,600 (= .80 × $12,000), which results only if accumulated depreciation equals $2,400, so that book value equals $9,600 (= $12,000 − $2,400). But the sum of the depreciation charges equals only $2,100 (= $1,000 + $1,100). The *journal entry* to increase the accumulated depreciation account requires a *credit* to that account of $300. The backlog depreciation question arises: what account do we debit? Some theorists would *debit* an *income* account, and others would *debit* a *balance sheet owners' equity* account without reducing current-period earnings. The answer to the question of what to debit interrelates with how the firm records the *holding gains* on the asset. When the firm debits the asset account for $2,000 to increase the recorded amount from $10,000 to $12,000, it records a holding gain of $2,000 with a credit. Many theorists believe that whatever account the firm credits for the holding gain is the same account that the firm should debit for backlog depreciation. This is sometimes called "catch-up depreciation."

bad debt. An *uncollectible account;* see *bad debt expense* and *sales contra, estimated uncollectibles.*

bad debt expense. The name for an *account debited* in both the *allowance method* for *uncollectible accounts* and the *direct write-off method.* Under the allowance method, some prefer to treat the account as a revenue contra, not as an expense, and give it an account title such as Uncollectible Accounts Adjustment.

bad debt recovery. Collection, perhaps partial, of a specific account receivable previously written off as uncollectible. If a firm uses the *allowance method,* it will usually *credit* the *allowance* account, assuming that it has correctly assessed the amount of bad debts but has merely misjudged the identity of one of the nonpaying customers. If the firm decides that its charges for bad debts have been too large, it will credit the Bad Debt Expense account. If the firm uses the *direct write-off* method, it will credit a *revenue account.*

bailout period. In a *capital budgeting* context, the total time that elapses before accumulated cash inflows from a project, including the potential *salvage value* of assets at various times, equal or exceed the accumulated cash outflows. Contrast with *payback period,* which assumes completion of the project and uses terminal salvage value. Bailout, in contrast with payback, takes into account, at least to some degree, the *present value* of the cash flows after the termination date that the analyst is considering. The potential salvage value at any time includes some estimate of the flows that can occur after that time.

balance. As a noun, the opening balance in an *account* plus the amounts of increases less the amounts of decreases. (In the absence of a modifying adjective, the term means closing balance, in contrast to opening balance. The closing balance for a period becomes the opening balance for the next period.) As a verb, "balance" means to find the value of the arithmetic expression described above.

balance sheet. Statement of financial position that shows Total *Assets* = Total *Liabilities* + *Owners' Equity.* The *balance sheet* usually classifies Total Assets as (1) *current assets,* (2) *investments,* (3) *property, plant, and equipment,* or (4) *intangible assets.* The balance sheet accounts composing Total Liabilities usually appear under the headings Current Liabilities and Long-term Liabilities.

balance sheet account. An account that can appear on a balance sheet; a *permanent account.* Contrast with *temporary account.*

balanced scorecard. A set of performance targets, not all expressed in dollar amounts, for setting an organization's goals for its individual employees or groups or divisions. A community relations employee might, for example, set targets in terms of number of employee hours devoted to local charitable purposes.

balloon. Most *mortgage* and *installment loans* require relatively equal periodic payments. Sometimes the loan requires relatively equal periodic payments with a large final payment. Usage calls the large final payment a "balloon" payment and the loan, a "balloon" loan. Although a coupon bond meets this definition, usage seldom, if ever, applies this term to bond loans.

bank balance. The amount of the balance in a checking account shown on the *bank statement.* Compare with *adjusted bank balance of cash,* and see *bank reconciliation schedule.*

bank prime rate. See *prime rate.*

bank reconciliation schedule. A schedule that explains the difference between the book balance of the cash in a bank account and the bank's statement of that amount; takes into account the amount of items such as checks that have not cleared or deposits that have not been recorded by the bank, as well as errors made by the bank or the firm.

bank statement. A statement sent by the bank to a checking account customer showing deposits, checks cleared, and service charges for a period, usually one month.

bankrupt. Occurs when a company's *liabilities* exceed its *assets* and the firm or one of its creditors has filed a legal petition that the bankruptcy court has accepted under the bankruptcy law. A bankrupt firm is usually, but need not be, *insolvent.*

base stock method. A method of inventory valuation that assumes that a firm must keep on hand at all times a minimum normal, or base stock, of goods for effective continuity of operations. The firm values this base quantity at *acquisition cost* of the inventory on hand in the earliest period when inventory was on hand. Firms may not use this method, either for financial reporting or for tax reporting, but most theorists consider it to be the forerunner of the *LIFO* cost flow assumption.

basic accounting equation. *Accounting equation.*

basic cost-flow equation. *Cost-flow equation.*

basic earnings per share (BEPS). *Net income* to *common shareholders,* divided by the weighted average number of common shares *outstanding* during the period. Required by *SFAS No. 128* and by *IASC.* See *primary earnings per share (PEPS)* for contrast. Because BEPS does not deal with *common-stock equivalents,* it will almost always give a larger earnings-per-share figure than PEPS.

basis. *Acquisition cost,* or some substitute therefor, of an *asset* or *liability* used in computing gain or loss on disposition or retirement; *attribute measured.* This term appears in both *financial* and *tax reporting,* but the basis of a given item need not be the same for both purposes.

basket purchase. Purchase of a group of *assets* (and *liabilities*) for a single price; the acquiring firm must assign *costs* to each item so that it can record the individual items with their separate amounts in the *accounts.*

bear. One who believes that security prices will fall. A "bear market" refers to a time when stock prices are generally declining. Contrast with *bull.*

bearer bond. See *registered bond* for contrast and definition.

beginning inventory. Valuation of *inventory* on hand at the beginning of the *accounting period,* equals *ending inventory* from the preceding period.

behavioral congruence. *Goal congruence.*

benchmarking. Process of measuring a firm's performance, products, and services against standards based on best levels of performance achievable or, sometimes, achieved by other firms.

BEPS. *Basic earnings per share.*

betterment. An *improvement,* usually *capitalized,* not *expensed.*

bid. An offer to purchase, or the amount of the offer.

big bath. A *write-off* of a substantial amount of costs previously treated as *assets;* usually occurs when a corporation drops a business line that earlier required a large investment but that proved to be unprofitable. The term is sometimes used to describe a situation in which a corporation takes a large write-off in one period in order to free later periods of gradual write-offs of those amounts. In this sense it frequently occurs when the top management of the firm changes.

Big 5. The five largest U.S. *public accounting* partnerships; in alphabetical order: Arthur Andersen & Co.; Deloitte & Touche; Ernst & Young; KPMG Peat Marwick; and PricewaterhouseCoopers. See *Big N.*

Big N. The largest U.S. *public accounting* partnerships. When we first prepared this glossary, there were eight such partnerships, referred to as the "Big 8." See *Big 5.* The term "Big N" came into use when various of the *Big 8* proposed to merge with each other and the ultimate number of large partnerships was in doubt, which it still is.

bill. An *invoice* of charges and *terms of sale* for *goods* and *services;* also, a piece of currency.

bill of materials. A specification of the quantities of *direct materials* that a firm expects to use to produce a given job or quantity of output.

blocked currency. Currency that the holder, by law, cannot withdraw from the issuing country or exchange for the currency of another country.

board. *Board of directors.*

board of directors. The governing body of a corporation; elected by the shareholders.

bond. A certificate to show evidence of debt. The *par value* is the *principal* or face amount of the bond payable at maturity. The *coupon rate* is the amount of the yearly payments divided by the principal amount. Coupon bonds have attached coupons that the holder can redeem at stated dates. Increasingly, firms issue not coupon bonds but registered bonds; the firm or its agent keeps track of the owners of registered bonds. Normally, bonds call for semi-annual payments.

bond conversion. The act of exchanging *convertible bonds* for *preferred* or *common shares.*

bond discount. From the standpoint of the issuer of a *bond* at the issue date, the excess of the *par value* of a bond over its initial sales price and, at later dates, the excess of par over the sum of the following two amounts: initial issue price and the portion of discount already *amortized;* from the standpoint of a bondholder, the difference between par value and selling price when the bond sells below par.

bond indenture. The contract between an issuer of *bonds* and the bondholders.

bond premium. Exactly parallel to *bond discount* except that the issue price (or current selling price) exceeds *par value.*

bond ratings. Corporate and *municipal bond* issue ratings, based on the issuer's existing *debt* level, its previous record of payment, the *coupon rate* on the bonds, and the safety of the *assets* or *revenues* that are committed to paying off *principal* and *interest.* Moody's Investors Service and Standard & Poor's Corporation publish bond ratings: Moody's top rating is Aaa; Standard & Poor's is AAA.

bond redemption. Retirement of *bonds.*

bond refunding. To incur *debt,* usually through the issue of new *bonds,* intending to use the proceeds to retire an *outstanding* bond issue.

bond sinking fund. See *sinking fund.*

bond table. A table showing the current price of a *bond* as a function of the *coupon rate,* current (remaining) term *maturity,* and effective *yield to maturity* (or *effective rate*).

bonus. Premium over normal *wage* or *salary,* paid usually for meritorious performance.

bonus method. One of two methods to recognize an excess, say $10,000, when a *partnership* admits a new partner and when the new partner's capital account is to show an amount larger than the amount of *tangible* assets that he or she contributes. First, the old partners may transfer $10,000 from themselves to the new partner. This is the bonus method. Second, the partnership may recognize goodwill in the amount of $10,000, with the credit to the new partner's capital account. This is the *goodwill method.* (Notice that the new partner's percentage of total ownership differs under the two methods.) If the new partner's capital account is to show an amount smaller than the tangible assets that he or she contributed, then the old partners will receive bonus or goodwill, depending on the method.

book. As a verb, to record a transaction; as a noun, usually plural, the *journals* and *ledgers*; as an adjective, see *book value.*

book cost. *Book value.*

book inventory. An *inventory* amount that results not from physical count but from the amount of beginning inventory plus *invoice* amounts of net purchases less invoice amounts of *requisitions* or withdrawals; implies a *perpetual inventory* method.

book of original entry. *Journal.*

book value. The amount shown in the books or in the *accounts* for an *asset, liability,* or *owners' equity* item. The term is generally used to refer to the *net* amount of an *asset* or group of assets shown in the account that records the asset

and reductions, such as for *amortization,* in its cost. Of a firm, it refers to the excess of total assets over total liabilities; *net assets.*

book value per share of common stock. Common *shareholders' equity* divided by the number of shares of common stock outstanding. See *ratio.*

bookkeeping. The process of analyzing and recording transactions in the accounting records.

boot. The additional cash paid (or received) along with a used item in a trade-in or exchange transaction for another item. See *trade-in.*

borrower. See *loan.*

branch. A sales office or other unit of an enterprise physically separated from the home office of the enterprise but not organized as a legally separate *subsidiary.* Writers seldom use this term to refer to manufacturing units.

branch accounting. An accounting procedure that enables the firm to report the financial position and operations of each *branch* separately but later combine them for published statements.

breakeven analysis. See *breakeven chart.*

breakeven chart. Two kinds of breakeven charts appear here. The charts use the following information for one month. Revenue is $30 per unit.

Cost Classification	Variable Cost, Per Unit	Fixed Cost, Per Month
Manufacturing costs:		
Direct material	$ 4	—
Direct labor	9	—
Overhead	4	$3,060
Total manufacturing costs	$17	$3,060
Selling, general, and administrative costs	5	1,740
Total costs	$22	$4,800

The cost-volume-profit graph presents the relation between changes in volume to the amount of *profit,* or *income.* Such a graph shows total *revenue* and total *costs* for each volume level, and the user reads profit or loss at any volume directly from the chart. The profit-volume graph does not show revenues and costs but more readily indicates profit (or loss) at various output levels. Keep in mind two caveats about these graphs:

1. Although the curve depicting *variable cost* and total cost appears as a straight line for its entire length, at low or high levels of output, variable cost will probably differ from $22 per unit. The variable cost figure usually results from studies of operations at some broad central area of production, called the *relevant range.* The chart will not usually provide accurate results for low (or high) levels of activity. For this

(a) Cost-Volume-Profit Graph

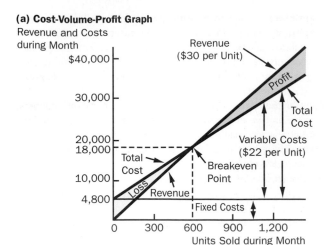

(b) Profit-Volume Graph

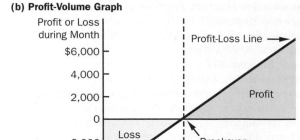

reason, the total cost and the profit-loss curves sometimes appear as dotted lines at lower (or higher) volume levels.

2. This chart, simplistically, assumes a single-product firm. For a multiproduct firm, the horizontal axis would have to be stated in dollars rather than in physical units of output. Breakeven charts for multiproduct firms necessarily assume that the firm sells constant proportions of the several products, so that changes in this mixture, as well as in costs or selling prices, invalidate such a chart.

breakeven point. The volume of sales required so that total *revenues* equals total *costs;* may be expressed in units (*fixed costs ÷ contribution per unit*) or in sales dollars [selling price per unit × (fixed costs ÷ contribution per unit)].

budget. A financial plan that a firm uses to estimate the results of future operations; frequently used to help control future operations. In governmental operations, budgets often become the law. See *standard costs* for further elaboration and contrast.

budgetary accounts. In governmental accounting, the accounts that reflect estimated operations and financial condition, as affected by estimated *revenues, appropriations,* and *encumbrances.* Contrast with *proprietary accounts,* which record the transactions.

budgetary control. Management of governmental (nongovernmental) unit in accordance with an official (approved) *budget* in order to keep total expenditures within authorized (planned) limits.

budgeted cost. See *standard costs* for definition and contrast.

budgeted statements. *Pro forma statements* prepared before the event or period occurs.

bull. One who believes that security prices will rise. A "bull market" refers to a time when stock prices are generally rising. Contrast with *bear.*

burden. See *overhead costs.*

burn rate. A new business usually begins life with cash-absorbing operating losses but with a limited amount of cash. The "burn rate" measures how long the new business

can survive before operating losses must stop or the firm must receive a new infusion of cash. Writers usually express the burn rate in months.

business combination. As defined in *APB Opinion No. 16,* the bringing together into a single accounting *entity* of two or more incorporated or unincorporated businesses. The new entity will account for the *merger* either with the *purchase method* or the *pooling-of-interests method.* See *conglomerate.*

business entity. *Entity; accounting entity.*

BV *(besloten vennootschap).* Netherlands: a private limited-liability company.

bylaws. The rules adopted by the shareholders of a corporation; specify the general methods for carrying out the functions of the corporation.

by-product. A *joint product* whose sales value is so small relative to the sales value of the other joint product(s) that it does not receive normal accounting treatment. The costs assigned to by-products reduce the costs of the main product(s). Accounting allocates by-products a share of joint costs such that the expected gain or loss at their sale is zero. Thus, by-products appear in the *accounts* at *net realizable value.*

C corporation. In tax terminology, a corporation paying its own income taxes. Contrast with *S corporation.*

CA. *Chartered accountant.*

call. An option to buy *shares* of a publicly traded corporation at a fixed price during a fixed time span. Contrast with *put.*

call premium. See *callable bond.*

call price. See *callable bond.*

callable bond. A *bond* for which the issuer reserves the right to pay a specific amount, the call price, to retire the obligation before its *maturity* date. If the issuer agrees to pay more than the *face amount* of the bond when called, the excess of the payment over the face amount is the "call premium."

called-up share capital. UK: *common stock* at *par value.*

Canadian Institute of Chartered Accountants. The national organization that represents *chartered accountants* in Canada. Web Site: www.cica.ca.

cancelable lease. See *lease.*

CAP. *Committee on Accounting Procedure.*

capacity. Stated in units of product, the amount that a firm can produce per unit of time; stated in units of input, such as *direct labor* hours, the amount of input that a firm can use in production per unit of time. A firm uses this measure of output or input in allocating *fixed costs* if the amounts producible are normal, rather than maximum, amounts.

capacity cost. A *fixed cost* incurred to provide a firm with the capacity to produce or to sell. Consists of *standby costs* and *enabling costs.* Contrast with *programmed costs.*

capacity variance. *Production volume variance.*

capital. *Owners' equity* in a business; often used, equally correctly, to mean the total assets of a business; sometimes used to mean *capital assets.*

capital asset. Properly used, a designation, for income tax purposes, that describes property held by a taxpayer except *cash,* inventoriable *assets,* goods held primarily for sale, most depreciable property, *real estate, receivables,* certain *intangibles,* and a few other items. Sometimes writers use this term imprecisely to describe *plant* and *equipment,* which are clearly not capital assets under the income-tax definition. Writers often use the term to refer to an *investment* in *securities.*

capital budget. Plan of proposed outlays for acquiring long-term *assets* and the means of *financing* the acquisition.

capital budgeting. The process of choosing *investment* projects for an enterprise by considering the *present value* of cash flows and deciding how to raise the funds the investment requires.

capital consumption allowance. The term used for *depreciation expense* in national income accounting and the reporting of funds in the economy.

capital contributed in excess of par (or stated) value. A preferred title for the account that shows the amount received by the issuer for *capital stock* in excess of *par (or stated) value.*

capital expenditure (outlay). An *expenditure* to acquire long-term *assets.*

capital gain. The excess of proceeds over *cost,* or other *basis,* from the sale of a *capital asset* as defined by the Internal Revenue Code. If the taxpayer has held the capital asset for a sufficiently long time before sale, then the gain is taxed at a rate lower than that used for other gains and ordinary income.

capital lease. A *lease* treated by the *lessee* as both the borrowing of funds and the acquisition of an *asset* to be *amortized.* The lessee (tenant) recognizes both the *liability* and the asset on its balance sheet. Expenses consist of *interest* on the *debt* and *amortization* of the asset. The *lessor* (landlord) treats the lease as the sale of the asset in return for a series of future cash receipts. Contrast with *operating lease.*

capital loss. A negative capital gain; see *capital gain.*

capital rationing. In a *capital budgeting* context, the imposition of constraints on the amounts of total capital expenditures in each period.

capital stock. The ownership shares of a corporation. Consists of all classes of *common* and *preferred shares.*

capital structure. The composition of a corporation's equities; the relative proportions of short-term debt, long-term debt, and *owners' equity.*

capital surplus. An inferior term for *capital contributed in excess of par (or stated) value.*

capitalization of a corporation. A term used by investment analysts to indicate *shareholders' equity* plus bonds outstanding.

capitalization of earnings. The process of estimating the *fair value* of a firm by computing the *net present value* of the predicted *net income* (not *cash flows*) of the firm for the future.

capitalization rate. An *interest rate* used to convert a series of payments or receipts or earnings into a single *present value.*

capitalize. To record an *expenditure* that may benefit a future period as an *asset* rather than to treat the expenditure as an *expense* of the period of its occurrence. Whether expenditures for advertising or for research and development should be capitalized is controversial, but *SFAS No. 2* forbids capitalizing *R&D* costs. We believe GAAP should allow firms to capitalize expenditures when they lead to future benefits and thus meet the criterion to be an asset.

carryback, carryforward, carryover. The use of losses or tax credits in one period to reduce income taxes payable in other periods. Two common kinds of carrybacks exist: for net operating losses and for *capital losses.* They apply against taxable income. In general, carrybacks are for three years, with the earliest year first. The taxpayer can carry forward operating losses for fifteen years. Corporate capital loss carryforwards are for five years. Individuals can carry forward capital losses indefinitely.

carrying cost. Costs (such as property taxes and insurance) of holding, or storing, *inventory* from the time of purchase until the time of sale or use.

carrying value (amount). *Book value.*

CASB (Cost Accounting Standards Board). A board authorized by the U.S. Congress to "promulgate cost-accounting standards designed to achieve uniformity and consistency in the cost-accounting principles followed by defense contractors and subcontractors under federal contracts." The *principles* the CASB promulgated since 1970 have considerable weight in practice wherever the *FASB* has not established a standard. Congress allowed the CASB to go out of existence in 1980 but reinstated it in 1990.

cash. Currency and coins, negotiable checks, and balances in bank accounts. For the *statement of cash flows,* "cash" also includes *marketable securities* held as *current assets.*

cash basis of accounting. In contrast to the *accrual basis of accounting,* a system of accounting in which a firm recognizes *revenues* when it receives *cash* and recognizes *expenses* as it makes *disbursements*. The firm makes no attempt to match *revenues* and *expenses* in measuring *income*. See *modified cash basis*.

cash budget. A schedule of expected cash *receipts* and *disbursements*.

cash change equation. For any *period*, the change in *cash* equals the change in *liabilities* plus the change in *owners' equity* minus the change in noncash *assets*.

cash collection basis. The *installment method* for recognizing *revenue*. Do not confuse with the *cash basis of accounting*.

cash conversion cycle. *Cash cycle*.

cash cycle. The period of time during which a firm converts *cash* into *inventories*, inventories into *accounts receivable*, and *receivables* back into cash. Sometimes called *earnings cycle*.

cash disbursements journal. A specialized *journal* used to record *expenditures* by *cash* and by *check*. If a *check register* is also used, a cash disbursements journal records only expenditures of currency and coins.

cash discount. A sales or purchase price reduction allowed for prompt payment.

cash dividend. See *dividend*.

cash equivalent. According to *SFAS No. 95,* "short-term, highly liquid investments that are both readily convertible to known amounts of cash [and] so near their maturity that they present insignificant risk of changes in value because of changes in interest rates. . . . Examples of items commonly considered to be cash equivalents are Treasury bills, commercial paper, [and] money market funds."

cash equivalent value. A term used to describe the amount for which an *asset* could be sold. Sometimes called *market value* or *fair market price (value)*.

cash flow. Cash *receipts* minus *disbursements* from a given *asset,* or group of assets, for a given period. Financial analysts sometimes use this term to mean *net income + depreciation + depletion + amortization*. See also *operating cash flow* and *free cash flow*.

cash flow from operations. Receipts from customers and from investments less expenditures for inventory, labor, and services used in the usual activities of the firm, less interest expenditures. See *statement of cash flows* and *operations*. Same as *cash provided by operations*.

cash-flow hedge. A hedge of an exposure to variability in the cash flows of a recognized *asset* or *liability* or of a forecasted transaction, such as expected future foreign sales.

cash flow statement. *Statement of cash flows*.

cash provided by operations. An important subtotal in the *statement of cash flows*. This amount equals the total of revenues producing *cash* less *expenses* requiring cash. Often, the amount appears as *net income* plus expenses not requiring cash (such as depreciation charges) minus revenues not producing cash (such as revenues recognized under the *equity method* of accounting for a long-term investment). The statement of cash flows maintains the same distinctions between *continuing operations, discontinued operations,* and *income* or *loss* from *extraordinary items* as does the *income statement*.

cash receipts journal. A specialized *journal* used to record all *receipts* of *cash*.

cash (surrender) value of life insurance. An amount equal not to the face value of the policy to be paid in the event of death but to the amount that the owner could realize by immediately canceling the policy and returning it to the insurance company for cash. A firm owning a life insurance policy reports it as an asset at an amount equal to this value.

cash yield. See *yield*.

cashier's check. A bank's own *check* drawn on itself and signed by the cashier or other authorized official. It is a direct obligation of the bank. Compare with *certified check*.

catch-up depreciation. *Backlog depreciation*.

CCA. *Current cost accounting; current value accounting*.

central corporate expenses. General *overhead expenses* incurred in running the corporate headquarters and related supporting activities of a corporation. Accounting treats these expenses as *period expenses*. Contrast with *manufacturing overhead*. *Line of business reporting* must decide how to treat these expenses—whether to allocate them to the individual segments and, if so, how to allocate them.

central processing unit (CPU). The computer system component that carries out the arithmetic, logic, and data transfer.

certificate. The document that is the physical embodiment of a *bond* or a *share of stock;* a term sometimes used for the *auditor's report*.

certificate of deposit. A form of *deposit* in a bank or thrift institution. Federal law constrains the rate of interest that banks can pay to their depositors. Current law allows banks to pay a rate higher than the one allowed on a *time deposit* if the depositor promises to leave funds on deposit for several months or more. When the bank receives such funds, it issues a certificate of deposit. The depositor can withdraw the funds before maturity by paying a penalty.

certified check. The *check* of a depositor drawn on a bank. The bank inserts the words "accepted" or "certified" on the face of the check, with the date and a signature of a bank official. The check then becomes an obligation of the bank. Compare with *cashier's check*.

certified financial statement. A financial statement attested to by an independent *auditor* who is a *CPA*.

certified internal auditor. See *CIA*.

certified management accountant. *CMA*.

certified public accountant (CPA). An accountant who has satisfied the statutory and administrative requirements of his or her jurisdiction to be registered or licensed as a public accountant. In addition to passing the Uniform CPA Examination administered by the *AICPA,* the CPA must meet certain educational, experience, and moral requirements that differ from jurisdiction to jurisdiction. The jurisdictions are the 50 states, the District of Columbia, Guam, Puerto Rico, and the Virgin Islands.

CGA (Certified General Accountant). Canada: an accountant who has satisfied the experience, education, and examination requirements of the Certified General Accountants' Association.

chain discount. A series of *discount* percentages. For example, if a chain discount of 10 and 5 percent is quoted, then the actual, or *invoice,* price is the nominal, or list, price times .90 times .95, or 85.5, percent of invoice price.

change fund. Coins and currency issued to cashiers, delivery drivers, and so on.

changes, accounting. See *accounting changes.*

changes in financial position. See *statement of cash flows.*

charge. As a noun, a *debit* to an account; as a verb, to debit.

charge off. To treat as a *loss* or *expense* an amount originally recorded as an *asset*; use of this term implies that the charge is not in accord with original expectations.

chart of accounts. A list of names and numbers, systematically organized, of *accounts.*

charter. Document issued by a state government authorizing the creation of a corporation.

chartered accountant(s) (CA). The title used in Australia, Canada, and Scotland for an accountant who has satisfied the requirements of the institute of his or her jurisdiction to be qualified to serve as a *public accountant.* In the UK other than Scotland, members use the initials ACA or FCA: *A* means Associate and *F* means Fellow; the Associate has less experience than does the Fellow. A partnership of chartered accountants signs its firm name with the letters *CA.* In Canada, each provincial institute or order has the right to administer the examination and set the standards of performance and ethics for Chartered Accountants in its province. For a number of years, however, the provincial organizations have pooled their rights to qualify new members through the Inter-provincial Education Committee, and the result is that there are nationally set and graded examinations given in English and French. Deviation from the pass/fail grade awarded by the Board of Examiners (a subcommittee of the Inter-provincial Education Committee) is rare.

check. The Federal Reserve Board defines a check as "a *draft* or order upon a bank or banking house purporting to be drawn upon a deposit of funds for the payment at all events of a certain sum of money to a certain person therein named or to him or his order or to bearer and payable instantly on demand." It must contain the phrase "pay to the order of." The amount shown on the check must be clearly readable, and the check must have the signature of the drawer. The drawer need not date the check. In the accounts, the drawer usually reduces the *balance* in the *cash account* when it issues the check, not later when the check clears the bank. See *remittance advice.*

check register. A *journal* to record *checks* issued.

CIA (Certified Internal Auditor). One who has satisfied certain requirements of the *Institute of Internal Auditors* including experience, ethics, education, and passing examinations.

CICA. *Canadian Institute of Chartered Accountants.*

CIF (cost, insurance, and freight). In contracts, a term used along with the name of a given port, such as New Orleans, to indicate that the quoted price includes insurance, handling, and freight charges up to delivery by the seller at the given port.

circulating capital. *Working capital.*

clean opinion. See *auditor's report.*

clean surplus concept. The notion that all entries to the *retained earnings* account must record *net income* and *dividends.* See *comprehensive income.* Contrast with *current operating performance concept.* This concept, with minor exceptions, now controls *GAAP.* (See *APB Opinions No. 9* and *No. 30.*)

clearing account. An account containing amounts to be transferred to another account(s) before the end of the *accounting period.* Examples are the *income summary* account (whose balance transfers to *retained earnings*) and the purchases account (whose balance transfers to *inventory* or to *cost of goods sold*).

close. As a verb, to transfer the *balance* of a *temporary* or *contra* or *adjunct account* to the main account to which it relates; for example, to transfer *revenue* and *expense* accounts directly, or through the *income summary* account, to an *owners' equity* account or to transfer *purchase discounts* to purchases.

closed account. An *account* with equal *debits* and *credits,* usually as a result of a *closing entry.* See *ruling an account.*

closing entries. The *entries* that accomplish the transfer of balances in *temporary accounts* to the related *balance sheet accounts.* See *work sheet.*

closing inventory. *Ending inventory.*

CMA (Certified Management Accountant) certificate. Awarded by the *Institute of Certified Management Accountants* of the *Institute of Management Accountants* to those who pass a set of examinations and meet certain experience and continuing-education requirements.

CoCoA. *Continuously Contemporary Accounting.*

coding of accounts. The numbering of *accounts,* as for a *chart of accounts,* that is necessary for computerized accounting.

coinsurance. Common condition of insurance policies that protect against hazards such as fire or water damage. These often specify that the owner of the property may not collect the full amount of insurance for a loss unless the insurance policy covers at least some specified "coinsurance" percentage, usually about 80 percent, of the *replacement cost* of the property. Coinsurance clauses induce the owner to carry full, or nearly full, coverage.

COLA. Cost-of-living adjustment. See *indexation.*

collateral. *Assets* pledged by a *borrower* who will surrender those assets if he or she fails to repay a *loan.*

collectible. Capable of being converted into *cash*—now if due, later otherwise.

collusion. Cooperative effort by employees to commit fraud or another unethical act.

combination. See *business combination.*

comfort letter. A letter in which an auditor conveys negative assurances as to unaudited financial statements in a prospectus or draft financial statements included in a preliminary prospectus.

commercial paper. Short-term notes issued by corporate borrowers.

commission. Employee remuneration, usually expressed as a percentage, based on an activity rate, such as sales.

committed costs. *Capacity costs.*

Committee on Accounting Procedure (CAP). Predecessor of the *APB*. The *AICPA*'s principles-promulgating body from 1939 through 1959. Its 51 pronouncements are *Accounting Research Bulletins.*

common cost. *Cost* resulting from the use of *raw materials,* a facility (for example, plant or machines), or a service (for example, fire insurance) that benefits several products or departments. A firm must allocate this cost to those products or departments. Common costs result when two or more departments produce multiple products together even though the departments could produce them separately; *joint costs* occur when two or more departments must produce multiple products together. Many writers use "common costs" and "joint costs" synonymously. See *joint cost, indirect costs, overhead;* and *sterilized allocation.*

common-dollar accounting. *Constant-dollar accounting.*

common monetary measuring unit. For U.S. corporations, the dollar. See also *stable monetary unit assumption* and *constant-dollar accounting.*

common shares. *Shares* representing the class of owners who have residual claims on the *assets* and *earnings* of a *corporation* after the firm meets all *debt* and *preferred shareholders'* claims.

common-size statement. A *percentage statement* usually based on total *assets* or *net sales* or *revenues.*

common-stock equivalent. A *security* whose primary value arises from its holder's ability to exchange it for *common shares;* includes *stock options, warrants,* and also *convertible bonds* or *convertible preferred stock* whose *effective interest rate* at the time of issue is less than two-thirds the average Aa corporate bond yield. See *bond ratings.*

company-wide control. See *control system.*

comparative (financial) statements. *Financial statements* showing information for the same company for different times, usually two successive years for balance sheets and three for *income* and *cash flow statements.* Nearly all published financial statements are in this form. Contrast with *historical summary.*

compensating balance. The amount required to be left on deposit for a loan. When a bank lends funds to customers, it often requires that the customers keep on deposit in their checking accounts an amount equal to some percentage—say, 20 percent—of the loan. Such amounts effectively increase the *interest rate.* The borrower must disclose the amounts of such balances in *notes* to the *financial statements.*

completed contract method. Recognizing *revenues* and *expenses* for a job or order only when the firm finishes it, except that when the firm expects a loss on the contract, the firm must recognize all revenues and expenses in the period when the firm first foresees a loss. Accountants generally use this term only for long-term contracts. This method is otherwise equivalent to the *sales basis of revenue recognition.*

completed sales basis. See *sales basis of revenue recognition.*

compliance audit. Objectively obtaining and evaluating evidence regarding assertions, actions, and events to ascertain the degree of correspondence between them and established performance criteria.

compliance procedure. An *audit* procedure used to gain evidence as to whether the prescribed internal controls are operating effectively.

composite cost of capital. See *cost of capital.*

composite depreciation or **composite life method.** *Group depreciation* when the items are of unlike kind. The term also applies when the firm depreciates as a whole a single item (for example, a crane, which consists of separate units with differing service lives, such as the chassis, the motor, the lifting mechanism, and so on), rather than treating each of its components separately.

compound entry. A *journal entry* with more than one *debit* or more than one *credit* or both. See *trade-in transaction* for an example.

compound interest. *Interest* calculated on *principal* plus previously undistributed interest.

compound interest depreciation. A method designed to hold the *rate of return* on an asset constant. First find the *internal rate of return* on the cash inflows and outflows of the asset. The periodic depreciation charge equals the cash flow for the period less the internal rate of return multiplied by the asset's book value at the beginning of the period. When the cash flows from the asset are constant over time, usage sometimes refers to the method as the "annuity method" of depreciation.

compounding period. The time period, usually a year or a portion of a year, for which a firm calculates *interest.* At the end of the period, the borrower may pay interest to the lender or may add the interest (that is, convert it) to the principal for the next interest-earning period.

comprehensive budget. *Master budget.*

comprehensive income. Defined in *SFAC No. 3* as "the change in equity (net assets) of an entity during a period from transactions and other events and circumstances from nonowner sources. It includes all changes in equity during a period except those resulting from investments by owners and distributions to owners." In this definition, "equity" means *owners' equity* or *shareholders' equity. SFAS No. 130* requires firms to report comprehensive income as part of a statement showing *earnings* (primarily from realized transactions), comprehensive income (with additions for all other changes in owners' equity, primarily *holding gains and losses* and *foreign exchange gains and losses*), and comprehensive income plus *accounting adjustments.* The *FASB* encourages the discontinuation of the term "net income." The terms "earnings" and "comprehensive income" denote different concepts, with totals different from that of the old "net income." *SFAS No. 130* requires that the firm report comprehensive income in a format having the same prominence as other *financial statements.* We cannot predict which "income total"—earnings or comprehensive income—users of financial statements will focus on. See Exhibits 12.3 and 12.7 for the three formats the FASB suggests firms use.

comptroller. Same meaning and pronunciation as *controller*.

conceptual framework. A coherent system of interrelated objectives and fundamentals, promulgated by the *FASB* primarily through its *SFAC* publications, expected to lead to consistent standards for *financial accounting* and reporting.

confidence level. The measure of probability that the actual characteristics of the population lie within the stated precision of the estimate derived from a sampling process. A sample estimate may be expressed in the following terms: "Based on the sample, we are 95 percent sure [confidence level] that the true population value is within the range of X to Y [precision]." See *precision*.

confirmation. A formal memorandum delivered by the customers or suppliers of a company to its independent *auditor* verifying the amounts shown as receivable or payable. The auditor originally sends the confirmation document to the customer. If the auditor asks that the customer return the document whether the *balance* is correct or incorrect, usage calls it a "positive confirmation." If the auditor asks that the customer return the document only if it contains an error, usage calls it a "negative confirmation."

conglomerate. *Holding company*. This term implies that the owned companies operate in dissimilar lines of business.

conservatism. A *reporting objective* that calls for anticipation of all *losses* and *expenses* but defers recognition of *gains* or *profits* until they are *realized* in *arm's-length* transactions. In the absence of certainty, report events to minimize cumulative income. Conservatism does not mean reporting low income in every *accounting period*. Over long-enough time spans, income is cash-in less cash-out. If a (conservative) reporting method shows low income in early periods, it must show higher income in some later period.

consignee. See *on consignment*.

consignment. See *on consignment*.

consignor. See *on consignment*.

consistency. Treatment of like *transactions* in the same way in consecutive periods so that financial statements will be more comparable than otherwise; the reporting policy implying that a reporting *entity*, once it adopts specified procedures, should follow them from period to period. See *accounting changes* for the treatment of inconsistencies.

consol. A *bond* that never matures; a *perpetuity* in the form of a bond; originally issued by Great Britain after the Napoleonic wars to consolidate debt issues of that period. The term arose as an abbreviation for "consolidated annuities."

consolidated financial statements. Statements that are issued by legally separate companies and that show financial position and income as they would appear if the companies were one economic *entity*.

constant dollar. A hypothetical unit of *general purchasing power*, denoted "C$" by the *FASB*.

constant-dollar accounting. Accounting that measures items in *constant dollars*. See *historical cost/constant-dollar accounting* and *current cost/nominal-dollar accounting*. Sometimes called "general price level-adjusted accounting" or "general purchasing-power accounting."

constant-dollar date. The time at which the *general purchasing power* of one *constant dollar* exactly equals the *general purchasing power* of one *nominal dollar*; that is, the date when C$1 = $1. When the constant-dollar date is midperiod, the nominal amounts of *revenues* and *expenses* spread evenly throughout the period equal their constant-dollar amounts but end-of-period *balance sheet* amounts measured in constant midperiod dollars differ from their nominal-dollar amounts. When the constant-dollar date is at the end of the period, the constant-dollar amounts equal the nominal-dollar amounts on a balance sheet for that date.

constrained share company. Canada: a public company whose *charter* specifies that people who are Canadian citizens or who are corporations resident in Canada must own a prescribed percentage of the shares.

constructive liability. *FASB's* term for an item recorded as an accounting *liability*, which the firm has no obligation to pay but intends to pay. An example is the liability with related *expense* that management establishes for future cash payments for severance payments for employees it intends to discharge in a restructuring.

constructive receipt. An item included in taxable income when the taxpayer can control funds whether or not it has received cash. For example, *interest* added to *principal* in a savings account is constructively received.

Consumer Price Index (CPI). A *price index* computed and issued monthly by the Bureau of Labor Statistics of the U.S. Department of Labor. The index attempts to track the price level of a group of goods and services purchased by the average consumer. The CPI is used in *constant-dollar accounting*.

contingency. A potential *liability*. If a specified event occurs, such as a firm's losing a lawsuit, it would recognize a liability. The notes disclose the contingency, but so long as it remains contingent, it does not appear in the balance sheet. *SFAS No. 5* requires treatment as a contingency until the outcome is "probable" and the amount of payment can be reasonably estimated, perhaps within a range. When the outcome becomes probable (the future event is "likely" to occur) and the firm can reasonably estimate the amount (using the lower end of a range if it can estimate only a range), then the firm recognizes a liability in the accounts, rather than just disclosing it. A *material* contingency may lead to a qualified, "*subject to*" auditor's opinion. Firms do not record *gain* contingencies in the accounts but merely disclose them in notes.

contingent annuity. An *annuity* whose number of payments depends on the outcome of an event whose timing is uncertain at the time the annuity begins; for example, an annuity payable until death of the *annuitant*. Contrast with *annuity certain*.

contingent issue (securities). Securities issuable to specific individuals at the occurrence of some event, such as the firm's attaining a specified level of earnings.

contingent liability. *Contingency*. Avoid this term because it refers to something not (yet) a *liability* on the *balance sheet*.

continuing appropriation. A governmental *appropriation* automatically renewed without further legislative action until altered or revoked or expended.

continuing operations. See *income from continuing operations.*

continuity of operations. The assumption in accounting that the business *entity* will continue to operate long enough to carry out its current plans. The *going-concern assumption.*

continuous budget. A *budget* that adds a future period as the current period ends. This budget, then, always reports on the same number of periods.

continuous compounding. *Compound interest* in which the *compounding period* is every instant of time. See *e* for the computation of the equivalent annual or periodic rate.

continuous improvement. Modern *total quality management (TQM)* practitioners believe that the process of seeking quality is never complete. This attitude reflects that assumption, seeking always to improve activities.

continuous inventory method. The *perpetual inventory* method.

Continuously Contemporary Accounting (CoCoA). A name coined by the Australian theorist Raymond J. Chambers to indicate a combination of *current value accounting* in which the *measuring unit* is *constant dollars* and the *attribute measured* is *exit value.*

contra account. An *account,* such as *accumulated depreciation,* that accumulates subtractions from another account, such as machinery. Contrast with *adjunct account.*

contributed capital. Name for the *owners' equity* account that represents amounts paid in, usually in *cash,* by owners; the sum of the balances in *capital stock* accounts plus *capital contributed in excess of par (or stated) value* accounts. Contrast with *donated capital.*

contributed surplus. An inferior term for *capital contributed in excess of par value.*

contribution approach. *Income statement* preparation method that reports *contribution margin,* by separating *variable costs* from *fixed costs,* in order to emphasize the importance of cost-behavior patterns for purposes of planning and control.

contribution margin. *Revenue* from *sales* less all variable *expenses.* Contrast with *gross margin.*

contribution margin ratio. *Contribution margin* divided by *net sales*; usually measured from the price and cost of a single unit; sometimes measured in total for companies with multiple products.

contribution per unit. Selling price less *variable costs* per unit.

contributory. Said of a *pension plan* in which employees, as well as employers, make payments to a pension *fund.* Note that the provisions for *vesting* apply only to the employer's payments. Whatever the degree of vesting of the employer's payments, employees typically get back all their payments, with interest, in case of death or other cessation of employment before retirement.

control (controlling) account. A summary *account* with totals equal to those of entries and balances that appear in individual accounts in a *subsidiary ledger.* Accounts Receivable is a control account backed up with an account for each customer. Do not change the balance in a control account unless you make a corresponding change in one of the subsidiary accounts.

control system. A device used by top management to ensure that lower-level management carries out its plans or to safeguard assets. Control designed for a single function within the firm is "operational control"; control designed for autonomous segments that generally have responsibility for both revenues and costs is "divisional control"; control designed for activities of the firm as a whole is "company-wide control." Systems designed for safeguarding *assets* are "internal control" systems.

controllable cost. A *cost* influenced by the way a firm carries out operations. For example, marketing executives control advertising costs. These costs can be *fixed* or *variable.* See *programmed costs* and managed costs.

controlled company. A company in which an individual or corporation holds a majority of the voting shares. An owner can sometimes exercise effective control even though it owns less than 50 percent of the shares.

controller. A title for the chief accountant of an organization; often spelled *comptroller.*

conversion. The act of exchanging a convertible security for another security.

conversion audit. An examination of changeover procedures, and new accounting procedures and files, that takes place when a significant change in the accounting system (e.g., a change from a manual to a computerized system or a change of computers) occurs.

conversion cost. *Direct labor* costs plus factory *overhead* costs incurred in producing a product; that is, the cost to convert raw materials to finished products. *Manufacturing cost.*

conversion period. *Compounding period;* also, period during which the holder of a *convertible bond* or *convertible preferred stock* can convert it into *common shares.*

convertible bond. A *bond* whose owner may convert it into a specified number of shares of *capital stock* during the *conversion period.*

convertible preferred stock. *Preferred shares* whose owner may convert them into a specified number of *common shares.*

cooperative. An incorporated organization formed for the benefit of its members (owners), who are either producers or consumers, in order to acquire for them profits or savings that otherwise accrue to middlemen. Members exercise control on the basis of one vote per member.

coproduct. A product sharing production facilities with another product. For example, if an apparel manufacturer produces shirts and jeans on the same line, these are coproducts. Distinguish coproducts from *joint products* and *by-products* that, by their very nature, a firm must produce together, such as the various grades of wood a lumber factory produces.

copyright. Exclusive right granted by the government to an individual author, composer, playwright, or the like for the life of the individual plus 50 years. If a firm receives the copyright, then the right extends 75 years after the original publication. The *economic life* of a copyright can be less than the legal life, such as, for example, the copyright of this book.

corner. The control, of a quantity of shares or a commodity, sufficiently large that the holder can control the market price.

corporation. A legal entity authorized by a state to operate under the rules of the entity's *charter*.

correcting entry. An *adjusting entry* that properly records a previously, improperly recorded *transaction*. Do not confuse with entries that correct *accounting errors*.

correction of errors. See *accounting errors*.

cost. The sacrifice, measured by the *price* paid or to be paid, to acquire *goods* or *services*. See *acquisition cost* and *replacement cost*. Terminology often uses "cost" when referring to the valuation of a good or service acquired. When writers use the word in this sense, a cost is an *asset*. When the benefits of the acquisition (the goods or services acquired) expire, the cost becomes an *expense* or *loss*. Some writers, however, use "cost" and "expense" as synonyms. Contrast with *expense*. The word "cost" appears in more than 50 accounting terms, each with sometimes subtle distinctions in meaning. See *cost terminology* for elaboration. Clarity requires that the user include with the word "cost" an adjective or phrase to be clear about intended meaning.

cost accounting. Classifying, summarizing, recording, reporting, and allocating current or predicted *costs;* a subset of *managerial accounting*.

Cost Accounting Standards Board. See *CASB*.

cost accumulation. Bringing together, usually in a single *account,* all *costs* of a specified activity. Contrast with *cost allocation*.

cost allocation. Assigning *costs* to individual products or time periods. Contrast with *cost accumulation*.

cost-based transfer price. A *transfer price* based on *historical costs*.

cost behavior. The functional relation between changes in activity and changes in *cost;* for example: *fixed* versus *variable costs*; *linear* versus *curvilinear cost*.

cost/benefit criterion. Some measure of *costs* compared with some measure of *benefits* for a proposed undertaking. If the costs exceed the benefits, then the analyst judges the undertaking not worthwhile. This criterion will not yield good decisions unless the analyst estimates all costs and benefits flowing from the undertaking.

cost center. A unit of activity for which a firm accumulates *expenditures* and *expenses*.

cost driver. A factor that causes an activity's costs. See *driver* and *activity basis*.

cost-effective. Among alternatives, the one whose benefit, or payoff, per unit of cost is highest; sometimes said of an action whose expected benefits exceed expected costs whether or not other alternatives exist with larger benefit-cost ratios.

cost estimation. The process of measuring the functional relation between changes in activity levels and changes in cost.

cost flow assumption. See *flow assumption*.

cost-flow equation. Beginning Balance + Transfers In = Transfers Out + Ending Balance; BB + TI = TO + EB.

cost flows. Costs passing through various classifications within an entity. See *flow of costs* for a diagram.

cost method (for investments). In accounting for an investment in the *capital stock* or *bonds* of another company, method in which the firm shows the investment at *acquisition cost* and treats only *dividends* declared or *interest receivable* as *revenue;* not allowed by *GAAP*.

cost method (for treasury stock). The method of showing *treasury stock* in a *contra account* to all other items of *shareholders' equity* in an amount equal to that paid to reacquire the stock.

cost object(ive). Any activity for which management desires a separate measurement of *costs*. Examples include departments, products, and territories.

cost of capital. *Opportunity cost* of funds invested in a business; the rate of return that rational owners require an asset to earn before they will devote that asset to a particular purpose; sometimes measured as the average annual rate that a company must pay for its *equities*. In *efficient capital markets,* this cost is the *discount rate* that equates the expected *present value* of all future cash flows to common shareholders with the market value of common stock at a given time. Analysts often measure the cost of capital by taking a *weighted average* of the firm's *debt* and various *equity securities*. We sometimes call the measurement so derived the "composite cost of capital," and some analysts confuse this measurement of the cost of capital with the cost of capital itself. For example, if the equities of a firm include substantial amounts for the *deferred income tax liability,* the composite cost of capital will underestimate the true cost of capital, the required rate of return on a firm's assets, because the deferred income tax liability has no explicit cost.

cost of goods manufactured. The sum of all costs allocated to products completed during a period, including materials, labor, and *overhead*.

cost of goods purchased. Net purchase price of goods acquired plus costs of storage and delivery to the place where the owner can productively use the items.

cost of goods sold. Inventoriable *costs* that firms *expense* because they sold the units; equals *beginning inventory* plus *cost of goods purchased* or *manufactured* minus *ending inventory*.

cost of sales. Generally refers to *cost of goods sold,* occasionally to *selling expenses*.

cost or market, whichever is lower. See *lower of cost or market*.

cost percentage. One less *markup percentage; cost* of *goods available for sale* divided by selling prices of goods available for sale (when FIFO is used); *cost* of *purchases* divided by selling prices of purchases (when LIFO is used). See *markup* for further detail on inclusions in the calculation of cost percentage.

cost pool. *Indirect cost pool;* groupings or aggregations of costs, usually for subsequent analysis.

cost principle. The *principle* that requires reporting *assets* at *historical* or *acquisition cost,* less accumulated *amortization.* This principle relies on the assumption that cost equals *fair market value* at the date of acquisition and that subsequent changes are not likely to be significant.

cost-recovery-first method. A method of *revenue* recognition that *credits inventory* as the firm receives cash collections and continues until the firm has collected cash equal to the sum of all costs. Only after the firm has collected cash equal to costs does it recognize *income.* A firm may not use this method in financial reporting unless the total amount of collections is highly uncertain. It is never allowed for income tax reporting. Contrast with the *installment method,* allowed for both book and tax, in which the firm credits constant proportions of each cash collection both to cost and to income.

cost sheet. Statement that shows all the elements composing the total cost of an item.

cost structure. For a given set of total costs, the percentages of fixed and variable costs, typically two percentages adding to 100 percent.

cost terminology. The word "cost" appears in many accounting terms. The accompanying exhibit classifies some of these terms according to the distinctions between the terms in accounting usage. Joel Dean was, to our knowledge, the first to attempt such distinctions; we have used some of his ideas here. We discuss some of the terms in more detail under their own listings.

Cost Terminology: Distinctions among Terms Containing the Word "Cost"

Terms (Synonyms Given in Parentheses)			Distinctions and Comments
			1. The following pairs of terms distinguish the basis measured in accounting.
Historical Cost (Acquisition Cost)	v.	Current Cost	A distinction used in financial accounting. Current cost can be used more specifically to mean replacement cost, net realizable value, or present value of cash flows. "Current cost" is often used narrowly to mean replacement cost.
Historical Cost (Actual Cost)	v.	Standard Cost	The distinction between historical and standard costs arises in product costing for inventory valuation. Some systems record actual costs; others record the standard costs.
			2. The following pairs of terms denote various distinctions among historical costs. For each pair of terms, the sum of the two kinds of costs equals total historical cost used in financial reporting.
Variable Cost	v.	Fixed Cost (Constant Cost)	Distinction used in breakeven analysis and in the design of cost accounting systems, particularly for product costing. See (4), below, for a further subdivision of fixed costs and (5), below, for the economic distinction between marginal and average cost closely paralleling this one.
Traceable Cost	v.	Common Cost (Joint Cost)	Distinction arises in allocating manufacturing costs to product. Common costs are allocated to product, but the allocations are more or less arbitrary. The distinction also arises in preparing segment reports and in separating manufacturing from nonmanufacturing costs.
Direct Cost	v.	Indirect Cost	Distinction arises in designing cost accounting systems and in product costing. Direct costs can be traced directly to a cost object (e.g., a product, a responsibility center), whereas indirect costs cannot.
Out-of-Pocket Cost (Outlay Cost; Cash Cost)	v.	Book Cost	Virtually all costs recorded in financial statements require a cash outlay at one time or another. The distinction here separates expenditures to occur in the future from those already made and is used in making decisions. Book costs, such as for depreciation, reduce income without requiring a future outlay of cash. The cash has already been spent. See future cost v. past cost in (5), below.
Incremental Cost (Marginal Cost; Differential Cost)	v.	Unavoidable Cost (Inescapable Cost; Sunk Cost)	Distinction used in making decisions. Incremental costs will be incurred (or saved) if a decision is made to go ahead (or to stop) some activity, but not otherwise. Unavoidable costs will be reported in financial statements whether the decision is made to go ahead or not, because cash has already been spent or committed. Not all unavoidable costs are book costs, such as, for example, a salary that is promised but not yet earned and that will be paid even if a no-go decision is made.

Terms (Synonyms Given in Parentheses)			**Distinctions and Comments**
			The economist restricts the term marginal cost to the cost of producing one more unit. Thus the next unit has a marginal cost; the next week's output has an incremental cost. If a firm produces and sells a new product, the related new costs would properly be called incremental, not marginal. If a factory is closed, the costs saved are incremental, not marginal.
Escapable Cost	v.	Inescapable Cost (Unavoidable Cost)	Same distinction as incremental cost v. unavoidable cost, but this pair is used only when the decision maker is considering stopping something—ceasing to produce a product, closing a factory, or the like. See next pair.
Avoidable Cost	v.	Unavoidable Cost	A distinction sometimes used in discussing the merits of variable and absorption costing. Avoidable costs are treated as product costs and unavoidable costs are treated as period expenses under variable costing.
Controllable Cost	v.	Uncontrollable Cost	The distinction here is used in assigning responsibility and in setting bonus or incentive plans. All costs can be affected by someone in the entity; those who design incentive schemes attempt to hold a person responsible for a cost only if that person can influence the amount of the cost.
			3. In each of the following pairs, used in historical cost accounting, the word "cost" appears in one of the terms where "expense" is meant.
Expired Cost	v.	Unexpired Cost	The distinction is between expense and asset.
Product Cost	v.	Period Cost	The terms distinguish product cost from period expense. When a given asset is used, is its cost converted into work-in-process and then finished goods on the balance sheet until the goods are sold, or is it an expense shown on this period's income statement? Product costs appear on the income statement as part of cost of goods sold in the period when the goods are sold. Period expenses appear on the income statement with an appropriate caption for the item in the period when the cost is incurred or recognized.
			4. The following subdivisions of fixed (historical) costs are used in analyzing operations. The relation between the components of fixed costs is as follows:

$$\text{Fixed Costs} \quad = \quad \text{Capacity Costs} \; + \; \text{Programmed Costs}$$

Semifixed Costs + "Pure" Fixed Costs	+	Fixed Portions of Semi-variable Costs	Standby Costs	+	Enabling Costs

Capacity Cost (Committed Cost)	v.	Programmed Cost (Managed Cost; Discretionary Cost)	Capacity costs give a firm the capability to produce or to sell. Programmed costs, such as for advertising or research and development, may not be essential, but once a decision to incur them is made, they become fixed costs.
Standby Cost	v.	Enabling Cost	Standby costs will be incurred whether capacity, once acquired, is used or not, such as property taxes and depreciation on a factory. Enabling costs, such as for a security force, can be avoided if the capacity is unused.
Semifixed Cost	v.	Semivariable Cost	A cost that is fixed over a wide range but that can change at various levels is a semifixed cost or "step cost." An example is the cost of rail lines from the factory to the main rail line, where fixed cost depends on whether there are one or two parallel lines but is independent of the number of trains run per day. Semivariable costs combine a strictly fixed component cost plus a variable component. Telephone charges usually have a fixed monthly component plus a charge related to usage.

Terms (Synonyms Given in Parentheses)			Distinctions and Comments
			5. The following pairs of terms distinguish among economic uses or decision-making uses or regulatory uses of cost terms.
Fully Absorbed Cost	v.	Variable Cost (Direct Cost)	Fully absorbed costs refer to costs where fixed costs have been allocated to units or departments as required by generally accepted accounting principles. Variable costs, in contrast, may be more relevant for making decisions, such as setting prices.
Fully Absorbed Cost	v.	Full Cost	In full costing, all costs, manufacturing costs as well as central corporate expenses (including financing expenses), are allocated to products or divisions. In full absorption costing, only manufacturing costs are allocated to products. Only in full costing will revenues, expenses, and income summed over all products or divisions equal corporate revenues, expenses, and income.
Opportunity Cost	v.	Outlay Cost (Out-of-Pocket Cost)	Opportunity cost refers to the economic benefit forgone by using a resource for one purpose instead of for another. The outlay cost of the resource will be recorded in financial records. The distinction arises because a resource is already in the possession of the entity with a recorded historical cost. Its economic value to the firm, opportunity cost, generally differs from the historical cost; it can be either larger or smaller.
Future Cost	v.	Past Cost	Effective decision making analyzes only present and future outlay costs, or out-of-pocket costs. Opportunity costs are relevant for profit maximizing; past costs are used in financial reporting.
Short-Run Cost	v.	Long-Run Cost	Short-run costs vary as output is varied for a given configuration of plant and equipment. Long-run costs can be incurred to change that configuration. This pair of terms is the economic analog of the accounting pair, see (2) above, variable and fixed costs. The analogy is not perfect because some short-run costs are fixed, such as property taxes on the factory, from the point of view of breakeven analysis.
Imputed Cost	v.	Book Cost	In a regulatory setting some costs, for example the cost of owners' equity capital, are calculated and used for various purposes; these are imputed costs. Imputed costs are not recorded in the historical costs accounting records for financial reporting. Book costs are recorded.
Average Cost	v.	Marginal Cost	The economic distinction equivalent to fully absorbed cost of product and variable cost of product. Average cost is total cost divided by number of units. Marginal cost is the cost to produce the next unit (or the last unit).
Differential Cost (Incremental Cost)	v.	Variable Cost	Whether a cost changes or remains fixed depends on the activity basis being considered. Typically, but not invariably, costs are said to be variable or with respect to an activity basis such as changes in production levels. Typically, but not invariably, costs are said to be incremental or not with respect to an activity basis such as the undertaking of some new venture. For example, consider the decision to undertake the production of food processors, rather than food blenders, which the manufacturer has been making. To produce processors requires the acquisition of a new machine tool. The cost of the new machine tool is incremental with respect to a decision to produce food processors instead of food blenders but, once acquired, becomes a fixed cost of producing food processors. If costs of direct labor hours are going to be incurred for the production of food processors or food blenders, whichever is produced (in a scenario when not both are to be produced), such costs are variable with respect to production measured in units but are not incremental with respect to the decision to produce processors rather than blenders. This distinction is often blurred in practice, so a careful understanding of the activity basis being considered is necessary to understand the concepts being used in a particular application.

cost-to-cost. The *percentage-of-completion method* in which the firm estimates the fraction of completion as the ratio of costs incurred to date divided by the total costs the firm expects to incur for the entire project.

cost-volume-profit analysis. A study of the sensitivity of *profits* to changes in units sold (or produced) or costs or prices.

cost-volume-profit graph (chart). A graph that shows the relation between *fixed costs, contribution per unit, breakeven point,* and *sales.* See *breakeven chart.*

costing. The process of calculating the cost of activities, products, or services; the British word for *cost accounting.*

counterparty. The term refers to the opposite party in a legal contract. In accounting and finance, a frequent usage arises when an entity purchases (or sells) a *derivative* financial contract, such as an *option, forward contract,* and *futures contract.*

coupon. That portion of a *bond* document redeemable at a specified date for payments. Its physical form resembles a series of tickets; each coupon has a date, and the holder either deposits it at a bank, just like a check, for collection or mails it to the issuer's agent for collection.

coupon rate. Of a *bond,* the amount of annual coupons divided by par value. Contrast with *effective rate.*

covenant. A promise with legal validity. A loan covenant specifies the terms under which the lender can force the borrower to repay funds otherwise not yet due. For example, a *bond* covenant might say that the *principal* of a bond issue falls due on December 31, 2010, unless the firm's *debt-equity ratio* falls below 40 percent, in which case the amount becomes due immediately.

CPA. See *certified public accountant.* The *AICPA* suggests that no periods appear in the abbreviation.

CPI. *Consumer price index.*

CPP. Current purchasing power; usually used, primarily in the UK, as an adjective modifying the word "accounting" to mean the accounting that produces *constant-dollar financial statements.*

Cr. Abbreviation for *credit,* always with initial capital letter. Quiz: what do you suppose *Cr.* stands for? For the answer, see *Dr.*

creative accounting. Selection of *accounting principles* and interpretation of transactions or events designed to manipulate, typically to increase but sometimes merely to smooth, reported *income from continuing operations;* one form of *fraudulent financial reporting.* Many attempts at creative accounting involve premature *revenue recognition.*

credit. As a noun, an entry on the right-hand side of an *account;* as a verb, to make an entry on the right-hand side of an account; records increases in *liabilities, owners' equity, revenues,* and *gains*; records decreases in *assets* and *expenses.* See *debit and credit conventions.* This term also refers to the ability or right to buy or borrow in return for a promise to pay later.

credit bureau. An organization that gathers and evaluates data on the ability of a person to meet financial obligations and sells this information to its clients.

credit loss. The amount of accounts receivable that the firm finds, or expects to find, *uncollectible.*

credit memorandum. A document used by a seller to inform a buyer that the seller is crediting (reducing) the buyer's account receivable because of *errors, returns,* or *allowances;* also, the document provided by a bank to a depositor to indicate that the bank is increasing the depositor's balance because of some event other than a deposit, such as the collection by the bank of the depositor's *note receivable.*

creditor. One who lends. In the UK, *account payable.*

critical path method (CPM). A method of *network analysis* in which the analyst estimates normal duration time for each activity within a project. The critical path identifies the shortest completion period based on the most time-consuming sequence of activities from the beginning to the end of the network. Compare *PERT.*

cross-reference (index). A number placed beside each *account* in a *journal entry* indicating the *ledger* account to which the record keeper posted the entry and placing in the ledger the page number of the journal where the record keeper first recorded the journal entry; used to link the *debit* and *credit* parts of an entry in the ledger accounts back to the original entry in the journal. See *audit trail.*

cross-section analysis. Analysis of *financial statements* of various firms for a single period of time; contrast with *time-series analysis,* in which analysts examine statements of a given firm for several periods of time.

Crown corporation. Canada and UK: a corporation that is ultimately accountable, through a minister of the Crown, to Parliament or a legislature for the conduct of its affairs.

cum div. (dividend). The condition of shares whose quoted market price includes a declared but unpaid dividend. This condition pertains between the declaration date of the dividend and the record date. Compare *ex div. (dividend).*

cum rights. The condition of securities whose quoted market price includes the right to purchase new securities. Compare *ex rights.*

cumulative dividend. Preferred stock *dividends* that, if not paid, accrue as a commitment that the firm must pay before it can declare dividends to common shareholders.

cumulative preferred shares. *Preferred* shares with *cumulative dividend* rights.

current assets. *Cash* and other *assets* that a firm expects to turn into cash, sell, or exchange within the normal operating cycle of the firm or one year, whichever is longer. One year is the usual period for classifying asset balances on the balance sheet. Current assets include *cash, marketable securities, receivables, inventory,* and *current prepayments.*

current cost. *Cost* stated in terms of current values (of *productive capacity*) rather than in terms of *acquisition cost.* See *net realizable value* and *current selling price.*

current cost accounting. The *FASB's* term for *financial statements* in which the *attribute measured* is *current cost.*

current cost/nominal-dollar accounting. Accounting based on *current cost* valuations measured in *nominal dollars.*

Components of *income* include an *operating margin* and *holding gains and losses.*

current exchange rate. The rate at which the holder of one unit of currency can convert it into another at the end of the *accounting period* being reported on or, for *revenues, expenses, gains,* and *losses,* the date of recognition of the transaction.

current exit value. *Exit value.*

current fund. In governmental accounting, a synonym for *general fund.*

current funds. *Cash* and other assets readily convertible into cash; in governmental accounting, funds spent for operating purposes during the current period; includes *general,* special revenue, *debt service,* and *enterprise funds.*

current (gross) margin. See *operating margin based on current costs.*

current liability. A debt or other obligation that a firm must discharge within a short time, usually the *earnings cycle* or one year, normally by expending *current assets.*

current operating performance concept. The notion that reported *income* for a period ought to reflect only ordinary, normal, and recurring operations of that period. A consequence is that *extraordinary* and nonrecurring items are entered directly in the Retained Earnings account. Contrast with *clean surplus concept.* This concept is no longer acceptable. (See *APB Opinion No. 9* and *No. 30.*)

current ratio. Sum of *current assets* divided by sum of *current liabilities.* See *ratio.*

current realizable value. *Realizable value.*

current replacement cost. Of an *asset,* the amount currently required to acquire an identical asset (in the same condition and with the same service potential) or an asset capable of rendering the same service at a current *fair market price.* If these two amounts differ, use the lower. Contrast with *reproduction cost.*

current selling price. The amount for which an *asset* could be sold as of a given time in an *arm's-length* transaction rather than in a forced sale.

current service costs. *Service costs* of a *pension plan.*

current value accounting. The form of accounting in which all assets appear at *current replacement cost (entry value)* or *current selling price* or *net realizable value (exit value)* and all *liabilities* appear at *present value.* Entry and exit values may differ from each other, so theorists have not agreed on the precise meaning of "current value accounting."

current yield. Of a *bond,* the annual amount of *coupons* divided by the current market price of the bond. Contrast with *yield to maturity.*

currently attainable standard cost. *Normal standard cost.*

curvilinear (variable) cost. A continuous, but not necessarily linear (straight-line), functional relation between activity levels and *costs.*

customers' ledger. The *ledger* that shows *accounts receivable* of individual customers. It is the *subsidiary ledger* for the *control account* Accounts Receivable.

cutoff rate. *Hurdle rate.*

D

data bank. An organized file of information, such as a customer name and address file, used in and kept up-to-date by a processing system.

database. A comprehensive collection of interrelated information stored together in computerized form to serve several applications.

database management system. Generalized software programs used to handle physical storage and manipulation of databases.

days of average inventory on hand. See *ratio.*

days of grace. The days allowed by law or contract for payment of a debt after its due date.

DCF. *Discounted cash flow.*

DDB. *Double declining-balance depreciation.*

debenture bond. A *bond* not secured with *collateral.*

debit. As a noun, an entry on the left-hand side of an *account;* as a verb, to make an entry on the left-hand side of an account; records increases in *assets* and *expenses;* records decreases in *liabilities, owners' equity,* and *revenues.* See *debit and credit conventions.*

debit and credit conventions. The conventional use of the *T-account* form and the rules for debit and credit in *balance sheet accounts* (see below). The equality of the two sides of the *accounting equation* results from recording equal amounts of *debits* and *credits* for each *transaction.*

Typical Asset Account

Opening Balance Increase + Dr. Ending Balance	Decrease − Cr.

Typical Liability Account

Decrease − Dr.	Opening Balance Increase + Cr. Ending Balance

Typical Owners' Equity Account

Decrease − Dr.	Opening Balance Increase + Cr. Ending Balance

Revenue and expense accounts belong to the owners' equity group. The relation and the rules for debit and credit in these accounts take the following form:

Owners' Equity	
Decrease	Increase
−	+
Dr.	Cr.

Expenses		Revenues	
Dr.	Cr.	Dr.	Cr.
+	−	−	+
*			*

*Normal balance before closing

debit memorandum. A document used by a seller to inform a buyer that the seller is debiting (increasing) the amount of the buyer's *accounts receivable.* Also, the document provided by a bank to a depositor to indicate that the bank is decreasing the depositor's *balance* because of some event other than payment for a *check,* such as monthly service charges or the printing of checks.

debt. An amount owed. The general name for *notes, bonds, mortgages,* and the like that provide evidence of amounts owed and have definite payment dates.

debt capital. *Noncurrent liabilities.* See *debt financing,* and contrast with *equity financing.*

debt-equity ratio. Total *liabilities* divided by total equities. See *ratio.* Some analysts put only total shareholders' equity in the denominator. Some analysts restrict the numerator to *long-term debt.*

debt financing. *Leverage.* Raising *funds* by issuing *bonds, mortgages,* or *notes.* Contrast with *equity financing.*

debt guarantee. See *guarantee.*

debt ratio. *Debt-equity ratio.*

debt service fund. In governmental accounting, a *fund* established to account for payment of *interest* and *principal* on all general-obligation *debt* other than that payable from special *assessments.*

debt service payment. The payment required by a lending agreement, such as periodic coupon payment on a bond or installment payment on a loan or a lease payment. It is sometimes called "interest payment," but this term will mislead the unwary. Only rarely will the amount of a debt service payment equal the interest expense for the period preceding the payment. A debt service payment will always include some amount for interest, but the payment will usually differ from the interest expense.

debt service requirement. The amount of cash required for payments of *interest,* current maturities of *principal* on outstanding *debt,* and payments to *sinking funds* (corporations) or to the debt service fund (governmental).

debtor. One who borrows; in the UK, *account receivable.*

decentralized decision making. Management practice in which a firm gives a manager of a business unit responsibility for that unit's *revenues* and *costs,* freeing the manager to make decisions about prices, sources of supply, and the like, as though the unit were a separate business that the manager owns. See *responsibility accounting* and *transfer price.*

declaration date. Time when the *board of directors* declares a *dividend.*

declining-balance depreciation. The method of calculating the periodic *depreciation* charge by multiplying the *book value* at the start of the period by a constant percentage. In pure declining-balance depreciation, the constant percentage is $1 - ns/c$, where n is the *depreciable life, s* is *salvage value,* and c is *acquisition cost.* See *double declining-balance depreciation.*

deep discount bonds. Said of *bonds* selling much below (exactly how much is not clear) *par value.*

defalcation. Embezzlement.

default. Failure to pay *interest* or *principal* on a *debt* when due.

defeasance. Transaction with the economic effect of *debt retirement* that does not retire the debt. When *interest rates* increase, many firms find that the *market value* of their outstanding *debt* has dropped substantially below its *book value.* In *historical cost accounting* for debt retirements, retiring debt with a *cash* payment less than the book value of the debt results in a gain (generally, an *extraordinary item*). Many firms would like to retire the outstanding debt issues and report the gain. Two factors impede doing so: (1) the gain can be a taxable event generating adverse *income tax* consequences; and (2) the transaction costs in retiring all the debt can be large, in part because the firm cannot easily locate all the debt holders or persuade them to sell back their bonds to the issuer. The process of "defeasance" serves as the economic equivalent to retiring a debt issue while it saves the issuer from experiencing adverse tax consequences and from actually having to locate and retire the bonds. The process works as follows. The debt-issuing firm turns over to an independent trustee, such as a bank, amounts of cash or low-risk government bonds sufficient to make all debt service payments on the outstanding debt, including bond retirements, in return for the trustee's commitment to make all debt service payments. The debt issuer effectively retires the outstanding debt. It debits the liability account, credits Cash or Marketable Securities as appropriate, and credits Extraordinary Gain on Debt Retirement. The trustee can retire debt or make debt service payments, whichever it chooses. For income tax purposes, however, the firm's debt remains outstanding. The firm will have taxable interest *deductions* for its still-outstanding debt and taxable interest *revenue* on the investments held by the trustee for debt service. In law, the term "defeasance" means "a rendering null and void." This process renders the outstanding debt economically null and void, without causing a taxable event.

defensive interval. A financial *ratio* equal to the number of days of normal cash *expenditures* covered by *quick assets.* It is defined as follows:

$$\frac{\text{Quick Assets}}{\text{(All Expenses Except Amortization and Others Not Using Funds} \div 365)}$$

The denominator of the ratio is the cash expenditure per day. Analysts have found this ratio useful in predicting *bankruptcy.*

deferral. The accounting process concerned with past *cash receipts* and *payments;* in contrast to *accrual;* recognizing a liability resulting from a current cash receipt (as for magazines to be delivered) or recognizing an asset from a current cash payment (as for prepaid insurance or a long-term depreciable asset).

deferral method. See *flow-through method* (of accounting for the *investment credit*) for definition and contrast.

deferred annuity. An *annuity* whose first payment occurs sometime after the end of the first period.

deferred asset. *Deferred charge.*

deferred charge. *Expenditure* not recognized as an *expense* of the period when made but carried forward as an *asset* to be *written off* in future periods, such as for advance rent payments or insurance premiums. See *deferral.*

deferred cost. *Deferred charge.*

deferred credit. Sometimes used to indicate *advances from customers.*

deferred debit. *Deferred charge.*

deferred expense. *Deferred charge.*

deferred gross margin. *Unrealized gross margin.*

deferred income. *Advances from customers.*

deferred income tax (liability). An *indeterminate-term liability* that arises when the pretax income shown on the tax return is less than what it would have been had the firm used the same *accounting principles* and *cost basis* for *assets* and *liabilities* in tax returns as it used for financial reporting. *SFAS No. 109* requires that the firm debit income tax *expense* and credit deferred income tax with the amount of the taxes delayed by using accounting principles in tax returns different from those used in financial reports. See *temporary difference, timing difference, permanent difference,* and *installment sales.* If, as a result of temporary differences, cumulative taxable income exceeds cumulative reported income before taxes, the deferred income tax account will have a *debit* balance, which the firm will report as a *deferred charge.*

deferred revenue. Sometimes used to indicate *advances from customers.*

deferred tax. See *deferred income tax.*

deficit. A *debit balance* in the Retained Earnings account; presented on the balance sheet in a *contra account* to shareholders' equity; sometimes used to mean negative *net income* for a period.

defined-benefit plan. A *pension plan* in which the employer promises specific dollar amounts to each eligible employee; the amounts usually depend on a formula that takes into account such things as the employee's earnings, years of employment, and age. The employer adjusts its cash contributions and pension expense to *actuarial* experience in the eligible employee group and investment performance of the pension *fund.* This is sometimes called a "fixed-benefit" pension plan. Contrast with *money purchase plan.*

defined-contribution plan. A *money purchase (pension) plan* or other arrangement, based on formula or discretion, in which the employer makes cash contributions to eligible individual employee *accounts* under the terms of a written plan document. The trustee of the funds in the account manages the funds, and the employee-beneficiary receives at retirement (or at some other agreed time) the amount in the fund. The employer makes no promise about that amount. Profit-sharing pension plans are of this type.

deflation. A period of declining *general price-level changes.*

demand deposit. *Funds* in a *checking account* at a bank.

demand loan. See *term loan* for definition and contrast.

denial of opinion. Canada: the statement that an *auditor,* for reasons arising in the *audit,* is unable to express an opinion on whether the *financial statements* provide *fair presentation.*

denominator volume. Capacity measured in the number of units the firm expects to produce this period; when divided into *budgeted fixed costs,* results in fixed costs applied per unit of product.

department(al) allocation. Obtained by first accumulating *costs* in *cost pools* for each department and then, using separate rates, or sets of rates, for each department, allocating from each cost pool to products produced in that department.

dependent variable. See *regression analysis.*

depletion. Exhaustion or *amortization* of a *wasting asset* or *natural resource.* Also see *percentage depletion.*

depletion allowance. See *percentage depletion.*

deposit, sinking fund. Payments made to a *sinking fund.*

deposit method (of revenue recognition). A method of *revenue* recognition that is the same as the *completed sale* or *completed contract method.* In some contexts, such as when the customer has the right to return goods for a full refund or in retail land sales, the customer must make substantial payments while still having the right to back out of the deal and receive a refund. When the seller cannot predict with reasonable precision the amount of cash it will ultimately collect and when it will receive cash, the seller must *credit* Deposits, a *liability account,* rather than *revenue.* (In this regard, the accounting differs from that in the completed contract method, in which the account credited offsets the *Work-in-Process* inventory account.) When the *sale* becomes complete, the firm credits a revenue account and *debits* the Deposits account.

deposits (by customers). A *liability* that the firm *credits* when receiving *cash* (as in a bank, or in a grocery store when the customer pays for soda-pop bottles with cash to be repaid when the customer returns the bottles) and when the firm intends to discharge the liability by returning the cash. Contrast with the liability account *Advances from Customers,* which the firm credits on receipt of cash, expecting later to discharge the liability by delivering goods or services. When the firm delivers the goods or services, it credits a *revenue* account.

deposits in transit. Deposits made by a firm but not yet reflected on the *bank statement.*

depreciable cost. That part of the *cost* of an asset, usually *acquisition cost* less *salvage value,* that the firm will charge off over the life of the asset through the process of *depreciation.*

depreciable life. For an *asset,* the time period or units of activity (such as miles driven for a truck) over which the firm allocates the *depreciable cost.* For tax returns, depreciable life may be shorter than estimated *service life.*

depreciation. *Amortization of plant assets;* the process of allocating the cost of an asset to the periods of benefit—the *depreciable life;* classified as a *production cost* or a *period expense,* depending on the asset and whether the firm uses *full absorption* or *variable costing.* Depreciation methods described in this glossary include the *annuity method, appraisal method, composite method, compound interest method, declining-balance method, production method, replacement method, retirement method, straight-line method, sinking fund method,* and *sum-of-the-years'-digits method.*

depreciation reserve. An inferior term for *accumulated depreciation.* See *reserve.* Do not confuse with a replacement *fund.*

derivative (financial instrument). A financial instrument, such as an option to purchase a share of stock, created from another, such as a share of stock; an instrument, such as a *swap,* whose value depends on the value of another asset: for example, the right to receive the difference between the interest payments on a fixed-rate five-year loan for $1 million annd the interest payments on a floating-rate five-year loan for $1 million. To qualify as a derivative under *FASB* rules, *SFAS No. 133,* the instrument has one or more underlyings, and one or more notional amounts or payment provisions or both, it does not require an initial net investment (or only one smaller than would be required for other types of contracts expected to have a similar response to changes in market factors), and its terms permit settlement for cash in lieu of physical delivery or the instrument itself trades on an exchange. See also *forward contract* and *futures contract.*

Descartes' rule of signs. In a *capital budgeting* context, a rule that says a series of cash flows will have a nonnegative number of *internal rates of return.* The number equals the number of variations in the sign of the cash flow series or is less than that number by an even integer. Consider the following series of cash flows, the first occurring now and the others at subsequent yearly intervals: $-100, -100, +50, +175, -50, +100.$ The internal rates of return are the numbers for r that satisfy the following equation:

$$-100 - \frac{100}{(1+r)} + \frac{50}{(1+r)^2} + \frac{175}{(1+r)^3} - \frac{50}{(1+r)^4} + \frac{100}{(1+r)^5} = 0$$

The series of cash flows has three variations in sign: a change from minus to plus, a change from plus to minus, and a change from minus to plus. The rule says that this series must have either one or three internal rates of return; in fact, it has only one, about 12 percent. But also see *reinvestment rate.*

detective controls. *Internal controls* designed to detect, or maximize the chance of detection of, errors and other irregularities.

determination. See *determine.*

determine. A term often used (in our opinion, overused) by accountants and those who describe the accounting process. A leading dictionary associates the following meanings with the verb "determine": settle, decide, conclude, ascertain, cause, affect, control, impel, terminate, and decide upon. In addition, accounting writers can mean any one of the following: measure, allocate, report, calculate, compute, observe, choose, and legislate. In accounting, there are two distinct sets of meanings: those encompassed by the synonym "cause or legislate" and those encompassed by the synonym "measure." The first set of uses conveys the active notion of causing something to happen, and the second set of uses conveys the more passive notion of observing something that someone else has caused to happen. An accountant who speaks of cost or income "determination" generally means measurement or observation, not causation; management and economic conditions cause costs and income to be what they are. One who speaks of accounting principles "determination" can mean choosing or applying (as in "determining depreciation charges" from an allowable set) or causing to be acceptable (as in the *FASB*'s "determining" the accounting for *leases*). In the long run, income is cash-in less cash-out, so management and economic conditions "determine" (cause) income to be what it is. In the short run, reported income is a function of accounting principles chosen and applied, so the accountant "determines" (measures) income. A question such as "Who determines income?" has, therefore, no unambiguous answer. The meaning of "an accountant determining acceptable accounting principles" is also vague. Does the clause mean merely choosing one principle from the set of generally acceptable principles, or does it mean using professional judgment to decide that some of the generally accepted principles are not correct under the current circumstances? We try never to use "determine" unless we mean "cause." Otherwise we use "measure," "report," "calculate," "compute," or whatever specific verb seems appropriate. We suggest that careful writers will always "determine" to use the most specific verb to convey meaning. "Determine" seldom best describes a process in which those who make decisions often differ from those who apply technique. The term *predetermined (factory) overhead rate* contains an appropriate use of the word.

development stage enterprise. As defined in *SFAS No. 7,* a firm whose planned principal *operations* have not commenced or, having commenced, have not generated significant *revenue.* The financial statements should identify such enterprises, but no special *accounting principles* apply to them.

diagnostic signal. See *warning signal* for definition and contrast.

differentiable cost. The cost increments associated with infinitesimal changes in volume. If a total cost curve is smooth (in mathematical terms, differentiable), then we say that the curve graphing the derivative of the total cost curve shows differentiable costs.

differential. An adjective used to describe the change (increase or decrease) in a *cost, expense, investment, cash flow, revenue, profit,* and the like as the firm produces or sells one or more additional (or fewer) units or undertakes (or ceases) an activity. This term has virtually the same meaning as *incremental,* but if the item declines, "decremental" better describes the change. Contrast with *marginal,* which means the change in cost or other item for a small (one unit or even less) change in number of units produced or sold.

differential analysis. Analysis of *differential costs, revenues, profits, investment, cash flow,* and the like.

differential cost. See *differential.*

dilution. A potential reduction in *earnings per share* or *book value* per share by the potential *conversion* of securities or by the potential exercise of *warrants* or *options.*

dilutive. Said of a *security* that will reduce *earnings per share* if it is exchanged for *common shares.*

dip(ping) into LIFO layers. See *LIFO inventory layer.*

direct access. Access to computer storage where information can be located directly, regardless of its position in the storage file. Compare *sequential access.*

direct cost. Cost of *direct material* and *direct labor* incurred in producing a product. See *prime cost.* In some accounting literature, writers use this term to mean the same thing as *variable cost.*

direct costing. Another, less-preferred, term for *variable costing.*

direct-financing (capital) lease. See *sales-type (capital) lease* for definition and contrast.

direct labor (material) cost. Cost of labor (material) applied and assigned directly to a product; contrast with *indirect labor (material).*

direct labor variance. Difference between actual and *standard direct labor* allowed.

direct method. See *statement of cash flows.*

direct posting. A method of bookkeeping in which the firm makes *entries* directly in *ledger accounts,* without using a *journal.*

direct write-off method. See *write-off method.*

disbursement. Payment by *cash* or by *check.* See *expenditure.*

DISC (domestic international sales corporation). A U.S. *corporation,* usually a *subsidiary,* whose *income* results primarily from exports. The parent firm usually defers paying *income tax* on 50 percent of a DISC's income for a long period. Generally, this results in a lower overall corporate tax for the *parent* than would otherwise be incurred.

disclaimer of opinion. An *auditor's report* stating that the auditor cannot give an opinion on the *financial statements.* Usually results from *material* restrictions on the scope of the audit or from material uncertainties, which the firm has been unable to resolve by the time of the audit, about the accounts.

disclosure. The showing of facts in *financial statements, notes* thereto, or the *auditor's report.*

discontinued operations. See *income from discontinued operations.*

discount. In the context of *compound interest, bonds* and *notes,* the difference between *face amount* (or *future value*) and *present value* of a payment; in the context of *sales* and *purchases,* a reduction in price granted for prompt payment. See also *chain discount, quantity discount,* and *trade discount.*

discount factor. The reciprocal of one plus the *discount rate.* If the discount rate is 10 percent per period, the discount factor for three periods is $1/(1.10)^3 = (1.10)^{-3} = 0.75131.$

discount rate. *Interest rate* used to convert future payments to *present values.*

discounted bailout period. In a *capital budgeting* context, the total time that must elapse before discounted value of net accumulated cash flows from a project, including potential *salvage value* at various times of assets, equals or exceeds the *present value* of net accumulated cash outflows. Contrast with *discounted payback period.*

discounted cash flow (DCF). Using either the *net present value* or the *internal rate of return* in an analysis to measure the value of future expected cash *expenditures* and *receipts* at a common date. In discounted cash flow analysis, choosing the alternative with the largest *internal rate of return* may yield wrong answers given *mutually exclusive projects* with differing amounts of initial investment for two of the projects. Consider, to take an unrealistic example, a project involving an initial investment of $1, with an *IRR* of 60 percent, and another project involving an initial investment of $1 million, with an IRR of 40 percent. Under most conditions, most firms will prefer the second project to the first, but choosing the project with the larger IRR will lead to undertaking the first, not the second. Usage calls this shortcoming of choosing between alternatives based on the magnitude of the internal rate of return, rather than based on the magnitude of the *net present value* of the cash flows, the "scale effect."

discounted payback period. The shortest amount of time that must elapse before the discounted *present value* of cash inflows from a project, excluding potential *salvage value,* equals the discounted present value of the cash outflows.

discounting a note. See *note receivable discounted* and *factoring.*

discounts lapsed (lost). The sum of *discounts* offered for prompt payment that the purchaser did not take because the discount period expired. See *terms of sale.*

discovery sampling. Acceptance sampling in which the analyst accepts an entire population if and only if the sample contains no disparities.

discovery value accounting. See *reserve recognition accounting.*

discretionary cost center. See *engineered cost center* for definition and contrast.

discretionary costs. *Programmed costs.*

Discussion Memorandum. A neutral discussion of all the issues concerning an accounting problem of current concern to the *FASB*. The publication of such a document usually signals that the FASB will consider issuing an *SFAS* or *SFAC* on this particular problem. The discussion memorandum brings together material about the particular problem to facilitate interaction and comment by those interested in the matter. A public hearing follows before the FASB will issue an *Exposure Draft*.

dishonored note. A *promissory note* whose maker does not repay the loan at *maturity,* for a *term loan,* or on demand, for a *demand loan.*

disintermediation. Moving funds from one interest-earning account to another, typically one promising a higher rate. Federal law regulates the maximum *interest rate* that both banks and savings-and-loan associations can pay for *time deposits.* When free-market interest rates exceed the regulated interest ceiling for such time deposits, some depositors withdraw their funds and invest them elsewhere at a higher interest rate. This process is known as "disintermediation."

distributable income. The portion of conventional accounting net income that the firm can distribute to owners (usually in the form of *dividends*) without impairing the physical capacity of the firm to continue operations at current levels. Pretax distributable income is conventional pretax income less the excess of *current cost* of goods sold and *depreciation* charges based on the replacement cost of *productive capacity* over cost of goods sold and depreciation on an *acquisition cost basis*. Contrast with *sustainable income*. See *inventory profit*.

distributable surplus. Canada and UK: the statutory designation to describe the portion of the proceeds of the issue of shares without *par value* not allocated to share capital.

distributed processing. Processing in a computer information network in which an individual location processes data relevant to it while the operating system transmits information required elsewhere, either to the central computer or to another local computer for further processing.

distribution expense. *Expense* of selling, advertising, and delivery activities.

dividend. A distribution of assets generated from *earnings* to owners of a corporation. The firm may distribute cash (cash dividend), stock (stock dividend), property, or other securities (dividend in kind). Dividends, except stock dividends, become a legal liability of the corporation when the corporation's board declares them. Hence, the owner of stock ordinarily recognizes *revenue* when the board of the corporation declares the dividend, except for stock dividends. See also *liquidating dividend* and *stock dividend*.

dividend yield. *Dividends* declared for the year divided by market price of the stock as of the time for which the analyst computes the yield.

dividends in arrears. Dividends on *cumulative preferred stock* that the corporation's board has not yet declared in accordance with the preferred stock contract. The corporation must usually clear such arrearages before it can declare dividends on *common shares*.

dividends in kind. See *dividend*.

division. A more or less self-contained business unit that is part of a larger family of business units under common control.

divisional control. See *control system*.

divisional reporting. See *segment reporting*.

dollar sign rules. In accounting statements or schedules, place a dollar sign beside the first figure in each column and beside any figure below a horizontal line drawn under the preceding figure.

dollar-value LIFO method. A form of *LIFO* inventory accounting with inventory quantities (*layers*) measured in dollar, rather than physical, terms. The method adjusts for changing prices by using specific price indexes appropriate for the kinds of items in the inventory.

domestic international sales corporation. See *DISC*.

donated capital. A *shareholders' equity* account credited when the company receives gifts, such as land or buildings, without issuing shares or other owners' equity interest in return. A city might donate a plant site hoping the firm will build a factory and employ local residents. Do not confuse with *contributed capital*.

double declining-balance depreciation (DDB). *Declining-balance depreciation* in which the constant percentage used to multiply by book value in computing the depreciation charge for the year is $2/n,$ where n is the *depreciable life* in periods. Omit *salvage value* from the depreciable amount. Thus if the asset cost $100 and has a depreciable life of five years, the depreciation in the first year would be $40 = 2/5 \times \$100$, in the second year would be $24 = 2/5 \times (\$100 - \$40)$, and in the third year would be $14.40 = 2/5 \times (\$100 - \$40 - \$24)$. By the fourth year, the remaining undepreciated cost could be depreciated under the straight-line method at $10.80 = \frac{1}{2} \times (\$100 - \$40 - \$24 - \$14.40)$ per year for tax purposes. Note that salvage value does not affect these computations except that the method will not depreciate the book value below salvage value.

double entry. In recording transactions, a system that maintains the equality of the accounting equation or the balance sheet. Each entry results in recording equal amounts of *debits* and *credits*.

double T-account. *T-account* with an extra horizontal line showing a change in the account balance to be explained by the subsequent entries into the account.

Plant	
42,000	

This account shows an increase in the asset account, plant, of $42,000 to be explained. Such accounts are useful in preparing the *statement of cash flows*; they are not a part of the formal record-keeping process.

double taxation. Occurs when the taxing authority (U.S. or state) taxes corporate income as earned (first tax) and then the same taxing authority taxes the aftertax income, distributed to owners as dividends, again as personal income tax (second tax).

doubtful accounts. *Accounts receivable* that the firm estimates to be *uncollectible*.

Dr. The abbreviation for *debit,* always with the initial capital letter. *Dr.* is a shortened from of the word *debitor,* and *Cr.* comes from the word *creditor.* In the early days of double-entry record keeping in the UK, the major asset was accounts receivable, called *creditors,* and the major liability was accounts payable, called *debitors.* Thus the *r* in *Cr.* does not refer to the *r* in *credit* but to the second *r* in *creditor.*

draft. A written order by the first party, called the drawer, instructing a second party, called the drawee (such as a bank) to pay a third party, called the payee. See also *check, cashier's check, certified check, NOW account, sight draft,* and *trade acceptance.*

drawee. See *draft.*

drawer. See *draft.*

drawing account. A *temporary account* used in *sole proprietorships* and *partnerships* to record payments to owners or partners during a period. At the end of the period, the firm closes the drawing account by crediting it and debiting the owner's or partner's share of income or, perhaps, his or her capital account.

drawings. Payments made to a *sole proprietor* or to a *partner* during a period. See *drawing account.*

driver, cost driver. A cause of costs incurred. Examples include processing orders, issuing an engineering change order, changing the production schedule, and stopping production to change machine settings. The notion arises primarily in product costing, particularly *activity-based costing.*

drop ship(ment). Occurs when a distributor asks a manufacturer to send an order directly to the customer (ordinarily a manufacturer sends goods to a distributor, who sends the goods to its customer). Usage calls the shipment a "drop shipment" and refers to the goods as "drop shipped."

dry-hole accounting. See *reserve recognition accounting* for definition and contrast.

dual-transactions assumption (fiction). Occurs when an analyst, in understanding cash flows, views transactions not involving *cash* as though the firm first generated cash and then used it. For example, the analyst might view the issue of *capital stock* in return for the *asset* land as though the firm issued stock for *cash* and then used cash to acquire the land. Other examples of transactions that could involve the dual-transaction assumption are the issue of a *mortgage* in return for a noncurrent asset and the issue of stock to bondholders on *conversion* of their *convertible bonds.*

dual transfer prices. Occurs when the *transfer price charged* to the buying *division* differs from that *credited* to the sell-ing division. Such prices make sense when the selling division has excess capacity and, as usual, the *fair market value* exceeds the *incremental cost* to produce the goods or services being transferred.

duality. The *double entry* record-keeping axiom that every *transaction* must result in equal *debit* and *credit* amounts.

dumping. A foreign firm's selling a good or service in the United States at a price below market price at home or, in some contexts, below some measure of cost (which concept is not clearly defined). The practice is illegal in the United States if it harms (or threatens to harm) a U.S. industry.

E

e. The base of natural logarithms; 2.71828. . . . If *interest* compounds continuously during a period at stated rate of *r* per period, then the effective *interest rate* is equivalent to interest compounded once per period at rate *i* where $i = e^r - 1$. Tables of e^r are widely available. If 12 percent annual interest compounds continuously, the effective annual rate is $e^{.12} - 1 = 12.75$ percent. Interest compounded continuously at rate *r* for *d* days is $e^{rd/365} - 1$. For example, interest compounded for 92 days at 12 percent is $e^{.12 \times 92/365} - 1 = 3.07$ percent.

earn-out. For two merging firms, an agreement in which the amount paid by the acquiring firm to the acquired firm's shareholders depends on the future earnings of the acquired firm or, perhaps, of the *consolidated entity.*

earned surplus. A term that writers once used, but no longer use, for *retained earnings.*

earnings. A term with no precise meaning but used to mean *income* or sometimes *profit.* The *FASB,* in requiring that firms report *comprehensive income,* encouraged firms to use the term "earnings" for the total formerly reported as *net income.* Firms will likely only slowly change from using the term "net income" to the term "earnings."

earnings, retained. See *retained earnings.*

earnings cycle. The period of time, or the series of transactions, during which a given firm converts *cash* into *goods* and *services,* then sells goods and services to customers, and finally collects cash from customers. *Cash cycle.*

earnings per share (of common stock). *Net income* to common shareholders (net income minus *preferred dividends*) divided by the average number of *common shares* outstanding; see also *primary earnings per share* and *fully diluted earnings per share.* See *ratio.*

earnings per share (of preferred stock). *Net income* divided by the average number of *preferred shares* outstanding during the period. This ratio indicates how well income covers (or protects) the preferred dividends; it does not indicate a legal share of *earnings.* See *ratio.*

earnings statement. *Income statement.*

easement. The acquired right or privilege of one person to use, or have access to, certain property of another. For example, a public utility's right to lay pipes or lines under the property of another and to service those facilities.

EBIT. *Earnings* before *income taxes;* acronym used by analysts.

EBITDA. *Earnings* before *income taxes, depreciation,* and *amortization;* acronym used by analysts to focus on a particular measure of *cash flow* used in valuation. This is not the same as, but is similar in concept to, *cash flow from operations.* Some analysts exclude *nonrecurring* items from this total.

economic consequences. The *FASB* says that in setting *accounting principles,* it should take into account the real effects on various participants in the business world. It calls these effects "economic consequences."

economic depreciation. Decline in *current cost* (or *fair value*) of an *asset* during a period.

economic entity. See *entity.*

economic life. The time span over which the firm expects to receive the benefits of an *asset.* The economic life of a *patent, copyright,* or *franchise* may be less than the legal life. *Service life.*

economic order quantity (EOQ). In mathematical *inventory* analysis, the optimal amount of stock to order when demand reduces inventory to a level called the "reorder point." If A represents the *incremental cost* of placing a single order, D represents the total demand for a period of time in units, and H represents the incremental holding cost during the period per unit of inventory, then the economic order quantity is $EOQ = \sqrt{2AD/H}$. Usage sometimes calls *EOQ* the "optimal lot size."

ED. *Exposure Draft.*

EDGAR. Electronic Data, Gathering, Analysis, and Retrieval system; rules and systems adopted by the *SEC* in 1993 to ensure that all the paperwork involved in the filings submitted by more than 15,000 public companies are electronically submitted.

EDP. *Electronic data processing.*

effective interest method. In computing *interest expense* (or *revenue*), a systematic method that makes the interest expense (revenue) for each period divided by the amount of the net *liability (asset)* at the beginning of the period equal to the *yield rate* on the liability (asset) at the time of issue (acquisition). Interest for a period is the yield rate (at time of issue) multiplied by the net liability (asset) at the start of the period. The *amortization* of discount or premium is the *plug* to give equal *debits* and *credits.* (Interest expense is a debit, and the amount of debt service payment is a credit.)

effective (interest) rate. Of a liability such as a bond, the *internal rate of return* or *yield to maturity* at the time of issue. Contrast with *coupon rate.* If the borrower issues the bond for a price below *par,* the effective rate is higher than the coupon rate; if it issues the bond for a price greater than par, the effective rate is lower than the coupon rate. In the context of *compound interest,* the effective rate occurs when the *compounding period* on a *loan* differs from one year, such as a nominal interest rate of 12 percent compounded monthly. The effective interest is the single rate that one could use at the end of the year to multiply the *principal* at the beginning of the year and give the same amount as results from compounding interest each period during the year. For example, if 12 percent per year compounds monthly, the effective annual interest rate is 12.683 percent. That is, if you compound $100 each month at 1 percent per month, the $100 will grow to $112.68 at the end of the year. In general, if the nominal rate of r percent per year compounds m times per year, then the effective rate is $(1 + r/m)^m - 1$.

efficiency variance. A term used for the *quantity variance* for materials or labor or *variable overhead* in a *standard costing system.*

efficient capital market. A market in which security prices reflect all available information and react nearly instantaneously and in an unbiased fashion to new information.

efficient market hypothesis. The finance supposition that security prices trade in *efficient capital markets.*

EITF. *Emerging Issues Task Force.*

electronic data processing. Performing computations and other data-organizing steps in a computer, in contrast to doing these steps by hand or with mechanical calculators.

eligible. Under income tax legislation, a term that restricts or otherwise alters the meaning of another tax or accounting term, generally to signify that the related assets or operations may receive a specified tax treatment.

eliminations. In preparing *consolidated statements, work sheet* entries made to avoid duplicating the amounts of *assets, liabilities, owners' equity, revenues,* and *expenses* of the consolidated *entity* when the firm sums the accounts of the *parent* and *subsidiaries.*

Emerging Issues Task Force (EITF). A group convened by the *FASB* to deal more rapidly with accounting issues than the FASB's due-process procedures can allow. The task force comprises about 20 members from public accounting, industry, and several trade associations. It meets every six weeks. Several FASB board members usually attend and participate. The chief accountant of the *SEC* has indicated that the SEC will require that published financial statements follow guidelines set by a consensus of the EITF. The EITF requires that nearly all its members agree on a position before that position receives the label of "consensus." Such positions appear in *Abstracts of the EITF,* published by the FASB. Since 1984, the EITF has become one of the promulgators of *GAAP.*

employee stock option. See *stock option.*

Employee Stock Ownership Trust (or Plan). See *ESOT.*

employer, employee payroll taxes. See *payroll taxes.*

enabling costs. A type of *capacity cost* that a firm will stop incurring if it shuts down operations completely but will incur in full if it carries out operations at any level. Examples include costs of a security force or of a quality-control inspector for an assembly line. Contrast with *standby costs.*

encumbrance. In governmental accounting, an anticipated *expenditure* or *funds* restricted for an anticipated expenditure, such as for outstanding purchase orders. *Appropriations* less expenditures less outstanding encumbrances yields unencumbered balance.

ending inventory. The *cost* of *inventory* on hand at the end of the *accounting period;* often called "closing inventory." Ending inventory from the end of one period becomes the *beginning inventory* for the next period.

endorsee. See *endorser.*

endorsement. See *draft.* The *payee* signs the draft and transfers it to a fourth party, such as the payee's bank.

endorser. A *note* or *draft payee,* who signs the note after writing "Pay to the order of X," transfers the note to person X, and presumably receives some benefit, such as cash, in return. Usage refers to person X as the "endorsee." The endorsee then has the rights of the payee and may in turn become an endorser by endorsing the note to another endorsee.

engineered cost center. Responsibility center with sufficiently well-established relations between inputs and outputs that the analyst, given data on inputs, can predict the outputs or, conversely, given the outputs, can estimate the amounts of inputs that the process should have used. Consider the relation between pounds of flour (input) and loaves of bread (output). Contrast discretionary cost center, where such relations are so imprecise that analysts have no reliable way to relate inputs to outputs. Consider the relation between advertising the corporate logo or trademark (input) and future revenues (output).

engineering method (of cost estimation). To estimate unit cost of product from study of the materials, labor, and *overhead* components of the production process.

enterprise. Any business organization, usually defining the accounting *entity.*

enterprise fund. A *fund* that a governmental unit establishes to account for acquisition, operation, and maintenance of governmental services that the government intends to be self-supporting from user charges, such as for water or airports and some toll roads.

entity. A person, *partnership, corporation,* or other organization. The *accounting entity* that issues accounting statements may not be the same as the entity defined by law. For example, a *sole proprietorship* is an accounting entity, but the individual's combined business and personal assets are the legal entity in most jurisdictions. Several affiliated corporations may be separate legal entities but issue *consolidated financial statements* for the group of companies operating as a single economic entity.

entity theory. The corporation view that emphasizes the form of the *accounting equation* that says *assets = equities.* Contrast with *proprietorship theory.* The entity theory focuses less on the distinction between *liabilities* and *shareholders' equity* than does the proprietorship theory. The entity theory views all equities as coming to the corporation from outsiders who have claims of differing legal standings. The entity theory implies using a *multiple-step* income statement.

entry value. The *current cost* of acquiring an asset or service at a *fair market price. Replacement cost.*

EOQ. *Economic order quantity.*

EPS. *Earnings per share.*

EPVI. *Excess present value index.*

equalization reserve. An inferior title for the allowance or *estimated liability* account when the firm uses the *allowance method* for such things as maintenance expenses. Periodically, the accountant will debit maintenance *expense* and credit the allowance. As the firm makes *expenditures* for maintenance, it will debit the allowance and credit cash or the other asset used in maintenance.

equities. *Liabilities* plus *owners' equity.* See *equity.*

equity. A claim to *assets;* a source of assets. *SFAC No. 3* defines equity as "the residual interest in the assets of an entity that remains after deducting its liabilities." Thus, many knowledgeable people use "equity" to exclude liabilities and count only owners' equities. We prefer to use the term to mean all liabilities plus all owners' equity because there is no other single word that serves this useful purpose. We fight a losing battle.

equity financing. Raising *funds* by issuing *capital stock.* Contrast with *debt financing.*

equity method. In accounting for an *investment* in the stock of another company, a method that debits the proportionate share of the earnings of the other company to the investment account and credits that amount to a *revenue* account as earned. When the investor receives *dividends,* it debits *cash* and credits the investment account. An investor who owns sufficient shares of stock of an unconsolidated company to exercise significant control over the actions of that company must use the equity method. It is one of the few instances in which the firm recognizes revenue without an increase in *working capital.*

equity ratio. *Shareholders' equity* divided by total *assets.* See *ratio.*

equivalent production. *Equivalent units.*

equivalent units (of work). The number of units of completed output that would require the same costs that a firm would actually incur for the production of completed and partially completed units during a period. For example, if at the beginning of a period the firm starts 100 units and by the end of the period has incurred costs for each of these equal to 75 percent of total costs to complete the units, then the equivalent units of work for the period would be 75. This is used primarily in *process costing* calculations to measure in uniform terms the output of a continuous process.

ERISA (Employee Retirement Income Security Act of 1974). The federal law that sets most *pension plan* requirements.

error accounting. See *accounting errors.*

escalator clause. Inserted in a purchase or rental contract, a clause that permits, under specified conditions, upward adjustments of price.

escapable cost. *Avoidable cost.*

ESOP (Employee Stock Ownership Plan). See *ESOT.*

ESOT (Employee Stock Ownership Trust). A trust *fund* that is created by a corporate employer and that can provide certain tax benefits to the corporation while providing for employee stock ownership. The corporate employer can contribute up to 25 percent of its payroll per year to the trust. The corporation may deduct the amount of the contribution from otherwise taxable income for federal *income tax* purposes. The trustee of the assets must use them for the benefit of employees—for example, to fund death or retirement benefits. The assets of the trust are usually the *common shares,* sometimes nonvoting, of the corporate employer. For an example of the potential *tax shelter,* consider the case of a corporation with $1 million of *debt* outstanding, which it wants to retire, and an annual payroll of $2 million. The corporation sells $1 million of common stock to the ESOT. The ESOT borrows $1 million with the loan guaranteed by, and therefore a *contingency* of, the corporation. The corporation uses the $1 million proceeds of the stock issue to retire its outstanding debt. (The debt of the corporation has been replaced with the debt of the ESOT.) The corporation can contribute $500,000 (= .25 × $2 million payroll) to the ESOT each year and treat the contribution as a deduction for tax purposes. After a little more than two years, the ESOT has received sufficient funds to retire its loan. The corporation has effectively repaid its original $1 million debt with pretax dollars. Assuming an income tax rate of 40 percent, it has saved $400,000 (= .40 × $1 million) of aftertax dollars *if* the $500,000 expense for the contribution to the ESOT for the pension benefits of employees would have been made, in one form or another, anyway. Observe that the corporation could use the proceeds ($1 million in the example) of the stock issued to the ESOT for any of several different purposes: financing expansion, replacing plant assets, or acquiring another company. Basically this same form of pretax-dollar financing through pensions is available with almost any corporate pension plan, with one important exception. The trustees of an ordinary pension trust must invest the assets prudently, and if they do not, they are personally liable to the employees. Current judgment about prudent investment requires diversification—trustees should invest pension trust assets in a wide variety of investment opportunities. (The trustee may not ordinarily invest more than 10 percent of a pension trust's assets in the parent's common stock.) Thus the ordinary pension trust cannot, in practice, invest all, or even most, of its assets in the parent corporation's stock. This constraint does not apply to the investments of an ESOT. The trustee may invest all ESOT assets in the parent company's stock. The ESOT also provides a means for closely held corporations to achieve wider ownership of shares without *going public.* The laws enabling ESOTs provide for the independent professional appraisal of shares not traded in public markets and for transactions between the corporation and the ESOT or between the ESOT and the employees to be based on the appraised values of the shares.

estate planning. The arrangement of an individual's affairs to facilitate the passage of assets to beneficiaries and to minimize taxes at death.

estimated expenses. See *after cost.*

estimated liability. The preferred terminology for estimated costs the firm will incur for such uncertain things as repairs under *warranty.* An estimated liability appears on the *balance sheet.* Contrast with *contingency.*

estimated revenue. A term used in governmental accounting to designate revenue expected to accrue during a period independent of whether the government will collect it during the period. The governmental unit usually establishes a *budgetary account* at the beginning of the budget period.

estimated salvage value. Synonymous with *salvage value* of an *asset* before its retirement.

estimates, changes in. See *accounting changes.*

estimation sampling. The use of sampling technique in which the sampler infers a qualitative (e.g., fraction female) or quantitative (e.g., mean weight) characteristic of the population from the occurrence of that characteristic in the sample drawn. See *attribute(s) sampling; variables sampling.*

EURL (entreprise unipersonnelle à responsabilité limitée). France: similar to *SARL* but having only one shareholder.

ex div. (dividend). Said of *shares* whose market price quoted in the market has been reduced by a *dividend* already declared but not yet paid. The *corporation* will send the dividend to the person who owned the share on the *record date.* One who buys the share ex dividend will not receive the dividend although the corporation has not yet paid it.

ex rights. The condition of securities whose quoted market price no longer includes the right to purchase new securities, such rights having expired or been retained by the seller. Compare *cum rights.*

except for. Qualification in *auditor's report,* usually caused by a change, approved by the auditor, from one acceptable accounting principle or procedure to another.

excess present value. In a *capital budgeting* context, *present value* (of anticipated net cash inflows minus cash outflows including initial cash outflow) for a project. The analyst uses the *cost of capital* as the *discount rate.*

excess present value index. *Present value* of future *cash* inflows divided by initial cash outlay.

exchange. The generic term for a transaction (or, more technically, a reciprocal transfer) between one entity and another; in another context, the name for a market, such as the New York Stock Exchange.

exchange gain or loss. The phrase used by the *FASB* for *foreign exchange gain or loss.*

exchange rate. The *price* of one country's currency in terms of another country's currency. For example, the British pound sterling might be worth U.S.$1.60 at a given time. The exchange rate would be stated as "one pound is worth one dollar and sixty cents" or "one dollar is worth £.625" (= £1/$1.60).

excise tax. Tax on the manufacture, sale, or consumption of a commodity.

executory contract. A mere exchange of promises; an agreement providing for payment by a payor to a payee on the performance of an act or service by the payee, such as a labor contract. Accounting does not recognize benefits arising from executory contracts as *assets,* nor does it recognize obligations arising from such contracts as *liabilities.* See *partially executory contract.*

exemption. A term used for various amounts subtracted from gross income in computing taxable income. Usage does not call all such subtractions "exemptions." See *tax deduction.*

exercise. Occurs when owners of an *option* or *warrant* purchase the security that the option entitles them to purchase.

exercise price. See *option.*

exit value. The proceeds that would be received if assets were disposed of in an *arm's-length transaction. Current selling price; net realizable value.*

expected value. The mean or arithmetic *average* of a statistical distribution or series of numbers.

expected value of (perfect) information. Expected *net benefits* from an undertaking with (perfect) information minus expected net benefits of the undertaking without (perfect) information.

expendable fund. In governmental accounting, a *fund* whose resources, *principal,* and earnings the governmental unit may distribute.

expenditure. Payment of *cash* for goods or services received. Payment may occur at the time the purchaser receives the goods or services or at a later time. Virtually synonymous with *disbursement* except that disbursement is a broader term and includes all payments for goods or services. Contrast with *expense.*

expense. As a noun, a decrease in *owners' equity* accompanying the decrease in *net assets* caused by selling goods or rendering services or by the passage of time; a "gone" (net) asset; an expired cost. Measure expense as the *cost* of the (net) assets used. Do not confuse with *expenditure* or *disbursement,* which may occur before, when, or after the firm recognizes the related expense. Use the word "cost" to refer to an item that still has service potential and is an asset. Use the word "expense" after the firm has used the asset's service potential. As a verb, "expense" means to designate an expenditure—past, current, or future—as a current expense.

expense account. An *account* to accumulate *expenses*; *closed* to *retained earnings* at the end of the accounting period; a *temporary owners' equity* account; also used to describe a listing of expenses that an employee submits to the employer for reimbursement.

experience rating. A term used in insurance, particularly unemployment insurance, to denote changes from ordinary rates to reflect extraordinarily large or small amounts of claims over time by the insured.

expired cost. An *expense* or a *loss.*

Exposure Draft (ED). A preliminary statement of the *FASB* (or the *APB* between 1962 and 1973) showing the contents of a pronouncement being considered for enactment by the board.

external reporting. Reporting to shareholders and the public, as opposed to internal reporting for management's benefit. See *financial accounting,* and contrast with *managerial accounting.*

extraordinary item. A *material expense* or *revenue* item characterized both by its unusual nature and by its infrequency of occurrence; appears along with its income tax effects separately from ordinary income and *income from discontinued operations* on the *income statement.* Accountants would probably classify a *loss* from an earthquake as an extraordinary item. Accountants treat gain (or loss) on the retirement of *bonds* as an extraordinary item under the terms of *SFAS No. 4.*

F

face amount (value). The nominal amount due at *maturity* from a *bond* or *note* not including the contractual periodic payment that may also come due on the same date. Good usage calls the corresponding amount of a stock certificate the *par* or *stated value,* whichever applies.

factoring. The process of buying *notes* or *accounts receivable* at a *discount* from the holder owed the debt; from the holder's point of view, the selling of such notes or accounts. When the transaction involves a single note, usage calls the process "discounting a note."

factory. Used synonymously with *manufacturing* as an adjective.

factory burden. *Manufacturing overhead.*

factory cost. *Manufacturing cost.*

factory expense. *Manufacturing overhead. Expense* is a poor term in this context because the item is a *product cost.*

factory overhead. Usually an item of *manufacturing cost* other than *direct labor* or *direct materials.*

fair market price (value). See *fair value.*

fair presentation (fairness). One of the qualitative standards of financial reporting. When the *auditor's report* says that the *financial statements* "present fairly . . . ," the auditor means that the accounting alternatives used by the entity all comply with *GAAP.* In recent years, however, courts have ruled that conformity with *generally accepted accounting principles* may be insufficient grounds for an opinion that the statements are fair. *SAS No. 5* requires that the auditor judge the accounting principles used in the statements to be "appropriate in the circumstances" before attesting to fair presentation.

fair value, fair market price (value). Price (value) negotiated at *arm's length* between a willing buyer and a willing seller, each acting rationally in his or her own self-interest. The accountant may estimate this amount in the absence of a monetary transaction. This is sometimes measured as the present value of expected cash flows.

fair-value hedge. A hedge of an exposure to changes in the *fair value* of a recognized *asset* or *liability* or of an unrecognized firm commitment.

FASAC. *Financial Accounting Standards Advisory Council.*

FASB (Financial Accounting Standards Board). An independent board responsible, since 1973, for establishing *generally accepted accounting principles.* Its official pronouncements are *Statements of Financial Accounting Concepts (SFAC), Statements of Financial Accounting Standards (SFAS),* and *FASB Interpretations.* See also *Discussion Memorandum* and *Technical Bulletin.* Web Site: www.fasb.org.

FASB Interpretation. An official *FASB* statement interpreting the meaning of *Accounting Research Bulletins, APB Opinions,* and *Statements of Financial Accounting Standards.*

FASB Technical Bulletin. See *Technical Bulletin.*

favorable variance. An excess of actual *revenues* over expected revenues; an excess of *standard cost* over actual cost.

federal income tax. *Income tax* levied by the U.S. government on individuals and corporations.

Federal Insurance Contributions Act. See *FICA.*

Federal Unemployment Tax Act. See *FUTA.*

feedback. The process of informing employees about how their actual performance compares with the expected or desired level of performance, in the hope that the information will reinforce desired behavior and reduce unproductive behavior.

FEI. *Financial Executives Institute.*

FICA (Federal Insurance Contributions Act). The law that sets *Social Security taxes* and benefits.

fiduciary. Someone responsible for the custody or administration of property belonging to another; for example, an executor (of an estate), agent, receiver (in *bankruptcy*), or trustee (of a trust).

FIFO (first-in, first-out). The *inventory flow assumption* that firms use to compute *ending inventory* cost from most recent purchases and *cost of goods sold* from oldest purchases including beginning inventory. FIFO describes cost flow from the viewpoint of the income statement. From the balance sheet perspective, *LISH* (last-in, still-here) describes this same cost flow. Contrast with *LIFO.*

finance. As a verb, to supply with *funds* through the *issue* of stocks, bonds, notes, or mortgages or through the retention of earnings.

financial accounting. The accounting for *assets, equities, revenues,* and *expenses* of a business; primarily concerned with the historical reporting, to external users, of the *financial position* and operations of an *entity* on a regular, periodic basis. Contrast with *managerial accounting.*

Financial Accounting Foundation. The independent foundation (committee), governed by a board of trustees, that raises funds to support the *FASB* and *GASB.*

Financial Accounting Standards Advisory Council (FASAC). A committee of academics, preparers, attestors, and users giving advice to the *FASB* on matters of strategy and emerging issues. The council spends much of each meeting learning about current developments in standard-setting from the FASB staff.

Financial Accounting Standards Board. *FASB.*

Financial Executives Institute (FEI). An organization of financial executives, such as chief accountants, *controllers,* and treasurers, of large businesses. In recent years, the FEI has been a critic of the FASB because it views many of

the FASB requirements as burdensome while not *cost-effective.*

financial expense. An *expense* incurred in raising or managing *funds.*

financial flexibility. As defined by *SFAC No. 5,* "the ability of an entity to take effective actions to alter amounts and timing of cash flows so it can respond to unexpected needs and opportunities."

financial forecast. See *financial projection* for definition and contrast.

financial instrument. The *FASB* defines this term as follows.: "Cash, evidence of an ownership interest in an entity, or a contract that both:

[a] imposes on one entity a contractual obligation (1) to deliver cash or another financial instrument to a second entity or (2) to exchange financial instruments on potentially unfavorable terms with the second entity, and

[b] conveys to that second entity a contractual right (1) to receive cash or another financial instrument from the first entity or (2) to exchange other financial instruments on potentially favorable terms with the first entity."

financial leverage. See *leverage.*

financial position (condition). Statement of the *assets* and *equities* of a firm; displayed as a *balance sheet.*

financial projection. An estimate of *financial position,* results of *operations,* and changes in cash flows for one or more future periods based on a set of assumptions. If the assumptions do not represent the most likely outcomes, then *GAAS* call the estimate a "projection." If the assumptions represent the most probable outcomes, then *GAAS* call the estimate a "forecast." "Most probable" means that management has evaluated the assumptions and that they are management's judgment of the most likely set of conditions and most likely outcomes.

financial ratio. See *ratio.*

financial reporting objectives. Broad objectives that are intended to guide the development of specific *accounting standards;* set out by *FASB SFAC No. 1.*

Financial Reporting Release. Series of releases, issued by the SEC since 1982; replaces the *Accounting Series Release.* See *SEC.*

financial statements. The *balance sheet, income statement, statement of retained earnings, statement of cash flows,* statement of changes in *owners' equity accounts,* statement of *comprehensive income,* and *notes* thereto.

financial structure. *Capital structure.*

financial vice-president. Person in charge of the entire accounting and finance function; typically one of the three most influential people in the company.

financial year. Australia and UK: term for *fiscal year.*

financing activities. Obtaining resources from (a) owners and providing them with a return on and a return of their *investment* and (b) *creditors* and repaying amounts borrowed (or otherwise settling the obligation). See *statement of cash flows.*

financing lease. *Capital lease.*

finished goods (inventory account). Manufactured product ready for sale; a *current asset* (inventory) account.

firm. Informally, any business entity. (Strictly speaking, a firm is a *partnership*.)

firm commitment. The *FASB*, in *SFAS No. 133*, defines this as "an agreement with an unrelated party, binding on both parties and usually legally enforceable," which requires that the firm promise to pay a specified amount of a currency and that the firm has sufficient disincentives for nonpayment that the firm will probably make the payment. A firm commitment resembles a *liability*, but it is an *executory contract*, so is not a liability. *SFAS No. 133* allows the firm to recognize certain financial *hedges* in the balance sheet if they hedge firm commitments. The *FASB* first used the term in *SFAS No. 52* and *No. 80* but made the term more definite and more important in *SFAS No. 133*. This is an early, perhaps the first, step in changing the recognition criteria for assets and liabilities to exclude the test that the future benefit (asset) or obligation (liability) not arise from an executory contract.

first-in, first-out. See *FIFO*.

fiscal year. A period of 12 consecutive months chosen by a business as the *accounting period* for *annual reports*, not necessarily a *natural business year* or a calendar year.

FISH. An acronym, conceived by George H. Sorter, for *first-in, still-here*. FISH is the same cost flow assumption as *LIFO*. Many readers of accounting statements find it easier to think about inventory questions in terms of items still on hand. Think of LIFO in connection with *cost of goods sold* but of FISH in connection with *ending inventory*. See *LISH*.

fixed assets. *Plant assets*.

fixed assets turnover. *Sales* divided by average total *fixed assets*.

fixed benefit plan. A *defined-benefit plan*.

fixed budget. A plan that provides for specified amounts of *expenditures* and *receipts* that do not vary with activity levels; sometimes called a "static budget." Contrast with *flexible budget*.

fixed charges earned (coverage) ratio. *Income* before *interest expense* and *income tax expense* divided by interest expense.

fixed cost (expense). An *expenditure* or *expense* that does not vary with volume of activity, at least in the short run. See *capacity costs*, which include *enabling costs* and *standby costs*, and *programmed costs* for various subdivisions of fixed costs. See *cost terminology*.

fixed interval sampling. A method of choosing a sample: the analyst selects the first item from the population randomly, drawing the remaining sample items at equally spaced intervals.

fixed liability. *Long-term* liability.

fixed manufacturing overhead applied. The portion of *fixed manufacturing overhead cost* allocated to units produced during a period.

fixed overhead variance. Difference between *actual fixed manufacturing costs* and fixed manufacturing costs applied to production in a *standard costing system*.

flexible budget. *Budget* that projects receipts and expenditures as a function of activity levels. Contrast with *fixed budget*.

flexible budget allowance. With respect to manufacturing overhead, the total cost that a firm should have incurred at the level of activity actually experienced during the period.

float. *Checks* whose amounts the bank has *added* to the depositor's bank account but whose amounts the bank has not yet reduced from the *drawer's* bank account.

flow. The change in the amount of an item over time. Contrast with *stock*.

flow assumption. An assumption used when the firm makes a *withdrawal* from *inventory*. The firm must compute the cost of the withdrawal by a flow assumption if the firm does not use the *specific identification* method. The usual flow assumptions are *FIFO*, *LIFO*, and *weighted average*.

flow of costs. *Costs* passing through various classifications within an *entity* engaging, at least in part, in manufacturing activities. See the accompanying diagram for a summary of *product* and *period cost* flows.

flow-through method. Accounting for the *investment credit* to show all income statement benefits of the credit in the year of acquisition rather than spreading them over the life of the asset acquired (called the "deferral method"). The *APB* preferred the deferral method in *Opinion No. 2* (1962) but accepted the flow-through method in *Opinion No. 4* (1964). The term also applies to *depreciation* accounting in which the firm uses the *straight-line method* for financial reporting and an *accelerated depreciation* method for tax reporting. Followers of the flow-through method would not recognize a *deferred tax liability*. *APB Opinion No. 11* prohibits the use of the flow-through approach in financial reporting, although some regulatory commissions have used it.

FOB. Free on board some location (for example, FOB shipping point, FOB destination). The *invoice* price includes delivery at seller's expense to that location. Title to goods usually passes from seller to buyer at the FOB location.

folio. A page number or other identifying reference used in posting to indicate the source of entry.

footing. Adding a column of figures.

footnotes. More detailed information than that provided in the *income statement, balance sheet, statement of retained earnings,* and *statement of cash flows*. These are an integral part of the statements, and the *auditor's report* covers them. They are sometimes called "notes."

forecast. See *financial projection* for definition and contrast.

foreclosure. Occurs when a lender takes possession of property for his or her own use or sale after the borrower fails to make a required payment on a *mortgage*. Assume that the lender sells the property but that the proceeds of the sale are too small to cover the outstanding balance on the loan at the time of foreclosure. Under the terms of most mortgages, the lender becomes an unsecured creditor of the borrower for the still-unrecovered balance of the loan.

foreign currency. For *financial statements* prepared in a given currency, any other currency.

Flow of Costs (and Sales Revenue)

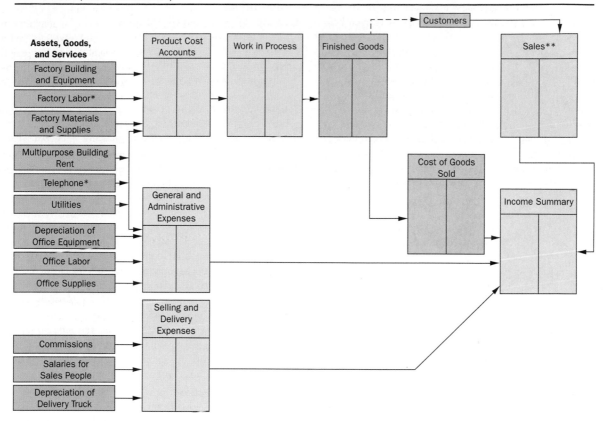

*The credit In the entry to record these items is usually to a payable, for all others, the credit is usually to an asset, or to an asset contra account.

**When the firm records sales to customers, it credits the Sales account. The debit is usually to Cash or Accounts Receivable.

foreign currency translation. Reporting in the currency used in financial statements the amounts denominated or measured in a different currency.

foreign exchange gain or loss. Gain or loss from holding *net* foreign *monetary items* during a period when the *exchange rate* changes.

foreign sales corporation. See *FSC.*

forfeited share. A share to which a subscriber has lost title because of nonpayment of a *call.*

Form 10-K. See *10-K.*

Form 20-F. See *20-F.*

forward contract. An agreement to purchase or sell a specific commodity or financial instrument for a specified price, the *forward price,* at a specified date. Contrast with *futures contract.* Typically, forward contracts are not traded on organized exchanges (unlike *futures contract*), so the parties to the agreement sacrifice liquidity but gain flexibility in setting contract quantities, qualities, and settlement dates.

forward-exchange contract. An agreement to exchange at a specified future date currencies of different countries at a specified rate called the "forward rate."

forward price. The price of a commodity for delivery at a specified future date; in contrast to the "spot price," the price of that commodity on the day of the price quotation.

franchise. A privilege granted or sold, such as to use a name or to sell products or services.

fraudulent conveyance. A transfer of goods or cash that a court finds illegal. *Creditors* of a *bankrupt* firm usually receive less than the firm owed them. For example, a creditor of a bankrupt firm might collect from the trustee of the bankrupt firm only $.60 for every dollar the bankrupt firm owed. Creditors, anticipating bankruptcy, sometimes attempt to persuade the firm to pay the debt in full before the firm declares bankruptcy, reducing the net assets available to other creditors. Bankruptcy laws have rules forbidding such transfers from a near-bankrupt firm to some of its creditors. Such a transfer is called a "fraudulent conveyance." Courts sometimes ask accountants to judge whether a firm had liabilities exceeding assets even before the firm went into bankruptcy. When the court can find that economic bankruptcy occurred before legal bankruptcy, it will declare transfers of assets to creditors after economic bankruptcy to be fraudulent conveyances and have the assets returned to the trustees (or to a legal entity called the "bankrupt's estate") for redistribution to all creditors.

fraudulent financial reporting. Intentional or reckless conduct that results in materially misleading *financial statements*. See *creative accounting*.

free cash flow. Financial statement analysts' term meaning *cash flow from operations + interest expense + income tax expense*.

free on board. *FOB*.

freight-in. The *cost* of freight or shipping incurred in acquiring *inventory*, preferably treated as a part of the cost of *inventory*; often shown temporarily in an *adjunct account* that the acquirer closes at the end of the period with other purchase accounts to the inventory account.

freight-out. The *cost* of freight or shipping incurred in selling *inventory*, treated by the seller as a selling *expense* in the period of sale.

FSC (foreign sales corporation). A foreign *corporation* engaging in certain export activities, some of whose *income* the United States exempts from federal *income tax*. A U.S. corporation need pay no income taxes on *dividends* distributed by an FSC out of *earnings* attributable to certain foreign income.

full absorption costing. The *costing* method that assigns all types of manufacturing costs (*direct material, direct labor, fixed* and *variable overhead*) to units produced; required by *GAAP;* also called "absorption costing." Contrast with *variable costing*.

full costing, full costs. The total cost of producing and selling a unit; often used in *long-term* profitability and pricing decisions. Full cost per unit equals *full absorption cost* per unit plus *marketing, administrative, interest,* and other *central corporate expenses,* per unit. The sum of full costs for all units equals total costs of the firm.

full disclosure. The reporting policy requiring that all significant or *material* information appear in the financial statements. See *fair presentation*.

fully diluted earnings per share. For *common stock,* smallest *earnings per share* figure that one can obtain by computing an earnings per share for all possible combinations of assumed *exercise* or *conversion* of *potentially dilutive securities*. This figure must appear on the *income statement* if it is less than 97 percent of earnings available to common shareholders divided by the average number of common shares outstanding during the period.

fully vested. Said of a *pension plan* when an employee (or his or her estate) has rights to all the benefits purchased with the employer's contributions to the plan even if the employee does not work for this employer at the time of death or retirement.

function. In governmental accounting, said of a group of related activities for accomplishing a service or regulatory program for which the governmental unit has responsibility; in mathematics, a rule for associating a number, called the dependent variable, with another number (or numbers), called independent variable(s).

functional classification. *Income statement* reporting form that classifies *expenses* by function, that is, cost of goods sold, administrative expenses, financing expenses, selling expenses. Contrast with *natural classification*.

functional currency. Currency in which an entity carries out its principal economic activity.

fund. An *asset* or group of assets set aside for a specific purpose. See also *fund accounting*.

fund accounting. The accounting for resources, obligations, and *capital* balances, usually of a not-for-profit or governmental *entity,* which the entity has segregated into *accounts* representing logical groupings based on legal, donor, or administrative restrictions or requirements. The groupings are "funds." The accounts of each fund are *self-balancing,* and from them one can prepare a *balance sheet* and an operating statement for each fund. See *fund* and *fund balance*.

fund balance. In governmental accounting, the excess of assets of a *fund* over its liabilities and reserves; the not-for-profit equivalent of *owners' equity*.

funded. Said of a *pension plan* or other obligation when the firm has set aside *funds* for meeting the obligation when it comes due. The federal law for pension plans requires that the firm fund all *normal costs* when it recognizes them as expenses. In addition, the firm must fund *prior service cost* of pension plans over 30 or over 40 years, depending on the circumstances.

funding. Replacing *short-term* liabilities with *long-term* debt.

funds. Generally *working capital*; current assets less current liabilities; sometimes used to refer to *cash* or to cash and *marketable securities*.

funds provided by operations. See *cash provided by operations*.

funds statement. An informal name often used for the *statement of cash flows*.

funny money. Said of securities, such as *convertible preferred stock, convertible bonds, options,* and *warrants,* that have aspects of *common shares* but that did not reduce reported *earnings per share* before the issuance of *APB Opinion No. 9* in 1966 and *No. 15* in 1969.

FUTA (Federal Unemployment Tax Act). Provides for taxes to be collected at the federal level, to help subsidize the individual states' administration of their unemployment compensation programs.

future value. Value at a specified future date of a sum increased at a specified *interest rate*.

futures contract. An agreement to purchase or sell a specific commodity or financial instrument for a specified price, at a specific future time or during a specified future period. Contrast with *forward contract.* When traded on an organized exchange, the exchange sets the minimum contract size and expiration date(s). The exchange requires that the holder of the contract settle in cash each day the fluctuations in the value of the contract. That is, each day, the exchange marks the contract to market value, called the "(daily) settlement price." A contract holder who has lost during the day must put up more cash, and a holder who has gained receives cash.

G

GAAP. *Generally accepted accounting principles;* a plural noun. In the UK and elsewhere, this means "generally accepted accounting practices."

GAAS. *Generally accepted auditing standards;* a plural noun. Do not confuse with *GAS.*

gain. Increase in *owners' equity* caused by a transaction that is not part of a firm's typical, day-to-day operations and not part of owners' *investment* or *withdrawals.* Accounting distinguishes the meaning of the term "gain" (or *loss*) from that of related terms. First, gains (and losses) generally refer to nonoperating, incidental, peripheral, or nonroutine transactions: gain on sale of land in contrast to *gross margin* on *sale* of *inventory.* Second, gains and losses are *net* concepts, not gross concepts: gain or loss results from subtracting some measure of *cost* from the measure of inflow. *Revenues* and *expenses,* on the other hand, are gross concepts; their difference is a net concept. Gain is nonroutine and net, *profit* or *margin* is routine and net; revenue from *continuing operations* is routine and gross; revenue from *discontinued operations* is nonroutine and gross. Loss is net but can be either routine ("loss on sale of inventory") or not ("loss on disposal of segment of business").

gain contingency. See *contingency.*

GAS. *Goods available for sale.* Do not confuse with *GAAS.*

GASB (Governmental Accounting Standards Board). An independent body responsible, since 1984, for establishing accounting standards for state and local government units. It is part of the *Financial Accounting Foundation,* parallel to the *FASB,* and currently consists of five members.

GbR (Gesellschaft des bürgerlichen Rechtes). Germany: a *partnership* whose members agree to share in specific aspects of their own separate business pursuits, such as an office. This partnership has no legal form and is not a separate accounting *entity.*

GDP Implicit Price Deflator (index). A *price index* issued quarterly by the Office of Business Economics of the U.S. Department of Commerce. This index attempts to trace the price level of all *goods and services* composing the *gross domestic product.* Contrast with *Consumer Price Index.*

gearing. UK: *financial leverage.*

gearing adjustment. A *revenue* representing part of a *holding gain.* Consider a firm that has part of its assets financed by

noncurrent liabilities and that has experienced *holding gains* on its *assets* during a period. All the increase in wealth caused by the holding gains belongs to the owners; none typically belongs to the lenders. Some British accounting authorities believe that published *income statements* should show part of the holding gain in *income* for the period. The part they would report in income is the fraction of the gain equal to the fraction that debt composes of total financing; for example, if debt equals 40 percent of total equities and the holding gain equals $100 for the period, the amount to appear in income for the period would be $40. Usage calls that part the "gearing adjustment."

general debt. A governmental unit's debt legally payable from general revenues and backed by the full faith and credit of the governmental unit.

general expenses. *Operating expenses* other than those specifically identified as cost of goods sold, selling, and administration.

general fixed asset (group of accounts). Accounts showing a governmental unit's long-term assets that are not accounted for in *enterprise, trust,* or intragovernmental service funds.

general fund. A nonprofit entity's assets and liabilities not specifically earmarked for other purposes; the primary operating fund of a governmental unit.

general journal. The formal record in which the firm records transactions, or summaries of similar transactions, in *journal entry* form as they occur. Use of the adjective "general" usually implies that the journal has only two columns for cash amounts or that the firm also uses various *special journals,* such as a *check register* or *sales journal.*

general ledger. The name for the formal *ledger* containing all the financial statement accounts. It has equal debits and credits, as evidenced by the *trial balance.* Some of the accounts in the general ledger may be *control accounts,* supported by details contained in *subsidiary ledgers.*

general partner. *Partnership* member who is personally liable for all debts of the partnership; contrast with *limited partner.*

general price index. A measure of the aggregate prices of a wide range of goods and services in the economy at one time relative to the prices during a base period. See *Consumer Price Index* and *GDP Implicit Price Deflator.* Contrast with *specific price index.*

general price level-adjusted statements. See *constant-dollar accounting.*

general price-level changes. Changes in the aggregate prices of a wide range of goods and services in the economy. These price measurements result from using a *general price index.* Contrast with *specific price changes.*

general purchasing power. The command of the dollar over a wide range of goods and services in the economy. The general purchasing power of the dollar is inversely related to changes in a general price index. See *general price index.*

general purchasing-power accounting. See *constant-dollar accounting.*

generally accepted accounting principles (GAAP). As previously defined by the *CAP, APB,* and now the *FASB,* the conventions, rules, and procedures necessary to define accepted accounting practice at a particular time; includes both broad guidelines and relatively detailed practices and procedures. In the United States the FASB defines GAAP to include accounting pronouncements of the *SEC* and other government agencies as well as a variety of authoritative sources, such as this book.

generally accepted auditing standards (GAAS). The standards, as opposed to particular procedures, that are promulgated by the *AICPA* (in *Statements on Auditing Standards*) and that concern "the auditor's professional quantities" and "the judgment exercised by him in the performance of his examination and in his report." Currently, there are ten such standards: three general ones (concerned with proficiency, independence, and degree of care to be exercised), three standards of field work, and four standards of reporting. The first standard of reporting requires that the *auditor's report* state whether the firm prepared the *financial statements* in accordance with *generally accepted accounting principles*. Thus the typical auditor's report says that the auditor conducted the examination in accordance with generally accepted auditing standards and that the firm prepared the statements in accordance with generally accepted accounting principles. See *auditor's report*.

geographic segment. A single operation or a group of operations that are located in a particular geographic area and that generate revenue, incur costs, and have assets used in or associated with generating such revenue.

G4+1. A group concerned with unifying accounting standards across countries. It originally comprised the *FASB, CICA* (Canada), the Accounting Standards Board (UK), and the Australian Accounting Standards Board, plus the *IASC*. Hence, the name: a group of four national standard-setters plus the *IASC*. The group now includes participants from New Zealand.

GIE (groupement d'intérêt économique). France: a joint venture, normally used for exports and research-and-development pooling.

GmbH (Gesellschaft mit beschränkter Haftung). Germany: a private company with an unlimited number of shareholders. Transfer of ownership can take place only with the consent of other shareholders. Contrast with *AG*.

goal congruence. The idea that all members of an organization have incentives to perform for a common interest, such as *shareholder* wealth maximization for a *corporation*.

going-concern assumption. For accounting purposes, accountants' assumption that a business will remain in operation long enough to carry out all its current plans. This assumption partially justifies the *acquisition cost* basis, rather than a *liquidation* or *exit value* basis, of accounting.

going public. Said of a business when its *shares* become widely traded rather than being closely held by relatively few shareholders; issuing shares to the general investing public.

goods. Items of merchandise, supplies, raw materials, or finished goods. Sometimes the meaning of "goods" is extended to include all *tangible* items, as in the phrase "goods and services."

goods available for sale. The sum of *beginning inventory* plus all acquisitions of merchandise or finished goods during an *accounting period*.

goods-in-process. *Work-in-process*.

goodwill. The excess of cost of an acquired firm (or operating unit) over the current *fair market value* of the separately identifiable *net assets* of the acquired unit. Before the acquiring firm can recognize goodwill, it must assign a *fair market value* to all identifiable assets, even when not recorded on the books of the acquired unit. For example, if a firm has developed a *patent* that does not appear on its books because of *SFAS No. 2,* if another company acquires the firm, the acquirer will recognize the patent at an amount equal to its estimated fair market value. The acquirer will compute the amount of goodwill only after assigning values to all assets it can identify. Informally, the term indicates the value of good customer relations, high employee morale, a well-respected business name, and so on, all of which the firm or analyst expects to result in greater-than-normal earning power.

goodwill method. A method of accounting for the *admission* of a new partner to a *partnership* when the new partner will receive a portion of capital different from the value of the *tangible* assets contributed as a fraction of tangible assets of the partnership. See *bonus method* for a description and contrast.

Governmental Accounting Standards Advisory Council. A group that consults with the *GASB* on agenda, technical issues, and the assignment of priorities to projects. It comprises more than a dozen members representing various areas of expertise.

Governmental Accounting Standards Board. *GASB*.

GPL (general price level). Usually used as an adjective modifying the word "accounting" to mean *constant-dollar accounting*.

GPLA (general price level-adjusted accounting). *Constant-dollar accounting*.

GPP (general purchasing power). An adjective modifying the word "accounting" to mean *constant-dollar accounting*.

graded vesting. Said of a *pension plan* in which not all employees currently have fully *vested* benefits. By law, the benefits must vest according to one of several formulas as time passes.

grandfather clause. An exemption in new accounting *pronouncements* exempting transactions that occurred before a given date from the new accounting treatment. For example, *APB Opinion No. 17,* adopted in 1970, exempted *goodwill* acquired before 1970 from required *amortization*. The term "grandfather" appears in the title to *SFAS No. 10*.

gross. Not adjusted or reduced by deductions or subtractions. Contrast with *net,* and see *gain* for a description of how the difference between net and gross affects usage of the terms *revenue, gain, expense,* and *loss.*

gross domestic product (GDP). The market value of all goods and services produced by capital or labor within a country, regardless of who owns the capital or of the nationality of the labor; most widely used measure of production within a country. Contrast with gross national product (GNP), which measures the market value of all goods and services produced with capital owned by, and labor services supplied by, the residents of that country regardless of where they work or where they own capital. In the United States in recent years, the difference between GDP and GNP equals about two-tenths of 1 percent of GDP.

gross margin. *Net sales* minus *cost of goods sold.*

gross margin percent. $100 \times (1 - cost\ of\ goods\ sold/net\ sales) = 100 \times (gross\ margin/net\ sales).$

gross national product (GNP). See *gross domestic product* for definition and contrast.

gross price method (of recording purchase or sales discounts). The firm records the *purchase* (or *sale*) at the *invoice price,* not deducting the amounts of *discounts* available. Later, it uses a *contra* account to purchases (or sales) to record the amounts of discounts taken. Since information on discounts lapsed will not emerge from this system, most firms should prefer the *net price method* of recording purchase discounts.

gross profit. *Gross margin.*

gross profit method. A method of estimating *ending inventory* amounts. First, the firm measures *cost of goods sold* as some fraction of sales; then, it uses the *inventory equation* to value *ending inventory.*

gross profit ratio. *Gross margin* divided by *net sales.*

gross sales. All *sales* at *invoice* prices, not reduced by *discounts, allowances, returns,* or other adjustments.

group depreciation. In calculating *depreciation* charges, a method that combines similar assets rather than depreciating them separately. It does not recognize gain or loss on retirement of items from the group until the firm sells or retires the last item in the group. See *composite life method.*

Group of 4 Plus 1. See *G4+1.*

guarantee. A promise to answer for payment of debt or performance of some obligation if the person liable for the debt or obligation fails to perform. A guarantee is a *contingency* of the *entity* making the promise. Often, writers use the words "guarantee" and "warranty" to mean the same thing. In precise usage, however, "guarantee" means some person's promise to perform a contractual obligation such as to pay a sum of cash, whereas "warranty" refers to promises about pieces of machinery or other products. See *warranty.*

H

half-year convention. In *tax accounting* under *ACRS,* and sometimes in *financial accounting,* an assumption that the firm acquired *depreciable assets* at midyear of the year of acquisition. When the firm uses this convention, it computes the *depreciation charge* for the year as one-half the charge that it would have used if it had acquired the assets at the beginning of the year.

hardware. The physical equipment or devices forming a computer and peripheral equipment.

hash total. Used to establish accuracy of data processing; a control that takes the sum of data items not normally added together (e.g., the sum of a list of part numbers) and subsequently compares that sum with a computer-generated total of the same values. If the two sums are identical, then the analyst takes some comfort that the two lists are identical.

Hasselback. An annual directory of accounting faculty at colleges and universities; gives information about the faculty's training and fields of specialization. James R. Hasselback, of Florida State University, has compiled the directory since the 1970s; Prentice-Hall distributes it. On-line, you can find it at the Rutgers University accounting Web Site: www.rutgers.edu/Accounting/.

hedge. To reduce, perhaps cancel altogether, one risk the entity already bears, by purchasing a security or other financial instrument. For example, a farmer growing corn runs the risk that corn prices may decline before the corn matures and can be brought to market. Such a farmer can arrange to sell the corn now for future delivery, hedging the risk of corn price changes. A firm may have a *receivable* denominated in German marks due in six months. It runs the risk that the exchange rate between the dollar and the mark will change and the firm will receive a smaller number of dollars in the future than it would receive from the same number of marks received today. Such a firm may hedge its exposure to risk of changes in the exchange rate between dollars and German marks in a variety of ways.

held-to-maturity securities. *Marketable debt securities* that a firm expects to, and has the ability to, hold to *maturity;* a classification important in *SFAS No. 115,* which generally requires the owner to carry marketable securities on the balance sheet at market value, not at cost. Under *SFAS No. 115,* the firm may show held-to-maturity debt securities at *amortized cost.* If the firm lacks either the expectation or the intent to hold the debt security to its maturity, then the firm will show that security at market value as a security *available for sale.*

hidden reserve. An amount by which a firm has understated *owners' equity,* perhaps deliberately. The understatement arises from an undervaluation of *assets* or overvaluation of *liabilities.* By undervaluing assets on this period's *balance sheet,* the firm can overstate *net income* in some future period by disposing of the asset: actual *revenues* less artificially low cost of assets sold yields artificially high net income. No *account* in the *ledger* has this title.

hire-purchase agreement (contract). UK: a *lease* containing a purchase *option.*

historical cost. *Acquisition cost; original cost;* a *sunk cost.*

historical cost/constant-dollar accounting. Accounting based on *historical cost* valuations measured in *constant dollars.* The method restates *nonmonetary items* to reflect changes in the *general purchasing power* of the dollar since the time the firm acquired specific *assets* or incurred specific *liabilities.* The method recognizes a *gain* or *loss* on *monetary items* as the firm holds them over time periods when the general purchasing power of the dollar changes.

historical exchange rate. The rate at which one currency converts into another at the date a transaction took place. Contrast with *current exchange rate.*

historical summary. A part of the *annual report* that shows items, such as *net income, revenues, expenses, asset* and *equity* totals, *earnings per share,* and the like, for five or ten periods including the current one. Usually not as much detail appears in the historical summary as in *comparative statements,* which typically report as much detail for the two preceding years as for the current year. Annual reports may contain both comparative statements and a historical summary.

holdback. Under the terms of a contract, a portion of the progress payments that the customer need not pay until the contractor has fulfilled the contract or satisfied financial obligations to subcontractors.

holding company. A company that confines its activities to owning *stock* in, and supervising management of, other companies. A holding company usually owns a controlling interest in—that is, more than 50 percent of the voting stock of—the companies whose stock it holds. Contrast with *mutual fund.* See *conglomerate.* In British usage, the term refers to any company with controlling interest in another company.

holding gain or loss. Difference between end-of-period price and beginning-of-period price of an asset held during the period. The financial statements ordinarily do not separately report realized holding gains and losses. Income does not usually report unrealized gains at all, except on *trading securities.* See *lower of cost or market.* See *inventory profit* for further refinement, including *gains* on *assets* sold during the period.

holding gain or loss net of inflation. Increase or decrease in the *current cost* of an asset while it is held; measured in units of *constant dollars.*

horizontal analysis. *Time-series analysis.*

horizontal integration. An organization's extension of activity in the same general line of business or its expansion into supplementary, complementary, or compatible products. Compare *vertical integration.*

house account. An account with a customer who does not pay sales commissions.

human resource accounting. A term used to describe a variety of proposals that seek to report the importance of human resources—knowledgeable, trained, and loyal employees—in a company's earning process and total assets.

hurdle rate. Required rate of return in a *discounted cash flow* analysis.

hybrid security. *Security,* such as a *convertible bond,* containing elements of both *debt* and *owners' equity.*

hypothecation. The *pledging* of property, without transfer of title or possession, to secure a loan.

I

IAA. *Interamerican Accounting Association.*

IASC. *International Accounting Standards Committee.*

ICMA (Institute of Certified Management Accountants). See *CMA* and *Institute of Management Accountants.*

ideal standard costs. *Standard costs* set equal to those that a firm would incur under the best-possible conditions.

IIA. *Institute of Internal Auditors.*

IMA. *Institute of Management Accountants.*

impairment. Reduction in *market value* of an *asset.* When the firm has information indicating that its long-lived *assets,* such as *plant,* identifiable *intangibles,* and *goodwill,* have declined in *market value* or will provide a smaller future benefit that originally anticipated, it tests to see if the decline in value is so drastic that the expected future cash flows from the asset have declined below *book value.* If then-current book value exceeds the sum of expected cash flows, an asset impairment has occurred. At the time the firm judges that an impairment has occurred, the firm writes down the book value of the asset to its then-current *fair value,* which is the market value of the asset or, if the firm cannot assess the market value, the expected *net present value* of the future cash flows.

implicit interest. *Interest* not paid or received. See *interest, imputed.* All transactions involving the deferred payment or receipt of cash involve interest, whether explicitly stated or not. The implicit interest on a single-payment *note* equals the difference between the amount collected at maturity and the amount lent at the start of the loan. One can compute the implicit *interest rate* per year for loans with a single cash inflow and a single cash outflow from the following equation:

$$\left[\frac{\text{Cash Received at Maturity}}{\text{Cash Lent}} \right]^{(1/t)} - 1$$

where t is the term of the loan in years; t need not be an integer.

imprest fund. *Petty cash fund.*

improvement. An *expenditure* to extend the useful life of an *asset* or to improve its performance (rate of output, cost) over that of the original asset; sometimes called "betterment." The firm capitalizes such expenditures as part of the asset's cost. Contrast with *maintenance* and *repair.*

imputed cost. A cost that does not appear in accounting records, such as the *interest* that a firm could earn on cash spent to acquire inventories rather than, say, government bonds. Or, consider a firm that owns the buildings it occupies. This firm has an imputed cost for rent in an amount equal to what it would have to pay to use similar buildings owned by another or equal to the amount it could collect from someone renting the premises from the firm. *Opportunity cost.*

imputed interest. See *interest, imputed.*

in the black (red). Operating at a profit (loss).

in-process R&D. When one firm acquires another, the acquired firm will often have *research and development* activities under way that, following *GAAP,* it has *expensed.* The acquiring firm will pay for these activities to the extent they have value and will then, following GAAP, write off the activities. For each dollar of in-process R&D the acquiring firm identifies and immediately *expenses,* it will have one less dollar of *goodwill* or other assets to *amortize.* Some acquirers have overstated the valuations of acquired in-process R&D in order to increase immediate *write-offs* and subsequent, recurring *income.*

incentive compatible compensation. Said of a compensation plan that induces managers to act for the interests of owners while acting also in their own interests. For example, consider that a time of rising prices and increasing inventories when using a *LIFO* cost flow assumption implies paying lower *income taxes* than using *FIFO.* A bonus scheme for managers based on accounting *net income* is not incentive-compatible because owners likely benefit more under LIFO, whereas managers benefit more if they report using FIFO. See *LIFO conformity rule* and *goal congruence.*

income. *Excess of revenues* and *gains* over *expenses* and *losses* for a period; *net income.* The term is sometimes used with an appropriate modifier to refer to the various intermediate amounts shown in a *multiple-step income statement* or to refer to revenues, as in "rental income." See *comprehensive income.*

income accounts. *Revenue* and *expense accounts.*

income before taxes. On the *income statement,* the difference between all *revenues* and *expenses* except *income tax* expense. Contrast with *net income.*

income determination. See *determine.*

income distribution account. *Temporary account* sometimes debited when the firm declares *dividends*; closed to *retained earnings.*

income from continuing operations. As defined by *APB Opinion No. 30,* all *revenues* less all *expenses* except for the following: results of operations (including *income tax* effects) that a firm has discontinued or will discontinue; *gains* or *losses,* including income tax effects, on disposal of segments of the business; gains or losses, including income tax effects, from *extraordinary items*; and the cumulative effect of *accounting changes.*

income from discontinued operations. *Income,* net of tax effects, from parts of the business that the firm has discontinued during the period or will discontinue in the near future. Accountants report such items on separate lines of the *income statement,* after *income from continuing operations* but before *extraordinary items.*

income (revenue) bond. See *special revenue debt.*

income smoothing. A method of timing business *transactions* or choosing *accounting principles* so that the firm reports smaller variations in *income* from year to year than it otherwise would. Although some managements set income smoothing as an objective, no standard-setter does.

income statement. The statement of *revenues, expenses, gains,* and *losses* for the period, ending with *net income* for the period. Accountants usually show the *earnings-per-share* amount on the income statement; the *reconciliation* of beginning and ending balances of *retained earnings* may also appear in a combined statement of income and retained earnings. See *income from continuing operations, income from discontinued operations, extraordinary items, multiple-step,* and *single-step.*

income summary. In problem solving, an *account* that serves as a surrogate for the *income statement.* In using an income summary, close all *revenue* accounts to the Income Summary as *credits* and all *expense* accounts as *debits.* The *balance* in the account, after you make all these *closing entries,* represents income or loss for the period. Then, close the income summary balance to retained earnings.

income tax. An annual tax levied by the federal and other governments on the income of an entity.

income tax allocation. See *deferred income tax (liability)* and *tax allocation:intra-statement.*

incremental. An adjective used to describe the increase in *cost, expense, investment, cash flow, revenue, profit,* and the like if the firm produces or sells one or more units or if it undertakes an activity. See *differential.*

incremental cost. See *incremental.*

incur. Said of an obligation of a firm, whether or not that obligation is *accrued.* For example, a firm incurs interest expense on a loan as time passes but accrues that interest only on payment dates or when it makes an *adjusting entry.*

indenture. See *bond indenture.*

independence. The mental attitude required of the *CPA* in performing the *attest* function. It implies that the CPA is impartial and that the members of the auditing CPA firm own no stock in the corporation being audited.

independent accountant. The *CPA* who performs the *attest* function for a firm.

independent variable. See *regression analysis.*

indeterminate-term liability. A *liability* lacking the criterion of being due at a definite time. This term is our own coinage to encompass the *minority interest.*

indexation. An attempt by lawmakers or parties to a contract to cope with the effects of *inflation.* Amounts fixed in law or contracts are "indexed" when these amounts change as a given measure of price changes. For example, a so-called escalator clause (COLA—cost of living allowance or adjustment) in a labor contract might provide that hourly wages will be increased as the *Consumer Price Index* increases. Many economists have suggested the indexation of numbers fixed in the *income tax* laws. If, for example, the personal *exemption* is $2,500 at the start of the period, if prices rise by 10 percent during the period, and if the personal exemption is indexed, then the personal exemption would automatically rise to $2,750 (= $2,500 + .10 × $2,500) at the end of the period.

indirect cost pool. Any grouping of individual costs that a firm does not identify with a *cost objective*.

indirect costs. Production costs not easily associated with the production of specific goods and services; *overhead costs*. Accountants may *allocate* them on some *arbitrary* basis to specific products or departments.

indirect labor (material) cost. An *indirect cost* for labor (material), such as for supervisors (supplies).

indirect method. See *statement of cash flows*.

individual proprietorship. *Sole proprietorship*.

Industry Audit Guides. A series of *AICPA* publications providing specific accounting and *auditing principles* for specialized situations. Audit guides have been issued covering government contractors, state and local government units, investment companies, finance companies, brokers and dealers in securities, and many other subjects.

inescapable cost. A *cost* that the firm or manager cannot avoid (see *avoidable*) because of an action. For example, if management shuts down two operating rooms in a hospital but still must employ security guards in unreduced numbers, the security costs are "inescapable" with respect to the decision to close the operating rooms.

inflation. A time of generally rising prices.

inflation accounting. Strictly speaking, *constant-dollar accounting*. Some writers incorrectly use the term to mean *current cost accounting*.

information circular. Canada: a document, accompanying the notice of a shareholders' meeting, prepared in connection with the solicitation of proxies by or on behalf of the management of the corporation. It contains information concerning the people making the solicitation, election of directors, appointment of auditors, and other matters to be acted on at the meeting.

information system. A system, sometimes formal and sometimes informal, for collecting, processing, and communicating data that are useful for the managerial functions of decision making, planning, and control and for financial reporting under the *attest* requirement.

inherent interest rate. *Implicit interest* rate.

insolvent. Unable to pay debts when due; said of a company even though *assets* exceed *liabilities*.

installment. Partial payment of a debt or partial collection of a receivable, usually according to a contract.

installment contracts receivable. The name used for *accounts receivable* when the firm uses the *installment method* of recognizing revenue. Its *contra account, unrealized gross margin,* appears on the balance sheet as a subtraction from the amount receivable.

installment sales. Sales on account when the buyer promises to pay in several separate payments, called *installments*. The seller may, but need not, account for such sales using the *installment method*. If the seller accounts for installment sales with the sales *basis of revenue recognition* for finan-

cial reporting but with the installment method for income tax returns, then it will have *deferred income tax (liability)*.

installment (sales) method. Recognizing *revenue* and *expense* (or *gross margin*) from a sales transaction in proportion to the fraction of the selling price collected during a period; allowed by the *IRS* for income tax reporting but acceptable in *GAAP* (*APB Opinion No. 10*) only when the firm cannot estimate cash collections with reasonable precision. See *realized* (and *unrealized*) *gross margin*.

Institute of Certified Management Accountants (ICMA). See *CMA* and *Institute of Management Accountants*.

Institute of Internal Auditors (IIA). The national association of accountants who are engaged in internal auditing and are employed by business firms; administers a comprehensive professional examination. Those who pass the exam qualify to be designated *CIA* (Certified Internal Auditor).

Institute of Management Accountants (IMA). Formerly, the National Association of Accountants, NAA; a society open to those engaged in management accounting; parent organization of the *ICMA,* which oversees the *CMA* program.

insurance. A contract for reimbursement of specific losses; purchased with insurance premiums. "Self-insurance" is not insurance but is merely the noninsured's willingness to assume the risk of incurring losses while saving the premium.

intangible asset. A nonphysical right that gives a firm an exclusive or preferred position in the marketplace. Examples are *copyright, patent, trademark, goodwill, organization costs, capitalized* advertising cost, computer programs, licenses for any of the preceding, government licenses (e.g., broadcasting or the right to sell liquor), *leases,* franchises, mailing lists, exploration permits, import and export permits, construction permits, and marketing quotas. Commonly, accountants define "intangible" using a "for example" list, as we have just done, because accounting has been unable to devise a definition of "intangible" that will include items such as those listed above but exclude stock and bond certificates. Accountants classify these items as tangibles, even though they give their holders a preferred position in receiving dividends and interest payments.

Interamerican Accounting Association (IAA). An organization, headquartered in Miami, devoted to facilitating interaction between accounting practitioners in the Americas.

intercompany elimination. See *eliminations*.

intercompany profit. Profit within an organization. If one *affiliated company* sells to another, and the goods remain in the second company's *inventory* at the end of the period, then the first company has not yet realized a *profit* by a sale to an outsider. The profit is "intercompany profit," and the accountant eliminates it from net *income* when preparing *consolidated income statements* or when the firm uses the *equity method*.

intercompany transaction. *Transaction* between a *parent company* and a *subsidiary* or between subsidiaries in a *consolidated entity;* the accountant must eliminate the effects of such a transaction when preparing *consolidated financial statements*. See *intercompany profit*.

intercorporate investment. Occurs when a given *corporation* owns *shares* or *debt* issued by another.

interdepartment monitoring. An *internal control* device. The advantage of allocating *service department costs* to *production departments* stems from the incentives that this gives those charged with the costs to control the costs incurred in the service department. That process of having one group monitor the performance of another is interdepartment monitoring.

interest. The charge or cost for using cash, usually borrowed funds. Interest on one's own cash used is an *opportunity cost, imputed interest.* The amount of interest for a loan is the total amount paid by a borrower to a lender less the amount paid by the lender to the borrower. Accounting seeks to allocate that interest over the time of the loan so that the interest rate (= interest charge/amount borrowed) stays constant each period See *interest rate* for discussion of the quoted amount. See *effective interest rate* and *nominal interest rate.*

interest, imputed. The difference between the face amount and the present value of a promise. If a borrower merely promises to pay a single amount, sometime later than the present, then the face amount the borrower will repay at *maturity* will exceed the present value (computed at a *fair market* interest rate, called the "imputed interest rate") of the promise. See also *imputed cost.*

interest factor. One plus the *interest* rate.

interest method. See *effective interest method.*

interest rate. A basis used for computing the cost of borrowing funds; usually expressed as a ratio between the number of currency units (e.g., dollars) charged for a period of time and the number of currency units borrowed for that same period of time. When the writers and speakers do not state a period, they almost always mean a period of one year. See *interest, simple interest, compound interest, effective (interest) rate,* and *nominal interest rate.*

interest rate swap. See *swap.*

interfund accounts. In governmental accounting, the accounts that show transactions between funds, especially interfund receivables and payables.

interim statements. Statements issued for periods less than the regular, annual *accounting period.* The *SEC* requires most corporations to issue interim statements on a quarterly basis. In preparing interim reports, a problem arises that the accountant can resolve only by understanding whether interim reports should report on the interim period (1) as a self-contained accounting period or (2) as an integral part of the year so that analysts can make forecasts of annual performance. For example, assume that at the end of the first quarter, a retailer has dipped into old LIFO layers, depleting its *inventory,* so that it computes *LIFO cost of goods sold* artificially low and *net income* artificially high, relative to the amounts the firm would have computed if it had made the "normal" purchases, equal to or greater than sales. The retailer expects to purchase inventory sufficiently large so that when it computes cost of goods sold for the year,

there will be no *dips into old LIFO layers* and income will not be artificially high. The first approach will compute the quarterly income from low cost of goods sold using data for the dips that have actually occurred by the end of the quarter. The second approach will compute quarterly income from cost of goods sold assuming that purchases were equal to "normal" amounts and that the firm did not dip into old LIFO layers. *APB Opinion No. 28* and the *SEC* require that interim reports be constructed largely to satisfy the second purpose.

internal audit, internal auditor. An *audit* conducted by the firm's own employees, called "internal auditors," to ascertain whether the firm's *internal control* procedures work as planned. Contrast with an external audit conducted by a *CPA.*

internal controls. Policies and procedures designed to provide management with reasonable assurances that employees behave in a way that enables the firm to meet its organizational goals. See *control system.*

internal rate of return (IRR). The discount rate that equates the net *present value* of a stream of cash outflows and inflows to zero.

internal reporting. Reporting for management's use in planning and control. Contrast with *external reporting* for financial statement users.

Internal Revenue Service (IRS). Agency of the U.S. Treasury Department responsible for administering the Internal Revenue Code and collecting income and certain other taxes.

International Accounting Standards Committee (IASC). An organization that promotes the international harmonization of accounting standards. Web Site: www.iasc.org.uk.

International Organization of Securities Commissions. *IOSCO.*

interperiod tax allocation. See *deferred income tax (liability).*

interpolation. The estimation of an unknown number intermediate between two (or more) known numbers.

Interpretations. See *FASB Interpretation.*

intrastatement tax allocation. See *tax allocation: intrastatement.*

inventoriable costs. *Costs* incurred that the firm adds to the cost of manufactured products; *product costs (assets)* as opposed to *period expenses.*

inventory. As a noun, the *balance* in an asset *account,* such as raw materials, supplies, work-in-process, and finished goods; as a verb, to calculate the *cost* of goods on hand at a given time or to count items on hand physically.

inventory equation. *Beginning inventory* + net additions − withdrawals = *ending inventory.* Ordinarily, additions are net purchases, and withdrawals are *cost of goods sold.* Notice that ending inventory, appearing on the balance sheet, and cost of goods sold, appearing on the income statement, must add to a fixed sum. The larger is one; the smaller must be the other. In valuing inventories, the firm usually knows beginning inventory and net purchases. Some inventory methods (for example, some applications of the *retail inventory method*) measure costs of goods sold and use the equation to find the cost of ending inventory. Most methods measure cost of ending inventory and use the equation to find the cost of goods sold (withdrawals). In *current cost* (in contrast to *historical cost) accounting,* additions (in the equation) include holding gains, whether realized or not. Thus the current cost inventory equation is as follows: Beginning Inventory (at Current Cost) + Purchases (where Current Cost is Historical Cost) + Holding Gains (whether Realized or Not) − Ending Inventory (at Current Cost) = Cost of Goods Sold (Current Cost).

inventory holding gains. See *inventory profit.*

inventory layer. See *LIFO inventory layer.*

inventory profit. A term with several possible meanings. Consider the data in the accompanying illustration. The firm uses a *FIFO cost flow assumption* and derives its *historical cost* data. The assumed *current cost* data resemble those that the FASB suggested in *SFAS No. 89.* The term *income from continuing operations* refers to revenues less expenses based on current, rather than historical, costs. To that subtotal, add realized holding gains to arrive at realized (conventional) income. To that, add unrealized holding gains to

arrive at economic income. The term "inventory profit" often refers (for example in some *SEC* releases) to the realized holding gain, $110 in the illustration. The amount of inventory profit will usually be material when the firm uses FIFO and when prices rise. Other analysts, including us, prefer to use the term "inventory profit" to refer to the total *holding gain,* $300 (= $110 + $190, both realized and unrealized), but writers use this meaning less often. In periods of rising prices and increasing inventories, the realized holding gains under a FIFO cost flow assumption will exceed those under LIFO. In the illustration, for example, assume under LIFO that the historical cost of goods sold is $4,800, that historical LIFO cost of beginning inventory is $600, and that historical LIFO cost of ending inventory is $800. Then income from continuing operations, based on current costs, remains $350 (= $5,200 − $4,850), realized holding gains are $50 (= $4,850 − $4,800), realized income is $400 (= $350 + $50), the unrealized holding gain for the year is $250 [= ($1,550 − $800) − ($1,100 − $600)], and economic income is $650 (= $350 + $50 + $250). The cost flow assumption has only one real effect on this series of calculations: the split of the total holding gain into realized and unrealized portions. Thus, economic income does not depend on the cost flow assumption. Holding gains total $300 in the illustration. The choice of cost flow assumption determines the portion reported as realized.

inventory turnover. Number of times the firm sells the average *inventory* during a period; *cost of goods sold* for a period divided by average inventory for the period. See *ratio.*

invested capital. *Contributed capital.*

investee. A company in which another entity, the "investor," owns stock.

investing activities. Lending funds and collecting *principal* (but not *interest,* which is an *operating activity*) on those loans; acquiring and selling *securities* or productive *assets* expected to produce *revenue* over several *periods.*

investment. An *expenditure* to acquire property or other *assets* in order to produce *revenue*; the asset so acquired; hence a *current* expenditure made in anticipation of future income; said of other companies' *securities* held for the long term and appearing in a separate section of the *balance sheet*; in this context, contrast with *marketable securities.*

investment center. A *responsibility center,* with control over *revenues, costs,* and *assets.*

investment credit. A reduction in income tax liability sometimes granted by the federal government to firms that buy new equipment. This item is a credit in that the taxpayer deducts it from the tax bill, not from pretax income. The tax credit has been a given percentage of the purchase price of the assets purchased. The government has changed the actual rules and rates over the years. As of 1999, there is no investment credit. See *flow-through method* and *carryforward.*

investment decision. The decision whether to undertake an action involving production of goods or services; contrast with financing decision.

Inventory Profit Illustration

	(Historical) Acquisition Cost Assuming FIFO	Current Cost
ASSUMED DATA		
Inventory, 1/1	$ 900	$1,100
Inventory, 12/31	1,160	1,550
Cost of Goods Sold for the Year	4,740	4,850
Sales for the Year	$5,200	$5,200
INCOME STATEMENT FOR THE YEAR		
Sales	$5,200	$5,200
Cost of Goods Sold	4,740	4,850
(1) Income from Continuing Operations		$ 350
Realized Holding Gains		110[a]
(2) Realized Income = Conventional Net Income (under FIFO)	$ 460	$ 460
Unrealized Holding Gain		190[b]
(3) Economic Income		$ 650

[a]Realized holding gain during a period is current cost of goods sold less historical cost of goods sold; for the year the realized holding gain under FIFO is $110 = $4,850 − $4,740. Some refer to this as "inventory profit."

[b]The total unrealized holding gain at any time is current cost of inventory on hand at that time less historical cost of that inventory. The unrealized holding gain during a period is unrealized holding gain at the end of the period less the unrealized holding gain prior to this year is: $200 = $1,100 − $900. Unrealized holding gain during the year = ($1,550 − $1,160) − ($1,100 − 900) = $390 − $200 = $190.

investment tax credit. *Investment credit.*

investment turnover ratio. A term that means the same thing as *total assets turnover ratio.*

investments. A balance sheet heading for tangible assets held for periods longer than the operating cycle and not used in revenue production (assets not meeting the definitions of *current assets* or *property, plant, and equipment*).

invoice. A document showing the details of a sale or purchase *transaction.*

IOSCO (International Organization of Securities Commissions). The name, since 1983, of a confederation of regulators of securities and futures markets. Members come from over 80 countries. The IOSCO encourages the *IASC* to eliminate accounting alternatives and to ensure that accounting standards are detailed and complete, with adequate disclosure requirements, and that financial statements are user-friendly.

I.O.U. An informal document acknowledging a debt, setting out the amount of the debt and signed by the debtor.

IRR. *Internal rate of return.*

IRS. *Internal Revenue Service.*

isoprofit line. On a graph showing feasible production possibilities of two products that require the use of the same, limited resources, a line showing all feasible production possibility combinations with the same *profit* or, perhaps, *contribution margin.*

issue. A corporation exchange of its stock (or *bonds*) for cash or other *assets.* Terminology says the corporation "issues," not "sells," that stock (or bonds). Also used in the context of withdrawing supplies or materials from inventory for use in operations and of drawing a *check.*

issued shares. Those shares of *authorized capital stock* that a *corporation* has distributed to the shareholders. See *issue.* Shares of *treasury stock* are legally issued but are not *outstanding* for the purpose of voting, *dividend declarations,* and *earnings-per-share* calculations.

J

JIT. See *just-in-time inventory.*

job cost sheet. A schedule showing actual or budgeted inputs for a special order.

job development credit. The name used for the *investment credit* in the 1971 tax law, since repealed, on this subject.

job (-order) costing. Accumulation of *costs* for a particular identifiable batch of product, known as a job, as it moves through production.

joint cost. Cost of simultaneously producing or otherwise acquiring two or more products, called joint products, that a firm must, by the nature of the process, produce or acquire together, such as the cost of beef and hides of cattle. Generally, accounting allocates the joint costs of production to the individual products in proportion to their respective sales value (or, sometimes and usually not preferred, their respective physical quantities) at the *split-off* point. Other

examples include *central corporate expenses* and *overhead* of a department when it manufactures several products. See *common cost* and *sterilized allocation.*

joint cost allocation. See *joint cost.*

joint product. One of two or more outputs with significant value that a firm must produce or acquire simultaneously. See *by-product* and *joint cost.*

journal. The place where the firm records transactions as they occur; the book of original entry.

journal entry. A dated *journal* recording, showing the accounts affected, of equal *debits* and *credits,* with an explanation of the *transaction,* if necessary.

Journal of Accountancy. A monthly publication of the *AICPA.*

Journal of Accounting and Economics. Scholarly journal published by the William E. Simon Graduate School of Business Administration of the University of Rochester.

Journal of Accounting Research. Scholarly journal containing articles on theoretical and empirical aspects of accounting; published by the Graduate School of Business of the University of Chicago.

journal voucher. A *voucher* documenting (and sometimes authorizing) a *transaction,* leading to an entry in the *journal.*

journalize. To make an entry in a *journal.*

judgment(al) sampling. A method of choosing a sample in which the analyst subjectively selects items for examination, in contrast to selecting them by statistical methods. Compare *random sampling.*

junk bond. A low-rated *bond* that lacks the merit and characteristics of an investment-grade bond. It offers high yields, typically in excess of 15 percent per year, but also possesses high risk of default. Sometimes writers, less pejoratively, call these "high-yield bonds." No clear line separates junk from nonjunk bonds.

just-in-time inventory (production) (JIT). In managing *inventory* for manufacturing, system in which a firm purchases or manufactures each component just before the firm uses it. Contrast with systems in which firms acquire or manufacture many parts in advance of needs. JIT systems have much smaller carrying costs for inventory, ideally none, but run higher risks of incurring *stockout* costs.

K

k. Two to the tenth power (2^{10} or 1,024), when referring to computer storage capacity. The one-letter abbreviation derives from the first letter of the prefix "kilo-" (which means 1,000 in decimal notation).

Kaizen costing. A management concept that seeks continuous improvements, likely occurring in small incremental amounts, by refinements of all components of a production process.

KG (Kommanditgesellschaft). Germany: similar to a general partnership (*OHG*) except that some of its members may limit their liability. One of the partners must be a *general partner* with unlimited liability.

kiting. A term with slightly different meanings in banking and auditing contexts. In both, however, it refers to the wrongful practice of taking advantage of the *float,* the time that elapses between the deposit of a *check* in one bank and its collection at another. In the banking context, an individual deposits in Bank A a check written on Bank B. He (or she) then writes checks against the deposit created in Bank A. Several days later, he deposits in Bank B a check written on Bank A, to cover the original check written on Bank B. Still later, he deposits in Bank A a check written on Bank B. The process of covering the deposit in Bank A with a check written on Bank B and vice versa continues until the person can arrange an actual deposit of cash. In the auditing context, kiting refers to a form of *window dressing* in which the firm makes the amount of the account Cash in Bank appear larger than it actually is by depositing in Bank A a check written on Bank B without recording the check written on Bank B in the *check register* until after the close of the *accounting period.*

know-how. Technical or business information that is of the type defined under *trade secret* but that a firm does not maintain as a secret. The rules of accounting for this *asset* are the same as for other *intangibles.*

L

labor variances. The *price* (or *rate*) and *quantity* (or *usage*) *variances* for *direct labor* inputs in a *standard costing system.*

laid-down cost. Canada and UK: the sum of all direct costs incurred for procurement of goods up to the time of physical receipt, such as invoice cost plus customs and excise duties, freight and cartage.

land. An *asset* shown at *acquisition cost* plus the *cost* of any nondepreciable *improvements;* in accounting, implies use as a plant or office site rather than as a *natural resource,* such as timberland or farmland.

lapping (accounts receivable). The theft, by an employee, of cash sent in by a customer to discharge the latter's *payable.* The employee conceals the theft from the first customer by using cash received from a second customer. The employee conceals the theft from the second customer by using cash received from a third customer, and so on. The process continues until the thief returns the funds or can make the theft permanent by creating a fictitious *expense* or receivable write-off or until someone discovers the fraud.

lapse. To expire; said of, for example, an insurance policy or discounts that are made available for prompt payment and that the purchaser does not take.

last-in, first-out. See *LIFO.*

layer. See *LIFO inventory layer.*

lead time. The time that elapses between placing an order and receiving the *goods* or *services* ordered.

learning curve. A mathematical expression of the phenomenon that incremental unit costs to produce decrease as managers and labor gain experience from practice.

lease. A contract calling for the lessee (user) to pay the lessor (owner) for the use of an asset. A cancelable lease allows the lessee to cancel at any time. A noncancelable lease requires payments from the lessee for the life of the lease and usually shares many of the economic characteristics of *debt financing.* Most long-term noncancelable leases meet the usual criteria for classifying them as *liabilities,* and GAAP require the firm to show them as liabilities. *SFAS No. 13* and the *SEC* require disclosure, in notes to the financial statements, of the commitments for long-term noncancelable leases. See *capital lease* and *operating lease.*

leasehold. The *asset* representing the right of the lessee to use leased property. See *lease* and *leasehold improvement.*

leasehold improvement. An *improvement* to leased property. The firm should *amortize* it over the *service life* or the life of the lease, whichever is shorter.

least and latest rule. Paying the least amount of taxes as late as possible within the law to minimize the *present value* of tax payments for a given set of operations. Sensible taxpayers will follow this rule. When a taxpayer knows that tax rates will increase later, the taxpayer may reduce the present value of the tax burden by paying smaller taxes sooner. Each set of circumstances requires its own computations.

ledger. A book of accounts; book of final entry. See *general ledger* and *subsidiary ledger.* Contrast with *journal.*

legal capital. The amount of *contributed capital* that, according to state law, the firm must keep permanently in the firm as protection for creditors.

legal entity. See *entity.*

lender. See *loan.*

lessee. See *lease.*

lessor. See *lease.*

letter stock. Privately placed *common shares;* so called because the *SEC* requires the purchaser to sign a letter of intent not to resell the shares.

leverage. More than proportional result from extra effort or financing. Some measure of output increases faster than the measure of input. "Operating leverage" refers to the tendency of *net income* to rise at a faster rate than sales in the presence of *fixed costs.* A doubling of sales, for example, usually implies a more than doubling of net income. "Financial leverage" (or "capital leverage") refers to an increase in rate of return larger than the increase in explicit financing costs—the increased rate of return on *owners' equity* (see *ratio*) when an *investment* earns a return larger than the after-tax *interest rate* paid for *debt* financing. Because the interest charges on debt usually do not change, any *incremental* income benefits owners and none benefits debtors. When writers use the term "leverage" without a qualifying adjective, the term usually refers to financial leverage, the use of *long-term* debt in securing *funds* for the *entity.*

leveraged lease. A special form of lease involving three parties: a *lender,* a *lessor,* and a *lessee.* The lender, such as a bank or insurance company, lends a portion, say 80 percent, of the cash required for acquiring the *asset.* The lessor puts up the remainder, 20 percent, of the cash required. The lessor acquires the asset with the cash, using the asset as security for the loan, and leases it to the lessee on a *noncancelable* basis. The lessee makes periodic lease payments to the lessor, who in turn makes payments on the loan to the lender. Typically, the lessor has no obligation for the debt to the lender other than transferring a portion of the receipts from the lessee. If the lessee should default on the required lease payments, then the lender can repossess the leased asset. The lessor usually has the right to benefit from the tax deductions for *depreciation* on the asset, for *interest expense* on the loan from the lender, and for any *investment credit*. The lease is leveraged in the sense that the lessor, who takes most of the risks and enjoys most of the rewards of ownership, usually borrows most of the funds needed to acquire the asset. See *leverage*.

liability. An obligation to pay a definite (or reasonably definite) amount at a definite (or reasonably definite) time in return for a past or current benefit (that is, the obligation arises from a transaction that is not an *executory contract*); a probable future sacrifice of economic benefits arising from present obligations of a particular *entity* to *transfer assets* or to provide services to other entities in the future as a result of past *transactions* or events. *SFAC No. 6* says that "probable" refers to that which we can reasonably expect or believe but that is neither certain nor proved. A liability has three essential characteristics: (1) the obligation to transfer assets or services has a specified or knowable date, (2) the entity has little or no discretion to avoid the transfer, and (3) the event causing the obligation has already happened, that is, it is not executory.

lien. The right of person A to satisfy a claim against person B by holding B's property as security or by seizing B's property.

life annuity. A *contingent annuity* in which payments cease at the death of a specified person(s), usually the *annuitant(s)*.

LIFO (last-in, first-out). An *inventory* flow assumption in which the *cost of goods sold* equals the cost of the most recently acquired units and a firm computes the *ending inventory cost* from the costs of the oldest units. In periods of rising prices and increasing inventories, LIFO leads to higher reported expenses and therefore lower reported income and lower balance sheet inventories than does FIFO. Contrast with *FIFO*. See *FISH* and *inventory profit*.

LIFO conformity rule. The *IRS* rule requiring that companies that use a *LIFO cost flow assumption* for *income taxes* must also use LIFO in computing *income* reported in *financial statements* and forbidding the disclosure of pro forma results from using any other cost flow assumption.

LIFO, dollar-value method. See *dollar-value LIFO method*.

LIFO inventory layer. A portion of LIFO inventory cost on the *balance sheet*. The *ending inventory* in physical quantity will usually exceed the *beginning inventory*. The *LIFO cost flow assumption* assigns to this increase in physical quantities a cost computed from the prices of the earliest purchases during the year. The LIFO inventory then consists of layers, sometimes called "slices," which typically consist of relatively small amounts of physical quantities from each of the past years when purchases in physical units exceeded sales in units. Each layer carries the prices from near the beginning of the period when the firm acquired it. The earliest layers will typically (in periods of rising prices) have prices much less than current prices. If inventory quantities should decline in a subsequent period—a "dip into old LIFO layers"—the latest layers enter cost of goods sold first.

LIFO reserve. *Unrealized holding gain* in *ending inventory*: current or *FIFO historical* cost of ending inventory less LIFO *historical cost*. A better term for this concept is "excess of current cost over LIFO historical cost." See *reserve*.

limited liability. The legal concept that shareholders of corporations are not personally liable for debts of the company.

limited partner. A *partnership* member who is not personally liable for debts of the partnership. Every partnership must have at least one *general partner*, who is fully liable.

line-of-business reporting. See *segment reporting*.

line of credit. An agreement with a bank or set of banks for short-term borrowings on demand.

linear programming. A mathematical tool for finding profit-maximizing (or cost-minimizing) combinations of products to produce when a firm has several products that it can produce but faces linear constraints on the resources available in the production processes or on maximum and minimum production requirements.

liquid. Said of a business with a substantial amount (the amount is unspecified) of *working capital,* especially *quick assets*.

liquid assets. *Cash, current marketable securities,* and sometimes, *current receivables*.

liquidating dividend. A *dividend* that a firm declares in the winding up of a business to distribute its assets to the shareholders. Usually the recipient treats this as a return of *investment,* not as *revenue*.

liquidation. Payment of a debt; sale of assets in closing down a business or a segment thereof.

liquidation value per share. The amount each *share* of stock will receive if the *board* dissolves a corporation; for *preferred stock* with a liquidation preference, a stated amount per share.

liquidity. Refers to the availability of *cash,* or near-cash resources, for meeting a firm's obligations.

LISH. An acronym, conceived by George H. Sorter, for *last-in, still-here.* LISH is the same cost flow assumption as *FIFO.* Many readers of accounting statements find it easier to think about inventory questions in terms of items still on hand. Think of FIFO in connection with *cost of goods sold* but of LISH in connection with *ending inventory.* See *FISH*.

list price. The published or nominally quoted price for goods.

list price method. See *trade-in transaction*.

loan. An arrangement in which the owner of property, called the lender, allows someone else, called the borrower, the use of the property for a period of time, which the agreement setting up the loan usually specifies. The borrower promises to return the property to the lender and, often, to make a payment for the use of the property. This term is generally used when the property is *cash* and the payment for its use is *interest*.

LOCOM. *Lower of cost or market.*

long-lived (term) asset. An asset whose benefits the firm expects to receive over several years; a *noncurrent* asset, usually includes *investments, plant assets,* and *intangibles*.

long-term (construction) contract accounting. The *percentage-of-completion method* of *revenue* recognition; sometimes used to mean the *completed contract method*.

long-term debt ratio. *Noncurrent liabilities* divided by total *assets*.

long-term liability (debt). *Noncurrent liability*.

long-term, long-run. A term denoting a time or time periods in the future. How far in the future depends on context. For some securities traders, "long-term" can mean anything beyond the next hour or two. For most managers, it means anything beyond the next year or two. For government policymakers, it can mean anything beyond the next decade or two. For geologists, it can mean millions of years.

long-term solvency risk. The risk that a firm will not have sufficient *cash* to pay its *debts* sometime in the *long run*.

loophole. Imprecise term meaning a technicality allowing a taxpayer (or *financial statements*) to circumvent the intent, without violating the letter, of the law (or *GAAP*).

loss. Excess of *cost* over net proceeds for a single transaction; negative *income* for a period; a cost expiration that produced no *revenue*. See *gain* for a discussion of related and contrasting terms and how to distinguish loss from *expense*.

loss contingency. See *contingency*.

lower of cost or market (LOCOM). A basis for valuation of *inventory*. This basis sets inventory value at the lower of *acquisition cost* or *current replacement cost* (market), subject to the following constraints. First, the market value of an item used in the computation cannot exceed its *net realizable value*—an amount equal to selling price less reasonable costs to complete production and to sell the item. Second, the market value of an item used in the computation cannot be less than the net realizable value minus the normal *profit* ordinarily realized on disposition of completed items of this type. The basis chooses the lower-of-cost-or-market valuation as the lower of acquisition *cost* or replacement cost *(market)* subject to the upper and lower bounds on replacement cost established in the first two steps. Thus,

Market Value = Midvalue of (Replacement Cost, Net Realizable Value, Net Realizable Value Less Normal Profit Margin)

Lower of Cost or Market Valuation = Minimum (Acquisition Cost, Market Value)

The accompanying exhibit illustrates the calculation of the lower-of-cost-or-market valuation for four inventory items. Notice that each of the four possible outcomes occurs once in measuring lower of cost or market. Item 1 uses acquisition cost; item 2 uses net realizable value; item 3 uses replacement cost; and item 4 uses net realizable value less normal profit margin.

	Item			
	1	**2**	**3**	**4**
Calculation of Market Value				
(a) Replacement Cost	$92	$96	$92	$96
(b) Net Realizable Value	95	95	95	95
(c) Net Realizable Value Less Normal Profit Margin [= (b) − $9]	86	86	86	86
(d) Market = Midvalue [(a), (b), (c)]	92	95	92	95
Calculation of Lower of Cost or Market				
(e) Acquisition Cost	90	97	96	90
(f) Market [= (d)]	92	95	92	95
(g) Lower of Cost or Market = Minimum [(e), (f)]	90	95	92	90

A taxpayer may not use the lower-of-cost-or-market basis for inventory on tax returns in a combination with a *LIFO cost flow assumption*. In the context of inventory, once the firm writes down the asset, it establishes a new "original cost" basis and ignores subsequent increases in market value in the accounts.

The firm may apply lower of cost or market to individual items of inventory or to groups (usually called *pools*) of items. The smaller the group, the more *conservative* the resulting valuation.

Omit hyphens when you use the term as a noun, but use them when you use the term as an adjectival phrase.

Ltd., Limited. UK: a private limited corporation. The name of a private limited company must include the word "Limited" or its abbreviation "Ltd."

lump-sum acquisition. *Basket purchase*.

M

MACRS. *Modified Accelerated Cost Recovery System.* See *Accelerated Cost Recovery System*. Since 1986, MACRS has been the accelerated depreciation method required for U.S. income tax purposes.

maintenance. *Expenditures* undertaken to preserve an *asset's* service potential for its originally intended life. These expenditures are *period expenses* or *product costs*. Contrast with *improvement*, and see *repair*.

make-or-buy decision. A managerial decision about whether the firm should produce a product internally or purchase it from others. Proper make-or-buy decisions in the short run result only when a firm considers *incremental costs* in the analysis.

maker (of note) (of check). One who signs a *note* to borrow; one who signs a *check*; in the latter context, synonymous with "drawer." See *draft*.

management. Executive authority that operates a business.

management accounting. See *managerial accounting*.

Management Accounting. Monthly publication of the *IMA*.

management audit. An audit conducted to ascertain whether a firm or one of its operating units properly carries out its objectives, policies, and procedures; generally applies only to activities for which accountants can specify qualitative standards. See *audit* and *internal audit*.

management by exception. A principle of management in which managers focus attention on performance only if it differs significantly from that expected.

management by objective (MBO). A management approach designed to focus on the definition and attainment of overall and individual objectives with the participation of all levels of management.

management information system (MIS). A system designed to provide all levels of management with timely and reliable information required for planning, control, and evaluation of performance.

management's discussion and analysis (MD&A). A discussion of management's views of the company's performance; required by the *SEC* to be included in the *10-K* and in the *annual report* to shareholders. The information typically contains discussion of such items as liquidity, results of *operations, segments,* and the effects of *inflation*.

managerial (management) accounting. Reporting designed to enhance the ability of management to do its job of decision making, planning, and control. Contrast with *financial accounting*.

manufacturing cost. Cost of producing goods, usually in a factory.

manufacturing expense. An imprecise, and generally incorrect, alternative title for *manufacturing overhead*. The term is generally incorrect because these costs are usually *product costs,* not expenses.

manufacturing overhead. General manufacturing *costs* that are not directly associated with identifiable units of product and that the firm incurs in providing a capacity to carry on productive activities. Accounting treats *fixed* manufacturing overhead cost as a *product cost* under *full absorption costing* but as an *expense* of the period under *variable costing*.

margin. *Revenue* less specified expenses. See *contribution margin, gross margin,* and *current margin*.

margin of safety. Excess of actual, or budgeted, sales over *breakeven* sales; usually expressed in dollars but may be expressed in units of product.

marginal cost. The *incremental cost* or *differential cost* of the last unit added to production or the first unit subtracted from production. See *cost terminology* and *differential* for contrast.

marginal costing. *Variable costing.*

marginal revenue. The increment in *revenue* from the sale of one additional unit of product.

marginal tax rate. The amount, expressed as a percentage, by which income taxes increase when taxable income increases by one dollar. Contrast with *average tax rate*.

markdown. See *markup* for definition and contrast.

markdown cancellation. See *markup* for definition and contrast.

market-based transfer price. A *transfer price* based on external market data rather than internal company data.

market price. See *fair value.*

market rate. The rate of *interest* a company must pay to borrow *funds* currently. See *effective rate.*

market value. *Fair market value.*

marketable equity securities. *Marketable securities* representing *owners' equity* interest in other companies, rather than *loans* to them.

marketable securities. Other companies' *stocks* and *bonds* held that can be readily sold on stock exchanges or over-the-counter markets and that the company plans to sell as cash is needed; classified as *current assets* and as part of "cash" in preparing the *statement of cash flows*. If the firm holds these same securities for *long-term* purposes, it will classify them as *noncurrent assets*. *SFAS No. 115* requires that all marketable equity and all debt securities (except those debt securities the holder has the ability and intent to hold to maturity) appear at market value on the balance sheet. The firm reports changes in market value in income for *trading securities* but debits holding losses (or credits holding gains) directly to owners' equity accounts for *securities available for sale*.

marketing costs. Costs incurred to sell; includes locating customers, persuading them to buy, delivering the goods or services, and collecting the sales proceeds.

markon. See *markup* for definition and contrast.

markup. The difference between the original selling price of items acquired for *inventory* and the cost. Precise usage calls this "markon," although many businesspeople use the term "markup." Because of confusion of this use of "markup" with its precise definition (see below), terminology sometimes uses "original markup." If the originally established retail price increases, the precise term for the amount of price increase is "markup," although terminology sometimes uses "additional markup." If a firm reduces selling price, terminology uses the terms "markdown" and "markup cancellation." "Markup cancellation" refers to reduction in price following "additional markups" and can, by definition, be no more than the amount of the additional markup; "cancellation of additional markup," although not used, is descriptive. "Markdown" refers to price reductions from the original retail price. A price increase after a markdown is a "markdown cancellation." If original cost is $12 and original selling price is $20, then markon (original markup) is $8; if the firm later increases the price to $24, the $4 increase is markup (additional markup); if the firm later lowers the price to $21, the $3 reduction is markup cancellation; if the firm further lowers the price to $17, the $4 reduction comprises $1 markup cancellation and $3 markdown; if the firm later increases the price to $22, the $5 increase comprises $3 of markdown cancellation and $2 of markup (additional markup). Accountants track markup cancellations and markdowns separately because they deduct the former (but not the latter) in computing the selling prices of goods available for sale for the denominator of the *cost percentage* used in the conventional *retail inventory method.*

markup cancellation. See *markup* for definition and contrast.

markup percentage. *Markup* divided by (acquisition cost plus *markup*).

master budget. A *budget* projecting all *financial statements* and their components.

matching convention. The concept of recognizing cost expirations *(expenses)* in the same accounting period during which the firm recognizes related *revenues;* combining or simultaneously recognizing the revenues and expenses that jointly result from the same *transactions* or other events.

material. As an adjective, it means relatively important, capable of influencing a decision (see *materiality*); as a noun, *raw material.*

materiality. The concept that accounting should disclose separately only those events that are relatively important (no operable definition yet exists) for the business or for understanding its statements. *SFAC No. 2* suggests that accounting information is material if "the judgment of a reasonable person relying on the information would have been changed or influenced by the omission or misstatement."

materials variances. *Price* and *quantity variances* for *direct materials* in *standard costing systems;* difference between actual cost and standard cost.

matrix. A rectangular array of numbers or mathematical symbols.

matrix inverse. For a given square *matrix* **A,** the matrix, $\mathbf{A}^{-1}$ such that $\mathbf{AA}^{-1} = \mathbf{A}^{-1}\mathbf{A} = \mathbf{I}$, the identity matrix. Not all square matrices have inverses. Those that do not are "singular"; those that do are nonsingular.

maturity. The date at which an obligation, such as the *principal* of a *bond* or a *note,* becomes due.

maturity value. The amount expected to be collected when a loan reaches *maturity*. Depending on the context, the amount may be *principal* or principal and *interest.*

MBO. *Management by objective.*

MD&A. *Management's discussion and analysis* section of the *annual report.*

measuring unit. See *attribute measured* for definition and contrast.

merchandise. *Finished goods* bought by a retailer or wholesaler for resale; contrast with finished goods of a manufacturing business.

merchandise costs. Costs incurred to sell a product, such as commissions and advertising.

merchandise turnover. *Inventory turnover* for merchandise. See *ratio.*

merchandising business. As opposed to a manufacturing or service business, one that purchases (rather than manufactures) *finished goods* for resale.

merger. The joining of two or more businesses into a single *economic entity.* See *holding company.*

minority interest. A *balance sheet account* on *consolidated statements* showing the *equity* in a less-than-100-percent-owned *subsidiary* company; equity allocable to those who are not part of the controlling (majority) interest; may be classified either as shareholders' equity or as a liability of *indeterminate term* on the consolidated balance sheet. The *income statement* must subtract the minority interest in the current period's income of the less-than-100-percent-owned subsidiary to arrive at consolidated *net income* for the period.

minority investment. A holding of less than 50 percent of the *voting stock* in another corporation; accounted for with the *equity method* when the investor owns sufficient shares that it can exercise "significant influence" and as *marketable securities* otherwise. See *mutual fund.*

minutes book. A record of all actions authorized at corporate *board of directors* or shareholders' meetings.

MIS. *Management information system.*

mix variance. One of the *manufacturing variances.* Many *standard cost* systems specify combinations of inputs—for example, labor of a certain skill and materials of a certain quality grade. Sometimes combinations of inputs used differ from those contemplated by the standard. The mix variance attempts to report the cost difference caused by those changes in the combination of inputs.

mixed cost. A *semifixed* or a *semivariable* cost.

Modified Accelerated Cost Recovery System (MACRS). Name used for the *Accelerated Cost Recovery System,* originally passed by Congress in 1981 and amended by Congress in 1986.

modified cash basis. The *cash basis of accounting* with long-term assets accounted for using the *accrual basis of accounting.* Most users of the term "cash basis of accounting" actually mean "modified cash basis."

monetary assets and liabilities. See *monetary items.*

monetary gain or loss. The firm's *gain* or *loss* in *general purchasing power* as a result of its holding *monetary assets* or liabilities during a period when the *general purchasing power of the dollar* changes; explicitly reported in *constant-dollar accounting.* During periods of *inflation,* holders of net monetary assets lose, and holders of net monetary liabilities gain, general purchasing power. During periods of *deflation,* holders of net monetary assets gain, and holders of net monetary liabilities lose, general purchasing power.

monetary items. Amounts fixed in terms of dollars by statute or contract; *cash, accounts receivable, accounts payable,* and *debt*. The distinction between monetary and nonmonetary items is important for *constant-dollar accounting* and for *foreign exchange gain or loss* computations. In the foreign exchange context, account amounts denominated in dollars are not monetary items, whereas amounts denominated in any other currency are monetary.

monetary-nonmonetary method. *Foreign currency translation* that translates all *monetary items* at the *current exchange rate* and translates all *nonmonetary items* at the *historical rate*.

money. A word seldom used with precision in accounting, at least in part because economists have not yet agreed on its definition. Economists use the term to refer to both a medium of exchange and a store of value. See *cash* and *monetary items*.

money purchase plan. A *pension plan* in which the employer contributes a specified amount of cash each year to each employee's pension fund; sometimes called a *defined-contribution plan;* contrast with *defined-benefit plan*. The plan does not specify the benefits ultimately received by the employee, since these benefits depend on the rate of return on the cash invested. As of the mid-1990s, most corporate pension plans were defined-benefit plans because both the law and *generally accepted accounting principles* for pensions made defined-benefit plans more attractive than money purchase plans. *ERISA* makes money purchase plans relatively more attractive than they had been. We expect the relative number of money purchase plans to continue to increase.

mortality table. Data of life expectancies or probabilities of death for persons of specified age and sex.

mortgage. A claim given by the borrower (mortgagor) to the lender (mortgagee) against the borrower's property in return for a loan.

moving average. An *average* computed on observations over time. As a new observation becomes available, analysts drop the oldest one so that they always compute the average for the same number of observations and use only the most recent ones.

moving average method. *Weighted-average inventory method*.

multiple-step. Said of an *income statement* that shows various subtotals of *expenses* and *losses* subtracted from *revenues* to show intermediate items such as *operating income,* income of the enterprise (operating income plus *interest* income), income to investors (income of the enterprise less *income taxes*), net income to shareholders (income to investors less interest charges), and income retained (net income to shareholders less dividends). See *entity theory*.

municipal bond. A *bond* issued by a village, town, or city. *Interest* on such bonds is generally exempt from federal *income taxes* and from some state income taxes. Because bonds issued by state and county governments often have these characteristics, terminology often calls such bonds "municipals" as well. These are also sometimes called "tax-exempts."

mutual fund. An investment company that issues its own stock to the public and uses the proceeds to invest in securities of other companies. A mutual fund usually owns less than 5 or 10 percent of the stock of any one company and accounts for its investments using current *market values*. Contrast with *holding company*.

mutually exclusive (investment) projects. Competing investment projects in which accepting one project eliminates the possibility of undertaking the remaining projects.

N

NAARS. *National Automated Accounting Research System*.

NASDAQ (National Association of Securities Dealers Automated Quotation System). A computerized system to provide brokers and dealers with price quotations for securities traded *over the counter* as well as for some *NYSE* securities.

National Association of Accountants (NAA). Former name for the *Institute of Management Accountants (IMA)*.

National Automated Accounting Research System (NAARS). A computer-based information-retrieval system containing, among other things, the complete text of most public corporate annual reports and *Forms 10-K*. Users may access the system through the *AICPA*.

natural business year. A 12-month period chosen as the reporting period so that the end of the period coincides with a low point in activity or inventories. See *ratio* for a discussion of analyses of financial statements of companies using a natural business year.

natural classification. *Income statement* reporting form that classifies *expenses* by nature of items acquired, that is, materials, wages, salaries, insurance, and taxes, as well as depreciation. Contrast with *functional classification*.

natural resources. Timberland, oil and gas wells, ore deposits, and other products of nature that have economic value. Terminology uses the term *depletion* to refer to the process of *amortizing* the cost of natural resources. Natural resources are "nonrenewable" (for example, oil, coal, gas, ore deposits) or "renewable" (timberland, sod fields); terminology often calls the former "wasting assets." See also *reserve recognition accounting* and *percentage depletion*.

negative confirmation. See *confirmation*.

negative goodwill. See *goodwill*. When a firm acquires another company, and the *fair market value* of the *net assets* acquired exceeds the purchase price, *APB Opinion No. 16* requires that the acquiring company reduce the valuation of noncurrent assets (except *investments* in *marketable securities*) until the purchase price equals the adjusted valuation of the fair market value of net assets acquired. If, after the acquiring company reduces the valuation of noncurrent assets to zero, the valuation of the remaining net assets acquired still exceeds the purchase price, then the difference appears as a credit balance on the balance sheet as negative goodwill. For negative goodwill to exist, someone must be willing to sell a company for less than the fair market value of net current assets and marketable securities. Because such bargain purchases are rare, one seldom sees negative goodwill in the financial statements. When it does appear, it generally signals unrecorded obligations, such as a contingency related to a pending lawsuit.

negotiable. Legally capable of being transferred by *endorsement*. Usually said of *checks* and *notes* and sometimes of *stocks* and *bearer bonds*.

negotiated transfer price. A *transfer price* set jointly by the buying and the selling divisions.

net. Reduced by all relevant deductions.

net assets. Total *assets* minus total *liabilities;* equals the amount of *owners' equity*. Often, we find it useful to split the balance sheet into two parts: owners' equity and all the rest. The "rest" is total assets less total liabilities. To take an example, consider one definition of *revenue*: the increase in owners' equity accompanying the net assets increase caused by selling goods or rendering services. An alternative, more cumbersome way to say the same thing is: the increase in owners' equity accompanying the assets increase or the liabilities decrease, or both, caused by selling goods or rendering services. Consider the definition of *goodwill*: the excess of purchase price over the fair market value of identifiable net assets acquired in a purchase transaction. Without the phrase "net assets," the definition might be as follows: the excess of purchase price over the fair market value of identifiable assets reduced by the fair market value of identifiable liabilities acquired in a purchase transaction.

net bank position. From a firm's point of view, *cash* in a specific bank less *loans* payable to that bank.

net current asset value (per share). *Working capital* divided by the number of common shares outstanding. Some analysts think that when a common share trades in the market for an amount less than net current asset value, the shares are undervalued and investors should purchase them. We find this view naive because it ignores, generally, the efficiency of capital markets and, specifically, unrecorded obligations, such as for executory contracts and contingencies, not currently reported as *liabilities* in the *balance sheet* under *GAAP*.

net current assets. *Working capital = current assets − current liabilities*.

net income. The excess of all *revenues* and *gains* for a period over all *expenses* and *losses* of the period. The FASB is proposing to discontinue use of this term and substitute *earnings*. See *comprehensive income*.

net loss. The excess of all *expenses* and *losses* for a period over all *revenues* and *gains* of the period; negative *net income*.

net markup. In the context of *retail inventory methods, markups* less markup cancellations; a figure that usually ignores *markdowns* and markdown cancellations.

net of tax method. A nonsanctioned method for dealing with the problem of *income tax allocation*; described in *APB*

Opinion No. 11. The method subtracts deferred tax items from specific *asset* amounts rather than showing them as a deferred credit or *liability*.

net of tax reporting. Reporting, such as for *income from discontinued operations, extraordinary items,* and *prior-period adjustments,* in which the firm adjusts the amounts presented in the *financial statements* for all income tax effects. For example, if an extraordinary loss amounted to $10,000, and the marginal tax rate was 40 percent, then the extraordinary item would appear "net of taxes" as a $6,000 loss. Hence, not all a firm's income taxes necessarily appear on one line of the income statement. The reporting allocates the total taxes among *income from continuing operations, income from discontinued operations, extraordinary items,* cumulative effects of *accounting changes,* and *prior-period adjustments*.

net operating profit. *Income from continuing operations*.

net present value. Discounted or *present value* of all cash inflows and outflows of a project or of an *investment* at a given *discount rate*.

net price method (of recording purchase or sales discounts). Method that records a *purchase* (or *sale*) at its *invoice* price less all *discounts* made available, under the assumption that the firm will take nearly all discounts offered. The purchaser debits, to an *expense* account, discounts lapsed through failure to pay promptly. For purchases, management usually prefers to know about the amount of discounts lost because of inefficient operations, not the amounts taken, so that most managers prefer the net price method to the *gross price method*.

net realizable (sales) value. Current selling price less reasonable costs to complete production and to sell the item. Also, a method for *allocating joint costs* in proportion to *realizable values* of the joint products. For example, joint products A and B together cost $100; A sells for $60, whereas B sells for $90. Then a firm would allocate to A ($60/$150) × $100 = .40 × $100 = $40 of cost while it would allocate to B ($90/$150) × $100 = $60 of cost.

net sales. Sales (at gross invoice amount) less *returns, allowances,* freight paid for customers, and *discounts* taken.

net working capital. *Working capital;* the term "net" is redundant in accounting. Financial analysts sometimes mean *current assets* when they speak of working capital, so for them the "net" is not redundant.

net worth. A misleading term with the same meaning as *owners' equity*. Avoid using this term; accounting valuations at historical cost do not show economic worth.

network analysis. A project planning and scheduling method, usually displayed in a diagram, that enables management to identify the interrelated sequences that it must accomplish to complete the project.

New York Stock Exchange (NYSE). A public market in which those who own seats (a seat is the right to participate) trade various corporate *securities*.

next-in, first-out. See *NIFO*.

NIFO (next-in, first-out). A *cost flow assumption,* one not allowed by GAAP. In making decisions, many managers consider *replacement costs* (rather than *historical costs*) and refer to them as NIFO costs.

no par. Said of *stock* without a *par value.*

nominal accounts. *Temporary accounts,* such as *revenue* and *expense* accounts; contrast with *balance sheet accounts.* The firm *closes* all nominal accounts at the end of each *accounting period.*

nominal amount (value). An amount stated in dollars, in contrast to an amount stated in *constant dollars.* Contrast with *real amount (value).*

nominal dollars. The measuring unit giving no consideration to differences in the *general purchasing power of the dollar* over time. The face amount of currency or coin, a *bond,* an *invoice,* or a *receivable* is a nominal-dollar amount. When the analyst adjusts that amount for changes in *general purchasing power,* it becomes a *constant-dollar* amount.

nominal interest rate. A rate specified on a *debt* instrument; usually differs from the market or *effective rate;* also, a rate of *interest* quoted for a year. If the interest compounds more often than annually, then the *effective interest rate* exceeds the nominal rate.

noncancelable. See *lease.*

nonconsolidated subsidiary. An *intercorporate investment* in which the parent owns more than 50 percent of the shares of the *subsidiary* but accounts for the investment with the *cost method.*

noncontributory. Said of a *pension plan* in which only the employer makes payments to a pension *fund.* Contrast with *contributory.*

noncontrollable cost. A cost that a particular manager cannot *control.*

noncurrent. Of a *liability,* due in more than one year (or more than one *operating cycle*); of an *asset,* the firm will enjoy the future benefit in more than one year (or more than one operating cycle).

nonexpendable fund. A governmental fund whose *principal,* and sometimes earnings, the entity may not spend.

noninterest-bearing note. A *note* that does not specify explicit interest. The *face value* of such a note will exceed its *present value* at any time before *maturity* value so long as *interest rates* are positive. *APB Opinion No. 21* requires that firms report the present value, not face value, of long-term noninterest-bearing notes as the *asset* or *liability* amount in financial statements. For this purpose, the firm uses the *historical interest rate.* See *interest, imputed.*

nonmanufacturing costs. All *costs* incurred other than those necessary to produce goods. Typically, only manufacturing firms use this designation.

nonmonetary items. All items that are not monetary. See *monetary items.*

nonoperating. In the *income statement* context, said of *revenues* and *expenses* arising from *transactions* incidental to the company's main line(s) of business; in the *statement of cash flows* context, said of all financing and investing sources or uses of cash in contrast to cash provided by operations. See *operations.*

nonprofit corporation. An incorporated *entity,* such as a hospital, with owners who do not share in the earnings. It usually emphasizes providing services rather than maximizing income.

nonrecurring. Said of an event that is not expected to happen often for a given firm. *APB Opinion No. 30* requires firms to disclose separately the effects of such events as part of *ordinary* items unless the event is also unusual. See *extraordinary* item.

nonvalue-added activity. An activity that causes costs without increasing a product's or service's value to the customer.

normal cost. Former name for *service cost* in accounting for pensions and other postemployment benefits.

normal costing. Method of charging costs to products using actual *direct materials,* actual *direct labor,* and predetermined *factory overhead* rates.

normal costing system. *Costing* based on *actual material* and *labor* costs but using *predetermined overhead* rates per unit of some *activity* basis (such as *direct labor hours* or machine hours) to apply overhead to production. Management decides the rate to charge to production for overhead at the start of the period. At the end of the period the accounting multiplies this rate by the actual number of units of the base activity (such as actual direct labor hours worked or actual machine hours used during the period) to apply overhead to production.

normal spoilage. Costs incurred because of ordinary amounts of spoilage. Accounting prorates such costs to units produced as *product costs.* Contrast with *abnormal spoilage.*

normal standard cost, normal standards. The *cost* a firm expects to incur under reasonably efficient operating conditions with adequate provision for an average amount of rework, spoilage, and the like.

normal volume. The level of production that will, over a time span, usually one year, satisfy purchasers' demands and provide for reasonable *inventory* levels.

note. An unconditional written promise by the maker (borrower) to pay a certain amount on demand or at a certain future time.

note receivable discounted. A *note* assigned by the holder to another. The new holder of the note typically pays the old holder an amount less than the *face value* of the note, hence the word "discounted." If the old holder assigns the note to the new holder with recourse, the old holder has a *contingent liability* until the maker of the note pays the debt. See *factoring.*

notes. Some use this word instead of *footnotes* when referring to the detailed information included by management as an integral part of the *financial statements* and covered by the *auditor's report.*

NOW (negotiable order of withdrawal) account. Negotiable order of withdrawal. A *savings account* whose owner can draw an order to pay, much like a *check* but technically not a check, and give it to others, who can redeem the order at the savings institution.

number of days sales in inventory (or receivables). Days of average inventory on hand (or average collection period for receivables). See *ratio.*

NV (naamloze vennootschap). Netherlands: a public limited liability company.

NYSE. *New York Stock Exchange.*

O

OASD(H)I. *Old Age, Survivors, Disability, and (Hospital) Insurance.*

objective. See *reporting objectives* and *objectivity.*

objective function. In *linear programming,* the name of the profit (or cost) criterion the analyst wants to maximize (or minimize).

objectivity. The reporting policy implying that the firm will not give formal recognition to an event in financial statements until the firm can measure the magnitude of the events with reasonable accuracy and check that amount with independent verification.

obsolescence. An asset's *market value* decline caused by improved alternatives becoming available that will be more *cost-effective.* The decline in market value does not relate to physical changes in the asset itself. For example, computers become obsolete long before they wear out. See *partial obsolescence.*

Occupational Safety and Health Act. *OSHA.*

off-balance-sheet financing. A description often used for an obligation that meets all the tests to be classified a liability except that the obligation arises from an *executory contract* and, hence, is not a *liability.* Consider the following example. Miller Corporation desires to acquire land costing $25 million, on which it will build a shopping center. It could borrow the $25 million from its bank, paying interest at 12 percent, and buy the land outright from the seller. If so, both an asset and a liability will appear on the balance sheet. Instead, it borrows $5 million and purchases for $5 million from the seller an *option* to buy the land from the seller at any time within the next six years for a price of $20 million. The option costs Miller Corporation $5 million immediately and provides for continuing "option" payments of $2.4 million per year, which precisely equal Miller Corporation's borrowing rate multiplied by the remaining purchase price of the land: $2.4 million = .12 × $20 million. Although Miller Corporation need not continue payments and can let the option lapse at any time, it also has an obligation to begin developing on the site immediately. Because Miller Corporation has invested a substantial sum in the option, will invest more, and will begin immediately developing the land, Miller Corporation will almost certainly exercise its option before expiration. The seller of the land can take the option contract to the bank and borrow $20

million, paying interest at Miller Corporation's borrowing rate, 12 percent per year. The continuing option payments from Miller Corporation will be sufficient to enable the seller to make its payments to the bank. *Generally accepted accounting principles* view Miller Corporation as having acquired an option for $5 million rather than having acquired land costing $25 million in return for $25 million of debt. The firm will not recognize debt on the balance sheet until it borrows more funds to exercise the option.

off-balance-sheet risk. A contract that exposes an entity to the possibility of loss but that does not appear in the financial statements. For example, a *forward-exchange contract* generally does not appear on the balance sheet because it is an *executory contract.* The contract may reduce or increase the entity's exposure to foreign-exchange risk (the chance of loss due to unfavorable changes in the foreign-exchange rate). It may also expose the entity to credit risk (the chance of loss that occurs when the *counterparty* to the contract cannot fulfill the contract terms). *SFAS No. 105* requires entities to describe contracts with off-balance-sheet risk.

OHG (Offene Handelsgesellschaft). Germany: a general *partnership.* The partners have unlimited *liability.*

Old Age, Survivors, Disability, and (Hospital) Insurance, or OASD(H)I. The technical name for Social Security under the Federal Insurance Contributions Act (*FICA*).

on consignment. Said of goods delivered by the owner (the consignor) to another (the consignee) to be sold by the consignee. The arrangement entitles the owner either to the return of the property or to payment of a specified amount. The goods are *assets* of the consignor. Such arrangements provide the consignor with better protection than an outright *sale on account* to the consignee in case the consignee becomes bankrupt. In event of *bankruptcy,* the ordinary seller, holding an account receivable, has no special claim to the return of the goods, whereas a consignor can reclaim the goods without going through bankruptcy proceedings, from which the consignor might recover only a fraction of the amounts owed to it.

on (open) account. Said of a *purchase* (or *sale*) when the seller expects payment sometime after delivery and the purchaser does not give a *note* evidencing the *debt.* The purchaser has generally signed an agreement sometime in the past promising to pay for such purchases according to an agreed time schedule. When the firm sells (purchases) on open account, it *debits* (*credits*) *Accounts Receivable (Payable).*

one-line consolidation. Said of an *intercorporate investment* accounted for with the *equity method.* With this method, the *income* and *balance sheet* total *assets* and *equities* amounts are identical to those that would appear if the parent consolidated the investee firm, even though the income from the investment appears on a single line of the income statement and the net investment appears on a single line in the Assets section of the balance sheet.

one-write system. A system of bookkeeping that produces several records, including original documents, in one operation by the use of reproductive paper and equipment that provides for the proper alignment of the documents.

open account. Any *account* with a nonzero *debit* or *credit balance.* See *on (open) account.*

operating. An adjective used to refer to *revenue* and *expense* items relating to the company's main line(s) of business. See *operations.*

operating accounts. *Revenue, expense,* and *production cost accounts.* Contrast with *balance sheet accounts.*

operating activities. For purposes of the *statement of cash flows,* all *transactions* and *events* that are neither *financing activities* nor *investing activities.* See *operations.*

operating budget. A formal *budget* for the *operating cycle* or for a year.

operating cash flow. *Cash flow from operations.* Financial statement analysts sometimes use this term to mean *cash flow from operations − capital expenditures − dividends.* This usage leads to such ambiguity that the reader should always confirm the definition that the writer uses before drawing inferences from the reported data.

operating cycle. *Earnings cycle.*

operating expenses. *Expenses* incurred in the course of *ordinary* activities of an *entity;* frequently, a classification including only *selling, general,* and *administrative expenses,* thereby excluding *cost of goods sold, interest,* and *income tax* expenses. See *operations.*

operating lease. A *lease* accounted for by the *lessee* without showing an *asset* for the lease rights *(leasehold)* or a *liability* for the lease payment obligations. The lessee reports only rental payments during the period, as *expenses* of the period. The asset remains on the lessor's *books,* where rental collections appear as *revenues.* Contrast with *capital lease.*

operating leverage. Usually said of a firm with a large proportion of *fixed costs* in its *total costs.* Consider a book publisher or a railroad: such a firm has large costs to produce the first unit of service; then, the *incremental costs* of producing another book or transporting another freight car are much less than the *average cost,* so the *gross margin* on the sale of the subsequent units is relatively large. Contrast this situation with that, for example, of a grocery store, where the *contribution margin* equals less than 5 percent of the selling price. For firms with equal profitability, however defined, we say that the one with the larger percentage increase in income from a given percentage increase in dollar sales has the larger operating leverage. See *leverage* for contrast of this term with "financial leverage." See *cost terminology* for definitions of terms involving the word "cost."

operating margin. *Revenues* from *sales* minus *cost of goods sold* and *operating expenses.*

operating margin based on current costs. *Revenues* from *sales* minus *current cost* of goods sold; a measure of operating efficiency that does not depend on the *cost flow assumption* for *inventory;* sometimes called "current (gross) margin." See *inventory profit* for illustrative computations.

operating ratio. See *ratio.*

operational control. See *control system.*

operations. A word not precisely defined in *accounting.* Generally, analysts distinguish operating activities (producing and selling *goods* or *services*) from financing activities (raising funds) and *investing activities.* Acquiring goods on account and then paying for them one month later, though generally classified as an operating activity, has the characteristics of a financing activity. Or consider the transaction of selling plant assets for a price in excess of book value. On the *income statement,* the gain appears as part of income from operations ("continuing operations" or "discontinued" operations, depending on the circumstances), but the *statement of cash flows* reports all the funds received below the Cash from Operations section, as a nonoperating source of cash, "disposition of noncurrent assets." In income tax accounting, an "operating loss" results whenever deductions exceed taxable revenues.

opinion. The *auditor's report* containing an attestation or lack thereof; also, *APB Opinion.*

opinion paragraph. Section of *auditor's report,* generally following the *scope paragraph* and giving the auditor's conclusion that the *financial statements* are (rarely, are not) in accordance with *GAAP* and present fairly the *financial position,* changes in financial position, and the results of *operations.*

opportunity cost. The *present value* of the *income* (or *costs*) that a firm could earn (or save) from using an *asset* in its best alternative use to the one under consideration.

opportunity cost of capital. *Cost of capital.*

option. The legal right to buy or sell something during a specified period at a specified price, called the *exercise* price. If the right exists during a specified time interval, it is known as an "American option." If it exists for only one specific day, it is known as a "European option." Do not confuse employee stock options with *put* and *call* options, traded in various public markets.

ordinary annuity. An *annuity in arrears.*

ordinary income. For income tax purposes, reportable *income* not qualifying as *capital gains.*

organization costs. The *costs* incurred in planning and establishing an *entity;* example of an *intangible* asset. The firm must treat these costs as *expenses* of the period, even though the *expenditures* clearly provide future benefits and meet the test to be *assets.*

original cost. *Acquisition cost;* in public utility accounting, the acquisition cost of the *entity* first devoting the *asset* to public use. See *aboriginal cost.*

original entry. Entry in a *journal.*

OSHA (Occupational Safety and Health Act). The federal law that governs working conditions in commerce and industry.

other comprehensive income. According to the FASB, *comprehensive income* items that are not themselves part of earnings. See *comprehensive income.* To define comprehensive income does not convey its essence. To understand comprehensive income, you need to understand how it differs from *earnings* (or *net income*), the concept measured in the *earnings (income) statement*. The term *earnings* (or *net income*) refers to the sum of all components of comprehensive income *minus* the components of other comprehensive income.

outlay. The amount of an *expenditure*.

outlier. Said of an observation (or data point) that appears to differ significantly in some regard from other observations (or data points) of supposedly the same phenomenon; in a *regression analysis,* often used to describe an observation that falls far from the fitted regression equation (in two dimensions, line).

out-of-pocket. Said of an *expenditure* usually paid for with cash; an *incremental* cost.

out-of-stock cost. The estimated decrease in future *profit* as a result of losing customers because a firm has insufficient quantities of *inventory* currently on hand to meet customers' demands.

output. Physical quantity or monetary measurement of *goods* and *services* produced.

outside director. A corporate board of directors member who is not a company officer and does not participate in the corporation's day-to-day management.

outstanding. Unpaid or uncollected; when said of *stock,* refers to the shares issued less *treasury stock;* when said of *checks,* refers to a check issued that did not clear the *drawer's* bank prior to the *bank statement* date.

over-and-short. Title for an *expense account* used to account for small differences between book balances of cash and actual cash and vouchers or receipts in *petty cash* or *change funds.*

overapplied (overabsorbed) overhead. Costs applied, or *charged,* to product and exceeding actual *overhead costs* during the period; a *credit balance* in an overhead account after overhead is assigned to product.

overdraft. A *check* written on a checking account that contains funds less than the amount of the check.

overhead costs. Any *cost* not directly associated with the production or sale of identifiable goods and services; sometimes called "burden" or "indirect costs" and, in the UK, "oncosts"; frequently limited to manufacturing overhead. See *central corporate expenses* and *manufacturing overhead.*

overhead rate. Standard, or other predetermined rate, at which a firm applies *overhead costs* to products or to services.

over-the-counter. Said of a *security* traded in a negotiated transaction, as on *NASDAQ,* rather than in an auctioned one on an organized stock exchange, such as the *New York Stock Exchange.*

owners' equity. *Proprietorship; assets* minus *liabilities; paid-in capital* plus *retained earnings* of a corporation; partners' capital accounts in a *partnership*; owner's capital account in a *sole proprietorship.*

P

paid-in capital. Sum of balances in *capital stock* and *capital contributed in excess of par (or stated) value* accounts;

same as *contributed capital* (minus *donated capital*). Some use the term to mean only *capital contributed in excess of par (or stated value).*

paid-in surplus. See *surplus.*

P&L. Profit-and-loss statement; *income statement.*

paper profit. A *gain* not yet realized through a *transaction;* an *unrealized holding gain.*

par. See *at par* and *face amount.*

par value. *Face amount* of a *security.*

par value method. In accounting for *treasury stock,* method that *debits* a common stock account with the *par value* of the shares required and allocates the remaining debits between the *Additional Paid-in Capital* and *Retained Earnings* accounts. Contrast with *cost method.*

parent company. Company owning more than 50 percent of the voting shares of another company, called the *subsidiary.*

Pareto chart. A graph of a skewed statistical distribution. In many business settings, a relatively small percentage of the potential population causes a relatively large percentage of the business activity. For example, some businesses find that the top 20 percent of the customers buy 80 percent of the goods sold. Or, the top 10 percent of products account for 60 percent of the revenues or 70 percent of the profits. The statistical distribution known as the Pareto distribution has this property of skewness, so a graph of a phenomenon with such skewness has come to be known as a Pareto chart, even if the underlying data do not actually well fit the Pareto distribution. Practitioners of *total quality management* find that in many businesses, a small number of processes account for a large fraction of the quality problems, so they advocate charting potential problems and actual occurrences of problems to identify the relatively small number of sources of trouble. They call such a chart a "Pareto chart."

partial obsolescence. One cause of decline in *market value* of an *asset.* As technology improves, the economic value of existing *assets* declines. In many cases, however, it will not pay a firm to replace the existing asset with a new one, even though it would acquire the new type rather than the old if it did make a new acquisition currently. In these cases, the accountant should theoretically recognize a loss from partial obsolescence from the firm's owning an old, out-of-date asset, but *GAAP* do not permit recognition of partial obsolescence until the sum of future cash flows from the asset total less than book value; see *impairment.* The firm will carry the old asset at *cost* less *accumulated depreciation* until the firm retires it from service so long as the *undiscounted* future *cash flows* from the asset exceed its book value. Thus management that uses an asset subject to partial obsolescence reports results inferior to those reported by a similar management that uses a new asset. See *obsolescence.*

partially funded. Said of a *pension plan* in which the firm has not funded all earned benefits. See *funded* for funding requirements.

partially vested. Said of a *pension plan* in which not all employee benefits have *vested.* See *graded vesting.*

participating dividend. *Dividend* paid to preferred shareholders in addition to the minimum preferred dividends when the *preferred stock* contract provides for such sharing in earnings. Usually the contract specifies that dividends on *common shares* must reach a specified level before the preferred shares receive the participating dividend.

participating preferred stock. *Preferred stock* with rights to *participating dividends.*

partner's drawing. A payment made to a partner and debited against his or her share of income or capital. The name of a *temporary account,* closed to the partner's capital account, to record the debits when the partner receives such payments.

partnership. Contractual arrangement between individuals to share resources and operations in a jointly run business. See *general* and *limited partner* and *Uniform Partnership Act.*

patent. A right granted for up to 20 years by the federal government to exclude others from manufacturing, using, or selling a claimed design, product, or plant (e.g., a new breed of rose) or from using a claimed process or method of manufacture; an *asset* if the firm acquires it by purchase. If the firm develops it internally, current *GAAP* require the firm to *expense* the development costs when incurred.

payable. Unpaid but not necessarily due or past due.

pay-as-you-go. Said of an *income tax* scheme in which the taxpayer makes periodic payments of income taxes during the period when it earns the income to be taxed; in contrast to a scheme in which the taxpayer owes no payments until the end of, or after, the period when it earned the income being taxed (called PAYE—pay-as-you-earn—in the UK). The phrase is sometimes used to describe an *unfunded pension plan,* or retirement benefit plan, in which the firm makes payments to pension plan beneficiaries from general corporate funds, not from cash previously contributed to a fund. Under this method, the firm debits expense as it makes payments, not as it incurs the obligations. This is not acceptable as a method of accounting for pension plans, under *SFAS No. 87,* or as a method of *funding,* under *ERISA.*

payback period. Amount of time that must elapse before the cash inflows from a project equal the cash outflows.

payback reciprocal. One divided by the *payback period.* This number approximates the *internal rate of return* on a project when the project life exceeds twice the payback period and the cash inflows are identical in every period after the initial period.

PAYE (pay-as-you-earn). See *pay-as-you-go* for contrast.

payee. The person or entity who receives a cash payment or who will receive the stated amount of cash on a *check.* See *draft.*

payout ratio. *Common stock dividends* declared for a year divided by net *income* to common stock for the year; a term used by financial analysts. Contrast with *dividend yield.*

payroll taxes. Taxes levied because the taxpayer pays salaries or wages; for example, *FICA* and unemployment compensation insurance taxes. Typically, the employer pays a portion and withholds part of the employee's wages.

P/E ratio. *Price-earnings ratio.*

Pension Benefit Guarantee Corporation (PBGC). A federal corporation established under *ERISA* to guarantee basic pension benefits in covered pension plans by administering terminated pension plans and placing *liens* on corporate assets for certain unfunded pension liabilities.

pension fund. *Fund,* the assets of which the trustee will pay to retired ex-employees, usually as a *life annuity;* generally held by an independent trustee and thus not an *asset* of the employer.

pension plan. Details or provisions of employer's contract with employees for paying retirement *annuities* or other benefits. See *funded, vested, service cost, prior service cost, money purchase plan,* and *defined-benefit plan.*

per books. An expression used to refer to the *book value* of an item at a specific time.

percent. Any number, expressed as a decimal, multiplied by 100.

percentage depletion (allowance). Deductible *expense* allowed in some cases by the federal *income tax* regulations; computed as a percentage of gross income from a *natural resource* independent of the unamortized cost of the *asset.* Because the amount of the total deductions for tax purposes usually exceeds the cost of the asset being *depleted,* many people think the deduction is an unfair tax advantage or *loophole.*

percentage-of-completion method. Recognizing *revenues* and *expenses* on a job, order, or contract (1) in proportion to the *costs* incurred for the period divided by total costs expected to be incurred for the job or order ("cost to cost") or (2) in proportion to engineers' or architects' estimates of the incremental degree of completion of the job, order, or contract during the period. Contrast with *completed contract method.*

percentage statement. A statement containing, in addition to (or instead of) dollar amounts, ratios of dollar amounts to some base. In a percentage *income statement,* the base is usually either *net sales* or total *revenues,* and in a percentage *balance sheet,* the base is usually total *assets.*

period. *Accounting period.*

period cost. An inferior term for *period expense.*

period expense (charge). *Expenditure,* usually based on the passage of time, charged to operations of the accounting period rather than *capitalized* as an asset. Contrast with *product cost.*

periodic inventory. In recording *inventory,* a method that uses data on beginning inventory, additions to inventories, and ending inventory to find the cost of withdrawals from inventory. Contrast with *perpetual inventory.*

periodic procedures. The process of making *adjusting entries* and *closing entries* and preparing the *financial statements,* usually by use of *trial balances* and *work sheets.*

permanent account. An account that appears on the *balance sheet.* Contrast with *temporary account.*

permanent difference. Difference between reported income and taxable income that will never reverse and, hence, requires no entry in the *deferred income tax (liability)* account;

for example, nontaxable state and municipal *bond* interest that will appear on the financial statements. Contrast with *temporary difference*. See *deferred income tax liability*.

permanent file. The file of working papers that are prepared by a public accountant and that contain the information required for reference in successive professional engagements for a particular organization, as distinguished from working papers applicable only to a particular engagement.

perpetual annuity. *Perpetuity*.

perpetual inventory. *Inventory* quantity and amount records that the firm changes and makes current with each physical addition to or withdrawal from the stock of goods; an inventory so recorded. The records will show the physical quantities and, frequently, the dollar valuations that should be on hand at any time. Because the firm explicitly computes *cost of goods sold*, it can use the *inventory equation* to compute an amount for what *ending inventory* should be. It can then compare the computed amount of ending inventory with the actual amount of ending inventory as a *control* device to measure the amount of *shrinkages*. Contrast with *periodic inventory*.

perpetuity. An *annuity* whose payments continue forever. The *present value* of a perpetuity in *arrears* is *p/r* where *p* is the periodic payment and *r* is the *interest rate* per period. If a perpetuity promises $100 each year, in arrears, forever and the interest rate is 8 percent per year, then the perpetuity has a value of $1,250 = $100/.08.

perpetuity growth model. See *perpetuity*. A *perpetuity* whose cash flows grow at the rate *g* per period and thus has *present value* of $1/(r - g)$. Some call this the "Gordon Growth Model" because Myron Gordon wrote about applications of this formula and its variants in the 1950s. John Burr Williams wrote about them in the 1930s.

personal account. *Drawing account*.

PERT (Program Evaluation and Review Technique). A method of *network analysis* in which the analyst makes three time estimates for each activity—the optimistic time, the most likely time, and the pessimistic time—and gives an expected completion date for the project within a probability range.

petty cash fund. Currency and coins maintained for expenditures that the firm makes with cash on hand.

physical units method. A method of allocating a *joint cost* to the *joint products* based on a physical measure of the joint products; for example, allocating the cost of a cow to sirloin steak and to hamburger, based on the weight of the meat. This method usually provides nonsensical (see *sterilized allocation*) results unless the physical units of the joint products tend to have the same value.

physical verification. *Verification*, by an *auditor*, performed by actually inspecting items in *inventory, plant assets*, and the like, in contrast to merely checking the written records. The auditor may use statistical sampling procedures.

planning and control process. General name for the management techniques comprising the setting of organizational goals and *strategic plans, capital budgeting, operations*

budgeting, comparison of plans with actual results, performance evaluation and corrective action, and revisions of goals, plans, and budgets.

plant. *Plant assets*.

plant asset turnover. Number of dollars of *sales* generated per dollar of *plant assets;* equal to sales divided by average *plant assets*.

plant assets. *Assets* used in the revenue-production process. Plant assets include buildings, machinery, equipment, land, and natural resources. The phrase "property, plant, and equipment" (though often appearing on balance sheets) is therefore a redundancy. In this context, "plant" used alone means buildings.

plantwide allocation method. A method for *allocating overhead costs* to product. First, use one *cost pool* for the entire plant. Then, allocate all costs from that pool to products using a single overhead *allocation* rate, or one set of rates, for all the products of the plant, independent of the number of departments in the plant.

PLC (public limited company). UK: a publicly held *corporation*. Contrast with *Ltd*.

pledging. The borrower assigns *assets* as security or *collateral* for repayment of a loan.

pledging of receivables. The process of using expected collections on *accounts receivable* as *collateral* for a loan. The borrower remains responsible for collecting the receivable but promises to use the proceeds for repaying the debt.

plow back. To retain *assets* generated by earnings for continued investment in the business.

plug. Process for finding an unknown amount. For any *account*, beginning balance + additions − deductions = ending balance; if you know any three of the four items, you can find the fourth with simple arithmetic, called "plugging." In making a *journal entry*, often you know all *debits* and all but one of the *credits* (or vice versa). Because *double-entry* bookkeeping requires equal debits and credits, you can compute the unknown quantity by subtracting the sum of the known credits from the sum of all the debits (or vice versa), also called "plugging." Accountants often call the unknown the "plug." For example, in amortizing a *discount* on *bonds payable* with the *straight-line depreciation* method, *interest expense* is a plug: interest expense = interest payable + *discount amortization*. See *trade-in transaction* for an example. The term sometimes has a bad connotation for accountants because plugging can occur in a slightly different context. During the process of preparing a *preclosing trial balance* (or *balance sheet*), often the sum of the debits does not equal the sum of the credits. Rather than find the error, some accountants are tempted to force equality by changing one of the amounts, with a plugged debit or credit to an account such as Other Expenses. No harm results from this procedure if the amount of the error is small compared with asset totals, since spending tens or hundreds of dollars in a bookkeeper's or accountant's time to find an error of a few dollars will not be *cost-effective*. Still, most accounting teachers rightly disallow this use of plugging because exercises and problems set for students provide enough information not to require it.

point of sale. The time, not the location, at which a *sale* occurs.

pooling-of-interests method. Accounting for a *business combination* by adding together the *book value* of the *assets* and *equities* of the combined firms; generally leads to a higher reported *net income* for the combined firms than results when the firm accounts for the business combination as a purchase because the *market values* of the merged assets generally exceed their book values. *APB Opinion No. 16* states the conditions that, when met, require the pooling-of-interests treatment. Contrast with *purchase method.* Called *uniting-of-interests method* by the *IASC.*

population. The entire set of numbers or items from which the analyst samples or performs some other analysis.

positive confirmation. See *confirmation.*

post. To record entries in an *account* to a *ledger,* usually as transfers from a *journal.*

post-closing trial balance. *Trial balance* taken after the accountant has *closed* all *temporary accounts.*

post-statement events. Events that have *material* impact and that occur between the end of the *accounting period* and the formal publication of the *financial statements.* Even though the events occur after the end of the period being reported on, the firm must disclose such events in notes if the auditor is to give a *clean opinion.*

potentially dilutive. A *security* that its holder may convert into, or exchange for, common stock and thereby reduce reported *earnings per share; options, warrants, convertible bonds,* and *convertible preferred stock.*

PPB. *Program budgeting.* The second "P" stands for "plan."

practical capacity. Maximum level at which a plant or department can operate efficiently.

precision. The degree of accuracy for an estimate derived from a sampling process, usually expressed as a range of values around the estimate. The analyst might express a sample estimate in the following terms: "Based on the sample, we are 95 percent sure [confidence level] that the true population value is within the range of X to Y [precision]." See *confidence level.*

preclosing trial balance. *Trial balance* taken at the end of the period before *closing entries;* in this sense, an *adjusted trial balance;* sometimes taken before *adjusting entries* and then synonymous with *unadjusted trial balance.*

predatory prices. Setting prices below some measure of cost in an effort to drive out competitors with the hope of recouping losses later by charging monopoly prices. Illegal in the United States if the prices set are below long-run variable costs. We know of no empirical evidence that firms are successful at recoupment.

predetermined (factory) overhead rate. Rate used in applying *overhead costs* to products or departments developed at the start of a period. Compute the rate as estimated overhead cost divided by the estimated number of units of the overhead allocation base (or *denominator volume*) activity. See *normal costing.*

preemptive right. The privilege of a *shareholder* to maintain a proportionate share of ownership by purchasing a proportionate share of any new stock issues. Most state corporation laws allow corporations to pay shareholders to waive their preemptive rights or state that preemptive rights exist only if the *corporation charter* explicitly grants them. In practice, then, preemptive rights are the exception rather than the rule.

preference as to assets. The rights of *preferred shareholders* to receive certain payments before common shareholders receive payments in case the board dissolves the corporation.

preferred shares. *Capital stock* with a claim to *income* or *assets* after *bondholders* but before *common shares. Dividends* on preferred shares are *income distributions,* not *expenses.* See *cumulative preferred stock.*

premium. The excess of issue (or market) price over *par value.* For a different context, see *insurance.*

premium on capital stock. Alternative but inferior title for *capital contributed in excess of par (or stated) value.*

prepaid expense. An *expenditure* that leads to a *deferred charge* or *prepayment.* Strictly speaking, this is a contradiction in terms because an *expense* is a gone asset, and this title refers to past *expenditures,* such as for rent or insurance premiums, that still have future benefits and thus are *assets.* We try to avoid this term and use "prepayment" instead.

prepaid income. An inferior alternative title for *advances from customers.* Do not call an item *revenue* or *income* until the firm earns it by delivering goods or rendering services.

prepayments. *Deferred charges; assets* representing *expenditures* for future benefits. Rent and insurance premiums paid in advance are usually current prepayments.

present value. Value today (or at some specific date) of an amount or amounts to be paid or received later (or at other, different dates), discounted at some *interest* or *discount rate;* an amount that, if invested today at the specified rate, will grow to the amount to be paid or received in the future.

price. The quantity of one *good* or *service,* usually *cash,* asked in return for a unit of another good or service. See *fair value.*

price-earnings (P/E) ratio. At a given time, the market value of a company's *common share,* per share, divided by the *earnings per* common *share* for the past year. The analyst usually bases the denominator on *income from continuing operations* or, if the analyst thinks the current figure for that amount does not represent a usual situation—such as when the number is negative or, if positive, close to zero—on some estimate of the number. See *ratio.*

price index. A series of numbers, one for each period, that purports to represent some *average* of prices for a series of periods, relative to a base period.

price level. The number from a *price index* series for a given period or date.

price level-adjusted statements. *Financial statements* expressed in terms of dollars of uniform purchasing power. The statements restate *nonmonetary* items to reflect changes in general *price levels* since the time the firm acquired specific *assets* and incurred *liabilities*. The statements recognize a *gain* or *loss* on *monetary items* as the firm holds them over time periods when the general *price level changes*. Conventional financial statements show *historical costs* and ignore differences in purchasing power in different periods.

price variance. In accounting for *standard costs,* an amount equal to (actual cost per unit − standard cost per unit) times actual quantity.

primary earnings per share (PEPS). Net *income* to common shareholders plus *interest* (net of tax effects) or *dividends* paid on *common-stock equivalents* divided by (weighted average of common shares outstanding plus the net increase in the number of common shares that would become *outstanding* if the holders of all common stock equivalents were to exchange them for common shares with cash proceeds, if any, used to retire common shares). As of 1997 and *SFAS No. 128,* replaced with *basic earnings per share.*

prime cost. Sum of *direct materials* plus *direct labor* costs assigned to product.

prime rate. The loan rate charged by commercial banks to their creditworthy customers. Some customers pay even less than the prime rate and others, more. The *Federal Reserve Bulletin* is the authoritative source of information about historical prime rates.

principal. An amount on which *interest* accrues, either as *expense* (for the borrower) or as *revenue* (for the lender); the *face amount* of a *loan;* also, the absent owner (principal) who hires the manager (agent) in a "principal-agent" relationship.

principle. See *generally accepted accounting principles.*

prior-period adjustment. A *debit* or *credit* that is made directly to *retained earnings* (and that does not affect *income* for the period) to adjust earnings as calculated for prior periods. Such adjustments are now rare. Theory suggests that accounting should correct for errors in accounting estimates (such as the *depreciable life* or *salvage value* of an asset) by adjusting retained earnings so that statements for future periods will show correct amounts. But *GAAP* require that corrections of such estimates flow through current, and perhaps future, *income statements*. See *accounting changes* and *accounting errors*.

prior service cost. *Present value* at a given time of a *pension plan's* retroactive *benefits.* "Unrecognized prior service cost" refers to that portion of prior service cost not yet *debited* to *expense.* See *actuarial accrued liability* and *funded.* Contrast with *normal cost.*

pro forma statements. Hypothetical statements; financial statements as they would appear if some event, such as a *merger* or increased production and sales, had occurred or were to occur; sometimes spelled as one word, "proforma."

probable. In many of its definitions, the *FASB* uses the term "probable." See, for example, *asset, firm commitment, liability.* A survey of practicing accountants revealed that the average of the probabilities that those surveyed had in mind when they used the term "probable" was 85 percent. Some

accountants think that any event whose outcome is greater than 50 percent should be called "probable." The FASB uses the phrase "more likely than not" when it means greater than 50 percent.

proceeds. The *funds* received from the disposition of assets or from the issue of securities.

process costing. A method of *cost accounting* based on average costs (total cost divided by the *equivalent units* of work done in a period); typically used for assembly lines or for products that the firm produces in a series of steps that are more continuous than discrete.

product. *Goods* or *services* produced.

product cost. Any *manufacturing cost* that the firm can—or, in some contexts, should—debit to an *inventory* account. See *flow of costs,* for example. Contrast with *period expenses.*

product life cycle. Time span between initial concept (typically starting with research and development) of a good or service and the time when the firm ceases to support customers who have purchased the good or service.

production cost. *Manufacturing cost.*

production cost account. A *temporary account* for accumulating *manufacturing costs* during a period.

production department. A department producing salable *goods* or *services;* contrast with *service department.*

production method (depreciation). One form of *straight-line depreciation.* The firm assigns to the depreciable asset (e.g., a truck) a *depreciable life* measured not in elapsed time but in units of output (e.g., miles) or perhaps in units of time of expected use. Then the *depreciation* charge for a period is a portion of depreciable cost equal to a fraction computed as the actual output produced during the period divided by the expected total output to be produced over the life of the asset. This method is sometimes called the "units-of-production (or output) method."

production method (revenue recognition). *Percentage-of-completion method* for recognizing *revenue.*

production volume variance. Standard fixed *overhead* rate per unit of normal *capacity* (or base activity) times (units of base activity budgeted or planned for a period minus actual units of base activity worked or assigned to product during the period); often called a "volume variance."

productive capacity. One *attribute measured* for *assets.* The *current cost* of *long-term assets* means the cost of reproducing the productive capacity (for example, the ability to manufacture one million units a year), not the cost of reproducing the actual physical assets currently used (see *reproduction cost*). *Replacement cost* of productive capacity will be the same as reproduction cost of assets only in the unusual case when no technological improvement in production processes has occurred and the relative prices of goods and services used in production have remained approximately the same as when the firm acquired the currently used goods and services.

profit. Excess of *revenues* over *expenses* for a *transaction;* sometimes used synonymously with *net income* for the period.

profit and loss account. UK: *retained earnings.*

profit-and-loss sharing ratio. The fraction of *net income* or loss allocable to a partner in a *partnership;.* need not be the same fraction as the partner's share of capital.

profit-and-loss statement. *Income statement.*

profit center. A *responsibility center* for which a firm accumulates both *revenues* and *expenses*. Contrast with *cost center.*

profit margin. *Sales* minus all *expenses.*

profit margin percentage. *Profit margin* divided by *net sales.*

profit maximization. The doctrine that the firm should account for a given set of operations so as to make reported *net income* as large as possible; contrast with *conservatism.* This concept in accounting differs from the profit-maximizing concept in economics, which states that the firm should manage operations to maximize the present value of the firm's wealth, generally by equating *marginal costs* and *marginal revenues.*

profit-sharing plan. A *defined-contribution plan* in which the employer contributes amounts based on *net income.*

profit variance analysis. Analysis of the causes of the difference between budgeted profit in the *master budget* and the profits earned.

profit-volume analysis (equation). Analysis of effects, on *profits,* caused by changes in volume or *contribution margin* per unit or *fixed costs.* See *breakeven chart.*

profit-volume graph. See *breakeven chart.*

profit-volume ratio. *Net income* divided by net sales in dollars.

profitability accounting. *Responsibility accounting.*

program budgeting (PPB). Specification and analysis of inputs, outputs, costs, and alternatives that link plans to *budgets.*

programmed cost. A *fixed cost* not essential for carrying out operations. For example, a firm can control costs for research and development and advertising designed to generate new business, but once it commits to incur them, they become fixed costs. These costs are sometimes called managed costs or *discretionary costs.* Contrast with *capacity costs.*

progressive tax. Tax for which the rate increases as the taxed base, such as income, increases. Contrast with *regressive tax.*

project financing arrangement. As defined by *SFAS No. 47,* the financing of an investment project in which the lender looks principally to the *cash flows* and *earnings* of the project as the source of funds for repayment and to the *assets* of the project as *collateral* for the loan. The general *credit* of the project entity usually does not affect the terms of the financing either because the borrowing entity is a *corporation* without other assets or because the financing provides that the lender has no direct *recourse* to the entity's owners.

projected benefit obligation. The *actuarial present value* at a given date of all pension benefits attributed by a *defined-benefit pension* formula to employee service rendered before that date. The analyst measures the obligation using assumptions as to future compensation levels if the formula incorporates future compensation, as happens, for example, when the plan bases the eventual pension benefit on wages of the last several years of employees' work lives. Contrast to "accumulated benefit obligation," where the analyst mea-

sures the obligation using employee compensation levels at the time of the measurement date.

projected financial statement. *Pro forma* financial statement.

projection. See *financial projection* for definition and contrast.

promissory note. An unconditional written promise to pay a specified sum of cash on demand or at a specified date.

proof of journal. The process of checking the arithmetic accuracy of *journal entries* by testing for the equality of all *debits* and all *credits* since the last previous proof.

property dividend. A *dividend in kind.*

property, plant, and equipment. See *plant assets.*

proportionate consolidation. Canada: a presentation of the *financial statements* of any investor-investment relationship, whereby the investor's pro rata share of each *asset, liability, income* item, and *expense* item appears in the *financial statements* of the investor under the various *balance sheet* and *income statement* headings.

proprietary accounts. See *budgetary accounts* for definition and contrast in the context of governmental accounting.

proprietorship. *Assets* minus *liabilities* of an *entity;* equals *contributed capital* plus *retained earnings.*

proprietorship theory. The corporation view that emphasizes the form of the *accounting equation* that says *assets − liabilities = owners' equity;* contrast with *entity theory.* The major implication of a choice between these theories deals with the treatment of *subsidiaries.* For example, the proprietorship theory views *minority interest* as an *indeterminate-term liability.* The proprietorship theory implies using a *single-step income statement.*

prorate. To *allocate* in proportion to some base; for example, to allocate *service department* costs in proportion to hours of service used by the benefited department or to allocate *manufacturing variances* to product sold and to product added to *ending inventory.*

prorating variances. See *prorate.*

prospectus. Formal written document describing *securities* a firm will issue. See *proxy.*

protest fee. Fee charged by banks or other financial agencies when the bank cannot collect items (such as *checks*) presented for collection.

provision. Part of an *account* title. Often the firm must recognize an *expense* even though it cannot be sure of the exact amount. The entry for the estimated expense, such as for *income taxes* or expected costs under *warranty,* is as follows:

Expense (Estimated)	X	
Liability (Estimated)		X

American terminology often uses "provision" in the expense account title of the above entry. Thus, Provision for Income Taxes means the estimate of income tax expense. (British terminology uses "provision" in the title for the estimated liability of the above entry, so that Provision for Income Taxes is a balance sheet account.)

proxy. Written authorization given by one person to another so that the second person can act for the first, such as to vote shares of stock; of particular significance to accountants because the *SEC* presumes that management distributes financial information along with its proxy solicitations.

public accountant. Generally, this term is synonymous with *certified public accountant*. Some jurisdictions, however, license individuals who are not CPAs as public accountants.

public accounting. That portion of accounting primarily involving the *attest* function, culminating in the *auditor's report*.

PuPU. Acronym for *purchasing power unit*; conceived by John C. Burton, former chief accountant of the *SEC*. Those who think that *constant-dollar accounting* is not particularly useful poke fun at it by calling it "PuPU accounting."

purchase allowance. A reduction in sales *invoice price* usually granted because the purchaser received *goods* not exactly as ordered. The purchaser does not return the goods but agrees to keep them for a price lower than originally agreed upon.

purchase discount. A reduction in purchase *invoice price* granted for prompt payment. See *sales discount* and *terms of sale*.

purchase investigation. An investigation of the financial affairs of a company for the purpose of disclosing matters that may influence the terms or conclusion of a potential acquisition.

purchase method. Accounting for a *business combination* by adding the acquired company's assets at the price paid for them to the acquiring company's assets. Contrast with *pooling-of-interests method*. The firm adds the acquired assets to the books at current values rather than original costs; the subsequent *amortization expenses* usually exceed those (and reported income is smaller than that) for the same business combination accounted for as a pooling of interests. *GAAP* require that the acquirer use the purchase method unless the acquisition meets all the pooling criteria in *APB Opinion No. 16*.

purchase order. Document issued by a buyer authorizing a seller to deliver goods, with the buyer to make payment later.

purchasing power gain or loss. *Monetary gain or loss.*

push-down accounting. An accounting method used in some *purchase transactions*. Assume that Company A purchases substantially all the *common shares* of Company B but that Company B must still issue its own *financial statements*. The question arises, shall Company B change the *basis* for its *assets* and *equities* on its own books to the same updated amounts at which they appear on Company A's *consolidated financial statements*? Company B uses "push-down accounting" when it shows the new asset and equity bases reflecting Company A's purchase, because the method "pushes down" the new bases from Company A (where *GAAP* require them) to Company B (where the new bases would not appear in *historical cost accounting*). Since 1983, the *SEC* has required push-down accounting under some circumstances.

put. An option to sell *shares* of a publicly traded corporation at a fixed price during a fixed time span. Contrast with *call*.

Q

qualified report (opinion). *Auditor's report* containing a statement that the auditor was unable to complete a satisfactory examination of all things considered relevant or that the auditor has doubts about the financial impact of some *material* item reported in the financial statements. See *except for* and *subject to*.

quality. In modern usage, a product or service has quality to the extent it conforms to specifications or provides customers the characteristics promised them.

quality of earnings. A phrase with no single, agreed-upon meaning. Some who use the phrase use it with different meanings on different occasions. "Quality of earnings" has an accounting aspect and a business cycle aspect.

In its accounting aspect, managers have choices in measuring and reporting *earnings*. This discretion can involve any of the following: selecting *accounting principles* or standards when *GAAP* allow a choice; making estimates in the application of accounting principles; and timing transactions to allow recognizing *nonrecurring* items in earnings. In some instances the range of choices has a large impact on reported earnings and in others, small. (1) Some use the phrase "quality of earnings" to mean the degree to which management can affect reported income by its choices of accounting estimates even though the choices recur every period. These users judge, for example, insurance companies to have low-quality earnings. Insurance company management must reestimate its liabilities for future payments to the insured each period, thereby having an opportunity to report periodic earnings within a wide range. (2) Others use the phrase to mean the degree to which management actually takes advantage of its flexibility. For them, an insurance company that does not vary its methods and estimating techniques, even though it has the opportunity to do so, has high-quality earnings. (3) Some have in mind the proximity in time between *revenue* recognition and cash collection. For them, the smaller the time delay, the higher will be the quality. (4) Still others use the phrase to mean the degree to which managers who have a choice among the items with large influence on earnings choose the ones that result in income measures that are more likely to recur. For them, the more likely an item of earnings is to recur, the higher will be its quality. Often these last two groups trade off with each other. Consider a dealer leasing a car on a long-term *lease*, receiving monthly collections. The dealer who uses *sales-type lease* accounting scores low on proximity of revenue recognition (all at the time of signing the lease) to cash collection but highlights the nonrepetitive nature of the transaction. The leasing dealer who uses *operating lease* accounting has perfectly matching revenue recognition and cash collection, but the *recurring* nature of the revenue gives a misleading picture of a repetitive transaction. The phrase "item of earnings" in (4) is ambiguous. The writer could mean the underlying economic event (which occurs when the lease for the car is signed) or the revenue recognition (which occurs every time the dealer using operating lease accounting receives cash). Hence, you should try to understand what other speakers and writers mean by "quality of earnings" when you interpret what they say and write. Some who refer to "earnings quality" suspect that managers will usually make choices that enhance current earnings and present the firm in the best light, independent of the ability of the firm to generate similar earnings in the future.

In the business cycle aspect, management's action often has no impact on the stability and recurrence of earnings. Compare a company that sells consumer products and likely has sales repeating every week with a construction company that builds to order. Companies in noncyclical businesses, such as some public utilities, likely have more stable earnings than ones in cyclical businesses, such as steel. Some use "quality of earnings" to refer to the stability and recurrence of basic revenue-generating activities. Those who use the phrase this way rarely associate earnings quality with accounting issues.

quality of financial position. Because of the *articulation* of the *income statement* with the *balance sheet,* the factors that imply a high (or low) *quality of earnings* also affect the balance sheet. Users of this phrase have in mind the same accounting issues as they have in mind when they use the phrase "quality of earnings."

quantitative performance measure. A measure of output based on an objectively observable quantity, such as units produced or *direct costs* incurred, rather than on an unobservable quantity or a quantity observable only nonobjectively, like quality of service provided.

quantity discount. A reduction in purchase price as quantity purchased increases. The Robinson-Patman Act constrains the amount of the discount. Do not confuse with *purchase discount.*

quantity variance. *Efficiency variance;* in *standard cost* systems, the standard price per unit times (actual quantity used minus standard quantity that should be used).

quasi-reorganization. A *reorganization* in which no new company emerges or no court has intervened, as would happen in *bankruptcy.* The primary purpose is to rid the balance sheet of a *deficit* (negative *retained earnings*) and give the firm a "fresh start."

quick assets. *Assets* readily convertible into *cash*; includes cash, current marketable securities, and current receivables.

quick ratio. Sum of (cash, current marketable securities, and current receivables) divided by *current liabilities;* often called the "acid test ratio." The analyst may exclude some nonliquid receivables from the numerator. See *ratio.*

R

R^2. The proportion of the statistical variance of a *dependent variable* explained by the equation fit to *independent variable(s)* in a *regression analysis.*

Railroad Accounting Principles Board (RAPB). A board brought into existence by the Staggers Rail Act of 1980 to advise the Interstate Commerce Commission on accounting matters affecting railroads. The RAPB was the only cost-accounting body authorized by the government during the decade of the 1980s (because Congress ceased funding the CASB during the 1980s). The RAPB incorporated the pronouncements of the CASB and became the government's authority on cost accounting principles.

R&D. See *research and development.*

random number sampling. For choosing a sample, a method in which the analyst selects items from the *population* by using a random number table or generator.

random sampling. For choosing a sample, a method in which all items in the population have an equal chance of being selected. Compare *judgment(al) sampling.*

RAPB. *Railroad Accounting Principles Board.*

rate of return on assets. *Return on assets.*

rate of return on common stock equity. See *ratio.*

rate of return on shareholders' (owners') equity. See *ratio.*

rate of return (on total capital). See *ratio* and *return on assets.*

rate variance. *Price variance,* usually for *direct labor costs.*

ratio. The number resulting when one number divides another. Analysts generally use ratios to assess aspects of profitability, solvency, and liquidity. The commonly used financial ratios fall into three categories: (1) those that summarize some aspect of *operations* for a period, usually a year, (2) those that summarize some aspect of *financial position* at a given moment—the moment for which a balance sheet reports, and (3) those that relate some aspect of operations to some aspect of financial position. Exhibit 5.11 lists the most common financial ratios and shows separately both the numerator and the denominator for each ratio.

For all ratios that require an average balance during the period, the analyst often derives the average as one half the sum of the beginning and the ending balances. Sophisticated analysts recognize, however, that particularly when companies use a fiscal year different from the calendar year, this averaging of beginning and ending balances may mislead. Consider, for example, the rate of *return on assets* of Sears, Roebuck & Company, whose fiscal year ends on January 31. Sears chooses a January 31 closing date at least in part because inventories are at a low level and are therefore easy to count—it has sold the Christmas merchandise, and the Easter merchandise has not yet all arrived. Furthermore, by January 31, Sears has collected for most Christmas sales, so receivable amounts are not unusually large. Thus at January 31, the amount of total assets is lower than at many other times during the year. Consequently, the denominator of the rate of return on assets, total assets, for Sears more likely represents the smallest amount of total assets on hand during the year rather than the average amount. The return on assets rate for Sears and other companies that choose a fiscal year-end to coincide with low points in the inventory cycle is likely to exceed the ratio measured with a more accurate estimate of the average amounts of total assets.

raw material. Goods purchased for use in manufacturing a product.

reacquired stock. *Treasury shares.*

real accounts. *Balance sheet accounts,* as opposed to *nominal accounts.* See *permanent accounts.*

real amount (value). An amount stated in *constant dollars.* For example, if the firm sells an investment costing $100 for $130 after a period of 10 percent general *inflation,* the *nominal amount* of *gain* is $30 (= $130 − $100) but the real amount of gain is C$20 (= $130 − 1.10 × $100), where "C$" denotes constant dollars of purchasing power on the date of sale.

real estate. *Land* and its *improvements,* such as landscaping and roads, but not buildings.

real interest rate. Interest rate reflecting the productivity of capital, not including a premium for inflation anticipated over the life of the loan.

realizable value. *Fair value* or, sometimes, *net realizable (sales) value.*

realization convention. The accounting practice of delaying the recognition of *gains* and *losses* from changes in the market price of *assets* until the firm sells the assets. However, the firm recognizes unrealized losses on *inventory* (or *marketable securities* classified as *trading securities*) prior to sale when the firm uses the *lower-of-cost-or-market* valuation basis for inventory (or the *fair value* basis for marketable securities).

realize. To convert into *funds;* when applied to a *gain* or *loss,* implies that an *arm's-length transaction* has taken place. Contrast with *recognize;* the firm may recognize a loss (as, for example, on *marketable equity securities*) in the financial statements even though it has not yet realized the loss via a transaction.

realized gain (or loss) on marketable equity securities. An income statement account title for the difference between the proceeds of disposition and the *original cost* of *marketable equity securities.*

realized holding gain. See *inventory profit* for definition and an example.

rearrangement costs. Costs of reinstalling assets, perhaps in a different location. The firm may, but need not, *capitalize* them as part of the assets cost, just as is done with original installation cost. The firm will *expense* these costs if they merely maintain the asset's future benefits at their originally intended level before the relocation.

recapitalization. *Reorganization.*

recapture. Name for one kind of tax payment. Various provisions of the *income tax* rules require a refund by the taxpayer (recapture by the government) of various tax advantages under certain conditions. For example, the taxpayer must repay tax savings provided by *accelerated depreciation* if the taxpayer prematurely retires the item providing the tax savings.

receipt. Acquisition of *cash.*

receivable. Any *collectible,* whether or not it is currently due.

receivable turnover. See *ratio.*

reciprocal holdings. Company A owns stock of Company B, and Company B owns stock of Company A; or Company B owns stock of Company C, which owns stock of Company A.

recognize. To enter a transaction in the accounts; not synonymous with *realize.*

reconciliation. A calculation that shows how one balance or figure derives from another, such as a reconciliation of retained earnings or a *bank reconciliation schedule.* See *articulate.*

record date. The date at which the firm pays *dividends* on payment date to those who own the stock.

recourse. The rights of the lender if a borrower does not repay as promised. A recourse loan gives the lender the right to take any of the borrower's assets not exempted from such taking by the contract. See also *note receivable discounted.*

recovery of unrealized loss on trading securities. An *income statement account title* for the *gain* during the current period on *trading securities.*

recurring. Occurring again; occurring repetitively; in accounting, an adjective often used in describing *revenue* or *earnings.* In some contexts, the term "recurring revenue" is ambiguous. Consider a construction contractor who accounts for a single long-term project with the *installment method,* with revenue recognized at the time of each cash collection from the customer. The recognized revenue is recurring, but the transaction leading to the revenue is not. See *quality of earnings.*

redemption. Retirement by the issuer, usually by a purchase or *call,* of *stocks* or *bonds.*

redemption premium. *Call premium.*

redemption value. The price a corporation will pay to retire *bonds* or *preferred stock* if it calls them before *maturity.*

refinancing. An adjustment in the *capital structure* of a *corporation,* involving changes in the nature and amounts of the various classes of *debt* and, in some cases, *capital* as well as other components of *shareholders' equity.* *Asset* carrying values in the accounts remain unchanged.

refunding bond issue. Said of a *bond* issue whose proceeds the firm uses to retire bonds already *outstanding.*

register. A collection of consecutive entries, or other information, in chronological order, such as a check register or an insurance register that lists all insurance policies owned. If the firm records entries in the register, it can serve as a *journal.*

registered bond. A bond for which the issuer will pay the *principal* and *interest,* if registered as to interest, to the owner listed on the books of the issuer; as opposed to a bearer bond, in which the issuer must pay the possessor of the bond.

registrar. An *agent,* usually a bank or trust company, appointed by a corporation to keep track of the names of shareholders and distributions to them.

registration statement. Required by the Securities Act of 1933, statement of most companies that want to have owners of their securities trade the securities in public markets. The statement discloses financial data and other items of interest to potential investors.

regression analysis. A method of *cost estimation* based on statistical techniques for fitting a line (or its equivalent in higher mathematical dimensions) to an observed series of data points, usually by minimizing the sum of squared deviations of the observed data from the fitted line. Common usage calls the cost that the analysis explains the "dependent variable"; it calls the variable(s) we use to estimate cost behavior "independent variable(s)." If we use more than one independent variable, the term for the analysis is "multiple regression analysis." See R^2, *standard error,* and *t-value.*

regressive tax. Tax for which the rate decreases as the taxed base, such as income, increases. Contrast with *progressive tax.*

Regulation S-K. The *SEC*'s standardization of nonfinancial statement disclosure requirements for documents filed with the SEC.

Regulation S-T. The *SEC*'s regulations specifying formats for electronic filing and the *EDGAR* system.

Regulation S-X. The *SEC*'s principal accounting regulation, which specifies the form and content of financial reports to the SEC.

rehabilitation. The improving of a used *asset* via an extensive repair. Ordinary *repairs* and *maintenance* restore or maintain expected *service potential* of an asset, and the firm treats them as *expenses.* A rehabilitation improves the asset beyond its current service potential, enhancing the service potential to a significantly higher level than before the rehabilitation. Once rehabilitated, the asset may be better, but need not be, than it was when new. The firm will *capitalize expenditures* for rehabilitation, like those for *betterments* and *improvements.*

reinvestment rate. In a *capital budgeting* context, the rate at which the firm invests cash inflows from a project occurring before the project's completion. Once the analyst assumes such a rate, no project can ever have multiple *internal rates of return.* See *Descartes' rule of signs.*

relative performance evaluation. Setting performance targets and, sometimes, compensation in relation to the performance of others, perhaps in different firms or divisions, who face a similar environment.

relative sales value method. See *net realizable (sales) value.*

relevant cost. Cost used by an analyst in making a decision. *Incremental cost; opportunity cost.*

relevant range. Activity levels over which costs are linear or for which *flexible budget* estimates and *breakeven charts* will remain valid.

remit earnings. An expression likely to confuse a reader without a firm understanding of accounting basics. A firm generates *net assets* by earning *income* and retains net assets if it does not declare *dividends* in the amount of net income. When a firm declares dividends and pays the cash (or other net assets), some writers would say the firm "remits earnings." We think the student learns better by conceiving

earnings as a *credit balance.* When a firm pays dividends it sends net assets, things with debit balances, not something with a credit balance, to the recipient. When writers say firms "remit earnings," they mean the firms send assets (or net assets) that previous earnings have generated and reduce *retained earnings.*

remittance advice. Information on a *check stub,* or on a document attached to a check by the *drawer,* that tells the *payee* why a payment is being made.

rent. A charge for use of land, buildings, or other assets.

reorganization. In the *capital structure* of a corporation, a major change that leads to changes in the rights, interests, and implied ownership of the various security owners; usually results from a *merger* or an agreement by senior security holders to take action to forestall *bankruptcy.*

repair. An *expenditure* to restore an *asset's* service potential after damage or after prolonged use. In the second sense, after prolonged use, the difference between repairs and maintenance is one of degree and not of kind. A repair is treated as an *expense* of the period when incurred. Because the firm treats repairs and maintenance similarly in this regard, the distinction is not important. A repair helps to maintain capacity at the levels planned when the firm acquired the *asset.* Contrast with *improvement.*

replacement cost. For an asset, the current fair market price to purchase another, similar asset (with the same future benefit or service potential). *Current cost.* See *reproduction cost* and *productive capacity.* See also *distributable income* and *inventory profit.*

replacement cost method of depreciation. Method in which the analyst augments the original-cost *depreciation* charge with an amount based on a portion of the difference between the *current replacement cost* of the asset and its *original cost.*

replacement system of depreciation. See *retirement method of depreciation* for definition and contrast.

report. *Financial statement; auditor's report.*

report form. *Balance sheet* form that typically shows *assets* minus *liabilities* as one total. Then, below that total appears the components of *owners' equity* summing to the same total. Often, the top section shows *current* assets less current liabilities before *noncurrent assets* less noncurrent liabilities. Contrast with *account form.*

reporting objectives (policies). The general purposes for which the firm prepares *financial statements.* The *FASB* has discussed these in *SFAC No. 1.*

representative item sampling. Sampling in which the analyst believes the sample selected is typical of the entire population from which it comes. Compare *specific item sampling.*

reproduction cost. The *cost* necessary to acquire an *asset* similar in all physical respects to another asset for which the analyst requires a *current value.* See *replacement cost* and *productive capacity* for contrast.

required rate of return (RRR). *Cost of capital.*

requisition. A formal written order or request, such as for withdrawal of supplies from the storeroom.

resale value. *Exit value; net realizable value.*

research and development (R&D). A form of economic activity with special accounting rules. Firms engage in research in hopes of discovering new knowledge that will create a new product, process, or service or of improving a present product, process, or service. Development translates research findings or other knowledge into a new or improved product, process, or service. *SFAS No. 2* requires that firms expense costs of such activities as incurred on the grounds that the future benefits are too uncertain to warrant *capitalization* as an asset. This treatment seems questionable to us because we wonder why firms would continue to undertake R&D if there was no expectation of future benefit; if future benefits exist, then R&D *costs* should be assets that appear, like other assets, at *historical cost.*

reserve. The worst word in accounting because almost everyone not trained in accounting, and some who are, misunderstand it. The common confusion is that "reserves" represent a pool of *cash* or other *assets* available when the firm needs them. Wrong. Cash always has a *debit balance.* Reserves always have a *credit* balance. When properly used in accounting, "reserves" refer to an account that appropriates *retained earnings* and restricts dividend declarations. Appropriating retained earnings is itself a poor and vanishing practice, so the word should seldom appear in accounting. In addition, "reserve" was used in the past to indicate an asset *contra account* (for example, "reserve for depreciation") or an *estimated liability* (for example, "reserve for warranty costs"). In any case, reserve accounts have *credit* balances and are not pools of *funds,* as the unwary reader might infer. If a company has set aside a pool of *cash* (or *marketable securities*) to serve some specific purpose such as paying for a new factory, then it will call that cash a *fund.* No other word in accounting causes so much misunderstanding by nonexperts as well as by "experts" who should know better. A leading unabridged dictionary defines "reserve" as "cash, or assets readily convertible into cash, held aside, as by a corporation, bank, state or national government, etc. to meet expected or unexpected demands." This definition is absolutely wrong in accounting. Reserves are not funds. For example, the firm creates a contingency fund of $10,000 by depositing cash in a fund and makes the following entry:

Dr. Contingency Fund	10,000	
Cr. Cash		10,000

The following entry may accompany the previous entry, if the firm wants to appropriate retained earnings:

Dr. Retained Earnings	10,000	
Cr. Reserve for Contingencies		10,000

The transaction leading to the first entry has economic significance. The second entry has little economic impact for most firms. The problem with the word "reserve" arises because the firm can make the second entry without the first— a company can create a reserve, that is, appropriate retained earnings, without creating a fund. The problem results, at least in part, from the fact that in common usage, "reserve" means a pool of assets, as in the phrase "oil reserves." The *Internal Revenue Service* does not help in dispelling confusion about the term "reserves." The federal *income tax* return for corporations uses the title "Reserve for Bad Debts" to mean "Allowance for Uncollectible Accounts" and speaks of the "Reserve Method" in referring to the *allowance method* for estimating *revenue* or *income* reductions from estimated *uncollectibles.*

reserve recognition accounting (RRA). One form of *accounting* for natural resources. In exploration for natural resources, the problem arises of how to treat the expenditures for exploration, both before the firm knows the outcome of the efforts and after it knows the outcome. Suppose that the firm spends $10 million to drill 10 holes ($1 million each) and that nine of them are dry whereas one is a gusher containing oil with a *net realizable value* of $40 million. Dry hole, or *successful efforts,* accounting would expense $9 million and *capitalize* $1 million, which the firm will *deplete* as it lifts the oil from the ground. *SFAS No. 19,* now suspended, required *successful efforts costing.* Full costing would expense nothing but would capitalize the $10 million of drilling costs that the firm will deplete as it lifts the oil from the single productive well. Reserve recognition accounting would capitalize $40 million, which the firm will deplete as it lifts the oil, with a $30 million *credit* to *income* or *contributed capital.* The *balance sheet* shows the *net realizable value* of proven oil and gas reserves. The *income statement* has three sorts of items: (1) current income resulting from production or "lifting profit," which is the *revenue* from sales of oil and gas less the expense based on the current valuation amount at which these items have appeared on the balance sheet, (2) profit or loss from exploration efforts in which the current value of new discoveries is revenue and all the exploration cost is expense, and (3) gain or loss on changes in current value during the year, which accountants in other contexts call a *holding gain or loss.*

reset bond. A bond, typically a *junk bond,* that specifies that periodically the issuer will reset the coupon rate so that the bond sells at *par* in the market. Investment bankers created this type of instrument to help ensure the purchasers of such bonds of getting a fair rate of return, given the riskiness of the issuer. If the issuer gets into financial trouble, its bonds will trade for less than par in the market. The issuer of a reset bond promises to raise the interest rate and preserve the value of the bond. Ironically, the reset feature has often had just the opposite effect. The default risk of many issuers of reset bonds has deteriorated so much that the bonds have dropped to less than 50 percent of par. To raise the value to par, the issuer would have to raise the interest rate to more than 25 percent per year. That rate is so large that issuers have declared bankruptcy rather than attempt to make the new large interest payments; this then reduces the market value of the bonds rather than increases them.

residual income. In an external reporting context, a term that refers to *net income* to *common shares* (= net income less *preferred stock dividends*). In *managerial accounting*, this term refers to the excess of income for a *division* or *segment* of a company over the product of the *cost of capital* for the company multiplied by the average amount of capital invested in the division during the period over which the division earned the income.

residual security. A *potentially dilutive security. Options, warrants, convertible bonds,* and *convertible preferred stock.*

residual value. At any time, the estimated or actual *net realizable value* (that is, proceeds less removal costs) of an *asset,* usually a depreciable *plant asset.* In the context of depreciation accounting, this term is equivalent to *salvage value* and is preferred to *scrap value* because the firm need not scrap the asset. It is sometimes used to mean net *book value.* In the context of a *noncancelable* lease, it is the estimated value of the leased asset at the end of the lease period. See *lease.*

resources supplied. *Expenditures* made for an activity.

resources used. *Cost driver* rate times cost driver volume.

responsibility accounting. Accounting for a business by considering various units as separate entities, or *profit centers,* giving management of each unit responsibility for the unit's *revenues* and *expenses.* See *transfer price.*

responsibility center. An organization part or *segment* that top management holds accountable for a specified set of activities. Also called "accountability center." See *cost center, investment center, profit center,* and *revenue center.*

restricted assets. Governmental resources restricted by legal or contractual requirements for specific purpose.

restricted retained earnings. That part of *retained earnings* not legally available for *dividends.* See *retained earnings, appropriated.* Bond indentures and other loan contracts can curtail the legal ability of the corporation to declare dividends without formally requiring a retained earnings appropriation, but the firm must disclose such restrictions.

retail inventory method. Ascertaining cost amounts of *ending inventory* as follows (assuming *FIFO*): cost of ending inventory = (selling price of *goods available for sale* − sales) × *cost percentage.* The analyst then computes cost of goods sold from the inventory equation; costs of beginning inventory, purchases, and ending inventory are all known. (When the firm uses *LIFO,* the method resembles the *dollar-value LIFO method.*) See *markup.*

retail terminology. See *markup.*

retained earnings. Net *income* over the life of a corporation less all *dividends* (including capitalization through *stock dividends*); *owners' equity* less *contributed capital.*

retained earnings, appropriated. An *account* set up by crediting it and debiting *retained earnings;* used to indicate that a portion of retained earnings is not available for dividends. The practice of appropriating retained earnings is misleading unless the firm marks all capital with its use, which is not practicable, nor sensible, since capital is fungible—all the *equities* jointly fund all the *assets.* The use of formal retained earnings appropriations is declining.

retained earnings statement. A *reconciliation* of the beginning and the ending balances in the *retained earnings account;* required by *generally accepted accounting principles* whenever the firm presents *comparative balance sheets* and an *income statement.* This reconciliation can appear in a separate statement, in a combined statement of income and retained earnings, or in the balance sheet.

retirement method of depreciation. A method in which the firm records no entry for *depreciation expense* until it retires an *asset* from service. Then, it makes an entry *debiting* depreciation expense and *crediting* the asset account for the cost of the asset retired. If the retired asset has a *salvage value,* the firm reduces the amount of the debit to depreciation expense by the amount of salvage value with a corresponding debit to cash, receivables, or salvaged materials. The "replacement system of depreciation" is similar, except that the debit to depreciation expense equals the cost of the new asset less the salvage value, if any, of the old asset. Some public utilities used these methods. For example, if the firm acquired ten telephone poles in Year 1 for $60 each and replaces them in Year 10 for $100 each when the salvage value of the old poles is $5 each, the accounting would be as follows:

Retirement Method

Plant Assets	600	
Cash		600
To acquire assets in Year 1.		
Depreciation Expense	550	
Salvage Receivable	50	
Plant Assets		600
To record retirement and depreciation in Year 10.		
Plant Assets	1,000	
Cash		1,000
To record acquisition of new assets in Year 10.		

Replacement Method

Plant Assets	600	
Cash		600
To acquire assets in Year 1.		
Depreciation Expense	950	
Salvage Receivable	50	
Cash		1,000
To record depreciation on old asset in amount quantified by net cost of replacement asset in Year 10.		

The retirement method is like *FIFO* in that it records the cost of the first assets as depreciation and puts the cost of the second assets on the balance sheet. The replacement method is like *LIFO* in that it records the cost of the second assets as depreciation expense and leaves the cost of the first assets on the balance sheet.

retirement plan. *Pension plan.*

retroactive benefits. In initiating or amending a *defined-benefit pension plan,* benefits that the benefit formula attributes to employee services rendered in periods prior to the initiation or amendment. See *prior service costs.*

return. A schedule of information required by governmental bodies, such as the tax return required by the *Internal Revenue Service;* also the physical return of merchandise. See also *return on investment.*

return on assets (ROA). *Net income* plus after-tax *interest charges* plus *minority interest* in income divided by average total *assets;* perhaps the single most useful ratio for assessing management's overall operating performance. Most financial economists would subtract average noninterest-bearing *liabilities* from the denominator. Economists realize that when liabilities do not provide for explicit interest charges, the creditor adjusts the terms of contract, such as setting a higher selling price or lower discount, to those who do not pay cash immediately. (To take an extreme example, consider how much higher salary a worker who receives a salary once per year, rather than once per month, would demand.) This ratio requires in the numerator the income amount before the firm accrues any charges to suppliers of funds. We cannot measure the interest charges implicit in the noninterest-bearing liabilities because they cause items such as cost of goods sold and salary expense to be somewhat larger, since the interest is implicit. Subtracting their amounts from the denominator adjusts for their implicit cost. Such subtraction assumes that assets financed with noninterest-bearing liabilities have the same rate of return as all the other assets.

return on investment (ROI), return on capital. *Income* (before distributions to suppliers of capital) for a period; as a rate, this amount divided by average total assets. The analyst should add back *interest,* net of tax effects, to *net income* for the numerator. See *ratio.*

revenue. The *owners' equity* increase accompanying the *net assets* increase caused by selling goods or rendering services; in short, a service rendered; *sales* of products, merchandise, and services and earnings from *interest, dividends, rents,* and the like. Measure revenue as the expected *net present value* of the net assets the firm will receive. Do not confuse with *receipt* of *funds,* which may occur before, when, or after revenue is recognized. Contrast with *gain* and *income.* See also *holding gain.* Some writers use the term *gross income* synonymously with *revenue;* avoid such usage.

revenue center. Within a firm, a *responsibility center* that has control only over revenues generated. Contrast with *cost center.* See *profit center.*

revenue expenditure. A term sometimes used to mean an *expense,* in contrast to a capital *expenditure* to acquire an *asset* or to discharge a *liability.* Avoid using this term; use *period expense* instead.

revenue received in advance. An inferior term for *advances from customers.*

reversal (reversing) entry. An *entry* in which all *debits* and *credits* are the credits and debits, respectively, of another entry, and in the same amounts. The accountant usually records a reversal entry on the first day of an *accounting period* to reverse a previous *adjusting entry,* usually an *accrual.* The purpose of such entries is to make the bookkeeper's tasks easier. Suppose that the firm pays salaries every other Friday, with paychecks compensating employees for the two weeks just ended. Total salaries accrue at the rate of $5,000 per five-day workweek. The bookkeeper is accustomed to making the following entry every other Friday:

(1) Salary Expense	10,000	
Cash		10,000
To record salary expense and salary payments.		

If the firm delivers paychecks to employees on Friday, November 25, then the *adjusting entry* made on November 30 (or perhaps later) to record accrued salaries for November 28, 29, and 30 would be as follows:

(2) Salary Expense	3,000	
Salaries Payable		3,000
To charge November operations with all salaries earned in November.		

The firm would close the Salary Expense account as part of the November 30 closing entries. On the next payday, December 9, the salary entry would be as follows:

(3) Salary Expense	7,000	
Salaries Payable	3,000	
Cash		10,000
To record salary payments split between expense for December (seven days) and liability carried over from November.		

To make entry (3), the bookkeeper must look back into the records to see how much of the debit is to Salaries Payable accrued from the previous month in order to split the total debits between December expense and the liability carried over from November. Notice that this entry forces the bookkeeper both (a) to refer to balances in old accounts and (b) to make an entry different from the one customarily made, entry (1). The reversing entry, made just after the books have been closed for the second quarter, makes the salary entry for December 9 the same as that made on all other Friday paydays. The reversing entry merely *reverses* the adjusting entry (2):

(4) Salaries Payable	3,000	
Salary Expense		3,000
To reverse the adjusting entry.		

This entry results in a zero balance in the Salaries Payable account and a credit balance in the Salary Expense account. If the firm makes entry (4) just after it closes the books for November, then the entry on December 9 will be the customary entry (1). Entries (4) and (1) together have exactly the same effect as entry (3).

The procedure for using reversal entries is as follows: the firm makes the required adjustment to record an accrual (*payable* or *receivable*) at the end of an *accounting period*; it makes the closing entry as usual; as of the first day of the following period, it makes an entry reversing the adjusting entry; when the firm makes (or receives) a payment, it records the entry as though it had not recorded an adjusting entry at the end of the preceding period. Whether a firm uses reversal entries affects the record-keeping procedures but not the financial statements.

This term is also used to describe the entry reversing an incorrect entry before recording the correct entry

reverse stock split. A stock split in which the firm decreases the number of shares *outstanding*. See *stock split*.

revolving fund. A fund whose amounts the firm continually spends and replenishes; for example, a *petty cash fund*.

revolving loan. A *loan* that both the borrower and the lender expect to renew at *maturity*.

right. The privilege to subscribe to new *stock* issues or to purchase stock. Usually, securities called *warrants* contain the rights, and the owner of the warrants may sell them. See also *preemptive right*.

risk. A measure of the variability of the *return on investment*. For a given expected amount of return, most people prefer less risk to more risk. Therefore, in rational markets, investments with more risk usually promise, or investors expect to receive, a higher rate of return than investments with lower risk. Most people use "risk" and "uncertainty" as synonyms. In technical language, however, these terms have different meanings. We use "risk" when we know the probabilities attached to the various outcomes, such as the probabilities of heads or tails in the flip of a fair coin. "Uncertainty" refers to an event for which we can only estimate the probabilities of the outcomes, such as winning or losing a lawsuit.

risk-adjusted discount rate. Rate used in discounting cash flows for projects more or less risky than the firm's average. In a *capital budgeting* context, a decision analyst compares projects by comparing their net *present values* for a given *interest* rate, usually the cost of capital. If the analyst considers a given project's outcome to be much more or much less risky than the normal undertakings of the company, then the analyst will use a larger interest rate (if the project is riskier) or a smaller interest rate (if less risky) in discounting, and the rate used is "risk-adjusted."

risk-free rate. An interest rate reflecting only the pure interest rate plus an amount to compensate for inflation anticipated over the life of a loan, excluding a premium for the risk of default by the borrower. Financial economists usually measure the risk-free rate in the United States from U.S. government securities, such as Treasury bills and notes.

risk premium. Extra compensation paid to employees or extra *interest* paid to lenders, over amounts usually considered normal, in return for their undertaking to engage in activities riskier than normal.

ROA. *Return on assets.*

ROI. *Return on investment*; usually used to refer to a single project and expressed as a ratio: *income* divided by average *cost* of *assets* devoted to the project.

royalty. Compensation for the use of property, usually a patent, copyrighted material, or natural resources. The amount is often expressed as a percentage of receipts from using the property or as an amount per unit produced.

RRA. *Reserve recognition accounting.*

RRR. Required rate of return. See *cost of capital*.

rule of 69. Rule stating that an amount of cash invested at r percent per period will double in $69/r + .35$ periods. This approximation is accurate to one-tenth of a period for interest rates between 1/4 and 100 percent per period. For example, at 10 percent per period, the rule says that a given sum will double in $69/10 + .35 = 7.25$ periods. At 10 percent per period, a given sum actually doubles in 7.27+ periods.

rule of 72. Rule stating that an amount of cash invested at r percent per period will double in $72/r$ periods. A reasonable approximation for interest rates between 4 and 10 percent but not nearly as accurate as the *rule of 69* for interest rates outside that range. For example, at 10 percent per period, the rule says that a given sum will double in $72/10 = 7.2$ periods.

rule of 78. The rule followed by many finance companies for allocating earnings on *loans* among the months of a year on the sum-of-the-months'-digits basis when the borrower makes equal monthly payments to the lender. The sum of the digits from 1 through 12 is 78, so the rule allocates 12/78 of the year's earnings to the first month, 11/78 to the second month, and so on. This approximation allocates more of the early payments to interest and less to principal than does the correct, compound-interest method. Hence, lenders still use this method even though present-day computers can make the compound-interest computation as easily as they can carry out the approximation. See *sum-of-the-years'-digits depreciation*.

ruling (and balancing) an account. The process of summarizing a series of entries in an *account* by computing a new *balance* and drawing double lines to indicate that the new balance summarizes the information above the double lines. An illustration appears below. The steps are as follows: (1) Compute the sum of all *debit* entries including opening debit balance, if any—$1,464.16. (2) Compute the sum of all credit entries including opening credit balance, if any—$413.57. (3) If the amount in (1) exceeds the amount in (2), then write the excess as a credit with a checkmark—$1,464.16 − $413.57 = $1,050.59. (4) Add both debit and credit columns, which should both now sum to the same amount, and show that identical total at the foot of both columns. (5) Draw double lines under those numbers and write the excess of debits over credits as the new debit balance with a checkmark. (6) If the amount in (2) exceeds the amount in (1), then write the excess as a debit with a checkmark. (7) Do steps (4) and (5) except that the excess becomes the new credit balance. (8) If the amount in (1) equals the amount in (2), then the balance is zero, and only the totals with the double lines beneath them need appear.

Rutgers Accounting Web Site. See http://www.rutgers.edu/ Accounting/ for a useful compendium of accounting information.

S

S corporation. A corporation taxed like a *partnership*. Corporation (or partnership) agreements allocate the periodic *income* to the individual shareholders (or partners) who report these amounts on their individual *income tax* returns. Contrast with *C corporation*.

SA (société anonyme). France: A *corporation*.

SAB. Staff Accounting Bulletin of the SEC.

safe-harbor lease. A form of *tax-transfer lease*.

safety stock. Extra items of *inventory* kept on hand to protect against running out.

salary. Compensation earned by managers, administrators, and professionals, not based on an hourly rate. Contrast with *wage*.

sale. A *revenue* transaction in which the firm delivers *goods* or *services* to a customer in return for cash or a contractual obligation to pay.

sale and leaseback. A *financing* transaction in which the firm sells improved property but takes it back for use on a long-term *lease*. Such transactions often have advantageous income tax effects but usually have no effect on *financial statement income*.

sales activity variance. *Sales volume variance.*

sales allowance. A sales *invoice* price reduction that a seller grants to a buyer because the seller delivered *goods* different from, perhaps because of damage, those the buyer ordered. The seller often accumulates amounts of such adjustments in a temporary *revenue contra account* having this, or a similar, title. See *sales discount*.

sales basis of revenue recognition. Recognition of *revenue* not when a firm produces goods or when it receives orders but only when it has completed the sale by delivering the goods or services and has received cash or a claim to cash. Most firms recognize revenue on this basis. Compare with the *percentage-of-completion method* and the *installment method*. This is identical with the *completed contract method*, but the latter term ordinarily applies only to *long-term* construction projects.

sales contra, estimated uncollectibles. A title for the contra-revenue account to recognize estimated reductions in income caused by *accounts receivable* that will not be collected. See *bad debt expense, allowance for uncollectibles,* and *allowance method*.

sales discount. A sales *invoice* price reduction usually offered for prompt payment. See *terms of sale* and *2/10, n/30*.

sales return. The physical return of merchandise. The seller often accumulates amounts of such returns in a temporary revenue contra account.

An Open Account, Ruled and Balanced
(Steps indicated in parentheses correspond to steps described in "ruling an account.")

	Date 2000	Explanation	Ref.	Debit (1)	Date 2000	Explanation	Ref.	Credit (2)	
	Jan. 2	Balance	√	100.00					
	Jan. 13		VR	121.37	Sept. 15		J	.42	
	Mar. 20		VR	56.42	Nov. 12		J	413.15	
	June 5		J	1,138.09	Dec. 31	Balance	√	1,050.59	(3)
	Aug. 18		J	1.21					
	Nov. 20		VR	38.43					
	Dec, 7		VR	8.64					
(4)	2001			1,464.16	2001			1,464.16	(4)
(5)	Jan. 1	Balance	√	1,050.59					

sales-type (capital) lease. A form of *lease.* See *capital lease.* When a manufacturer (or other firm) that ordinarily sells goods enters a capital lease as *lessor,* the lease is a "sales-type lease." When a financial firm, such as a bank or insurance company or leasing company, acquires the asset from the manufacturer and then enters a capital lease as lessor, the lease is a "direct-financing-type lease." The manufacturer recognizes its ordinary profit (sales price less *cost of goods sold,* where sales price is the *present value* of the contractual lease payments plus any down payment) on executing the sales-type capital lease, but the financial firm does not recognize profit on executing a capital lease of the direct-financing type.

sales value method. *Relative sales value method.* See *net realizable value method.*

sales volume variance. Budgeted *contribution margin* per unit times (planned sales volume minus actual sales volume).

salvage value. Actual or estimated selling price, net of removal or disposal costs, of a used *plant asset* that the firm expects to sell or otherwise retire. See *residual value.*

SAR. *Summary annual report.*

SARL (société à responsabilité limitée). France: a *corporation* with limited liability and a life of no more than 99 years; must have at least two and no more than 50 *shareholders.*

SAS. *Statement on Auditing Standards* of the *AICPA.*

scale effect. See *discounted cash flow.*

scatter diagram. A graphic representation of the relation between two or more variables within a population.

schedule. A supporting set of calculations, with explanations, that show how to derive figures in a *financial statement* or tax return.

scientific method. *Effective interest method* of *amortizing bond discount* or *premium.*

scrap value. *Salvage value* assuming the owner intends to junk the item. A *net realizable value. Residual value.*

SEC (Securities and Exchange Commission). An agency authorized by the U.S. Congress to regulate, among other things, the financial reporting practices of most public corporations. The SEC has indicated that it will usually allow the *FASB* to set accounting principles, but it often requires more disclosure than the FASB requires. The SEC states its accounting requirements in its *Accounting Series Releases (ASR), Financial Reporting Releases, Accounting and Auditing Enforcement Releases, Staff Accounting Bulletins* (these are, strictly speaking, interpretations by the accounting staff, not rules of the commissioners themselves), and *Regulations S-X.* See also *registration statement, 10-K,* and *20-F.*

secret reserve. *Hidden reserve.*

Securities and Exchange Commission. *SEC.*

security. Document that indicates ownership, such as a *share* of *stock,* or indebtedness, such as a *bond,* or potential ownership, such as an *option* or *warrant.*

security available for sale. According to *SFAS No. 115* (1993), a *debt* or *equity security* that is not a *trading security,* or a debt security that is not a *security held to maturity.*

security held to maturity. According to *SFAS No. 115* (1993), a *debt security* the holder has both the ability and the intent to hold to *maturity;* valued in the *balance sheet* at amortized acquisition cost: the book value of the security at the end of each period is the book value at the beginning of the period multiplied by the historical *yield* on the security (measured as of the time of purchase) less any cash the holder receives at the end of this period from the security.

segment (of a business). As defined by *APB Opinion No. 30,* "a component of an *entity* whose activities represent a separate major line of business or class of customer. . . . [It may be] a *subsidiary,* a division, or a department, . . . provided that its *assets,* results of *operations,* and activities can be clearly distinguished, physically and operationally for financial reporting purposes, from the other assets, results of operations, and activities of the entity." In *SFAS No. 14,* a segment is defined as a "component of an enterprise engaged in promoting a product or service or a group of related products and services primarily to unaffiliated customers . . . for a profit." *SFAS No. 131* defines operating segments using the "management approach" as components of the enterprise engaging in revenue- and expense-generating business activities "whose operating results are regularly reviewed by the enterprise's chief operating decision maker to make decisions about resources . . . and asset performance."

segment reporting. Reporting of *sales, income,* and *assets* by *segments of a business,* usually classified by nature of products sold but sometimes by geographical area where the firm produces or sells goods or by type of customers; sometimes called "line of business reporting." The accounting for segment income does not allocate *central corporate expenses* to the segments.

self-balancing. A set of records with equal *debits* and *credits* such as the *ledger* (but not individual accounts), the *balance sheet,* and a *fund* in nonprofit accounting.

self-check(ing) digit. A digit forming part of an account or code number, normally the last digit of the number, which is mathematically derived from the other numbers of the code and is used to detect errors in transcribing the code number. For example, assume the last digit of the account number is the remainder after summing the preceding digits and dividing that sum by nine. Suppose the computer encounters the account numbers 7027261-7 and 9445229-7. The program can tell that something has gone wrong with the encoding of the second account number because the sum of the first seven digits is 35, whose remainder on division by 9 is 8, not 7. The first account number does not show such an error because the sum of the first seven digits is 25, whose remainder on division by 9 is, indeed, 7. The first account number may be in error, but the second surely is.

self-insurance. See *insurance.*

self-sustaining foreign operation. A foreign operation both financially and operationally independent of the reporting enterprise (owner) so that the owner's exposure to exchange-rate changes results only from the owner's net investment in the foreign entity.

selling and administrative expenses. *Expenses* not specifically identifiable with, or assigned to, production.

semifixed costs. *Costs* that increase with activity as a step function.

semivariable costs. *Costs* that increase strictly linearly with activity but that are positive at zero activity level. Royalty fees of 2 percent of sales are variable; royalty fees of $1,000 per year plus 2 percent of sales are semivariable.

senior securities. *Bonds* as opposed to *preferred stock; preferred stock* as opposed to *common stock*. The firm must meet the senior security claim against *earnings* or *assets* before meeting the claims of less-senior securities.

sensitivity analysis. A study of how the outcome of a decision-making process changes as one or more of the assumptions change.

sequential access. Computer-storage access in which the analyst can locate information only by a sequential search of the storage file. Compare *direct access*.

serial bonds. An *issue* of *bonds* that mature in part at one date, another part on another date, and so on. The various maturity dates usually occur at equally spaced intervals. Contrast with *term bonds*.

service basis of depreciation. *Production method*.

service bureau. A commercial data-processing center providing service to various customers.

service cost, (current) service cost. *Pension plan expenses incurred* during an *accounting period* for employment services performed during that period. Contrast with *prior service cost*. See *funded*.

service department. A department, such as the personnel or computer department, that provides services to other departments rather than direct work on a salable product. Contrast with *production department*. A firm must allocate costs of service departments whose services benefit manufacturing operations to *product costs* under *full absorption costing*.

service life. Period of expected usefulness of an asset; may differ from *depreciable life* for income tax purposes.

service potential. The future benefits that cause an item to be classified as an *asset*. Without service potential, an item has no future benefits, and accounting will not classify the item as an asset. *SFAC No. 6* suggests that the primary characteristic of service potential is the ability to generate future net cash inflows.

services. Useful work done by a person, a machine, or an organization. See *goods*.

setup. The time or costs required to prepare production equipment for doing a job.

SFAC. *Statement of Financial Accounting Concepts* of the *FASB*.

SFAS. *Statement of Financial Accounting Standards*. See *FASB*.

shadow price. An opportunity cost. A *linear programming* analysis provides as one of its outputs the potential value of having available more of the scarce resources that constrain the production process, for example, the value of having more time available on a machine tool critical to the production of two products. Common terminology refers to this value as the "shadow price" or the "dual value" of the scarce resource.

share. A unit of *stock* representing ownership in a corporation.

share premium. UK: *additional paid-in capital* or *capital contributed in excess of par value*.

shareholders' equity. *Proprietorship* or *owners' equity* of a corporation. Because *stock* means inventory in Australia, the UK, and Canada, their writers use the term "shareholders' equity" rather than the term "stockholders' equity."

short-run. The opposite of *long-run* or *long-term*.

short-term. Current; ordinarily, due within one year.

short-term liquidity risk. The risk that an *entity* will not have enough *cash* in the *short run* to pay its *debts*.

shrinkage. An excess of *inventory* shown on the *books* over actual physical quantities on hand; can result from theft or shoplifting as well as from evaporation or general wear and tear. Some accountants, in an attempt to downplay their own errors, use the term to mean record-keeping mistakes that they later must correct, with some embarrassment, and that result in material changes in reported income. One should not use the term "shrinkage" for the correction of mistakes because adequate terminology exists for describing mistakes.

shutdown cost. Those fixed costs that the firm continues to incur after it has ceased production; the costs of closing down a particular production facility.

sight draft. A demand for payment drawn by Person A to whom Person B owes cash. Person A presents the *draft* to Person B's (the debtor's) bank in expectation that Person B will authorize his or her bank to disburse the funds. Sellers often use such drafts when selling goods to a new customer in a different city. The seller is uncertain whether the buyer will pay the bill. The seller sends the *bill* of lading, or other evidence of ownership of the goods, along with a sight draft to the buyer's bank. Before the warehouse holding the goods can release them to the buyer, the buyer must instruct its bank to honor the sight draft by withdrawing funds from the buyer's account. Once the bank honors the sight draft, it hands to the buyer the bill of lading or other document evidencing ownership, and the goods become the property of the buyer.

simple interest. *Interest* calculated on *principal* where interest earned during periods before maturity of the loan does not increase the principal amount earning interest for the subsequent periods and the lender cannot withdraw the funds before maturity. Interest = principal × interest rate × time, where the rate is a rate per period (typically a year) and time is expressed in units of that period. For example, if the *rate* is annual and the time is two months, then in the formula, use 2/12 for *time*. Simple interest is seldom used in economic calculations except for periods of less than one year and then only for computational convenience. Contrast with *compound interest*.

single-entry accounting. Accounting that is neither *self-balancing* nor *articulated*. That is, it does not rely on equal *debits* and *credits*. The firm makes no *journal entries* and must *plug* to derive *owners' equity* for the *balance sheet*.

single proprietorship. *Sole proprietorship.*

single-step. Said of an *income statement* in which *ordinary revenue* and *gain* items appear first, with their total. Then come all ordinary *expenses* and *losses,* with their total. The difference between these two totals, plus the effect of *income from discontinued operations* and *extraordinary items,* appears as *net income.* Contrast with *multiple-step* and see *proprietorship theory.*

sinking fund. *Assets* and their earnings earmarked for the retirement of bonds or other long-term obligations. Earnings of sinking fund investments become taxable income of the company.

sinking fund method of depreciation. Method in which the periodic charge is an equal amount each period so that the *future value* of the charges, considered as an *annuity,* will accumulate at the end of the depreciable life to an amount equal to the *acquisition cost* of the asset. The firm does not necessarily, or even usually, accumulate a *fund* of cash. Firms rarely use this method.

skeleton account. *T-account.*

slide. The name of the error made by a bookkeeper in recording the digits of a number correctly with the decimal point misplaced; for example, recording $123.40 as $1,234.00 or as $12.34. If the only errors in a *trial balance* result from one or more slides, then the difference between the sum of the *debits* and the sum of the *credits* will be divisible by nine. Not all such differences divisible by nine result from slides. See *transposition error.*

SMAC (Society of Management Accountants of Canada). The national association of accountants whose provincial associations engage in industrial and governmental accounting. The association undertakes research and administers an educational program and comprehensive examinations; those who pass qualify to be designated CMA (Certified Management Accountants), formerly called RIA (Registered Industrial Accountant).

SNC (société en nom collectif). France: a *partnership.*

soak-up method. The *equity method.*

Social Security taxes. Taxes levied by the federal government on both employers and employees to provide *funds* to pay retired persons (or their survivors) who are entitled to receive such payments, either because they paid Social Security taxes themselves or because Congress has declared them eligible. Unlike a *pension plan,* the Social Security system does not collect funds and invest them for many years. The tax collections in a given year pay primarily for benefits distributed that year. At any given time the system has a multi-trillion-dollar unfunded obligation to current workers for their eventual retirement benefits. See *Old Age, Survivors, Disability, and (Hospital) Insurance.*

software. The programming aids, such as compilers, sort and report programs, and generators, that extend the capabilities of and simplify the use of the computer, as well as certain operating systems and other control programs. Compare *hardware.*

sole proprietorship. A firm in which all *owners' equity* belongs to one person.

solvent. Able to meet debts when due.

SOP. *Statement of Position* (of the *AcSEC* of the *AICPA*).

sound value. A phrase used mainly in appraisals of *fixed assets* to mean *fair market price (value)* or *replacement cost* in present condition.

source of funds. Any *transaction* that increases *cash* and *marketable securities* held as *current assets.*

sources and uses statement. *Statement of cash flows.*

SOYD. *Sum-of-the years'-digits depreciation.*

SP (société en participation). France: a silent *partnership* in which the managing partner acts for the partnership as an individual in transacting with others who need not know that the person represents a partnership.

special assessment. A compulsory levy made by a governmental unit on property to pay the costs of a specific improvement or service presumed not to benefit the general public but only the owners of the property so assessed; accounted for in a special assessment fund.

special journal. A *journal,* such as a sales journal or cash disbursements journal, to record *transactions* of a similar nature that occur frequently.

special revenue debt. A governmental unit's debt backed only by revenues from specific sources, such as tolls from a bridge.

specific identification method. Method for valuing *ending inventory* and *cost of goods sold* by identifying actual units sold and remaining in inventory and summing the actual costs of those individual units; usually used for items with large unit values, such as precious jewelry, automobiles, and fur coats.

specific item sampling. Sampling in which the analyst selects particular items because of their nature, value, or method of recording. Compare *representative item sampling.*

specific price changes. Changes in the market prices of specific *goods* and *services.* Contrast with *general price-level changes.*

specific price index. A measure of the price of a specific good or service, or a small group of similar goods or services, at one time relative to the price during a base period. Contrast with *general price index.* See *dollar-value LIFO method.*

spending variance. In *standard cost systems,* the *rate* or *price variance* for *overhead costs.*

split. *Stock split.* Sometimes called "split-up."

split-off point. In accumulating and allocating costs for *joint products,* the point at which all costs are no longer *joint costs* but at which an analyst can identify costs associated with individual products or perhaps with a smaller number of *joint products.*

spoilage. See *abnormal spoilage* and *normal spoilage.*

spot price. The price of a commodity for delivery on the day of the price quotation. See *forward price* for contrast.

spreadsheet. For many years, a term that referred specifically to a *work sheet* organized like a *matrix* that provides a two-way classification of accounting data. The rows and columns both have labels, which are *account* titles. An entry in a row represents a *debit,* whereas an entry in a column represents a *credit.* Thus, the number "100" in the "cash" row and the "accounts receivable" column records an entry debiting cash and crediting accounts receivable for $100. A given row total indicates all debit entries to the account represented by that row, and a given column total indicates the sum of all credit entries to the account represented by the column. Since personal-computer software has become widespread, this term has come to refer to any file created by programs such as Lotus 1-2-3® and Microsoft Excel®. Such files have rows and columns, but they need not represent debits and credits. Moreover, they can have more than two dimensions.

squeeze. A term sometimes used for *plug.*

SSARS. *Statement on Standards for Accounting and Review Services.*

stabilized accounting. *Constant-dollar accounting.*

stable monetary unit assumption. In spite of *inflation,* which appears to be a way of life, the assumption that underlies historical cost/nominal-dollar accounting—namely that one can meaningfully add together current dollars and dollars of previous years. The assumption gives no specific recognition to changing values of the dollar in the usual *financial statements.* See *constant-dollar accounting.*

Staff Accounting Bulletin. An interpretation issued by the staff of the Chief Accountant of the *SEC* "suggesting" how the accountants should apply various *Accounting Series Releases* in practice. The suggestions are part of *GAAP.*

stakeholder. An individual or group, such as employees, suppliers, customers, and shareholders, who have an interest in the corporation's activities and outcomes.

standard cost. Anticipated *cost* of producing a unit of output; a predetermined cost to be assigned to products produced. Standard cost implies a norm—what costs should be. Budgeted cost implies a forecast—something likely, but not necessarily, a "should," as implied by a norm. Firms use standard costs as the benchmark for gauging good and bad performance. Although a firm may similarly use a budget, it need not. A budget may be a planning document, subject to changes whenever plans change, whereas standard costs usually change annually or when technology significantly changes or when costs of labor and materials significantly change.

standard costing. *Costing* based on *standard costs.*

standard costing system. *Product costing* using *standard costs* rather than actual costs. The firm may use either *full absorption* or *variable costing* principles.

standard error (of regression coefficients). A measure of the uncertainty about the magnitude of the estimated parameters of an equation fit with a *regression analysis.*

standard manufacturing overhead. *Overhead costs* expected to be incurred per unit of time and per unit produced.

standard price (rate). Unit price established for materials or labor used in *standard cost systems.*

standard quantity allowed. The direct material or direct labor (inputs) quantity that production should have used if it had produced the units of output in accordance with preset *standards.*

standby costs. A type of *capacity cost,* such as property taxes, incurred even if a firm shuts down operations completely. Contrast with *enabling costs.*

stated capital. Amount of capital contributed by shareholders; sometimes used to mean *legal capital.*

stated value. A term sometimes used for the *face amount of capital stock,* when the *board* has not designated a *par value.* Where there is stated value per share, capital *contributed in excess of stated value* may come into being.

statement of affairs. A *balance sheet* showing immediate *liquidation* amounts rather than *historical costs,* usually prepared when *insolvency* or *bankruptcy* is imminent. Such a statement specifically does not use the *going-concern assumption.*

statement of cash flows. A schedule of *cash receipts* and *payments,* classified by *investing, financing,* and *operating activities;* required by the *FASB* for all for-profit companies. Companies may report operating activities with either the direct method (which shows only receipts and payments of cash) or the indirect method (which starts with *net income* and shows adjustments for *revenues* not currently producing cash and for *expenses* not currently using cash). "Cash" includes cash equivalents such as Treasury bills, commercial paper, and *marketable securities* held as *current assets.* This is sometimes called the "funds statement." Before 1987, the FASB required the presentation of a similar statement called the *statement of changes in financial position,* which tended to emphasize *working capital,* not cash.

statement of changes in financial position. As defined by *APB Opinion No. 19,* a statement that explains the changes in *working capital* (or cash) balances during a period and shows the changes in the working capital (or cash) accounts themselves. The *statement of cash flows* has replaced this statement.

statement of charge and discharge. A financial statement, showing *net assets* or *income,* drawn up by an executor or administrator, to account for receipts and dispositions of cash or other assets in an estate or trust.

Statement of Financial Accounting Concepts (SFAC). One of a series of *FASB* publications in its *conceptual framework* for *financial accounting* and reporting. Such statements set forth objectives and fundamentals to be the basis for specific financial accounting and reporting standards.

Statement of Financial Accounting Standards (SFAS). See *FASB.*

statement of financial position. *Balance sheet.*

Statement of Position (SOP). A recommendation, on an emerging accounting problem, issued by the *AcSEC* of the *AICPA.* The AICPA's Code of Professional Ethics specifically states that *CPAs* need not treat *SOPs* as they do rules from the *FASB,* but a CPA would be wary of departing from the recommendations of a *SOP.*

statement of retained earnings (income). A statement that reconciles the beginning-of-period and the end-of-period balances in the *retained earnings* account. It shows the effects of *earnings, dividend declarations,* and *prior-period adjustments.*

statement of significant accounting policies (principles). A summary of the significant *accounting principles* used in compiling an *annual report;* required by *APB Opinion No. 22.* This summary may be a separate exhibit or the first *note* to the financial statements.

Statement on Auditing Standards (SAS). A series addressing specific auditing standards and procedures. *No. 1* (1973) of this series codifies all statements on auditing standards previously promulgated by the *AICPA.*

Statement on Standards for Accounting and Review Services (SSARS). Pronouncements issued by the *AICPA* on unaudited *financial statements* and unaudited financial information of nonpublic entities.

static budget. *Fixed budget.* Budget developed for a set level of the driving variable, such as production or sales, which the analyst does not change if the actual level deviates from the level set at the outset of the analysis.

status quo. Events or cost incurrences that will happen or that a firm expects to happen in the absence of taking some contemplated action.

statutory tax rate. The tax rate specified in the *income tax* law for each type of income (for example, *ordinary income, capital gain or loss*).

step allocation method. *Step-down method.*

step cost. *Semifixed cost.*

step-down method. In *allocating service department* costs, a method that starts by allocating one service department's costs to *production departments* and to all other service departments. Then the firm allocates a second service department's costs, including costs allocated from the first, to production departments and to all other service departments except the first one. In this fashion, a firm may allocate all service departments costs, including previous allocations, to production departments and to those service departments whose costs it has not yet allocated.

step(ped) cost. *Semifixed cost.*

sterilized allocation. Desirable characteristics of cost allocation methods. Optimal decisions result from considering *incremental costs* only. Optimal decisions never require *allocations* of *joint* or *common costs.* A "sterilized allocation" causes the optimal decision choice not to differ from the one that occurs when the accountant does not allocate joint or common costs "sterilized" with respect to that decision. Arthur L. Thomas first used the term in this context. Because *absorption costing* requires that product costs absorb all manufacturing costs and because some allocations can lead to bad decisions, Thomas (and we) advocate that the analyst choose a sterilized allocation scheme that will not alter the otherwise optimal decision. No single

allocation scheme is always sterilized with respect to all decisions. Thus, Thomas (and we) advocate that decisions be made on the basis of incremental costs before any allocations.

stewardship. Principle by which management is accountable for an *entity's* resources, for their efficient use, and for protecting them from adverse impact. Some theorists believe that accounting has as a primary goal aiding users of *financial statements* in their assessment of management's performance in stewardship.

stock. A measure of the amount of something on hand at a specific time. In this sense, contrast with *flow.* See *inventory* and *capital stock.*

stock appreciation rights. An employer's promise to pay to the employee an amount of *cash* on a certain future date, with the amount of cash being the difference between the *market value* of a specified number of *shares* of *stock* in the employer's company on the given future date and some base price set on the date the rights are granted. Firms sometimes use this form of compensation because changes in tax laws in recent years have made *stock options* relatively less attractive. *GAAP* compute compensation based on the difference between the market value of the shares and the base price set at the time of the grant.

stock dividend. A so-called *dividend* in which the firm distributes additional *shares* of *capital stock* without cash payments to existing shareholders. It results in a *debit* to *retained earnings* in the amount of the market value of the shares issued and a *credit* to *capital stock* accounts. Firms ordinarily use stock dividends to indicate that they have permanently reinvested earnings in the business. Contrast with a *stock split,* which requires no entry in the capital stock accounts other than a notation that the *par* or *stated value* per share has changed.

stock option. The right to purchase or sell a specified number of shares of *stock* for a specified price at specified times. Employee stock options are purchase rights granted by a corporation to employees, a form of compensation. Traded stock options are *derivative* securities, rights created and traded by investors, independent of the corporation whose stock is optioned. Contrast with *warrant.*

stock right. See *right.*

stock split(-up). Increase in the number of common shares outstanding resulting from the issuance of additional shares to existing shareholders without additional capital contributions by them. Does not increase the total *value* (or *stated value*) of *common shares* outstanding because the *board* reduces the par (or stated) value per share in inverse proportion. A three-for-one stock split reduces par (or stated) value per share to one-third of its former amount. A stock split usually implies a distribution that increases the number of shares outstanding by 20 percent or more. Compare with *stock dividend.*

stock subscriptions. See *subscription* and *subscribed stock.*

stock warrant. See *warrant.*

stockholders' equity. See *shareholders' equity.*

stockout. Occurs when a firm needs a unit of *inventory* to use in production or to sell to a customer but has none available.

stockout costs. *Contribution margin* or other measure of *profits* not earned because a seller has run out of *inventory* and cannot fill a customer's order. A firm may incur an extra cost because of delay in filling an order.

stores. *Raw materials,* parts, and supplies.

straight-debt value. An estimate of the *market value* of a *convertible bond* if the bond did not contain a conversion privilege.

straight-line depreciation. Method in which, if the *depreciable life* is *n* periods, the periodic *depreciation* charge is 1/*n* of the *depreciable cost;* results in equal periodic charges. Accountants sometimes call it "straight-time depreciation."

strategic plan. A statement of the method for achieving an organization's goals.

stratified sampling. In choosing a *sample,* a method in which the investigator first divides the entire *population* into relatively homogeneous subgroups (strata) and then selects random samples from these subgroups.

street security. A stock certificate in immediately transferable form, most commonly because the issuing firm has registered it in the name of the broker, who has endorsed it with "payee" left blank.

Subchapter S corporation. A firm legally organized as a *corporation* but taxed as if it were a *partnership.* Tax terminology calls the corporations paying their own income taxes *C corporations.*

subject to. In an *auditor's report,* qualifications usually caused by a *material* uncertainty in the valuation of an item, such as future promised payments from a foreign government or outcome of pending litigation.

subordinated. *Debt* whose claim on income or assets has lower priority than claims of other debt.

subscribed stock. A *shareholders' equity* account showing the capital that the firm will receive as soon as the share-purchaser pays the subscription price. A subscription is a legal contract, so once the share-purchaser signs it, the firm makes an entry *debiting* an *owners' equity contra account* and *crediting* subscribed stock.

subscription. Agreement to buy a *security* or to purchase periodicals, such as magazines.

subsequent events. *Poststatement events.*

subsidiary. A company in which another company owns more than 50 percent of the voting shares.

subsidiary ledger. The *ledger* that contains the detailed accounts whose total appears in a *controlling account* of the *general ledger.*

subsidiary (ledger) accounts. The *accounts* in a *subsidiary ledger.*

successful efforts costing. In petroleum accounting, the *capitalization* of the drilling costs of only those wells that contain gas or oil. See *reserve recognition accounting* for an example.

summary annual report (SAR). Condensed financial statements distributed in lieu of the usual *annual report.* Since 1987, the *SEC* has allowed firms to include such statements in the annual report to shareholders as long as the firm includes full, detailed statements in SEC filings and in *proxy* materials sent to shareholders.

summary of significant accounting principles. *Statement of significant accounting policies (principles).*

sum-of-the-years'-digits depreciation (SYD, SOYD). An *accelerated depreciation* method for an asset with *depreciable life* of *n* years where the charge in period *i* ($i = 1, \ldots, n$) is the fraction $(n + 1 - i)/[n(n + 1)/2]$ of the *depreciable cost.* If an asset has a depreciable cost of \$15,000 and a five-year depreciable life, for example, the depreciation charges would be \$5,000 ($= 5/15 \times \$15,000$) in the first year, \$4,000 in the second, \$3,000 in the third, \$2,000 in the fourth, and \$1,000 in the fifth. The name derives from the fact that the denominator in the fraction is the sum of the digits 1 through *n*.

sunk cost. Past *costs* that current and future decisions cannot affect and, hence, that are irrelevant for decision making aside from *income tax* effects. Contrast with *incremental costs* and *imputed costs.* For example, the *acquisition cost* of machinery is irrelevant to a decision of whether to scrap the machinery. The current *exit value* of the machinery is the *opportunity cost* of continuing to own it, and the cost of, say, the electricity to run the machinery is an incremental cost of its operation. Sunk costs become relevant for decision making when the analysis requires taking *income taxes* (*gain* or *loss* on disposal of asset) into account, since the cash payment for income taxes depends on the tax basis of the asset. Avoid this term in careful writing because it is ambiguous. Consider, a machine costing \$100,000, for example, with current *salvage* value of \$20,000. Some (including us) would say that \$100,000 (*gross* amount) is "sunk"; others would say that only \$80,000 (*net* amount) is "sunk."

supplementary statements (schedules). Statements (schedules) in addition to the four basic *financial statements (balance sheet, income statement, statement of cash flows,* and the *statement of retained earnings).*

surplus. A word once used but now considered poor terminology; prefaced by "earned" to mean *retained earnings* and prefaced by "capital" to mean *capital contributed in excess of par (or stated) value.*

surplus reserves. *Appropriated retained earnings.* A phrase with nothing to recommend it: of all the words in accounting, *reserve* is the most objectionable, and *surplus* is the second-most objectionable.

suspense account. A *temporary account* used to record part of a transaction before final analysis of that transaction. For example, if a business regularly classifies all sales into a dozen or more different categories but wants to deposit the proceeds of cash sales every day, it may credit a sales suspense account pending detailed classification of all sales into Durable Goods Sales, Women's Clothing Sales, Men's Clothing Sales, Housewares Sales, and so on.

sustainable income. The part of *distributable income* (computed from *current cost* data) that the firm can expect to earn in the next accounting period if it continues operations at the same levels as were maintained during the current period. *Income from discontinued operations,* for example, may be distributable but not sustainable.

swap. A currency swap is a financial instrument in which the holder promises to pay to (or receive from) the *counterparty* the difference between *debt* denominated in one currency (such as U.S. dollars) and the payments on debt denominated in another currency (such as German marks). An interest-rate swap typically obligates the party and counterparty to exchange the difference between fixed- and floating-rate interest payments on otherwise similar loans.

S-X. See *Regulation S-X.*

SYD. *Sum-of-the-years'-digits depreciation.*

T

T-account. Account form shaped like the letter T with the title above the horizontal line. *Debits* appear on the left of the vertical line, *credits* on the right.

take-home pay. The amount of a paycheck; earned wages or *salary* reduced by deductions for *income taxes, Social Security taxes,* contributions to fringe-benefit plans, union dues, and so on. Take-home pay might be as little as half of earned compensation.

take-or-pay contract. As defined by *SFAS No. 47,* a purchaser-seller agreement that provides for the purchaser to pay specified amounts periodically in return for products or services. The purchaser must make specified minimum payments even if it does not take delivery of the contracted products or services.

taking a bath. To incur a large loss. See *big bath.*

tangible. Having physical form. Accounting has never satisfactorily defined the distinction between tangible and intangible assets. Typically, accountants define intangibles by giving an exhaustive list, and everything not on the list is defined as tangible. See *intangible asset* for such a list.

target cost. *Standard cost.* Sometimes, target price less expected profit margin.

target price. Selling price based on customers' value in use of a good or service, constrained by competitors' prices of similar items.

tax. A nonpenal, but compulsory, charge levied by a government on income, consumption, wealth, or other basis, for the benefit of all those governed. The term does not include fines or specific charges for benefits accruing only to those paying the charges, such as licenses, permits, special assessments, admission fees, and tolls.

tax allocation: interperiod. See *deferred income tax liability.*

tax allocation: intrastatement. The showing of income tax effects on *extraordinary items, income from discontinued operations,* and *prior-period adjustments,* along with these items, separately from income taxes on other income. See *net-of-tax reporting.*

tax avoidance. See *tax shelter* and *loophole.*

tax basis of assets and liabilities. A concept important for applying *SFAS No. 109* on *deferred income taxes.* Two *assets* will generally have different *book values* if the firm paid different amounts for them, *amortizes* them on a different schedule, or both. Similarly a single asset will generally have a book value different from what it will have for tax purposes if the firm recorded different *acquisition* amounts for the asset for book and for tax purposes, amortizes it differently for book and for tax purposes, or both. The difference between financial book value and income tax basis becomes important in computing deferred income tax amounts. The adjusted cost in the financial records is the "book basis," and the adjusted amount in the tax records is the "tax basis." Differences between book and tax basis can arise for *liabilities* as well as for assets.

tax credit. A subtraction from taxes otherwise payable. Contrast with *tax deduction.*

tax deduction. A subtraction from *revenues* and *gains* to arrive at taxable income. Tax deductions differ technically from tax *exemptions,* but both reduce gross income in computing taxable income. Both differ from *tax credits,* which reduce the computed tax itself in computing taxes payable. If the tax rate is the fraction t of pretax income, then a *tax credit* of $1 is worth $1/t$ of *tax deductions.*

tax evasion. The fraudulent understatement of taxable revenues or overstatement of deductions and expenses or both. Contrast with *tax shelter* and *loophole.*

tax-exempts. See *municipal bonds.*

tax shelter. The legal avoidance of, or reduction in, *income taxes* resulting from a careful reading of the complex income-tax regulations and the subsequent rearrangement of financial affairs to take advantage of the regulations. Often writers use the term pejoratively, but the courts have long held that a taxpayer has no obligation to pay taxes any larger than the legal minimum. If the public concludes that a given tax shelter is "unfair," then Congress can, and has, changed the laws and regulations. The term is sometimes used to refer to the investment that permits tax avoidance. See *loophole.*

tax shield. The amount of an *expense,* such as *depreciation,* that reduces taxable income but does not require *working capital.* Sometimes this term includes expenses that reduce taxable income and use working capital. A depreciation deduction (or *R&D expense* in the expanded sense) of $10,000 provides a tax shield of $3,700 when the marginal tax rate is 37 percent.

taxable income. *Income* computed according to *IRS* regulations and subject to *income taxes.* Contrast with income, net income, income before taxes (in the *income statement*), and *comprehensive income* (a *financial reporting* concept). Use the term "pretax income" to refer to income before taxes on the income statement in financial reports.

tax-transfer lease. One form of *capital lease.* Congress has in the past provided business with an incentive to invest in qualifying *plant and equipment* by granting an *investment credit,* which, though it occurs as a reduction in *income* *taxes* otherwise payable, effectively reduces the purchase price of the assets. Similarly, Congress continues to grant an incentive to acquire such assets by allowing the *Modified Accelerated Cost Recovery System* (*MACRS,* form of unusually *accelerated depreciation*). Accelerated depreciation for tax purposes allows a reduction of taxes paid in the early years of an asset's life, providing the firm with an increased *net present value* of *cash flows.* The *IRS* administers both of these incentives through the income tax laws, rather than paying an outright cash payment. A business with no taxable income in many cases had difficulty reaping the benefits of the investment credit or of accelerated depreciation because Congress had not provided for tax refunds to those who acquire qualifying assets but who have no taxable income. In principle, a company without taxable income could lease from another firm with taxable income an asset that it would otherwise purchase. The second firm acquires the asset, gets the tax-reduction benefits from the acquisition, and becomes a lessor, leasing the asset (presumably at a lower price reflecting its own costs lowered by the tax reductions) to the unprofitable company. Before 1981, tax laws discouraged such leases. That is, although firms could enter into such leases, they could not legally transfer the tax benefits. Under certain restrictive conditions, the tax law now allows a profitable firm to earn tax credits and take deductions while leasing to the firm without tax liability in such leases. These are sometimes called "safe-harbor leases."

Technical Bulletin. The *FASB* has authorized its staff to issue bulletins to provide guidance on financial accounting and reporting problems. Although the FASB does not formally approve the contents of the bulletins, their contents are part of *GAAP*.

technology. The sum of a firm's technical *trade secrets* and *know-how,* as distinct from its *patents*.

temporary account. *Account* that does not appear on the *balance sheet; revenue* and *expense* accounts, their *adjuncts* and *contras, production cost accounts, dividend distribution accounts,* and purchases-related accounts (which close to the various inventories); sometimes called a "nominal account."

temporary difference. According to the *SFAS No. 109* (1992) definition: "A difference between the tax basis of an asset or liability and its reported amount in the financial statements that will result in taxable or deductible amounts in future years." Temporary differences include *timing differences* and differences between *taxable income* and pretax income caused by different cost bases for assets. For example, a plant asset might have a cost of $10,000 for financial reporting but a basis of $7,000 for income tax purposes. This temporary difference might arise because the firm has used an accelerated depreciation method for tax but straight-line for book, or the firm may have purchased the asset in a transaction in which the fair value of the asset exceeded its tax basis. Both situations create a temporary difference.

temporary investments. Investments in *marketable securities* that the owner intends to sell within a short time, usually one year, and hence classifies as *current assets*.

10-K. The name of the annual report that the *SEC* requires of nearly all publicly held corporations.

term bonds. A *bond issue* whose component bonds all mature at the same time. Contrast with *serial bonds*.

term loan. A loan with a *maturity* date, as opposed to a demand loan, which is due whenever the lender requests payment. In practice, bankers and auditors use this phrase only for loans for a year or more.

term structure. A phrase with different meanings in *accounting* and *financial economics*. In accounting, it refers to the pattern of times that must elapse before *assets* turn into, or produce, *cash* and the pattern of times that must elapse before *liabilities* require cash. In financial economics, the phrase refers to the pattern of interest rates as a function of the time that elapses for loans to come due. For example, if six-month loans cost 6 percent per year and 10-year loans cost 9 percent per year, this is called a "normal" term structure because the longer-term loan carries a higher rate. If the six-month loan costs 9 percent per year and the 10-year loan costs 6 percent per year, the term structure is said to be "inverted."

terms of sale. The conditions governing payment for a sale. For example, the terms *2/10, n(et)/30* mean that if the purchaser makes payment within 10 days of the invoice date, it can take a *discount* of 2 percent from *invoice* price; the purchaser must pay the invoice amount, in any event, within 30 days, or it becomes overdue.

theory of constraints (TOC). Concept of improving operations by identifying and reducing bottlenecks in process flows.

thin capitalization. A state of having a high *debt-equity ratio*. Under income tax legislation, the term has a special meaning.

throughput contract. As defined by *SFAS No. 47,* an agreement that is signed by a shipper (processor) and by the owner of a transportation facility (such as an oil or natural gas pipeline or a ship) or a manufacturing facility and that provides for the shipper (processor) to pay specified amounts periodically in return for the transportation (processing) of a product. The shipper (processor) must make cash payments even if it does not ship (process) the contracted quantities.

throughput contribution. Sales dollars minus the sum of all short-run variable costs.

tickler file. A collection of *vouchers* or other memoranda arranged chronologically to remind the person in charge of certain duties to make payments (or to do other tasks) as scheduled.

time-adjusted rate of return. *Internal rate of return*.

time cost. *Period cost*.

time deposit. Cash in bank earning interest. Contrast with *demand deposit*.

time-series analysis. See *cross-section analysis* for definition and contrast.

times-interest (charges) earned. Ratio of pretax *income* plus *interest* charges to interest charges. See *ratio*.

timing difference. The major type of *temporary difference* between taxable income and pretax income reported to shareholders; reverses in a subsequent period and requires an entry in the *deferred income tax* account; for example, the use of *accelerated depreciation* for tax returns and *straight-line depreciation* for financial reporting. Contrast with *permanent difference*.

Toronto Stock Exchange (TSE). A public market where various corporate securities trade.

total assets turnover. *Sales* divided by average total *assets*.

total quality management (TQM). Concept of organizing a company to excel in all its activities in order to increase the quality of products and services.

traceable cost. A *cost* that a firm can identify with or assign to a specific product. Contrast with a *joint cost*.

trade acceptance. A *draft* that a seller presents for signature (acceptance) to the buyer at the time it sells goods. The draft then becomes the equivalent of a *note receivable* of the seller and a *note payable* of the buyer.

trade credit. Occurs when one business allows another to buy from it in return for a promise to pay later. Contrast with "consumer credit," which occurs when a business extends a retail customer the privilege of paying later.

trade discount. A *list price discount* offered to all customers of a given type. Contrast with a *discount* offered for prompt payment and with *quantity discount*.

trade-in. Acquiring a new *asset* in exchange for a used one and perhaps additional cash. See *boot* and *trade-in transaction*.

trade-in transaction. The accounting for a trade-in; depends on whether the firm receives an asset "similar" to (and used in the same line of business as) the asset traded in and whether the accounting is for *financial statements* or for *income tax* returns. Assume that an old asset cost $5,000, has $3,000 of *accumulated depreciation* (after recording depreciation to the date of the trade-in), and hence has a *book value* of $2,000. The old asset appears to have a market value of $1,500, according to price quotations in used asset markets. The firm trades in the old asset on a new asset with a list price of $10,000. The firm gives up the old asset and $5,500 cash *(boot)* for the new asset. The generic entry for the trade-in transaction is as follows:

New Asset	A		
Accumulated Depreciation (Old Asset)	3,000		
Adjustment on Exchange of Asset	B	or	B
Old Asset			5,000
Cash			5,500

(1) The *list price* method of accounting for trade-ins rests on the assumption that the list price of the new asset closely approximates its market value. The firm records the new asset at its list price (A = $10,000 in the example); B is a *plug* (= $2,500 credit in the example). If B requires a *debit* plug, the Adjustment on Exchange of Asset is a *loss*; if B requires a *credit* plug (as in the example), the adjustment is a *gain*.

(2) Another theoretically sound method of accounting for trade-ins rests on the assumption that the price quotation from used-asset markets gives a market value of the old asset that is a more reliable measure than the market value of the new asset determined by list price. This method uses the *fair market price (value)* of the old asset, $1,500 in the example, to determine B (= $2,000 book value − $1,500 assumed proceeds on disposition = $500 debit or loss). The exchange results in a loss if the book value of the old asset exceeds its market value and in a gain if the market value exceeds the book value. The firm records the new asset on the books by plugging for A (= $7,000 in the example).

(3) For income tax reporting, the taxpayer must recognize neither gain nor loss on the trade-in. Thus the taxpayer records the new asset for tax purposes by assuming B is zero and plugging for A (= $7,500 in the example). In practice, firms that want to recognize the loss currently will sell the old asset directly, rather than trading it in, and acquire the new asset entirely for cash.

(4) *Generally accepted accounting principles (APB Opinion No. 29)* require a variant of these methods. The basic method is (1) or (2), depending on whether the list price of the new asset (1) or the quotation of the old asset's market value (2) provides the more reliable indication of market value. If the basic method requires a debit entry, or loss, for the Adjustment on Exchange of Asset, then the firm records the trade-in as in (1) or (2) and recognizes the full amount of the loss currently. If, however, the basic method requires a credit entry, or gain, for the Adjustment on Exchange of Asset, then the firm recognizes the gain currently if the old asset and the new asset are not "similar." If the assets are similar and the party trading in receives no cash, then it recognizes no gain and the treatment resembles that in (3); that is B = 0, plug for A. If the assets are similar and the firm trading in receives cash—a rare case—then it recognizes a portion of the gain currently. The portion of the gain recognized currently is the fraction cash received/fair market value of total consideration received. (When the firm uses the list price method, (1), it assumes that the market value of the old asset is the list price of the new asset plus the amount of cash received by the party trading in.)

A summary of the results of applying *GAAP* to the example follows.

More Reliable Information As to Fair Market Value	Old Asset Compared with New Asset	
	Similar	Not Similar
New Asset List Price	A = $7,500 B = 0	A = $10,000 B = 2,500 gain
Old Asset Market Price	A = $7,000 B = 500 loss	A = $ 7,000 B = 500 loss

trade payables (receivables). *Payables (receivables)* arising in the ordinary course of business transactions. Most *accounts payable (receivable)* are of this kind.

trade secret. Technical or business information such as formulas, recipes, computer programs, and marketing data not generally known by competitors and maintained by the firm as a secret; theoretically capable of having an indefinite, finite life. A famous example is the secret process for Coca-Cola® (a registered *trademark* of the company). Compare with *know-how*. The firm will capitalize this intangible asset only if purchased and then will amortize it over a period not to exceed 40 years. If the firm develops the intangible internally, the firm will *expense* the costs as incurred and show no asset.

trademark. A distinctive word or symbol that is affixed to a product, its package, or its dispenser and that uniquely identifies the firm's products and services. See *trademark right*.

trademark right. The right to exclude competitors in sales or advertising from using words or symbols that are so similar to the firm's *trademarks* as possibly to confuse consumers. Trademark rights last as long as the firm continues to use the trademarks in question. In the United States, trademark rights arise from use and not from government registration. They therefore have a legal life independent of the life of a registration. Registrations last 20 years, and the holder may renew them as long as the holder uses the trademark. Although a trademark right might have an indefinite life, *GAAP* require amortization over some estimate of its life, not to exceed 40 years. Under *SFAS No. 2,* the firm must *expense* internally developed trademark rights.

trading on the equity. Said of a firm engaging in *debt financing*; frequently said of a firm doing so to a degree considered abnormal for a firm of its kind. *Leverage*.

trading securities. *Marketable securities* that a firm holds and expects to sell within a relatively short time; a classification important in *SFAS No. 115,* which requires the owner to carry marketable equity securities on the balance sheet at market value, not at cost. Contrast with *available for sale, securities* and *held-to-maturity securities*. Under *SFAS No. 115,* the balance sheet reports trading securities at market value on the balance sheet date, and the income statement reports *holding gains and losses* on trading securities. When the firm sells the securities, it reports realized gain or loss as the difference between the selling price and the market value at the last balance sheet date.

transaction. A *transfer* (of more than promises—see *executory contract*) between the accounting *entity* and another party or parties.

transfer. Under *SFAC No. 6,* consists of two types: "reciprocal" and "nonreciprocal." In a reciprocal transfer, or "exchange," the entity both receives and sacrifices. In a nonreciprocal transfer, the entity sacrifices but does not receive (examples include gifts, distributions to owners) or receives but does not sacrifice (investment by owner in entity). *SFAC No. 6* suggests that the term "internal transfer" is self-contradictory and that writers should use the term "internal event" instead.

transfer agent. Usually a bank or trust company designated by a corporation to make legal transfers of *stock (bonds)* and, perhaps, to pay *dividends (coupons)*.

transfer price. A substitute for a *market,* or *arm's-length, price* used in *profit,* or *responsibility center, accounting* when one segment of the business "sells" to another segment. Incentives of profit center managers will not coincide with the best interests of the entire business unless a firm sets transfer prices properly.

transfer-pricing problem. The problem of setting *transfer prices* so that both buyer and seller have *goal congruence* with respect to the parent organization's goals.

translation adjustment. The effect of *exchange-rate* changes caused by converting the value of a net investment denominated in a *foreign currency* to the entity's reporting currency. *SFAS No. 52* requires firms to translate their net investment in relatively self-contained foreign operations at the *balance sheet* date. Year-to-year changes in value caused by exchange-rate changes accumulate in an *owners' equity* account, sometimes called the "cumulative translation adjustment."

translation gain (or loss). *Foreign exchange gain (or loss).*

transportation-in. *Freight-in.*

transposition error. An error in record keeping resulting from reversing the order of digits in a number, such as recording "32" for "23." If the only errors in a *trial balance* result from one or more transposition errors, then the difference between the sum of the *debits* and the sum of the *credits* will be divisible by nine. Not all such differences result from transposition errors. See *slide*.

treasurer. The financial officer responsible for managing cash and raising funds.

treasury bond. A bond issued by a corporation and then reacquired. Such bonds are treated as retired when reacquired, and an *extraordinary gain or loss* on reacquisition is recognized. This term also refers to a *bond* issued by the U.S. Treasury Department.

treasury shares. *Capital stock* issued and then reacquired by the corporation. Such reacquisitions result in a reduction of *shareholders' equity* and usually appear on the balance sheet as contra to shareholders' equity. Accounting recognizes neither *gain* nor *loss* on transactions involving treasury stock. The accounting debits (if positive) or credits (if negative) any difference between the amounts paid and received for treasury stock transactions to *additional paid-in capital.* See *cost method* and *par value method.*

treasury stock. *Treasury shares.*

trial balance. A two-column listing of *account balances.* The left-hand column shows all accounts with *debit* balances and their total. The right-hand column shows all accounts with *credit* balances and their total. The two totals should be equal. Accountants compute trial balances as a partial check of the arithmetic accuracy of the entries previously made. See *adjusted, preclosing, post-closing, unadjusted trial balance, plug, slide,* and *transposition error.*

troubled debt restructuring. As defined in *SFAS No. 15,* a concession (changing of the terms of a *debt*) that is granted by a *creditor* for economic or legal reasons related to the *debtor's* financial difficulty and that the creditor would not otherwise consider.

TSE. *Toronto Stock Exchange.*

t-statistic. For an estimated *regression* coefficient, the estimated coefficient divided by the *standard error* of the estimate.

turnover. The number of times that *assets,* such as *inventory* or *accounts receivable,* are replaced on average during the period. Accounts receivable turnover, for example, is total sales on account for a period divided by the average accounts receivable balance for the period. See *ratio.* In the UK, "turnover" means *sales.*

turnover of plant and equipment. See *ratio.*

t-value. In *regression analysis,* the ratio of an estimated regression coefficient divided by its *standard error.*

20-F. Form required by the *SEC* for foreign companies issuing or trading their securities in the United States. This form reconciles the foreign accounting amounts resulting from using foreign *GAAP* to amounts resulting from using U.S. GAAP.

two T-account method. A method for computing either (1) *foreign-exchange gains and losses* or (2) *monetary gains or losses* for *constant-dollar accounting statements.* The left-hand *T-account* shows actual net balances of *monetary items,* and the right-hand T-account shows implied (common) dollar amounts.

2/10, n(et)/30. See *terms of sale.*

U

unadjusted trial balance. *Trial balance* taken before the accountant makes *adjusting* and *closing entries* at the end of the period.

unappropriated retained earnings. *Retained earnings* not appropriated and therefore against which the *board* can declare *dividends* in the absence of retained earnings restrictions. See *restricted retained earnings.*

unavoidable cost. A *cost* that is not an *avoidable cost.*

uncertainty. See *risk* for definition and contrast.

uncollectible account. An *account receivable* that the *debtor* will not pay. If the firm uses the preferable *allowance method,* the entry on judging a specific account to be uncollectible *debits* the allowance for uncollectible accounts and *credits* the specific account receivable. See *bad debt expense* and *sales contra, estimated uncollectibles.*

unconsolidated subsidiary. A *subsidiary* not consolidated and, hence, not accounted for in the *equity method.*

uncontrollable cost. The opposite of *controllable cost.*

underapplied (underabsorbed) overhead. An excess of actual *overhead costs* for a period over costs applied, or charged, to products produced during the period; a *debit balance* remaining in an overhead account after the accounting assigns overhead to product.

underlying document. The record, memorandum, *voucher,* or other signal that is the authority for making an *entry* into a *journal.*

underwriter. One who agrees to purchase an entire *security issue* for a specified price, usually for resale to others.

undistributed earnings. *Retained earnings.* Typically, this term refers to that amount retained for a given year.

unearned income (revenue). *Advances from customers;* strictly speaking, a contradiction in terms because the terms "income" and "revenue" mean earned.

unemployment tax. See *FUTA.*

unencumbered appropriation. In governmental accounting, portion of an *appropriation* not yet spent or encumbered.

unexpired cost. An *asset.*

unfavorable variance. In *standard cost* accounting, an excess of expected revenue over actual revenue or an excess of actual cost over standard cost.

unfunded. Not *funded.* An obligation or *liability,* usually for *pension costs,* exists, but no *funds* have been set aside to discharge the obligation or liability.

Uniform Partnership Act. A model law, enacted by many states, to govern the relations between partners when the *partnership* agreement fails to specify the agreed-upon treatment.

unissued capital stock. *Stock* authorized but not yet issued.

uniting-of-interests method. Term for the *pooling-of-interests method* used by the *IASC.* The IASC allows uniting of interests only when the merging firms are roughly equal in size and the shareholders retain substantially the same, relative to each other, voting rights and interests in the combined entity after the combination as before.

units-of-production method. The *production method of depreciation.*

unlimited liability. The legal obligation of *general partners* or the sole proprietor for all debts of the *partnership* or *sole proprietorship.*

unqualified opinion. See *auditor's report.*

unrealized appreciation. An *unrealized holding gain;* frequently used in the context of *marketable securities.*

unrealized gain (loss) on marketable securities. An *income statement account* title for the amount of *gain (loss)* during the current period on the portfolio of *marketable securities* held as *trading securities. SFAS No. 115* requires the firm to recognize, in the income statement, gains and losses caused by changes in market values, even though the firm has not yet *realized* them.

unrealized gross margin (profit). A *contra account* to *installment accounts receivable* used with the *installment method* of revenue recognition; shows the amount of profit that the firm will eventually realize when it collects the receivable. Some accountants show this account as a *liability*.

unrealized holding gain. See *inventory profit* for the definition and an example.

unrecovered cost. *Book value* of an *asset*.

unused capacity. The difference between resources supplied and resources used.

usage variance. *Efficiency variance*.

use of funds. Any transaction that reduces funds (however "funds" is defined).

useful life. *Service life*.

V

valuation account. A *contra account* or *adjunct account*. When the firm reports *accounts receivable* at expected collectible amounts, it will credit any expected uncollectible amounts to the *allowance for uncollectibles,* a valuation account. In this way, the firm can show both the gross receivables amount and the amount it expects to collect. *SFAC No. 6* says a valuation account is "a separate item that reduces and increases the carrying amount" of an asset (or liability). The accounts are part of the related assets (or liabilities) and are not assets (or liabilities) in their own right.

value. Monetary worth. This term is usually so vague that you should not use it without a modifying adjective unless most people would agree on the amount. Do not confuse with cost. See *fair market price (value), entry value,* and *exit value*.

value added. *Cost* of a product or *work-in-process* minus the cost of the material purchased for the product or work-in-process.

value-added activity. Any activity that increases the usefulness to a customer of a product or service.

value chain. The set of business functions that increase the usefulness to the customer of a product or service; typically including research and development, design of products and services, production, marketing, distribution, and customer service.

value engineering. An evaluation of the activities in the value chain to reduce costs.

value variance. *Price variance*.

variable annuity. An *annuity* whose periodic payments depend on some uncertain outcome, such as stock market prices.

variable budget. *Flexible budget*.

variable costing. In allocating costs, a method that assigns only *variable manufacturing costs* to products and treats *fixed manufacturing costs* as *period expenses*. Contrast with *full absorption costing*.

variable costs. *Costs* that change as activity levels change. Strictly speaking, variable costs are zero when the activity level is zero. See *semivariable costs*. In accounting, this term most often means the sum of *direct costs* and variable *overhead*.

variable overhead variance. Difference between actual and *standard variable overhead costs*.

variable rate debt. *Debt* whose interest rate results from the periodic application of a formula, such as "three-month LIBOR [London Interbank Offered Rate] plus 1 percent [one hundred basis points] set on the 8th day of each February, May, August, and November."

variables sampling. The use of a sampling technique in which the sampler infers a particular quantitative characteristic of an entire population from a sample (e.g., mean amount of accounts receivable). See also *estimation sampling*. See *attribute(s) sampling* for contrast and further examples.

variance. Difference between actual and *standard costs* or between *budgeted* and actual *expenditures* or, sometimes, *expenses*. The word has completely different meanings in accounting and in statistics, where it means a measure of dispersion of a distribution.

variance analysis. *Variance investigation*. This term's meaning differs in statistics.

variance investigation. A step in managerial control processes. *Standard costing systems* produce *variance* numbers of various sorts. These numbers seldom exactly equal to zero. Management must decide when a variance differs sufficiently from zero to study its cause. This term refers both to the decision about when to study the cause and to the study itself.

variation analysis. Analysis of the causes of changes in financial statement items of interest such as *net income* or *gross margin*.

VAT (Value-added tax). A tax levied on the market value of a firm's outputs less the market value of its purchased inputs.

vendor. A seller; sometimes spelled "vender."

verifiable. A qualitative *objective* of financial reporting specifying that accountants can trace items in *financial statements* back to *underlying documents*—supporting *invoices,* canceled *checks,* and other physical pieces of evidence.

verification. The auditor's act of reviewing or checking items in *financial statements* by tracing back to *underlying documents*—supporting *invoices,* canceled *checks,* and other business documents—or sending out *confirmations* to be returned. Compare with *physical verification*.

vertical analysis. Analysis of the financial statements of a single firm or across several firms for a particular time, as opposed to *horizontal* or *time-series analysis,* in which the analyst compares items over time for a single firm or across firms.

vertical integration. The extension of activity by an organization into business directly related to the production or distribution of the organization's end products. Although a firm may sell products to others at various stages, a vertically integrated firm devotes the substantial portion of the output at each stage to the production of the next stage or to end products. Compare *horizontal integration.*

vested. An employee's *pension plan* benefits that are not contingent on the employee's continuing to work for the employer.

visual curve fitting method. One crude form of cost *estimation.* Sometimes, when a firm needs only rough approximations of the amounts of *fixed* and *variable costs,* management need not perform a formal *regression analysis* but can plot the data and draw a line that seems to fit the data. Then it can use the parameters of that line for the rough approximations.

volume variance. *Production volume variance;* less often, used to mean *sales volume variance.*

voucher. A document that signals recognition of a *liability* and authorizes the disbursement of cash; sometimes used to refer to the written evidence documenting an *accounting entry,* as in the term *journal voucher.*

voucher system. In controlling *cash,* a method that requires someone in the firm to authorize each *check* with an approved *voucher.* The firm makes no *disbursements* of currency or coins except from *petty cash funds.*

vouching. The function performed by an *auditor* to ascertain that underlying data or documents support a *journal entry.*

W

wage. Compensation of employees based on time worked or output of product for manual labor. But see *take-home pay.*

warning signal. Tool used to identify quality-control problems; only signals a problem. Contrast with *diagnostic signal,* which both signals a problem and suggests its cause.

warrant. A certificate entitling the owner to buy a specified number of shares at a specified time(s) for a specified price; differs from a *stock option* only in that the firm grants options to employees and issues warrants to the public. See *right.*

warranty. A promise by a seller to correct deficiencies in products sold. When the seller gives warranties, proper accounting practice recognizes an estimate of warranty *expense* and an *estimated liability* at the time of sale. See *guarantee* for contrast in proper usage.

wash sale. The sale and purchase of the same or similar *asset* within a short time period. For *income tax* purposes, the taxpayer may not recognize *losses* on a sale of stock if the taxpayer purchases equivalent stock within 30 days before or after the date of sale.

waste. Material that is a residue from manufacturing operations and that has no sale value. Frequently, this has negative value because a firm must incur additional costs for disposal.

wasting asset. A *natural resource* that has a limited *useful life* and, hence, is subject to *amortization,* called *depletion.* Examples are timberland, oil and gas wells, and ore deposits.

watered stock. Shares issued for *assets* with *fair market price (value)* less than *par* or *stated value.* The firm records the

assets on the books at the overstated values. In the law, for shares to be considered watered, the *board of directors* must have acted in bad faith or fraudulently in issuing the shares under these circumstances. The term originated from a former practice of cattle owners who fed cattle ("stock") large quantities of salt to make them thirsty. The cattle then drank much water before their owner took them to market. The owners did this to make the cattle appear heavier and more valuable than otherwise.

weighted average. An average computed by counting each occurrence of each value, not merely a single occurrence of each value. For example, if a firm purchases one unit for $1 and two units for $2 each, then the simple average of the purchase prices is $1.50, but the weighted average price per unit is $5/3 = $1.67. Contrast with *moving average.*

weighted-average inventory method. Valuing either *withdrawals* or *ending inventory* at the *weighted-average* purchase price of all units on hand at the time of withdrawal or of computation of ending inventory. The firm uses the *inventory equation* to calculate the other quantity. If a firm uses the *perpetual inventory* method, accountants often call it the *moving average method.*

where-got, where-gone statement. A term allegedly used in the 1920s by W. M. Cole for a statement much like the *statement of cash flows.* Noted accounting historian S. Zeff reports that Cole actually used the term "where-got-gone" statement.

wind up. To bring to an end, such as the life of a corporation. The *board* winds up the life of a corporation by following the winding-up provisions of applicable statutes, by surrendering the charter, or by following *bankruptcy* proceedings. See also *liquidation.*

window dressing. The attempt to make financial statements show *operating* results, or a *financial position,* more favorable than they would otherwise show.

with recourse. See *note receivable discounted.*

withdrawals. *Assets* distributed to an owner. *Partner's drawings.* See *inventory equation* for another context.

withholding. Deductions that are taken from *salaries* or *wages,* usually for *income taxes,* and that the employer remits, in the employee's name, to the taxing authority.

without recourse. See *note receivable discounted.*

work sheet (program). (1) A computer program designed to combine explanations and calculations. This type of program helps in preparing *financial statements* and *schedules.* (2) A tabular schedule for convenient summary of *adjusting* and *closing entries.* The work sheet usually begins with an *unadjusted trial balance.* Adjusting entries appear in the next two columns, one for *debits* and one for *credits.* The work sheet carries the horizontal sum of each line to the right into either the *income statement* or the *balance sheet* column, as appropriate. The *plug* to equate the income statement column totals is, if a debit, the income or, if a credit, a loss for the period. That income will close retained earnings on the balance sheet. The income statement credit columns are the revenues for the period, and the debit columns are the expenses (and revenue contras) that appear on the income statement. "Work sheet" also refers to *schedules* for ascertaining other items that appear on the *financial statements* and that require adjustment or compilation.

working capital. *Current assets* minus *current liabilities;* sometimes called "net working capital" or "net current assets."

work(ing) papers. The schedules and analyses prepared by the *auditor* in carrying out investigations before issuing an *opinion* on *financial statements.*

work-in-process (inventory account). Partially completed product; appears on the balance sheet as *inventory.*

worth. *Value.* See *net worth.*

worth-debt ratio. Reciprocal of the *debt-equity ratio.* See *ratio.*

write down. To *write off,* except that the firm does not charge all the *asset*'s cost to *expense* or *loss;* generally used for nonrecurring items.

write off. To *charge* an *asset* to *expense* or *loss*; that is, to *debit* expense (or loss) and *credit* the asset.

write-off method. For treating *uncollectible accounts,* a method that *debits bad debt expense* and *credits* accounts receivable of specific customers as the firm identifies specific accounts as uncollectible. The firm cannot use this method when it can estimate uncollectible amounts and they are significant. See *bad debt expense, sales contra, estimated uncollectibles,* and the *allowance method* for contrast.

write up. To increase the recorded *cost* of an *asset* with no corresponding *disbursement* of *funds*; that is, to *debit* asset and *credit revenue* or, perhaps, *owners' equity;* seldom done in the United States because currently accepted accounting principles await actual transactions before recording asset increases. An exception occurs in accounting for *marketable equity securities.*

Y

yield. *Internal rate of return* of a stream of cash flows. Cash yield is cash flow divided by book value. See also *dividend yield.*

yield to maturity. At a given time, the *internal rate of return* of a series of cash flows; usually said of a *bond;* sometimes called the "effective rate."

yield variance. Measures the input-output relation while holding the standard mix of inputs constant: (standard price multiplied by actual amount of input used in the standard mix) − (standard price multiplied by standard quantity allowed for the actual output). It is the part of the *efficiency variance* not called the *mix variance.*

Z

zero-base(d) budgeting (ZBB). One philosophy for setting budgets. In preparing an ordinary *budget* for the next period, a manager starts with the budget for the current period and makes adjustments as seem necessary because of changed conditions for the next period. Since most managers like to increase the scope of the activities managed and since most prices increase most of the time, amounts in budgets prepared in the ordinary, incremental way seem to increase period after period. The authority approving the budget assumes that managers will carry out operations in the same way as in the past and that next period's expenditures will have to be at least as large as those of the current period. Thus, this authority tends to study only the increments to the current period's budget. In ZBB, the authority questions the process for carrying out a program and the entire budget for the next period. The authority studies every dollar in the budget, not just the dollars incremental to the previous period's amounts. The advocates of ZBB claim that in this way, (1) management will more likely delete programs or divisions of marginal benefit to the business or governmental unit, rather than continuing with costs at least as large as the present ones, and (2) management may discover and implement alternative, more cost-effective ways of carrying out programs. ZBB implies questioning the existence of programs and the fundamental nature of the way that firms carry them out, not merely the amounts used to fund them. Experts appear to divide evenly as to whether the middle word should be "base" or "based."

INDEX

Callable preferred shares, defined, 679–81

Called-up share capital, defined, 72

Canada, accounting principles in, 776

Capital contributed in excess of par (stated) value, account, 67

Capital contributions, 682–9
  effect on statement of cash flows, 706

Capital expenditures, defined, 429

Capital lease method, 541–3
  conditions requiring, 544–5
  generally accepted accounting principles on, 779

Capital markets, efficiency of, 21–2

Capital reserve, defined, 70

Capital stock contract, defined, 678

Capital surplus. *See* Capital contributed in excess of par (stated) value

Capital transactions, defined, 667

Capitalization. *See* Amortization

Capitalize, defined, 436

Capitalized lease obligations, as liability account, 67

Capitalizing earnings, defined, 839

Casey, Cornelius, 254n

Cash
  as asset account, 65
  basis of accounting, 103–5
  change equation, 174
  collection basis. *See* Revenue recognition, installment method
  dividends, 697
  equivalents, defined, 729
  flow
    defined, 730
    from financing activities, 170–1, 198–200, 749
    from investing activities, 170, 198–200, 749
    from operations, 170, 198–200, 749
      relation to net income, 748–9
    from operations to current liabilities ratio, 254, 261
    from operations to total liabilities ratio, 258, 261
    statement of. *See* Statement of cash flows
  inflows and outflows, illustrated, 15

Cash-flow hedge
  defined, 560
  journal entries for, 562–3

Central vs. peripheral activities, 670

Certificate. *See* Auditor's opinion

Certificate (bond), defined, 496

Changes in accounting principles, adjustments for, 673

Changes in shareholders' equity, disclosure of, 700–2

Charge, defined, 58

Charter, defined, 678

Closing
  entries, defined, 115
  process, 113

Collateral, defined, 490

Columnar worksheet, illustrated, 174–6, 180–2

Common shareholders equity. *See* Shareholders' equity

Common size balance sheet, 68–70

Common size income statement, 135–6
  illustrated, 239

Common stock
  acquisition of, on statement of cash flows, 743
  as owners' equity account, 67
  defined, 680–1

Comparative balance sheets, illustrated, 9, 26, 71–3, 175, 181, 197, 235, 783

Comparative income statements, illustrated, 234, 782

Comparative statements of cash flow, illustrated, 236, 784

Completed contract method of revenue recognition, 322

Completed sale method. *See* Revenue recognition

Compound interest
  defined, 826
  power of, 826–7

Comprehensive income reporting, 674–6

Conceptual framework of FASB, 773

Conformity of financial reporting to income tax reporting, 20

Conservatism
  criterion in financial statements, 790–1
  in accounting, 49, 366n

Consolidated balance sheet, illustrated, 613, 732, 733

Consolidated financial statements. *See* Consolidated statements; specific statements

Consolidated income, 610

Consolidated income statement, illustrated, 613, 731

Consolidated statement of cash flows, illustrated, 734

Consolidated statements
  compared to other methods, 613

defined, 604
  disclosure of, 606–7
  effects on statement of cash flows, 630–1
  generally accepted accounting principles on, 776–7
  illustrating purchase and pooling-of-interest methods, 625
  international perspective on, 614
  limitations of, 612
  preparation of, 617–22
  purpose of, 605–6
  understanding, 607–12
  when acquisition price exceeds book value, 621–2
  See also Balance sheet, consolidated; Income statement, consolidated; Statement of cash flows, consolidated

Consolidation, one line, 611

Consolidation policy, defined, 606

Constructive liabilities, 482–3

Contingencies, defined, 480–2

Contingent liability, defined, 482

Contingent obligations, 538–9

Continuous inventory method. *See* Perpetual inventory system

Contra accounts
  defined, 115
  for merchandise purchase adjustments, 356

Contra-asset account for leases, 542

Contracts
  accounting for, 493–6
  executory, 479, 537–8
  interest imputation, 493–5
  partially executed, 479
  throughput, 479
  take-or-pay, 479

Contributed capital
  defined, 10
  on pro forma balance sheet, 269

Contribution, defined, 678

Contributions in excess of par value. *See* Additional paid-in capital

Conversion of debt into equity, on statement of cash flows, 745

Convertible bonds
  accounting for, 688–9
  defined, 497
  effect on statement of cash flows, 706
  payable, as liability account, 67

Convertible preferred shares
  accounting for, 688–9